The History of Economic Thought: A Reader

Edited by
Steven G. Medema and
Warren J. Samuels

Routledge
Taylor & Francis Group

LONDON AND NEW YORK

First published 2003 by Routledge
11 New Fetter Lane, London EC4P 4EE

Simultaneously published in the USA and Canada
by Routledge
29 West 35th Street, New York, NY 10001

Routledge is an imprint of the Taylor & Francis Group

Typeset in Baskerville by
Newgen Imaging Systems (P) Ltd, Chennai, India
Printed and bound in Great Britain by
TJ International Ltd, Padstow, Cornwall

British Library Cataloguing in Publication Data
A catalogue record for this book is available from the British Library

Library of Congress Cataloging in Publication Data
A catalog record for this book has been requested

ISBN 0–415–20551–4 (hbk)
ISBN 0–415–20550–6 (pbk)

**For Alex and Christopher,
and for Michelle,
in the hope that they, too,
will come to love the world of ideas**

Contents

Preface

The following pages contain some of the great literature in the history of economic ideas. The task of putting together a reader such as this is like confronting an endless smorgasbord of delights when on a highly restrictive diet – so many good things to sample and so little room to actually indulge. It should be obvious that reading the selections contained herein is no substitute for reading the original works in their entirety. However, we hope that the reader will find our selections sufficient to provide a useful overview of some of the major themes in the history of economic thought as they were developed in the hands of the giants in the field.

No "reader" can pretend to be comprehensive in its coverage. The scholars chosen for inclusion, and the passages excerpted from their works, will no doubt please some greatly and disappoint others. For the latter, we apologize. In putting together this reader, we have relied on a broad survey of course reading lists in the field, conversations with various colleagues, and our own instincts and intuition regarding topics usually covered in courses on history of economic thought. We have tried both to present the central ideas of each epoch within economic thought and to avoid overlap across writers. In doing so, we have also paid attention to the fact that certain of these classic works (e.g. Adam Smith's *The Wealth of Nations*) are readily available in inexpensive paperback editions should the reader wish to examine them further. Thus, the length of the excerpts from, for example, Smith and Keynes reprinted here are perhaps rather more brief than what their stature in the history of economic ideas would suggest. We have also endeavored to provide sufficient introductory material[1] for each section and each entry to provide a bit of background and plenty of suggestions for additional reading. There are many ways of doing history, and many ways of teaching the history of economic thought. We have tried to be sensitive to this in the preparation of this volume, and we are hopeful that all readers/students/scholars with interest in the history of economic ideas will find useful things to take from this volume.

While we anticipate that the primary market for this book will be students in history of economic thought courses, some of you may be reading this book simply because you have an interest in the history of ideas – economic or otherwise. For those who are new to the history of economic thought and wish to supplement their reading with secondary analysis, we refer you to Roger Backhouse's *The Ordinary Business of Life* (*The Penguin History of Economics* in the UK), Robert Heilbroner's *The Worldly Philosophers*, or the excellent textbooks in the field by Mark Blaug, Robert Ekelund and Robert Hébert, Harry Landreth and David Colander, Henry Spiegel, and Ingrid Rima. If you would like to "sit a course of lectures" in the field from your easy chair, you may consult Lionel Robbins' *A History of Economic Thought: The LSE Lectures*.

---

1 We would like to acknowledge the fact that we have drawn heavily on Mark Blaug's *Great Economists Before Keynes* for the biographical information contained in these introductory materials.

For various reasons, this project has had a rather long gestation process. We are most grateful to Alan Jarvis, Allison Kirk, and, especially, Robert Langham of Routledge for their strong interest in this project and their patience in seeing it through to completion. We would also like to thank all those who gave us advice along the way, including Roger Backhouse, Bill Barber, and several anonymous reviewers of this proposal, as well as Matt Powers, who provided invaluable research assistance, and Brian Duncan for technical assistance. Finally, we would like to thank the various publishers who have graciously allowed us to reprint the works included in this volume.

Steven G. Medema
Warren J. Samuels

Acknowledgments

The authors and publishers would like to thank the following for granting permission to reproduce material in this work.

The National Portrait Gallery, London for permission to reproduce images of Sir William Petty, John Locke, John Maynard Keynes, William Godwin, Henry Thornton, Jeremy Bentham, Alfred Marshall, and Francis Ysidro Edgeworth.

Corbis for permission to reproduce images of Aristotle and Plato, St Thomas Aquinas, and Thorstein Veblen.

Manuscripts and Archives, Yale University Library for permission to reproduce the image of Irving Fisher.

Every effort has been made to contact copyright holders for their permission to reprint material in this book. The publishers would be grateful to hear from any copyright holder who is not here acknowledged and will undertake to rectify any errors or omissions in future editions of this book.

Part 1

Pre-Classical Thought

Introduction

It is a widely held, and probably substantially correct, view that the emergence and development of modern economic thought was correlative with the emergence of a commercial, eventually industrial, capitalist market economy. It is this economic system, especially as it arose in Western Europe in the eighteenth century, that economics attempts to describe, interpret, and explain, as well as to justify. This economic thought was both positive and normative, that is, it combined efforts to objectively describe and explain with those to justify and/or to prescribe (such as policy). As a positive, scientific discipline, it combined two modes of thought: (1) empirical observation, dependent upon some more or less implicit theoretical or interpretive schema, and (2) logical analysis of the relationships between variables, dependent upon some more or less conscious generalization of interpreted observations.

Prior to this time, speaking generally, there were markets and market relationships but not market economies as the latter came to be understood after roughly the eighteenth century. While modern economic theory did not exist, thinkers of various types did speculate about a set of more or less clearly identified "economic" topics, such as trade, value, money, production, and so on. These speculations are found in documents emanating from the ancient civilizations, such as Sumeria, Babylonia, Assyria, Egypt, Persia, Israel, and the Hittite empire. Some of these documents are literary or historical; others are legal; still others arose out of business and family matters; and others involved speculation about current and/or perennial events and problems. It is clear that economic activity, especially that having to do with trade, both local and between distant lands, was engaged in by households and specialized enterprises, and gave rise to various forms of economic "analysis."

These documents seem not to have contained anything like what we now recognize as theoretical or empirical economics. But they do indicate several important concerns, centering on the general problem of the organization and control of economic activity: problems of class and of hierarchy versus equality, problems of continuity versus change of existing arrangements, problems of reconciling interpersonal conflicts of interest, problems of the nature and place of the institution of private property in the social structure, problems of the distributions of income and taxes, and so on, all interrelated. Much of the speculation related to current issues rather than to abstract generalizations, but the latter are not absent.

Early economic thought had two other characteristics: One was the mythopoeic nature of description and explanation: explication through the creation of stories involving either the gods or, eventually, God, or an anthropomorphic characterization of nature as involving spirits and transcendental forces. The other was the subordination of economic thinking to theology and organized religion and, especially, the superimposition of a system of morals upon economic (and other forms of) activity. The former remains in the form of the concept of the "invisible hand;" the latter, in the felt need for the social control of both individual economic activity and the organization of markets.

"Modern" philosophy in the West traces back to the Greeks during the fifth and fourth centuries BC. Mythopoetry does not disappear but, one might sense, reaches its highest levels of sophistication, and, especially, existing alongside of self-conscious and self-reflective philosophical inquiry, the latter becoming increasingly independent – though not without tension and conflict. The development of philosophy is facilitated and motivated by (1) the postulation of the existence of principles of an intellectual order in the universe (in nature and in society), (2) the growing belief in the opportunity accorded by God to study the nature of things without such activity being deemed an intrusion upon the domain of God, and *inter alia* (3) the development of principles of observation, logic, and epistemology.

In the eighth century BC, Hesiod wrote several works, one of which, *Ode to Work* (or *Works and Days*), identified the role of hard, honest labor in production and the studied approach to husbandry and farming, the latter couched in terms of proceeding in the manner desired by deified forces of nature, including the seasons. This work was cited three centuries later by Plato and Aristotle. One of their contemporaries was Xenophon (430–355 BC), whose *Oeconomicus* dealt with household management (most production was undertaken by households) and with analyses of the division of labor, money, and the responsibilities of the wealthy. Xenophon's *Revenue of Athens* was a brilliant analysis of the means that could be employed by the organized city-state to increase both the prosperity of the people and the revenues of their government, an analysis combined with the injunction, once the program of measures of economic development had been worked out, to consult the oracles of Dodona and Delphi if such a program was indeed going to be advantageous.

But it is with Plato (427–347 BC), notably in his *Republic* and *The Laws*, and with Aristotle (384–322 BC), in his *Politics* and *Nichomachean Ethics*, that more elaborate and more sophisticated economic analysis takes place. Both Plato and Aristotle were concerned with (1) aspects of the relation of knowledge to social action; (2) topics of political economy, such as the nature and implications of "justice" for the organization and control of the economy, including issues of private property versus communism and/or its social control; and (3) more technical topics of economics, such as self-sufficiency versus trade, the consequences of specialization and division of labor (including their relation to trade), the desirable-necessary location of the city-state, the nature and role of exchange, the roles of money and money demand, interest on loans, the question of population, prices and price levels, and the meaning and source of "value." Their discussions of these topics reflect the social (read: class) organization of Athens, the deep philosophical positions they held on a variety of topics, the economic development of Athens and its trading partners, and how they worked out solutions to serious, perennial problems of social order. In terms of the canon of Western economic thinking, economic analysis largely disappeared for roughly a millennium-and-a-half subsequent to the death of Aristotle, not to reappear in a significant way until the scholastic writers beginning in the thirteenth century AD.

The readings that follow in this part trace the development of economic thought from the Greeks through the late eighteenth century. Along the way, the reader will be introduced to classic writings in scholasticism, mercantilism, and physiocracy, as well as works that mark a turn in economic thinking toward a more systematic, and some would say scientific, method of analysis. While economics, throughout this period, was primarily considered to be, and analyzed from the perspective of, larger systems of social and philosophical thought, the economic system increasingly came to be recognized as a sphere that embodied its own particular set of laws, worthy of analysis in its own right. The reader will also notice an increasing recognition over this period of the interdependent nature of economic phenomena and thus the tendency of the authors to increasingly treat the economic system as an interrelated whole as opposed to engaging in piecemeal analysis of particular aspects of economic activity.

References and further reading

Blaug, Mark, ed. (1991) *Preclassical Economists*, Aldershot: Edward Elgar Publishing.
Hutchison, Terence (1988) *Before Adam Smith: The Emergence of Political Economy, 1662–1776*, Oxford: Basil Blackwell.
Letwin, William (1964) *The Origins of Scientific Economics*, Garden City, NY: Doubleday & Co.
Lowry, S. Todd, ed. (1987) *Pre-Classical Economic Thought: From the Greeks to the Scottish Enlightenment*, Boston: Kluwer.
Rothbard, Murray (1995) *Economic Thought Before Adam Smith*, Aldershot: Edward Elgar Publishing.
Spengler, Joseph J. (1980) *Origins of Economic Thought and Justice*, Carbondale: Southern Illinois University Press.

ARISTOTLE (384–322 BC)

Aristotle with Plato, by courtesy of Corbis, www.corbis.com.

Aristotle was born in Stagira and spent some twenty years studying under the tutelage of Plato in Athens. After a number of years of travel and serving as tutor to the young man who would later become Alexander the Great, Aristotle returned to Athens and established his own school, the Lyceum, in 335 BC.

The works of Aristotle span virtually the entire breadth of human knowledge – logic, epistemology, metaphysics, ethics, the natural sciences, rhetoric, politics, and aesthetics. While only a small fraction of his writings deal with economics, he did see matters economic as an important aspect of the social fabric and thus as necessary elements of a larger social-philosophical system of thought. Aristotle's writings had a profound influence on Aquinas and, through Aquinas, on subsequent scholastic thinking. Indeed, Aristotle's influence continues to be present in modern economic theory.

In the excerpts from Aristotle's *Politics* and *Nichomachean Ethics* provided next, we are introduced to his theories of the natural division of labor within society, household management (œconomicus) and wealth acquisition (chrematistics), private property versus communal property, and of the exchange process. The reader may wish to take particular note of the "reciprocal needs" basis of Aristotle's division of labor, his view that wealth acquisition is "unnatural" because it knows no natural limits, his strong defense of private property (as against his teacher, Plato), and his theory of reciprocity in exchange.

References and further reading

Finley, M.I. (1970) "Aristotle and Economic Analysis," *Past and Present* 47 (May): 3–25.
—— (1973) *The Ancient Economy*, Berkeley: University of California Press.
—— (1987) "Aristotle," in John Eatwell, Murray Milgate, and Peter Newman (eds), *The New Palgrave: A Dictionary of Economics*, Vol. 1, London: Macmillan, 112–13.

Gordon, Barry (1975) *Economic Analysis Before Adam Smith: Hesiod to Lessius*, New York: Barnes and Noble.

Laistner, M.L.W. (1923) *Greek Economics: Introduction and Translation*, New York: E.P. Dutton & Co.

Langholm, Odd (1979) *Price and Value Theory in the Aristotelian Tradition*, Bergen: Universitetsforlaget.

——(1983) *Wealth and Money in the Aristotelian Tradition*, Bergen: Universitetsforlaget.

——(1984) *The Aristotelian Analysis of Usury*, Bergen: Universitetsforlaget.

Lowry, S. Todd (1969) "Aristotle's Mathematical Analysis of Exchange," *History of Political Economy* 1 (Spring): 44–66.

——(1979) "Recent Literature on Ancient Greek Economic Thought," *Journal of Economic Literature* 17: 65–86.

——(1987) *The Archaeology of Economic Ideas: The Greek Classical Tradition*, Durham, NC: Duke University Press.

Soudek, Josef (1952) "Aristotle's Theory of Exchange: An Enquiry into the Origin of Economic Analysis," *Proceedings of the American Philosophical Society* 96: 45–75.

Spengler, Joseph J. (1955) "Aristotle on Economic Imputation and Related Matters," *Southern Economic Journal* 21 (April): 371–89.

——(1980) *Origins of Economic Thought and Justice*, Carbondale, IL: Southern Illinois University Press.

Worland, Stephen T. (1984) "Aristotle and the Neoclassical Tradition: The Shifting Ground of Complementarity," *History of Political Economy* 16: 107–34.

Politics*

Book I

Part I

Every state is a community of some kind, and every community is established with a view to some good; for mankind always act in order to obtain that which they think good. But, if all communities aim at some good, the state or political community, which is the highest of all, and which embraces all the rest, aims at good in a greater degree than any other, and at the highest good.

Some people think that the qualifications of a statesman, king, householder, and master are the same, and that they differ, not in kind, but only in the number of their subjects. For example, the ruler over a few is called a master; over more, the manager of a household; over a still larger number, a statesman or king, as if there were no difference between a great household and a small state. The distinction which is made between the king and the statesman is as follows: When the government is personal, the ruler is a king; when, according to the rules of the political science, the citizens rule and are ruled in turn, then he is called a statesman.

But all this is a mistake; for governments differ in kind, as will be evident to any one who considers the matter according to the method which has hitherto guided us. As in other departments of science, so in politics, the compound should always be resolved into the simple elements or least parts of the whole. We must, therefore, look at the elements of which the state is composed, in order that we may see in what the different kinds of rule differ from one another, and whether any scientific result can be attained about each one of them.

Part II

He who thus considers things in their first growth and origin, whether a state or anything else, will obtain the clearest view of them. In the first place there must be a union of those who cannot exist without each other; namely of male and female, that the race may continue (and this is a union which is formed, not of deliberate purpose, but because, in common with other animals and with plants, mankind have a natural desire to leave behind them an image of themselves), and of natural ruler and subject, that both may be preserved. For that which can foresee by the exercise of mind is by nature intended to be lord and master, and that which can with its body give effect to such foresight is a subject, and by nature a slave; hence master and slave have the same interest. Now nature has distinguished between the female and the slave. For she is not niggardly, like the smith who fashions the Delphian knife for many uses; she makes each thing for a single use, and every instrument is best made when intended for one and not for many uses.

---

* Translated by Benjamin Jowett.

But among barbarians no distinction is made between women and slaves, because there is no natural ruler among them: they are a community of slaves, male and female. Wherefore the poets say, "It is meet that Hellenes should rule over barbarians;" as if they thought that the barbarian and the slave were by nature one.

Out of these two relationships between man and woman, master and slave, the first thing to arise is the family, and Hesiod is right when he says, "First house and wife and an ox for the plow" for the ox is the poor man's slave. The family is the association established by nature for the supply of men's everyday wants, and the members of it are called by Charondas "companions of the cupboard," and by Epimenides the Cretan, "companions of the manger." But when several families are united, and the association aims at something more than the supply of daily needs, the first society to be formed is the village. And the most natural form of the village appears to be that of a colony from the family, composed of the children and grandchildren, who are said to be suckled "with the same milk." And this is the reason why Hellenic states were originally governed by kings; because the Hellenes were under royal rule before they came together, as the barbarians still are. Every family is ruled by the eldest, and therefore in the colonies of the family the kingly form of government prevailed because they were of the same blood. As Homer says: "Each one gives law to his children and to his wives." For they lived dispersedly, as was the manner in ancient times. Wherefore men say that the Gods have a king, because they themselves either are or were in ancient times under the rule of a king. For they imagine, not only the forms of the Gods, but their ways of life to be like their own.

When several villages are united in a single complete community, large enough to be nearly or quite self-sufficing, the state comes into existence, originating in the bare needs of life, and continuing in existence for the sake of a good life. And therefore, if the earlier forms of society are natural, so is the state, for it is the end of them, and the nature of a thing is its end. For what each thing is when fully developed, we call its nature, whether we are speaking of a man, a horse, or a family. Besides, the final cause and end of a thing is the best, and to be self-sufficing is the end and the best.

…

Further, the state is by nature clearly prior to the family and to the individual, since the whole is of necessity prior to the part; for example, if the whole body be destroyed, there will be no foot or hand, except in an equivocal sense, as we might speak of a stone hand; for when destroyed the hand will be no better than that. But things are defined by their working and power; and we ought not to say that they are the same when they no longer have their proper quality, but only that they have the same name. The proof that the state is a creation of nature and prior to the individual is that the individual, when isolated, is not self-sufficing; and therefore he is like a part in relation to the whole. But he who is unable to live in society, or who has no need because he is sufficient for himself, must be either a beast or a God: he is no part of a state. A social instinct is implanted in all men by nature, and yet he who first founded the state was the greatest of benefactors. For man, when perfected, is the best of animals, but, when separated from law and justice, he is the worst of all; since armed injustice is more dangerous, and he is equipped at birth with arms, meant to be used by intelligence and virtue, which he may use for the worst ends. Wherefore, if he have not virtue, he is the most unholy and the most savage of animals, and the most full of lust and gluttony. But justice is the bond of men in states, for the administration of justice, which is the determination of what is just, is the principle of order in political society.

Part III

Seeing then that the state is made up of households, before speaking of the state we must speak of the management of the household. The parts of household management correspond to the persons who compose the household, and a complete household consists of slaves and freemen. Now we should begin by examining everything in its fewest possible elements; and the first and fewest possible parts of a family are master and slave, husband and wife, father and children. We have, therefore, to consider what each of these three relations is and ought to be: I mean the relation of master and servant, the marriage relation (the conjunction of man and wife has no name of its own), and third, the procreative relation (this also has no proper name). And there is another element of a household, the so-called art of getting wealth, which, according to some, is identical with household management, according to others, a principal part of it; the nature of this art will also have to be considered by us.

Let us first speak of master and slave, looking to the needs of practical life and also seeking to attain some better theory of their relation than exists at present. For some are of the opinion that the rule of a master is a science, and that the management of a household, and the mastership of slaves, and the political and royal rule, as I was saying at the outset, are all the same. Others affirm that the rule of a master over slaves is contrary to nature, and that the distinction between slave and freeman exists by law only, and not by nature; and being an interference with nature is, therefore, unjust.

Part IV

Property is a part of the household, and the art of acquiring property is a part of the art of managing the household; for no man can live well, or indeed live at all, unless he be provided with necessaries. And as in the arts which have a definite sphere the workers must have their own proper instruments for the accomplishment of their work, so it is in the management of a household. Now instruments are of various sorts; some are living, others lifeless; in the rudder the pilot of a ship has a lifeless instrument, in the look-out man, a living instrument; for in the arts the servant is a kind of instrument. Thus, too, a possession is an instrument for maintaining life. And so, in the arrangement of the family, a slave is a living possession, and property a number of such instruments; and the servant is himself an instrument which takes precedence of all other instruments. For if every instrument could accomplish its own work, obeying or anticipating the will of others, like the statues of Daedalus, or the tripods of Hephaestus, which, says the poet, "of their own accord entered the assembly of the Gods;" if, in like manner, the shuttle would weave and the plectrum touch the lyre without a hand to guide them, chief workmen would not want servants, nor masters slaves. Here, however, another distinction must be drawn; the instruments, commonly so called, are instruments of production, whilst a possession is an instrument of action. The shuttle, for example, is not only of use; but something else is made by it, whereas of a garment or of a bed there is only the use. Further, as production and action are different in kind, and both require instruments, the instruments which they employ must likewise differ in kind. But life is action and not production, and therefore the slave is the minister of action. Again, a possession is spoken of as a part is spoken of; for the part is not only a part of something else, but wholly belongs to it; and this is also true of a possession. The master is only the master of the slave; he does not belong to him, whereas the slave is not only the slave of his master, but wholly belongs to him. Hence, we see what is the nature and office of a slave; he who is by nature not his own but another's man, is by nature a slave; and he may be said to be another's man who, being a human being, is also a possession. And a possession may be defined as an instrument of action, separable from the possessor.

Part VIII

Let us now inquire into property generally, and into the art of getting wealth, in accordance with our usual method, for a slave has been shown to be a part of property. The first question is whether the art of getting wealth is the same with the art of managing a household or a part of it, or instrumental to it; and if the last, whether in the way that the art of making shuttles is instrumental to the art of weaving, or in the way that the casting of bronze is instrumental to the art of the statuary, for they are not instrumental in the same way, but the one provides tools and the other material; and by material I mean the substratum out of which any work is made; thus, wool is the material of the weaver, bronze of the statuary. Now it is easy to see that the art of household management is not identical with the art of getting wealth, for the one uses the material which the other provides. For the art which uses household stores can be no other than the art of household management. There is, however, a doubt whether the art of getting wealth is a part of household management or a distinct art. If the getter of wealth has to consider whence wealth and property can be procured, but there are many sorts of property and riches, then are husbandry, and the care and provision of food in general, parts of the wealth-getting art or distinct arts? Again, there are many sorts of food, and therefore there are many kinds of lives both of animals and men; they must all have food, and the differences in their food have made differences in their ways of life. For of beasts, some are gregarious, others are solitary; they live in the way which is best adapted to sustain them, accordingly as they are carnivorous or herbivorous or omnivorous: and their habits are determined for them by nature in such a manner that they may obtain with greater facility the food of their choice. But, as different species have different tastes, the same things are not naturally pleasant to all of them; and therefore the lives of carnivorous or herbivorous animals further differ among themselves. In the lives of men too there is a great difference. The laziest are shepherds, who lead an idle life, and get their subsistence without trouble from tame animals; their flocks having to wander from place to place in search of pasture, they are compelled to follow them, cultivating a sort of living farm. Others support themselves by hunting, which is of different kinds. Some, for example, are brigands, others, who dwell near lakes or marshes or rivers or a sea in which there are fish, are fishermen, and others live by the pursuit of birds or wild beasts. The greater number obtain a living from the cultivated fruits of the soil. Such are the modes of subsistence which prevail among those whose industry springs up of itself, and whose food is not acquired by exchange and retail trade – there is the shepherd, the husbandman, the brigand, the fisherman, the hunter. Some gain a comfortable maintenance out of two employments, eking out the deficiencies of one of them by another: thus, the life of a shepherd may be combined with that of a brigand, the life of a farmer with that of a hunter. Other modes of life are similarly combined in any way which the needs of men may require. Property, in the sense of a bare livelihood, seems to be given by nature herself to all, both when they are first born, and when they are grown up. For some animals bring forth, together with their offspring, so much food as will last until they are able to supply themselves; of this the vermiparous or oviparous animals are an instance; and the viviparous animals have up to a certain time a supply of food for their young in themselves, which is called milk. In like manner we may infer that, after the birth of animals, plants exist for their sake, and that the other animals exist for the sake of man, the tame for use and food, the wild, if not all at least the greater part of them, for food, and for the provision of clothing and various instruments. Now if nature makes nothing incomplete, and nothing in vain, the inference must be that she has made all animals for the sake of man. And so, in one point of view, the art of war is a natural art of acquisition, for the art of acquisition includes hunting, an art which we ought to practice against wild beasts, and against men who, though intended by nature to be governed, will not submit; for war of such a kind is naturally just.

Of the art of acquisition then there is one kind which by nature is a part of the management of a household, in so far as the art of household management must either find ready to hand, or itself provide, such things necessary to life, and useful for the community of the family or state, as can be stored. They are the elements of true riches; for the amount of property which is needed for a good life is not unlimited, although Solon in one of his poems says that "No bound to riches has been fixed for man." But there is a boundary fixed, just as there is in the other arts; for the instruments of any art are never unlimited, either in number or size, and riches may be defined as a number of instruments to be used in a household or in a state. And so we see that there is a natural art of acquisition which is practiced by managers of households and by statesmen, and what is the reason of this.

Part IX

There is another variety of the art of acquisition which is commonly and rightly called an art of wealth-getting, and has in fact suggested the notion that riches and property have no limit. Being nearly connected with the preceding, it is often identified with it. But though they are not very different, neither are they the same. The kind already described is given by nature, the other is gained by experience and art.

Let us begin our discussion of the question with the following considerations: Of everything which we possess there are two uses: both belong to the thing as such, but not in the same manner, for one is the proper, and the other the improper or secondary use of it. For example, a shoe is used for wear, and is used for exchange; both are uses of the shoe. He who gives a shoe in exchange for money or food to him who wants one, does indeed use the shoe as a shoe, but this is not its proper or primary purpose, for a shoe is not made to be an object of barter. The same may be said of all possessions, for the art of exchange extends to all of them, and it arises at first from what is natural, from the circumstance that some have too little, others too much. Hence, we may infer that retail trade is not a natural part of the art of getting wealth; had it been so, men would have ceased to exchange when they had enough. In the first community, indeed, which is the family, this art is obviously of no use, but it begins to be useful when the society increases. For the members of the family originally had all things in common; later, when the family divided into parts, the parts shared in many things, and different parts in different things, which they had to give in exchange for what they wanted, a kind of barter which is still practiced among barbarous nations who exchange with one another the necessaries of life and nothing more; giving and receiving wine, for example, in exchange for coin, and the like. This sort of barter is not part of the wealth-getting art and is not contrary to nature, but is needed for the satisfaction of men's natural wants. The other or more complex form of exchange grew, as might have been inferred, out of the simpler. When the inhabitants of one country became more dependent on those of another, and they imported what they needed, and exported what they had too much of, money necessarily came into use. For the various necessaries of life are not easily carried about, and hence men agreed to employ in their dealings with each other something which was intrinsically useful and easily applicable to the purposes of life, for example, iron, silver, and the like. Of this the value was at first measured simply by size and weight, but in process of time they put a stamp upon it, to save the trouble of weighing and to mark the value.

When the use of coin had once been discovered, out of the barter of necessary articles arose the other art of wealth-getting, namely retail trade; which was at first probably a simple matter, but became more complicated as soon as men learned by experience whence and by what exchanges the greatest profit might be made. Originating in the use of coin, the art of getting wealth is generally thought to be chiefly concerned with it, and to be the art which produces riches and wealth; having to consider how they may be accumulated. Indeed, riches is assumed by many to be only a quantity of coin, because the arts of getting wealth and retail trade are concerned with coin. Others maintain that coined money is a mere sham, a thing not natural, but conventional only, because, if the users substitute another commodity for it, it is worthless, and because it is not useful as a means to any of the necessities of life, and, indeed, he who is rich in coin may often be in want of necessary food. But how can that be wealth of which a man may have a great abundance and yet perish with hunger, like Midas in the fable, whose insatiable prayer turned everything that was set before him into gold?

Hence, men seek after a better notion of riches and of the art of getting wealth than the mere acquisition of coin, and they are right. For natural riches and the natural art of wealth-getting are a different thing; in their true form they are part of the management of a household; whereas retail trade is the art of producing wealth, not in every way, but by exchange. And it is thought to be concerned with coin; for coin is the unit of exchange and the measure or limit of it. And there is no bound to the riches which spring from this art of wealth-getting. As in the art of medicine there is no limit to the pursuit of health, and as in the other arts there is no limit to the pursuit of their several ends, for they aim at accomplishing their ends to the uttermost (but of the means there is a limit, for the end is always the limit), so, too, in this art of wealth-getting there is no limit of the end, which is riches of the spurious kind, and the acquisition of wealth. But the art of wealth-getting which consists in household management, on the other hand, has a limit; the unlimited acquisition of wealth is not its business. And, therefore, in one point of view, all riches must have a limit; nevertheless, as a matter of fact, we find the opposite to be the case; for all get-ters of wealth increase their hoard of coin without limit. The source of the confusion is the near connection between the two kinds of wealth-getting; in either, the instrument is the same, although the use is different, and so they pass into one another; for each is a use of the same property, but with a difference: accumulation is the end in one case, but there is a further end in the other. Hence, some persons are led to believe that getting wealth is the object of household management, and the whole idea of their lives is that they ought either to increase their money without limit, or at any rate not to lose it. The origin of this disposition in men is that they are intent upon living only, and not upon living well; and as their desires are unlimited they also desire that the means of gratifying them should be without limit. Those who do aim at a good life seek the means of obtaining bodily pleasures; and, since the enjoyment of these appears to depend on property, they are absorbed in getting wealth: and so there arises the second species of wealth-getting. For, as their enjoyment is in excess, they seek an art which produces the excess of enjoyment; and, if they are not able to supply their pleasures by the art of getting wealth, they try other arts, using in turn every faculty in a manner contrary to nature. The quality of courage, for example, is not intended to make wealth, but to inspire confidence; neither is this the aim of the general's or of the physician's art; but the one aims at victory and the other at health. Nevertheless, some men turn every quality or art into a means of getting wealth; this they conceive to be the end, and to the promotion of the end they think all things must contribute.

Thus, then, we have considered the art of wealth-getting which is unnecessary, and why men want it; and also the necessary art of wealth-getting, which we have seen to be different from the other, and to be a natural part of the art of managing a household, concerned with the provision of food, not, however, like the former kind, unlimited, but having a limit.

Part X

And we have found the answer to our original question, whether the art of getting wealth is the business of the manager of a household and of the statesman or not their business? Namely that wealth is presupposed by them. For as political science does not make men, but takes them from nature and uses them, so too nature provides them with earth or sea, or the like as a source of food. At this stage begins the duty of the manager of a household, who has to order the things which nature supplies; he may be compared to the weaver who has not to make but to use wool, and to know, too, what sort of wool is good and serviceable or bad and unserviceable. Were this otherwise, it would be difficult to see why the art of getting wealth is a part of the management of a household and the art of medicine not; for surely the members of a household must have health just as they must have life or any other necessary. The answer is that as from one point of view the master of the house and the ruler of the state have to consider about health, from another point of view not they but the physician; so in one way the art of household management, in another way the subordinate art, has to consider about wealth. But, strictly speaking, as I have already said, the means of life must be provided beforehand by nature; for the business of nature is to furnish food to that which is born, and the food of the offspring is always what remains over of that from which it is produced. Wherefore the art of getting wealth out of fruits and animals is always natural.

There are two sorts of wealth-getting, as I have said; one is a part of household management, the other is retail trade: the former necessary and honorable, while that which consists in exchange is justly censured; for it is unnatural, and a mode by which men gain from one another. The most hated sort, and with the greatest reason, is usury, which makes a gain out of money itself, and not from the natural object of it. For money was intended to be used in exchange, but not to increase at interest. And this term interest, which means the birth of money from money, is applied to the breeding of money because the offspring resembles the parent. Wherefore of all modes of getting wealth this is the most unnatural.

Part XI

Enough has been said about the theory of wealth-getting; we will now proceed to the practical part. The discussion of such matters is not unworthy of philosophy, but to be engaged in them practically is illiberal and irksome. The useful parts of wealth-getting are, first, the knowledge of livestock – which are most profitable, and where, and how – as, for example, what sort of horses or sheep or oxen or any other animals are most likely to give a return. A man ought to know which of these pay better than others, and which pay best in particular places, for some do better in one place and some in another. Second, husbandry, which may be either tillage or planting, and the keeping of bees and of fish, or fowl, or of any animal which may be useful to man. These are the divisions of the true or proper art of wealth-getting and come first. Of the other, which consists in exchange, the first and most important division is commerce (of which there are three kinds – the provision of a ship, the conveyance of goods, exposure for sale – these again differing as they are safer or more profitable), the second is usury, the third, service for hire – of this, one kind is employed in the mechanical arts, the other in unskilled and bodily labor. There is still a third sort of wealth-getting, intermediate between this and the first or natural mode which is partly natural, but is also concerned with exchange, namely the industries that make their profit from the earth, and from things growing from the earth which, although they bear no fruit, are nevertheless profitable; for example, the cutting of timber and all mining. The art of mining, by which minerals are obtained, itself has many branches, for there are various kinds of things dug out of the earth. Of the several divisions of wealth-getting I now speak generally; a minute consideration of them might be useful in practice, but it would be tiresome to dwell upon them at greater length now.

Those occupations are most truly arts in which there is the least element of chance; they are the meanest in which the body is most deteriorated, the most servile in which there is the greatest use of the body, and the most illiberal in which there is the least need of excellence.

Works have been written upon these subjects by various persons; for example, by Chares the Parian, and Apollodorus the Lemnian, who have treated of Tillage and Planting, while others have treated of other branches; any one who cares for such matters may refer to their writings. It would be well also to collect the scattered stories of the ways in which individuals have succeeded in amassing a fortune; for all this is useful to persons who value the art of getting wealth. There is the anecdote of Thales the Milesian and his financial device, which involves a principle of universal application, but is attributed to him on account of his reputation for wisdom. He was reproached for his poverty, which was supposed to show that philosophy was of no use. According to the story, he knew by his skill in the stars while it was yet winter that there would be a great harvest of olives in the coming year; so, having a little money, he gave deposits for the use of all the olive-presses in Chios and Miletus, which he hired at a low price because no one bid against him. When the harvest-time came, and many were wanted all at once and of a sudden, he let them out at any rate which he pleased, and made a quantity of money. Thus, he showed the world that philosophers can easily be rich if they like, but that their ambition is of another sort. He is supposed to have given a striking proof of his wisdom, but, as I was saying, his device for getting wealth is of universal application, and is nothing but the creation of a monopoly. It is an art often practiced by cities when they are want of money; they make a monopoly of provisions.

There was a man of Sicily, who, having money deposited with him, bought up an the iron from the iron mines; afterwards, when the merchants from their various markets came to buy, he was the only seller, and without much increasing the price he gained 200 per cent. Which when Dionysius heard, he told him that he might take away his money, but that he must not remain at Syracuse, for he thought that the man had discovered a way of making money which was injurious to his own interests. He made the same discovery as Thales; they both contrived to create a monopoly for themselves. And statesmen as well ought to know these things; for a state is often as much in want of money and of such devices for obtaining it as a household, or even more so; hence some public men devote themselves entirely to finance.

Book II

Part V

Next let us consider what should be our arrangements about property: should the citizens of the perfect state have their possessions in common or not? This question may be discussed separately from the enactments about women and children. Even supposing that the women and children belong to individuals, according to the custom which is at present universal, may there not be an advantage in having and using possessions in common? Three cases are possible: (1) the soil may be appropriated, but the produce may be thrown for consumption into the common stock; and this is the practice of some nations. Or (2), the soil may be common, and may be cultivated in common, but the produce divided among individuals for their private use; this is a form of common property which is said to exist among certain barbarians. Or (3), the soil and the produce may be alike common.

When the husbandmen are not the owners, the case will be different and easier to deal with; but when they till the ground for themselves the question of ownership will give a world of trouble. If they do not share equally enjoyments and toils, those who labor much and get little will necessarily complain of those who labor little and receive or consume much. But indeed there is always a difficulty in men living together and having all human relations in common, but especially in their having common property. The partnerships of fellow-travelers are an example to the point; for they generally fall out over everyday matters and quarrel about any trifle which turns up. So with servants: we are most able to take offense at those with whom we most frequently come into contact in daily life.

These are only some of the disadvantages which attend the community of property; the present arrangement, if improved as it might be by good customs and laws, would be far better, and would have the advantages of both systems. Property should be in a certain sense common, but, as a general rule, private; for, when everyone has a distinct interest, men will not complain of one another, and they will make more progress, because every one will be attending to his own business. And yet by reason of goodness, and in respect of use, "Friends," as the proverb says, "will have all things common." Even now there are traces of such a principle, showing that it is not impracticable, but, in well-ordered states, exists already to a certain extent and may be carried further. For, although every man has his own property, some things he will place at the disposal of his friends, while of others he shares the use with them. The Lacedaemonians, for example, use one another's slaves, and horses, and dogs, as if they were their own; and when they lack provisions on a journey, they appropriate what they find in the fields throughout the country. It is clearly better that property should be private, but the use of it common; and the special business of the legislator is to create in men this benevolent disposition. Again, how immeasurably greater is the pleasure, when a man feels a thing to be his own; for surely the love of self is a feeling implanted by nature and not given in vain, although selfishness is rightly censured; this, however, is not the mere love of self, but the love of self in excess, like the miser's love of money; for all, or almost all, men love money and other such objects in a measure. And further, there is the greatest pleasure in doing a kindness or service to friends or guests or companions, which can only be rendered when a man has private property. These advantages are lost by excessive unification of the state. The exhibition of two virtues, besides, is visibly annihilated in such a state: first, temperance towards women (for it is an honorable action to abstain from another's wife for temperance' sake); second, liberality in the matter of property. No one, when men have all things in common, will any longer set an example of liberality or do any liberal action; for liberality consists in the use which is made of property.

Such legislation may have a specious appearance of benevolence; men readily listen to it, and are easily induced to believe that in some wonderful manner everybody will become everybody's friend, especially when some one is heard denouncing the evils now existing in states, suits about contracts, convictions for perjury, flatteries of rich men and the like, which are said to arise out of the possession of private property. These evils, however, are due to a very different cause – the wickedness of human nature. Indeed, we see that there is much more quarreling among those who have all things in common, though there are not many of them when compared with the vast numbers who have private property.

Nichomachean Ethics (350 BC)*

Book V

Part 5

Some think that reciprocity is without qualification just, as the Pythagoreans said; for they defined justice without qualification as reciprocity. Now 'reciprocity' fits neither distributive nor rectificatory justice – yet people want even the justice of Rhadamanthus to mean this: Should a man suffer what he did, right justice would be done – for in many cases reciprocity and rectificatory justice are not in accord; for example, (1) if an official has inflicted a wound, he should not be wounded in return, and if some one has wounded an official, he ought not to be wounded only but punished in addition. Further (2) there is a great difference between a voluntary and an involuntary act. But in associations for exchange this sort of justice does hold men together – reciprocity in accordance with a proportion and not on the basis of precisely equal return. For it is by proportionate requital that the city holds together. Men seek to return either evil for evil – and if they cannot do so, think their position mere slavery – or good for good – and if they cannot do so there is no exchange, but it is by exchange that they hold together. This is why they give a prominent place to the temple of the Graces – to promote the requital of services; for this is characteristic of grace – we should serve in return one who has shown grace to us, and should another time take the initiative in showing it.

   Now proportionate return is secured by cross-conjunction. Let A be a builder, B a shoemaker, C a house, D a shoe. The builder, then, must get from the shoemaker the latter's work, and must himself give him in return his own. If, then, first there is proportionate equality of goods, and then reciprocal action takes place, the result we mention will be effected. If not, the bargain is not equal, and does not hold; for there is nothing to prevent the work of the one being better than that of the other; they must therefore be equated. (And this is true of the other arts also; for they would have been destroyed if what the patient suffered had not been just what the agent did, and of the same amount and kind.) For it is not two doctors that associate for exchange, but a doctor and a farmer, or in general people who are different and unequal; but these must be equated. This is why all things that are exchanged must be somehow comparable. It is for this end that money has been introduced, and it becomes in a sense an intermediate; for it measures all things, and therefore the excess and the defect – how many shoes are equal to a house or to a given amount of food. The number of shoes exchanged for a house (or for a given amount of food) must therefore correspond to the ratio of builder to shoemaker. For if this be not so, there will be no exchange and no intercourse. And this proportion will not be effected unless the goods are

* Translated by W.D. Ross.

somehow equal. All goods must therefore be measured by some one thing, as we said before. Now this unit is in truth demand, which holds all things together (for if men did not need one another's goods at all, or did not need them equally, there would be either no exchange or not the same exchange); but money has become by convention a sort of representative of demand; and this is why it has the name 'money' (nomisma) – because it exists not by nature but by law (nomos) and it is in our power to change it and make it useless. There will, then, be reciprocity when the terms have been equated so that as farmer is to shoemaker, the amount of the shoemaker's work is to that of the farmer's work for which it exchanges. But we must not bring them into a figure of proportion when they have already exchanged (otherwise one extreme will have both excesses), but when they still have their own goods. Thus, they are equals and associates just because this equality can be effected in their case. Let A be a farmer, C food, B a shoemaker, D his product equated to C. If it had not been possible for reciprocity to be thus effected, there would have been no association of the parties. That demand holds things together as a single unit is shown by the fact that when men do not need one another, that is, when neither needs the other or one does not need the other, they do not exchange, as we do when some one wants what one has one-self, for example, when people permit the exportation of corn in exchange for wine. This equa-tion therefore must be established. And for the future exchange – that if we do not need a thing now we shall have it if ever we do need it – money is as it were our surety; for it must be possible for us to get what we want by bringing the money. Now the same thing happens to money itself as to goods – it is not always worth the same; yet it tends to be steadier. This is why all goods must have a price set on them; for then there will always be exchange, and if so, association of man with man. Money, then, acting as a measure, makes goods commensurate and equates them; for neither would there have been association if there were not exchange, nor exchange if there were not equality, nor equality if there were not commensurability. Now in truth it is impossible that things differing so much should become commensurate, but with reference to demand they may become so sufficiently. There must, then, be a unit, and that fixed by agreement (for which reason it is called money); for it is this that makes all things commensurate, since all things are measured by money. Let A be a house, B ten minae, C a bed. A is half of B, if the house is worth five minae or equal to them; the bed, C, is a tenth of B; it is plain, then, how many beds are equal to a house, namely five. That exchange took place thus before there was money is plain; for it makes no difference whether it is five beds that exchange for a house, or the money value of five beds.

ST THOMAS AQUINAS (1225–1274)

St Thomas Aquinas, by courtesy of Corbis, www.corbis.com.

By the thirteenth century, the Roman Catholic church – for our purposes the Scholastic writers – had achieved considerable if not essentially complete hegemony in Western Europe. The fundamental premises of Catholic socio-economic thought were the necessity of superimposing a system of values – deemed more or less final – upon economic life and the subordination of economic activity to the domain deemed more important by the Church, namely salvation of souls. The practical effect of this intellectual activity was to construct the framework of a system of thought within which economic concepts, relations, issues and problems might be discussed and worked out. This system of thought has persisted to the present day. Although it often postulated a stable social order, and the maintenance of stable social structures as a Christian duty, the structure of both mediaeval organized life and that system of thought, we now know in abundance, exhibited – then and now – considerable diversity, conflict and change.

The leading figure of the scholastic period was St Thomas Aquinas (1225–1274). Aquinas was a member of the Dominican order, studied under Albertus Magnus, and spent much of his life teaching and writing at various institutions of higher learning. His writings are incredibly extensive, and attempt to integrate and reconcile the teachings of the Scriptures, the church fathers, and the recently rediscovered Aristotle. Aquinas, like the Greeks before him, did not construct a cohesive body of economic theory. Rather, his economics was just one facet of his larger moral philosophy. As relations between man and man (including those economic), and the justice thereof, are an aspect of the relationship between man and God, economic matters naturally enter into Aquinas's theology. His major work, *Summa Theologica*, is a comprehensive exposition of Christian theology and philosophy, and this, along with Aquinas's various other writings, set the tone of discussion and debate for subsequent centuries of scholastic thought and analysis.

Aquinas and the Scholastics were overwhelmingly concerned with questions of the organization and control of economic life – in regard to which they adopted laws and principles which severely restricted entrepreneurial activity. They were also necessarily concerned with two great issues: the "just price" and interest on loans, the two topics of analysis in the excerpts from Aquinas's *Summa Theologica* are reprinted here.

The approaches taken to the just price by civil and, especially, canonical courts included emphases, respectively, on the intrinsic nature or quality of a good, its scarcity, its cost of production, subjective tastes and protection of social structure. Inasmuch as litigation involves disputed transactions in particular social contexts, it is likely that the price in dispute would be compared by a court with prevalent prices for the good in the area. It is also likely that over the centuries, with the further extension of markets and of trade, that the price in question increasingly became that of the "competitive market," whatever that might have meant in practice. Still, while some modern historians of thought have emphasized the increasing secularization of Church doctrinal practice, others have argued that Church figures had no meaningful idea of a self-regulating market system and were deeply influenced by then-traditional modes of theological reasoning.

The charging of interest on loans – usury *per se* – was conspicuously forbidden by the Church, which was driven by such ideas as the importance, indeed the obligation, of Christian charity and the sterility of money. In time, however, distinctions were effectively made between loans for consumption and loans for business purposes and between consumption loans due to necessity and consumption loans for conveniences and luxuries. And in time, it was held not only that some justification for the charging and paying of interest likely existed in the case of typical loans, but that administrators of Church monies were obligated to invest them (at interest). But how interest, and prices, were treated during the mediaeval period by local canonical and other tribunals remains unknown.

References and further reading

Baldwin, John W. (1959) "The Medieval Theories of Just Price," *Transactions of the American Philosophical Society* NS 49(4): 15–92.

De Roover, Raymond (1955) "Scholastic Economics: Survival and Lasting Influence from the Sixteenth Century to Adam Smith," *Quarterly Journal of Economics* 69 (May): 161–90.

—— (1958) "The Concept of the Just Price: Theory and Economic Policy," *Journal of Economic History* 18 (December): 418–34.

—— (1967) *San Bernardino of Siena and Sant' Antonino of Florence: The Two Great Economic Thinkers of the Middle Ages*, Boston: Baker Library, Harvard Graduate School of Business Administration.

Gordon, Barry (1975) *Economic Analysis Before Adam Smith: Hesiod to Lessius*, New York: Barnes and Noble.

—— (1987) "Aquinas, St. Thomas," in John Eatwell, Murray Milgate, and Peter Newman (eds), *The New Palgrave: A Dictionary of Economics*, Vol. 1, London: Macmillan, 99–100.

Grice-Hutchison, M. (1978) *Early Economic Thought in Spain, 1177–1740*, London: Allen & Unwin.

Hollander, Samuel (1965) "On the Interpretation of the Just Price," *Kyklos* 18(4): 615–34.

Langholm, Odd (1979) *Price and Value Theory in the Aristotelian Tradition*, Bergen: Universitetsforlaget.

—— (1983) *Wealth and Money in the Aristotelian Tradition*, Bergen: Universitetsforlaget.

—— (1984) *The Aristotelian Analysis of Usury*, Bergen: Universitetsforlaget.

—— (1998) *The Legacy of Scholasticism in Economic Thought: Antecedents of Choice and Power*, Cambridge: Cambridge University Press.

Lapidus, André (1997) "Metal, Money, and the Prince: John Buridan and Nicholas Oresme after Thomas Aquinas," *History of Political Economy* 29 (Spring): 21–53.

Noonan, J.T. (1957) *The Scholastic Analysis of Usury*, Cambridge, MA: Harvard University Press.

Spiegel, Henry W. (1987) "Scholastic Economic Thought," in John Eatwell, Murray Milgate and Peter Newman (eds), *The New Palgrave: A Dictionary of Economics*, Vol. 4, London: Macmillan, 259–61.

Viner, Jacob (1978) *Religious Thought and Economic Society*, Durham, NC: Duke University Press.

Worland, Stephen T. (1967) *Scholasticism and Welfare Economics*, Notre Dame, IN: University of Notre Dame Press.

Summa Theologica (1267–1273)*

Second part of the second part

(D) By sins committed in buying and selling (Question [77])
Of cheating, which is committed in buying and selling (four articles)

We must now consider those sins which relate to voluntary commutations. First, we shall consider cheating, which is committed in buying and selling: second, we shall consider usury, which occurs in loans. In connection with the other voluntary commutations no special kind of sin is to be found distinct from rapine and theft.

Under the first head there are four points of inquiry:

1   Of unjust sales as regards the price; namely whether it is lawful to sell a thing for more than its worth?
2   Of unjust sales on the part of the thing sold;
3   Whether the seller is bound to reveal a fault in the thing sold?
4   Whether it is lawful in trading to sell a thing at a higher price than was paid for it?

Article 1: Whether it is lawful to sell a thing for more than its worth?

Objection 1: It would seem that it is lawful to sell a thing for more than its worth. In the commutations of human life, civil laws determine that which is just. Now according to these laws it is just for buyer and seller to deceive one another (Cod. IV, xliv, De Rescind. Vend. 8,15): and this occurs by the seller selling a thing for more than its worth, and the buyer buying a thing for less than its worth. Therefore, it is lawful to sell a thing for more than its worth.

Objection 2: Further, that which is common to all would seem to be natural and not sinful. Now Augustine relates that the saying of a certain jester was accepted by all, "You wish to buy for a song and to sell at a premium," which agrees with the saying of Prov. 20:14, "It is naught, it is naught, saith every buyer: and when he is gone away, then he will boast." Therefore, it is lawful to sell a thing for more than its worth.

Objection 3: Further, it does not seem unlawful if that which honesty demands be done by mutual agreement. Now, according to the Philosopher (Ethic. viii, 13), in the friendship which is based on utility, the amount of the recompense for a favor received should depend on the utility accruing to the receiver: and this utility sometimes is worth more than the thing given, for instance if the receiver be in great need of that thing, whether for the purpose of avoiding a danger, or of deriving some particular benefit. Therefore, in contracts of buying and selling, it is lawful to give a thing in return for more than its worth.

* Benziger Bros. edition, 1947. Translated by Fathers of the English Dominican Province.

On the contrary, it is written (Mt. 7:12): "All things … whatsoever you would that men should do to you, do you also to them." But no man wishes to buy a thing for more than its worth. Therefore, no man should sell a thing to another man for more than its worth.

I answer that, It is altogether sinful to have recourse to deceit in order to sell a thing for more than its just price, because this is to deceive one's neighbor so as to injure him. Hence, Tully says (De Offic. iii, 15): "Contracts should be entirely free from double-dealing: the seller must not impose upon the bidder, nor the buyer upon one that bids against him."

But, apart from fraud, we may speak of buying and selling in two ways. First, as considered in themselves, and from this point of view, buying and selling seem to be established for the common advantage of both parties, one of whom requires that which belongs to the other, and vice versa, as the Philosopher states (Polit. i, 3). Now whatever is established for the common advantage, should not be more of a burden to one party than to another, and consequently all contracts between them should observe equality of thing and thing. Again, the quality of a thing that comes into human use is measured by the price given for it, for which purpose money was invented, as stated in Ethic. v, 5. Therefore if either the price exceed the quantity of the thing's worth, or, conversely, the thing exceed the price, there is no longer the equality of justice: and consequently, to sell a thing for more than its worth, or to buy it for less than its worth, is in itself unjust and unlawful.

Second we may speak of buying and selling, considered as accidentally tending to the advantage of one party, and to the disadvantage of the other: for instance, when a man has great need of a certain thing, while another man will suffer if he be without it. In such a case the just price will depend not only on the thing sold, but on the loss which the sale brings on the seller. And thus it will be lawful to sell a thing for more than it is worth in itself, though the price paid be not more than it is worth to the owner. Yet, if the one man derive a great advantage by becoming possessed of the other man's property, and the seller be not at a loss through being without that thing, the latter ought not to raise the price, because the advantage accruing to the buyer, is not due to the seller, but to a circumstance affecting the buyer. Now no man should sell what is not his, though he may charge for the loss he suffers.

On the other hand, if a man find that he derives great advantage from something he has bought, he may, of his own accord, pay the seller something over and above: and this pertains to his honesty.

Reply to Objection 1: As stated above (FS, Question [96], Article [2]) human law is given to the people among whom there are many lacking virtue, and it is not given to the virtuous alone. Hence, human law was unable to forbid all that is contrary to virtue; and it suffices for it to prohibit whatever is destructive of human intercourse, while it treats other matters as though they were lawful, not by approving of them, but by not punishing them. Accordingly, if without employing deceit the seller disposes of his goods for more than their worth, or the buyer obtain them for less than their worth, the law looks upon this as licit, and provides no punishment for so doing, unless the excess be too great, because then even human law demands restitution to be made, for instance if a man be deceived in regard to more than half the amount of the just price of a thing [*Cod. IV, xliv, De Rescind. Vend. 2,8].

On the other hand, the Divine law leaves nothing unpunished that is contrary to virtue. Hence, according to the Divine law, it is reckoned unlawful if the equality of justice be not observed in buying and selling: and he who has received more than he ought must make compensation to him that has suffered loss, if the loss be considerable. I add this condition, because the just price of things is not fixed with mathematical precision, but depends on a kind of estimate, so that a slight addition or subtraction would not seem to destroy the equality of justice.

Reply to Objection 2: As Augustine says "this jester, either by looking into himself or by his experience of others, thought that all men are inclined to wish to buy for a song and sell at a premium. But since in reality this is wicked, it is in every man's power to acquire that justice whereby he may resist and overcome this inclination." And then he gives the example of a man who gave the just price for a book to a man who through ignorance asked a low price for it. Hence, it is evident that this common desire is not from nature but from vice, wherefore it is common to many who walk along the broad road of sin.

Reply to Objection 3: In commutative justice we consider chiefly real equality. On the other hand, in friendship based on utility we consider equality of usefulness, so that the recompense should depend on the usefulness accruing, whereas in buying it should be equal to the thing bought.

Article 2: Whether a sale is rendered unlawful through a fault in the thing sold?

Objection 1: It would seem that a sale is not rendered unjust and unlawful through a fault in the thing sold. For less account should be taken of the other parts of a thing than of what belongs to its substance. Yet, the sale of a thing does not seem to be rendered unlawful through a fault in its substance: for instance, if a man sell instead of the real metal, silver or gold produced by some chemical process, which is adapted to all the human uses for which silver and gold are necessary, for instance in the making of vessels and the like. Much less therefore will it be an unlawful sale if the thing be defective in other ways.

Objection 2: Further, any fault in the thing, affecting the quantity, would seem chiefly to be opposed to justice which consists in equality. Now quantity is known by being measured: and the measures of things that come into human use are not fixed, but in some places are greater, in others less, as the Philosopher states (Ethic. v, 7). Therefore just as it is impossible to avoid defects on the part of the thing sold, it seems that a sale is not rendered unlawful through the thing sold being defective.

Objection 3: Further, the thing sold is rendered defective by lacking a fitting quality. But in order to know the quality of a thing, much knowledge is required that is lacking in most buyers. Therefore, a sale is not rendered unlawful by a fault (in the thing sold).

On the contrary, Ambrose says (De Offic. iii, 11): "It is manifestly a rule of justice that a good man should not depart from the truth, nor inflict an unjust injury on anyone, nor have any connection with fraud."

I answer that, a threefold fault may be found pertaining to the thing which is sold. One, in respect of the thing's substance: and if the seller be aware of a fault in the thing he is selling, he is guilty of a fraudulent sale, so that the sale is rendered unlawful. Hence, we find it written against certain people (Is. 1:22), "Thy silver is turned into dross, thy wine is mingled with water": because that which is mixed is defective in its substance.

Another defect is in respect of quantity which is known by being measured: wherefore if anyone knowingly make use of a faulty measure in selling, he is guilty of fraud, and the sale is illicit. Hence, it is written (Dt. 25:13,14): "Thou shalt not have divers weights in thy bag, a greater and a less: neither shall there be in thy house a greater bushel and a less," and further on (Dt. 25:16): "For the Lord ... abhorreth him that doth these things, and He hateth all injustice."

A third defect is on the part of the quality, for instance, if a man sell an unhealthy animal as being a healthy one: and if anyone do this knowingly he is guilty of a fraudulent sale, and the sale, in consequence, is illicit.

In all these cases not only is the man guilty of a fraudulent sale, but he is also bound to restitution. But if any of the foregoing defects be in the thing sold, and he knows nothing about this, the seller does not sin, because he does that which is unjust materially, nor is his deed unjust, as shown above (Question [59], Article [2]). Nevertheless, he is bound to compensate the buyer, when the defect comes to his knowledge. Moreover what has been said of the seller applies equally to the buyer. For sometimes it happens that the seller thinks his goods to be specifically of lower value, as when a man sells gold instead of copper, and then if the buyer be aware of this, he buys it unjustly and is bound to restitution: and the same applies to a defect in quantity as to a defect in quality.

Reply to Objection 1: Gold and silver are costly not only on account of the usefulness of the vessels and other like things made from them, but also on account of the excellence and purity of their substance. Hence, if the gold or silver produced by alchemists has not the true specific nature of gold and silver, the sale thereof is fraudulent and unjust, especially as real gold and silver can produce certain results by their natural action, which the counterfeit gold and silver of alchemists cannot produce. Thus, the true metal has the property of making people joyful, and is helpful medicinally against certain maladies. Moreover, real gold can be employed more frequently, and lasts longer in its condition of purity than counterfeit gold. If, however, real gold were to be produced by alchemy, it would not be unlawful to sell it for the genuine article, for nothing prevents art from employing certain natural causes for the production of natural and true effects, as Augustine says (De Trin. iii, 8) of things produced by the art of the demons.

Reply to Objection 2: The measures of salable commodities must needs be different in different places, on account of the difference of supply: because where there is greater abundance, the measures are wont to be larger. However, in each place those who govern the state must determine the just measures of things salable, with due consideration for the conditions of place and time. Hence, it is not lawful to disregard such measures as are established by public authority or custom.

Reply to Objection 3: As Augustine says (De Civ. Dei xi, 16) the price of things salable does not depend on their degree of nature, since at times a horse fetches a higher price than a slave; but it depends on their usefulness to man. Hence, it is not necessary for the seller or buyer to be cognizant of the hidden qualities of the thing sold, but only of such as render the thing adapted to man's use, for instance, that the horse be strong, run well and so forth. Such qualities the seller and buyer can easily discover.

Article 3: Whether the seller is bound to state the defects of the thing sold?

Objection 1: It would seem that the seller is not bound to state the defects of the thing sold. Since the seller does not bind the buyer to buy, he would seem to leave it to him to judge of the goods offered for sale. Now judgment about a thing and knowledge of that thing belong to the same person. Therefore, it does not seem imputable to the seller if the buyer be deceived in his judgment, and be hurried into buying a thing without carefully inquiring into its condition.

Objection 2: Further, it seems foolish for anyone to do what prevents him carrying out his work. But if a man states the defects of the goods he has for sale, he prevents their sale: wherefore Tully (De Offic. iii, 13) pictures a man as saying: "Could anything be more absurd than for a public crier, instructed by the owner, to cry: 'I offer this unhealthy horse for sale?'" Therefore, the seller is not bound to state the defects of the thing sold.

Objection 3: Further, man needs more to know the road of virtue than to know the faults of things offered for sale. Now one is not bound to offer advice to all or to tell them the truth about matters pertaining to virtue, though one should not tell anyone what is false. Much less therefore is a seller bound to tell the faults of what he offers for sale, as though he were counseling the buyer.

Objection 4: Further, if one were bound to tell the faults of what one offers for sale, this would only be in order to lower the price. Now sometimes the price would be lowered for some other reason, without any defect in the thing sold: for instance, if the seller carry wheat to a place where wheat fetches a high price, knowing that many will come after him carrying wheat; because if the buyers knew this they would give a lower price. But apparently the seller need not give the buyer this information. Therefore, in like manner, neither need he tell him the faults of the goods he is selling.

On the contrary, Ambrose says (De Offic. iii, 10): "In all contracts the defects of the salable commodity must be stated; and unless the seller make them known, although the buyer has already acquired a right to them, the contract is voided on account of the fraudulent action."

I answer that, It is always unlawful to give anyone an occasion of danger or loss, although a man need not always give another the help or counsel which would be for his advantage in any way; but only in certain fixed cases, for instance, when someone is subject to him, or when he is the only one who can assist him. Now the seller who offers goods for sale, gives the buyer an occasion of loss or danger, by the very fact that he offers him defective goods, if such defect may occasion loss or danger to the buyer – loss, if, by reason of this defect, the goods are of less value, and he takes nothing off the price on that account – danger, if this defect either hinder the use of the goods or render it hurtful, for instance, if a man sells a lame for a fleet horse, a tottering house for a safe one, rotten or poisonous food for wholesome. Wherefore if such like defects be hidden, and the seller does not make them known, the sale will be illicit and fraudulent, and the seller will be bound to compensation for the loss incurred.

On the other hand, if the defect be manifest, for instance if a horse have but one eye, or if the goods though useless to the buyer, be useful to someone else, provided the seller take as much as he ought from the price, he is not bound to state the defect of the goods, since perhaps on account of that defect the buyer might want him to allow a greater rebate than he need. Wherefore the seller may look to his own indemnity, by withholding the defect of the goods.

Reply to Objection 1: Judgment cannot be pronounced save on what is manifest: for "a man judges of what he knows" (Ethic. i, 3). Hence, if the defects of the goods offered for sale be hidden, judgment of them is not sufficiently left with the buyer unless such defects be made known to him. The case would be different if the defects were manifest.

Reply to Objection 2: There is no need to publish beforehand by the public crier the defects of the goods one is offering for sale, because if he were to begin by announcing its defects, the bidders would be frightened to buy, through ignorance of other qualities that might render the thing good and serviceable. Such defect ought to be stated to each individual that offers to buy: and then he will be able to compare the various points, one with the other, the good with the bad: for nothing prevents that which is defective in one respect being useful in many others.

Reply to Objection 3: Although a man is not bound strictly speaking to tell everyone the truth about matters pertaining to virtue, yet he is so bound in a case when, unless he tells the truth, his conduct would endanger another man in detriment to virtue: and so it is in this case.

Reply to Objection 4: The defect in a thing makes it of less value now than it seems to be: but in the case cited, the goods are expected to be of less value at a future time, on account of the arrival of other merchants, which was not foreseen by the buyers. Wherefore the seller, since he sells his goods at the price actually offered him, does not seem to act contrary to justice through not stating what is going to happen. If however he were to do so, or if he lowered his price, it would be exceedingly virtuous on his part: although he does not seem to be bound to do this as a debt of justice.

Article 4: Whether, in trading, it is lawful to sell a thing at a higher price than what was paid for it?

Objection 1: It would seem that it is not lawful, in trading, to sell a thing for a higher price than we paid for it. For Chrysostom [*Hom. xxxviii in the Opus Imperfectum, falsely ascribed to St John Chrysostom] says on Mt. 21:12: "He that buys a thing in order that he may sell it, entire and unchanged, at a profit, is the trader who is cast out of God's temple." Cassiodorus speaks in the same sense in his commentary on Ps. 70:15, "Because I have not known learning, or trading" according to another version [*The Septuagint]: "What is trade," says he, "but buying at a cheap price with the purpose of retailing at a higher price?" and he adds: "Such were the tradesmen whom Our Lord cast out of the temple." Now no man is cast out of the temple except for a sin. Therefore, such like trading is sinful.

Objection 2: Further, it is contrary to justice to sell goods at a higher price than their worth, or to buy them for less than their value, as shown above (Article [1]). Now if you sell a thing for a higher price than you paid for it, you must either have bought it for less than its value, or sell it for more than its value. Therefore, this cannot be done without sin.

Objection 3: Further, Jerome says (Ep. ad Nepot. lii): "Shun, as you would the plague, a cleric who from being poor has become wealthy, or who, from being a nobody has become a celebrity." Now trading would net seem to be forbidden to clerics except on account of its sinfulness. Therefore, it is a sin in trading, to buy at a low price and to sell at a higher price.

On the contrary, Augustine commenting on Ps. 70:15, "Because I have not known learning," [*Cf. OBJ 1] says: "The greedy tradesman blasphemes over his losses; he lies and perjures himself over the price of his wares. But these are vices of the man, not of the craft, which can be exercised without these vices." Therefore, trading is not in itself unlawful.

I answer that, a tradesman is one whose business consists in the exchange of things. According to the Philosopher (Polit. i, 3), exchange of things is twofold; one, natural as it were, and necessary, whereby one commodity is exchanged for another, or money taken in exchange for a commodity, in order to satisfy the needs of life. Such like trading, properly speaking, does not belong to tradesmen, but rather to housekeepers or civil servants who have to provide the household or the state with the necessaries of life. The other kind of exchange is either that of money for money, or of any commodity for money, not on account of the necessities of life, but for profit, and this kind of exchange, properly speaking, regards tradesmen, according to the Philosopher (Polit. i, 3). The former kind of exchange is commendable because it supplies a natural need: but the latter is justly deserving of blame, because, considered in itself, it satisfies the greed for gain, which knows no limit and tends to infinity. Hence, trading, considered in itself, has a certain debasement attaching thereto, in so far as, by its very nature, it does not imply a virtuous or necessary end. Nevertheless, gain which is the end of trading, though not implying, by its nature, anything virtuous or necessary, does not, in itself, connote anything sinful or contrary to virtue: wherefore nothing prevents gain from being directed to some necessary or even virtuous end, and thus trading becomes lawful. Thus, for instance, a man may intend the moderate gain which he seeks to acquire by trading for the upkeep of his household, or for the assistance of the needy: or again, a man may take to trade for some public advantage, for instance, lest his country lack the necessaries of life, and seek gain, not as an end, but as payment for his labor.

Reply to Objection 1: The saying of Chrysostom refers to the trading which seeks gain as a last end. This is especially the case where a man sells something at a higher price without its undergoing any change. For if he sells at a higher price something that has changed for the better, he would seem to receive the reward of his labor. Nevertheless, the gain itself may be lawfully intended, not as a last end, but for the sake of some other end which is necessary or virtuous, as stated above.

Reply to Objection 2: Not everyone that sells at a higher price than he bought is a tradesman, but only he who buys that he may sell at a profit. If, on the contrary, he buys not for sale but for possession, and afterwards, for some reason wishes to sell, it is not a trade transaction even if he sell at a profit. For he may lawfully do this, either because he has bettered the thing, or because the value of the thing has changed with the change of place or time, or on account of the danger he incurs in transferring the thing from one place to another, or again in having it carried by another. In this sense neither buying nor selling is unjust.

Reply to Objection 3: Clerics should abstain not only from things that are evil in themselves, but even from those that have an appearance of evil. This happens in trading, both because it is directed to worldly gain, which clerics should despise, and because trading is open to so many vices, since "a merchant is hardly free from sins of the lips" [*A merchant is hardly free from negligence, and a huckster shall not be justified from the sins of the lips'] (Ecclus. 26:28). There is also another reason, because trading engages the mind too much with worldly cares, and consequently withdraws it from spiritual cares; wherefore the Apostle says (2Tim. 2:4): "No man being a soldier to God entangleth himself with secular businesses." Nevertheless, it is lawful for clerics to engage in the first mentioned kind of exchange, which is directed to supply the necessaries of life, either by buying or by selling.

(E) By sins committed in loans (Question [78])
Of the sin of usury (four articles)

We must now consider the sin of usury, which is committed in loans: and under this head there are four points of inquiry:

1   Whether it is a sin to take money as a price for money lent, which is to receive usury?
2   Whether it is lawful to lend money for any other kind of consideration, by way of payment for the loan?
3   Whether a man is bound to restore just gains derived from money taken in usury?
4   Whether it is lawful to borrow money under a condition of usury?

Article 1: Whether it is a sin to take usury for money lent?

Objection 1: It would seem that it is not a sin to take usury for money lent. For no man sins through following the example of Christ. But Our Lord said of Himself (Lk. 19:23): "At My coming I might have exacted it," that is, the money lent, "with usury." Therefore, it is not a sin to take usury for lending money.

Objection 2: Further, according to Ps. 18:8, "The law of the Lord is unspotted," because, to wit, it forbids sin. Now usury of a kind is allowed in the Divine law, according to Dt. 23:19,20: "Thou shalt not fenerate to thy brother money, nor corn, nor any other thing, but to the stranger": nay more, it is even promised as a reward for the observance of the Law, according to Dt. 28:12: "Thou shalt fenerate* to many nations, and shalt not borrow of any one." [*"Faeneraberis" – "Thou shalt lend upon usury." The Douay version has simply "lend." The objection lays stress on the word "faeneraberis": hence the necessity of rendering it by "fenerate."] Therefore, it is not a sin to take usury.

Objection 3: Further, in human affairs justice is determined by civil laws. Now civil law allows usury to be taken. Therefore, it seems to be lawful.

Objection 4: Further, the counsels are not binding under sin. But, among other counsels we find (Lk. 6:35): "Lend, hoping for nothing thereby." Therefore, it is not a sin to take usury.

Objection 5: Further, it does not seem to be in itself sinful to accept a price for doing what one is not bound to do. But one who has money is not bound in every case to lend it to his neighbor. Therefore, it is lawful for him sometimes to accept a price for lending it.

Objection 6: Further, silver made into coins does not differ specifically from silver made into a vessel. But it is lawful to accept a price for the loan of a silver vessel. Therefore, it is also lawful to accept a price for the loan of a silver coin. Therefore, usury is not in itself a sin.

Objection 7: Further, anyone may lawfully accept a thing which its owner freely gives him. Now he who accepts the loan, freely gives the usury. Therefore, he who lends may lawfully take the usury.

On the contrary, It is written (Ex. 22:25): "If thou lend money to any of thy people that is poor, that dwelleth with thee, thou shalt not be hard upon them as an extortioner, nor oppress them with usuries."

I answer that, to take usury for money lent is unjust in itself, because this is to sell what does not exist, and this evidently leads to inequality which is contrary to justice. In order to make this evident, we must observe that there are certain things the use of which consists in their consumption: thus we consume wine when we use it for drink and we consume wheat when we use it for food. Wherefore in such like things the use of the thing must not be reckoned apart from the thing itself, and whoever is granted the use of the thing, is granted the thing itself and for this reason, to lend things of this kind is to transfer the ownership. Accordingly if a man wanted to sell wine separately from the use of the wine, he would be selling the same thing twice, or he would be selling what does not exist, wherefore he would evidently commit a sin of injustice. In like manner he commits an injustice who lends wine or wheat, and asks for double payment, namely one, the return of the thing in equal measure, the other, the price of the use, which is called usury.

On the other hand, there are things the use of which does not consist in their consumption: thus to use a house is to dwell in it, not to destroy it. Wherefore in such things both may be granted: for instance, one man may hand over to another the ownership of his house while reserving to himself the use of it for a time, or vice versa, he may grant the use of the house, while retaining the ownership. For this reason a man may lawfully make a charge for the use of his house, and, besides this, revendicate the house from the person to whom he has granted its use, as happens in renting and letting a house.

Now money, according to the Philosopher (Ethic. v, 5; Polit. i, 3) was invented chiefly for the purpose of exchange: and consequently the proper and principal use of money is its consumption or alienation whereby it is sunk in exchange. Hence, it is by its very nature unlawful to take payment for the use of money lent, which payment is known as usury: and just as a man is bound to restore other ill-gotten goods, so is he bound to restore the money which he has taken in usury.

Reply to Objection 1: In this passage usury must be taken figuratively for the increase of spiritual goods which God exacts from us, for He wishes us ever to advance in the goods which we receive from Him: and this is for our own profit not for His.

Reply to Objection 2: The Jews were forbidden to take usury from their brethren, that is, from other Jews. By this we are given to understand that to take usury from any man is evil simply, because we ought to treat every man as our neighbor and brother, especially in the state of the Gospel, whereto all are called. Hence, it is said without any distinction in Ps. 14:5: "He that hath not put out his money to usury," and (Ezech. 18:8): "Who hath not taken usury [*Vulg.: 'If a man … hath not lent upon money, nor taken any increase … he is just.']." They were permitted, however, to take usury from foreigners, not as though it were lawful, but in order to avoid a greater evil, lest, to wit, through avarice to which they were prone according to Is.56:11, they should take usury from the Jews who were worshippers of God.

Where we find it promised to them as a reward, "Thou shalt fenerate to many nations," etc., fenerating is to be taken in a broad sense for lending, as in Ecclus. 29:10, where we read: "Many have refused to fenerate, not out of wickedness," that is, they would not lend. Accordingly the Jews are promised in reward an abundance of wealth, so that they would be able to lend to others.

Reply to Objection 3: Human laws leave certain things unpunished, on account of the condition of those who are imperfect, and who would be deprived of many advantages, if all sins were strictly forbidden and punishments appointed for them. Wherefore human law has permitted usury, not that it looks upon usury as harmonizing with justice, but lest the advantage of many should be hindered. Hence, it is that in civil law [*Inst. II, iv, de Usufructu] it is stated that "those things according to natural reason and civil law which are consumed by being used, do not admit of usufruct," and that "the senate did not (nor could it) appoint a usufruct to such things, but established a quasi-usufruct," namely by permitting usury. Moreover the Philosopher, led by natural reason, says (Polit. i, 3) that "to make money by usury is exceedingly unnatural."

Reply to Objection 4: A man is not always bound to lend, and for this reason it is placed among the counsels. Yet, it is a matter of precept not to seek profit by lending: although it may be called a matter of counsel in comparison with the maxims of the Pharisees, who deemed some kinds of usury to be lawful, just as love of one's enemies is a matter of counsel. Or again, He speaks here not of the hope of usurious gain, but of the hope which is put in man. For we ought not to lend or do any good deed through hope in man, but only through hope in God.

Reply to Objection 5: He that is not bound to lend, may accept repayment for what he has done but he must not exact more. Now he is repaid according to equality of justice if he is repaid as much as he lent. Wherefore if he exacts more for the usufruct of a thing which has no other use but the consumption of its substance, he exacts a price of something non-existent: and so his exaction is unjust.

Reply to Objection 6: The principal use of a silver vessel is not its consumption, and so one may lawfully sell its use while retaining one's ownership of it. On the other hand, the principal use of silver money is sinking it in exchange, so that it is not lawful to sell its use and at the same time expect the restitution of the amount lent. It must be observed, however, that the secondary use of silver vessels may be an exchange, and such use may not be lawfully sold. In like manner there may be some secondary use of silver money; for instance, a man might lend coins for show, or to be used as security.

Reply to Objection 7: He who gives usury does not give it voluntarily simply, but under a certain necessity, in so far as he needs to borrow money which the owner is unwilling to lend without usury.

Article 2: Whether it is lawful to ask for any other kind of consideration for money lent?

Objection 1: It would seem that one may ask for some other kind of consideration for money lent. For everyone may lawfully seek to indemnify himself. Now sometimes a man suffers loss through lending money. Therefore, he may lawfully ask for or even exact something else besides the money lent.

Objection 2: Further, as stated in Ethic. v, 5, one is in duty bound by a point of honor, to repay anyone who has done us a favor. Now to lend money to one who is in straits is to do him a favor for which he should be grateful. Therefore, the recipient of a loan, is bound by a natural debt to repay something. Now it does not seem unlawful to bind oneself to an obligation of the natural law. Therefore, it is not unlawful, in lending money to anyone, to demand some sort of compensation as condition of the loan.

Objection 3: Further, just as there is real remuneration, so is there verbal remuneration, and remuneration by service, as a gloss says on Is. 33:15, "Blessed is he that shaketh his hands from all bribes [*Vulg.: 'Which of you shall dwell with everlasting burnings? ... He that shaketh his hands from all bribes.']." Now it is lawful to accept service or praise from one to whom one has lent money. Therefore, in like manner it is lawful to accept any other kind of remuneration.

Objection 4: Further, seemingly the relation of gift to gift is the same as of loan to loan. But it is lawful to accept money for money given. Therefore, it is lawful to accept repayment by loan in return for a loan granted.

Objection 5: Further, the lender, by transferring his ownership of a sum of money removes the money further from himself than he who entrusts it to a merchant or craftsman. Now it is lawful to receive interest for money entrusted to a merchant or craftsman. Therefore, it is also lawful to receive interest for money lent.

Objection 6: Further, a man may accept a pledge for money lent, the use of which pledge he might sell for a price: as when a man mortgages his land or the house wherein he dwells. Therefore, it is lawful to receive interest for money lent.

Objection 7: Further, it sometimes happens that a man raises the price of his goods under guise of loan, or buys another's goods at a low figure; or raises his price through delay in being paid, and lowers his price that he may be paid the sooner. Now in all these cases there seems to be payment for a loan of money: nor does it appear to be manifestly illicit. Therefore, it seems to be lawful to expect or exact some consideration for money lent.

On the contrary, among other conditions requisite in a just man it is stated (Ezech. 18:17) that he "hath not taken usury and increase."

I answer that, according to the Philosopher (Ethic. iv, 1), a thing is reckoned as money "if its value can be measured by money." Consequently, just as it is a sin against justice, to take money, by tacit or express agreement, in return for lending money or anything else that is consumed by being used, so also is it a like sin, by tacit or express agreement to receive anything whose price can be measured by money. Yet, there would be no sin in receiving something of the kind, not as exacting it, nor yet as though it were due on account of some agreement tacit or expressed, but as a gratuity: since, even before lending the money, one could accept a gratuity, nor is one in a worse condition through lending.

On the other hand, it is lawful to exact compensation for a loan, in respect of such things as are not appreciated by a measure of money, for instance, benevolence, and love for the lender, and so forth.

Reply to Objection 1: A lender may without sin enter an agreement with the borrower for compensation for the loss he incurs of something he ought to have, for this is not to sell the use of money but to avoid a loss. It may also happen that the borrower avoids a greater loss than the lender incurs, wherefore the borrower may repay the lender with what he has gained. But the lender cannot enter an agreement for compensation, through the fact that he makes no profit out of his money: because he must not sell that which he has not yet and may be prevented in many ways from having.

Reply to Objection 2: Repayment for a favor may be made in two ways. In one way, as a debt of justice; and to such a debt a man may be bound by a fixed contract; and its amount is measured according to the favor received. Wherefore the borrower of money or any such thing the use of which is its consumption is not bound to repay more than he received in loan: and consequently it is against justice if he be obliged to pay back more. In another way a man's obligation to repayment for favor received is based on a debt of friendship, and the nature of this debt depends more on the feeling with which the favor was conferred than on the greatness of the favor itself. This debt does not carry with it a civil obligation, involving a kind of necessity that would exclude the spontaneous nature of such a repayment.

Reply to Objection 3: If a man were, in return for money lent, as though there had been an agreement tacit or expressed, to expect or exact repayment in the shape of some remuneration of service or words, it would be the same as if he expected or exacted some real remuneration, because both can be priced at a money value, as may be seen in the case of those who offer for hire the labor which they exercise by work or by tongue. If on the other hand, the remuneration by service or words be given not as an obligation, but as a favor, which is not to be appreciated at a money value, it is lawful to take, exact, and expect it.

Reply to Objection 4: Money cannot be sold for a greater sum than the amount lent, which has to be paid back: nor should the loan be made with a demand or expectation of aught else but of a feeling of benevolence which cannot be priced at a pecuniary value, and which can be the basis of a spontaneous loan. Now the obligation to lend in return at some future time is repugnant to such a feeling, because again an obligation of this kind has its pecuniary value. Consequently it is lawful for the lender to borrow something else at the same time, but it is unlawful for him to bind the borrower to grant him a loan at some future time.

Reply to Objection 5: He who lends money transfers the ownership of the money to the borrower. Hence, the borrower holds the money at his own risk and is bound to pay it all back: wherefore the lender must not exact more. On the other hand, he that entrusts his money to a merchant or craftsman so as to form a kind of society, does not transfer the ownership of his money to them, for it remains his, so that at his risk the merchant speculates with it, or the craftsman uses it for his craft, and consequently he may lawfully demand as something belonging to him, part of the profits derived from his money.

Reply to Objection 6: If a man in return for money lent to him pledges something that can be valued at a price, the lender must allow for the use of that thing towards the repayment of the loan. Else if he wishes the gratuitous use of that thing in addition to repayment, it is the same as if he took money for lending, and that is usury, unless perhaps it were such a thing as friends are wont to lend to one another gratis, as in the case of the loan of a book.

Reply to Objection 7: If a man wish to sell his goods at a higher price than that which is just, so that he may wait for the buyer to pay, it is manifestly a case of usury: because this waiting for the payment of the price has the character of a loan, so that whatever he demands beyond the just price in consideration of this delay, is like a price for a loan, which pertains to usury. In like manner if a buyer wishes to buy goods at a lower price than what is just, for the reason that he pays for the goods before they can be delivered, it is a sin of usury; because again this anticipated payment of money has the character of a loan, the price of which is the rebate on the just price of the goods sold. On the other hand, if a man wishes to allow a rebate on the just price in order that he may have his money sooner, he is not guilty of the sin of usury.

Article 3: Whether a man is bound to restore whatever profits he has made out of money gotten by usury?

Objection 1: It would seem that a man is bound to restore whatever profits he has made out of money gotten by usury. For the Apostle says (Rm. 11:16): "If the root be holy, so are the branches." Therefore, likewise if the root be rotten so are the branches. But the root was infected with usury. Therefore, whatever profit is made therefrom is infected with usury. Therefore, he is bound to restore it.

Objection 2: Further, it is laid down (Extra, De Usuris, in the Decretal: 'Cum tu sicut asseris'): "Property accruing from usury must be sold, and the price repaid to the persons from whom the usury was extorted." Therefore, likewise, whatever else is acquired from usurious money must be restored.

Objection 3: Further, that which a man buys with the proceeds of usury is due to him by reason of the money he paid for it. Therefore, he has no more right to the thing purchased than to the money he paid. But he was bound to restore the money gained through usury. Therefore, he is also bound to restore what he acquired with it.

On the contrary, a man may lawfully hold what he has lawfully acquired. Now that which is acquired by the proceeds of usury is sometimes lawfully acquired. Therefore, it may be lawfully retained.

I answer that, as stated above (Article [1]), there are certain things whose use is their consumption, and which do not admit of usufruct, according to law (ibid., ad 3). Wherefore if such like things be extorted by means of usury, for instance money, wheat, wine and so forth, the lender is not bound to restore more than he received (since what is acquired by such things is the fruit not of the thing but of human industry), unless indeed the other party by losing some of his own goods be injured through the lender retaining them: for then he is bound to make good the loss.

On the other hand, there are certain things whose use is not their consumption: such things admit of usufruct, for instance, house or land property and so forth. Wherefore if a man has by usury extorted from another his house or land, he is bound to restore not only the house or land but also the fruits accruing to him therefrom, since they are the fruits of things owned by another man and consequently are due to him.

Reply to Objection 1: The root has not only the character of matter, as money made by usury has; but has also somewhat the character of an active cause, in so far as it administers nourishment. Hence, the comparison fails.

Reply to Objection 2: Further, property acquired from usury does not belong to the person who paid usury, but to the person who bought it. Yet, he that paid usury has a certain claim on that property just as he has on the other goods of the usurer. Hence, it is not prescribed that such property should be assigned to the persons who paid usury, since the property is perhaps worth more than what they paid in usury, but it is commanded that the property be sold, and the price be restored, of course according to the amount taken in usury.

Reply to Objection 3: The proceeds of money taken in usury are due to the person who acquired them not by reason of the usurious money as instrumental cause, but on account of his own industry as principal cause. Wherefore he has more right to the goods acquired with usurious money than to the usurious money itself.

Article 4: Whether it is lawful to borrow money under a condition of usury?

Objection 1: It would seem that it is not lawful to borrow money under a condition of usury. For the Apostle says (Rm. 1:32) that they "are worthy of death … not only they that do" these sins, "but they also that consent to them that do them." Now he that borrows money under a condition of usury consents in the sin of the usurer, and gives him an occasion of sin. Therefore, he sins also.

Objection 2: Further, for no temporal advantage ought one to give another an occasion of committing a sin: for this pertains to active scandal, which is always sinful, as stated above (Question [43], Article [2]). Now he that seeks to borrow from a usurer gives him an occasion of sin. Therefore, he is not to be excused on account of any temporal advantage.

Objection 3: Further, it seems no less necessary sometimes to deposit one's money with a usurer than to borrow from him. Now it seems altogether unlawful to deposit one's money with a usurer, even as it would be unlawful to deposit one's sword with a madman, a maiden with a libertine, or food with a glutton. Neither, therefore, is it lawful to borrow from a usurer.

On the contrary, he that suffers injury does not sin, according to the Philosopher (Ethic. v, 11), wherefore justice is not a mean between two vices, as stated in the same book (ch. 5). Now a usurer sins by doing an injury to the person who borrows from him under a condition of usury. Therefore, he that accepts a loan under a condition of usury does not sin.

I answer that, it is by no means lawful to induce a man to sin, yet it is lawful to make use of another's sin for a good end, since even God uses all sin for some good, since He draws some good from every evil as stated in the Enchiridion (xi). Hence, when Publicola asked whether it were lawful to make use of an oath taken by a man swearing by false gods (which is a manifest sin, for he gives Divine honor to them) Augustine (Ep. xlvii) answered that he who uses, not for a bad but for a good purpose, the oath of a man that swears by false gods, is a party, not to his sin of swearing by demons, but to his good compact whereby he kept his word. If, however, he were to induce him to swear by false gods, he would sin.

Accordingly, we must also answer to the question in point that it is by no means lawful to induce a man to lend under a condition of usury: yet it is lawful to borrow for usury from a man who is ready to do so and is a usurer by profession; provided the borrower have a good end in view, such as the relief of his own or another's need. Thus too it is lawful for a man who has fallen among thieves to point out his property to them (which they sin in taking) in order to save his life, after the example of the ten men who said to Ismahel (Jer. 41:8): "Kill us not: for we have stores in the field."

Reply to Objection 1: He who borrows for usury does not consent to the usurer's sin but makes use of it. Nor is it the usurer's acceptance of usury that pleases him, but his lending, which is good.

Reply to Objection 2: He who borrows for usury gives the usurer an occasion, not for taking usury, but for lending; it is the usurer who finds an occasion of sin in the malice of his heart. Hence, there is passive scandal on his part, while there is no active scandal on the part of the person who seeks to borrow. Nor is this passive scandal a reason why the other person should desist from borrowing if he is in need, since this passive scandal arises not from weakness or ignorance but from malice.

Reply to Objection 3: If one were to entrust one's money to a usurer lacking other means of practising usury; or with the intention of making a greater profit from his money by reason of the usury, one would be giving a sinner matter for sin, so that one would be a participator in his guilt. If, on the other hand, the usurer to whom one entrusts one's money has other means of practising usury, there is no sin in entrusting it to him that it may be in safer keeping, since this is to use a sinner for a good purpose.

THOMAS MUN (1571–1641)

By the seventeenth century the spread of production for market, the extension of markets, and the growth of commerce throughout Europe had accelerated from ancient, if gradual, beginnings and from their marked establishment between the thirteenth and fifteenth centuries. Organized religion – still widely Catholic on the mainland but eventually Anglican in England and also Protestant in various areas after the mid-sixteenth century) – remained strong. But new values were coming to dominate life, including spiritual approval of work and the accumulation of wealth, altogether a preoccupation with personal material success in this world. One result was a set of practices and an associated belief system now called Mercantilism.

Mercantilism was a complex attitude of mind and practice which had several elements centering on the exercise of government authority, now doing on the national level what local governments had long been undertaking among and against each other, to promote internal economic interests by adopting policies aimed at generating a favorable balance of payments, for the purposes of business profit, royal revenue, and economic prosperity. The means included tariff protection against imports; selective subsidies of production and exports; the acquisition of colonies, which provided raw materials and a workforce of settlers and native peoples at low cost, a market for the mother country's finished goods, a monopoly of colonial trade and shipping, and a direct contribution to the power and prestige of empire; the development of naval power; and measures to minimize the cost of maintaining the domestic population, such as low agricultural prices, low wages, fisheries for cheap food, and so on. Doctrinal emphases on the utility of poverty and on the importance of gold holdings served instrumental purposes for those seeking power and profit.

These ideas are easily lambasted; for example, competitive protectionism is a basis for neither world order nor economic growth. But the variety of Mercantilist authors and pamphleteers constituted the first major group of economic thinkers, the first group to envision an increase of wealth as either a good in itself or a means to a related end, and to develop a corpus of analysis on that basis. Theirs was, given their felt interests, a high level of analysis of both processes and means–ends relations. They generally understood both the relationship of the quantity of money to the level of prices and the (related) working of the specie-flow mechanism between countries, their understanding adjusted, as it were, to their point of view. All of this was correlative with the growth of commerce and, especially, a money economy. Mercantilism, or the commercial system, was the first stage of the modern economy and was the policy of early modern states.

Thomas Mun (1571–1641) was a wealthy merchant and a director of the East India Company, and his *England's Treasure by Forraign Trade* was one of the most sophisticated works affirming Mercantilist policy. The East India Company's activities were controversial because their purchases of goods from the East Indies resulted in outflows of bullion – contrary to mercantilist precepts. Mun's emphasis on the net inflow of specie that resulted from the larger body of international trade set him apart from many other mercantilist writers who saw a ban on bullion exports as a key to the promotion of national welfare – and, in the hands of some, national wealth. In the excerpts from *England's Treasure* provided here, we see some of the classic mercantilist themes: the issue of the relationship between national wealth and bullion ("treasure"), the maximization of net exports, the virtues of the re-export trade and the implications for bullion export restrictions, the rationale for bullion accumulation by the crown, and the measurement of the gains from trade.

References and further reading

Allen, William R. (1987) "Mercantilism," in John Eatwell, Murray Milgate, and Peter Newman (eds), *The New Palgrave: A Dictionary of Economics*, Vol. 3, London: Macmillan, 445–49.

Beer, Max (1938) *Early British Economics*, London: George Allen & Unwin.

Coleman, D.C., ed. (1969) *Revisions in Mercantilism*, London: Methuen.

Eltis, Walter (1987) "Mun, Thomas," in John Eatwell, Murray Milgate, and Peter Newman (eds), *The New Palgrave: A Dictionary of Economics*, Vol. 3, London: Macmillan, 576–77.

Grampp, W.D. (1952) "The Liberal Elements in English Mercantilism," *Quarterly Journal of Economics* 66 (November): 465–502.

Heckscher, Eli F. (1935) *Mercantilism*, London: George Allen & Unwin. Reprinted with a new introduction by Lars Magnusson, London: Routledge, 1994.

Letwin, William (1964) *The Origins of Scientific Economics*, Garden City, New York: Doubleday & Co.

Magnusson, Lars (1993a) *Mercantilism: The Shaping of Economic Language*, London: Routledge.

——ed. (1993b) *Mercantilist Economics*, Boston: Kluwer.

Malynes, Gerrard de (1601) *A Treatise of the Canker of England's Common Wealth*, London.

——(1622) *Consuetudo, vel, Lex Mercatoria*, London.

——(1623) *The Center of the Circle of Commerce*, London.

Misselden, Edward (1623) *The Circle of Commerce*, London.

Schmoller, Gustav (1897) *The Mercantile System*, New York: Macmillan.

Viner, Jacob (1930) "English Theories of Foreign Trade Before Adam Smith," *Journal of Political Economy* 38: 249–310, 404–57. Reprinted as chapts. I and II in *Studies in the Theory of International Trade*, New York: Harper & Row, 1937.

England's Treasure by Forraign Trade or the Ballance of our Forraign Trade is the Rule of our Treasure (1664)*

Chapter 2: The Means to enrich this Kingdom, and to encrease our Treasure

Although a Kingdom may be enriched by gifts received, or by purchase taken from some other Nations, yet these are things uncertain and of small consideration when they happen. The ordinary means therefore to encrease our wealth and treasure is by Forraign Trade, wherein wee must ever observe this rule; to sell more to strangers yearly than wee consume of theirs in value. For suppose that when this Kingdom is plentifully served with the Cloth, Lead, Tinn, Iron, Fish and other native commodities, we doe yearly export the overplus to forraign Countries to the value of twenty two hundred thousand pounds; by which means we are enabled beyond the Seas to buy and bring in forraign wares for our use and Consumption, to the value of twenty hundred thousand pounds; By this order duly kept in our trading, we may rest assured that the Kingdom shall be enriched yearly two hundred thousand pounds, which must be brought to us in so much Treasure; because that part of our stock which is not returned to us in wares must necessarily be brought home in treasure.

For in this case it cometh to pass in the stock of a Kingdom, as in the estate of a private man; who is supposed to have one thousand pounds yearly revenue and two thousand pounds of ready money in his Chest: If such a man through excess shall spend one thousand five hundred pounds per annum, all his ready mony will be gone in four years; and in the like time his said money will be doubled if he take a Frugal course to spend but five hundred pounds per annum; which rule never faileth likewise in the Commonwealth, but in some cases (of no great moment) which I will hereafter declare, when I shall shew by whom and in what manner this ballance of the Kingdoms account ought to be drawn up yearly, or so often as it shall please the State to discover how much we gain or lose by trade with forraign Nations. But first I will say something concerning those ways and means which will encrease our exportations and diminish our importations of wares; which being done, I will then set down some other arguments both affirmative and negative to strengthen that which is here declared, and thereby to shew that all the other means which are commonly supposed to enrich the Kingdom with Treasure are altogether insufficient and meer fallacies.

Chapter 3: The particular ways and means to encrease the exportation of our commodities, and to decrease our Consumption of forraign wares

The revenue or stock of a Kingdom by which it is provided of forraign wares is either Natural or Artificial. The Natural wealth is so much only as can be spared from our own use and necessities

* Written by Thomas Mun of Lond. Merchant, and now published for the Common good by his son John Mun of Bearsted in the County of Kent, Esquire. London, Printed by J.G. for Thomas Clark, and are to be sold at his Shop at the South entrance of the Royal Exchange, 1664.

to be exported unto strangers. The Artificial consists in our manufactures and industrious trading with forraign commodities, concerning which I will set down such particulars as may serve for the cause we have in hand.

1. First, although this Realm be already exceeding rich by nature, yet might it be much encreased by laying the waste grounds (which are infinite) into such employments as should no way hinder the present revenues of other manufactured lands, but hereby to supply our selves and prevent the importations of Hemp, Flax, Cordage, Tobacco, and divers other things which now we fetch from strangers to our great impoverishing.

2. We may likewise diminish our importations, if we would soberly refrain from excessive consumption of forraign wares in our diet and rayment, with such often change of fashions as is used, so much the more to encrease the waste and charge; which vices at this present are more notorious amongst us than in former ages. Yet might they easily be amended by enforcing the observation of such good laws as are strictly practised in other Countrey against the said excesses; where likewise by commanding their own manufactures to be used, they prevent the coming in of others, without prohibition, or offence to strangers in their mutual commerce.

3. In our exportations we must not only regard our own superfluities, but also we must consider our neighbours necessities, that so upon the wares which they cannot want, nor yet be furnished thereof elsewhere, we may (besides the vent of the Materials) gain so much of the manufacture as we can, and also endeavour to sell them dear, so far forth as the high price cause not a less vent in the quantity. But the superfluity of our commodities which strangers use, and may also have the same from other Nations, or may abate their vent by the use of some such like wares from other places, and with little inconvenience; we must in this case strive to sell as cheap as possible we can, rather than to lose the utterance of such wares. For we have found of late years by good experience, that being able to sell our Cloth cheap in Turkey, we have greatly encreased the vent thereof, and the Venetians have lost as much in the utterance of theirs in those Countreys, because it is dearer. And on the other side, a few years past, when by excessive price of Wools our Cloth was exceeding dear, we lost at the least half our clothing for forraign parts, which since is no otherwise (well neer) recovered again than by the great fall of price for Wools and Cloth. We find that twenty five in the hundred less in the price of these and some other Wares, to the loss of private mens revenues, may raise above fifty upon the hundred in the quantity vented to the benefit of the publique. For when Cloth is dear, other Nations doe presently practise clothing, and we know they want neither art nor materials to this performance. But when by cheapness we drive them from this employment, and so in time obtain our dear price again, then do they also use their former remedy. So that by these alterations we learn, that it is in vain to expect a greater revenue of our wares than their condition will afford, but rather it concerns us to apply our endeavours to the times with care and diligence to help our selves the best we may, by making our cloth and other manufactures without deceit, which will encrease their estimation and use.

4. The value of our exportations likewise may be much advanced when we perform it our selves in our own Ships, for then we get only not the price of our wares as they are worth here, but also the Merchants gains, the changes of ensurance, and fraight to carry them beyond the seas. As for example, if the Italian Merchants should come hither in their own shipping to fetch our Corn, our red Herrings or the like, in the case the Kingdom should have ordinarily but twenty-five shillings for a quarter of Wheat, and twenty shillings for a barrel of red herrings, whereas if we carry these wares our selves into Italy upon the said rates, it is likely that wee shall obtain fifty shillings for the first, and forty shillings for the last, which is a great difference in the utterance or vent of the Kingdoms stock. And although it is true that the commerce ought to be free to strangers to bring in and carry out at their pleasure, yet nevertheless in many places the exportation of victuals and munition are either prohibited, or at least limited to be done onely by the people and Shipping of those places where they abound.

5. The frugal expending likewise of our own natural wealth might advance much yearly to be exported unto strangers; and if in our rayment we will be prodigal, yet let this be done with our own materials and manufactures, as Cloth, Lace, Imbroderies, Cutworks and the like, where the excess of the rich may be the employment of the poor, whose labours notwithstanding of this kind, would be more profitable for the Commonwealth, if they were done to the use of strangers.

6. The Fishing in his Majesties seas of England, Scotland and Ireland is our natural wealth, and would cost nothing but labour, which the Dutch bestow willingly, and thereby draw yearly a very great profit to themselves by serving many places of Christendom with our Fish, for which they return and supply their wants both of forraign Wares and Mony, besides the multitude of Mariners and Shipping, which hereby are maintain'd, whereof a long discourse might be made to shew the particular manage of this important business. Our Fishing plantation likewise in New England, Virginia, Groenland, the Summer Islands and the New-found-land, are of the like nature, affording much wealth and employments to maintain a great number of poor, and to encrease our decaying trade.

7. A Staple or Magazin for forraign Corn, Indico, Spices, Raw-silks, Cotton wool or any other commodity whatsoever, to be imported will encrease Shipping, Trade, Treasure, and the Kings customes, by exporting them again where need shall require, which course of Trading, hath been the chief means to raise Venice, Genoa, the low-Countreys, with some others; and for such a purpose England stands most commodiously, wanting nothing to this performance but our own diligence and endeavour.

8. Also wee ought to esteem and cherish those trades which we have in remote or far Countreys, for besides the encrease of Shipping and Mariners thereby, the wares also sent thither and receiv'd from thence are far more profitable unto the kingdom than by our trades neer at hand: As for example; suppose Pepper to be worth here two Shillings the pound constantly, if then it be brought from the Dutch at Amsterdam, the Merchant may give there twenty pence the pound, and gain well by the bargain; but if he fetch this Pepper from the East-Indies, he must not give above three pence the pound at the most, which is a mighty advantage, not only in that part which serveth for our own use, but also for that great quantity which (from hence) we transport yearly unto divers other Nations to be sold at a higher price: whereby it is plain, that we make a far greater stock by gain upon these Indian Commodities, than those Nations doe where they grow, and to whom they properly appertain, being the natural wealth of their Countrey. But for the better understanding of this particular, we must ever distinguish between the gain of the Kingdom, and the profit of the Merchant; for although the Kingdom payeth no more for this Pepper than is before supposed, nor for any other commodity bought in forraign parts more than the stranger receiveth from us for the same, yet the Merchant payeth not only that price, but also the fraight, ensurance, customes and other charges which are exceeding great in these long voyages; but yet all these in the Kingdoms accompt are but commutations among our selves, and no Privation of the Kingdoms stock, which being duly considered, together with the support also of our other trades in our best Shipping to Italy, France, Turkey, and East Countreys and other places, by transporting and venting the wares which we bring yearly from the East Indies; It may well stir up our utmost endeavours to maintain and enlarge this great and noble business, so much importing the Publique wealth, Strength, and Happiness. Neither is there less honour and judgment by growing rich (in this manner) upon the stock of other Nations, than by an industrious encrease of our own means, especially when this later is advanced by the benefit of the former, as we have found in the East Indies by sale of much of our Tin, Cloth, Lead, and other Commodities, the vent whereof doth daily encrease in those Countreys which formerly had no use of our wares.

9. It would be very beneficial to export money as well as wares, being done in trade only, it would encrease our Treasure; but of this I write more largely in the next chapter to prove it plainly.

10. It were policie and profit for the State to suffer manufactures made of forraign Materials to be exported custome-free, as Velvets and all other wrought Silks, Fustians, thrown Silks and the like, it would employ very many poor people, and much encrease the value of our stock yearly issued into other Countreys, and it would (for this purpose) cause the more forraign Materials to be brought in, to the improvement of His Majesties Customes. I will here remember a notable encrease in our manufacture of winding and twisting only of forraign raw Silk, which within 35 years to my knowledge did not employ more than 300 people in the City and suburbs of London, where at this present time it doth set on work above fourteen thousand souls, as upon diligent enquiry hath been credibly reported unto His Majesties Commissioners for Trade. and it is certain, that if the raid forraign Commodities might be exported from hence, free of custome, this manufacture would yet encrease very much, and decrease as fast in Italy and in the Netherlands. But if any man allege the Dutch proverb, Live and let others live; I answer, that the Dutchmen notwithstanding their own Proverb, doe not onely in these Kingdoms, encroach upon our livings, but also in other forraign parts of our trade (where they have power) they do hinder and destroy us in our lawful course of living, hereby taking the bread out of our mouth, which we shall never prevent by plucking the pot from their nose, as of late years too many of us do practise to the great hurt and dishonour of this famous Nation; We ought rather to imitate former times in taking sober and worthy courses more pleasing to God and suitable to our ancient reputation.

11. It is needful also not to charge the native commodities with too great customes, lest by indearing them to the strangers use, it hinder their vent. And especially forraign wares brought in to be transported again should be favoured, for otherwise that manner of trading (so much importing the good of the Commonwealth) cannot prosper nor subsist. But the Consumption of such forraign wares in the Realm may be the more charged, which will turn to the profit of the kingdom in the Ballance of the Trade, and thereby also enable the King to lay up the more Treasure out of his yearly incomes, as of this particular I intend to write more fully in his proper place, where I shall shew how much money a Prince may conveniently lay up without the hurt of his subjects.

12. Lastly, in all things we must endeavour to make the most we can of our own, whether it be Natural or Artificial, And forasmuch as the people which live by the Arts are far more in number than they who are masters of the fruits, we ought the more carefully to maintain those endeavours of the multitude, in whom doth consist the greatest strength and riches both of the King and Kingdom: for where the people are many, and the arts good, there the traffique must be great, and the Countrey rich. The Italians employ a greater number of people; and get more money by their industry and manufactures of the raw Silks of the Kingdom of Cicilia, than the King of Spain and his Subjects have by the revenue of this rich commodity. But what need we fetch the example so far, when we know that our own natural wares doe not yeild us so much profit as our industry? For Iron oar in the Mines is of no great worth, when it is compared with the employment and advantage it yields being digged, tried, transported, brought, sold, cast into Ordnance, Muskets, and many other instruments of war for offence and defence, wrought into Anchors, bolts, spikes, nayles and the like, for the use of Ships, Houses, Carts, Coaches, Ploughs, and other instruments for Tillage. Compare our Fleece-wools with our Cloth, which requires shearing, washing, carding, spinning, Weaving, fulling, dying, dressing and other trimmings, and we shall find these Arts more profitable than the natural wealth, whereof I might instance other examples, but I will not be more tedious, for if I would amplify upon this and the other particulars before written, I might find matter sufficient to make a large volume, but my desire in all is only to prove what I propound with breviity and plainness.

Chapter 4: The Exportation of our Moneys in Trade of Merchandize is a means to encrease our Treasure

This Position is so contrary to the common opinion, that it will require many and strong arguments to prove it before it can be accepted of the Multitude, who bitterly exclaim when they see any monies carried out of the Realm; affirming thereupon that wee have absolutely lost so much Treasure, and that this is an act directly against the long continued laws made and confirmed by the wisdom of this Kingdom in the High Court of Parliament, and that many places, nay Spain it self which is the Fountain of Mony, forbids the exportation thereof, some cases only excepted. To all which I might answer, that Venice, Florence, Genoa, the Low Countreys and divers other places permit it, their people applaud it, and find great benefit by it; but all this makes a noise and proves nothing, we must therefore come to those reasons which concern the business in question.

First, I will take that for granted which no man of judgment will deny, that we have no other means to get Treasure but by forraign trade, for Mines wee have none which do afford it, and how this mony is gotten in the managing of our said Trade I have already shewed, that it is done by making our commodities which are exported yearly to over ballance in value the forraign wares which we consume; so that it resteth only to shew how our monyes may be added to our commodities, and being jointly exported may so much the more encrease our Treasure.

We have already supposed our yearly consumption of forraign wares to be for the value of twenty hundred thousand pounds, and our exportations to exceed that two hundred thousand pounds, which sum wee have thereupon affirmed is brought to us in treasure to ballance accompt. But now if we add three thousand pounds mor in ready mony unto our former exportations in wares, what profit can we have (will some men say) although by this means we should bring in so much ready mony more than wee did before, seeing that wee have carried out the like value.

To this the answer is, that when wee have prepared our exportations of wares, and sent out as much of every thing as wee can spare or vent abroad: It is not therefore said that then we should add our money thereunto to fetch in the more mony immediately, but rather first to enlarge our trade by enabling us to bring in more forraign wares, which being sent out again will in due time much encrease our Treasure.

For although in this manner wee do yearly multiply our importation to the maintenance of more Shipping and Mariners, improvement of His Majesties Customs and other benefits: yet our consumption of those forraign wares is no more than it was before; so that all the said encrease of commodities brought in by the means of our ready mony sent out as is afore written, doth in the end become an exportation unto us of a far greater value than our said moneys were, which is proved by three several examples following.

1. For I suppose that hundred thousand livres being sent in our Shipping to the East Countreys, will buy there one hundred thousand quarters of wheat cleer aboard the Ships, which being after brought into England and housed, to export the same at the best time for vent thereof in Spain or Italy, it cannot yield less in those parts than two hundred thousand pounds to make the Merchant but a saver, yet by this reckning wee see the Kingdom hath doubled that Treasure.

2. Again this profit will be far greater when wee trade thus in remote Countreys, as for example, if wee send one hundred thousand pounds into the East-Indies to buy Pepper there, and bring it hither, and from hence send it for Italy or Turkey, it must yield seven hundred thousand pounds at least in those places, in regard of the excessive charge which the Merchant disburseth in those long voyages in Shipping, Wages, Victuals, Insurance, Interest, Customes, Imposts, and the like, all which notwithstanding the King and the Kingdom gets.

3. But where the voyages are short and the wares rich, which therefore will not employ much Shipping, the profit will be far less. As when another hundred thousand pounds shall be employed in Turkey in raw Silks, and brought hither to be after transported from hence into France, the Low Countreys, or Germany, the Merchant shall have good gain, although he sell it there but for one hundred and fifty thousand pounds: and thus take the voyages altogether in their Medium, the moneys exported will be returned unto us more than Trebled. But if any man will yet object, that these returns come to us in wares, and not really in mony as they were issued out.

The answer is (keeping our first ground) that if our consumption of forraign wares be no more yearly than is already supposed, and that our exportations be so mightly encreased by this manner of Trading with ready money as is before declared: It is not then possible but that all the over-ballance or difference should return either in mony or in such wares as we must export again, which, as is already plainly shewed will be still a greater means to encrease our Treasure.

For it is in the stock of the Kingdom as in the estates of private men, who having store of wares, doe not therefore say that they will not venture out or trade with their mony (for this were ridiculous) but do also turn that into wares, whereby they multiply their Mony, and so by a continual and orderly change of one into the other grow rich, and when they please turn all their estates into Treasure; for they that have Wares cannot want mony.

Neithr is it said that Mony is the Life of Trade, as if it could not subsist without the same; for wee know that there was great trading by way of commutation or bartr when there was little mony stirring in the world. The Italians and some other Nations have such remedies against this want, that it can neither decay nor hinder their trade, for they transfer bills of debt, and have Banks both publick and private, wherein they do assign their credits from one to another daily for very great sums with ease and satisfaction by writings only, whilst in the mean time the Mass of Treasure which gave foundation to these credits is employed in Forraign Trade as a Merchandize, and by the said means they have little other use of money in those countrerys more than for their ordinary expences. It is not therefore the keeping of our mony in the Kingdom, but the necessity and use of our wares in forraign Countrey, and our want of their commodities that causeth the vent and consumption on all sides, which makes a quick and ample Trade. If wee were once poor, and now having gained some store of mony by trade with resolution to keep it still in the Realm; shall this cause other Nations to spend more of our commodities than formerly they have done, whereby we might say that our trade is Quickned and Enlarged? No verily, it will produce no such good effect: but rather according to the alteration of times by their true causes we may expect the contrary; for all men do consent that plenty of mony in a Kingdom doth make the native commodities dearer, which as it is to the profit of some private men in their revenues, so is it directly against the benefit of the Publique in the quantity of the trade; for as plenty of mony makes wares dearer, so dear wares decline their use and consumption, as hath been already plainly shewed in the last chapter upon that particular of our cloth; and although this is a very hard lesson for some great landed men to learn, yet I am sure it is a true lesson for all the land to observe, lest when wee have gained some store of mony by trade, wee lose it again by not trading with our mony. I know a Prince in Italy (of famous memory) Ferdinando the first, great Duke of Tuscanie, who being very rich in Treasure, endevoured therewith to enlarge his trade by issuing out to his Merchants great sums of money for very small profit; I my self had forty thousand crowns of him gratis for a whole year, although he knew that I would presently send it away in Specie for the parts of Turkey to be employed in wares for his Countries, he being well assured that in this course of trade it would return again (according to the old saying) with a Duck in the mouth. This noble and industrious Prince by his care and diligence to countenance and favour Merchants in their affairs, did so encrease the practice thereof, that there is scarce a Nobleman or Gentleman in all his dominions that doth not Merchandize eithr by himself or in partnership with others, whereby within these thirty years the trade to his port of Leghorn is so much encreased, that of a poor little town (as I my self knew it) it is now become a fair and strong City,

being one of the most famous places for trade in all Christendom. And yet it is worthy our observation, that the multitude of Ships and wares which come thither from England, the Low
Countreys, and other places, have little or no means to make their returns from thence but only
in ready mony, which they may and do carry away freely at all times, to the incredible advantage
of the said great Duke of Tuscanie and his subjects, who are much enriched by the continual
great concourse of Merchants from all the States of the neighbour Princes, bringing them plenty
of mony daily to supply their wants of the said wares. And thus we see that the current of
Merchandize which carries away their Treasure, becomes a flowing stream to fill them again in
a greater measure with mony.

There is yet an objection or two as weak as all the rest: that is, if wee trade with our Mony wee
shall issue out the less wares; as if a man should say, those Countreys which heretofore had occasion to consume our Cloth, Lead, Tin, Iron, Fish, and the like, shall now make use of our monies
in the place of those necessaries, which were most absurd to affirm, or that the Merchant had not
rather carry our wares by which there is ever some gains expected, than to export money which is
still but the same without any encrease.

But on the contrary there are many Countreys which may yield us very profitable trade for our
mony, which otherwise afford us no trade at all, because they have no use of our wares, as namely
the East-Indies for one in the first beginning thereof, although since by industry in our commerce
with those Nations we have brought them into the use of much of our Lead, Cloth, Tin, and
other things, which is a good addition to the former vent of our commodities.

Again, some men have alleged that those Countrey which permit mony to be carried out, do it
because they have few or no wares to trade withall: but wee have great store of commodities, and
therefore their action ought not to be our example.

To this the answer is briefly, that if we have such a quantity of wares as doth fully provided us
of all things needful from beyond the seas: why should we then doubt that our monys sent out in
trade, must not necessarily come back again in treasure; together with the great gains which it
may procure in such manner as is before set down? And on the other side, if those Nations which
send out their monies do it because they have but few wares of their own, how come they then to
have so much Treasure as we ever see in those places which suffer it freely to be exported at all
times and by whomsoever? I answer, Even by trading with their Moneys; for by what other means
can they get it, having no Mines of Gold or Silver?

Thus may we plainly see, that when this weighty business is duly considered in his end, as
all our humane actions ought well to be weighed, it is found much contrary to that which
most men esteem thereof, because they search no further than the beginning of the work, which
mis-informs their judgments, and leads them into error: For if we only behold the actions of
the husbandman in the seed-time when he casteth away much good corn into the ground, we
will rathr accompt him a mad man than a husbandman: but when we consider his labours in the
harvest which is the end of his endeavours, we find the worth and plentiful encrease of his actions.

Chapter 10: The observation of the Statute of Imployments to be made by strangers, cannot encrease, nor yet preserve our Treasure

To keep our money in the Kingdom is a work of no less skill and difficulty than to augment our
treasure: for the causes of their preservation and production are the same in nature. The statute
for employment of strangers wares into our commodities seemeth at the first to be a good and a
lawful way leading to those ends; but upon the examination of the particulars, we shall find that
it cannot produce such good effects.

For as the use of forraign trade is alike unto all Nations, so may we easily perceive what will be
done therein by strangers, when we do but observe our own proceedings in this waighty business,

by which we do not only seek with the vent of our own commodities to supply our wants of for-raign wares, but also to enrich our selves with treasure: all which is done by a different manner of trading according to our own occasions and the nature of the places whereunto we do trade; as namely in some Countreys we sell our commodities and bring away their wares, or part in mony; in other Countreys we sell our goods and take their money, because they have little or no wares that fits our turns: again in some places we have need of their commodities, but they have little use of ours; so they take our mony which we get in other Countreys: And thus by a course of traffick (which changeth according to the accurrents of time) the particular members do accom-modate each other, and all accomplish the whole body of the trade, which will ever languish if the harmony of her health be distempered by the diseases of excess at home, violence abroad, charges, and restrictions at home or abroad: but in this place I have occasion to speak only of restriction, which I will perform briefly.

There are three ways by which a Merchant may make the returns of his wares from beyond the Seas, that is to say in mony, in commodities, or by Exchange. But the Statute of employment doth not only restrain mony (in which there is a seeming providence and Justice) but also the use of the Exchange by bills, which doth violate the Law of Commerce, and is indeed an Act without example in any place of the world where we have trade, and therefore to be considered, that whatsoever (in this kind) we shall impose upon strangers here, will presently be made a Law for us in their Countreys, expecially where we have our greatest trade with our vigilant neighbours, who omit no care nor occasion to support their traffique in equal privileges with other Nations. And thus in the first place we should be deprived of that freedom and means which now we have to bring Treasure into the Kingdom, and therewith likewise we should lose the vent of much wares which we carry to divers places, whereby our trade and our Treasure would decay together.

Second, if by the said Statute we thrust the exportation of our wares (more than ordinary) upon the stranger, we must then take it from the English, which were injurious to our Merchants, Marriners and Shipping, besides the hurt to the Commonwealth in venting the Kingdoms stock to the stranger at far lower rates here than we must do if we sold it to them in their own Countreys, as is proved in the third chapter.

Third, whereas we have already sufficiently shewed, that if our commodities be over ballance in value by forraign wares, our mony must be carried out. How is it possible to prevent this by tying the Strangers' hands, and leaving the English loose? Shall not the same reason and advan-tage cause that to be done by them now, that was done by the other before? Or if we will make a statute (without example) to prevent both alike, shall we not then overthrow all at once? The King in his customes and the Kingdom in her profits; for such a restriction must of necessity destroy much trade, because the diversity of occasions and places which make an ample trade require that some men should both export and import wares; some export only, others import, some deliver out their monies by exchange, others take it up; some carry out mony, others bring it in, and this in a greater or lesser quantity according to the good husbandry or excess in the Kingdom, over which only if we keep a strict law, it will rule all the rest, and without this all other Statutes are no rules either to keep or procure us Treasure.

Lastly, to leave no Objection unansweered, if it should be said that a Statute comprehending the English as well as the stranger must needs keep our money in the Kingdom. What shall we get by this, if it hinder the coming in of money by the decay of that ample Trade which we enjoyed in the freedom thereof? Is not the Remedy far worse than the disease? Shall we not life more like Irishmen than Englishmen, when the Kings revenues, our Merchants, Marriners, Shipping, Arts, Lands, Riches, and all decay together with our Trade?

Yea but, say some men, we have better hopes than so; for th' intent of the Statute is, that as all the forraign wares which are brought in shall be imployed in our commodities, thereby to keep our money in the Kingdom: So we doubt not but send out a sufficient quantity of our own wares over and above to bring in the value thereof in ready money.

Although this is absolutely denied by the reasons afore written, yet now we will grant it, because we desire to end the dispute: For if this be true, that other Nations will vent more of our commodities than we consume of theirs in value, then I affirm that the overplus must necessarily return unto us in treasure without the use of the Statute, which is therefore not onely fruitless but hurtful, as some other like restrictions are found to be when they are fully discovered.

Chapter 11: It will not increase our treasure to enjoyn the Merchant that exporteth Fish, Corn, or Munition, to return all or part of the value in Money

Victuals and Munition for war are so pretious in a Commonwealth, that either it seemeth necesary to restrain the exportation altogether, or (if the plenty permits it) to require the return thereof in so much treasure; which appeareth to be reasonable and without difficulty, because Spain and other Countries do willingly part with their money for such wares, although in other occasions of trade they straightly prohibit the exportation thereof: all which I grant to be true, yet notwithstanding we must consider that all the ways and means which (in course of trade) force treasure into the Kingdom, do not therefore make it ours: for this can be done onely by a lawful gain, and this gain is no way to be accomplished but by the overballance of our trade, and this overballance is made less by restrictions: therefore such restrictions do hinder the increase of our treasure. The Argument is plain, and needs no other reasons to strengthen it, except any man be so vain to think that restrictions would not cause the less wares to be exported. But if this likewise should be granted, yet to enjoyn the Merchant to bring in money for Victuals and Munition carried out, will not cause us to have one peny the more in the Kingdom at the years end; for whatsoever is forced in one way must out again another way: because onely so much will remain and abide withus as is gained and incorporated into the estate of the Kingdom by the overballance of the trade.

This may be made plain by an example taken from an Englishman, who had occasion to buy and consume the wares of divers strangers for the value of six hundred pounds, and having wares of his own for the value of one thousand pounds, he sold them to the said strangers, and presently forced all the mony from them into his own power; yet upon cleering of the reckoning between them there remained onely four hundred pounds to the said Englishman for overballance of the wares bought and sold; so the rest which he had received was returned back from whence he forced it. And this shall suffice to shew that whatsoever courses we take to force money into the Kingdom, yet so much onely will remain with us as we shall gain by the ballance of our trade.

Chapter 17: Whether it be necessary for great Princes to lay up store of Treasure

Before we set down the quantity of Treasure which Princes may conveniently lay up yearly without hurting the Common-wealth, it will be fit to examine whether the act it self of Treasuring be necessary: for in common conference we ever find some men who do so much dote or hope upon the Liberality of Princes, that they term it baseness, and conceive it needless for them to lay up store of Treasure, accounting the honour and safety of great Princes to consist more in their Bounty, than in their Money, which they labour to confirm by the examples of Caesar, Alexander, and others, who hating covetousness, atchieved many acts and victories by lavish gifts and liberal expences. Unto which they add also the little fruit which came by that great summ of money which King David laid up and left to his son Solomon, who notwithstanding this, and all his other rich Presents and wealthy Traffique in a quiet reign, consumed all with pomp and vain delights, excepting only that which was spent in building of the Temple. Whereupon (say they) if so much treasure gathered by so just a King, effect so little, what shall we hope for by the endeavours of this kind in other Princes? Sardanapalus left ten millions of pounds to them that slew him. Darius left twenty millions of pounds to Alexander that took him; Nero being left rich, and extoring much from his best Subjects, gave away above twelve millions of pounds to his base flatterers and such unworthy persons, which caused Galba after him to revoke those gifts. A Prince who hath store of mony hates peace, despiseth the friendship of his Neighbours and Allies, enters not only into unnecessary, but also into dangerous Wars, to the ruin and over-throw (sometimes) of his own estate: All which, with divers other weak arguments of this kind, (which for brevity I omit) make nothing against the lawful gathering and massing up of Treasure by wise and provident Princes, if they be rightly understood.

For first, concerning those worthies who have obtained to the highest top of honour and dignity, by their great gifts and expences, who know not that this hath been done rather upon the spoils of their Enemies than out of their own Cofers, which is indeed a Bounty that causeth neither loss nor peril? Whereas on the countrary, those Princes which do not providently lay up Treasure, or do imoderately consume the same when they have it, will sodainly come to want and misery; for there is nothing doth so soon decay as Excessive Bounty, in using whereof they want the means to use it. And this was King Solomon's case, notwithstanding, his infinite Treasure, which made him overburthen his Subjects in such a manner, that (for this cause) many of them rebelled against his Son Rehoboam, who thereby lost a great part of his dominions, being so grosly mis-led by his young Counsellors. Therefore a Prince that will not oppress his people, and yet be able to maintain his Estate, and defend his Right, that will not run himself into Poverty, Contempt, Hate, and Danger, must lay up treasure, and be thrifty, for further proof whereof I might yet produce some other examples, which here I do omit as needless.

Only I will add this as a necessary rule to be observed, that when more treasure must be raised than can be received by the ordinary taxes, it ought ever to be done with equality to avoid the hate of the people, who are never pleased except their contributions be granted by general consent: For which purpose the invention of Parliaments is an excellent policie of Government, to keep a sweet concord between a King and his Subjects, by restraining the Insolency of the Nobility, and redressing the Injuries of the Commons, without engaging a Prince to adhere to either party, but indifferently to favour both. There could nothing be devised with more judgement for the common quiet of a Kingdom, or with greater care for the safety of a King, who hereby hath also good means to dispatch those things by others, which will move envy, and to execute that himself which will merit thanks.

Chapter 18: How much Treasure a Prince may conveniently lay up yearly

Thus far we have shewed the ordinary and extraordinary incomes of Princes, the conveniency thereof, and to whom only it doth necessarily and justly belong, to take the extraordinary contributions of their Subjects. It resteth now to examine what proportion of treasure each particular Prince may conveniently lay up yearly. This business doth seem at the first to be very plain and easy, for if a Prince have two millions yearly revenue, and spend but one, why should he not lay up the other? Indeed I must confess that this course is ordinary in the means and gettings of private men, but in the affairs of Princes it is far different, there are other circumstances to be considered; for although the revenue of a King should be very great, yet if the gain of the Kingdom be but small, this latter must ever give rule and proportion to that Treasure, which may conveniently be laid up yearly, for if he should mass up more money than is gained by the over-ballance of his Forraign Trade, he shall not Fleece, but Flea his Subjects, and so with their ruin overthrow himself for want of future sheerings. To make this plain, suppose a Kingdom to be so rich by nature and art, that it may supply it self of forraign wares by trade, and yet advance yearly two hundred thousand livres in ready mony: Next suppose all the Kings revenues to be nine hundred thousand livres and his expences but four hundred thousand livres whereby he may lay up thirty thousand livres more in his Coffers yearly than the whole Kingdom gains from strangers by forraign trade; who sees not then that all the mony in such a State, would suddenly be drawn into the Princes treasure, whereby the life of lands and arts must fail and fall to the ruin both of the publick and private wealth? So that a King who desires to lay up much mony must endeavour by all good means to maintain and encrease his forraign trade, because it is the sole way not only to lead him to his own ends, but also to enrich his Subjects to his farther benefit: for a Prince is esteemed no less powerful by having many rich and well affected Subjects, than by possessing much treasure in his Coffers.

But here we must meet with an Objection, which peradventure may be made concerning such States (whereof I have formerly spoken) which are of no great extent, and yet bordering upon mighty Princes, are therefore constrained to lay extraordinary taxes upon their subjects, whereby they procure to themselves very great incomes yearly, and are richly provided against any Forraign Invasions; yet have they no such great trade with Strangers, as that the overbalance or gain of the same may suffice to lay up the one half of that which they advance yearly, besides their own expences.

To this answer is, that stil the gain of their Forraign Trade must be the rule of laying up their treasure, the which although it should not be much yearly, yet in the time of a long continued peace, and being well managed to advantage, it wil become a great summe of mony, able to make a long defence, which may end or divert the war. Neither are all the advances of Princes strictly tied to be massed up in treasure, for they have other no less necessary and profitable wayes to make them rich and powerfull, by issuing out continually a great part of the mony of their yearly Incomes to their subjects from whom it was first taken; as namely, by employing them to make Ships of War, with all the provisions thereunto belonging, to build and repair Forts, to buy and store up Corn in the Granaries of each Province for a years use (at least) aforehand, to serve in occasion of Dearth, which cannot be neglected by a State but with great danger, to erect Banks with their money for the encrease of their subjects trade, to maintain in their pay, Collonels, Captains, Souldiers, Commanders, Mariners, and others, both by Sea and Land, with good discipline, to fill their Store-houses (in sundry strong places) and to abound in Gunpowder, Brimstone, Saltpeter, Shot, Ordnance, Musquets, Swords, Pikes, Armours, Horses, and in many other such like Provisions fitting War; all which will make them to be feared abroad, and loved at home, especially if care be taken that all (as neer as possible) be made out of the Matter and Manufacture of their own subjects, which bear the burden of the yearly Contributions; for a Prince (in this case) is like the stomach in the body, which if it cease to digest and distribute to the other members, it doth no sooner corrupt them, but it destroyes it self.

Thus we have seen that a small State may lay up a great wealth in necessary provisions, which are Princes Jewels, no less precious than their Treasure, for in time of need they are ready, and cannot otherwise be had (in some places) on the suddain, whereby a State may be lost, whilst Munition is in providing: so that we may account that Prince as poor who can have no wares to buy at his need, as he that hath no money to buy wares; for although Treasure is said to be the sinews of the War, yet this is so because it doth provide, unite, and move the power of men, victuals, and munition where and when the cause doth require; but if these things be wanting in due time, what shall we then do with our money? The consideration of this, doth cause divers well-governed States to be exceeding provident and well furnished of such provisions, especially those Granaries and Storehouses with that famous Arsenal of the Venetians, are to be admired for the magnificence of the buildings, the quantity of the Munitions and Stores both for Sea and

Land, the multitude of the workmen, the diversity and excellency of the Arts, with the order of the government. They are rare and worthy things for Princes to behold and imitate; for Majesty without providence of competent force, and ability of necessary provisions is unassured.

Chapter 20: The order and means whereby we may draw up the ballance of our Forraign Trade

Now, that we have sufficiently proved the Ballance of our Forraign Trade to be the true rule of our Treasure; It resteth that we shew by whom and in what manner the said ballance may be drawn up at all times, when it shall please the State to discover how we prosper or decline in this great and weighty business, wherein the Officers of his Majesties Customes are the onely Agents to be employed, because they have the accounts of all the wares which are issued out or brought into the Kingdome; and although (it is true) they cannot exactly set down the cost and charges of other mens goods bought here or beyond the seas; yet nevertheless, if they ground themselves upon the book of Rates, they shall be able to make such an estimate as may well satisfie this enquiry: for it is not expected that such an account can possible be drawn up to a just ballance, it will suffice onely that the difference be not over great.

First therefore, concerning our Exportations, when we have valued their first cost, we must add 25 per cent thereunto for the charges here, for fraight of Ships, ensurance of the Adventure, and the Merchants Gains; and for our Fishing Trades, which pay no Customs to his Majesty, the value of such Exportations may be easily esteem'd by good observations which have been made, and may continually be made, according to the increase or decrease of those affairs, the present estate of this commodity being valued at one hundred and forty thousand pounds issued yearly. Also we must add to our Exportations all the moneys which are carried out in Trade by license from his Majesty.

Secondly, for our Importations of Forraign Wares, the Custome-books serve onely to direct us concerning the quantity, for we must not value them as they are rated here, but as they cost us with all charges laden into our Ships beyond the Seas, in the respective places where they are bought: for the Merchants gain, the charges of Insurance, Fraight of Ships, Customes, Imposts, and other Duties here, which doe greatly indear them unto our use and consumption, are not withstanding but Commutations amongst our selves, for the Stranger hath no part thereof: wherefore our said Importations ought to be valued at 25 per cent less than they are rated to be worth here. And although this may seem to be too great allowance upon many rich Commodities, which come but from the Low Countreys and other places neer hand, yet will it be found reasonable, when we consider it in gross Commodities, and upon Wares laden in remote Countreys, as our Pepper, which cost us, with charges, but four pence the pound: so that when all is brought into a medium, the valuation ought to be made as afore-written. And therefore, the order which hath been used to multiply the full rates upon wares inwards by twenty, would produce a very great errour in the Ballance, for in this manner the ten thousand bags of Pepper, which this year we have brought hither from the East Indies, should be valued at very near two hundred and fifty thousand pounds, whereas all this Pepper in the Kingdomes accompt, cost not above fifty thousand pounds, because the Indians have had no more of us, although we paid them extraordinary dear prices for the same. All the other charges (as I have said before) is but a charge of effects amongst our selves, and from the Subject to the King, which cannot impoverish the Common-wealth. But it is true, that whereas nine thousand bags of the said Pepper are already shipped out for divers forraign parts; These and all other Wares, forraign or domestick, which are thus transported Outwards, ought to be cast up by the rates of his Majesties Custome-money, multiplyed by twenty, or rather by twenty five (as I conceive) which will come neerer the reckoning, when we consider all our Trades to bring them into a medium.

Thirdly, we must remember, that all Wares exported or imported by Strangers (in their shipping) be esteemed by themselves, for what they carry out, the Kingdom hath only the first cost and the custom: And what they bring in, we must rate it as it is worth here, the Custom, Impost, and petty charges only deducted.

Lastly, there must be good notice take of all the great losses which we receive at Sea in our Shipping either outward or homeward bound: for the value of the one is to be deducted from our Exportations, and the value of the other is to be added to our Importations: for to lose and to consume doth produce one and the same reckoning. Likewise if it happen that His Majesty doth make over any great sums of mony by Exchange to maintain a forraign war, where we do not feed and clothe the Souldiers, and Provide the armies, we must deduct all this charge out of our Exportations or add it to our Importations; for this expence doth either carry out or hinder the coming in of so much Treasure. And here we must remember the great collections of mony which are supposed to be made throughout the Realm yearly from our Recusants by Priests and Jesuits, who secretly convey the same unto their Colleges, Cloysters, and Nunneries beyond the Seas, from whence it never returns to us again in any kind; therefore if this mischief cannot be prevented, yet it must be esteemed and set down as a cleer loss to the Kingdome, except (to ballance this) we will imagine that as great a value may perhaps come in from forraign Princes to their Pensioners here for Favours or Intelligence, which some States account good Policy, to purchase with great Liberality; the receipt whereof notwithstanding is plain Treachery.

There are yet some other petty things which seem to have reference to this Ballance, of which the said Officers of His Majesties Customs can take no notice, to bring them into the accompt. As namely the expences of travailers, the gifts to Ambassadors and Strangers, the fraud of some rich goods not entred into the Custom-house, the gain which is made here by Strangers by change and re-change, Interest of mony, ensurance upon English mens goods and their lives: which can be little when the charges of their living here is deducted; besides that the very like advantages are as amply ministred unto the English in forraign Countreys, which doth counterpoize all these things, and therefore they are not considerable in the drawing up of the said Ballance.

WILLIAM PETTY (1623–1687)

Sir William Petty, Artist: Issac Fuller (1606–1672), by courtesy of the National Portrait Gallery, London.

Sir William Petty was educated in medicine and anatomy and, after holding positions of Professor of Anatomy at Oxford and Professor of Music at Gresham College, London, was appointed chief medical officer to the Cromwell's army in Ireland in 1651. Here, he was responsible for overseeing a survey of Irish lands (1655–1658) that would be turned over to Cromwell's soldiers and financiers as compensation for their efforts and, in the process, became a major landholder himself. Much of the remainder of his life was spent in management of and litigation over his various landholdings.

Petty was substantially influenced by the Baconian empirical approach to science, and he was part of a group, including many of the leading scientists of the day, that founded the Royal Society for the Improving of Natural Knowledge in 1662. The Royal Society championed the Baconian method, both within and without the natural sciences. The influence of this methodology is evidenced throughout Petty's writings, but perhaps nowhere better than in the preface to his *Political Arithmetick*, where he states that "instead of using only comparative and superlative Words, and intellectual Arguments, I have taken the course ... to express my self in Terms of *Number, Weight* or *Measure*; to use only Arguments of Sense, and to consider only such Causes, as have visible Foundations in Nature; leaving those that depend upon the mutable Minds, Opinions, Appetites and Passions of particular men, to the consideration of others ..."

Petty wrote on numerous subjects, including medicine, fortifications, and religion, but is best known as a father of statistics for his quantitative empirical emphasis on number, weight, and measure. He wrote widely on economic subjects, including the division of labor, the theory of value, and distribution theory. He was also an imperialist mercantilist.

Petty's *A Treatise of Taxes and Contributions* is really the first treatise on public finance in the economics literature. Although written with a view to illustrating how the crown might most effectively finance its operations, the *Treatise* also contains a number of fundamental advances in economic analysis. In the excerpts reprinted here, we find Petty laying out his view of the appropriate role for the state, his commentary on the system of taxation, his introduction into economic analysis of the notion of rents – which later played a central role in physiocratic and classical thinking – and the valuation of these for tax purposes, and his defense of usury. In his analysis of rents and his defense of usury, we see a clear premonition of the idea that rates of return will equalize across sectors, as with his valuation of land rents and his belief that the rate of interest will approximate the rate of return on land over a given time period.

References and further reading

Aspromourgos, Tony (1988) "The Life of William Petty in Relation to His Economics: A Tercentenary Interpretation," *History of Political Economy* 20 (Fall): 337–56.

——(1996) *On the Origins of Classical Economics: Distribution and Value from William Petty to Adam Smith*, London: Routledge.

Fitzmaurice, Lord Edmond (1895) *Life of Sir William Petty*, London: John Murray.

Hutchison, Terence (1988) *Before Adam Smith: The Emergence of Political Economy, 1662–1776*, Oxford: Basil Blackwell.

Letwin, William (1964) *The Origins of Scientific Economics*, Garden City, NY: Doubleday & Co.

Petty, William (1899) *The Economic Writings of Sir William Petty*, edited by Charles Henry Hull, Cambridge: Cambridge University Press.

Roncaglia, Alessandro (1985) *Petty: The Origins of Political Economy*, New York: M.E. Sharpe.

——(1987) "Petty, William," in John Eatwell, Murray Milgate, and Peter Newman (eds), *The New Palgrave: A Dictionary of Economics*, Vol. 3, London: Macmillan, 853–55.

A Treatise of Taxes and Contributions (1662)

Chapter 1: Of the several sorts of Publick Charges

The Publick Charges of a State, are, that of its Defence by Land and Sea, of its Peace at home and abroad, as also of its honourable vindication from the injuries of other States; all which we may call the Charge of the Militia, which commonly is in ordinary as great as any other Branch of the whole; but extraordinary (i.e. in time of War, or fear of War) is much the greatest.

2. Another branch of the Publick Charge is, the Maintenance of the Governours, Chief and Subordinate; I mean, such not onely as spend their whole time in the Execution of their respective Offices, but also who spent much in fitting themselves as well with abilities to that end, as in begetting an opinion in their Superiors of such their ability and trustworthiness.

3. Which Maintenance of the Governours is to be in such a degree of plenty and splendour, as private Endeavours and Callings seldom reach unto: To the end, that such Governours may have the natural as well as the artificial Causes of Power to act with.

4. For if a great multitude of men should call one of their number King, unless this instituted Prince, appear in greater visible splendour then others, can reward those that obey and please him, and do the contrary to others; his Institution signifies little, even although he chance to have greater corporal or mental faculties, than any other of the number.

5. There be Offices which are but πάρεργα, as Sheriffs, Justices of the Peace, Constables, Churchwardens, etc. which men may attend without much prejudice to their ordinary wayes of livelihood, and for which the honour of being trusted, and the pleasure of being feared, hath been thought a competent Reward.

6. Unto this head, the Charge of the administring justice may be referred, as well between man and man, as between the whole State or Commonalty and particularly members of it; as well that of righting and punishing past injuries and crimes, as of preventing the same in time to come.

7. A third branch of the Publick Charge is, that of the Pastorage of mens Souls, and the guidance of their Consciences; which, one would think (because it respects another world, and but the particular interest of each man there) should not be a publick Charge in this: Nevertheless, if we consider how easie it is to elude the Laws of man, to commit unproveable crimes, to corrupt and divert Testimonies, to wrest the sense and meaning of the Laws, etc. there follows a necessity of contributing towards a publick Charge, wherewith to have men instructed in the Laws of God, that take notice of evil thoughts and designs, and much more of secret deeds, and that punisheth eternally in another world, what man can but slightly chastise in this.

8. Now those who labour in this publick Service, must also be maintained in a proportionable splendour; and must withall have the means to allure men with some kinde of reward, even in this life; forasmuch, as many heretofore followed even Christ himself, but for the Loaves he gave them.

9. Another branch is, the Charge of Schools and Universities, especially for so much as they teach above Reading, Writing and Arithmetick; these being of particular use to every man, as

being helps and substitutes of Memory and Reason, Reckoning being of the latter, as Writing and Reading are of the former; for whether Divinity, etc. ought to be made a private Trade, is to me a question.

10. 'Tis true, that Schools and Colledges are now for the most part but the Donations of particular men, or places where particular men spend their money and time upon their own private accounts; but no doubt it were not amiss, if the end of them were to furnish all imaginable helps unto the highest and finest Natural Wits, towards the discovery of Nature in all its operations; in which sense they ought to be a publick Charge: The which Wits should not be selected for that work, according to the fond conceits of their own Parents and Friends, (Crows that think their own Birds ever fairest) but rather by the approbation of others more impartial; such as they are, who pick from out of the Christians Children the ablest Instruments and Support of the Turkish Governments. Of which Selections more hereafter.

11. Another branch, is that of the Maintenance of Orphans, found and exposed Children, which also are Orphans; as also of Impotents of all sorts, and moreover such as want employment.

12. For the permitting of any to beg is a more chargeable way of maintaining them whom the law of Nature will not suffer to starve, where food may possibly be had: Besides, it is unjust to let any starve, when we think it just to limit the wages of the poor, so as they can lay up nothing against the time of their impotency and want of work.

13. A last Branch may be, the Charge of High-wayes, Navigable Rivers, Aquaeducts, Bridges, Havens, and other things of universal good and concernment.

14. Other Branches may be thought on, which let other men either refer unto these, or adde over and above. For it suffices for my purpose to have for the present set down these the chief and most obvious of all the rest.

Chapter 3: How the causes of the unquiet bearing of taxes may be lessened

We have slightly gone through all the six branches of the Publick Charge, and have (though imperfectly and in haste) shewn what would encrease, and what would abate them.

We come next to take away some of the general Causes of the unquiet bearing of Taxes, and yielding to Contributions, namely

2.1. That the people think, the Sovereign askes more then he needs. To which we answer, 1. That if the Sovereign were sure to have what he wanted in due time, it were his own great dammage to draw away the money out of his Subjects hands, who by trade increase it, and to hoard it up in his own Coffers, where 'tis of no use even to himself, but lyable to be begged or vainly expended.

3.2. Let the Tax be never so great, if it be proportionable unto all, then no man suffers the loss of any Riches by it. For men (as we said but now) if the Estates of them all were either halfed or doubled, would in both cases remain equally rich. For they would each man have his former state, dignity and degree; and moreover, the Money leavied not going out of the Nation, the same also would remain as rich in comparison of any other Nation; onely the Riches of the Prince and People would differ for a little while, namely until the money leavied from some, were again refunded upon the same, or other persons that paid it: In which case every man also should have his change and opportunity to be made the better or worse by the new distribution; or if he lost by one, yet to gain by another.

4.3. Now that which angers men most, is to be taxed above their Neighbours. To which I answer, that many times these surmizes are mistakes, many times they are chances, which in the next Tax may run more favourable; and if they be by design, yet it cannot be imagined, that it was by design of the Sovereign, but of some temporary Assessor, whose turn it may be to receive the Talio upon the next occasion from the very man he has wronged.

5.4. Men repine much, if they think the money leavyed will be expended on Entertainments, magnificent Shews, triumphal Arches, etc. To which I answer, that the same is a refunding of said moneys to the Tradesmen who work upon those things; which Trades though they seem vain and onely of orniment, yet they refund presently to the most useful; namely to Brewers, Bakers, Taylours, Shoemakers, etc. Moreover, the Prince hath no more pleasure in these Shews and Entertainments than 100,000 others of his meanest Subjects have, whom, for all their grumbling, we see to travel many miles to be spectators of these mistaken and distasted vanities.

6.5. The people often complain, that the King bestows the money he raises from the people upon his Favourites: To which we answer; that what is given to Favourites, may at the next step or transmigration, come into our own hands, or theirs unto whom we wish well, and think do deserve it.

7. Second, as this man is a Favourite to day, so another, or our selves, may be hereafter; favour being of a very slippery and moveable nature, and not such a thing as we need much to envy; for the same way that – leads up a hill, leads also down the same. Besides there is nothing in the Lawes or Customes of England, which excludes any the meanest mans Childe, from arriving to the highest Offices in the this Kingdom, much less debars him from the Personall kindness of his Prince.

8. All these imaginations (whereunto the vulgar heads are subject) do cause a backwardness to pay, and that necessitates the Prince to severity. Now this lighting upon some poor, though stubborn, stiffnecked Refuser, charged with Wife and Children, gives the credulous great occasion to complain of Oppression, and breeds ill blood as to all other matters; feeding the ill humours already in being.

9.6. Ignorance of the Number, Trade, and Wealth of the people, is often the reason why the said people are needlesly troubled, namely with the double charge and vexation of two, or many Levies, when one might have served: Examples whereof have been seen in late Poll-moneys; in which (by reason of not knowing the state of the people, namely how many there were of each Taxable sort, and the want of sensible markes whereby to rate men, and the confounding of Estates with Titles and Offices) great mistakes were committed.

10. Besides, for not knowing the Wealth of the people, the Prince knows not what they can bear; and for not knowing the Trade, he can make no Judgment of the proper season when to demand his Exhibitions.

11.7. Obscurities and doubts, about the right of imposing, hath been the cause of great and ugly Reluctancies in the people, and of Involuntary Severities in the Prince; an eminent Example whereof was the Ship-money, no small cause of twenty years calamity to the whole Kingdom.

12.8. Fewness of people, is real poverty; and a Nation wherein are Eight Millions of people, are more than twice as rich as the same scope of Land wherein are but Four; For the same Governours which are the great charge, may serve near as well, for the greater, as the lesser number.

13. Secondly, If the people be so few, as that they can live, *Ex sponte Creatis*, or with little labour, such as is Grazing, etc. they become wholly without Art. No man that will not exercise his hands, being able to endure the tortures of the mind, which much thoughtfullness doth occasion.

14.9. Scarcity of money, is another cause of the bad payment of Taxes; for if we consider, that of all the wealth of this Nation, namely Lands, Housing, Shipping, Commodities, Furniture, Plate, and Money, that scarce one part of an hundred is Coin; and that perhaps there is scarce six millions of Pounds now in England, that is but twenty shillings a head for every head in the Nation. We may easily judge, how difficult it is for men of competent estates, to pay a Summe of money on a sudden; which if they cannot compass, Severities, and Charges ensue; and that with reason, though unluckie enough, it being more tolerable to undoe one particular Member, then to endanger the whole, nothwithstanding indeed it be more tolerable for one particular Member to be undone with the whole, then alone.

15.10. It seems somewhat hard, that all Taxes should be paid in money, that is, (when the King hath occasion to Victual his Ships at Portsmouth) that Fat Oxen, and Corn should not be received in kind, but that Farmers must first carry their corn perhaps ten Miles to sell, and turn into money; which being paid to the King, is again reconverted into Corn, fetcht many miles further.

16. Moreover, the Farmer for haste is force to undersell his Corn, and the King for haste likewise, is forced to over-buy his provisions. Whereas the paying in kinde, Pro Hic & Nunc, would lessen a considerable grievance to the poor people.

17. The next consideration shall be of the consequences, and effects of too great a Tax, not in respect of particular men, of which we have spoken before, but to the whole people in general: To which I say, that there is a certain measure, and proportion of money requisite to drive the trade of a Nation, more or less then which would prejudice the same. Just as there is a certain proportion of Farthings necessary in a small retail Trade, to change silver money, and to even such reckonings, as cannot be adjusted with the smallest silver pieces. For money, (made of Gold and silver) is to the $τάχρήσα$ (i.e. to the matter of our Food and Covering) but as Farthings, and other local extrinsick money, is to the Gold and Silver species.

18. Now as the proportion of the number of Farthings requisite in comerse is to be taken from the number of people, the frequency of their exchanges; as also, and principally from the value of the smallest silver pieces of money; so in like maner, the proportion of money requisite to our Trade, is to be likewise taken from the frequency of commutations, and from the bigness of the payments, that are by law or custome usually made otherwise. From whence it follows, that where there are Registers of Lands, whereby the just value of each man's interest in them may be well known; and where there are Depositories of the $τάχρήσα$, as of Metals, Cloth, Linnen, Leather, and other Usefuls; and where there are Banks of money also, there less money is necessary to drive the Trade. For if all the greatest payments be made in Lands, and the other perhaps down to ten pound, or twenty pound be made by credit in Lombars or Money-Banks: It follows, that there needs only money to pay sums less than those aforementioned; just as fewer Farthings are requisite for change, where there be plenty of silver two Pences, then where the least silver piece is six Pence.

19. To apply all this, I say, that if there be too much money in a Nation, it were good for the Commonalty, as well as the King, and no harm even to particular men, if the King had in his Coffers, all that is superfluos, no more than if men were permitted to pay their Taxes in any thing they could best spare.

20. On the other side, if the largeness of a publick Exhibition should leave less money than is necessary to drive the nations Trade, then the mischief thereof would be the doing of less work, which is the same as lessening the people, or their Art and Industry; for a hundred pound passing a hundred hands for Wages, causes a 10,000 livres worth of Commodities to be produced, which hands would have been idle and useless, had there not been this continual motive to their employment.

21. Taxes if they be presently expended upon our own domestick Commodities, seem to me, to do little harm to the whole Body of the people, onely they work a change in the Riches and Fortunes of particular men; and particulary by transferring the same from the Landed and Lazy, to the Crafty and Industrious. As for example, if a Gentleman have let his Lands to Farm for a hundred pound per annum, for several years or lives, and he be taxed twenty pound per annum, to maintain a Navy; then the effect hereof will be, that this Gentlemans twenty pounds per annum, will be distributed amongst Seamen, Ship-Carpenters, and other Trades relating to Naval matters; but if the Gentleman had his Land in his own hands, then being taxed a Fifth part, he would raise his Rents near the same proportion upon his under Tenants, or would sell his Cattle, Corn and Wooll a Fifth part dearer; the like also would all other subdependents on him do; and thereby recover in some measure, what he paid. Last, but if all the money levied were thrown into the Sea, then the ultimate effect would onely be, that every man must work a fifth part the harder, or retrench a fifth part of his consumptions, namely the former, if forreign Trade be improveable, and the latter, if it be not.

22. This, I conceive, were the worst of Taxes in a well policyed State; but in other States, where is not a certain prevention of Beggary and Theevery, that is a sure livelihood for men, wanting imployment; there, I confess, an excessive Taxe, causes excessive and insuperable want, even of natural necessities, and that on a sudden, so as ignorant particular persons, cannot finde out what way to subsist by; and this, by the law of Nature, must cause sudden effects to relieve it self, that is, Rapines, Frauds; and this again must bring Death, Mutilations, and Imprisonments, according to the present Laws which are Mischiefs, and Punishments, as well unto the State, as to the particular sufferers of them.

Chapter 4: Of the Several wayes of Taxe, and first, of setting a part, a proportion of the whole Territory for Publick uses, in the nature of Crown Lands; and secondly, by way of Assessement, or Land-taxe

But supposing, that the several causes of Publick Charge are lessened, as much as may be, and that the people be well satisfied, and contented to pay their just shares of what is needfull for their Government and Protection, as also for the Honour of their Prince and Countrey: It follows now to propose the several wayes, and expedients, how the same may be most easily, speedily, and insensibly collected. The which I shall do, by exposing the conveniences and inconveniences of some of the principal wayes of Levyings, used of later years within the several States of Europe: unto which others of smaller and more rare use may be referred.

2. Imagine then, a number of people, planted in a Territory, who had upon Computation concluded, that two Millions of pounds per annum, is necessary to the publick charges. Or rather, who going more wisely to work, had computed a twenty-fifth part of the proceed of all their Lands and Labours, were to be the Excisium, or the part to be cut out, and laid aside for publick uses. Which proportions perhaps are fit enough to the affairs of England, but of that hereafter.

3. Now the question is, how the one or the other shall be raised. The first way we propose, is, to Excize the very Land it self in kinde; that is, to cut out of the whole twenty five Millions, which are said to be in England and Wales, as much Land in specie, as whereof the Rack-rent would be two Millions, namely about four Millions of Acres, which is about a sixth part of the whole; making the said four Millions to be Crown Lands, and as the four Counties intended to be reserved in Ireland upon the forfeitures were. Or else to excize a sixth part of the rent of the whole, which is about the proportion, that the Adventurers and Souldiers in Ireland retribute to the King, as Quit Rents. Of which two wayes, the latter is manifestly the better, the King having more security, and more obliges; provided the trouble and charge of this universal Collection, exceed not that of the other advantage considerably.

4. This way in a new State would be good, being agreed upon, as it was in Ireland, before men had even the possession of any Land at all; wherefore whosoever buyes Land in Ireland hereafter, is no more concerned with the Quit Rents wherewith they are charged, then if the Acres were so much the fewer; or then men are, who buy Land, out of which they know Tythes are to be paid. And truly that Countrey is happy, in which by Original Accord, such a Rent is reserved, as whereby the Publick Charge may be born, without contingent, sudden, superadditions, in which lies the very Ratio of the burthen of all Contributions and Exactions. For in such cases, as was said before, it is not onely the Landlord payes, but every man who eats but an Egg, or an Onion of the growth of his Lands; or who useth the help of any Artisan, which feedeth on the same.

5. But if the same were propounded in England, namely if an aliquot part of every Landlords Rent were excinded or retrenched, then those whose Rents were settled, and determined for long times to come, would chiefly bear the burthen of such an Imposition, and others have a benefit thereby. For suppose A, and B, have each of them a parcel of Land, of equal goodness and value; suppose also that A hath let his parcel for twenty one years at twenty pound per annum, but that B is free; now there comes out a Taxe of a fifth part; hereupon B will not let under 25 livres that his remainder may be twenty, whereas A must be contented with sixteen neat; nevertheless the Tenants of A will sell the proceed of their bargain at the same rate, that the Tenants of B shall do. The effect of all this is; First, that the Kings fifth part of B his Farm shall be greater then before. Second, that the Farmer to B shall gain more then before the Taxe. Third, that the Tenant or Farmer of A shall gain as much as the King and Tenant to B both. Fourth, the Taxe doth ultimately light upon the Landlord A and the Consumptioners. From whence it follows, that a Land-taxe resolves into an irregular Excize upon consumptions, that those, bear it most, who least complain. And lastly, that some. Landlords may gain, and onely such whose Rents are predetermined shall loose; and that doubly, namely one way by the raising of their revenues, and the other by exhausting the prices of provisions upon them.

6. Another way is an Excisum out of the Rent of Houseing, which is much more uncertain then that of Land. For an House is of a double nature, namely one, wherein it is a way and means of expence; the other, as 'tis an Instrument and Tool of gain: for a Shop in London of less capacity and less charge in building then a fair Dining-room in the same House unto which both do belong, shall nevertheless be of the greater value; so also shall a Dungeon, Sellar, then a pleasant Chamber; because the one is expence, the other profit. Now the way Land-taxe rates housing, as of the latter nature, but the Excize, as of the former.

7. We might sometimes adde hereunto, that housing is sometimes disproportionately taxed to discourage Building, especially upon new Foundations, thereby to prevent the growth of a City; suppose London, such excessive and overgrown Cities being dangerous to Monarchy, though the more secure when the supremacy is in Citizens of such places themselves, as in Venice.

8. But we say, that such checking of new Buildings signifies nothing to this purpose; forasmuch as Buildings do not encrease, until the People already have increased: but the remedy of the above mentioned dangers is to be sought in the causes of the encrease of People, the which if they can be nipt, the other work will necessarily be done.

But what then is the true effect of forbidding to build upon new foundations? I answer to keep and fasten the City to its old seat and ground-plot, the which encouragement for new Buildings will remove, as it comes to pass almost in all great Cities, though insensibly, and not under many years progression.

9. The reason whereof is, because men are unwilling to build new houses at the charge of pulling down their old, where both the old house it self, and the ground it stands upon do make a much dearer ground-plot for a new house, and yet far less free and convenient; wherefore men build upon new free foundations, and cobble up old houses, until they become fundamentally irreparable, at which time they become either the dwelling of the Rascality, or in process of time return to waste and Gardens again, examples whereof are many even about London.

Now if great Cities are naturally apt to remove their Seats, I ask which way? I say, in the case of London, it must be Westward, because the Windes blowing near 3/4 of the year from the West, the dwellings of the West end are so much the more free from the fumes, steams, and stinks of the whole Easterly Pyle; which where Seacoal is burnt is a great matter. Now if it follow from hence, that the Pallaces of the greatest men will remove Westward, it will also naturally follow, that the dwellings of others who depend upon them will creep after them. This we see in

London, where the Noblemen's ancient houses are not become Halls for Companies, or turned into Tenements, and all the Pallaces are gotten Westward; Insomuch, as I do not doubt but that five hundred years hence, the King's Pallace will be near Chelsey, and the old building of Whitehall converted to uses more answerable to their quality. For to build a new Royal Pallace upon the same ground will be too great a confinement, in respect of Gardens and other magnificencies, and withall a disaccommodation in the time of the work; but it rather seems to me, that the next Pallace will be buildt from the whole present contignation of houses at such a distance as the old Pallace of Westminster was from the City of London, when the Archers began to bend their bowes just without Ludgate, and when all the space between the Thames, Fleet-Street, and Holborn was as Finsbury-Fields are now.

10. This digression I confess to be both impertinent to the business of Taxes, and in itself almost needless; for why should we trouble our selves what shall be five hundred years hence, not knowing what a day may bring forth; and since 'tis not unlikely, but that before that time we may be all transplanted from hence into America, these Countreys being overrun with Turks, and made waste, as the Seats of the famous Eastern Empires at this day are.

11. Onely I think 'tis certain, that while ever there are people in England, the greatest cohabitation of them will be about the place which is now London, the Thames being the most commodious River of this Island, and the seat of London the most commodious part of the Thames; so much doth the means of facilitating Carriage greaten a City, which may put us in minde of employing our idle hands about mending the High-wayes, making Bridges, Cawseys, and Rivers navigable: Which considerations brings me back round into my way of Taxes, from whence I digrest.

12. But before we talk too much of Rents, we should endeavour to explain the mysterious nature of them, with reference as well to Money, the rent of which we call usury; as to that of Lands and Houses, afore-mentioned.

13. Suppose a man could with his own hands plant a certain scope of Land with Corn, that is, could Digg, or Plough, Harrow, Weed, Reap, Carry home, Tresh, and Winnow so much as the Husbandry of this Land requires; and had withal Seed wherewith to sowe the same. I say, that when this man hath subducted his seed out of the proceed of his Harvest, and also, what himself hath both eaten and given to others in exchange for Clothes, and other Natural necessaries; that the remainder of Corn is the natural and true Rent of the Land for that year; and the medium of seven years, or rather of so many years as makes up the Cycle, within which Dearths and Plenties make their revolution, doth give the ordinary Rent of Land in Corn.

14. But a further, though collateral question may be, how much English money this Corn or Rent is worth? I answer, so much as the money, which another single man can save, within the same time, over and above his expence, if he imployed himself wholly to produce and make it; namely let another man go travel into a Countrey where is Silver, there Dig it, Refine it, bring it to the same place where the other man planted his Corn; Coyne it, etc. the same person, all the while of his working for Silver, gathering also food for his necessary livelihood, and procuring himself covering, etc. I say, the Silver of the one, must be esteemed of equal value with the Corn of the other: the one being perhaps twenty Ounces and the other twenty Bushels. From whence it follows, that the price of a Bushel of this Corn to be an Ounce of Silver.

15. And forasmuch as possible there may be more Art and Hazzard in working about the Silver, then about the Corn, yet all comes to the same pass; for let a hundred men work ten years upon Corn, and the same number of men, the same time, upon Silver; I say, that the neat proceed of the Silver is the price of the whole neat proceed of the Corn, and like parts of the one, the price of like parts of the other. Although not so many of those who wrought in Silver, learned the Art of refining and coining, or out-lived the dangers and diseases of working in the Mines. And this also is the way of pitching the true proportion, between the values of Gold and Silver, which many times is set but by popular errour, sometimes more, sometimes less, diffused in the world; which errour (by the way) is the cause of our having been pestred with too much Gold heretofore, and wanting it now.

16. This, I say, to be the foundation of equallizing and ballancing of values; yet in the super-structures and practices hereupon, I confess there is much variety, and intricacy; of which hereafter.

17. The world measures things by Gold and Silver, but principally the latter; for there may not be two measures, and consequently the better of many must be the onely of all; that is, by fine silver of a certain weight: but now if it be hard to measure the weight and fineness of silver, as by the different reports of the ablest Saymasters I have known it to be; and if silver granted to be of the same fineness and weight, rise and fall in its price, and be more worth at one place than another, not onely for being father from the Mines, but for other accidents, and may be more worth at present, then a moneth or other small time hence; and if it differ in its proportion unto the several things valued by it, in several ages upon the increase and diminution thereof, we shall endeavour to examine some other natural Standards and Measures, without derogating from the excellent use of these.

18. Our Silver and Gold we call by severall names, as in England by pounds, shillings, and pence, all which may be called and understood by either of the three. But that which I would say upon this matter is, that all things ought to be valued by two natural Denominations, which is Land and Labour; that is, we ought to say, a Ship or garment is worth such a measure of Land, with such another measure of Labour; forasmuch as both Ships and Garments were the creatures of Lands and men's Labours thereupon; This being true, we should be glad to finde out a natural Par between Land and Labour, so as we might express the value by either of them alone as well or better then by both, and reduce pence into pounds. Wherefore we would be glad to finde the natural values of the Fee simple of Land, though but no better then we have done that of the *usus fructus* above-mentioned, which we attempt as followeth.

19. Having found the Rent or value of the *usus fructus* per annum, the question is, how many years purchase (as we usually say) is the Fee simple naturally worth? If we say an infinite number, then an Acre of Land would be equal in value to a thousand Acres of the same Land; which is absurd, an infinity of unites being equal to an infinity of thousands. Wherefore we must pitch upon some limited number, and that I apprehend to be the number of years, which I conceive one man of fifty years old, another of twenty eight, and another of seven years old, all being alive together may be thought to live; that is to say, of a Grandfather, Father, and Childe; few men having reason to take care of more remote Posterity: for if a man be a great Grandfather, he himself is so much the nearer his end, so as there are but three in a continual line of descent usually co-existing together; and as some are Grandfathers at forty years, yet as many are not till above sixty, and *sic de eteteris*.

20. Wherefore I pitch the number of years purchase, that any Land is naturally worth, to be the ordinary extent of three such persons their lives. Now in England we esteem three lives equal to one and twenty years, and consequently the value of Land, to be about the same number of years purchase. Possibly if they thought themselves mistaken in the one, (as the observator on the Bills of Mortality thinks they are) they would alter in the other, unless the consideration of the force of popular errour and dependance of things already concatenated, did hinder them.

21. This I esteem to be the number of years purchase where Titles are good, and where there is a moral certainty of enjoying the purchase. But in other Countreys Lands are worth nearer thirty years purchase, by reason of the better Titles, more people, and perhaps truer opinion of the value and duration of three lives.

22. And in some places, Lands are worth yet more years purchase by reason of some special honour, pleasures, priviledge or jurisdiction annexed unto them.

23. On the other hand, Lands are worth fewer years purchase (as in Ireland) for the following reasons, which I have here set down, as unto the like whereof the cause of the like cheapness in any other place may be imputed.

First, In Ireland, by reason of the frequent Rebellions, (in which if you are conquered, all is lost; or if you conquer, yet you are subject to swarms of thieves and robbers) and the envy which precedent missions of English have against the subsequent, perpetuity it self is but forty years long, as within which time some ugly disturbance hath hitherto happened almost ever since the first coming of the English thither.

24.2. The Claims upon Claims which each hath to the others Estates, and the facility of making good any pretence whatsoever by the favour of some one or other of the many Governours and Ministers which within forty years shall be in power there; as also by the frequency of false testimonies, and abuse of solemn Oaths.

25.3. The paucity of Inhabitants, there being not above the 1/5th part so many as the Territory would maintain, and of those but a small part do work at all, and yet a smaller work so much as in other Countreys.

26.4. That a great part of the Estates, both real and personal in Ireland, are owned by Absentees, and such as draw over the profits raised out of Ireland refunding nothing; so as Ireland exporting more then it imports doth yet grow poorer to a paradox.

27.5. The difficulty of executing justice, so many of those in power being themselves protected by Offices, and protecting others. Moreover, the number of criminous and indebted persons being great, they favour their like in Juries, Offices, and wheresoever they can: Besides, the Countrey is seldom enough to give due encouragement to profound Judges and Lawyers, which makes judgements very casual; ignorant men being more bold to be apt and arbitrary, then such as understand the dangers of it. But all this with a little care in due season might remedy, so as to bring Ireland in a few years to the same level of values with other places; but of this also elsewhere more at large, for in the next place we shall come to Usury.

Chapter 5: Of Usury

What reason there is for taking or giving Interest or Usury for any thing which we may certainly have again whensoever we call for it, I see not; nor why Usury should be scrupled, where money or other necessaries valued by it, is lent to be paid at such a time and place as the Borrower chuseth, so as the Lender cannot have his money paid him back where and when himself pleaseth, I also see not. Wherefore when a man giveth out his money upon condition that he may not demand it back until a certain time to come, whatsoever his own necessities shall be in the mean time, he certainly may take a compensation for this inconvenience which he admits against himself: And this allowance is that we commonly call Usury.

2. And when one man furnisheth another with money at some distant place, and engages under great Penalties to pay him there, and at a certain day besides; the consideration for this, is that we call Exchange or local Usury.

As for example, if a man wanting money at Carlisle in the heat of the late Civil Wars, when the way was full of Souldiers and Robbers, and the passage by Sea very long troublesome, and dangerous, and seldom passed; why might not another take much more than an 100 livres at London for warranting the like Summe to be paid at Carlisle on a certain day?

3. Now the Questions arising hence are; what are the natural Standards of Usury and Exchange? As for Usury, the least that can be, is the Rent of so much Land as the money lent will buy, where the security is undoubted; but where the security is casual, then a kinde of ensurance must be enterwoven with the simple natural Interest, which may advance the Usury very conscionably unto any height below the Principal it self. Now if things are so in England, that really there is no such security as abovementioned, but that all are more or less hazardous, troublesome, or chargeable to make, I see no reason for endouvering to limit Usury upon time, any more than that upon place, which the practice of the world doth not, unless it be that those who make such Laws were rather Borrowers then Lenders: But of the vanity and fruitlessness of making Civil Positive Laws against the Laws of Nature, I have spoken elsewhere, and instanced in several particulars.

4. As for the natural measures of Exchange, I say, that in times of Peace, the greatest Exchange can be but the labour of carrying the money in specie, but where are hazards emergent uses for money in one place then another, etc. or opinions of these true or false, the Exchange will be governed by them.

5. Parallel unto this, is something which we omit concerning the price of Land; for as great need of money heightens Exchange, so doth great need of Corn raise the price of that likewise, and consequently of the Rent of the Land that bears Corn, and lastly of the Land it self; as for example, if the Corn which feedeth London, or an Army, be brought forty miles thither, then the Corn growing within a mile of London, or the quarters of such Army, shall have added unto its natural price, so much as the charge of bringing it thirty miles doth amount unto: And unto perishable Commodities, as fresh fish, fruits, etc. the ensurance upon the hazard of corrupting, etc. shall be added also; and finally, unto him that eats these things there (suppose in Taverns) shall be added the charge of all the circumstancial appurtenances of House-rent, Furniture, Attendance, and the Cooks skill as well as his labour to accompany the same.

6. Hence it comes to pass, that Lands intrinsically alike near populous places, such as where the perimeter of the Area that feeds them is great, will not onely yield more Rent for these Reasons, but also more years purchase then in remote places, by reason of the pleasure and honour extraordinary of having Lands there; for – *Omne tulit penctum qui miscuit utile dulci.*

JOHN LOCKE (1632–1704)

John Locke, Artist: Unknown, by courtesy of the National Portrait Gallery, London.

John Locke was educated at Oxford, where he first studied the classics and later, like Petty, medicine. He became the personal physician to Anthony Ashley Cooper, who later became the first Earl of Shaftsbury and, from 1672 to 1674, served as Chancellor of the Exchequer. Locke served as Shaftsbury's secretary and assistant at the Exchequer, and it was through this connection, and subsequent work as secretary to the Council of Trade and Plantations (1673–1674) and later as a Commissioner for Trade, that he developed an interest in economic issues.

Locke was a major philosopher, not only through his theories of property and government, of modern Western civilization, but of empiricism, psychology, and utilitarianism. He developed a labor theory of property and of value and was a foremost articulator of the quantity theory of money in its most sophisticated form, all the while supporting mercantilist policies. His theories of property and government made him the premier philosopher of non-landed property, government as responsive to the felt interests of the middle class, and of the central role of the legislature dominated by property owners.

The excerpts from Locke's writings reprinted here are taken from his *Of Civil Government* and *Some Considerations of the Consequences of the Lowering of Interest, and Raising the Value of Money*. In the former we find Locke's defense of private property based on the application of labor effort, an idea that, among other things, served to ground later writers' attempts to put forth a labor theory of value. In *Considerations*, Locke treats the question of whether the rate of interest can be regulated by governmental authorities and offers a defense of the proposition that it cannot be, because the forces of the market are more powerful than those of the law. Locke applies basic notions of supply and demand to illustrate that the price of money (interest) is determined in a manner akin to the prices of other goods – making the rate of interest a function of the overall profitability of investment rather than something that can be fixed by law. Locke then proceeds to argue that the value of money, or its purchasing power, is a function of the quantity of money in circulation – an idea later to be known as the quantity theory of money – and to apply this theory to the international monetary arena.

References and further reading

Eltis, Walter (1995) "John Locke, the Quantity Theory of Money and the Establisment of a Sound Currency," in Mark Blaug *et al.* (eds), *The Quantity Theory of Money: From Locke to Keynes and Friedman*, Aldershot: Edward Elgar.

Hutchison, Terence (1988) *Before Adam Smith: The Emergence of Political Economy, 1662–1776*, Oxford: Basil Blackwell.

Laslett, P. (1957) "John Locke, the Great Recoinage, and the Origins of the Board of Trade," *William and Mary Quarterly* 14 (July): 370–92.

Leigh, A.H. (1974) "John Locke and the Quantity Theory of Money," *History of Political Economy* 6 (Summer): 200–19.

Letwin, William (1964) *The Origins of Scientific Economics*, Garden City, NY: Doubleday & Co.

Locke, John (1823) *The Works of John Locke*, London: Thomas Tegg.

Vaughn, Karen I. (1980) *John Locke: Economist and Social Scientist*, Chicago: University of Chicago Press.

——(1987) "Locke, John," in John Eatwell, Murray Milgate, and Peter Newman (eds), *The New Palgrave: A Dictionary of Economics*, Vol. 3, London: Macmillan, 229–30.

Of Civil Government (1690)*

Chapter V: Of property

25. Whether we consider natural reason, which tells us, that men, being once born, have a right to their preservation, and consequently to meat and drink, and such other things as nature affords for their subsistence; or revelation, which gives us an account of those grants God made of the world to Adam, and to Noah, and his sons; it is very clear, that God, as king David says, Psal. cxv. 16, 'has given the earth to the children of men'; given it to mankind in common. But this being supposed, it seems to some a very great difficulty how any one should ever come to have a property in any thing: I will not content myself to answer, that if it be difficult to make out property, upon a supposition that God gave the world to Adam and his posterity in common, it is impossible that any man, but one universal monarch, should have any property, upon a supposition that God gave the world to Adam, and his heirs in succession, exclusive of all the rest of his posterity. But I shall endeavour to show how men might come to have a property in several parts of that which God gave to mankind in common, and that without any express compact of all the commoners.

26. God, who hath given the world to men in common, hath also given them reason to make use of it to the best advantage of life and convenience. The earth, and all that is therein, is given to men for the support and comfort of their being. And though all the fruits it naturally produces, and beasts it feeds, belong to mankind in common, as they are produced by the spontaneous hand of nature; and nobody has originally a private dominion, exclusive of the rest of mankind, in any of them, as they are thus in their natural state: yet being given for the use of men, there must of necessity be a means to appropriate them some way or other before they can be of any use, or at all beneficial to any particular man. The fruit, or venison, which nourishes the wild Indian, who knows no enclosure, and is still a tenant in common, must be his, and so his, that is, a part of him, that another can no longer have any right to it, before it can do him any good for the support of his life.

27. Though the earth, and all inferior creatures, be common to all men, yet every man has a property in his own person: this nobody has any right to but himself. The labour of his body, and the work of his hands, we may say, are properly his. Whatsoever then he removes out of the state that nature hath provided, and left it in, he hath mixed his labour with, and joined to it something that is his own, and thereby makes it his property. It being by him removed from the common state nature hath placed it in, it hath by this labour something annexed to it that excludes the common right of other men. For this labour being the unquestionable property of

* *Two Treatises of Government.* London, 1764. Taken from: *The Works of John Locke*, A New Edition, Corrected, Vol. V. London: Printed for Thmas Tegg; W. Sharpe and Son; G. Offor; G. and J. Robinson; J. Evans and Co.: Also R. Griffin and Co. Glasgow; and J. Cumming, Dublin. 1823. Pp. 207–485. Reprinted Germany: Scientia Verlag Aalen, 1963.

the labourer, no man but he can have a right to what that is once joined to, at least where there is enough, and as good, left in common for others.

28. He that is nourished by the acorns he picked up under an oak, or the apples he gathered from the trees in the wood, has certainly appropriated them to himself. Nobody can deny but the nourishment is his. I ask then, when did they begin to be his? When he digested? Or when he ate? Or when he boiled? Or when he brought them home? Or when he picked them up? And it is plain, if the first gathering made them not his, nothing else could. That labour put a distinction between them and common: that added something to them more than nature, the common mother of all, had done; and so they became his private right. And will any one say, he had no right to those acorns or apples he thus appropriated, because he had not the consent of all mankind to make them his? Was it a robbery thus to assume to himself what belonged to all in common? If such a consent as that was necessary, man had starved, notwithstanding the plenty God had given him. We see in commons, which remain so by compact, that it is the taking any part of what is common, and removing it out of the state nature leaves it in, which begins the property; without which the common is of no use. And the taking of this or that part does not depend on the express consent of all the commoners. Thus the grass my horse has bit; the turfs my servant has cut; and the ore I have digged in any place, where I have a right to them in common with others; become my property, without the assignation or consent of any body. The labour that was mine, removing them out of that common state they were in, hath fixed my property in them.

29. By making an explicit consent of every commoner necessary to any one's appropriating to himself any part of what is given in common, children or servants could not cut the meat, which their father or master had provided for them in common, without assigning to every one his peculiar part. Though the water running in the fountain be every one's, yet who can doubt but that in the pitcher is his only who drew it out? His labour hath taken it out of the hands of nature, where it was common, and belonged equally to all her children, and hath thereby appropriated it to himself.

...

31. It will perhaps be objected to this, that 'if gathering the acorns, or other fruits of the earth, &c. makes a right to them, then any one may engross as much as he will'. To which I answer, Not so. The same law of nature, that does by this means give us property, does also bound that property too. 'God has given us all things richly', I Tim. vi. 17, is the voice of reason confirmed by inspiration. But how far has he given it us? To enjoy. As much as any one can make use of to any advantage of life before it spoils, so much he may by his labour fix a property in: whatever is beyond this, is more than his share, and belongs to others. Nothing was made by God for man to spoil or destroy. And thus, considering the plenty of natural provisions there was a long time in the world, and the few spenders; and to how small a part of that provision the industry of one man could extend itself, and engross it to the prejudice of others; especially keeping within the bounds, set by reason, of what might serve for his use; there could be then little room for quarrels or contentions about property so established.

32. But the chief matter of property being now not the fruits of the earth, and the beasts that subsist on it, but the earth itself; as that which takes in, and carries with it all the rest; I think it is plain, that property in that too is acquired as the former. As much land as a man tills, plants, improves, cultivates, and can use the product of, so much is his property. He by his labour does, as it were, enclose it from the common. Nor will it invalidate his right, to say every body else has an equal title to it, and therefore he cannot appropriate, he cannot enclose, without the consent of all his fellow-commoners, all mankind. God, when he gave the world in common to all mankind, commanded man also to labour, and the penury of his condition required it of him. God and his reason commanded him to subdue the earth, that is, improve it for the benefit of life, and therein lay out something upon it that was his own, his labour. He that, in obedience to this command of God, subdued, tilled, and sowed any part of it, thereby annexed to it something that was his property, which another had no title to, nor could without injury take from him.

33. Nor was this appropriation of any parcel of land, by improving it, any prejudice to any other man, since there was still enough, and as good left; and more than the yet unprovided could use. So that, in effect, there was never the less left for others because of his enclosure for himself: for he that leaves as much as another can make use of, does as good as take nothing at all. Nobody could think himself injured by the drinking of another man, though he took a good draught, who had a whole river of the same water left him to quench his thirst; and the case of land and water, where there is enough of both, is perfectly the same.

34. God gave the world to men in common; but since he gave it them for their benefit, and the greatest conveniencies of life they were capable to draw from it, it cannot be supposed he meant it should always remain common and uncultivated. He gave it to the use of the industrious and rational (and labour was to be his title to it), not to the fancy or covetousness of the quarrelsome and contentious. He that had as good left for his improvement as was already taken up, needed not complain, ought not to meddle with what was already improved by another's labour: if he did, it is plain he desired the benefit of another's pains, which he had no right to, and not the ground which God had given him in common with others to labour on, and whereof there was as good left as that already possessed, and more than he knew what to do with, or his industry could reach to.

...

37. This is certain, that in the beginning, before the desire of having more than man needed had altered the intrinsic value of things, which depends only on their usefulness to the life of man; or had agreed, that a little piece of yellow metal, which would keep without wasting or decay, should be worth a great piece of flesh, or a whole heap of corn; though men had a right to appropriate, by their labour, each one to himself, as much of the things of nature as he could use: yet this could not be much, nor to the prejudice of others, where the same plenty was still left to those who would use the same industry. To which let me add, that he who appropriates land to himself by his labour, does not lessen, but increase the common stock of mankind: for the provisions serving to the support of human life, produced by one acre of enclosed and cultivated land, are (to speak much within compass) ten times more than those which are yielded by an acre of land of an equal richness lying waste in common. And therefore he that encloses land, and has a greater plenty of the conveniencies of life from ten acres, than he could have from an hundred left to nature, may truly be said to give ninety acres to mankind: for his labour now supplies him with provisions out of ten acres, which were by the product of an hundred lying in common. I have here rated the improved land very low, in making its product but as ten to one, when it is much nearer an hundred to one: for I ask, whether in the wild woods and uncultivated waste of America, left to nature, without any improvement, tillage, or husbandry, a thousand acres yield the needy and wretched inhabitants as many conveniencies of life as ten acres equally fertile land do in Devonshire, where they are well cultivated?

Before the appropriation of land, he who gathered as much of the wild fruit, killed, caught, or tamed, as many of the beasts, as he could; he that so employed his pains about any of the spontaneous products of nature, as any way to alter them from the state which nature put them in, by placing any of his labour on them, did thereby acquire a propriety in them: but if they perished, in his possession, without their due use; if the fruits rotted, or the venison putrefied, before he could spend it, he offended against the common law of nature, and was liable to be punished; he invaded his neighbour's share, for he had no right, farther than his use called for any of them, and they might serve to afford him conveniencies of life.

...

40. Nor is it so strange, as perhaps before consideration it may appear, that the property of labour should be able to overbalance the community of land: for it is labour indeed that put the difference of value on every thing; and let any one consider what the difference is between an acre of land planted with tobacco or sugar, sown with wheat or barley, and an acre of the same land lying in common, without any husbandry upon it, and he will find, that the improvement of labour makes the far greater part of the value. I think it will be but a very modest computation to say, that of the products of the earth useful to the life of man, nine-tenths are the effects of labour: nay, if we will rightly estimate things as they come to our use, and cast up the several expenses about them, what in them is purely owing to nature, and what to labour, we shall find, that in most of them ninety-nine-hundredths are wholly to be put on the account of labour.

41. There cannot be a clearer demonstration of any thing, than several nations of the Americans are of this, who are rich in land, and poor in all the comforts of life; whom nature having furnished as liberally as any other people with the materials of plenty, that is, a fruitful soil, apt to produce in abundance what might serve for food, raiment, and delight; yet, for want of improving it by labour, have not one-hundredth part of the conveniencies we enjoy: and a king of a large and fruitful territory there feeds, lodges, and is clad worse than a day-labourer in England.

42. To make this a little clear, let us but trace some of the ordinary provisions of life, through their several progresses, before they come to our use, and see how much of their value they receive from human industry. Bread, wine, and cloth, are things of daily use, and great plenty; yet notwithstanding, acorns, water, and leaves, or skins, must be our bread, drink, and clothing, did not labour furnish us with these more useful commodities: for whatever bread is more worth than acorns, wine than water, and cloth or silk than leaves, skins, or moss, that is wholly owing to labour and industry; the one of these being the food and raiment which unassisted nature furnishes us with; the other, provisions which our industry and pains prepare for us; which, how much they exceed the other in value, when any one hath computed, he will then see how much labour makes the far greatest part of the value of things we enjoy in this world: and the ground which produces the materials is scarce to be reckoned in as any, or, at most, but a very small part of it; so little, that even amongst us, land that is left wholly to nature, that hath no improvement of pasturage, tillage, or planting, is called, as indeed it is, waste; and we shall find the benefit of it amount to little more than nothing.

Some Considerations of the Consequences of the Lowering of Interest, and Raising the Value of Money (1691)*

Sir,

I have so little concern in paying or receiving of 'interest', that were I in no more danger to be misled by inability and ignorance, than I am to be biassed by interest and inclination, I might hope to give you a very perfect and clear account of the consequences of a law to reduce interest to 4 per cent. But, since you are pleased to ask my opinion, I shall endeavour fairly to state this matter of use, with the best of my skill.

The first thing to be considered is, 'Whether the price of the hire of money can be regulated by law?' And to that I think, generally speaking, one may say, it is manifest it cannot. For since it is impossible to make a law, that shall hinder a man from giving away his money or estate to whom he pleases, it will be impossible, by any contrivance of law, to hinder men, skilled in the power they have over their own goods, and the ways of conveying them to others, to purchase money to be lent them, at what rate soever their occasions shall make it necessary for them to have it; for it is to be remembered, that no man borrows money, or pays use, out of mere pleasure: it is the want of money drives men to that trouble and charge of borrowing; and proportionably to this want, so will every one have it, whatever price it cost him. Wherein the skilful, I say, will always so manage it, as to avoid the prohibition of your law, and keep out of its penalty, do what you can. What then will be the unavoidable consequences of such a law?

1. It will make the difficulty of borrowing and lending much greater, whereby trade (the foundation of riches) will be obstructed.

2. It will be a prejudice to none, but those who most need assistance and help; I mean widows and orphans, and others uninstructed in the arts and management of more skilful men, whose estates lying in money, they will be sure, especially orphans, to have no more profit of their money, than what interest the law barely allows.

3. It will mightily increase the advantage of bankers and scriveners, and other such expert brokers, who, skilled in the arts of putting out money, according to the true and natural value, which the present state of trade, money, and debts, shall always raise interest to, they will infallibly get what the true value of interest shall be above the legal; for men, finding the convenience of lodging their money in hands, where they can be sure of it, at short warning, the ignorant and lazy will be forwardest to put it into these men's hands, who are known willingly to receive it, and where they can, readily have the whole, or part, upon any sudden occasion, that may call for it.

---

* *Some Considerations of the Consequences of the Lowering of Interest and Raising the Value of Money*. In a letter sent to a Member of Parliament, 1691 London Printed for Awnsham and John Churchill, at the Black Swan in Pater-Noster-Row. Taken from: *The Works of John Locke*, A New Edition, Corrected, Vol. V. London: Printed for Thmas Tegg; W. Sharpe and Son; G. Offor; G. and J. Robinson; J. Evans and Co.: Also R. Griffin and Co. Glasgow; and J. Cumming, Dublin. 1823. Pp. 3–130. Reprinted Germany: Scientia Verlag Aalen, 1963.

4. I fear I may reckon it as one of the probable consequences of such a law, that it is likely to cause great perjury in the nation; a crime, than which nothing is more carefully to be prevented by law-makers, not only by penalties, that shall attend apparent and proved perjury, but by avoiding and lessening, as much as may be, the temptations to it; for where those are strong (as they are, where men shall swear for their own advantage) there the fear of penalties to follow will have little restraint, especially if the crime be hard to be proved; all which, I suppose, will happen in this case, where ways will be found out to receive money upon other pretences than for use, to evade the rule and rigour of the law: and there will be secret trusts and collusions amongst men, that though they may be suspected, can never be proved, without their own confession. …

But that law cannot keep men from taking more use than you set (the want of money being that alone which regulates its price) will perhaps appear, if we consider how hard it is to set a price upon wine, or silks, or other unnecessary commodities: but how impossible it is to set a rate upon victuals, in a time of famine; for money being a universal commodity, and as necessary to trade as food is to life, every body must have it, at what rate they can get it; and unavoidably pay dear, when it is scarce; and debts, no less than trade, have made borrowing in fashion. The bankers are a clear instance of this: for some years since, the scarcity of money having made it in England worth really more than 6 per cent, most of those that had not the skill to let it for more than 6 per cent, and secure themselves from the penalty of the law, put it in the bankers' hands, where it was ready at their call, when they had an opportunity of greater improvement; so that the rate you set, profits not the lenders; and very few of the borrowers, who are fain to pay the price for money, that commodity would bear, were it left free; and the gain is only to the banker: and should you lessen the use to 4 per cent, the merchant or tradesman that borrows would not have it one jot cheaper than he has now; but probably these two ill effects would follow: first, that he would pay dearer; and, second, that there would be less money left in the country to drive the trade: for the bankers, paying at most but 4 per cent and receiving from 6–10 per cent or more, at that low rate could be content to have more money lie dead by them, than now, when it is higher; by which means there would be less money stirring in trade, and a greater scarcity, which would raise it upon the borrower by this monopoly; and what a part of our treasure their skill and management, joined with others' laziness, or want of skill, is apt to draw into their hands, is to be known by those vast sums of money they were found to owe, at shutting up of the Exchequer: and though it be very true, yet it is almost beyond belief, that one private goldsmith of London should have credit, upon his single security (being usually nothing but a note, under one of his servants' hands) for above eleven hundred thousand pounds at once. The same reasons, I suppose, will still keep on the same trade; and when you have taken it down by law to that rate, nobody will think of having more than 4 per cent of the banker; though those who have need of money, to employ it in trade, will not then, any more than now, get it under 5 or 6, or as some pay, 7 or 8. And if they had then, when the law permitted men to make more profit of their money, so large a proportion of the cash of the nation in their hands, who can think but that, by this law, it should be more driven into Lombard-street now? There being many now, who lend them at 4 or 5 per cent who would not lend to others at 6. It would therefore, perhaps, bring down the rate of money to the borrower, and certainly distribute it better to the advantage of trade in the country, if the legal use were kept pretty near to the natural; (by natural use, I mean that rate of money, which the present scarcity of it makes it naturally at, upon an equal distribution of it) for then men, being licensed by the law to take near the full natural use, will not be forward to carry it to London, to put it into the banker's hands; but will lend it to their neighbours in the country, where it is convenient for trade it should be. But, if you lessen the rate of use, the lender, whose interest it is to keep up the rate of money, will rather lend it to the banker, at the legal interest, than to the tradesman, or gentleman, who, when the law is broken, shall be sure to pay the full natural interest, or more; because of the engrossing by the banker, as well as the risque in transgressing the law: whereas, were the natural use, suppose 7 per cent and the legal 6; first, the owner would not venture the penalty of the law, for the gaining 1 in 7, that being the utmost his money would yield: nor would the banker venture to borrow, where his gains would be but 1 per cent, nor the moneyed man lend him what he could make better profit of legally at home. All the danger lies in this; that your trade should suffer, if your being behind hand has made the natural use so high, that your tradesman cannot live upon his labour, but that your rich neighbours will so undersell you, that the return you make will not amount to pay the use, and afford a livelihood. There is no way to recover from this, but by a general frugality and industry; or by being masters of the trade of some commodity, which the world must have from you at your rate, because it cannot be otherwhere supplied.

Now, I think, the natural interest of money is raised two ways: first, when the money of a country is but little, in proportion to the debts of the inhabitants, one amongst another. For, suppose ten thousand pounds were sufficient to manage the trade of Bermudas, and that the ten first planters carried over twenty thousand pounds, which they lent to the several tradesmen and inhabitants of the country, who living above their gains, had spent ten thousand pounds of this money, and it were gone out of the island; it is evident, that, should all the creditors at once call in their money, there would be a great scarcity of money, when that, employed in trade, must be taken out of the tradesmen's hands to pay debts; or else the debtors want money, and be exposed to their creditors, and so interest will be high. But this seldom happening, that all, or the greatest part, of the creditors do at once call for their money, unless it be in some great and general danger, is less and seldomer felt than the following, unless where the debts of the people are grown to a greater proportion; for that, constantly causing more borrowers than there can be lenders, will make money scarce, and consequently interest high. Second, that, which constantly raises the natural interest of money, is, when money is little, in proportion to the trade of a country. For in trade every body calls for money, according as he wants it, and this disproportion is always felt. For, if Englishmen owed in all but one million, and there were millions of money in England, the money would be well enough proportioned to the debts: but, if two millions were necessary to carry on the trade, there would be a million wanting, and the price of money would be raised, as it is of any other commodity in a market, where the merchandize will not serve half the customers, and there are two buyers for one seller.

It is in vain, therefore, to go about effectually to reduce the price of interest by a law; and you may as rationally hope to set a fixed rate upon the hire of houses, or ships, as of money. He that wants a vessel, rather than lose his market, will not stick to have it at the market-rate, and find ways to do it with security to the owner, though the rate were limited by law: and he that wants money, rather than lose his voyage, or his trade, will pay the natural interest for it; and submit to such ways of conveyance, as shall keep the lender out of the reach of the law. So that your act, at best, will serve only to increase the arts of lending, but not at all lessen the charge of the borrower: he, it is likely, shall, with more trouble, and going farther about, pay also the more for his money; unless you intend to break in only upon mortgages and contracts already made, and (which is not to be supposed) by law, *post factum*, void bargains lawfully made, and give to Richard what is Peter's due, for no other reason, but because one was borrower, and the other lender.

But, supposing the law reached the intention of the promoters of it; and that this act be so contrived, that it fixed the natural price of money, and hindered its being, by any body, lent at a higher use than 4 per cent, which is plain it cannot: let us, in the next place, see what will be the consequences of it.

1. It will be a loss to widows, orphans, and all those who have their estates in money, one-third of their estates; which will be a very hard case upon a great number of people: and it is warily to be considered, by the wisdom of the nation, whether they will thus, at one blow, fine and impoverish a great and innocent part of the people, who having their estates in money, have as much right to make as much of the money as it is worth (for more they cannot) as the landlord has to let his land for as much as it will yield. To fine men one-third of their estates, without any crime, or offence committed, seems very hard.

2. As it will be a considerable loss and injury to the moneyed man, so it will be no advantage at all to the kingdom. For, so trade be not cramped, and exportation of our native commodities and manufactures not hindered, it will be no matter to the kingdom, who amongst ourselves gets or loses: only common charity teaches, that those should be most taken care of by the law, who are least capable of taking care for themselves.

3. It will be a gain to the borrowing merchant. For if he borrow at 4 per cent, and his returns be 12 per cent, he will have 8 per cent, and the lender 4; whereas now they divide the profit equally at 6 per cent. But this neither gets, nor loses, to the kingdom, in your trade, supposing the merchant and lender to be both Englishmen; only it will, as I have said, transfer a third part of the moneyed man's estate, who had nothing else to live on, into the merchant's pocket; and that without any merit in the one, or transgression in the other. Private men's interests ought not thus to be neglected, nor sacrificed to any thing, but the manifest advantage of the public. But, in this case, it will be quite the contrary. This loss to the moneyed men will be a prejudice to trade: since it will discourage lending at such a disproportion of profit to risque; as we shall see more by and by, when we come to consider of what consequence it is to encourage lending, that so none of the money of the nation may lie dead, and thereby prejudice trade.

4. It will hinder trade. For, there being a certain proportion of money necessary for driving such a proportion of trade, so much money of this as lies still, lessens so much of the trade. Now it cannot be rationally expected, but that, where the venture is great and the gains small, (as it is in lending in England, upon low interest) many will choose rather to hoard up their money, than venture it abroad, on such terms. This will be a loss to the kingdom, and such a loss, as, here in England, ought chiefly to be looked after: for, we having no mines, nor any other way of getting, or keeping of riches amongst us, but by trade; so much of our trade as is lost, so much of our riches must necessarily go with it; and the over-balancing of trade, between us and our neighbours, must inevitably carry away our money, and quickly leave us poor and exposed. Gold and silver, though they serve for few, yet they command all the conveniencies of life, and therefore in a plenty of them consist riches.

…

In a country not furnished with mines, there are but two ways of growing rich, either conquest or commerce. By the first the Romans made themselves masters of the riches of the world; but I think that, in our present circumstances, nobody is vain enough to entertain a thought of our reaping the profits of the world with our swords, and making the spoil and tribute of vanquished nations the fund for the supply of the charges of the government, with an overplus for the wants, and equally craving luxury, and fashionable vanity of the people.

Commerce, therefore, is the only way left to us, either for riches, or subsistence: for this the advantages of our situation as well as the industry and inclination of our people, bold and skilful at sea, do naturally fit us: by this the nation of England has been hitherto supported, and trade left almost to itself, and assisted only by the natural advantages above-mentioned, brought us in plenty of riches, and always set this kingdom in a rank equal, if not superior to any of its neighbours; and would no doubt, without any difficulty, have continued it so, if the more enlarged and better understood interest of trade, since the improvement of navigation, had not raised us many rivals; and the amazing politics of some late reigns let in other competitors with us for the sea, who will be sure to seize to themselves whatever parts of trade our mismanagement, or want of money, shall let slip out of our hands: and when it is once lost, it will be too late to hope, by a mistimed care, easily to retrieve it again. For the currents of trade, like those of waters, make themselves channels, out of which they are afterwards as hard to be diverted, as rivers that have worn themselves deep within their banks.

Trade, then, is necessary to the producing of riches, and money necessary to the carrying on of trade. This is principally to be looked after, and taken care of. For if this be neglected, we shall in vain by contrivances amongst ourselves, and shuffling the little money we have, from one another's hands, endeavour to prevent our wants: decay of trade will quickly waste all the remainder; and then the landed-man, who thinks, perhaps, by the fall of interest to raise the value of his land, will find himself cruelly mistaken; when the money being gone, (as it will be, if our trade be not kept up) he can get neither farmer to rent, nor purchaser to buy his land. Whatsoever, therefore, binders the lending of money, injures trade; and so the reducing of money to 4 per cent, which will discourage men from lending, will be a loss to the kingdom, in stopping so much of the current money, which turns the wheels of trade. But all this upon a supposition, that the lender and borrower are both Englishmen.

...

The necessity of a certain proportion of money to trade (I conceive) lies in this, that money, in its circulation, driving the several wheels of trade, whilst it keeps in that channel (for some of it will unavoidably be drained into standing pools) is all shared between the landholder, whose land affords the materials; the labourer, who works them; the broker, that is, the merchant and shop-keeper, who distributes them to those that want them; and the consumer who spends them. Now money is necessary to all these sorts of men, as serving both for counters and for pledges' and so carrying with it even reckoning, and security, that he that receives it shall have the same value for it again, of other things that he wants, whenever he pleases. The one of these it does by its stamp and denomination; the other by its intrinsic value, which is its quantity.

For mankind, having consented to put an imaginary value upon gold and silver, by reason of their durableness, scarcity, and not being very liable to be counterfeited, have made them, by general consent, the common pledges, whereby men are assured, in exchange for them, to receive equally valuable things, to those they parted with, for any quantity of these metals; by which means it comes to pass, that the intrinsic value, regarded in these metals, made the common barter, is nothing but the quantity which men give or receive of them; for they having, as money, no other value, but as pledges to procure what one wants or desires, and they procuring what we want or desire only by their quantity, it is evident that the intrinsic value of silver and gold, used in commerce, is nothing but their quantity.

...

To return to the business in hand, and show the necessity of a proportion of money to trade. Every man must have at least so much money, or so timely recruits, as may in hand, or in a short distance of time, satisfy his creditor who supplies him with the necessaries of life, or of his trade. For nobody has any longer these necessary supplies than he has money, or credit, which is nothing else but an assurance of money, in some short time. So that it is requisite to trade, that there should be so much money as to keep up the landholder's, labourer's, and broker's, credit: and therefore ready money must be constantly exchanged for wares and labour, or follow within a short time after.

This shows the necessity of some proportion of money to trade: but what proportion that is, is hard to determine; because it depends not barely on the quantity of money, but the quickness of its circulation. The very same shilling may, at one time, pay twenty men in twenty days: at another, rest in the same hands one hundred days together. This makes it impossible exactly to estimate the quantity of money needful in trade; but, to make some probable guess, we are to consider how much money it is necessary to suppose must rest constantly in each man's hands, as requisite to the carrying on of trade.

...

There is another seeming consequence of the reducing of money to a low price, which at first sight has such an appearance of truth in it, that I have known it to impose upon very able men, and I guess it has no small influence, at this time, in promoting this alteration; and that is, that the lowering of interest will raise the value of all other things in proportion. For money being the counter-balance to all other things purchaseable by it, and lying, as it were, in the opposite scale of commerce, it looks like a natural consequence, that as much as you take off from the value of money, so much you add to the price of other things which are exchanged for it; the raising of the price of any thing being no more but the addition to its value in respect of money, or, which is all one, lessening the value of money. For example: should the value of gold be brought down to that of silver, one hundred guineas would purchase little more corn, wool, or land, than one hundred shillings; and so, the value of money being brought lower, say they, the price of other things will rise, and the falling of interest from six pounds to four pounds per cent is taking away so much of the price of money, and so consequently the lessening its value.

The mistake of this plausible way of reasoning will be easily discovered, when we consider that the measure of the value of money, in proportion to any thing purchaseable by it, is the quantity of the ready money we have in comparison with the quantity of that thing, and its vent; or, which amounts to the same thing, the price of any commodity rises or falls, by the proportion of the number of buyers and sellers: this rule holds universally in all things that are to be bought and sold, bating now and then an extravagant fancy of some particular person, which never amounts to so considerable a part of trade, as to make any thing in the account worthy to be thought an exception to this rule.

The vent of any thing depends upon its necessity or usefulness; as convenience, or opinion, guided by fancy, or fashion, shall determine.

The vent of any commodity comes to be increased, or decreased, as a greater part of the running cash of the nation is designed to be laid out, by several people at the same time, rather in that than another; as we see in the change of fashions.

I shall begin first with the necessaries, or conveniencies of life, and the consumable commodities subservient thereunto; and show, that the value of money, in respect of those, depends only on the plenty or scarcity of money, in proportion to the plenty and scarcity of those things; and not on what interest shall, by necessity, law, or contract, be at that time laid on the borrowing of money; and then afterwards I shall show that the same holds in land.

There is nothing more confirmed, by daily experience, than that men give any portion of money, for whatsoever is absolutely necessary, rather than go without it. And in such things, the scarcity of them alone makes their prices. As for example: let us suppose half an ounce of silver, or half a crown now in England, is worth a bushel of wheat: but should there be next year a great scarcity of wheat in England, and a proportionable want of all other food, five ounces of silver would, perhaps, in exchange purchase but one bushel of wheat: so that money would be then nine-tenths less worth in respect of food, though at the same value it was before, in respect of other things, that kept their former proportion, in their quantity and consumption.

...

The fall, therefore, or rise of interest, making immediately, by its change, neither more nor less land, money, or any sort of commodity in England, than there was before, alters not at all the value of money, in reference to commodities. Because the measure of that is only the quantity and vent, which are not immediately changed by the change of interest. So far as the change of interest conduces, in trade, to the bringing in, or carrying out money, or commodities, and so in time to the varying their proportions here in England, from what it was before; so far the change of interest, as all other things that promote or hinder trade, may alter the value of money, in reference to commodities. But that is not in this place to be considered.

...

2. Money has a value, as it is capable, by exchange, to procure us the necessaries or conveniencies of life, and in this it has the nature of a commodity; only with this difference, that it serves us commonly by its exchange, never almost by its consumption. But though the use men make of money be not in its consumption, yet it has not at all a more standing, settled value, in exchange with any other thing, than any other commodity has; but a more known one, and better fixed by name, number, and weight, to enable us to reckon what the proportion of scarcity and vent of one commodity is to another. For supposing, as before, that half an ounce of silver would last year exchange for one bushel of wheat, or for 15 lb weight of lead; if this year wheat be ten times scarcer, and lead in the same quantity to its vent as it was, is it not evident, that half an ounce of silver will still exchange for 15 lb of lead, though it will exchange but for one-tenth of a bushel of wheat? And he that has use of lead will as soon take 15 lb weight of lead as half an ounce of silver, for one-tenth of a bushel of wheat, and no more. So that if you say, that money now is nine-tenths less worth than it was the former year, you must say so of lead too, and all other things, that keep the same proportion to money which they had before. The variation, indeed, is first and most taken notice of in money: because that is the universal measure by which people reckon, and used by every body in the valuing of all things. For calling that half an ounce of silver half a crown, they speak properly, and are readily understood, when they say, half a crown, or two shillings and six-pence, will now buy one-tenth of a bushel of wheat, but do not say, that 15 lb of lead will now buy one-tenth of a bushel of wheat, because it is not generally used to this sort of reckoning; nor do they say, lead is less worth than it was, though, in respect of wheat, lead be nine-tenths worse than it was, as well as silver; only by the tale of shillings we are better enabled to judge of it: because these are measures, whose ideas by constant use are settled in every Englishman's mind.

This, I suppose, is the true value of money, when it passes from one to another, in buying and selling; where it runs the same changes of higher, or lower, as any other commodity doth: for one equal quantity whereof you shall receive in exchange more or less of another commodity, at one time, than you do at another. For a farmer that carries a bushel of wheat to market, and a labourer that carries half a crown, shall find that the money of one, as well as corn of the other, shall at some times purchase him more or less leather, or salt, according as they are in greater plenty, and scarcity, one to another. So that in exchanging coined silver for any other commodity, (which is buying and selling) the same measure governs the proportion you receive, as if you exchanged lead, or wheat, or any other commodity. That which regulates the price, that is, the quantity given for money (which is called buying and selling) for another commodity (which is called bartering) is nothing else but their quantity in proportion to their vent. If then lowering of use makes not your silver more in specie, or your wheat or other commodities less, it will not have any influence at all to make it exchange for less of wheat or any other commodity, than it will have on lead, to make it exchange for less wheat, or any other commodity.

...

He that will justly estimate the value of any thing, must consider its quantity in proportion to its vent, for this alone regulates the price. The value of any thing, compared with itself or with a standing measure, is greater, as its quantity is less in proportion to its vent: but, in comparing it, or exchanging it with any other thing, the quantity and vent of that thing too must be allowed for, in the computation of their value. But, because the desire of money is constantly almost every where the same, its vent varies very little, but as its greater scarcity enhances its price, and increases the scramble: there being nothing else that does easily supply the want of it: the lessening its quantity, therefore, always increases its price, and makes an equal portion of it exchange for a greater of any other thing. Thus it comes to pass, that there is no manner of settled proportion between the value of an ounce of silver and any other commodity: for, either varying its quantity in that country, or the commodity changing its quantity in proportion to its vent, their respective values change, that is, less of one will barter for more of the other: though, in the ordinary way of speaking, it is only said, that the price of the commodity, not of the money, is changed. For example, half an ounce of silver in England will exchange sometimes for a whole bushel of wheat, sometimes for half, sometimes but a quarter, and this it does equally, whether by use it be apt to bring in to the owner six in the hundred of its own weight per annum, or nothing at all: it being only the change of the quantity of wheat to its vent, supposing we have still the same sum of money in the kingdom; or else the change of the quantity of our money in the kingdom, supposing the quantity of wheat, in respect to its vent, be the same too, that makes the change in the price of wheat. For if you alter the quantity, or vent, on either side, you presently alter the price, but no other way in the world.

…

I have met with patrons of 4 per cent who (amongst many other fine things they tell us of) affirm, 'That if interest were reduced to four per cent. then some men would borrow money at this low rate, and pay their debts; others would borrow more than they now do, and improve their land; others would borrow more, and employ it in trade and manufacture'. Gilded words indeed, were there any thing substantial in them! These men talk as if they meant to show us not only the wisdom, but the riches of Solomon, and would make gold and silver as common as stones in the street: but at last, I fear, it will be but wit without money, and I wish it amount to that. It is without question, that could the countryman and the tradesman take up money cheaper than now they do, every man would be forward to borrow, and desire that he might have other men's money to employ to his advantage. I confess, those who contend for 4 per cent have found out a way to set men's mouths a watering for money at that rate, and to increase the number of borrowers in England, if any body can imagine it would be an advantage to increase them. But to answer all their fine projects, I have but this one short question to ask them: Will 4 per cent increase the number of the lenders? If it will not, as any man at the very first hearing will shrewdly suspect it will not, then all the plenty of money, these conjurers bestow upon us, for improvement of land, paying of debts, and advancement of trade, is but like the gold and silver which old women believe other conjurers bestow sometimes, by whole lapfuls, on poor credulous girls, which, when they bring to the light, is found to be nothing but withered leaves; and the possessors of it are still as much in want of money as ever.

Indeed, I grant it would be well for England, and I wish it were so, that the plenty of money were so great amongst us, that every man could borrow as much as he could use in trade for 4 per cent; nay, that men could borrow as much as they could employ for 6 per cent. But even at that rate, the borrowers already are far more than the lenders. Why else doth the merchant, upon occasion, pay 6 per cent and often above that rate, for brokerage? And why doth the country gentleman of 1000*l.* per annum find it so difficult, with all the security he can bring, to take up 1000? All which proceeds from the scarcity of money and bad security; two causes which will not be less powerful to hinder borrowing, after the lowering of interest; and I do not see how any one can imagine that reducing use to 4 per cent should abate their force, or how lessening the reward of the lender, without diminishing his risk, should make him more forward and ready to lend. So that these men, whilst they talk that at 4 per cent men would take up and employ more money to the public advantage, do but pretend to multiply the number of borrowers among us, of which it is certain we have too many already. While they thus set men a longing for the golden days of 4 per cent, methinks they use the poor indigent debtor, and needy tradesman, as I have seen prating jackdaws do sometimes their young, who, kawing and fluttering about the nest, set all their young ones a gaping, but, having nothing in their empty mouths but noise and air, leave them as hungry as before.

It is true these men have found out by a cunning project how, by the restraint of a law, to make the price of money one-third cheaper, and then they tell John a Nokes that he shall have 10,000 *l* of it to employ in merchandize, or clothing; and John a Stiles shall have 20,000 *l* more to pay his debts; and so distribute this money as freely as Diego did his legacies, which they are to have, even where they can get them. But till these men can instruct the forward borrowers where they shall be furnished, they have perhaps done something to increase men's desire, but not made money one jot easier to come by; and, till they do that, all this sweet jingling of money, in their discourses, goes just to the tune of 'If all the world were oatmeal'. Methinks these undertakers, whilst they have put men in hopes of borrowing more plentifully, at easier rates, for the supply of their wants and trades, had done better to have bethought themselves of a way how men need not borrow upon use at all: for this would be much more advantageous, and altogether as feasible. It is as easy to distribute twenty pair of shoes amongst thirty men, if they pay nothing for them at all, as if they paid 4*s* a pair; ten of them (notwithstanding the statute-rate should be reduced from 6*s* to 4*s* a pair) will be necessitated to sit still barefoot, as much as if they were to pay nothing for shoes at all. Just so it is in a country that wants money in proportion to trade. It is as easy to contrive how every man shall be supplied with what money he needs (i.e. can employ in improvement of land, paying his debts, and returns of his trade) for nothing, as for 4 per cent. Either we have already more money than the owners will lend, or we have not. If part of the money, which is now in England, will not be let at the rate interest is at present at, will men be more ready to lend, and borrowers be furnished for all those brave purposes more plentifully, when money is brought to 4 per cent? If people do already lend all the money they have, above their own occasions, whence are those who will borrow more at 4 per cent to be supplied? Or is there such plenty of money, and scarcity of borrowers, that there needs the reducing of interest to 4 per cent to bring men to take it?

…

Of raising our coin

Being now upon the consideration of interest and money, give me leave to say one word more on this occasion, which may not be wholly unseasonable at this time. I hear a talk up and down of raising our money, as a means to retain our wealth, and keep our money from being carried away. I wish those that use the phrase of raising our money had some clear notion annexed to it; and that then they would examine, 'Whether, that being true, it would at all serve to those ends for which it is proposed?'

The raising of money, then, signifies one of these two things; either raising the value of our money, or raising the denomination of our coin.

The raising the value of money, or any thing else, is nothing but the making a less quantity of it exchange for any other thing than would have been taken for it before; for example, If 5*s*. will exchange for, or (as we call it) buy a bushel of wheat; if you can make 4*s*. buy another bushel of the same wheat, it is plain the value of your money is raised, in respect of wheat, one-fifth. But thus nothing can raise or fall the value of your money, but the proportion of its plenty, or scarcity, in proportion to the plenty, scarcity, or vent of any other commodity with which you compare it, or for which you would exchange it. And thus silver, which makes the intrinsic value of money, compared with itself, under any stamp or denomination of the same or different countries, cannot be raised. For an ounce of silver, whether in pence, groats, or crown-pieces, stivers, or ducatoons, or in bullion, is, and always eternally will be, of equal value to any other ounce of silver, under what stamp or denomination soever; unless it can be shown that any stamp can add any new or better qualities to one parcel of silver, which another parcel of silver wants.

Silver, therefore, being always of equal value to silver, the value of coin, compared with coin, is greater, less, or equal, only as it has more, less, or equal silver in it: and in this respect, you can by no manner of way raise or fall your money. …

All then that can be done in this great mystery of raising money, is only to alter the denomination, and call that a crown now, which before, by the law, was but a part of a crown. For example: supposing, according to the standard of our law, 5s. or a crown, were to weigh an ounce (as it does now, wanting about 16 grains) whereof one-twelfth were copper, and eleven-twelfths silver (for thereabouts it is) it is plain here, it is the quantity of silver gives the value to it. For let another piece be coined of the same weight, wherein half the silver is taken out, and copper, or other alloy, put into the place, every one knows it will be worth but half as much. For the value of the alloy is so inconsiderable as not to be reckoned. This crown now must be raised, and from henceforth our crown-pieces coined one-twentieth lighter; which is nothing but changing the denomination, calling that a crown now, which yesterday was but a part, namely nineteen-twentieths of a crown; whereby you have only raised 19 parts to the denomination formerly given to 20. For I think nobody can be so senseless as to imagine that 19 grains or ounces of silver can be raised to the value of 20; or that 19 grains or ounces of silver shall at the same time exchange for, or buy as much corn, oil, or wine, as 20; which is to raise it to the value of 20. For if 19 ounces of silver can be worth 20 ounces of silver, or pay for as much of any other commodity, then 18, 10, or 1 ounce may do the same. For if the abating one-twentieth of the quantity of the silver of any coin, does not lessen its value, the abating nineteen-twentieths of the quantity of the silver of any coin will not abate its value. And so a single three pence, or a single penny, being called a crown, will buy as much spice, or silk, or any other commodity, as a crown-piece, which contains 20 or 60 times as much silver; which is an absurdity so great, that I think nobody will want eyes to see, and sense to disown.

Now this raising your money, or giving a less quantity of silver the stamp and denomination of a greater, may be done two ways.

1   By raising one species of your money.
2   By raising all your silver coin, at once proportionably; which is the thing, I suppose, now proposed.

1. The raising of one species of your coin, beyond its intrinsic value, is done by coining any one species (which in account bears such a proportion to the other species of your coin) with less silver in it than is required by that value it bears in your money.

For example: a crown with us goes for 60 pence, a shilling for 12 pence, a tester for 6 pence, and a groat for 4 pence; and accordingly, the proportion of silver in each of them, ought to be as 60, 12, 6, and 4. Now, if in the mint there should be coined groats, or testers, that, being of the same alloy with our other money, had but two-thirds of the weight that those species are coined at now; or else, being of the same weight, were so alloyed, as to have one-third of the silver, required by the present standard, changed into copper, and should thus, by law, be made current; (the rest of your silver money being kept to the present standard in weight and fineness) it is plain, those species would be raised one-third part; that passing for 6d. which had but the silver of *4d.* in it; and would be all one, as if a groat should by law be made current for 6d. and every 6d. in payment pass for 9d. This is truly raising these species: but is no more in effect, than if the mint should coin clipped money; and has, besides the cheat that is put by such base, or light money, on every particular man that receives it, that he wants one-third of that real value, which the public ought to secure him, in the money it obliges him to receive, as lawful and current. It has, I say, this great and unavoidable inconvenience to the public, that, besides the opportunity it gives to domestic coiners to cheat you with lawful money, it puts it into the hands of foreigners to fetch away your money, without any commodities for it. For if they find that two-penny weight of silver, marked with a certain impression, shall here in England be equivalent to 3d. weight, marked with another impression, they will not fail to stamp pieces of that fashion; and so importing that base and low coin, will here in England, receive 3d. for 2d. and quickly carry away your silver in exchange for copper, or barely the charge of coinage.

...

The quantity of silver, that is in each piece, or species of coin, being that which makes its real and intrinsic value, the due proportions of silver ought to be kept in each species, according to the respective rate, set on each of them by law. And, when this is ever varied from, it is but a trick to serve some present occasion; but is always with loss to the country where the trick is played.

2. The other way of raising money is by raising all your silver coin at once, the proportion of a crown, a shilling, and a penny, in reference to one another, being still kept (namely that a shilling shall weigh one-fifth of a crown-piece, and a penny-weight one-twelfth of a shilling, in standard silver) but out of every one of these you abate one-twentieth of the silver they were wont to have in them.

If all the species of money be, as it is called, raised, by making each of them to have one-twentieth less of silver in them than formerly, and so your whole money be lighter than it was; these following will be some of the consequences of it.

1. It will rob all creditors of one-twentieth (or 5 per cent) of their debts, and all landlords one-twentieth of their quit-rents for ever; and in all other rents, as far as their former contracts reach, (of 5 per cent) of their yearly income; and this without any advantage to the debtor, or farmer. For he, receiving no more pounds sterling for his land, or commodities, in this new lighter coin, than he should have done of your old and weightier money, gets nothing by it. If you say, yes, he will receive more crown, half-crown, and shilling pieces, for what he now sells for new money, than he should have done, if the money of the old standard had continued; you confess your money is not raised in value, but in denomination: since what your new pieces want in weight must now be made up in their number. But, which way soever this falls, it is certain the public (which most men think ought to be the only reason of changing a settled law, and disturbing the common current course of things) receives not the least profit by it. Nay, as we shall see by and by, it will be a great charge and loss to the kingdom. But this, at first sight, is visible. That in all payments to be received upon precedent contracts, if your money be in effect raised, the receiver will lose 5 per cent. For money having been lent, and leases and other bargains made, when money was of the same weight and fineness that it is now, upon confidence that under the same names of pounds, shillings, and pence, they should receive the same value, that is, the same quantity of silver, by giving the denomination now to less quantities of silver by one-twentieth, you take from them 5 per cent of their due.

When men go to market, to buy any other commodities with their new, but lighter money, they will find 20*s.* of their new money will buy no more of any commodity than 19 would before. For it not being the denomination, but the quantity of silver, that gives the value to any coin, 19 grains, or parts, of silver, however denominated or marked, will no more be worth, or pass for, or buy so much of any other commodity, as 20 grains of silver will, than 19*s.* will pass for 20*s.* If any one thinks a shilling, or a crown in name, has its value from the denomination, and not from the quantity of silver in it, let it be tried; and hereafter let a penny be called a shilling, or a shilling be called a crown. I believe nobody would be content to receive his debts or rents in such money: which, though the law should raise thus, yet he foresees he should lose eleven-twelfths by the one, and by the other four-fifths of the value he received; and would find his new shilling, which had no more silver in it than one-twelfth of what a shilling had before, would buy him of corn, cloth, or wine, but one-twelfth of what an old shilling would. This is as plainly so in the raising, as you call it, your crown to 5*s.* and 3*d.* or (which is the same thing) making your crown one-twentieth lighter in silver. The only difference is, that the loss is so great (it being eleven-twelfths) that every body sees, and abhors it at first proposal; but, in the other (it being but one-twentieth, and covered with the deceitful name of raising our money) people do not readily observe it. If it be good to raise the crown-piece this way one-twentieth this week, I suppose it will be as good and profitable to raise it as much again the next week. For there is no reason, why it will not be as good, to raise it again, another one-twentieth, the next week, and so on; wherein, if you proceed but ten weeks successively, you will, by new-year's day next, have every half-crown raised to a crown, to the loss of one-half of people's debts and rents, and the king's revenue, besides the confusion of all your affairs: and, if you please to go on in this beneficial way of raising your money, you may, by the same art, bring a penny-weight of silver to be a crown.

Silver, that is, the quantity of pure silver, separable from the alloy, makes the real value of money. If it does not, coin copper with the same stamp and denomination, and see whether it will be of the same value. I suspect your stamp will make it of no more worth than the copper money of Ireland is, which is its weight in copper, and no more. That money lost so much to Ireland as it passed for above the rate of copper. But yet I think nobody suffered so much by it as he by whose authority it was made current.

If silver give the value, you will say, what need is there then of the charge of coinage? May not men exchange silver by weight for other things; make their bargains and keep their accounts in silver by weight? This might be done, but it has these inconveniencies:

1. The weighing of silver to every one we had occasion to pay it to would be very troublesome, for every one most carry about scales in his pocket.

2. Scales would not do the business; for, in the next place, every one cannot distinguish between fine and mixed silver: so that though he received the full weight, he was not sure he received the full weight of silver, since there might be a mixture of some of the baser metals, which he was not able to discern. Those who have had the care and government of politic societies introduced coinage, as a remedy to those two inconveniencies. The stamp was a warranty of the public, that, under such a denomination, they should receive a piece of such a weight, and such a fineness; that is, they should receive so much silver. And this is the reason why the counterfeiting the stamp is made the highest crime, and has the weight of treason laid upon it: because the stamp is the public voucher of the intrinsic value. The royal authority gives the stamp, the law allows and confirms the denomination, and both together give, as it were, the public faith, as a security, that sums of money contracted for under such denominations shall be of such a value, that is, shall have in them so much silver; for it is silver, and not names, that pays debts, and purchases commodities. If therefore I have contracted for twenty crowns, and the law then has required that each of those crowns should have an ounce of silver; it is certain my bargain is not made good; I am defrauded (and whether the public faith be not broken with me, I leave to be considered) if, paying me twenty crowns, the law allots them to be such as have but nineteen-twentieths of the silver they ought to have, and really had in them, when I made my contract.

[3.] It diminishes all the king's revenue 5 per cent. For though the same number of pounds, shillings, and pence are paid into the exchequer as were wont, yet these names being given to coin that have each of them one-twentieth less of silver in them; and that being not a secret concealed from strangers, no more than from his own subjects; they will sell the king no more pitch, tar, or hemp, for 20*s.*, after the raising your money, than they would before for 19; or, to speak in the ordinary phrase, they will raise their commodities 5 per cent as you have raised your money 5 per cent. And it is well if they stop there. For usually in such change, an outcry being made of you, lessening your coin, those, who have to deal with your taking the advantage, of the alarm, to secure themselves from any loss by your new trick, raise their price even beyond the par of your lessening your coin.

···

It will possibly be here objected to me, That we see 100*l.* of clipped money, above 5 per cent lighter than the standard, will buy as much corn, cloth, or wine, as 100*l.* in milled money, which is above one-twentieth heavier: whereby it is evident that my rule fails, and that it is not the quantity of silver that gives the value to money, but its stamp and denomination. To which I answer, that men make their estimate and contracts according to the standard, upon supposition they shall receive good and lawful money, which is that of full weight: and so in effect they do, whilst they receive the current money of the country. For since 100*l.* of clipped money will pay a debt of 100*l.* as well as the weightiest milled money; and a new crown out of the mint will pay for no more flesh, fruit, or cloth, than five clipped shillings; it is evident that they are equivalent as to the purchase of any thing here at home, whilst nobody scruples to take five clipped shillings in exchange for a weighty milled crown. But this will be quite otherwise as soon as you change your coin, and (to raise it as you call it) make your money one-twentieth lighter in the mint; for then nobody will any more give an old crown of the former standard for one of the new, than he will now give you 5*s.* and 3*d.* for a crown: for so much then his old crown will yield him at the mint.

Clipped and unclipped money will always buy an equal quantity of any thing else, as long as they will without scruple change one for another. And this makes that the foreign merchant, who comes to sell his goods to you, always counts upon the value of your money, by the silver that is in it, and estimates the quantity of silver by the standard of your mint; though perhaps by reason of clipped or worn money amongst it, any sum that is ordinarily received is much lighter than the standard, and so has less silver in it than what is in a like sum, new coined in the mint. But whilst clipped and weighty money will equally change one for another, it is all one to him, whether he receives his money in clipped money or no, so it be but current. For if he buy other commodities here with his money, whatever sum he contracts for, clipped as well as weighty money equally pays for it. If he would carry away the price of his commodity in ready cash, it is easily changed into weighty money: and then he has not only the sum in tale that he contracted for, but the quantity of silver he expected, for his commodities, according to the standard of our mint. If the quantity of your clipped money be once grown so great, that the foreign merchant cannot (if he has a mind to it) easily get weighty money for it, but having sold his merchandize, and received clipped money, finds a difficulty to procure what is weight for it; he will, in selling his goods, either contract to be paid in weighty money, or else raise the price of his commodity, according to the diminished quantity of silver in your current coin.

...

By this example, in a neighbour country, we may see how our new milled money goes away. When foreign trade imports more than our commodities will pay for, it is certain we must contract debts beyond sea, and those must be paid with money, when either we cannot furnish, or they will not take our goods to discharge them. To have money beyond sea to pay our debts, when our commodities do not raise it, there is no other way but to send it thither. And since a weighty crown costs no more here than a light one, and our coin beyond sea is valued no otherwise than according to the quantity of silver it has in it, whether we send it in specie, or whether we melt it down here to send it in bullion (which is the safest way, as not being prohibited) the weightiest is sure to go. But when so great a quantity of your money is clipped, or so great a part of your weighty money is carried away, that the foreign merchant, or his factor here, cannot have his price paid in weighty money, or such as will easily be changed into it, then every one will see (when men will no longer take five clipped shillings for a milled or weighty crown) that it is the quantity of silver that buys commodities and pays debts, and not the stamp and denomination which is put upon it. And then too it will be seen what a robbery is committed on the public by clipping. Every grain diminished from the just weight of our money is so much loss to the nation, which will one time or other be sensibly felt; and which, if it be not taken care of, and speedily stopped, will, in that enormous course it is now in, quickly, I fear, break out into open ill effects, and at one blow deprive us of a great part (perhaps near one-fourth) of our money. For that will be really the case, when the increase of clipped money makes it hard to get weighty: when men begin to put a difference of value between that which is weighty and light money; and will not sell their commodities, but for money that is weight, and will make their bargains accordingly.

…

Hitherto we have only considered the raising of silver coin, and that has been only by coining it with less silver in it, under the same denomination. There is another way yet of raising money, which has something more of reality, though as little good in it as the former. This too, now that we are upon the chapter of raising money, it may not be unseasonable to open a little. The raising I mean is, when either of the two richer metals (which money is usually made of) is by law raised above its natural value, in respect of the other. Gold and silver have, in almost all ages and parts of the world (where money was used) generally been thought the fittest materials to make it of. But there being a great disproportion in the plenty of these metals in the world, one has always been valued much higher than the other; so that one ounce of gold has exchanged for several ounces of silver…

…

The effect indeed, and ill consequence of raising either of these two metals, in respect of the other, is more easily observed, and sooner found in raising gold than silver coin: because your accounts being kept, and your reckonings all made in pounds, shillings, and pence, which are denominations of silver coins, or numbers of them; if gold be made current at a rate above the free and market value of those two metals, every one will easily perceive the inconvenience. But there being a law for it, you cannot refuse the gold in payment for so much. And all the money, or bullion, people will carry beyond sea from you, will be in silver; and the money, or bullion, brought in, will be in gold. And just the same will happen, when your silver is raised and gold debased, in respect of one another, beyond their true and natural proportion: (natural proportion or value I call that respective rate they find, any where, without the prescription of law). For then silver will be that which is brought in, and gold will be carried out; and that still with loss to the kingdom, answerable to the over-value set by the law. Only as soon as the mischief is felt, people will (do what you can) raise the gold to its natural value. For your accounts and bargains being made in the denomination of silver money, if, when gold is raised above its proportion, by the law, you cannot refuse it in payment (as if the law should make a guinea current at 22*s*. 6*d*.) you are bound to take it at that rate in payment. But if the law should make guineas current at 20*s*., he that has them is not bound to pay them away at that rate, but may keep them, if he pleases, or get more for them, if he can; yet, from such a law, one of these things will follow. Either, first, the law forces them to go at 20*s*. and then being found passing at that rate, foreigners make their advantage of it: Or, second, people keep them up, and will not part with them at the legal rate, understanding them really to be worth more, and then all your gold lies dead, and is of no more use to trade than if it were all gone out of the kingdom: Or, third, it passes for more than the law allows, and then your law signifies nothing, and had been better let alone. Which way soever it succeeds, it proves either prejudicial or ineffectual. If the design of your law takes place, the kingdom loses by it: if the inconvenience be felt and avoided, your law is eluded.

Money is the measure of commerce, and of the rate of every thing, and therefore ought to be kept (as all other measures) as steady and invariable as may be. But this cannot be, if your money be made of two metals, whose proportion, and, consequently, whose price, constantly varies in respect to one another. Silver, for many reasons, is the fittest of all metals to be this measure; and therefore generally made use of for money. But then it is very unfit and inconvenient that gold, or any other metal, should be made current, legal money, at a standing, settled rate. This is to set a rate upon the varying value of things by law, which justly cannot be done; and is, as I have showed, as far as it prevails, a constant damage and prejudice to the country, where it is practised. …

What then! (will you be ready to say) Would you have gold kept out of England? Or, being here, would you have it useless to trade; and must there be no money made of it? I answer, quite the contrary. It is fit the kingdom should make use of the treasure it has. It is necessary your gold should be coined, and have the king's stamp upon it, to secure men in receiving it, that there is so much gold in each piece. But it is not necessary that it should have a fixed value set on it by public authority: it is not convenient that it should in its varying proportion, have a settled price. Let gold, as other commodities, find its own rate. And when, by the king's image and inscription, it carries with it a public assurance of its weight and fineness; the gold money, so coined, will never fail to pass at the known market rates, as readily as any other species of your money. Twenty guineas, though designed at first for 20*l.*, go now as current for 21*l.* 10*s.* as any other money, and sometimes for more, as the rate varies. The value, or price, of any thing, being only the respective estimate it bears to some other, which it comes in competition with, can only be known by the quantity of the one which will exchange for a certain quantity of the other. There being no two things in nature whose proportion and use does not vary, it is impossible to set a standing, regular price between them. The growing plenty, or scarcity, of either in the market (whereby I mean the ordinary place where they are to be had in traffic) or the real use, or changing fashion of the place, bringing either of them more into demand than formerly, presently varies the respective value of any two things. You will as fruitlessly endeavour to keep two different things steadily at the same price one with another, as to keep two things in an equilibrium, where their varying weights depend on different causes. Put a piece of sponge in one scale, and an exact counterpoise of silver in the other; you will be mightily mistaken if you imagine, that because they are to-day equal, they shall always remain so. The weight of the sponge varying with every change of moisture in the air, the silver, in the opposite scale, will sometimes rise and sometimes fall. This is just the state of silver and gold, in regard of their mutual value. Their proportion, or use, may, nay constantly does vary, and with it their price, For, being estimated one in reference to the other, they are, as it were, put in opposite scales; and as the one rises the other falls, and so on the contrary.

Farthings, made of a baser metal, may on this account too deserve your consideration. For whatsoever coin you make current, above the intrinsic value, will always be damage to the public, whoever get by it. But of this I shall not, at present, enter into a more particular inquiry; only this I will confidently affirm, that it is the interest of every country, that all the current money of it should he of one and the same metal; that the several species should be of the same alloy, and none of a baser mixture: and that the standard, once thus settled, should be inviolably and immutably kept to perpetuity. For whenever that is altered, upon what pretence soever, the public will lose by it.

...

RICHARD CANTILLON (1680?–1734)

Richard Cantillon (was an Irishman who spent most of his life in Paris as a successful merchant banker and speculator in commodities and foreign exchange. His *Essay on the Nature of Commerce in General* was one of, if not the most sophisticated treatises in economics in the eighteenth century. He was considered by William Stanley Jevons to have been the "first economist," and by Joseph J. Spengler to have been the principal forerunner of both the classical and neoclassical schools. Cantillon provided a general model of a market economy, emphasizing general interdependence, the circulation of money income, a self-adjusting equilibrium system inclusive of both domestic and foreign trade, and the critical roles of both the price mechanism and the entrepreneurial class. He worked out theories of money, price levels, value and price, and distribution. He, too, was something of a Mercantilist but emphasized the role of an export surplus in promoting prosperity, not the accumulation of gold, recognizing the role of the specie-flow mechanism in governing relative price levels between countries through the equation of exchange-quantity theory of money. He also was concerned about over-population.

The excerpts from Cantillon's *Essai* reprinted here deal with Cantillon's goods-based definition of wealth, his input-cost-based theory of what he calls "intrinsic value" and the distinction between this and the supply-and-demand-determined market price, the role of risk in price determination, Cantillon's elaboration and qualification of Locke's linkage between the money stock and the price level, and his supply-and-demand-based theory of interest rate determination.

References and further reading

Aspromourgos, Tony (1996) *On the Origins of Classical Economics: Distribution and Value from William Petty to Adam Smith*, London: Routledge.

Bordo, Michael David (1983) "Some Aspects of the Monetary Economics of Richard Cantillon," *Journal of Monetary Economics* 12 (August): 235–58.

Brewer, Anthony (1988) "Cantillon and Mercantilism," *History of Political Economy* 20 (Fall): 447–60.

——(1992a) "Petty and Cantillon," *History of Political Economy* 24 (Fall): 711–28.

——(1992b) *Richard Cantillon: A Pioneer of Economic Theory*, London: Routledge.

Hutchison, Terence (1988) *Before Adam Smith: The Emergence of Political Economy, 1662–1776*, Oxford: Basil Blackwell.

Jevons, W.S. (1881) "Richard Cantillon and the Nationality of Political Economy," reprinted in *Richard Cantillon, Essai sur la nature du commerce en général*, edited by Henry Higgs, London: Macmillan, 1931.

Murphy, Antoin E. (1984) "Richard Cantillon – An Irish Banker in Paris," in Antoin E. Murphy (ed.), *Economists and the Irish Economy from the Eighteenth Century to the Present Day*, Dublin: Irish Academic Press in Association with Hermathena, Trinity College, Dublin, 45–74.

Spengler, Joseph J. (1954) "Richard Cantillon: First of the Moderns," *Journal of Political Economy* 62 (August and October): 281–95, 406–24.

Walsh, Vivian (1987) "Cantillon, Richard," in John Eatwell, Murray Milgate, and Peter Newman (eds), *The New Palgrave: A Dictionary of Economics*, Vol. 1, London: Macmillan, 317–20.

Essay on the Nature of Commerce in General (1755)

Part one

Chapter one: On wealth

The land is the source or matter from whence all wealth is produced. The labour of man is the form which produces it: and wealth in itself is nothing but the maintenance, conveniencies and superfluities of life.

Land produces herbage, roots, corn, flax, cotton, hemp, shrubs and timber of several kinds, with divers sorts of fruits, bark and foliage like that of the mulberry-tree for silkworms; it supplies mines and minerals. To all this the labour of man gives the form of wealth.

Rivers and seas supply fish for the food of man, and many other things for his enjoyment. But these seas and rivers belong to the adjacent lands or are common to all, and the labour of man extracts from them the fish and other advantages.

Chapter nine: The number of labourers, handicraftsmen and others, who work in a state is naturally proportioned to the demand for them

If all the labourers in a village breed up several sons to the same work there will be too many labourers to cultivate the lands belonging to the village, and the surplus adults must go to seek a livelihood elsewhere, which they generally do in cities: if some remain with their fathers, as they will not all find sufficient employment they will live in great poverty and will not marry for lack of means to bring up children, or if they marry, the children who come will soon die of starvation with their parents, as we see every day in France.

Therefore if the village continue in the same situation as regards employment, and derives its living from cultivating the same portion of land, it will not increase in population in a thousand years.

The women and girls of this village can, it is true, when they are not working in the fields, busy themselves in spinning, knitting or other work which can be sold in the cities; but this rarely suffices to bring up the extra children, who leave the village to seek their fortune elsewhere.

The same may be said of the tradesmen of a village. If a tailor makes all the cloths there and breeds up three sons to the same trade, as there is but work enough for one successor to him the two others must go to seek their livelihood elsewhere: if they do not find enough employment in the neighbouring town they must go further afield or change their occupations to get a living and become lackeys, soldiers, sailors, etc.

By the same process of reasoning it is easy to conceive that the labourers, handicraftsmen and others who gain their living by work, must proportion themselves in number to the employment and demand for them in market towns and cities.

But if four tailors are enough to make all the cloths for a town and a fifth arrives he may attract some custom at the expense of the other four; so if the work is divided between the five tailors none of them will have enough employment, and each one will live more poorly.

It often happens that labourers and handicraftsmen have not enough employment when there are too many of them to share the business. It happens also that they are deprived of work by accidents and by variations in demand, or that they are overburdened with work according to circumstances. Be that as it may, when they have no work they quit the villages, towns or cities where they live in such numbers that those who remain are always proportioned to the employment which suffices to maintain them; when there is a continuous increase of work there is gain to be made and enough others arrive to share in it.

From this it is easy to understand that the Charity Schools in England and the proposals in France to increase the number of handicraftsmen, are useless. If the King of France sent 100,000 of his subjects at his expense into Holland to learn seafaring, they would be of no use on their return if no more vessels were sent to sea than before. It is true that it would be a great advantage to a state to teach its subjects to produce the manufactures which are customarily drawn from abroad, and all the other articles bought there, but I am considering only at present a state in relation to itself.

As the handicraftsmen earn more than the labourers they are better able to bring up their children to crafts; and there will never be a lack of craftsmen in a state when there is enough work for their constant employment.

Chapter ten: The price and intrinsic value of a thing in general is the measure of the land and labour which enter into its production

One acre of land produces more corn or feeds more sheep than another. The work of one man is dearer than that of another, as I have already explained, according to the superior skill and occurrences of the times. If 2 acres of land are of equal goodness, one will feed as many sheep and produce as much wool as the other, supposing the labour to be the same, and the wool produced by 1 acre will be the same, and the wool produced by 1 acre will sell at the same price as that produced by the other.

If the wool of the 1 acre is made into a suit of coarse cloth and the wool of the other into a suit of fine cloth, as the latter will require more work and dearer workmanship it will be sometimes ten times dearer, though both contain the same quantity and quality of wool. The quantity of the produce of the land and the quantity as well as the quality of the labour, will of necessity enter into the price.

A pound of flax wrought into fine Brussels lace requires the labour of 14 persons for a year or of one person for 14 years, as may be seen from a calculation of the different processes in the supplement, where we also see that the price obtained for the lace suffices to pay for the maintenance of one person for 14 years as well as the profits of all the undertakers and merchants concerned.

The fine steel spring which regulates an English watch is generally sold at a price which makes the proportion of material to labour, or of steel to spring, one to one million so that in this case labour makes up nearly all the value of the spring. See the calculation in the supplement.

On the other hand, the price of the hay in a field, on the spot, or a wood which it is proposed to cut down, is fixed by the matter or produce of the land, according to its goodness.

The price of a pitcher of Seine water is nothing, because there is an immense supply which does not dry up; but in the streets of Paris people give a sol for it – the price or measure of the labour of the water carrier.

By these examples and inductions it will, I think, be understood that the price or intrinsic value of a thing is the measure of the quantity of land and of labour entering into its production, having regard to the fertility or produce of the land and to the quality of the labour.

But it often happens that many things which have actually this intrinsic value are not sold in the market according to that value: that will depend on the humours and fancies of men and on their consumption.

If a gentleman cuts canals and erects terraces in his garden, their intrinsic value will be proportionable to the land and labour; but the price in reality will not always follow this proportion. If he offers to sell the garden possibly no one will give him half the expense he has incurred. It is also possible that if several persons desire it he may be given double the intrinsic value, that is twice the value of the land and the expense he has incurred.

If the farmers in a state sow more corn than usual, much more than is needed for the year's consumption, the real and intrinsic value of the corn will correspond to the land and labour which enter into its production; but as there is too great an abundance of it and there are more sellers than buyers the market price of the corn will necessarily fall below the intrinsic price or value. If, on the contrary, the farmers sow less corn than is needed for consumption there will be more buyers than sellers and the market price of corn will rise above its intrinsic value.

There is never a variation in intrinsic values, but the impossibility of proportioning the production of merchandise and produce in a state to their consumption causes a daily variation, and a perpetual ebb and flow in market prices. However, in well-organized societies the market prices of articles whose consumption is tolerably constant and uniform do not vary much from the intrinsic value; and when there are no years of too scanty or too abundant production the magistrates of the city are able to fix the market prices of many things, like bread and meat, without any one having cause to complain.

Land is the matter and labour the form of all produce and merchandise, and as those who labour must subsist on the produce of the land it seems that some relation might be found between the value of labour and that of the produce of the land: this will form the subject of the next chapter.

Chapter eleven: *Of the par or relation between the value of land and labour*

It does not appear that Providence has given the right of the possession of land to one man preferably to another: the most ancient titles are founded on violence and conquest. The lands of Mexico now belong to the Spaniards and those at Jerusalem to the Turks. But howsoever people come to the property and possession of land we have already observed that it always falls into the hands of a few in proportion to the total inhabitants.

If the proprietor of a great estate keeps it in his own hands he will employ slaves or free men to work upon it. If he has many slaves he must have overseers to keep them at work: he must likewise have slave craftsmen to supply the needs and conveniencies of life for himself and his workers, and must have trades taught to others in order to carry on the work.

In this economy he must allow his labouring slaves their subsistence and wherewithal to bring up their children. The overseers must allow advantages proportionable to the confidence and authority which he gives them. The slaves who have been taught a craft must be maintained without any return during the time of their apprenticeship and the artisan slaves and their overseers who should be competent in the crafts must have a better subsistence than the labouring slaves, etc. since the loss of an artisan would be greater than that of a labourer and more care must be taken of him having regard to the expense of training another to take his place.

On this assumption the labour of an adult slave of the lowest class is worth at least as much as the quantity of land which the proprietor is obliged to allot for his food and necessaries and also to double the land which serves to breed a child up till he is of age fit for labour, seeing half the children that are born die before the age of 17, according to the calculations and observations of the celebrated Dr Halley. So that two children must be reared up to keep one of them till working age and it would seem that even this would not be enough to ensure a continuance of labour since adult men die at all ages.

It is true that the one-half of the children who die before 17 die faster in the first years after birth than in the following, since a good third of those who are born die in their first year. This seems to diminish the cost of raising a child to working age, but as the mothers lose much time in nursing their children in illness and infancy and the daughters even when grown up are not the equals of the males in work and barely earn their living, it seems that to keep one of two children to manhood or working age as much land must be employed as for the subsistence of an adult slave, whether the proprietor raises them himself in his house or has the children raised there or that the father brings them up in a house or hamlet apart. Thus, I conclude that the daily labour of the meanest slave corresponds in value to double the produce of the land required to maintain him, whether the proprietor give it him for his subsistence and that of his family or provides him and his family subsistence in his own house. It does not admit of exact calculation, and exactitude is not very necessary; it suffices to be near enough to the truth.

If the proprietor employ the labour of vassals or free peasants he will probably maintain them upon a better foot than slaves according to the custom of the place he lives in, yet in this case also the labour of a free labourer ought to correspond in value to double the produce of land needed for his maintenance. But it will always be more profitable to the proprietor to keep slaves than to keep free peasants, because when he has brought up a number too large for his requirements he can sell the surplus slaves as he does his cattle and obtain for them a price proportionable to what he has spent in rearing them to manhood or working age, except in cases of old age or infirmity.

In the same way one may appraise the labour of slave craftsmen at twice the produce of the land which they consume. Overseers likewise, allowing for the favours and privileges given to them above those who work under them.

When the artisans or labourers have their double portion at their own disposal they employ one part of it for their own upkeep if they are married and the other for their children. If they are unmarried they set aside a little of their double portion to enable them to marry and to make a little store for housekeeping; but most of them will consume the double portion for their own maintenance.

For example the married labourer will content himself with bread, cheese, vegetables, etc., will rarely eat meat, will drink little wine or beer, and will have only old and shabby clothes which he will wear as long as he can. The surplus of his double portion he will employ in raising and keeping his children, while the unmarried labourer will eat meat as often as he can, will treat himself to new clothes, etc. and employ his double portion on his own requirements. Thus, he will consume twice as much personally of the produce of the land as the married man.

I do not here take into account the expense of the wife. I suppose that her labour barely suffices to pay for her own living, and when one sees a large number of little children in one of these poor families I suppose that charitable persons contribute somewhat to their maintenance, otherwise the parents must deprive themselves of some of their necessaries to provide a living for their children.

For the better understanding of this it is to be observed that a poor labourer may maintain himself, at the lowest computation, upon the produce of an acre and a half of land if he lives on bread and vegetables, wears hempen garments, wooden shoes, etc., while if he can allow himself wine, meat, woollen clothes, etc. he may without drunkenness or gluttony or excess of any kind consume the produce of 4–10 acres of land of ordinary goodness, such as most of the land in Europe taking part with another. I have caused some figures to be drawn up which will be found in the supplement, to determine the amount of land of which one man can consume the produce under each head of food, clothing and other necessaries of life in a single year, according to the mode of living in Europe where the peasants of divers countries are often nourished and maintained very differently.

For this reason I have not determined to how much land the labour of the meanest peasant corresponds in value when I laid down that it is worth double the produce of the land which serves to maintain him: because this varies according to the mode of living in different countries. In some provinces of France the peasant keeps himself on the produce of 1 acre and a half of land and the value of his labour may be reckoned equal to the product of 3 acres. But in the county of Middlesex the peasant usually spends the produce of 5–8 acres of land and his labour may be valued at twice as much as this.

In the country of the Iroquois where the inhabitants do not plough the land and live entirely by hunting, the meanest hunter may consume the produce of 50 acres of land since it probably requires so much to support the animals he eats in one year, especially as these savages have not the industry to grow grass by cutting down the trees but leave everything to nature. The labour of this hunter may then be reckoned equal in value to the product of 100 acres of land. In the southern provinces of China the land yields rice up to three crops in one year and a hundred times as much as is sown, owing to the great care which they have of agriculture and the fertility of the soil which is never fallow. The peasants who work there almost naked live only on rice and drink only rice water, and it appears that 1 acre will support there more than 10 peasants. It is not surprising, therefore, that the population is prodigious in number. In any case it seems from these examples that nature is altogether indifferent whether that earth produce grass, trees, or grain or maintains a large or small number of vegetables, animals, or men.

Farmers in Europe seem to correspond to overseers of labouring slaves in other countries, and the master tradesmen who employ several journeymen to the overseers of artisan slaves. These masters know pretty well how much work a journeyman artisan can do in a day in each craft, and often pay them in proportion to the work they do, so that the journeymen work for their own interest as hard as they can without further inspection.

As the farmers and masters of crafts in Europe are all undertakers working at a risk, some get rich and gain more than a double subsistence, others are ruined and become bankrupt, as will be explained more in detail in treating of undertakers; but the majority support themselves and their families from day to day, and their labour or superintendence may be valued at about thrice the produce of the land which serves for their maintenance.

Evidently these farmers and master craftsmen, if they superintend the labour of 10 labourers or journeymen, would be equally capable of superintending the labour of twenty, according to the size of their farms or the number of their customers, and this renders uncertain the value of their labour or superintendence.

By these examples and others which might be added in the same sense, it is seen that the value of the day's work has a relation to the produce of the soil, and that the intrinsic value of any thing may be measured by the quantity of land used in its production and the quantity of labour which enters into it, in other words by the quantity of land of which the produce is allotted to those who have worked upon it; and as all the land belongs to the prince and the landowners all things which have this intrinsic value have it only at their expense.

The money or coin which finds the proportion of values in exchange is the most certain measure for judging of the par between land and labour and the relation of one to the other in different countries where this par varies according to the greater or less produce of the land allotted to those who labour.

If, for example, one man earn an ounce of silver every day by his work, and another in the same place earn only half an ounce, one can conclude that the first has as much again of the produce of the land to dispose of as the second.

Sir William Petty, in a little manuscript of the year 1685, considers this par, or equation between land and labour, as the most important consideration in political arithmetic, but the research which he has made into it in passing is fanciful and remote from natural laws, because he has attached himself not to causes and principles but only to effects, as Mr Locke, Mr Davenant and all the other English authors who have written on this subject have done after him.

Chapter thirteen: *The circulation and exchange of goods and merchandise as well as their production are carried on in Europe by Undertakers, and at a risk*

The farmer is an undertaker who promises to pay to the landowner, for his farm or land, a fixed sum of money (generally supposed to be equal in value to the third of the produce) without assurance of the profit he will derive from this enterprise. He employs part of the land to feed flocks, produce corn, wine, hay, etc. according to his judgement without being able to foresee which of these will pay best. The price of these products will depend partly on the weather, partly on the demand; if corn is abundant relatively to consumption it will be dirt cheap, if there is scarcity it will be dear. Who can foresee the increase or reduction of expense which may come about in the families? And yet the price of the farmer's produce depends naturally upon these unforeseen circumstances, and consequently he conducts the enterprise of his farm at an uncertainty.

The city consumes more than half the farmer's produce. He carries it to market there or sells it in the market of the nearest town, or perhaps a few individuals set up as carriers themselves. These bind themselves to pay the farmer a fixed price for his produce, that of the market price of the day, to get in the city an uncertain price which should however defray the cost of carriage and leave them a profit. But the daily variation in the price of produce in the city, though not considerable, makes their profit uncertain.

The undertaker or merchant who carries the products of the country to the city cannot stay there to sell retail as they are consumed. No city family will burden itself with the purchase all at once of the produce it may need, each family being susceptible of increase or decrease in number and in consumption or at least varying in the choice of produce it will consume. Wine is almost the only article of consumption stocked in a family. In any case the majority of citizens who live from day to day and yet are the largest consumers cannot lay in a stock of country produce.

For this reason many people set up in a city as merchants or undertakers, to buy the country produce from those who bring it or to order it to be brought on their account. They pay a certain price following that of the place where they purchase it, to resell wholesale or retail at an uncertain price.

Such undertakers are the wholesalers in wool and corn, bakers, butchers, manufacturers and merchants of all kinds who buy country produce and materials to work them up and resell them gradually as the inhabitants require them.

These undertakers can never know how great will be the demand in their city, nor how long their customers will buy of them since their rivals will try all sorts of means to attract customers from them. All this causes so much uncertainty among these undertakers that every day one sees some of them become bankrupt.

The manufacturer who has bought wool from the merchant or direct from the farmer cannot foretell the profit he will make in selling his cloths and stuffs to the merchant tailor. If the latter have not a reasonable sale he will not load himself with the cloths and stuffs of the manufacturer, especially if those stuffs cease to be in the fashion.

The draper is an undertaker who buys cloths and stuffs from the manufacturer at a certain price to sell them again at an uncertain price, because he cannot foresee the extent of the demand. He can of course fix a price and stand out against selling unless he gets it, but if his customers leave him to buy cheaper from another, he will be eaten up by expenses while waiting to sell at the price he demands, and that will ruin him as soon as or sooner than if he sold without profit.

Shopkeepers and retailers of every kind are undertakers who buy at a certain price and sell in their shops or the markets at an uncertain price. What encourages and maintains these undertakers in a state is that the consumers who are their customers prefer paying a little more to get what they want ready to hand in small quantities rather than lay in a stock and that most of them have not the means to lay in such a stock by buying at first hand.

All these undertakers become consumers and customers one in regard to the other, the draper of the wine merchant and vice versa. They proportion themselves in a state to the customers or consumption. If there are too many hatters in a city or in a street for the number of people who buy hats there, some who are least patronised must become bankrupt: if they be too few it will be a profitable undertaking which will encourage new hatters to open shops there and so it is that the undertakers of all kinds adjust themselves to risks in a state.

All the other undertakers like those who take charge of mines, theatres, building, etc., the merchants by sea and land, etc., cook-shop keepers, pastry cooks, innkeepers, etc. as well as the undertakers of their own labour who need no capital to establish themselves, like journeymen artisans, coppersmiths, needlewomen, chimney sweeps, water carriers, live at uncertainty and proportion themselves to their customers. Master craftsmen like shoemakers, tailors, carpenters, wigmakers, etc. who employ journeymen according to the work they have, live at the same uncertainty since their customers may foresake them from one day to another: the undertakers of their own labour in art and science, like painters, physicians, lawyers, etc. live in the like uncertainty. If one attorney or barristers earn 5000 pounds sterling yearly in the service of his clients or in his practice and another earn only 500 they may be considered as having so much uncertain wages from those who employ them.

It may perhaps be urged that undertakers seek to snatch all they can in their calling and to get the better of their customers, but this is outside my subject.

By all these inductions and many others which might be made in a topic relating to all the inhabitants of a state, it may be laid down that except the prince and the proprietors of land, all the inhabitants of a state are dependent; that they can be divided into two classes, undertakers and hired people; and that all the undertakers are as it were on unfixed wages and the others on wages fixed so long as they receive them though their functions and ranks may be very unequal. The general who has his pay, the courtier his pension and the domestic servant who has wages all fall into this last class. All the rest are undertakers, whether they set up with a capital to conduct their enterprise, or are undertakers of their own labour without capital, and they may be regarded as living at uncertainty; the beggars even and the robbers are undertakers of this class. Finally all the inhabitants of a state derive their living and their advantages from the property of the landowners and are dependent.

It is true, however, that if some person on high wages or some large undertaker has saved capital or wealth, that is, if he have stores of corn, wool, copper, gold, silver or some produce or merchandise in constant use or vent in a state, having an intrinsic or a real value, he may be justly considered independent so far as this capital goes. He may dispose of it to acquire a mortgage, and interest from land and from public loans secured upon land: he may live still better than the small landowners and even buy the property of some of them.

But produce and merchandise, even gold and silver, are much more subject to accident and loss than the ownership of land; and however one may have gained or saved them they are always derived from the land of actual proprietors either by gain or by saving of the wages destined for one's subsistence.

The number of proprietors of money in a large state is often considerable enough; and though the value of all the money which circulates in the state barely exceeds the ninth or tenth part of the value of the produce drawn from the soil yet, as the proprietors of money lend considerable amounts for which they receive interest either by mortgage or the produce and merchandise of the state, the sums due to them usually exceed all the money in the state, and they often become so powerful a body that they could in certain cases rival the proprietors of lands if these last were not often equally proprietors of money, and if the owners of large sums of money did not always seek to become landowners themselves.

It is nevertheless always true that all the sums gained or saved have been drawn from the land of the actual proprietors; but as many of these ruin themselves daily in a state and the others who acquire the property of their land take their place, the independence given by the ownership of land applies only to those who keep the possession of it; and as all land has always an actual Master or Owner, I presume that it is from their property that all the inhabitants of the state derive their living and all their wealth. If these proprietors confined themselves to living on their rents it would be beyond question, and in that case it would be much more difficult for the other inhabitants to enrich themselves at their expense.

I will then lay it down as a principle that the proprietors of land alone are naturally independent in a state: that all the other classes are dependent whether undertakers or hired, and that all the exchange and circulation of the state is conducted by the medium of these undertakers.

Part two

Chapter one: Of barter

In Part one an attempt was made to prove that the real value of everything used by man is proportionate to the quantity of land used for its production and for the upkeep of those who have fashioned it. In this second part, after summing up the different degrees of fertility of the land in several countries and the different kinds of produce it can bring forth with greater abundance according to its intrinsic quality, and assuming the establishment of towns and their markets to facilitate the sale of these products, it will be shewn by comparing exchanges which may be made, wine for cloth, corn for shoes, hats, etc. and by the difficulty which the transport of these different products or merchandises would involve, that it was impossible to fix their respective intrinsic value, and there was absolute necessity for man to find a substance easily transportable, not perishable, and having by weight a proportion or value equal to the different products and merchandises, necessary or convenient. Thence arose the choice of gold and silver for large business and of copper for small traffic.

These metals are not only durable and easily transported but correspond to the employment of a large area of land for their production, which gives them the real value desirable in exchange.

Mr Locke who, like all the English writers on this subject, has looked only to market prices, lays down that the value of all things is proportionable to their abundance or scarcity, and the abundance or scarcity of the silver for which they are exchanged. It is generally known that the prices of produce and merchandise have been raised in Europe since so great a quantity of silver has been brought thither from the West Indies.

But I consider that we must not suppose as a general rule that the market prices of things should be proportionable to their quantity and to that of the silver actually circulating in one place, because the products and merchandise sent away to be sold elsewhere do not influence the price of those which remain. If, for example, in a market town where there is twice as much corn as is consumed there, we compared the whole quantity of corn to that of silver, the corn would be more abundant in proportion than the silver destined for its purchase; the market price, however, will be maintained just as if there were only half the quantity of corn, since the other half can be and even must be, sent into the city, and the cost of transport will be included in the city price which is always higher than that of the town. But apart from the case of hoping to sell in another market, I consider that Mr Locke's idea is correct in the sense of the following chapter, and not otherwise.

Chapter two: Of market prices

Suppose the butchers on one side and the buyers on the other. The price of meat will be settled after some altercations, and a pound of beef will be in value to a piece of silver pretty nearly as the whole beef offered for sale in the market is to all the silver brought there to buy beef.

This proportion is come at by bargaining. The butcher keeps up his price according to the number of buyers he sees; the buyers, on their side, offer less according as they think the butcher will have less sale: the price set by some is usually followed by others. Some are more clever in puffing up their wares, other in running them down. Though this method of fixing market prices has no exact or geometrical foundation, since it often depends upon the eagerness or easy temperament of a few buyers or sellers, it does not seem that it could be done in any more convenient way. It is clear that the quantity of produce or of merchandise offered for sale, in proportion to the demand or number of buyers, is the basis on which is fixed or always supposed to be fixed the actual market prices; and that in general these prices do not vary much from the intrinsic value.

Let us take another case. Several *maître d'hôtels* have been told to buy green peas when they first come in. One master has ordered the purchase of 10 litrons for 60 livres, another 10 litrons for 50 livres, a third 10 for 40 livres and a fourth 10 litrons for 30 livres. If these orders are to be carried out there must be 40 litrons of green peas in the market. Suppose there are only 20. The vendors, seeing many buyers, will keep up their prices, and the buyers will come up to the prices prescribed to them: so that those who offer 60 livres for 10 litrons will be the first served. The sellers, seeing later that no one will go above 50, will let the other 10 litrons go at that price. Those who had orders not to exceed 40 and 30 livres will go away empty.

If instead of 40 litrons there were 400, not only would the *maître d'hôtels* get the new peas much below the sums laid down for them, but the sellers in order to be preferred one to the other by the few buyers will lower their new peas almost to their intrinsic value, and in that case many *maîtres d'hôtels* who had no orders will buy some.

It often happens that sellers who are too obstinate in keeping up their price in the market, miss the opportunity of selling their produce or merchandise to advantage and are losers thereby. It also happens that by sticking to their prices they may be able to sell more profitably another day.

Distant markets may always effect the prices of the market where one is: if corn is extremely dear in France it will go up in England and in other neighbouring countries.

Chapter six: Of the increase and decrease in the quantity of hard money in a state

If mines of gold or silver be found in a state and considerable quantities of minerals drawn from them, the proprietors of these mines, the undertaker, and all those who work there, will not fail to increase their expenses in proportion to the wealth and profit they make: they will also lend at interest the sums of money which they have over and above what they need to spend.

All this money, whether lent or spent, will enter into circulation and will not fail to raise the price of products and merchandise in all the channels of circulation which it enters. Increased money will bring about increased expenditure and this will cause an increase of market prices in the highest years of exchange and gradually in the lowest.

Everybody agrees that the abundance of money or its increase in exchange, raises the price of everything. The quantity of money brought from America to Europe for the last two centuries justifies this truth by experience.

Mr Locke lays it down as a fundamental maxim that the quantity of produce and merchandise in proportion to the quantity of money serves as the regulator of market price. I have tried to elucidate his idea in the preceding chapters: he has clearly seen that the abundance of money makes everything dear, but he has not considered how it does so. The great difficulty of this question consists in knowing in what way and in what proportion the increase of money raises prices.

I have already remarked that an acceleration or greater rapidity in circulation of money in exchange, is equivalent to an increase of actual money up to a point. I have also observed that the increase or decrease of prices in a distant market, home or foreign, influences the actual market prices. On the other hand, money flows in detail through so many channels that it seems impossible not to lose sight of it seeing that having been amassed to make large sums it is distributed in little rills of exchange, and then gradually accumulated again to make large payments. For these operations it is constantly necessary to change coins of gold, silver and copper according to the activity of exchange. It is also usually the case that the increase or decrease of actual money in a state is not perceived because it flows abroad, or is brought into the state, by such imperceptible means and proportions that it is impossible to know exactly the quantity which enters or leaves the state.

However, all these operations pass under our eyes and everybody takes part in them. I may therefore venture to offer a few observations on the subject, even though I may not be able to give an account which is exact and precise.

I consider in general that an increase of actual money causes in a state a corresponding increase of consumption which gradually brings about increased prices.

If the increase of actual money comes from mines of gold or silver in the state the owner of these mines, the adventurers, the smelters, refiners and all the other workers will increase their expenses in proportion to their gains. They will consume in their households more meat, wine or beer than before, will accustom themselves to wear better cloaths, finer linen, to have better furnished houses and other choicer commodities. They will consequently give employment to several mechanics who had not so much to do before and who for the same reason will increase their expenses: all this increase of expense in meat, wine, wool, etc. diminishes of necessity the share of the other inhabitants of the state who do not participate at first in the wealth of the mines in question. The altercations of the market, or the demand for meat, wine, wool, etc. being more intense than usual, will not fail to raise their prices. These high prices will determine the farmers to employ more land to produce them in another year: these same farmers will profit by this rise of prices and will increase the expenditure of their families like the others. Those then who will suffer from this dearness and increased consumption will be first of all the landowners, during the term of their leases, then their domestic servants and all the workmen or fixed wage-earners who support their families on their wages. All these must diminish their expenditure in proportion to the new consumption, which will compel a large number of them to emigrate to seek a living elsewhere. The landowners will dismiss many of them, and the rest will demand an increase of wages to enable them to live as before. It is thus, approximately, that a considerable increase of money from the mines increases consumption, and by diminishing the number of inhabitants entails a greater expense among those who remain.

If more money continues to be drawn from the mines all prices will owing to this abundance rise to such a point that not only will the landowners raise their rents considerably when the leases expire and resume their old style of living, increasing proportionably the wages their servants, but the mechanics and workmen will raise the prices of their articles so high that there will be a considerable profit in buying them from the foreigner who makes them much more cheaply. This will naturally induce several people to import many articles made in foreign countries, where they will be found very cheap: this will gradually ruin the mechanics and manufacturers of the state who will not be able to maintain themselves there by working at such low prices owing to the dearness of living.

When the excessive abundance of money from the Mines has diminished the inhabitants of a state, accustomed those who remain to a too large expenditure, raised produce of the land and the labour of workmen to excessive prices, ruined the manufactures of the state by use of foreign productions on the part of landlords and mine workers, the money produced by the mines will necessarily go abroad to pay for the imports: this will gradually impoverish the state and render it in some sort dependent on the Foreigner to whom it is obliged to send money every year as it is drawn from the mines. The great circulation of money, which was general at the beginning, ceases: poverty and misery follow and the labour of the mines appears to be only to the advantage of those employed upon them and the Foreigners who profit thereby.

This is approximately what has happened to Spain since the discovery of the Indies. As to the Portuguese, since the discovery of the gold mines of Brazil, they have nearly always made use of foreign articles and manufactures; and it seems that they work at the mines only for the account and advantage of foreigners. All the gold and silver which these two states extract from the mines does not supply them in circulation with more precious metal than others. England and France have even more as a rule.

Now if the increase of money in the state proceeds from a balance of foreign trade (i.e. from sending abroad articles and manufactures in greater value and quantity than is imported and consequently receiving the surplus in money) this annual increase of money will enrich a great number of merchants and Undertakers in the state, and will give employment to numerous mechanics and workmen who furnish the commodities sent to the Foreigner from whom the money is drawn. This will increase gradually the consumption of these industrial inhabitants and will raise the price of land and labour. But the industrious who are eager to acquire property will not at first increase their expense: they will wait till they have accumulated a good sum from which they can draw an assured interest, independently of their trade. When a large number of the inhabitants have acquired considerable fortunes from this money, which enters the state regularly and annually, they will, without fail, increase their consumption and raise the price of everything. Though this dearness involves them in a greater expense than they at first contemplated they will for the most part continue so long as their capital lasts; for nothing is easier or more agreeable than to increase the family expenses, nothing more difficult or disagreeable than to retrench them.

If an annual and continuous balance has brought about in a state a considerable increase of money it will not fail to increase consumption, to raise the price of every thing and even to diminish the number of inhabitants unless additional produce is drawn from abroad proportionable to the increased consumption. Moreover, it is usual in states which have acquired a considerable abundance of money to draw many things from neighbouring countries where money is rare and consequently everything is cheap: but as money must be sent for this the balance of trade will become smaller. The cheapness of land and labour in the foreign countries where money is rare will naturally cause the erection of manufactories and works similar to those of the state, but which will not at first be so perfect nor so highly valued.

In this situation the state may subsist in abundance of money, consume all its own produce and also much foreign produce and over and above all this maintain a small balance of trade against the Foreigner or at least keep the balance level for many years, that is import in exchange for its work and manufactures as much money from these foreign countries as it has to send them for the commodities or products of the land it takes from them. If the state is a maritime state the facility and cheapness of its shipping for the transport of its work and manufactures into foreign countries may compensate in some sort the high price of labour caused by the too great abundance of money; so that the work and manufactures of this state, dear though they be, will sell in foreign countries cheaper sometimes than the manufactures of another state where labour is less highly paid.

The cost of transport increases a good deal the prices of things sent to distant countries; but these costs are very moderate in maritime states, where there is regular shipping to all foreign ports so that Ships are nearly always found there ready to sail which take on board all cargoes confided to them at a very reasonable freight.

It is not so in states where navigation does not Nourish. There it is necessary to build ships expressly for the carrying trade and this sometimes absorbs all the profit; and navigation there is always very expensive, which entirely discourages trade.

England today consumes not only the greatest part of its own small produce but also much foreign produce, such as Silks, Wines, Fruit, Linen in great quantity, etc. while she sends abroad only the produce of her mines, her work and manufactures for the most part, and dear though labour be owing to the abundance of money, she does not fail to sell her articles in distant countries, owing to the advantage of her shipping, at prices as reasonable as in France where these same articles are much cheaper.

The increased quantity of money in circulation in a state may also be caused, without balance of trade, by subsidies paid to this state by foreign powers, by the expenses of several ambassadors, or of travellers whom political reasons or curiosity or pleasure may induce to reside there for some time, by the transfer of the property and fortune of some Families who from motives of religious liberty or other causes quit their own country to settle down in this state. In all these cases the sums which come into the state always cause an increased expense and consumption there and consequently raise the prices of all things in the channels of exchange into which money enters.

Suppose a quarter of the inhabitants of the state consume daily meat, wine, beer, etc. and supply themselves frequently with cloaths, linen, etc. before the increase in money, but that after the increase a third or half of the inhabitants consume these same things, the prices of them will not fail to rise, and the dearness of meat will induce several of those who formed a quarter of the state to consume less of it than usual. A man who eats three pounds of meat a day will manage with two pounds, but he feels the reduction, while the other half of the inhabitants who ate hardly any meat will not feel the reduction. Bread will in truth go up gradually because of this increased consumption, as I have often suggested, but it will be less dear in proportion than meat. The increased price of meat causes diminished consumption on the part of a small section of the people, and so is felt; but the increased price of bread diminishes the share of all the inhabitants, and so is less felt. If 100,000 extra people come to live in a state of 10 millions of inhabitants, their extra consumption of bread will amount to only 1 pound in 100 which must be subtracted from the old inhabitants; but when a man instead of 100 pounds of bread consumes 99 for his subsistence he hardly feels this reduction.

When the consumption of meat increases the farmers add to their pastures to get more meat, and this diminishes the arable land and consequently the amount of corn. But what generally causes meat to become dearer in proportion than Bread is that ordinarily the free import of foreign corn is permitted while the import of Cattle is absolutely forbidden, as in England, or heavy import duties are imposed as in other states. This is the reason why the rents of meadows and pastures go up in England, in the abundance of money, to three times more than the rents of arable land.

There is no doubt that Ambassadors, Travellers, and Families who come to settle in the state, increase consumption there and that prices rise in all the channels of exchange where money is introduced.

As to subsidies which the state has received from foreign powers, either they are hoarded for state necessities or are put into circulation. If we suppose them hoarded they do not concern my argument for I am considering only money in circulation. Hoarded money, plate, Church treasures, etc. are wealth which the state turns to service in extremity, but are of no present utility. If the state puts into circulation the subsidies in question it can only be by spending them and this will very certainly increase consumption and send up all prices. Whoever receives this money will set it in motion in the principal affair of life, which is the food, either of himself or of some other, since to this everything corresponds directly or indirectly.

Chapter seven: Continuation of the same subject

As gold, silver and copper have an intrinsic value proportionable to the land and labour which enter into their production at the mines added to the cost of their importation or introduction into states which have no mines, the quantity of money, as of all other commodities, determines its value in the bargaining of the market against other things.

If England begins for the first time to make use of gold, silver and copper in exchanges, money will be valued according to the quantity of it in circulation proportionably to its power of exchange against all other merchandise and produce, and their value will be arrived at roughly by the altercations of the markets. On the footing of this estimation the landowners and Undertakers will fix the wages of their Domestic Servants and Workmen at so much a day or a year, so that they and their families may be able to live on the wages they receive.

Suppose now that the residence of Ambassadors and foreign travellers in England have introduced as much money into the circulation there as there was before; this money will at first pass into the hands of various mechanics, Domestic Servants, Undertakers and others who have had a share in providing the equipages, amusements, etc. of these Foreigners; the manufacturers, farmers, and other Undertakers will feel the effect of this increase of money which will habituate a great number of people to a larger expense than before, and this will in consequence send up market prices. Even the children of these Undertakers and mechanics will embark upon new expense: in this abundance of money their Fathers will give them a little money for their petty pleasures, and with this they will buy cakes and patties, and this new quantity of money will spread itself in such a way that many who lived without handling money will now have some. Many purchases which used to be made on credit will now be made for cash, and there will therefore be greater rapidity in the circulation of money in England than there was before.

From all this I conclude that by doubling the quantity of money in a state the prices of products and merchandise are not always doubled. A River which runs and winds about in its bed will not flow with double the speed when the amount of its water is doubled.

The proportion of the dearness which the increased quantity of money brings about in the state will depend on the turn which this money will impart to consumption and circulation. Through whatever hands the money which is introduced may pass it will naturally increase the consumption; but this consumption will be more or less great according to circumstances. It will be directed more or less to certain kinds of products or merchandise according to the idea of those who acquire the money. Market prices will rise more for certain things than for others however abundant the money may be. In England the price of meat might be tripled while the price of corn went up only one-fourth.

In England it is always permitted to bring in corn from foreign countries, but not cattle. For this reason however great the increase of hard money may be in England the price of corn can only be raised above the price in other countries where money is scarce by the cost and risks of importing corn from these foreign countries.

It is not the same with the price of Cattle, which will necessarily be proportioned to the quantity of money offered for meat in proportion to the quantity of meat and the number of Cattle bred there.

An ox weighing 800 pounds sells in Poland and Hungary for two or three ounces of silver, but commonly sells in the London market for more than 40. Yet, the bushel of flour does not sell in London for double the price in Poland and Hungary.

Increase of money only increases the price of products and merchandise by the difference of the cost of transport, when this transport is allowed. But in many cases the carriage would cost more than the thing is worth, and so timber is useless in many places. This cost of carriage is the reason why milk, fresh butter, salads, game, etc. are almost given away in the provinces distant from the capital.

I conclude that an increase of money circulating in a state always causes there an increase of consumption and a higher standard of expense. But the dearness caused by this money does not affect equally all the kinds of products and merchandise, proportionably to the quantity of money, unless what is added continues in the same circulation as the money before, that is to say unless those who offer in the market one ounce of silver be the same and only ones who now offer two ounces when the amount of money in circulation is doubled in quantity, and that is hardly ever the case. I conceive that when a large surplus of money is brought into a state the new money gives a new turn to consumption and even a new speed to circulation. But it is not possible to say exactly to what extent.

Chapter nine: Of the interest of money and its causes

Just as the prices of things are fixed in the altercations of the market by the quantity of things offered for sale in proportion to the quantity of money offered for them, or, what comes to the same thing, by the proportionate number of sellers and buyers, so in the same way the interest of money in a state is settled by the proportionate number of lenders and borrowers.

Though money passes for a pledge in exchange it does not multiply itself or beget an interest in simple circulation. The needs of man seem to have introduced the usage of interest. A man who lends his money on good security or on mortgage runs at least the risk of the ill will of the borrower, or of expenses, lawsuits and losses. But when he lends without security he runs the risk of losing everything. For this reason needy men must in the beginning have tempted lenders by the bait of a profit. And this profit must have been proportionate to the needs of the borrowers and the fear and avarice of the lenders. This seems to me the origin of interest. But its constant usage in states seems based upon the profits which the Undertakers can make out of it.

The land naturally produces, aided by human labour, 4, 10, 20, 50, 100, 150 times the amount of corn sown upon it, according to the fertility of the soil and the industry of the inhabitants. It multiplies fruits and cattle. The farmer who conducts the working of it has generally two-thirds of the produce, one-third pays his expenses and upkeep, the other remains for the profit of his enterprise.

If the farmer have enough capital to carry on his enterprise, if he have the needful tools and instruments, horses for ploughing, cattle to make the land pay, etc. he will take for himself after paying all expenses a third of the produce of his farm. But if a competent labourer who lives from day to day on his wages and has no capital, can find some one willing to lend him land or money to buy some, he will be able to give the lender all the third rent, or third part of the produce of a farm of which he will become the farmer or Undertaker. However, he will think his position improved since he will find in the second rent and will become master instead man. If by great economy and pinching himself somewhat of his necessities he can gradually accumulate some little capital, he will have every year less to borrow, and will at last arrive at keeping the whole of his third rent.

If this new Undertaker finds means to buy corn or cattle on credit, to be paid off at a long date when he can make money by the sale of his farm produce, he will gladly pay more than the market price for ready money. The result will be the same as if he borrowed cash to buy corn for ready money, paying as interest the difference between the cash price and the price payable at a future date. But whether he borrow cash or goods there must be enough left to him for upkeep or he will become bankrupt. The risk of this is the reason why he will be required to pay 20 or 30 per cent profit or interest on the amount of money or value of the produce or merchandise lent to him.

Again, a master hatter who has capital to carry on his manufacture of hats, either to rent a house, buy beaver, wool, dye, etc. or to pay for the subsistence of his workmen every week, ought not only to find his upkeep in this enterprise, but also a profit like that of the farmer who has his third part for himself. This upkeep and the profit should come from the sale of the hats whose price ought to cover not only the materials but also the upkeep of the hatter and his workmen and also the profit in question.

But a capable journeyman hatter with no capital may undertake the same manufacture by borrowing money and materials and abandoning the profit to anybody who is willing to lend him the money or entrust him with the beaver, wool, etc. for which he will pay only some time later when he has sold his hats. If when his bills are due the lender requires his capital back, or if the wool merchant and other lenders will not grant him further credit be must give up his business, in which case he may prefer to go bankrupt. But if he is prudent and industrious he may be able to prove to his creditors that he has in cash or in hats about the value of what he has borrowed and they will probably choose to continue to give him credit and be satisfied for the present with their interest or profit. In this way he will carry on and will perhaps gradually save some capital by retrenching a little upon his necessities. With the aid of this he will have every year less to borrow, and when he has collected a capital sufficient to conduct his manufacture, which will always be proportionable to his sales, the profit will remain to him entirely and he will grow rich if he does not increase his expenditure.

It is well to observe that the upkeep of such a manufacturer is small compared with the sums he borrows in his trade or with the materials entrusted to him, and therefore the lenders run no great risk of losing their capital if he is respectable and hard working: but as it is quite possible that he is not so the lenders always require from him a profit or interest of 20–30 per cent of the value of their loan. Even then only those who have a good opinion of him will trust him. The same inductions may be made with regard to all the masters, artisans, manufacturers and other Undertakers in the state who carry on enterprises in which the capital considerably exceeds the value of their annual upkeep.

But if a water-carrier in Paris sets up as the Undertaker of his own work, all the capital he needs will be the price of two buckets which he can buy for an ounce of silver and then all his gains are profit. If by his labour he gains 50 ounces of silver a year, the amount of his capital or borrowing will be to that of his profit as 1–50. That is he will gain 5000 per cent while the hatter will gain only 50 per cent and will also have to pay 20 or 30 per cent to the lender.

Nevertheless, a money lender will prefer to lend 1000 ounces of silver to a hatmaker at 20 per cent interest rather than to lend 1000 ounces to 1000 water carriers at 500 per cent interest. The water carriers will quickly spend on their maintenance not only the money they gain by their daily labour but all that which is lent to them. These capitals lent to them are small compared with what they need for their maintenance: whether they be much or little employed they can easily spend all they earn. Therefore, it is hardly possible to arrive at the profits of these little Undertakers. It might well be that a water carrier gains 5000 per cent of the value of the buckets which serve as his capital, even 10,000 per cent if by hard work he gains 100 ounces of silver a year. But as he may spend on his living 100 ounces just as well as 50, it is only by knowing what he devotes to his upkeep that we can find how much he has of clear profit.

The subsistence and upkeep of Undertakers must always be deducted before arriving at their profit. We have done this in the example of the farmer and of the hatmaker, but it can hardly be determined in the case of the petty Undertakers, who are for the most part insolvent when they are in debt.

It is customary for the London brewers to lend a few barrels of beer to the keepers of ale-houses, and when these pay for the first barrels to continue to lend them more. If these ale-houses do a brisk business the brewers sometimes make a profit of 500 per cent per annum; and I have heard that the big brewers grow rich when no more than half the ale-houses go bankrupt upon them in the course of the year.

All the merchants in a state are in the habit of lending merchandise or produce for a time to retailers, and proportion the rate of their profit or interest to that of their risk. This risk is always great because of the high proportion of the borrower's upkeep to the loan. For if the borrower or retailer have not a quick turnover in small business he will quickly go to ruin and will spend all he has borrowed on his own subsistence and will therefore be forced into bankruptcy.

The fishwives, who buy fish at Billingsgate in London to sell again in the other quarters of the City, generally pay under a contract made by an expert scrivener, 1 shilling per guinea, or 2 shillings, interest per week, which amounts to 260 per cent per annum. The market-women at Paris, whose business is smaller, pay 5 sols for the week's interest on an écu of 3 livres, which exceeds 430 per cent per annum. And yet there are few lenders who make a fortune from such high interest.

These high rates of interest are not only permitted but are in a way useful and necessary in a state. Those who buy fish in the streets pay these high interest charges in the increased price. It suits them and they do not feel it. In like manner an artisan who drinks a pot of beer and pays for it a price which enables the brewer to get his 500 per cent profit, is satisfied with this convenience and does not feel the loss in so small a detail.

The Casuists, who seem hardly suitable people to judge the nature of interest and of matters of trade, have invented a term, *damnum emergens*, by whose aid they consent to tolerate these high rates of interest; and rather than upset the custom and convenience of society, they have agreed and allowed to those who lend at great risk to exact in proportion a high rate of interest: and this without limit, for they would be hard put to it to find any certain limit since the business depends in reality on the fears of the lenders and the needs of the borrowers.

Maritime merchants are praised when they can make a profit on their Adventures, even though it be 10,000 per cent; and whatever profit wholesale merchants may make or stipulate for in Selling on long credit produce or merchandise to smaller retail merchants, I have not heard that the Casuists make it a crime. They are or seem to be a little more scrupulous about loans in hard cash though it is essentially the same thing. Yet, they tolerate even these loans by a distinction, *lucrum cessans*, which they have invented. I understand this to mean that a man who has been in the habit of making his money bring in 500 per cent in his trade may demand this profit when he lends it to another. Nothing is more amusing than the multitude of laws and canons made in every age on the subject of the interest of money, always by wiseacres who were hardly acquainted with trade and always without effect.

From these examples and inductions it seems that there are in a state many classes and channels of interest or profit, that in the lowest classes interest is always highest in proportion to the greater risk, and that it diminishes from class to class up to the highest which is that of merchants who are rich and reputed solvent. The interest demanded in this class is called the current rate of interest in the state and differs little from interest on the mortgage of land. The bill of a solvent and solid merchant is as much esteemed, at least for a short date, as a lien upon land, because the possibility of a lawsuit or a dispute on this last makes up for the possibility of the bankruptcy of the merchant.

If there were in a state no Undertakers who could make a profit on the money or goods which they borrow, the use of interest would probably be less frequent than it is. Only extravagant and prodigal people would contract loans. But accustomed as every one is to make use of Undertakers there is a constant source for Loans and therefore for interest. They are the Undertakers who cultivate the land and supply bread, meat, clothes, etc. to all the inhabitants of a city. Those who work on wages for these Undertakers seek also to set themselves up as Undertakers, in emulation of each other. The multitude of Undertakers is much greater among the Chinese, and as they all have lively intelligence, a genius for enterprise, and great perseverance in carrying it out, there are among them many Undertakers who are among us people on fixed wages. They supply labourers with meals, even in the fields. It is perhaps this multitude of small Undertakers and others, from class to class, who finding the means to gain a good deal by ministering to consumption without its being felt by the consumers, keep up the rate of interest in the highest class at 30 per cent while it hardly exceeds 5 per cent in our Europe. At Athens in the time of Solon interest was at 18 per cent. In the Roman Republic it was most commonly 12 per cent, but has been known to be 48, 20, 8, 6 and at the lowest 4 per cent. It was never so low in the free market as towards the end of the Republic and under Augustus after the conquest of Egypt. The Emperor Antoninus and Alexander Severus only reduced interest to 4 per cent by lending public money on the mortgage of land.

FRANÇOIS QUESNAY (1694–1774)

François Quesnay, by courtesy of The Warren J. Samuels Portrait Collection at Duke University.

Like William Petty and Locke, François Quesnay (1694–1774) was also a physician, in the French court under Louis XV, and the driving force behind the Physiocratic school of economic thought and analysis. His doctrines emphasized both the application of capitalist methods and the dedication of government policy to the promotion of agriculture, as against the mercantilist policies of the French finance minister, Colbert. Quesnay argued that agriculture alone produced a surplus (in physiocratic terms, a net product) over and above its inputs; manufacturing was said to be sterile. All taxation ultimately was paid from this surplus, which should be taxed directly. Maximization of the surplus required adequate investment in agriculture, large-scale farming, and high prices for agricultural goods, which in turn required an appropriate level and structure of spending. Given the extent of the mercantilist policies promoting manufacturing at the expense of agriculture and the antiquated nature of agricultural production in France during this period, the physiocrats program of reform represented a substantial departure from the status quo.

A defining feature of the larger body of physiocratic thought is its identification with the natural order. Physiocracy meant the rule of nature – to be promoted by a government that followed Quesnay's principles, the optimal form of which, according to Quesnay, was monarchy. Although Quesnay did not use the term, the tone of his work is that of laissez faire, but it means not some notion of minimal government but, rather, government policy following the natural laws of the natural order; which in practice means activist government promotion of an agricultural kingdom. Interestingly, Quesnay was one of the earliest writers to identify the possibility of economic instability, which he attributed to an inadequate level and an improper structure of spending, and called for governmental policy to promote stability.

Quesnay's *Tableau Économique* offers a hypothetical diagrammatic representation of his ideas. Society is divided into three classes; only agriculture creates a net product; and a circular flow of spending and income, and thereby reproduction, takes place. Quesnay offered many versions and revisions of the *Tableau* over time, using it to illustrate a variety of issues of theory and policy. Reprinted here is the third edition of the *Tableau*, along with Quesnay's explanatory notes.

References and further reading

Beer, Max (1939) *An Inquiry into Physiocracy*, London: Allen & Unwin.

Eltis, Walter A. (1975) "François Quesnay: Reinterpretation 1, The Tableau Economique," *Oxford Economic Papers* 27 (July): 167–200.

—— (1975) "François Quesnay: Reinterpretation 2, The Theory of Economic Growth," *Oxford Economic Papers* 27 (November): 327–51.

Eltis, Walter *et al.* (2002) "Mini-Symposium on Physiocracy," *Journal of the History of Economic Thought* 24 (March): 39–110.

Fox-Genovese, E. (1976) *The Origins of Physiocracy: Economic Revolution and Social Order in Eighteenth Century France*, Ithaca: Cornell University Press.

Higgs, Henry (1897) *The Physiocrats*, London: Macmillan.

Kuczynski, M. and Meek, R.L. (1972) *Quesnay's Tableau Économique*, London: Macmillan.

Meek, R.L. (1962) *The Economics of Physiocracy: Essays and Translations*, London: George Allen & Unwin.

Mirabeau, V.R. (1758–60) *L'ami des Hommes, ou Traité de la Population*, Aalen: Scientia Verlag, 1970.

—— (1760) *Theorie de l'impôt*, Aalen: Scientia Verlag, 1972.

—— (1764) *Philosophie Rurale*, Aalen: Scientia Verlag, 1972.

Phillips, A. (1955) "The Tableau Economique as a Simple Leontief Model," *Quarterly Journal of Economics* 69 (February): 137–44.

Samuels, Warren J. (1962) "The Physiocratic Theory of Economic Policy," *Quarterly Journal of Economics* 76 (February): 145–62.

Vaggi, G. (1987a) "Physiocrats," in John Eatwell, Murray Milgate, and Peter Newman (eds), *The New Palgrave: A Dictionary of Economics*, Vol. 3, London: Macmillan, 869–75.

—— (1987b) "Quesnay, François," in John Eatwell, Murray Milgate, and Peter Newman (eds), *The New Palgrave: A Dictionary of Economics*, Vol. 4, London: Macmillan, 22–9.

—— (1987c) *The Economics of François Quesnay*, London: Macmillan.

*Tableau Économique**

Objects to be considered: (1) three kinds of expenditure; (2) their source; (3) their advances; (4) their distribution; (5) their effects; (6) their reproduction; (7) their relations with one another; (8) their relations with the population; (9) with agriculture; (10) with industry; (11) with trade; (12) with the total wealth of a nation.

Productive expenditure	Expenditure of the revenue	Sterile expenditure
Relative to agriculture, etc.	After deduction of taxes, is divided between productive expenditure and sterile expenditure	Relative to industry, etc.
Annual advances required to produce a revenue of 600*l* are 600*l*	Annual revenue	Annual advances for the works of sterile expenditure are

600*l* produce net ·········:600*l*   300*l*

one-half goes here   *one-half goes here*

Products   Works, etc.

300*l* reproduce net *one-half* ····300*l*   *one-half goes here* ····300*l*

150*l* reproduce net ···········150   *one-half, etc.* ·····150

one-half etc.

75 reproduce net ·············75   75

37..10 reproduce net ·········37..10   37..10

18..15 reproduce net ··········18..15   18..15

9... 7 ... 6*d* reproduce net ·······9...7...6*d*   9 ... 7 ... 6*d*

4..13 ... 9 reproduce net ········4..13 ... 9   4..13 ... 9

2 ... 6..10 reproduce net ·······2 ... 6..10   2 ... 6..10

1 ... 3 ... 5 reproduce net ·······1 ... 3 ... 5   1 ... 3 ... 5

0..11 ... 8 reproduce net ·······0..11 ... 8   0..11 ... 8

0... 5.. 10 reproduce net ·······0 ... 5..10   0 ... 5..10

0 ... 2..11 reproduce net ·······0 ... 2..11   0 ... 2..11

0 ... 1 ... 5 reproduce net ·······0 ... 1 ... 5   0 ... 1 ... 5

Total reproduced 600*l* of revenue; in addition, the annual costs of 600*l* and the interest on the original advances of the husbandman amounting to 300*l*, which the land restores. Thus the reproduction is 1500*l*, including the revenue of 600*l* which forms the base of the calculation, abstraction being made of the taxes deducted and of the advances which their annual reproduction entails, etc. See the Explanation on the following page.

* The 'Third Edition' of the *TABLEAU ÉCONOMIQUE* Facsimile Reproduction and English Translation, in *Quesnay's Tableau Économique*, edited, with new material, translations and notes by Marguerite Kuczynski and Ronald L. Meek. London: Macmillan and New York: Augustus M. Kelley for The Royal Economic Society and The American Economic Association, 1972.

Explanation of the *tableau économique*

Productive expenditure is employed in agriculture, grasslands, pastures, forests, mines, fishing, etc., in order to perpetuate wealth in the form of corn, drink, wood, livestock, raw materials for manufactured goods, etc.

Sterile expenditure is on manufactured commodities, house-room, clothing, interest on money, servants, commercial costs, foreign produce, etc. The sale of the net product which the cultivator has generated in the previous year, by means of the *annual advances* of 600 livres employed in cultivation by the farmer, results in the payment to the proprietor of a *revenue* of 600 livres.

The *annual advances* of the sterile expenditure class, amounting to 300 livres, are employed for the capital and costs of trade, for the purchase of raw materials for manufactured goods, and for the subsistence and other needs of the artisan until he has completed and sold his work.

Of the *600 livres of revenue*, one-half is spent by the proprietor in purchasing bread, wine, meat, etc., from the productive expenditure class, and the other half in purchasing clothing, furnishings, utensils, etc., from the sterile expenditure class.

This expenditure may go more or less to one side or the other, according as the man who engages in it goes in more or less for luxury in the way of subsistence or for luxury in the way of ornamentation. We assume here a medium situation in which the reproductive expenditure renews the same revenue from year to year. But it is easy to estimate the changes which would take place in the annual reproduction of revenue, according as sterile expenditure or productive expenditure preponderated to a greater or lesser degree. It is easy to estimate them, I say, simply from the changes which would occur in the order of the *tableau*. Suppose, for example, that luxury in the way of ornamentation increased by one-sixth in the case of the proprietor, by one-sixth in the case of the artisan, and by one-sixth in the case of the cultivator. Then the revenue reproduced, which is now 600 livres, would be reduced to 400 livres.[1] Suppose, on the other hand, that an increase of the same degree took place in expenditure on the consumption or export of raw produce. Then the revenue reproduced would increase from 600 to 800 livres,[2] and so on in progression. Thus, it can be seen that an opulent nation which indulges in excessive luxury in the way of ornamentation can very quickly be overwhelmed by its sumptuousness.

The 300 livres of revenue which according to the order of the *tableau* have passed into the hands of the class of productive expenditure, return to this class its *advances* in the form of money. These advances reproduce 300 livres net, which represents the reproduction of part of the proprietor's revenue; and it is by means of the remainder of the distribution of the sums of money which are returned to this same class that the total revenue is reproduced each year. These 300 livres, I say, which are returned at the beginning of the process to the productive expenditure class, by means of the sale of the products which the proprietor buys from it, are spent by the farmer, one-half in the consumption of products provided by this class itself, and the other half in keeping itself in clothing, utensils, implements, etc., for which it makes payment to the sterile expenditure class. And the 300 livres are regenerated with the net product.

The 300 livres of the proprietor's revenue which have passed into the hands of the sterile expenditure class are spent by the artisan, as to one-half, in the purchase of products for his subsistence, for raw materials for his work, and for foreign trade, from the productive expenditure class; and the other half is distributed among the sterile expenditure class itself for its maintenance and for the restitution of its *advances*. This circulation and mutual distribution are continued in the same way by means of sub-divisions down to the last penny of the sums of money which mutually pass from the hands of one expenditure class into those of the other.

Circulation brings 600 livres to the sterile expenditure class, from which 300 livres have to be kept back for the *annual advances*, which leaves 300 livres for wages. These wages are equal to the 300 livres which this class receives from the productive expenditure class, and the advances are equal to the 300 livres of revenue which pass into the hands of this same sterile expenditure class.

The products of the other class amount to 1200 livres, abstracting from taxes, tithes and interest on the husbandman's advances, which will be considered separately in order not to complicate the order of expenditure too much. The 1200 livres' worth of product are disposed of as follows: The proprietor of the revenue buys 300 livres' worth of them. Three hundred livres' worth passes into the hands of the sterile expenditure class, of which one-half, amounting to 150 livres, is consumed for subsistence within this class, and the other half, amounting to 150 livres, is taken for external trade, which is included in this same class. Finally, 300 livres' worth are consumed within the productive expenditure class by the men who cause them to be generated; and 300 livres' worth are used for the feeding and maintenance of livestock. Thus, of the 1200 livres' worth of product, 600 are consumed by this class, and its *advances* of 600 livres are returned to it in the form of money through the sales which it makes to the proprietor and to the sterile expenditure class. One-eighth of the total of this product enters into external trade, either as exports or as raw materials and subsistence for the country's workers who sell their goods to other nations. The sales of the merchant counterbalance the purchases of the commodities and bullion which are obtained from abroad.

Such is the order of the distribution and consumption of raw produce as between the different classes of citizens; and such is the view which we ought to take of the use and extent of external trade in a flourishing agricultural nation.

Mutual sales from one expenditure class to the other distribute the revenue of 600 livres to both sides, giving 300 livres to each, in addition to the advances which are maintained intact. The proprietor subsists by means of the 600 livres which he spends. The 300 livres distributed to each expenditure class, together with the product of the taxes, the tithes, etc., which is added to them, can support one man in each: thus 600 livres of revenue together with the appurtenant sums can enable three heads of families to subsist. On this basis 600 millions of revenue can enable 3 million families to subsist, estimated at four persons of all ages per family.

The costs provided for by the *annual advances* of the productive expenditure class, which are also regenerated each year, and of which one-half is spent on the feeding of livestock and the other half in paying wages to the men engaged in the work carried on by this class, add 300 millions of expenditure to the total; and this, together with the share of the other products which are added to them, can enable another 1 million heads of families to subsist.

Thus, these 900 millions, which, abstracting from taxes, tithes, and interest on the annual advances and original advances of the husbandman, would be annually regenerated from landed property, could enable 16 million people of all ages to subsist according to this order of circulation and distribution of the annual revenue.

By circulation is here meant the purchases at first hand, paid for by the revenue which is shared out among all classes of men, abstracting from trade, which multiplies sales and purchases without multiplying things, and which represents nothing but an addition to sterile expenditure.

The *wealth of the productive expenditure class*, in a nation where the proprietors of land regularly receive a revenue of 600 millions, can be worked out as follows:

A revenue of 600 millions for the proprietors presupposes an extra 300 millions for taxes; and 150 millions for tithes on the annual product, all charges included, which are levied on the tithable branches of cultivation. This makes a total of 1050 millions, including the revenue. Add to these the reproduction of 1050 millions of annual advances, and 110 millions of interest on these advances at 10 per cent, and the grand total becomes 2,210,000,000 livres.

In a kingdom with many vineyards, forests, meadows, etc., only about two-thirds of these 2210 millions would be obtained by means of ploughing. Assuming a satisfactory state of affairs in which large-scale cultivation was being carried on with the aid of horses, this portion would require the employment of 333,334 ploughs at 120 *arpents* of land per plough; 333,334 men to drive them; and 40 million *arpents* of land.

With advances amounting to five or six milliards, it would be possible for this type of cultivation to be extended in France to more than 60 million *arpents*.

We are not speaking here of small-scale cultivation carried on with the aid of oxen, in which more than a million ploughs and about 2 million men would be required to work 40 million *arpents* of land, and which would bring in only two-fifths of the product yielded by large-scale cultivation. This small-scale cultivation, to which cultivators are reduced owing to their lack of the wealth necessary to make the original advances, and in which the land is largely employed merely to cover the costs, is carried on at the expense of landed property itself, and involves an excessive annual expenditure for the subsistence of the great numbers of men engaged in this type of cultivation, which absorbs almost the whole of the product. This thankless type of cultivation, which reveals the poverty and ruin of those nations in which it predominates, has no connection with the order of the *tableau*, which is worked out on the basis of half the employment of a plough of land, where the annual advances are able, with the aid of the fund of original advances, to produce 100 per cent.

The full total of the original advances required for putting a plough of land under large-scale cultivation, for the first fund of expenditure on livestock, implements, seed, food, upkeep, wages, etc., in the course of two years' labour prior to the first harvest, is estimated at 10,000 livres. Thus, the total for 333,334 ploughs is 3,333,340,000 livres. (See the articles Farm, Farmers, Corn in the Encyclopedia.)

The interest on these advances ought to amount to 10 per cent at least, since the products of agriculture are subject to disastrous accidents which, over a period often years, destroy at least the value of one year's harvest. Moreover, these advances require a great deal of upkeep and renewal. Thus, the total interest on the original advances required for setting up the husbandmen is 333,322,000 livres.

Meadows, vineyards, ponds, forests, etc., do not require very great original advances on the part of the farmers. The value of these advances, including in them the original expenditure on plantations and other work carried out at the expense of the proprietors, can be reduced to 1,000,000,000 livres.

But vineyards and gardens require large annual advances which, taken together with those of the other branches, may on the average be included in the total of annual advances set out above.

The total annual reproduction of net product, of annual advances with the interest thereon, and of interest on the original advances, worked out in accordance with the order of the tableau, is 2,543,322,000 livres.

The territory of France, given advances and markets, could produce as much as this and even a great deal more.

Of this sum of 2,543,322,000 livres, 525 millions constitutes that half of the reproduction of the annual advances which is employed in feeding livestock. There remains (if the whole of the taxes go back into circulation, and if they do not encroach upon the advances of the husbandmen) 2,018,322,000 livres.

That makes, *for men's expenditure*, 504,580,500 livres on the average for each million heads of families, or 562 livres for each individual head of family, which accidents reduce to about 530 livres. On this basis a state is strong in taxable capacity and resources, and its people live in easy circumstances.

The stock of land which annually produces for the benefit of men 2,018,322,000 livres, of which 1,050,000,000 take the form of net product, when evaluated at the rate of 1 in 30, constitutes from this point of view wealth amounting to 33,455,000,000 livres, to which must be added the original advances of 4,333,340,000 livres, making a total of 36,788,340,000. Adding to this the 2,543,322,000 livres of annual product, *the total, costs included, of the wealth of the productive expenditure class will be* 40,331,662,000 livres.

The value and the product of livestock have not been separately calculated, since they have been included in the advances of the farmers and in the total of the annual product.

We include the land here because, relatively to its market value, it can be considered in something the same way as movable property, since its price is dependent upon changes in the other items of wealth required for cultivation. For land deteriorates, and the proprietors lose on the market value of their landed property, to the extent that the wealth of their farmers is wasted away.

The *wealth of the sterile expenditure class* consists of:

1. The total of the annual sterile advances 525,000,000 livres.
2. The original advances of this class for setting up manufactures, for tools, machines, mills, forges, and other works, etc. 2,000,000,000 livres.
3. The coined money or money stock of an opulent agricultural nation is about equal to the net product which it obtains annually from its landed property through the medium of trade. Thus, it is 1,000,000,000 livres.
4. The capital value of 4 million houses or dwelling-places for 4 million families, each house being valued on the average at 1500 livres, comes to 6,000,000,000 livres.
5. The value of the furnishings and utensils of 4 million houses, estimated on the average at about 1 year's revenue or gain of 4 million heads of families, comes to 3,000,000,000 livres.
6. The value of silver plate, jewellery, precious stones, mirrors, pictures, books, and other durable manufactured products, which are purchased or inherited, may in a wealthy nation amount to 3,000,000,000 livres.
7. The value of merchant and military shipping, and their appurtenances, in the case of a maritime nation; in addition, the artillery, weapons, and other durable products required for land warfare; the buildings, ornamental structures, and other durable public works: all these things taken together can be valued at 2,000,000,000 livres.

We do not take account here of the manufactured commodities and produce which are exported and imported, and which are stored in the shops and warehouses of the merchants and destined for annual use or consumption, since they are included and taken account of in the figures of annual product and expenditure, in conformity with the order set out in the *tableau*.

The total of the wealth of the sterile expenditure class may amount to about   18,000,000,000 livres.
Grand total   59,000,000,000 livres.
That is, assuming a possible error of one-twentieth either way   55–60,000,000,000 livres.

We are speaking here of an opulent nation with a territory and advances which yield it annually and without any abatement a net product of 1050 millions. But all these items of wealth, which are successively maintained by this annual product, may be destroyed or lose their value if an agricultural nation falls into a state of decline, simply through the wasting away of the advances required for productive expenditure. This wasting away can make considerable head-way in a short time for eight principal reasons:

1   A bad system of tax-assessment, which encroaches upon the cultivators' advances. *Noli me tangere* – that is the motto for these advances.
2   An extra burden of taxation due to the costs of collection.
3   An excess of luxury in the way of ornamentation.
4   Excessive expenditure on litigation.
5   A lack of external trade in the products of landed property.
6   A lack of freedom of internal trade in raw produce, and in cultivation.
7   The personal harassment of the inhabitants of the countryside.
8   Failure of the annual net product to return to the productive expenditure class.

Notes

1 Erratum: for '400 livres' read '500 livres'.
2 Erratum: for '800 livres' read '700 livres'.

ANNE ROBERT JACQUES TURGOT (1727–1781)

Anne Robert Jacques Turgot, by courtesy of The Warren J. Samuels Portrait Collection at Duke University.

Anne Robert Jacques Turgot, a Frenchman and prominent physiocrat, was educated for the church but eventually decided to enter government service. He served as a provincial administrator under Louis XV and as Minister of Finance under Louis XVI. Echoing some of Quesnay's ideas, Turgot attempted to reform both the administration of taxation and welfare programs. Because he engendered opposition from adversely affected interests, his tenure as Minister of Finance was short-lived. It is widely felt that if the monarchy had adopted the tone and substance of Turgot's reform program, the French Revolution might have been averted, though that is highly problematic.

His *Reflections on the Formation and Distribution of Wealth* ranks in importance almost as high as Cantillon's *Essay* as a pre-Adam Smith treatise on political economy. In many ways, the structure of *Reflections* parallels that of Smith's *Wealth of Nations*. While far less grand and sweeping in his analysis, Turgot's work is perhaps no less insightful than Smith's, and his theory of capital, contained in the excerpts reprinted here, represented a landmark advance in that area.

References and further reading

Brewer, Anthony (1987) "Turgot: Founder of Classical Economics," *Economica* 54 (November): 417–28.

Groenewegen, Peter D. (1977) *The Economics of A.R.J. Turgot*, The Hague: Martinus Nijhoff.

——(1987) "Turgot, Anne Robert Jacques, Baron de L'Aulne," in John Eatwell, Murray Milgate, and Peter Newman (eds), *The New Palgrave: A Dictionary of Economics*, Vol. 4, London: Macmillan, 707–12.

Hutchison, Terence (1988) *Before Adam Smith: The Emergence of Political Economy, 1662–1776*, Oxford: Basil Blackwell.

Meek, Ronald L. (1973) *Turgot on Progress, Sociology and Economics*, New York: Cambridge University Press.

Rothschild, Emma (1992) "Commerce and the State: Turgot, Condorcet and Smith," *Economic Journal* 102 (September): 1197–210.

Reflections on the Formation and Distribution of Wealth (1770)*

Section 49

Of the excess of annual produce accumulated to form capitals.

As soon as men are found, whose property in land assures them an annual revenue more than sufficient to satisfy all their wants, among them there are some, who, either uneasy respecting the future, or, perhaps, only provident, lay by a portion of what they gather every year, either with a view to guard against possible accidents, or to augment their enjoyments. When the commodities they have gathered are difficult to preserve, they ought to procure themselves in exchange, such objects of a more durable nature, and such as will not decrease in their value by time, or those that may be employed in such a manner, as to procure such profits as will make good the decrease with advantage.

Section 50

Personal property, accumulation of money.

This species of possession, resulting from the accumulation of annual produce, not consumed, is known by the name of personal property. Household goods, houses, merchandise in store, utensils of trade, and cattle are under this denomination. It is evident men must have toiled hard to procure themselves as much as they could of this kind of wealth, before they became acquainted, but it is not less evident that, as with the use of money, soon as it was known, that it was the least liable to alteration of all the objects of commerce and the most easy to preserve without trouble, it would be principally sought after by whoever wished to accumulate. It was not only the proprietors of land who thus accumulated their superfluity. Although the profits of industry are not, like the revenue of lands, a gift of nature; and the industrious man draws from his labour only the price which is given him by the persons who pay him his wages; although the latter is as frugal as he can of his salary, and that a competition obliges an industrious man to content himself with a less price than he otherwise would do, it is yet certain that these competitions have neither been so numerous or strong in any species of labour, but that a man more expert, more active, and who practises more œconomy than others in his personal expences, has been able, at all times, to gain a little more than sufficient to support him and his family, and reserve his surplus to form a little hoard.

---

* *Reflections on the Formation and Distribution of Wealth* by M. Turgot, Comptroller General of the Finances of France, in 1774, 1775 and 1776. Translated from the French. London: Printed by E. Spragg, For J. Good, Bookseller, No. 159, New Bond Street; John Anderson, No. 62, Holborn Hill; and W. Richardson, Royal Exchange. 1793.

Section 51

Circulating wealth is an indispensible requisite for all lucrative works.

It is even necessary, that in every trade the workmen, or those who employ them, possess a certain quantity of circulating wealth, collected beforehand. We here again are obliged to go back to a retrospect of many things which have been as yet only hinted at, after we have spoken of the division of different professions, and of the different methods by which the proprietors of capitals may render them of value; because, otherwise, we should not be able to explain them properly, without interrupting the connection of our ideas.

Section 52

Necessity of advances for cultivation.

Every species of labour, of cultivation, of industry, or of commerce, require advances. When people cultivate the ground, it is necessary to sow before they can reap; they must also support themselves until after the harvest. The more cultivation is brought to perfection and enlivened, the more considerable these advances are. Cattle, utensils for farming, buildings to hold the cattle, to store the productions, a number of persons, in proportion to the extent of the undertaking, must be paid and subsisted until the harvest. It is only by means of considerable advances, that we obtain rich harvests, and that lands produce a large revenue. In whatever business they engage, the workman must be provided with tools, must have a sufficient quantity of such materials as the object of his labour requires; and he must subsist until the sale of his goods.

Section 53

First advance furnished by the land although uncultivated.

The earth was ever the first and the only source of all riches; it is that which by cultivation produces all revenue; it is that which has afforded the first fund for advances, anterior to all cultivation. The first cultivator has taken the grain he has sown from such productions as the land had spontaneously produced; while waiting for the harvest, he has supported himself by hunting, by fishing, or upon wild fruits. His tools have been the branches of trees, procured in the forests, and cut with stones sharpened upon other stones; the animals wandering in the woods he has taken in the chace, caught them in his traps, or has subdued them unawares. At first he has made use of them for food, afterwards to help him in his labours. These first funds or capital have increased by degrees. Cattle were in early times the most sought after of all circulating property; and were also the easiest to accumulate; they perish, but they also breed, and this sort of riches is in some respects unperishable. This capital augments by generation alone, and affords an annual produce, either in milk, wool, leather, and other materials, which, with wood taken in the forest, have effected the first foundations for works of industry.

Section 54

Cattle – a circulating wealth, even before the cultivation of the earth.

In times when there was yet a large quantity of uncultivated land, and which did not belong to any individual, cattle might be maintained without having a property in land. It is even probable, that mankind have almost every where began to collect flocks and herds, and to live on what they produced, before they employed themselves in the more laborious occupation of cultivating the ground. It seems that those nations who first cultivated the earth, are those who found in their country such sorts of animals as were the most susceptible of being tamed, and that they have by this been drawn from the wandering and restless life of hunters and fishers, to the more tranquil enjoyment of pastoral pursuits. Pastoral life requires a longer residence in the same place, affords more leisure, more opportunities to study the difference of lands, to observe the ways of nature in the production of such plants as serve for the support of cattle. Perhaps it is for this reason that the Asiatic nations have first cultivated the earth, and that the inhabitants of America have remained so long in a savage state.

Section 55

Another species of circulating wealth, and advances necessary for cultivation, slaves.

The slaves were another kind of personal property, which at first were procured by violence, and afterwards by way of commerce and exchange. Those that had many, employed them not only in the culture of land, but in various other channels of labour. The facility of accumulating, almost without measure, those two sources of riches, and of making use of them abstractedly from the land, caused the land itself to be estimated, and the value compared to moveable riches.

Section 56

Personal property has an exchangeable value, even for land itself.

A man that would have been possessed of a quantity of lands without cattle or slaves, would undoubtedly have made an advantageous bargain, in yielding a part of his land, to a person that would have offered him in exchange, cattle and slaves to cultivate the rest. It is chiefly by this principle that property in land entered likewise into commerce, and had a comparative value with that of all the other goods. If four bushels of corn, the net produce of an acre of land, was worth six sheep, the acre itself that feeds them could have been given for a certain value, greater indeed, but always easy to settle by the same way, as the price of other wares. Namely, at first by debates among the two contractors, next, by the current price established by the agreement of those who exchange land for cattle, or the contrary. It is by the scale of this current specie that lands are appraised, when a debtor is prosecuted by his creditor, and is constrained to yield up his property.

Section 57

Valuations of lands by the proportion of their revenue, with the sum of personal property, or the value for which they are exchanged: this proportion is called the price of lands.

It is evident that if land which produces a revenue equivalent to six sheep, can be sold for a certain value, which may always be expressed by a number of sheep equivalent to that value; this number will bear a fixed proportion with that of six, and will contain it a certain number of times. Thus the price of an estate is nothing else but its revenue multiplied a certain number of times; twenty times if the price is a hundred and twenty sheep; thirty times if one hundred and eighty sheep. And so the current price of land is reckoned by the proportion of the value of the revenue; and the number of times, that the price of the sale contains that of the revenue, is called so many years purchase of the land. They are sold at the price of twenty, thirty, or forty years purchase, when on purchasing them we pay twenty, thirty, or forty times their revenue. It is also not less evident, that this price must vary according to the number of purchasers, or sellers of land, in the same manner as other goods vary in a ratio to the different proportion between the offer and the demand.

Section 58

***All capital in money, and all amounts of value, are equivalent to land
producing a revenue equal to some portion of that capital or value.
First employment of capitals. Purchase of lands.***

Let us now go back to the time after the introduction of money. The facility of accumulating it
has soon rendered it the most desirable part of personal property, and has afforded the means of
augmenting, by economy, the quantity of it without limits. Whoever, either by the revenue of his
land or by the salary of his labour or industry, receives every year a higher income than he needs
to spend, may lay up the residue and accumulate it: these accumulated values are what we name
a capital. The pusillanimous miser, that keeps his money with the mere view of soothing his
imagination against apprehension of distress in the uncertainty of futurity, keeps his money in a
hoard. If the dangers he had foreseen should eventually take place, and he in his poverty be
reduced to live every year upon the treasure, or a prodigal successor lavish it by degrees, this treasure would soon be exhausted, and the capital totally lost to the possessor. The latter can draw a
far greater advantage from it; for an estate in land of a certain revenue, being but an equivalent
of a sum of value equal to the revenue, taken a certain number of times, it follows, that any sum
whatsoever of value is equivalent to an estate in land, producing a revenue equal to a fixed proportion of that sum. It is perfectly the same whether the amount of this capital consists in a mass
of metal, or any other matter, since money represents all kinds of value, as well as all kinds
of value represent money. By these means the possessor of a capital may at first employ it in the
purchase of lands; but he is not without other resources.

Section 59

***Another employment for money in advances for enterprizes
of manufacture or industry.***

I have already observed, that all kinds of labour, either of cultivation or industry, required
advances. And I have shewn how the earth, by the fruits and herbages it spontaneously produces
for the nourishment of men and animals, and by the trees, of which man has first formed his
utensils, had furnished the first advances for cultivation; and even of the first manual works a
man can perform for his own service. For instance, it is the earth that provides the stone, clay, and
wood, of which the first houses were built; and, before the division of professions, when the same
man that cultivated the earth provided also for his other wants by his own labour, there was no
need of other advances. But when a great part of society began to have no resource but in their
hands, it was necessary that those who lived thus upon salaries, should have somewhat before
hand, that they might either procure themselves the materials on which they laboured, or subsist
during the time they were waiting for their salary.

Section 60

***Explanation of the use of the advances of capitals in enterprizes of industry;
on their returns and the profits they ought to produce.***

In early times, he that employed labouring people under him, furnished the materials himself,
and paid from day to day the salaries of the workmen. It was the cultivator or the owner himself
that gave to the spinner the hemp he had gathered, and he maintained her during the time of her
working. Thence he passed the yarn to a weaver, to whom he gave every day the salary agreed
upon. But those slight daily advances can only take place in the coarsest works. A vast number of

arts, and even of those arts indispensable for the use of the most indigent members of society, require that the same materials should pass through many different hands, and undergo, during a considerable space of time, difficult and various operations. I have already mentioned the preparation of leather, of which shoes are made. Whoever has seen the workhouse of a tanner, cannot help feeling the absolute impossibility of one, or even several indigent persons providing themselves with leather, lime, tan, utensils, and so on, and causing the requisite buildings to be erected to put the tan house to work, and of their living during a certain space of time, till their leather can be sold. In this art, and many others, must not those that work on it have learned the craft before they presume to touch the materials, lest they should waste them in their first trials? Here then is another absolute necessity of advances. Who shall now collect the materials for the manufactory, the ingredients, the requisite utensils for their preparation? Who is to construct canals, markets, and buildings of every denomination? How shall that multitude of workmen subsist till the time of their leather being sold, and of whom none individually would be able to prepare a single skin; and where the emolument of the sale of a single skin could not afford subsistence to any one of them? Who shall defray the expences for the instruction of the pupils and apprentices? Who shall maintain them until they are sufficiently instructed, guiding them gradually from an easy labour proportionate to their age, to works that demand more vigour and ability? It must then be one of those proprietors of capitals, or moveable accumulated property that must employ them, supplying them with advances in part for the construction and purchase of materials, and partly for the daily salaries of the workmen that are preparing them. It is he that must expect the sale of the leather, which is to return him not only his advances, but also an emolument sufficient to indemnify him for what his money would have procured him, had he turned it to the acquisition of lands, and moreover of the salary due to his troubles and care, to his risque, and even to his skill; for surely, upon equal profits, he would have preferred living without solicitude, on the revenue of land, which he could have purchased with the same capital. In proportion as this capital returns to him by the sale of his works, he employs it in new purchases for supporting his family and maintaining his manufactory; by this continual circulation, he lives on his profits, and lays by in store what he can spare to increase his stock, and to advance his enterprize by augmenting the mass of his capital, in order proportionably to augment his profits.

Section 61

Subdivisions of the industrious stipendiary class, in undertaking capitalists and simple workmen.

Thus the whole class employed in supplying the different wants of society, with an immense variety of works of industry, is, if I may speak thus, subdivided into two classes. The one, of the undertakers, manufacturers and masters, all proprietors of large capitals, which they avail themselves of, by furnishing work to the other class, composed of artificers, destitute of any property but their hands, who advance only their daily labour, and receive no profits but their salaries.

Section 62

Another employment of capitals, in advances towards undertakings of agriculture. Observations on the use, and indispensable profits of capitals in undertakings of agriculture.

In speaking first of the placing of capitals in manufacturing enterprizes, I had in view to adduce a more striking example, of the necessity and effect of large advances, and of the course of their circulation. But I have reversed the natural order, which seemed to require that I should rather begin to speak of enterprizes of agriculture, which also can neither be performed, nor extended, nor afford any profit, but by means of considerable advances. It is the proprietors of great capitals, who, in order to make them productive in undertakings of agriculture, take leases of lands, and pay to the owners large rents, taking on themselves the whole burthen of advances. Their case must necessarily be the same as that of the undertakers of manufactures. Like them, they are obliged to make the first advances towards the undertaking, to provide themselves with cattle, horses, utensils of husbandry, to purchase the first seeds; like them they must maintain and nourish their carters, reapers, threshers, servants, and labourers, of every denomination, who subsist only by their hands, who advance only their labour, and reap only their salaries. Like them, they ought to have not only their capital, I mean, all their prior and annual advances returned, but, first, a profit equal to the revenue they could have acquired with their capital, exclusive of any fatigue; second, the salary, and the price of their own trouble, of their risk, and their industry; third, an emolument to enable them to replace the effects employed in their enterprize, and the loss by waste, cattle dying, and utensils wearing out, and so on, all which ought to be first charged on the products of the earth. The overplus will serve the cultivator to pay to the proprietor, for the permission he has given him to make use of his field in the accomplishing of his enterprize; that is, the price of the leasehold, the rent of the proprietor and the clear product: for all that the land produces, until reimbursement of the advances, and profits of every kind to him that has made these advances, cannot be looked upon as a revenue, but only as a reimbursement of the expences of the cultivation, since if the cultivator could not obtain them, he would be loath to risk his wealth and trouble in cultivating the field of another.

Section 63

The competition between the capitalists, undertakers of cultivation, fixes the current price of leases of lands.

The competition between rich undertakers of cultivation fixes the current price of leases, in proportion to the fertility of the soil, and of the rate at which its productions are sold, always according to the calculation which farmers make both of their expenditures, and of the profits they ought to draw from their advances. They cannot give to the owners more than the overplus. But when the competition among them happens to be more animated, they sometimes render him the whole overplus, the proprietor leasing his land to him that offers the greatest rent.

Section 64

The default of capitalists, undertakers, limits the cultivation of lands to a small extent.

When, on the contrary, there are no rich men that possess capitals large enough to embark in enterprizes of agriculture; when, through the low rate of the productions of the earth, or any other cause, the crops are not sufficient to ensure to the undertakers, besides the reimbursement of their capital, emoluments adequate at least to those they would derive from their money, by employing it in some other channel; there are no farmers that offer to lease lands, the proprietors are constrained to hire mercenaries or metayers, which are equally unable to make any advances, or duly to cultivate it. The proprietor himself makes moderate advances, which only produce him an indifferent revenue: if the land happens to belong to an owner, poor, negligent, and in debt, to a widow, or a minor, it remains unmanured; such is the principle of the difference I have observed between provinces, where the lands are cultivated by opulent farmers, as in Normandy and the Isle de France, and those where they are cultivated only by indigent mercenaries, as in Limousin, Angoumois, Bourbonnois, and several others.

Section 65

Subdivisions of the class of cultivators into undertakers, or farmers, and hired persons, servants, and day-labourers.

Hence it follows, that the class of cultivators may be divided, like that of manufacturers, into two branches, the one of undertakers or capitalists, who make the advances, the other of simple stipendiary workmen. It results also, that capitals alone can form and support great enterprizes of agriculture, that give to the lands an unvariable value, if I may use the expression, and that secure to the proprietors a revenue always equal, and the largest possible.

Section 66

Fourth employment of capitals, in advances for enterprizes of commerce. Necessity of the interposition of merchants, properly so called, between the producers of the commodities and the consumers.

The undertakers either in cultivation or manufacture, draw their advances and profits only from the sale of the fruits of the earth, or the commodities fabricated. It is always the wants and the ability of the consumer that sets the price on the sale; but the consumer does not want the produce prepared or fitted up at the moment of the crop, or the perfection of the work. However, the undertakers want their stocks immediately and regularly reimbursed, to embark in fresh enterprizes: the manuring and the seed ought to succeed the crops without interruption. The workmen of a manufacture are unceasingly to be employed in beginning other works, in proportion as the first are distributed, and to replace the materials in proportion as they are consumed. It would not be advisable to stop short in an enterprize once put in execution, nor is it to be presumed that it can be begun again at any time. It is then the strictest interest of the undertaker, to have his capital quickly reimbursed by the sale of his crop or commodities. On the other hand, it is the consumers interest to find, when and where he wishes it, the things he stands in need of; it would be extremely inconvenient for him to be necessitated to make, at the time of the crop, his provision for the whole course of a year. Among the objects of usual consumption, there are many that require long and expensive labours, labours that cannot be undertaken with profit, except on a large quantity of materials, and on such as the consumption of a small number of inhabitants of a limited district, may not be sufficient for even the sale of the work of a single manufactory. Undertakings of this kind must then necessarily be in a reduced number, at a considerable distance from each other, and consequently very distant from the habitations of the greater number of consumers. There is no man, not oppressed under the extremest misery, that is not in a situation to consume several things, which are neither gathered nor fabricated, except in places considerably distant from him, and not less distant from each other. A person that could not procure himself the objects of his consumption but in buying it directly from the hand of him that gathers or works it, would be either unprovided with many commodities, or pass his life in wandering after them.

This double interest which the person producing and the consumer have, the former to find a purchaser, the other to find where to purchase, and yet not to waste useful time in expecting a purchaser, or in finding a seller, has given the idea to a third person to stand between the one and the other. And it is the object of the mercantile profession, who purchase goods from the hands of the person who produces them, to store them in warehouses, whither the consumer comes to make his purchase. By these means the undertaker, assured of the sale and the re-acquisition of his funds, looks undisturbed and indefatigably out for new productions, and the consumer finds within his reach and at once, the objects of which he is in want.

Section 67

Different orders of merchants. They all have this in common, that they purchase to sell again; and that their traffic is supported by advances which are to revert with a profit, to be engaged in new enterprizes.

From the green-woman who exposes her ware in a market, to the merchants of Nantz or Cadiz, who traffic even to India and America, the profession of a trader, or what is properly called commerce, divides into an infinity of branches, and it may be said of degrees. One trader confines himself to provide one or several species of commodities which he sells in his shop to those who chuse; another goes with certain commodities to a place where they are in demand, to bring from thence in exchange, such things as are produced there, and are wanted in the place from whence he departed: one makes his exchanges in his own neighbourhood, and by himself, another by means of correspondents, and by the interposition of carriers, whom he pays, employs, and sends from one province to another, from one kingdom to another, from Europe to Asia, and from Asia back to Europe. One sells his merchandize by retail to those who use them, another only sells in large parcels at a time, to other traders who retail them out to the consumers: but all have this in common that they buy to sell again, and that their first purchases are advances which are returned to them only in course of time. They ought to be returned to them, like those of the cultivators and manufacturers, not only within a certain time, to be employed again in new purchases, but also, (1) with an equal revenue to what they could acquire with their capital without any labour; (2) with the value of their labour, of their risk, and of their industry. Without being assured of this return, and of these indispensable profits, no trader would enter into business, nor could any one possibly continue therein: tis in this view he governs himself in his purchases, on a calculation he makes of the quantity and the price of the things, which he can hope to dispose of in a certain time: the retailer learns from experience, by the success of limited trials made with precaution, what is nearly the wants of those consumers who deal with him. The merchant learns from his correspondents, of the plenty or scarcity, and of the price of merchandize in those different countries to which his commerce extends; he directs his speculations accordingly, he sends his goods from the country where they bear a low price to those where they are sold dearer, including the expence of transportation in the calculation of the advances he ought to be reimbursed. Since trade is necessary, and it is impossible to undertake any commerce without advances proportionable to its extent, we here see another method of employing personal property, a new use that the possessor of a parcel of commodities reserved and accumulated, of a sum of money, in a word, of a capital, may make of it to procure himself subsistence, and to augment, his riches.

Section 68

The true idea of the circulation of money.

We see by what has been just now said, how the cultivation of lands, manufactures of all kinds, and all the branches of trade, depend on a mass of capital, or the accumulation of personal property, which, having been at first advanced by the undertakers, in each of these different branches, ought to return to them again every year with a regular profit; that is, the capital to be again invested, and advanced in the continuation of the same enterprizes, and the profits employed for the greater or less subsistence of the undertakers. It is this continued advance and return which constitutes what ought to be called the circulation of money: this useful and fruitful circulation, which animates all the labour of society, which supports all the motion, and is the life of the body politic, and which is with great reason compared to the circulation of the blood in the human body. For, if by any disorder in the course of the expenses of the different orders of society, the undertakers cease to draw back their advances with such profit as they have a right to expect; it is evident they will be obliged to reduce their undertakings; that the total of the labour, of the consumption of the fruits of the earth, of the productions and of the revenue would be equally diminished; that poverty will succeed to riches, and that the common workman, ceasing to find employ, will fall into the deepest misery.

Section 69

All extensive undertakings, particularly those of manufactures and of commerce, must indispensibly have been very confined, before the introduction of gold and silver in trade.

It is almost unnecessary to remark, that undertakings of all kinds, but especially those of manufactures, and above all those of commerce, must, unavoidably be very confined, before the introduction of gold and silver in trade; since it was almost impossible to accumulate considerable capitals, and yet more difficult, to multiply and divide payments so much as is necessary, to facilitate and increase the exchanges to that extent, which a spirited commerce and circulation require. The cultivation of the land only may support itself to a certain degree, because the cattle are the principal cause of the advances required therein, and it is very probable, there is then no other adventurer in cultivation but the proprietor. As to arts of all kinds, they must necessarily have been in the greatest languor before the introduction of money; they were confined to the coarsest works, for which the proprietors supported the advances, by nourishing the workmen, and furnishing them with materials, or they caused them to be made in their own houses by their servants.

Section 70

Capitals being as necessary to all undertakings as labour and industry, the industrious man shares voluntarily the profit of his enterprize with the owner of the capital who furnishes him the funds he is in need of.

Since capitals are the indispensable foundation of all lucrative enterprizes; since with money we can furnish means for culture, establish manufactures, and raise a commerce, the profits of which being accumulated and frugally laid up, will become a new capital: since, in a word, money is the principal means to beget money; those who with industry and the love of labour are destitute of capital, and have not sufficient for the undertaking they wish to embark in, have no difficulty in resolving to give up to the proprietors of such capital or money, who are willing to trust them, a portion of the profits which they are in expectation of gaining, over and above their advances.

Section 71

Fifth employment of capitals, lending on interest; nature of a loan.

The possessors of money balance the risk their capital may run, if the enterprize does not succeed, with the advantage of enjoying a constant profit without toil; and regulate themselves thereby, to require more or less profit or interest for their money, or to consent to lend it for such an interest as the borrower offers. Here another opportunity opens to the possessor of money, namely, lending on interest, or the commerce of money. Let no one mistake me here, lending on interest is only a trade, in which the lender is a man who sells the use of his money, and the borrower one who buys; precisely the same as the proprietor of an estate, or the person who farms it, buys and sells respectively the use of the hired land. The Latin term for a loan of money or interest, expresses it exactly, *usura pecuniae*, a word which adopted into the French language is become odious, by a consequence of false ideas being adopted on the interest of money.

Section 74

True foundation of interest of money.

A man then may lend his money as lawfully as he may sell it; and the possessor of money may either do one or the other, not only because money is equivalent to a revenue, and a means to procure a revenue: not only because the lender loses, during the continuance of the loan, the revenue he might have procured by it; not only because he risks his capital; not only because the borrower can employ it in advantageous acquisitions, or in undertakings from whence he will draw a large profit; the proprietor of money may lawfully receive the interest of it, by a more general and decisive principle. Even if none of these circumstances should take place, he will not have the less right to require an interest for his loan, for this reason only, that his money is his own. Since it is his own, he has a right to keep it, nothing can imply a duty in him to lend it; if then he does lend, he may annex such a condition to the loan as he chuses, in this he does no injury to the borrower, since the latter agrees to the conditions, and has no sort of right over the sum lent. The profit which money can procure the borrower, is doubtless one of the most prevailing motives to determine him to borrow on interest; it is one of the means which facilitates his payment of the interest, but this is by no means that which gives a right to the lender to require it; it is sufficient for him that his money is his own, and this is a right inseparable from property. He who buys bread, does it for his support, but the right the baker has to exact a price is totally independent of the use of bread; the same right he would possess in the sale of a parcel of stones, a right founded on this principle only, that the bread is his own, and no one has any right to oblige him to give it up for nothing.

Section 76

The rate of interest ought to be fixed, as the price of every other merchandize, by the course of trade alone.

I have already said, that the price of money borrowed, is regulated like the price of all other merchandize, by the proportion of the money at market with the demand for it: thus, when there are many borrowers who are in want of money, the interest of money rises; when there are many possessors who are ready to lend, it falls. It is therefore an error to believe that the interest of money in trade ought to be fixed by the laws of prices. It has a current price fixed like that of all other merchandize. This price varies a little, according to the greater or less security which the lender has; but on equal security, he ought to raise and fall his price in proportion to the abundance of the demand, and the law no more ought to fix the interest of money than it ought to regulate the price of any other merchandizes which have a currency in trade.

Section 80

***The price of interest depends immediately on the proportion of the demand
of the borrowers, with the offer of the lenders, and this proportion depends
principally on the quantity of personal property, accumulated by an excess
of revenue and of the annual produce to form capitals, whether these
capitals exist in money or in any other kind of effects having a value
in commerce.***

The price of silver in circulation has no influence but with respect to the quantity of this metal
employed in common circulation; but the rate of interest is governed by the quantity of property
accumulated and laid by to form a capital. It is indifferent whether this property is in metal or
other effects, provided these effects, are easily convertible into money. It is far from being the case,
that the mass of metal existing in a state, is as large as the amount of the property lent on interest in the course of a year; but all the capitals in furniture, merchandize, tools, and cattle, supply
the place of silver and represent it. A paper signed by a man, who is known to be worth 100,000
livres, and who promises to pay 100 marks in a certain time is worth that sum; the whole property
of the man who has signed this note is answerable for the payment of it, in whatever the nature
of these effects consists, provided they are in value 100,000 livres. It is not therefore the quantity of
silver existing as merchandize which causes the rate of interest to rise or fall, or which brings
more money in the market to be lent; it is only the capitals existing in commerce, that is to say, the
actual value of personal property of every kind accumulated, successively saved out of the
revenues and profits to be employed by the possessors to procure them new revenues and new
profits. It is these accumulated savings which are offered to the borrowers, and the more there are
of them, the lower the interest of money will be, at least if the number of borrowers is not
augmented in proportion.

Section 81

***The spirit of oeconomy continually augments the amount of capitals,
luxury continually tends to destroy them.***

The spirit of œconomy in any nation tends incessantly to augment the amount of the capitals, to
increase the number of lenders, and to diminish that of the borrowers. The habit of luxury has
precisely a contrary effect, and by what has been already remarked on the use of capitals in all
undertakings, whether of cultivation, manufacture, or commerce, we may judge if luxury
enriches a nation, or impoverishes it.

Section 82

***The lowering of interest proves that in Europe œconomy has in
general prevailed over luxury.***

Since the interest of money has been constantly diminishing in Europe for several centuries, we
must conclude, that the spirit of œconomy has been more general than the spirit of luxury. It is
only people of fortune who run into luxury, and among the rich, the sensible part of them confine their expences within their incomes, and pay great attention not to touch their capital. Those
who wish to become rich are far more numerous in a nation than those which are already so.
Now, in the present state of things, as all the land is occupied, there is but one way to become
rich; it is either to possess, or to procure in some way or other, a revenue or an annual profit

above what is absolutely necessary for subsistence, and to lay up every year in reserve to form a capital, by means of which they may obtain an increase of revenue or annual profit, which will again produce another saving, and become capital. There are consequently a great number of men interested and employed in amassing capitals.

Section 84

The influence which the different methods of employing money have on each other.

It is evident that the annual returns, which capitals, placed in different employs, will produce, are proportionate to each other, and all have relation to the actual rate of the interest of money.

Section 85

Money invested in land, necessarily produces the least.

The person who invests his money in land let to a solvent tenant, procures himself a revenue which gives him very little trouble in receiving, and which he may dispose of in the most agreeable manner, by indulging all his inclinations. There is a greater advantage in the purchase of this species of property, than of any other, since the possession of it is more guarded against accidents. We must therefore purchase a revenue in land at a higher price, and must content ourselves with a less revenue for an equal capital.

Section 86

Money on interest ought to bring a little more income than land purchased with an equal capital.

He who lends his money on interest, enjoys it still more peaceably and freely than the possessor of land, but the insolvency of his debtor may endanger the loss of his capital. He will not therefore content himself with an interest equal to the revenue of the land which he could buy with an equal capital. The interest of money lent, must consequently be larger than the revenue of an estate purchased with the same capital; for if the proprietor could find an estate to purchase of an equal income, he would prefer that.

Section 87

Money employed in cultivation, manufactures, or commerce, ought to produce more than the interest of money on loan.

By a like reason, money employed in agriculture, in manufactures, or in commerce, ought to produce a more considerable profit than the revenue of the same capital employed in the purchase of lands, or the interest of money on loan: for these undertakings, besides the capital advanced, require much care and labour, and if they were not more lucrative, it would be much better to secure an equal revenue, which might be enjoyed without labour. It is necessary then, that, besides the interest of the capital, the undertaker should draw every year a profit to recompence him for his care, his labour, his talents, the risque he runs, and to replace the wear and tear of that portion of his capital which he is obliged to invest in effects capable of receiving injury, and exposed to all kinds of accidents.

Section 88

Meantime the freedom of these various employments are limited by each other, and maintain, notwithstanding their inequality, a species of equilibrium.

The different uses of the capitals produce very unequal profits; but this inequality does not prevent them from having a reciprocal influence on each other, nor from establishing a species of equilibrium among themselves, like that between two liquors of unequal gravity, and which communicate with each other by means of a reversed syphon, the two branches of which they fill; there can be no height to which the one can rise or fall, but the liquor in the other branch will be affected in the same manner.

I will suppose, that on a sudden, a great number of proprietors of lands are desirous of selling them. It is evident that the price of lands will fall, and that with a less sum we may acquire a larger revenue; this cannot come to pass without the interest of money rising, for the possessors of money would chuse rather to buy lands, than to lend at a lower interest than the revenue of the lands they could purchase. If, then, the borrowers want to have money, they will be constrained to pay a greater rate. If the interest of the money increases, they will prefer lending it, to setting out in a hazardous manner on enterprizes of agriculture, industry, and commerce: and they will be aware of any enterprizes but those that produce, besides the retribution for their trouble, an emolument by far greater than the rate of the lender's produce. In a word, if the profits, springing from an use of money, augment or diminish, the capitals are converted by withdrawing them from other employments, or are withdrawn by converting them to other ends, which necessarily alters, in each of those employments, the proportion of profits on the capital to the annual product. Generally, money converted into property in land, does not bring in so much as money on interest; and money on interest brings less than money used in laborious enterprizes: but the produce of money laid out in any way whatever, cannot augment or decrease without implying a proportionate augmentation, or decrease in other employments of money.

Section 89

The current interest of money is the standard by which the abundance or scarcity of capitals may be judged; it is the scale on which the extent of a nation's capacity for enterprizes in agriculture, manufactures, and commerce, may be reckoned.

Thus the current interest of money may be considered as a standard of the abundance or scarcity of capitals in a nation, and of the extent of enterprizes of every denomination, in which she may embark: it is manifest, that the lower the interest of money is, the more valuable is the land. A man that has an income of 50,000 livres, if the land is sold but at the rate of 20 years purchase is an owner of only 1 million; he has 2 millions, if the land is sold at the rate of forty. If the interest is at 5 per cent any land to be brought into cultivation would continue fallow, if, besides the recovery of the advances, and the retribution due to the care of the cultivator, its produce would not afford 5 per cent. No manufactory, no commerce can exist, that does not bring in 5 per cent exclusively of the salary and equivalents for the risque and trouble of the undertaker. If there is a neighbouring nation in which the interest stands only at 2 per cent not only will it engross all the branches of commerce, from which the nation where an interest at 5 per cent is established, is excluded, but its manufacturers and merchants, enabled to satisfy themselves with a lower interest, will also sell their goods at a more moderate price, and will attract the almost exclusive commerce of all articles, which they are not prevented to sell by particular circumstances of excessive dearth, and expences of carriages, from the nation in which the interest bears 5 per cent.

Section 90

Influence of the rate of interest of money on all lucrative enterprizes.

The price of the interest may be looked upon as a kind of level, under which all labour, culture, industry, or commerce, acts. It is like a sea expanded over a vast country, the tops of the mountains rise above the surface of the water, and form fertile and cultivated islands. If this sea happens to give way, in proportion as it descends, sloping ground, then plains and vallies appear, which cover themselves with productions of every kind. It wants no more than a foot elevation, or falling, to inundate or to restore culture to unmeasurable tracts of land. It is the abundance of capitals that animates enterprize; and a low interest of money is at the same time the effect and a proof of the abundance of capitals.

Section 93

In which of the three classes of society the lenders of money are to be ranked.

Let us see now, how what we have just discussed about the different ways of employing capitals, agrees with what we have before established about the division of all the members of society into three classes, the one the productive class of husbandmen, the industrious or trading class, and the disposing class, or the class of proprietors.

Section 94

The lender of money belongs, as to his persons, to the disposing class.

We have seen that every rich man is necessarily a possessor either of a capital in moveable riches, or funds equivalent to a capital. Any estate in land is of equal value with a capital; consequently every proprietor is a capitalist, but not every capitalist a proprietor of a real estate; and the possessor of a moveable capital may chuse to confer it on acquiring funds, or to improve it in enterprizes of the cultivating class, or of the industrious class. The capitalist, turned an undertaker in culture or industry, is no more of the disposing class, than the simple workmen in those two lines; they are both taken up in the continuation of their enterprizes. The capitalist who keeps to the lending money, lends it either to a proprietor or to an undertaker. If he lends it to a proprietor, he seems to belong to the class of proprietors, and he becomes co-partitioner in the property; the income of the land is destined to the payment of the interest of his trust; the value of the funds is equal to the security of his capital.

If the money-lender has lent to an undertaker, it is certain that his person belongs to the disposing class; but his capital continues destined to the advances of the enterprizer, and cannot be withdrawn without hurting the enterprize, or without being replaced by a capital of equal value.

Section 95

The use which the money-lender makes of his interest.

Indeed, the interest he draws from that capital seems to make him of the disposing class, since the undertaker and the enterprize may shift without it. It seems also we may form an inference, that in the profits of the two laborious classes, either in the culture of the earth or industry, there is a disposable portion, namely, that which answers to the interest of the advances, calculated on the current rate of interest of money lent; it appears also that this conclusion seems to agree with what we have said, that the mere class of proprietors had a revenue properly so called, a disposing revenue, and that all the members of the other classes had only salaries or profits. This merits some future inquiry. If we consider the 1000 crowns that a man receives annually, who has lent 60,000 livres, to a merchant, in respect to the use he may make of it, there is no doubt of this being perfectly disposable, since the enterprize may subsist without it.

Section 96

The interest of the money is not disposable in one sense, namely, so as the state may be authorized to appropriate, without any inconvenience, a part to supply its wants.

But it does not ensue that they are of the disposing class in such a sense, that the state can appropriate to itself with propriety a portion for the public wants. Those 1000 crowns are not a retribution, which culture or commerce bestows gratuitously on him that makes the advance; it is the price and the condition of this advance, independently of which the enterprize could not subsist. If this retribution is diminished, the capitalist will withdraw his money, and the undertaking will cease. This retribution ought then to be inviolable, and enjoy an entire immunity, because it is the price of an advance made for the enterprize, without which the enterprize could not exist. To encroach upon it, would cause an augmentation in the price of advances in all enterprizes, and consequently diminish the enterprizes themselves, that is to say, cultivation, industry, and commerce.

This answer should lead us to infer, that if we have said, that the capitalist who had lent money to a proprietor, seemed to belong to the class of proprietors, this appearance had somewhat equivocal in it which wanted to be elucidated. In fact, it is strictly true, that the interest of his money is not more disposable, that is, it is not more susceptible of retrenchment, than that of money lent to the undertakers in agriculture and commerce. But the interest is equally the price of the free agreement, and they cannot retrench any part of it without altering or changing the price of the loan.

For it imports little to whom the loan has been made: if the price decreases or augments for the proprietor of lands, it will also decrease and augment for the cultivator, the manufacturer, and the merchant. In a word, the proprietor who lends money ought to be considered, as a dealer in a commodity absolutely necessary for the production of riches, and which cannot be at too low a price. It is also as unreasonable to charge this commerce with duties as it would be to lay a duty on a dunghill which serves to manure the land. Let us conclude from hence, that the person who lends money belongs properly to the disposable class as to his person, because he has nothing to do; but not as to the nature of his property, whether the interest of his money is paid by the proprietor of land out of a portion of his income, or whether it is paid by an undertaker, out of a part of his profits designed to pay the interest of his advances.

BERNARD MANDEVILLE (1670–1733)

Bernard Mandeville practiced medicine in Holland and became a celebrated literary figure in England. He is best known in economics for his *Fable of the Bees, or Private Vices Public Benefits*, which, in literary form, argues that behavior hitherto deemed sinful by religion is actually responsible for the prosperity which people are coming to enjoy. His position obviously reflects the change in moral views and ideology as between pre-market and market economies. Mandeville emphasizes individual psychology, especially self-love; a utilitarian approach to ethics; and the growing materialism, namely, the view that living standards, not salvation as prescribed by theology, are the central focus of life. Egoism and spontaneous, individual activity are both described and implicitly lauded as the basis of the social system. Mandeville coupled his egoism and individualism with the Mercantilism of his day, however much it might seem to compromise his argument that pursuit of individual material self-interest conduces to public economic welfare.

The *Fable* began with Mandeville's writing of *The Grumbling Hive: Or, Knaves Turn'd Honest* in 1714, upon which he published a greatly extended commentary some eight years later. It is this original poem that is reprinted here, and the reader is encouraged to consult the larger work for Mandeville's elaboration of its basic lessons.

References and further reading

Chalk, A. (1966) "Mandeville's *Fable of the Bees*: A Reappraisal," *Southern Economic Journal* 33 (July): 1–6.

Hayek, Friedrich A. (1949) "Individualism: True and False," in *Individualism and Economic Order*, London: Routledge & Kegan Paul.

——(1978) "Dr. Bernard Mandeville," in *New Studies in Philosophy, Politics, Economics, and the History of Ideas*, Chicago: University of Chicago Press.

Hutchison, Terence (1988) *Before Adam Smith: The Emergence of Political Economy, 1662–1776*, Oxford: Basil Blackwell.

Landreth, Harry (1975) "The Economic Thought of Bernard Mandeville," *History of Political Economy* 7 (Summer): 193–208.

Mandeville, Bernard (1732) *The Fable of the Bees: Or, Private Vices, Public Benefits*, reprinted in two volumes with commentary by F.B. Kaye, Oxford: Oxford University Press, 1924.

Rosenberg, Nathan (1963) "Mandeville and Laissez-Faire," *Journal of the History of Ideas* 24 (April–June): 183–96.

——(1987) "Mandeville, Bernard," in John Eatwell, Murray Milgate, and Peter Newman (eds), *The New Palgrave: A Dictionary of Economics*, Vol. 3, London: Macmillan, 297–8.

Scott-Taggart, M.J. (1966) "Mandeville: Cynic or Fool," *Philosophical Quarterly* 16 (July): 221–32.

Viner, Jacob (1953) "Introduction," in Bernard Mandeville (ed.), *A Letter to Dion* (1732), Berkeley and Los Angeles: University of California and Augustan Reprint Society Publication 41. Reprinted in Jacob Viner (ed.), *Essays on the Intellectual History of Economics*, Princeton: Princeton University Press, 1991, 176–88.

The Grumbling Hive: or, Knaves Turn'd Honest

A Spacious Hive well stockt with Bees,
That liv'd in Luxury and Ease;
And yet as fam'd for Laws and Arms,
As yielding large and early Swarms;
Was counted the great Nursery
Of Sciences and Industry.
No Bees had better government,
More Fickleness, or less Content:
They were not Slaves to Tyranny,
Nor rul'd by wild *Democracy*;
But Kings, that could not wrong, because
Their Power was circumscrib'd by Laws.

Those Insects liv'd like Men, and all
Our Actions they perform'd in small:
They did whatever's done in Town,
And what belongs to Sword or Gown:
Tho' th' Artful works, by nimble Slight
Of minute Limbs, 'scap'd Human Sight;
Yet we've no Engines, Labourers,
Ships, Castles, Arms, Artificers,
Craft, Science, Shop, or Instrument,
But they had an Equivalent:
Which, since their Language is unknown,
Must be call'd, as we do our own.
As grant, that among other Things,
They wanted Dice, yet they had Kings;
And those had Guards; from whence we may
Justly conclude, they had some Play;
Unless a Regiment be shewn
Of Soldiers, that make use of none.

Vast Numbers throng'd the fruitful Hive;
Yet those vast Numbers made 'em thrive;
Millions endeavouring to supply
Each other's Lust and Vanity;
While other Millions were employ'd,
To see their Handy-works destroy'd;

They furnish'd half the Universe;
Yet had more Work than Labourers.
Some with vast Stocks, and little Pains,
Jump'd into Business of great Gains;
And some were damn'd to Sythes and Spades,
And all those hard laborious Trades;
Where willing Wretches daily sweat,
And wear out Strength and Limbs to eat:
While others follow'd Mysteries,
To which few Folks bind 'Prentices;
That want no Stock, but that of Brass,
And may set up without a Cross;
As Sharpers, Parasites, Pimps, Players,
Pick-pockets, Coiners, Quacks, Sooth-sayers,
And all those, that in Enmity,
With downright Working, cunningly
Convert to their own Use the Labour
Of their good-natur'd heedless Neighbour.
These were call'd Knaves, but bar the Name,
The grave Industrious were the same:
All Trades and Places knew some Cheat,
No Calling was without Deceit.

 THE Lawyers, of whose Art the Basis
Was raising Feuds and splitting Cases,
Oppos'd all Registers, that Cheats
Might make more Work with dipt Estates;
As wer't unlawful, that one's own,
Without a Law-Suit, should be known.
They kept off Hearings wilfully,
To finger the refreshing Fee;
And to defend a wicked Cause,
Examin'd and survey'd the Laws,
As Burglars Shops and Houses do,
To find out, where they'd best break through.

 PHYSICIANS valu'd Fame and Wealth
Above the drooping Patient's Health,
Or their own Skill: The greatest Part
Study'd, instead of Rules of Art,
Grave pensive Looks and dull Behaviour,
To gain th' Apothecary's Favour;
The Praise of Midwives, Priests, and all
That serv'd at Birth or Funeral.
To bear with th' ever-talking Tribe,
And hear my Lady's Aunt prescribe;
With formal Smile, and kind How d'ye,
To fawn on all the Family;
And, which of all the greatest Curse is,
T' endure th' Impertinence of Nurses.

AMONG the many Priests of *Jove*,
Hir'd to draw Blessings from Above,
Some few were Learn'd and Eloquent,
But thousands Hot and Ignorant:
Yet all pass'd Muster that could hide
Their Sloth, Lust, Avarice and Pride;
For which they were as fam'd as Tailors
For Cabbage, or for Brandy Sailors:
Some, meagre-lookd, and meanly clad,
Would mystically pray for Bread,
Meaning by that an ample Store,
Yet lit'rally received no more;
And, while these holy Drudges starv'd,
The lazy Ones, for which they serv'd,
Indulg'd their Ease, with all the Graces
Of Health and Plenty in their Faces.

THE Soldiers, that were forc'd to fight,
If they surviv'd, got Honour by't;
Tho' some, that shunn'd the bloody Fray,
Had Limbs shot off, that ran away:
Some valiant Gen'rals fought the Foe;
Others took Bribes to let them go:
Some ventur'd always where 'twas warm,
Lost now a Leg, and then an Arm;
Till quite disabled, and put by,
They liv'd on half their Salary
While others never came in Play,
And staid at Home for double Pay.

THEIR Kings were serv'd, but Knavishly,
Cheated by their own Ministry;
Many, that for their Welfare slaved,
Robbing the very Crown they saved:
Pensions were small, and they liv'd high,
Yet boasted of their Honesty.
Calling, whene'er they strain'd their Right,
The slipp'ry Trick a Perquisite;
And when Folks understood their Cant,
They chang'd that for Emolument;
Unwilling to be short or plain,
In any thing concerning Gain;
For there was not a Bee but would
Get more, I won't say, than he should;
But than he dar'd to let them know,
That pay'd for't; as your Gamesters do,
That, tho' at fair Play, ne'er will own
Before the Losers what they've won.

BUT who can all their Frauds repeat?
The very Stuff, which in the Street
They sold for Dirt t'enrich the Ground,
Was often by the Buyers found
Sophisticated with a quarter
Of good-for-nothing Stones and Mortar
Tho' *Flail* had little Cause to mutter,
Who sold the other Salt for Butter.

JUSTICE her self, fam'd for fair Dealing,
By Blindness had not lost her Feeling;
Her Left Hand, which the Scales should hold,
Had often dropt 'em, brib'd with Gold;
And, tho' she seem'd Impartial,
Where Punishment was corporal,
Pretended to a reg'lar Course,
In Murther, and all Crimes of Force;
Tho' some, first pillory'd for Cheating,
Were hang'd in Hemp of their own beating;
Yet, it was thought, the Sword she bore
Check'd but the Desp'rate and the Poor;
That, urg'd by mere Necessity,
Were ty'd up to the wretched Tree
For Crimes, which not deserv'd that Fate,
But to secure the Rich and Great.

THUS every Part was full of Vice,
Yet the whole Mass a Paradise;
Flatter'd in Peace, and fear'd in Wars,
They were th' Esteem of Foreigners,
And lavish of their Wealth and Lives,
The Balance of all other Hives.
Such were the Blessings of that State
Their Crimes conspir'd to make them Great
And Virtue, who from Politicks
Had learn'd a Thousand Cunning Tricks,
Was, by their happy Influence,
Made Friends with Vice: And ever since,
The worst of all the Multitude
Did something for the Common Good.

THIS was the State's Craft, that maintain'd
The Whole of which each Part complain'd:
This, as in Musick Harmony,
Made Jarrings in the main agree;
Parties directly opposite,
Assist each other, as 'twere for Spight;
And Temp'rance with Sobriety,
Serve Drunkenness and Gluttony.

THE Root of Evil, Avarice,
That damn'd ill-natur'd baneful Vice,
Was Slave to Prodigality,
That noble Sin; whilst Luxury
Employ'd a Million of the Poor,
And odious Pride a Million more:
Envy it self, and Vanity,
Were Ministers of Industry;
Their darling Folly, Fickleness,
In Diet, Furniture and Dress,
That strange ridic'lous Vice, was made
The very Wheel that turn'd the Trade.
Their Laws and Clothes were equally
Objects of Mutability;
For, what was well done for a time,
In half a Year became a Crime;
Yet while they alter'd thus their Laws,
Still finding and correcting Flaws,
They mended by Inconstancy
Faults, which no Prudence could foresee.

THUS Vice nurs'd Ingenuity,
Which join'd with Time and Industry,
Had carry'd Life's Conveniencies,
It's real Pleasures, Comforts, Ease,
To such a Height, the very Poor
Liv'd better than the Rich before,
And nothing could be added more.

HOW Vain is Mortal Happiness!
Had they but known the Bounds of Bliss
And that Perfection here below
Is more than Gods can well bestow;
The Grumbling Brutes had been content
With Ministers and Government.
But they, at every ill Success,
Like Creatures lost without Redress,
Curs'd Politicians, Armies, Fleets;
While every one cry'd, *Damn the Cheats*,
And would, tho' conscious of his own,
In others barb'rously bear none.

ONE, that had got a Princely Store,
By cheating Master, King and Poor,
Dar'd cry aloud, *The Land must sink
For all its Fraud*; And whom d'ye think
The Sermonizing Rascal chid?
A Glover that sold Lamb for Kid.

THE least thing was not done amiss,
Or cross'd the Publick Business;
But all the Rogues cry'd brazenly,
Good Gods, Had we but Honesty!
Merc'ry smil'd at th' Impudence,
And others call'd it want of Sense,
Always to rail at what they lov'd
But *Jove* with Indignation mov'd,
At last in Anger swore, *He'd rid*
The bawling Hive of Fraud; and did.
The very Moment it departs,
And Honesty fills all their Hearts
There shews 'em, like th' Instructive Tree,
Those Crimes which they're asham'd to see;
Which now in Silence they confess,
By blushing at their Ugliness:
Like Children, that would hide their Faults,
And by their Colour own their Thoughts:
Imag'ning, when they're look'd upon,
That others see what they have done.

BUT, Oh ye Gods! What Consternation,
How vast and sudden was th' Alteration!
In half an Hour, the Nation round,
Meat fell a Penny in the Pound.
The Mask Hypocrisy's flung down,
From the great Statesman to the Clown:
And some in borrow'd Looks well known,
Appear'd like Strangers in their own.
The Bar was silent from that Day;
For now the willing Debtors pay,
Ev'n what's by Creditors forgot;
Who quitted them that had it not.
Those, that were in the Wrong, stood mute,
And dropt the patch'd vexatious Suit:
On which since nothing less can thrive,
Than Lawyers in an honest Hive,
All, except those that got enough,
With Inkhorns by their sides troop'd off.

JUSTICE hang'd some, set others free;
And after Goal delivery,
Her Presence being no more requir'd,
With all her Train and Pomp retir'd.
First march'd some Smiths with Locks and Grates,
Fetters, and Doors with Iron Plates:
Next Goalers, Turnkeys and Assistants:
Before the Goddess, at some distance,
Her chief and faithful Minister,

'Squire CATCH, the Law's great Finisher,
Bore not th' imaginary Sword,
But his own Tools, an Ax and Cord:
Then on a Cloud the Hood-wink'd Fair,
JUSTICE her self was push'd by Air
About her Chariot, and behind,
Were Serjeants, Bums of every kind,
Tip-staffs, and all those Officers,
That squeeze a Living out of Tears.

THO' Physick liv'd, while Folks were ill,
None would prescribe, but Bees of skill,
Which through the Hive dispers'd so wide,
That none of them had need to ride;
Wav'd vain Disputes, and strove to free
The Patients of their Misery;
Left Drugs in cheating Countries grown,
And us'd the Product of their own;
Knowing the Gods sent no Disease
To Nations without Remedies.

THEIR Clergy rous'd from Laziness,
Laid not their Charge on Journey-Bees;
But serv'd themselves, exempt from Vice,
The Gods with Pray'r and Sacrifice;
All those, that were unfit, or knew
Their Service might be spar'd, withdrew:
Nor was there Business for so many,
(if th' Honest stand in need of any,)
Few only with the High-Priest staid,
To whom the rest Obedience paid:
Himself employ'd in Holy Cares,
Resign'd to others State-Affairs.
He chas'd no Starv'ling from his Door,
Nor pinch'd the Wages of the Poor;
But at his House the Hungry's fed,
The Hireling finds unmeasur'd Bread,
The needy Trav'ler Board and Bed.

AMONG the King's great Ministers,
And all th' inferior Officers
The Change was great; for frugally
They now liv'd on their Salary:
That a poor Bee should ten times come
To ask his Due, a trifling Sum,
And by some well-hir'd Clerk be made
To give a Crown, or ne'er be paid,
Would now be call'd a downright Cheat,
Tho' formerly a Perquisite.

All Places manag'd first by Three,
Who watch'd each other's Knavery,
And often for a Fellow-feeling,
Promoted one another's stealing,
Are happily supply'd by One,
By which some thousands more are gone.

No Honour now could be content,
To live and owe for what was spent;
Liv'ries in Brokers Shops are hung,
They part with Coaches for a Song;
Sell stately Horses by whole Sets;
And Country-Houses, to pay Debts.

Vain Cost is shunn'd as much as Fraud;
They have no Forces kept Abroad;
Laugh at th' Esteem of Foreigners,
And empty Glory got by Wars;
They fight, but for their Country's sake,
When Right or Liberty's at Stake.

Now mind the glorious Hive, and see
How Honesty and Trade agree.
The Shew is gone, it thins apace;
And looks with quite another Face.
For 'twas not only that They went,
By whom vast Sums were Yearly spent;
But Multitudes that liv'd on them,
Were daily forc'd to do the same.
In vain to other Trades they'd fly;
All were o'er-stock'd accordingly.

The Price of Land and Houses falls;
Mirac'lous Palaces, whose Walls,
Like those of *Thebes*, were rais'd by Play,
Are to be let; while the once gay,
Well-seated Houshold Gods would be
More pleas'd to expire in Flames, than see
The mean Inscription on the Door
Smile at the lofty ones they bore.
The building Trade is quite destroy'd,
Artificers are not employ'd;
No Limner for his Art is fam'd,
Stone-cutters, Carvers are not nam'd.

Those, that remain'd, grown temp'rate, strive,
Not how to spend, but how to live,
And, when they paid their Tavern Score,
Resolv'd to enter it no more:

No Vintner's jilt in all the Hive
Could wear now Cloth of Gold, and thrive;
Nor *Torcol* such vast Sums advance,
For *Burgundy* and *Ortelans*;
The Courtier's gone, that with his Miss
Supp'd at his House on *Christmas* Peas;
Spending as much in two Hours stay,
As keeps a Troop of Horse a Day.

    THE haughty *Chloe*, to live Great,
Had made her Husband rob the State:
But now she sells her Furniture,
Which th' *Indies* had been ransack'd for;
Contracts th' expensive Bill of Fare,
And wears her strong Suit a whole Year:
The slight and fickle Age is past;
And Clothes, as well as Fashions, last.
Weavers, that join'd rich Silk with Plate,
And all the Trades subordinate,
Are gone. Still Peace and Plenty reign,
And every Thing is cheap, tho' plain:
Kind Nature, free from Gard'ners Force,
Allows all Fruits in her own Course;
But Rarities cannot be had,
Where Pains to get them are not paid.

    As Pride and Luxury decrease,
So by degrees they leave the Seas.
Not Merchants now, but Companies
Remove whole Manufactories.
All Arts and Crafts neglected lie;
Content, the Bane of Industry,
Makes 'em admire their homely Store,
And neither seek nor covet more.

    SO few, in the vast Hive remain,
The hundredth Part they can't maintain
Against th' Insults of numerous Foes;
Whom yet they valiantly oppose:
'Till some well-fenc'd Retreat is found,
And here they die or stand their Ground.
No Hireling in their Army's known;
But bravely fighting for their own,
Their Courage and Integrity
At last were crown'd with Victory.

    THEY triumph'd not without their Cost,
For many Thousand Bees were lost.
Hard'ned with Toils and Exercise,

They counted Ease it self a Vice;
Which so improv'd their Temperance;
That, to avoid Extravagance,
They flew into a hollow Tree,
Blest with Content and Honesty.

The moral

THEN leave Complaints: Fools only strive
To make a Great an Honest Hive.
T' enjoy the World's Conveniencies,
Be fam'd in War, yet live in Ease,
Without great Vices, is a vain
EUTOPIA seated in the Brain.
Fraud, Luxury and Pride must live,
While we the Benefits receive:
Hunger's a dreadful Plague, no doubt,
Yet who digests or thrives without?
Do we not owe the Growth of Wine
To the dry shabby crooked Vine?
Which, while its Shoots neglected stood,
Chok'd other Plants, and ran to Wood;
But blest us with its noble Fruit,
As soon as it was ty'd and cut:
So Vice is beneficial found,
When it's by Justice lopt and bound;
Nay, where the People would be great,
As necessary to the State,
As Hunger is to make 'em eat.
Bare Virtue can't make Nations live
In Splendor; they, that would, revive
A Golden Age, must be as free,
For Acorns, as for Honesty.

Finis

Part 2

The Classical School

Introduction

English Classical Political Economy was the dominant school of economics from the late eighteenth century until the last quarter of the nineteenth century. Its major figures were Adam Smith, David Ricardo, Thomas Robert Malthus, James Mill, Jeremy Bentham and John Stuart Mill. The English Classicists were the first major school to explicate a modern market, capitalist economy. Two of their most distinctive doctrines – Malthus's law of population and Ricardo's principle of diminishing returns – led to the portrayal of economics as the "dismal science." Because of the centrality of the two doctrines to their system of thought, that view is not altogether erroneous. But the adverse portrayal was also due to both the economists' treatment of these doctrines as ontologically given, transcendent and inescapable, and the use of the doctrines to challenge economic and political reforms. As it turned out, the classicists' doctrines had to be understood both within their larger system of thought and in the context of their approach to abstract theory; the doctrines worked out through human institutions, they did not dictate human arrangements.

The core of English Classical Political Economy is derived from the world view of a modern market, capitalist economy. Its program was to promote the further development of such an economy, in part through political reform and the adoption of suitable government policy. Most of the Classical Economists after Smith, with the notable exception of Malthus, supported the transformation of the combined English economy and policy from an agricultural one dominated by the landowning class to one increasingly both representative of and promotive of the interests and world view of the middle class, that is, of businessmen of all types. The characteristic, indeed, dominant issue involved the Corn Laws, legislation which worked to restrict the importation of agricultural products, thus promoting the high price of food and the high rent of the landowning class. Higher aggregate rents meant less national income was available for the business and wage-earning classes; it also meant "subsidization" of the landed ruling class, in the sense of government policy skewed to their interests, the class whose position the rising middle class was seeking to either replace or join in forming government policy and thereby the institutions through which economic "laws" operated and worked out.

The specific theories of the classical school included, in addition to the laws of population and of diminishing returns, the labor theory of value, the theory of Ricardian rent, the division of labor, the role of the market in price determination and resource allocation, the Ricardian theory of comparative advantage explaining international trade and capital flows, the quantity theory of money, and theories of wages and profits. The dominant Ricardian model was the long-run performance of the economic system, largely in terms of distribution: the tendency of rent to increase, of wages to gravitate to a socially determined minimum of subsistence, and of profits to fall – together underscoring a dismal future.

The negative implications of the laws of population, diminishing returns and the falling rate of profit (largely driven by the first two) were a matter of working out the logical implications of the Classicists' premises. Their actual attitude was largely anything but dismal. They both accepted and lauded the industrial market capitalist system and, while they could have had a more dramatic place for technological change in their analyses, they were personally optimistic about the future. The three laws were to them both constraints upon optimism and conditions under which institutions operated – and they were insistent upon the promulgation of the institutions of a business, rather than a mediaeval agrarian, society. Thus, they accepted and lauded the allocation of resources through markets at the same time they understood the importance of government action in providing the necessary framing institutions of a market economy, in exercising social control, and in serving as an agent of social change – again, not laissez faire in the sense of minimal and passive government but a government promotive of and operating within a market or business economy. Like the Physiocrats, the Classical Economists took their desired system as given, and their prescribed economic role of government was tailored to achieve their system.

The entries reprinted in this section have been selected with a view to giving the reader a sense for these major themes, as discussed by the classical thinkers themselves, along with some sense for the differences of opinions that characterized the theoretical and policy debates within classical political economy.

For further reading

Bharadwaj, Krishna (1987) "Wages in Classical Economics," in John Eatwell, Murray Milgate, and Peter Newman (eds), *The New Palgrave: A Dictionary of Economics*, Vol. 4, London: Macmillan, 843–6.

Blaug, Mark (1987) "Classical Economics," in John Eatwell, Murray Milgate, and Peter Newman (eds), *The New Palgrave: A Dictionary of Economics*, Vol. 1, London: Macmillan, 434–45.

Cannan, Edwin (1917) *A History of the Theories of Production and Distribution from 1776 to 1848*, 3rd edn, London: Staples Press, 1953.

Dobb, Maurice (1973) *Theories of Value and Distribution Since Adam Smith: Ideology and Economic Theory*, Cambridge: Cambridge University Press.

Eatwell, John (1987) "Competition: Classical Conceptions," in John Eatwell, Murray Milgate, and Peter Newman (eds), *The New Palgrave: A Dictionary of Economics*, Vol. 1, London: Macmillan, 537–40.

Eltis, Walter (1984) *The Classical Theory of Economic Growth*, London: Macmillan.

Gilibert, Giorgio (1987) "Production: Classical Theories," in John Eatwell, Murray Milgate, and Peter Newman (eds), *The New Palgrave: A Dictionary of Economics*, Vol. 3, London: Macmillan, 990–2.

Green, Roy (1987) "Classical Theory of Money," in John Eatwell, Murray Milgate, and Peter Newman (eds), *The New Palgrave: A Dictionary of Economics*, Vol. 1, London: Macmillan, 449–51.

Harris, Donald J. (1987) "Classical Growth Models," in John Eatwell, Murray Milgate, and Peter Newman (eds), *The New Palgrave: A Dictionary of Economics*, Vol. 1, London: Macmillan, 445–9.

Hollander, Samuel (1992) *Classical Economics*, Toronto: University of Toronto Press.

Irwin, Douglas A. (1996) *Against the Tide: An Intellectual History of Free Trade*, Princeton: Princeton University Press.

Kurz, Heinz D. and Salvadori, Neri (1998) *The Elgar Companion to Classical Economics*, Cheltenham: Edward Elgar Publishing.

O'Brien, D.P. (1975) *The Classical Economists*, Oxford: Oxford University Press.

Pivetti, Massimo (1987) "Distribution Theories: Classical," in John Eatwell, Murray Milgate, and Peter Newman (eds), *The New Palgrave: A Dictionary of Economics*, Vol. 1, London: Macmillan, 872–6.

Robbins, Lionel (1952) *The Theory of Economic Policy in English Classical Political Economy*, London: Macmillan.

Samuels, Warren J. (1966) *The Classical Theory of Economic Policy*, Cleveland, World.

Samuelson, P.A. (1978) "The Canonical Classical Model of Political Economy," *Journal of Economic Literature* 16 (December): 1415–34.

Sowell, Thomas (1974) *Classical Economics Reconsidered*, Princeton: Princeton University Press.

Tucker, G.S.L. (1960) *Progress and Profits in British Economic Thought, 1650–1850*, London: Cambridge University Press.

Viner, Jacob (1937) *Studies in the Theory of International Trade*, New York: Harper & Row.

DAVID HUME (1711–1776)

David Hume, by courtesy of The Warren J. Samuels Portrait Collection at Duke University.

David Hume was one of history's eminent philosophers. He was a Scot, a close friend of Adam Smith, and devoted the majority of his life to study and writing. Hume wrote on questions of human nature-psychology and epistemology-theory of knowledge. Like the other writers, Hume represented the modern Enlightenment orientation with its emphasis on reason, secularism, individualism, materialism, politicization – all with their policy-conscious emphasis on the role of social choice in the social construction of reality, albeit within the constraints of physical nature and of received institutions and systems. His willingness to confront the received wisdom of his time, particularly on matters relating to religion, engendered considerable antipathy in some quarters. Hume also wrote essays on political philosophy and on increasingly conspicuous topics of economics: money, interest, trade, taxation, and population growth. In many of these respects, Hume was either more advanced and/or more articulate than his close friend Adam Smith.

Reprinted here are Hume's three classic essays on money, interest, and the balance of trade. These essays reflect Hume's adoption of the quantity theory of money and his application of it to the analysis of the then dominant mercantilist ideas. "Of Money" examines the relationship between the money supply and economic growth, discussing conditions under which an increase in the money supply can stimulate economic activity. "Of Interest" attempts to refute the notion that the rate of interest is determined by the money supply, arguing, instead, that the interest rate is a function of the supply of real capital. Finally, "Of the Balance of Trade" examines the specie flow mechanism and argues that restrictions on trade to promote specie accumulation will be counterproductive because bullion inflows will raise domestic prices relative to those abroad, thereby reducing exports and increasing imports – the net effect of which is an outflow of specie.

References and further reading

Arkin, Marcus (1956) "The Economic Writings of David Hume – A Reassessment," *South African Journal of Economics* 24 (September): 204–20. Reprinted in J.J. Spengler and W.R. Allen (eds), *Essays in Economic Thought*, Skokie, IL Rand McNally, 1960, 141–60.

Hume, David (1955) *Writings on Economics*, edited by Eugene Rotwein, Madison: University of Wisconsin Press; London: Nelson.

——(1987) *Essays Moral, Political, and Literary*, edited with a Foreword, Notes, and Glossary by Eugene F. Miller, Revised edition, Indianapolis: Liberty Classics.

Hutchison, Terence (1988) *Before Adam Smith: The Emergence of Political Economy, 1662–1776*, Oxford: Basil Blackwell.

Mayer, Thomas (1980) "David Hume and Monetarism," *Quarterly Journal of Economics* 95 (August): 89–101.

Rotwein, Eugene (1987) "Hume, David," in John Eatwell, Murray Milgate, and Peter Newman (eds), *The New Palgrave: A Dictionary of Economics*, Vol. 2, London: Macmillan, 692–5.

Skinner, Andrew S. (1996) "David Hume: Economic Writings," in *A System of Social Science: Papers Relating to Adam Smith*, 2nd edn, Oxford: Clarendon Press.

Wood, Geoffrey E. (1995) "The Quantity Theory in the 1980s: Hume, Thornton, Friedman and the Relation Between Money and Inflation," in Mark Blaug *et al.* (eds), *The Quantity Theory of Money: From Locke to Keynes and Friedman*, Aldershot: Edward Elgar Publishing.

Political Discources (1752)

"Of Money"

Money is not, properly speaking, one of the subjects of commerce; but only the instrument which men have agreed upon to facilitate the exchange of one commodity for another. It is none of the wheels of trade: It is the oil which renders the motion of the wheels more smooth and easy. If we consider any one kingdom by itself, it is evident, that the greater or less plenty of money is of no consequence; since the prices of commodities are always proportioned to the plenty of money, and a crown in *Harry VII*'s time served the same purpose as a pound does at present. It is only the public which draws any advantage from the greater plenty of money; and that only in its wars and negociations with foreign states. And this is the reason, why all rich and trading countries from *Carthage* to *Great Britain* and *Holland*, have employed mercenary troops, which they hired from their poorer neighbours. Were they to make use of their native subjects, they would find less advantage from their superior riches, and from their great plenty of gold and silver; since the pay of all their servants must rise in proportion to the public opulence. Our small army of 20,000 men is maintained at as great expence as a *French* army twice as numerous. The *English* fleet, during the late war, required as much money to support it as all the *Roman* legions, which kept the whole world in subjection, during the time of the emperors.

The greater number of people and their greater industry are serviceable in all cases; at home and abroad, in private, and in public. But the greater plenty of money, is very limited in its use, and may even sometimes be a loss to a nation in its commerce with foreigners.

There seems to be a happy concurrence of causes in human affairs, which checks the growth of trade and riches, and hinders them from being confined entirely to one people; as might naturally at first be dreaded from the advantages of an established commerce. Where one nation has gotten the start of another in trade, it is very difficult for the latter to regain the ground it has lost; because of the superior industry and skill of the former, and the greater stocks, of which its merchants are possessed, and which enable them to trade on so much smaller profits. But these advantages are compensated, in some measure, by the low price of labour in every nation which has not an extensive commerce, and does not much abound in gold and silver. Manufactures, therefore gradually shift their places, leaving those countries and provinces which they have already enriched, and flying to others, whither they are allured by the cheapness of provisions and labour; till they have enriched these also, and are again banished by the same causes. And, in general, we may observe, that the dearness of every thing, from plenty of money, is a disadvantage, which attends an established commerce, and sets bounds to it in every country, by enabling the poorer states to undersell the richer in all foreign markets.

This has made me entertain a doubt concerning the benefit of banks and paper-credit, which are so generally esteemed advantageous to every nation. That provisions and labour should become dear by the encrease of trade and money, is, in many respects, an inconvenience; but an inconvenience that is unavoidable, and the effect of that public wealth and prosperity which are the end of all our wishes. It is compensated by the advantages, which we reap from the possession of these precious metals, and the weight, which they give the nation in all foreign wars and nego- ciations. But there appears no reason for encreasing that inconvenience by a counterfeit money, which foreigners will not accept of in any payment, and which any great disorder in the state will reduce to nothing. There are, it is true, many people in every rich state, who having large sums of money, would prefer paper with good security; as being of more easy transport and more safe custody. If the public provide not a bank, private bankers will take advantage of this circum- stance; as the goldsmiths formerly did in *London*, or as the bankers do at present in *Dublin*: And therefore it is better, it may be thought, that a public company should enjoy the benefit of that paper-credit, which always will have place in every opulent kingdom. But to endeavour artifi- cially to encrease such a credit, can never be the interest of any trading nation; but must lay them under disadvantages, by encreasing money beyond its natural proportion to labour and com- modities, and thereby heightening their price to the merchant and manufacturer. And in this view, it must be allowed, that no bank could be more advantageous, than such a one as locked up all the money it received, and never augmented the circulating coin, as is usual, by returning part of its treasure into commerce. A public bank, by this expedient, might cut off much of the deal- ings of private bankers and money-jobbers; and though the state bore the charge of salaries to the directors and tellers of this bank (for, according to the preceding supposition, it would have no profit from its dealings), the national advantage, resulting from the low price of labour and the destruction of paper-credit, would be a sufficient compensation. Not to mention, that so large a sum, lying ready at command, would be a convenience in times of great public danger and distress; and what part of it was used might be replaced at leisure, when peace and tranquillity was restored to the nation.

But of this subject of paper-credit we shall treat more largely hereafter. And I shall finish this essay on money, by proposing and explaining two observations, which may, perhaps, serve to employ the thoughts of our speculative politicians.

I. It was a shrewd observation of *Anacharsis* the *Scythian*, who had never seen money in his own country, that gold and silver seemed to him of no use to the *Greeks*, but to assist them in numera- tion and arithmetic. It is indeed evident, that money is nothing but the representation of labour and commodities, and serves only as a method of rating or estimating them. Where coin is in greater plenty; as a greater quantity of it is required to represent the same quantity of goods; it can have no effect, either good or bad, taking a nation within itself; any more than it would make an alteration on a merchant's books, if, instead of the *Arabian* method of notation, which requires few characters, he should make use of the *Roman*, which requires a great many. Nay, the greater quantity of money, like the *Roman* characters, is rather inconvenient, and requires greater trouble both to keep and transport it. But notwithstanding this conclusion, which must be allowed just, it is certain, that, since the discovery of the mines in *America*, industry has encreased in all the nations of *Europe*, except in the possessors of those mines; and this may justly be ascribed, amongst other reasons, to the encrease of gold and silver. Accordingly we find, that, in every kingdom, into which money begins to flow in greater abundance than formerly, every thing takes a new face: labour and industry gain life; the merchant becomes more enterprising, the manu- facturer more diligent and skilful, and even the farmer follows his plough with greater alacrity and attention. This is not easily to be accounted for, if we consider only the influence which a greater abundance of coin has in the kingdom itself, by heightening the price of Commodities, and obliging every one to pay a greater number of these little yellow or white pieces for every thing he purchases. And as to foreign trade, it appears, that great plenty of money is rather disadvantageous, by raising the price of every kind of labour.

To account, then, for this phenomenon, we must consider, that though the high price of commodities be a necessary consequence of the encrease of gold and silver, yet it follows not immediately upon that encrease; but some time is required before the money circulates through the whole state, and makes its effect be felt on all ranks of people. At first, no alteration is perceived; by degrees the price rises, first of one commodity, then of another; till the whole at last reaches a just proportion with the new quantity of specie which is in the kingdom. In my opinion, it is only in this interval or intermediate situation, between the acquisition of money and rise of prices, that the encreasing quantity of gold and silver is favourable to industry. When any quantity of money is imported into a nation, it is not at first dispersed into many hands; but is confined to the coffers of a few persons, who immediately seek to employ it to advantage. Here are a set of manufacturers or merchants, we shall suppose, who have received returns of gold and silver for goods which they sent to *Cadiz*. They are thereby enabled to employ more workmen than formerly, who never dream of demanding higher wages, but are glad of employment from such good paymasters. If workmen become scarce, the manufacturer gives higher wages, but at first requires an encrease of labour; and this is willingly submitted to by the artisan, who can now eat and drink better, to compensate his additional toil and fatigue. He carries his money to market, where he finds every thing at the same price as formerly, but returns with greater quantity and of better kinds, for the use of his family. The farmer and gardener, finding, that all their commodities are taken off, apply themselves with alacrity to the raising more; and at the same time can afford to take better and more cloths from their tradesmen, whose price is the same as formerly, and their industry only whetted by so much new gain. It is easy to trace the money in its progress through the whole commonwealth; where we shall find, that it must first quicken the diligence of every individual, before it encrease the price of labour.

And that the specie may encrease to a considerable pitch, before it have this latter effect, appears, amongst other instances, from the frequent operations of the *French* king on the money; where it was always found, that the augmenting of the numerary value did not produce a proportional rise of the prices, at least for some time. In the last year of *Louis XIV*, money was raised three-sevenths, but prices augmented only one. Corn in *France* is now sold at the same price, or for the same number of livres, it was in 1683; though silver was then at 30 livres the mark, and is now at 50. Not to mention the great addition of gold and silver, which may have come into that kingdom since the former period.

From the whole of this reasoning we may conclude, that it is of no manner of consequence, with regard to the domestic happiness of a state, whether money be in a greater or less quantity. The good policy of the magistrate consists only in keeping it, if possible, still encreasing; because, by that means, he keeps alive a spirit of industry in the nation, and encreases the stock of labour, in which consists all real power and riches. A nation, whose money decreases, is actually, at that time, weaker and more miserable than another nation, which possesses no more money, but is on the encreasing hand. This will be easily accounted for, if we consider, that the alterations in the quantity of money, either on one side or the other, are not immediately attended with proportionable alterations in the price of commodities. There is always an interval before matters be adjusted to their new situation; and this interval is as pernicious to industry, when gold and silver are diminishing, as it is advantageous when these metals are encreasing. The workman has not the same employment from the manufacturer and merchant; though he pays the same price for every thing in the market. The farmer cannot dispose of his corn and cattle; though he must pay the same rent to his landlord. The poverty, and beggary, and sloth, which must ensue, are easily foreseen.

II. The second observation which I proposed to make with regard to money, may be explained after the following manner. There are some kingdoms, and many provinces in *Europe* (and all of them were once in the same condition) where money is so scarce, that the landlord can get none at all from his tenants; but is obliged to take his rent in kind, and either to consume it himself, or transport it to places where he may find a market. In those countries, the prince can levy few or no taxes, but in the same manner: And as he will receive small benefit from impositions so paid, it is evident that such a kingdom has little force even at home; and cannot maintain fleets and armies to the same extent, as if every part of it abounded in gold and silver. There is surely a greater disproportion between the force of *Germany*, at present, and what it was three centuries ago, than there is in its industry, people, and manufactures. The *Austrian* dominions in the empire are in general well peopled and well cultivated, and are of great extent; but have not a proportionable weight in the balance of *Europe*; proceeding, as is commonly supposed, from the scarcity of money. How do all these facts agree with that principle of reason, that the quantity of gold and silver is in itself altogether indifferent? According to that principle wherever a sovereign has numbers of subjects, and these have plenty of commodities, he should of course be great and powerful, and they rich and happy, independent of the greater or lesser abundance of the precious metals. These admit of divisions and subdivisions to a great extent; and where the pieces might become so small as to be in danger of being lost, it is easy to mix the gold or silver with a baser metal, as is practised in some countries of *Europe*; and by that means raise the pieces to a bulk more sensible and convenient. They still serve the same purposes of exchange, whatever their number may be, or whatever colour they may be supposed to have.

To these difficulties I answer, that the effect, here supposed to flow from scarcity of money, really arises from the manners and customs of the people; and that we mistake, as is too usual, a collateral effect for a cause. The contradiction is only apparent; but it requires some thought and reflection to discover the principles, by which we can reconcile reason to experience.

It seems a maxim almost self-evident, that the prices of every thing depend on the proportion between commodities and money, and that any considerable alteration on either has the same effect, either of heightening or lowering the price. Encrease the commodities, they become cheaper; encrease the money, they rise in their value. As, on the other hand, a diminution of the former, and that of the latter, have contrary tendencies.

It is also evident, that the prices do not so much depend on the absolute quantity of commodities and that of money, which are in a nation, as on that of the commodities, which come or may come to market, and of the money which circulates. If the coin be locked up in chests, it is the same thing with regard to prices, as if it were annihilated; if the commodities be hoarded in magazines and granaries, a like effect follows. As the money and commodities, in these cases, never meet, they cannot affect each other. Were we, at any time, to form conjectures concerning the price of provisions, the corn, which the farmer must reserve for seed and for the maintenance of himself and family, ought never to enter into the estimation. It is only the overplus, compared to the demand, that determines the value.

To apply these principles, we must consider, that, in the first and more uncultivated ages of any state, ere fancy has confounded her wants with those of nature, men, content with the produce of their own fields, or with those rude improvements which they themselves can work upon them, have little occasion for exchange, at least for money, which, by agreement, is the common measure of exchange. The wool of the farmer's own flock, spun in his own family, and wrought by a neighbouring weaver, who receives his payment in corn or wool, suffices for furniture and cloathing. The carpenter, the smith, the mason, the tailor, are retained by wages of a like nature; and the landlord himself, dwelling in the neighbourhood, is content to receive his rent in the commodities raised by the farmer. The greater part of these he consumes at home, in rustic hospitality: The rest, perhaps, he disposes of for money to the neighbouring town, whence he draws the few materials of his expence and luxury.

But after men begin to refine on all these enjoyments, and live not always at home, nor are content with what can be raised in their neighbourhood, there is more exchange and commerce of all kinds, and more money enters into that exchange. The tradesmen will not be paid in corn; because they want something more than barely to eat. The farmer goes beyond his own parish for the commodities he purchases, and cannot always carry his commodities to the merchant who supplies him. The landlord lives in the capital, or in a foreign country; and demands his rent in gold and silver, which can easily be transported to him. Great undertakers, and manufacturers, and merchants, arise in every commodity; and these can conveniently deal in nothing but in specie. And consequently, in this situation of society, the coin enters into many more contracts, and by that means is much more employed than in the former.

The necessary effect is, that, provided the money encrease not in the nation, every thing must become much cheaper in times of industry and refinement, than in rude, uncultivated ages. It is the proportion between the circulating money, and the commodities in the market, which determines the prices. Goods, that are consumed at home, or exchanged with other goods in the neighbourhood, never come to market; they affect not in the least the current specie; with regard to it they are as if totally annihilated; and consequently this method of using them sinks the proportion on the side of the commodities, and encreases the prices. But after money enters into all contracts and sales, and is every where the measure of exchange, the same national cash has a much greater task to perform; all commodities are then in the market; the sphere of circulation is enlarged; it is the same case as if that individual sum were to serve a larger kingdom; and therefore, the proportion being here lessened on the side of the money, every thing must become cheaper, and the prices gradually fall.

By the most exact computations, that have been formed all over *Europe*, after making allowance for the alteration in the numerary value or the denomination, it is found, that the prices of all things have only risen three, or at most, four times, since the discovery of the *West Indies*. But will any one assert, that there is not much more than four times the coin in *Europe*, that was in the fifteenth century, and the centuries preceding it? The *Spaniards* and *Portuguese* from their mines, the *English*, *French*, and *Dutch*, by their *African* trade, and by their interlopers in the *West Indies*, bring home about six millions a year, of which not above a third goes to the *East-Indies*. This sum alone, in ten years, would probably double the ancient stock of money in *Europe*. And no other satisfactory reason can be given, why all prices have not risen to a much more exorbitant height, except that which is derived from a change of customs and manners. Besides that more commodities are produced by additional industry, the same commodities come more to market, after men depart from their ancient simplicity of manners. And though this encrease has not been equal to that of money, it has, however, been considerable, and has preserved the proportion between coin and commodities nearer the ancient standard.

Were the question proposed, which of these methods of living in the people, the simple or refined, is the most advantageous to the state or public? I should, without much scruple, prefer the latter, in a view to politics at least; and should produce this as an additional reason for the encouragement of trade and manufactures.

While men live in the ancient simple manner, and supply all their necessaries from domestic industry or from the neighbourhood, the sovereign can levy no taxes in money from a considerable part of his subjects; and if he will impose on them any burthens, he must take payment in commodities, with which alone they abound; a method attended with such great and obvious inconveniencies, that they need not here be insisted on. All the money he can pretend to raise, must be from his principal cities, where alone it circulates; and these, it is evident, cannot afford him so much as the whole state could, did gold and silver circulate throughout the whole. But besides this obvious diminution of the revenue, there is another cause of the poverty of the public in such a situation. Not only the sovereign receives less money, but the same money goes not so far as in times of industry and general commerce. Every thing is dearer, where the gold and silver are supposed equal; and that because fewer commodities come to market, and the whole coin bears a higher proportion to what is to be purchased by it; whence alone the prices of every thing are fixed and determined.

Here then we may learn the fallacy of the remark, often to be met with in historians, and even in common conversation, that any particular state is weak, though fertile, populous, and well cultivated, merely because it wants money. It appears, that the want of money can never injure any state within itself: For men and commodities are the real strength of any community. It is the simple manner of living which here hurts the public, by confining the gold and silver to few hands, and preventing its universal diffusion and circulation. On the contrary, industry and refinements of all kinds incorporate it with the whole state, however small its quantity may be: They digest it into every vein, so to speak; and make it enter into every transaction and contract. No hand is entirely empty of it. And as the prices of every thing fall by that means, the sovereign has a double advantage: He may draw money by his taxes from every part of the state; and what he receives, goes farther in every purchase and payment.

We may infer, from a comparison of prices, that money is not more plentiful in *China*, than it was in *Europe* three centuries ago: But what immense power is that empire possessed of, if we may judge by the civil and military establishment maintained by it? *Polybius* tells us, that provisions were so cheap in *Italy* during his time, that in some places the stated price for a meal at the inns was a semis a head, little more than a farthing! Yet the *Roman* power had even then subdued the whole known world. About a century before that period, the *Carthaginian* ambassador said, by way of raillery, that no people lived more sociably amongst themselves than the *Romans*; for that, in every entertainment, which, as foreign ministers, they received, they still observed the same plate at every table. The absolute quantity of the precious metals is a matter of great indifference. There are only two circumstances of any importance, namely, their gradual encrease, and their thorough concoction and circulation through the state; and the influence of both these circumstances has here been explained.

In the following essay we shall see an instance of a like fallacy as that above mentioned; where a collateral effect is taken for a cause, and where a consequence is ascribed to the plenty of money; though it be really owing to a change in the manners and customs of the people.

"Of Interest"

Nothing is esteemed a more certain sign of the flourishing condition of any nation than the lowness of interest: And with reason; though I believe the cause is somewhat different from what is commonly apprehended. Lowness of interest is generally ascribed to plenty of money. But money, however plentiful, has no other effect, if fixed, than to raise the price of labour. Silver is more common than gold; and therefore you receive a greater quantity of it for the same commodities. But do you pay less interest for it? Interest in *Batavia* and *Jamaica* is at 10 per cent in *Portugal* at 6; though these places, as we may learn from the prices of every thing, abound more in gold and silver than either *London* or *Amsterdam*.

Were all the gold in *England* annihilated at once, and one and twenty shillings substituted in the place of every guinea, would money be more plentiful or interest lower? No surely: We should only use silver instead of gold. Were gold rendered as common as silver, and silver as common as copper; would money be more plentiful or interest lower? We may assuredly give the same answer. Our shillings would then be yellow, and our halfpence white; and we should have no guineas. No other difference would ever be observed; no alteration on commerce, manufactures, navigation, or interest; unless we imagine, that the colour of the metal is of any consequence.

Now, what is so visible in these greater variations of scarcity or abundance in the precious metals, must hold in all inferior changes. If the multiplying of gold and silver fifteen times makes no difference, much less can the doubling or tripling them. All augmentation has no other effect than to heighten the price of labour and commodities; and even this variation is little more than that of a name. In the progress towards these changes, the augmentation may have some influence, by exciting industry; but after the prices are settled, suitably to the new abundance of gold and silver, it has no manner of influence.

An effect always holds proportion with its cause. Prices have risen near four times since the discovery of the *Indies*; and it is probable gold and silver have multiplied much more: But interest has not fallen much above half. The rate of interest, therefore, is not derived from the quantity of the precious metals.

Money having chiefly a fictitious value, the greater or less plenty of it is of no consequence, if we consider a nation within itself; and the quantity of specie, when once fixed, though ever so large, has no other effect, than to oblige every one to tell out a greater number of those shining bits of metal, for clothes, furniture or equipage, without encreasing any one convenience of life. If a man borrow money to build a house, he then carries home a greater load; because the stone, timber, lead, glass, and so on with the labour of the masons and carpenters, are represented by a greater quantity of gold and silver. But as these metals are considered chiefly as representations, there can no alteration arise, from their bulk or quantity, their weight or colour, either upon their real value or their interest. The same interest, in all cases, bears the same proportion to the sum. And if you lent me so much labour and so many commodities; by receiving five per cent you always receive proportional labour and commodities, however represented, whether by yellow or white coin, whether by a pound or an ounce. It is in vain, therefore, to look for the cause of the fall or rise of interest in the greater or less quantity of gold and silver, which is fixed in any nation.

High interest arises from three circumstances: A great demand for borrowing; little riches to supply that demand; and great profits arising from commerce: And these circumstances are a clear proof of the small advance of commerce and industry, not of the scarcity of gold and silver. Low interest, on the other hand, proceeds from the three opposite circumstances: A small demand for borrowing; great riches to supply that demand; and small profits arising from commerce: And these circumstances are all connected together, and proceed from the encrease of industry and commerce, not of gold and silver. We shall endeavour to prove these points; and shall begin with the causes and the effects of a great or small demand for borrowing.

When a people have emerged ever so little from a savage state, and their numbers have encreased beyond the original multitude, there must immediately arise an inequality of property; and while some possess large tracts of land, others are confined within narrow limits, and some are entirely without any landed property. Those who possess more land than they can labour, employ those who possess none, and agree to receive a determinate part of the product. Thus the landed interest is immediately established; nor is there any settled government, however rude, in which affairs are not on this footing. Of these proprietors of land, some must presently discover themselves to be of different tempers from others; and while one would willingly store up the produce of his land for futurity, another desires to consume at present what should suffice for many years. But as the spending of a settled revenue is a way of life entirely without occupation; men have so much need of somewhat to fix and engage them, that pleasures, such as they are, will be the pursuit of the greater part of the landholders, and the prodigals among them will always be more numerous than the misers. In a state, therefore, where there is nothing but a landed interest, as there is little frugality, the borrowers must be very numerous, and the rate of interest must hold proportion to it. The difference depends not on the quantity of money, but on the habits and manners which prevail. By this alone the demand for borrowing is encreased or diminished. Were money so plentiful as to make an egg be sold for sixpence; so long as there are only landed gentry and peasants in the state, the borrowers must be numerous, and interest high. The rent for the same farm would be heavier and more bulky: But the same idleness of the landlord, with the higher price of commodities, would dissipate it in the same time, and produce the same necessity and demand for borrowing.

Nor is the case different with regard to the second circumstance which we proposed to consider, namely, the great or little riches to supply the demand. This effect also depends on the habits and way of living of the people, not on the quantity of gold and silver. In order to have, in any state, a great number of lenders, it is not sufficient nor requisite, that there be great abundance of the precious metals. It is only requisite, that the property or command of that quantity, which is in the state, whether great or small, should be collected in particular hands, so as to form considerable sums, or compose a great monied interest. This begets a number of lenders, and sinks the rate of usury; and this I shall venture to affirm, depends not on the quantity of specie, but on particular manners and customs, which make the specie gather into separate sums or masses of considerable value.

For suppose, that, by miracle, every man in *Great Britain* should have five pounds slipt into his pocket in one night; this would much more than double the whole money that is at present in the kingdom; yet there would not next day, nor for some time, be any more lenders, nor any variation in the interest. And were there nothing but landlords and peasants in the state, this money, however abundant, could never gather into sums; and would only serve to encrease the prices of every thing, without any farther consequence. The prodigal landlord dissipates it, as fast as he receives it; and the beggarly peasant has no means, nor view, nor ambition of obtaining above a bare livelihood. The overplus of borrowers above that of lenders continuing still the same, there will follow no reduction of interest. That depends upon another principle; and must proceed from an encrease of industry and frugality, of arts and commerce.

Every thing useful to the life of man arises from the ground; but few things arise in that condition which is requisite to render them useful. There must, therefore, beside the peasants and the proprietors of land, be another rank of men, who receiving from the former the rude materials, work them into their proper form, and retain part for their own use and subsistence. In the infancy of society, these contracts between the artisans and the peasants, and between one species of artisans and another are commonly entered into immediately by the persons themselves, who, being neighbours, are easily acquainted with each other's necessities, and can lend their mutual assistance to supply them. But when men's industry encreases, and their views enlarge, it is found, that the most remote parts of the state can assist each other as well as the more contiguous, and that this intercourse of good offices may be carried on to the greatest extent and intricacy. Hence the origin of merchants, one of the most useful races of men, who serve as agents between those parts of the state, that are wholly unacquainted, and are ignorant of each other's necessities. Here are in a city fifty workmen in silk and linen, and a thousand customers; and these two ranks of men, so necessary to each other, can never rightly meet, till one man erects a shop, to which all the workmen and all the customers repair. In this province, grass rises in abundance: The inhabitants abound in cheese, and butter, and cattle; but want bread and corn, which, in a neighbouring province, are in too great abundance for the use of the inhabitants. One man discovers this. He brings corn from the one province and returns with cattle; and supplying the wants of both, he is, so far, a common benefactor. As the people encrease in numbers and industry, the difficulty of their intercourse encreases: The business of the agency or merchandize becomes more intricate; and divides, subdivides, compounds, and mixes to a greater variety. In all these transactions, it is necessary, and reasonable, that a considerable part of the commodities and labour should belong to the merchant, to whom, in a great measure, they are owing. And these commodities he will sometimes preserve in kind, or more commonly convert into money, which is their common representation. If gold and silver have encreased in the state together with the industry, it will require a great quantity of these metals to represent a great quantity of commodities and labour. If industry alone has encreased, the prices of every thing must sink, and a small quantity of specie will serve as a representation.

There is no craving or demand of the human mind more constant and insatiable than that for exercise and employment; and this desire seems the foundation of most of our passions and pursuits. Deprive a man of all business and serious occupation, he runs restless from one amusement to another; and the weight and oppression, which he feels from idleness, is so great, that he forgets the ruin which must follow him from his immoderate expences. Give him a more harmless way of employing his mind or body, he is satisfied, and feels no longer that insatiable thirst after pleasure. But if the employment you give him be lucrative, especially if the profit be attached to every particular exertion of industry, he has gain so often in his eye, that he acquires, by degrees, a passion for it, and knows no such pleasure as that of seeing the daily encrease of his fortune. And this is the reason why trade encreases frugality, and why, among merchants, there is the same overplus of misers above prodigals, as, among the possessors of land, there is the contrary.

Commerce encreases industry, by conveying it readily from one member of the state to another, and allowing none of it to perish or become useless. It encreases frugality, by giving occupation to men, and employing them in the arts of gain, which soon engage their affection, and remove all relish for pleasure and expence. It is an infallible consequence of all industrious professions, to beget frugality, and make the love of gain prevail over the love of pleasure. Among lawyers and physicians who have any practice, there are many more who live within their income, than who exceed it, or even live up to it. But lawyers and physicians beget no industry; and it is even at the expence of others they acquire their riches; so that they are sure to diminish the possessions of some of their fellow-citizens, as fast as they encrease their own. Merchants, on the contrary, beget industry, by serving as canals to convey it through every corner of the state: And at the same time, by their frugality, they acquire great power over that industry, and collect a large property in the labour and commodities, which they are the chief instruments in producing. There is no other profession, therefore, except merchandize, which can make the monied interest considerable, or, in other words, can encrease industry, and, by also encreasing frugality, give a great command of that industry to particular members of the society. Without commerce, the state must consist chiefly of landed gentry, whose prodigality and expence make a continual demand for borrowing; and of peasants, who have no sums to supply that demand. The money never gathers into large stocks or sums, which can be lent at interest. It is dispersed into number-less hands, who either squander it in idle show and magnificence, or employ it in the purchase of the common necessaries of life. Commerce alone assembles it into considerable sums; and this effect it has merely from the industry which it begets, and the frugality which it inspires, inde-pendent of that particular quantity of precious metal which may circulate in the state.

Thus an encrease of commerce, by a necessary consequence, raises a great number of lenders, and by that means produces lowness of interest. We must now consider how far this encrease of commerce diminishes the profits arising from that profession, and gives rise to the third circumstance requisite to produce lowness of interest.

It may be proper to observe on this head, that low interest and low profits of merchandize are two events, that mutually forward each other, and are both originally derived from that extensive commerce, which produces opulent merchants, and renders the monied interest considerable. Where merchants possess great stocks, whether represented by few or many pieces of metal, it must frequently happen, that, when they either become tired of business, or leave heirs unwilling or unfit to engage in commerce, a great proportion of these riches naturally seeks an annual and secure revenue. The plenty diminishes the price, and makes the lenders accept of a low interest. This consideration obliges many to keep their stock employed in trade, and rather be content with low profits than dispose of their money at an undervalue. On the other hand, when com-merce has become extensive, and employs large stocks, there must arise rivalships among the merchants, which diminish the profits of trade, at the same time that they encrease the trade itself. The low profits of merchandize induce the merchants to accept more willingly of a low interest, when they leave off business, and begin to indulge themselves in ease and indolence. It is needless, therefore, to enquire which of these circumstances, to wit, low interest or low prof-its, is the cause, and which the effect? They both arise from an extensive commerce, and mutually forward each other. No man will accept of low profits, where he can have high interest; and no man will accept of low interest, where he can have high profits. An extensive commerce, by producing large stocks, diminishes both interest and profits; and is always assisted, in its diminution of the one, by the proportional sinking of the other. I may add, that, as low profits arise from the encrease of commerce and industry, they serve in their turn to its farther encrease, by rendering the commodities cheaper, encouraging the consumption, and heightening the industry. And thus, if we consider the whole connexion of causes and effects, interest is the barometer of the state, and its lowness is a sign almost infallible of the flourishing condition of a people. It proves the encrease of industry, and its prompt circulation through the whole state, little inferior to a demonstration. And though, perhaps, it may not be impossible but a sudden and a great check to commerce may have a momentary effect of the same kind, by throwing so many stocks out of trade; it must be attended with such misery and want of employment in the poor, that, besides its short duration, it will not be possible to mistake the one case for the other.

Those who have asserted, that the plenty of money was the cause of low interest, seem to have taken a collateral effect for a cause; since the same industry, which sinks the interest, commonly acquires great abundance of the precious metals. A variety of fine manufactures, with vigilant enterprising merchants, will soon draw money to a state, if it be anywhere to be found in the world. The same cause, by multiplying the conveniencies of life, and encreasing industry, collects great riches into the hands of persons, who are not proprietors of land, and produces, by that means, a lowness of interest. But though both these effects, plenty of money and low interest, naturally arise from commerce and industry, they are altogether independent of each other. For suppose a nation removed into the Pacific ocean, without any foreign commerce, or any knowledge of navigation: Suppose, that this nation possesses always the same stock of coin, but is continually encreasing in its numbers and industry: It is evident, that the price of every commodity must gradually diminish in that kingdom; since it is the proportion between money and any species of goods, which fixes their mutual value; and, upon the present supposition, the conveniencies of life become every day more abundant, without any alteration in the current specie. A less quantity of money, therefore, among this people, will make a rich man, during the times of industry, than would suffice to that purpose, in ignorant and slothful ages. Less money will build a house, portion a daughter, buy an estate, support a manufactory, or maintain a family and equipage. These are the uses for which men borrow money; and therefore, the greater or less quantity of it in a state has no influence on the interest. But it is evident, that the greater or less stock of labour and commodities must have a great influence; since we really and in effect borrow these, when we take money upon interest. It is true, when commerce is extended all over the globe, the most industrious nations always abound most with the precious metals: So that low interest and plenty of money are in fact almost inseparable. But still it is of consequence to know the principle whence any phenomenon arises, and to distinguish between a cause and a concomitant effect. Besides that the speculation is curious, it may frequently be of use in the conduct of public affairs. At least, it must be owned, that nothing can be of more use than to improve, by practice, the method of reasoning on these subjects, which of all others are the most important; though they are commonly treated in the loosest and most careless manner.

Another reason of this popular mistake with regard to the cause of low interest, seems to be the instance of some nations; where, after a sudden acquisition of money or of the precious metals, by means of foreign conquest, the interest has fallen, not only among them, but in all the neighbouring states, as soon as that money was dispersed, and had insinuated itself into every corner. Thus, interest in *Spain* fell near a half immediately after the discovery of the *West Indies*, as we are informed by *Garcilasso de la Vega*: And it has been ever since gradually sinking in every kingdom of *Europe*. Interest in *Rome*, after the conquest of *Egypt*, fell from 6 to 4 per cent as we learn from *Dion*.

The causes of the sinking of interest, upon such an event, seem different in the conquering country and in the neighbouring states; but in neither of them can we justly ascribe that effect merely to the encrease of gold and silver.

In the conquering country, it is natural to imagine, that this new acquisition of money will fall into a few hands, and be gathered into large sums, which seek a secure revenue, either by the purchase of land or by interest; and consequently the same effect follows, for a little time, as if there had been a great accession of industry and commerce. The encrease of lenders above the borrowers sinks the interest; and so much the faster, if those, who have acquired those large sums, find no industry or commerce in the state, and no method of employing their money but by lending it at interest. But after this new mass of gold and silver has been digested, and has circulated through the whole state, affairs will soon return to their former situation; while the landlords and new money-holders, living idly, squander above their income; and the former daily contract debt, and the latter encroach on their stock till its final extinction. The whole money may still be in the state, and make itself felt by the encrease of prices: But not being now collected into any large masses or stocks, the disproportion between the borrowers and lenders is the same as formerly, and consequently the high interest returns.

Accordingly we find, in *Rome*, that, so early as *Tiberius's* time, interest had again mounted to 6 per cent though no accident had happened to drain the empire of money. In *Trajan's* time, money lent on mortgages in *Italy*, bore 6 per cent on common securities in *Bithynia*, 12 per cent. And if interest in *Spain* has not risen to its old pitch; this can be ascribed to nothing but the continuance of the same cause that sunk it, to wit, the large fortunes continually made in the *Indies*, which come over to *Spain* from time to time, and supply the demand of the borrowers. By this accidental and extraneous cause, more money is to be lent in *Spain*, that is, more money is collected into large sums than would otherwise be found in a state, where there are so little commerce and industry.

As to the reduction of interest, which has followed in *England*, *France*, and other kingdoms of *Europe*, that have no mines, it has been gradual; and has not proceeded from the encrease of money, considered merely in itself; but from that of industry, which is the natural effect of the former encrease, in that interval, before it raises the price of labour and provisions. For to return to the foregoing supposition; if the industry of *England* had risen as much from other causes (and that rise might easily have happened, though the stock of money had remained the same) must not all the same consequences have followed, which we observe at present? The same people would, in that case, be found in the kingdom, the same commodities, the same industry, manufactures, and commerce; and consequently the same merchants, with the same stocks, that is, with the same command over labour and commodities, only represented by a smaller number of white or yellow pieces; which being a circumstance of no moment, would only affect the waggoner, porter, and trunk-maker. Luxury, therefore, manufactures, arts, industry, frugality, flourishing equally as at present, it is evident, that interest must also have been as low; since that is the necessary result of all these circumstances; so far as they determine the profits of commerce, and the proportion between the borrowers and lenders in any state.

"Of the Balance of Trade"

It is very usual, in nations ignorant of the nature of commerce, to prohibit the exportation of commodities, and to preserve among themselves whatever they think valuable and useful. They do not consider, that, in this prohibition, they act directly contrary to their intention; and that the more is exported of any commodity, the more will be raised at home, of which they themselves will always have the first offer.

It is well known to the learned, that the ancient laws of *Athens* rendered the exportation of figs criminal; that being supposed a species of fruit so excellent in *Attica*, that the *Athenians* deemed it too delicious for the palate of any foreigner. And in this ridiculous prohibition they were so much in earnest, that informers were thence called sycophants among them, from two *Greek* words, which signify figs and discoverer. There are proofs in many old acts of parliament of the same ignorance in the nature of commerce, particularly in the reign of *Edward III.* And to this day, in *France*, the exportation of corn is almost always prohibited; in order, as they say, to prevent famines; though it is evident, that nothing contributes more to the frequent famines, which so much distress that fertile country.

The same jealous fear, with regard to money, has also prevailed among several nations; and it required both reason and experience to convince any people, that these prohibitions serve to no other purpose than to raise the exchange against them, and produce a still greater exportation.

These errors, one may say, are gross and palpable: But there still prevails, even in nations well acquainted with commerce, a strong jealousy with regard to the balance of trade, and a fear, that all their gold and silver may be leaving them. This seems to me, almost in every case, a groundless apprehension; and I should as soon dread, that all our springs and rivers should be exhausted, as that money should abandon a kingdom where there are people and industry. Let us carefully preserve these latter advantages; and we need never be apprehensive of losing the former.

It is easy to observe, that all calculations concerning the balance of trade are founded on very uncertain facts and suppositions. The custom-house books are allowed to be an insufficient ground of reasoning; nor is the rate of exchange much better; unless we consider it with all nations, and know also the proportions of the several sums remitted; which one may safely pronounce impossible. Every man, who has ever reasoned on this subject, has always proved his theory, whatever it was, by facts and calculations, and by an enumeration of all the commodities sent to all foreign kingdoms.

The writings of Mr *Gee* struck the nation with an universal panic, when they saw it plainly demonstrated, by a detail of particulars, that the balance was against them for so considerable a sum as must leave them without a single shilling in five or six years. But luckily, twenty years have since elapsed, with an expensive foreign war; yet is it commonly supposed, that money is still more plentiful among us than in any former period.

Nothing can be more entertaining on this head than Dr *Swift*; an author so quick in discerning the mistakes and absurdities of others. He says, in his short view of the state of *Ireland*, that the whole cash of that kingdom formerly amounted but to 500,000 livres; that out of this the *Irish* remitted every year a neat million to *England*, and had scarcely any other source from which they could compensate themselves, and little other foreign trade than the importation of *French* wines, for which they paid ready money. The consequence of this situation, which must be owned to be disadvantageous, was, that, in a course of three years, the current money of *Ireland*, from 500,000 livres was reduced to less than two. And at present, I suppose, in a course of 30 years it is absolutely nothing. Yet I know not how, that opinion of the advance of riches in *Ireland*, which gave the Doctor so much indignation, seems still to continue, and gain ground with every body.

In short, this apprehension of the wrong balance of trade, appears of such a nature, that it discovers itself, wherever one is out of humour with the ministry, or is in low spirits; and as it can never be refuted by a particular detail of all the exports, which counterbalance the imports, it may here be proper to form a general argument, that may prove the impossibility of this event, as long as we preserve our people and our industry.

Suppose four-fifths of all the money in *Great Britain* to be annihilated in one night, and the nation reduced to the same condition, with regard to specie, as in the reigns of the *Harrys* and *Edwards*, what would be the consequence? Must not the price of all labour and commodities sink in proportion, and every thing be sold as cheap as they were in those ages? What nation could then dispute with us in any foreign market, or pretend to navigate or to sell manufactures at the same price, which to us would afford sufficient profit? In how little time, therefore, must this bring back the money which we had lost, and raise us to the level of all the neighbouring nations? Where, after we have arrived, we immediately lose the advantage of the cheapness of labour and commodities; and the farther flowing in of money is stopped by our fulness and repletion.

Again, suppose, that all the money of *Great Britain* were multiplied fivefold in a night, must not the contrary effect follow? Must not all labour and commodities rise to such an exorbitant height, that no neighbouring nations could afford to buy from us; while their commodities, on the other hand, became comparatively so cheap, that, in spite of all the laws which could be formed, they would be run in upon us, and our money flow out; till we fall to a level with foreigners, and lose that great superiority of riches, which had laid us under such disadvantages?

Now, it is evident, that the same causes, which would correct these exorbitant inequalities, were they to happen miraculously, must prevent their happening in the common course of nature, and must for ever, in all neighbouring nations, preserve money nearly proportionable to the art and industry of each nation. All water, wherever it communicates, remains always at a level. Ask naturalists the reason; they tell you, that, were it to be raised in any one place, the superior gravity of that part not being balanced, must depress it, till it meet a counterpoise; and that the same cause, which redresses the inequality when it happens, must for ever prevent it, without some violent external operation.

Can one imagine, that it had ever been possible, by any laws, or even by any art or industry, to have kept all the money in *Spain*, which the galleons have brought from the *Indies*? Or that all commodities could be sold in *France* for a tenth of the price which they would yield on the other side of the *Pyrenees*, without finding their way thither, and draining from that immense treasure? What other reason, indeed, is there, why all nations, at present, gain in their trade with *Spain* and *Portugal*; but because it is impossible to heap up money, more than any fluid, beyond its proper level? The sovereigns of these countries have shown, that they wanted not inclination to keep their gold and silver to themselves, had it been in any degree practicable.

But as any body of water may be raised above the level of the surrounding element, if the former has no communication with the latter; so in money, if the communication be cut off, by any material or physical impediment (for all laws alone are ineffectual) there may, in such a case, be a very great inequality of money. Thus the immense distance of *China*, together with the monopolies of our *India* companies, obstructing the communication, preserve in *Europe* the gold and silver, especially the latter, in much greater plenty than they are found in that kingdom. But, notwithstanding this great obstruction, the force of the causes abovementioned is still evident. The skill and ingenuity of *Europe* in general surpasses perhaps that of *China*, with regard to manual arts and manufactures; yet are we never able to trade thither without great disadvantage. And were it not for the continual recruits, which we receive from *America*, money would soon sink in *Europe*, and rise in *China*, till it came nearly to a level in both places. Nor can any reasonable man doubt, but that industrious nation, were they as near us as *Poland* or *Barbary*, would drain us of the overplus of our specie, and draw to themselves a larger share of the *West Indian* treasures. We need not have recourse to a physical attraction, in order to explain the necessity of this operation. There is a moral attraction, arising from the interests and passions of men, which is full as potent and infallible.

How is the balance kept in the provinces of every kingdom among themselves, but by the force of this principle, which makes it impossible for money to lose its level, and either to rise or sink beyond the proportion of the labour and commodities which are in each province? Did not long experience make people easy on this head, what a fund of gloomy reflections might calculations afford to a melancholy *Yorkshireman*, while he computed and magnified the sums drawn to *London* by taxes, absentees, commodities, and found on comparison the opposite articles so much inferior? And no doubt, had the Heptarchy subsisted in *England*, the legislature of each state had been continually alarmed by the fear of a wrong balance; and as it is probable that the mutual hatred of these states would have been extremely violent on account of their close neighbour-hood, they would have loaded and oppressed all commerce, by a jealous and superfluous caution. Since the union has removed the barriers between *Scotland* and *England*, which of these nations gains from the other by this free commerce? Or if the former kingdom has received any encrease of riches, can it reasonably be accounted for by anything but the encrease of its art and industry? It was a common apprehension in *England*, before the union, as we learn from *L'Abbé du Bos*, that *Scotland* would soon drain them of their treasure, were an open trade allowed; and on the other side the *Tweed* a contrary apprehension prevailed: With what justice in both, time has shown.

What happens in small portions of mankind, must take place in greater. The provinces of the *Roman* empire, no doubt, kept their balance with each other, and with *Italy*, independent of the legislature; as much as the several counties of *Great Britain*, or the several parishes of each county. And any man who travels over *Europe* at this day, may see, by the prices of commodities, that money, in spite of the absurd jealousy of princes and states, has brought itself nearly to a level; and that the difference between one kingdom and another is not greater in this respect, than it is often between different provinces of the same kingdom. Men naturally flock to capital cities, sea-ports, and navigable rivers. There we find more men, more industry, more commodities, and consequently more money; but still the latter difference holds proportion with the former, and the level is preserved.

Our jealousy and our hatred of *France* are without bounds; and the former sentiment, at least, must be acknowledged reasonable and well-grounded. These passions have occasioned innumer-able barriers and obstructions upon commerce, where we are accused of being commonly the aggressors. But what have we gained by the bargain? We lost the *French* market for our woollen manufactures, and transferred the commerce of wine to *Spain* and *Portugal*, where we buy worse liquor at a higher price. There are few *Englishmen* who would not think their country absolutely ruined, were *French* wines sold in *England* so cheap and in such abundance as to supplant, in some measure, all ale, and home-brewed liquors: But would we lay aside prejudice, it would not be difficult to prove, that nothing could be more innocent, perhaps advantageous. Each new acre of vineyard planted in *France*, in order to supply *England* with wine, would make it requisite for the *French* to take the produce of an *English* acre, sown in wheat or barley, in order to subsist them-selves; and it is evident, that we should thereby get command of the better commodity.

There are many edicts of the *French* king, prohibiting the planting of new vineyards, and order-ing all those which are lately planted to be grubbed up: So sensible are they, in that country, of the superior value of corn, above every other product.

Mareschal *Vauban* complains often, and with reason, of the absurd duties which load the entry of those wines of *Languedoc, Guienne*, and other southern provinces, that are imported into *Britanny* and *Normandy*. He entertained no doubt but these latter provinces could preserve their balance, notwithstanding the open commerce which he recommends. And it is evident, that a few leagues more navigation to *England* would make no difference; or if it did, that it must operate alike on the commodities of both kingdoms.

There is indeed one expedient by which it is possible to sink, and another by which we may raise money beyond its natural level in any kingdom; but these cases, when examined, will be found to resolve into our general theory, and to bring additional authority to it.

I scarcely know any method of sinking money below its level, but those institutions of banks, funds, and paper-credit, which are so much practised in this kingdom. These render paper equiv-alent to money, circulate it throughout the whole state, make it supply the place of gold and silver, raise proportionably the price of labour and commodities, and by that means either banish a great part of those precious metals, or prevent their farther encrease. What can be more short-sighted than our reasonings on this head? We fancy, because an individual would be much richer, were his stock of money doubled, that the same good effect would follow were the money of every one encreased; not considering, that this would raise as much the price of every commodity, and reduce every man, in time, to the same condition as before. It is only in our public negociations and transactions with foreigners, that a greater stock of money is advantageous; and as our paper is there absolutely insignificant, we feel, by its means, all the ill effects arising from a great abundance of money, without reaping any of the advantages.

Suppose that there are 12 millions of paper, which circulate in the kingdom as money (for we are not to imagine, that all our enormous funds are employed in that shape) and suppose the real cash of the kingdom to be 18 millions: Here is a state which is found by experience to be able to hold a stock of 30 millions. I say, if it be able to hold it, it must of necessity have acquired it in gold and silver, had we not obstructed the entrance of these metals by this new invention of paper. Whence would it have acquired that sum? From all the kingdoms of the world. But why? Because, if you remove these 12 millions, money in this state is below its level, compared with our neighbours; and we must immediately draw from all of them, till we be full and saturate, so to speak, and can hold no more. By our present politics, we are as careful to stuff the nation with this fine commodity of bank-bills and chequer-notes, as if we were afraid of being overburthened with the precious metals.

It is not to be doubted, but the great plenty of bullion in *France* is, in a great measure, owing to the want of paper-credit. The *French* have no banks: Merchants bills do not there circulate as with us: Usury or lending on interest is not directly permitted; so that many have large sums in their coffers: Great quantities of plate are used in private houses; and all the churches are full of it. By this means, provisions and labour still remain cheaper among them, than in nations that are not half so rich in gold and silver. The advantages of this situation, in point of trade as well as in great public emergencies, are too evident to be disputed.

The same fashion a few years ago prevailed in *Genoa*, which still has place in *England* and *Holland*, of using services of *China*-ware instead of plate; but the senate, foreseeing the consequence, prohibited the use of that brittle commodity beyond a certain extent; while the use of silverplate was left unlimited. And I suppose, in their late distresses, they felt the good effect of this ordinance. Our tax on plate is, perhaps, in this view, somewhat impolitic.

Before the introduction of paper-money into our colonies, they had gold and silver sufficient for their circulation. Since the introduction of that commodity, the least inconveniency that has followed is the total banishment of the precious metals. And after the abolition of paper, can it be doubted but money will return, while these colonies possess manufactures and commodities, the only thing valuable in commerce, and for whose sake alone all men desire money.

What pity *Lycurgus* did not think of paper-credit, when he wanted to banish gold and silver from *Sparta*! It would have served his purpose better than the lumps of iron he made use of as money and would also have prevented more effectually all commerce with strangers, as being of so much less real and intrinsic value.

It must, however, be confessed, that, as all these questions of trade and money are extremely complicated, there are certain lights, in which this subject may be placed, so as to represent the advantages of paper-credit and banks to be superior to their disadvantages. That they banish specie and bullion from a state is undoubtedly true; and whoever looks no farther than this circumstance does well to condemn them; but specie and bullion are not of so great consequence as not to admit of a compensation, and even an overbalance from the encrease of industry and of credit, which may be promoted by the right use of paper-money. It is well known of what advantage it is to a merchant to be able to discount his bills upon occasion; and every thing that facilitates this species of traffic is favourable to the general commerce of a state. But private bankers are enabled to give such credit by the credit they receive from the depositing of money in their shops; and the bank of *England* in the same manner, from the liberty it has to issue its notes in all payments. There was an invention of this kind, which was fallen upon some years ago by the banks of *Edinburgh*; and which, as it is one of the most ingenious ideas that has been executed in commerce, has also been thought advantageous to *Scotland*. It is there called a *Bank-Credit*; and is of this nature. A man goes to the bank and finds surety to the amount, we shall suppose, of a 1000 pounds. This money, or any part of it, he has the liberty of drawing out whenever he pleases, and he pays only the ordinary interest for it, while it is in his hands. He may, when he pleases, repay any sum so small as 20 pounds, and the interest is discounted from the very day of the repayment. The advantages, resulting from this contrivance, are manifold. As a man may find surety nearly to the amount of his substance, and his bank-credit is equivalent to ready money, a merchant does hereby in a manner coin his houses, his household furniture, the goods in his warehouse, the foreign debts due to him, his ships at sea; and can, upon occasion, employ them in all payments, as if they were the current money of the country. If a man borrow a 1000 pounds from a private hand, besides that it is not always to be found when required, he pays interest for it, whether he be using it or not: His bank-credit costs him nothing except during the very moment, in which it is of service to him: And this circumstance is of equal advantage as if he had borrowed money at much lower interest. Merchants, likewise, from this invention, acquire a great facility in supporting each other's credit, which is a considerable security against bankruptcies. A man, when his own bank-credit is exhausted, goes to any of his neighbours who is not in the same condition; and he gets the money, which he replaces at his convenience.

After this practice had taken place during some years at *Edinburgh*, several companies of merchants at *Glasgow* carried the matter farther. They associated themselves into different banks, and issued notes so low as 10 shillings, which they used in all payments for goods, manufactures, tradesmen's labour of all kinds; and these notes, from the established credit of the companies, passed as money in all payments throughout the country. By this means, a stock of 5000 pounds was able to perform the same operations as if it were 6 or 7; and merchants were thereby enabled to trade to a greater extent, and to require less profit in all their transactions. But whatever other advantages result from these inventions, it must still be allowed that, besides giving too great facility to credit, which is dangerous, they banish the precious metals; and nothing can be a more evident proof of it, than a comparison of the past and present condition of *Scotland* in that particular. It was found, upon the recoinage made after the union, that there was near a million of specie in that country: But notwithstanding the great encrease of riches, commerce and manufactures of all kinds, it is thought, that, even where there is no extraordinary drain made by *England*, the current specie will not now amount to a third of that sum.

But as our projects of paper-credit are almost the only expedient, by which we can sink money below its level; so, in my opinion, the only expedient, by which we can raise money above it, is a practice which we should all exclaim against as destructive, namely, the gathering of large sums into a public treasure, locking them up, and absolutely preventing their circulation. The fluid, not communicating with the neighbouring element, may, by such an artifice, be raised to what height we please. To prove this, we need only return to our first supposition, of annihilating the half or any part of our cash; where we found, that the immediate consequence of such an event would be the attraction of an equal sum from all the neighbouring kingdoms. Nor does there seem to be any necessary bounds set, by the nature of things, to this practice of hoarding. A small city, like *Geneva*, continuing this policy for ages, might engross nine-tenths of the money of *Europe*. There seems, indeed, in the nature of man, an invincible obstacle to that immense growth of riches. A weak state, with an enormous treasure, will soon become a prey to some of its poorer, but more powerful neighbours. A great state would dissipate its wealth in dangerous and ill-concerted projects; and probably destroy, with it, what is much more valuable, the industry, morals, and numbers of its people. The fluid, in this case, raised to too great a height, bursts and destroys the vessel that contains it; and mixing itself with the surrounding element, soon falls to its proper level.

So little are we commonly acquainted with this principle, that, though all historians agree in relating uniformly so recent an event, as the immense treasure amassed by *Harry VII* (which they make amount to 2,700,000 pounds) we rather reject their concurring testimony, than admit of a fact, which agrees so ill with our inveterate prejudices. It is indeed probable, that this sum might be three-fourths of all the money in *England*. But where is the difficulty in conceiving, that such a sum might be amassed in 20 years, by a cunning, rapacious, frugal, and almost absolute monarch? Nor is it probable, that the diminution of circulating money was ever sensibly felt by the people, or ever did them any prejudice. The sinking of the prices of all commodities would immediately replace it, by giving *England* the advantage in its commerce with the neighbouring kingdoms.

Have we not an instance, in the small republic of *Athens* with its allies, who, in about fifty years, between the *Median* and *Peloponnesian* wars, amassed a sum not much inferior to that of *Harry VII*? For all the *Greek* historians and orators agree, that the *Athenians* collected in the citadel more than 10,000 talents, which they afterwards dissipated to their own ruin, in rash and imprudent enterprizes. But when this money was set a running, and began to communicate with the surrounding fluid; what was the consequence? Did it remain in the state? No. For we find, by the memorable census mentioned by *Demosthenes* and *Polybius*, that, in about fifty years afterwards, the whole value of the republic, comprehending lands, houses, commodities, slaves, and money, was less than 6000 talents.

What an ambitious high-spirited people was this, to collect and keep in their treasury, with a view to conquests, a sum, which it was every day in the power of the citizens, by a single vote, to distribute among themselves, and which would have gone near to triple the riches of every individual! For we must observe, that the numbers and private riches of the *Athenians* are said, by ancient writers, to have been no greater at the beginning of the *Peloponnesian* war, than at the beginning of the *Macedonian*.

Money was little more plentiful in *Greece* during the age of *Philip* and *Perseus*, than in *England* during that of *Harry VII*. Yet these two monarchs in thirty years collected from the small kingdom of *Macedon*, a larger treasure than that of the *English* monarch. *Paulus Aemilius* brought to *Rome* about 1,700,000 pounds Sterling. *Pliny* says, 2,400,000. And that was but a part of the *Macedonian* treasure. The rest was dissipated by the resistance and flight of *Perseus*.

We may learn from *Stanian*, that the canton of *Berne* had 300,000 pounds lent at interest, and had above six times as much in their treasury. Here then is a sum hoarded of 1,800,000 pounds Sterling, which is at least quadruple what should naturally circulate in such a petty state; and yet no one, who travels in the *Pais de Vaux*, or any part of that canton, observes any want of money more than could be supposed in a country of that extent, soil, and situation. On the contrary, there are scarce any inland provinces in the continent of *France* or *Germany*, where the inhabitants are at this time so opulent, though that canton has vastly encreased its treasure since 1714, the time when *Stanian* wrote his judicious account of *Switzerland*.

The account given by *Appian* of the treasure of the *Ptolemies*, is so prodigious, that one cannot admit of it; and so much the less, because the historian says, that the other successors of *Alexander* were also frugal, and had many of them treasures not much inferior. For this saving humour of the neighbouring princes must necessarily have checked the frugality of the *Egyptian* monarchs, according to the foregoing theory. The sum he mentions is 740,000 talents, or 191,166,666 pounds 13 shillings and 4 pence, according to *Dr Arbuthnot's* computation. And yet *Appian* says, that he extracted his account from the public records; and he was himself a native of *Alexandria*.

From these principles we may learn what judgment we ought to form of those numberless bars, obstructions, and imposts, which all nations of *Europe*, and none more than *England*, have put upon trade; from an exorbitant desire of amassing money, which never will heap up beyond its level, while it circulates; or from an ill-grounded apprehension of losing their specie, which never will sink below it. Could any thing scatter our riches, it would be such impolitic contrivances. But this general ill effect, however, results from them, that they deprive neighbouring nations of that free communication and exchange which the Author of the world has intended, by giving them soils, climates, and geniuses, so different from each other.

Our modern politics embrace the only method of banishing money, the using of paper-credit; they reject the only method of amassing it, the practice of hoarding; and they adopt a hundred contrivances, which serve to no purpose but to check industry, and rob ourselves and our neighbours of the common benefits of art and nature.

All taxes, however, upon foreign commodities, are not to be regarded as prejudicial or useless, but those only which are founded on the jealousy abovementioned. A tax on *German* linen encourages home manufactures, and thereby multiplies our people and industry. A tax on brandy encreases the sale of rum, and supports our southern colonies. And as it is necessary, that imposts should be levied, for the support of government, it may be thought more convenient to lay them on foreign commodities, which can easily be intercepted at the port, and subjected to the impost. We ought, however, always to remember the maxim of *Dr Swift*, that, in the arithmetic of the customs, two and two make not four, but often make only one. It can scarcely be doubted, but if the duties on wine were lowered to a third, they would yield much more to the government than at present: Our people might thereby afford to drink commonly a better and more wholesome liquor; and no prejudice would ensue to the balance of trade, of which we are so jealous. The manufacture of ale beyond the agriculture is but inconsiderable, and gives employment to few hands. The transport of wine and corn would not be much inferior.

But are there not frequent instances, you will say, of states and kingdoms, which were formerly rich and opulent, and are now poor and beggarly? Has not the money left them, with which they formerly abounded? I answer, If they lose their trade, industry, and people, they cannot expect to keep their gold and silver: For these precious metals will hold proportion to the former advantages. When *Lisbon* and *Amsterdam* got the *East-India* trade from *Venice* and *Genoa*, they also got the profits and money which arose from it. Where the seat of government is transferred, where expensive armies are maintained at a distance, where great funds are possessed by foreigners; there naturally follows from these causes a diminution of the specie. But these, we may observe, are violent and forcible methods of carrying away money, and are in time commonly attended with the transport of people and industry. But where these remain, and the drain is not continued, the money always finds its way back again, by a hundred canals, of which we have no notion or suspicion. What immense treasures have been spent, by so many nations, in *Flanders*, since the revolution, in the course of three long wars? More money perhaps than the half of what is at present in *Europe*. But what has now become of it? Is it in the narrow compass of the *Austrian* provinces? No, surely: It has most of it returned to the several countries whence it came, and has followed that art and industry, by which at first it was acquired. For above a thousand years, the money of *Europe* has been flowing to *Rome*, by an open and sensible current; but it has been emptied by many secret and insensible canals: And the want of industry and commerce renders at present the papal dominions the poorest territory in all *Italy*.

In short, a government has great reason to preserve with care its people and its manufactures. Its money, it may safely trust to the course of human affairs, without fear or jealousy. Or if it ever give attention to this latter circumstance, it ought only to be so far as it affects the former.

ADAM SMITH (1723–1790)

Adam Smith, by courtesy of The Warren J. Samuels Portrait Collection at Duke University.

Adam Smith was born in the small fishing village of Kircaldy, Scotland. He received his MA from the University of Glasgow at age 17 and then spent six unhappy years at Balliol College, Oxford. He was elected to a professorship in Logic at Glasgow in 1751 and shortly thereafter was elected to the chair in Moral Philosophy. In 1763, he resigned his professorship to become a tutor to the Duke of Buccleuch and spent nearly three years accompanying the young Duke on a tour of Europe. Some of this time was spent in France, where Smith made the acquaintance of leading physiocratic thinkers, including Quesnay and Turgot. Upon his return to Britain in 1766, Smith devoted his efforts to writing *The Wealth of Nations* and, shortly after its publication in 1776, he was appointed Commissioner of Customs for Scotland. Smith died in Edinburgh in 1790.

Smith's *Inquiry into the Nature and Causes of the Wealth of Nations* has a simple argument. Wealth consists of goods which either can be consumed directly or used in the production of such goods. The production of wealth is promoted by taking advantage of the division of labor, which in turn is facilitated by the wide extent of the market, the use of money, the accumulation of capital, and free trade both domestic and international. Along with this central argument Smith presents analyses of how markets work in allocating resources through the price mechanism, the labor theory of value, government taxation, the psychological foundations of economic activity, competition, income, wealth, income distribution, the history of British economic institutions, capital, and so on. There are also critiques of both Mercantilism and the Physiocrats' agricultural system.

The tendency acquired from looking solely at *The Wealth of Nations* is to think of the economy as a system unto itself. For Smith, however, his economic theory was part of a larger, tripartite system of social science. One part was presented in his *Theory of Moral Sentiments*, in which he explored the roles, first, of sympathy, or fellow feeling, in motivating behavior and, second, of moral rules in the social control of that behavior. Like both Hume and his teacher, Frances Hutcheson, Smith envisioned a secular process through which moral rules were generated by human beings, driven by people's tendency to approve or disapprove of the actions of both themselves and others. A second part was the role of law – of government and jurisprudence – in working out the legal relations between and among people, including the legal institutions serving as the foundations of the economic system. Smith never published his projected work in this area, but two sets of lectures on the subject have been found and published. The third is his analysis of the economy, with its emphasis on the role of self-interest in market behavior transactions.

Accordingly, the total Smithian system comprises sympathy, moral rules, self-interested economic action, markets, and legal social control. This is his picture of the modern economic system, to be distinguished from that of the feudal and post-feudal system.

Smith's total system of thought is made complicated by his particular combination of philosophical positions. Smith had his feet, so to say, in several different paradigms: supernaturalism, naturalism, rationalism, materialism, empiricism, pragmatism, and individualism. Depending upon which of these elements one chooses to emphasize, the nuances and overall meaning of Smith varies among writers. Smith's "simple and obvious system of natural liberty" is thus simultaneously a rhetorical device with which to critique the extraordinary encouragements and restrictions that constituted Mercantilism, a projection onto nature of his notion of an ideal market economy, and a forerunner of the twentieth century model of a transcendent pure abstract conceptual a-institutional market economy, each to be distinguished from the actual world of markets which are formed and structured by institutions, notably but not solely legal institutions, which operate through the markets they have been used to create. On the one hand, one finds naturalism, perhaps even supernaturalism, and pure rationalism; on the other, secularism, empiricism, and pragmatism.

The excerpts from *The Wealth of Nations* reprinted here highlight a number of the major themes in Smith's work: the key role played by the division of labor in economic growth, his theory of natural (cost-based) versus market prices, his scathing critique of mercantilist trade policy, and his view of the market as a self-adjusting mechanism, guided by the "invisible hand," that will tend to promote the greatest level of national wealth.

References and further reading

Blaug, Mark, ed. (1991) *Adam Smith (1723–1790)*, Aldershot: Edward Elgar Publishing.

Bloomfield, A.I. (1975) "Adam Smith and the Theory of International Trade," in A.S. Skinner and T. Wilson (eds), *Essays on Adam Smith*, Oxford: Clarendon Press.

Clark, J.M. *et al.* (1928) *Adam Smith, 1776–1926: Lectures to Commemorate the Sesqui-Centennial of the Publication of The Wealth of Nations*, Chicago: University of Chicago Press.

Hollander, Samuel (1973) *The Economics of Adam Smith*, Toronto: University of Toronto Press.

Laidler, David (1981) "Adam Smith as a Monetary Economist," *Canadian Journal of Economics* 14 (May): 187–200.

Rae, John (1895) *The Life of Adam Smith*, London: Macmillan.

Rosenberg, Nathan (1960) "Some Institutional Aspects of the Wealth of Nations," *Journal of Political Economy* 68: 557–70.

Ross, Ian Simpson (1995) *The Life of Adam Smith*, Oxford: Clarendon Press.

Rothschild, Emma (2001) *Economic Sentiments: Adam Smith, Condorcet, and the Enlightenment*, Cambridge, MA: Harvard University Press.

Skinner, Andrew S. (1987) "Smith, Adam," in John Eatwell, Murray Milgate, and Peter Newman (eds), *The New Palgrave: A Dictionary of Economics*, Vol. 4, London: Macmillan, 357–75.

Skinner, A.S. and Wilson, T. (eds), *Essays on Adam Smith*, Oxford: Clarendon Press.

Smith, Adam (1759) *The Theory of Moral Sentiments*, edited by D.D. Raphael and A.L. Macfie, Oxford: Clarendon Press, 1976.

——(1776) *An Inquiry into the Nature and Causes of the Wealth of Nations*, edited by R.H. Campbell, A.S. Skinner, and W.B. Todd, Oxford: Clarendon Press, 1976.

——(1977) *Correspondence of Adam Smith*, edited by E.C. Mossner and I.S. Ross, Oxford: Clarendon Press.

——(1978) *Lectures on Jurisprudence*, edited by R.L. Meek, P.G. Stein, and D.D. Raphael, Oxford: Clarendon Press.

——(1980) *Essays on Philosophical Subjects*, edited by D.D. Raphael and A.S. Skinner, Oxford: Clarendon Press.

——(1983) *Lectures on Rhetoric and Belles Lectures*, edited by J.C. Bryce, general editor A.S. Skinner, Oxford: Clarendon Press.

Stewart, Dugald (1793) *Biographical Memoir of Adam Smith*. Edinburgh: Thomas Constable & Co. Reprinted by Augustus M. Kelley, 1966.

Viner, Jacob (1928) "Adam Smith and Laissez Faire," in Douglas A. Irwin (ed.), *Essays on the Intellectual History of Economics*, Princeton: Princeton University Press, 1991, 85–113.

West, E.G. (1964) "Adam Smith's Two Views on the Division of Labor," *Economica* 31 (February): 23–32.

——(1976) "Adam Smith's Economics of Politics," *History of Political Economy* 8 (Winter): 515–39.

Winch, Donald (1978) *Adam Smith's Politics: An Essay in Historiographic Revision*, Cambridge: Cambridge University Press.

Wood, John C., ed. (1984) *Adam Smith: Critical Assessments*, London: Croon Helm.

An Inquiry into the Nature and Causes of the Wealth of Nations (1776)

Book one: Of the causes of improvement in the productive powers of labour, and of the order according to which its produce is naturally distributed among the different ranks of the people

Chapter I: Of the division of labour

The greatest improvement in the productive powers of labour, and the greater part of the skill, dexterity, and judgment with which it is anywhere directed, or applied, seem to have been the effects of the division of labour.

The effects of the division of labour, in the general business of society, will be more easily understood by considering in what manner it operates in some particular manufactures. It is commonly supposed to be carried furthest in some very trifling ones; not perhaps that it really is carried further in them than in others of more importance: but in those trifling manufactures which are destined to supply the small wants of but a small number of people, the whole number of workmen must necessarily be small; and those employed in every different branch of the work can often be collected into the same workhouse, and placed at once under the view of the spectator. In those great manufactures, on the contrary, which are destined to supply the great wants of the great body of the people, every different branch of the work employs so great a number of workmen that it is impossible to collect them all into the same workhouse. We can seldom see more, at one time, than those employed in one single branch. Though in such manufactures, therefore, the work may really be divided into a much greater number of parts than in those of a more trifling nature, the division is not near so obvious, and has accordingly been much less observed.

To take an example, therefore, from a very trifling manufacture; but one in which the division of labour has been very often taken notice of, the trade of the pin-maker; a workman not educated to this business (which the division of labour has rendered a distinct trade), nor acquainted with the use of the machinery employed in it (to the invention of which the same division of labour has probably given occasion), could scarce, perhaps, with his utmost industry, make one pin in a day, and certainly could not make twenty. But in the way in which this business is now carried on, not only the whole work is a peculiar trade, but it is divided into a number of branches, of which the greater part are likewise peculiar trades. One man draws out the wire, another straights it, a third cuts it, a fourth points it, a fifth grinds it at the top for receiving, the head; to make the head requires two or three distinct operations; to put it on is a peculiar business, to whiten the pins is another; it is even a trade by itself to put them into the paper; and the important business of making a pin is, in this manner, divided into about eighteen distinct operations, which, in some manufactories, are all performed by distinct hands, though in others the same man will sometimes perform two or three of them. I have seen a small manufactory of this kind where ten men only were employed, and where some of them consequently performed two or three distinct operations. But though they were very poor, and therefore but indifferently accommodated with the necessary machinery, they could, when they exerted themselves, make among them about twelve pounds of pins in a day. There are in a pound upwards of four thousand pins of a middling size. Those ten persons, therefore, could make among them upwards of forty-eight thousand pins in a day. Each person, therefore, making a tenth part of forty-eight thousand pins, might be considered as making four thousand eight hundred pins in a day. But if they had all wrought separately and independently, and without any of them having been educated to this peculiar business, they certainly could not each of them have made twenty, perhaps not one pin in a day; that is, certainly, not the two hundred and fortieth, perhaps not the four thousand eight hundredth part of what they are at present capable of performing, in consequence of a proper division and combination of their different operations.

In every other art and manufacture, the effects of the division of labour are similar to what they are in this very trifling one; though, in many of them, the labour can neither be so much subdivided, nor reduced to so great a simplicity of operation. The division of labour, however, so far as it can be introduced, occasions, in every art, a proportionable increase of the productive powers of labour. The separation of different trades and employments from one another seems to have taken place in consequence of this advantage. This separation, too, is generally called furthest in those countries which enjoy the highest degree of industry and improvement; what is the work of one man in a rude state of society being generally that of several in an improved one. In every improved society, the farmer is generally nothing but a farmer; the manufacturer, nothing but a manufacturer. The labour, too, which is necessary to produce any one complete manufacture is almost always divided among a great number of hands. How many different trades are employed in each branch of the linen and woollen manufactures from the growers of the flax and the wool, to the bleachers and smoothers of the linen, or to the dyers and dressers of the cloth! The nature of agriculture, indeed, does not admit of so many subdivisions of labour, nor of so complete a separation of one business from another, as manufactures. It is impossible to separate so entirely the business of the grazier from that of the corn-farmer as the trade of the carpenter is commonly separated from that of the smith. The spinner is almost always a distinct person from the weaver; but the ploughman, the harrower, the sower of the seed, and the reaper of the corn, are often the same. The occasions for those different sorts of labour returning with the different seasons of the year, it is impossible that one man should be constantly employed in any one of them. This impossibility of making so complete and entire a separation of all the different branches of labour employed in agriculture is perhaps the reason why the improvement of the productive powers of labour in this art does not always keep pace with their improvement in manufactures. The most opulent nations, indeed, generally excel all their neighbours in agriculture as well as in manufactures; but they are commonly more distinguished by their superiority in the latter than in the former. Their lands are in general better cultivated, and having more labour and expense bestowed upon them, produce more in proportion to the extent and natural fertility of the ground. But this superiority of produce is seldom much more than in proportion to the superiority of labour and expense. In agriculture, the labour of the rich country is not always much more productive than that of the poor; or, at least, it is never so much more productive as it commonly is in manufactures. The corn of the rich country, therefore, will not always, in the same degree of goodness, come cheaper to market than that of the poor. ...

This great increase of the quantity of work which, in consequence of the division of labour, the same number of people are capable of performing, is owing to three different circumstances; first, to the increase of dexterity in every particular workman; second, to the saving of the time which is commonly lost in passing from one species of work to another; and lastly, to the invention of a great number of machines which facilitate and abridge labour, and enable one man to do the work of many.

First, the improvement of the dexterity of the workman necessarily increases the quantity of the work he can perform; and the division of labour, by reducing every man's business to some one simple operation, and by making this operation the sole employment of his life, necessarily increases very much dexterity of the workman. A common smith, who, though accustomed to handle the hammer, has never been used to make nails, if upon some particular occasion he is obliged to attempt it, will scarce, I am assured, be able to make above two or three hundred nails in a day, and those too very bad ones. A smith who has been accustomed to make nails, but whose sole or principal business has not been that of a nailer, can seldom with his utmost diligence make more than eight hundred or a thousand nails in a day. I have seen several boys under 20 years of age who had never exercised any other trade but that of making nails, and who, when they exerted themselves, could make, each of them, upwards of two thousand three hundred nails in a day. The making of a nail, however, is by no means one of the simplest operations. The same person blows the bellows, stirs or mends the fire as there is occasion, heats the iron, and forges every part of the nail: in forging the head too he is obliged to change his tools. The different operations into which the making of a pin, or of a metal button, is subdivided, are all of them much more simple, and the dexterity of the person, of whose life it has been the sole business to perform them, is usually much greater. The rapidity with which some of the operations of those manufacturers are performed, exceeds what the human hand could, by those who had never seen them, be supposed capable of acquiring.

Second, the advantage which is gained by saving the time commonly lost in passing from one sort of work to another is much greater than we should at first view be apt to imagine it. It is impossible to pass very quickly from one kind of work to another that is carried on in a different place and with quite different tools. A country weaver, who cultivates a small farm, must lose a good deal of time in passing from his loom to the field, and from the field to his loom. When the two trades can be carried on in the same workhouse, the loss of time is no doubt much less. It is even in this case, however, very considerable. A man commonly saunters a little in turning his hand from one sort of employment to another. When he first begins the new work he is seldom very keen and hearty; his mind, as they say, does not go to it, and for some time he rather trifles than applies to good purpose. The habit of sauntering and of indolent careless application, which is naturally, or rather necessarily acquired by every country workman who is obliged to change his work and his tools every half hour, and to apply his hand in twenty different ways almost every day of his life, renders him almost always slothful and lazy, and incapable of any vigorous application even on the most pressing occasions. Independent, therefore, of his deficiency in point of dexterity, this cause alone must always reduce considerably the quantity of work which he is capable of performing.

Third, and last, everybody must be sensible how much labour is facilitated and abridged by the application of proper machinery. It is unnecessary to give any example. I shall only observe, therefore, that the invention of all those machines by which labour is so much facilitated and abridged seems to have been originally owing to the division of labour. Men are much more likely to discover easier and readier methods of attaining any object when the whole attention of their minds is directed towards that single object than when it is dissipated among a great variety of things. But in consequence of the division of labour, the whole of every man's attention comes naturally to be directed towards some one very simple object. It is naturally to be expected, there-fore, that some one or other of those who are employed in each particular branch of labour should soon find out easier and readier methods of performing their own particular work, wher-ever the nature of it admits of such improvement. A great part of the machines made use of in those manufactures in which labour is most subdivided, were originally the inventions of com-mon workmen, who, being each of them employed in some very simple operation, naturally turned their thoughts towards finding out easier and readier methods of performing it. Whoever has been much accustomed to visit such manufactures must frequently have been shown very pretty machines, which were the inventions of such workmen in order to facilitate and quicken their particular part of the work. ...

All the improvements in machinery, however, have by no means been the inventions of those who had occasion to use the machines. Many improvements have been made by the ingenuity of the makers of the machines, when to make them became the business of a peculiar trade; and some by that of those who are called philosophers or men of speculation, whose trade it is not to do anything, but to observe everything; and who, upon that account, are often capable of combining together the powers of the most distant and dissimilar objects. In the progress of society, philosophy or speculation becomes, like every other employment, the principal or sole trade and occupation of a particular class of citizens. Like every other employment too, it is subdivided into a great number of different branches, each of which affords occupation to a peculiar tribe or class of philosophers; and this subdivision of employment in philosophy, as well as in every other business, improves dexterity, and saves time. Each individual becomes more expert in his own peculiar branch, more work is done upon the whole, and the quantity of science is considerably increased by it.

It is the great multiplication of the productions of all the different arts, in consequence of the division of labour, which occasions, in a well-governed society, that universal opulence which extends itself to the lowest ranks of the people. Every workman has a great quantity of his own work to dispose off beyond what he himself has occasion for; and every other workman being exactly in the same situation, he is enabled to exchange a great quantity of his own goods for a great quantity, or, what comes to the same thing, for the price of a great quantity of theirs. He supplies them abundantly with what they have occasion for, and they accommodate him as amply with what he has occasion for, and a general plenty diffuses itself through all the different ranks of the society.

...

Chapter II: Of the principle which gives occasion to the division of labour

This division of labour, from which so many advantages are derived, is not originally the effect of any human wisdom, which foresees and intends that general opulence to which it gives occasion. It is the necessary, though very slow and gradual consequence of a certain propensity in human nature which has in view no such extensive utility; the propensity to truck, barter, and exchange one thing for another.

Whether this propensity be one of those original principles in human nature of which no further account can be given; or whether, as seems more probable, it be the necessary consequence of the faculties of reason and speech, it belongs not to our present subject to inquire. It is common to all men, and to be found in no other race of animals, which seem to know neither this nor any other species of contracts. Two greyhounds, in running down the same hare, have sometimes the appearance of acting in some sort of concert. Each turns her towards his companion, or endeavours to intercept her when his companion turns her towards himself. This, however, is not the effect of any contract, but of the accidental concurrence of their passions in the same object at that particular time. Nobody ever saw a dog make a fair and deliberate exchange of one bone for another with another dog. Nobody ever saw one animal by its gestures and natural cries signify to another, this is mine, that yours; I am willing to give this for that. When an animal wants to obtain something either of a man or of another animal, it has no other means of persuasion but to gain the favour of those whose service it requires. A puppy fawns upon its dam, and a spaniel endeavours by a thousand attractions to engage the attention of its master who is at dinner, when it wants to be fed by him. Man sometimes uses the same arts with his brethren, and when he has no other means of engaging them to act according to his inclinations, endeavours by every servile and fawning attention to obtain their good will. He has not time, however, to do this upon every occasion. In civilised society he stands at all times in need of the cooperation and assistance of great multitudes, while his whole life is scarce sufficient to gain the friendship of a few persons. In almost every other race of animals each individual, when it is grown up to maturity, is entirely independent, and in its natural state has occasion for the assistance of no other living creature. But man has almost constant occasion for the help of his brethren, and it is in vain for him to expect it from their benevolence only. He will be more likely to prevail if he can interest their self-love in his favour, and show them that it is for their own advantage to do for him what he requires of them. Whoever offers to another a bargain of any kind, proposes to do this. Give me that which I want, and you shall have this which you want, is the meaning of every such offer; and it is in this manner that we obtain from one another the far greater part of those good offices which we stand in need of. It is not from the benevolence of the butcher, the brewer, or the baker that we expect our dinner, but from their regard to their own interest. We address ourselves, not to their humanity but to their self-love, and never talk to them of our own necessities but of their advantages. Nobody but a beggar chooses to depend chiefly upon the benevolence of his fellow-citizens. Even a beggar does not depend upon it entirely. The charity of well-disposed people, indeed, supplies him with the whole fund of his subsistence. But though this principle ultimately provides him with all the necessaries of life which he has occasion for, it neither does nor can provide him with them as he has occasion for them. The greater part of his occasional wants are supplied in the same manner as those of other people, by treaty, by barter, and by purchase. With the money which one man gives him he purchases food. The old clothes which another bestows upon him he exchanges for other old clothes which suit him better, or for lodging, or for food, or for money, with which he can buy either food, clothes, or lodging, as he has occasion.

As it is by treaty, by barter, and by purchase that we obtain from one another the greater part of those mutual good offices which we stand in need of, so it is this same trucking disposition which originally gives occasion to the division of labour. In a tribe of hunters or shepherds a particular person makes bows and arrows, for example, with more readiness and dexterity than any other. He frequently exchanges them for cattle or for venison with his companions; and he finds at last that he can in this manner get more cattle and venison than if he himself went to the field to catch them. From a regard to his own interest, therefore, the making of bows and arrows grows to be his chief business, and he becomes a sort of armourer. Another excels in making the frames and covers of their little huts or movable houses. He is accustomed to be of use in this way to his neighbours, who reward him in the same manner with cattle and with venison, till at last he finds it his interest to dedicate himself entirely to this employment, and to become a sort of house-carpenter. In the same manner a third becomes a smith or a brazier, a fourth a tanner or dresser of hides or skins, the principal part of the nothing of savages. And thus the certainty of being able to exchange all that surplus part of the produce of his own labour, which is over and above his own consumption, for such parts of the produce of other men's labour as he may have occasion for, encourages every man to apply himself to a particular occupation, and to cultivate and bring to perfection whatever talent or genius he may possess for that particular species of business.

The difference of natural talents in different men is, in reality, much less than we are aware of; and the very different genius which appears to distinguish men of different professions, when grown up to maturity, is not upon many occasions so much the cause as the effect of the division of labour. The difference between the most dissimilar characters, between a philosopher and a common street porter, for example, seems to arise not so much from nature as from habit, custom, and education. When they came into the world, and for the first 6 or 8 years of their existence, they were perhaps very much alike, and neither their parents nor playfellows could perceive any remarkable difference. About that age, or soon after, they come to be employed in very different occupations. The difference of talents comes then to be taken notice of, and widens by degrees, till at last the vanity of the philosopher is willing to acknowledge scarce any resemblance. But without the disposition to truck, barter, and exchange, every man must have procured to himself every necessary and conveniency of life which he wanted. All must have had the same duties to perform, and the same work to do, and there could have been no such difference of employment as could alone give occasion to any great difference of talents.

. . .

Chapter III: That the division of labour is limited by the extent of the market

As it is the power of exchanging that gives occasion to the division of labour, so the extent of this division must always be limited by the extent of that power, or, in other words, by the extent of the market. When the market is very small, no person can have any encouragement to dedicate himself entirely to one employment, for want of the power to exchange all that surplus part of the produce of his own labour, which is over and above his own consumption, for such parts of the produce of other men's labour as he has occasion for.

There are some sorts of industry, even of the lowest kind, which can be carried on nowhere but in a great town. A porter, for example, can find employment and subsistence in no other place. A village is by much too narrow a sphere for him; even an ordinary market town is scarce large enough to afford him constant occupation. In the lone houses and very small villages which are scattered about in so desert a country as the Highlands of Scotland, every farmer must be butcher, baker, and brewer for his own family. In such situations we can scarce expect to find even a smith, a carpenter, or a mason, within less than twenty miles of another of the same trade. The scattered families that live at eight or ten miles distance from the nearest of them must learn to perform themselves a great number of little pieces of work, for which, in more populous countries, they would call in the assistance of those workmen. Country workmen are almost everywhere obliged to apply themselves to all the different branches of industry that have so much affinity to one another as to be employed about the same sort of materials. A country carpenter deals in every sort of work that is made of wood: a country smith in every sort of work that is made of iron. The former is not only a carpenter, but a joiner, a cabinet-maker, and even a carver in wood, as well as a wheel-wright, a plough-wright, a cart, and waggon-maker. The employments of the latter are still more various. It is impossible there should be such a trade as even that of a nailer in the remote and inland parts of the Highlands of Scotland. Such a workman at the rate of a 1000 nails a day, and 300 working days in the year, will make 300,000 nails in the year. But in such a situation it would be impossible to dispose off 1000, that is, of one day's work in the year.

As by means of water-carriage a more extensive market is opened to every sort of industry than what land-carriage alone can afford it, so it is upon the sea-coast, and along the banks of navigable rivers that industry of every kind naturally begins to subdivide and improve itself, and it is frequently not till a long time after that those improvements extend themselves to the inland parts of the country. . . .

Chapter VI: Of the component parts of the price of commodities

In that early and rude state of society which precedes both the accumulation of stock and the appropriation of land, the proportion between the quantities of labour necessary for acquiring different objects seems to be the only circumstance which can afford any rule for exchanging them for one another. If among a nation of hunters, for example, it usually costs twice the labour to kill a beaver which it does to kill a deer, one beaver should naturally exchange for or be worth two deer. It is natural that what is usually the produce of two days' or two hours' labour, should be worth double of what is usually the produce of one day's or one hour's labour.

If the one species of labour should be more severe than the other, some allowance will naturally be made for this superior hardship; and the produce of one hour's labour in the one way may frequently exchange for that of two hours' labour in the other.

Or if the one species of labour requires an uncommon degree of dexterity and ingenuity, the esteem which men have for such talents will naturally give a value to their produce, superior to what would be due to the time employed about it. Such talents can seldom be acquired but in consequence of long application, and the superior value of their produce may frequently be no more than a reasonable compensation for the time and labour which must be spent in acquiring them. In the advanced state of society, allowances of this kind, for superior hardship and superior skill, are commonly made in the wages of labour; and something of the same kind must probably have taken place in its earliest and rudest period.

In this state of things, the whole produce of labour belongs to the labourer; and the quantity of labour commonly employed in acquiring or producing any commodity is the only circumstance which can regulate the quantity of labor which it ought commonly to purchase, command, or exchange for.

As soon as stock has accumulated in the hands of particular persons, some of them will naturally employ it in setting to work industrious people, whom they will supply with materials and subsistence, in order to make a profit by the sale of their work, or by what their labour adds to the value of the materials. In exchanging the complete manufacture either for money, for labour, or for other goods, over and above what may be sufficient to pay the price of the materials, and the wages of the workmen, something must be given for the profits of the undertaker of the work who hazards his stock in this adventure. The value which the workmen add to the materials, therefore, resolves itself in this case into two parts, of which the one pays their wages, the other the profits of their employer upon the whole stock of materials and wages which he advanced. He could have no interest to employ them, unless he expected from the sale of their work something more than what was sufficient to replace his stock to him; and he could have no interest to employ a great stock rather than a small one, unless his profits were to bear some proportion to the extent of his stock.

. . .

As soon as the land of any country has all become private property, the landlords, like all other men, love to reap where they never sowed, and demand a rent even for its natural produce. The wood of the forest, the grass of the field, and all the natural fruits of the earth, which, when land was in common, cost the labourer only the trouble of gathering them, come, even to him, to have an additional price fixed upon them. He must then pay for the licence to gather them; and must give up to the landlord a portion of what his labour either collects or produces. This portion, or, what comes to the same thing, the price of this portion, constitutes the rent of land, and in the price of the greater part of commodities makes a third component part.

The real value of all the different component parts of price, it must be observed, is measured by the quantity of labour which they can, each of them, purchase or command. Labour measures the value not only of that part of price which resolves itself into labour, but of that which resolves itself into rent, and of that which resolves itself into profit.

In every society the price of every commodity finally resolves itself into some one or other, or all of those three parts; and in every improved society, all the three enter more or less, as component parts, into the price of the far greater part of commodities.

. . .

As the price or exchangeable value of every particular commodity, taken separately, resolves itself into some one or other or all of those three parts; so that of all the commodities which compose the whole annual produce of the labour of every country, taken complexly, must resolve itself into the same three parts, and be parcelled out among different inhabitants of the country, either as the wages of their labour, the profits of their stock, or the rent of their land. The whole of what is annually either collected or produced by the labour of every society, or what comes to the same thing, the whole price of it, is in this manner originally distributed among some of its different members. Wages, profit, and rent, are the three original sources of all revenue as well as of all exchangeable value. All other revenue is ultimately derived from some one or other of these.

...

Chapter VII: Of the natural and market price of commodities

There is in every society or neighbourhood an ordinary or average rate both of wages and profit in every different employment of labour and stock. This rate is naturally regulated, as I shall show hereafter, partly by the general circumstances of the society, their riches or poverty, their advancing, stationary, or declining condition; and partly by the particular nature of each employment.

There is likewise in every society or neighbourhood an ordinary or average rate of rent, which is regulated too, as I shall show hereafter, partly by the general circumstances of the society or neighbourhood in which the land is situated, and partly by the natural or improved fertility of the land.

These ordinary or average rates may be called the natural rates of wages, profit, and rent, at the time and place in which they commonly prevail.

When the price of any commodity is neither more nor less than what is sufficient to pay the rent of the land, the wages of the labour, and the profits of the stock employed in raising, preparing, and bringing it to market, according to their natural rates, the commodity is then sold for what may be called its natural price.

The commodity is then sold precisely for what it is worth, or for what it really costs the person who brings it to market; for though in common language what is called the prime cost of any commodity does not comprehend the profit of the person who is to sell it again, yet if he sell it at a price which does not allow him the ordinary rate of profit in his neighbourhood, he is evidently a loser by the trade; since by employing his stock in some other way he might have made that profit. His profit, besides, is his revenue, the proper fund of his subsistence. As, while he is preparing and bringing the goods to market, he advances to his workmen their wages, or their subsistence; so he advances to himself, in the same manner, his own subsistence, which is generally suitable to the profit which he may reasonably expect from the sale of his goods. Unless they yield him this profit, therefore, they do not repay him what they may very properly be said to have really cost him.

Though the price, therefore, which leaves him this profit is not always the lowest at which a dealer may sometimes sell his goods, it is the lowest at which he is likely to sell them for any considerable time; at least where there is perfect liberty, or where he may change his trade as often as he pleases.

The actual price at which any commodity is commonly sold is called its market price. It may either be above, or below, or exactly the same with its natural price.

The market price of every particular commodity is regulated by the proportion between the quantity which is actually brought to market, and the demand of those who are willing to pay the natural price of the commodity, or the whole value of the rent, labour, and profit, which must be paid in order to bring it thither. Such people may be called the effectual demanders, and their demand the effectual demand; since it may be sufficient to effectuate the bringing of the commodity to market. It is different from the absolute demand. A very poor man may be said in some sense to have a demand for a coach and six; he might like to have it; but his demand is not an effectual demand, as the commodity can never be brought to market in order to satisfy it.

When the quantity of any commodity which is brought to market falls short of the effectual demand, all those who are willing to pay the whole value of the rent, wages, and profit, which must be paid in order to bring it thither, cannot be supplied with the quantity which they want. Rather than want it altogether, some of them will be willing to give more. A competition will immediately begin among them, and the market price will rise more or less above the natural price, according as either the greatness of the deficiency, or the wealth and wanton luxury of the competitors, happen to animate more or less the eagerness of the competition. Among competitors of equal wealth and luxury the same deficiency will generally occasion a more or less eager competition, according as the acquisition of the commodity happens to be of more or less importance to them. Hence, the exorbitant price of the necessaries of life during the blockade of a town or in a famine.

When the quantity brought to market exceeds the effectual demand, it cannot be all sold to those who are willing to pay the whole value of the rent, wages, and profit, which must be paid in order to bring it thither. Some part must be sold to those who are willing to pay less, and the low price which they give for it must reduce the price of the whole. The market price will sink more or less below the natural price, according as the greatness of the excess increases more or less the competition of the sellers, or according as it happens to be more or less important to them to get immediately rid of the commodity. The same excess in the importation of perishable, will occasion a much greater competition than in that of durable commodities; in the importation of oranges, for example, than in that of old iron.

When the quantity brought to market is just sufficient to supply the effectual demand, and no more, the market price naturally comes to be either exactly, or as nearly as can be judged of, the same with the natural price. The whole quantity upon hand can be disposed of for this price, and cannot be disposed of for more. The competition of the different dealers obliges them all to accept of this price, but does not oblige them to accept of less.

The quantity of every commodity brought to market naturally suits itself to the effectual demand. It is the interest of all those who employ their land, labour, or stock, in bringing any commodity to market, that the quantity never should exceed the effectual demand; and it is the interest of all other people that it never should fall short of that demand.

If at any time it exceeds the effectual demand, some of the component parts of its price must be paid below their natural rate. If it is rent, the interest of the landlords will immediately prompt them to withdraw a part of their land; and if it is wages or profit, the interest of the labourers in the one case, and of their employers in the other, will prompt them to withdraw a part of their labour or stock from this employment. The quantity brought to market will soon be no more than sufficient to supply the effectual demand. All the different parts of its price will rise to their natural rate, and the whole price to its natural price.

If, on the contrary, the quantity brought to market should at any time fall short of the effectual demand, some of the component parts of its price must rise above their natural rate. If it is rent, the interest of all other landlords will naturally prompt them to prepare more land for the raising of this commodity; if it is wages or profit, the interest of all other labourers and dealers will soon prompt them to employ more labour and stock in preparing and bringing it to market. The quantity brought thither will soon be sufficient to supply the effectual demand. All the different parts of its price will soon sink to their natural rate, and the whole price to its natural price.

The natural price, therefore, is, as it were, the central price, to which the prices of all commodities are continually gravitating. Different accidents may sometimes keep them suspended a good deal above it, and sometimes force them down even somewhat below it. But whatever may be the obstacles which hinder them from settling in this centre of repose and continuance, they are constantly tending towards it.

The whole quantity of industry annually employed in order to bring any commodity to market naturally suits itself in this manner to the effectual demand. It naturally aims at bringing always that precise quantity thither which may be sufficient to supply, and no more than supply, that demand.

...

But though the market price of every particular commodity is in this manner continually gravitating, if one may say so, towards the natural price, yet sometimes particular accidents, sometimes natural causes, and sometimes particular regulations of police, may, in many commodities, keep up the market price, for a long time together, a good deal above the natural price.

...

The market price of any particular commodity, though it may continue long above, can seldom continue long below its natural price. Whatever part of it was paid below the natural rate, the persons whose interest it affected would immediately feel the loss, and would immediately withdraw either so much land, or so much labour, or so much stock, from being employed about it, that the quantity brought to market would soon be no more than sufficient to supply the effectual demand. Its market price, therefore, would soon rise to the natural price. This at least would be the case where there was perfect liberty.

...

Book four: Of systems of political economy

Introduction

Political economy, considered as a branch of the science of a statesman or legislator, proposes two distinct objects: first, to provide a plentiful revenue or subsistence for the people, or more properly to enable them to provide such a revenue or subsistence for themselves; and second, to supply the state or commonwealth with a revenue sufficient for the public services. It proposes to enrich both the people and the sovereign.

The different progress of opulence in different ages and nations has given occasion to two different systems of political economy with regard to enriching the people. The one may be called the system of commerce, the other that of agriculture. I shall endeavour to explain both as fully and distinctly as I can, and shall begin with the system of commerce. It is the modern system, and is best understood in our own country and in our own times.

Chapter II: Of restraints upon the importation from foreign countries of such goods as can be produced at home

By restraining, either by high duties or by absolute prohibitions, the importation of such goods from foreign countries as can be produced at home, the monopoly of the home market is more or less secured to the domestic industry employed in producing them. Thus, the prohibition of importing either live cattle or salt provisions from foreign countries secures to the graziers of Great Britain the monopoly of the home market for butcher's meat. The high duties upon the importation of corn, which in times of moderate plenty amount to a prohibition, give a like advantage to the growers of that commodity. The prohibition of the importation of foreign woollens is equally favourable to the woollen manufacturers. The silk manufacture, though altogether employed upon foreign materials, has lately obtained the same advantage. The linen manufacture has not yet obtained it, but is making great strides towards it. Many other sorts of manufacturers have, in the same manner, obtained in Great Britain, either altogether or very nearly, a monopoly against their countrymen. The variety of goods of which the importation into Great Britain is prohibited, either absolutely, or under certain circumstances, greatly exceeds what can easily be suspected by those who are not well acquainted with the laws of the customs.

That this monopoly of the home market frequently gives great encouragement to that particular species of industry which enjoys it, and frequently turns towards that employment a greater share of both the labour and stock of the society than would otherwise have gone to it, cannot be doubted. But whether it tends either to increase the general industry of the society, or to give it the most advantageous direction, is not, perhaps, altogether so evident.

The general industry of the society never can exceed what the capital of the society can employ. As the number of workmen that can be kept in employment by any particular person must bear a certain proportion to his capital, so the number of those that can be continually employed by all the members of a great society must bear a certain proportion to the whole capital of that society, and never can exceed that proportion. No regulation of commerce can increase the quantity of industry in any society beyond what its capital can maintain. It can only divert a part of it into a direction into which it might not otherwise have gone; and it is by no means certain that this artificial direction is likely to be more advantageous to the society than that into which it would have gone of its own accord.

Every individual is continually exerting himself to find out the most advantageous employment for whatever capital he can command. It is his own advantage, indeed, and not that of the society, which he has in view. But the study of his own advantage naturally, or rather necessarily, leads him to prefer that employment which is most advantageous to the society. First, every individual endeavours to employ his capital as near home as he can, and consequently as much as he can in the support of domestic industry; provided always that he can thereby obtain the ordinary, or not a great deal less than the ordinary profits of stock.

Thus, upon equal or nearly equal profits, every wholesale merchant naturally prefers the home trade to the foreign trade of consumption, and the foreign trade of consumption to the carrying trade. In the home trade his capital is never so long out of his sight as it frequently is in the foreign trade of consumption. He can know better the character and situation of the persons whom he trusts, and if he should happen to be deceived, he knows better the laws of the country from which he must seek redress. In the carrying trade, the capital of the merchant is, as it were, divided between two foreign countries, and no part of it is ever necessarily brought home, or placed under his own immediate view and command. … The merchant, in order to save a second loading and unloading, endeavours always to sell in the home market as much of the goods of all those different countries as he can, and thus, so far as he can, to convert his carrying trade into a foreign trade of consumption. A merchant, in the same manner, who is engaged in the foreign trade of consumption, when he collects goods for foreign markets, will always be glad, upon equal or nearly equal profits, to sell as great a part of them at home as he can. He saves himself the risk and trouble of exportation, when, so far as he can, he thus converts his foreign trade of consumption into a home trade. Home is in this manner the centre, if I may say so, round which the capitals of the inhabitants of every country are continually circulating, and towards which they are always tending, though by particular causes they may sometimes be driven off and repelled from it towards more distant employments. But a capital employed in the home trade, it has already been shown, necessarily puts into motion a greater quantity of domestic industry, and gives revenue and employment to a greater number of the inhabitants of the country, than an equal capital employed in the foreign trade of consumption: and one employed in the foreign trade of consumption has the same advantage over an equal capital employed in the carrying trade. Upon equal, or only nearly equal profits, therefore, every individual naturally inclines to employ his capital in the manner in which it is likely to afford the greatest support to domestic industry, and to give revenue and employment to the greatest number of people of his own country.

Second, every individual who employs his capital in the support of domestic industry, necessarily endeavours so to direct that industry that its produce may be of the greatest possible value.

The produce of industry is what it adds to the subject or materials upon which it is employed. In proportion as the value of this produce is great or small, so will likewise be the profits of the employer. But it is only for the sake of profit that any man employs a capital in the support of industry; and he will always, therefore, endeavour to employ it in the support of that industry of which the produce is likely to be of the greatest value, or to exchange for the greatest quantity either of money or of other goods.

But the annual revenue of every society is always precisely equal to the exchangeable value of the whole annual produce of its industry, or rather is precisely the same thing with that exchangeable value. As every individual, therefore, endeavours as much as he can both to employ his capital in the support of domestic industry, and so to direct that industry that its produce may be of the greatest value; every individual necessarily labours to render the annual revenue of the society as great as he can. He generally, indeed, neither intends to promote the public interest, nor knows how much he is promoting it. By preferring the support of domestic to that of foreign industry, he intends only his own security; and by directing that industry in such a manner as its produce may be of the greatest value, he intends only his own gain, and he is in this, as in many other cases, led by an invisible hand to promote an end which was no part of his intention. Nor is it always the worse for the society that it was no part of it. By pursuing his own interest he frequently promotes that of the society more effectually than when he really intends to promote it. I have never known much good done by those who affected to trade for the public good. It is an affectation, indeed, not very common among merchants, and very few words need be employed in dissuading them from it.

What is the species of domestic industry which his capital can employ, and of which the produce is likely to be of the greatest value, every individual, it is evident, can, in his local situation, judge much better than any statesman or lawgiver can do for him. The statesman who should attempt to direct private people in what manner they ought to employ their capitals would not only load himself with a most unnecessary attention, but assume an authority which could safely be trusted, not only to no single person, but to no council or senate whatever, and which would nowhere be so dangerous as in the hands of a man who had folly and presumption enough to fancy himself fit to exercise it.

To give the monopoly of the home market to the produce of domestic industry, in any particular art or manufacture, is in some measure to direct private people in what manner they ought to employ their capitals, and must, in almost all cases, be either a useless or a hurtful regulation. If the produce of domestic can be brought there as cheap as that of foreign industry, the regulation is evidently useless. If it cannot, it must generally be hurtful. It is the maxim of every prudent master of a family never to attempt to make at home what it will cost him more to make than to buy. The tailor does not attempt to make his own shoes, but buys them of the shoemaker. The shoemaker does not attempt to make his own clothes, but employs a tailor. The farmer attempts to make neither the one nor the other, but employs those different artificers. All of them find it for their interest to employ their whole industry in a way in which they have some advantage over their neighbours, and to purchase with a part of its produce, or what is the same thing, with the price of a part of it, whatever else they have occasion for.

What is prudence in the conduct of every private family can scarce be folly in that of a great kingdom. If a foreign country can supply us with a commodity cheaper than we ourselves can make it, better buy it of them with some part of the produce of our own industry employed in a way in which we have some advantage. The general industry of the country, being always in proportion to the capital which employs it, will not thereby be diminished, no more than that of the above-mentioned artificers; but only left to find out the way in which it can be employed with the greatest advantage. It is certainly not employed to the greatest advantage when it is thus directed towards an object which it can buy cheaper than it can make. The value of its annual produce is certainly more or less diminished when it is thus turned away from producing commodities evidently of more value than the commodity which it is directed to produce. According to the supposition, that commodity could be purchased from foreign countries cheaper than it can be made at home. It could, therefore, have been purchased with a part only of the commodities, or, what is the same thing, with a part only of the price of the commodities, which the industry employed by an equal capital would have produced at home, had it been left to follow its natural course. The industry of the country, therefore, is thus turned away from a more to a less advantageous employment, and the exchangeable value of its annual produce, instead of being increased, according to the intention of the lawgiver, must necessarily be diminished by every such regulation.

By means of such regulations, indeed, a particular manufacture may sometimes be acquired sooner than it could have been otherwise, and after a certain time may be made at home as cheap or cheaper than in the foreign country. But though the industry of the society may be thus carried with advantage into a particular channel sooner than it could have been otherwise, it will by no means follow that the sum total, either of its industry, or of its revenue, can ever be augmented by any such regulation. The industry of the society can augment only in proportion as its capital augments, and its capital can augment only in proportion to what can be gradually saved out of its revenue. But the immediate effect of every such regulation is to diminish its revenue, and what diminishes its revenue is certainly not very likely to augment its capital faster than it would have augmented of its own accord had both capital and industry been left to find out their natural employments.

Though for want of such regulations the society should never acquire the proposed manufacture, it would not, upon that account, necessarily be the poorer in any one period of its duration. In every period of its duration its whole capital and industry might still have been employed, though upon different objects, in the manner that was most advantageous at the time. In every period its revenue might have been the greatest which its capital could afford, and both capital and revenue might have been augmented with the greatest possible rapidity.

The natural advantages which one country has over another in producing particular commodities are sometimes so great that it is acknowledged by all the world to be in vain to struggle with them. By means of glasses, hotbeds, and hot walls, very good grapes can be raised in Scotland, and very good wine too can be made of them at about thirty times the expense for which at least equally good can be brought from foreign countries. Would it be a reasonable law to prohibit the importation of all foreign wines merely to encourage the making of claret and burgundy in Scotland? But if there would be a manifest absurdity in turning towards any employment thirty times more of the capital and industry of the country than would be necessary to purchase from foreign countries an equal quantity of the commodities wanted, there must be an absurdity, though not altogether so glaring, yet exactly of the same kind, in turning towards any such employment a thirtieth, or even a three-hundredth part more of either. Whether the advantages which one country has over another be natural or acquired is in this respect of no consequence. As long as the one country has those advantages, and the other wants them, it will always be more advantageous for the latter rather to buy of the former than to make. It is an acquired advantage only, which one artificer has over his neighbour, who exercises another trade; and yet they both find it more advantageous to buy of one another than to make what does not belong to their particular trades.

Merchants and manufacturers are the people who derive the greatest advantage from this monopoly of the home market. The prohibition of the importation of foreign cattle, and of salt provisions, together with the high duties upon foreign corn, which in times of moderate plenty amount to a prohibition, are not near so advantageous to the graziers and farmers of Great Britain as other regulations of the same kind are to its merchants and manufacturers. Manufactures, those of the finer kind especially, are more easily transported from one country to another than corn or cattle. It is in the fetching and carrying manufactures, accordingly, that foreign trade is chiefly employed. In manufactures, a very small advantage will enable foreigners to undersell our own workmen, even in the home market. It will require a very great one to enable them to do so in the rude produce of the soil. If the free importation of foreign manufactures were permitted, several of the home manufactures would probably suffer, and some of them, perhaps, go to ruin altogether, and a considerable part of the stock and industry at present employed in them would be forced to find out some other employment. But the freest importation of the rude produce of the soil could have no such effect upon the agriculture of the country.

...

Country gentlemen and farmers are, to their great honour, of all people, the least subject to the wretched spirit of monopoly. The undertaker of a great manufactory is sometimes alarmed if another work of the same kind is established within twenty miles of him. The Dutch undertaker of the woollen manufacture at Abbeville stipulated that no work of the same kind should be established within thirty leagues of that city. Farmers and country gentlemen, on the contrary, are generally disposed rather to promote than to obstruct the cultivation and improvement of their neighbours' farms and estates. They have no secrets such as those of the greater part of manufacturers, but are generally rather fond of communicating to their neighbours and of extending as far as possible any new practice which they have found to be advantageous. *Pius Questus, says old Cato, stabilissimusque, minimeque invidiosus; minimeque male cogitantes sunt, qui in eo studio occupati sunt.* Country gentlemen and farmers, dispersed in different parts of the country, cannot so easily combine as merchants and manufacturers, who, being collected into towns, and accustomed to that exclusive corporation spirit which prevails in them, naturally endeavour to obtain against all their countrymen the same exclusive privilege which they generally possess against the inhabitants of their respective towns. They accordingly seem to have been the original inventors of those restraints upon the importation of foreign goods which secure to them the monopoly of the home market. It was probably in imitation of them, and to put themselves upon a level with those who, they found, were disposed to oppress them, that the country gentlemen and farmers of Great Britain in so far forgot the generosity which is natural to their station as to demand the exclusive privilege of supplying their countrymen with corn and butcher's meat. They did not perhaps take time to consider how much less their interest could be affected by the freedom of trade than that of the people whose example they followed. To prohibit by a perpetual law the importation of foreign corn and cattle is in reality to enact that the population and industry of the country shall at no time exceed what the rude produce of its own soil can maintain.

There seem, however, to be two cases in which it will generally be advantageous to lay some burden upon foreign for the encouragement of domestic industry.

The first is, when some particular sort of industry is necessary for the defence of the country. The defence of Great Britain, for example, depends very much upon the number of its sailors and shipping. The Act of Navigation, therefore, very properly endeavours to give the sailors and shipping of Great Britain the monopoly of the trade of their own country in some cases by absolute prohibitions and in others by heavy burdens upon the shipping of foreign countries. ...

The second case, in which it will generally be advantageous to lay some burden upon foreign for the encouragement of domestic industry is, when some tax is imposed at home upon the produce of the latter. In this case, it seems reasonable that an equal tax should be imposed upon the like produce of the former. This would not give the monopoly of the home market to domestic industry, nor turn towards a particular employment a greater share of the stock and labour of the country than what would naturally go to it. It would only hinder any part of what would naturally go to it from being turned away by the tax into a less natural direction, and would leave the competition between foreign and domestic industry, after the tax, as nearly as possible upon the same footing as before it. In Great Britain, when any such tax is laid upon the produce of domestic industry, it is usual at the same time, in order to stop the clamorous complaints of our merchants and manufacturers that they will be undersold at home, to lay a much heavier duty upon the importation of all foreign goods of the same kind.

This second limitation of the freedom of trade according to some people should, upon some occasions, be extended much farther than to the precise foreign commodities which could come into competition with those which had been taxed at home. When the necessaries of life have been taxed any country, it becomes proper, they pretend, to tax not only the like necessaries of life imported from other countries, but all sorts of foreign goods which can come into competition with anything that is the produce of domestic industry. Subsistence, they say, becomes necessarily dearer in consequence of such taxes; and the price of labour must always rise with the price of the labourers' subsistence. Every commodity, therefore, which is the produce of domestic industry, though not immediately taxed itself, becomes dearer in consequence of such taxes, because the labour which produces it becomes so. Such taxes, therefore, are really equivalent, they say, to a tax upon every particular commodity produced at home. In order to put domestic upon the same footing with foreign industry, therefore, it becomes necessary, they think, to lay some duty upon every foreign commodity equal to this enhancement of the price of the home commodities with which it can come into competition.

Whether taxes upon the necessaries of life, such as those in Great Britain upon soap, salt, leather, candles, etc., necessarily raise the price of labour, and consequently that of all other commodities, I shall consider hereafter when I come to treat of taxes. Supposing, however, in the meantime, that they have this effect, and they have it undoubtedly, this general enhancement of the price of all commodities, in consequence of that of labour, is a case which differs in the two following respects from that of a particular commodity of which the price was enhanced by a particular tax immediately imposed upon it.

First, it might always be known with great exactness how far the price of such a commodity could be enhanced by such a tax: but how far the general enhancement of the price of labour might affect that of every different commodity about which labour was employed could never be known with any tolerable exactness. It would be impossible, therefore, to proportion with any tolerable exactness the tax upon every foreign to this enhancement of the price of every home commodity.

Second, taxes upon the necessaries of life have nearly the same effect upon the circumstances of the people as a poor soil and a bad climate. Provisions are thereby rendered dearer in the same manner as if it required extraordinary labour and expense to raise them. As in the natural scarcity arising from soil and climate it would be absurd to direct the people in what manner they ought to employ their capitals and industry, so is it likewise in the artificial scarcity arising from such taxes. To be left to accommodate, as well as they could, their industry to their situation, and to find out those employments in which, notwithstanding their unfavourable circumstances, they might have some advantage either in the home or in the foreign market, is what in both cases would evidently be most for their advantage. To lay a new tax upon them, because they are already overburdened with taxes, and because they already pay too dear for the necessaries of life, to make them likewise pay too dear for the greater part of other commodities, is certainly a most absurd way of making amends.

Such taxes, when they have grown up to a certain height, are a curse equal to the barrenness of the earth and the inclemency of the heavens; and yet it is in the richest and most industrious countries that they have been most generally imposed. No other country could support so great a disorder. As the strongest bodies only can live and enjoy health under an unwholesome regimen, so the nations only that in every sort of industry have the greatest natural and acquired advantages can subsist and prosper under such taxes. Holland is the country in Europe in which they abound most, and which from peculiar circumstances continues to prosper, not by means of them, as has been most absurdly supposed, but in spite of them.

As there are two cases in which it will generally be advantageous to lay some burden upon foreign for the encouragement of domestic industry, so there are two others in which it may sometimes be a matter of deliberation; in the one, how far it is proper to continue the free importation of certain foreign goods; and in the other, how far, or in what manner, it may be proper to restore that free importation after it has been for some time interrupted.

The case in which it may sometimes be a matter of deliberation how far it is proper to continue the free importation of certain foreign goods is, when some foreign nation restrains by high duties or prohibitions the importation of some of our manufactures into their country. Revenge in this case naturally dictates retaliation, and that we should impose the like duties and prohibitions upon the importation of some or all of their manufactures into ours. Nations, accordingly, seldom fail to retaliate in this manner. ...

There may be good policy in retaliations of this kind, when there is a probability that they will procure the repeal of the high duties or prohibitions complained of. The recovery of a great foreign market will generally more than compensate the transitory inconveniency of paying dearer during a short time for some sorts of goods. To judge whether such retaliations are likely to produce such an effect does not, perhaps, belong so much to the science of a legislator, whose deliberations ought to be governed by general principles which are always the same, as to the skill of that insidious and crafty animal, vulgarly called a statesman or politician, whose councils are directed by the momentary fluctuations of affairs. When there is no probability that any such repeal can be procured, it seems a bad method of compensating the injury done to certain classes of our people to do another injury ourselves, not only to those classes, but to almost all the other classes of them. When our neighbours prohibit some manufacture of ours, we generally prohibit, not only the same, for that alone would seldom affect them considerably, but some other manufacture of theirs. This may no doubt give encouragement to some particular class of workmen among ourselves, and by excluding some of their rivals, may enable them to raise their price in the home market. Those workmen, however, who suffered by our neighbours' prohibition will not be benefited by ours. On the contrary, they and almost all the other classes of our citizens will thereby be obliged to pay dearer than before for certain goods. Every such law, therefore, imposes a real tax upon the whole country, not in favour of that particular class of workmen who were injured by our neighbours' prohibition, but of some other class.

The case in which it may sometimes be a matter of deliberation, how far, or in what manner, it is proper to restore the free importation of foreign goods, after it has been for some time interrupted, is, when particular manufactures, by means of high duties or prohibitions upon all foreign goods which can come into competition with them, have been so far extended as to employ a great multitude of hands. Humanity may in this case require that the freedom of trade should be restored only by slow gradations, and with a good deal of reserve and circumspection. Were those high duties and prohibitions taken away all at once, cheaper foreign goods of the same kind might be poured so fast into the home market as to deprive all at once many thousands of our people of their ordinary employment and means of subsistence. The disorder which this would occasion might no doubt be very considerable. It would in all probability, however, be much less than is commonly imagined, for the two following reasons:

First, all those manufactures, of which any part is commonly exported to other European countries without a bounty, could be very little affected by the freest importation of foreign goods. Such manufactures must be sold as cheap abroad as any other foreign goods of the same quality and kind, and consequently must be sold cheaper at home. They would still, therefore, keep possession of the home market, and though a capricious man of fashion might sometimes prefer foreign wares, merely because they were foreign, to cheaper and better goods of the same kind that were made at home, this folly could, from the nature of things, extend to so few that it could make no sensible impression upon the general employment of the people. But a great part of all the different branches of our woollen manufacture, of our tanned leather, and of our hardware, are annually exported to other European countries without any bounty, and these are the manufactures which employ the greatest number of hands. The silk, perhaps, is the manufacture which would suffer the most by this freedom of trade, and after it the linen, though the latter much less than the former.

Second, though a great number of people should, by thus restoring the freedom of trade, be thrown all at once out of their ordinary employment and common method of subsistence, it would by no means follow that they would thereby be deprived either of employment or subsistence. By the reduction of the army and navy at the end of the late war, more than a hundred thousand soldiers and seamen, a number equal to what is employed in the greatest manufactures, were all at once thrown out of their ordinary employment; but, though they no doubt suffered some inconveniency, they were not thereby deprived of all employment and subsistence. The greater part of the seamen, it is probable, gradually betook themselves to the merchant-service as they could find occasion, and in the meantime both they and the soldiers were absorbed in the great mass of the people, and employed in a great variety of occupations. Not only no great convulsion, but no sensible disorder arose from so great a change in the situation of more than a hundred thousand men, all accustomed to the use of arms, and many of them to rapine and plunder. The number of vagrants was scarce anywhere sensibly increased by it, even the wages of labour were not reduced by it in any occupation, so far as I have been able to learn, except in that of seamen in the merchant service. But if we compare together the habits of a soldier and of any sort of manufacturer, we shall find that those of the latter do not tend so much to disqualify him from being employed in a new trade, as those of the former from being employed in any. The manufacturer has always been accustomed to look for his subsistence from his labour only: the soldier to expect it from his pay. Application and industry have been familiar to the one; idleness and dissipation to the other. But it is surely much easier to change the direction of industry from one sort of labour to another than to turn idleness and dissipation to any. To the greater part of manufactures besides, it has already been observed, there are other collateral manufactures of so similar a nature that a workman can easily transfer his industry from one of them to another. The greater part of such workmen too are occasionally employed in country labour. The stock which employed them in a particular manufacture before will still remain in the country to employ an equal number of people in some other way. The capital of the country remaining the same, the demand for labour will likewise be the same, or very nearly the same, though it may be exerted in different places and for different occupations. Soldiers and seamen, indeed, when discharged from the king's service, are at liberty to exercise any trade, within any town or place of Great Britain or Ireland. Let the same natural liberty of exercising what species of industry they please, be restored to all his Majesty's subjects, in the same manner as to soldiers and seamen; that is, break down the exclusive privileges of corporations, and repeal the Statute of Apprenticeship, both which are real encroachments upon natural liberty, and add to these the repeal of the Law of Settlements, so that a poor workman, when thrown out of employment either in one trade or in one place, may seek for it in another trade or in another place without the fear either of a prosecution or of a removal, and neither the public nor the individuals will suffer much more from the occasional disbanding of some particular classes of manufacturers than from that of soldiers. Our manufacturers have no doubt great merit with their country, but they cannot have more than those who defend it with their blood, nor deserve to be treated with more delicacy.

To expect, indeed, that the freedom of trade should ever be entirely restored in Great Britain is as absurd as to expect that an Oceana or Utopia should ever be established in it. Not only the prejudices of the public, but what is much more unconquerable, the private interests of many individuals, irresistibly oppose it. Were the officers of the army to oppose with the same zeal and unanimity any reduction in the numbers of forces with which master manufacturers set themselves against every law that is likely to increase the number of their rivals in the home market; were the former to animate their soldiers in the same manner as the latter enflame their workmen to attack with violence and outrage the proposers of any such regulation, to attempt to reduce the army would be as dangerous as it has now become to attempt to diminish in any respect the monopoly which our manufacturers have obtained against us. This monopoly has so much increased the number of some particular tribes of them that, like an overgrown standing army, they have become formidable to the government, and upon many occasions intimidate the legislature. The Member of Parliament who supports every proposal for strengthening this monopoly is sure to acquire not only the reputation of understanding trade, but great popularity and influence with an order of men whose numbers and wealth render them of great importance. If he opposes them, on the contrary, and still more if he has authority enough to be able to thwart them, neither the most acknowledged probity, nor the highest rank, nor the greatest public services can protect him from the most infamous abuse and detraction, from personal insults, nor sometimes from real danger, arising from the insolent outrage of furious and disappointed monopolists.

The undertaker of a great manufacture, who, by the home markets being suddenly laid open to the competition of foreigners, should be obliged to abandon his trade, would no doubt suffer very considerably. That part of his capital which had usually been employed in purchasing materials and in paying his workmen might, without much difficulty, perhaps, find another employment. But that part of it which was fixed in workhouses, and in the instruments of trade, could scarce be disposed of without considerable loss. The equitable regard, therefore, to his interest requires that changes of this kind should never be introduced suddenly, but slowly, gradually, and after a very long warning. The legislature, were it possible that its deliberations could be always directed, not by the clamorous importunity of partial interests, but by an extensive view of the general good, ought upon this very account, perhaps, to be particularly careful neither to establish any new monopolies of this kind, nor to extend further those which are already established. Every such regulation introduces some degree of real disorder into the constitution of the state, which it will be difficult afterwards to cure without occasioning another disorder.

How far it may be proper to impose taxes upon the importation of foreign goods, in order not to prevent their importation but to raise a revenue for government, I shall consider hereafter when I come to treat of taxes. Taxes imposed with a view to prevent, or even to diminish importation, are evidently as destructive of the revenue of the customs as of the freedom of trade.

Chapter VIII: Conclusion of the mercantile system

The laudable motive of all these regulations is to extend our own manufactures, not by their own improvement, but by the depression of those of all our neighbours, and by putting an end, as much as possible, to the troublesome competition of such odious and disagreeable rivals. Our master manufacturers think it reasonable that they themselves should have the monopoly of the ingenuity of all their countrymen. Though by restraining, in some trades, the number of apprentices which can be employed at one time, and by imposing the necessity of a long apprenticeship in all trades, they endeavour, all of them, to confine the knowledge of their respective employments to as small a number as possible; they are unwilling, however, that any part of this small number should go abroad to instruct foreigners.

Consumption is the sole end and purpose of all production; and the interest of the producer ought to be attended to only so far as it may be necessary for promoting that of the consumer. The maxim is so perfectly self evident that it would be absurd to attempt to prove it. But in the mercantile system the interest of the consumer is almost constantly sacrificed to that of the producer; and it seems to consider production, and not consumption, as the ultimate end and object of all industry and commerce.

In the restraints upon the importation of all foreign commodities which can come into competition with those of our own growth or manufacture, the interest of the home consumer is evidently sacrificed to that of the producer. It is altogether for the benefit of the latter that the former is obliged to pay that enhancement of price which this monopoly almost always occasions.

It is altogether for the benefit of the producer that bounties are granted upon the exportation of some of his productions. The home consumer is obliged to pay, first, the tax which is necessary for paying the bounty, and second, the still greater tax which necessarily arises from the enhancement of the price of the commodity in the home market.

Chapter IX: Of the agricultural systems, or of those systems of political economy which represent the produce of land as either the sole or the principal source of the revenue and wealth every country

The agricultural systems of political economy will not require so long an explanation as that which I have thought it necessary to bestow upon the mercantile or commercial system.

That system which represents the produce of land as the sole source of the revenue and wealth of every country has, so far as I know, never been adopted by any nation, and it at present exists only in the speculations of a few men of great learning and ingenuity in France. It would not, surely, be worth while to examine at great length the errors of a system which never has done, and probably never will do, any harm in any part of the world. I shall endeavour to explain, however, as distinctly as I can, the great outlines of this very ingenious system.

Mr Colbert, the famous minister of Louis XIV, was a man of probity, of great industry and knowledge of detail, of great experience and acuteness in the examination of public accounts, and of abilities, in short, every way fitted for introducing method and good order into the collection and expenditure of the public revenue. That minister had unfortunately embraced all the prejudices of the mercantile system, in its nature and essence a system of restraint and regulation, and such as could scarce fail to be agreeable to a laborious and plodding man of business, who had been accustomed to regulate the different departments of public offices, and to establish the necessary checks and controls for confining each to its proper sphere. The industry and commerce of a great country he endeavoured to regulate upon the same model as the departments of a public office; and instead of allowing every man to pursue his own interest in his own way, upon the liberal plan of equality, liberty, and justice, he bestowed upon certain branches of industry extraordinary privileges, while he laid others under as extraordinary restraints. He was not only disposed, like other European ministers, to encourage more the industry of the towns than that of the country; but, in order to support the industry of the towns, he was willing even to depress and keep down that of the country. In order to render provisions cheap to the inhabitants of the towns, and thereby to encourage manufactures and foreign commerce, he prohibited altogether the exportation of corn, and thus excluded the inhabitants of the country from every foreign market for by far the most important part of the produce of their industry. This prohibition, joined to the restraints imposed by the ancient provincial laws of France upon the transportation of corn from one province to another, and to the arbitrary and degrading taxes which are levied upon the cultivators in almost all the provinces, discouraged and kept down the agriculture of that country very much below the state to which it would naturally have risen in so very fertile a soil and so very happy a climate. This state of discouragement and depression was felt more or less in every different part of the country, and many different inquiries were set on foot concerning the causes of it. One of those causes appeared to be the preference given, by the institutions of Mr Colbert, to the industry of the towns above that of the country.

If the rod be bent too much one way, says the proverb, in order to make it straight you must bend it as much the other. The French philosophers, who have proposed the system which represents agriculture as the sole source of the revenue and wealth of every country, seem to have adopted this proverbial maxim; and as in the plan of Mr Colbert the industry of the towns was certainly overvalued in comparison with that of the country; so in their system it seems to be as certainly undervalued.

...

Some speculative physicians seem to have imagined that the health of the human body could be preserved only by a certain precise regimen of diet and exercise, of which every, the smallest, violation necessarily occasioned some degree of disease or disorder proportioned to the degree of the violation. Experience, however, would seem to show that the human body frequently preserves, to all appearances at least, the most perfect state of health under a vast variety of different regimens; even under some which are generally believed to be very far from being perfectly wholesome. But the healthful state of the human body, it would seem, contains in itself some unknown principle of preservation, capable either of preventing or of correcting, in many respects, the bad effects even of a very faulty regimen. Mr Quesnai, who was himself a physician, and a very speculative physician, seems to have entertained a notion of the same kind concerning the political body, and to have imagined that it would thrive and prosper only under a certain precise regimen, the exact regimen of perfect liberty and perfect justice. He seems not to have considered that, in the political body, the natural effort which every man is continually making to better his own condition is a principle of preservation capable of preventing and correcting, in many respects, the bad effects of a political economy, in some degree, both partial and oppressive. Such a political economy, though it no doubt retards more or less, is not always capable of stopping altogether the natural progress of a nation towards wealth and prosperity, and still less of making it go backwards. If a nation could not prosper without the enjoyment of perfect liberty and perfect justice, there is not in the world a nation which could ever have prospered. In the political body, however, the wisdom of nature has fortunately made ample provision for remedying many of the bad effects of the folly and injustice of man, in the same manner as it has done in the natural body for remedying those of his sloth and intemperance.

The capital error of this system, however, seems to lie in its representing the class of artificers, manufacturers, and merchants as altogether barren and unproductive. The following observations may serve to show the impropriety of this representation.

First, this class, it is acknowledged, reproduces annually the value of its own annual consumption, and continues, at least, the existence of the stock or capital which maintains and employs it. But upon this account alone the denomination of barren or unproductive should seem to be very improperly applied to it. We should not call a marriage barren or unproductive though it produced only a son and a daughter, to replace the father and mother, and though it did not increase the number of the human species, but only continued it as it was before. Farmers and country labourers, indeed, over and above the stock which maintains and employs them, reproduce annually a net produce, a free rent to the landlord. As a marriage which affords three children is certainly more productive than one which affords only two; so the labour of farmers and country labourers is certainly more productive than that of merchants, artificers, and manufacturers. The superior produce of the one class, however, does not render the other barren or unproductive.

Second, it seems, upon this account, altogether improper to consider artificers, manufacturers, and merchants in the same light as menial servants. The labour of menial servants does not continue the existence of the fund which maintains and employs them. Their maintenance and employment is altogether at the expense of their masters, and the work which they perform is not of a nature to repay that expense. That work consists in services which perish generally in the very instant of their performance, and does not fix or realize itself in any vendible commodity which can replace the value of their wages and maintenance. The labour, on the contrary, of artificers, manufacturers, and merchants naturally does fix and realize itself in some such vendible commodity. It is upon this account that, in the chapter in which I treat of productive and unproductive labour, I have classed artificers, manufacturers, and merchants among the productive labourers, and menial servants among the barren or unproductive.

Third, it seems upon every supposition improper to say that the labour of artificers, manufacturers, and merchants does not increase the real revenue of the society. Though we should suppose, for example, as it seems to be supposed in this system, that the value of the daily, monthly, and yearly consumption of this class was exactly equal to that of its daily, monthly, and yearly production, yet it would not from thence follow that its labour added nothing to the real revenue, to the real value of the annual produce of the land and labour of the society. An artificer, for example, who, in the first six months after harvest, executes ten pounds' worth of work, though he should in the same time consume ten pounds' worth of corn and other necessaries, yet really adds the value of ten pounds to the annual produce of the land and labour of the society. While he has been consuming a half-yearly revenue of ten pounds' worth of corn and other necessaries, he has produced an equal value of work capable of purchasing, either to himself or some other person, an equal half-yearly revenue. The value, therefore, of what has been consumed and produced during these six months is equal, not to ten, but to twenty pounds. It is possible, indeed, that no more than ten pounds' worth of this value may ever have existed at any one moment of time. But if the ten pounds' worth of corn and other necessaties, which were consumed by the artificer, had been consumed by a soldier or by a menial servant, the value of that part of the annual produce which existed at the end of the six months would have been ten pounds less than it actually is in consequence of the labour of the artificer. Though the value of what the artificer produces, therefore, should not at any one moment of time be supposed greater than the value he consumes, yet at every moment of time the actually existing value of goods in the market is, in consequence of what he produces, greater than it otherwise would be.

When the patrons of this system assert that the consumption of artificers, manufacturers, and merchants is equal to the value of what they produce, they probably mean no more than that their revenue, or the fund destined for their consumption, is equal to it. But if they had expressed themselves more accurately, and only asserted that the revenue of this class was equal to the value of what they produced, it might readily have occurred to the reader that what would naturally be saved out of this revenue must necessarily increase more or less the real wealth of the society. In order, therefore, to make out something like an argument, it was necessary that they should express themselves as they have done; and this argument, even supposing things actually were as it seems to presume them to be, turns out to be a very inconclusive one.

Fourth, farmers and country labourers can no more augment, without parsimony, the real revenue, the annual produce of the land and labour of their society, than artificers, manufacturers, and merchants. The annual produce of the land and labour of any society can be augmented only in two ways; either, first, by some improvement in the productive powers of the useful labour actually maintained within it; or, second, by some increase in the quantity of that labour.

The improvement in the productive powers of useful labour depend, first, upon the improvement in the ability of the workman; and, secondly, upon that of the machinery with which he works. But the labour of artificers and manufacturers, as it is capable of being more subdivided, and the labour of each workman reduced to a greater simplicity of operation than that of farmers and country labourers, so it is likewise capable of both these sorts of improvements in a much higher degree. In this respect, therefore, the class of cultivators can have no sort of advantage over that of artificers and manufacturers.

The increase in the quantity of useful labour actually employed within any society must depend altogether upon the increase of the capital which employs it; and the increase of that capital again must be exactly equal to the amount of the savings from the revenue, either of the particular persons who manage and direct the employment of that capital, or of some other persons who lend it to them. If merchants, artificers, and manufacturers are, as this system seems to suppose, naturally more inclined to parsimony and saving than proprietors and cultivators, they are, so far, more likely to augment the quantity of useful labour employed within their society, and consequently to increase its real revenue, the annual produce of its land and labour.

Fifth and last, though the revenue of the inhabitants of every country was supposed to consist altogether, as this system seems to suppose, in the quantity of subsistence which their industry could procure to them; yet, even upon this supposition, the revenue of a trading and manufacturing country must, other things being equal, always be much greater than that of one without trade or manufactures. By means of trade and manufactures, a greater quantity of subsistence can be annually imported into a particular country than what its own lands, in the actual state of their cultivation, could afford. The inhabitants of a town, though they frequently possess no lands of their own, yet draw to themselves by their industry such a quantity of the rude produce of the lands of other people as supplies them, not only with the materials of their work, but with the fund of their subsistence. What a town always is with regard to the country in its neighbourhood, one independent state or country may frequently be with regard to other independent states or countries. It is thus that Holland draws a great part of its subsistence from other countries; live cattle from Holstein and Jutland, and corn from almost all the different countries of Europe. A small quantity of manufactured produce purchases a great quantity of rude produce. A trading and manufacturing country, therefore, naturally purchases with a small part of its manufactured produce a great part of the rude produce of other countries; while, on the contrary, a country without trade and manufactures is generally obliged to purchase, at the expense of a great part of its rude produce, a very small part of the manufactured produce of other countries. The one exports what can subsist and accommodate but a very few, and imports the subsistence and accommodation of a great number. The other exports the accommodation and subsistence of a great number, and imports that of a very few only. The inhabitants of the one must always enjoy a much greater quantity of subsistence than what their own lands, in the actual state of their cultivation, could afford. The inhabitants of the other must always enjoy a much smaller quantity.

This system, however, with all its imperfections is, perhaps, the nearest approximation to the truth that has yet been published upon the subject of political economy, and is upon that account well worth the consideration of every man who wishes to examine with attention the principles of that very important science. Though in representing the labour which is employed upon land as the only productive labour, the notions which it inculcates are perhaps too narrow and confined; yet in representing the wealth of nations as consisting, not in the unconsumable riches of money, but in the consumable goods annually reproduced by the labour of the society, and in representing perfect liberty as the only effectual expedient for rendering this annual reproduction the greatest possible, its doctrine seems to be in every respect as just as it is generous and liberal. Its followers are very numerous; and as men are fond of paradoxes, and of appearing to understand what surpasses the comprehension of ordinary people, the paradox which it maintains, concerning the unproductive nature of manufacturing labour, has not perhaps contributed a little to increase the number of its admirers. They have for some years past made a pretty considerable sect, distinguished in the French republic of letters by the name of The Economists. Their works have certainly been of some service to their country; not only by bringing into general discussion many subjects which had never been well examined before, but by influencing in some measure the public administration in favour of agriculture. It has been in consequence of their representations, accordingly, that the agriculture of France has been delivered from several of the oppressions which it before laboured under. The term during which such a lease can be granted, as will be valid against every future purchaser or proprietor of the land, has been prolonged from nine to twenty-seven years. The ancient provincial restraints upon the transportation of corn from one province of the kingdom to another have been entirely taken away, and the liberty of exporting it to all foreign countries has been established as the common law of the kingdom in all ordinary cases. This sect, in their works, which are very numerous, and which treat not only of what is properly called Political Economy, or of the nature and causes of the wealth of nations, but of every other branch of the system of civil government, all follow implicitly and without any sensible variation, the doctrine of Mr Quesnai. There is upon this account little variety in the greater part of their works. The most distinct and best connected account of this doctrine is to be found in a little book written by Mr Mercier de la Riviere, some time intendant of Martinico, entitled, The Natural and Essential Order of Political Societies. The admiration of this whole sect for their master, who was himself a man of the greatest modesty and simplicity, is not inferior to that of any of the ancient philosophers for the founders of their respective systems. 'There have been, since the world began', says a very diligent and respectable author, the Marquis de Mirabeau, 'three great inventions which have principally given stability to political societies, independent of many other inventions which have enriched and adorned them. The first is the invention of writing, which alone gives human nature the power of transmitting, without alteration, its laws, its contracts, its annals, and its discoveries. The second is the invention of money, which binds together all the relations between civilised societies. The third is the Economical Table, the result of the other two, which completes them both by perfecting their object; the great discovery of our age, but of which our posterity will reap the benefit'.

...

The greatest and most important branch of the commerce of every nation, it has already been observed, is that which is carried on between the inhabitants of the town and those of the country. The inhabitants of the town draw from the country the rude produce which constitutes both the materials of their work and the fund of their subsistence; and they pay for this rude produce by sending back to the country a certain portion of it manufactured and prepared for immediate use. The trade which is carried on between these two different sets of people consists ultimately in a certain quantity of rude produce exchanged for a certain quantity of manufactured produce. The dearer the latter, therefore, the cheaper the former; and whatever tends in any country to raise the price of manufactured produce tends to lower that of the rude produce of the land, and thereby to discourage agriculture. The smaller the quantity of manufactured produce which any given quantity of rude produce, or, what comes to the same thing, which the price of any given quantity of rude produce is capable of purchasing, the smaller the exchangeable value of that given quantity of rude produce, the smaller the encouragement which either the landlord has to increase its quantity by improving or the farmer by cultivating the land. Whatever, besides, tends to diminish in any country the number of artificers and manufacturers, tends to diminish the home market, the most important of all markets for the rude produce of the land, and thereby still further to discourage agriculture.

Those systems, therefore, which, preferring agriculture to all other employments, in order to promote it, impose restraints upon manufactures and foreign trade, act contrary to the very end which they propose, and indirectly discourage that very species of industry which they mean to promote. They are so far, perhaps, more inconsistent than even the mercantile system. That system, by encouraging manufactures and foreign trade more than agriculture, turns a certain portion of the capital of the society from supporting a more advantageous, to support a less advantageous species of industry. But still it really and in the end encourages that species of industry which it means to promote. Those agricultural systems, on the contrary, really and in the end discourage their own favourite species of industry.

It is thus that every system which endeavours, either by extraordinary encouragements to draw towards a particular species of industry a greater share of the capital of the society than what would naturally go to it, or, by extraordinary restraints, force from a particular species of industry some share of the capital which would otherwise be employed in it, is in reality subversive of the great purpose which it means to promote. It retards, instead of accelerating, the progress of the society towards real wealth and greatness; and diminishes, instead of increasing, the real value of the annual produce of its land and labour.

All systems either of preference or of restraint, therefore, being thus completely taken away, the obvious and simple system of natural liberty establishes itself of its own accord. Every man, as long as he does not violate the laws of justice, is left perfectly free to pursue his own interest his own way, and to bring both his industry and capital into competition with those of any other man, or order of men. The sovereign is completely discharged from a duty, in attempting to perform which he must always be exposed to innumerable delusions, and for the proper performance of which no human wisdom or knowledge could ever be sufficient; the duty of superintending the industry of private people, and of directing it towards the employments most suitable to the interest of the society. According to the system of natural liberty, the sovereign has only three duties to attend to; three duties of great importance, indeed, but plain and intelligible to common understandings: first, the duty of protecting the society from violence and invasion of other independent societies; second, the duty of protecting, as far as possible, every member of the society from the injustice or oppression of every other member of it, or the duty of establishing an exact administration of justice; and, third, the duty of erecting and maintaining certain public works and certain public institutions which it can never be for the interest of any individual, or small number of individuals, to erect and maintain; because the profit could never repay the expense to any individual or small number of individuals, though it may frequently do much more than repay it to a great society.

...

JEREMY BENTHAM (1748–1832)

Jeremy Bentham, Artist: Thomas Frye (1710–1762), by courtesy of the National Portrait Gallery, London.

Jeremy Bentham was the model of the Enlightenment mind. He was individualist, secularist, materialist, and pragmatic. He believed that while people were influenced by received moral rules and religious beliefs, these rules and beliefs, no matter what people said, were filtered through their dominant utilitarian approach to life. Whereas Smith's model of human nature was both more complex and more finely textured and nuanced, Bentham's approach was that people generally rationally calculated their pleasures and pains, more interested in the consequences of action for their self-interests than in obediently and blindly giving effect to received morality. Bentham's utilitarianism, therefore, not only finessed the role of received morality, subjugating it – as an empirical matter, he believed – to calculations of advantage, it ended up as something of a tautology, at least insofar as it might serve as an predictive device. But his philosophy of methodological individualism and the felicific calculus served to give credibility to a more secular and more materialist mode of reasoning, effectively endorsing an ubiquitous benefit–cost mode of decision making in both private and public affairs.

The other element of his philosophy, the greatest happiness principle, was perhaps equally revolutionary – and even more resented by established powers. For Bentham argued that government policy should be driven not by the interests of either a monarch or a narrow ruling class but by the interests of all people. The problem here was to be seen as how maximization was to weigh the utility of those relatively most benefited against the utility of those relatively least benefited, that is, the relative weights to be assigned to the intensive and extensive margins, whether to maximize happiness by maximizing the utility/welfare of those most benefited or of the number benefited. This problem of measuring and weighing the elements of "the greatest happiness for the greatest number" led to two grand traditions: the bourgeois and the socialist traditions, or the Benthamite right versus the Benthamite left.

As history transpired, Bentham could meaningfully be declared the father of both British individualism and British collectivism: of British individualism insofar as he (and/or his disciples) promoted the extension of the rights, participation and benefits of citizenship to ever-increasing numbers of people, ultimately to all people; and of British collectivism insofar as once the masses received the right to vote they sought to use government in analytically the same way as the upper classes had done – though without the decorative rhetoric of identifying their system with the natural order of things, instead the agenda being given the designation of collectivism and/or welfare state, terms laudatory to some and malodorous to others. The use of government to promote middle-class interests became nineteenth-century liberalism and that to promote working class and consumer interests became twentieth-century liberalism. The "radicalism" of the middle class was now supplanted by the "radicalism" of the working class.

Which serves to indicate that by the third decade of the nineteenth century, or thereabouts, the historic conflict between landed property and nonlanded property (capitalist) interests would be resolved along the following general lines (epitomized by the Reform Act of 1832): the landed interests retained their land, their titles (where relevant), control over the House of Lords, and the monarchy; whereas the nonlanded interests came to dominate the House of Commons and had their desires enacted into law, as the economy proceeded apace from a rural and agricultural type to an urban, commercial and industrial type. Not coincidentally, it was roughly at this same time that the first major organized stirrings of the working class were being felt, and increasingly the conflict over the control of government was less between two different types of actual and would-be property claimants and more between those who had and those who did not have property, the latter of whom increasingly sought the advancement of their interests along lines more or less analytically equivalent to property, in social and regulatory legislation.

So Bentham promoted a more clear cut and explicit, conscious making of personal and collective policy decisions. He also, by his three doctrines gave political economy a confidence that an economic science could be built on secure philosophical foundations. His secular, utilitarian approach also tended, but only tended, to enable collective decision making – the economic role of government – to be treated relatively objectively as a mode of social control; but it truly only tended to do so, inasmuch as various forms of political-economic ideology continued to function, and even increased in magnitude and reason-disrupting dissimulation.

Although his writings are voluminous, Bentham actually published very little of this material during his lifetime. Much of his influence on contemporary and immediately subsequent economic thinking was personal, and his disciples included David Ricardo, James Mill, and John Stuart Mill.

In the excerpts from Bentham's work reprinted here, we see shades of several major themes that appear in the larger corpus of in his his writings: utilitarianism, the greatest happiness principle, and the relationship between government and individual rights.

References and further reading

Bentham, Jeremy (1952) *Jeremy Bentham's Economic Writings*, 3 Vols, edited by W. Stark, London: George Allen and Unwin for The Royal Economic Society.

Blaug, Mark, ed. (1991) *Henry Thornton (1760–1815), Jeremy Bentham (1748–1832), James Lauderdale (1759–1839), Simonde de Sismondi (1773–1842)*, Aldershot: Edward Elgar Publishing.

Harrison, Ross (1983) *Bentham*, London: Routledge and Kegan Paul.

——(1987) "Bentham, Jeremy," in John Eatwell, Murray Milgate, and Peter Newman (eds), *The New Palgrave: A Dictionary of Economics*, Vol. 1, London: Macmillan, 226–29.

Halévy, Élie (1928) *The Growth of Philosophical Radicalism*, translated by Mary Morris, London: Faber & Faber.

Hutchison, T.W. (1956) "Bentham as Economist," *Economic Journal* 66 (June): 288–306.

Petrella, F. 1977) "Benthamism and the Demise of Classical Economic Ordnungs Politik," *History of Political Economy* 9 (Summer): 215–36.

Robbins, Lionel (1964) "Bentham in the Twentieth Century," reprinted in Lionel Robbins, *The Evolution of Modern Economic Theory and Other Papers on the History of Economic Thought*, London: Macmillan, 1970, 73–84.

Stark, W. (1941) "Liberty and Equality, or Bentham as an Economist: I. Bentham's Doctrine," *Economic Journal* 51 (April): 56–79.

—— (1946) "Liberty and Equality, or Bentham as an Economist: II. Bentham's Influence," *Economic Journal* 56 (December): 583–608.

Viner, Jacob (1949) "Bentham and J.S. Mill: The Utilitarian Background," *American Economic Review* 39 (March): 360–82.

Warke, Tom (2000) "Mathematical Fitness in the Evolution of the Utility Concept from Bentham to Jevons to Marshall," *Journal of the History of Economic Thought* 22 (March): 5–27.

An Introduction to the Principles of Morals and Legislation (1789)

Chapter 1: Of the principle of utility

Nature has placed mankind under the governance of two sovereign masters, *pain* and *pleasure*. It is for them alone to point out what we ought to do, as well as to determine what we shall do. On the other hand, the standard of right and wrong, on the other chain of causes and effects, are fastened to their throne. They govern us in all we do, in all we say, in all we think: every effort we can make to throw off our subjection, will serve but to demonstrate and confirm it. In words a man may pretend to abjure their empire: but in reality he will remain subject to it all the while. The *principle of utility* recognises this subjection, and assumes it for the foundation of that system, the object of which is to rear the fabric of felicity by the hands of reason and of law. Systems which attempt to question it, deal in sounds instead of sense, in caprice instead of reason, in darkness instead of light.

But enough of metaphor and declamation: it is not by such means that moral science is to be improved.

II. The principle of utility is the foundation of the present work: it will be proper therefore at the outset to give an explicit and determinate account of what is meant by it. By the principle of utility is meant that principle which approves or disapproves of every action whatsoever, according to the tendency which it appears to have to augment or diminish the happiness of the party whose interest is in question: or, what is the same thing in other words, to promote or to oppose that happiness. I say of every action whatsoever; and therefore not only of every action of a private individual, but of every measure of government.

III. By utility is meant that property in any object, whereby it tends to produce benefit, advantage, pleasure, good, or happiness (all this in the present case comes to the same thing), or (what comes again to the same thing) to prevent the happening of mischief, pain, evil, or unhappiness to the party whose interest is considered: if that party be the community in general, then the happiness of the community: if a particular individual, then the happiness of that individual.

IV. The interest of the community is one of the most general expressions that can occur in the phraseology of morals: no wonder that the meaning of it is often lost. When it has a meaning, it is this. The community is a fictitious *body*, composed of the individual persons who are considered as constituting as it were its *members*. The interest of the community then is, what? – the sum of the interest of the several members who compose it.

V. It is in vain to talk of the interest of the community, without understanding what is the interest of the individual. A thing is said to promote the interest, or to be *for* the interest, of an individual, when it tends to add to the sum total of his pleasures: or, what comes to the same thing, to diminish the sum total of his pains.

VI. An action then may be said to be conformable to the principle of utility, or, for shortness sake, to utility (meaning with respect to the community at large), when the tendency it has to augment the happiness of the community is greater than any it has to diminish it.

VII. A measure of government (which is but a particular kind of action, performed by a particular person or persons) may be said to be conformable to or dictated by the principle of utility, when in like manner the tendency which it has to augment the happiness of the community is greater then any which it has to diminish it.

VIII. When an action, or in particular a measure of government, is supposed by a man to be conformable to the principle of utility, it may be convenient, for the purposes of discourse, to imagine a kind of law or dictate, called a law or dictate of utility; and to speak of the action in question, as being conformable to such law or dictate.

IX. A man may be said to be a partizan of the principle of utility, when the approbation or disapprobation he annexes to any action, or to any measure, is determined by and proportioned to the tendency which he conceives it to have to augment or to diminish the happiness of the community: or in others words, to its conformity or unconformity to the laws or dictates of utility.

X. Of an action that is conformable to the principle of utility, one may always say either that it is one that ought to be done, or at least that it is not one that ought not to be done. One may say also, that it is right it should be done; at least that it is not wrong it should be done: that it is a right action; at least that it is not a wrong action. When thus interpreted, the words *ought*, and *right* and *wrong*, and others of that stamp, have a meaning: when otherwise, they have none.

XI. Has the rectitude of this principle been ever formally contested? It should seem that it had, by those who have not known what they have been meaning. Is it susceptible of any direct proof? It should seem not: for that which is used to prove every thing else, cannot itself be proved: a chain of proofs must have their commencement somewhere. To give such proof is as impossible as it is needless.

XII. Not that there is or ever has been that human creature breathing, however stupid or perverse, who has not on many, perhaps on most occasions of his life, deferred to it. By the natural constitution of the human frame, on most occasions of their lives men in general embrace this principle, without thinking of it: if not for the ordering of their own actions, yet for the trying of their own actions, as well as of those of other men. There have been, at the same time, not many, perhaps, even of the most intelligent, who have been disposed to embrace it purely and without reserve. There are even few who have not taken some occasion or other to quarrel with it, either on account of their not understanding always how to apply it, or on account of some prejudice or other which they were of afraid to examine into, or could not bear to part with. For such is the stuff that man is made of: in principle and in practice, in a right track and in a wrong one, the rarest of all human qualities is consistency.

XIII. When a man attempts to combat the principle of utility, it is with reasons drawn, without his being aware of it, from that very principle itself. His arguments, if they prove any thing, prove not that the principle is *wrong*, but that, according to the applications he supposes is to be made of it, it is misapplied. Is it possible for a man to move the earth? Yes; but he must first find out another earth to stand upon.

XIV. To disprove the propriety of it by arguments is impossible; but, from the causes that have been mentioned, or from some confused or partial view of it, a man may happen to be disposed not to relish it. Where this is the case, if he thinks the settling of his opinions on such a subject worth the trouble, let him take the following steps, and at length, perhaps, he may come to reconcile himself to it.

1. Let him settle with himself, whether he would wish to discard this principle altogether; if so, let him consider what it is that all his reasonings (in matters of politics especially) can amount to?

2. If he would, let him settle with himself, whether he would judge and act without any principle, or whether there is any other he would judge and act by?

3. If there be, let him examine and satisfy himself whether the principle he thinks he has found is really any separate intelligible principle; or whether it be not a mere principle in words, a kind of phase, which at bottom expresses neither more or less than the mere averment of his own unfounded sentiments; that is, what in another person he might be apt to call caprice?

4. If he is inclined to think that his own approbation or disapprobation, annexed to the idea of an act, without any regard to its consequences, is a sufficient foundation for him to judge and act upon, let him ask himself whether his sentiment is to be a standard of right and wrong, with respect to every other man, or whether every man's sentiment has the same privilege of being a standard to itself?

5. In the first case, let him ask himself whether his principle is not despotical, and hostile to all the rest of human race?

6. In the second case, whether it is not anarchial, and whether at this rate there are not as many different standards of right and wrong as there are men? And whether even to the same man, the same thing, which is right to-day, may not (without the least change in its nature) be wrong to-morrow? And whether the same thing is not right and wrong in the same place at the same time? And in either case, whether all argument is not at an end? And whether, when two men have said, 'I like this,' and 'I don't like it,' they can (upon such a principle) have any thing more to say.

7. If he should have said to himself, No: for that the sentiment which he proposes as a standard must be grounded on reflection, let him say on what particulars the reflection is to turn? If on particulars having relation to the utility of the act, then let him say whether this is not deserting his own principle, and borrowing assistance from that very one in opposition to which he sets it up: or if not on those particulars on what other particulars?

8. If he should be for compounding the matter, and adopting his own principle in part, and the principle of utility in part, let him say how far he will adopt it?

9. When he has settled with himself where he will stop, then let him ask himself how he justifies to himself the adopting it so far? And why he will not adopt it any farther?

10. Admitting any other principle than the principle of utility to be a right principle, a principle that it is right for a man to pursue; admitting (what is not true) that the word right can have a meaning without reference to utility let him say whether there is any such thing as a motive that a man can have to pursue the dictates of it: if there is, let him say what that motive is, and how it is to be distinguished from those which enforce the dictates of utility: if not, then lastly let him say what it is this other principle can be good for?

A Manual of Political Economy (1795)

Chapter I: Introduction

Political Economy is at once a *science* and an *art*. The value of the science has for its efficient cause and measure, its subserviency to the art.

According to the principle of utility in every branch of the art of legislation, the object or end in view should be the production of the maximum of happiness in a given time in the community in question.

In the instance of this branch of the art, the object or end in view should be the production of that maximum of happiness, in so far as this more general end is promoted by the production of the maximum of wealth and the maximum of population.

The practical questions, therefore, are – How far the measures respectively suggested by these two branches of the common end agree? – How far they differ, and which requires the preference? – How far the end in view is best promoted by individuals acting for themselves? And in what cases these ends may be best promoted by the hands of government?

Those cases in which, and those measures or operations by which, the end is promoted by individuals acting for themselves, and without any special interference exercised with this special view on the part of government, beyond the distribution made and maintained, and the protection afforded by the civil and penal branches of the law, may be said to arise *sponte acta*.

What the legislator and the minister of the interior have it in their power to do towards increase either of wealth or population, is as nothing in comparison with what is done of course, and without thinking of it, by the judge, and his assistant the minister of police.

The cases in which, and the measures by which, the common end may be promoted by the hands of government, may be termed *agenda*.

With the view of causing an increase to take place in the mass of national wealth, or with a view to increase of the means either of subsistence or enjoyment, without some special reason, the general rule is, that nothing ought to be done or attempted by government. The motto, or watchword of government, on these occasions, ought to be – *Be quiet*.

For this quietism there are two main reasons:

1. Generally speaking, any interference for this purpose on the part of government is *needless*. The wealth of the whole community is composed of the wealth of the several individuals belonging to it taken together. But to increase his particular portion is, generally speaking, among the constant objects of each individual's exertions and care. Generally speaking, there is no one who knows what is for your interest, so well as yourself – no one who is disposed with so much ardour and constancy to pursue it.

2. Generally speaking, it is moreover likely to be pernicious, namely by being unconducive, or even obstructive, with reference to the attainment of the end in view. Each individual bestowing more time and attention upon the means of preserving and increasing his portion of wealth, than is or can be bestowed by government, is likely to take a more effectual course than what, in his instance and on his behalf, would be taken by government.

It is, moreover, universally and constantly pernicious in another way, by the restraint or constraint imposed on the free agency of the individual. Pain is the general concomitant of the sense of such restraint, wherever it is experienced.

Without being productive of such coercion, and thereby of such, pain – in such a way more or less direct – more or less perceptible, with this or any other view, the interposition of government can hardly take place. If the coercion be not applied to the very individual whose conduct is endeavoured to be made immediately subservient to this purpose, it is at any rate applied to others – indeed, to the whole community taken together.

In coercive measures, so called, it is only to the individual that the coercion is applied. In the case of measures of encouragement, the field of coercion is vastly more extensive. Encouragements are grants of money or money's worth, applied in some shape or other to this purpose. But for this, any more than any other purpose, money is not raised but by taxes, and taxes are the produce of coercive laws applied to the most coercive purpose.

This would not be the less true, though the individual pieces of money thus applied happened to come from a source which had not been fed by any such means. In all communities, by far the greatest share of the money disposed of by government being supplied by taxes, whether this or that particular portion of money so applied, be supplied from that particular source, makes no sort of difference.

To estimate the good expected from the application of any particular mass of government money, compare it always with the mischief produced by the extraction of an equal sum of money by the most burthensome species of tax; since, by forbearing to make application of that sum of money, you might forbear levying the amount of that same sum of money by that tax, and thereby forbear imposing the mass of burthen that results from it.

Anarchical Fallacies (1795)

Specimens of a criticism of the French declarations of rights

Article I – Men (all men) are born and remain free,
and equal in respect of rights.
Social distinctions cannot be founded, but upon common utility

In this article are contained, grammatically speaking, two distinct sentences. The first is full of error, the other of ambiguity.

In the first are contained four distinguishable propositions, all of them false – all of them notoriously and undeniably false:

1   That all men are born free.
2   That all men remain free.
3   That all men are born equal in rights.
4   That all men remain (i.e. remain for ever, for the proposition is indefinite and unlimited) equal in rights.

All men are born free? All men remain free? No, not a single man: not a single man that ever was, or is, or will be, All men, on the contrary, are born in subjection, and the most absolute subjection – the subjection of a helpless child to the parents on whom he depends every moment for his existence. In this subjection every man is born – in this subjection he continues for years – for a great number of years – and the existence of the individual and of the species depends upon his so doing.

What is the state of things to which the supposed existence of these supposed rights is meant to bear reference? – a state of things prior to the existence of government, or a state of things subsequent to the existence of government? If to a state prior to the existence of government, what would the existence of such rights as these be to the purpose, even if it were true, in any country where there is such a thing as government? If to a state of things subsequent to the formation of government – if in a country where there is a government, in what single instance – in the instance of what single government, is it true? Setting aside the case of parent and child, let any man name that single government under which any such equality is recognized.

All men born free? Absurd and miserable nonsense! When the great complaint – a complaint made perhaps by the very same people at the same time, is – that so many men are born slaves. Oh! but when we acknowledge them to be born slaves, we refer to the laws in being; which laws being void, as being contrary to those laws of nature which are the efficient causes of those rights of man that we are declaring, the men in question are free in one sense, though slaves in another; – slaves, and free, at the same time: free in respect of the laws of nature – slaves in respect of the pretended human laws, which, though called laws, are no laws at all, as being contrary to the laws of nature. For such is the difference – the great and perpetual difference, betwixt the good subject, the rational censor of the laws, and the anarchist – between the moderate man and the man of violence. The rational censor, acknowledging the existence of the law he disapproves, proposes the repeal of it: the anarchist, setting up his will and fancy for a law before which all mankind are called upon to bow down at the first word – the anarchist, trampling on truth and decency, denies the validity of the law in question, – denies the existence of it in the character of a law, and calls upon all mankind to rise up in a mass, and resist the execution of it.

. . .

Article II – The end in view of every political association is the preservation of the natural and imprescriptible rights of man. These rights are liberty, property, security, and resistance to oppression

Sentence 1. The end in view of every political association, is the preservation of the natural and imprescriptible rights of man.

More confusion – more nonsense – and the nonsense, as usual, dangerous nonsense. The words can scarcely be said to have a meaning: but if they have, or rather if they had a meaning, these would be the propositions either asserted or implied:

1. That there are such things as rights anterior to the establishment of governments: for nat-ural, as applied to rights, if it mean anything, is meant to stand in opposition to legal – to such rights as are acknowledged to owe their existence to government, and are consequently posterior in their date to the establishment of government.

2. That these rights *can not* be abrogated by government; for *can not* is implied in the form of the word imprescriptible, and the sense it wears when so applied, is the cut-throat sense above explained.

3. That the governments that exist derive their origin from formal associations, or what are now called *conventions*: associations entered into by a partnership contract, with all the members for partners, – entered into at a day prefixed, for a predetermined purpose, the formation of a new government where there was none before (for as to formal meetings holden under the control of an existing government, they are evidently out of question here) in which it seems again to be implied in the way of inference, though a necessary and unavoidable inference, that all governments (i.e. self-called governments, knots of persons exercising the power of govern-ment) that have had any other origin than an association of the above description, are illegal, that is, no governments at all; resistance to them, and subversion of them, lawful and commendable; and so on.

Such are the notions implied in this first of the article. How stands the truth of things? That there are no such things as natural rights – no such things as rights anterior to the establishment of government – no such things as natural rights opposed to, in contradistinction to, legal; that the expression is merely figurative; that when used, in the moment you attempt to give it a literal meaning, it leads to error, and to that sort of error that leads to mischief – to the extremity of mischief.

We know what it is for men to live without government – and living without government, to live without rights: we know what it is for men to live without government, for we see instances of such a way of life – we see it in many savage nations, or rather races of mankind; for instance, among the savages of New South Wales, whose way of living is so well known to us; no habit of obedience, and thence no government – no government, and thence no laws – no laws, and thence no such things as rights – no security – no property: liberty, as against regular control, the control of laws and government – perfect but as against all irregular control, the mandates of stronger individuals, none. In this state at a time earlier than the commencement of history – in this same state, judging from analogy, we, the inhabitants of the part of the globe we call Europe, were; no government, consequently no rights: no rights, consequently no property – no legal security – no legal liberty: security not more than belongs to beasts – forecast and sense of insecurity keener consequently in point of happiness below the level of the brutal race.

In proportion to the want of happiness resulting from the want of rights, a reason exists for wishing that there were such things as rights. But reasons for wishing there were such things as rights, are not rights: a reason for wishing that a certain right were established, is not that right – want is not supply – hunger is not bread.

That which has not existence cannot be destroyed – that which cannot be destroyed cannot require anything to preserve it from destruction. *Natural rights is* simple nonsense: natural and imprescriptible rights, rhetorical nonsense – nonsense upon stilts. But this rhetorical nonsense ends in the old strain of mischievous nonsense: for immediately a list of these pretended natural rights is given, and those are so expressed as to present to view legal rights. And of these rights, whatever they are, there is not, it seems, any one of which any government can, upon any occasion whatever, abrogate the smallest particle.

So much for terrorist language. What is the language of reason and plain sense upon this same subject? That in proportion as it is right or proper, that is, advantageous to the society in question, that this or that right – a right to this or that effect – should be established and maintained, in that same proportion it is *wrong* that is should be abrogated: but, that as there is no *right*, which ought not to be maintained so long as it is upon the whole advantageous to society that it should be maintained, so there is no right which, when the abolition of it is advantageous to society, should not be abolished. To know whether it would be more for the advantage of society that this or that right should be maintained or abolished, the time at which the question about maintaining or abolishing is proposed, must be given, and the circumstances under which it is proposed to maintain or abolish it; the right itself must be specifically described, not jumbled with an undistinguishable heap of others, under any such vague general terms as property, liberty, and the like.

One thing, in the midst of all this confusion, is but too plain. They know not of what they are talking under the name of natural rights, and yet they would have the imprescriptible – proof against all the power of the laws – pregnant with occasions summoning the members of the community to rise up in resistance against those laws. What, then, was their object in declaring the existence of imprescriptible rights, and without specifying a single one by any such mark as it could be known by? This, and no other – to excite and keep up a spirit of resistance to all laws – a spirit of insurrection against all governments – against the governments of all other nations instantly – against the government of their own nation – against the government they themselves were pretending to establish – even that, as soon as their own reign should be at an end. In us is the perfection of virtue and wisdom: in all mankind besides, the extremity of wickedness and folly. Our will shall consequently reign without control, and for ever: reign now, we are living – reign after we are dead.

All nations – all future ages – shall be, for they are predestined to be, our slaves.

Future governments will not have honesty enough to be trusted with the determination of what rights shall be maintained, what abrogated – what laws kept in force, what repealed. Future subjects (I should say future citizens, for French government does not admit of subjects) will not have wit enough to be trusted with the choice whether to submit to the determination of the government of their time, or to resist it. Governments, citizens – all to the end of time – all must be kept in chains.

Such are their maxims – such their premises: for it is by such premises only that the doctrine of imprescriptible rights and unrepealable laws can be supported.

What is the real source of these imprescriptible rights – these unrepealable laws? Power turned blind by looking from its own height: self-conceit and tyranny exalted into insanity. No man was to have any other man for a servant, yet all men were for ever to be *their* slaves. Making laws with imposture in their mouths, under pretence of declaring them – giving for laws any thing that came uppermost, and these unrepealable ones, on pretence of finding them ready made. Made by what? Not by God – they allow of none; but by their goddess, Nature.

The origination of governments from a contract is a pure fiction; or, in other words, a falsehood. It never has been known to be true in any instance; the allegation of it does mischief, by involving the subject in error and confusion, and is neither necessary nor useful to any good purpose.

All governments that we have any account of have been gradually established by habit, after having formed by force; unless in the instance of governments formed by individuals who have been emancipated, or have emancipated themselves from governments already formed, the governments under which they were born – a rare case, and from which nothing follows with regard to the rest. What signifies it how governments are formed? Is it the less proper – the less conducive to the happiness of society – that the happiness of society should be the one object kept in view by the members of the government in all their measures? Is it the less the interest of men to be happy – less to be wished that they may be so – less the moral duty of their governors to make them so, so far as they can, at Magadore than at Philadelphia?

Whence is it, but from government, that contracts derive their binding force? Contracts came from government, not government from contracts. It is from the habit of enforcing contracts, and seeing them enforced, that governments are chiefly indebted for whatever disposition they have to observe them.

Principles of the Civil Code (1802)

Chapter VI: Propositions of pathology upon which the advantage of equality is founded

1   Each portion of wealth is connected with a corresponding portion of happiness.
2   Of two individuals, possessed of unequal fortunes, he who possesses the greatest wealth will possess the greatest happiness.
3   The excess of happiness on the part of the most wealthy will not be so great as the excess of his wealth.
4   For the same reason, the greater the disproportion between the two masses of wealth, the less the probability that there exists an equally great disproportion between the masses of happiness.
5   The more nearly the actual proportion approaches to equality, the greater will be the total mass of happiness.

THOMAS ROBERT MALTHUS (1766–1834)

Thomas Robert Malthus, by courtesy of The Warren J. Samuels Portrait Collection at Duke University.

Thomas Robert Malthus studied Mathematics at Jesus College, Cambridge, graduating in 1788. He entered the church shortly after his graduation and held the office of Minister of the Church of England for the remainder of his life. In 1805, Malthus was appointed "Professor of General History, Politics, Commerce and Finance," which later was changed to "Professor of History and Political Economy" – this latter title making him the first person, in England at least, to hold the title of "Professor of Political Economy." Malthus died in Bath in 1834 and is buried in Bath Abbey.

The problem of population pressure had been stressed for some time, even by the ancient Greek philosophers – though not by all writers, for some saw in growing population more hands for the farm, factory and military. In 1798, Malthus published his *Essay on the Principle of Population, As It Affects the Future Improvement of Society; With Remarks on the Speculations of Mr Godwin, M. Condorcet, and Other Writers*, in an attempt to dispel the utopian ideals of Godwin, Condorcet, etc. It proved to be a momentous event, influencing or at least framing debate on a vast variety of economic issues and proposals of social reform for over a century. Although some took Malthus's argument as a prediction of the future and others saw it as both a matter of conflicting tendencies and as a condition with which human action and government policy would have to deal, and although the treatment of methods of birth control was muted for over a century and a half, his "law" of population, or at least the "problem" of population became a focal consideration of Classical Political Economy. The impact of and on population became a matter of central interest for almost every public issue. Conservatives could point to over-reproduction among the masses as the cause of their poverty, and liberals could point to institutions which channeled income toward upper classes, but the logic of population pressure, even with changes in institutions – which was, after all, the point at issue – was very powerful. As it turned out, in the two centuries after 1798 (1) real income levels increased in the industrialized countries and remained low in underdeveloped countries, thus demonstrating that the Malthusian tendency need not materialize, and (2) some people remained concerned about global over-population and others disputed that a serious problem existed.

Malthus argued that while population increased in a geometric ratio, the food supply could only increase at an arithmetic ratio – that is, the capacity to produce human beings was greater than the capacity to grow food, thereby placing pressure on the standard of living for most people. For him, population was necessarily limited by the means of subsistence, population increases when subsistence increases unless checked, and population tends to increase faster than the increase in subsistence. Average per capita incomes would thus strongly tend to gravitate toward the minimum-of-subsistence level.

The possible checks to population growth were of two types, the preventive and the positive. The preventive checks encompassed vice (sexual relations outside of marriage) and moral restraint (sexual abstinence within marriage, foregoing marriage, and perhaps birth control devices). The positive check involves increased death rates due to famine and epidemics, war, cannibalism, infanticide, and geriatricide. All of this ultimately devolved to, as Malthus put it, "misery and vice" – not the utopian perfectibility of Godwin and others. As it turned out, whereas Malthus initially seemed to stress the positive checks, a dismal picture indeed, he later stressed moral restraint – in effect recognizing Godwin's argument about the role of the intellect vis-à-vis the desire for sex.

Actually, Malthus's analysis stressed three consequences of population pressure. One was downward pressure on living standards. The other two were negative effects on the quality of life and the need to resort to greater formal, that is, legal, social control – both due to great numbers of people, greater density of population, and greater interaction among people.

Malthus's law of population served as a basis for the theory of rent developed by him and several others, notably David Ricardo. Rent was the sum of the supramarginal returns on land that was more fertile and/or better situated; it was driven by population growth and was differential as between lands of different grade. Malthus invoked the theory of rent in support of the Corn Laws, reasoning that they served to support the politically and socially important landowning class, with which he identified. The same theory of rent was used by Ricardo to support doing away with the Corn Laws, because they served to raise the wages paid by business, the class with which he identified. This episode in the history of economic thought illustrates how readily a theory can be combined with different additional assumptions to generate different analytical and policy implications. The meaning of a theory depends on its use, which is often a matter of implicit antecedent premises as to whose interests are to count.

Malthus's *Essay* went through six editions between 1798 and 1827. The first revision, published in 1803, was greatly enlarged and reflected Malthus's observations made during European travels as well as other data and information that he felt supported his argument. This edition had one other key difference from the first: the addition of a third restraint – the prudential check, meaning the deferral (rather than foregoing) of marriage, which, he said, did not involve either misery or vice.

The passages from Malthus's *Essay* reprinted here are from the first edition of 1798 and present Malthus's case for the population problem and his discussion of the preventive and postive checks to population growth.

References and further reading*

Bonar, J. (1924) *Malthus and His Work*, 2nd edn, London: George Allen and Unwin.
Eversley, D.E.C. (1959) *Social Theories of Fertility and the Malthusian Debate*, London: Oxford University Press.

---

* Further references to Malthus's life and work can be found in the introduction to the subsequent reading from his *Principles of Political Economy*.

James, Patricia (1979) *Population Malthus: His Life and Times*, London: Routledge and Kegan Paul.

Keynes, J.M. (1933) "Robert Malthus," in J.M. Keynes (ed.), *Essays in Biography*, London: Macmillan.

McCleary, G.F. (1953) *The Malthusian Population Theory*, London: Faber & Faber.

Petersen, William (1964) *The Politics of Population*, Garden City, NY: Doubleday.

Pullen, J.M. (1981) "Malthus' Theological Ideas and Their Influence on His Principle of Population," *History of Political Economy* 13 (Spring) 39–54.

——(1987) "Malthus, Thomas Robert," in John Eatwell, Murray Milgate, and Peter Newman (eds), *The New Palgrave: A Dictionary of Economics*, Vol. 3, London: Macmillan, 280–5.

Simon, Julian L. (1998) *The Economics of Population: Classic Writings*, New Brunswick, NJ: Transaction Publishers.

Spengler, J.J. (1972) *Population Economics: Selected Essays*, Durham, NC: Duke University Press.

Stangeland, Charles E. (1904) *Pre-Malthusian Doctrines of Population: A Study in the History of Economic Theory*, reprinted New York: Augustus M. Kelley, 1966.

Weir, D.R. (1987) "Malthus's Theory of Population," in John Eatwell, Murray Milgate, and Peter Newman (eds), *The New Palgrave: A Dictionary of Economics*, Vol. 3, London: Macmillan, 290–3.

An Essay on the Principle of Population (1798)*

Chapter 1

The great and unlooked for discoveries that have taken place of late years in natural philosophy, the increasing diffusion of general knowledge from the extension of the art of printing, the ardent and unshackled spirit of inquiry that prevails throughout the lettered and even unlettered world, the new and extraordinary lights that have been thrown on political subjects which dazzle and astonish the understanding, and particularly that tremendous phenomenon in the political horizon, the French Revolution, which, like a blazing comet, seems destined either to inspire with fresh life and vigour, or to scorch up and destroy the shrinking inhabitants of the earth, have all concurred to lead many able men into the opinion that we were touching on a period big with the most important changes, changes that would in some measure be decisive of the future fate of mankind.

It has been said that the great question is now at issue, whether man shall henceforth start forward with accelerated velocity towards illimitable, and hitherto unconceived improvement, or be condemned to a perpetual oscillation between happiness and misery, and after every effort remain still at an immeasurable distance from the wished-for goal.

Yet, anxiously as every friend of mankind must look forward to the termination of this painful suspense, and eagerly as the inquiring mind would hail every ray of light that might assist its view into futurity, it is much to be lamented that the writers on each side of this momentous question still keep far aloof from each other. Their mutual arguments do not meet with a candid examination. The question is not brought to rest on fewer points, and even in theory scarcely seems to be approaching to a decision.

The advocate for the present order of things is apt to treat the sect of speculative philosophers either as a set of artful and designing knaves who preach up ardent benevolence and draw captivating pictures of a happier state of society only the better to enable them to destroy the present establishments and to forward their own deep-laid schemes of ambition, or as wild and mad-headed enthusiasts whose silly speculations and absurd paradoxes are not worthy the attention of any reasonable man.

The advocate for the perfectibility of man, and of society, retorts on the defender of establishments a more than equal contempt. He brands him as the slave of the most miserable and narrow prejudices; or as the defender of the abuses of civil society only because he profits by them. He paints him either as a character who prostitutes his understanding to his interest, or as one whose powers of mind are not of a size to grasp any thing great and noble, who cannot see

* *An Essay on the Principle of Population, As It Affects the Future Improvement of Society With Remarks on the Speculations of Mr Godwin, M. Condorcet, and Other Writers*, London, Printed for Johnson, J. in St Paul's Church-Yard, 7 June 1798.

above five yards before him, and who must therefore be utterly unable to take in the views of the enlightened benefactor of mankind.

In this unamicable contest the cause of truth cannot but suffer. The really good arguments on each side of the question are not allowed to have their proper weight. Each pursues his own theory, little solicitous to correct or improve it by an attention to what is advanced by his opponents.

The friend of the present order of things condemns all political speculations in the gross. He will not even condescend to examine the grounds from which the perfectibility of society is inferred. Much less will he give himself the trouble in a fair and candid manner to attempt an exposition of their fallacy.

The speculative philosopher equally offends against the cause of truth. With eyes fixed on a happier state of society, the blessings of which he paints in the most captivating colours, he allows himself to indulge in the most bitter invectives against every present establishment, without applying his talents to consider the best and safest means of removing abuses and without seeming to be aware of the tremendous obstacles that threaten, even in theory, to oppose the progress of man towards perfection.

It is an acknowledged truth in philosophy that a just theory will always be confirmed by experiment. Yet so much friction, and so many minute circumstances occur in practice, which it is next to impossible for the most enlarged and penetrating mind to foresee, that on few subjects can any theory be pronounced just, till all the arguments against it have been maturely weighed and clearly and consistently refuted.

I have read some of the speculations on the perfectibility of man and of society with great pleasure. I have been warmed and delighted with the enchanting picture which they hold forth. I ardently wish for such happy improvements. But I see great, and, to my understanding, unconquerable difficulties in the way to them. These difficulties it is my present purpose to state, declaring, at the same time, that so far from exulting in them, as a cause of triumph over the friends of innovation, nothing would give me greater pleasure than to see them completely removed.

The most important argument that I shall adduce is certainly not new. The principles on which it depends have been explained in part by Hume, and more at large by Dr Adam Smith. It has been advanced and applied to the present subject, though not with its proper weight, or in the most forcible point of view, by Mr Wallace, and it may probably have been stated by many writers that I have never met with. I should certainly therefore not think of advancing it again, though I mean to place it in a point of view in some degree different from any that I have hitherto seen, if it had ever been fairly and satisfactorily answered.

The cause of this neglect on the part of the advocates for the perfectibility of mankind is not easily accounted for. I cannot doubt the talents of such men as Godwin and Condorcet. I am unwilling to doubt their candour. To my understanding, and probably to that of most others, the difficulty appears insurmountable. Yet these men of acknowledged ability and penetration scarcely deign to notice it, and hold on their course in such speculations with unabated ardour and undiminished confidence. I have certainly no right to say that they purposely shut their eyes to such arguments. I ought rather to doubt the validity of them, when neglected by such men, however forcibly their truth may strike my own mind. Yet, in this respect, it must be acknowledged that we are all of us too prone to err. If I saw a glass of wine repeatedly presented to a man, and he took no notice of it, I should be apt to think that he was blind or uncivil. A juster philosophy might teach me rather to think that my eyes deceived me and that the offer was not really what I conceived it to be.

In entering upon the argument I must premise that I put out of the question, at present, all mere conjectures, that is, all suppositions, the probable realization of which cannot be inferred upon any just philosophical grounds. A writer may tell me that he thinks man will ultimately become an ostrich. I cannot properly contradict him. But before he can expect to bring any reasonable person over to his opinion, he ought to shew that the necks of mankind have been gradually elongating, that the lips have grown harder and more prominent, that the legs and feet are daily altering their shape, and that the hair is beginning to change into stubs of feathers. And till the probability of so wonderful a conversion can be shewn, it is surely lost time and lost eloquence to expatiate on the happiness of man in such a state; to describe his powers, both of running and flying, to paint him in a condition where all narrow luxuries would be condemned, where he would be employed only in collecting the necessaries of life, and where, consequently, each man's share of labour would be light, and his portion of leisure ample.

I think I may fairly make two postulata.

First, that food is necessary to the existence of man.
Second, that the passion between the sexes is necessary and will remain nearly in its present state.

These two laws, ever since we have had any knowledge of mankind, appear to have been fixed laws of our nature, and, as we have not hitherto seen any alteration in them, we have no right to conclude that they will ever cease to be what they now are, without an immediate act of power in that Being who first arranged the system of the universe, and for the advantage of his creatures, still executes, according to fixed laws, all its various operations.

I do not know that any writer has supposed that on this earth man will ultimately be able to live without food. But Mr Godwin has conjectured that the passion between the sexes may in time be extinguished. As, however, he calls this part of his work a deviation into the land of conjecture, I will not dwell longer upon it at present than to say that the best arguments for the perfectibility of man are drawn from a contemplation of the great progress that he has already made from the savage state and the difficulty of saying where he is to stop. But towards the extinction of the passion between the sexes, no progress whatever has hitherto been made. It appears to exist in as much force at present as it did two thousand or four thousand years ago. There are individual exceptions now as there always have been. But, as these exceptions do not appear to increase in number, it would surely be a very unphilosophical mode of arguing to infer, merely from the existence of an exception, that the exception would, in time, become the rule, and the rule the exception.

Assuming then my postulata as granted, I say, that the power of population is indefinitely greater than the power in the earth to produce subsistence for man.

Population, when unchecked, increases in a geometrical ratio. Subsistence increases only in an arithmetical ratio. A slight acquaintance with numbers will shew the immensity of the first power in comparison of the second.

By that law of our nature which makes food necessary to the life of man, the effects of these two unequal powers must be kept equal.

This implies a strong and constantly operating check on population from the difficulty of subsistence. This difficulty must fall somewhere and must necessarily be severely felt by a large portion of mankind.

Through the animal and vegetable kingdoms, nature has scattered the seeds of life abroad with the most profuse and liberal hand. She has been comparatively sparing in the room and the nourishment necessary to rear them. The germs of existence contained in this spot of earth, with ample food, and ample room to expand in, would fill millions of worlds in the course of a few thousand years. Necessity, that imperious all pervading law of nature, restrains them within the prescribed bounds. The race of plants and the race of animals shrink under this great restrictive law. And the race of man cannot, by any efforts of reason, escape from it. Among plants and animals its effects are waste of seed, sickness, and premature death. Among mankind, misery and vice. The former, misery, is an absolutely necessary consequence of it. Vice is a highly probable consequence, and we therefore see it abundantly prevail, but it ought not, perhaps, to be called an absolutely necessary consequence. The ordeal of virtue is to resist all temptation to evil.

This natural inequality of the two powers of population and of production in the earth, and that great law of our nature which must constantly keep their effects equal, form the great difficulty that to me appears insurmountable in the way to the perfectibility of society. All other arguments are of slight and subordinate consideration in comparison of this. I see no way by which man can escape from the weight of this law which pervades all animated nature. No fancied equality, no agrarian regulations in their utmost extent, could remove the pressure of it even for a single century. And it appears, therefore, to be decisive against the possible existence of a society, all the members of which should live in ease, happiness, and comparative leisure; and feel no anxiety about providing the means of subsistence for themselves and families.

Consequently, if the premises are just, the argument is conclusive against the perfectibility of the mass of mankind.

I have thus sketched the general outline of the argument, but I will examine it more particularly, and I think it will be found that experience, the true source and foundation of all knowledge, invariably confirms its truth.

Chapter 2

I said that population, when unchecked, increased in a geometrical ratio, and subsistence for man in an arithmetical ratio.

Let us examine whether this position be just. I think it will be allowed, that no state has hitherto existed (at least that we have any account of) where the manners were so pure and simple, and the means of subsistence so abundant, that no check whatever has existed to early marriages, among the lower classes, from a fear of not providing well for their families, or among the higher classes, from a fear of lowering their condition in life. Consequently in no state that we have yet known has the power of population been left to exert itself with perfect freedom.

Whether the law of marriage be instituted or not, the dictate of nature and virtue seems to be an early attachment to one woman. Supposing a liberty of changing in the case of an unfortunate choice, this liberty would not affect population till it arose to a height greatly vicious; and we are now supposing the existence of a society where vice is scarcely known.

In a state therefore of great equality and virtue, where pure and simple manners prevailed, and where the means of subsistence were so abundant that no part of the society could have any fears about providing amply for a family, the power of population being left to exert itself unchecked, the increase of the human species would evidently be much greater than any increase that has been hitherto known.

In the United States of America, where the means of subsistence have been more ample, the manners of the people more pure, and consequently the checks to early marriages fewer, than in any of the modern states of Europe, the population has been found to double itself in twenty-five years.

This ratio of increase, though short of the utmost power of population, yet as the result of actual experience, we will take as our rule, and say, that population, when unchecked, goes on doubling itself every twenty-five years or increases in a geometrical ratio.

Let us now take any spot of earth, this Island for instance, and see in what ratio the subsistence it affords can be supposed to increase. We will begin with it under its present state of cultivation.

If I allow that by the best possible policy, by breaking up more land and by great encouragements to agriculture, the produce of this Island may be doubled in the first twenty-five years, I think it will be allowing as much as any person can well demand.

In the next twenty-five years, it is impossible to suppose that the produce could be quadrupled. It would be contrary to all our knowledge of the qualities of land. The very utmost that we can conceive, is, that the increase in the second twenty-five years might equal the present produce. Let us then take this for our rule, though certainly far beyond the truth, and allow that, by great exertion, the whole produce of the Island might be increased every twenty-five years, by a quantity of subsistence equal to what it at present produces. The most enthusiastic speculator cannot suppose a greater increase than this. In a few centuries it would make every acre of land in the Island like a garden.

Yet, this ratio of increase is evidently arithmetical.

It may be fairly said, therefore, that the means of subsistence increase in an arithmetical ratio. Let us now bring the effects of these two ratios together.

The population of the Island is computed to be about seven millions, and we will suppose the present produce equal to the support of such a number. In the first twenty-five years the population would be fourteen millions, and the food being also doubled, the means of subsistence would be equal to this increase. In the next twenty-five years the population would be twenty-eight millions, and the means of subsistence only equal to the support of twenty-one millions. In the next period, the population would be fifty-six millions, and the means of subsistence just sufficient for half that number. And at the conclusion of the first century the population would be one hundred and twelve millions and the means of subsistence only equal to the support of thirty-five millions, which would leave a population of seventy-seven millions totally unprovided for.

A great emigration necessarily implies unhappiness of some kind or other in the country that is deserted. For few persons will leave their families, connections, friends, and native land, to seek a settlement in untried foreign climes, without some strong subsisting causes of uneasiness where they are, or the hope of some great advantages in the place to which they are going.

But to make the argument more general and less interrupted by the partial views of emigration, let us take the whole earth, instead of one spot, and suppose that the restraints to population were universally removed. If the subsistence for man that the earth affords was to be increased every twenty-five years by a quantity equal to what the whole world at present produces, this would allow the power of production in the earth to be absolutely unlimited, and its ratio of increase much greater than we can conceive that any possible exertions of mankind could make it.

Taking the population of the world at any number, a thousand millions, for instance, the human species would increase in the ratio of – 1, 2, 4, 8, 16, 32, 64, 128, 256, 512, etc. and subsistence as – 1, 2, 3, 4, 5, 6, 7, 8, 9, 10, etc. In two centuries and a quarter, the population would be to the means of subsistence as 512 to 10: in three centuries as 4096 to 13, and in two thousand years the difference would be almost incalculable, though the produce in that time would have increased to an immense extent.

No limits whatever are placed to the productions of the earth; they may increase for ever and be greater than any assignable quantity. Yet still the power of population being a power of a superior order, the increase of the human species can only be kept commensurate to the increase of the means of subsistence by the constant operation of the strong law of necessity acting as a check upon the greater power.

The effects of this check remain now to be considered.

Among plants and animals the view of the subject is simple. They are all impelled by a powerful instinct to the increase of their species, and this instinct is interrupted by no reasoning or doubts about providing for their offspring. Wherever therefore there is liberty, the power of increase is exerted, and the superabundant effects are repressed afterwards by want of room and nourishment, which is common to animals and plants, and among animals by becoming the prey of others.

The effects of this check on man are more complicated. Impelled to the increase of his species by an equally powerful instinct, reason interrupts his career and asks him whether he may not bring beings into the world for whom he cannot provide the means of subsistence. In a state of equality, this would be the simple question. In the present state of society, other considerations occur. Will he not lower his rank in life? Will he not subject himself to greater difficulties than he at present feels? Will he not be obliged to labour harder? And if he has a large family, will his utmost exertions enable him to support them? May he not see his offspring in rags and misery, and clamouring for bread that he cannot give them? And may he not be reduced to the grating necessity of forfeiting his independence, and of being obliged to the sparing hand of charity for support?

These considerations are calculated to prevent, and certainly do prevent, a very great number in all civilized nations from pursuing the dictate of nature in an early attachment to one woman. And this restraint almost necessarily, though not absolutely so, produces vice. Yet, in all societies, even those that are most vicious, the tendency to a virtuous attachment is so strong that there is a constant effort towards an increase of population. This constant effort as constantly tends to subject the lower classes of the society to distress and to prevent any great permanent ameliora-tion of their condition.

The way in which, these effects are produced seems to be this. We will suppose the means of subsistence in any country just equal to the easy support of its inhabitants. The constant effort towards population, which is found to act even in the most vicious societies, increases the number of people before the means of subsistence are increased. The food therefore which before sup-ported seven millions must now be divided among seven millions and a half or eight millions. The poor consequently must live much worse, and many of them be reduced to severe distress. The number of labourers also being above the proportion of the work in the market, the price of labour must tend towards a decrease, while the price of provisions would at the same time tend to rise. The labourer therefore must work harder to earn the same as he did before. During this season of distress, the discouragements to marriage, and the difficulty of rearing a family are so great that population is at a stand. In the mean time the cheapness of labour, the plenty of labour-ers, and the necessity of an increased industry amongst them, encourage cultivators to employ more labour upon their land, to turn up fresh soil, and to manure and improve more completely what is already in tillage, till ultimately the means of subsistence become in the same proportion to the population as at the period from which we set out. The situation of the labourer being then again tolerably comfortable, the restraints to population are in some degree loosened, and the same retrograde and progressive movements with respect to happiness are repeated.

This sort of oscillation will not be remarked by superficial observers, and it may be difficult even for the most penetrating mind to calculate its periods. Yet that in all old states some such vibration does exist, though from various transverse causes, in a much less marked, and in a much more irregular manner than I have described it, no reflecting man who considers the subject deeply can well doubt.

···

The theory on which the truth of this position depends appears to me so extremely clear that I feel at a loss to conjecture what part of it can be denied.

That population cannot increase without the means of subsistence is a proposition so evident that it needs no illustration.

That population does invariably increase where there are the means of subsistence, the history of every people that have ever existed will abundantly prove.

And that the superior power of population cannot be checked without producing misery or vice, the ample portion of these too bitter ingredients in the cup of human life and the continu-ance of the physical causes that seem to have produced them bear too convincing a testimony.

···

Chapter 4

In examining the next state of mankind with relation to the question before us, the state of mixed pasture and tillage, in which with some variation in the proportions the most civilized nations must always remain, we shall be assisted in our review by what we daily see around us, by actual experience, by facts that come within the scope of every man's observation. ...

...

In examining the principal states of modern Europe, we shall find that though they have increased very considerably in population since they were nations of shepherds, yet that at present their progress is but slow, and instead of doubling their numbers every twenty-five years they require three or four hundred years, or more, for that purpose. Some, indeed, may be absolutely stationary, and others even retrograde. The cause of this slow progress in population cannot be traced to a decay of the passion between the sexes. We have sufficient reason to think that this natural propensity exists still in undiminished vigour. Why then do not its effects appear in a rapid increase of the human species? An intimate view of the state of society in any one country in Europe, which may serve equally for all, will enable us to answer this question, and to say that a foresight of the difficulties attending the rearing of a family acts as a preventive check, and the actual distresses of some of the lower classes, by which they are disabled from giving the proper food and attention to their children, act as a positive check to the natural increase of population.

England, as one of the most flourishing states of Europe, may be fairly taken for an example, and the observations made will apply with but little variation to any other country where the population increases slowly.

The preventive check appears to operate in some degree through all the ranks of society in England. There are some men, even in the highest rank, who are prevented from marrying by the idea of the expenses that they must retrench, and the fancied pleasures that they must deprive themselves of, on the supposition of having a family. These considerations are certainly trivial, but a preventive foresight of this kind has objects of much greater weight for its contemplation as we go lower.

A man of liberal education, but with an income only just sufficient to enable him to associate in the rank of gentlemen, must feel absolutely certain that if he marries and has a family he shall be obliged, if he mixes at all in society, to rank himself with moderate farmers and the lower class of tradesmen. The woman that a man of education would naturally make the object of his choice would be one brought up in the same tastes and sentiments with himself and used to the familiar intercourse of a society totally different from that to which she must be reduced by marriage. Can a man consent to place the object of his affection in a situation so discordant, probably, to her tastes and inclinations? Two or three steps of descent in society, particularly at this round of the ladder, where education ends and ignorance begins, will not be considered by the generality of people as a fancied and chimerical, but a real and essential evil. If society be held desirable, it surely must be free, equal, and reciprocal society, where benefits are conferred as well as received, and not such as the dependent finds with his patron or the poor with the rich.

These considerations undoubtedly prevent a great number in this rank of life from following the bent of their inclinations in an early attachment. Others, guided either by a stronger passion, or a weaker judgement, break through these restraints, and it would be hard indeed, if the gratification of so delightful a passion as virtuous love, did not, sometimes, more than counterbalance all its attendant evils. But I fear it must be owned that the more general consequences of such marriages are rather calculated to justify than to repress the forebodings of the prudent.

The sons of tradesmen and farmers are exhorted not to marry, and generally find it necessary to pursue this advice till they are settled in some business or farm that may enable them to support a family. These events may not, perhaps, occur till they are far advanced in life. The scarcity of farms is a very general complaint in England. And the competition in every kind of business is so great that it is not possible that all should be successful.

The labourer who earns eighteen pence a day and lives with some degree of comfort as a single man, will hesitate a little before he divides that pittance among four or five, which seems to be but just sufficient for one. Harder fare and harder labour he would submit to for the sake of living with the woman that he loves, but he must feel conscious, if he thinks at all, that should he have a large family, and any ill luck whatever, no degree of frugality, no possible exertion of his manual strength could preserve him from the heart-rending sensation of seeing his children starve, or of forfeiting his independence, and being obliged to the parish for their support. The love of independence is a sentiment that surely none would wish to be erased from the breast of man, though the parish law of England, it must be confessed, is a system of all others the most calculated gradually to weaken this sentiment, and in the end may eradicate it completely.

The servants who live in gentlemen's families have restraints that are yet stronger to break through in venturing upon marriage. They possess the necessaries, and even the comforts of life, almost in as great plenty as their masters. Their work is easy and their food luxurious compared with the class of labourers. And their sense of dependence is weakened by the conscious power of changing their masters, if they feel themselves offended. Thus comfortably situated at present, what are their prospects in marrying? Without knowledge or capital, either for business, or farming, and unused and therefore unable, to earn a subsistence by daily labour, their only refuge seems to be a miserable alehouse, which certainly offers no very enchanting prospect of a happy evening to their lives. By much the greater part, therefore, deterred by this uninviting view of their future situation, content themselves with remaining single where they are.

If this sketch of the state of society in England be near the truth, and I do not conceive that it is exaggerated, it will be allowed that the preventive check to population in this country operates, though with varied force, through all the classes of the community. The same observation will hold true with regard to all old states. The effects, indeed, of these restraints upon marriage are but too conspicuous in the consequent vices that are produced in almost every part of the world, vices that are continually involving both sexes in inextricable unhappiness.

Chapter 5

The positive check to population, by which I mean the check that represses an increase which is already begun, is confined chiefly, though not perhaps solely, to the lowest orders of society.

This check is not so obvious to common view as the other I have mentioned, and, to prove distinctly the force and extent of its operation would require, perhaps, more data than we are in possession of. But I believe it has been very generally remarked by those who have attended to bills of mortality that of the number of children who die annually, much too great a proportion belongs to those who may be supposed unable to give their offspring proper food and attention, exposed as they are occasionally to severe distress and confined, perhaps, to unwholesome habitations and hard labour. This mortality among the children of the poor has been constantly taken notice of in all towns. It certainly does not prevail in an equal degree in the country, but the subject has not hitherto received sufficient attention to enable anyone to say that there are not more deaths in proportion among the children of the poor, even in the country, than among those of the middling and higher classes. Indeed, it seems difficult to suppose that a labourer's wife who has six children, and who is sometimes in absolute want of bread, should be able always to give them the food and attention necessary to support life. The sons and daughters of peasants will not be found such rosy cherubs in real life as they are described to be in romances. It cannot fail to be remarked by those who live much in the country that the sons of labourers are very apt to be stunted in their growth, and are a long while arriving at maturity. Boys that you would guess to be fourteen or fifteen are, upon inquiry, frequently found to be eighteen or nineteen. And the lads who drive plough, which must certainly be a healthy exercise, are very rarely seen with any appearance of calves to their legs: a circumstance which can only be attributed to a want either of proper or of sufficient nourishment.

To remedy the frequent distresses of the common people, the poor laws of England have been instituted; but it is to be feared, that though they may have alleviated a little the intensity of individual misfortune, they have spread the general evil over a much larger surface. It is a subject often started in conversation and mentioned always as a matter of great surprise that, notwithstanding the immense sum that is annually collected for the poor in England, there is still so much distress among them. Some think that the money must be embezzled, others that the church-wardens and overseers consume the greater part of it in dinners. All agree that somehow or other it must be very ill-managed. In short the fact that nearly three millions are collected annually for the poor and yet that their distresses are not removed is the subject of continual astonishment. But a man who sees a little below the surface of things would be very much more astonished if the fact were otherwise than it is observed to be, or even if a collection universally of eighteen shillings in the pound, instead of four, were materially to alter it. I will state a case which I hope will elucidate my meaning.

Suppose that by a subscription of the rich the eighteen pence a day which men earn now was made up five shillings, it might be imagined, perhaps, that they would then be able to live comfortably and have a piece of meat every day for their dinners. But this would be a very false conclusion. The transfer of three shillings and sixpence a day to every labourer would not increase the quantity of meat in the country. There is not at present enough for all to have a decent share. What would then be the consequence? The competition among the buyers in the market of meat would rapidly raise the price from sixpence or sevenpence, to two or three shillings in the pound, and the commodity would not be divided among many more than it is at present. When an article is scarce, and cannot be distributed to all, he that can shew the most valid patent, that is, he that offers most money, becomes the possessor. If we can suppose the competition among the buyers of meat to continue long enough for a greater number of cattle to be reared annually, this could only be done at the expense of the corn, which would be a very disadvantagous exchange, for it is well known that the country could not then support the same population, and when subsistence is scarce in proportion to the number of people, it is of little consequence whether the lowest members of the society possess eighteen pence or five shillings. They must at all events be reduced to live upon the hardest fare and in the smallest quantity.

It will be said, perhaps, that the increased number of purchasers in every article would give a spur to productive industry and that the whole produce of the island would be increased. This might in some degree be the case. But the spur that these fancied riches would give to population would more than counterbalance it, and the increased produce would be to be divided among a more than proportionably increased number of people. All this time I am supposing that the same quantity of work would be done as before. But this would not really take place. The receipt of five shillings a day, instead of eighteen pence, would make every man fancy himself comparatively rich and able to indulge himself in many hours or days of leisure. This would give a strong and immediate check to productive industry, and, in a short time, not only the nation would be poorer, but the lower classes themselves would be much more distressed than when they received only eighteen pence a day.

A collection from the rich of eighteen shillings in the pound, even if distributed in the most judicious manner, would have a little the same effect as that resulting from the supposition I have just made, and no possible contributions or sacrifices of the rich, particularly in money, could for any time prevent the recurrence of distress among the lower members of society, whoever they were. Great changes might, indeed, be made. The rich might become poor, and some of the poor rich, but a part of the society must necessarily feel a difficulty of living, and this difficulty will naturally fall on the least fortunate members.

It may at first appear strange, but I believe it is true, that I cannot by means of money raise a poor man and enable him to live much better than he did before, without proportionably depressing others in the same class. If I retrench the quantity of food consumed in my house, and give him what I have cut off, I then benefit him, without depressing any but myself and family, who, perhaps, may be well able to bear it. If I turn up a piece of uncultivated land, and give him the produce, I then benefit both him and all the members of the society, because what he before consumed is thrown into the common stock, and probably some of the new produce with it. But if I only give him money, supposing the produce of the country to remain the same, I give him a title to a larger share of that produce than formerly, which share he cannot receive without diminishing the shares of others. It is evident that this effect, in individual instances, must be so small as to be totally imperceptible; but still it must exist, as many other effects do, which, like some of the insects that people the air, elude our grosser perceptions.

Supposing the quantity of food in any country to remain the same for many years together, it is evident that this food must be divided according to the value of each man's patent, or the sum of money that he can afford to spend on this commodity so universally in request. (Mr Godwin calls the wealth that a man receives from his ancestors a mouldy patent. It may, I think, very properly be termed a patent, but I hardly see the propriety of calling it a mouldy one, as it is an article in such constant use.) It is a demonstrative truth, therefore, that the patents of one set of men could not be increased in value without diminishing the value of the patents of some other set of men. If the rich were to subscribe and give five shillings a day to five hundred thousand men without retrenching their own tables, no doubt can exist, that as these men would naturally live more at their ease and consume a greater quantity of provisions, there would be less food remaining to divide among the rest, and consequently each man's patent would be diminished in value or the same number of pieces of silver would purchase a smaller quantity of subsistence.

An increase of population without a proportional increase of food will evidently have the same effect in lowering the value of each man's patent. The food must necessarily be distributed in smaller quantities, and consequently a day's labour will purchase a smaller quantity of provisions. An increase in the price of provisions would arise either from an increase of population faster than the means of subsistence, or from a different distribution of the money of the society. The food of a country that has been long occupied, if it be increasing, increases slowly and regularly and cannot be made to answer any sudden demands, but variations in the distribution of the money of a society are not infrequently occurring, and are undoubtedly among the causes that occasion the continual variations which we observe in the price of provisions.

The poor laws of England tend to depress the general condition of the poor in these two ways. Their first obvious tendency is to increase population without increasing the food for its support. A poor man may marry with little or no prospect of being able to support a family in independence. They may be said therefore in some measure to create the poor which they maintain, and as the provisions of the country must, in consequence of the increased population, be distributed to every man in smaller proportions, it is evident that the labour of those who are not supported by parish assistance will purchase a smaller quantity of provisions than before and consequently more of them must be driven to ask for support.

Second, the quantity of provisions consumed in workhouses upon a part of the society that cannot in general be considered as the most valuable part diminishes the shares that would otherwise belong to more industrious and more worthy members, and thus in the same manner forces more to become dependent. If the poor in the workhouses were to live better than they now do, this new distribution of the money of the society would tend more conspicuously to depress the condition of those out of the workhouses by occasioning a rise in the price of provisions.

Fortunately for England, a spirit of independence still remains among the peasantry. The poor laws are strongly calculated to eradicate this spirit. They have succeeded in part, but had they succeeded as completely as might have been expected their pernicious tendency would not have been so long concealed.

Hard as it may appear in individual instances, dependent poverty ought to be held disgraceful. Such a stimulus seems to be absolutely necessary to promote the happiness of the great mass of mankind, and every general attempt to weaken this stimulus, however benevolent its apparent intention, will always defeat its own purpose. If men are induced to marry from a prospect of parish provision, with little or no chance of maintaining their families in independence, they are not only unjustly tempted to bring unhappiness and dependence upon themselves and children, but they are tempted, without knowing it, to injure all in the same class with themselves. A labourer who marries without being able to support a family may in some respects be considered as an enemy to all his fellow-labourers.

I feel no doubt whatever that the parish laws of England have contributed to raise the price of provisions and to lower the real price of labour. They have therefore contributed to impoverish that class of people whose only possession is their labour. It is also difficult to suppose that they have not powerfully contributed to generate that carelessness and want of frugality observable among the poor, so contrary to the disposition frequently to be remarked among petty tradesmen and small farmers. The labouring poor, to use a vulgar expression, seem always to live from hand to mouth. Their present wants employ their whole attention, and they seldom think of the future. Even when they have an opportunity of saving they seldom exercise it, but all that is beyond their present necessities goes, generally speaking, to the ale-house. The poor laws of England may therefore be said to diminish both the power and the will to save among the common people, and thus to weaken one of the strongest incentives to sobriety and industry, and consequently to happiness.

...

To remove the wants of the lower classes of society is indeed an arduous task. The truth is that the pressure of distress on this part of a community is an evil so deeply seated that no human ingenuity can reach it. Were I to propose a palliative, and palliatives are all that the nature of the case will admit, it should be, in the first place, the total abolition of all the present parish-laws. This would at any rate give liberty and freedom of action to the peasantry of England, which they can hardly be said to possess at present. They would then be able to settle without interruption, wherever there was a prospect of a greater plenty of work and a higher price for labour. The market of labour would then be free, and those obstacles removed which, as things are now, often for a considerable time prevent the price from rising according to the demand.

Second, premiums might be given for turning up fresh land, and if possible encouragements held out to agriculture above manufactures, and to tillage above grazing. Every endeavour should be used to weaken and destroy all those institutions relating to corporations, apprenticeships, etc., which cause the labours of agriculture to be worse paid than the labours of trade and manufactures. For a country can never produce its proper quantity of food while these distinctions remain in favour of artisans. Such encouragements to agriculture would tend to furnish the market with an increasing quantity of healthy work, and at the same time, by augmenting the produce of the country, would raise the comparative price of labour and ameliorate the condition of the labourer. Being now in better circumstances, and seeing no prospect of parish assistance, he would be more able, as well as more inclined, to enter into associations for providing against the sickness of himself or family.

Lastly, for cases of extreme distress, county workhouses might be established, supported by rates upon the whole kingdom, and free for persons of all counties, and indeed of all nations. The fare should be hard, and those that were able obliged to work. It would be desirable that they should not be considered as comfortable asylums in all difficulties, but merely as places where severe distress might find some alleviation. A part of these houses might be separated, or others built for a most beneficial purpose, which has not been infrequently taken notice of, that of providing a place where any person, whether native or foreigner, might do a day's work at all times and receive the market price for it. Many cases would undoubtedly be left for the exertion of individual benevolence.

A plan of this kind, the preliminary of which should be an abolition of all the present parish laws, seems to be the best calculated to increase the mass of happiness among the common people of England. To prevent the recurrence of misery, is, alas! beyond the power of man. In the vain endeavour to attain what in the nature of things is impossible, we now sacrifice not only possible but certain benefits. We tell the common people that if they will submit to a code of tyrannical regulations, they shall never be in want. They do submit to these regulations. They perform their part of the contract, but we do not, nay cannot, perform ours, and thus the poor sacrifice the valuable blessing of liberty and receive nothing that can be called an equivalent in return.

Notwithstanding, then, the institution of the poor laws in England, I think it will be allowed that considering the state of the lower classes altogether, both in the towns and in the country, the distresses which they suffer from the want of proper and sufficient food, from hard labour and unwholesome habitations, must operate as a constant check to incipient population.

To these two great checks to population, in all long occupied countries, which I have called the preventive and the positive checks, may be added vicious customs with respect to women, great cities, unwholesome manufactures, luxury, pestilence, and war.

All these checks may be fairly resolved into misery and vice. And that these are the true causes of the slow increase of population in all the states of modern Europe, will appear sufficiently evident from the comparatively rapid increase that has invariably taken place whenever these causes have been in any considerable degree removed.

WILLIAM GODWIN (1756–1836)

William Godwin, Artist: James Northcote (1746–1831), by courtesy of the National Portrait Gallery, London.

William Godwin was in effect an advocate of reform along Bentham left/collectivist lines. He, too, not unlike the Philosophical Radicals whose membership included many of the English Classical economists, sought institutional reform to advance interests, in his case the interests of the masses, as a matter of political justice. Godwin recognized that an increase in the standard of living of the masses, which he hoped his system would engender, might lead to an increase of population of such a magnitude as to reduce that standard to something like a physical minimum of subsistence. The solution of Godwin and his followers to this problem was to project a change in the structure of human action, if not of human nature, specifically the eclipsing of the desire for sex by the development of intellectual pleasures.

Godwin espoused a labor theory of value and his ideas contain the seeds of a theory of exploitation. He believed that property should be held in common, advocated an economy based on small-scale production, and felt that technological advance would reduce production time sufficiently to allow people to further develop their intellectual and moral faculties – all of this culminating in a utopian society that might best be described as "voluntary communism." His work influenced early socialist thinkers such as Robert Owen and Thomas Hodgskin and was remarked upon favorably by Marx.

As noted in the introduction to the excerpts from (and, of course, the full title of) Malthus's *Essay on Population*, it was, in part, Godwin's ideas, first expressed in his *An Enquiry Concerning Political Justice and Its Influence on General Virtue and Happiness* (1793), to which Malthus's *Essay* constituted a response. Godwin's response to Malthus was *Of Population: An Enquiry Concerning the Power of Increase in the Numbers of Mankind*, published in 1820, and it is from this that the following excerpts are taken.

References and further reading

Clark, John P. (1977) *The Philosophical Radicalism of William Godwin*, Princeton: Princeton University Press.

Godwin, William (1793) *An Enquiry Concerning Political Justice and Its Influence on General Virtue and Happiness*, London: Robinson.

Locke, Don (1980) *A Fantasy of Reason: The Life and Thought of William Godwin*, London: Routledge & Kegan Paul.

Marshall, Peter (1987) "Godwin, William," in John Eatwell, Murray Milgate, and Peter Newman (eds), *The New Palgrave: A Dictionary of Economics*, Vol. 2, London: Macmillan, 534–5.

Monro, D.H. (1953) *Godwin's Moral Philosophy*, London: Oxford University Press.

Simon, Julian L. (1998) *The Economics of Population: Classic Writings*, New Brunswick, NJ: Transaction Publishers.

Of Population (1820)*

Preface

It happens to men sometimes, where they had it in their thoughts to set forward and advance some mighty benefit to their fellow creatures, not merely to fail in giving substance and efficacy to the sentiment that animated them, but also to realize and bring on some injury to the party they purposed to serve. Such is my case, if the speculations that have now been current for nearly twenty years, and which had scarcely been heard of before, are to be henceforth admitted, as forming an essential branch of the science of politics.

When I wrote my Enquiry concerning Political Justice, I flattered myself that there was no mean probability that I should render an important service to mankind. ...

The book I produced seemed for some time fully to answer in its effects the most sanguine expectations I had conceived from it. I could not complain that it 'fell dead-born from the press', or that it did not awaken a considerable curiosity among my countrymen. I was never weak enough to suppose, that it would immediately sweep away all error before it, like a mighty influx of the waves of the ocean. I hailed the opposition it encountered, direct and indirect, argumentative and scurrilous, as a symptom (we will suppose, not altogether unequivocal) of the result I so earnestly desired. Among other phenomena of the kind, I hailed the attack of Mr Malthus. I believed, that the Essay on Population, like other erroneous and exaggerated representations of things, would soon find its own level.

In this I have been hitherto disappointed. It would be easy to assign the causes of my disappointment; the degree in which, by the necessity of the case, the theory of this writer flattered the vices and corruption of the rich and great, and the eager patronage it might very naturally be expected to obtain from them: but this makes no part of what it is my purpose to say. Finding therefore, that whatever arguments have been produced against it by others, it still holds on its prosperous career, and has not long since appeared in the impressive array of a Fifth Edition, I cannot be contented to go out of the world, without attempting to put into a permanent form what has occurred to me on the subject. I was sometimes idle enough to suppose, that I had done my part, in producing the book that had given occasion to Mr Malthus's Essay, and that I might safely leave the comparatively easy task, as it seemed, of demolishing the 'Principle of Population', to some one of the men who have risen to maturity since I produced my most considerable performance. But I can refrain no longer. 'I will also answer my part; I likewise will shew my opinion: for I am full of matter; and the spirit within me constraineth me'.

---

* *Of Population: An Enquiry Concerning the Power of Increase in the Numbers of Mankind, Being an Answer to Mr Malthus's Essay on that Subject*, by William Godwin. London: Printed for Longman, Hurst, Rees, Orme and Brown, Paternoster Row, 1820.

This is a task in which I am the more bound to engage, because, as I have said, if the dogmas which are now afloat on the subject of population are to become permanent, I have, instead of contributing as I desired to the improvement of society, become, very unintentionally, the occasion of placing a bar upon all improvements to come, and bringing into discredit all improvements that are past. If Mr Malthus's way of reasoning only tended to the overthrow of what many will call 'the visionary speculations' of the Enquiry concerning Political Justice, the case would have been different. I might have gone to my grave with the disgrace, to whatever that might amount, of having erected castles in the air, for the benefit, not of myself, but of my species, and of then seeing them battered to pieces before my face. But I cannot consent to close my eyes for ever, with the judgment, as the matter now seems to stand, recorded on my tomb, that, in attempting one further advance in the route of improvement, I should have brought on the destruction of all that Solon, and Plato, and Montesquieu, and Sidney, in ancient times, and in a former age, had seemed to have effected for the redemption and the elevation of mankind.

It is not a little extraordinary, that Mr Malthus's book should now have been twenty years before the public, without any one, so far as I know, having attempted a refutation of his main principle. It was easy for men of a generous temper to vent their horror at the revolting nature of the conclusions he drew from his principle; and this is nearly all that has been done. That principle is delivered by him in the most concise and summary manner. He says, that he 'considered it as established in the first six pages. The American increase was related [in three lines]; and the geometrical ratio was proved'. Now, it stands out broadly to the common sense of mankind, that this was proving nothing. Population, and the descent, and increase or otherwise, of one generation of mankind after another, is not a subject of such wonderful simplicity, as to be thus established. It is in reality the complexity and thorniness of the question, that have had the effect of silencing Mr Malthus's adversaries respecting it. They seem with one consent to have shrunk from a topic, which required so much patient investigation. In the midst of this general desertion of the public interest, I have ventured to place myself in the breach. With what success it is for others to judge.

···

I beg leave to repeat one passage here from the ensuing volume, as containing a thought very proper to be presented to the reader in the outset of the enquiry. 'If America had never been discovered, the geometrical ratio, as applied to the multiplication of mankind, would never have been known. If the British colonies had never been planted, Mr Malthus would never have written. The human species might have perished of a long old age, a fate to which perhaps all sublunary things are subject at last, without one statesman or one legislator, through myriads of centuries, having suspected this dangerous tendency to increase, "in comparison with which human institutions, however they may appear to be causes of much mischief to society, are mere feathers"'.

In the following pages I confine myself strictly to Mr Malthus's book, and the question which he has brought under consideration. My bitterest enemy will hardly be able to find in this volume the author of the Enquiry concerning Political Justice. I have scarcely allowed myself to recollect the beautiful visions (if they shall turn out to be visions), which enchanted my soul, and animated my pen, while writing that work. I conceived that any distinct reference to what is there treated of, would be foreign to the subject which is now before me. The investigation of the power of increase in the numbers of mankind, must be interesting to every one to whom the human species and human society appear to be matters of serious concern: and I should have thought that I was guilty of a sort of treason against that interest, if I had unnecessarily obtruded into the discussion any thing that could shock the prejudices, or insult the views, of those whose conceptions of political truth mighty be most different from my own.

···

Enquiry concerning population

Book I: Of the population of Europe, Asia, Africa, and South America, in ancient times and modern times

Chapter I: Introduction

Mr Malthus has published what he calls an Essay on the Principle of Population, by which he undertakes to annul every thing that had previously been received, respecting the views that it is incumbent upon those who preside over political society to cherish, and the measures that may conduce to the happiness of mankind. His theory is evidently founded upon nothing. He says, that 'population, when unchecked, goes on doubling itself every twenty-five years, or increases in a geometrical ratio'. If we ask why we are to believe this, he answers that, 'in the northern states of America, the population has been found so to double itself for above a century and a half successively'. All this he delivers in an oraculous manner. He neither proves nor attempts to prove what he asserts. If Mr Malthus has taken a right view of the question, it is to be hoped that some author will hereafter arise, who will go into the subject and shew that it is so.

Mr Malthus having laid down a theory in this dogmatical manner, a sort of proceeding wholly unworthy of a reflecting nation or an enlightened age, it is time in reality that some one should sweep away this house of cards, and endeavour to ascertain whether anything is certainly known on the subject.

This is the design and the scheme of the present volume. I shall make no dogmatical assertions; or, at least I am sure I will make none respecting the proposition or propositions which form the basis of the subject. I shall call upon my reader for no implicit faith. I shall lay down no positions authoritatively, and leave him to seek for evidence, elsewhere, and as he can, by which they may be established. All that I deliver shall be accompanied by its proofs. My purpose is to engage in a train of patient investigation, and to lay before every one who will go along with me, the facts which satisfy my mind on the subject, and which I am desirous should convey similar satisfaction to the minds of others.

...

The first point then that I have to examine, and which will form the subject of Three of the Six Books into which my treatise is divided, is respecting the Power of Increase in the Numbers of the Human Species, and the Limitations of that Power. ...

The result of our investigations into the subject of population, I believe, will afford some presumption that there is in the constitution of the human species a power, absolutely speaking, of increasing its numbers. Mr Malthus says that the power is equal to the multiplication of mankind by a doubling every twenty-five years, that is, to an increase for ever in a geometrical series, of which the exponent is 2 – a multiplication, which it is difficult for human imagination, or (as I should have thought) for human credulity to follow: and therefore his theory must demand the most tremendous checks [their names in the Essay on Population are vice and misery] to keep the power in that state of neutrality, in which it is perhaps in almost all cases to be found in Europe. I think I shall be able to make out that the power of increase in the numbers of the human species is extremely small. But, be that as it may, it must be exceedingly interesting to assign the Causes by which this Power is Restrained from producing any absolute multiplication, from century to century, in those many countries where population appears to be at a stand: and I have accordingly endeavoured to take the question out of the occult and mystical state in which Mr Malthus has left it. ...

Chapter III: General views as to the alleged increase of mankind

To take a just view of any subject, one rule that is extremely worthy of our attention is, that we should get to a proper distance from it. The stranger to whom we would convey an adequate image of the city of London, we immediately lead to the top of St Paul's Church. And, if I may introduce an allusion to the records of the Christian religion, the devil took our Saviour 'up into an exceeding high mountain', when he would 'shew him all the kingdoms of the world, and the glory of them'.

Mr Malthus has taken his stand upon the reports of Dr Franklin, and Dr Ezra Styles. He repairs with them to the northern parts of the United States of America, and there he sees, or thinks he sees, 'the population doubling itself, for above a century and a half successively, in less than twenty-five years', and that 'from procreation only'. He does not discover an ample population even in this, his favourite country. Far from it. The reason why the population goes on so rapidly in North America is, according to him, because there is 'ample room and verge enough' for almost all the population that can be poured into it. He sees, in his prophetic conception, that country, some centuries hence, full of human inhabitants, even to overflowing, and groaning under the multitude of the tribes shall dwell in it.

Would it not have been fairer to have taken before him the globe of earth at one view, and from thence to have deduced the true 'Principle of Population', and the policy that ought to direct the measures of those who govern the world?

How long the race of man has subsisted, unless we derive our opinions on the subject from the light of revelation, no man knows. The Chinese, and the people of Indostan, carry back their chronology through millions of years. Even if we refer to the Bible, the Hebrew text, and the Samaritan which is perhaps of equal authority, differ most considerably and fundamentally from each other. But Mr Malthus is of the opinion, that, in reasoning on subjects of political economy, we are bound to regulate our ideas by statistical reports, and tables that have been scientifically formed by proficients in that study, and has accordingly confined himself to these.

But, though we know not how long the human race has existed, nor how extensive a period it has had to multiply itself in, we are able to form some rude notions respecting its present state. It has by some persons been made an objection to the Christian religion, that it has not become universal. It would perhaps be fairer, to make it an objection to the 'Principle of Population', as laid down by Mr Malthus, that the earth is not peopled.

If I were to say that the globe would maintain twenty times its present inhabitants, or, in other words, that for every human creature now called into existence, twenty might exist in a state of greater plenty and happiness than with our small number we do at present, I should find no one timid and saturnine enough to contradict me. In fact, he must be a literal and most uninventive speculator, who would attempt to set bounds to the physical powers of the earth to supply the means of human subsistence.

The first thing therefore that would occur to him who should survey 'all the kingdoms of the earth', and the state of their population, would be the thinness of their numbers, and the multitude and extent of their waste and desolate places. If his heart abounded with 'the milk of human kindness', he would not fail to contrast the present state of the globe with its possible state; he would see his species as a little remnant widely scattered over a fruitful and prolific surface, and would weep to think that the kindly and gracious qualities of our mother earth were turned to so little account. If he were more of a sober and reasoning, than of a tender and passionate temper, perhaps he would not weep, but I should think he would set himself seriously to enquire, how the populousness of nations might be increased, and the different regions of the globe replenished with a numerous and happy race.

Dr Paley's observations on this head are peculiarly to the purpose. 'The quantity of happiness', he says, 'in any given district, although it is possible it may be increased, the number of inhabitants remaining the same, is chiefly and most naturally affected by alteration of the numbers: consequently, *the decay of population is the greatest evil that a state can suffer*; and the improvement of it is the object, which ought in all countries to be aimed at, in preference to every other political purpose whatsoever'.

Such has been the doctrine, I believe, of every enlightened politician and legislator since the world began. But Mr Malthus has placed this subject in a new light. He thinks that there is a possibility that the globe of earth may at some time or other contain more human inhabitants than it can subsist; and he has therefore written a book, the direct tendency of which is to keep down the numbers of mankind. He has no consideration for the millions and millions of men, who might be conceived as called into existence, and made joint partakers with us in such happiness as a sublunary existence, with liberty and improvement, might impart; but, for the sake of a future possibility, would shut against them once for all the door of existence.

He says indeed, 'The difficulty, so far from being remote, is imminent and immediate. At every period during the progress of cultivation, from the present moment to the time when the whole earth was become like a garden, the distress for want of food would be constantly pressing on all mankind'. He adds it is true in this place, 'if they were equal'. But these words are plainly unnecessary, since it is almost the sole purpose of his book to shew, that, in all old established countries, 'the population is always pressing hard against the means of subsistence'.

This however – I mean the distress that must always accompany us in every step of our progress – is so palpably untrue, that I am astonished that any man should have been induced by the love of paradox, and the desire to divulge something new, to make the assertion. There is no principle respecting man and society more certain, than that every man in a civilized state is endowed with the physical power of producing more than shall suffice for his own subsistence. This principle lies at the foundation of all the history of all mankind. If it were otherwise, we should be all cultivators of the earth. We should none of us ever know the sweets of leisure: and all human science would be contained in the knowledge of seed-time and harvest. But no sooner have men associated in tribes and nations, than this great truth comes to be perceived, that comparatively a very small portion of labour on the part of the community, will subsist the whole. Hence it happens that even the farmer and the husbandman have leisure for their religion, their social pleasures, and their sports; and hence it happens, which is of infinitely more importance in the history of the human mind, that, while a minority of the community are employed in the labours indispensably conducive to the mere subsistence of the whole, the rest can devote themselves to art, to science, to literature, to contemplation, and even to all the wanton refinements of sensuality, luxury, and ostentation.

What is it then, we are naturally led to ask, that causes any man to starve, or prevents him from cultivating the earth, and subsisting upon its fruits, so long as there is a portion of soil in the country in which he dwells, that has not been applied to the producing as much of the means of human subsistence, as it is capable of producing? Mr Malthus says, it is ' "*the Law of Nature*". After the public notice which I have proposed, if any man chose to marry, without a prospect of being able to support a family, he should have the most perfect liberty to do so. Though to marry, in this case, is in my opinion clearly an immoral act, yet it is not one which society can justly take upon itself to prevent or punish. To the *punishment of Nature* therefore he should be left'. And elsewhere, 'A man who is born into a world already possessed, if he cannot get subsistence from his parents, and if the society do not want his labour, has no claim of right to the smallest portion of food, and in fact has no business to be where he is. At *Nature's mighty feast* there is no vacant cover for him. *She* tells him to be gone, and will quickly execute *her own* orders'.

Never surely was there so flagrant an abuse of terms, as in this instance. Mr Malthus is speaking of England, where there are many thousands of acres wholly uncultivated, and perhaps as many more scarcely employed in any effectual manner to increase the means of human subsistence;

for these passages occur in chapters of his Essay where he is treating of our Poor-laws, and the remedies that might be applied to the defects he imputes to them. I grant him then, that it is *Law* which condemns the persons he speaks of to starve. So far we are agreed. This Law Mr Malthus may affirm to be just, to be wise, to be necessary to the state of things as we find them. All this would be open to fair enquiry. Great and cogent no doubt are the reasons that have given so extensive a reign to this extreme inequality. But it is not *the Law of Nature*. It is *the Law of very artificial life*. It is the Law which 'heaps upon some few with vast excess' the means of every wanton expence and every luxury, while others, some of them not less worthy, are condemned to pine in want.

Compare this then with Mr Malthus's favourite position, in opposition to what he calls 'the great error under which Mr. Godwin labours', that 'political regulations and the established administration of property are in reality light and superficial causes of mischief to society, in comparison with those which result from the *Laws of Nature*'.

But to return, and resume the point with which this chapter commenced. If Mr Malthus's doctrine is true, why is the globe not peopled? If the human species has so strong a tendency to increase, that, unless the tendency were violently and calamitously counteracted, they would everywhere 'double their numbers in less than twenty-five years', and that for ever, how comes it that the world is a wilderness, a wide and desolate place, where men crawl about in little herds, comfortless, unable from the dangers of free-booters, and the dangers of wild beasts to wander from climate to climate, and without that mutual support and cheerfulness which a populous earth would most naturally afford? The man on the top of St Paul's would indeed form a conception of innumerable multitudes: but he who should survey 'all the kingdoms of the world', would receive a very different impression. On which side then lies the evidence? Do the numbers of mankind actually and in fact increase or decrease? If mankind has so powerful and alarming a tendency to increase, how is it that this tendency no where shews itself in general history? Mr Malthus and his followers are reduced to confess the broad and glaring fact that mankind do not increase, but he has found out a calculation, a geometrical ratio, to shew that they ought to do so, and then sits down to write three volumes, assigning certain obscure, vague, and undefinable causes, why his theory and the stream of ancient and modern history are completely at variance with each other.

Chapter IV: General view of the arguments against the increase of mankind

Mr Malthus's theory is certainly of a peculiar structure, and it is somewhat difficult to account for the success it has met with.

The subject is population.

It has been agreed among the best philosophers in Europe, especially from the time of Lord Bacon to the present day, that the proper basis of all our knowledge respecting man and nature, respecting what has been in times that are past, and what may be expected in time to come, is experiment. This standard is peculiarly applicable to the subject of population.

Mr Malthus seems in one respect fully to concur in this way of viewing the subject. There are two methods of approaching the question, the first, by deriving our ideas respecting it from the volumes of sacred writ, and the second, by having recourse to such enumerations, statistical tables, and calculations, as the industry of mere uninspired men has collected; and Mr Malthus has made his election for the latter. Dr Robert Wallace, an able writer on these subjects, whose works have lately engaged in a considerable degree the attention of curious enquirers, has taken the opposite road. He begins his 'Dissertation on the Numbers of Mankind in Ancient and Modern Times', printed in 1758, with the position that the whole human race is descended 'from a single pair', and, taking that for the basis of his theory, proceeds to calculate the periods of the multiplication of mankind.

Mr Malthus, on the contrary reposes throughout his Essay on the pure basis of human experience and unenlightened human reason; and I have undertaken to write a refutation of his theories. He has chosen his ground; and I follow him to the contest. He had made no allusion to Adam and Eve, and has written just as any speculator in political economy might have done, to whom the records of the Bible were unknown. If there is any thing irreverend in this, to Mr Malthus, and not to me, the blame is to be imputed. He has constructed his arguments upon certain *data*, and I have attempted nothing more than the demolishing of those arguments. If any one shall be of opinion that the whole question is in the jurisdiction of another court, the Treatise I am writing has nothing to do with this. I design nothing more than an investigation of mere human authorities, and an examination of the theories of the Essay on Population; and I leave the question in all other respects as I found it. To return.

It will appear, I think, in the course of our discussion, that population is a subject with which mankind as yet are very little acquainted. But let us first recollect what it is that we are supposed to know. And I will first state those things which are admitted by Mr Malthus, and which appear to make very little for the support of his system.

The globe we inhabit may be divided into the Old World and the New. Our knowledge of the history of Europe and Asia extends backward some thousand years. We know a little of the history of Africa. America was discovered about three hundred years ago, but has not in many of its parts been by any means so long a place of reception for European colonies. Mr Malthus does not venture to carry his appeal on the subject of population there, farther back than one hundred and fifty years.

Well then, how stands the question of population in the Old World? Mr Malthus freely and without hesitation admits, that on this side of the globe population is, and has long been, at a stand: he might safely have added that it has not increased as far back as any authentic records of profane history will carry us. He brings forward some memorable examples of a striking depopulation: he might have added many more: he would certainly have found it difficult to produce an example equally unequivocal, of an increase of population, in any quarter of the Old World.

As to South America, and the indigenous inhabitants of North America, it is hardly to be disputed, and Mr Malthus is very ready to admit, that they have sustained a melancholy diminution since the voyage of Columbus.

Such then is, so far, the foundation of our knowledge, as afforded us by experience, on the subject of population. Mr Malthus has brought forward an exception to all this, which I shall hereafter take occasion fully to examine, in a certain tract of the globe, now known by the name of the United States of America, and he affirms this exception to spread itself over a period of one hundred and fifty years. The entire foundation of his work lies in one simple sentence: 'In the Northern States of America, the population has been found to double itself for above a century and a half successively, in less than twenty-five years'.

The pith of Mr Malthus's book therefore, and a bolder design has seldom entered into the mind of man, is to turn the exception into the rule, and the whole stream of examples in every other case, into exceptions, that are to be accounted for without detracting from the authority of the rule.

The Essay on Population is the most oddly constructed, of any book, pretending to the character of science, that was perhaps ever given to the world.

...

The strength of Mr Malthus's writing wholly depends upon his intrenching himself in general statements. If we hope for any victory over him, it must be by drawing him out of his stronghold, and meeting him upon the fair ground of realities.

The hypothesis of the Essay on Population is this. The human species doubles itself in the United States of America every twenty-five years: therefore it must have an inherent tendency so to double itself: therefore it would so double itself in the Old World, were not the increase intercepted by causes which have not yet sufficiently engaged the attention of political enquirers.

To clear up this point let us consider how many children may be allowed to a marriage, upon the supposition that the object is barely to keep the numbers of the human species up to their present standard. In the first place it is clear, that every married pair may be allowed two upon an average, without any increase to the population, nay, with the certainty of diminution if they fall short of this. In the next place it is unquestionable, that every child that is born, does not live to years of maturity, so as to be able to propagate the kind; for this condition is necessary, the children who die in their nonage plainly contributing nothing to the keeping up the numbers of our species. I should have thought therefore, that we might safely allow of three children to every marriage, without danger of overstocking the community. It will hereafter appear that all political economists allow four, it being the result of various censuses and tables of population, that one-half of the born die under years of maturity. To this number of children to be allowed to every marriage upon an average, the purpose being barely to keep up the numbers of our species to the present standard, something must be added, in consideration of the known fact, that every man and woman do not marry, and thus put themselves in the road for continuing their species.

When Mr Malthus therefore requires us to believe in the geometrical ratio, or that the human species has a natural tendency to double itself every twenty-five years, he does nothing less in other words, than require us to believe that every marriage among human creatures produces upon an average, including the prolific marriages, those in which the husband or wife die in the vigour of their age or in the early years of their union, those in which the prolific power seems particularly limited, and the marriages that are totally barren, eight children.

All this Mr Malthus requires us to believe, because he wills it. Let it never again be made one of the reproaches of the present day, that we are fallen upon an age of incredulity. I am sure no false prophet, in the darkest ages of ignorance, could ever boast of a greater number of hoodwinked and implicit disciples, than Mr Malthus in this enlightened period.

How comes it, that neither this author, nor any one for him, has looked into this view of the question? There are such things as registers of marriages and births. To these it was natural for Mr Malthus to have recourse for a correlative argument to support his hypothesis. The writer of the Essay on Population has resorted to certain statements of the population of the United States, and from them has inferred that the number of its citizens have doubled every twenty-five years, and as he adds, 'by procreation only': that is, in other words, as we have shown, that every marriage in America, and by parity of reasoning, in all other parts of the world, produces upon an average eight children. For the difference between the United States and the Old World does not, I presume, lie in the superior fecundity of their women, but that a greater number of children are cut off in the Old World in years of nonage, by vice and misery. We double very successfully (if they double) in the first period; but we do not, like them, rear our children, to double over again in the second. Naturally therefore he would have produced a strong confirmation of his hypothesis, by shewing from the registers of different parts of the world, or of different countries of Europe, that every marriage does upon an average produce eight children: and if he had done this, I think he would have saved me the trouble of writing this volume. Something however has been done in the way of collating the registers of marriages and births; and of this I shall make full use in my Second Book.

It may however be objected, that there are two ways in which an increase of population may be intercepted; either by the number of children who shall perish in their nonage, through the powerful agency, as Mr Malthus informs us, of vice and misery; or by certain circumstances which shall cause a smaller number to be born: it may not therefore be merely by the ravages of an extensive mortality, that population in the Old World is kept down to its level.

Mr Malthus himself has furnished me with a complete answer to this objection. In the first edition of his book he sets out with what he called 'fairly making two *postulata:* first, that food is necessary to the existence of man: secondly, that the passion between the sexes is necessary, and will always remain nearly in its present state'.

This indeed is one of the 'passages, which the author has expunged in the later editions of his book, that he might not inflict an unnecessary violence upon the feelings of his readers', or, as he himself expresses it, is one of the places, in which, he 'has endeavoured to soften some of the harshest conclusions of his first Essay – in doing which he hopes he has not violated the principles of just reasoning'. But, as Mr Malthus has retained to the last all the conclusions drawn from these *postudata*, and as his argument respecting the impracticability of a permanent state of equality among human beings, founded upon the parity of these two propositions, stands in the Fifth Edition *verbatim* as it stood in the first, I cannot myself consent to his withdrawing his premises, at the same time that he retains the inferences built upon them.

Again: in compliance with 'the feelings of certain readers', Mr Malthus has added in his subsequent editions, to the two checks upon population, namely vice and misery, as they stood in the first, a third which he calls moral restraint. But then he expressly qualifies this by saying, 'the principle of moral restraint has undoubtedly in past ages operated with very inconsiderable force'; subjoining at the same time his protest against 'any opinion respecting the probable improvement of society, in which we are not borne out by the experience of the past'.

It is clearly therefore Mr Malthus's doctrine that population is kept down in the Old World, not by a smaller number of children being born among us, but by the excessive number of children that perish in their nonage through the instrumentality of vice and misery.

Let us then proceed to illustrate this proposition, in its application to our own beloved country of England. We will take its present population at ten millions. Of this population we will suppose five millions to be adults. There must then, according to the statement of Dr Franklin and other calculators, be ten millions of children, born and to be born from these five millions of adults, to give us a chance of keeping up the race of Englishmen. Of these ten millions five millions must be expected to die in their nonage, according to the constitution and course of nature. Surely this, together with the incessant uninterrupted mortality of the middle-aged, and of the more ancient members of society, may be regarded as sufficiently rendering the globe we inhabit 'a universe of death'.

But Mr Malthus demands from us, by virtue of his geometrical ratio, ten millions of children more than our unsuspecting ancestors ever dreamed of, that is, eight children for every pair of adults. I say eight, because, if in countries where they have room and every facility for rearing their children, two perish in their nonage out of the first four, there can be no reason that I can apprehend, why as many should not perish out of the second four. Thus it appears that, for every five millions that grow up to the estate of man and woman, twenty millions of children are born, of which fifteen millions, every where in the Old World, perish in their infancy. The first five millions of those who die in this manner, constitute a mortality that we must be contented to witness, since such, it seems, is the condition of our existence. But the next ten millions I should call a sort of superfetation of alternate births and deaths, purely for the benefit of the geometrical ratio.

But where is the record of all this? In most civilized countries some sort of register is kept of births, marriages, and deaths. I believe no trace of these additional births which Mr Malthus has introduced to our acquaintance, is anywhere to be found. Were all these children sent out of the world, without so much as the ceremonies of baptism? Were they exposed among the wilds of Mount Taygetus, or cast into the Barathrum, or hurled from the Tarpeian rock, or carelessly thrown forth, as Mr Malthus says the Chinese infants are in the streets of Peking? For my own part, I am disposed to require some further evidence on the subject, than merely to be told they must have been born and have died, in defiance of all received evidence on the subject, because such is the inference that follows from the principles of the Essay on Population.

In reality, if I had not taken up the pen with the express purpose of confuting all the errors of Mr Malthus's book, and of endeavouring to introduce other principles, more cheering, more favourable to the best interests of mankind, and better prepared to resist the inroads of vice and misery, I might close my argument here, and lay down the pen with this brief remark, that, when this author shall have produced from any country, the United States of North America not excepted, a register of marriages and births, from which it shall appear that there are on an average eight births to a marriage, then, and not till then, can I have any just reason to admit his doctrine of the geometrical ratio.

HENRY THORNTON (1760–1815)

Henry Thornton, engraving by James Ward after John Hoppner, by courtesy of the National Portrait Gallery, London.

Henry Thornton was a successful London banker and a Member of Parliament, and, as MP, devoted a great deal of effort to British currency and banking issues, including the controversy surrounding the Bank of England's suspension of the convertability of bank notes into gold as a response to the financial instability resulting from England's wars with France in the late eighteenth and early nineteenth centuries.

Thornton was, along with David Ricardo, a significant player in the debate that was known as "the bullion controversy." Thornton was on the "bullionist" side of this debate; that is, he was among the group that believed that the inflation that Britain was experiencing was caused by monetary expansion. The Bullion Report of a Select Committee of the House of Commons (1810), of which Committee Thornton was a prominent member, came down on the bullionist side, recommending the resumption of gold payments by the Bank of England to slow the rate of monetary expansion.

Thorton's *Inquiry Into the Nature and Effects of the Paper Credit of Great Britain* is regarded by some as the most significant work on monetary theory prior to Wicksell's *Interest and Prices* (1898) and, at the very least, puts him on a par with Hume in terms of insights into the workings of the monetary system during the classical period. Thornton's book analyzes the home and international effects of expansions and contractions in the money supply, emphasizing the link from money supply, through interest rates, to prices as well as the effect of the velocity of circulation and how this velocity differs across credit instruments.

References and further reading

Blaug, Mark, ed. (1991) *Henry Thornton (1760–1815), Jeremy Bentham (1748–1832), James Lauderdale (1759–1839), Simonde de Sismondi (1773–1842)*, Aldershot: Edward Elgar Publishing.

Cannan, Edwin, ed. (1919) *The Paper Pound of 1797–1821: The Bullion Report*, London P.S. King & Son.

Corry, B.A. (1962) *Money, Saving and Investment in British Economics, 1800–1850*, New York: St Martin's Press.

Hicks, J.R. (1967) "Thornton's Paper Credit," in J.R. Hicks (ed.), *Critical Essays in Monetary Theory*, London: Oxford University Press.

Laidler, David (1987) "Thornton, Henry," in John Eatwell, Murray Milgate, and Peter Newman (eds), *The New Palgrave: A Dictionary of Economics*, Vol. 4, London: Macmillan, 633–5.

Peake, Charles F. (1978) "Henry Thornton and the Development of Ricardo's Economic Thought," *History of Political Economy* 10 (Summer): 193–212.

Reisman, D.A. (1971) "Henry Thornton and Classical Monetary Economics," *Oxford Economic Papers* 23 (March): 70–89.

Skaggs, Neil T. (1995) "Henry Thornton and the Development of Classical Monetary Economics," *Canadian Journal of Economics* 28 (November): 1212–27.

Viner, Jacob (1937) *Studies in the Theory of International Trade*, New York: Harper & Row.

Wood, Geoffrey E. (1995) "The Quantity Theory in the 1980s: Hume, Thornton, Friedman and the Relation Between Money and Inflation," in Mark Blaug *et al.* (eds), *The Quantity Theory of Money: From Locke to Keynes and Friedman*, Aldershot: Edward Elgar Publishing.

An Enquiry into the Nature and Effects of the Paper Credit of Great Britain (1802)*

Chapter III

Of circulating Paper – of Bank Notes – of Bills Considered as circulating Paper – different Degrees of Rapidity in the Circulation of different Sorts of circulating Medium, and of the same Sort of circulating Medium at different Times. – Error of Dr A. Smith. – Difference in the Quantities wanted for effecting the Payments of a Country in Consequence of this Difference of Rapidity. – Proof of this taken from Events of 1793. – Fallacy involved in the Supposition that Paper Credit might lie abolished.

We proceed next to speak of circulating paper, and first of *Notes payable to Bearer on Demand*, whether issued by a public bank or by a private banker.

When confidence rises to a certain height in a country, it occurs to some persons, that profit may be obtained by issuing notes, which purport to be exchangeable for money; and which, through the known facility of thus exchanging them, may circulate in its stead; a part only of the money, of which the notes supply the place, being kept in store as a provision for the current payments. On the remainder interest is gained, and this interest constitutes the profit of the issuer. Some powerful and well accredited company will probably be the first issuers of paper of this sort, the numerous proprietors of the company exerting their influence for the sake of the dividends which they expect, in giving currency to the new paper credit. The establishment of a great public bank has a tendency to promote the institution of private banks. The public bank, obliged to provide itself largely with money for its own payments, becomes a reservoir of gold to which private banks may resort with little difficulty, expence, or delay, for the supply of their several necessities.

Dr A. Smith, in his chapter on Paper Credit, considers the national stock of money in the same light with those machines and instruments of trade which require a certain expence, first, to erect, and afterwards to support them. And he proceeds to observe, that the substitution of paper, in the room of gold and silver coin, serves to replace a very expensive instrument of commerce with one much less costly, and sometimes equally convenient. 'Thus', he says, 'a banker, by issuing 100,000 *l.* in notes, keeping 20,000 *l.* in hand for his current payments, causes 20,000 *l.* in gold and silver to perform all the functions which 100,000 *l.* would otherwise have performed; in

---

* *An Enquiry Into the Nature and Effects of the Paper credit of Great Britan*, by Henry Thornton. London: Printed for J. Hatchard, Bookseller to the Queen, Piccadilly; and Messrs. F. and C. Rivington, St Paul's Church Yard, 1802. Extracted from *An Enquiry Into the Nature and Effects of the Paper Credit of Great Britain (1802) by Henry Thornton, Together With His Evidence Given Before the Committees of Secrecy of the Two Houses of Parliament in the Bank of England, March and April, 1797, Some Manuscript Notes, and His Speeches on the Bullion Report, May 1811*, Edited with an Introduction by F.A. v. Hayek, London: George Allen & Unwin Ltd., 1939. Reprinted New York: Augustus M. Kelley, 1962.

consequence of which, 80,000 *l*. of gold and silver can be spared, which will not fail to be exchanged for foreign goods, and become a new fund for a new trade, producing profit to the country.'

Dr Smith, although he discusses at some length the subject of Paper Circulation, does not at all advert to the tendency of bills of exchange to spare the use of bank paper, or to their faculty of supplying its place in many cases.

In the former chapter it was shewn that bills, though professedly drawn for the purpose of exchanging a debt due to one person for a debt due to another, are, in fact, created rather for the sake of serving as a discountable article, and of forming a provision against contingencies; and that, by being at any time convertible into cash (i.e. into either money or bank notes) they render that supply of cash which is necessary to be kept in store much less considerable.

But they not only spare the use of ready money; they also occupy its place in many cases. Let us imagine a farmer in the country to discharge a debt of 10 *l*. to his neighbouring grocer, by giving to him a bill for that sum, drawn on his cornfactor in London for grain sold in the metropolis; and the grocer to transmit the bill, he having previously indorsed it, to a neighbouring sugar-baker, in discharge of a like debt; and the sugar-baker to send it, when again indorsed, to a West India merchant in an outport, and the West India merchant to deliver it to his country banker, who also indorses it, and sends it into further circulation. The bill in this case will have effected five payments exactly as if it were a 10 *l*. note payable to the bearer on demand. It will, however, have circulated in consequence chiefly of the confidence placed by each receiver of it in the last indorser, his own correspondent in trade; whereas, the circulation of a bank note is owing rather to the circumstance of the name of the issuer being so well known as to give to it an universal credit. A multitude of bills pass between trader and trader in the country in the manner which has been described; and they evidently form, in the strictest sense, a part of the circulating medium of the kingdom.

Bills, however, and especially those which are drawn for large sums, may be considered as in general circulating more slowly than either gold or bank notes, and for a reason which it is material to explain. Bank notes, though they yield an interest to the issuer, afford none to the man who detains them in his possession; they are to him as unproductive as guineas. The possessor of a bank note, therefore, makes haste to part with it. The possessor of a bill of exchange possesses, on the contrary, that which is always growing more valuable. The bill, when it is first drawn, is worth something less than a bank note, on account of its not being due until a distant day; and the first receiver of it may be supposed to obtain a compensation for the inferiority of its value in the price of the article with which the bill is purchased. When he parts with it, he may be considered as granting to the next receiver a like compensation, which is proportionate to the time which the bill has still to run. Each holder of a bill has, therefore, an interest in detaining it.

Bills, it is true, generally pass among traders in the country without there being any calculation or regular allowance of discount; the reason of which circumstance is, that there is a generally understood period of time for which those bills may have to run, which, according to the custom of traders, are accepted as current payment. If any bill given in payment has a longer time than usual to run, he who receives it is considered as so far favouring the person from whom he takes it; and the favoured person has to compensate for this advantage, not, perhaps, by a recompence of the same kind accurately calculated, but in the general adjustment of the pecuniary affairs of the two parties.

This quality in bills of exchange (and it might be added of interest notes, etc.) of occupying the place of bank paper, and of also throwing the interest accruing during their detention into the pocket of the *holder*, contributes greatly to the use of them. The whole trading world may be considered as having an interest in encouraging them. To possess some article which, so long as it is detained, shall produce a regular interest, which shall be subject to no fluctuations in price, which, by the custom of commerce, shall pass in certain cases as a payment, and shall likewise be convertible into ready money by the sacrifice of a small discount, is the true policy of the merchant. Goods will not serve this purpose, because they do not grow more valuable by detention; nor stocks, because, though they yield an interest, they fluctuate much in value, and, also, because the expence of brokerage is incurred in selling them, not to mention the inconveniences arising from the circumstance of their being transferable only in the books of the Bank of England. Stocks, however, by being at all times a saleable and ready money article, are, to a certain degree, held by persons in London on the same principle as bills, and serve, therefore, in some measure, like bills, if we consider these as a discountable article, to spare the use of bank notes. Exchequer bills will not fully answer the purpose, because there is a commission on the sale of these, as on the sale of stocks; and because, not to speak of some other inferior objections to them, they fluctuate, in some small degree, in price.

Bills, since they circulate chiefly among the trading world, come little under the observation of the public. The amount of bills in existence may yet, perhaps, be at all times greater than the amount of all the bank notes of every kind, and of all the circulating guineas.

The amount of what is called the circulating medium of a country has been supposed by some to bear a regular proportion to the quantity of trade and of payments. It has, however, been shewn, that such part of the circulating medium as yields an interest to the holder will effect much fewer payments, in proportion to its amount, than the part which yields to the holder no interest. A number of country bank notes, amounting to 100 *l.*, may, for instance, effect on an average one payment in three days; while a bill of 100 *l.* may, through the disposition of each holder to detain it, effect only one payment in nine days.

There is a passage in the work of Dr Adam Smith which serves to inculcate the error of which I have been speaking; a passage on which it may be useful to comment with some particularity. He says, 'The whole paper money of *every kind* which can *easily* circulate in any country, never can exceed the value of the gold and silver of which it supplies the place, or which (the commerce being supposed the same) would circulate there, if there was no paper money.'

Does Dr Smith mean to include, in his idea of 'the *whole* paper money of *every kind* which can easily circulate', all the bills of exchange of a country, or does he not? And does he also include interest notes, exchequer bills, and India bonds, and those other articles which very much resemble bills of exchange? In an earlier part of his chapter he has this observation – 'There are different sorts of paper money; but the circulating notes of banks and bankers are the species which is best known, and which seems best adapted for this purpose.' We are led to judge by this passage, and also by the term 'paper money of *every kind*' in the passage quoted before, that it was his purpose to include bills of exchange; on the other hand, if *all* the bills of exchange of a country are to be added to the bank notes which circulate, it becomes then so manifest, that the whole of the paper must be more than equal to the amount of the money which would circulate if there were no paper, that we feel surprised that the erroneousness of the position did not strike Dr Smith himself. He introduces, indeed, the qualifying word 'easily'; he speaks of 'the whole paper money of every kind which can *easily* circulate'. But this term, as I apprehend, is meant only to refer to an easy, in contradistinction to a forced, paper circulation; for it is on the subject of a forced circulation that a great part of his observations turn. He seems, on the other hand, to have paid no regard to the distinction on which I have dwelt, of a more slow and a more rapid circulation; a thing which is quite different from an easy and a difficult circulation. He appears, in short, not at all to have reflected how false his maxim is rendered (if laid down in the terms which he has used) both by the different degrees of rapidity of circulation which generally belong to the two different classes of paper of which I have spoken, and also by the different degrees of rapidity which may likewise belong to the circulation of the same kinds of paper, and even of the same guineas, at different times.

The error of Dr Smith, then, is this: – he represents the whole paper, which can easily circulate when there are no guineas, to be the same in quantity with the guineas which would circulate if there were no paper, whereas, it is the quantity not of 'the thing which circulates', that is, of the thing which is *capable* of circulation, but of the actual circulation which should rather be spoken of as the same in both cases. The quantity of circulating paper, that is, of paper capable of circulation, may be great, and yet the quantity of actual circulation may be small, or vice versa. The same note may either effect ten payments in one day, or one payment in ten days, and one note, therefore, will effect the same payments in the one case, which it would require a hundred notes to effect in the other.

I have spoken of the different degrees of rapidity in the circulation of *different kinds* of paper, and of the consequent difference of the quantity of each which is wanted in order to effect the same payments. I shall speak next of the different degrees of rapidity in the circulation of the *same* mediums at *different times*: and, first, of bank notes.

The causes which lead to a variation in the rapidity of the circulation of bank notes may be several. In general, it may be observed, that a high state of confidence serves to quicken their circulation, and this happens upon a principle which shall be fully explained. It must be premised, that by the phrase a more or less quick circulation of notes will be meant a more or less quick circulation of the whole of them on an average. Whatever encreases that reserve, for instance, of Bank of England notes which remains in the drawer of the London banker as his provision against contingencies, contributes to what will here be termed the less quick circulation of the whole. Now a high state of confidence contributes to make men provide less amply against contingencies. At such a time, they trust, that if the demand upon them for a payment, which is now doubtful and contingent, should actually be made, they shall be able to provide for it at the moment; and they are loth to be at the expence of selling an article, or of getting a bill discounted, in order to make the provision much before the period at which it shall be wanted. When, on the contrary, a season of distrust arises, prudence suggests, that the loss of interest arising from a detention of notes for a few additional days should not be regarded.

It is well known that guineas are hoarded, in times of alarm, on this principle. Notes, it is true, are not hoarded to the same extent; partly because notes are not supposed equally likely, in the event of any general confusion, to find their value, and partly because the class of persons who are the holders of notes is less subject to weak and extravagant alarms. In difficult times, however, the disposition to hoard, or rather to be largely provided with Bank of England notes, will, perhaps, prevail in no inconsiderable degree.

This remark has been applied to Bank of England notes, because these are always in high credit; and it ought, perhaps, to be chiefly confined to these. They constitute the coin in which the great mercantile payments in London, which are payments on account of the whole country, are effected. If, therefore, a difficulty in converting bills of exchange into notes is apprehended, the effect both on bankers, merchants, and tradesmen, is somewhat the same as the effect of an apprehension entertained by the lower class of a difficulty in converting Bank of England notes or bankers' notes into guineas. The apprehension of the approaching difficulty makes men eager to do that today, which otherwise they would do tomorrow.

The truth of this observation, as applied to Bank of England notes, as well as the importance of attending to it, may be made manifest by adverting to the events of the year 1793, when, through the failure of many country banks, much general distrust took place. The alarm, the first material one of the kind which had for a long time happened, was extremely great. It does not appear that the Bank of England notes, at that time in circulation, were fewer than usual. It is certain, however, that the existing number became, at the period of apprehension, insufficient for giving punctuality to the payments of the metropolis, and it is not to be doubted, that the insufficiency must have arisen, in some measure, from that slowness in the circulation of notes, naturally attending an alarm, which has been just described. Every one fearing lest he should not have his notes ready when the day of payment should come, would endeavour to provide himself with them somewhat beforehand. A few merchants, from a natural though hurtful timidity, would keep in their own hands some of those notes, which, in other times, they would have lodged with their bankers; and the effect would be, to cause the same quantity of bank paper to transact fewer payments, or, in other words, to lessen the rapidity of the circulation of notes on the whole, and thus to encrease the number of notes wanted. Probably, also, some Bank of England paper would be used as a substitute for country bank notes suppressed.

The success of the remedy which the parliament administered, denotes what was the nature of the evil. A loan of exchequer bills was directed to be made to as many mercantile persons, giving proper security, as should apply. It is a fact, worthy of serious attention, that the failures abated greatly, and mercantile credit began to be restored, not at the period when the exchequer bills were actually delivered, but at a time antecedent to that æra. It also deserves notice, that though the failures had originated in an extraordinary demand for guineas, it was not any supply of gold which effected the cure. That fear of not being able to obtain guineas, which arose in the country, led, in its consequences, to an extraordinary demand for bank notes in London; and the want of bank notes in London became, after a time, the chief evil. The very expectation of a supply of exchequer bills, that is, of a supply of an article which almost any trader might obtain, and which it was known that he might then sell, and thus turn into bank notes, and after turning into bank notes might also convert into guineas, created an idea of general solvency. This expectation cured, in the first instance, the distress of London, and it then lessened the demand for guineas in the country, through that punctuality in effecting the London payments which it produced, and the universal confidence which it thus inspired. The sum permitted by parliament to be advanced in exchequer bills was five millions, of which not one half was taken. Of the sum taken, no part was lost. On the contrary, the small compensation, or extra interest, which was paid to government for lending its credit (for it was mere credit, and not either money or bank notes that the government advanced), amounted to something more than was necessary to defray the charges, and a small balance of profit accrued to the public. For this seasonable interference, a measure at first not well understood and opposed at the time, chiefly on the ground of constitutional jealousy, the mercantile as well as the manufacturing interests of the country were certainly much indebted to the parliament, and to the government.

That a state of distrust causes a slowness in the circulation of *guineas*, and that at such a time a greater quantity of money will be wanted in order to effect only the same money payments, is a position which scarcely needs to be proved. Some observations, however, on this subject may not be useless. When a season of extraordinary alarm arises, and the money of the country in some measure disappears, the guineas, it is commonly said, are hoarded. In a certain degree this assertion may be literally true. But the scarcity of gold probably results chiefly from the circumstance of a considerable variety of persons, country bankers, shopkeepers, and others, augmenting, some in a smaller and some in a more ample measure, that supply which it had been customary to keep by them. The stock thus enlarged is not a fund which its possessor purposes, in no case, to diminish, but a fund which, if he has occasion to lessen it, he endeavours, as he has opportunity, to replace. It is thus that a more slow circulation of guineas is occasioned; and the slower the circulation, the greater the quantity wanted, in order to effect the same number of money payments.

Thus, then, it appears, that the sentiment which Dr Smith leads his readers to entertain, namely, that there is in every country a certain fixed quantity of paper, supplying the place of gold, which is all that 'can easily circulate' (or circulate without being *forced* into circulation), and which is all (for such, likewise, seems to be the intended inference) that should ever be allowed to be sent into circulation, is, in a variety of respects, incorrect. The existence of various hoards of gold in the coffers of bankers, and of the Bank of England, while there are no corresponding hoards of paper, would of itself forbid anything like accurate comparison between them. Many additional, though smaller, circumstances might be mentioned as contributing to prevent the quantity of notes which will circulate from being the same as the quantity of gold which would circulate if there were no notes; such as their superior convenience in a variety of respects, the facility of sending them by post, the faculty which they have of being either used as guineas, or of supplying the place of bills of exchange, and furnishing a remittance to distant places.

There is a further objection to the same remark of Dr Smith. It would lead an uninformed person to conceive, that the trade of a country, and of this country in particular, circumstanced as it now is, might be carried on altogether by guineas, if bank notes of all kinds were by any means annihilated. It may already have occurred, that if bank paper were abolished, a substitute for it would be likely to be found, to a certain degree, in bills of exchange; and that these, on account of their slower circulation, must, in that case, be much larger in amount than the notes of which they would take the place. But further, if bills and bank notes were extinguished, other substitutes than gold would unquestionably be found. Recourse would be had to devices of various kinds by which men would save themselves the trouble of counting, weighing, and transporting guineas, in all the larger operations of commerce, so that the amount of guineas brought into use would not at all correspond with the amount of the bills and notes suppressed. Banks would be instituted, not of the description which now exist, but of that kind and number which should serve best to spare both the trouble of gold, and the expence incurred by the loss of interest upon the quantity of it in possession. Merely by the transfer of the debts of one merchant to another, in the books of the banker, a large portion of what are termed cash payments is effected at this time without the use of any bank paper, and a much larger sum would be thus transferred, if guineas were the only circulating medium of the country. Credit would still exist; credit in books, credit depending on the testimony of witnesses, or on the mere verbal promise of parties. It might not be paper credit; but still it might be such credit as would spare, more or less, the use of guineas. It might be credit of a worse kind, less accurately dealt out in proportion to the desert of different persons, and therefore, in some instances, at least, still more extended; it might be credit less contributing to punctuality of payments, and to the due fulfillment of engagements; less conducive to the interests of trade, and to the cheapening of articles; and it would, perhaps, also be credit quite as liable to interruption on the occasion of any sudden alarm or material change in the commercial prospects and circumstances of the country.

Chapter VIII

Of the Tendency of a too great Issue of Bank Paper to produce an Excess of the Market Price above the Mint Price of Gold. – Of the Means by which it creates this Excess, namely, by its Operation on the Price of Goods and on the Course of Exchange. – Errors of Dr A. Smith on the Subject of excessive Paper. – Of the Manner in which the Limitation of the Quantity of the Bank of England Paper serves to limit the Quantity and sustain the Value of all the Paper of the Kingdom.

A third objection commonly made to country banks, is, the influence which their notes are supposed to have in raising the price of articles.

By the principles which shall be laid down in this chapter, I propose to prove, that, though a general encrease of paper has this tendency, the objection, when applied to the paper of country banks, is particularly ill founded.

It will be necessary, in the discussion which is now about to take place, to join the consideration of two subjects, that of the influence which an enlarged emission of paper has in lifting up the price of commodities, and that of its influence, also, in producing an excess of the market price above the mint price of gold, and in thus exposing the bank to failure, and the country to considerable inconvenience. It is through the medium of the enhanced price of commodities that I conceive the ill effect on the mint price of gold to be brought about. The discussion of these topics will best be introduced by a statement of the principle which regulates the value of all the articles of life.

The price of commodities in the market is formed by means of a certain struggle which takes place between the buyers and the sellers. It is commonly said, that the price of a thing is regulated by the proportion between the supply and the demand. This is, undoubtedly, true, and for the following reason. If the supply of an article or the demand for it is great, it is also known to be great, and if small, it is understood to be small. When, therefore, the supply, for example, is known to be less than the demand, the sellers judge that the buyers are in some degree at their mercy, and they insist on as favourable a price as their power over the buyers is likely to enable them to obtain. The price paid is not at all governed by the equity of the case, but entirely by the degree of command which the one party has over the other. When the demand is less than the supply, the buyers, in their turn, in some degree, command the market, giving not that sum which is calculated to indemnify the seller against loss, but so much only as they think that the seller will accept rather than not sell his article. The question of price is, therefore, in all cases, a question of power, and of power only. It is obvious, that a rise in the price of a scarce commodity will be more or less considerable in proportion as the article is felt to be one of more or less strict necessity.

The principle which has been laid down as governing the price of goods, must be considered as also regulating that of the paper for which they are sold; for it may as properly be said, on the occasion of a sale of goods, that paper is sold for goods, as that goods are sold for paper: thus the sale of a single commodity, as it is called, is a twofold transaction, though not commonly understood to be so: I mean, that the price at which the exchange (or sale) takes place depends on two facts; on the proportion between the supply of the particular commodity and the demand for it, which is one question; and on the proportion, also, between the state of the general supply of the circulating medium and that of the demand for it, which is another.

Paper, moreover (of which I shall here speak as if it were the only circulating medium, it being the only one used in the larger payments), is, to some persons, somewhat in the same manner as bread is to all, an article of necessity. It is necessary to traders, partly because they have come under engagements to make payments which are only to be effected by means of their own previous receipts; and partly because they hold goods which must, within no long time, be sold for money, that is to say, for paper, since a continually growing loss accrues from the detention of them. Paper, therefore, must be bought by the trader; and if there is a difficulty in obtaining it, the buyer of it is brought under the power of the seller, and, in that case, more goods must be given for it.

Let us, now, trace carefully the steps by which an encrease of paper serves to lift up the price of articles. Let us suppose, for example, an encreased number of Bank of England notes to be issued. In such case the traders in the metropolis discover that there is a more than usual facility of obtaining notes at the bank by giving bills for them, and that they may, therefore, rely on finding easy means of performing any pecuniary engagements into which they may enter. Every trader is encouraged by the knowledge of this facility of borrowing, a little to enlarge his speculations; he is rendered, by the plenty of money, somewhat more ready to buy, and rather less eager to sell; he either trusts that there will be a particular profit on the article which is the object of his speculation, or else he judges, that, by extending his general purchases, he shall at least have his share of the ordinary profit of commercial business, a profit which he considers to be proportioned to the quantity of it. The opinion of an encreased facility of effecting payments causes other traders to become greater buyers for the same reason, and at the same time. Thus an inclination to buy is created in all quarters, and an indisposition to sell. Now, since the cost of articles depends on the issue of that general conflict between the buyers and sellers, which was spoken of, it follows, that any circumstance which serves to communicate a greater degree of eagerness to the mind of the one party than to that of the other, will have an influence on price.

It is not necessary to suppose either a monopoly, or a combination, or the least unfairness, to exist, or even large and improper speculations. The encrease in the eagerness of each buyer may be trifling. The zeal to buy, being generally diffused, may, nevertheless, have a sensible operation on price.

That, on the other hand, a reduction of the quantity of paper causes a fall in the price of goods, is scarcely necessary to be proved. It may be useful, however, in some degree, to illustrate this point by facts. I understand, that at the time of the great failure of paper credit in 1795, the price of corn fell, in a few places, no less than 20 or 30 per cent. The fall arose from the necessity of selling corn under which some farmers were placed, in order to carry on their payments. Much of the circulating medium being withdrawn, the demand for it was in those places far greater than the supply; and the few persons, therefore, who were in possession of cash, or of what would pass as cash, having command of the market, obliged the farmers to sell at a price thus greatly reduced.

It was a new and sudden scarcity of cash, not any new plenty of corn, which caused the price of corn to drop. It has been already observed, that some few days antecedent to the suspension of the cash payments of the bank, exchequer bills, as well as stocks, when sold for ready money, that is to say, for bank notes, fell in price. Not many days afterwards, although no material event had occurred except that of the stoppage of the bank, they rose. This fall and rise in the price of government securities evidently did not result from any corresponding fluctuation in the national confidence in them; for the fall took place when the national credit would naturally be the highest, namely, when the bank was as yet paying in cash, and the approaching stoppage was not known; and the rise happened when the national credit would be the lowest, namely, within a few days after that discouraging event. The reason for each of the fluctuations unquestionably was the fluctuation in the quantity of the Bank of England notes, which, as it has since appeared, were, during the day or two which preceded the suspension, about a million less than they were either a short time before or a short time afterwards. The notes being fewer during those few days, the price of them was, at the same time, higher. It was, in fact, therefore, the price of notes which rose, rather than that of stocks which fell, on the days immediately preceding the suspension; and it was the price of notes which a few days afterwards fell, rather than that of stocks which rose.

I shall, for the present, consider the doctrine which has been laid down, as being sufficiently established, namely, that paper fluctuates in price on the same principles as any other article, its value rising as its quantity sinks, and vice versa, or, in other words, that an augmentation of it has a general tendency to raise, and a diminished issue to lower, the nominal cost of commodities, although, partly for reasons which have been already touched upon, and partly for some which shall be hereafter given, an exact correspondence between the quantity of paper and the price of commodities can by no means be expected always to subsist.

The reader possibly may think that, in treating of this subject, I have been mistaking the effect for the cause, an encreased issue of paper being, in his estimation, merely a consequence which follows a rise in the price of goods, and not the circumstance which produces it. That an enlarged emission of paper may often fairly be considered as only, or chiefly, an effect of high prices, is not meant to be denied. It is, however, intended to insist, that, unquestionably, in some cases at least, the greater quantity of paper is, more properly speaking, the cause. A fuller explanation of this apparently difficult and disputable position will be given in the further progress of this work.

I proceed, in the next place, to shew in what manner a general rise in the cost of commodities, whether proceeding from an extravagant issue of paper, or from any other circumstance, contributes to produce an excess of the market price above the mint price of gold.

It is obvious, that, in proportion as goods are rendered dear in Great Britain, the foreigner becomes unwilling to buy them, the commodities of other countries which come into competition with ours obtaining a preference in the foreign market; and, therefore, that in consequence of a diminution of orders from abroad, our exports will be diminished; unless we assume, as we shall find it necessary to do, that some compensation in the exchange is given to the foreigner for the disadvantage attending the purchase of our articles. But not only will our exports lessen in the case supposed; our imports also will encrease: for the high British price of goods will tempt foreign commodities to come in nearly in the same degree in which it will discourage British articles from going out. I mean only, that these two effects (that of a diminished export, and that of an encreased import) will follow, provided that we suppose, what is not supposable, namely, that, at the time when the price of goods is greatly raised in Great Britain, the course of exchange suffers no alteration. For the following reason, I have said that this is not supposable. Under the circumstances which have been described of a diminished export, and an encreased import, the balance of trade must unavoidably turn against us; the consequence of which must be, that the drawers of bills on Great Britain in foreign countries will become more in number than the persons having occasion to remit bills. This disparity between the number of individuals wanting to draw, and of those wanting to remit, as was remarked in a former chapter, must produce a fall in the price at which the overabundant bills on England sell in the foreign market. The fall in the selling price abroad of bills payable here, will operate as an advantage to the foreign buyer of our commodities in the computation of the exchangeable value of that circulating medium of his own country with which he discharges the debt in Britain contracted by his purchase. It will thus obviate the dearness of our articles: it will serve as a compensation to the foreigner for the loss which he would otherwise sustain by buying in our market. The fall of our exchange will, therefore, promote exportation and encourage importation. It will, in a great degree, prevent the high price of goods in Great Britain from producing that unfavourable balance of trade, which, for the sake of illustrating the subject was supposed to exist.

The compensation thus made to the foreigner for the high British price of all articles is necessary as an inducement to him to take them, somewhat in the same manner as a drawback or bounty on exportation is the necessary inducement to take those particular goods which have been rendered too dear for the foreign market by taxes laid on them in this country. In each case, the British consumer pays the high price, and the foreigner is spared, because otherwise he will not accept out commodities.

The fall in our exchange was just now defined to be an advantage gained in the computation of the exchangeable value of that foreign circulating medium with which the foreigner discharges his debt in Great Britain, a debt paid in the circulating medium of this country. It implies, therefore, a high valuation of his circulating medium, and a low valuation of ours; a low valuation, that is to say, both of our paper and of the coin which is interchanged with it.

Now, when coin is thus rendered cheap, it by no means follows that bullion is rendered cheap also. Coin is rendered cheap through its constituting a part of our circulating medium; but bullion does not constitute a part of it. Bullion is a commodity, and nothing but a commodity; and it rises and falls in value on the same principle as all other commodities. It becomes, like them, dear in proportion as the circulating medium for which it is exchanged is rendered cheap, and cheap in proportion as the circulating medium is rendered dear.

In the case, therefore, which has now been supposed, we are to consider coin as sinking below its proper and intrinsic worth, while bullion maintains its natural and accustomed price. Hence there arises that temptation, which was formerly noticed, either to convert back into bullion and then to export; or, which is the same thing, to export and then convert back into bullion; or, which is also the same thing, to convert back into bullion, and then sell to the bank, at the price which would be gained by exportation, that gold which the bank has purchased, and has converted from bullion into coin.

In this manner an encrease of paper, supposing it to be such as to raise the price of commodities in Britain above the price at which, unless there is some allowance afforded in the course of exchange, they will be received in foreign countries, contributes to produce an excess of the market price above the mint price of gold, and to prevent, therefore, the introduction of a proper supply of it into the Bank of England, as well as to draw out of its coffers that coin which the directors of the bank would wish to keep in them.

Dr Smith appears to me to have treated the important subject of the tendency of an excessive paper circulation to send gold out of a country, and thus to embarrass its banking establishments, in a manner which is particularly defective and unsatisfactory. It is true, that he blames the Bank of England for having contributed to bring on itself, during several successive years, a great expence in buying gold through a too great circulation of its paper; and that he also charges the Scotch banks with having had, through their excessive issues, a share in producing this evil. Thus, therefore, he seems to give to his reader some intimation of the tendency of an excessive issue of paper to create an excess of the market price above the mint price of gold.

It appears, however, in some degree, from the passage in question, though much more clearly from other parts of his work, that he considers every permanent excess, whether of the market price above the mint price, or of the mint price above the market price of gold, as entirely referable to 'something in the state of the coin'.

In one place he remarks, that a high price of bullion arises from the difference between the weight of our more light and that of our more heavy guineas; the value of the gold in the heavier guineas, as he represents the case, determining the general current value of both the lighter and the heavier pieces of coin; and the superior quantity of gold in the heavier guineas constituting, therefore, so much profit on the melting of those heavier pieces: a supposition manifestly erroneous, and contradicted by experience, for it implies that the excess of the market price above the mint price of gold both never is and never can be greater than the excess of the weight of the heavier above the lighter guineas, and, also, that the price of bullion cannot fluctuate while the state of our coinage remains in all respects the same. We have lately experienced fluctuations in our exchange, and correspondent variations in the market price, compared with the mint price of gold, amounting to no less than 8 or 10 per cent, the state of our coinage continuing, in all respects, the same.

Dr Smith recommends a seignorage, as tending to raise the value both of the lighter and heavier coin; and thus, also, to diminish, if not destroy, the excess of the market price above the mint price of gold.

It is remarkable, that this Writer does not, in any degree, advert either to that more immediate cause (a fall of our exchanges), from which I have, in this as well as in a former chapter, described the excess in question, as, in all cases, arising, or to that more remote one on which I have lately dwelt, namely, a too high price of goods, which produces a fall of our exchanges.

Dr Smith does not, in any of his observations on this subject, proceed sufficiently, as I conceive, on the practical principle of shewing how it is through the medium of prices (of the prices of goods in general, and of bullion in particular, compared with the price of the current circulating medium), that the operations of importing and exporting gold are brought about. He considers our coin as going abroad simply in consequence of our circulation at home being over full. Payment in coin, according to his doctrine, is demanded of every bank for as much of its paper as is excessive, because the excessive paper can neither be sent abroad nor turned to any use at home; whereas, when it is changed into coin, the coin may be transmitted to a foreign part, and may there be advantageously employed.

The reader will perceive, that, according to the principle which I have endeavoured to establish, coin does not merely leave the country because, the circulation being full, no use can be found at home for additional circulating medium; but that every encrease of paper has been represented as enhancing the price of goods, which advanced price of goods affords employment to a larger quantity of circulating medium, so that the circulation can never be said to be over full.

This advanced price of goods is the same thing as a reduced price of coin; the coin, therefore, in consequence of its reduced price, is carried out of the country for the sake of obtaining for it a better market. The heavier pieces, undoubtedly, will be preferred, if there is a facility of obtaining and transporting them; but the lighter guineas will also be exported, when the state of the exchange shall be sufficiently low to afford a profit on such a transaction. One of the consequences of Dr Smith's mode of treating the subject, is, that the reader is led into the error of thinking, that when, through an excessive issue of paper, gold has been made to flow away from us, the expence of restoring it consists merely in the charge of collecting it and transporting it from the place to which it is gone. It follows, on the contrary, from the principles which I have laid down, that, in order to bring back gold, the expence not only of importing it may be to be incurred, but that also of purchasing it at a loss, and at a loss which may be either more or less considerable: a circumstance of great importance in the question. If this loss should ever become extremely great, the difficulties of restoring the value of our paper might not easily be surmounted, and a current discount or difference between the coin and paper of the country would scarcely be avoidable.

Dr Smith, indeed, represents the expence of bringing back gold as considerable; but he seems to impute the greatness of it to the circumstance of its recurring again and again: and he describes it as continuing to recur in the case of each individual bank, whether in town or country, which persists in the false policy of issuing more paper than is sufficient to fill the circulation of the neighbouring district. I shall here take occasion to notice some great inaccuracies in one part of his reasoning upon this point.

He says, 'A banking company which issues more paper than can be employed in the circulation of the country, and of which the excess is continually returning upon them for payment, ought to encrease the quantity of gold and silver which they keep at all times in their coffers, not only in proportion to this excess, but to a much greater proportion. Suppose, for instance, all the paper of a particular bank, which the circulation of the country can easily absorb, amounts to forty thousand pounds, and the bank keeps usually ten thousand pounds in gold and silver for its occasional demands. If this bank should attempt to circulate forty-four thousand pounds, the excess of four thousand pounds will return as fast as it is issued. Fourteen thousand pounds must then be kept instead of ten thousand pounds, and the bank will gain nothing by the excessive circulation. On the contrary, it will lose the whole expence of continually collecting four thousand pounds in gold and silver, which will be continually going out of its coffers as fast as they are brought in.'

He then adds, 'Had every particular bank always understood and attended to its own interest, the circulation would never have been overstocked with paper money.'

There is, no doubt, some sort of ground for saying that an excess of paper will come back upon the banks which issue it, and that, in coming back, it will involve the issuing banks in expence. Much exception, however might be taken against Dr Smith's mode of estimating the expence which the quantity which would come back would bring upon the issuing banks. But the objection which I shall in the first place, urge against the remark of Dr Smith, is, that, even granting it to be just, it can be just only in a case which can scarcely ever occur among the country banks of this kingdom. I mean, that it can apply solely to the case of a single bank of which the paper circulates exclusively through a surrounding district: it obviously cannot hold in the case of many banks, the paper of all of which circulates in the same district.

In order to explain this clearly, let us make the following supposition. Let us imagine the circulation of country bank paper which a certain district will bear to be one hundred thousand pounds, and ten banks to be in that district, each usually circulating and able to keep in circulation ten thousand pounds. Let us also suppose an excessive issue of four thousand pounds, and let us allow the effect of this on the ten banks to be that which Dr Smith describes, a point which might certainly be disputed, namely, that a necessity will arise for *always* keeping (for this is what Dr Smith's language implies) an additional stock of gold amounting to exactly four thousand pounds, and also that a reiterated expence will be incurred (Dr Smith does not say how frequently reiterated) in collecting and transporting these four thousand pounds of gold. Still it must be observed, that we may suppose the issue of the four thousand pounds excessive paper to be made by some one only of the ten banks, while the charge incurred by such issue may be divided among them all. It may, therefore, on Dr Smith's own principles, answer to one of several banks emitting paper which circulates in the same place, to issue the paper which is considered by him as excessive, and the practice of doing so may be owing to the country banker's too well knowing his own interest, and not, as Dr Smith supposes, to his too ill understanding it.

But the case which I have supposed has been put merely by way of illustration. When many banks issue notes circulating over the same district, it is impossible to say whose paper constitutes the excess. Whatever temptation to excess exists, must be a general one. It is, however, counteracted not only by the charge of transporting gold, on which alone Dr Smith dwells, but likewise by all the other charges, as well as by all the risks to which country bank notes subject the issuers; not to mention the difficulty of finding a channel through which a quantity of paper much larger than common can be sent by the country bank into circulation.

Dr Smith supposes, in the passage which has just been quoted, that, when there is an excessive circulation of country bank paper, the excess returns upon the banks to be exchanged for gold and silver. The fact is, that it returns to be exchanged not for gold and silver only, but either for gold and silver, or for bills on London. A bill on London is an order to receive in London, after a certain interval, either gold or Bank of England notes. This order imposes on the country banker the task of providing a fund in London sufficient to answer his draft: it serves, however, to spare that expence of transporting gold, as well as to lessen that necessity of maintaining a stock of guineas, which Dr Smith assumes to be the consequence of every excessive emission of notes, and to be the certain means, if bankers do but understand their interest, of limiting their issue.

The remark which has just been made derives particular importance from the circumstances of the period through which we have passed. For, if the usual means of preventing an excess of country bank notes were nothing else than the liability of the issuers to be called upon for a money payment of them, it might fairly be assumed, that, at a time when the money payment of them has been suspended, we must necessarily have been exposed to the greatest inundation of country paper, and to a proportionate depreciation of it. The unbounded issue of country bank notes has been restrained by the obligation under which country bankers have considered themselves to be of granting bills on London; that is to say, orders to receive in London Bank of England paper in exchange for their notes, if required to do so: and it is certain that they would be required to do so whenever the quantity of their notes should be much greater in proportion to the occasion for them, than the quantity of the notes of the Bank of England in proportion to the occasion for those notes.

For the sake of explaining this, let it be admitted, for a moment, that a country bank has issued a very extraordinary quantity of notes. We must assume these to be employed by the holders of them in making purchases in the place in which alone the country bank paper passes, namely, in the surrounding district. The effect of such purchases, according to the principles established in this Chapter, must be a great local rise in the price of articles. But to suppose a great and merely local rise, is to suppose that which can never happen or which, at least, cannot long continue to exist, for every purchaser will discover that he can buy commodities elsewhere at a cheaper rate, and he will not fail to procure them in the quarter in which they are cheap, and to transport them to the spot in which they are dear, for the sake of the profit on the transaction. In order that he may be enabled to do this, he will demand to have the notes which pass current in the place in which we have supposed goods to have been rendered dear by the extraordinary emission of paper, converted into the circulating medium of the place in which goods are cheap: he will, therefore, require to have his country bank note turned into a Bank of England note, or into a bill on London, which is nearly the same thing, provided Bank of England notes are fewer in proportion to the occasion for them than the country bank notes; that is to say, provided Bank of

England notes have less lifted up the price of goods in London than country bank notes have lifted up the price of goods in the country.

This point may be still more fully illustrated in the following manner. Let us imagine a mercantile house to consist of two branches, the one placed in the metropolis, the other in the country, and each branch to be accustomed to make certain payments in the spot in which it is situated, each, however, to be in the habit of borrowing as largely as it is able, the one of a neighbouring country bank, the other of the Bank of England, and of applying these loans to the joint use of the trading concern. Let us next suppose an extraordinary facility of borrowing at the country bank to rise, while the opportunities of obtaining loans at the Bank of England remain the same. In such case the mercantile house, provided its London payments continue to bear the same proportion as before to its country payments, which will hardly fail to be the case, will exchange some part of its encreased loans in the country, consisting in country bank notes, for bills on London, or, in other words, for Bank of England notes. It will thus adjust, with the greatest nicety, the quantity of London and of country paper to the amount of the pecuniary demands upon it in each quarter; and, in doing so, it will contribute to prevent the supply of notes in either place from becoming greater in proportion to the demand than in the other. What has been supposed of one house, may be supposed of many similar ones; and not only of houses of the particular description which has been spoken of, but also of the several independent establishments in the two distant places which have pecuniary transactions together, and have an interest in accommodating each other. Their general operations, of a pecuniary kind, must be such as always to check a local rise in the price of commodities in either place, while it is as yet so small as to be scarcely perceptible. In this manner, therefore, the exchangeableness of country paper for London paper will never fail very nearly to equalize the value of them both. It is, moreover, important clearly to point out that their value will be equalized, or nearly equalized, not by a tendency in the London paper to partake in a low value which the country paper has acquired in consequence of its not being limited by any voluntary act of the issuers; nor by a tendency in each to approximate in value to the other; but by a tendency in the country paper to take exactly the high value which the London paper bears in consequence of its being restricted by the issuers. That this must be the case is plain, from the remark which has just been made; for it has been shewn, that the country paper, however it may fail to be limited in quantity by any moderation or prudence of the issuers, becomes no less effectually limited through the circumstance of their being compelled by the holders to exchange as much of it as is excessive for the London paper which is limited; which is limited, I mean, in consequence of a principle of limitation which the directors of the Bank of England have prescribed to themselves.

The country paper, let it then be observed, does not add any thing to the quantity of the London paper, for the effectual limitation of the London paper is the great point, which it must be borne in mind, that we have assumed. The country paper, therefore, does not in any degree diminish the price of the London paper; for its price must remain fixed so long as its quantity continues fixed, supposing, as we do in our present argument, that the demand for it is the same. It has been proved, however, that the country paper is rendered, by its exchangeableness with the London paper, almost exactly equal to it in value. It is, then, rendered almost exactly equal in value to a paper of which the value is completely sustained. Thus, therefore, the limitation of the supply of the single article of London paper, of which, however, we are taking for granted that the demand continues the same, is the means both of sustaining the value of London paper, and also of sustaining the value as well as limiting the quantity of the whole paper of the country.

It is, however, necessary here to point out to the reader, that, in the immediately preceding observations, we have assumed certain facts to exist, for the sake of stating clearly a general principle. It will be the object of a succeeding chapter to shew in what respects the case which has been supposed differs from the actual one.

DAVID RICARDO (1772–1823)

David Ricardo, by courtesy of The Warren J. Samuels Portrait Collection at Duke University.

David Ricardo was born in London and, at age 14, went to work for his father, who was a member of the London Stock Exchange. A falling out with his family over his marriage, outside of his Jewish faith, to a Quaker woman at age 21 caused him to go into business for himself. His success was such that, at age 42, he was able to retire from the business world and spend much of the remainder of his life in study and writing and, from 1819, holding a seat in the House of Commons and participating actively in parliamentary debates.

Ricardo's interest in economics was stimulated by his reading of Smith's *Wealth of Nations* in 1799 while staying for a time at the Bath spa. A decade later, he was very involved in the bullion controversy – including penning his classic tract on *The High Price of Bullion* – and, later, in the debate over the corn laws. Indeed, from about 1815 onward, he devoted the largest part of his effort to working on issues in political economy, culminating in the publication of his *Principles of Political Economy and Taxation* in 1817.

There are important commonalities between Ricardo's *The High Price of Bullion* and Thornton's *Paper Credit*. Both individuals took a bullionist approach to the controversy of the day, and their positions were validated by the report of the Committee. While Thornton's analysis represents a more nuanced view of the central issues of monetary theory and policy, it also more or less disappeared from the scholarly debates for a century. It was Ricardo's ideas that set the tone for nineteenth-century monetary theory.

References and further reading*

Cannan, Edwin, ed. (1919) *The Paper Pound of 1797–1821: The Bullion Report*, London: P.S. King & Son.

Corry, B.A. (1962) *Money, Saving and Investment in British Economics, 1800–1850*, New York: St Martin's.

De Vivo, G. (1987) "Ricardo, David," in John Eatwell, Murray Milgate, and Peter Newman (eds), *The New Palgrave: A Dictionary of Economics*, Vol. 3, London: Macmillan, 183–98.

Sayers, R.S. (1953) "Ricardo's Views on Monetary Questions," *Quarterly Journal of Economics* 67 (February): 30–49.

Viner, Jacob (1937) *Studies in the Theory of International Trade*, New York: Harper & Row.

---

* Further references to Ricardo's life and work can be found in the introduction to the subsequent reading from his *Principles of Political Economy and Taxation*.

The High Price of Bullion (1810)*

The precious metals employed for circulating the commodities of the world, previously to the establishment of banks, have been supposed by the most approved writers on political economy to have been divided into certain proportions among the different civilized nations of the earth, according to the state of their commerce and wealth, and therefore according to the number and frequency of the payments which they had to perform. While so divided they preserved everywhere the same value, and as each country had an equal necessity for the quantity actually in use, there could be no temptation offered to either for their importation or exportation.

Gold and silver, like other commodities, have an intrinsic value, which is not arbitrary, but is dependent on their scarcity, the quantity of labour bestowed in procuring them, and the value of the capital employed in the mines which produce them.

'The quality of utility, beauty, and scarcity', says Dr Smith, 'are the original foundation of the high price of those metals, or of the great quantity of other goods for which they can every where be exchanged. This value was antecedent to, and independent of their being employed as coin, and was the quality which fitted them for that employment'.

If the quantity of gold and silver in the world employed as money were exceedingly small, or abundantly great, it would not in the least affect the proportions in which they would be divided among the different nations – the variation in their quantity would have produced no other effect than to make the commodities for which they were exchanged comparatively dear or cheap. The smaller quantity of money would perform the functions of a circulating medium, as well as the larger. Ten millions would be as effectual for that purpose as one hundred millions. Dr Smith observes, 'that the most abundant mines of the precious metals would add little to the wealth of the world. A produce of which the value is principally derived from its scarcity is necessarily degraded by its abundance'.

If in the progress towards wealth, one nation advanced more rapidly than the others, that nation would require and obtain a greater proportion of the money of the world. Its commerce, its commodities, and its payments, would increase, and the general currency of the world would be divided according to the new proportions. All countries therefore would contribute their share to this effectual demand.

In the same manner, if any nation wasted part of its wealth, or lost part of its trade, it could not retain the same quantity of circulating medium which it before possessed. A part would be exported, and divided among the other nations till the usual proportions were re-established.

While the relative situation of countries continued unaltered, they might have abundant commerce with each other, but their exports and imports would on the whole be equal. England

* *The High Price of Bullion, a Proof of the Depreciation of Bank Notes*, London: Printed for John Murray, 32, Fleet Street; And Sold by Every Other Bookseller in Town and Country 1810.

might possibly import more goods from, than she would export to, France, but she would in consequence export more to some other country, and France would import more from that country; so that the exports and imports of all countries would balance each other; bills of exchange would make the necessary payments, but no money would pass, because it would have the same value in all countries.

If a mine of gold were discovered in either of these countries, the currency of that country would be lowered in value in consequence of the increased quantity of the precious metals brought into circulation, and would therefore no longer be of the same value as that of other countries. Gold and silver, whether in coin or in bullion, obeying the law which regulates all other commodities, would immediately become articles of exportation; they would leave the country where they were cheap, for those countries where they were dear, and would continue to do so, as long as the mine should prove productive, and till the proportion existing between capital and money in each country before the discovery of the mine, were again established, and gold and silver restored every where to one value. In return for the gold exported, commodities would be imported; and though what is usually termed the balance of trade would be against the country exporting money or bullion, it would be evident that she was carrying on a most advantageous trade, exporting that which was no way useful to her, for commodities which might be employed in the extension of her manufactures, and the increase of her wealth.

If instead of a mine being discovered in any country, a bank were established, such as the Bank of England, with the power of issuing its notes for a circulating medium; after a large amount had been issued either by way of loan to merchants, or by advances to government, thereby adding considerably to the sum of the currency, the same effect would follow as in the case of the mine. The circulating medium would be lowered in value, and goods would experience a proportionate rise. The equilibrium between that and other nations would only be restored by the exportation of part of the coin.

The establishment of the Bank and the consequent issue of its notes therefore, as well as the discovery of the mine, operate as an inducement to the exportation either of bullion or of coin, and are beneficial only in as far as that object may be accomplished. The Bank substitutes a currency of no value for one most costly, and enables us to turn the precious metals (which, though a very necessary part of our capital, yield no revenue) into a capital which will yield one. Dr A. Smith compares the advantages attending the establishment of a bank to those which would be obtained by converting our highways into pastures and corn-fields, and procuring a road through the air. The highways, like the coin, are highly useful, but neither yield any revenue. Some people might be alarmed at the specie leaving the country, and might consider that as a disadvantageous trade which required us to part with it; indeed the law so considers it by its enactments against the exportation of specie; but a very little reflection will convince us that it is our choice, and not our necessity, that sends it abroad; and that it is highly beneficial to us to exchange that commodity which is superfluous, for others which may be made productive.

The exportation of the specie may at all times be safely left to the discretion of individuals; it will not be exported more than any other commodity, unless its exportation should be advantageous to the country. If it be advantageous to export it, no laws can effectually prevent its exportation. Happily in this case, as well as in most others in commerce where there is free competition, the interests of the individual and that of the community are never at variance.

···

The Bank might continue to issue their notes, and the specie be exported with advantage to the country, while their notes were payable in specie on demand, because they could never issue more notes than the value of the coin which would have circulated had there been no bank.

If they attempted to exceed this amount, the excess would be immediately returned to them for specie; because our currency, being thereby diminished in value, could be advantageously exported, and could not be retained in our circulation. These are the means, as I have already explained, by which our currency endeavours to equalize itself with the currencies of other counties. As soon as this equality was attained, all advantage arising from exportation would cease; but if the Bank assuming, that because a given quantity of circulating medium had been necessary last year, therefore the same quantity must be necessary this, or for any other reason, continued to re-issue the returned notes, the stimulus which a redundant currency first gave to the exportation of the coin would be again renewed with similar effects; gold would be again demanded, the exchange would become unfavourable, and gold bullion would rise, in a small degree, above its mint price, because it is legal to export bullion, but illegal to export the coin, and the difference would be about equal to the fair compensation for the risk.

In this manner if the Bank persisted in returning their notes into circulation, every guinea might be drawn out of their coffers.

...

The Bank would be obliged therefore ultimately to adopt the only remedy in their power to put a stop to the demand for guineas. They would withdraw part of their notes from circulation, till they should have increased the value of the remainder to that of gold bullion, and consequently to the value of the currencies of other countries. All advantage from the exportation of gold bullion would then cease, and there would be no temptation to exchange bank-notes for guineas.

In this view of the subject, then, it appears, that the temptation to export money in exchange for goods, or what is termed an unfavourable balance of trade, never arises but from a redundant currency. But Mr Thornton, who has considered this subject very much at large, supposes that a very unfavourable balance of trade may be occasioned to this country by a bad harvest, and the consequent importation of corn; and that there may be at the same time an unwillingness in the country, to which we are indebted, to receive our goods in payment; the balance due to the foreign country must therefore be paid out of that part of our currency, consisting of coin, and that hence arises the demand for gold bullion and its increased price. He considers the Bank as affording considerable accommodation to the merchants, by supplying with their notes the void occasioned by the exportation of the specie.

...

It is evident, then, that a depreciation of the circulating medium is the necessary consequence of its redundance; and that in the common state of the national currency this depreciation is counteracted by the exportation of the precious metals.

Such, then, appear to me to be the laws that regulate the distribution of the precious metals throughout the world, and which cause and limit their circulation from one country to another, by regulating their value in each. But before I proceed to examine on these principles the main object of my enquiry, it is necessary that I should shew what is the standard measure of value in this country, and of which, therefore, our paper currency ought to be the representative, because it can only be by a comparison to this standard that its regularity, or its depreciation, may be estimated.

No permanent measure of value can be said to exist in any nation while the circulating medium consists of two metals, because they are constantly subject to variation in value with respect to each other. However exact the conductors of the mint may be, in proportioning the relative value of gold to silver in the coins, at the time when they fix the ratio, they cannot prevent one of these metals from rising, while the other remains stationary, or falls in value. Whenever this happens, one of the coins will be melted to be sold for the other. Mr Locke, Lord Liverpool, and many other writers, have ably considered this subject, and have all agreed, that the only remedy for the evils in the currency proceeding from this source, is the making of only one of the metals the standard measure of value. Mr Locke considered silver as the most proper metal for this purpose, and proposed that gold coins should be left to find their own value, and pass for a greater or lesser number of shillings, as the market price of gold might vary with respect to silver.

Lord Liverpool, on the contrary, maintained that gold was not only the most proper metal for a general measure of value in this country, but that, by the common consent of the people, it had become so, was so considered by foreigners, and that it was best suited to the increased commerce and wealth of England.

…

While the circulating medium consists, therefore, of coin undebased, or of paper-money immediately exchangeable for undebased coin, the exchange can never be more above, or more below, par, than the expences attending the transportation of the precious metals. But when it consists of a depreciated paper-money, it necessarily will fall according to the degree of the depreciation.

The exchange will, therefore, be a tolerably accurate criterion by which we may judge of the debasement of the currency, proceeding either from a clipped coinage, or a depreciated paper-money.

It is observed by Sir James Stuart, 'That if the foot measure was altered at once over all England, by adding to it, or taking from it, any proportional part of its standard length, the alteration would be best discovered, by comparing the new foot with that of Paris, or of any other country, which had suffered no alteration'.

'Just so, if the pound sterling, which is the English unit, shall be found any how changed; and if the variation it has met with be difficult to ascertain, because of a complication of circumstances; the best way to discover it will be to compare the former and the present value of it, with the money of other nations which has suffered no variation. This the exchange will perform with the greatest exactness'. The Edinburgh reviewers, in speaking of Lord King's pamphlet, observe, that 'it does not follow because our imports always consist partly of bullion, that the balance of trade is therefore permanently in our favour. Bullion', they say, 'is a commodity, for which, as for every other, there is a varying demand; and which, exactly like any other, may enter the catalogue either of imports or exports; and this exportation or importation of bullion will not affect the course of exchange in a different way from the exportation or importation of any other commodities'.

No person ever exports or imports bullion without first considering the rate of exchange. It is by the rate of exchange that he discovers the relative value of bullion in the two countries between which it is estimated. It is therefore consulted by the bullion-merchant in the same manner as the price-current is by other merchants, before they determine on the exportation or importation of other commodities. If eleven florins in Holland contain an equal quantity of pure silver as 20 standard shillings, silver bullion, equal in weight to 20 standard shillings, can never be exported from London to Amsterdam whilst the exchange is at par, or unfavourable to Holland. Some expence and risk must attend its exportation, and the very term par expresses that a quantity of silver bullion, equal to that weight and purity, is to be obtained in Holland by the purchase of a bill of exchange, free of all expence. Who would send bullion to Holland at an expence of 3 or 4 per cent when, by the purchase of a bill at par, he in fact obtains an order for the delivery to his correspondent in Holland of the same weight of bullion which he was about to export?

It would be as reasonable to contend, that when the price of corn is higher in England than on the Continent, corn would be sent, notwithstanding all the charges on its exportation, to be sold in the cheaper market.

…

We may therefore fairly conclude that this difference in the relative value, or, in other words, that this depreciation in the actual value of bank-notes has been caused by the too abundant quantity which the Bank has sent into circulation. The same cause which has produced a difference of from 15 to 20 per cent in bank-notes when compared with gold bullion, may increase it to 50 per cent. There can be no limit to the depreciation which may arise from a constantly increasing quantity of paper. The stimulus which a redundant currency gives to the exportation of the coin has acquired new force, but cannot, as formerly, relieve itself. We have paper-money only in circulation, which is necessarily confined to ourselves. Every increase in its quantity degrades it below the value of gold and silver bullion, below the value of the currencies of other counties.

The effect is the same as that which would have been produced from clipping our coins. If one-fifth were taken off from every guinea, the market price of gold bullion would rise one-fifth above the mint price. Forty-four guineas and a half (the number of guineas weighing a pound, and therefore called the mint price), would no longer weigh a pound, therefore a fifth more than that quantity, or about 56 l. would be the price of a pound of gold, and the difference between the market and the mint price, between 56 l. and 46 l. 14 s. 6 d. would measure the depreciation.

If such debased coin were to continue to be called by the name of guineas, and if the value of gold bullion and all other commodities were rated in the debased coin, a guinea fresh from the mint would be said to be worth 1 l. 5 s. and that sum would be given for it by the illicit trader; but it would not be the value of the new guinea which had increased, but that of the debased guineas which had fallen. This would immediately be evident, if a proclamation were issued, prohibiting the debased guineas from being current but by weight at the mint price of 3 l. 17 s. 10 1/2 d.; this would be constituting the new and heavy guineas, the standard measure of value, in lieu of the clipped and debased guineas. The latter would then pass at their true value, and be called 17 or 18 shilling-pieces. So if a proclamation to the same effect were now enforced, bank-notes would not be less current, but would pass only for the value of the gold bullion which they would purchase. A guinea would then no longer be said to be worth 1 l. 4 s. but a pound note would be current only for 16 or 17 shillings. At present the gold coin is only a commodity, and bank-notes are the standard measure of value, but in that case gold coin would be that measure, and bank-notes would be the marketable commodity.

'It is', says Mr Thornton, 'the maintenance of our general exchanges, or, in other words, it is the agreement of the mint price with the bullion price of gold, which seems to be the true proof that the circulating paper is not depreciated'. ...

It is contended, that the rate of interest, and not the price of gold or silver bullion, is the criterion by which we may, always judge of the abundance of paper-money; that if it were too abundant, interest would fall, and if not sufficiently so, interest would rise. It can, I think, be made manifest, that the rate of interest is not regulated by the abundance or scarcity of money, but by the abundance or scarcity of that part of capital, not consisting of money.

'Money', observes Dr A. Smith, 'the great wheel of circulation, the great instrument of commerce, like all other instruments of trade, though it makes a part, and a very valuable part of the capital, makes no part of the revenue of the society to which it belongs; and though the metal pieces of which it is composed, in the course of their annual circulation, distribute to every man the revenue which properly belongs to him, they make themselves no part of that revenue'.

'When we compute the quantity of industry which the circulating capital of any society can employ, we must always have regard to those parts of it only which consist in provisions, materials, and finished work: the other, which consists in money, and which serves only to circulate those three, must always be deducted. In order to put industry into motion, three things are requisite: materials to work upon, tools to work with, and the wages or recompense for the sake of which the work is done. Money is neither a material to work upon, nor a tool to work with; and though the wages of the workman are commonly paid to him in money, his real revenue, like that of all other men, consists not in money, but in money's worth; not in the metal pieces, but what can be got for them.'

And in other parts of his work, it is maintained, that the discovery of the mines in America, which so greatly increased the quantity of money, did not lessen the interest for the use of it: the rate of interest being regulated by the profits on the employment of capital, and not by the number or quality of the pieces of metal, which are used to circulate its produce.

Mr Hume has supported the same opinion. The value of the circulating medium of every country bears some proportion to the value of the commodities which it circulates. In some countries this proportion is much greater than in others, and varies, on some occasions, in the same country. It depends upon the rapidity of circulation, upon the degree of confidence and credit existing between traders, and above all, on the judicious operations of banking. In England so many means of economizing the use of circulating medium have been adopted, that its value, compared with the value of the commodities which it circulates, is probably (during a period of confidence) reduced to as small a proportion as is practicable.

What that proportion may be has been variously estimated. No increase or decrease of its quantity, whether consisting of gold, silver, or paper-money, can increase or decrease its value above or below this proportion. If the mines cease to supply the annual consumption of the precious metals, money will become more valuable, and a smaller quantity will be employed as a circulating medium. The diminution in the quantity will be proportioned to the increase of its value. In like manner, if new mines be discovered, the value of the precious metals will be reduced, and an increased quantity used in the circulation; so that in either case the relative value of money, to the commodities which it circulates, will continue as before.

If, whilst the Bank paid their notes on demand in specie, they were to increase their quantity, they would produce little permanent effect on the value of the currency, because nearly an equal quantity of the coin would be withdrawn from circulation and exported.

If the Bank were restricted from paying their notes in specie, and all the coin had been exported, any excess of their notes would depreciate the value of the circulating medium in proportion to the excess. If twenty millions had been the circulation of England before the restriction, and four millions were added to it, the twenty-four millions would be of no more value than the twenty were before, provided commodities had remained the same, and there had been no corresponding exportation of coins; and if the Bank were successively to increase it to fifty, or a hundred millions, the increased quantity would be all absorbed in the circulation of England, but would be, in all cases, depreciated to the value of the twenty millions.

I do not dispute, that if the Bank were to bring a large additional sum of notes into the market, and offer them on loan, but that they would for a time affect the rate of interest. The same effects would follow from the discovery of a hidden treasure of gold or silver coin. If the amount were large, the Bank, or the owner of the treasure, might not be able to lend the notes or the money at four, nor perhaps, above 3 per cent; but having done so, neither the notes, nor the money, would be retained unemployed by the borrowers; they would be sent into every market, and would everywhere raise the prices of commodities, till they were absorbed in the general circulation. It is only during the interval of the issues of the Bank, and their effect on prices, that we should be sensible of an abundance of money; interest would, during that interval, be under its natural level; but as soon as the additional sum of notes or of money became absorbed in the general circulation, the rate of interest would be as high, and new loans would be demanded with as much eagerness as before the additional issues.

The circulation can never be over-full. If it be one of gold and silver, any increase in its quantity will be spread over the world. If it be one of paper, it will diffuse itself only in the country where it is issued. Its effects on prices will then be only local and nominal, as a compensation by means of the exchange will be made to foreign purchasers.

To suppose that any increased issues of the Bank can have the effect of permanently lowering the rate of interest, and satisfying the demands of all borrowers, so that there will be none to apply for new loans, or that a productive gold or silver mine can have such an effect, is to attribute a power to the circulating medium which it can never possess. Banks would, if this were possible, become powerful engines indeed. By creating paper-money, and lending it at 3 or 2 per cent under the present market rate of interest, the Bank would reduce the profits on trade in the same proportion; and if they were sufficiently patriotic to lend their notes at an interest no higher than necessary to pay the expences of their establishment, profits would be still further reduced; no nation, but by similar means, could enter into competition with us, we should engross the trade of the world. To what absurdities would not such a theory lead us! Profits can only be lowered by a competition of capitals not consisting of circulating medium. As the increase of bank-notes does not add to this species of capital, as it neither increases our exportable commodities, our machinery, or our raw materials, it cannot add to our profits nor lower interest.

When any one borrows money for the purpose of entering into trade, he borrows it as a medium by which he can possess himself of 'materials, provisions, etc.' to carry on that trade; and it can be of little consequence to him, provided he obtain the quantity of materials, etc. necessary, whether he be obliged to borrow a thousand, or ten thousand pieces of money. If he borrows ten thousand, the produce of his manufacture will be ten times the nominal value of what it would have been, had one thousand been sufficient for the same purpose. The capital actually employed in the country is necessarily limited to the amount of the 'materials, provisions, etc.' and might be made equally productive, though not with equal facility, if trade were carried on wholly by barter. The successive possessors of the circulating medium have the command over this capi-tal: but however abundant may be the quantity of money or of bank-notes; though it may increase the nominal prices of commodities; though it may distribute the productive capital in different proportions; though the Bank, by increasing the quantity of their notes, may enable A to carry on part of the business formerly engrossed by B and C, nothing will be added to the real revenue and wealth of the country. B and C may be injured, and A and the Bank may be gainers, but they will gain exactly what B and C lose. There will be a violent and an unjust transfer of property, but no benefit whatever will be gained by the community.

For these reasons I am of opinion that the funds are not indebted for their high price to the depreciation of our currency. Their price must be regulated by the general rate of interest given for money. If before the depreciation I gave thirty years' purchase for land, and twenty-five for an annuity in the stocks, I can after the depreciation give a larger sum for the purchase of land, without giving more years' purchase, because the produce of the land will sell for a greater nominal value in consequence of the depreciation; but as the annuity in the funds is paid in the depreciated medium, there can be no reason why I should give a greater nominal value for it after than before the depreciation.

If guineas were degraded by clipping to half their present value, every commodity as well as land would rise to double its present nominal value; but as the interest of the stocks would be paid in the degraded guineas, they would, on that account, experience no rise.

The remedy which I propose for all the evils in our currency, is that the Bank should gradually decrease the amount of their notes in circulation until they shall have rendered the remainder of equal value with the coins which they represent, or, in other words, till the prices of gold and silver bullion shall be brought down to their mint price. I am well aware that the total failure of paper credit would be attended with the most disastrous consequences to the trade and commerce of the county, and even its sudden limitation would occasion so much ruin and distress, that it would be highly inexpedient to have recourse to it as the means of restoring our currency to its just and equitable value.

If the Bank were possessed of more guineas than they had notes in circulation, they could not, without great injury to the country, pay their notes in specie, while the price of gold bullion continued greatly above the mint price, and the foreign exchanges unfavourable to us. The excess of our currency would be exchanged for guineas at the Bank and exported, and would be suddenly withdrawn from circulation. Before therefore they can safely pay in specie, the excess of notes must be gradually withdrawn from circulation. If gradually done, little inconvenience would be felt; so that the principle were fairly admitted, it would be for future consideration whether the object should be accomplished in one year or in five. I am fully persuaded that we shall never restore our currency to its equitable state, but by this preliminary step, or by the total overthrow of our paper credit.

If the Bank directors had kept the amount of their notes within reasonable bounds; if they had acted up to the principle which they have avowed to have been that which regulated their issues when they were obliged to pay their notes in specie, namely, to limit their notes to that amount which should prevent the excess of the market above the mint price of gold, we should not have been now exposed to all the evils of a depreciated, and perpetually varying currency.

...

When the order of council for suspending the cash payments became necessary in 1797, the run upon the Bank was, in my opinion, caused by political alarm alone, and not by a superabundant, or a deficient quantity (as some have supposed) of their notes in circulation.

This is a danger to which the Bank, from the nature of its institution, is at all times liable. No prudence on the part of the directors could perhaps have averted it: but if their loans to government had been more limited; if the same amount of notes had been issued to the public through the medium of discounts; they would have been able, in all probability, to have continued their payments till the alarm had subsided. At any rate, as the debtors to the Bank would have been obliged to discharge their debts in the space of sixty days, that being the longest period for which any bill discounted by the Bank has to run, the directors would in that time, if necessary, have been enabled to redeem every note in circulation. It was then owing to the too intimate connection between the Bank and government that the restriction became necessary; it is to that cause too that we owe its continuance.

To prevent the evil consequences which may attend the perseverance in this system, we must keep our eyes steadily fixed on the repeal of the Restriction bill.

The only legitimate security which the public can possess against the indiscretion of the Bank is to oblige them to pay their notes on demand in specie; and this can only be effected by diminishing the amount of bank-notes in circulation till the nominal price of gold be lowered to the mint price.

Here I will conclude; happy if my feeble efforts should awaken the public attention to a due consideration of the state of our circulating medium. I am well aware that I have not added to the stock of information with which the public has been enlightened by many able writers on the same important subject. I have had no such ambition. My aim has been to introduce a calm and dispassionate enquiry into a question of great importance to the state, and the neglect of which may be attended with consequences which every friend of his country would deplore.

JEAN-BAPTISTE SAY (1767–1832)

Jean-Baptiste Say, by courtesy of The Warren J. Samuels Portrait Collection at Duke University.

Jean-Baptiste Say was born to a merchant family in Lyon, France. Much of his career was spent in the private and public sectors, including banking, insurance, newspaper work, and manufacturing, and it was not until 1815 that he began to lecture in political economy. In his later years he was appointed professor of industrial economics, culminating his appointment to the first Chair of Political Economy in France (at the Collège de France, Paris) in 1830.

Say published the first edition of his *Treatise on Political Economy* in 1803. The *Treatise* bears remarkable similarities to Smith's *Wealth of Nations* (which Say had read some fifteen years earlier) and did much to popularize Smith's ideas in particular and classical political economy in general on the European continent and in the United States. Say is often credited with advancing the theory of the role of the entreprenuer within economic activity (although some of this credit would seem to be misplaced, given his relatively narrow view of the entrepreneurial function), and he was an early and forceful advocate of the role of utility and demand in price determination, as against the British classical focus on costs of production. However, it is "Say's Law" of markets for which he is best known.

The "law of the market" with which Say is so closely associated actually seems to have been formulated first by James Mill in his *Commerce Defended* (1808) but is best known in the form given by and with the name of Jean-Baptiste Say (1767–1832). The law has been given several formulations. The conventional statement is that (1) supply creates its own demand. Others are (2) the presence of supply/suppliers in the market *per se* expresses a demand for other goods; (3) supply in the aggregate is its own demand; (4) consumption, in the sense of total use, is coextensive with production; and (5) income equals expenditures, that what is not spent for consumption is also spent, on investment. But in one form or another, Say's Law lies at the heart of classical macroeconomics and was the launching point for Keynes's critique of the classical view in his *General Theory* (1936).

The law has a number of assumptions, including that (1) money is only a medium of exchange – which, if true, would mean that it can only be spent; (2) people have insatiable wants, as to both consumption and investment – which means that there are no limits to spending; (3) the interest rate equates saving and investment – which means that consumption plus saving from one year's income equals consumption plus investment giving rise to the next year's income; and (4) all prices, including the wages of labor, are flexible – which means that all markets clear, without unsold items. The implications from such a construction are that (1) there is neither general overproduction nor general unemployment; (2) the economy always tends to equilibrium at full employment; (3) there is no such thing as a business cycle; and (4) any partial over- and underproduction offset each other and are temporary.

There are several problems with this construction; indeed, the assumptions rule out precisely the ways in which instability can arise. First, money is not only a medium of exchange, it is a store of value, such that people can defer spending and hold money; such holding of money is a leakage from the income stream. Second, although the subtleties of "insatiable wants" lead to no commonly held conclusion, it is abundantly clear that even if people had insatiable wants – to wit, a lust to consume goods and to accumulate capital – there are conditions in which people will currently refrain from consuming more (expectation of falling prices, fear of loss of job, greater uncertainty as to the future) or from investing more (inadequate expected returns, for a variety of possible reasons). Third, it is generally agreed that saving and investment are equated not by the rate of interest but by changes in income itself – the very category which the law concludes will be stable. And fourth, while economists do not agree about and seldom analyze the meaning of "flexible" and "inflexible" prices – which means that most if not all relevant statements are meaningless – some economists believe that prices are basically flexible, some believe they are basically inflexible, and others that prices are relatively flexible upwards and relatively inflexible downwards. The general result is that the assumptions of Say's Law are not correct and do not do what the law would have them do.

Furthermore, the statement that there is no overproduction is both ambiguous and misleading. The problem is not whether there is no general overproduction and/or no general unemployment (all people out of work, or all industries in decline?) but whether there is enough unemployment, etc. to constitute a problem. A typical recession is identified in terms of 7–9 percent unemployment; a depression, in terms of 10 plus percent unemployment.

Moreover, the law misconstrues the nature of the income mechanism, in part by neglecting the roles of changes in spending and in income and in part by neglecting the factors which can generate changes of spending and thereby of income; in short, the factors which can result in what John Maynard Keynes a century later called equilibrium at less than full employment.

Finally, the empirical record amply demonstrates a history of business cycles.

In the following excepts from his *Treatise*, we see Say making the case for utility in value determination and are introduced to his espousal of the ideas that came to be known as "Say's Law."

References and further reading

Baumol, William J. (1977) "Say's (At Least) Eight Laws, Or What Say and James Mill May Really Have Meant," *Economica* 44 (May): 145–62.

Becker, Gary and Baumol, William J. (1960) "The Classical Monetary Theory: The Outcome of the Discussion," in J.J. Spengler and W.R. Allen (eds), *Essays in Economic Thought*, Chicago: Rand McNally.

Gordon, Barry (1965) "Say's Law, Effective Demand, and the Contemporary British Periodicals," *Economica* 32 (November): 438–46.

Keynes, J.M. (1936) *The General Theory of Employment, Interest and Money*, London: Macmillan.

Lange, Oskar (1942) "Say's Law: A Restatement and Criticism," in Oskar Lange, Francis McIntyre, and Theodore, O. Yntema (eds), *Studies in Mathematical Economics and Econometrics: In Memory of Henry Schultz*, Chicago: University of Chicago Press, 49–68.

Sowell, Thomas (1972) *Say's Law: An Historical Analysis*, Princeton: Princeton University Press.

——(1987) "Say, Jean-Baptiste," in John Eatwell, Murray Milgate, and Peter Newman (eds), *The New Palgrave: A Dictionary of Economics*, Vol. 1, London: Macmillan, 249.

——(1987) "Say's Law," in John Eatwell, Murray Milgate, and Peter Newman (eds), *The New Palgrave: A Dictionary of Economics*, Vol. 1, London: Macmillan, 249–51.

Spengler, J.J. (1960) "The Physiocrats and Say's Law of Markets," in J.J. Spengler and W.R. Allen (eds), *Essays in Economic Thought*, Chicago: Rand McNally.

A Treatise on Political Economy

Book I: Of the production of wealth

Chapter I: Of what is to be understood by the term, production

If we take the pains to inquire what that is, which mankind in a social state of existence denominate wealth, we shall find the term employed to designate an indefinite quantity of objects bearing inherent value, as of land, of metal, of coin, of grain, of stuffs, of commodities of every description. When they further extend its signification to landed securities, bills, notes of hand, and the like, it is evidently so because they contain obligations to deliver things possessed of inherent value. In point of fact, wealth can only exist where there are things possessed of real and intrinsic value.

Wealth is proportionate to the quantum of that value; great, when the aggregate of component value is great; small, when that aggregate is small.

The value of a specific article is always vague and arbitrary, so long as it remains unacknowledged. Its owner is not a jot the richer, by setting a higher ratio upon it in his own estimation. But the moment that other persons are willing, for the purpose of obtaining it, to give in exchange a certain quantity of other articles, likewise bearing value, the one may then be said to be worth, or to be of equal value with, the other.

The quantity of money, which is readily parted with to obtain a thing, is called its *price. Current price*, at a given time and place, is that price which the owner is sure of obtaining for a thing, if he is inclined to part with it.[1]

The knowledge of the real nature of wealth, thus defined, of the difficulties that must be surmounted in its attainment, of the course and order of its distribution amongst the members of society, of the uses to which it may be applied, and, further, of the consequence resulting respectively from these several circumstances, constitutes that branch of science now entitled Political Economy.

The value that mankind attach to objects originates in the use it can make of them. Some afford sustenance; others serve for clothing; some defend them from the inclemencies of the season, as houses; others gratify their taste, or, at all events, their vanity, both of which are species of wants: of this class are all mere ornaments and decorations. It is universally true, that, when men attribute value to any thing, it is in consideration of its useful properties; what is good for nothing they set no price upon.[2] To this inherent fitness or capability of certain things to satisfy the various wants of mankind, I shall take leave to affix the name of utility. And I will go on to say, that, to create objects which have any kind of utility, is to create wealth; for the utility of things is the ground-work of their value, and their value constitutes wealth.

Objects, however, cannot be created by human means; nor is the mass of matter, of which this globe consists, capable of increase or diminution. All that man can do is, to re-produce existing materials under another form, which may give them a utility they did not before possess, or merely enlarge one they may have before presented. So that, in fact, there is a creation, not of matter, but of utility; and this I call *production of wealth*.

In this sense, then, the word production must be understood in political economy, and throughout the whole course of the present work. Production is the creation, not of matter, but of utility. It is not to be estimated by the length, the bulk, or the weight of the product, but by the utility it presents.

Although price is the measure of the value of things, and their value the measure of their utility, it would be absurd to draw the inference, that, by forcibly raising their price, their utility can be augmented. Exchangeable value, or price, is an index of the recognised utility of a thing, so long only as human dealings are exempt from every influence but that of the identical utility: in like manner as a barometer denotes the weight of the atmosphere, only while the mercury is submitted to the exclusive action of atmospheric gravity.

In fact, when one man sells any product to another, he sells him the utility vested in that product; the buyer buys it only for the sake of its utility, of the use he can make of it. If, by any cause whatever, the buyer is obliged to pay more than the value to himself of that utility, he pays for value that has no existence, and consequently which he does not receive.[3]

This is precisely the case, when authority grants to a particular class of merchants the exclusive privilege of carrying on a certain branch of trade, the India trade for instance; the price of Indian imports is thereby raised, without any accession to their utility or intrinsic value. This excess of price is nothing more or less than so much money transferred from the pockets of the consumers into those of the privileged traders, whereby the latter are enriched exactly as much as the former are unnecessarily impoverished. In like manner, when a government imposes on wine a tax, which raises to 15 cents the bottle what would otherwise be sold for 10 cents, what does it else, but transfer 5 cents per bottle from the hands of the producers or the consumers of wine to those of the tax-gatherer?[4] The particular commodity is here only the means resorted to for getting at the tax-payer with more or less convenience; and its current value is composed of two ingredients, namely (1) its real value originating in its utility; (2) the value of the tax that the government thinks fit to exact, for permitting its manufacture, transport, or consumption.

Wherefore, there is no actual production of wealth, without a creation or augmentation of utility. Let us see in what manner this utility is to be produced.

Chapter XV: Of the demand or market for products

It is common to hear adventurers in the different channels of industry assert, that their difficulty lies not in the production, but in the disposal of commodities; that products would always be abundant, if there were but a ready demand, or market for them. When the demand for their commodities is slow, difficult, and productive of little advantage, they pronounce money to be scarce; the grand object of their desire is, a consumption brisk enough to quicken sales and keep up prices. But ask them what peculiar causes and circumstances facilitate the demand for their products, and you will soon perceive that most of them have extremely vague notions of these matters; that their observation of facts is imperfect, and their explanation still more so; that they treat doubtful points as matter of certainty, often pray for what is directly opposite to their interests, and importunately solicit from authority a protection of the most mischievous tendency.

To enable us to form clear and correct practical notions in regard to markets for the products of industry, we must carefully analyse the best established and most certain facts, and apply to them the inferences we have already deduced from a similar way of proceeding; and thus perhaps we may arrive at new and important truths, that may serve to enlighten the views of the agents of industry, and to give confidence to the measures of governments anxious to afford them encouragement.

A man who applies his labour to the investing of objects with value by the creation of utility of some sort, can not expect such a value to be appreciated and paid for, unless where other men have the means of purchasing it. Now, of what do these means consist? Of other values of other products, likewise the fruits of industry, capital, and land. Which leads us to a conclusion that may at first sight appear paradoxical, namely that it is production which opens a demand for product.

Should a tradesman say, 'I do not want other products for my woollens, I want money', there could be little difficulty in convincing him that his customers could not pay him in money, without having first procured it by the sale of some other commodities of their own. 'Yonder farmer', he may be told, 'will buy your woollens, if his crops be good, and will buy more or less according to their abundance or scantiness; he can buy none at all, if his crops fail altogether. Neither can you buy his wool nor his corn yourself, unless you contrive to get woollens or some other article, to buy withal. You say, you only want money; I say, you want other commodities, and not money. For what, in point of fact, do you want the money? Is it not for the purchase of raw materials or stock for your trade, or victuals for your support?[5] Wherefore, it is products that you want, and not money. The silver coin you will have received on the sale of your own products, and given in the purchase of those of other people, will the next moment execute the same office between other contracting parties, and so from one to another to infinity; just as a public vehicle successively transports objects one after another. If you can not find a ready sale for your commodity, will you say, it is merely for want of a vehicle to transport it? For, after all, money is but the agent of the transfer of values. Its whole utility has consisted in conveying to your hands the value of the commodities, which your customer has sold, for the purpose of buying again from you; and the very next purchase you make, it will again convey to a third person the value of the products you may have sold to others. So that you will have bought, and every body must buy, the objects of want or desire, each with the value of his respective products transformed into money for the moment only. Otherwise, how could it be possible that there should now be bought and sold in France five or six times as any commodities, as in the miserable reign of Charles VI? Is it not obvious, that five or six times as many commodities must have been produced, and that they must have served to purchase one or the other?'

Thus, to say that sales are dull, owing to the scarcity of money is to mistake the means for the cause, an error that proceeds from the circumstance, that almost all produce is in the first instance exchanged for money, before it is ultimately converted into other produce: and the commodity, which recurs so repeatedly in use, appears to vulgar apprehensions the most important of commodities, and the end and object of all transactions, whereas it is only the medium. Sales cannot be said to be dull because money is scarce, but because other products are so. There is always money enough to conduct the circulation and mutual interchange of other values, when those values really exist. Should the increase of traffic require more money to facilitate it, the want is easily supplied, and is a strong indication of prosperity – a proof that a great abundance of values has been created, which it is wished to exchange for other values. In such cases, merchants know well enough how to find substitutes for the product serving as the medium of exchange or money:[6] and money itself soon pours in, for this reason, that all produce naturally gravitates to that place where it is most in demand. It is a good sign when the business is too great for the money; just in the same way as it is a good sign when the goods are too plentiful for the warehouses.

When a superabundant article can find no vent, the scarcity of money has so little to do with the obstruction of its sale, that the sellers would gladly receive its value in goods for their own consumption at the current price of the day: they would not ask for money, or have any occasion for that product, since the only use they could make of it would be to convert it forthwith into articles of their own consumption.[7]

This observation is applicable to all cases, where there is a supply of commodities or of services in the market. They will universally find the most extensive demand in those places, where the most of values are produced; because in no other places are the sole means of purchase created, that is, values. Money performs but a monetary function in this double exchange; and when the transaction is finally closed, it will always be found, that one kind of commodity has been exchanged for another.

It is worth while to remark, that a product is no sooner created, than it, from that instant, affords a market for other products to the full extent of its own value. When the producer has put the finishing hand to his product, he is most anxious to sell it immediately, lest its value should diminish in his hands. Nor is he less anxious to dispose of the money be may get for it; for the value of money is also perishable. But the only way of getting rid of money is in the purchase of some product or other. Thus, the mere circumstance of the creation of one product immediately opens a vent for other products.

For this reason, a good harvest is favourable, not only to the agriculturist, but likewise to the dealers in all commodities generally. The greater the crop, the larger are the purchases of the growers. A bad harvest, on the contrary, hurts the sale of commodities at large. And so it is also with the products of manufacture and commerce. The success of one branch of commerce supplies more ample means of purchase, and consequently opens a market for the products of all the other branches; on the other hand, the stagnation of one channel of manufacture, or of commerce, is felt in all the rest.

But it may be asked, if this be so, how does it happen, that there is at times so great a glut of commodities in the market, and so much difficulty in finding a vent for them? Why cannot one of these super-abundant commodities be exchanged for another? I answer that the glut of a particular commodity arises from its having outrun the total demand for it in one or two ways; either because it has been produced in excessive abundance, or because the production of other commodities has fallen short.

It is because the production of some commodities has declined, that other commodities are superabundant. To use a more hackneyed phrase, people have bought less, because they have made less profit;[8] and they have made less profit for one or two causes; either they have found difficulties in the employment of their productive means, or these means have themselves been deficient.

It is observable, moreover, that precisely at the same time that one commodity makes a loss, another commodity is making excessive profit.[9] And, since such profits must operate as a powerful stimulus to the cultivation of that particular kind of products, there must needs be some violent means, or some extraordinary cause, a political or natural convulsion, or the avarice or ignorance of authority, to perpetuate this scarcity on the one hand, and consequent glut on the other. No sooner is the cause of this political disease removed, than the means of production feel a natural impulse towards the vacant channels, the replenishment of which restores activity to all the others. One kind of production would seldom outstrip every other, and its products be disproportionately cheapened, were production left entirely free.[10]

Should a producer imagine, that many other classes, yielding no material products, are his customers and consumers equally with the classes that raise themselves a product of their own; as, for example, public functionaries, physicians, lawyers, churchmen, etc., and thence infer, that there is a class of demand other than that of the actual producers, he would but expose the shallowness and superficiality of his ideas. A priest goes to a shop to buy a gown or a surplice; he takes the value, that is to make the purchase, in the form of money. Whence had he that money? From some tax-gatherer who has taken it from a tax-payer. But whence did this latter derive it? From the value he has himself produced. This value, first produced by the tax-payer, and afterwards turned into money, and given to the priest for his salary, has enabled him to make the purchase. The priest stands in the place of the producer, who might himself have laid the value of his product on his

own account, in the purchase, perhaps, not of a gown or surplice, but of some other more serviceable product. The consumption of the particular product, the gown or surplice, has but supplanted that of some other product. It is quite impossible that the purchase of one product can
be affected, otherwise than by the value of another.[11]

From this important truth may be deduced the following important conclusions:

1. That, in every community the more numerous are the producers, and the more various
their productions, the more prompt, numerous, and extensive are the markets for those productions; and, by a natural consequence, the more profitable are they to the producers; for price rises
with the demand – but this advantage is to be derived from real production alone, and not from
a forced circulation of products; for a value once created is not augmented in its passage from
one hand to another, nor by being seized and expended by the government, instead of by
an individual. The man, that lives upon the productions of other people, originates no demand
for those productions; he merely puts himself in the place of the producer, to the great injury of
production, as we shall presently see.

2. That each individual is interested in the general prosperity of all, and that the success of
one branch of industry promotes that of all the others. In fact, whatever profession or line of
business a man may devote himself to, he is the better paid and the more readily finds employment, in proportion as he sees others thriving equally around him. A man of talent, that scarcely
vegetates in a retrograde state of society, would find a thousand ways of turning his faculties to
account in a thriving community that could afford to employ and reward his ability. A merchant
established in a rich and populous town, sells to a much larger amount than one who sets up in
a poor district, with a population sunk in indolence and apathy. What could an active manufacturer, or an intelligent merchant, do in a small deserted and semi-barbarous town in a remote
corner of Poland or Westphalia? Though in no fear of a competitor, he could sell but little,
because little was produced; whilst at Paris, Amsterdam, or London, in spite of the competition
of a hundred dealers in his own line, he might do business on the largest scale. The reason is
obvious: he is surrounded with people who produce largely in an infinity of ways, and who make
purchases, each with his respective products, that is to say, with the money arising from the sale of
what he may have produced.

This is the true source of the gains made by the towns' people out of the country people, and
again by the latter out of the former; both of them have wherewith to buy more largely, the more
amply they themselves produce. A city, standing in the centre of a rich surrounding country, feels
no want of rich and numerous customers and, on the other hand, the vicinity of an opulent city
gives additional value to the produce of the country. The division of nations into agricultural,
manufacturing, and commercial, is idle enough. For the success of a people in agriculture is
a stimulus to its manufacturing and commercial prosperity; and the flourishing condition of
its manufacture and commerce reflects a benefit upon its agriculture also.[12]

The position of a nation, in respect of its neighbours, is analogous to the relation of one of its
provinces to the others, or of the country to the town; it has an interest in their prosperity, being
sure to profit by their opulence. The government of the United States, therefore, acted most
wisely, in their attempt, about the year 1802, to civilize their savage neighbours, the Creek
Indians. The design was to introduce habits of industry amongst them, and make them producers capable of carrying on a barter trade with the States of the Union; for there is nothing to be
got by dealing with a people that have nothing to pay. It is useful and honourable to mankind,
that one nation among so many should conduct itself uniformly upon liberal principles. The brilliant results of this enlightened policy will demonstrate, that the systems and theories really
destructive and fallacious, are the exclusive and jealous maxims acted upon by the old European

governments, and by them most impudently styled *practical truths*, for no other reason, as it would seem, than because they have the misfortune to put them in practice. The United States will have the honour of proving experimentally, that true policy goes hand-in-hand with moderation and humanity.[13]

3. From this fruitful principle, we may draw this further conclusion, that it is no injury to the internal or national industry and production to buy and import commodities from abroad; for nothing can be bought from strangers, except with native products, which find a vent in this external traffic. Should it be objected, that this foreign produce may have been bought with specie, I answer, specie is not always a native product, but must have been bought itself with the products of native industry; so that, whether the foreign articles be paid for in specie or in home products, the vent for national industry is the same in both cases.[14]

4. The same principle leads to the conclusion, that the encouragement of mere consumption is no benefit to commerce; for the difficulty lies in supplying the means, not in stimulating the desire of consumption; and we have seen that production alone, furnishes those means. Thus, it is the aim of good government to stimulate production, of bad government to encourage consumption.

For the same reason that the creation of a new product is the opening of a new market for other products, the consumption or destruction of a product is the stoppage of a vent for them. This is no evil where the end of the product has been answered by its destruction, which end is the satisfying of some human want, or the creation of some new product designed for such a satisfaction. Indeed, if the nation be in a thriving condition, the gross national re-production exceeds the gross consumption. The consumed products have fulfilled their office, as it is natural and fitting they should; the consumption, however, has opened no new market, but just the reverse.[15]

Having once arrived at the clear conviction, that the general demand for products is brisk in proportion to the activity of production, we need not trouble ourselves much to inquire towards what channel of industry production may be most advantageously directed. The products created give rise to various degrees of demand, according to the wants, the manners, the comparative capital, industry, and natural resources of each country; the article most in request, owing to the competition of buyers, yields the best interest of money to the capitalist, the largest profits to the adventurer, and the best wages to the labourer; and the agency of their respective services is naturally attracted by these advantages towards those particular channels.

In a community, city, province, or nation, that produces abundantly, and adds every moment to the sum of its products, almost all the branches of commerce, manufacture, and generally of industry, yield handsome profits, because the demand is great, and because there is always a large quantity of products in the market, ready to bid for new productive services. And, vice versa, wherever, by reason of the blunders of the nation or its government, production is stationary, or does not keep pace with consumption, the demand gradually declines, the value of the product is less than the charges of its production; no productive exertion is properly rewarded; profits and wages decrease; the employment of capital becomes less advantageous and more hazardous; it is consumed piecemeal, not through extravagance, but through necessity, and because the sources of profit are dried up.[16] The labouring classes experience a want of work; families before in tolerable circumstances, are more cramped and confined; and those before in difficulties are left altogether destitute. Depopulation, misery, and returning barbarism, occupy the place of abundance and happiness.

Such are the concomitants of declining production, which are only to be remedied by frugality, intelligence, activity, and freedom.

Notes

1 The numerous and difficult points arising out of the confusion of positive and relative value are discussed in different parts of this work; particularly in the leading chapters of Book IL. Not to perplex the attention of the reader, I confine myself here to so much as is absolutely necessary to comprehend the phenomenon of the production of wealth.

2 It would be out of place here to examine, whether or no the value mankind attach to a thing be always proportionate to its actual utility. The accuracy of the estimate must depend upon the comparative judgment, intelligence, habits, and prejudices of those who make it. True morality, and the clear perception of their real interests, lead mankind to the just appreciation of benefits. Political economy takes this appreciation as it finds it – as one of the data of its reasonings; leaving to the moralist and the practical man, the several duties of' enlightening and of guiding their fellow-creatures, as well in this, as in other particulars of human conduct.

3 This position will hereafter be further illustrated. For the present it is enough to know, that, whatever be the state of society, current prices approximate to the real value of things, in proportion to the liberty of production and mutual dealing.

4 It will be shown in Book III of this work, what proportion of the tax is paid by the producer, and what by the consumer.

5 Even when money is obtained with a view to hoard or bury it, the ultimate object is always to employ it in a purchase of some kind. The heir of the lucky finder uses it in that way, if the miser do not; for money, as money, has no other use than to buy with.

6 By bills at sight, or after date, bank-notes, running-credits, write-offs, etc. as at London and Amsterdam.

7 I speak here of their aggregate consumption, whether unproductive and designed to satisfy the personal wants of themselves and their families, or expended in the sustenance of reproductive industry. The woollen or cotton manufacturer operates a two-fold consumption of wool and cotton: (1) For his personal wear; (2) for the supply of his manufacture; but, be the purpose of his consumption what it may, whether personal gratification or reproduction, he must needs buy what he consumes with what he produces.

8 Individual profits must, in every description of production, from the general merchant to the common artisan, be derived from the participation in the values produced. The ratio of that participation will form the subject of Book II, infra.

9 The reader may easily apply these maxims to any time or country he is acquainted with. We have had a striking instance in France during the years 1811, 1812, and 1813; when the high prices of colonial produce of wheat, and other articles, went hand-in-hand with the low price of many others that could find no advantageous market.

10 These considerations have hitherto been almost wholly overlooked, though forming the basis of correct conclusions in matters of commerce, and of its regulation by the national authority. The right course where it has, by good luck, been pursued, appears to have been selected by accident, or, at most, by a confused idea of its propriety, without either self-conviction, or the ability to convince other people. Sismondi, who seems not to have very well understood the principles laid down, in this and the three first chapters of Book II of this work, instances the immense quantity of manufactured products with which England has of late inundated the markets of other nations, as a proof, that it is impossible for industry to be too productive. (Nouv. Prin. liv. iv. c. 4.) But the glut thus occasioned proves nothing more than the feebleness of production in those countries that have been thus glutted with English manufactures. Did Brazil produce wherewithal to purchase the English goods exported thither, those goods would not glut her market. Were England to admit the import of the products of the, United States, she would find a better market for her own in those States. The English government, by the exorbitance of its taxation upon import and consumption, virtually interdicts to its subjects many kinds of importation, thus obliging the merchant to offer to foreign countries a higher price for those articles, whose import is practicable, as sugar, coffee, gold, silver, etc. for the price of the precious metals to them is enhanced by the low price of their commodities, which accounts, for the ruinous returns of their commerce.

I would not be understood to maintain in this chapter, that one product can not be raised in too great abundance, in relation to all others; but merely that nothing is more favourable to the demand of one product, than the supply of another; that the import of English manufactures into Brazil would cease to be excessive and, be rapidly absorbed, did Brazil produce on her side returns sufficiently ample; to which end it would be necessary that the legislative bodies of either country should consent, the one to free production, the other to free importation. In Brazil every thing is grasped by monopoly, and property is not exempt from the invasion of the government. In England, the heavy duties are a serious obstruction to the foreign commerce of the nation, inasmuch as they circumscribe the choice of returns.

I happen myself to know of a most valuable and scientific collection of natural history, which could not be imported from Brazil into England by reason of the exorbitant duties. (a) The views of Sismondi, in this particular, have been since adopted by our own Malthus, and those of our author by Ricardo. This difference of opinion has given rise to an interesting discussion between our author and Malthus, to whom he has recently addressed a correspondence on this and other parts of the science. Were any thing wanting to confirm the arguments of this chapter, it would be supplied by a reference to his *Lettre 1, a M Malthus*. Sismondi has vainly attempted to answer Ricardo, but has made no mention of his original antagonist. *Vide Annales* de Legislation, No. 1. art. 3. Geneve, 1820. T.

11 The capitalist, in spending the interest of his capital, spends his portion of the products raised by the employment of that capital. The general rules that regulate the ratio he receives will be investigated in Book II, infra. Should he ever spend the principal, still he consumes products only; for capital consists of products, devoted indeed to reproductive, but susceptible of unproductive consumption; to which it is in fact consigned whenever it is wasted or dilapidated.

12 A productive establishment on a large scale is sure to animate the industry – of the whole neighbourhood. 'In Mexico', says Humboldt, 'the best cultivated tract, and that which brings to the recollection of the traveller the most beautiful part of French scenery, is the level country extending from Salamanca as far as Silao, Guanaxuato, and Villa de Leon, and encircling the richest mines of the known world. Wherever the veins of precious metal have been discovered and worked, even in the most desert part of the Cordilleras, and in the most barren and insulated spots, the working of the mines, instead of interrupting the business of superficial cultivation, has given it more than usual activity. The opening of a considerable vein is sure to be followed by the immediate erection of a town; farming concerns are established in the vicinity; and the spot so lately insulated in the midst of wild and desert mountains, is soon brought into contact with the tracts before in tillage'. *Essai pol sur la Nouv Espagne.*

13 It is only by the recent advances of political economy, that these most important truths have been made manifest, not to vulgar apprehension alone, but even to the most distinguished and enlightened observers. We read in Voltaire that 'such is the lot of humanity, that the patriotic desire for one's country's grandeur, is but a wish for the humiliation of one's neighbours; that it is clearly impossible for one country to gain, except by the loss of another'. (*Dict. Phil. Art. Patrie.*) By a continuation of the same false reasoning, he goes on to declare, that a thorough citizen of the world cannot wish his country to be greater or less, richer or poorer. It is true, that he would not desire her to extend the limits of her dominion, because, in so doing, she might endanger her own well-being; but he will desire her to progress in wealth, for her progressive prosperity promotes that of all other nations.

14 This effect has been sensibly experienced in Brazil of late years. The large imports of European commodities, which the freedom of navigation directed to the markets of Brazil, has been so favourable to its native productions and commerce, that Brazilian products never found so good a sale. So there is an instance of a national benefit arising from importation. By the way, it might have perhaps been better for Brazil if the prices of her products and the profits of her producers had risen more slowly and gradually; for exorbitant prices never lead to the establishment of a permanent commercial intercourse; it is better to gain by the multiplication of one's own products than by their increased price.

15 If the barren consumption of a product be of itself adverse to re-production, and a diminution *pro tanto* of the existing demand or vent for produce, how shall we designate that degree of insanity, which would induce a government deliberately to burn and destroy the imports of foreign products, and thus to annihilate the sole advantage accruing from unproductive consumption, that is to say the gratification of the wants of the consumer?

16 Consumption of this kind gives no encouragement to future production, but devours products already in existence. No additional demand can be created until there be new products raised; there is only an exchange of one product for another. Neither can one branch of industry suffer without affecting the rest.

DAVID RICARDO (1772–1823)

David Ricardo was the first great self-conscious economic theorist. He used the premises of the theories of population and rent, coupled with the language of the labor theory of value, to generate a picture of long-run economic performance. The growth of population meant that the share of national income going to the landowners in the form of rent would increase; the per capita real income of labor would tend to the social minimum of subsistence (the physical minimum adjusted by custom and habit); so that the decreasing proportion of national income left after rent would leave a falling rate of profit, after the income of the working class (increased in number, times the social minimum of subsistence). This was, indeed, a dismal picture – for all but the landowners.

Classical economic theory can be understood as a paradigm founded on the concept of capital, by capital meaning both fixed (plant and equipment) and circulating (advances to workers during the production process). From Smith comes the idea that the source of capital is saving; accumulation is central. For all of the Classicists, the deployment of capital both generates the social organization for production and sets labor in motion. Commodities are produced by means of other commodities: capital goods and the wage goods in effect advanced to labor. Output is a function of capital; the capital stock is necessarily on hand prior to production. Decisions over the allocation of the total capital stock effectively govern the use of technology, the allocation of resources between goods, the substance and rate of economic growth, and the distribution of income. The principal decision over allocation of capital is between fixed and circulating capital. Circulating capital, it was hypothesized, went into the wages fund, from which labor was paid: the average wage rate depended directly upon the size of the wages fund and inversely upon the size of the labor force. The critical socioeconomic role is no longer that of the landowner but of the capitalist, who organizes production and provides the means of subsistence to the working class. It is clear that, however accurate or inaccurate, and however meaningful or meaningless, all this may be, the foregoing picture (and the related theories) derive from perceptions of the new urban, industrial, commercial capitalist market economy.

A great deal of controversy ensued, especially in the twentieth century, over the meaning of Ricardo's labor theory of value. His theory had pretty much all the trappings of a labor theory, but he modified it to take account of (1) variable ratios of fixed to circulating capital, (2) varying durability of fixed capital, and (3) varying rates of turnover of circulating capital. Ambiguity exists with regard to whether his theory is a theory of the measure or source of value, and whether, after his adjustments were made, his was an absolute or a relative labor theory of value. If one considers capital as so much stored-up labor, then everything is labor, and the adjustments are technical and not substantive. At any rate, for many later economists Ricardo's labor theory of value became transformed into a cost of production theory of value. Also relevant is the view that, as with Smith's labor theory of value, one could distinguish value from price, and market price was substantially to all these people a matter of demand and supply – though this was frequently eclipsed by focusing on value as such. Finally, in the late twentieth century, Piero Sraffa reformulated Ricardo's (and Marx's) labor theory of value in such a way that, among other things, argued the dependence of value on the distribution of income. Sraffa's analysis relied implicitly upon some construction of an invariable measure of value – a recognition which Ricardo had made and on which he was working at the end of his life.

Ricardo developed a number of other theories, some original, and others a continuation of received ideas. These included the quantity theory of money (as evidenced in the earlier reading from Ricardo), the comparative-advantage theory of international trade, and the theory of diminishing returns in agriculture – as well as the theory of rent.

Ricardo also became concerned about what later came to be called technological unemployment, namely, unemployment consequent to the introduction of machinery – a significant concern juxtaposed to James Mill and Jean Baptiste Say's "law of the market," which argued that there could be no general overproduction or unemployment. This traces back, in effect, to ideas in Smith's *Wealth of Nations*, wherein one finds both capital setting labor in motion and capital substituting for labor.

One has to comprehend Ricardo's impressive accomplishments as a theorist in the context of his political agenda. Along with most of the other Classical economists, Ricardo was seeking to revise the institutional, especially the legal, framework of the economy to facilitate the extension of a modern market economy. This explains, for example, his approach to the Corn Laws, that is, free trade, monetary and banking reform, population control, and so on.

The following excerpts from Ricardo's *Principles of Political Economy and Taxation* highlight the major themes in his analysis: the labor theory of value, rent, the theory of wages (with attendant commentary on the Poor Laws), the tendency toward a falling rate of profit, and the theory of comparative advantage in international trade – all of which very much set the tone for nineteenth-century classical economic thinking.

References and further reading*

Blaug, Mark (1958) *Ricardian Economics*, New Haven, CT: Yale University Press.
—— (1991) *David Ricardo (1772–1823)*, Aldershot: Edward Elgar Publishing.
Bloomfield, A.I. (1981) "British Thought on the Influence of Foreign Trade and Investment on Growth," *History of Political Economy* 13 (Spring): 95–120.
Fetter, Frank W. (1980) *The Economist in Parliament*, Durham, NC: Duke University Press.
Gordon, Barry (1969) "Criticism of Ricardian Views on Value and Distribution in the British Periodicals," *History of Political Economy* 1 (Fall): 370–87.
Henderson, John P. (1997) *The Life and Economics of David Ricardo*, with supplemental chapters by John B. Davis, edited by Warren J. Samuels and Gilbert B. Davis, Boston: Kluwer.
Hicks, J.R. and Hollander, S. (1977) "Mr. Ricardo and the Moderns," *Quarterly Journal of Economics* 91 (August): 351–69.
Hollander, Jacob H. (1910) *David Ricardo: A Centenary Estimate*, Baltimore, MD: Johns Hopkins Press.
Hollander, Samuel (1979) *The Economics of David Ricardo*, Toronto: University of Toronto Press.
Kurz, Heinz D. and Salvadori, Neri (1998) "Ricardo, David," in Heinz D. Kurz and Neri Salvadori (eds), *The Elgar Companion to Classical Economics*, Vol. 2, Cheltenham: Edward Elgar Publishing, 314–24.
Meek, Ronald L. (1973) *Studies in the Labour Theory of Value*, 2nd edn, London: Lawrence & Wishart.
Ricardo, David (1951–1955) *The Works and Correspondence of David Ricardo*, 10 Vols, edited by Piero Sraffa with the collaboration of M.H. Dobb, London: Cambridge University Press.
Skourtos, Michalis S. (1998) "Corn Model," in Heinz D. Kurz and Neri Salvadori (eds), *The Elgar Companion to Classical Economics*, Vol. 1, Cheltenham: Edward Elgar Publishing, 194–6.

* Further references to Ricardo's life and work can be found in the introduction to the previous reading from his *The High Price of Bullion*.

Sraffa, Piero (1951) "Introduction," in *The Works and Correspondence of David Ricardo*, Vol. 1, edited by Piero Sraffa with the collaboration of M.H. Dobb, London: Cambridge University Press, xiii–lxii.

Stigler, George J. (1952) "The Ricardian Theory of Value and Distribution," in George J. Stigler, *Essays in the History of Economics*, Chicago, University of Chicago Press, 1965.

——(1958) "Ricardo and the 93 Per Cent Labor Theory of Value," in George J. Stigler, *Essays in the History of Economics*, Chicago: University of Chicago Press, 1965.

Wood, John C. (1985) *David Ricardo: Critical Assessments*, London: Croom Helm.

Viner, Jacob (1937) *Studies in the Theory of International Trade*, New York: Harper & Row.

On the Principles of Political Economy and Taxation (1817)*

Chapter 1: On value

The value of a commodity, or the quantity of any other commodity for which it will exchange, depends on the relative quantity of labour which is necessary for its production, and not on the greater or less compensation which is paid for that labour.

It has been observed by Adam Smith that 'the word Value has two different meanings, and sometimes expresses the utility of some particular object, and sometimes the power of purchasing other goods which the possession of that object conveys. The one may be called value in use; the other value in exchange. The things', he continues, 'which have the greatest value in use, have frequently little or no value in exchange; and, on the contrary, those which have the greatest value in exchange, have little or no value in use'. Water and air are abundantly useful; they are indeed indispensable to existence, yet, under ordinary circumstances, nothing can be obtained in exchange for them. Gold, on the contrary, though of little use compared with air or water, will exchange for a great quantity of other goods.

Utility then is not the measure of exchangeable value, although it is absolutely essential to it. If a commodity were in no way useful – in other words, if it could in no way contribute to our gratification – it would be destitute of exchangeable value, however scarce it might be, or whatever quantity of labour might be necessary to procure it.

Possessing utility, commodities derive their exchangeable value from two sources: from their scarcity and from the quantity of labour required to obtain them.

There are some commodities, the value of which is determined by their scarcity alone. No labour can increase the quantity of such goods, and therefore their value cannot be lowered by an increased supply. Some rare statues and pictures, scarce books and coins, wines of a peculiar quality, which can be made only from grapes grown on a particular soil, of which there is a very limited quantity, are all of this description. Their value is wholly independent of the quantity of labour originally necessary to produce them, and varies with the varying wealth and inclinations of those who are desirous to possess them.

These commodities, however, form a very small part of the mass of commodities daily exchanged in the market. By far the greatest part of those goods which are the objects of desire, are procured by labour, and they may be multiplied, not in one country alone, but in many, almost without any assignable limit, if we are disposed to bestow the labour necessary to obtain them.

In speaking then of commodities, of their exchangeable value, and of the laws which regulate their relative prices, we mean always such commodities only as can be increased in quantity by the exertion of human industry, and on the production of which competition operates without restraint.

---

* London: John Murray, Albemarle-Street, 3rd edition, 1821.

In the early stages of society, the exchangeable value of these commodities, or the rule which determines how much of one shall be given in exchange for another, depends almost exclusively on the comparative quantity of labour expended on each.

'The real price of every thing', says Adam Smith, 'what every thing really costs to the man who wants to acquire it, is the toil and trouble of acquiring it. What every thing is really worth to it, or the man who has acquired it, and who wants to dispose of it, or exchange it for something else, is the toil and trouble which it can save to himself, and which it can impose upon other people'. 'Labour was the first price – the original purchase-money that was paid for all things'. Again, 'in that early and rude state of society, which precedes both the accumulation of stock and the appropriation of land, the proportion between the quantities of labour necessary for acquiring different objects seems to be the only circumstance which can afford any rule for exchanging them for one another. If among a nation of hunters, for example, it usually cost twice the labour to kill a beaver which it does to kill a deer, one beaver should naturally exchange for, or be worth two deer. It is natural that what is usually the produce of two days', or two hours' labour, should be worth double of what is usually the produce of one day's, or one hour's labour'.

That this is really the foundation of the exchangeable value of all things, excepting those which cannot be increased by human industry, is a doctrine of the utmost importance in political economy; for from no source do so many errors, and so much difference of opinion in that science proceed, as from the vague ideas which are attached to the word value.

If the quantity of labour realized in commodities, regulate their exchangeable value, every increase of the quantity of labour must augment the value of that commodity on which it is exercised, as every diminution must lower it.

Adam Smith, who so accurately defined the original source of exchangeable value, and who was bound in consistency to maintain, that all things became more or less valuable in proportion as more or less labour was bestowed on their production, has himself erected another standard measure of value, and speaks of things being more or less valuable, in proportion as they will exchange for more or less of this standard measure. Sometimes he speaks of corn, at other times of labour, as a standard measure; not the quantity of labour bestowed on the production of any object, but the quantity which it can command in the market: as if these were two equivalent expressions, and as if because a man's labour had become doubly efficient, and he could therefore produce twice the quantity of a commodity, he would necessarily receive twice the former quantity in exchange for it.

If this indeed were true, if the reward of the labourer were always in proportion to what he produced, the quantity of labour bestowed on a commodity, and the quantity of labour which that commodity would purchase, would be equal, and either might accurately measure the variations of other things: but they are not equal; the first is under many circumstances an invariable standard, indicating correctly the variations of other things; the latter is subject to as many fluctuations as the commodities compared with it. Adam Smith, after most ably showing the insufficiency of a variable medium, such as gold and silver, for the purpose of determining the varying value of other things, has himself, by fixing on corn or labour, chosen a medium no less variable.

Gold and silver are no doubt subject to fluctuations, from the discovery of new and more abundant mines; but such discoveries are rare, and their effects, though powerful, are limited to periods of comparatively short duration. They are subject also to fluctuation, from improvements in the skill and machinery with which the mines may be worked; as in consequence of such improvements, a greater quantity may be obtained with the same labour. They are further subject to fluctuation from the decreasing produce of the mines, after they have yielded a supply to the world, for a succession of ages. But from which of these sources of fluctuation is corn exempted? Does not that also vary, on one hand, from improvements in agriculture, from improved machinery and implements used in husbandry, as well as from the discovery of new tracts of fertile land, which in other countries may be taken into cultivation, and which will affect the value of corn in every market where importation is free? Is it not on the other hand subject to be enhanced in value from prohibitions of importation, from increasing population and wealth, and the greater difficulty of obtaining the increased supplies, on account of the additional quantity of labour which the cultivation of inferior lands requires? Is not the value of labour equally variable; being not only affected, as all other things are, by the proportion between the supply and demand, which uniformly varies with every change in the condition of the community, but also by the varying price of food and other necessaries, on which the wages of labour are expended?

In the same country double the quantity of labour may be required to produce a given quantity of food and necessaries at one time, that may be necessary at another, and a distant time; yet the labourer's reward may possibly be diminished very little. If the labourer's wages at the former period, were a certain quantity of food and necessaries, he probably could not have subsisted if that quantity had been reduced. Food and necessaries in this case will have risen 100 per cent if estimated by the *quantity* of labour necessary to their production, while they will scarcely have increased in value, if measured by the quantity of labour for which they will *exchange*.

...

If the shoes and clothing of the labourer, could, by improvements in machinery, be produced by one-fourth of the labour now necessary to their production, they would probably fall 75 per cent; but so far is it from being true, that the labourer would thereby be enabled permanently to consume four coats, or four pair of shoes, instead of one, that it is probable his wages would in no long time be adjusted by the effects of competition, and the stimulus to population, to the new value of the necessaries on which they were expended. If these improvements extended to all the objects of the labourer's consumption, we should find him probably at the end of a very few years, in possession of only a small, if any, addition to his enjoyments, although the exchangeable value of those commodities, compared with any other commodity, in the manufacture of which no such improvement were made, had sustained a very considerable reduction; and though they were the produce of a very considerably diminished quantity of labour.

It cannot then be correct, to say with Adam Smith, 'that as labour may sometimes purchase a greater, and sometimes a smaller quantity of goods, it is their value which varies, not that of the labour which purchases them'; and therefore, 'that labour alone never varying in its own value, is alone the ultimate and real standard by which the value of all commodities can at all times and places be estimated and compared'; but it is correct to say, as Adam Smith had said previously, 'that the proportion between the quantities of labour necessary for acquiring different objects seems to be the only circumstance which can afford any rule for exchanging them for one another'; or in other words, that it is the comparative quantity of commodities which labour will produce, that determines their present or past relative value, and not the comparative quantities of commodities, which are given to the labourer in exchange for his labour.

Two commodities vary in relative value, and we wish to know in which the variation has really taken place. If we compare the present value of one, with shoes, stockings, hats, iron, sugar, and all other commodities, we find that it will exchange for precisely the same quantity of all these things as before. If we compare the other with the same commodities, we find it has varied with respect to them all: we may then with great probability infer that the variation has been in this commodity, and not in the commodities with which we have compared it. If on examining still more particularly into all the circumstances connected with the production of these various commodities, we find that precisely the same quantity of labour and capital are necessary to the production of the shoes, stockings, hats, iron, sugar, and so on; but that the same quantity as before is not necessary to produce the single commodity whose relative value is altered, probability is changed into certainty, and we are sure that the variation is in the single commodity. We then discover also the cause of its variation.

If I found that an ounce of gold would exchange for a lesser quantity of all the commodities enumerated above, and many others; and if, moreover, I found that by the discovery of a new and more fertile mine, or by the employment of machinery to great advantage, a given quantity of gold could be obtained with a less quantity of labour, I should be justified in saying that the cause of the alteration in the value of gold, relative to other commodities, was the greater facility of its production, or the smaller quantity of labour necessary to obtain it. In like manner, if labour fell considerably in value, relative to all other things, and if I found that its fall was in consequence of an abundant supply, encouraged by the great facility with which corn, and the other necessaries of the labourer, were produced, it would, I apprehend, be correct for me to say that corn and necessaries had fallen in value in consequence of less quantity of labour being necessary to produce them, and that this facility of providing for the support of the labourer had been followed by a fall in the value of labour. No, say Adam Smith and Mr Malthus, in the case of the gold you were correct in calling its variation a fall of its value, because corn and labour had not then varied; and as gold would command a less quantity of them, as well as of all other things, than before, it was correct to say that all things had remained stationary, and that gold only had varied; but when corn and labour fall, things which we have selected to be our standard measure of value, notwithstanding all the variations to which we acknowledge they are subject, it would be highly improper to say so; the correct language will be to say, that corn and labour have remained stationary, and all other things have risen in value.

Now it is against this language that I protest. I find that precisely, as in the case of the gold, the cause of the variation between corn and other things, is the smaller quantity of labour necessary to produce it, and therefore, by all just reasoning, I am bound to call the variation of corn and labour a fall in their value, and not a rise in the value of the things with which they are compared. If I have to hire a labourer for a week, and instead of ten shillings I pay him eight, no variation having taken place in the value of money, the labourer can probably obtain more food and necessaries, with his eight shillings, than he before obtained for ten: but this is owing, not to a rise in the real value of his wages, as stated by Adam Smith, and more recently by Mr Malthus, but to a fall in the value of the things on which his wages are expended, things perfectly distinct; and yet for calling this a fall in the real value of wages, I am told that I adopt new and unusual language, not reconcileable with the true principles of the science. To me it appears that the unusual and, indeed, inconsistent language, is that used by my opponents.

Suppose a labourer to be paid a bushel of corn for a week's work, when the price of corn is 80s. per quarter, and that he is paid a bushel and a quarter when the price falls to 40s. Suppose, too, that he consumes half a bushel of corn in a week in his own family, and exchanges the remainder for other things, such as fuel, soap, candles, tea, sugar, salt, and the like; if the three-fourths of a bushel which will remain to him, in one case, cannot procure him as much of the above commodities as half a bushel did in the other, which it will not, will labour have risen or fallen in value? Risen, Adam Smith must say, because his standard is corn, and the labourer receives more corn for a week's labour. Fallen, must the same Adam Smith say, 'because the value of a thing depends on the power of purchasing other goods which the possession of that object conveys', and labour has less power of purchasing such other goods.

Section II

> *Labour of different qualities differently rewarded. This is no cause of variation in the relative value of commodities.*

In speaking, however, of labour, as being the foundation of all value, and the relative quantity of labour as almost exclusively determining the relative value of commodities, I must not be supposed to be inattentive to the different qualities of labour, and the difficulty of comparing an hour's or a day's labour, in one employment, with the same duration of labour in another. The estimation in which different qualities of labour are held, comes soon to be adjusted in the market with sufficient precision for all practical purposes, and depends much on the comparative skill of the labourer, and intensity of the labour performed. The scale, when once formed, is liable to little variation. If a day's labour of a working jeweller be more valuable than a day's labour of a common labourer, it has long ago been adjusted, and placed in its proper position in the scale of value.

In comparing therefore the value of the same commodity, at different periods of time, the consideration of the comparative skill and intensity of labour, required for that particular commodity, needs scarcely to be attended to, as it operates equally at both periods. One description of labour at one time is compared with the same description of labour at another; if a tenth, a fifth, or a fourth, has been added or taken away, an effect proportioned to the cause will be produced on the relative value of the commodity.

If a piece of cloth be now of the value of two pieces of linen, and if, in ten years hence, the ordinary value of a piece of cloth should be four pieces of linen, we may safely conclude, that either more labour is required to make the cloth, or less to make the linen, or that both causes have operated.

As the inquiry to which I wish to draw the reader's attention, relates to the effect of the variations in the relative value of commodities, and not in their absolute value, it will be of little importance to examine the comparative degree of estimation in which the different kinds of human labour are held. We may fairly conclude, that whatever inequality there might originally have been in them, whatever the ingenuity, skill, or time necessary for the acquirement of one species of manual dexterity more than another, it continues nearly the same from one generation to another; or at least, that the variation is very inconsiderable from year to year, and therefore, can have little effect, for short periods, on the relative value of commodities.

...

Section III

Not only the labour applied immediately to commodities affect their value, but the labour also which is bestowed on the complements, tools, and buildings, with which much labour is assisted.

Even in that early state to which Adam Smith refers, some capital, though possibly made and accumulated by the hunter himself, would be necessary to enable him to kill his game. Without some weapon, neither the beaver nor the deer could be destroyed, and therefore the value of these animals would be regulated, not solely by the time and labour necessary to their destruction, but also by the time and labour necessary for providing the hunter's capital, the weapon, by the aid of which their destruction was effected.

Suppose the weapon necessary to kill the beaver, was constructed with much more labour than that necessary to kill the deer, on account of the greater difficulty of approaching near the former animal, and the consequent necessity of its being more true to its mark; one beaver would naturally be of more value than two deer, and precisely for this reason, that more labour would, on the whole, be necessary to its destruction. Or suppose that the same quantity of labour was necessary to make both weapons, but that they were of very unequal durability; of the durable implement only a small portion of its value would be transferred to the commodity, a much greater portion of the value of the less durable implement would be realized in the commodity which it contributed to produce.

All the implements necessary to kill the beaver and deer might belong to one class of men, and the labour employed in their destruction might be furnished by another class; still, their comparative prices would be in proportion to the actual labour bestowed, both on the formation of the capital, and on the destruction of the animals. Under different circumstances of plenty or scarcity of capital, as compared with labour, under different circumstances of plenty or scarcity of the food and necessaries essential to the support of men, those who furnished an equal value of capital for either one employment or for the other, might have a half, a fourth, or an eighth of the produce obtained, the remainder being paid as wages to those who furnished the labour; yet this division could not affect the relative value of these commodities, since whether the profits of capital were greater or less, whether they were 50, 20, or 10 per cent or whether the wages of labour were high or low, they would operate equally on both employments.

If we suppose the occupations of the society extended, that some provide canoes and tackle necessary for fishing, others the seed and rude machinery first used in agriculture, still the same principle would hold true, that the exchangeable value of the commodities produced would be in proportion to the labour bestowed on their production; not on their immediate production only, but on all those implements or machines required to give effect to the particular labour to which they were applied.

If we look to a state of society in which greater improvements have been made, and in which arts and commerce flourish, we shall still find that commodities vary in value conformably with this principle: in estimating the exchangeable value of stockings, for example, we shall find that their value, compared with other things, depends on the total quantity of labour necessary to manufacture them, and bring them to market. First, there is the labour necessary to cultivate the land on which the raw cotton is grown; second, the labour of conveying the cotton to the country where the stockings are to be manufactured, which includes a portion of the labour bestowed in building the ship in which it is conveyed, and which is charged with the freight of the goods; third, the labour of the spinner and weaver; fourth, a portion of the labour of the engineer, smith, and carpenter, who erected the buildings and machinery, by the help of which they are made; fifth, the labour of the retail dealer, and of many others, whom it is unnecessary further to particularize. The aggregate sum of these various kinds of labour, determines the quantity of other things for which these stockings will exchange, while the same consideration of the various quantities of labour which have been bestowed on those other things, will equally govern the portion of them which will be given for the stockings.

To convince ourselves that this is the real foundation of exchangeable value, let us suppose any improvement to be made in the means of abridging labour in any one of the various processes through which the raw cotton must pass, before the manufactured stockings come to the market, to be exchanged for other things, and observe the effects which will follow. If fewer men were required to cultivate the raw cotton, or if fewer sailors were employed in navigating, or shipwrights in constructing the ship, in which it was conveyed to us; if fewer hands were employed in raising the buildings and machinery, or if these, when raised, were rendered more efficient, the stockings would inevitably fall in value, and consequently command less of other things. They would fall, because a lesser quantity of labour was necessary to their production, and would therefore exchange for a smaller quantity of those things in which no such abridgment of labour had been made.

Economy in the use of labour never fails to reduce the relative value of a commodity, whether the saving be in the labour necessary to the manufacture of the commodity itself, or in that necessary to the formation of the capital, by the aid of which it is produced. In either case the price of stockings would fall, whether there were fewer men employed as bleachers, spinners, and weavers, persons immediately necessary to their manufacture; or as sailors, carriers, engineers, and smiths, persons more indirectly concerned. In the one case, the whole saving of labour would fall on the stockings, because that portion of labour was wholly confined to the stockings; in the other, only a portion would fall on the stockings, the remainder being applied to all those other commodities, to the production of which the buildings, machinery, and carriage, were subservient.

Suppose that in the early stages of society, the bows and arrows of the hunter were of equal value, and of equal durability, with the canoe and implements of the fisherman, both being the produce of the same quantity of labour. Under such circumstances the value of the deer, the produce of the hunter's day's labour, would be exactly equal to the value of the fish, the produce of the fisherman's day's labour. The comparative value of the fish and the game, would be entirely regulated by the quantity of labour realized in each; whatever might be the quantity of production, or however high or low general wages or profits might be. If for example the canoes and implements of the fisherman were of the value of £100 and were calculated to last for ten years, and he employed ten men, whose annual labour cost £100 and who in one day obtained by their labour twenty salmon: if the weapons employed by the hunter were also of £100 value and calculated to last ten years, and if he also employed ten men, whose annual labour cost £100 and who in one day procured him ten deer, then the natural price of a deer would be two salmon, whether the proportion of the whole produce bestowed on the men who obtained it, were large or small. The proportion which might be paid for wages, is of the utmost importance in the question of profits; for it must at once be seen, that profits would be high or low, exactly in proportion as wages were low or high; but it could not in the least affect the relative value of fish and game, as wages would be high or low at the same time in both occupations. If the hunter urged the plea of his paying a large proportion, or the value of a large proportion of his game for wages, as an inducement to the fisherman to give him more fish in exchange for his game, the latter would state that he was equally affected by the same cause; and therefore under all variations of wages and profits, under all the effects of accumulation of capital, as long as they continued by a day's labour to obtain respectively the same quantity of fish, and the same quantity of game, the natural rate of exchange would be one deer for two salmon.

If with the same quantity of labour a less quantity of fish, or a greater quantity of game were obtained, the value of fish would rise in comparison with that of game. If, on the contrary, with the same quantity of labour a less quantity of game, or a greater quantity of fish was obtained, game would rise in comparison with fish.

If there was any other commodity which was invariable in its value, we should be able to ascertain, by comparing the value of fish and game with this commodity, how much of the variation was to be attributed to a cause which affected the value of fish, and how much to a cause which affected the value of game.

Suppose money to be that commodity. If a salmon were worth £1 and a deer £2 one deer would be worth two salmon. But a deer might become of the value of three salmon, for more labour might be required to obtain the deer, or less to get the salmon, or both these causes might operate at the same time. If we had this invariable standard, we might easily ascertain in what degree either of these causes operated. If salmon continued to sell for £1 whilst deer rose to £3 we might conclude that more labour was required to obtain the deer. If deer continued at the same price of £2 and salmon sold for 13s. 4d. we might then be sure that less labour was required to obtain the salmon; further if deer rose to £2 10s. and salmon fell to 16s. 8d. we should be convinced that both causes had operated in producing the alteration of the relative value of these commodities.

No alteration in the wages of labour could produce any alteration in the relative value of these commodities; for them to rise, no greater quantity of labour would be required in any of these occupations, but it would be paid for at a higher price, and the same reasons which should make the hunter and fisherman endeavour to raise the value of their game and fish, would cause the owner of the mine to raise the value of his gold. This inducement acting with the same force on all these three occupations, and the relative situation of those engaged in them being the same before and after the rise of wages, the relative value of game, fish, and gold, would continue unaltered.

Wages might rise 20 per cent, and profits consequently fall in a greater or lesser proportion, without occasioning the least alteration in the relative value of these commodities.

Now suppose, that with the same labour and fixed capital, more fish could be produced, but no more gold or game, the relative value of fish would fall in comparison with gold or game. If, instead of twenty salmon, twenty-five were the produce of one day's labour, the price of a salmon would be sixteen shillings instead of a pound, and two salmon and a half, instead of two salmon, would be given in exchange for one deer, but the price of deer would continue at £2 as before. In the same manner, if fewer fish could be obtained with the same capital and labour, fish would rise in comparative value. Fish then would rise or fall in exchangeable value, only because more or less labour was required to obtain a given quantity; and it never could rise or fall beyond the proportion of the increased or diminished quantity of labour required.

If we had then an invariable standard, by which to measure the variation in other commodities, we should find that the utmost limit to which they could permanently rise, if produced under the circumstances supposed, was proportioned to the additional quantity of labour required for their production; and that unless more labour were required for their production, they could not rise in any degree whatever. A rise in wages would not raise their money value, nor relatively to any other commodities, the production of which required no additional quantity of labour, which employed the same proportion of fixed and circulating capital, and fixed capital of the same durability. If more or less labour were required in the production of the other commodity, we have already stated that this will immediately occasion an alteration in its relative value, but such alteration is owing to the altered quantity of requisite labour, and not to the rise in wages.

Section IV

The principle that the quantity of labour bestowed on the production of commodities regulates their relative value, considerably modified by the employment of machinery and other fixed and durable capital.

In the former section we have supposed the implements and weapons necessary to kill the deer and salmon, to be equally durable, and to be the result of the same quantity of labour, and we have seen that the variations in the relative value of deer and salmon depended solely on the varying quantities of labour necessary to obtain them – but in every state of society, the tools, implements, buildings, and machinery employed in different trades may be of various degrees of durability, and may require different portions of labour to produce them. The proportions, too, in which the capital that is to support labour, and the capital that is invested in tools, machinery and buildings, may be variously combined. This difference in the degree of durability of fixed capital, and this variety in the proportions in which the two sorts of capital may be combined, introduce another cause, besides the greater or lesser quantity of labour necessary to produce commodities, for the variations in their relative value – this cause is the rise or fall in the value of labour.

The food and clothing consumed by the labourer, the buildings in which he works, the implements with which his labour is assisted, are all of a perishable nature. There is however a vast difference in the time for which these different capitals will endure: a steam engine will last longer than a ship, a ship than the clothing of the labourer, and the clothing of the labourer longer than the food which he consumes.

As capital is rapidly perishable, and requires to be frequently reproduced, or is of slow consumption, it is classed under the heads of circulating, or of fixed capital. A brewer, whose buildings and machinery are valuable and durable, is said to employ a large portion of fixed capital; on the contrary, a shoemaker, whose capital is chiefly employed in the payment of wages, which are expended on food and clothing, commodities more perishable than buildings and machinery, is said to employ a large proportion of his capital as circulating capital.

It is also to be observed that the circulating capital may circulate, or be returned to its employer, in very unequal times. The wheat bought by a farmer to sow is a fixed capital compared to the wheat purchased by a baker to make into loaves. One leaves it in the ground, and can obtain no return for a year; the other can get it ground into flour, sell it as bread to his customers, and have his capital free to renew the same, or commence any other employment in a week.

Two trades then may employ the same amount of capital; but it may be very differently divided with respect to the portion which is fixed, and that which is circulating.

In one trade very little capital may be employed as circulating capital, that is to say in the support of labour – it may be principally invested in machinery, implements, buildings, and the like, that is capital of a comparatively fixed and durable character. In another trade the same amount of capital may be used, but it may be chiefly employed in the support of labour, and very little may be invested in implements, machines, and buildings. A rise in the wages of labour cannot fail to affect unequally the commodities produced under such different circumstances.

Again two manufacturers may employ the same amount of fixed, and the same amount of circulating capital; but the durability of their fixed capitals may be very unequal. One may have steam engines of the value of £10,000, the other, ships of the same value.

If men employed no machinery in production but labour only, and were all the same length of time before they brought their commodities to market, the exchangeable value of their goods would be precisely in proportion to the quantity of labour employed.

If they employed fixed capital of the same value and of the same durability, then, too, the value of the commodities produced would be the same, and they would vary with the greater or lesser quantity of labour employed in their production.

But although commodities produced under similar circumstances, would not vary with respect to each other, from any cause but an addition or diminution of the quantity of labour necessary to produce one or other of them, yet compared with others not produced with the same proportionate quantity of fixed capital, they would vary from the other cause also which I have mentioned before, namely, a rise in the value of labour, although neither more nor less labour was employed in the production of either of them. Barley and oats would continue to bear the same relation to each other under any variation of wages. Cotton goods and cloth would do the same, if they also were produced under circumstances precisely similar to each other, but yet with a rise or fall of wages, barley might be more or less valuable compared with cotton goods, and oats compared with cloth.

Suppose two men employ one hundred men each for a year in the construction of two machines, and another man employs the same number of men in cultivating corn, each of the machines at the end of the year will be of the same value as the corn, for they will each be produced by the same quantity of labour. Suppose one of the owners of one of the machines to employ it, with the assistance of one hundred men, the following year in making cloth, and the owner of the other machine to employ his also, with the assistance likewise of one hundred men, in making cotton goods, while the farmer continues to employ one hundred men as before in the cultivation of corn. During the second year they will all have employed the same quantity of labour, but the goods and machine together of the clothier, and also of the cotton manufacturer, will be the result of the labour of two hundred men, employed for a year; or, rather, of the labour of one hundred men for two years; whereas the corn will be produced by the labour of one hundred men for one year, consequently if the corn be of the value of £500 the machine and cloth of the clothier together, ought to be of the value of £1,000 and the machine and cotton goods of the cotton manufacturer ought to be also of twice the value of the corn. But they will be of more than twice the value of the corn, for the profit on the clothier's and cotton manufacturer's capital for the first year has been added to their capitals, while that of the farmer has been expended and enjoyed. On account then of the different degrees of durability of their capitals, or, which is the same thing, on account of the time which must elapse before one set of commodities can be brought to market, they will be valuable, not exactly in proportion to the quantity of labour bestowed on them – they will not be as two to one, but something more, to compensate for the greater length of time which must elapse before the most valuable can be brought to market.

Suppose that for the labour of each workman £50 per annum were paid, or that £5,000 capital were employed and profits were 10 per cent, the value of each of the machines as well as of the corn, at the end of the first year, would be £5,500. The second year the manufacturers and farmer will again employ £5,000 each in the support of labour, and will therefore again sell their goods for £5,500, but the men using the machines, to be on a par with the farmer, must not only obtain £5,500, for the equal capitals of £5,000 employed on labour, but they must obtain a further sum of £550; for the profit on £5,500 which they have invested in machinery, and consequently their goods must sell for £6,050. Here then are capitalists employing precisely the same quantity of labour annually on the production of their commodities, and yet the goods they produce differ in value on account of the different quantities of fixed capital, or accumulated labour, employed by each respectively. The cloth and cotton goods are of the same value, because they are the produce of equal quantities of labour, and equal quantities of fixed capital; but corn is not of the same value as these commodities, because it is produced, as far as regards fixed capital, under different circumstances.

But how will their relative value be affected by a rise in the value of labour? It is evident that the relative values of cloth and cotton goods will undergo no change, for what affects one must equally affect the other, under the circumstances supposed: neither will the relative values of wheat and barley undergo any change, for they are produced under the same circumstances as far as fixed and circulating capital are concerned; but the relative value of corn to cloth, or to cotton goods, must be altered by a rise of labour.

There can be no rise in the value of labour without a fall of profits. If the corn is to be divided between the farmer and the labourer, the larger the proportion that is given to the latter, the lesser will remain for the former. So if cloth or cotton goods be divided between the workman and his employer, the larger the proportion given to the former, the less remains for the latter. Suppose then, that owing to a rise of wages, profits fall from 10 to 9 per cent, instead of adding £550 to the common price of their goods (to £5,500) for the profits on their fixed capital, the manufacturers would add only 9 per cent on that sum, or £495, consequently the price would be £5,995 instead of £6,050. As the corn would continue to sell for £5,500, the manufactured goods in which more fixed capital was employed, would fall relatively to corn or to any other goods in which a less portion of fixed capital entered. The degree of alteration in the relative value of goods, on account of a rise or fall of labour, would depend on the proportion which the fixed capital bore to the whole capital employed. All commodities which are produced by very valuable machinery, or in very valuable buildings, or which require a great length of time before they can be brought to market, would fall in relative value, while all those which were chiefly produced by labour, or which would be speedily brought to market would rise in relative value.

The reader, however, should remark, that this cause of the variation of commodities is comparatively slight in its effects. With such a rise of wages as should occasion a fall of 1 per cent in profits, goods produced under the circumstances I have supposed, vary in relative value only 1 per cent: they fall with so great a fall of profits from £6,050 to £5,995. The greatest effects which could be produced on the relative prices of these goods from a rise of wages, could not exceed 6 or 7 per cent; for profits could not, probably, under any circumstances, admit of a greater general and permanent depression than to that amount.

Not so with the other great cause of the variation in the value of commodities, namely, the increase or diminution in the quantity of labour necessary to produce them. If to produce the corn, eighty, instead of one hundred men, should be required, the value of the corn would fall 20 per cent or from £5,500 to £4,400. If to produce the cloth, the labour of eighty instead of one hundred men would suffice, cloth would fall from £6,050 to £4,950. An alteration in the permanent rate of profits, to any great amount, is the effect of causes which do not operate but in the course of years; whereas alterations in the quantity of labour necessary to produce commodities, are of daily occurrence. Every improvement in machinery, in tools, in buildings, in raising the raw material, saves labour, and enables us to produce the commodity to which the improvement is applied with more facility, and consequently its value alters. In estimating, then, the causes of the variations in the value of commodities, although it would be wrong wholly to omit the consideration of the effect produced by a rise or fall of labour, it would be equally incorrect to attach much importance to it; and consequently, in the subsequent part of this work, though I shall occasionally refer to this cause of variation, I shall consider all the great variations which take place in the relative value of commodities to be produced by the greater or lesser quantity of labour which may be required from time to time to produce them.

It is hardly necessary to say, that commodities which have the same quantity of labour bestowed on their production, will differ in exchangeable value, if they cannot be brought to market in the same time.

Suppose I employ 20 men at an expense of £1,000 for a year in the production of a commodity, and at the end of the year I employ twenty men again for another year, at a further expense of £1,000 in finishing or perfecting the same commodity, and that I bring it to market at the end of two years, if profits be 10 per cent, my commodity must sell for £2,310; for I have employed £1,000 capital for one year, and £2,100 capital for one year more. Another man employs precisely the same quantity of labour, but he employs it all in the first year; he employs forty men at an expense of £2,000, and at the end of the first year he sells it with 10 per cent profit, or for £2,200. Here then are two commodities having precisely the same quantity of labour bestowed on them, one of which sells for £2,310 – the other for £2,200.

This case appears to differ from the last, but is, in fact, the same. In both cases the superior price of one commodity is owing to the greater length of time which must elapse before it can be brought to market. In the former case the machinery and cloth were more than double the value of the corn, although only double the quantity of labour was bestowed on them. In the second case, one commodity is more valuable than the other, although no more labour was employed on its production. The difference in value arises in both cases from the profits being accumulated as capital, and is only a just compensation for the time that the profits were withheld.

It appears then that the division of capital into different proportions of fixed and circulating capital, employed in different trades, introduces a considerable modification to the rule, which is of universal application when labour is almost exclusively employed in production; namely, that commodities never vary in value, unless a greater or lesser quantity of labour be bestowed on their production, it being shown in this section that without any variation in the quantity of labour, the rise of its value merely will occasion a fall in the exchangeable value of those goods, in the production of which fixed capital is employed; the larger the amount of fixed capital, the greater will be the fall.

Section V

The principle that value does not vary with the rise or fall of wages, modified also by the unequal durability of capital, and by the unequal rapidity with which it is returned to its employer.

In the last section we have supposed that of two equal capitals in two different occupations, the proportions of fixed and circulating capitals were unequal, now let us suppose them to be in the same proportion but of unequal durability. In proportion as fixed capital is less durable, it approaches to the nature of circulating capital. It will be consumed and its value reproduced in a shorter time, in order to preserve the capital of the manufacturer. We have just seen, that in proportion as fixed capital preponderates in a manufacture, when wages rise, the value of commodities produced in that manufacture, is relatively lower than that of commodities produced in manufactures where circulating capital preponderates. In proportion to the less durability of fixed capital, and its approach to the nature of circulating capital, the same effect will be produced by the same cause.

...

It will be seen, then, that in the early stages of society, before much machinery or durable capital is used, the commodities produced by equal capitals will be nearly of equal value, and will rise or fall only relatively to each other on account of more or less labour being required for their production; but after the introduction of these expensive and durable instruments, the commodities produced by the employment of equal capitals will be of very unequal value; and although they will still be liable to rise or fall relatively to each other, as more or less labour becomes necessary to their production, they will be subject to another, though a minor variation, also, from the rise or fall of wages and profits. Since goods which sell for £5,000 may be the produce of a capital equal in amount to that from which are produced other goods which sell for £10,000, the profits on their manufacture will be the same; but those profits would be unequal, if the prices of the goods did not vary with a rise or fall in the rate of profits.

It appears, too, that in proportion to the durability of capital employed in any kind of production, the relative prices of those commodities on which such durable capital is employed, will vary inversely as wages; they will fall as wages rise, and rise as wages fall; and, on the contrary, those which are produced chiefly by labour with less fixed capital, or with fixed capital of a less durable character than the medium in which price is estimated, will rise as wages rise, and fall as wages fall.

Section VI

On an invariable measure of value.

When commodities varied in relative value, it would be desirable to have the means of ascertaining which of them fell and which rose in real value, and this could be effected only by comparing them one after another with some invariable standard measure of value, which should itself be subject to none of the fluctuations to which other commodities are exposed. Of such a measure it is impossible to be possessed, because there is no commodity which is not itself exposed to the same variations as the things, the value of which is to be ascertained; that is, there is none which is not subject to require more or less labour for its production. But if this cause of variation in the value of a medium could be removed – if it were possible that in the production of our money for instance, the same quantity of labour should at all times be required, still it would not be a perfect standard or invariable measure of value, because, as I have already endeavoured to explain, it would be subject to relative variations from a rise or fall of wages, on account of the different proportions of fixed capital which might be necessary to produce it, and to produce those other commodities whose alteration of value we wished to ascertain. It might be subject to variations too, from the same cause, on account of the different degrees of durability of the fixed capital employed on it, and the commodities to be compared with it – or the time necessary to bring the one to market, might be longer or shorter than the time necessary to bring the other commodities to market, the variations of which were to be determined; all of which circumstances disqualify any commodity that can be thought of from being a perfectly accurate measure of value.

If, for example, we were to fix on gold as a standard, it is evident that it is but a commodity obtained under the same contingencies as every other commodity, and requiring labour and fixed capital to produce it. Like every other commodity, improvements in the saving of labour might be applied to its production, and consequently it might fall in relative value to other things merely on account of the greater facility of producing it.

If we suppose this cause of variation to be removed, and the same quantity of labour to be always required to obtain the same quantity of gold, still gold would not be a perfect measure of value, by which we could accurately ascertain the variations in all other things, because it would not be produced with precisely the same combinations of fixed and circulating capital as all other things; nor with fixed capital of the same durability; nor would it require precisely the same length of time, before it could be brought to market. It would be a perfect measure of value for all things produced under the same circumstances precisely as itself, but for no others. If, for example, it were produced under the same circumstances as we have supposed necessary to produce cloth and cotton goods, it would be a perfect measure of value for those things, but not so for corn, for coals, and other commodities produced with either a lesser or a greater proportion of fixed capital, because, as we have shown, every alteration in the permanent rate of profits would have some effect on the relative value of all these goods, independently of any alteration in the quantity of labour employed on their production. If gold were produced under the same circumstances as corn, even if they never changed, it would not, for the same reasons, be at all times a perfect measure of the value of cloth and cotton goods. Neither gold then, nor any other commodity, can ever be a perfect measure of value for all things; but I have already remarked, that the effect on the relative prices of things, from a variation in profits, is comparatively slight; that by far the most important effects are produced by the varying quantities of labour required for production; and therefore, if we suppose this important cause of variation removed from the production of gold, we shall probably possess as near an approximation to a standard measure of value as can be theoretically conceived. May not gold be considered as a commodity produced with such proportions of the two kinds of capital as approach nearest to the the average quantity employed in the production of most commodities? May not these proportions be so nearly equally distant from the two extremes, the one where little fixed capital is used, the other where little labour is employed, as to form a just mean between them?

If, then, I may suppose myself to be possessed of a standard so nearly approaching to an invariable one, the advantage is, that I shall be enabled to speak of the variations of other things, without embarrassing myself on every occasion with the consideration of the possible alteration in the value of the medium in which price and value are estimated.

To facilitate, then, the object of this enquiry, although I fully allow that money made of gold is subject to most of the variations of other things, I shall suppose it to be invariable, and therefore all alterations in price to be occasioned by some alteration in the value of the commodity of which I may be speaking.

Before I quit this subject, it may be proper to observe, that Adam Smith, and all the writers who have followed him, have, without one exception that I know of, maintained that a rise in the price of labour would be uniformly followed by a rise in the price of all commodities. I hope I have succeeded in showing, that there are no grounds for such an opinion, and that only those commodities would rise which had less fixed capital employed upon them than the medium in which price was estimated, and that all those which had more, would positively fall in price when wages rose. On the contrary, if wages fell, those commodities only would fall, which had a less proportion of fixed capital employed on them, than the medium in which price was estimated; all those which had more, would positively rise in price.

It is necessary for me also to remark, that I have not said, because one commodity has so much labour bestowed upon it as will cost £1,000 and another so much as will cost £2,000 that therefore one would be of the value of £1,000 and the other of the value of £2,000 but I have said that their value will be to each other as two to one, and that in those proportions they will be exchanged. It is of no importance to the truth of this doctrine, whether one of these commodities sells for £1,100 and the other for £2,200, or one for £1,500 and the other for £3,000; into that question I do not at present enquire; I affirm only, that their relative values will be governed by the relative quantities of labour bestowed on their production.

Chapter 2: On rent

It remains however to be considered, whether the appropriation of land, and the consequent creation of rent, will occasion any variation in the relative value of commodities, independently of the quantity of labour necessary to production. In order to understand this part of the subject, we must enquire into the nature of rent, and the laws by which its rise or fall is regulated.

Rent is that portion of the produce of the earth, which is paid to the landlord for the use of the original and indestructible powers of the soil. It is often, however, confounded with the interest and profit of capital, and, in popular language, the term is applied to whatever is annually paid by a farmer to his landlord. If, of two adjoining farms of the same extent, and of the same natural fertility, one had all the conveniences of farming buildings, and, besides, were properly drained and manured, and advantageously divided by hedges, fences, and walls, while the other had none of these advantages, more remuneration would naturally be paid for the use of one, than for the use of the other; yet in both cases this remuneration would be called rent. But it is evident, that only a portion of the money annually to be paid for the improved farm, would be given for the original and indestructible powers of the soil; the other portion would be paid for the use of the capital which had been employed in ameliorating the quality of the land, and in erecting such buildings as were necessary to secure and preserve the produce. ... This is a distinction of great importance, in an enquiry concerning rent and profits; for it is found, that the laws which regulate the progress of rent, are widely different from those which regulate the progress of profits, and seldom operate in the same direction. In all improved countries, that which is annually paid to the landlord, partaking of both characters, rent, and profit, is sometimes kept stationary by the effects of opposing causes; at other times advances or recedes, as one or the other of these causes preponderates. In the future pages of this work, then, whenever I speak of the rent of land, I wish to be understood as speaking of that compensation, which is paid to the owner of land for the use of its original and indestructible powers.

On the first settling of a country, in which there is an abundance of rich and fertile land, a very small proportion of which is required to be cultivated for the support of the actual population, or indeed can be cultivated with the capital which the population can command, there will be no rent; for no one would pay for the use of land, when there was an abundant quantity not yet appropriated, and, therefore, at the disposal of whosoever might choose to cultivate it.

On the common principles of supply and demand, no rent could be paid for such land, for the reason stated why nothing is given for the use of air and water, or for any other of the gifts of nature which exist in boundless quantity. With a given quantity of materials, and with the assistance of the pressure of the atmosphere, and the elasticity of steam, engines may perform work, and abridge human labour to a very great extent; but no charge is made for the use of these natural aids, because they are inexhaustible, and at every man's disposal. In the same manner the brewer, the distiller, the dyer, make incessant use of the air and water for the production of their commodities; but as the supply is boundless, they bear no price. If all land had the same properties, if it were unlimited in quantity, and uniform in quality, no charge could be made for its use, unless where it possessed peculiar advantages of situation. It is only, then, because land is not unlimited in quantity and uniform in quality, and because in the progress of population, land of an inferior quality, or less advantageously situated, is called into cultivation, that rent is ever paid for the use of it. When in the progress of society, land of the second degree of fertility is taken into cultivation, rent immediately commences on that of the first quality, and the amount of that rent will depend on the difference in the quality of these two portions of land.

When land of the third quality is taken into cultivation, rent immediately commences on the second, and it is regulated as before, by the difference in their productive powers. At the same time, the rent of the first quality will rise, for that must always be above the rent of the second, by the difference between the produce which they yield with a given quantity of capital and labour. With every step in the progress of population, which shall oblige a country to have recourse to land of a worse quality, to enable it to raise its supply of food, rent, on all the more fertile land, will rise.

Thus suppose land – No. 1, 2, 3 – to yield, with an equal employment of capital and labour, a net produce of hundred, ninety, and eighty quarters of corn. In a new country, where there is an abundance of fertile land compared with the population, and where therefore it is only necessary to cultivate No. 1, the whole net produce will belong to the cultivator, and will be the profits of the stock which he advances. As soon as population had so far increased as to make it necessary to cultivate No. 2, from which ninety quarters only can be obtained after supporting the labourers, rent would commence on No. 1; for either there must be two rates of profit on agricultural capital, or ten quarters, or the value of ten quarters must be withdrawn from the produce of No. 1, for some other purpose. Whether the proprietor of the land, or any other person, cultivated No. 1, these ten quarters would equally constitute rent; for the cultivator of No. 2 would get the same result with his capital, whether he cultivated No. 1, paying ten quarters for rent, or continued to cultivate No. 2, paying no rent. In the same manner it might be shown that when No. 3 is brought into cultivation, the rent of No. 2 must be ten quarters, or the value of ten quarters, whilst the rent of No. 1 would rise to twenty quarters; for the cultivator of No. 3 would have the same profits whether he paid twenty quarters for the rent of No. 1, ten quarters for the rent of No. 2, or cultivated No. 3 free of all rent.

...

The most fertile, and most favourably situated, land will be first cultivated, and the exchangeable value of its produce will be adjusted in the same manner as the exchangeable value of all other commodities, by the total quantity of labour necessary in various forms, from first to last, to produce it, and bring it to market. When land of an inferior quality is taken into cultivation, the exchangeable value of raw produce will rise, because more labour is required to produce it.

The exchangeable value of all commodities, whether they be manufactured, or the produce of the mines, or the produce of land, is always regulated, not by the less quantity of labour that will suffice for their production under circumstances highly favourable, and exclusively enjoyed by those who have peculiar facilities of production; but by the greater quantity of labour necessarily bestowed on their production by those who have no such facilities; by those who continue to produce them under the most unfavourable circumstances; meaning – by the most unfavourable circumstances, the most unfavourable under which the quantity of produce required, renders it necessary to carry on the production.

...

It is true, that on the best land, the same produce would still be obtained with the same labour as before, but its value would be enhanced in consequence of the diminished returns obtained by those who employed fresh labour and stock on the less fertile land. Notwithstanding, then, that the advantages of fertile over inferior lands are in no case lost, but only transferred from the cultivator, or consumer, to the landlord, yet, since more labour is required on the inferior lands, and since it is from such land only that we are enabled to furnish ourselves with the additional supply of raw produce, the comparative value of that produce will continue permanently above its former level, and make it exchange for more hats, cloth, shoes, and the like in the production of which no such additional quantity of labour is required.

The reason then, why raw produce rises in comparative value, is because more labour is employed in the production of the last portion obtained, and not because a rent is paid to the landlord. The value of corn is regulated by the quantity of labour bestowed on its production on that quality of land, or with that portion of capital, which pays no rent. Corn is not high because a rent is paid, but a rent is paid because corn is high; and it has been justly observed, that no reduction would take place in the price of corn, although landlords should forego the whole of their rent. Such a measure would only enable some farmers to live like gentlemen, but would not diminish the quantity of labour necessary to raise raw produce on the least productive land in cultivation.

Nothing is more common than to hear of the advantages which the land possesses over every other source of useful produce, on account of the surplus which it yields in the form of rent. Yet when land is most abundant, when most productive, and most fertile, it yields no rent; and it is only when its powers decay, and less is yielded in return for labour, that a share of the original produce of the more fertile portions is set apart for rent. It is singular that this quality in the land, which should have been noticed as an imperfection, compared with the natural agents by which manufacturers are assisted, should have been pointed out as constituting its peculiar pre-eminence. If air, water, the elasticity of steam, and the pressure of the atmosphere, were of various qualities; if they could be appropriated, and each quality existed only in moderate abundance, they, as well as the land, would afford a rent, as the successive qualities were brought into use. With every worse quality employed, the value of the commodities in the manufacture of which they were used, would rise, because equal quantities of labour would be less productive. Man would do more by the sweat of his brow, and nature perform less; and the land would be no longer pre-eminent for its limited powers.

...

The rise of rent is always the effect of the increasing wealth of the country, and of the difficulty of providing food for its augmented population. It is a symptom, but it is never a cause of wealth; for wealth often increases most rapidly while rent is either stationary, or even falling. Rent increases most rapidly, as the disposable land decreases in its productive powers. Wealth increases most rapidly in those countries where the disposable land is most fertile, where importation is least restricted, and where through agricultural improvements, productions can be multiplied without any increase in the proportional quantity of labour, and where consequently the progress of rent is slow.

If the high price of corn were the effect, and not the cause of rent, price would be proportionally influenced as rents were high or low, and rent would be a component part of price. But that corn which is produced by the greatest quantity of labour is the regulator of the price of corn; and rent does not and cannot enter in the least degree as a component part of its price. Adam Smith, therefore, cannot be correct in supposing that the original rule which regulated the exchangeable value of commodities, namely, the comparative quantity of labour by which they were produced, can be at all altered by the appropriation of land and the payment of rent. Raw material enters into the composition of most commodities, but the value of that raw material, as well as corn, is regulated by the productiveness of the portion of capital last employed on the land, and paying no rent; and therefore rent is not a component part of the price of commodities.

...

Without multiplying instances, I hope enough has been said to show, that whatever diminishes the inequality in the produce obtained from successive portions of capital employed on the same or on new land, tends to lower rent; and that whatever increases that inequality, necessarily produces an opposite effect, and tends to raise it.

In speaking of the rent of the landlord, we have rather considered it as the proportion of the produce, obtained with a given capital on any given farm, without any reference to its exchangeable value; but since the same cause, the difficulty of production, raises the exchangeable value of raw produce, and raises also the proportion of raw produce paid to the landlord for rent, it is obvious that the landlord is doubly benefited by difficulty of production. First, he obtains a greater share, and second the commodity in which he is paid is of greater value.

Chapter 5: On wages

Labour, like all other things which are purchased and sold, and which may be increased or diminished in quantity, has its natural and its market price. The natural price of labour is that price which is necessary to enable the labourers, one with another, to subsist and to perpetuate their race, without either increase or diminution.

The power of the labourer to support himself, and the family which may be necessary to keep up the number of labourers, does not depend on the quantity of money which he may receive for wages, but on the quantity of food, necessaries, and conveniences become essential to him from habit, which that money will purchase. The natural price of labour, therefore, depends on the price of the food, necessaries, and conveniences required for the support of the labourer and his family. With a rise in the price of food and necessaries, the natural price of labour will rise; with the fall in their price, the natural price of labour will fall.

With the progress of society the natural price of labour always has a tendency to rise, because one of the principal commodities by which its natural price is regulated, has a tendency to become dearer, from the greater difficulty of producing it. As, however, the improvements in agriculture, the discovery of new markets, whence provisions may be imported, may for a time counteract the tendency to a rise in the price of necessaries, and may even occasion their natural price to fall, so will the same causes produce the correspondent effects on the natural price of labour.

The natural price of all commodities, excepting raw produce and labour, has a tendency to fall, in the progress of wealth and population; for though, on one hand, they are enhanced in real value, from the rise in the natural price of the raw material of which they are made, this is more than counterbalanced by the improvements in machinery, by the better division and distribution of labour, and by the increasing skill, both in science and art, of the producers.

The market price of labour is the price which is really paid for it, from the natural operation of the proportion of the supply to the demand; labour is dear when it is scarce, and cheap when it is plentiful. However much the market price of labour may deviate from its natural price, it has, like commodities, a tendency to conform to it.

It is when the market price of labour exceeds its natural price, that the condition of the labourer is flourishing and happy, that he has it in his power to command a greater proportion of the necessaries and enjoyments of life, and therefore to rear a healthy and numerous family. When, however, by the encouragement which high wages give to the increase of population, the number of labourers is increased, wages again fall to their natural price, and indeed from a reaction sometimes fall below it.

When the market price of labour is below its natural price, the condition of the labourers is most wretched: then poverty deprives them of those comforts which custom renders absolute necessaries. It is only after their privations have reduced their number, or the demand for labour has increased, that the market price of labour will rise to its natural price, and that the labourer will have the moderate comforts which the natural rate of wages will afford.

Notwithstanding the tendency of wages to conform to their natural rate, their market rate may, in an improving society, for an indefinite period, be constantly above it; for no sooner may the impulse, which an increased capital gives to a new demand for labour be obeyed, than another increase of capital may produce the same effect; and thus, if the increase of capital be gradual and constant, the demand for labour may give a continued stimulus to an increase of people.

...

Thus, then, with every improvement of society, with every increase in its capital, the market wages of labour will rise; but the permanence of their rise will depend on the question, whether the natural price of labour has also risen; and this again will depend on the rise in the natural price of those necessaries on which the wages of labour are expended.

It is not to be understood that the natural price of labour, estimated even in food and necessaries, is absolutely fixed and constant. It varies at different times in the same country, and very materially differs in different countries. It essentially depends on the habits and customs of the people. An English labourer would consider his wages under their natural rate, and too scanty to support a family, if they enabled him to purchase no other food than potatoes, and to live in no better habitation than a mud cabin; yet these moderate demands of nature are often deemed sufficient in countries where 'man's life is cheap', and his wants easily satisfied. Many of the conveniences now enjoyed in an English cottage, would have been thought luxuries at an earlier period of our history.

From manufactured commodities always falling, and raw produce always rising, with the progress of society, such a disproportion in their relative value is at length created, that in rich countries a labourer, by the sacrifice of a very small quantity only of his food, is able to provide liberally for all his other wants.

Independently of the variations in the value of money, which necessarily affect money wages, but which we have here supposed to have no operation, as we have considered money to be uniformly of the same value, it appears then that wages are subject to a rise or fall from two causes: first the supply and demand of labourers; and second the price of the commodities on which the wages of labour are expended.

In different stages of society, the accumulation of capital, or of the means of employing labour, is more or less rapid, and must in all cases depend on the productive powers of labour. The productive powers of labour are generally greatest when there is an abundance of fertile land: at such periods accumulation is often so rapid, that labourers cannot be supplied with the same rapidity as capital.

It has been calculated, that under favourable circumstances population may be doubled in twenty-five years; but under the same favourable circumstances, the whole capital of a country might possibly be doubled in a shorter period. In that case, wages during the whole period would have a tendency to rise, because the demand for labour would increase still faster than the supply.

In new settlements, where the arts and knowledge of countries far advanced in refinement are introduced, it is probable that capital has a tendency to increase faster than mankind: and if the deficiency of labourers were not supplied by more populous countries, this tendency would very much raise the price of labour. In proportion as these countries become populous, and land of a worse quality is taken into cultivation, the tendency to an increase of capital diminishes; for the surplus produce remaining, after satisfying the wants of the existing population, must necessarily be in proportion to the facility of production, namely to the smaller number of persons employed in production. Although, then, it is probable, that under the most favourable circumstances, the power of production is still greater than that of population, it will not long continue so; for the land being limited in quantity, and differing in quality, with every increased portion of capital employed on it, there will be a decreased rate of production, whilst the power of population continues always the same.

In those countries where there is abundance of fertile land, but where, from the ignorance, indolence, and barbarism of the inhabitants, they are exposed to all the evils of want and famine, and where it has been said that population presses against the means of subsistence, a very different remedy should be applied from that which is necessary in long-settled countries, where, from the diminishing rate of the supply of raw produce, all the evils of a crowded population are experienced. In the one case, the evil proceeds from bad government, from the insecurity of property, and from a want of education in all ranks of the people. To be made happier they require only to be better governed and instructed, as the augmentation of capital, beyond the augmentation of people, would be the inevitable result. No increase in the population can be too great, as the powers of production are still greater. In the other case, the population increases faster than the funds required for its support. Every exertion of industry, unless accompanied by a diminished rate of increase in the population, will add to the evil, for production cannot keep pace with it.

With a population pressing against the means of subsistence, the only remedies are either a reduction of people, or a more rapid accumulation of capital. In rich countries, where all the fertile land is already cultivated, the latter remedy is neither very practicable nor very desirable, because its effect would be, if pushed very far, to render all classes equally poor. But in poor countries, where there are abundant means of production in store, from fertile land not yet brought into cultivation, it is the only safe and efficacious means of removing the evil, particularly as its effect would be to elevate all classes of the people.

The friends of humanity cannot but wish that in all countries the labouring classes should have a taste for comforts and enjoyments, and that they should be stimulated by all legal means in their exertions to procure them. There cannot be a better security against a superabundant population. In those countries, where the labouring classes have the fewest wants, and are contented with the cheapest food, the people are exposed to the greatest vicissitudes and miseries. They have no place of refuge from calamity; they cannot seek safety in a lower station; they are already so low, that they can fall no lower. On any deficiency of the chief article of their subsistence, there are few substitutes of which they can avail themselves, and dearth to them is attended with almost all the evils of famine.

In the natural advance of society, the wages of labour will have a tendency to fall, as far as they are regulated by supply and demand; for the supply of labourers will continue to increase at the same rate, whilst the demand for them will increase at a slower rate. If, for instance, wages were regulated by a yearly increase of capital, at the rate of 2 per cent, they would fall when it accumulated only at the rate of 1.5 per cent. They would fall still lower when it increased only at the rate of 1, or 0.5 per cent, and would continue to do so until the capital became stationary, when wages also would become stationary, and be only sufficient to keep up the numbers of the actual population. I say that, under these circumstances, wages would fall, if they were regulated only by the supply and demand of labourers; but we must not forget, that wages are also regulated by the prices of the commodities on which they are expended.

As population increases, these necessaries will be constantly rising in price, because more labour will be necessary to produce them. If, then, the money wages of labour should fall, whilst every commodity on which the wages of labour were expended rose, the labourer would be doubly affected, and would be soon totally deprived of subsistence. Instead, therefore, of the money wages of labour falling, they would rise; but they would not rise sufficiently to enable the labourer to purchase as many comforts and necessaries as he did before the rise in the price of those commodities. If his annual wages were before £24, or six quarters of corn when the price was £4 per quarter, he would probably receive only the value of five quarters when corn rose to £5 per quarter.

But five quarters would cost £25; he would therefore receive an addition in his money wages, though with that addition he would be unable to furnish himself with the same quantity of corn and other commodities, which he had before consumed in his family.

Notwithstanding, then, that the labourer would be really worse paid, yet this increase in his wages would necessarily diminish the profits of the manufacturer; for his goods would sell at no higher price, and yet the expense of producing them would be increased. This, however, will be considered in our examination into the principles which regulate profits.

It appears, then, that the same cause which raises rent, namely, the increasing difficulty of providing an additional quantity of food with the same proportional quantity of labour, will also raise wages; and therefore if money be of an unvarying value, both rent and wages will have a tendency to rise with the progress of wealth and population.

But there is this essential difference between the rise of rent and the rise of wages. The rise in the money value of rent is accompanied by an increased share of the produce; not only is the landlord's money rent greater, but his corn rent also; he will have more corn, and each defined measure of that corn will exchange for a greater quantity of all other goods which have not been raised in value. The fate of the labourer will be less happy; he will receive more money wages, it is true, but his corn wages will be reduced; and not only his command of corn, but his general condition will be deteriorated, by his finding it more difficult to maintain the market rate of wages above their natural rate. While the price of corn rises 10 per cent, wages will always rise less than 10 per cent, but rent will always rise more; the condition of the labourer will generally decline, and that of the landlord will always be improved.

...

In proportion as corn became dear, he would receive less corn wages, but his money wages would always increase, whilst his enjoyments, on the above supposition, would be precisely the same. But as other commodities would be raised in price in proportion as raw produce entered into their composition, he would have more to pay for some of them. Although his tea, sugar, soap, candles, and house rent, would probably be no dearer, he would pay more for his bacon, cheese, butter, linen, shoes, and cloth; and therefore, even with the above increase of wages, his situation would be comparatively worse. But it may be said that I have been considering the effect of wages on price, on the supposition that gold, or the metal from which money is made, is the produce of the country in which wages varied; and that the consequences which I have deduced agree little with the actual state of things, because gold is a metal of foreign production. The circumstance, however, of gold being a foreign production, will not invalidate the truth of the argument, because it may be shewn, that whether it were found at home, or were imported from abroad, the effects ultimately and, indeed, immediately would be the same.

...

These then are the laws by which wages are regulated, and by which the happiness of far the greatest part of every community is governed. Like all other contracts, wages should be left to the fair and free competition of the market, and should never be controlled by the interference of the legislature.

The clear and direct tendency of the poor laws, is in direct opposition to these obvious principles: it is not, as the legislature benevolently intended, to amend the condition of the poor, but to deteriorate the condition of both poor and rich; instead of making the poor rich, they are calculated to make the rich poor; and whilst the present laws are in force, it is quite in the natural order of things that the fund for the maintenance of the poor should progressively increase, till it has absorbed all the net revenue of the country, or at least so much of it as the state shall leave to us, after satisfying its own never failing demands for the public expenditure.

This pernicious tendency of these laws is no longer a mystery, since it has been fully developed by the able hand of Mr Malthus; and every friend to the poor must ardently wish for their abolition. Unfortunately, however, they have been so long established, and the habits of the poor have been so formed upon their operation, that to eradicate them with safety from our political system, requires the most cautious and skilful management. It is agreed by all who are most friendly to a repeal of these laws, that if it be desirable to prevent the most overwhelming distress to those for whose benefit they were erroneously enacted, their abolition should be effected by the most gradual steps.

It is a truth which admits not a doubt, that the comforts and well-being of the poor cannot be permanently secured without some regard on their part, or some effort on the part of the legislature, to regulate the increase of their numbers, and to render less frequent among them early and improvident marriages. The operation of the system of poor laws has been directly contrary to this. They have rendered restraint superfluous, and have invited imprudence, by offering it a portion of the wages of prudence and industry.

The nature of the evil points out the remedy. By gradually contracting the sphere of the poor laws; by impressing on the poor the value of independence, by teaching them that they must look not to systematic or casual charity, but to their own exertions for support, that prudence and forethought are neither unnecessary nor unprofitable virtues, we shall by degrees approach a sounder and more healthful state.

No scheme for the amendment of the poor laws merits the least attention, which has not their abolition for its ultimate object; and he is the best friend to the poor, and to the cause of humanity, who can point out how this end can be attained with the most security, and at the same time with the least violence. It is not by raising in any manner different from the present, the fund from which the poor are supported, that the evil can be mitigated. It would not only be no improvement, but it would be an aggravation of the distress which we wish to see removed, if the fund were increased in amount, or were levied according to some late proposals, as a general fund from the country at large. The present mode of its collection and application has served to mitigate its pernicious effects. Each parish raises a separate fund for the support of its own poor. Hence it becomes an object of more interest and more practicability to keep the rates low, than if one general fund were raised for the relief of the poor of the whole kingdom. A parish is much more interested in an economical collection of the rate, and a sparing distribution of relief, when the whole saving will be for its own benefit, than if hundreds of other parishes were to partake of it.

It is to this cause, that we must ascribe the fact of the poor laws not having yet absorbed all the net revenue of the country; it is to the rigour with which they are applied, that we are indebted for their not having become overwhelmingly oppressive. If by law every human being wanting support could be sure to obtain it, and obtain it in such a degree as to make life tolerably comfortable, theory would lead us to expect that all other taxes together would be light compared with the single one of poor rates. The principle of gravitation is not more certain than the tendency of such laws to change wealth and power into misery and weakness; to call away the exertions of labour from every object, except that of providing mere subsistence; to confound all intellectual distinction; to busy the mind continually in supplying the body's wants; until at last all classes should be infected with the plague of universal poverty. Happily these laws have been in operation during a period of progressive prosperity, when the funds for the maintenance of labour have regularly increased, and when an increase of population would be naturally called for. But if our progress should become more slow; if we should attain the stationary state, from which I trust we are yet far distant, then will the pernicious nature of these laws become more manifest and alarming; and then, too, will their removal be obstructed by many additional difficulties.

Chapter 6: On profits

The profits of stock, in different employments, having been shewn to bear a proportion to each other, and to have a tendency to vary all in the same degree and in the same direction, it remains for us to consider what is the cause of the permanent variations in the rate of profit, and the consequent permanent alterations in the rate of interest.

We have seen that the price of corn is regulated by the quantity of labour necessary to produce it, with that portion of capital which pays no rent. We have seen, too, that all manufactured commodities rise and fall in price, in proportion as more or less labour becomes necessary to their production. Neither the farmer who cultivates that quantity of land, which regulates price, nor the manufacturer, who manufactures goods, sacrifice any portion of the produce for rent. The whole value of their commodities is divided into two portions only: one constitutes the profits of stock, the other the wages of labour.

Supposing corn and manufactured goods always to sell at the same price, profits would be high or low in proportion as wages were low or high. But suppose corn to rise in price because more labour is necessary to produce it; that cause will not raise the price of manufactured goods in the production of which no additional quantity of labour is required. If, then, wages continued the same, the profits of manufacturers would remain the same; but if, as is absolutely certain, wages should rise with the rise of corn, then their profits would necessarily fall.

If a manufacturer always sold his goods for the same money, for £1,000, for example, his profits would depend on the price of the labour necessary to manufacture those goods. His profits would be less when wages amounted to £800 than when he paid only £600. In proportion then as wages rose, would profits fall. But if the price of raw produce would increase, it may be asked, whether the farmer at least would not have the same rate of profits, although he should pay an additional sum for wages? Certainly not: for he will not only have to pay, in common with the manufacturer, an increase of wages to each labourer he employs, but he will be obliged either to pay rent, or to employ an additional number of labourers to obtain the same produce; and the rise in the price of raw produce will be proportioned only to that rent, or that additional number, and will not compensate him for the rise of wages.

If both the manufacturer and farmer employed ten men, on wages rising from £24 to £25 per annum per man, the whole sum paid by each would be £250 instead of £240. This is, however, the whole addition that would be paid by the manufacturer to obtain the same quantity of commodities; but the farmer on new land would probably be obliged to employ an additional man, and therefore to pay an additional sum of £25 for wages; and the farmer on the old land would be obliged to pay precisely the same additional sum of £25 for rent; without which additional labour, corn would not have risen, nor rent have been increased. One will therefore have to pay £275 for wages alone, the other, for wages and rent together; each £25 more than the manufacturer: for this latter £25 the farmer is compensated by the addition to the price of raw produce, and therefore his profits still conform to the profits of the manufacturer. …

…

There are few commodities which are not more or less affected in their price by the rise of raw produce, because some raw material from the land enters into the composition of most commodities. Cotton goods, linen, and cloth, will all rise in price with the rise of wheat; but they rise on account of the greater quantity of labour expended on the raw material from which they are made, and not because more was paid by the manufacturer to the labourers whom he employed on those commodities.

In all cases, commodities rise because more labour is expended on them, and not because the labour which is expended on them is at a higher value. Articles of jewellery, of iron, of plate, and of copper, would not rise, because none of the raw produce from the surface of the earth enters into their composition.

It may be said that I have taken it for granted, that money wages would rise with a rise in the price of raw produce, but that this is by no means a necessary consequence, as the labourer may be contented with fewer enjoyments. It is true that the wages of labour may previously have been at a high level, and that they may bear some reduction. If so, the fall of profits will be checked; but it is impossible to conceive that the money price of wages should fall, or remain stationary with a gradually increasing price of necessaries; and therefore it may be taken for granted that, under ordinary circumstances, no permanent rise takes place in the price of necessaries, without occasioning, or having been preceded by a rise in wages.

The effects produced on profits would have been the same, or nearly the same, if there had been any rise in the price of those other necessaries, besides food, on which the wages of labour are expended. The necessity under which the labourer would be paying an increased price for such necessaries, would oblige him to demand more wages; and whatever increases wages, necessarily reduces profits. But suppose the price of silks, velvets, furniture, and any other commodities, not required by the labourer, to rise in consequence of more labour being expended on them, would not that affect profits? Certainly not: for nothing can affect profits but a rise in wages; silks and velvets are not consumed by the labourer, and therefore cannot raise wages.

It is to be understood that I am speaking of profits generally. I have already remarked, that the market price of a commodity may exceed its natural or necessary price, as it may be produced in less abundance than the new demand for it requires. This, however, is but a temporary effect. The high profits on capital employed in producing that commodity, will naturally attract capital to that trade; and as soon as the requisite funds are supplied, and the quantity of the commodity is duly increased, its price will fall, and the profits of the trade will conform to the general level. A fall in the general rate of profits is by no means incompatible with a partial rise of profits in particular employments. It is through the inequality of profits, that capital is moved from one employment to another. Whilst then general profits are falling, and gradually setting at a lower level in consequence of the rise of wages, and the increasing difficulty of supplying the increasing population with necessaries, the profits of the farmer may, for an interval of some little duration, be above the former level. An extraordinary stimulus may also be given for a certain time, to a particular branch of foreign and colonial trade; but the admission of this fact by no means invalidates the theory, that profits depend on high or low wages, wages on the price of necessaries, and the price of necessaries chiefly on the price of food, because all other requisites may be increased almost without limit.

It should be recollected that prices always vary in the market, and in the first instance, through the comparative state of demand and supply. Although cloth could be furnished at 40s. per yard, and give the usual profits of stock, it may rise to 60 or 80s. from a general change of fashion, or from any other cause which should suddenly and unexpectedly increase the demand, or diminish the supply of it. The makers of cloth will for a time have unusual profits, but capital will naturally flow to that manufacture, till the supply and demand are again at their fair level, when the price of cloth will again sink to 40s., its natural or necessary price. In the same manner, with every increased demand for corn, it may rise so high as to afford more than the general profits to the farmer. If there be plenty of fertile land, the price of corn will again fall to its former standard, after the requisite quantity of capital has been employed in producing it, and profits will be as before; but if there be not plenty of fertile land, if, to produce this additional quantity, more than the usual quantity of capital and labour be required, corn will not fall to its former level. Its natural price will be raised, and the farmer, instead of obtaining permanently larger profits, will find himself obliged to be satisfied with the diminished rate which is the inevitable consequence of the rise of wages, produced by the rise of necessaries.

The natural tendency of profits then is to fall; for in the progress of society and wealth, the additional quantity of food required is obtained by the sacrifice of more and more labour. This tendency, this gravitation as it were of profits, is happily checked at repeated intervals by the improvements in machinery, connected with the production of necessaries, as well as by discoveries in the science of agriculture which enable us to relinquish a portion of labour before required, and therefore to lower the price of the prime necessary of the labourer. The rise in the price of necessaries and in the wages of labour is however limited; for as soon as wages should be equal (as in the case formerly stated) to £720, the whole receipts of the farmer, there must be an end of accumulation; for no capital can then yield any profit whatever, and no additional labour can be demanded, and consequently population will have reached its highest point. Long indeed before this period, the very low rate of profits will have arrested all accumulation, and almost the whole produce of the country, after paying the labourers, will be the property of the owners of land and the receivers of tithes and taxes.

...

Chapter 7: On foreign trade

No extension of foreign trade will immediately increase the amount of value in a country, although it will very powerfully contribute to increase the mass of commodities, and therefore the sum of enjoyments. As the value of all foreign goods is measured by the quantity of the produce of our land and labour, which is given in exchange for them, we should have no greater value, if by the discovery of new markets, we obtained double the quantity of foreign goods in exchange for a given quantity of ours. If by the purchase of English goods to the amount of £1,000, a merchant can obtain a quantity of foreign goods, which he can sell in the English market for £1,200, he will obtain 20 per cent profit by such an employment of his capital; but neither his gains, nor the value of the commodities imported, will be increased or diminished by the greater or smaller quantity of foreign goods obtained. Whether, for example, he imports twenty-five or fifty pipes of wine, his interest can be no way affected, if at one time the twenty-five pipes, and at another the fifty pipes, equally sell for £1,200. In either case his profit will be limited to £200, or 20 per cent on his capital; and in either case the same value will be imported into England. If the fifty pipes sold for more than £1,200, the profits of this individual merchant would exceed the general rate of profits, and capital would naturally flow into this advantageous trade, till the fall of the price of wine had brought every thing to the former level.

It has indeed been contended, that the great profits which are sometimes made by particular merchants in foreign trade, will elevate the general rate of profits in the country, and that the abstraction of capital from other employments, to partake of the new and beneficial foreign commerce, will raise prices generally, and thereby increase profits. It has been said, by high authority, that less capital being necessarily devoted to the growth of corn, to the manufacture of cloth, hats, shoes, and so on, while the demand continues the same, the price of these commodities will be so increased, that the farmer, hatter, clothier, and shoemaker, will have an increase of profits, as well as the foreign merchant.

They who hold this argument agree with me, that the profits of different employments have a tendency to conform to one another; to advance and recede together. Our variance consists in this: they contend, that the equality of profits will be brought about by the general rise of profits; and I am of opinion, that the profits of the favoured trade will speedily subside to the general level.

For, first, I deny that less capital will necessarily be devoted to the growth of corn, to the manufacture of cloth, hats, shoes, and so on unless the demand for these commodities be diminished; and if so, their price will not rise. In the purchase of foreign commodities, either the same, a larger, or a lesser portion of the produce of the land and labour of England will be employed.

If the same portion be so employed, then will the same demand exist for cloth, shoes, corn, and hats, as before, and the same portion of capital will be devoted to their production. If, in consequence of the price of foreign commodities being cheaper, a lesser portion of the annual produce of the land and labour of England is employed in the purchase of foreign commodities, more will remain for the purchase of other things. If there be a greater demand for hats, shoes, corn, and the like than before, which there may be, the consumers of foreign commodities having an additional portion of their revenue disposable, the capital is also disposable with which the greater value of foreign commodities was purchased before; so that with the increased demand for corn, shoes, and so on there exists also the means of procuring an increased supply, and therefore neither prices nor profits can permanently rise. If more of the produce of the land and labour of England be employed in the purchase of foreign commodities, less can be employed in the purchase of other things, and therefore fewer hats, shoes, and so on will be required. At the same time that capital is liberated from the production of shoes, hats, and so on more must be employed in manufacturing those commodities with which foreign commodities are purchased; and consequently in all cases the demand for foreign and home commodities together, as far as regards value, is limited by the revenue and capital of the country. If one increases, the other must diminish. If the quantity of wine, imported in exchange for the same quantity of English commodities, be doubled, the people of England can either consume double the quantity of wine that they did before, or the same quantity of wine and a greater quantity of English commodities. If my revenue had been £1,000, with which I purchased annually one pipe of wine for £100 and a certain quantity of English commodities for £900; when wine fell to £50 per pipe, I might lay out the £50 saved, either in the purchase of an additional pipe of wine, or in the purchase of more English commodities. If I bought more wine, and every wine drinker did the same, the foreign trade would not be in the least disturbed; the same quantity of English commodities would be exported in exchange for wine, and we should receive double the quantity, though not double the value of wine. But if I, and others, contented ourselves with the same quantity of wine as before, fewer English commodities would be exported, and the wine drinkers might either consume the commodities which were before exported, or any others for which they had an inclination. The capital required for their production would be supplied by the capital liberated from the foreign trade.

There are two ways in which capital may be accumulated: it may be saved either in consequence of increased revenue, or of diminished consumption. If my profits are raised from £1,000 to £1,200 while my expenditure continues the same, I accumulate annually £200 more than I did before. If I save £200 out of my expenditure, while my profits continue the same, the same effect will be produced; £200 per annum will be added to my capital. The merchant who imported wine after profits had been raised from 20 to 40 per cent, instead of purchasing his English goods for £1,000 must purchase them for £857 2s. 10d., still selling the wine which he imports in return for those goods for £1,200; or, if he continued to purchase his English goods for £1,000 must raise the price of his wine to £1,400; he would thus obtain 40 instead of 20 per cent profit on his capital; but if, in consequence of the cheapness of all the commodities on which his revenue was expended, he and all other consumers could save the value of £200 out of every £1,000 they expended before, they would more effectually add to the real wealth of the country; in one case, the savings would be made in consequence of an increase of revenue, in the other, in consequence of diminished expenditure.

If, by the introduction of machinery, the generality of the commodities on which revenue was expended fell 20 per cent in value, I should be enabled to save as effectually as if my revenue had been raised 20 per cent; but in one case the rate of profits is stationary, in the other it is raised 20 per cent. If, by the introduction of cheap foreign goods, I can save 20 per cent from my expenditure, the effect will be precisely the same as if machinery had lowered the expense of their production, but profits would not be raised.

It is not, therefore, in consequence of the extension of the market that the rate of profit is raised, although such extension may be equally efficacious in increasing the mass of commodities, and may thereby enable us to augment the funds destined for the maintenance of labour, and the materials on which labour may be employed. It is quite as important to the happiness of mankind, that our enjoyments should be increased by the better distribution of labour, by each country producing those commodities for which by its situation, its climate, and its other natural or artificial advantages, it is adapted, and by their exchanging them for the commodities of other countries, as they should be augmented by a rise in the rate of profits.

It has been my endeavour to shew throughout this work, that the rate of profits can never be increased but by a fall in wages, and that there can be no permanent fall of wages but in consequence of a fall of the necessaries on which wages are expended. If, therefore, by the extension of foreign trade, or by improvements in machinery, the food and necessaries of the labourer can be brought to market at a reduced price, profits will rise. If, instead of growing our own corn, or manufacturing the clothing and other necessaries of the labourer, we discover a new market from which we can supply ourselves with these commodities at a cheaper price, wages will fall and profits rise; but if the commodities obtained at a cheaper rate, by the extension of foreign commerce, or by the improvement of machinery, be exclusively the commodities consumed by the rich, no alteration will take place in the rate of profits. The rate of wages would not be affected, although wine, velvets, silks, and other expensive commodities should fall 50 per cent, and consequently profits would continue unaltered.

Foreign trade, then, though highly beneficial to a country, as it increases the amount and variety of the objects on which revenue may be expended, and affords, by the abundance and cheapness of commodities, incentives to saving, and to the accumulation of capital, has no tendency to raise the profits of stock, unless the commodities imported be of that description on which the wages of labour are expended.

The remarks which have been made respecting foreign trade, apply equally to home trade. The rate of profits is never increased by a better distribution of labour, by the invention of machinery, by the establishment of roads and canals, or by any means of abridging labour either in the manufacture or in the conveyance of goods. These are causes which operate on price, and never fail to be highly beneficial to consumers; since they enable them with the same labour, or with the value of the produce of the same labour, to obtain in exchange a greater quantity of the commodity to which the improvement is applied; but they have no effect whatever on profit. On the other hand, every diminution in the wages of labour raises profits, but produces no effect on the price of commodities. One is advantageous to all classes, for all classes are consumers; the other is beneficial only to producers; they gain more, but every thing remains at its former price. In the first case they get the same as before; but every thing on which their gains are expended, is diminished in exchangeable value.

The same rule which regulates the relative value of commodities in one country, does not regulate the relative value of the commodities exchanged between two or more countries.

Under a system of perfectly free commerce, each country naturally devotes its capital and labour to such employments as are most beneficial to each. This pursuit of individual advantage is admirably connected with the universal good of the whole. By stimulating industry, by rewarding ingenuity, and by using most efficaciously the peculiar powers bestowed by nature, it distributes labour most effectively and most economically; while, by increasing the general mass of productions, it diffuses general benefit, and binds together by one common tie of interest and intercourse, the universal society of nations throughout the civilized world. It is this principle which determines that wine shall be made in France and Portugal, that corn shall be grown in America and Poland, and that hardware and other goods shall be manufactured in England.

In one and the same country, profits are, generally speaking, always on the same level; or differ only as the employment of capital may be more or less secure and agreeable. It is not so between different countries. If the profits of capital employed in Yorkshire, should exceed those of capital employed in London, capital would speedily move from London to Yorkshire, and an equality of profits would be effected; but if in consequence of the diminished rate of production in the lands of England, from the increase of capital and population, wages should rise, and profits fall, it would not follow that capital and population would necessarily move from England to Holland, or Spain, or Russia, where profits might be higher.

If Portugal had no commercial connexion with other countries, instead of employing a great part of her capital and industry in the production of wines, with which she purchases for her own use the cloth and hardware of other countries, she would be obliged to devote a part of that capital to the manufacture of those commodities, which she would thus obtain probably inferior in quality as well as quantity.

The quantity of wine which she shall give in exchange for the cloth of England, is not determined by the respective quantities of labour devoted to the production of each, as it would be, if both commodities were manufactured in England, or both in Portugal.

England may be so circumstanced, that to produce the cloth may require the labour of 100 men for one year; and if she attempted to make the wine, it might require the labour of 120 men for the same time. England would therefore find it her interest to import wine, and to purchase it by the exportation of cloth.

To produce the wine in Portugal, might require only the labour of 80 men for one year, and to produce the cloth in the same country, might require the labour of 90 men for the same time. It would therefore be advantageous for her to export wine in exchange for cloth. This exchange might even take place, notwithstanding that the commodity imported by Portugal could be produced there with less labour than in England. Though she could make the cloth with the labour of 90 men, she would import it from a country where it required the labour of 100 men to produce it, because it would be advantageous to her rather to employ her capital in the production of wine, for which she would obtain more cloth from England, than she could produce by diverting a portion of her capital from the cultivation of vines to the manufacture of cloth.

Thus England would give the produce of the labour of 100 men, for the produce of the labour of 80. Such an exchange could not take place between the individuals of the same country. The labour of one hundred Englishmen cannot be given for that of 80 Englishmen, but the produce of the labour of 100 Englishmen may be given for the produce of the labour of 80 Portuguese, 60 Russians, or 120 East Indians. The difference in this respect, between a single country and many, is easily accounted for, by considering the difficulty with which capital moves from one country to another, to seek a more profitable employment, and the activity with which it invariably passes from one province to another in the same country.

It would undoubtedly be advantageous to the capitalists of England, and to the consumers in both countries, that under such circumstances, the wine and the cloth should both be made in Portugal, and therefore that the capital and labour of England employed in making cloth, should be removed to Portugal for that purpose. In that case, the relative value of these commodities would be regulated by the same principle, as if one were the produce of Yorkshire, and the other of London: and in every other case, if capital freely flowed towards those countries where it could be most profitably employed, there could be no difference in the rate of profit, and no other difference in the real or labour price of commodities, than the additional quantity of labour required to convey them to the various markets where they were to be sold.

Experience, however, shews, that the fancied or real insecurity of capital, when not under the immediate control of its owner, together with the natural disinclination which every man has to quit the country of his birth and connexions, and intrust himself with all his habits fixed, to a strange government and new laws, checks the emigration of capital. These feelings, which I should be sorry to see weakened, induce most men of property to be satisfied with a low rate of profits in their own country, rather than seek a more advantageous employment for their wealth in foreign nations.

Gold and silver having been chosen for the general medium of circulation, they are, by the competition of commerce, distributed in such proportions amongst the different countries of the world, as to accommodate themselves to the natural traffic which would take place if no such metals existed, and the trade between countries were purely a trade of barter.

Thus, cloth cannot be imported into Portugal, unless it sell there for more gold than it cost in the country from which it was imported; and wine cannot be imported into England, unless it will sell for more there than it cost in Portugal. If the trade were purely a trade of barter, it could only continue whilst England could make cloth so cheap as to obtain a greater quantity of wine with a given quantity of labour, by manufacturing cloth than by growing vines; and also whilst the industry of Portugal were attended by the reverse effects. Now suppose England to discover a process for making wine, so that it should become her interest rather to grow it than import it; she would naturally divert a portion of her capital from the foreign trade to the home trade; she would cease to manufacture cloth for exportation, and would grow wine for herself. The money price of these commodities would be regulated accordingly; wine would fall here while cloth continued at its former price, and in Portugal no alteration would take place in the price of either commodity. Cloth would continue for some time to be exported from this country, because its price would continue to be higher in Portugal than here; but money instead of wine would be given in exchange for it, till the accumulation of money here, and its diminution abroad, should so operate on the relative value of cloth in the two countries, that it would cease to be profitable to export it. If the improvement in making wine were of a very important description, it might become profitable for the two countries to exchange employments; for England to make all the wine, and Portugal all the cloth consumed by them; but this could be effected only by a new distribution of the precious metals, which should raise the price of cloth in England, and lower it in Portugal. The relative price of wine would fall in England in consequence of the real advantage from the improvement of its manufacture; that is to say, its natural price would fall; the relative price of cloth would rise there from the accumulation of money.

Thus, suppose before the improvement in making wine in England, the price of wine here were £50 per pipe, and the price of a certain quantity of cloth were £45, whilst in Portugal the price of the same quantity of wine was £45, and that of the same quantity of cloth £50; wine would be exported from Portugal with a profit of £5 and cloth from England with a profit of the same amount.

Suppose that, after the improvement, wine falls to £45 in England, the cloth continuing at the same price. Every transaction in commerce is an independent transaction. Whilst a merchant can buy cloth in England for £45 and sell it with the usual profit in Portugal, he will continue to export it from England. His business is simply to purchase English cloth, and to pay for it by a bill of exchange, which he purchases with Portuguese money. It is to him of no importance what becomes of this money, he has discharged his debt by the remittance of the bill. His transaction is undoubtedly regulated by the terms on which he can obtain this bill, but they are known to him at the time; and the causes which may influence the market price of bills, or the rate of exchange, is no consideration of his.

If the markets be favourable for the exportation of wine from Portugal to England, the exporter of the wine will be a seller of a bill, which will be purchased either by the importer of the cloth, or by the person who sold him his bill; and thus without the necessity of money passing from either country, the exporters in each country will be paid for their goods. Without having any direct transaction with each other, the money paid in Portugal by the importer of cloth will be paid to the Portuguese exporter of wine; and in England by the negotiation of the same bill, the exporter of the cloth will be authorized to receive its value from the importer of wine.

But if the prices of wine were such that no wine could be exported to England, the importer of cloth would equally purchase a bill; but the price of that bill would be higher, from the knowledge which the seller of it would possess, that there was no counter bill in the market by which he could ultimately settle the transactions between the two countries; he might know that the gold or silver money which he received in exchange for his bill, must be actually exported to his correspondent in England, to enable him to pay the demand which he had authorized to be made upon him, and he might therefore charge in the price of his bill all the expenses to be incurred, together with his fair and usual profit.

If then this premium for a bill on England should be equal to the profit on importing cloth, the importation would of course cease; but if the premium on the bill were only 2 per cent, if to be enabled to pay a debt in England of £100, £102 should be paid in Portugal, whilst cloth which cost £45 would sell for £50, cloth would be imported, bills would be bought, and money would be exported, till the diminution of money in Portugal, and its accumulation in England, had produced such a state of prices as would make it no longer profitable to continue these transactions.

But the diminution of money in one country, and its increase in another, do not operate on the price of one commodity only, but on the prices of all, and therefore the price of both wine and cloth will be raised in England, and lowered in Portugal. The price of cloth, from being £45 in one country and £50 in the other, would probably fall to £49 or £48 in Portugal, and rise to £46 or £47 in England, and not afford a sufficient profit after paying a premium for a bill to induce any merchant to import that commodity.

It is thus that the money of each country is apportioned to it in such quantities only as may be necessary to regulate a profitable trade of barter. England exported cloth in exchange for wine, because, by so doing her industry was rendered more productive to her; she had more cloth and wine than if she had manufactured both for herself; and Portugal imported cloth and exported wine, because the industry of Portugal could be more beneficially employed for both countries in producing wine. Let there be more difficulty in England in producing cloth, or in Portugal in producing wine, or let there be more facility in England in producing wine, or in Portugal in producing cloth, and the trade must immediately cease.

No change whatever takes place in the circumstances of Portugal; but England finds that she can employ her labour more productively in the manufacture of wine, and instantly the trade of barter between the two countries changes. Not only is the exportation of wine from Portugal stopped, but a new distribution of the precious metals takes place, and her importation of cloth is also prevented.

Both countries would probably find it their interest to make their own wine and their own cloth; but this singular result would take place: in England, though wine would be cheaper, cloth would be elevated in price, more would be paid for it by the consumer; while in Portugal the consumers, both of cloth and of wine, would be able to purchase those commodities cheaper. In the country where the improvement was made, prices would be enhanced; in that where no change had taken place, but where they had been deprived of a profitable branch of foreign trade, prices would fall.

This, however, is only a seeming advantage to Portugal, for the quantity of cloth and wine together produced in that country would be diminished, while the quantity produced in England would be increased. Money would in some degree have changed its value in the two countries, it would be lowered in England and raised in Portugal. Estimated in money, the whole revenue of Portugal would be diminished; estimated in the same medium, the whole revenue of England would be increased.

Thus then it appears, that the improvement of a manufacture in any country tends to alter the distribution of the precious metals amongst the nations of the world: it tends to increase the quantity of commodities, at the same time that it raises general prices in the country where the improvement takes place.

To simplify the question, I have been supposing the trade between two countries to be confined to two commodities – to wine and cloth; but it is well known that many and various articles enter into the list of exports and imports. By the abstraction of money from one country, and the accumulation of it in another, all commodities are affected in price, and consequently encouragement is given to the exportation of many more commodities besides money, which will therefore prevent so great an effect from taking place on the value of money in the two countries as might otherwise be expected.

Besides the improvements in arts and machinery, there are various other causes which are constantly operating on the natural course of trade, and which interfere with the equilibrium, and the relative value of money. Bounties on exportation or importation, new taxes on commodities, sometimes by their direct, and at other times, by their indirect operation, disturb the natural trade of barter, and produce a consequent necessity of importing or exporting money, in order that prices may be accommodated to the natural course of commerce; and this effect is produced not only in the country where the disturbing cause takes place, but, in a greater or less degree, in every country of the commercial world.

This will in some measure account for the different value of money in different countries; it will explain to us why the prices of home commodities, and those of great bulk, though of comparatively small value, are, independently of other causes, higher in those countries where manufactures flourish. Of two countries having precisely the same population, and the same quantity of land of equal fertility in cultivation, with the same knowledge too of agriculture, the prices of raw produce will be highest in that where the greater skill, and the better machinery is used in the manufacture of exportable commodities. The rate of profits will probably differ but little; for wages, or the real reward of the labourer, may be the same in both; but those wages, as well as raw produce, will be rated higher in money in that country, into which, from the advantages attending their skill and machinery, an abundance of money is imported in exchange for their goods.

Of these two countries, if one had the advantage in the manufacture of goods of one quality, and the other in the manufacture of goods of another quality, there would be no decided influx of the precious metals into either; but if the advantage very heavily preponderated in favour of either, that effect would be inevitable.

In the former part of this work, we have assumed, for the purpose of argument, that money always continued of the same value; we are now endeavouring to shew that besides the ordinary variations in the value of money, and those which are common to the whole commercial world, there are also partial variations to which money is subject in particular countries; and in fact, that the value of money is never the same in any two countries, depending as it does on relative taxation, on manufacturing skill, on the advantages of climate, natural productions, and many other causes.

Although, however, money is subject to such perpetual variations, and consequently the prices of the commodities which are common to most countries, are also subject to considerable difference, yet no effect will be produced on the rate of profits, either from the influx or efflux of money. Capital will not be increased, because the circulating medium is augmented. If the rent paid by the farmer to his landlord, and the wages to his labourers, be 20 per cent higher in one country than another, and if at the same time the nominal value of the farmer's capital be 20 per cent more, he will receive precisely the same rate of profits, although he should sell his raw produce 20 per cent higher.

Profits, it cannot be repeated too often, depend on wages; not on nominal, but real wages; not on the number of pounds that may be annually paid to the labourer, but on the number of days' work, necessary to obtain those pounds. Wages may therefore be precisely the same in two countries; they may bear too the same proportion to rent, and to the whole produce obtained from the land, although in one of those countries the labourer should receive 10s. per week, and in the other twelve.

In the early states of society, when manufactures have made little progress, and the produce of all countries is nearly similar, consisting of the bulky and most useful commodities, the value of money in different countries will be chiefly regulated by their distance from the mines which supply the precious metals; but as the arts and improvements of society advance, and different nations excel in particular manufactures, although distance will still enter into the calculation, the value of the precious metals will be chiefly regulated by the superiority of those manufactures.

Suppose all nations to produce corn, cattle, and coarse clothing only, and that it was by the exportation of such commodities that gold could be obtained from the countries which produced them, or from those who held them in subjection; gold would naturally be of greater exchangeable value in Poland than in England, on account of the greater expense of sending such a bulky commodity as corn the more distant voyage, and also the greater expense attending the conveying of gold to Poland.

This difference in the value of gold, or which is the same thing, this difference in the price of corn in the two countries, would exist, although the facilities of producing corn in England should far exceed those of Poland, from the greater fertility of the land, and the superiority in the skill and implements of the labourer.

If however Poland should be the first to improve her manufactures, if she should succeed in making a commodity which was generally desirable, including great value in little bulk, or if she should be exclusively blessed with some natural production, generally desirable, and not possessed by other countries, she would obtain an additional quantity of gold in exchange for this commodity, which would operate on the price of her corn, cattle, and coarse clothing. The disadvantage of distance would probably be more than compensated by the advantage of having an exportable commodity of great value, and money would be permanently of lower value in Poland than in England. If, on the contrary, the advantage of skill and machinery were possessed by England, another reason would be added to that which existed before, why gold should be less valuable in England than in Poland, and why corn, cattle, and clothing, should be at a higher price in the former country.

These I believe to be the only two causes which regulate the comparative value of money in the different countries of the world; for although taxation occasions a disturbance of the equilibrium of money, it does so by depriving the country in which it is imposed of some of the advantages attending skill, industry, and climate.

It has been my endeavour to distinguish carefully between a low value of money, and a high value of corn, or any other commodity with which money may be compared. These have been generally considered as meaning the same thing; but it is evident, that when corn rises from 5 to 10s. a bushel, it may be owing either to a fall in the value of money, or to a rise in the value of corn. Thus we have seen, that from the necessity of having recourse successively to land of a worse and worse quality, in order to feed an increasing population, corn must rise in relative value to other things. If therefore money continues permanently of the same value, corn will exchange for more of such money, that is to say, it will rise in price. The same rise in the price of corn will be produced by such improvement of machinery in manufactures, as shall enable us to manufacture commodities with peculiar advantages: for the influx of money will be the consequence; it will fall in value, and therefore exchange for less corn. But the effects resulting from a high price of corn when produced by the rise in the value of corn, and when caused by a fall in the value of money, are totally different. In both cases the money price of wages will rise, but if it be in consequence of the fall in the value of money, not only wages and corn, but all other commodities will rise. If the manufacturer has more to pay for wages, he will receive more for his manufactured goods, and the rate of profits will remain unaffected. But when the rise in the price of corn is the effect of the difficulty of production, profits will fall; for the manufacturer will be obliged to pay more wages, and will not be enabled to remunerate himself by raising the price of his manufactured commodity.

...

THOMAS ROBERT MALTHUS (1766–1834)

Malthus saw himself as a disciple of Adam Smith, but he had a very close friendship with David Ricardo, and their debates on the fundamental questions of political economy, many of which are reflected in their private correspondence, shed a most interesting light on the development of economic ideas in the first part of the nineteenth century.

One aspect of the debate between Malthus and Ricardo was what we now know as Say's Law. Malthus raised serious concerns about the possibility of overproduction, and thereby gluts, in the market, in effect joining Quesnay in pointing to the possibility of instability in the economy and in providing theoretical explanations for it. Keynes hailed Malthus as a kindred spirit for this theory a century later, although a close reading of Malthus and Keynes calls into question the extent to which Malthus actually anticipated certain of Keynes's central ideas on this score. Malthus was also different from Ricardo in another important respect: he rejected the labor theory of value, and even the idea of a transcendent "value" toward which price gravitated, and adopted an essentially demand and supply theory of price.

In the passages from Malthus's *Principle of Political Economy* excerpted here, we find Malthus defending his thesis about the possibility of a general overproduction based on a deficiency of effective demand and laying out potential prescriptions for dealing with these problems.

References and further reading

Blaug, Mark (1991) *Thomas Robert Malthus (1766–1834) and John Stuart Mill (1806–1873)*, Aldershot: Edward Elgar Publishing.

Bleaney, Michael F. (1976) *Underconsumption Theories: A History and Critical Analysis*, New York: International Publishers.

Corry, B.A. (1958) "The Theory of the Economic Effects of Government in English Classical Political Economy," *Economica* 25 (February): 34–48.

Eltis, Walter (1980) "Malthus's Theory of Effective Demand Growth," *Oxford Economic Papers* 32 (March): 19–56.

Grampp, William D. (1956) "Malthus on Money Wages and Welfare," *American Economic Review* 46 (December): 924–36.

Hollander, Samuel (1997) *The Economics of Thomas Robert Malthus*, Toronto: University of Toronto Press.

Lambert, P. (1966) "Lauderdale, Malthus, and Keynes," *Annals of Public and Cooperative Economy* 37 (January): 3–23.

Malthus, Thomas Robert (1815) *An Inquiry into the Nature and Progress of Rent*, London: John Murray.

——(1827) *Definitions in Political Economy*, London: John Murray.

Paglin, M. (1961) *Malthus and Lauderdale: The Anti-Ricardian Tradition*, New York: Augustus M. Kelley.

Pullen, J.M. (1987) "Malthus, Thomas Robert," in John Eatwell, Murray Milgate, and Peter Newman (eds), *The New Palgrave: A Dictionary of Economics*, Vol. 3, London: Macmillan, 280–85.

Rashid, Salim (1977) "Malthus' Model of a General Glut," *History of Political Economy* 9 (Fall): 366–83.

Rashid, Salim (1987) "Malthus and Classical Economics," in John Eatwell, Murray Milgate, and Peter Newman (eds), *The New Palgrave: A Dictionary of Economics*, Vol. 3, London: Macmillan, 285–90.

Rutherford, R.P. (1987) "Malthus and Keynes," *Oxford Economic Papers* 39 (March) 175–89.

Sowell, Thomas (1963) "The General Glut Controversy Reconsidered," *Oxford Economic Papers* NS 15 (November): 193–203.

Wood, John C. (1986) *Thomas Robert Malthus: Critical Assessments*, London: Croon Helm.

Principles of Political Economy (1820)*

Chapter VII: On the immediate causes of the progress of wealth

Section I: Statement of the particular object of inquiry

There is scarcely any inquiry more curious, or, from its importance, more worthy of attention, than that which traces the causes which practically check the progress of wealth in different countries, and stop it, or make it proceed very slowly, while the power of production remains comparatively undiminished, or at least would furnish the means of a great and abundant increase of produce and population.

In a former work I endeavoured to trace the causes which practically keep down the population of a country to the level of its actual supplies. It is now my object to shew what are the causes which chiefly influence these supplies, or call forth the powers of production into the shape of increasing wealth.

Among the primary and most important causes which influence the wealth of nations, must unquestionably be placed, those which come under the head of politics and morals. Security of property, without a certain degree of which there can be no encouragement to individual industry, depends mainly upon the political constitution of a country, the excellence of its laws and the manner in which they are administered. And those habits which are the most favourable to regular exertions as well as to general rectitude of character, and are consequently most favourable to the production and maintenance of wealth, depend chiefly upon the same causes, combined with moral and religious instruction. It is not however my intention at present to enter fully into these causes, important and effective as they are; but to confine myself chiefly to the more immediate and proximate causes of increasing wealth, whether they may have their origin in these political and moral sources, or in any others more specifically and directly within the province of political economy.

It is obviously true that there are many countries, not essentially different either in the degree of security which they afford to property, or in the moral and religious instruction received by the people, which yet, with nearly equal natural capabilities, make a very different progress in wealth. It is the principal object of the present inquiry to explain this; and to furnish some solution of certain phenomena frequently obtruded upon our attention, whenever we take a view of the different states of Europe, or of the world; namely, countries with great powers of production comparatively poor, and countries with small powers of production comparatively rich.

If the actual riches of a country not subject to repeated violences and a frequent destruction of produce, be not after a certain period in some degree proportioned to its power of producing riches, this deficiency must have arisen from the want of an adequate stimulus to continued production. The practical question then for our consideration is, what are the most immediate and effective stimulants to the continued creation and progress of wealth.

---

* *Principles of Political Economy Considered with a View to Their Practical Application*, London: John Murray 1820.

Section II: *Of the increase of population considered as a stimulus to the continued increase of wealth*

Many writers have been of the opinion that an increase of population is the sole stimulus necessary to the increase of wealth, because population, being the great source of consumption, must in their opinion necessarily keep up the demand for an increase of produce, which will naturally be followed by a continued increase of supply.

That a permanent increase of population is a powerful and necessary element of increasing demand, will be most readily allowed; but that the increase of population alone, or, more properly speaking, the pressure of the population hard against the limits of subsistence, does not furnish an effective stimulus to the continued increase of wealth, is not only evident in theory, but is confirmed by universal experience. If want alone, or the desire of the labouring classes to possess the necessaries and conveniences of life, were a sufficient stimulus to production, there is no state in Europe, or in the world, that would have found any other practical limit to its wealth than its power to produce; and the earth would probably before this period have contained, at the very least, ten times as many inhabitants as are supported on its surface at present.

But those who are acquainted with the nature of effective demand, will be fully aware that, where the right of private property is established, and the wants of society are supplied by industry and barter, the desire of any individual to possess the necessary conveniences and luxuries of life, however intense, will avail nothing towards their production, if there be nowhere a reciprocal demand for something which he possesses. A man whose only possession is his labour has, or has not, an effective demand for produce according as his labour is, or is not, in demand by those who have the disposal of produce. And no productive labour will ever be in demand unless the produce when obtained is of greater value than the labour which obtained it. No fresh hands can be employed in any sort of industry merely in consequence of the demand for its produce occasioned by the persons employed. No farmer will take the trouble of superintending the labour of ten additional men merely because his whole produce will then sell in the market at an advanced price just equal to what he had paid his additional labourers. There must be something in the previous state of the demand and supply of the commodity in question, or in its price, antecedent to and independently of the demand occasioned by the new labourers, in order to warrant the employment of an additional number of people in its production.

It will be said perhaps that the increase of population will lower wages, and, by thus diminishing the costs of production, will increase the profits of the capitalists and the encouragement to produce. Some temporary effect of this kind may no doubt take place, but it is evidently very strictly limited. The fall of wages cannot go on beyond a certain point without not only stopping the progress of the population but making it even retrograde; and before this point is reached, it will probably happen that the increase of produce occasioned by the labour of the additional number of persons will have so lowered its value, as more than to counterbalance the fall of wages, and thus to diminish instead of increase the profits of the capitalists and the power and will to employ more labour.

It is obvious then in theory that an increase of population, when an additional quantity of labour is not wanted, will soon be checked by want of employment, and the scanty support of those employed, and will not furnish the required stimulus to an increase of wealth proportioned to the power of production.

But, if any doubts should remain with respect to the *theory* on the subject, they will surely be dissipated by a reference to *experience*. It is scarcely possible to cast our eyes on any nation of the world without seeing a striking confirmation of what has been advanced. Almost universally, the actual wealth of all the states with which we are acquainted is very far short of their powers of production; and almost universally among those states, the slowest progress in wealth is made where the stimulus arising from population alone is the greatest, that is, where the population presses the hardest against the limits of subsistence. It is quite evident that the only fair way, indeed the only way, by which we can judge the practical effect of population alone as a stimulus to wealth, is to refer to those countries where, from the excess of population above the funds applied to the maintenance of labour, the stimulus of want is the greatest. And if in these countries, which still have great powers of production, the progress of wealth is very slow, we have certainly all the evidence which experience can possibly give us, that population alone cannot create an effective demand for wealth.

To suppose an actual and permanent increase of population is to beg the question. We may as well suppose at once an increase of wealth; because an actual and permanent increase of population cannot take place without a proportionate or nearly proportionate increase of wealth. The question really is, whether encouragements to population, or even the natural tendency of population to increase beyond the funds for its maintenance, so as to press hard against the limits of subsistence, will, or will not, alone furnish an adequate stimulus to the increase of wealth. And this question, Spain, Portugal, Poland, Hungary, Turkey, and many other countries in Europe, together with nearly the whole of Asia and Africa, and the greatest part of America, distinctly answer in the negative.

Section III: Of accumulation, or the saving from revenue to add to capital, considered as a stimulus to the increase of wealth

Those who reject mere population as an adequate stimulus to the increase of wealth, are generally disposed to make everything depend upon accumulation. It is certainly true that no permanent and continued increase of wealth can take place without a continued increase of capital; and I cannot agree with Lord Lauderdale in thinking that this increase can be effected in any other way than by saving from the stock which might have been destined for immediate consumption, and adding it to that which is to yield a profit; or in other words, by the conversion of revenue into capital.

But we have yet to inquire what is the state of things which generally disposes a nation to accumulate; and further, what is the state of things which tends to make that accumulation the most effective, and lead to a further and continued increase of capital and wealth.

It is undoubtedly possible by parsimony to devote at once a much larger share than usual of the produce of any country to the maintenance of productive labour; and it is quite true that the labourers so employed are consumers as well as unproductive labourers; and as far as the labourers are concerned, there would be no diminution of consumption or demand. But it has already been shewn that the consumption and demand occasioned by the persons employed in productive labour can never alone furnish a motive to the accumulation and employment of capital; and with regard to the capitalists themselves, together with the landlords and other rich persons, they have, by the supposition, agreed to be parsimonious, and by depriving themselves of their usual conveniences and luxuries to save from their revenue and add to their capital. Under these circumstances, I would ask, how it is possible to suppose that the increased quantity of commodities, obtained by the increased number of productive labourers, should find purchasers, without such a fall of price as would probably sink their value below the costs of production, or, at least, very greatly diminish both the power and the will to save.

It has been thought by some very able writers that although there may easily be a glut of particular commodities, there cannot possibly be a glut of commodities in general; because, according to their view of the subject, commodities being always exchanged for commodities, one-half will furnish a market for the other half, and production being thus the sole source of demand, an excess in the supply of one article merely proves a deficiency in the supply of some other, and a general excess is impossible. M. Say, in his distinguished work on political economy, has indeed gone so far as to state that the consumption of a commodity by taking it out of the market diminishes demand, and the production of a commodity proportionably increases it.

This doctrine, however, to the extent in which it has been applied, appears to me to be utterly unfounded, and completely to contradict the great principles which regulate supply and demand.

It is by no means true, as a matter of fact, that commodities are always exchanged for commodities. The great mass of commodities is exchanged directly for labour, either productive or unproductive; and it is quite obvious that this mass of commodities, compared with the labour with which it is to be exchanged, may fall in value from a glut just as any one commodity falls in value from an excess of supply, compared either with labour or money.

In the case supposed there would evidently be an unusual quantity of commodities of all kinds in the market, owing to the unproductive labourers of the country having been converted, by the accumulation of capital, into productive labourers; while the number of labourers altogether being the same, and the power and will to purchase for consumption among landlords and capitalists being by supposition diminished, commodities would necessarily fall in value, compared with labour, so as to lower profits almost to nothing, and to check for a time further production. But this is precisely what is meant by the term glut, which, in this case, is evidently general not partial.

M. Say, Mr Mill, and Mr Ricardo, the principal authors of the new doctrines on profits, appear to me to have fallen into some fundamental errors in the view which they have taken of this subject.

In the first place, they have considered commodities as if they were so many mathematical figures, or arithmetical characters, the relations of which were to be compared, instead of articles of consumption, which must of course be referred to the numbers and wants of the consumers.

If commodities were only to be compared and exchanged with each other, then indeed it would be true that, if they were all increased in their proper proportions to any extent, they would continue to bear among themselves the same relative value; but, if we compare them, as we certainly ought to do, with the numbers and wants of the consumers, then a great increase of produce with comparatively stationary numbers and with wants diminished by parsimony, must necessarily occasion a great fall of value estimated in labour, so that the same produce, though it might have *cost* the same quantity of labour as before, would no longer *command* the same quantity; and both the power of accumulation and the motive to accumulate would be strongly checked.

It is asserted that effectual demand is nothing more than the offering of one commodity in exchange for another. But is this all that is necessary to effectual demand? Though each commodity may have cost the same quantity of labour and capital in its production, and they may be exactly equivalent to each other in exchange, yet why may not both be so plentiful as not to command more labour, or very little more than they have cost; and in this case, would the demand for them be effectual? Would it be such as to encourage their continued production? Unquestionably not. Their relation to each other may not have changed; but their relation to the wants of the society, their relation to bullion, and their relation to domestic and foreign labour, may have experienced a most important change.

It will be readily allowed that a new commodity thrown into the market, which, in proportion to the labour employed upon it, is of higher exchangeable value than usual, is precisely calculated to increase demand; because it implies, not a mere increase of quantity, but a better adaptation of the produce to the tastes, wants, and consumption of the society. But to fabricate or procure commodities of this kind is the grand difficulty; and they certainly do not naturally and necessarily follow an accumulation of capital and increase of commodities, most particularly when such accumulation and increase have been occasioned by economy of consumption, or a discouragement to the indulgence of those tastes and wants, which are the very elements of demand.

Mr Ricardo, though he maintains as a general position that capital cannot be redundant, is obliged to make the following concession. He says, 'There is only one case, and that will be temporary, in which the accumulation of capital with a low price of food may be attended with a fall of profits; and that is, when the funds for the maintenance of labour increase much more rapidly than population; – wages will then be high and profits low. If every man were to forego the use of luxuries and be intent only on accumulation, a quantity of necessaries might be produced for which there could not be any immediate consumption. Of commodities so limited in number, there might undoubtedly be an universal glut; and consequently there might neither be demand for an additional quantity of such commodities, nor profits on the employment of more capital. If men ceased to consume, they would cease to produce'. Mr Ricardo then adds, 'This admission does not impugn the general principle'. In this remark I cannot quite agree with him. As, from the nature of population, an increase of labourers cannot be brought into the market, in consequence of a particular demand, till after the lapse of sixteen or eighteen years, and the conversion of revenue into capital may take place much more rapidly; a country is always liable to an increase of the funds for the maintenance of labour faster than the increase of population. But if, whenever this occurs, there may be a universal glut of commodities, how can it be maintained, as a general position, that capital is never redundant; and that because commodities may retain the same relative values, a glut can only be partial, not general?

Another fundamental error into which the above-mentioned writers and their followers appear to have fallen is, the not taking into consideration the influence of so general and important a principle in human nature, as indolence or the love of ease.

It has been supposed that, if a certain number of farmers and a certain number of manufacturers had been exchanging their surplus food and clothing with each other, and their powers of production were suddenly so increased that both parties could, with the same labour, produce luxuries in addition to what they had before obtained, there could be no sort of difficulty with regard to demand, as part of the luxuries which the farmer produced would be exchanged against part of the luxuries produced by the manufacturer; and the only result would be, the happy one of both parties being better supplied and having more enjoyments.

But in this intercourse of mutual gratifications, two things are taken for granted, which are the very points in dispute. It is taken for granted that luxuries are always preferred to indolence, and that the profits of each party are consumed as revenue. What would be the effect of a desire to save under such circumstances, shall be considered presently. The effect of a preference of indolence to luxuries would evidently be to occasion a want of demand for the returns of the increased powers of production supposed, and to throw labourers out of employment. The cultivator, being now enabled to obtain the necessaries and conveniences to which he had been accustomed, with less toil and trouble, and his tastes, for ribands, lace, and velvet not being fully formed, might be very likely to indulge himself in indolence, and employ less labour on the land; while the manufacturer, finding his velvets rather heavy of sale, would be led to discontinue their manufacture, and to fall almost necessarily into the same indolent system as the farmer. That an efficient taste for luxuries, that is, such a taste as will properly stimulate industry, instead of being ready to appear at the moment it is required, is a plant of slow growth, the history of human society sufficiently shews; and that it is a most important error to take for granted, that mankind will produce and consume all that they have the power to produce and consume, and will never prefer indolence to the rewards of industry, will sufficiently appear from a slight review of some of the nations with which we are acquainted. But I shall have occasion for a review of this kind in the next section; and to this I refer the reader.

A third very serious error of the writers referred to above, and practically the most important of the three, consists in supposing that accumulation ensures demand; or that the consumption of the labourers employed by those whose object is to save, will create such an effectual demand for commodities as to encourage a continued increase of produce.

Mr Ricardo observes, that 'If 10,000 *l.* were given to a man having 100,000 *l.* per annum, he would not lock it up in a chest, but would either increase his expenses by 10,000 *l*, employ it himself productively, or lend it to some other person for that purpose; in either case demand would be increased, although it would be for different objects. If he increased his expenses, his effectual demand might probably be for buildings, furniture, or some such enjoyment. If he employed his 10,000 *l.* productively, his effectual demand would be for food, clothing, and raw materials, which might set new labourers to work. But still it would be *demand*'.

Upon this principle it is supposed that if the richer portion of society were to forego their accustomed conveniences and luxuries with a view to accumulation, the only effect would be a direction of nearly the whole capital of the country to the production of necessaries, which would lead to a great increase of cultivation and population. But, without supposing an entire change in the usual motives to accumulation, this could not possibly happen. The usual motives for accumulation are, I conceive, either the future wealth and enjoyment of the individual who accumulates, or of those to whom he means to leave his property. And with these motives it could never answer to the possessor of land to employ nearly all the labour which the soil could support in cultivation; as by so doing he would necessarily destroy his neat rent, and render it impossible for him, without subsequently dismissing the greatest part of his workmen and occasioning the most dreadful distress, either to give himself the means of greater enjoyment at a future distant period, or to transmit such means to his posterity.

The very definition of fertile land is, land that will support a much greater number of persons than are necessary to cultivate it; and if the landlord, instead of spending this surplus in conveniences, luxuries, and unproductive consumers, were to employ it in setting to work on the land as many labourers as his savings could support, it is quite obvious that, instead of being enriched, he would be impoverished by such a proceeding, both at first and in future. Nothing could justify such a conduct but a different motive for accumulation; that is, a desire to increase the population – not the love of wealth and enjoyment; and till such a change takes place in the passions and propensities of mankind, we may be quite sure that the landlords and cultivators will not go on employing labourers in this way.

What then would happen? As soon as the landlords and cultivators found that they could not realize their increasing produce in some way which would give them a command of wealth in future, they would cease to employ more labour upon the land; and if the business of that part of the society which was not engaged in raising raw produce, consisted merely in preparing the other simple necessaries of life, the number required for this purpose being inconsiderable, the rest of those whom the soil could support would be thrown out of work. Having no means of legally demanding a portion of the raw produce, however plentiful it might be at first, they would gradually decrease in numbers; and the failure of effective demand for the produce of the soil would necessarily diminish cultivation, and throw a still greater number of persons out of employment. This action and reaction would thus go on till the balance of produce and consumption was restored in reference to the new tastes and habits which were established: and it is obvious that without an expenditure which will encourage commerce, manufactures, and unproductive consumers, or an Agrarian law calculated to change the usual motives for accumulation, the possessors of land would have no sufficient stimulus to cultivate well; and a country such as our own, which had been rich and populous, would, with such parsimonious habits, infallibly become poor, and comparatively unpeopled.

The same kind of reasoning will obviously apply to the case noticed before. While the farmers were disposed to consume the luxuries produced by the manufacturers, and the manufacturers those produced by the farmers, all would go on smoothly; but if either one or both of the parties were disposed to save with a view of bettering their condition, and providing for their families in future, the state of things would be very different. The farmer, instead of indulging himself in ribands, lace, and velvets, would be disposed to be satisfied with more simple clothing, but by this economy he would disable the manufacturer from purchasing the same amount of his produce; and for the returns of so much labour employed upon the land, and all greatly increased in productive power, there would evidently be no market. The manufacturer, in like manner, instead of indulging himself in sugar, grapes, and tobacco, might be disposed to save with a view to the future, but would be totally unable to do so, owing to the parsimony of the farmers and the want of demand for manufactures.

An accumulation, to a certain extent, of common food and common clothing might take place on both sides; but the amount must necessarily be extremely confined. It would be of no sort of use to the farmer to go on cultivating his land with a view merely to give food and clothing to his labourers. He would be doing nothing either for himself or family, if he neither consumed the surplus of what they produced himself, nor could realize it in a shape that might be transmitted to his descendants. If he were a tenant, such additional care and labour would be entirely thrown away; and if he were a landlord, and were determined, without reference to markets, to cultivate his estate in such a way as to make it yield the greatest neat surplus with a view to the future, it is quite certain that the large portion of this surplus which was not required either for his own consumption, or to purchase clothing for himself and his labourers, would be absolutely wasted. If he did not choose to use it in the purchase of luxuries or the maintenance of unproductive labourers, it might as well be thrown into the sea. To save it, that is to use it in employing more labourers upon the land would, as I said before, be to impoverish both himself and his family.

It would be still more useless to the manufacturers to go on producing clothing beyond what was wanted by the agriculturists and themselves. Their numbers indeed would entirely depend upon the demands of the agriculturists, as they would have no means of purchasing subsistence, but in proportion as there was a reciprocal want of their manufactures. The population required to provide simple clothing for such a society with the assistance of good machinery would be inconsiderable, and would absorb but a small portion of the proper surplus of rich and well cultivated land. There would evidently therefore be a general want of demand, both for produce and population; and while it is quite certain that an adequate passion for consumption may fully keep up the proper proportion between supply and demand, whatever may be the powers of production, it appears to be quite as certain that a passion for accumulation must inevitably lead to a supply of commodities beyond what the structure and habits of such a society will permit to be consumed.

But if this be so, surely it is a most important error to couple the passion for expenditure and the passion for accumulation together, as if they were of the same nature; and to consider the demand for the food and clothing of the labourer, who is to be employed productively, as securing such a general demand for commodities and such a rate of profits for the capital employed in producing them, as will adequately call forth the powers of the soil, and the ingenuity of man in procuring the greatest quantity both of raw and manufactured produce.

Perhaps it may be asked by those who have adopted Mr Ricardo's view of profits – what becomes of the division of that which is produced, when population is checked merely by want of demand? It is acknowledged that the powers of production have not begun to fail; yet, if labour produces largely and yet is ill paid, it will be said that profits must be high.

I have already stated in a former chapter, that the value of the materials of capital very frequently do not fall in proportion to the fall in the value of the produce of capital, and this alone will often account for low profits. But independently of this consideration, it is obvious that in the production of any other commodities than necessaries, the theory is perfectly simple. From want of demand, such commodities may be very low in price, and a large portion of the whole value produced may go to the labourer, although in necessaries he may be ill paid, and his wages, both with regard to the quantity of food which he receives and the labour required to produce it, may be decidedly low.

If it be said, that on account of the large portion of the value of manufactured produce which on this supposition is absorbed by wages, it may be affirmed that the cause of the fall of profits is high wages, I should certainly protest against so manifest an abuse of words. The only justifiable ground for adopting a new term, or using an old one in a new sense, is, to convey more precise information to the reader; but to refer to high wages in this case, instead of to a fall of commodities, would be to proceed as if the specific intention of the writer were to keep his reader as much as possible in the dark as to the real state of things.

In the production of necessaries however, it will be allowed, that the answer to the question is not quite so simple, yet still it may be made sufficiently clear. Mr Ricardo acknowledges that there may be a limit to the employment of capital upon the land from the limited wants of society, independently of the exhaustion of the soil. In the case supposed, this limit must necessarily be very narrow, because there would be comparatively no population besides the agriculturists to make an effective demand for produce. Under such circumstances corn might be produced, which would lose the character and quality of wealth; and, as I before observed in a note, all the parts of the same produce would not be of the same value. The actual labourers employed might be tolerably well fed, as is frequently the case, practically, in those countries where the labourers are fed by the farmers, but there would be little work or food for their grown up sons; and from varying markets and varying crops, the profits of the farmer might be the lowest at the very time when, according to the division of the produce, it ought to be the highest, that is, when there was the greatest proportionate excess of produce above what was paid to the labourer. The wages of the labourer cannot sink below a certain point, but a part of the produce, from excess of supply, may for a time be absolutely useless, and permanently it may so fall from competition as to yield only the lowest profits.

I would observe further, that if in consequence of a diminished demand for corn, the cultivators were to withdraw their capitals so as better to proportion their supplies to the quantity that could be properly paid for; yet if they could not employ the capital they had withdrawn in any other way, which, according to the preceding supposition, they could not, it is certain that, though they might for a time make fair profits of the small stock which they still continued to employ in agriculture, the consequences to them as cultivators would be, to all intents and purposes, the same as if a general fall had taken place on all their capital.

If, in the process of saving, all that was lost by the capitalist was gained by the labourer, the check to the progress of wealth would be but temporary, as stated by Mr Ricardo; and the consequences need not be apprehended. But if the conversion of revenue into capital pushed beyond a certain point will, by diminishing the effectual demand for produce, throw the labouring classes out of employment, it is obvious that the adoption of parsimonious habits in too great a degree may be accompanied by the most distressing effects at first, and by a marked depression of wealth and population permanently.

It is not, of course, meant to be stated that parsimony, or even a temporary diminution of consumption, is not often in the highest degree useful, and sometimes absolutely necessary to the progress of wealth. A state may certainly be ruined by extravagance; and a diminution of the actual expenditure may not only be necessary on this account, but when the capital of a country is deficient, compared with the demand for its products, a temporary economy of consumption is required, in order to provide that supply of capital which can alone furnish the means of an increased consumption in future. All that I mean to say is, that no nation can *possibly* grow rich by an accumulation of capital, arising from a permanent diminution of consumption; because, such accumulation being greatly beyond what is wanted, in order to supply the effective demand for produce, a part of it would very soon lose both its use and its value, and cease to possess the character of wealth.

On the supposition indeed of a *given* consumption, the accumulation of capital beyond a certain point must appear at once to be perfectly futile. But, even taking into consideration the increased consumption likely to arise among the labouring classes from the abundance and cheapness of commodities, yet as this cheapness must be at the expense of profits, it is obvious that the limits to such an increase of capital from parsimony, as shall not be attended by a very rapid diminution of the motive to accumulate, are very narrow, and may very easily be passed.

The laws which regulate the rate of profits and the progress of capital, bear a very striking and singular resemblance to the laws which regulate the rate of wages and the progress of population.

Mr Ricardo has very clearly shewn that the rate of profits must diminish, and the progress of accumulation be finally stopped, under the most favourable circumstances, by the increasing difficulty of procuring the food of the labourer. I, in like manner, endeavoured to shew in my 'Essay on the Principle of Population' that, under circumstances the most favourable to cultivation which could possibly be supposed to operate in the actual state of the earth, the wages of the labourer would become more scanty, and the progress of population be finally stopped by the increasing difficulty of procuring the means of subsistence.

But Mr Ricardo has not been satisfied with proving the position just stated. He has not been satisfied with shewing that the difficulty of procuring the food of the labourer is the only *absolutely necessary* cause of the fall of profits, in which I am ready fully and entirely to agree with him: but he has gone on to say, that there is *no other cause* of the fall of profits in the actual state of things that has any degree of permanence. In this latter statement he appears to me to have fallen into precisely the same kind of error as I should have fallen into, if, after having shewn that the unrestricted power of population was beyond comparison greater than the power of the earth to produce food under the most favourable circumstances possible, I had allowed that population could not be redundant unless the powers of the earth to keep up with the progress of population had been tried to the uttermost. But I all along said, that population might be redundant, and greatly redundant, compared with the demand for it and the actual means of supporting it, although it might most properly be considered as deficient, and greatly deficient, compared with the extent of territory, and the powers of such territory to produce additional means of subsistence; that, in such cases, notwithstanding the acknowledged deficiency of population, and the obvious desirableness of having it greatly increased, it was useless and foolish directly to encourage the birth of more children, as the effect of such encouragement, without a demand for labour and the means of paying it properly, could only be increased misery and mortality with little or no final increase of population.

Though Mr Ricardo has taken a very different course, I think that the same kind of reasoning ought to be applied to the rate of profits and the progress of capital. Fully acknowledging that there is hardly a country in the four quarters of the globe where capital is not deficient, and in most of them very greatly deficient, compared with the territory and even the number of people; and fully allowing at the same time the extreme desirableness of an increase of capital, I should say that, where the demand for commodities was not such as to afford fair profits to the producer, and the capitalists were at a loss where and how to employ their capitals to advantage, the saving from revenue to add still more to these capitals would only tend prematurely to diminish the motive to accumulation, and still further to distress the capitalists, with little increase of a wholesome and effective capital.

The first thing wanted in both these cases of deficient capital and deficient population, is an effective demand for commodities, that is, a demand by those who are able and willing to pay an adequate price for them; and though high profits are not followed by an increase of capital, so certainly as high wages are by an increase of population, yet I believe that they are so followed more generally than they appear to be, because, in many countries, as I have before intimated, profits are often thought to be high, owing to the high interest of money, when they are really low; and because, universally, risk in employing capital has precisely the same effect in diminishing the motive to accumulate and the reward of accumulation, as low profits. At the same time it will be allowed that determined extravagance, and a determined indisposition to save, may keep profits permanently high. The most powerful stimulants may, under peculiar circumstances, be resisted; yet still it will not cease to be true that the natural and legitimate encouragement to the increase of capital is that increase of the power and will to save which is held out by high profits; and under circumstances in any degree similar, such increase of power and will to save must almost always be accompanied by a proportionate increase of capital.

One of the most striking instances of the truth of this remark, and a further proof of a singular resemblance in the laws that regulate the increase of capital and of population, is to be found in the rapidity with which the loss of capital is recovered during a war which does not interrupt commerce. The loans to government convert capital into revenue, and increase demand at the same time that they at first diminish the means of supply. The necessary consequence must be an increase of profits. This naturally increases both the power and the reward of accumulation; and if only the same habits of saving prevail among the capitalists as before, the recovery of the lost stock must be rapid, just for the same kind of reason that the a recovery of population is so rapid when, by some cause or other, it has been suddenly destroyed.

It is now fully acknowledged that it would be a gross error in the latter case, to imagine that, with out the previous diminution of the population, the same rate of increase would still have taken place because it is precisely the high wages occasioned by the demand for labour, which produce the effect of so rapid an increase of population. On the same principle it appears to me as gross an error to suppose that, without the previous loss of capital occasioned by the expenditure in question, capital should be as rapidly accumulated; because it is precisely the high profits of stock occasioned by the demand for commodities, and the consequent demand for the means of producing them, which at once give the power and the will to accumulate.

Though it may be allowed therefore that the laws which regulate the increase of capital are not quite so distinct as those which regulate the increase of population, yet they are certainly just of the same kind; and it is equally vain, with a view to the permanent increase of wealth, to continue converting revenue into capital, when there is no adequate demand for the products of such capital, as to continue encouraging marriage and the birth of children without a demand for labour and an increase of the funds for its maintenance.

Section IX: Of the distribution occasioned by unproductive consumers, considered as the meant of increasing the exchangeable value of the whole produce

The third main cause which tends to keep up and increase the value of produce by favouring its distribution is the employment of unproductive labour, or the maintenance of an adequate proportion of unproductive consumers.

It has been already shewn that, under a rapid accumulation of capital, or, more properly speaking, a rapid conversion of unproductive into productive labour, the demand, compared with the supply of material products, would prematurely fail, and the motive to further accumulation be checked, before it was checked by the exhaustion of the land. It follows that, without supposing the productive classes to consume much more than they are found to do by experience, particularly when they are rapidly saving from revenue to add to their capitals, it is absolutely necessary that a country with great powers of production should possess a body of unproductive consumers.

In the fertility of the soil, in the powers of man to apply machinery as a substitute for labour, and in the motives to exertion under a system of private property, the great laws of nature have provided for the leisure of a certain portion of society; and if this beneficent offer be not accepted by an adequate number of individuals, not only will a positive good, which might have been so attained, be lost, but the rest of the society, so far from being benefited by such self-denial, will be decidedly injured by it.

What the proportion is between the productive and unproductive classes of a society, which affords the greatest encouragement to the continued increase of wealth, it has before been said that the resources of political economy are unequal to determine. It must depend upon a great variety of circumstances, particularly upon fertility of soil and the progress of invention in machinery. A fertile soil and an ingenious people can not only support a considerable proportion of unproductive consumers without injury, but may absolutely require such a body of demanders, in order to give effect to their powers of production. While, with a poor soil and a people of little ingenuity, an attempt to support such a body would throw land out of cultivation, and lead infallibly to impoverishment and ruin.

Another cause, which makes it impossible to say what proportion of the unproductive to the productive classes is most favourable to the increase of wealth, is the difference in the degrees of consumption which may prevail among the producers themselves.

Perhaps it will be said that there can be no occasion for unproductive consumers, if a consumption sufficient to keep up the value of the produce takes place among those who are engaged in production.

With regard to the capitalists who are so engaged, they have certainly the power of consuming their profits, or the revenue which they make by the employment of their capitals; and if they were to consume it, with the exception of what could be beneficially added to their capitals, so as to provide in the best way both for an increased production and increased consumption, there might be little occasion for unproductive consumers. But such consumption is not consistent with the actual habits of the generality of capitalists. The great object of their lives is to save a fortune, both because it is their duty to make a provision for their families, and because they cannot spend an income with so much comfort to themselves, while they are obliged perhaps to attend a counting-house for seven or eight hours a day.

It has been laid down as a sort of axiom among some writers that the wants of mankind may be considered as at all times commensurate with their powers; but this position is not always true, even in those cases where a fortune comes without trouble; and in reference to the great mass of capitalists, it is completely contradicted by experience. Almost all merchants and manufacturers save, in prosperous times, much more rapidly than it would be possible for the national capital to increase, so as to keep up the value of the produce. But if this be true of them as a body, taken one with another, it is quite obvious that, with their actual habits, they could not afford an adequate market to each other by exchanging their several products.

There must therefore be a considerable class of other consumers, or the mercantile classes could not continue extending their concerns, and realizing their profits. In this class the landlords no doubt stand pre-eminent; but if the powers of production among capitalists are considerable, the consumption of the landlords, in addition to that of the capitalists themselves and of their workmen, may still be insufficient to keep up and increase the exchangeable value of the whole produce, that is, to make the increase of quantity more than counterbalance the fall of price. And if this be so, the capitalists cannot continue the same habits of saving. They must either consume more, or produce less; and when the mere pleasure of present expenditure, without the accompaniments of an improved local situation and an advance in rank, is put in opposition to the continued labour of attending to business during the greatest part of the day, the probability is that a considerable body of them will be induced to prefer the latter alternative, and produce less. But if, in order to balance the demand and supply, a permanent diminution of production takes place, rather than an increase of consumption, the whole of the national wealth, which consists of what is produced and consumed, and not of the excess of produce above consumption, will be decidedly diminished.

Mr Ricardo frequently speaks, as if saving were an end instead of a means. Yet even with regard to individuals, where this view of the subject is nearest the truth, it must be allowed that the final object in saving is expenditure and enjoyment. But, in reference to national wealth, it can never be considered either immediately or permanently in any other light than as a means. It may be true that, by the cheapness of commodities, and the consequent saving of expenditure in consumption, the same surplus of produce above consumption may be obtained as by a great rise of profits with an undiminished consumption; and, if saving were an end, the same end would be accomplished. But saving is the means of furnishing an increasing supply for the increasing national wants. If however commodities are already so plentiful that an adequate portion of them is not consumed, the capital so saved, the office of which is still further to increase the plenty of commodities, and still further to lower already low profits, can be comparatively of little use. On the other hand, if profits are high, it is a sure sign that commodities are scarce, compared with the demand for them, that the wants of the society are clamorous for a supply, and that an increase in the means of production, by saving a considerable part of the new revenue created by the high profits, and adding it to capital, will be specifically and permanently beneficial.

National saving, therefore, considered as the means of increased production, is confined within much narrower limits than individual saving. While some individuals continue to spend, other individuals may continue to save to a very great extent; but the national saving, or the balance of produce above consumption, in reference to the whole mass of producers and consumers, must necessarily be limited by the amount which can be advantageously employed in supplying the demand for produce; and to create this demand, there must be an adequate consumption either among the producers themselves, or other classes of consumers.

Adam Smith has observed 'that the desire of food is limited in every man by the narrow capacity of the human stomach; but the desire of the conveniences and ornaments of building, dress, equipage, and household furniture, seems to have no limit or certain boundary'. That it has no *certain* boundary is unquestionably true; that it has no limit must be allowed to be too strong an expression, when we consider how it will be practically limited by the countervailing luxury of indolence, or by the general desire of mankind to better their condition, and make a provision for a family; a principle which, as Adam Smith himself states, is on the whole stronger than the principle which prompts to expense. But surely it is a glaring misapplication of this statement in any sense in which it can be reasonably understood, to say, that there is no limit to the saving and employment of capital except the difficulty of procuring food. It is to find a doctrine upon the unlimited desire of mankind to consume; then to suppose this desire limited in order to save capital, and thus completely alter the premises; and yet still to maintain that the doctrine is true. Let a sufficient consumption always take place, whether by the producers or others, to keep up and increase most effectually the exchangeable value of the whole produce; and I am perfectly ready to allow that, to the employment of a national capital, increasing only at such a rate, there is no other limit than that which bounds the power of maintaining population. But it appears to me perfectly clear in theory, and universally confirmed by experience, that the employment of a capital, too rapidly increased by parsimonious habits, may find a limit, and does, in fact, often find a limit, long before there is any real difficulty in procuring the means of subsistence; and that both capital and population may be at the same time, and for a period of great length, redundant, compared with the effective demand for produce.

Of the wants of mankind in general, it may be further observed, that it is a partial and narrow view of the subject, to consider only the propensity to spend what is actually possessed. It forms but a very small part of the question to determine that if a man has a hundred thousand a year, he will not decline the offer of ten thousand more; or to lay down generally that mankind are never disposed to refuse the means of increased power and enjoyment. The main part of the question respecting the wants of mankind, relates to their power of calling forth the exertions necessary to acquire the means of expenditure. It is unquestionably true that wealth produces wants; but it is a still more important truth, that wants produce wealth. Each cause acts and reacts upon the other, but the order, both of precedence and of importance, is with the wants which stimulate to industry; and with regard to these, it appears that, instead of being always ready to second the physical powers of man, they require for their development, 'all appliances and means to boot'. The greatest of all difficulties in converting uncivilized and thinly peopled countries into civilized and populous ones, is to inspire them with the wants best calculated to excite their exertions in the production of wealth. One of the greatest benefits which foreign commerce confers, and the reason why it has always appeared an almost necessary ingredient in the progress of wealth, is, its tendency to inspire new wants, to form new tastes, and to furnish fresh motives for industry. Even civilized and improved countries cannot afford to lose any of these motives. It is not the most pleasant employment to spend eight hours a day in a counting-house. Nor will it be submitted to after the common necessaries and conveniences of life are attained, unless adequate motives are presented to the mind of the man of business. Among these motives is undoubtedly the desire of advancing his rank, and contending with the landlords in the enjoyment of leisure, as well as of foreign and domestic luxuries.

But the desire to realize a fortune as a permanent provision for a family is perhaps the most general motive for the continued exertions of those whose incomes depend upon their own personal skill and efforts. Whatever may be said of the virtue of parsimony or saving, as a *public* duty, there cannot be a doubt that it is, in numberless cases, a most sacred and binding *private* duty; and were this legitimate and praiseworthy motive to persevering industry in any degree weakened, it is impossible that the wealth and prosperity of the country should not most materially suffer. But if, from the want of other consumers, the capitalists were obliged to consume all that could not be advantageously added to the national capital, the motives which support them in their daily tasks must essentially be weakened, and the same powers of production would not be called forth.

It has appeared then that, in the ordinary state of society, the master producers and capitalists, though they may have the power, have not the will, to consume to the necessary extent. And with regard to their workmen, it must be allowed that, if they possessed the will, they have not the power. It is indeed most important to observe that no power of consumption on the part of the labouring classes can ever, according to the common motives which influence mankind, alone furnish an encouragement to the employment of capital. As I have said before, nobody will ever employ capital merely for the sake of the demand occasioned by those who work for him. Unless they produce an excess of value above what they consume, which he either wants himself in kind, or which he can advantageously exchange for something which he desires, either for present or future use, it is quite obvious that his capital will not be employed in maintaining them. When indeed this further value is created and affords a sufficient excitement to the saving and employment of stock, then certainly the power of consumption possessed by the workmen will greatly add to the whole national demand, and make room for the employment of a much greater capital.

It is most desirable that the labouring classes should be well paid, for a much more important reason than any that can relate to wealth; namely, the happiness of the great mass of society. But to those who are inclined to say that unproductive consumers cannot be necessary as a stimulus to the increase of wealth, if the productive classes do but consume a fair proportion of what they produce, I would observe that as a great increase of consumption among the working classes must greatly increase the cost of production, it must lower profits, and diminish or destroy the motive to accumulate, before agriculture, manufactures, and commerce have reached any considerable degree of prosperity. If each labourer was actually to consume double the quantity of corn which he does at present, such a demand, instead of giving a stimulus to wealth, would probably throw a great quantity of land out of cultivation, and greatly diminish both internal and external commerce.

There is certainly however very little danger of a diminution of wealth from this cause. Owing to the principle of population, all the tendencies are the other way; and there is much more reason to fear that the working classes will consume too little for their own happiness, than that they will consume too much to allow of an adequate increase of wealth. I only adverted to the circumstance to shew that, supposing so impossible a case as a very great consumption among the working producers, such consumption would not be of the kind to push the wealth of a country to its greatest extent.

It may be said, perhaps, that owing to the laws which regulate the increase of population, it is in no respect probable that the corn wages of labour should continue permanently very high, yet the same consumption would take place if the labouring classes did not work so many hours in the day, and it was necessary to employ a greater number in each occupation. I have always thought and felt that many among the labouring classes in this country work too hard for their health, happiness, and intellectual improvement; and, if a greater degree of relaxation from severe toil could be given to them with a tolerably fair prospect of its being employed in innocent amusements and useful instruction, I should consider it as very cheaply purchased, by the sacrifice of a portion of the national wealth and populousness. But I see no probability, or even possibility, of accomplishing this object. To interfere generally with persons who have arrived at years of discretion in the command of the main property which they possess, namely their labour, would be an act of gross injustice; and the attempt to legislate directly in the teeth of one of the most general principles by which the business of society is carried on, namely, the principle of competition, must inevitably and necessarily fail. It is quite obvious that nothing could be done in this way, but by the labouring classes themselves; and even in this quarter we may perhaps much more reasonably expect that such a degree of prudence will prevail among them as to keep their wages permanently high, than that they should not enter into a competition with each other in working. A man who is prudent before marriage, and saves something for a family, reaps the benefit of his conduct, although others do not follow his example; but, without a simultaneous resolution on the part of all the labouring classes to work fewer hours in the day, the individual who should venture so to limit his exertions would necessarily reduce himself to comparative want and wretchedness. If the supposition made here were accomplished, not by a simultaneous resolution, which is scarcely possible, but by those general habits of indolence and ignorance, which so frequently prevail in the less improved stages of society, it is well known that such leisure would be of little value; and that while these habits would prematurely check the rate of profits and the progress of population, they would bring with them nothing to compensate the loss.

It is clear therefore that, with the single exception of the increased degree of prudence to be expected among the labouring classes of society from the progress of education and general improvement, which may occasion a greater consumption among the working producers, all the other tendencies are precisely in an opposite direction; and that, generally, all such increased consumption, whether desirable or not on other grounds, must always have the specific effect of preventing the wealth and population of a country, under a system of private property, from being pushed so far, as it might have been, if the costs of production had not been so increased.

It may be thought perhaps that the landlords could not fail to supply any deficiency of demand and consumption among the producers, and that between them there would be little chance of any approach towards redundancy of capital. What might be the result of the most favourable distribution of landed property it is not easy to say from experience; but experience certainly tells us that, under the distribution of land which actually takes place in most of the countries in Europe, the demands of the landlords, added to those of the producers, have not always been found sufficient to prevent any difficulty in the employment of capital. In the instance alluded to in a former chapter, which occurred in this country in the middle of the last century, there must have been considerable difficulty in finding employment for capital, or the national creditors would rather have been paid off than have submitted to a reduction of interest from 4 per cent to 3.5 per cent, and afterwards to 3. And that this fall in the rate of interest and profits arose from a redundancy of capital and a want of demand for produce, rather than from the difficulty of production on the land, is fully evinced by the low price of corn at the time, and the very different state of interest and profits which has occurred since.

A similar instance took place in Italy in 1685, when, upon the Pope's reducing the interest of his debts from 4 to 3 per cent, the value of the principal rose afterwards to 112, and yet the pope's territories have at no time been so cultivated as to occasion such a low rate of interest and profits from the difficulty of procuring the food of the labourer. Under a more favourable distribution of property, there cannot be a doubt that such a demand for produce, agricultural, manufacturing, and mercantile, might have been created, as to have prevented for many many years the interest of money from falling below 3 per cent. In both these cases, the demands of the landlords were added to those of the productive classes.

But if the master-producers, from the laudable desire they feel of bettering their condition, and providing for a family, do not consume sufficiently to give an adequate stimulus to the increase of wealth; if the working producers, by increasing their consumption, supposing them to have the means of so doing, would impede the growth of wealth more by diminishing the power of production, than they could encourage it by increasing the demand for produce; and if the expenditure of the landlords, in addition to the expenditure of the two preceding classes, be found insufficient to keep up and increase the value of that which is produced, where are we to look for the consumption required but among the unproductive labourers of Adam Smith?

Every society must have a body of unproductive labourers; as every society, besides the menial servants that are required, must have statesmen to govern it, soldiers to defend it, judges and lawyers to administer justice and protect the rights of individuals, physicians and surgeons to cure diseases and heal wounds, and a body of clergy to instruct the ignorant, and administer the consolations of religion. No civilized state has ever been known to exist without a certain portion of all these classes of society in addition to those who are directly employed in production. To a certain extent therefore they appear to be absolutely necessary. But it is perhaps one of the most important practical questions that can possibly be brought under our view, whether, however necessary and desirable they may be, they must be considered as detracting so much from the material products of a country, and its power of supporting an extended population; or whether they furnish fresh motives to production, and tend to push the wealth of a country farther than it would go without them.

The solution of this question evidently depends, first, upon the solution of the main practical question, whether the capital of a country can or cannot be redundant; that is, whether the motive to accumulate may be checked or destroyed by the want of effective demand long before it is checked by the difficulty of procuring the subsistence of the labourer. And second, whether, allowing the *possibility* of such a redundance, there is sufficient reason to believe that, under the actual habits of mankind, it is a probable occurrence.

In the chapter on Profits, but more particularly in the third section of the present chapter, where I have considered the effect of accumulation as a stimulus to the increase of wealth, I trust that the first of these questions has been satisfactorily answered. And in the present section it has been shewn that the actual habits and practice of the productive classes, in the most improved societies, do not lead them to consume so large a proportion of what they produce, even though assisted by the landlords, as to prevent their finding frequent difficulties in the employment of their capitals. We may conclude therefore, with little danger of error, that such a body of persons as I have described is not only necessary to the government, protection, health, and instruction of a country, but is also necessary to call forth those exertions which are required to give full play to its physical resources.

With respect to the persons constituting the unproductive classes, and the modes by which they should be supported, it is probable that those which are paid voluntarily by individuals, will be allowed by all to be the most likely to be useful in exciting industry, and the least likely to be prejudicial by interfering with the costs of production. It may be presumed that a person will not take a menial servant, unless he can afford to pay him; and that he is as likely to be excited to industry by the prospect of this indulgence, as by the prospect of buying ribands and laces. Yet to shew how much the wealth of nations depends upon the proportion of parts, rather than on any positive rules respecting the advantages of productive or unproductive labour generally, it may be worth while to remind the reader that, though the employment of a certain number of persons in menial service is in every respect desirable, there could hardly be a taste more unfavourable to the progress of wealth than a strong preference of menial service to material products. We may however, for the most part, trust to the inclinations of individuals in this respect; and it will be allowed generally, that there is little difficulty in reference to those classes which are supported voluntarily, though there may be much with regard to those which must be supported by taxation.

With regard to these latter classes, such as statesmen, soldiers, sailors, and those who live upon the interest of a national debt, it cannot be denied that they contribute powerfully to distribution and demand; they frequently occasion a division of property more favourable to the progress of wealth than would otherwise have taken place; they ensure that consumption which is necessary to give the proper stimulus to production; and the desire to pay a tax, and yet enjoy the same means of gratification, must often operate to excite the exertions of industry quite as effectually as the desire to pay a lawyer or physician. Yet to counterbalance these advantages, which so far are unquestionable, it must be acknowledged that injudicious taxation might stop the increase of wealth at almost any period of its progress, early or late, and that the most judicious taxation might ultimately be so heavy as to clog all the channels of foreign and domestic trade, and almost prevent the possibility of accumulation.

The effect therefore on national wealth of those classes of unproductive labourers which are supported by taxation, must be very various in different countries, and must depend entirely upon the powers of production, and upon the manner in which the taxes are raised in each country. As great powers of production are neither likely to be called into action, or, when once in action, kept in activity without great consumption, I feel very little doubt that instances have practically occurred of national wealth being greatly stimulated by the consumption of those who have been supported by taxes. Yet taxation is a stimulus so liable in every way to abuse, and it is so absolutely necessary for the general interests of society to consider private property as sacred, that one should be extremely cautious of trusting to any government the means of making a different distribution of wealth, with a view to the general good. But when, either from necessity or error, a different distribution has taken place, and the evil, as far as it regards private property, has actually been committed, it would surely be most unwise to attempt, at the expense of a great temporary sacrifice, a return to the former distribution, without very fully considering whether, if it were effected, it would be really advantageous; that is, whether, in the actual circumstances of the country, with reference to its powers of production, more would not be lost by the want of consumption than gained by the diminution of taxation.

If there could be no sort of difficulty in finding employment for capital, provided the price of labour were sufficiently low, the way to national wealth, though it might not always be easy, would be quite straight, and our only object need be to save from revenue, and repress unproductive consumers. But, if it has appeared that the greatest powers of production are rendered comparatively unless without adequate consumption, and that a proper distribution of the produce is as necessary to the continued increase of wealth as the means of producing it, it follows that, in cases of this kind, the question depends upon proportions; and it would be the height of rashness to determine, under all circumstances, that the diminution of a national debt and the removal of taxation must necessarily tend to increase the national wealth, and provide employment for the labouring classes.

If we were to suppose the powers of production in a rich and well-peopled country to be so increased that the whole of what it produced could be obtained by one-third of the labour before applied, can there be a reasonable doubt that the principal difficulty would be to effect such a distribution of the produce, as to call forth these great powers of production? To consider the gift of such powers as an evil would indeed be most strange; but they would be an evil, and practically a great and grievous one, if the effect were to be an increase of the neat produce at the expense of the gross produce, and of the population. But if, on the other hand, a more favourable distribution of the abundant produce were to take place; if the more intelligent among the working classes were raised into overseers of works, clerks of various kinds, and retail dealers, while many who had been in these situations before, together with numerous others who had received a tolerable education, were entitled to an income from the general produce, and could live nearly at leisure upon their mortgages; what an improved structure of society would this state of things present; while the value of the gross produce, and the numbers of the people would be increasing with rapidity! As I have said before, it would not be possible, under the principle of competition, (which can never be got rid of) to secure much more leisure to those actually engaged in manual labour; but the very great increase in the number of prizes which would then be attainable by industrious and intelligent exertion, would most essentially improve their condition; and, on the whole, the society would have gained a great accession of comfort and happiness. It is not meant to be stated that such a distribution of the produce could be easily effected; but merely that, *with* such a distribution, the powers supposed would confer a prodigious benefit on the society, and *without* such a distribution, or such a change of tastes as would secure an equivalent consumption, the powers supposed might be worse than thrown away.

Now the question is, whether this country, in its actual state, with the great powers of production which it unquestionably possesses, does not bear some slight resemblance to the case here imagined; and whether, without such a body of unproductive consumers as these who live upon the interest of the national debt, the same stimulus would have been given to production, and the same powers would have been called forth. Under the actual division of landed property which now takes place in this country, I feel no sort of doubt that the incomes which are received and spent by the national creditors are more favourable to the demand for the great mass of manufactured products, and tend much more to increase the happiness and intelligence of the whole society, than if they were returned to the landlords.

I am far, however, from being insensible to the evils of a great national debt. Though, in many respects, it maybe a useful instrument of distribution, it must be allowed to be a very cumbersome and very dangerous instrument. In the first place, the revenue necessary to pay the interest of such a debt can only be raised by taxation; and, as this taxation, if pushed to any considerable extent, can hardly fail of interfering with the powers of production, there is always danger of impairing one element of wealth, while we are improving another. A second important objection to a large national debt, is the feeling which prevails so very generally among all those not immediately concerned in it, and consequently among the great mass of the population, that they would be immediately and greatly relieved by its extinction; and, whether this impression be well founded or not, it cannot exist without rendering such revenue in some degree insecure, and exposing a country to the risk of a great convulsion of property. A third objection to such a debt is, that it greatly aggravates the evils arising from changes in the value of money. When the currency falls in value, the annuitants, as owners of fixed incomes, are most unjustly deprived of their proper share of the national produce; when the currency rises in value, the pressure of the taxation necessary to pay the interest of the debt, may become suddenly so heavy as greatly to distress the productive classes; and this kind of sudden pressure must very much enhance the insecurity of property vested in public funds.

On these and other accounts it might be desirable slowly to diminish the debt, and to discourage the growth of it in future, even though it were allowed that its past effects had been favourable to wealth, and that the advantageous distribution of produce which it had occasioned, had, under the actual circumstances, more than counterbalanced the obstructions which it might have given to commerce. Security with moderate wealth is a wiser choice, and better calculated for peace and happiness than insecurity with greater wealth. But, unfortunately, a country accustomed to a distribution of produce which has at once excited and given full play to great powers of production, cannot withdraw into a less ambitious path without passing through a period of very great distress.

It is, I know, generally thought that all would be well, if we could but be relieved from the heavy burden of our debt. And yet I feel perfectly convinced that, if a spunge could be applied to it tomorrow, and we could put out of our consideration the poverty and misery of the public creditors, by supposing them to be supported comfortably in some other country, the rest of the society, as a nation, instead of being enriched, would be impoverished. It is the greatest mistake to suppose that the landlords and capitalists would either at once, or in a short time, be prepared for so great an additional consumption as such a change would require; and if they adopted the alternative suggested by Mr Ricardo in a former instance, of saving, and lending their increased incomes, the evil would be aggravated tenfold. The new distribution of produce would diminish the demand for the results of productive labour; and if, in addition to this, more revenue were converted into capital, profits would fall to nothing, and a much greater quantity of capital would emigrate, or be destroyed at home, and a much greater number of persons would be starving for want of employment, than before the extinction of the debt. It would signify little to be able to export cheap goods. If the distribution of property at home were not such as to occasion an adequate power and will to purchase and consume the returns for these goods, the quantity of capital which could be employed in the foreign trade of consumption would be diminished instead of increased. Of this we may be convinced if we look to India, where low wages appear to be of little use in commerce, while there are no middle classes of society to afford a market for any considerable quantity of foreign goods.

The landlords, in the event supposed, not being inclined to an adequate consumption of the results of productive labour, would probably employ a greater number of menial servants; and perhaps, in the actual circumstances, this would be the best thing that could be done, and indeed the only way of preventing great numbers of the labouring classes from being starved for want of work. It is by no means likely, however, that it should soon take place to a sufficient extent; but if it were done completely, and the landlords paid as much in wages to menial servants as they had before paid to the national creditors, could we for a moment compare the state of society which would ensue to that which had been destroyed?

With regard to the capitalists, though they would be relieved from a great portion of their taxes, yet there is every probability that their habits of saving, combined with the diminution in the number of effective demanders, would occasion such a fall in the prices of commodities as greatly to diminish that part of the national income which depends upon profits; and I feel very little doubt that, in five years from the date of such an event, not only would the exchangeable value of the whole produce, estimated in domestic and foreign labour, be decidedly diminished, but a smaller absolute quantity of corn would be grown, and fewer manufactured and foreign commodities would be brought to market than before.

It is not of course meant to be said that a country with a large quantity of land, labour, and capital, has not the means of gradually recovering from any shock, however great, which it may experience; and after such an event, it might certainly place itself in a situation in which its property would be more secure than with a large national debt. All that I mean to say is, that it would pass through a period, probably of considerable duration, in which the diminution of effective demand from an unfavourable distribution of the produce would more than counterbalance the increased power of production occasioned by the relief from taxation; and it may fairly be doubted whether finally it would attain a great degree of wealth, or call forth, as it ought, a great degree of skill in agriculture, manufactures, and commerce, without possessing, in some way or other, a large body of unproductive consumers, or supplying this deficiency by a much greater tendency to consume the results of productive labour than is generally observed to prevail in society.

It has been repeatedly conceded, that the productive classes have the power of consuming all that they produce; and, if this power were adequately exercised, there might be no occasion, with a view to wealth, for unproductive consumers. But it is found by experience that, though there may be the power, there is not the will; and it is to supply this will that a body of unproductive consumers is necessary. Their specific use in encouraging wealth is, to maintain such a balance between produce and consumption as to give the greatest exchangeable value to the results of the national industry. If unproductive labour were to predominate, the comparatively small quantity of material products brought to market would keep down the value of the whole produce, from the deficiency of quantity. If the productive classes were in excess, the value of the whole produce would fall from excess of supply. It is obviously a certain proportion between the two which will yield the greatest value, and command the greatest quantity of domestic and foreign labour; and we may safely conclude that, among the causes necessary to that distribution, which will keep up and increase the exchangeable value of the whole produce, we must place the maintenance of a certain body of unproductive consumers. This body, to make it effectual as a stimulus to wealth, and to prevent it from being prejudicial, as a clog to it, should vary in different countries, and at different times, according to the powers of production; and the most favourable result evidently depends upon the proportion between productive and unproductive consumers, being best suited to the natural resources of the soil, and the acquired tastes and habits of the people.

JAMES MILL (1773–1836)

James Mill was a prominent follower of both Jeremy Bentham and of David Ricardo, whom he prodded into writing his *Principles of Political Economy and Taxation* and whose economics he helped to popularize. However, he is probably best known as the father of John Stuart Mill and for his most interesting approach to the education of his brilliant son. Educated at the University of Edinburgh, Mill entered the (Scottish) church for a time, but eventually moved to London where he pursued a career in journalism – focusing largely on political and economic issues. As a leader of the Benthamite philosophical radicals, Mill pushed for reforms of British institutions along the lines of utilitarian thinking. His *History of British India* (1817) gave him wide exposure and led to an appointment with the East India Company (for which his son also later worked) from 1819 until his death.

Mill's *Commerce Defended* (1808) was an attack on physiocracy and contains the first strong statement of what came to be known as Say's Law. His *Elements of Political Economy* reflects the influence of Ricardo on his thinking. It was really the first "textbook" in economics – Ricardo for everyman, if you will, and is essentially a record of the instruction in political economy that James Mill gave to his son in his early teens. In the excerpts reprinted here, the reader will note the simplified (and some would say, simplistic) treatment of the issues at hand – specifically here, the wages fund theory and the cost-of-production theory of value – reflecting the popular nature of the work.

References and further reading

Bain, A. (1882) *James Mill: A Biography*, London: Longmans.

Barber, William J. (1969) "James Mill and the Theory of Economic Policy in India," *History of Political Economy* 1 (Spring): 85–100.

De Marchi, Neil (1983) "The Case for James Mill," in A.W. Coats (ed.) *Methodological Controversy in Economics: Historical Essays in Honor of T.W. Hutchison*, Greenwich, CT: JAI Press.

Thweatt, W.O. (1976) "James Mill and the Early Development of Comparative Advantage," *History of Political Economy* 8 (Summer): 207–34.

Winch, Donald (1966) *James Mill: Selected Economic Writings*, Edinburgh: Oliver & Boyd.

—— (1987) "Mill, James," in John Eatwell, Murray Milgate, and Peter Newman (eds), *The New Palgrave: A Dictionary of Economics*, Vol. 3, London: Macmillan, 465–6.

Elements of Political Economy (1821)*

Introduction

The subject – its limits – and division

Political Economy is to the State, what domestic economy is to the family.

The family consumes; and, in order to consume, it must supply.

Domestic economy has, therefore, two grand objects; the consumption and supply of the family. The consumption being a quantity always indefinite, for there is no end to the desire of enjoyment, the grand concern is, to increase the supply.

Those things, which are produced, in sufficient abundance for the satisfaction of all, without the intervention of human labour; as air, the light of the sun, water, and so on; are not objects of care or providence; and therefore, accurately speaking, do not form part of the subject of domestic economy. The art of him, who manages a family, consists in regulating the supply and consumption of those things, which cannot be obtained but with cost; in other words, with human labour, 'the original purchase money, which is given for every thing'.

The same is the case with Political Economy. It also has two grand objects, the Consumption of the Community, and that Supply upon which the consumption depends. Those things, which are supplied without the intervention of human labour, as nothing is required in order to obtain them, need not be taken into account. Had every thing, desired for consumption, existed without human labour, there would have been no place for Political Economy. Science is not implied in putting forth the hand, and using. But when labour is to be employed, and the objects of desire can be multiplied only by a preconcerted plan of operations, it becomes an object of importance to ascertain completely the means of that multiplication, and to frame a system of rules for applying them with greatest advantage to the end.

It is not pretended, that writers on Political Economy have always limited their disquisitions to this object. It seems, however, important to detach the science from all considerations not essential to it. The Reader is therefore requested to observe that, in the following pages, I have it merely in view, to ascertain the laws, according to which the production and consumption are regulated of those commodities, which the intervention of human labour is necessary to procure.

The Science of Political Economy, thus defined, divides itself into two grand inquiries; that which relates to Production, and that which relates to Consumption.

But, after things are produced, it is evident, that, before they are consumed, they must be distributed. The laws of distribution, therefore, constitute an intermediate inquiry.

When commodities are produced, and distributed, it is highly convenient, for the sake, both of reproduction and consumption, that portions of them should be exchanged for one another.

* Originally published in 1821. The extract reprinted here is from the third edition of 1844, London: H.G. Bohn.

To ascertain, therefore, the laws, according to which commodities are exchanged for one another, is a second inquiry, preceding that which relates to the last great topic of Political Economy, Consumption.

It thus appears, that four inquiries are comprehended in this science.

First, what are the laws, which regulate the production of commodities; second, what are the laws, according to which the commodities, produced by the labour of the community, are distributed; third, what are the laws, according to which commodities are exchanged for one another; fourth, what are the laws, which regulate consumption.

Chapter 2: Distribution

Section II: Wages

Production is performed by labour. Labour, however, receives the raw material which it fashions, and the machinery by which it is aided, from capital, or more properly speaking, these articles are the capital.

...

That the rate of wages depends on the proportion between population, and employment, in other words, capital

We come now to the question as to what determines the share of the labourer, or the proportion in which the commodity, or its worth, is divided between him and the capitalist. Whatever the share of the labourer, such is the rate of wages; and, vice versa whatever the rate of wages, such is the share of the commodity, or commodity's worth, which the labourer receives.

It is very evident, that the share of the two parties is the subject of a bargain between them; and if there is a bargain, it is not difficult to see on what the terms of the bargain must depend. All bargains, when made in freedom, are determined by competition, and the terms alter according to the state of supply and demand.

Let us begin by supposing that there is a certain number of capitalists, with a certain quantity of food, raw material, and instruments, or machinery; that there is also a certain number of labourers; and that the proportion, in which the commodities produced are divided between them, has fixed itself at some particular point.

Let us next suppose, that the labourers have increased in number one half, without any increase in the quantity of capital. There is the same quantity of the requisites for the employment of labour; that is, of food, tools, and material, as there was before; but for every 100 labourers there are now 150. There will be 50 men, therefore, in danger of being left out of employment. To prevent their being left out of employment they have but one resource; they must endeavour to supplant those who have forestalled the employment; that is, they must offer to work for a smaller reward. Wages, therefore, decline.

If we suppose, on the other hand, that the quantity of capital has increased, while the number of labourers remains the same, the effect will be reversed. The capitalists have a greater quantity than before of the means of employment; of capital, in short; from which they wish to derive advantage. To derive this advantage they must have more labourers. To obtain them, they also have but one resource, to offer higher wages. But the masters by whom the labourers are now employed are in the same predicament, and will of course offer higher to induce them to remain. This competition is unavoidable, and the necessary effect of it is a rise of wages.

It thus appears, that, if population increases, without an increase of capital, wages fall; and that, if capital increases, without an increase of population, wages rise. It is evident, also, that if both increase, but one faster than the other, the effect will be the same as if the one had not increased at all, and the other had made an increase equal to the difference. Suppose, for example, that population has increased one-eighth, and capital one-eighth; this is the same thing as if they had stood still, with regard to the effect upon labour. But suppose that, in addition to the above-mentioned one-eighth, population had increased another eighth, the effect, in that case, upon wages, would be the same as if capital had not increased at all, and population had increased one-eighth.

Universally, then, we may affirm, that, other things remaining the same, if the ratio which capital and population bear to one another remains the same, wages will remain the same; if the ratio which capital bears to population increases, wages will rise; if the ratio which population bears to capital increases, wages will fall.

From this law, clearly understood, it is easy to trace the circumstances which, in any country, determine the condition of the great body of the people. If that condition is easy and comfortable, all that is necessary to keep it so, is, to make capital increase as fast as population; or, on the other hand, to prevent population from increasing faster than capital. If that condition is not easy and comfortable, it can only be made so, by one of two methods; either by quickening the rate at which capital increases, or retarding the rate at which population increases; augmenting, in short, the ratio which the means of employing the people bear to the number of people.

If it were the natural tendency of capital to increase faster than population, there would be no difficulty in preserving a prosperous condition of the people. If, on the other hand, it were the natural tendency of population to increase faster than capital, the difficulty would be very great. There would be a perpetual tendency in wages to fall. The progressive fall of wages would produce a greater and a greater degree of poverty among the people, attended with its inevitable consequences, misery and vice. As poverty, and its consequent misery increased, mortality would also increase. Of a numerous family born, a certain number only, from want of the means of well-being, would be reared. By whatever proportion the population tended to increase faster than capital, such a proportion of those who were born would die: the ratio of increase in capital and population would then remain the same, and the fall of wages would proceed no farther.

That population has a tendency to increase faster, than, in most places, capital has actually increased, is proved, incontestably, by the condition of the population in most parts of the globe. In almost all countries, the condition of the great body of the people is poor and miserable. This would have been impossible, if capital had increased faster than population. In that case wages must have risen; and high wages would have placed the labourer above the miseries of want.

This general misery of mankind is a fact, which can be accounted for, upon one only of two suppositions: either that there is a natural tendency in population to increase faster than capital, or that capital has, by some means, been prevented from increasing so fast as it has a tendency to increase. This, therefore, is an inquiry of the highest importance.

Chapter 3: Interchange

Section II: What determines the quantity in which commodities exchange for one another

When a certain quantity of one commodity is exchanged for a certain quantity of another commodity; a certain quantity of cloth, for example, for a certain quantity of corn; there is something which determines the owner of the cloth to accept for it such and such a quantity of corn; and, in like manner, the owner of the corn to accept such and such a quantity of cloth.

This is, evidently, the principle of demand and supply, in the first instance. If a great quantity of corn comes to market to be exchanged for cloth, and only a small quantity of cloth to be exchanged for corn, a great quantity of corn will be given for a small quantity of cloth. If the quantity of cloth, which thus comes to market, is increased, without any increase in the quantity of corn, the quantity of corn which is exchanged for a given quantity of cloth will be proportionally diminished.

This answer, however, does not resolve the whole of the question. The quantity in which commodities exchange for one another depends upon the proportion of supply to demand. It is evidently therefore necessary to ascertain upon what that proportion depends. What are the laws according to which supply is furnished to demand, is one of the most important inquiries in Political Economy.

Demand creates, and the loss of demand annihilates, supply. When an increased demand arises for any commodity, an increase of supply, if the supply is capable of increase, follows, as a regular effect. If the demand for any commodity altogether ceases, the commodity is no longer produced.

The connexion here, or causes and effects, is easily explained. If corn is brought to market, the cost of bringing it has been so much. If cloth is brought to market, the cost of bringing it has been so much. For the benefit of simplicity, the number of commodities in the market is here supposed to be two: it is of no consequence, with regard to the result, whether they are understood to be few or many.

The cost of bringing the corn to market has been either equal to that of bringing the cloth, or unequal. If it has been equal, there is no motive, to those who bring the cloth or the corn, for altering the quantity of either. They cannot obtain more of the commodity which they receive in exchange, by transferring their labour to its production. If the cost has been unequal, there immediately arises a motive for altering the proportions. Suppose that the cost of bringing, the whole of the corn has been greater than that of bringing the whole of the cloth; and that the whole of the one is exchanged against the whole of the other, either at once, or in parts: the persons who brought the cloth have in that case possessed themselves of a quantity of corn at less cost, than that at which it was brought to market, by those who produced it; those, on the other hand, who brought the corn have possessed themselves of a quantity of cloth, at a greater cost than that at which it can be made and brought to market.

Here motives arise, to diminish the quantity of corn, and increase the quantity of cloth; because the men who have been producing corn, and purchasing cloth, can obtain more cloth, by transferring their means of production from the one to the other. As soon, again, as no more cloth can be obtained by applying the same amount of means to the production of cloth, than by applying them to corn, and exchanging it for cloth, all motive to alter the quantity of the one as compared with that of the other is at an end. Nothing is to be gained by producing corn rather than cloth, or cloth rather than corn. The cost of production on both sides is equal.

It thus appears that the relative value of commodities, or in other words, the quantity of one which exchanges for a given quantity of another, depends upon demand and supply, in the first instance; but upon cost of production, ultimately; and hence, in accurate language, upon cost of production, entirely. An increase or diminution of demand or supply, may temporarily increase or diminish, beyond the point of productive cost, the quantity of one commodity which exchanges for a given quantity of another; but the law of competition, wherever it is not obstructed, tends invariably to bring it to that point, and to keep it there.

Cost of production, then, regulates the exchangeable value of commodities. But cost of production is itself involved in some obscurity.

NASSAU W. SENIOR (1790–1864)

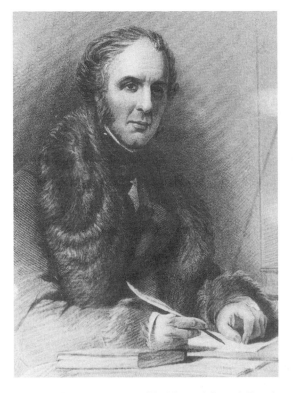

Nassau W. Senior, by courtesy of The Warren J. Samuels Portrait Collection at Duke University.

Nassau William Senior was educated at Oxford and at Lincoln's Inn and spent his early career practicing law and writing on economic subjects. He was appointed to the Drummond Chair of Political Economy at Oxford from 1825–1830 and again from 1847–1852, having devoted the intervening years to public service.

Senior's greatest impact was not academic. He was the first political economist to engage in extensive service as a policy advisor, providing regular counsel to Whig politicians and serving on four Royal Commissions – the Poor Laws, the Factory Acts, Distress of the Hand-loom Weavers, and Popular Education – between 1834 and 1857. He was a major figure on these commissions, writing most or all of their reports and lobbying extensively for the recommendations these commissions outlined. He is perhaps best known on policy front for his work as primary architect of the reform of the Poor Laws, which had the effect of replacing aid to the able-bodied with a new scheme that provided relief to those who were sick, aged, and poverty-stricken.

Senior made a number of important contributions to political economy, including expanding the Ricardian notion of rent to what might be called an unearned increment accruing to any factor of production (that is, not just land) that is in fixed supply, sketching the principle of diminishing marginal utility, and providing useful insights into the relationship between the balance of payments and relative international wages and prices. Like Say, Senior devoted more attention than many classical thinkers to the influence of demand on price, including extending the role of costs of production in price determination to the demand side. In his view, the producer's costs of production set the lower bound on price. However, he said, if the price rises sufficiently high, it will be more economical for the buyers of the good to produce it themselves. Thus, costs of production to the buyer set the upper bound on price.

Senior may well be best known, however, for his abstinence theory of profits, the notion that profits are a legitimate reward to the capitalist for abstaining from current consumption during the time when his capital is invested. This theory had the unfortunate effect of stimulating people to question how much pain was endured by the wealthy in their 'abstinence' and provided nice cannon fodder for Marx's later critique of what he saw as classical apologia for the bourgeois class. Senior also drew an important methodological distinction between the 'science' of political economy and the 'art' of political economy – what we would now call 'positive' versus 'normative' economics.

Senior's approach to value and price determination, his abstinence theory of profits, and his extension of the notion of rent are set out in the passages reprinted here from his *Outline of the Science of Political Economy* (1836).

References and further reading

Bowley, Marian (1937) *Nassau Senior and Classical Economics*, London: Allen & Unwin.

De Marchi, N. (1987) "Senior, Nassau William," in John Eatwell, Murray Milgate, and Peter Newman (eds), *The New Palgrave: A Dictionary of Economics*, Vol. 4, London: Macmillan, 303–5.

Johnson, Orace (1969) "The 'Last Hour' of Senior and Marx," *History of Political Economy* 1 (Fall): 359–69.

Pullen, John M. (1989) "In Defence of Senior's Last Hour-And-Twenty-Five-Minutes," *History of Political Economy* 21 (Summer): 299–312.

Senior, Nassau W. (1831) *Three Lectures on the Rate of Wages*, London: J. Murray.

——(1928) *Industrial Efficiency and Social Economy*, in S. Leon Levy(ed.), New York: Henry Holt.

——(1965) *Selected Writings on Economics: A Volume of Pamphlets, 1827–1852*, New York: Augustus M. Kelley.

Stigler, George J. (1950) "The Classical Economists: An Alternative View," in George J. Stigler, *Five Lectures on Economic Problems*, New York: Macmillan, 25–36.

An Outline of the Science of Political Economy (1836)*

Nature of wealth

Value

Value defined

Our definition of Wealth, as comprehending all those things, and those things only which have *Value*, requires us to explain at some length the signification which we attribute to the word Value; especially as the meaning of that word has been the subject of long and eager controversy. We have already stated that we use the word Value in its popular acceptation, as signifying *that quality in any thing which fits it to be given and received in Exchange*; or, in other words, to be lent or sold, hired or purchased.

So defined, Value denotes a relation reciprocally existing between two objects, and the precise relation which it denotes is the quantity of the one which can be obtained in exchange for a given quantity of the other. It is impossible, therefore, to predicate value of any object, without referring; expressly or tacitly, to some other objects in which its value is to be estimated; or, in other words, of which a certain quantity can be obtained in exchange for a certain quantity of the object in question.

We have already observed that the substance which at present is most desired, or, in other words, possesses the highest degree of value, is the diamond. By this we meant to express that there is no substance of which a given quantity will exchange for so large a quantity of every other commodity. When we wished to state the value of the king of Persia's bracelet, we stated first the amount of gold, and afterwards of English labour, which it would command in exchange. If we had attempted to give a perfect account of its value, we could have done so only by enumerating separately the quantity of every other article of wealth which could be obtained in exchange for it. Such an enumeration, if it could have been given, would have been a most instructive commercial lesson; for it would have shown not only the value of the diamond in all other commodities, but the reciprocal value of all other commodities in one another. If we had ascertained that a diamond weighing an ounce would exchange for one million five hundred thousand tons of Hepburn coal, or one hundred thousand tons of Essex wheat, or two thousand five hundred tons of English foolscap paper, we might have inferred that the coal, wheat, and paper would mutually exchange in the same proportions in which they were exchangeable for the diamond, and that a given weight of paper would purchase six hundred times as much coal, and forty times as much wheat.

Demand and Supply

The causes which determine the reciprocal values of commodities, or, in other words, which determine that a given quantity of one shall exchange for a given quantity of another, must be

* Nassau W. Senior, *An Outline of the Science of Political Economy*, London: W. Clowes and Sons, 1836.

divided into two sets: those which occasion the one to be limited in supply and useful, (using that word to express the power of occasioning pleasure and preventing pain), and those which occasion those attributes to belong to the other. In ordinary language, the *force* of the causes which give utility to a commodity is generally indicated by the word *Demand*; and the *weakness* of the obstacles which limit the quantity of a commodity by the word Supply.

Thus the common statement that commodities exchange in proportion to the Demand and Supply of each, means that they exchange in proportion to the force of weakness of the causes which give utility to them respectively, and to the weakness or force of the obstacles by which they are respectively limited in supply.

Unfortunately, however, the words Demand and Supply have not been always so used. Demand is sometimes used as synonymous with consumption, as when an increased production is said to generate an increased demand; sometimes it is used to express not only the desire to obtain a commodity, but the power to give the holder of it something which will induce him to part with it. 'A Demand', says Mr Mill (*Political Economy*, p. 23, 3rd edition) 'means the will to purchase and the power of purchasing'. Mr Malthus (Definitions in *Political Economy*, p. 244) states that 'Demand for commodities has two distinct meanings: one in regard to its extent, or the quantity of commodities purchased; the other in regard to its intensity, or the sacrifice which the demanders are able and willing to make in order to satisfy their wants'.

Demand

Neither of these expressions appears to be consistent with common usage. It must be admitted that the word Demand is used in its ordinary sense when we say that a deficient wheat harvest increases the Demand for oats and barley. But this proposition is not true if we use the word Demand in any other sense than as expressing the increased utility of oats and barley; or, in other words, the increased desire of the community to obtain them. The deficiency of wheat would not give to the consumers of oats and barley any increased power of purchasing them, nor would the quantity purchased or consumed be increased. The mode of consumption would be altered; instead of being applied to the feeding of horses, or to the supply of stimulant liquids, a certain portion of them would be used as human food. And, as the desire to eat is more urgent than the desire to feed horses, or drink beer or spirits, the desire to obtain, oats and barley, or, in other words, the pleasure given, or the pain averted, by the possesion of a given quantity of them or, in other words, the utility of a given quantity of them, would increase. A fact, which, in ordinary language, would be expressed by saying, that the demand for them was increased.

But though the vagueness with which the word Demand has been used renders it an objectionable term, it is too useful and concise to be given up; but we shall endeavour never to use it in any other signification than as expressing the utility of a commodity; or, what is the same, for we have seen that all utility is relative, the degree in which its possession is desired.

Supply

We cannot complain of equal vagueness in the use of the word Supply. In ordinary language, as well as in the writings of Political Economists, it is used to signify the quantity of a commodity actually brought to market. The complaint is, not that the word Supply has been used in this sense, but that, when used in this sense, it has been considered as a cause of value, except in a few cases, or for very short periods. We have shown, in the examples of coats and waistcoats, and gold and silver, that the reciprocal value of any two commodities depends, not on the quantity of each brought to market, but on the comparative force of, the obstacles which in each case oppose any increase in that quantity. When, therefore, we represent increase or diminution of supply as affecting value, we must be understood to mean not a mere positive increase or diminution, but an increase or diminution occasioned by a diminution or increase of the obstacles by which the supply is limited.

Intrinsic and extrinsic causes of the Value of a commodity

To revert to our original proposition, the reciprocal Values of any two commodities must be determined by two sets of causes; those which determine the Demand and Supply of the one, and those which determine the Demand and Supply of the other. The causes which give utility to a commodity and limit it in supply may be called the *intrinsic* causes of its value; those which limit the supply and occasion the utility of the commodities for which it is to be exchanged, may be called the *extrinsic* causes of its value. Gold and silver are now exchanged for one another in Europe in the proportion of one ounce of gold for about sixteen ounces of silver. This proportion must arise partly from the causes which give utility to gold and limit its supply, and partly from those which create the utility and limit the supply of silver. When talking of the value of gold we may consider the first set of causes affect gold only so far as it said to be exchanged for silver, which may be called one of its special values; the aggregate of its specific values forming its general value. If while the causes which give utility to silver and limit it in supply were unaltered, those which affect gold should vary; if, for instance, fashion should require every well-dressed man to have all his buttons of pure gold, or the disturbances in South America should perma-nently stop all the gold works of Brazil and Columbia, and thus (as would be the case) intercept five-sixths of our supplies of gold, the reciprocal values of gold and silver would in time be mate-rially varied. Though silver would be unaltered both as to its utility and as to its limitation in supply, a given quantity of it would exchange for a less quantity of gold, in the proportion per-haps of twenty to one, instead of sixteen to one. As between one another the rise and fall of gold and silver would precisely correspond, silver would fall and gold would rise one-fourth. But the fall of silver would not be general but specific; though fallen as estimated in gold, it would com-mand precisely the same quantities as before of all other commodities. The rise of gold would be more general; a given quantity of it would command one-fourth more not only of silver, but of all other commodities. The holder of a given quantity of silver would be just as rich as before for all purposes except the purchase of gold; the holder of a given quantity of gold would be richer than before for all purposes.

The circumstances by which each different class of commodities is invested with utility and limited in supply are subject to perpetual variation. Sometimes one of the causes alone varies. Sometimes they both vary in the same direction; sometimes in opposite directions. In the last case the opposite variations, wholly or partially neutralize one another.

The effects of an increased Demand concurrent with increased obstacles to Supply, and of diminished Demand concurrent with increased facility of Supply, are well exemplified by hemp. Its average price before the revolutionary war, exclusive of duty, did not exceed £30 per ton. The increased Demand, occasioned by a maritime war, and the natural obstacles to a proportionate increase of Supply, raised it, in the year 1796, to above £50 a ton; at about which price it continued during the next twelve years. But in 1808, the rupture between England and the Baltic powers, the principal source of our supplies, suddenly raised it to £118 a ton, being nearly four times the average price in peace. At the close of the war, both the extraordinary demand and the extraor-dinary obstacles to the supply ceased together, and the price fell to about its former average.

We have already stated that the utility of a commodity, in our extended sense of the term util-ity, or, in other words, the demand for it as an object of purchase or hire, is principally dependent on the obstacles which limit its supply. But there are many cases in which, while the existing obstacles remain unaltered, the demand is affected by the slightest suspicion that their force may at a future period be increased or diminished. This occurs with respect to those commodities of which the supply is not susceptible of accurate regulation, but is afforded either in uncertain quantities and at stated periods, between which it cannot be increased or diminished – in the case for instance of the annual products of the earth – or is dependent on our relations with foreign Countries. If a harvest deficient by one-third should occur, that deficiency must last for a whole year, or be supplied from abroad at an extravagant cost. If we should go to war with Russia, the obstacles to the supply of hemp would be increased while the war lasted. In either case the holders of corn or hemp would obtain great profits. In all rich Countries, and particularly in our own, there is a great number of persons who have large masses of wealth capable of being suddenly applied to the purchase of any given objects. The instant such persons suspect that the obstacles to the supply of any article are likely to be increased, they are anxious to become holders of it. They enter the market as new demanders; the price rises, and the mere fact that it has risen is a cause of its rising further. The details of commerce are so numerous, the difficulty of obtaining early and accurate information is so great, and the facts themselves are so constantly changing, that the most cautious merchants are often forced to act upon very doubtful premises; and the imprudent, dazzled by the chance of an enormous gain, which will be their own, and little restrained by the fear of a loss which may principally fall upon their creditors, are often ready to act upon scarcely any premises at all. They see that the price of some article has risen, and they suppose that there must be some good cause for it. They see that if they had purchased a month ago, they would have been gainers now, and conclude that if they purchase now they will be gainers a month hence. So far is this reasoning, if it can be called reasoning, carried, that a rise in the price of any one important commodity is generally found to occasion a rise in the price of many others. 'A' (thinks a speculator) 'bought hemp before the price had risen, and has resold it at a profit. Cotton has not yet risen, nor do I see clearly why it should rise, any more than I see why hemp should have risen, but it probably will rise like hemp, therefore I will purchase'.

...

When we consider that the supply of large classes of commodities is dependent on our amicable or hostile relations with foreign States, and on the commercial and financial legislation both of those States and of our own Country, and that the supply of still larger classes is dependent not only on those contingencies, but on the accidents of the seasons – and when we consider how the demand is affected not merely by the existing, or the anticipated obstacles to the supply, but often by a spirit of speculation as blind as that of a gambler ignorant of the odds and even of the principles of his game – it is obvious that the general value of all commodities, the quantity of each which will exchange for a given quantity of every other, can never remain the same for a single day. Every day there will be a variation in the demand or the supply of one or more of the innumerable classes of commodities which are the objects of exchange in a commercial Country. A given quantity of the commodity which has varied will consequently exchange for a greater or a less quantity of all other commodities. All other commodities, therefore, will have varied in value as estimated in the first-mentioned commodity. It is as impossible for one commodity to remain perfectly unaltered in value while any other is altered, as it would be for a lighthouse to keep at the same distance from all the ships in a harbour while any one of them should approach it or recede.

Steadiness in Value, on what it depends

But it may be asked, what do we mean when we say that a commodity has, for a given period, remained *steady* in value?

The question must be answered by referring to the different effects produced on the value of a commodity by an alteration in the intrinsic, or an alteration in the extrinsic, causes on which value depends. If the causes which give utility to a commodity and limit its supply, and which we have called the intrinsic causes of its value, are altered, the rise or fall in its value will be general.

A given quantity of it will exchange for a greater or a less quantity than before of every other commodity which has not also varied at the same time, in the same direction, and in the same degree; a coincidence which rarely occurs. Every other commodity must also rise or fall in value as estimated in the first-mentioned commodity, but not generally.

The fluctuations in value to which a commodity is subject by alternations, in what we have called the extrinsic causes of its value, or, in other words, by alterations in the demand or supply of other commodities, have a tendency, like all other extensive combinations of chances, to neutralize one another. It may be said, without impropriety, therefore, to remain steady in value. But the rise or fall in value which a commodity experiences in consequence of an alteration in its utility, or in the obstacles to its supply, is, in fact, entirely uncompensated. It is compensated only with regard to those commodities of which the utility or the supply has also varied at the same time and in the same direction. And as quite as many are likely to experience a similar variation, but in an opposite direction, there is really no compensation. A commodity, therefore, which is strikingly subject to such variations, is properly said to be unsteady in value.

But we may be asked to account for another and not unfrequent statement, that at particular periods all commodities have been observed to rise or fall in value. Literally taken, this statement involves a contradiction in terms, since it is impossible that a given quantity of every commodity should exchange for a greater or a less quantity of every other. When those who make this statement have any meaning, they always tacitly exclude some one commodity, and estimate in that the rise or fall of all others. The excluded commodity is, in general, money or labour.

Estimated in labour, all commodities, money included, have fallen in value in England since the sixteenth century. It is scarcely possible to mention one of which a given quantity will not purchase less labour than it did at the close of Elizabeth's reign; estimated in money, almost all commodities, labour included, have fallen in England since the termination of the late war.

The last remark which we shall now make on value is, that, with a very few exceptions, it is strictly local. A ton of coal at the bottom of the pit near Newcastle is perhaps worth 2 s. 6 d., at the pit's mouth it is perhaps worth 5 s., at ten miles off 7 s., at Hull 10 s. By the time the collier has reached the Pool, its cargo is seldom worth less than 16 s. a ton; and the inhabitant of Grosvenor Square may perhaps think himself fortunate if he can fill his coal cellars at 25 s. a ton. A ton of coal, though physically identical, must be considered, for economical purposes, as a different commodity at the bottom of the pit and at its mouth, in Hull and in Grosvenor Square. At every different stage of its progress it is limited in supply by different obstacles, and consequently exchangeable for different things and in different proportions. Supposing that at Newcastle a ton of the best wheat is now worth about twenty tons of the best coal: the same wheat and coal at the west end of London may probably exchange in the proportions of about four tons of coal for one of wheat. At Odessa, they may perhaps exchange about weight for weight.

Whenever, therefore, we speak of the value of a commodity, it is necessary to state the locality both of the commodity in question, and of the commodity in which its value is estimated. And in most cases we shall find their respective proximity to the places where they are respectively to be made use of one of the principal constituents of their respective values. The purchaser of the distant commodity has to consider the labour of transporting it to the place of consumption, the time for which that labour must be paid in advance, and the taxation, and the risk of injury or loss to which it may be subject in its transit. Nor is this all. He must also consider the danger that its quality may not correspond with the description or sample which guided him in making the purchase. The whole expense and risk attending the transport of a diamond from Edinburgh to London are but trifling; but its value is so dependent on its form and lustre, and those are qualities as to which it is so difficult to satisfy any purchaser who cannot ascertain them by inspection, that it would be difficult to obtain in London a fair price for a diamond in Edinburgh. Again, though a given quantity of coal from a given mine is generally of an ascertained quality, yet the expense, loss of time, risk, and taxation, which must be incurred in its transport from Newcastle to Grosvenor Square, are such, that a ton of coal, when it has reached Grosvenor Square, may be of nearly five times the value which it bore at Newcastle.

Statement of the four elementary propositions of the science of political economy

Instruments of Production

Having explained the nature of Production and Consumption, we now proceed to consider the Agents by whose intervention Production takes place.

I. Labour

The primary Instruments of Production are Labour, and those Agents of which nature, unaided by man, affords us the assistance.

Labour is the voluntary exertion of bodily or mental faculties for the purpose of, Production. It may appear unnecessary to define a term having a meaning so precise and so generally understood. Peculiar notions respecting the causes of value have, however, led some Economists to employ the term labour in senses so different from its common acceptation, that for some time to come it will be dangerous to use the word without explanation. We have already observed that many recent writers have considered value as solely dependent on labour. When pressed to explain how wine in a cellar, or an oak in its progress from a sapling to a tree, could, on this principle, increase in value, they replied that they considered the improvement of the wine and the growth of the tree as so much additional labour bestowed on each. We do not quite understand the meaning of this reply; but we have given a definition of labour, lest we should be supposed to include in it the unassisted operations of nature. It may also be well to remind our readers that this definition excludes all those exertions which are not intended, immediately or through their products, to be made the subjects of exchange. A hired messenger and a person walking for his amusement, a sportsman and a gamekeeper, the ladies at an English ball and a company of Natch girls in India, undergo the same fatigues; but ordinary language does not allow us to consider those as undergoing labour who exert themselves for the mere purpose of amusement.

II. Natural Agents

Under the term 'the Agents offered to us by nature', or, to use a shorter expression, 'Natural Agents', we include every productive agent so far as it does not derive its powers from the act of man.

The term 'Natural Agent' is far from being a convenient designation, but we have adopted it partly because it has been already made use of in this sense by eminent writers, and partly because we have not been able to find one less objectionable. The principal of these agents is the land, with its mines, its rivers, its natural forests with their wild inhabitants, and, in short, all its spontaneous productions. To these must be added the ocean, the atmosphere, light and heat, and even those physical laws, such as gravitation and electricity, by the knowledge of which we are able to vary the combinations of matter. All these productive agents have in general, by what appears to be an inconvenient synecdoche, been designated by the term *land*; partly because the land, as a source of profit, is the most important of those which are susceptible of appropriation, but chiefly because its possession generally carries with it the command over most of the others. And it is to be remembered that, though the powers of nature are necessary to afford a substratum for the other instruments of production to work upon, they are not of themselves, when universally accessible, causes of value. Limitation in supply is, as we have seen, a necessary constituent of value; and what is universally accessible is practically unlimited in supply.

III. Abstinence

But although Human Labour, and the Agency of Nature, independently of that of man, are the primary Productive Powers, they require the concurrence of a Third Productive Principle to give to them complete efficiency. The most laborious population, inhabiting the most fertile territory, if they devoted all their labour to the production of immediate results, and consumed its produce as it arose, would soon find their utmost exertions insufficient to produce even the mere necessaries of existence.

To the Third Principle, or Instrument of Production, without which the two others are inefficient, we shall give the name of *Abstinence:* a term by which we express the conduct of a person who either abstains from the unproductive use of what he can command, or designedly prefers the production of remote to that of immediate results.

It was to the effects of this Third Instrument of Production that we adverted when we laid down, as the third of our elementary propositions, *that the Powers of Labour and of the other Instruments which produce Wealth, may be indefinitely increased by using their Products as the means of further Production.* All our subsequent remarks on abstinence are a development and illustration, because it can scarcely be said to require formal proof.

The division of the Instruments of Production into three great branches has long been familiar to Economists. Those branches they have generally termed Labour, Land, and Capital. In the principle of this division we agree; though we have substituted different expressions for the second and third branches. We have preferred the term Natural Agents to that of Land, to avoid designating a whole genus by the name of one of its species a practice which has occasioned the other cognate species to be generally slighted and often forgotten. We have substituted the term Abstinence for that of Capital on different grounds.

The term Capital has been so variously defined that it may be doubtful whether it have any generally received meaning. We think, however, that, in popular acceptation, and in that of Economists themselves, when they are not reminded of their definitions, that word signifies *an article of wealth, the result of human exertion, employed in the production or distribution of wealth.* We say the result of human exertion, in order to exclude those productive instruments to which we have given the name of natural agents, and which afford not profit, in the scientific sense of that word, but rent.

It is evident that Capital, thus defined, is not a simple productive instrument; it is in most cases the result of all the three productive instruments combined. Some natural agent must have afforded the material, some delay of enjoyment must in general have reserved it from unproductive use, and some labour must in general have been employed to prepare and preserve it. *By the word Abstinence, we wish to express that agent, distinct from labour and the agency of nature, the concurrence of which is necessary to the existence of Capital, and which stands in the same relation to Profit as Labour does to Wages.* We are aware that we employ the word Abstinence in a more extensive sense than is warranted by common usage. Attention is usually drawn to abstinence only when it is not united with labour. It is recognized instantly in the conduct of a man who allows a tree or a domestic animal to attain its full growth; but it is less obvious when he plants the sapling or sows the seed corn. The observer's attention is occupied by the labour, and he omits to consider the additional sacrifice made when labour is undergone for a distant object. This additional sacrifice we comprehend under the term Abstinence; not because Abstinence is an unobjectionable expression for it, but because we have not been able to find one to which there are not still greater objections. We once thought of using 'providence'; but providence implies no self-denial, and has no necessary connection with profit. To take out an umbrella is provident, but not in the usual sense of the word profitable. We afterwards proposed 'frugality', but frugality implies some care and attention, that is to say, some labour; and though in practice Abstinence is almost always accompanied by some degree of labour, it is obviously necessary to keep them separate in an analysis of the instruments of production.

It may be said that pure Abstinence, being a mere negation, cannot produce positive effects; the same remark might as well be applied to intrepidity, or even to liberty; but who ever objected to their being considered as equivalent to active agents? To abstain from the enjoyment which is in our power, or to seek distant rather than immediate results, are among the most painful exertions of the human will. It is true that such exertions are made, and indeed are frequent in every state of society, except perhaps in the very lowest, and have been made in the very lowest, for society could not otherwise have improved; but of all the means by which man can be raised in the scale of being, abstinence, as it is perhaps the most effective, is the slowest in its increase, and the least generally diffused. Among nations, those that are the least civilized, and among the different classes of the same nation those which are the worst educated, are always the most improvident, and consequently the least abstinent.

...

Distribution of wealth

Society divided into three classes: Labourers, Capitalists, and Proprietors of Natural Agents

According to the usual language of Political Economists, Labour, Capital, and Land are the three Instruments of Production; Labourers, Capitalists, and Landlords are the three classes of Producers; and the whole Produce is divided into Wages, Profits, and Rent: the first designating the Labourer's share, the second that of the Capitalist, and the third that of the Landlord. We approve, on the whole, of the principles on which this classification is founded, but we have been forced, much against our will, to make considerable alterations in the language in which it has been usually expressed; to add some new terms, and to enlarge or contract the signification of some others.

It appears to us that, to have a nomenclature which should fully and precisely indicate the facts of the case, not less than *twelve* distinct terms would be necessary. For each class there ought to be a name for the *Instrument* employed or exercised, a name for the *Class of persons* who employ or exercise it, a name for the *Act* of employing or exercising it, and a name for the *Share* of the produce by which that act is remunerated. Of these terms we have not much more than half, as will appear if we examine each class separately.

Nomenclature applicable to the first class, the Labourers

For the first class we have the terms 'to Labour', 'a Labourer', and 'Wages'. None of these terms expresses the instruments of production: the substantive 'labour', and the verb 'to labour', express merely an act. 'A labourer' is an agent, and wages are a result: but what is the thing employed? What is it that the labourer exerts? Clearly his mental or bodily faculties. With the addition of this term the nomenclature of the first class will be complete. To Labour is to employ strength of body or mind for the purpose of Production; the person who does so is a Labourer, and Wages are his remuneration.

Nomenclature applicable to the second class, the Capitalists

In the second class we have the words Capital, Capitalist, and Profit. These terms express the instrument, the person who employs or exercises it, and his remuneration; but there is no familiar term to express the act, the conduct of which profit is the reward, and which bears the same relation to profit which labour does to wages. To this conduct we have already given the name of

Abstinence. The addition of this term will complete the nomenclature of the second class. Capital is an article of wealth, the result of human exertion, employed in the production or distribution of Wealth. Abstinence expresses both the act of abstaining from the unproductive use of capital, and also the similar conduct of the man who devotes his labour to the production of remote rather than of immediate results. The person who so acts is a Capitalist, the reward of his conduct is Profit.

Nomenclature applicable to the third class, the Proprietors of Natural Agents

The defectiveness of the established nomenclature is more striking when we come to the third class. Wages and profits are the creation of man. They are the recompense for the sacrifice made in the one case, of ease, in the other, of immediate enjoyment. But a considerable part of the produce of every country is the recompense of no sacrifice whatever; is received by those who neither labour nor put by, but merely hold out their hands to accept the offerings of the rest of the community.

...

Of the Agents afforded by nature, the principal is the Land, with its Rivers, Ports, and Mines. In the rare cases in which the quantity of useful land is practically unlimited, a state of things which occurs only in the early stages of colonization, Land is an agent universally accessible, and, as nothing is paid for its use, the whole produce belongs to the cultivators, and is divided, under the names of wages and profit, between the capitalists and the labourers, of whose abstinence and industry it is the result.

But in all old Countries, and even in colonies within a very few years after their foundation, certain Lands, from peculiar advantages of soil or situation, are found to make more than the average return to a given expenditure of capital and industry. The proprietor of such lands, if he cultivate them himself, receives a surplus after having paid the wages of his labourers and deducted the profit to which he is entitled on his capital. He of course receives the same surplus if, instead of cultivating them himself, he lets them out to some other capitalist. The tenant receives the same profit, and the labourers receive the same wages as if they were employed on land possessing merely average natural advantages; the surplus forms the rent of the proprietor, or, as we usually term him, the landlord. The whole produce, instead of two, is divided into three shares – Rent, Profit, and Wages. If the owner is also the capitalist or farmer, he receives two of these shares, both the profit and the rent. If he allow it to be cultivated by the capital of another, he receives only rent. But rent, with or without profit, he necessarily receives. And when the whole of a Country has been appropriated, though it be true, as will be shown hereafter, that some of the produce is raised by the application of additional capital without payment of additional rent, and may therefore be said to be raised rent free, yet it is equally true that a rent is received from every cultivated acre; a rent rising or falling according to the accidents of soil and situation, but the necessary result of limited extent and productive power.

It is obvious, however, as we have already stated, that land, though the principal, is not the only natural agent that can be appropriated. The mere knowledge of the operations of nature, as long as the use of that knowledge can be confined either by secrecy or by law, creates a revenue to its possessor analogous to the rent of land. The knowledge of the effect on the fibres of cotton of rollers moving with different velocities, enabled a village barber to found in a very few years a more than aristocratic fortune. Still greater wealth might probably have been acquired by Dr Jenner, if he could have borne somewhat to limit the benefits which he has conferred on mankind.

When the author of a useful discovery puts it himself in practice, he is like a proprietor farming his own property; the produce, after paying average wages for the labour, and average profits for the capital, employed, affords a still further revenue, the effect not of that capital or of that labour, but of the discovery, the creation not of man but of nature. If, instead of using it himself, he let out to another the privilege of using it, be obtains a revenue so precisely resembling the rent of land, that it often receives the same name. The payment made by a manufacturer to a patentee for the privilege of using the patent process, is usually termed, in commercial language, a *Rent*; and under the same head must be ranked all the peculiar advantages of situation or connection, and all extraordinary qualities of body and mind. The surplus revenue which they occasion beyond average wages and profits is a revenue for which no additional sacrifice has been made. The proprietor of these advantages differs from a landlord only in the circumstance that he cannot in general let them out to be used by another, and must consequently either allow them to be useless or turn them to account himself. He is forced, therefore, always to employ on them his own industry, and generally his own capital, and receives not only rent, but wages and profit. If, therefore, the established division is adhered to, and all that is produced is to be divided into rent, profit, and wages – and certainly that appears to be the most convenient classification; and if wages and profit are to be considered as the rewards of peculiar sacrifices, the former the remuneration for labour, and the latter for abstinence from immediate enjoyment, it is clear that under the term 'rent' must be included all that is obtained without any sacrifice; or, which is the same thing, beyond the remuneration for that sacrifice; all that nature or fortune bestows either without any exertion on the part of the recipient, or in addition to the average remuneration for the exercise of industry or the employment of capital.

But though we see no objection to this extension of the word rent, the terms land and landlord are too precise to admit of being equally extended. It would be too great an innovation to include under the term land every natural agent which is capable of appropriation, or under the term landlord every proprietor of such an agent. For these terms we must substitute those of *natural agent*, and *proprietor of a natural agent*. And the third class will then have a term for the third instrument of production a term for the owner of that instrument, and a term for the share which he receives of the produce: terms corresponding with the terms faculties of body and mind, labourer, and wages, as applied to the first class, and with capital, capitalist, and profit, as applied to the second. We shall still want a term corresponding with labour and abstinence – a term indicating the *conduct* which enables the proprietor of a natural agent to receive a rent. But as this conduct implies no sacrifice – as it consists merely in not suffering the instrument of which he is the owner to be useless, it perhaps does not require a distinct designation. When a man possesses an estate, we take it for granted that he does not allow it to lie waste, but either uses it himself, or lets it to a tenant. In ordinary language, the receipt of rent is included under the term ownership. There will therefore be little danger of obscurity if we consider the word 'possess', when applied to the proprietor of a natural agent, as implying the receipt of the advantages afforded by that agent, or, in other words, of rent. Talents, indeed, often lie idle, but in that case they may be considered for economical purposes as not possessed. In fact, unaccompanied by the will to use them, they are useless.

...

In most cases a considerable interval elapses between the period at which the natural agent and the labourer are first employed, and the completion of the product. In this climate the harvest is seldom reaped until nearly a year after it has been sown; a still longer time is required for the maturity of oxen; and longer still for that of a horse; and sixty or seventy years may pass between the commencement of a plantation, and the time at which the timber is saleable. It is obvious that neither the landlord nor the labourer, as such, can wait during all this interval for their remuneration. The doing so would, in fact, be an act of abstinence. It would be the employment of land and labour in order to obtain remote results. This sacrifice is made by the capitalist, and he is repaid for it by his appropriate remuneration, profit. He advances to the landlord and the labourer, and in most cases to some previous capitalist, the price of their respective assistance; or, in other words, the hire of the land and capital belonging to one, and of the mental and bodily powers of another, and becomes solely entitled to the whole of the product. The success of his operations depends on the proportion which the value of that produce, (or, in commercial language, the value of his returns), bears to the value of his advances, taking into consideration the time for which those advances have been made. If the value of the return is inferior to that of the advance, he is obviously a loser; he is a loser if it be merely equal, as he has incurred abstinence without profit, or, in ordinary language, has lost the interest on his capital. He is a loser even if the value of his returns do not exceed that of his advances by an amount equal to the current rate of profit for the period during which the advance has been made. In any of these cases the product is sold, so far as the capitalist is concerned, for less than the cost of its production. The employment of capital, therefore, is necessarily a speculation; it is the purchase of so much productive power which may or may not occasion a remunerative return.

The common language of Economists, therefore, which describes the landlord, the capitalist, and the labourer as sharers of the produce, is a fiction. Almost all that is produced is in the first instance the property of the capitalist; he has purchased it by having previously paid the rent and wages, and incurred or paid for the abstinence, which were necessary to its production. A portion of it, but generally a small portion, he consumes himself, in the state in which he receives it; the remainder he sells. He may, if he think fit, employ the price of all that he sells in purchases for his own gratification; but he cannot remain a capitalist unless he consent to employ some portion of it in the hire of the land and labour, by the assistance of which the process of production is to be continued or recommenced. He cannot, generally speaking, fully retain his situation as a capitalist unless he employ some portion of it in the hire of the land and labour, by the assistance of which the process of production is to be continued or recommenced. He cannot, generally speaking, fully retain his situation as a capitalist unless he employ enough to hire as much land and labour as before; and if he wish to raise himself in the world, he must, generally speaking, not merely keep up, but increase the sum which he devotes to the purchase of productive force.

...

Exchange

Having made this general classification of the parties among whom the results of the different productive instruments are divided, we now proceed to consider the general laws which regulate the proportions in which those results are exchanged for one another. To a certain degree this question was considered when we treated of value; but not having at that time explained the words production, wages, profit, or rent, we were unable to do more than to state and illustrate the following propositions:

First, that all those things, and those things only, are susceptible of exchange, which, being transferable, are limited in supply, and are capable, directly or indirectly, of affording pleasure or preventing pain; a capacity to which we have affixed the name of utility. Second, that the reciprocal values of any two things, or, in other words, the quantity of the one which will exchange for a given quantity of the other, depend on two sets of causes; those which occasion the utility and limit the supply of the one, and those which limit the supply and occasion the utility of the other. The causes which occasion the utility and limit the supply of any given commodity or service, we denominate the *intrinsic* causes of its value. Those which limit the supply and occasion the utility of the commodities or services for which it is capable of being exchanged, we denominate the *extrinsic* causes of its value. And, third, that comparative limitation of supply, or, to speak more familiarly, though less philosophically, comparative scarcity, though not sufficient to constitute value, is by far its most important element; utility, or, in other words, demand, being mainly dependent on it. We had not then shown the means by which supply is effected. Having done this, having shown that human Labour and Abstinence, and the spontaneous agency of Nature, are the three instruments of production, we are at liberty to explain what are the obstacles which limit the supply of all that is produced, and the mode in which those obstacles affect the reciprocal values of the different subjects of exchange.

Price

In the following discussion, however, we shall in general substitute price or value in money for general value.

The general value of any commodity, that is, the quantity of all the other subjects of exchange which might be obtained in return for a given quantity of it, is incapable of being ascertained. Its specific value in any other commodity may be ascertained by the experiment of an exchange; the anxiety of each party in the exchange to give as little, and obtain as much as possible, leading him to investigate, as accurately as he can, the intrinsic causes giving value to each of the articles to be exchanged. This is, however, a troublesome operation, and many expedients are used to diminish its frequency. The most obvious one is to consider a single exchange, or the mean of a few exchanges, as a model for subsequent exchanges of a similar nature. By an extension of this expedient it may become a model for exchanges not of a similar nature. If given quantities of two different articles are each found by experience to exchange for a given quantity of a third article, the proportionate value of the two first-mentioned articles may, of course, be inferred. It is *measured* by the third. Hence arise the advantages of selecting, as one of the subjects of every exchange, a single commodity, or, more correctly, a species of commodities constituted of individuals of precisely similar qualities. In the first place, all persons can ascertain, with tolerable accuracy, the intrinsic causes which give value to the selected commodity, so that one half the trouble of an exchange is ready performed. And, second, if an exchange is to be effected between any other two commodities, the quantity of each that is usually exchanged for a given quantity of the third commodity is ascertained, and their relative value is inferred. The commodity thus selected as the general instrument of exchange, whatever be its substance, whether salt, as in Abyssinia, cowries, on the Coast of Guinea, or the precious metals, as in Europe, is money. When the use of such a commodity, or, in other words, of *money*, has become established, value in money, or price, is the only value familiarly contemplated. The scarcity and durability of gold and silver (the substances used as money by all civilized nations) make them peculiarly unsusceptible of alteration in value from intrinsic causes. On these accounts we think it better, in the following discussion, to refer rather to *price* than to general value, and to consider the value of money, so far as it depends on intrinsic causes, to be unvarying.

We must preface our explanation of the effect on price of the causes limiting supply, by a remark which may appear self-evident, but which must always be kept in recollection, namely that *Where the only natural agents employed are those which are universally accessible, and therefore are practically unlimited in supply, the utility of the produce, or, in other words, its power, directly or indirectly, of producing gratification, or preventing pain, must be in proportion to the sacrifices made to produce it, unless the producer has misapplied his exertions; since no man would willingly employ a given amount of labour or abstinence in producing one commodity, if he could obtain more gratification by devoting them to the production of another.*

We now revert to the causes which limit supply.

There are some commodities the results of agents no longer in existence, or acting at remote and uncertain periods, the supply of which cannot be increased, or cannot be reckoned upon. Antiques and relics belong to the first class, and all the very rare productions of Nature of Art, such as diamonds of extraordinary size, or pictures, or statues of extraordinary beauty, to the second. The values of such commodities are subject to no definite rules, and depend altogether on the wealth and taste of the community. In common language, they are said to bear a fancy price, that is, a price depending principally on the caprice or fashion of the day. The Boccaccio, which a few years ago sold for £2,000, and after a year or two's interval for £700, may, perhaps, fifty years hence, be purchased for a shilling. Relics which, in the ninth century, were thought too valuable to admit of a definite price, would now be thought equally incapable of price in consequence of their utter worthlessness. In the following discussion we shall altogether omit such commodities and confine our attention to those of which the supply is capable of increase, either regular, or sufficiently approaching to regularity, to admit of calculation.

The obstacle to the supply of those commodities which are produced by labour and abstinence, with that assistance only from nature which every one can command, consists solely in the difficulty of finding persons ready to submit to the labour and abstinence necessary to their production. In other words, their supply is limited by the cost of their production.

$$\ldots$$

Cost of Production defined

By *Cost of Production*, then, we mean the sum of the labour and abstinence necessary to production. But cost of production, thus, defined must be divided into the cost of production, on the part of the producer or seller, and the cost of production on the part of the consumer or purchaser. The first is of course the amount of labour and abstinence which must be undergone by him who offers for sale a given class of commodities or services in order to enable him to continue to produce them. The second is, the amount of the labour and abstinence which must be undergone by those to whom a given commodity or service is offered for sale, if, instead of purchasing, they themselves, or some of them on the behalf of themselves and the others, were to produce it. The first is equal to the minimum, the second to the maximum, of price. For, on the one hand, no man would continue to buy what they themselves, or some of them on behalf of themselves and the others, could produce at less expense. With respect to those commodities, or, to speak more accurately, with respect to the value of those parts or attributes of commodities, which are the subjects of equal competition, which may be produced by all persons with equal advantages, the cost of production to the producer and the cost of production to consumer are the same. Their price, therefore, represents the aggregate amount of the labour and abstinence necessary to continue their production. If their price should fall lower, the wages or the profits of those employed in their production must fall below the average remuneration of the labour and abstinence that must be undergone if their production is to be continued. In time, therefore, it is discontinued or diminished, until the value of the product has been raised by the diminution of the supply. If the price should rise beyond the cost of their production, the producers must receive more than an average remuneration for their sacrifices. As soon as this has been discovered, capital and industry flow towards the employment which, by this supposition, offers extraordinary advantages. Those who formerly were purchasers, or persons on their behalf, turn producers themselves, until the increased supply has equalized the price with the cost of production.

Some years ago London depended for water on the New River Company. As the quantity which they can supply is limited, the price rose with the extension of buildings, until it so far exceeded the cost of production as to induce some of the consumers to become producers. Three new Water Companies were established, and the price fell as the supply increased, until the shares in the New River Company fell to nearly one-fourth of their former value; from £15,000 to £4,000. If the metropolis should continue to increase, these transactions will recur. The price of water will increase and exceed the cost at which it could be afforded. New Companies will arise, and, unless the additional supply is checked by greater natural obstacles than those which the existing Companies have to surmount, the price will again fall to its present level.

But though, under free competition, cost of production is the regulator of price, its influence is subject to much occasional interruption. Its operation can be supposed to be perfect only if we suppose that there are no disturbing causes, that capital and labour can be at once transferred, and without loss, from one employment to another, and that every producer has full information of the profit to be derived from every mode of production. But it is obvious that these suppositions have no resemblance to the truth. A large portion of the capital essential to production consists of buildings, machinery, and other implements, the results of much time and labour, and of little service for any except their existing purposes. A still larger portion consists of knowledge and of intellectual and bodily dexterity, applicable only to the processes in which those qualities were originally acquired. Again, the advantage derived from any given business depends so much upon the dexterity and the judgment with which it is managed, that few capitalists can estimate, except upon an average of some years, the amount of their own profits, and still fewer can estimate those of their neighbours. Established businesses, therefore, may survive the causes in which they originated, and become gradually extinguished as their comparative unprofitableness is discovered, and the labourers and capital engaged in them wear away without being replaced; and, on the other hand, other employments are Inadequately supplied with the capital and industry which they could profitably absorb. During the interval, the products of the one sell for less, and those of the others for more, than their cost of production. Political Economy does not deal with particular facts but with general tendencies, and when we assign to cost of production the power of regulating price in cases of equal competition, we mean to describe it not as a point to which price is attached, but as a centre of oscillation which it is always endeavouring to approach.

We have seen that, under circumstances of equal competition, or, in other words, where all persons can become producers, and that with equal advantages, the cost of production on the part of the producer or seller, and the cost production on the part of the consumer or purchaser, are the same, and that the commodity thus produced sells for its cost of production; or, in other words, at a price equal to the sum of the labour and abstinence which its production requires; or, to use a more familiar expression, at a price equal to the amount of the wages and profits which must be paid to induce the producers to continue their exertions. It has lately been a general opinion that the bulk of commodities is produced under circumstances of equal competition. 'By far the greater part of those goods', says Mr Ricardo (Principles, p. 3) 'which are the objects of desire, are produced by labour, and may be multiplied almost without any assignable limit, if we are disposed to bestow the labour necessary to obtain them. In speaking then of commodities, of their exchangeable value, and of the laws which regulate their relative prices, we always mean such commodities only as can be increased in quantity by the exertion of human industry, and in the production of which competition operates without restraint'.

Now it is clear that the production in which no appropriated natural agent has concurred, is the only production which has been made under circumstances of perfectly equal competition. And how few are the commodities of which the production has in no stage been assisted by peculiar advantages of soil, or situation, or by extraordinary talent of body or mind, or by processes generally unknown, or protected by law from imitation. Where the assistance of these agents, to which we have given the general name of natural agents, has been obtained, the result is more than the result of equal labour and abstinence unassisted by similar aids. A commodity thus produced is called the subject of a *monopoly*; and the person who has appropriated such a natural agent, a *monopolist*.

JOHN STUART MILL (1806–1873)

John Stuart Mill, by courtesy of The Warren J. Samuels Portrait Collection at Duke University.

John Stuart Mill was a child prodigy. Educated under the strict direction of his father, James Mill, John Stuart Mill was studying Greek at age 3 and had progressed through Latin, mathematics, literature, history, the natural sciences, logic, and political economy by his early teen years. He assumed a position with the East India Company at age 16 and remained there for thirty-six years. By the time of his death, Mill, who had been raised to have the brightest and best-trained mind of his generation, had made fundamentally important contributions to philosophy, politics, and economics. From the literary perspective, his *Autobiography* is a classic of that genre and provides an excellent depiction of the childhood that Mill said was lived "in the absence of love and in the presence of fear."

Not surprisingly, given his father's strong Benthamite leanings, J.S. Mill, too, became a disciple of Bentham in his early years. However, a nervous breakdown and subsequent period of severe depression, followed by an encounter with the poetry of Wordsworth and Coleridge in his early twenties, resulted in his adoption of a more critical approach to the Benthamite position. He came to believe that the cool calculus of utilitarianism needed to be tempered by moral and spiritual concerns, recognizing that the type and quality of pleasure also matter. His ideas mixed the British empirical position with elements of French historical thinking a la Saint-Simon and August Comte. His relationship with Harriet Taylor, whom he met in his twenties and married some twenty years later when she became a widow, had a significant effect on his life, including prompting something of a flirtation with socialism.

Mill is unquestionably one of the, if not *the*, towering intellectual figures of his age. His seminal works range from political economy to philosophy and logic to political theory. His *A System of Logic* became a classic in the field, and his *On Liberty* has become one of the definitive defenses of the virtues of individual freedom. Mill's early forays into political economy can be seen in his book, *Essays on Some Unsettled Questions of Political Economy*, but his thinking reaches full flower in his *Principles of Political Economy, With Some of Their Applications to Social Philosophy* (1848). The *Principles*, which went through several editions during Mill's lifetime, evidences both the fleshing out of Ricardian political economy, tempered by the important insights of his own and others regarding certain flaws in Ricardo's analysis, and close attention to historical and contemporary illustrations.

The *Principles* was more than just a crowning summation of classical thinking; it also contained a number of fundamental theoretical advances – for example, in demand and supply analysis, in international trade and finance, and in the analysis of labor markets. Mill also presented a view of the economic role of government that was at once cognizant of the benefits of individual liberty and recognized that Smith's "invisible hand" did not always result in the individual pursuit of self-interest generating a maximum of social welfare. While a staunch adherent of the Malthusian theory of population, Mill was also of the mind that arrival of the stationary state was less problematic than previously thought. His distinction between the fixed laws of production and the malleable laws of distribution left open the door for governmental policies that could delay the arrival of the stationary state for a period of time and make life in the stationary state much more pleasant than thought by previous commentators.

In the following excerpts from Mill's *Principles*, the reader is treated to his attempt to distinguish between the laws of production and distribution, his discussion of the wages fund doctrine of wage determination, his extension of Ricardo's doctrine of comparative costs in international trade to include the effects of reciprocal demands on the terms of trade, an analysis of life in the stationary state, and his view of the appropriate role for government within the economic system.

References and further reading

Anschutz, R.P. (1953) *The Philosophy of J.S. Mill*, London: Oxford University Press.

Bladen, V.W. (1949) "John Stuart Mill's *Principles*: A Centenary Estimate," *American Economic Review* 39 (May): 1–12.

Blaug, Mark (1991) *Thomas Robert Malthus (1766–1834) and John Stuart Mill (1806–1873)*, Aldershot: Edward Elgar Publishing.

Breit, William (1967) "The Wages Fund Controversy: A Diagrammatic Exposition," *Canadian Journal of Economics* 33 (November): 523–8.

Chipman, John S. (1965) "A Survey on the Theory of International Trade: Part 1: The Classical Theory," *Econometrica* 33 (July): 477–519.

Hollander, Samuel (1985) *The Economics of John Stuart Mill*, Oxford: Basil Blackwell.

——(1987) "Mill, John Stuart, as Economic Theorist," in John Eatwell, Murray Milgate, and Peter Newman (eds), *The New Palgrave: A Dictionary of Economics*, Vol. 3, London: Macmillan, 471–6.

Mill, John Stuart (1844) *Essays on Some Unsettled Questions of Political Economy*, London: Parker.

——(1887) *On Liberty*, London: Longmans, Green.

——(1924) *Autobiography*, New York: Columbia University Press.

——(1963–85) *The Collected Works of John Stuart Mill*, edited by J.M. Robson, Toronto: University of Toronto Press.

Ryan, Alan (1974) *J.S. Mill*, London: Routledge and Kegan Paul.

——(1987) "Mill, John Stuart," in John Eatwell, Murray Milgate, and Peter Newman (eds), *The New Palgrave: A Dictionary of Economics*, Vol. 3, London: Macmillan, 466–71.

Taussig, F.W. (1898) Wages and Capital: An Examination of the Wages Fund Doctrine, New York: D. Appleton and Company.

Viner, Jacob (1937) *Studies in the Theory of International Trade*, New York: Harper & Row.

——(1949) "Bentham and J.S. Mill: The Utilitarian Background," *American Economic Review* 39 (March): 360–82.

Wood, John C. (1987) *John Stuart Mill: Critical Assessments*, London: Croom Helm.

Principles of Political Economy (1848)*

Book II: Distribution

Chapter I: Of property

1. The principles which have been set forth in the first part of this treatise, are, in certain respects, strongly distinguished from those on the consideration of which we are now about to enter. The laws and conditions of the Production of wealth partake of the character of physical truths. There is nothing optional or arbitrary in them. Whatever mankind produce, must be produced in the modes, and under the conditions, imposed by the constitution of external things, and by the inherent properties of their own bodily and mental structure. Whether they like it or not, their productions will be limited by the amount of their previous accumulation, and, that being given, it will be proportional to their energy, their skill, the perfection of their machinery, and their judicious use of the advantages of combined labour. Whether they like it or not, a double quantity of labour will not raise, on the same land, a double quantity of food, unless some improvement takes place in the processes of cultivation. Whether they like it or not, the unproductive expenditure of individuals will *pro tanto* tend to impoverish the community, and only their productive expenditure will enrich it. The opinions, or the wishes, which may exist on these different matters, do not control the things themselves. We cannot, indeed, foresee to what extent the modes of production may be altered, or the productiveness of labour increased, by future extensions of our knowledge of the laws of nature, suggesting new processes of industry of which we have at present no conception. But howsoever we may succeed, in making for ourselves more space within the limits set by the constitution of things, we know that there must be limits. We cannot alter the ultimate properties either of matter or mind, but can only employ those properties more or less successfully, to bring about the events in which we are interested.

It is not so with the Distribution of wealth. That is a matter of human institution solely. The things once there, mankind, individually or collectively, can do with them as they like. They can place them at the disposal of whomsoever they please, and on whatever terms. Further, in the social state, in every state except total solitude, any disposal whatever of them can only take place by the consent of society, or rather of those who dispose of its active force. Even what a person has produced by his individual toil, unaided by any one, he cannot keep, unless by the permission of society. Not only can society take it from him, but individuals could and would take it from him, if society only remained passive; if it did not either interfere *en masse*, or employ and pay people for the purpose of preventing him from being disturbed in the possession. The distribution of wealth, therefore, depends on the laws and customs of society. The rules by which it is

* *Principles of Political Economy With Some of Their Applications of Social Philosophy*, edited with an introduction by W.J. Ashley, London: Longmans, Green, and Co., 1909.

determined are what the opinions and feelings of the ruling portion of the community make them, and are very different in different ages and countries; and might be still more different, if mankind so chose.

The opinions and feelings of mankind, doubtless, are not a matter of chance. They are consequences of the fundamental laws of human nature, combined with the existing state of knowledge and experience, and the existing condition of social institutions and intellectual and moral culture. But the laws of the generation of human opinions are not within our present subject. They are part of the general theory of human progress, a far larger and more difficult subject of inquiry than political economy. We have here to consider, not the causes, but the consequences, of the rules according to which wealth may be distributed. Those, at least, are as little arbitrary, and have as much the character of physical laws, as the laws of production. Human beings can control their own acts, but not the consequences of their acts either to themselves or to others. Society can subject the distribution of wealth to whatever rules it thinks best: but what practical results will flow from the operation of those rules must be discovered, like any other physical or mental truths, by observation and reasoning.

We proceed, then, to the consideration of the different modes of distributing the produce of land and labour, which have been adopted in practice, or may be conceived in theory. Among these, our attention is first claimed by that primary and fundamental institution, on which, unless in some exceptional and very limited cases, the economical arrangements of society have always rested, though in its secondary features it has varied, and is liable to vary. I mean, of course, the institution of individual property.

Chapter XI: Of wages

1. Under the head of Wages are to be considered, first, the causes which determine or influence the wages of labour generally, and second, the differences that exist between the wages of different employments. It is convenient to keep these two classes of considerations separate; and in discussing the law of wages, to proceed in the first instance as if there were no other kind of labour than common unskilled labour of the average degree of hardness and disagreeableness.

Wages, like other things, may be regulated either by competition or by custom. In this country there are few kinds of labour of which the remuneration would not be lower than it is, if the employer took the full advantage of competition. Competition, however, must be regarded, in the present state of society, as the principal regulator of wages, and custom or individual character only as a modifying circumstance, and that in a comparatively slight degree.

Wages, then, depend mainly upon the demand and supply of labour; or, as it is often expressed, on the proportion between population and capital. By population is here meant the number only of the labouring class, or rather of those who work for hire; and by capital only circulating capital, and not even the whole of that, but the part which is expended in the direct purchase of labour. To this, however, must be added all funds which, without forming a part of capital, are paid in exchange for labour, such as the wages of soldiers, domestic servants, and all other unproductive labourers. There is unfortunately no mode of expressing by one familiar term, the aggregate of what has been called the wages-fund of a country: and as the wages of productive labour form nearly the whole of that fund, it is usual to overlook the smaller and less important part, and to say that wages depend on population and capital. It will be convenient to employ this expression, remembering, however, to consider it as elliptical, and not as a literal statement of the entire truth.

With these limitations of the terms, wages not only depend upon the relative amount of capital and population, but cannot, under the rule of competition, be affected by anything else. Wages (meaning, of course, the general rate) cannot rise, but by an increase of the aggregate funds employed in hiring labourers, or a diminution in the number of the competitors for hire; nor fall, except either by a diminution of the funds devoted to paying labour, or by an increase in the number of labourers to be paid.

Book III: Exchange

Chapter XVIII: Of international values

1. The values of commodities produced at the same place, or in places sufficiently adjacent for capital to move freely between them – let us say, for simplicity, of commodities produced in the same country – depend (temporary fluctuations apart) upon their cost of production. But the value of a commodity brought from a distant place, especially from a foreign country, does not depend on its cost of production in the place from whence it comes. On what, then, does it depend? The value of a thing in any place depends on the cost of its acquisition in that place; which, in the case of an imported article, means the cost of production of the thing which is exported to pay for it.

Since all trade is in reality barter, money being a mere instrument for exchanging things against one another, we will, for simplicity, begin by supposing the international trade to be in form, what it always is in reality, an actual trucking of one commodity against another. As far as we have hitherto proceeded, we have found all the laws of interchange to be essentially the same, whether money is used or not; money never governing, but always obeying, those general laws.

If, then, England imports wine from Spain, giving for every pipe of wine a bale of cloth, the exchange value of a pipe of wine in England will not depend upon what the production of the wine may have cost in Spain, but upon what the production of the cloth has cost in England. Though the wine may have cost in Spain the equivalent of only ten days' labour, yet, if the cloth costs in England twenty days' labour, the wine, when brought to England, will exchange for the produce of twenty days' English labour, *plus* the cost of carriage; including the usual profit on the importer's capital, during the time it is locked up, and withheld from other employment.

The value, then, in any country, of a foreign commodity, depends on the quantity of home produce which must be given to the foreign country in exchange for it. In other words, the values of foreign commodities depend on the terms of international exchange. What, then, do these depend upon? What is it which, in the case supposed, causes a pipe of wine from Spain to be exchanged with England for exactly that quantity of cloth? We have seen that it is not their cost of production. If the cloth and the wine were both made in Spain, they would exchange at their cost of production in Spain; if they were both made in England, they would exchange at their cost of production in England: but all the cloth being made in England, and all the wine in Spain, they are in circumstances to which we have already determined that the law of cost of production is not applicable. We must accordingly, as we have done before in a similar embarrassment, fall back upon an antecedent law, that of supply and demand: and in this we shall again find the solution of our difficulty.

I have discussed this question in a separate Essay, already once referred to; and a quotation of part of the exposition then given will be the best introduction to my present view of the subject. I must give notice that we are now in the region of the most complicated questions which political economy affords; that the subject is one which cannot possibly be made elementary; and that a more continuous effort of attention than has yet been required will be necessary to follow the series of deductions. The thread, however, which we are about to take in hand, is in itself very simple and manageable; the only difficulty is in following it through the windings and entanglements of complex international transactions.

2. 'When the trade is established between the two countries, the two commodities will exchange for each other at the same rate of interchange in both countries – bating the cost of carriage, of which, for the present, it will be more convenient to omit the consideration. Supposing, therefore, for the sake of argument, that the carriage of the commodities from one country to the other could be effected without labour and without cost, no sooner would the trade be opened than the value of the two commodities, estimated in each other, would come to a level in both countries.

'Suppose that 10 yards of broadcloth cost in England as much labour as 15 yards of linen, and in Germany as much as 20'. In common with most of my predecessors, I find it advisable, in these intricate investigations, to give distinctness and fixity to the conception by numerical examples. These examples must sometimes, as in the present case, be purely supposititious. I should have preferred real ones; but all that is essential is, that the numbers should be such as admit of being easily followed through the subsequent combinations into which they enter.

This supposition then being made, it would be the interest of England to import linen from Germany, and of Germany to import cloth from England. 'When each country produced both commodities for itself, 10 yards of cloth exchanged for 15 yards of linen in England, and for 20 in Germany. They will now exchange for the same number of yards of linen in both. For what number? If for 15 yards, England will be just as she was, and Germany will gain all. If for 20 yards, Germany will be as before, and England will derive the whole of the benefit. If for any number intermediate between 15 and 20, the advantage will be shared between the two countries. If, for example, 10 yards of cloth exchange for 18 of linen, England will gain an advantage of 3 yards on every 15, Germany will save 2 out of every 20. The problem is, what are the causes which determine the proportion in which the cloth of England and the linen of Germany will exchange for each other.

As exchange value, in this case as in every other, is proverbially fluctuating, it does not matter what we suppose it to be when we begin: we shall soon see whether there be any fixed point above which it oscillates, which it has a tendency always to approach to, and to remain at. Let us suppose, then, that by the effect of what Adam Smith calls the higgling of the market, 10 yards of cloth in both countries exchange for 17 yards of linen.

The demand for a commodity, that is, the quantity of it which can find a purchaser, varies, as we have before remarked, according to the price. In Germany the price of 10 yards of cloth is now 17 yards of linen, or whatever quantity of money is equivalent in Germany to 17 yards of linen. Now, that being the price, there is some particular number of yards of cloth, which will be in demand, or will find purchasers, at that price. There is some given quantity of cloth, more than which could not be disposed of at that price; less than which, at that price, would not fully satisfy the demand. Let us suppose this quantity to be 1000 times 10 yards.

Let us now turn our attention to England. There, the price of 17 yards of linen is 10 yards of cloth, or whatever quantity of money is equivalent in England to 10 yards of cloth. There is some particular number of yards of linen which, at that price, will exactly satisfy the demand, and no more. Let us suppose that this number is 1000 times 17 yards.

As 17 yards of linen are to 10 yards of cloth, so are 1000 times 17 yards to 1000 times 10 yards. At the existing exchange value, the linen which England requires will exactly pay for the quantity of cloth which, on the same terms of interchange, Germany requires. The demand on each side is precisely sufficient to carry off the supply on the other. The conditions required by the principle of demand and supply are fulfilled, and the two commodities will continue to be interchanged, as we supposed them to be, in the ratio of 17 yards of linen for 10 yards of cloth.

But our suppositions might have been different. Suppose that, at the assumed rate of interchange, England has been disposed to consume no greater quantity of linen than 800 times 17 yards: it is evident that, at the rate supposed, this would not have sufficed to pay for the 1000 times 10 yards of cloth which we have supposed Germany to require at the assumed value. Germany would be able to procure no more than 800 times 10 yards at that price. To procure the remaining 200, which she would have no means of doing but by bidding higher for them, she would offer more than 17 yards of linen in exchange for 10 yards of cloth: let us suppose her to offer 18. At this price, perhaps, England would be inclined to purchase a greater quantity of linen. She would consume, possibly, at that price, 900 times 18 yards. On the other hand, cloth having risen in price, the demand of Germany for it would probably have diminished. If, instead of 1000 times 10 yards, she is now contented with 900 times 10 yards, these will exactly pay for the 900 times 18 yards of linen which England is willing to take at the altered price: the demand on each side will again exactly suffice to take off the corresponding supply; and 10 yards for 18 will be the rate at which, in both countries, cloth will exchange for linen.

The converse of all this would have happened, if, instead of 800 times 17 yards, we had supposed that England, at the rate of 10 for 17, would have taken 1200 times 17 yards of linen. In this case, it is England whose demand is not fully supplied; it is England who, by bidding for more linen, will alter the rate of interchange to her own disadvantage; and 10 yards of cloth will fall, in both countries, below the value of 17 yards of linen. By this fall of cloth, or, what is the same thing, this rise of linen, the demand of Germany for cloth will increase, and the demand of England for linen will diminish, till the rate of interchange has so adjusted itself that the cloth and the linen will exactly pay for one another; and when once this point is attained, values will remain without further alteration.

It may be considered, therefore, as established, that when two countries trade together in two commodities, the exchange value of these commodities relatively to each other will adjust itself to the inclinations and circumstances of the consumers on both sides, in such manner that the quantities required by each country, of the articles which it imports from its neighbour, shall be exactly sufficient to pay for one another. As the inclinations and circumstances of consumers cannot be reduced to any rule, so neither can the proportions in which the two commodities will be interchanged. We know that the limits, within which the variation is confined, are the ratio between their costs of production in the one country, and the ratio between their costs of production in the other. Ten yards of cloth cannot exchange for more than 20 yards of linen, nor for less than 15. But they may exchange for any intermediate number. The ratios, therefore, in which the advantage of the trade may be divided between the two nations are various. The circumstances on which the proportionate share of each country more remotely depends, admit only of a very general indication.

It is even possible to conceive an extreme case, in which the whole of the advantage resulting from the interchange would be reaped by one party, the other country gaining nothing at all. There is no absurdity in the hypothesis that, of some given commodity, a certain quantity is all that is wanted at any price; and that, when that quantity is obtained, no fall in the exchange value would induce other consumers to come forward, or those who are already supplied to take more. Let us suppose that this is the case in Germany with cloth. Before her trade with England commenced, when 10 yards of cloth cost her as much labour as 20 yards of linen, she nevertheless consumed as much cloth as she wanted under any circumstances, and, if she could obtain it at the rate of 10 yards of cloth for 15 of linen, she would not consume more. Let this fixed quantity be 1000 times 10 yards. At the rate, however, of 10 for 20, England would want more linen than would be equivalent to this quantity of cloth. She would, consequently, offer a higher value for linen; or, what is the same thing, she would offer her cloth at a cheaper rate. But, as by no lowering of the value could she prevail on Germany to take a greater quantity of cloth, there would be no limit to the rise of linen or fall of cloth, until the demand of England for linen was reduced by the rise of its value, to the quantity which 1000 times 10 yards of cloth would purchase. It might be, that to produce this diminution of the demand a less fall would not suffice than that which would make 10 yards of cloth exchange for 15 of linen. Germany would then gain the whole of the advantage, and England would be exactly as she was before the trade commenced. It would be for the interest, however, of Germany herself to keep her linen a little below the value at which it could be produced in England, in order to keep herself from being supplanted by the home producer. England, therefore, would always benefit in some degree by the existence of the trade, though it might be a very trifling one.

In this statement, I conceive, is contained the first elementary principle of International Values. I have, as is indispensable in such abstract and hypothetical cases, supposed the circumstances to be much less complex than they really are: in the first place, by suppressing the cost of carriage; next, by supposing that there are only two countries trading together; and lastly, that they trade only in two commodities. To render the exposition of the principle complete it is necessary to restore the various circumstances thus temporarily left out to simplify the argument. Those who are accustomed to any kind of scientific investigation will probably see, without formal proof, that the introduction of these circumstances cannot alter the theory of the subject. Trade among any number of countries, and in any number of commodities, must take place on the same essential principles as trade between two countries and in two commodities. Introducing a greater number of agents precisely similar cannot change the law of their action, no more than putting additional weights into the two scales of a balance alters the law of gravitation. It alters nothing but the numerical results. For more complete satisfaction, however, we will enter into the complex cases with the same particularity with which we have stated the simpler one.

3. First, let us introduce the element of cost of carriage. The chief difference will then be, that the cloth and the linen will no longer exchange for each other at precisely the same rate in both countries. Linen, having to be carried to England, will be dearer there by its cost of carriage; and cloth will be dearer in Germany by the cost of carrying it from England. Linen, estimated in cloth, will be dearer in England than in Germany, by the cost of carriage of both articles: and so will cloth in Germany, estimated in linen. Suppose that the coat of carriage of each is equivalent to 1 yard of linen; and suppose that, if they could have been carried without cost, the terms of interchange would have been 10 yards of cloth for 17 of linen. It may seem at first that each country will pay its own cost of carriage; that is, the carriage of the article it imports; that in Germany 10 yards of cloth will exchange for 18 of linen, namely the original 17, and 1 to cover the cost of carriage of the cloth; while in England, 10 yards of cloth will only purchase 16 of linen, 1 yard being deducted for the cost of carriage of the linen. This, however, cannot be affirmed with certainty; it will only be true, if the linen which the English consumers would take at the price of 10 for 16, exactly pays for the cloth which the German consumers would take at 10 for 18. The values, whatever they are, must establish this equilibrium. No absolute rule, therefore, can be laid down for the division of the cost, no more than for the division of the advantage: and it does not follow that in whatever ratio the one is divided, the other will be divided in the same. It is impossible to say, if the cost of carriage could be annihilated, whether the producing or the importing country would be most benefited. This would depend on the play of international demand.

Cost of carriage has one effect more. But for it, every commodity would (if trade be supposed free) be either regularly imported or regularly exported. A country would make nothing for itself which it did not also make for other countries. But in consequence of cost of carriage there are many things, especially bulky articles, which every, or almost every, country produces within itself. After exporting the things in which it can employ itself most advantageously, and importing those in which it is under the greatest disadvantage, there are many lying between, of which the relative cost of production in that and in other countries differs so little, that the cost of carriage would absorb more than the whole saving in cost of production which would be obtained by importing one and exporting another. This is the case with numerous commodities of common consumption; including the coarser qualities of many articles of food and manufacture, of which, the finer kinds are the subject of extensive international traffic.

4. Let us now introduce a greater number of commodities than the two we have hitherto supposed. Let cloth and linen, however, be still the articles of which the comparative cost of

production in England and in Germany differs the most; so that, if they were confined to two commodities, these would be the two which it would be most their interest to exchange. We will now again omit cost of carriage, which, having been shown not to affect the essentials of the question, does but embarrass unnecessarily the statement of it. Let us suppose, then, that the demand of England for linen is either so much greater than that of Germany for cloth, or so much more extensible by cheapness, that if England had no commodity but cloth which Germany would take, the demand of England would force up the terms of interchange to 10 yards of cloth for only 16 of linen, so that England would gain only the difference between 15 and 16, Germany the difference between 16 and 20. But let us now suppose that England has also another commodity, say iron, which is in demand in Germany, and that the quantity of iron which is of equal value in England with 10 yards of cloth (let us call this quantity a hundred-weight) will, if produced in Germany, cost as much labour as 18 yards of linen, so that if offered by England for 17 it will undersell the German producer. In these circumstances, linen will not be forced up to the rate of 16 yards for 10 of cloth, but will stop, suppose at 17; for although, at that rate of interchange, Germany will not take enough cloth to pay for all the linen required by England, she will take iron for the remainder, and it is the same thing to England whether she gives a hundredweight of iron or 10 yards of cloth, both being made at the same cost. If we now superadd coals or cottons on the side of England, and wine, or corn, or timber, on the side of Germany, it will make no difference in the principle. The exports of each country must exactly pay for the imports; meaning now the aggregate exports and imports, not those of particular commodities taken singly. The produce of fifty days' English labour, whether in cloth, coals, iron, or any other exports, will exchange for the produce of forty, or fifty, or sixty days' German labour, in linen, wine, corn, or timber, according to the international demand. There is some proportion at which the demand of the two countries for each other's products will exactly correspond: so that the things supplied by England to Germany will be completely paid for, and no more, by those supplied by Germany to England. This accordingly will be the ratio in which the produce of English and the produce of German labour will exchange for one another.

If, therefore, it be asked what country draws to itself the greatest share of the advantage of any trade it carries on, the answer is, the country for whose productions there is in other countries the greatest demand, and a demand the most susceptible of increase from additional cheapness. In so far as the productions of any country possess this property, the country obtains all foreign commodities at less cost. It gets its imports cheaper, the greater the intensity of the demand in foreign countries for its exports. It also gets its imports cheaper, the less the extent and intensity of its own demand for them. The market is cheapest to those whose demand is small. A country which desires few foreign productions, and only a limited quantity of them, while its own commodities are in great request in foreign countries, will obtain its limited imports at extremely small cost, that is, in exchange for the produce of a very small quantity of its labour and capital.

Lastly, having introduced more than the original two commodities into the hypothesis, let us also introduce more than the original two countries. After the demand of England for the linen of Germany has raised the rate of interchange to 10 yards of cloth for 16 of linen, suppose a trade opened between England and some other country which also exports linen. And let us suppose that, if England had no trade but with the third country, the play of international demand would enable her to obtain from it, for 10 yards of cloth or its equivalent, 17 yards of linen. She evidently would not go on buying linen from Germany at the former rate: Germany would be undersold, and must consent to give 17 yards, like the other country. In this case, the circumstances of production and of demand in the third country are supposed to be in themselves more advantageous to England than the circumstances of Germany; but this supposition is not necessary: we might suppose that if the trade with Germany did not exist, England would be obliged to give to the other country the same advantageous terms which she gives to Germany; 10 yards of cloth for 16, or even less than 16, of linen. Even so, the opening of the third country makes a great difference in favour of England. There is now a double market for English export, while the demand of England for linen is only what it was before. This necessarily obtains for England more advantageous terms of interchange. The two countries, requiring much more of her produce than was required by either alone, must, in order to obtain it, force an increased demand for their exports, by offering them at a lower value.

It deserves notice, that this effect in favour of England from the opening of another market for her exports, will equally be produced even though the country from which the demand comes should have nothing to sell which England is willing to take. Suppose that the third country, though requiring cloth or iron from England, produces no linen, nor any other article which is in demand there. She however produces exportable articles, or she would have no means of paying for imports: her exports, though not suitable to the English consumer, can find a market somewhere. As we are only supposing three countries, we must assume her to find this market in Germany, and to pay for what she imports from England by orders on her German customers. Germany, therefore, besides having to pay for her own imports, now owes a debt to England on account of the third country, and the means for both purposes must be derived from her exportable produce. She must therefore tender that produce to England on terms sufficiently favourable to force a demand equivalent to this double debt. Everything will take place precisely as if the third country had bought German produce with her own goods, and offered that produce to England in exchange for hers. There is an increased demand for English goods, for which German goods have to furnish the payment; and this can only be done by forcing an increased demand for them in England, that is, by lowering their value. Thus, an increase of demand for a country's exports in any foreign country enables her to obtain more cheaply even those imports which she procures from other quarters. And conversely, an increase of her own demand for any foreign commodity compels her, *cæteris paribus*, to pay dearer for all foreign commodities.

The law which we have now illustrated, may be appropriately named, the Equation of International Demand. It may be concisely stated as follows. The produce of a country exchanges for the produce of other countries, at such values as are required in order that the whole other exports may exactly pay for the whole of her imports. This law of International Values is but an extension of the more general law of Value, which we called the Equation of Supply and Demand. We have seen that the value of a commodity always so adjusts itself as to bring the demand to the exact level of the supply, but all trade, either between nations or individuals, is an interchange of commodities, in which the things that they respectively have to sell constitute also their means of purchase: the supply brought by the one constitutes his demand for what is brought by the other. So that supply and demand are but another expression for reciprocal demand: and to say that value will adjust itself so as to equalize demand with supply, is in fact to say that it will adjust itself so as to equalize the demand on one side with the demand on the other.

5. To trace the consequences of this law of International Values through their wide ramifications, would occupy more space than can be here devoted to such a purpose. But there is one of its applications which I will notice, as being in itself not unimportant, as bearing on the question which will occupy us in the next chapter, and especially as conducing to the more full and clear understanding of the law itself.

We have seen that the value at which a country purchases a foreign commodity does not conform to the cost of production in the country from which the commodity comes. Suppose now a change in that cost of production; an improvement, for example, in the process of manufacture. Will the benefit of the improvement be fully participated in by other countries? Will the commodity be sold as much cheaper to foreigners, as it is produced cheaper at home? This question, and the considerations which must be entered into in order to resolve it, are well adapted to try the worth of the theory.

Let us first suppose, that the improvement is of a nature to create a new branch of export: to make foreigners resort to the country for a commodity which they had previously produced at home. On this supposition, the foreign demand for the productions of the country is increased; which necessarily alters the international values to its advantage, and to the disadvantage of foreign countries, who, therefore, though they participate in the benefit of the new product, must purchase that benefit by paying for all the other productions of the country at a dearer rate than before. How much dearer, will depend on the degree necessary for re-establishing, under these new conditions, the Equation of International Demand. These consequences follow in a very obvious manner from the law of international values, and I shall not occupy space in illustrating them, but shall pass to the more frequent case, of an improvement which does not create a new article of export, but lowers the cost of production of something which the country already exported.

It being advantageous, in discussions of this complicated nature, to employ definite numerical amounts, we shall return to our original example. Ten yards of cloth, if produced in Germany, would require the same amount of labour and capital as 20 yards of linen; but by the play of international demand, they can be obtained from England for 17. Suppose now, that by a mechanical improvement made in Germany, and not capable of being transferred to England, the same quantity of labour and capital which produced 20 yards of linen, is enabled to produce 30. Linen falls one-third in value in the German market, as compared with other commodities produced in Germany. Will it also fall one-third as compared with English cloth, thus giving to England, in common with Germany, the full benefit of the improvement? Or (ought we not rather to say), since the cost to England of obtaining linen was not regulated by the cost to Germany of producing it, and since England, accordingly, did not get the entire benefit even of the 20 yards which Germany could have given for 10 yards of cloth, but only obtained 17 – why should she now obtain more, merely because this theoretical limit is removed 10 degrees further off?

It is evident that, in the outset, the improvement will lower the value of linen in Germany, in relation to all other commodities in the German market, including, among the rest, even the imported commodity, cloth. If 10 yards of cloth previously exchanged for 17 yards of linen, they will now exchange for half as much more, or 25$^1/_2$ yards. But whether they will continue to do so will depend on the effect which this increased cheapness of linen produces on the international demand. The demand for linen in England could scarcely fail to be increased. But it might be increased either in proportion to the cheapness, or in a greater proportion than the cheapness, or in a less proportion.

If the demand was increased in the same proportion with the cheapness, England would take as many times 25$^1/_2$ yards of linen, as the number of times 17 yards which she took previously. She would expend in linen exactly as much of cloth, or of the equivalents of cloth, as much in short of the collective income of her people, as she did before. Germany, on her part, would probably require, at that rate of interchange, the same quantity of cloth as before, because it would in reality cost her exactly as much; 25$^1/_2$ yards of linen being now of the same value in her market as 17 yards were before. In this case, therefore, 10 yards of cloth for 25$^1/_2$ of linen is the rate of interchange which under these new conditions would restore the equation of international demand; and England would obtain linen one-third cheaper than before, being the same advantage as was obtained by Germany.

It might happen, however, that this great cheapening of linen would increase the demand for it in England in a greater ratio than the increase of cheapness; and that, if she before wanted 1000 times 17 yards, she would now require more than 1000 times 25$^1/_2$ yards to satisfy her demand. If so, the equation of international demand cannot establish itself at that rate of interchange; to pay for the linen England must offer cloth on more advantageous terms; say, for example, 10 yards for 21 of linen; so that England will not have the full benefit of the improvement in the production of linen, while Germany, in addition to that benefit, will also pay less for cloth. But again, it is possible that England might not desire to increase her consumption of linen in even so great a proportion as that of the increased cheapness; she might not desire so great a quantity as 1000 times 25½ yards: and in that case Germany must force a demand by offering more than 25½ yards of linen for 10 of cloth; linen will be cheapened in England in a still greater degree than in Germany; while Germany will obtain cloth on more unfavourable terms; and at a higher exchange value than before.

After what has already been said, it is not necessary to particularize the manner in which these results might be modified by introducing into the hypothesis other countries and other commodities. There is a further circumstance by which they may also be modified. In the case supposed the consumers of Germany have had a part of their incomes set at liberty by the increased cheapness of linen, which they may indeed expend in increasing their consumption of that article, but which they may likewise expend in other articles, and among others, in cloth or other imported commodities. This would be an additional element in the international demand, and would modify more or less the terms of interchange.

Of the three possible varieties in the influence of cheapness on demand, which is the more probable – that the demand would be increased more than the cheapness, as much as the cheapness, or less than the cheapness? This depends on the nature of the particular commodity, and on the tastes of purchasers. When the commodity is one in general request, and the fall of its price brings it within reach of a much larger class of incomes than before, the demand is often increased in a greater ratio than the fall of price, and a larger sum of money is on the whole expended in the article. Such was the case with coffee, when its price was lowered by successive reductions of taxation; and such would probably be the case with sugar, wine, and a large class of commodities which, though not necessaries, are largely consumed, and in which many consumers indulge when the articles are cheap and economize when they are dear. But it more frequently happens that when a commodity falls in price, less money is spent in it than before: a greater quantity is consumed, but not so great a value. The consumer who saves money by the cheapness of the article, will be likely to expend part of the saving in increasing his consumption of other things: and unless the low price attracts a large class of new purchasers who were either not customers of the article at all, or only in small quantity and occasionally, a less aggregate sum will be expended on it. Speaking generally, therefore, the third of our three cases is the most probable: and an improvement in an exportable article is likely to be as beneficial (if not more beneficial) to foreign countries, as to the country where the article is produced.

6. Thus far had the theory of international values been carried in the first and second editions of this work. But intelligent criticisms (chiefly those of my friend Mr William Thornton), and subsequent further investigation, have shown that the doctrine stated in the preceding pages, though correct as far as it goes, is not yet the complete theory of the subject matter.

It has been shown that the exports and imports between the two countries (or, if we suppose more than two, between each country and the world) must in the aggregate pay for each other, and must therefore be exchanged for one another at such values as will be compatible with the equation of international demand. That this, however, does not furnish the complete law of the phenomenon, appears from the following consideration: that several different rates of international value may all equally fulfil the conditions of this law.

The supposition was, that England could produce 10 yards of cloth with the same labour as 15 of linen, and Germany with the same labour as 20 of linen; that a trade was opened between the two countries; that England thenceforth confined her production to cloth, and Germany to linen; and, that if 10 yards of cloth should thenceforth exchange for 17 of linen, England and Germany would exactly supply each other's demand: that, for instance, if England wanted at that price 17,000 yards of linen, Germany would want exactly the 10,000 yards of cloth, which, at that price, England would be required to give for the linen. Under these suppositions it appeared, that 10 cloth for 17 linen would be, in point of fact, the international values.

But it is quite possible that some other rate, such as 10 cloth for 18 linen, might also fulfil the conditions of the equation of international demand. Suppose that, at this last rate, England would want more linen than at the rate of 10 for 17, but not in the ratio of the cheapness; that she would not want the 18,000 which she could now buy with 10,000 yards of cloth, but would be content with 17,500, for which she would pay (at the new rate of 10 for 18) 9722 yards of cloth. Germany, again, having to pay dearer for cloth than when it could be bought at 10 for 17, would probably reduce her consumption to an amount below 10,000 yards, perhaps to the very same number, 9722. Under these conditions the Equation of International Demand would still exist. Thus, the rate of 10 for 17, and that of 10 for 18, would equally satisfy the Equation of Demand: and many other rates of interchange might satisfy it in like manner. It is conceivable that the conditions might be equally satisfied by every numerical rate which could be supposed. There is still therefore a portion of indeterminateness in the rate at which the international values would adjust themselves; showing that the whole of the influencing circumstances cannot yet have been taken into account.

7. It will be found that, to supply this deficiency, we must take into consideration not only, as we have already done, the quantities demanded in each country of the imported commodities; but also the extent of the means of supplying that demand which are set at liberty in each country by the change in the direction of its industry.

To illustrate this point it will be necessary to choose more convenient numbers than those which we have hitherto employed. Let it be supposed that in England 100 yards of cloth, previously to the trade, exchanged for 100 of linen, but that in Germany 100 of cloth exchanged for 200 of linen. When the trade was opened, England would supply cloth to Germany, Germany linen to England, at an exchange value which would depend partly on the element already discussed, namely the comparative degree in which, in the two countries, increased cheapness operates in increasing the demand; and partly on some other element not yet taken into account. In order to isolate this unknown element, it will be necessary to make some definite and invariable supposition in regard to the known element. Let us therefore assume, that the influence of cheapness on demand conforms to some simple law, common to both countries and to both commodities. As the simplest and most convenient, let us suppose that in both countries any given increase of cheapness produces an exactly proportional increase of consumption; or, in other words, that the value expended in the commodity, the cost incurred for the sake of obtaining it, is always the same, whether that cost affords a greater or a smaller quantity of the commodity.

Let us now suppose that England, previously to the trade, required a million of yards of linen, which were worth, at the English cost of production, a million yards of cloth. By turning all the labour and capital with which that linen was produced to the production of cloth, she would produce for exportation a million yards of cloth. Suppose that this is the exact quantity which Germany is accustomed to consume. England can dispose of all this cloth in Germany at the German price; she must consent indeed to take a little less until she has driven the German producer from the market, but as soon as this is effected, she can sell her million of cloth for two millions of linen; being the quantity that the German clothiers are enabled to make by transferring their whole labour and capital from cloth to linen. Thus, England would gain the whole benefit of the trade, and Germany nothing. This would be perfectly consistent with the equation of international demand: since England (according to the hypothesis in the preceding paragraph) now requires two millions of linen (being able to get them at the same cost at which she previously obtained only one), while, the prices in Germany not being altered, Germany requires as before exactly a million of cloth, and can obtain it by employing the labour and capital set at liberty from the production of cloth, in producing the two millions of linen required by England.

Thus far we have supposed that the additional cloth which England could make, by transferring to cloth the whole of the capital previously employed in making linen, was exactly sufficient to supply the whole of Germany's existing demand. But suppose next that it is more than sufficient. Suppose that while England could make with her liberated capital a million yards of cloth for exportation, the cloth which Germany had heretofore required was 800,000 yards only, equivalent at the German cost of production to 1,600,000 yards of linen. England therefore could not dispose of a whole million of cloth in Germany at the German prices. Yet she wants, whether cheap or dear (by our supposition), as much linen as can be bought for a million of cloth: and since this can only be obtained from Germany, or by the more expensive process of production at home, the holders of the million of cloth will be forced by each other's competition to offer it to Germany on any terms (short of the English cost of production) which will induce Germany to take the whole. What these terms would be, the supposition we have made enables us exactly to define. The 800,000 yards of cloth which Germany consumed, cost her the equivalent of 1,600,000 linen, and that invariable cost is what she is willing to expend in cloth, whether the quantity it obtains for her be more or less. England therefore, to induce Germany to take a million of cloth, must offer it for 1,600,000 of linen. The international values will thus be 100 cloth for 160 linen, intermediate between the ratio of the costs of production in England, and that of the costs of production in Germany: and the two countries will divide the benefit of the trade, England gaining in the aggregate 600,000 yards of linen, and Germany being richer by 200,000 additional yards of cloth.

Let us now stretch the last supposition still farther, and suppose that the cloth previously consumed by Germany, was not only less than the million yards which England is enabled to furnish by discontinuing her production of linen, but less in the full proportion of England's advantage in the production, that is, that Germany only required half a million. In this case, by ceasing altogether to produce cloth, Germany can add a million, but a million only, to her production of linen; and this million, being the equivalent of what the half million previously cost her, is all that she can be induced by any degree of cheapness to expend in cloth. England will be forced by her own competition to give a whole million of cloth for this million of linen, just as she was forced in the preceding case to give it for 1,600,000. But England could have produced at the same cost a million yards of linen for herself. England therefore derives, in this case, no advantage from the international trade. Germany gains the whole; obtaining a million of cloth instead of half a million, at what the half million previously cost her. Germany, in short, is, in this third case, exactly in the same situation as England was in the first case; which may easily be verified by reversing the figures.

As the general result of the three cases, it may be laid down as a theorem, that under the supposition we have made of a demand exactly in proportion to the cheapness, the law of international values will be as follows:

The whole of the cloth which England can make with the capital previously devoted to linen, will exchange for the whole of the linen which Germany can make with the capital previously devoted to cloth.

Or, still more generally, the whole of the commodities which the two countries can respectively make for exportation, with the labour and capital thrown out of employment by importation, will exchange against one another.

This law, and the three different possibilities arising from it in respect to the division of the advantage, may be conveniently generalized by means of algebraical symbols, as follows:

Let the quantity of cloth which England can make with the labour and capital withdrawn from the production of linen, be $= n$.

Let the cloth previously required by Germany (at the German cost of production) be $= m$.

Then n of cloth will always exchange for exactly $2\,m$ of linen.

Consequently if $n = m$, the whole advantage will be on the side of England.

If $n = 2m$, the whole advantage will be on the side of Germany.

If n be greater than m, but less than $2m$, the two countries will share the advantage; England getting $2m$ of linen where she before got only n; Germany getting n of cloth where she before got only m.

It is almost superfluous to observe that the figure '2' stands where it does only because it is the figure which expresses the advantage of Germany over England in linen as estimated in cloth, and (what is the same thing) of England over Germany in cloth as estimated in linen. If we had supposed that in Germany, before the trade, 100 of cloth exchanged for 1000 instead of 200 of linen, then (after the trade commenced) would have exchanged for $10m$ instead of $2m$. If instead of 1000 or 200 we had supposed only 150, n would have exchanged for only $(3/2)m$. If (in fine) the cost value of cloth (as estimated in linen) in Germany exceeds the cost value similarly estimated in England, in the ratio of p to q, then will n, after the opening of the trade, exchange for $(p/q)m$.

8. We have now arrived at what seems a law of International Values of great simplicity and generality. But we have done so by setting out from a purely arbitrary hypothesis respecting the relation between demand and cheapness. We have assumed their relation to be fixed, though it is essentially variable. We have supposed that every increase of cheapness produces an exactly proportional extension of demand; in other words, that the same invariable value is laid out in a commodity whether it be cheap or dear; and the law which we have investigated holds good only on this hypothesis, or some other practically equivalent to it. Let us now, therefore, combine the two variable elements of the question, the variations of each of which we have considered separately. Let us suppose the relation between demand and cheapness to vary, and to become such as would prevent the rule of interchange laid down in the last theorem from satisfying the conditions of the Equation of International Demand. Let it be supposed, for instance, that the demand of England for linen is exactly proportional to the cheapness, but that of Germany for cloth, not proportional. To revert to the second of our three cases, the case in which England by discontinuing the production of linen could produce for exportation a million yards of cloth, and Germany by ceasing to produce cloth could produce an additional 1,600,000 yards of linen. If the one of these quantities exactly exchanged for the other, the demand of England would on our present supposition be exactly satisfied, for she requires all the linen which can be got for a million yards of cloth: but Germany perhaps, though she required 800,000 cloth at a cost equivalent to 1,600,000 linen, yet when she can get a million of cloth at the same cost, may not require the whole million; or may require more than a million. First, let her not require so much; but only as much as she can now buy for 1,500,000 linen. England will still offer a million for these 1,500,000; but even this may not induce Germany to take so much as a million; and if England continues to expend exactly the same aggregate cost on linen whatever be the price, she will have to submit to take for her million of cloth any quantity of linen (not less than a million) which may be requisite to induce Germany to take a million of cloth. Suppose this to be 1,400,000 yards. England has now reaped from the trade a gain not of 600,000 but only of 400,000 yards; while Germany, besides having obtained an extra 200,000 yards of cloth, has obtained it with only seven-eighths of the labour and capital which she previously expended in supplying herself with cloth, and may expend the remainder in increasing her own consumption of linen, or of any other commodity.

Suppose on the contrary that Germany, at the rate of a million cloth for 1,600,000 linen, requires more than a million yards of cloth. England having only a million which she can give without trenching upon the quantity she previously reserved for herself, Germany must bid for the extra cloth at a higher rate than 160 for 100, until she reaches a rate (say 170 for 100) which will either bring down her own demand for cloth to the limit of a million, or else tempt England to part with some of the cloth she previously consumed at home.

Let us next suppose that the proportionality of demand to cheapness, instead of holding good in one country but not in the other, does not hold good in either country, and that the deviation is of the same kind in both; that, for instance, neither of the two increases its demand in a degree equivalent to the increase of cheapness. On this supposition, at the rate of one million cloth for 1,600,000 linen, England will not want so much as 1,600,000 linen, nor Germany so much as a million cloth: and if they fall short of that amount in exactly the same degree: if England only wants linen to the amount of nine-tenths of 1,600,000 (1,440,000), and Germany only 900,000 of cloth, the interchange will continue to take place at the same rate. And so if England wants a tenth more than 1,600,000, and Germany a tenth more than 1,000,000. This coincidence (which, it is to be observed, supposes demand to extend cheapness in a corresponding, but not in an equal degree) evidently could not exist unless by mere accident: and, in any other case, the equation of international demand would require a different adjustment of international values.

The only general law, then, which can be laid down, is this. The values at which a country exchanges its produce with foreign countries depend on two things: first, on the amount and extensibility of their demand for its commodities, compared with its demand for theirs; and second, on the capital which it has to spare from the production of domestic commodities for its own consumption. The more the foreign demand for its commodities exceeds its demand for foreign commodities, and the less capital it can spare to produce for foreign markets, compared with what foreigners spare to produce for its markets, the more favourable to it will be the terms of interchange: that is, the more it will obtain of foreign commodities in return for a given quantity of its own.

But these two influencing circumstances are in reality reducible to one: for the capital which a country has to spare from the production of domestic commodities for its own use is in proportion to its own demand for foreign commodities: whatever proportion of its collective income it expends in purchases from abroad, that same proportion of its capital is left without a home market for its productions. The new element, therefore, which for the sake of scientific correctness we have introduced into the theory of international values, does not seem to make any very material difference in the practical result. It still appears, that the countries which carry on their foreign trade on the most advantageous terms, are those whose commodities are most in demand by foreign countries, and which have themselves the least demand for foreign commodities. From which, among other consequences, it follows, that the richest countries, *cæteris paribus*, gain the least by a given amount of foreign commerce: since, having a greater demand for commodities generally, they are likely to have a greater demand for foreign commodities, and thus modify the terms of interchange to their own disadvantage. Their aggregate gains by foreign trade, doubtless, are generally greater than those of poorer countries, since they carry on a greater amount of such trade, and gain the benefit of cheapness on a larger consumption: but their gain is less on each individual article consumed.

9. We now pass to another essential part of the theory of the subject. There are two senses in which a country obtains commodities cheaper by foreign trade; in the sense of Value, and in the sense of Cost. It gets them cheaper in the first sense, by their falling in value relatively to other things: the same quantity of them exchanging, in the country, for a smaller quantity than before of the other produce of the country. To revert to our original figures; in England, all consumers of linen obtained, after the trade was opened, 17 or some greater number of yards for the same quantity of all other things for which they before obtained only 15. The degree of cheapness, in this sense of the term, depends on the laws of International Demand, so copiously illustrated in the preceding sections. But in the other sense, that of Cost, a country gets a commodity cheaper when it obtains a greater quantity of the commodity with the same expenditure of labour

and capital. In this sense of the term, cheapness in a great measure depends upon a cause of a different nature: a country gets its imports cheaper, in proportion to the general productiveness of its domestic industry; to the general efficiency of its labour. The labour of one country may be, as a whole, much more efficient than that of another; all or most of the commodities capable of being produced in both, may be produced in one at less absolute cost than in the other; which, as we have seen, will not necessarily prevent the two countries from exchanging commodities. The things which the more favoured country will import from others, are of course those in which it is least superior; but by importing them it acquires, even in those commodities, the same advantage which it possesses in the articles it gives in exchange for them. Thus, the countries which obtain their own productions at least cost, also get their imports at least cost.

This will be made still more obvious if we suppose two competing countries. England sends cloth to Germany, and gives 10 yards of it for 17 yards of linen, or for something else which in Germany is the equivalent of those 17 yards. Another country, as for example France, does the same. The one giving 10 yards of cloth for a certain quantity of German commodities, so must the other: if, therefore, in England, these 10 yards are produced by only half as much labour as that by which they are produced in France, the linen or other commodities of Germany will cost to England only half the amount of labour which they will cost to France. England would thus obtain her imports at less cost than France, in the ratio of the greater efficiency of her labour in the production of cloth: which might be taken, in the case supposed, as an approximate estimate of the efficiency of her labour generally; since France, as well as England, by selecting cloth as her article of export, would have shown that with her also it was the commodity in which labour was relatively the most efficient. It follows, therefore, that every country gets its imports at less cost, in proportion to the general efficiency of its labour.

This proposition was first clearly seen and expounded by Mr Senior, but only as applicable to the importation of the precious metals. I think it important to point out that the proposition holds equally true of all other imported commodities; and further, that it is only a portion of the truth. For, in the case supposed, the cost to England of the linen which she pays for with 10 yards of cloth, does not depend solely upon the cost to herself of 10 yards of cloth, but partly also upon how many yards of linen she obtains in exchange for them. What her imports cost to her is a function of two variables; the quantity of her own commodities which she gives for them, and the cost of those commodities. Of these, the last alone depends on the efficiency of her labour: the first depends on the law of international values; that is, on the intensity and extensibility of the foreign demand for her commodities, compared with her demand for foreign commodities.

In the case just now supposed, of a competition between England and France, the state of international values affected both competitors alike, since they were supposed to trade with the same country, and to export and import the same commodities. The difference, therefore, in what their imports cost them, depended solely on the other cause, the unequal efficiency of their labour. They gave the same quantities; the difference could only be in the cost of production. But if England traded to Germany with cloth, and France with iron, the comparative demand in Germany for those two commodities would bear a share in determining the comparative cost, in labour and capital, with which England and France would obtain German products. If iron were more in demand in Germany than cloth, France would recover, through that channel, part of her disadvantage; if less, her disadvantage would be increased. The efficiency, therefore, of a country's labour, is not the only thing which determines even the *cost* at which that country obtains imported commodities – while it has no share whatever in determining either their exchange *value*, or, as we shall presently see, their *price*.

Book IV: Influence of the progress of society on production and distribution

Chapter VI: Of the stationary state

1. The preceding chapters comprise the general theory of the economical progress of society, in the sense in which those terms are commonly understood; the progress of capital, of population, and of the productive arts. But in contemplating any progressive movement, not in its nature unlimited, the mind is not satisfied with merely tracing the laws of the movement; it cannot but ask the further question, to what goal? Towards what ultimate point is society tending by its industrial progress? When the progress ceases, in what condition are we to expect that it will leave mankind?

It must always have been seen, more or less distinctly, by political economists, that the increase of wealth is not boundless: that at the end of what they term the progressive state lies the stationary state, that all progress in wealth is but a postponement of this, and that each step in advance is an approach to it. We have now been led to recognise that this ultimate goal is at all times near enough to be fully in view; that we are always on the verge of it, and that if we have not reached it long ago, it is because the goal itself flies before us. The richest and the most prosperous countries would very soon attain the stationary state, if no further improvements were made in the productive arts, and if there were a suspension of the overflow of capital from those countries into the uncultivated or ill-cultivated regions of the earth.

This impossibility of ultimately avoiding the stationary state – this irresistible necessity that the stream of human industry should finally spread itself out into an apparently stagnant sea – must have been, to the political economists of the last two generations, an unpleasing and discouraging prospect; for the tone and tendency of their speculations goes completely to identify all that is economically desirable with the progressive state, and with that alone. With Mr McCulloch, for example, prosperity does not mean a large production and a good distribution of wealth, but a rapid increase of it; his test of prosperity is high profits; and as the tendency of that very increase of wealth, which he calls prosperity, is towards low profits, economical progress, according to him, must tend to the extinction of prosperity. Adam Smith always assumes that the condition of the mass of the people, though it may not be positively distressed, must be pinched and stinted in a stationary condition of wealth, and can only be satisfactory in a progressive state. The doctrine that, to however distant a time incessant struggling may put off our doom, the progress of society must 'end in shallows and in miseries', far from being, as many people still believe, a wicked invention of Mr Malthus, was either expressly or tacitly affirmed by his most distinguished predecessors, and can only be successfully combated on his principles. Before attention had been directed to the principle of population as the active force in determining the remuneration of labour, the increase of mankind was virtually treated as a constant quantity; it was, at all events, assumed that in the natural and normal state of human affairs population must constantly increase, from which it followed that a constant increase of the means of support was essential to the physical comfort of the mass of mankind. The publication of Mr Malthus' *Essay* is the era from which better views of this subject must be dated; and notwithstanding the acknowledged errors of his first edition, few writers have done more than himself, in the subsequent editions, to promote these juster and more hopeful anticipations.

Even in a progressive state of capital, in old countries, a conscientious or prudential restraint on population is indispensable, to prevent the increase of numbers from outstripping the increase of capital, and the condition of the classes who are at the bottom of society from being deteriorated. Where there is not, in the people, or in some very large proportion of them, a resolute resistance to this deterioration – a determination to preserve an established standard of comfort – the condition of the poorest class sinks, even in a progressive state, to the lowest point which they will consent to endure. The same determination would be equally effectual to keep up their condition in the stationary state, and would be quite as likely to exist. Indeed, even now, the countries in which the greatest prudence is manifested in the regulating of population are often those in which capital increases least rapidly. Where there is an indefinite prospect of employment for increased numbers, there is apt to appear less necessity for prudential restraint. If it were evident that a new hand could not obtain employment but by displacing, or succeeding to, one already employed, the combined influences of prudence and public opinion might in some measure be relied on for restricting the coming generation within the numbers necessary for replacing the present.

2. I cannot, therefore, regard the stationary state of capital and wealth with the unaffected aversion so generally manifested towards it by political economists of the old school. I am inclined to believe that it would be, on the whole, a very considerable improvement on our present condition. I confess I am not charmed with the ideal of life held out by those who think that the normal state of human beings is that of struggling to get on; that the trampling, crushing, elbowing, and treading on each other's heels, which form the existing type of social life, are the most desirable lot of human kind, or anything but the disagreeable symptoms of one of the phases of industrial progress. It may be a necessary stage in the progress of civilization, and those European nations which have hitherto been so fortunate as to be preserved from it, may have it yet to undergo. It is an incident of growth, not a mark of decline, for it is not necessarily destructive of the higher aspirations and the heroic virtues; as America, in her great civil war, has proved to the world, both by her conduct as a people and by numerous splendid individual examples, and as England, it is to be hoped, would also prove, on an equally trying and exciting occasion. But it is not a kind of social perfection which philanthropists to come will feel any very eager desire to assist in realizing. Most fitting, indeed, is it, that while riches are power, and to grow as rich as possible the universal object of ambition, the path to its attainment should be open to all, without favour or partiality. But the best state for human nature is that in which, while no one is poor, no one desires to be richer, nor has any reason to fear being thrust back by the efforts of others to push themselves forward.

That the energies of mankind should be kept in employment by the struggle for riches, as they were formerly by the struggle of war, until the better minds succeed in educating the others into better things, is undoubtedly more desirable than that they should rust and stagnate. While minds are coarse they require coarse stimuli, and let them have them. In the mean time, those who do not accept the present very early stage of human improvement as its ultimate type, may be excused for being comparatively indifferent to the kind of economical progress which excites the congratulations of ordinary politicians; the mere increase of production and accumulation. For the safety of national independence it is essential that a country should not fall much behind its neighbours in these things. But in themselves they are of little importance, so long as either the increase of population or anything else prevents the mass of the people from reaping any part of the benefit of them. I know not why it should be a matter of congratulation that persons who are already richer than any one needs to be, should have doubled their means of consuming things which give little or no pleasure except as representative of wealth; or that numbers of individuals should pass over, every year, from the middle classes into a richer class, or from the class of the occupied rich to that of the unoccupied. It is only in the backward countries of the world that increased production is still an important object: in those most advanced, what is economically needed is a better distribution, of which one indispensable means is a stricter restraint on population. Levelling institutions, either of a just or of an unjust kind, cannot alone accomplish it; they may lower the heights of society, but they cannot, of themselves, permanently raise the depths.

On the other hand, we may suppose this better distribution of property attained, by the joint effect of the prudence and frugality of individuals, and of a system of legislation favouring equality of fortunes, so far as is consistent with the just claim of the individual to the fruits, whether great or small, of his or her own industry. We may suppose, for instance (according to the suggestion thrown out in a former chapter), a limitation of the sum which any one person may acquire by gift or inheritance to the amount sufficient to constitute a moderate independence. Under this two-fold influence society would exhibit these leading features: a well-paid and affluent body of labourers; no enormous fortunes, except what were earned and accumulated during a single life-time; but a much larger body of persons than at present, not only exempt from the coarser toils, but with sufficient leisure, both physical and mental, from mechanical details, to cultivate freely the graces of life, and afford examples of them to the classes less favourably circumstanced for their growth. This condition of society, so greatly preferable to the present, is not only perfectly compatible with the stationary state, but, it would seem, more naturally allied with that state than with any other.

There is room in the world, no doubt, and even in old countries, for a great increase of population, supposing the arts of life to go on improving, and capital to increase. But even if innocuous, I confess I see very little reason for desiring it. The density of population necessary to enable mankind to obtain, in the greatest degree, all the advantages both of co-operation and of social intercourse, has, in all the most populous countries, been attained. A population may be too crowded, though all be amply supplied with food and raiment. It is not good for man to be kept perforce at all times in the presence of his species. A world from which solitude is extirpated is a very poor ideal. Solitude, in the sense of being often alone, is essential to any depth of meditation or of character; and solitude in the presence of natural beauty and grandeur, is the cradle of thoughts and aspirations which are not only good for the individual, but which society could ill do without. Nor is there much satisfaction in contemplating the world with nothing left to the spontaneous activity of nature; with every rood of land brought into cultivation, which is capable of growing food for human beings; every flowery waste or natural pasture ploughed up, all quadrupeds or birds which are not domesticated for man's use exterminated as his rivals for food, every hedgerow or superfluous tree rooted out, and scarcely a place left where a wild shrub or flower could grow without being eradicated as a weed in the name of improved agriculture. If the earth must lose that great portion of its pleasantness which it owes to things that the unlimited increase of wealth and population would extirpate from it, for the mere purpose of enabling it to support a larger, but not a better or a happier population, I sincerely hope, for the sake of posterity, that they will be content to be stationary, long before necessity compels them to it.

It is scarcely necessary to remark that a stationary condition of capital and population implies no stationary state of human improvement. There would be as much scope as ever for all kinds of mental culture, and moral and social progress; as much room for improving the Art of Living, and much more likelihood of its being improved, when minds ceased to be engrossed by the art of getting on. Even the industrial arts might be as earnestly and as successfully cultivated, with this sole difference, that instead of serving no purpose but the increase of wealth, industrial improvements would produce their legitimate effect, that of abridging labour. Hitherto [1848] it is questionable if all the mechanical inventions yet made have lightened the day's toil of any human being. They have enabled a greater population to live the same life of drudgery and imprisonment, and an increased number of manufacturers and others to make fortunes. They have increased the comforts of the middle classes. But they have not yet begun to effect those great changes in human destiny, which it is in their nature and in their futurity to accomplish. Only when, in addition to just institutions, the increase of mankind shall be under the deliberate guidance of judicious foresight, can the conquests made from the powers of nature by the intellect and energy of scientific discoverers become the common property of the species, and the means of improving and elevating the universal lot.

Book V: On the influence of government

Chapter XI: Of the grounds and limits of the laisser-faire *or non-interference principle*

1. We have now reached the last part of our undertaking; the discussion, so far as suited to this treatise (i.e. so far as it is a question of principle, not detail), of the limits of the province of government: the question, to what objects governmental intervention in the affairs of society may or should extend, over and above those which necessarily appertain to it. No subject has been more keenly contested in the present age: the contest, however, has chiefly taken place round certain select points, with only flying excursions into the rest of the field. Those indeed who have discussed any particular question of government interference, such as state education (spiritual or secular), regulation of hours of labour, a public provision for the poor, etc., have often dealt largely in general arguments, far outstretching the special application made of them, and have shown a sufficiently strong bias either in favour of letting things alone, or in favour of meddling; but have seldom declared, or apparently decided in their own minds, how far they would carry either principle. The supporters of interference have been content with asserting a general right and duty on the part of government to intervene, wherever its intervention would be useful: and when those who have been called the *laisser-faire* school have attempted any definite limitation of the province of government, they have usually restricted it to the protection of person and property against force and fraud; a definition to which neither they nor any one else can deliberately adhere, since it excludes, as has been shown in a preceding chapter, some of the most indispensable and unanimously recognized of the duties of government.

Without professing entirely to supply this deficiency of a general theory, on a question, which does not, as I conceive; admit of any universal solution, I shall attempt to afford some little aid towards the resolution of this class of questions as they arise, by examining, in the most general point of view in which the subject can be considered, what are the advantages, and what the evils or inconveniences, of government interference.

We must set out by distinguishing between two kinds of intervention by the government, which, though they may relate to the same subject, differ widely in their nature and effects, and require, for their justification, motives of a very different degree of urgency. The intervention may extend to controlling the free agency of individuals. Government may interdict all persons from doing certain things; or from doing them without its authorization; or may prescribe to them certain things to be done, or a certain manner of doing things which it is left optional with them to do or to abstain from. This is the *authoritative* interference of government. There is another kind of intervention which is not authoritative: when a government, instead of issuing a command and enforcing it by penalties, adopts the course so seldom resorted to by governments, and of which such important use might be made, that of giving advice, and promulgating information; or when, leaving individuals free to use their own means of pursuing any object of general interest, the government, not meddling with them, but not trusting the object solely to their care, establishes, side by side with their arrangements, an agency of its own for a like purpose. Thus, it is one thing to maintain a Church Establishment, and another to refuse toleration to other religions, or to persons professing no religion. It is one thing to provide schools or colleges, and another to require that no person shall act as an instructor of youth without a government licence. There might be a national bank, or a government manufactory, without any monopoly against private banks and manufactories. There might be a post-office, without penalties against the conveyance of letters by other means. There may be a corps of government engineers for civil purposes, while the profession of a civil engineer is free to be adopted by every one. There may be public hospitals, without any restriction upon private medical or surgical practice.

2. It is evident, even at first sight, that the authoritative form of government intervention has a much more limited sphere of legitimate action than the other. It requires a much stronger necessity to justify it in any case; while there are large departments of human life from which it must be unreservedly and imperiously excluded. Whatever theory we adopt respecting the foundation of the social union, and under whatever political institutions we live, there is a circle around every individual human being which no government, be it that of one, of a few, or of the many, ought to be permitted to overstep: there is a part of the life of every person who has come to years of discretion, within which the individuality of that person ought to reign uncontrolled either by any other individual or by the public collectively. That there is, or ought to be, some space in human existence thus entrenched around, and sacred from authoritative intrusion, no one who professes the smallest regard to human freedom or dignity will call in question: the point to be determined is, where the limit should be placed; how large a province of human life this reserved territory should include. I apprehend that it ought to include all that part which concerns only the life, whether inward or outward, of the individual, and does not affect the interests of others, or affects them only through the moral influence of example. With respect to the domain of the inward consciousness, the thoughts and feelings, and as much of external conduct as is personal only, involving no consequences, none at least of a painful or injurious kind, to other people; I hold that it is allowable in all, and in the more thoughtful and cultivated often a duty, to assert and promulgate, with all the force they are capable of, their opinion of what is good or bad, admirable or contemptible, but not to compel others to conform to that opinion; whether the force used is that of extra-legal coercion, or exerts itself by means of the law.

Even in those portions of conduct which do affect the interest of others, the onus of making out a case always lies on the defenders of legal prohibitions. It is not a merely constructive or presumptive injury to others which will justify the interference of law with individual freedom. To be prevented from doing what one is inclined to, or from acting according to one's own judgment of what is desirable, is not only always irksome, but always tends, *pro tanto*, to starve the development of some portion of the bodily or mental faculties, either sensitive or active; and unless the conscience of the individual goes freely with the legal restraint, it partakes, either in a great or in a small degree, of the degradation of slavery. Scarcely any degree of utility, short of absolute necessity, will justify a prohibitory regulation, unless it can also be made to recommend itself to the general conscience; unless persons of ordinary good intentions either believe already, or can be induced, to believe, that the thing prohibited is a thing which they ought not to wish to do.

It is otherwise with governmental interferences which do not restrain individual free agency. When a government provides means for fulfilling a certain end, leaving individuals free to avail themselves of different means if in their opinion preferable, there is no infringement of liberty, no irksome or degrading restraint. One of the principal objections to government interference is then absent. There is, however, in almost all forms of government agency, one thing which is compulsory; the provision of the pecuniary means. These are derived from taxation; or, if existing in the form of an endowment derived from public property, they are still the cause of as much compulsory taxation as the sale or the annual proceeds of the property would enable to be dispensed with. And the objection necessarily attaching to compulsory contributions, is almost always greatly aggravated by the expensive precautions and onerous restrictions which are indispensable to prevent evasion of a compulsory tax.

3. A second general objection to government agency is that every increase of the functions devolving on the government is an increase of its power, both in the form of authority, and still more, in the indirect form of influence. The importance of this consideration, in respect to political freedom, has in general been quite sufficiently recognized, at least in England; but many, in latter times, have been prone to think that limitation of the powers of the government is only essential when the government itself is badly constituted; when it does not represent the people, but is the organ of a class, or coalition of classes: and that a government of sufficiently popular constitution might be trusted with any amount of power over the nation, since its power would be only that of the nation over itself. This might be true, if the nation, in such cases, did not practically mean a mere majority of the nation, and if minorities were only capable of oppressing, but not of being oppressed. Experience, however, proves that the depositaries of power who are mere delegates of the people, that is of a majority, are quite as ready (when they think they can count on popular support) as any organs of oligarchy to assume arbitrary power, and encroach unduly on the liberty of private life. The public collectively is abundantly ready to impose, not only its generally narrow views of its interests, but its abstract opinions, and even its tastes, as laws binding upon individuals. And the present civilization tends so strongly to make the power of persons acting in masses the only substantial power in society, that there never was more necessity for surrounding individual independence of thought, speech, and conduct, with the most powerful defences, in order to maintain that originality of mind and individuality of character, which are the only source of any real progress, and of most of the qualities which make the human race much superior to any herd of animals. Hence, it is no less important in a democratic than in any other government, that all tendency on the part of public authorities to stretch their interference, and assume a power of any sort which can easily be dispensed with, should be regarded with unremitting jealousy. Perhaps this is even more important in a democracy than in any other form of political society; because, where public opinion is sovereign, an individual who is oppressed by the sovereign does not, as in most other states of things, find a rival power to which he can appeal for relief, or, at all events, for sympathy.

4. A third general objection to government agency rests on the principle of the division of labour. Every additional function undertaken by the government is a fresh occupation imposed upon a body already overcharged with duties. A natural consequence is that most things are ill done; much not done at all, because the government is not able to do it without delays which are fatal to its purpose; that the more troublesome, and less showy, of the functions undertaken, are postponed or neglected, and an excuse is always ready for the neglect; while the heads of the administration have their minds so fully taken up with official details, in however perfunctory a manner superintended, that they have no time or thought to spare for the great interests of the state, and the preparation of enlarged measures of social improvement.

But these inconveniences, though real and serious, result much more from the bad organization of governments, than from the extent and variety of the duties undertaken by them. Government is not a name for some one functionary, or definite number of functionaries: there may be almost any amount of division of labour within the administrative body itself. The evil in question is felt in great magnitude under some of the governments of the Continent, where six or eight men, living at the capital and known by the name of ministers, demand that the whole public business of the country shall pass, or be supposed to pass, under their individual eye. But the inconvenience would be reduced to a very manageable compass, in a country in which there was a proper distribution of functions between the central and local officers of government, and in which the central body was divided into a sufficient number of departments. When Parliament thought it expedient to confer on the government an inspecting and partially controlling authority over railways, it did not add railways to the department of the Home Minister, but created a Railway Board. When it determined to have a central superintending authority for pauper administration, it established the Poor Law Commission. There are few countries in which a greater number of functions are discharged by public officers, than in some states of the American Union, particularly the New England States: but the division of labour in public business is extreme; most of these officers being not even amenable to any common superior, but performing their duties freely, under the double check of election by their townsmen, and civil as well as criminal responsibility to the tribunals.

It is, no doubt, indispensable to good government that the chiefs of the administration, whether permanent or temporary, should extend a commanding, though general, view over the *ensemble* of all the interests confided, in any degree, to the responsibility of the central power. But with a skilful internal organization of the administrative machine, leaving to subordinates, and as far as possible, to local subordinates, not only the execution, but to a great degree the control, of details; holding them accountable for the results of their acts rather than for the acts themselves; except where these come within the cognizance of the tribunals; taking the most effectual securities for honest and capable appointments; opening a broad path to promotion from the inferior degrees of the administrative scale to the superior; leaving, at each step, to the functionary, a wider range in the origination of measures, so that, in the highest grade of all, deliberation might be concentrated on the great collective interests of the country in each department; if all this were done, the government would not probably be over-burthened by any business, in other respects fit to be undertaken by it; though the over-burthening would remain, as a serious addition to the inconveniences incurred by its undertaking any which was unfit.

5. But though a better organization of governments would greatly diminish the force of the objection to the mere multiplication of their duties, it would still remain true that in all the more advanced communities the great majority of things are worse done by the intervention of government, than the individuals most interested in the matter would do them, or cause them to be done, if left to themselves. The grounds of this truth are expressed with tolerable exactness in the popular dictum, that people understand their own business and their own interests better, and care for them more, than the government does, or can be expected to do. This maxim holds true throughout the greatest part of the business of life, and wherever it is true we ought to condemn every kind of government intervention that conflicts with it. The inferiority of government agency, for example, in any of the common operations of industry or commerce, is proved by the fact, that it is hardly ever able to maintain itself in equal competition with individual agency, where the individuals possess the requisite degree of industrial enterprise, and can command the necessary assemblage of means. All the facilities which a government enjoys of access to information; all the means which it possesses of remunerating, and therefore of commanding, the best available talent in the market – are not an equivalent for the one great disadvantage of an inferior interest in the result.

It must be remembered, besides, that even if a government were superior in intelligence and knowledge to any single individual in the nation, it must be inferior to all the individuals of the nation taken together. It can neither possess in itself, nor enlist in its service, more than a portion of the acquirements and capacities which the country contains, applicable to any given purpose. There must be many persons equally qualified for the work with those whom the government employs, even if it selects its instruments with no reference to any consideration but their fitness. Now these are the very persons into whose hands, in the cases of most common occurrence, a system of individual agency naturally tends to throw the work, because they are capable of doing it better or on cheaper terms than any other persons. So far as this is the case, it is evident that government, by excluding or even by superseding individual agency, either substitutes a less qualified instrumentality for one better qualified, or at any rate substitutes its own mode of accomplishing the work, for all the variety of modes which would be tried by a number of equally qualified persons aiming at the same end; a competition by many degrees more propitious to the progress of improvement than any uniformity of system.

6. I have reserved for the last place one of the strongest of the reasons against the extension of government agency. Even if the government could comprehend within itself, in each department, all the most eminent intellectual capacity and active talent of the nation, it would not be the less desirable that the conduct of a large portion of the affairs of the society should be left in the hands of the persons immediately interested in them. The business of life is an essential part

of the practical education of a people; without which, book and school instruction, though most necessary and salutary, does not suffice to qualify them for conduct, and for the adaptation of means to ends. Instruction is only one of the desiderata of mental improvement; another, almost as indispensable, is a vigorous exercise of the active energies; labour, contrivance, judgment, self-control: and the natural stimulus to these is the difficulties of life. This doctrine is not to be confounded with the complacent optimism, which represents the evils of life as desirable things, because they call forth qualities adapted to combat with evils. It is only because the difficulties exist, that the qualities which combat with them are of any value. As practical beings it is our business to free human life from as many as possible of its difficulties, and not to keep up a stock of them as hunters preserve game for the exercise of pursuing it. But since the need of active talent and practical judgment in the affairs of life can only be diminished, and not, even on the most favourable supposition, done away with, it is important that those endowments should be cultivated not merely in a select few, but in all, and that the cultivation should be more varied and complete than most persons are able to find in the narrow sphere of their merely individual interests. A people among whom there is no habit of spontaneous action for a collective interest – who look habitually to their government to command or prompt them in all matters of joint concern – who expect to have everything done for them, except what can be made an affair of mere habit and routine – have their faculties only half developed; their education is defective in one of its most important branches.

Not only is the cultivation of the active faculties by exercise, diffused through the whole community, in itself one of the most valuable of national possessions: it is rendered, not less, but more necessary, when a high degree of that indispensable culture is systematically kept up in the chiefs and functionaries of the state. There cannot be a combination of circumstances more dangerous to human welfare, than that in which intelligence and talent are maintained at a high standard within a governing corporation, but starved and discouraged outside the pale. Such a system, more completely than any other, embodies the idea of despotism, by arming with intellectual superiority as an additional weapon those who have already the legal power. It approaches as nearly as the organic difference between human beings and other animals admits, to the government of sheep by their shepherd without anything like so strong an interest as the shepherd has in the thriving condition of the flock. The only security against political slavery is the check maintained over governors by the diffusion of intelligence, activity, and public spirit among the governed. Experience proves the extreme difficulty of permanently keeping up a sufficiently high standard of those qualities; a difficulty which increases, as the advance of civilization and security removes one after another of the hardships, embarrassments, and dangers against which individuals had formerly no resource but in their own strength, skill, and courage. It is therefore of supreme importance that all classes of the community, down to the lowest, should have much to do for themselves; that as great a demand should be made upon their intelligence and virtue as it is in any respect equal to; that the government should not only leave as far as possible to their own faculties the conduct of whatever concerns themselves alone, but should suffer them, or rather encourage them, to manage as many as possible of their joint concerns by voluntary co-operation; since this discussion and management of collective interests is the great school of that public spirit, and the great source of that intelligence of public affairs, which are always regarded as the distinctive character of the public of free countries.

A democratic constitution, not supported by democratic institutions in detail, but confined to the central government, not only is not political freedom, but often creates a spirit precisely the reverse, carrying down to the lowest grade in society the desire and ambition of political domination. In some countries the desire of the people is for not being tyrannized over, but in others it is merely for an equal chance to everybody of tyrannizing. Unhappily this last state of the desires is fully as natural to mankind as the former, and in many of the conditions even of civilized humanity is far more largely exemplified. In proportion as the people are accustomed to manage their affairs by their own active intervention, instead of leaving them to the government, their desires will turn to repelling tyranny, rather than to tyrannizing: while in proportion as all real initiative and direction resides in the government, and individuals habitually feel and act as under its perpetual tutelage, popular institutions develop in them not the desire of freedom, but an unmeasured appetite for place and power; diverting the intelligence and activity of the country from its principal business to a wretched competition for the selfish prizes and the petty vanities of office.

7. The preceding are the principal reasons, of a general character, in favour of restricting to the narrowest compass the intervention of a public authority in the business of the community: and few will dispute the more than sufficiency of these reasons, to throw, in every instance, the burthen of making out a strong case, not on those who resist, but on those who recommend, government interference. *Laisser-faire*, in short, should be the general practice: every departure from it, unless required by some great good, is a certain evil.

The degree in which the maxim, even in the cases to which it is most manifestly applicable, has heretofore been infringed by governments, future ages will probably have difficulty in crediting. …

…

… But we must now turn to the second part of our task, and direct our attention to cases, in which some of those general objections are altogether absent, while those which can never be got rid of entirely are overruled by counter-considerations of still greater importance.

We have observed that, as a general rule, the business of life is better performed when those who have an immediate interest in it are left to take their own course, uncontrolled either by the mandate of the law or by the meddling of any public functionary. The persons, or some of the persons, who do the work, are likely to be better judges than the government, of the means of attaining the particular end at which they aim. Were we to suppose, what is not very probable, that the government has possessed itself of the best knowledge which had been acquired up to a given time by the persons most skilled in the occupation; even then the individual agents have so much stronger and more direct an interest in the result, that the means are far more likely to be improved and perfected if left to their uncontrolled choice. But if the workman is generally the best selector of means, can it be affirmed with the same universality, that the consumer, or person served, is the most competent judge of the end? Is the buyer always qualified to judge of the commodity? If not, the presumption in favour of the competition of the market does not apply to the case; and if the commodity be one in the quality of which society has much at stake, the balance of advantages may be in favour of some mode and degree of intervention by the authorized representatives of the collective interest of the state.

8. Now, the proposition that the consumer is a competent judge of the commodity, can be admitted only with numerous abatements and exceptions. He is generally the best judge (though even this is not true universally) of the material objects produced for his use. These are destined to supply some physical want, or gratify some taste or inclination, respecting which wants or inclinations there is no appeal from the person who feels them; or they are the means and appliances of some occupation, for the use of the persons engaged in it, who may be presumed to be judges of the things required in their own habitual employment. But there are other things, of the worth of which the demand of the market is by no means a test; things of which the utility does not consist in ministering to inclinations, nor in serving the daily uses of life, and the want of which is least felt where the need is greatest. This is peculiarly true of those things which are chiefly useful as tending to raise the character of human beings. The uncultivated cannot be competent judges of cultivation. Those who most need to be made wiser and better, usually desire it least, and, if they desired it, would be incapable of finding the way to it by their own

lights. It will continually happen, on the voluntary system, that, the end not being desired, the means will not be provided at all, or that, the persons requiring improvement having an imperfect or altogether erroneous conception of what they want, the supply called forth by the demand of the market will be anything but what is really required. Now any well-intentioned and tolerably civilized government may think, without presumption, that it does or ought to possess a degree of cultivation above the average of the community which it rules, and that it should therefore be capable of offering better education and better instruction to the people, than the greater number of them would spontaneously demand. Education, therefore, is one of those things which it is admissible in principle that a government should provide for the people. The case is one to which the reasons of the non-interference principle do not necessarily or universally extend.

...

One thing must be strenuously insisted on; that the government must claim no monopoly for its education, either in the lower or in the higher branches; must exert neither authority nor influence to induce the people to resort to its teachers in preference to others, and must confer no peculiar advantages on those who have been instructed by them. Though the government teachers will probably be superior to the average of private instructors, they will not embody all the knowledge and sagacity to be found in all instructors taken together, and it is desirable to leave open as many roads as possible to the desired end. It is not endurable that a government should, either *de jure* or *de facto*, have a complete control over the education of the people. To possess such a control, and actually exert it, is to be despotic. A government which can mould the opinions and sentiments of the people from their youth upwards, can do with them whatever it pleases. Though a government, therefore, may, and in many cases ought to, establish schools and colleges, it must neither compel nor bribe any person to come to them; nor ought the power of individuals to set up rival establishments to depend in any degree upon its authorization. It would be justified in requiring from all the people that they shall possess instruction in certain things, but not in prescribing to them how or from whom they shall obtain it.

9. In the matter of education, the intervention of government is justifiable, because the case is not one in which the interest and judgment of the consumer are a sufficient security for the goodness of the commodity. Let us now consider another class of cases, where there is no person in the situation of a consumer, and where the interest and judgment to be relied on are those of the agent himself; as in the conduct of any business in which he is exclusively interested, or in entering into any contract or engagement by which he himself is to be bound.

The ground of the practical principle of non-interference must here be, that most persons take a juster and more intelligent view of their own interest, and of the means of promoting it, than can either be prescribed to them by a general enactment of the legislature, or pointed out in the particular case by a public functionary. The maxim is unquestionably sound as a general rule; but there is no difficulty in perceiving some very large and conspicuous exceptions to it. These may be classed under several heads.

First: The individual who is presumed to be the best judge of his own interests may be incapable of judging or acting for himself; may be a lunatic, an idiot, an infant: or though not wholly incapable, may be of immature years and judgment. In this case the foundation of the *laisser-faire* principle breaks down entirely. The person most interested is not the best judge of the matter, nor a competent judge at all. Insane persons are everywhere regarded as proper objects of the care of the state. In the case of children and young persons, it is common to say, that though they cannot judge for themselves, they have their parents or other relatives to judge for them. But this removes the question into a different category; making it no longer a question whether the government should interfere with individuals in the direction of their own conduct and interests, but whether it should leave absolutely in their power the conduct and interests of somebody else. Parental power is as susceptible of abuse as any other power, and is, as a matter of fact, constantly abused. If laws do not succeed in preventing parents from brutally ill-treating, and even from murdering their children, far less ought it to be presumed that the interests of children will never be sacrificed, in more commonplace and less revolting ways, to the selfishness or the ignorance of their parents. Whatever it can be clearly seen that parents ought to do or forbear for the interests of children, the law is warranted, if it is able, in compelling to be done or forborne, and is generally bound to do so. To take an example from the peculiar province of political economy; it is right that children and young persons not yet arrived at maturity should be protected, so far as the eye and hand of the state can reach, from being over-worked. Labouring for too many hours in the day, or on work beyond their strength, should not be permitted to them, for if permitted it may always be compelled. Freedom of contract, in the case of children, is but another word for freedom of coercion. Education also, the best which circumstances admit of their receiving, is not a thing which parents or relatives, from indifference, jealousy, or avarice, should have it in their power to withhold.

The reasons for legal intervention in favour of children, apply not less strongly to the case of those unfortunate slaves and victims of the most brutal part of mankind, the lower animals. It is by the grossest misunderstanding of the principles of liberty, that the infliction of exemplary punishment on ruffianism practised towards these defenceless creatures has been treated as a meddling by government with things beyond its province; an interference with domestic life. The domestic life of domestic tyrants is one of the things which it is the most imperative on the law to interfere with; and it is to be regretted that metaphysical scruples respecting the nature and source of the authority of government should induce many warm supporters of laws against cruelty to animals to seek for a justification of such laws in the incidental consequences of the indulgence of ferocious habits to the interests of human beings, rather than in the intrinsic merits of the case itself. What it would be the duty of a human being, possessed of the requisite physical strength, to prevent by force if attempted in his presence, it cannot be less incumbent on society generally to repress. The existing laws of England on the subject are chiefly defective in the trifling, often almost nominal, maximum, to which the penalty even in the worst cases is limited.

Among those members of the community whose freedom of contract ought to be controlled by the legislature for their own protection, on account (it is said) of their dependent position, it is frequently proposed to include women: and in the existing Factory Acts their labour, in common with that of young persons, has been placed under peculiar restrictions. But the classing together, for this and other purposes, of women and children, appears to me both indefensible in principle and mischievous in practice. Children below a certain age cannot judge or act for themselves; up to a considerably greater age they are inevitably more or less disqualified for doing so; but women are as capable as men of appreciating and managing their own concerns, and the only hindrance to their doing so arises from the injustice of their present social position. When the law makes everything which the wife acquires, the property of the husband, while by compelling her to live with him it forces her to submit to almost any amount of moral and even physical tyranny which he may choose to inflict, there is some ground for regarding every act done by her as done under coercion: but it is the great error of reformers and philanthropists in our time to nibble at the consequences of unjust power, instead of redressing the injustice itself. If women had as absolute a control as men have, over their own persons and their own patrimony or acquisitions, there would be no plea for limiting their hours of labouring for themselves, in order that they might have time to labour for the husband, in what is called, by the advocates of restriction, *his* home. Women employed in factories are the only women in the labouring rank of life whose position is not that of slaves and drudges; precisely because they cannot easily be compelled to work and earn wages in factories against their will. For improving the condition of women, it should, on the contrary, be an object to give them the readiest access to independent industrial employment, instead of closing, either entirely or partially, that which is already open to them.

10. A second exception to the doctrine that individuals are the best judges of their own interest, is when an individual attempts to decide irrevocably now what will be best for his interest at some future and distant time. The presumption in favour of individual judgment is only legitimate, where the judgment is grounded on actual, and especially on present, personal experience; not where it is formed antecedently to experience, and not suffered to be reversed even after experience has condemned it. When persons have bound themselves by a contract, not simply to do some one thing, but to continue doing something for ever or for a prolonged period, without any power of revoking the engagement, the presumption which their perseverance in that course of conduct would otherwise raise in favour of its being advantageous to them, does not exist; and any such presumption which can be grounded on their having voluntarily entered into the contract, perhaps at an early age, and without any real knowledge of what they undertook, is commonly next to null. The practical maxim of leaving contracts free is not applicable without great limitations in case of engagements in perpetuity; and the law should be extremely jealous of such engagements; should refuse its sanction to them, when the obligations they impose are such as the contracting party cannot be a competent judge of; if it ever does sanction them, it should take every possible security for their being contracted with foresight and deliberation; and in compensation for not permitting the parties themselves to revoke their engagement, should grant them a release from it, on a sufficient case being made out before an impartial authority. These considerations are eminently applicable to marriage, the most important of all cases of engagement for life.

11. The third exception which I shall notice, to the doctrine that government cannot manage the affairs of individuals as well as the individuals themselves, has reference to the great class of cases in which the individuals can only manage the concern by delegated agency, and in which the so-called private management is, in point of fact, hardly better entitled to be called management by the persons interested than administration by a public officer. Whatever, if left to spontaneous agency, can only be done by joint-stock associations, will often be as well, and sometimes better done, as far as the actual work is concerned, by the state. Government management is, indeed, proverbially jobbing, careless, and ineffective, but so likewise has generally been joint-stock management. The directors of a joint-stock company, it is true, are always shareholders; but also the members of a government are invariably taxpayers; and in the case of directors, no more than in that of governments, is their proportional share of the benefits of good management equal to the interest they may possibly have in mis-management, even without reckoning the interest of their case. It may be objected, that the shareholders, in their collective character, exercise a certain control over the directors, and have almost always full power to remove them from office. Practically, however, the difficulty of exercising this power is found to be so great, that it is hardly ever exercised except in cases of such flagrantly unskilful, or, at least, unsuccessful management, as would generally produce the ejection from office of managers appointed by the government. Against the very ineffectual security afforded by meetings of shareholders, and by their individual inspection and inquiries, may be placed the greater publicity and more active discussion and comment, to be expected in free countries with regard to affairs in which the general government takes part. The defects, therefore, of government management do not seem to be necessarily much greater, if necessarily greater at all, than those of management by joint-stock.

The true reasons in favour of leaving to voluntary associations all such things as they are competent to perform would exist in equal strength if it were certain that the work itself would be as well or better done by public officers. These reasons have been already pointed out: the mischief of overloading the chief functionaries of government with demands on their attention, and diverting them from duties which they alone can discharge, to objects which can be sufficiently well attained without them; the danger of unnecessarily swelling the direct power and indirect influence of government, and multiplying occasions of collision between its agents and private citizens; and the inexpediency of concentrating in a dominant bureaucracy all the skill and experience in the management of large interests, and all the power of organized action, existing in the community; a practice which keeps the citizens in a relation to the government like that of children to their guardians, and is a main cause of the inferior capacity for political life which has hitherto characterized the over-governed countries of the Continent, whether with or without the forms of representative government.

But although, for these reasons, most things which are likely to be even tolerably done by voluntary associations should, generally speaking, be left to them; it does not follow that the manner in which those associations perform their work should be entirely uncontrolled by the government. There are many cases in which the agency, of whatever nature, by which a service is performed, is certain, from the nature of the case, to be virtually single; in which a practical monopoly, with all the power it confers of taxing the community, cannot be prevented from existing. I have already more than once adverted to the case of the gas and water companies, among which, though perfect freedom is allowed to competition, none really takes place, and practically they are found to be even more irresponsible, and unapproachable by individual complaints, than the government. There are the expenses without the advantages of plurality of agency; and the charge made for services which cannot be dispensed with, is, in substance, quite as much compulsory taxation as if imposed by law; there are few householders who make any distinction between their 'water-rate' and their other local taxes. In the case of these particular services, the reasons preponderate in favour of their being performed, like the paving and cleansing of the streets, not certainly by the general government of the state, but by the municipal authorities of the town, and the expense defrayed, as even now it in fact is, by a local rate. But in the many analogous cases which it is best to resign to voluntary agency, the community needs some other security for the fit performance of the service than the interest of the managers; and it is the part of government, either to subject the business to reasonable conditions for the general advantage, or to retain such power over it that the profits of the monopoly may at least be obtained for the public. This applies to the case of a road, a canal, or a railway. These are always, in a great degree, practical monopolies; and a government which concedes such monopoly unreservedly to a private company does much the same thing as if it allowed an individual or an association to levy any tax they chose, for their own benefit, on all the malt produced in the country, or on all the cotton imported into it. To make the concession for a limited time is generally justifiable, on the principle which justifies patents for inventions: but the state should either reserve to itself a reversionary property in such public works, or should retain, and freely exercise, the right of fixing a maximum of fares and charges, and, from time to time, varying that maximum. It is perhaps necessary to remark, that the state may be the proprietor of canals or railways without itself working them; and that they will almost always be better worked by means of a company renting the railway or canal for a limited period from the state.

12. To a fourth case of exception I must request particular attention, it being one to which, as it appears to me, the attention of political economists has not yet been sufficiently drawn. There are matters in which the interference of law is required, not to overrule the judgment of individuals respecting their own interest, but to give effect to that judgment: they being unable to give effect to it except by concert, which concert again cannot be effectual unless it receives validity and sanction from the law. For illustration, and without prejudging the particular point, I may advert to the question of diminishing the hours of labour. Let us suppose, what is at least supposable, whether it be the fact or not – that a general reduction of the hours of factory labour, say from ten to nine, would be for the advantage of the workpeople: that they would receive as high wages, or nearly as high, for nine hours' labour as they receive for ten. If this would be the result, and if the operatives generally are convinced that it would, the limitation, some may say, will be adopted spontaneously. I answer, that it will not be adopted unless the body of operatives bind themselves to one another to abide by it. A workman who refused to work more than nine hours while there were others who worked ten, would either not be employed at all, or if employed, must submit to lose one-tenth of his wages. However convinced, therefore, he may be that it is the interest of the class to work short time, it is contrary to his own interest to set the example, unless he is well assured that all or most others will follow it. But suppose a general agreement of the whole class: might not this be effectual without the sanction of law? Not unless enforced, by opinion, with a rigour practically equal to that of law. For however beneficial the observance of the regulation might be to the class collectively, the immediate interest of every individual would lie in violating it: and the more numerous those who adhered to the rule, the more would individuals gain by departing from it. If nearly all restricted themselves to nine hours, those who chose to work for ten would gain all the advantages of the restriction, together with the profit of infringing it; they would get ten hours' wages for nine hours' work, and an hour's wages besides. I grant that if a large majority adhered to the nine hours, there would be no harm done: the benefit would be, in the main, secured to the class, while those individuals who preferred to work harder and earn more, would have an opportunity of doing so. This certainly would be the state of things to be wished for; and assuming that a reduction of hours without any diminution of wages could take place without expelling the commodity from some of its markets – which is in every particular instance a question of fact, not of principle – the manner in which it would be most desirable that this effect should be brought about, would be by a quiet change in the general custom of the trade; short hours becoming, by spontaneous choice, the general practice, but those who chose to deviate from it having the fullest liberty to do so. Probably, however, so many would prefer the ten hours' work on the improved terms, that the limitation could not be maintained as a general practice: what some did from choice, others would soon be obliged to do from necessity, and those who had chosen long hours for the sake of increased wages, would be forced in the end to work long hours for no greater wages than before. Assuming then that it really would be the interest of each to work only nine hours if he could be assured that all others would do the same, there might be no means of their attaining this object but by converting their supposed mutual agreement into an engagement under penalty, by consenting to have it enforced by law. I am not expressing any opinion in favour of such an enactment, which has never in this country been demanded, and which I certainly should not, in present circumstances, recommend: but it serves to exemplify the manner in which classes of persons may need the assistance of law, to give effect to their deliberate collective opinion of their own interest, by affording to every individual a guarantee that his competitors will pursue the same course, without which he cannot safely adopt it himself.

...

13. Fifthly; the argument against government interference grounded on the maxim that individuals are the best judges of their own interest, cannot apply to the very large class of cases, in which those acts of individuals with which the government claims to interfere, are not done by those individuals for their own interest, but for the interest of other people. This includes, among other things, the important and much agitated subject of public charity. Though individuals should, in general, be left to do for themselves whatever it can reasonably be expected that they should be capable of doing, yet when they are at any rate not to be left to themselves, but to be helped by other people, the question arises whether it is better that they should receive this help exclusively from individuals, and therefore uncertainly and casually, or by systematic arrangements, in which society acts through its organ, the state.

This brings us to the subject of Poor Laws; a subject which would be of very minor importance if the habits of all classes of the people were temperate and prudent, and the diffusion of property satisfactory; but of the greatest moment in a state of things so much the reverse of this, in both points, as that which the British Islands present.

Apart from any metaphysical considerations respecting the foundation of morals or of the social union, it will be admitted to be right that human beings should help one another; and the more so, in proportion to the urgency of the need: and none needs help so urgently as one who is starving. The claim to help, therefore, created by destitution, is one of the strongest which can exist; and there is *primâ facie* the amplest reason for making the relief of so extreme an exigency as certain to those who require it as by any arrangements of society it can be made.

On the other hand, in all cases of helping, there are two sets of consequences to be considered; the consequences of the assistance itself, and the consequences of relying on the assistance. The former are generally beneficial, but the latter, for the most part, injurious; so much so, in many cases, as greatly to outweigh the value of the benefit. And this is never more likely to happen than in the very cases where the need of help is the most intense. There are few things for which it is more mischievous that people should rely on the habitual aid of others, than for the means of subsistence, and unhappily there is no lesson which they more easily learn. The problem to be solved is therefore one of peculiar nicety as well as importance; how to give the greatest amount of needful help, with the smallest encouragement to undue reliance on it.

Energy and self-dependence are, however, liable to be impaired by the absence of help, as well as by its excess. It is even more fatal to exertion to have no hope of succeeding by it, than to be assured of succeeding without it. When the condition of any one is so disastrous that his energies are paralyzed by discouragement, assistance is a tonic, not a sedative: it braces instead of deadening the active faculties: always provided that the assistance is not such as to dispense with self-help, by substituting itself for the person's own labour, skill, and prudence, but is limited to affording him a better hope of attaining success by those legitimate means. This accordingly is a test to which all plans of philanthropy and benevolence should be brought, whether intended for the benefit of individuals or of classes, and whether conducted on the voluntary or on the government principle.

In so far as the subject admits of any general doctrine or maxim, it would appear to be this – that if assistance is given in such a manner that the condition of the person helped is as desirable as that of the person who succeeds in doing the same thing without help, the assistance, if capable of being previously calculated on, is mischievous: but if, while available to everybody, it leaves to every one a strong motive to do without it if he can, it is then for the most part beneficial. This principle, applied to a system of public charity, is that of the Poor Law of 1834. If the condition of a person receiving relief is made as eligible as that of the labourer who supports himself by his own exertions, the system strikes at the root of all individual industry and self-government; and, if fully acted up to, would require as its supplement an organized system of compulsion for governing and setting to work like cattle those who had been removed from the influence of the motives that act on human beings. But if, consistently with guaranteeing all persons against absolute want, the condition of those who are supported by legal charity can be kept considerably less desirable than the condition of those who find support for themselves, none but beneficial consequences can arise from a law which renders it impossible for any person, except by his own choice, to die from insufficiency of food. That in England at least this supposition can be realized, is proved by the experience of a long period preceding the close of the last century, as well as by that of many highly pauperized districts in more recent times, which have been dispauperized by adopting strict rules of poor-law administration, to the great and permanent benefit of the whole labouring class. There is probably no country in which, by varying the means suitably to the character of the people, a legal provision for the destitute might not be made compatible with the observance of the conditions necessary to its being innocuous.

Subject to these conditions, I conceive it to be highly desirable that the certainty of subsistence should be held out by law to the destitute able-bodied, rather than that their relief should depend on voluntary charity. In the first place, charity almost always does too much or too little: it lavishes its bounty in one place, and leaves people to starve in another. Second, since the state must necessarily provide subsistence for the criminal poor while undergoing punishment, not to do the same for the poor who have not offended is to give a premium on crime. And lastly, if the poor are left to individual charity, a vast amount of mendicity is inevitable. What the state may and should abandon to private charity, is the task of distinguishing between one case of real necessity and another. Private charity can give more to the more deserving. The state must act by general rules. It cannot undertake to discriminate between the deserving and the undeserving indigent. It owes no more than subsistence to the first, and can give no less to the last. What is said about the injustice of a law which has no better treatment for the merely unfortunate poor than for the ill-conducted, is founded on a misconception of the province of law and public authority. The dispensers of public relief have no business to be inquisitors. Guardians and over-seers are not fit to be trusted to give or withhold other people's money according to their verdict on the morality of the person soliciting it; and it would show much ignorance of the ways of mankind to suppose that such persons, even in the almost impossible case of their being quali-fied, will take the trouble of ascertaining and sifting the past conduct of a person in distress, so as to form a rational judgment on it. Private charity can make these distinctions; and in bestowing its own money, is entitled to do so according to its own judgment. It should understand that this is its peculiar and appropriate province, and that it is commendable on the contrary, as it exer-cises the function with more or less discernment. But the administrators of a public fund ought not to be required to do more for anybody, than that minimum which is due even to the worst. If they are, the indulgence very speedily becomes the rule, and refusal the more or less capricious or tyrannical exception.

...

15. The same principle which points out colonization, and the relief of the indigent, as cases to which the principal objection to government interference does not apply, extends also to a variety of cases, in which important public services are to be performed, while yet there is no individual specially interested in performing them, nor would any adequate remuneration natu-rally or spontaneously attend their performance. Take for instance a voyage of geographical or scientific exploration. The information sought may be of great public value, yet no individual would derive any benefit from it which would repay the expense of fitting out the expedition; and there is no mode of intercepting the benefit on its way to those who profit by it, in order to levy a toll for the remuneration of its authors. Such voyages are, or might be, undertaken by private subscription; but this is a rare and precarious resource. Instances are more frequent in which the expense has been borne by public companies or philanthropic associations; but in general such enterprises have been conducted at the expense of government, which is thus enabled to entrust them to the persons in its judgment best qualified for the task. Again, it is a proper office of gov-ernment to build and maintain lighthouses, establish buoys, etc., for the security of navigation: for since it is impossible that the ships at sea which are benefited by a lighthouse should be made to pay a toll on the occasion of its use, no one would build lighthouses from motives of personal interest, unless indemnified and rewarded from a compulsory levy made by the state. There are many scientific researches, of great value to a nation and to mankind, requiring assiduous devotion of time and labour, and not unfrequently great expense, by persons who can obtain a high price for their services in other ways. If the government had no power to grant indemnity for expense, and remuneration for time and labour thus employed, such researches could only be undertaken by the very few persons who, with an independent fortune, unite technical knowledge, laborious habits, and either great public spirit, or an ardent desire of scientific celebrity.

Connected with this subject is the question of providing by means of endowments or salaries, for the maintenance of what has been called a learned class. The cultivation of speculative knowledge, though one of the most useful of all employments, is a service rendered to a community collectively, not individually, and one consequently for which it is, *primâ facie*, reasonable that the community collectively should pay; since it gives no claim on any individual for a pecuniary remuneration; and unless a provision is made for such services from some public fund, there is not only no encouragement to them, but there is as much discouragement as is implied in the impossibility of gaining a living by such pursuits, and the necessity consequently imposed on most of those who would be capable of them to employ the greatest part of their time in gaining a subsistence. The evil, however, is greater in appearance than in reality. The greatest things, it has been said, have generally been done by those who had the least time at their disposal; and the occupation of some hours every day in a routine employment, has often been found compatible with the most brilliant achievements in literature and philosophy. Yet, there are investigations and experiments which require not only a long but a continuous devotion of time and attention: there are also occupations which so engross and fatigue the mental faculties, as to be inconsistent with any vigorous employment of them upon other subjects, even in intervals of leisure. It is highly desirable, therefore, that there should be a mode of insuring to the public the services of scientific discoverers, and perhaps of some other classes of savants, by affording them the means of support consistently with devoting a sufficient portion of time to their peculiar pursuits. The fellowships of the Universities are an institution excellently adapted for such a purpose; but are hardly ever applied to it, being bestowed, at the best, as a reward for past proficiency, in committing to memory what has been done by others, and not as the salary of future labours in the advancement of knowledge. In some countries, Academies of science, antiquities, history, etc., have been formed with emoluments annexed. The most effectual plan, and at the same time least liable to abuse, seems to be that of conferring Professorships, with duties of instruction attached to them. The occupation of teaching a branch of knowledge, at least in its higher departments, is a help rather than an impediment to the systematic cultivation of the subject itself. The duties of a professorship almost always leave much time for original researches; and the greatest advances which have been made in the various sciences, both moral and physical, have originated with those who were public teachers of them; from Plato and Aristotle to the great names of the Scotch, French, and German Universities. I do not mention the English, because until very lately their professorships have been, as is well known, little more than nominal. In the case, too, of a lecturer in a great institution of education, the public at large has the means of judging, if not the quality of the teaching, at least the talents and industry of the teacher; and it is more difficult to misemploy the power of appointment to such an office, than to job in pensions and salaries to persons not so directly before the public eye.

It may be said generally, that anything which it is desirable should be done for the general interests of mankind or of future generations, or for the present interests of those members of the community who require external aid, but which is not of a nature to remunerate individuals or associations for undertaking it, is in itself a suitable thing to be undertaken by government: though, before making the work their own, governments ought always to consider if there be any rational probability of its being done on what is called the voluntary principle, and if so, whether it is likely to be done in a better or more effectual manner by government agency, than by the zeal and liberality of individuals.

16. The preceding heads comprise, to the best of my judgment, the whole of the exceptions to the practical maxim, that the business of society can be best performed by private and voluntary agency. It is, however, necessary to add, that the intervention of government cannot always practically stop short at the limit which defines the cases intrinsically suitable for it. In the particular circumstances of a given age or nation, there is scarcely anything really important to the general interest, which it may not be desirable, or even necessary, that the government should take upon itself, not because private individuals cannot effectually perform it, but because they will not. At some times and places there will be no roads, docks, harbours, canals, works of irrigation, hospitals, schools, colleges, printing-presses, unless the government establishes them; the public being either too poor to command the necessary resources, or too little advanced in intelligence to appreciate the ends, or not sufficiently practised in joint action to be capable of the means. This is true, more or less, of all countries inured to despotism, and particularly of those in which there is a very wide distance in civilization between the people and the government: as in those which have been conquered and are retained in subjection by a more energetic and more cultivated people. In many parts of the world, the people can do nothing for themselves which requires large means and combined action: all such things are left undone, unless done by the state. In these cases, the mode in which the government can most surely demonstrate the sincerity with which it intends the greatest good of its subjects, is by doing the things which are made incumbent on it by the helplessness of the public, in such a manner as shall tend not to increase and perpetuate, but to correct that helplessness. A good government will give all its aid in such a shape as to encourage and nurture any rudiments it may find of a spirit of individual exertion. It will be assiduous in removing obstacles and discouragements to voluntary enterprise, and in giving whatever facilities and whatever direction and guidance may be necessary: its pecuniary means will be applied, when practicable, in aid of private efforts rather than in supercession of them, and it will call into play its machinery of rewards and honours to elicit such efforts. Government aid, when given merely in default of private enterprise, should be so given as to be as far as possible a course of education for the people in the art of accomplishing great objects by individual energy and voluntary co-operation.

I have not thought it necessary here to insist on that part of the functions of government which all admit to be indispensable, the function of prohibiting and punishing such conduct on the part of individuals in the exercise of their freedom as is clearly injurious to other persons, whether the case be one of force, fraud, or negligence Even in the best state which society has yet reached, it is lamentable to think how great a proportion of all the efforts and talents in the world are employed in merely neutralizing one another. It is the proper end of government to reduce this wretched waste to the smallest possible amount, by taking such measures as shall cause the energies now spent by mankind in injuring one another, or in protecting themselves against injury, to be turned to the legitimate employment of the human faculties, that of compelling the powers of nature to be more and more subservient to physical and moral good.

Part 3

The Marxian Challenge

Karl Marx, by courtesy of The Warren J. Samuels Portrait Collection at Duke University.

Introduction

By the second quarter of the nineteenth century the middle class of businessmen and others was well along the way to cementing its transformation of society, polity, and economy, in England and elsewhere, from a rural, agricultural to an urban, industrial system. Conceptions of life, morality, politics, and indeed, every aspect of individual and organized living had undergone and were still undergoing more or less radical transformation.

When the business class offered justification for its program, they tended to speak and write in universalist terms: what was good for the landed upper class was not only also good for the middle class but for all people, at least all men, inasmuch as women were excluded from consideration by most spokesmen. In time, however, the middle class wrested power from the hitherto ruling class, coming to share control of government, and of government policy, with the landed interests. Their revolution was successful.

Spokesmen for the working class, however, felt that not much had changed for the masses. The social order was still in the hands of a small privileged minority, only now it comprised the owners of both landed and nonlanded property. Whereas special privilege hitherto had been based on birth, now it was based on both birth and wealth. And it seemed that the hitherto revolutionary middle class, now ensconced in power, was prepared to fight to conserve the status quo against any challenge from below, pretty much as the landed interests had sought to defend their order from the challenge brought by the middle class. One difference was that the old system of rulership by ennobled lords was relatively closed, whereas the new system of rulership by wealth was relatively open, so that its defenders could appeal to notions of self-help and opportunity. Still, spokesmen for the nonpropertied working class understood that power was important, that government power was especially important, and sought access to and participation in government by representatives of the working class so that government would become responsive to its interests as defined by them. For all practical purposes, though "socialism" later came to mean public ownership of the major means of production, central planning of one type or another, and, *inter alia*, the welfare state, one can best comprehend the historic meaning of socialism if one sees it as a movement seeking to bring about broadened participation by the masses in both economy and government, with both government and economy conducted toward broader objectives than those of the landed and nonlanded propertied classes.

The socialists had several interpretive and/or strategic problems. These included (1) whether to accept industrialism as a desirable and perhaps irreversible process or to reject and reverse it; (2) whether to accept or reject liberalism – the philosophy and institutions of personal freedom – as a value and as a limitation on political action; and (3) whether to accept or reject the newly developing labor movement, a choice which turned on one's attitude toward revolutionary versus "business" unionism, the former seeking radical and perhaps violent transformation of society, the latter seeking to improve wages and hours and conditions of work for workers within the existing capitalist economy. Accordingly, and not surprisingly, the socialist movement took many different forms with a variety of desired end-states – though all of them contemplated a great place in the sun for the working class. In other words, the leaders of the working class tried to do for it what the leaders of the middle class had succeeded in doing for it, differing as to means.

There were, of course, other reactions to the emergence of the new economic order, though no excerpts from those writings are included here. The English and German Romantics rejected the new system on the grounds that it violated the values of the old system. The Anarchists rejects organized society, especially the concentration of economic and political power in the hands of the wealthy, and sought the destruction of received institutions, generally seeking a new order with power diffused at the local level.

The general socialist movement embraced a number of economic theories, the specific content of each of which varied among authors – and were often shared by anarchist writers. These economic theories included: a labor theory of value; an exploitation theory of property, state, class, and income and wealth distributions; an underconsumption theory of the business cycle; the view that competition was destructive of itself and corrosive of human beings; and so on. As for distribution, some critics of the status quo argued that under capitalism income is distributed in such a way and with such a result as to be inconsistent with ethics and justice, that is, that institutionally produced inequality – which these critics thought prevalent – is unjust, and that poverty is inherently wrong and morally offensive in the face of great concentrated wealth. These arguments turn on at least three points: (1) whether the wrong people get the larger incomes; (2) whether the shape of the distribution is wrong; and/or (3) whether the process of distribution itself is wrong.

The principal theorist of socialism was Karl Marx. Marx was born in Germany and educated at the Universities of Bonn, Berlin, and Jena, receiving his doctorate in philosophy from Jena at age 23. His Hegelian philosophical outlook, and his association with the "Young Hegelians" and their strident social critiques, kept Marx from pursuing an academic career. He instead turned his energies to journalism, but the government outlawed the newspaper Marx was editing, and he was forced to leave Germany and spend the rest of his life in exile. Marx eventually settled in London in 1848, and he lived there until his death in 1883.

If it was Hegel who served to define Marx's intellectual perspective, it was his friendship with Friedrich Engels that situated its practical application. Engels encouraged Marx to explore political economy, and it was Engels' financial support that supplemented Marx's small journalism income and enabled him to devote his time to research, writing, and organizing those sympathetic to communist ideas. Their collaboration on the *Communist Manifesto* (1848) gives a clear and concise statement of a number of the central themes that would appear in Marx's later writings.

It was Marx's name and ideas – variously interpreted – that became a movement of world-historic proportions. Given Marx's emphasis on history as a dialectical process, it is either ironic or illustrative of his overall position that the Soviet Union, which adopted an ideology it identified with Marx, turned out to be destructive of the values which Marx supported; and that Marx's claim that socialism and, eventually, communism could only arise in an advanced capitalist nation was contradicted by (1) the failure of socialist revolutions in those countries to materialize, (2) the adoption of Marxism in the last essentially feudal nation in Europe, and (3) the adoption of Marxism as apparently the ideology of choice, perhaps the only available revolutionary ideology, in Third World countries seeking to overthrow either colonialism and/or feudal-like ruling classes.

Marx's basic doctrines are as follows. Marx believed in dialectical (or historical) materialism. The dialectical element signifies that development involves an interaction/conflict between and eventual synthesis of opposites, with any synthesis eventually engendering its own antithesis, leading to a new conflict, a new synthesis, a new antithesis, and so on. The materialist element signifies that the, or a major, driving force is the mode of production, by which Marx meant, in present-day terms, technology plus the social relations of production engendered by technology. The evolving mode of production, in his view, was the foundation of society and of history. Upon it was erected a superstructure of correlative belief systems and institutions. At any point in time there was a dominant mode of production (foundation 1, or $F1$) to which corresponded its derivative superstructure (superstructure 1, or $S1$). One facet of this situation is the hegemony of a particular ruling class (class 1, $RC1$). But in time, says Marx, the mode of production changes and becomes $F2$. The old superstructure, $S1$, with its ruling class, $RC1$, remain in power only to come into conflict with the burgeoning new superstructure corresponding to the new mode of production, $S2$, with its pretender to ruling class status, $RC2$. What is manifestly visible in all this, argues Marx, is the conflict between old and new ruling classes, between $RC1$ and $RC2$. History, he writes, is the history of class struggle. But this conflict is only the visible manifestation of the underlying conflict, which is between $F1$ and $S2$, on the one hand, and $F2$ and $S2$ on the other. This process continues, according to Marx, with the rise of $F3$ and $S3$, and the conflict between $RC2$ and $RC3$. It is Marx's view, however, that capitalism and its immediate successor in his system are the last such conflictual stages; communism, in his system, has no classes, hence no class struggle, and, since the state is defined as an instrument of class domination, in the absence of both class and class domination, there is no state, only administrative apparatus.

In one group of writings, Marx explicated this situation in terms of a theory of alienation, in which individuals under capitalism (and earlier forms of society) are alienated from each other, from the products they use, and from their "authentic" selves. Some Marxists elevate this theory above the theory found in another group of writings, writings much better known, such as *Capital*, in which an exploitation paradigm – actually a vast corpus of economic theory – is advanced. Other Marxists prefer the latter to the former; and still others feel that the two are complementary, or at least not mutually exclusive.

Marx's economic theory, his exploitation paradigm, is developed along the following lines. The labor theory of value, as a source (not mere measure) of value, is adopted and stated in a very sophisticated form: commodities are said to exchange in proportion to the average socially necessary abstract labor power embodied in them. Critical to his further theorizing are his beliefs that (1) labor gets paid the value of its labor power, that is, the value, in terms of labor, of the commodities necessary to maintain and reproduce the worker and his family and (2) labor gets paid, thereby, less than the value of what labor produces. The crux of the matter, therefore, is that labor is coerced, by fear of unemployment and starvation, to work a number of hours each day longer than the number of hours necessary to repay the employer for the value of labor power advanced (paid) to labor. The value created by labor in those extra hours and appropriated by the employer, Marx calls surplus value. Surplus value is the source of all nonlabor income (all this, therefore, is the core of Marx's theory of income distribution). Its creation and extraction is the heart of capitalism as an exploitative system. It is a class phenomenon, reflective of the power of the capitalist class, that is, of capital as a social and not merely technical economic category.

Marx goes further than this in an attempt to put his finger on the "laws of motion" of capitalism. Here he feels he has identified the falling rate of profit and the inherent contradictions of capitalism.

Before examining the falling rate of profit, several key relationships identified by Marx must be seen. Marx identifies constant capital (C) as plant and equipment, which can only transfer to their final products the value embodied in them; "constant" capital in the sense that its value is constant, and involves no accretion. Labor, however, is designated variable capital (V), capital in the Classicists' general sense of advances to workers (as above), and variable in the sense that because of the coerced length of the working day, labor can create a value greater than its own value, something which constant capital cannot do. This accretion is surplus value, or S. Now, since surplus value arises only from variable capital, S is a function of V, and only V. The value of any commodity (its embodied labor, as above) has these three parts: C plus V plus S.

Marx's law of the falling rate of profit derives from the quest for super-profits, which leads businesses to innovate, thus substituting capital for labor – or, in Marx's language, constant capital for variable capital. The ratio of C to V (the organic composition of capital) rises. But surplus value derives only from variable capital; and as V falls in relation to C, given the rate of exploitation (the ratio of S to V), the rate of profit will fall. Businesses can take apparent countermeasures to the falling rate of profit (e.g. increasing the rate of exploitation by lengthening the working day, depressing wages below the value of labor power; the charging of monopoly prices to consumers, that is, prices above the labor value of goods; and exporting capital to colonies to practice the foregoing against both the indigenous and the colonizing populations). But these only exacerbate the conflicts within the economy and do not seriously impede the continued decline of the rate of profit and the turmoil it engenders in business circles.

The dynamics of capitalism also encompasses, for Marx, these inherent contradictions of capitalism, contradictions which he felt engendered its doom. First, the concentration of capital and the centralization of production in ever fewer hands, generated by the quest for super-profits if not also for power, meant for Marx that capitalism was socializing itself from within; the revolution for which Marx called would only take over – nationalize and make responsible to all – an already socialist organization of production.

Second, the increasing misery of labor through falling wages, generated by the substitution of capital for labor and the creation of a reserve army of the unemployed, would exacerbate the relations between employees and employers and thereby between the nonpropertied, who had only their labor to sell, and the propertied, who were in a position to put labor to work, but only on terms propitious to themselves. In the face of increasing real living standards by the end of the nineteenth century, Marxists revised this theory of an absolute fall in wages into a relative fall in wages, wherein the increase in real wages by labor was minor relative to the accumulation of wealth by the propertied capitalist and monied classes.

Third, Marx identified economic instability in three ways: He argued that business cycles, or crises, were inherent in capitalism. He identified an array of theories explaining how capitalism was unstable: for example, anarchy of production, disproportionality between the growth of productive capacity and the buying power of the consuming masses, and so on. He argued that business cycles and crises not only existed but were becoming increasingly severe.

For all these reasons, Marx believed that capitalism, itself an advance – in terms of its ability to generate output – over previous economic systems, was only a transitory stage in human history and therefore doomed to extinction. This would happen, on the one hand, of its own accord, through the working of the laws of motion of capitalism; and, on the other, through timely revolutionary activity on the part of the enemies of capitalism.

The immediate foregoing raises a serious problem: How much capitalism's extinction is due to the laws of motion of history, and how much to revolutionary activity. This is the question of determinism which arises in connection with Marx's entire system. Accordingly, two different versions of Marx's fundamental position have emerged, each traceable to his, or to his and Friedrich Engel's, writings. The deterministic interpretation holds that the dialectical materialist process generating transformation of the mode of production, superstructure, and class struggle, will inevitably result in the classless communist society. This interpretation makes everything follow, albeit with lags, from the changing mode of production. The conditionistic interpretation holds that while Marx stressed the changing mode of production, such stress was because of its neglect by others; and that even to argue that the mode of production is the ultimate determining factor would not mean it was the only determining factor, that is, there is also a place for superstructure forces and for human consciousness (however much ultimately derivative of material conditions) and human action.

This brings the account of Marx's ideas to his theory of the state. V.I. Lenin's (1870–1924) later exposition seems to crystallize what is either explicit and/or implicit in Marx's own works. The theory has four steps, or rather stages, to it.

1   The class domination theory of the state in which society is divided into classes and the state, by definition, is an instrument of ruling-class domination, oppression, and exploitation. In capitalism, the state is, as it were, the executive committee for managing the common affairs of the bourgeoisie. It serves to administer, legitimize, and protect ruling-class hegemony and to facilitate the accumulation of capital, through exploitation, by the bourgeoisie. Even in formally democratic systems, the state is a plutocratic regime, one in which the wealthy rule indirectly but all the more safely and effectively through the alliance of government and business, corruption, and the financing of political careers and election campaigns.

2   When the productive forces have sufficiently matured, that is, when the contradictions inherent in capitalism have come to fruition and revolutionary volition has matured, revolution overthrows the bourgeois state. Revolution, not reform, is the order of the day. The power of the state is captured, the old-state's machinery either destroyed or taken over.

3   The revolution reverses the respective power positions of the bourgeoisie and the proletariat: the dictatorship of the bourgeoisie is replaced with the dictatorship of the proletariat. The state remains an instrument of class domination, but now the loci of dominated and dominator have been turned upside down. The state represses the bourgeoisie, preventing their counter-revolution; takes over and either replaces or revises the old administrative machinery; and works to establish "socialism," the centralization of the instruments of production in the hands of the state and the promotion of the expansion of productive forces as rapidly as possible.

4   Gradually, as the foregoing is achieved, a classless society emerges and the state as an instrument of domination withers away, leaving only administrative machinery performing only economic, and not repressive, functions. (The state will continue as an institution of social control, for example, resolving conflicts, but these conflicts will be interpersonal and not a matter of economic class.)

Looked at somewhat differently, the Marxian theory of the state is one part of what amounts to his political theory, meaning by "political" having to do with power. First, the state is indeed an instrument of a ruling class; under capitalism, the ruling class is the propertied, especially the capitalist class. Second, the economy is a system of nominally private power under capitalism. Capitalism is a system of the will to power via money, economic organization, and economic rulership. The production process is a prime field of power, hence political, relations. The state is only a part of the total system of power.

In the excerpts from Marx's writing reprinted here, we see a number of the central themes of his thinking, including his materialist conception of history, nicely elaborated in his Preface to the *Critique of Political Economy*, as well as the labor theory of value, his assessment of the capitalist process and the labor process, his theory of exploitation and the creation of surplus value, and his analysis of the accumulation process as set forth in his magnum opus, *Das Kapital*.

References and further reading

Arato, Andrew (1987) "Marxism," in John Eatwell, Murray Milgate, and Peter Newman (eds), *The New Palgrave: A Dictionary of Economics*, Vol. 3, London: Macmillan, 387–90.

Berlin, Isaiah (1996) *Karl Marx: His Life and Environment*, 4th edn, New York: Oxford University Press.

Böhm-Bawerk, Eugen von (1949) *Karl Marx and the Close of His System*, New York: Augustus M. Kelley.

Bottomore, Tom, ed. (1983) *A Dictionary of Marxist Thought*, Cambridge: Harvard University Press.

Brewer, Anthony (1984) *A Guide to Marx's Capital*, New York: Cambridge University Press.

Elster, Jon (1985) *Making Sense of Marx*, Cambridge: Cambridge University Press.

Glyn, Andrew (1987) "Marxist Economics," in John Eatwell, Murray Milgate, and Peter Newman (eds), *The New Palgrave: A Dictionary of Economics*, Vol. 3, London: Macmillan, 390–5.

Hayek, F.A. von (1944) *The Road to Serfdom*, Chicago: University of Chicago Press.

Horowitz, D., ed. (1968) *Marx and Modern Economists*, London: MacGibbon & Kee.

Howard, Michael C. and King, John (1975) *The Political Economy of Karl Marx*, New York: Longman, Inc.

Lange, O. and Taylor, F.M. (1938) *On the Economic Theory of Socialism*, 2 vols., Minneapolis: University of Minnesota Press.

Mandel, Ernest (1968) *Marxist Economic Theory*, 2 vols, translated by B. Pearce, London: Merlin Press.

——(1987) "Marx, Karl Heinrich," in John Eatwell, Murray Milgate, and Peter Newman (eds), *The New Palgrave: A Dictionary of Economics*, Vol. 3, London: Macmillan, 367–83.

——and Freeman, A., eds (1984) *Ricardo, Marx, Sraffa*, London: Verso.

Marx, Karl (1858) *Grundrisse (Foundations of the Critique of Political Economy)*, London: Penguin, 1973.

——(1963) *Theories of Surplus Value*, Moscow: Progress Publishers.

Marx, Karl and Engels, Friedrich (1848) *Manifesto of the Communist Party*, Chicago: C.H. Kerr, 1947.

Meek, Ronald L. (1973) *Studies in the Labour Theory of Value*, 2nd edn, London: Lawrence & Wishart.

Morishima, M. (1973) *Marx's Economics*, Cambridge: Cambridge University Press.

Popper, Karl (1945) *The Open Society and Its Enemies*, 2 vols, London: Routledge.

Robinson, Joan (1966) *An Essay on Marxian Economics*, 2nd edn, London: Macmillan.

Roemer, J.E. (1987) "Marxian Value Analysis," in John Eatwell, Murray Milgate, and Peter Newman (eds), *The New Palgrave: A Dictionary of Economics*, Vol. 3, London: Macmillan, 383–7.

——(1988) *Free to Lose: An Introduction to Marxist Economic Philosophy*, Cambridge: Harvard University Press.

Sraffa, Piero (1960) *Production of Commodities by Means of Commodities*, Cambridge: Cambridge University Press.

Steedman, Ian (1977) *Marx After Sraffa*, London: New Left Books.

Tucker, Robert C., ed. (1978) *The Marx–Engels Reader*, 2nd edn, New York: W.W. Norton.

A Contribution to the Critique of Political Economy (1859)

Preface

I examine the system of bourgeois economy in the following order: capital, landed property, wage-labour; the State, foreign trade, world market. The economic conditions of existence of the three great classes into which modern bourgeois society is divided are analysed under the first three headings; the interconnection of the other three headings is self-evident. The first part of the first book, dealing with Capital, comprises the following chapters: 1. The commodity; 2. Money or simple circulation; 3. Capital in general. The present part consists of the first two chapters. The entire material lies before me in the form of monographs, which were written not for publication but for self-clarification at widely separated periods; their remoulding into an integrated whole according to the plan I have indicated will depend upon circumstances.

A general introduction, which I had drafted, is omitted, since on further consideration it seems to me confusing to anticipate results which still have to be substantiated, and the reader who really wishes to follow me will have to decide to advance from the particular to the general. A few brief remarks regarding the course of my study of political economy are appropriate here.

Although I studied jurisprudence, I pursued it as a subject subordinated to philosophy and history. In the year 1842–1843, as editor of the *Rheinische Zeitung*, I first found myself in the embarrassing position of having to discuss what is known as material interests. The deliberations of the Rhenish Landtag on forest thefts and the division of landed property; the officials polemic started by Herr von Schaper, then Oberprasident of the Rhine Province, against the *Rheinische Zeitung* about the condition of the Moselle peasantry, and finally the debates on free trade and protective tariffs caused me in the first instance to turn my attention to economic questions. On the other hand, at that time when good intentions 'to push forward' often took the place of factual knowledge, an echo of French socialism and communism, slightly tinged by philosophy, was noticeable in the *Rheinische Zeitung*. I objected to this dilettantism, but at the same time frankly admitted in a controversy with the *Allgemeine Augsburger Zeitung* that my previous studies did not allow me to express any opinion on the content of the French theories. When the publishers of the *Rheinische Zeitung* conceived the illusion that by a more compliant policy on the part of the paper it might be possible to secure the abrogation of the death sentence passed upon it, I eagerly grasped the opportunity to withdraw from the public stage to my study.

The first work which I undertook to dispel the doubts assailing me was a critical re-examination of the Hegelian philosophy of law; the introduction to this work being published in the *Deutsch-Französische Jahrbucher* issued in Paris in 1844. My inquiry led me to the conclusion that neither legal relations nor political forms could be comprehended whether by themselves or on the basis of a so-called general development of the human mind, but that on the contrary they originate in the material conditions of life, the totality of which Hegel, following the example of English and French thinkers of the eighteenth century, embraces within the term 'civil society'; that the anatomy of this civil society, however, has to be sought in political economy. The study of this, which I began in Paris, I continued in Brussels, where I moved owing to an expulsion order issued by M. Guizot. The general conclusion at which I arrived and which, once reached, became the guiding principle of my studies can be summarized as follows. In the social production of their existence, men inevitably enter into definite relations, which are independent of their will, namely relations of production appropriate to a given stage in the development of their material forces of production. The totality of these relations of production constitutes the economic structure of society, the real foundation, on which arises a legal and political superstructure and to which correspond definite forms of social consciousness. The mode of production of material life conditions the general process of social, political and intellectual life. It is not the consciousness of men that determines their existence, but their social existence that determines their consciousness. At a certain stage of development, the material productive forces of society come into conflict with the existing relations of production or – this merely expresses the same thing in legal terms – with the property relations within the framework of which they have operated hitherto. From forms of development of the productive forces these relations turn into their fetters. Then begins an era of social revolution. The changes in the economic foundation led sooner or later to the transformation of the whole immense superstructure. In studying such transformations it is always necessary to distinguish between the material transformation of the economic conditions of production, which can be determined with the precision of natural science, and the legal, political, religious, artistic or philosophic – in short, ideological forms in which men become conscious of this conflict and fight it out. Just as one does not judge an individual by what he thinks about himself, so one cannot judge such a period of transformation by its consciousness, but, on the contrary, this consciousness must be explained from the contradictions of material life, from the conflict existing between the social forces of production and the relations of production. No social order is ever destroyed before all the productive forces for which it is sufficient have been developed, and new superior relations of production never replace older ones before the material conditions for their existence have matured within the framework of the old society. Mankind thus inevitably sets itself only such tasks as it is able to solve, since closer examination will always show that the problem itself arises only when the material conditions for its solution are already present or at least in the course of formation. In broad outline, the Asiatic, ancient, feudal and modern bourgeois modes of production may be designated as epochs marking progress in the economic development of society. The bourgeois mode of production is the last antagonistic form of the social process of production – antagonistic not in the sense of individual antagonism but of an antagonism that emanates from the individuals' social conditions of existence – but the productive forces developing within bourgeois society create also the material conditions for a solution of this antagonism. The prehistory of human society accordingly closes with this social formation.

Frederick Engels, with whom I maintained a constant exchange of ideas by correspondence since the publication of his brilliant essay on the critique of economic categories, printed in the *Deutsch-Französische Jahrbücher*, arrived by another road (compare his *Lage der arbeitenden Klasse in England*) at the same result as I, and when in the spring of 1845 he too came to live in Brussels, we decided to set forth together our conception as opposed to the ideological one of German philosophy, in fact to settle accounts with our former philosophical conscience. The intention was carried out in the form of a critique of post-Hegelian philosophy. The manuscript [*The German Ideology*], two large octavo volumes, had long ago reached the publishers in Westphalia when we were informed that owing to changed circumstances it could not be printed. We abandoned the manuscript to the gnawing criticism of the mice all the more willingly since we had achieved our main purpose – self-clarification. Of the scattered works in which at that time we presented one or another aspect of our views to the public, I shall mention only the *Manifesto of the Communist Party*, jointly written by Engels and myself, and a *Discours sur le libre échange*, which I myself published.

The salient points of our conception were first outlined in an academic, although polemical, form in my *Misère de la philosophie* ..., this book which was aimed at Proudhon appeared in 1847. The publication of an essay on *Wage-Labour* [*Wage-Labor and Capital*] written in German in which I combined the lectures I had held on this subject at the German Workers' Association in Brussels, was interrupted by the February Revolution and my forcible removal from Belgium in consequence.

The publication of the *Neue Rheinische Zeitung* in 1848 and 1849 and subsequent events cut short my economic studies, which I could only resume in London in 1850. The enormous amount of material relating to the history of political economy assembled in the British Museum, the fact that London is a convenient vantage point for the observation of bourgeois society, and finally the new stage of development which this society seemed to have entered with the discovery of gold in California and Australia, induced me to start again from the very beginning and to work carefully through the new material. These studies led partly of their own accord to apparently quite remote subjects on which I had to spend a certain amount of time. But it was in particular the imperative necessity of earning my living which reduced the time at my disposal. My collaboration, continued now for eight years, with the *New York Tribune*, the leading Anglo-American newspaper, necessitated an excessive fragmentation of my studies, for I wrote only exceptionally newspaper correspondence in the strict sense. Since a considerable part of my contributions consisted of articles dealing with important economic events in Britain and on the continent, I was compelled to become conversant with practical detail which, strictly speaking, lie outside the sphere of political economy.

This sketch of the course of my studies in the domain of political economy is intended merely to show that my views – no matter how they may be judged and how little they conform to the interested prejudices of the ruling classes – are the outcome of conscientious research carried on over many years. At the entrance to science, as at the entrance to hell, the demand must be made:

> Qui si convien lasciare ogni sospetto
> Ogni vilta convien che qui sia morta.

[From Dante, *Divina Commedia*:

> Here must all distrust be left;
> All cowardice must here be dead.]

Das Kapital (1867)*

Part I: Commodities and money

Chapter I: Commodities

Section 1: The two factors of a commodity: use-value and value
(the substance of value and the magnitude of value)

The wealth of those societies in which the capitalist mode of production prevails, presents itself as 'an immense accumulation of commodities', its unit being a single commodity. Our investigation must therefore begin with the analysis of a commodity.

A commodity is, in the first place, an object outside us, a thing that by its properties satisfies human wants of some sort or another. The nature of such wants, whether, for instance, they spring from the stomach or from fancy, makes no difference. Neither are we here concerned to know how the object satisfies these wants, whether directly as means of subsistence, or indirectly as means of production.

Every useful thing, as iron, paper, etc., may be looked at from the two points of view of quality and quantity. It is an assemblage of many properties, and may therefore be of use in various ways. To discover the various uses of things is the work of history. So also is the establishment of socially recognized standards of measure for the quantities of these useful objects. The diversity of these measures has its origin partly in the diverse nature of the objects to be measured, partly in convention.

The utility of a thing makes it a use-value. But this utility is not a thing of air. Being limited by the physical properties of the commodity, it has no existence apart from that commodity. A commodity, such as iron, corn, or a diamond, is therefore, so far as it is a material thing, a use-value, something useful. This property of a commodity is independent of the amount of labour required to appropriate its useful qualities. When treating of use-value, we always assume to be dealing with definite quantities, such as dozens of watches, yards of linen, or tons of iron. The use-values of commodities furnish the material for a special study, that of the commercial knowledge of commodities. Use-values become a reality only by use or consumption: they also constitute the substance of all wealth, whatever may be the social form of that wealth. In the form of society we are about to consider, they are, in addition, the material depositories of exchange-value.

Exchange-value, at first sight, presents itself as a quantitative relation, as the proportion in which values in use of one sort are exchanged for those of another sort, a relation constantly

* Karl Marx, *Capital: A Critique of Political Economy. Volume 1: The Process of Capitalist Production*, edited by Frederick Engels, translated from the third German edition by Samuel Moore and Edward Aveling. New York: International Publishers, 1967.

changing with time and place. Hence exchange-value appears to be something accidental and purely relative, and consequently an intrinsic value, that is, an exchange-value that is inseparably connected with, inherent in commodities, seems a contradiction in terms. Let us consider the matter a little more closely.

A given commodity, for example, a quarter of wheat is exchanged for x blacking, y silk, or z gold, etc. – in short, for other commodities in the most different proportions. Instead of one exchange-value, the wheat has, therefore, a great many. But since x blacking, y silk, or z gold etc., each represents the exchange-value of one quarter of wheat, x blacking, y silk, z gold, etc., must, as exchange-values, be replaceable by each other, or equal to each other. Therefore, first: the valid exchange-values of a given commodity express something equal; second, exchange-value, generally, is only the mode of expression, the phenomenal form, of something contained in it, yet distinguishable from it.

Let us take two commodities, for example, corn and iron. The proportions in which they are exchangeable, whatever those proportions may be, can always be represented by an equation in which a given quantity of corn is equated to some quantity of iron: for example, 1 quarter corn = x cwt. iron. What does this equation tell us? It tells us that in two different things – in 1 quarter of corn and x cwt. of iron, there exists in equal quantities something common to both. The two things must therefore be equal to a third, which in itself is neither the one nor the other. Each of them, so far as it is exchange-value, must therefore be reducible to this third.

A simple geometrical illustration will make this clear. In order to calculate and compare the areas of rectilinear figures, we decompose them into triangles. But the area of the triangle itself is expressed by something totally different from its visible figure, namely by half the product of the base multiplied by the altitude. In the same way the exchange-values of commodities must be capable of being expressed in terms of something common to them all, of which thing they represent a greater or less quantity.

This common 'something' cannot be either a geometrical, a chemical, or any other natural property of commodities. Such properties claim our attention only in so far as they affect the utility of those commodities, make them use-values. But the exchange of commodities is evidently an act characterised by a total abstraction from use-value. Then one use-value is just as good as another, provided only it be present in sufficient quantity. Or, as old Barbon says, 'one sort of wares are as good as another, if the values be equal. There is no difference or distinction in things of equal value. ... An hundred pounds' worth of lead or iron, is of as great value as one hundred pounds' worth of silver or gold'. As use-values, commodities are, above all, of different qualities, but as exchange-values they are merely different quantities, and consequently do not contain an atom of use-value.

If then we leave out of consideration the use-value of commodities, they have only one common property left, that of being products of labour. But even the product of labour itself has undergone a change in our hands. If we make abstraction from its use-value, we make abstraction at the same time from the material elements and shapes that make the product a use-value; we see in it no longer a table, a house, yarn, or any other useful thing. Its existence as a material thing is put out of sight. Neither can it any longer be regarded as the product of the labour of the joiner, the mason, the spinner, or of any other definite kind of productive labour. Along with the useful qualities of the products themselves, we put out of sight both the useful character of the various kinds of labour embodied in them, and the concrete forms of that labour; there is nothing left but what is common to them all; all are reduced to one and the same sort of labour, human labour in the abstract.

Let us now consider the residue of each of these products; it consists of the same unsubstantial reality in each, a mere congelation of homogeneous human labour, of labour-power expended without regard to the mode of its expenditure. All that these things now tell us is, that human labour-power has been expended in their production, that human labour is embodied in them. When looked at as crystals of this social substance, common to them all, they are – Values.

We have seen that when commodities are exchanged, their exchange-value manifests itself as something totally independent of their use-value. But if we abstract from their use-value, there remains their Value as defined above. Therefore, the common substance that manifests itself in the exchange-value of commodities, whenever they are exchanged, is their value. The progress of our investigation will show that exchange-value is the only form in which the value of commodities can manifest itself or be expressed. For the present, however, we have to consider the nature of value independently of this, its form.

A use-value, or useful article, therefore, has value only because human labour in the abstract has been embodied or materialised in it. How, then, is the magnitude of this value to be measured? Plainly, by the quantity of the value-creating substance, the labour, contained in the article. The quantity of labour, however, is measured by its duration, and labour-time in its turn finds its standard in weeks, days, and hours.

Some people might think that if the value of a commodity is determined by the quantity of labour spent on it, the more idle and unskilful the labourer, the more valuable would his commodity be, because more time would be required in its production. The labour, however, that forms the substance of value, is homogeneous human labour, expenditure of one uniform labour-power. The total labour-power of society, which is embodied in the sum total of the values of all commodities produced by that society, counts here as one homogeneous mass of human labour-power, composed though it be of innumerable individual units. Each of these units is the same as any other, so far as it has the character of the average labour-power of society, and takes effect as such; that is, so far as it requires for producing a commodity, no more time than is needed on an average, no more than is socially necessary. The labour-time socially necessary is that required to produce an article under the normal conditions of production, and with the average degree of skill and intensity prevalent at the time. The introduction of power-looms into England probably reduced by one-half the labour required to weave a given quantity of yarn into cloth. The hand-loom weavers, as a matter of fact, continued to require the same time as before; but for all that, the product of one hour of their labour represented after the change only half an hour's social labour, and consequently fell to one-half its former value.

We see then that that which determines the magnitude of the value of any article is the amount of labour socially necessary, or the labour-time socially necessary for its production. Each individual commodity, in this connexion, is to be considered as an average sample of its class. Commodities, therefore, in which equal quantities of labour are embodied, or which can be produced in the same time, have the same value. The value of one commodity is to the value of any other, as the labour-time necessary for the production of the one is to that necessary for the production of the other. 'As values, all commodities are only definite masses of congealed labour-time'.

The value of a commodity would therefore remain constant, if the labour-time required for its production also remained constant. But the latter changes with every variation in the productiveness of labour. This productiveness is determined by various circumstances, amongst others, by the average amount of skill of the workmen, the state of science, and the degree of its practical application, the social organisation of production, the extent and capabilities of the means of production, and by physical conditions. For example, the same amount of labour in favourable seasons is embodied in 8 bushels of corn, and in unfavourable, only in 4. The same labour extracts from rich mines more metal than from poor mines. Diamonds are of very rare occurrence on the earth's surface, and hence their discovery costs, on an average, a great deal of labour-time. Consequently much labour is represented in a small compass. Jacob doubts whether gold has ever been paid for at its full value. This applies still more to diamonds. According to Eschwege, the total produce of the Brazilian diamond mines for the eighty years, ending in 1823, had not realised the price of one and-a-half years' average produce of the sugar and coffee plantations of the same country, although the diamonds cost much more labour, and therefore represented more value. With richer mines, the same quantity of labour would embody itself in more diamonds, and their value would fall. If we could succeed at a small expenditure of labour, in converting carbon into diamonds, their value might fall below that of bricks. In general, the greater the productiveness of labour, the less is the labour-time required for the production of an article, the less is the amount of labour crystallised in that article, and the less is its value; and vice versâ, the less the productiveness of labour, the greater is the labour-time required for the production of an article, and the greater is its value. The value of a commodity, therefore, varies directly as the quantity, and inversely as the productiveness, of the labour incorporated in it.

A thing can be a use-value, without having value. This is the case whenever its utility to man is not due to labour. Such are air, virgin soil, natural meadows, etc. A thing can be useful, and the product of human labour, without being a commodity. Whoever directly satisfies his wants with the produce of his own labour, creates, indeed, use-values, but not commodities. In order to produce the latter, he must not only produce use-values, but use-values for others, social use-values. (And not only for others, without more. The mediaeval peasant produced quit-rent-corn for his feudal lord and tithe-corn for his parson. But neither the quit-rent-corn nor the tithe-corn became commodities by reason of the fact that they had been produced for others. To become a commodity a product must be transferred to another, whom it will serve as a use-value, by means of an exchange.) Lastly nothing can have value, without being an object of utility. If the thing is useless, so is the labour contained in it; the labour does not count as labour, and therefore creates no value.

Part II: The transformation of money into capital

Chapter IV: The general formula for capital

The circulation of commodities is the starting-point of capital. The production of commodities, their circulation, and that more developed form of their circulation called commerce, these form the historical ground-work from which it rises. The modern history of capital dates from the creation in the sixteenth century of a world-embracing commerce and a world-embracing market. If we abstract from the material substance of the circulation of commodities, that is, from the exchange of the various use-values, and consider only the economic forms produced by this process of circulation, we find its final result to be money: this final product of the circulation of commodities is the first form in which capital appears.

As a matter of history, capital, as opposed to landed property, invariably takes the form at first of money; it appears as moneyed wealth, as the capital of the merchant and of the usurer. But we have no need to refer to the origin of capital in order to discover that the first form of appearance of capital is money. We can see it daily under our very eyes. All new capital, to commence with, comes on the stage, that is, on the market, whether of commodities, labour, or money, even in our days, in the shape of money that by a definite process has to be transformed into capital.

The first distinction we notice between money that is money only, and money that is capital, is nothing more than a difference in their form of circulation. The simplest form of the circulation of commodities is C–M–C, the transformation of commodities into money, and the change of the money back again into commodities; or selling in order to buy. But alongside of this form we find another specifically different form: M–C–M, the transformation of money into commodities, and the change of commodities back again into money; or buying in order to sell. Money that circulates in the latter manner is thereby transformed into, becomes capital, and is already potentially capital.

Now let us examine the circuit M–C–M a little closer. It consists, like the other, of two anti-thetical phases. In the first phase, M–C, or the purchase, the money is changed into a commodity. In the second phase, C–M, or the sale, the commodity is changed back again into money. The combination of these two phases constitutes the single movement whereby money is exchanged for a commodity, and the same commodity is again exchanged for money; whereby a commodity is bought in order to be sold, or, neglecting the distinction in form between buying and selling, whereby a commodity is bought with money, and then money is bought with a commodity. The result, in which the phases of the process vanish, is the exchange of money for money, M–M. If I purchase 2,000 lbs of cotton for £100, and resell the 2,000 lbs of cotton for £110, I have, in fact, exchanged £100 for £110, money for money.

Now it is evident that the circuit M–C–M would be absurd and without meaning if the inten-tion were to exchange by this means two equal sums of money, £100 for £100. The miser's plan would be far simpler and surer; he sticks to his £100 instead of exposing it to the dangers of cir-culation. And yet, whether the merchant who has paid £100 for his cotton sells it for £110, or lets it go for £100, or even £50, his money has, at all events, gone through a characteristic and original movement, quite different in kind from that which it goes through in the hands of the peasant who sells corn, and with the money thus set free buys clothes. We have therefore to exam-ine first the distinguishing characteristics of the forms of the circuits M–C–M and C–M–C, and in doing this the real difference that underlies the mere difference of form will reveal itself.

Let us see, in the first place, what the two forms have in common. Both circuits are resolvable into the same two antithetical phases, C–M, a sale, and M–C, a purchase. In each of these phases the same material elements – a commodity, and money, and the same economic dramatis per-sonae, a buyer and a seller – confront one another. Each circuit is the unity of the same two anti-thetical phases, and in each case this unity is brought about by the intervention of three contracting parties, of whom one only sells, another only buys, while the third both buys and sells.

What, however, first and foremost distinguishes the circuit C–M–C from the circuit M–C–M, is the inverted order of succession of the two phases. The simple circulation of commodities begins with a sale and ends with a purchase, while the circulation of money as capital begins with a purchase and ends with a sale. In the one case both the starting-point and the goal are com-modities, in the other they are money. In the first form the movement is brought about by the intervention of money, in the second by that of a commodity.

In the circulation C–M–C, the money is in the end converted into a commodity, that serves as a use-value; it is spent once for all. In the inverted form, M–C–M, on the contrary, the buyer lays out money in order that, as a seller, he may recover money. By the purchase of his commodity he throws money into circulation, in order to withdraw it again by the sale of the same commodity. He lets the money go, but only with the sly intention of getting it back again. The money, there-fore, is not spent, it is merely advanced.

In the circuit C–M–C, the same piece of money changes its place twice. The seller gets it from the buyer and pays it away to another seller. The complete circulation, which begins with the receipt, concludes with the payment, of money for commodities. It is the very contrary in the cir-cuit M–C–M. Here it is not the piece of money that changes its place twice, but the commodity. The buyer takes it from the hands of the seller and passes it into the hands of another buyer. Just as in the simple circulation of commodities the double change of place of the same piece of money effects its passage from one hand into another, so here the double change of place of the same commodity brings about the reflux of the money to its point of departure.

Such reflux is not dependent on the commodity being sold for more than was paid for it. This circumstance influences only the amount of the money that comes back. The reflux itself takes place, so soon as the purchased commodity is resold, in other words, so soon as the circuit

M–C–M is completed. We have here, therefore, a palpable difference between the circulation of money as capital, and its circulation as mere money.

The circuit C–M–C comes completely to an end, so soon as the money brought in by the sale of one commodity is abstracted again by the purchase of another. If, nevertheless, there follows a reflux of money to its starting-point, this can only happen through a renewal or repetition of the operation. If I sell a quarter of corn for £3, and with this £3 buy clothes, the money, so far as I am concerned, is spent and done with. It belongs to the clothes merchant. If I now sell a second quarter of corn, money indeed flows back to me, not however as a sequel to the first transaction, but in consequence of its repetition. The money again leaves me, so soon as I complete this second transaction by a fresh purchase. Therefore, in the circuit C–M–C, the expenditure of money has nothing to do with its reflux. On the other hand, in M–C–M, the reflux of the money is conditioned by the very mode of its expenditure. Without this reflux, the operation fails, or the process is interrupted and incomplete, owing to the absence of its complementary and final phase, the sale.

The circuit C–M–C starts with one commodity, and finishes with another, which falls out of circulation and into consumption. Consumption, the satisfaction of wants, in one word, use-value, is its end and aim. The circuit M–C–M, on the contrary, commences with money and ends with money. Its leading motive, and the goal that attracts it, is therefore mere exchange-value.

In the simple circulation of commodities, the two extremes of the circuit have the same economic form. They are both commodities, and commodities of equal value. But they are also use-values differing in their qualities, as, for example, corn and clothes. The exchange of products, of the different materials in which the labour of society is embodied, forms here the basis of the movement. It is otherwise in the circulation M–C–M, which at first sight appears purposeless, because tautological. Both extremes have the same economic form. They are both money, and therefore are not qualitatively different use-values; for money is but the converted form of commodities, in which their particular use-values vanish. To exchange £100 for cotton, and then this same cotton again for £100, is merely a roundabout way of exchanging money for money, the same for the same, and appears to be an operation just as purposeless as it is absurd. One sum of money is distinguishable from another only by its amount. The character and tendency of the process M–C–M, is therefore not due to any qualitative difference between its extremes, both being money, but solely to their quantitative difference. More money is withdrawn from circulation at the finish than was thrown into it at the start. The cotton that was bought for £100 is perhaps resold for £100 + £10 or £110. The exact form of this process is therefore M–C–M′, where M′ = M + ΔM = the original sum advanced, plus an increment. This increment or excess over the original value I call 'surplus-value'. The value originally advanced, therefore, not only remains intact while in circulation, but adds to itself a surplus-value or expands itself. It is this movement that converts it into capital.

Of course, it is also possible, that in C–M–C, the two extremes C–C, say corn and clothes, may represent different quantities of value. The farmer may sell his corn above its value, or may buy the clothes at less than their value. He may, on the other hand, 'be done' by the clothes merchant. Yet, in the form of circulation now under consideration, such differences in value are purely accidental. The fact that the corn and the clothes are equivalents, does not deprive the process of all meaning, as it does in M–C–M. The equivalence of their values is rather a necessary condition to its normal course.

The repetition or renewal of the act of selling in order to buy, is kept within bounds by the very object it aims at, namely consumption or the satisfaction of definite wants, an aim that lies altogether outside the sphere of circulation. But when we buy in order to sell, we, on the contrary, begin and end with the same thing, money, exchange-value; and thereby the movement becomes interminable. No doubt, M becomes M + ΔM, £100 become £110. But when viewed in their qualitative aspect alone, £110 are the same as £100, namely money; and considered quantitatively, £110 is, like £100, a sum of definite and limited value. If now, the £110 be spent as money, they cease to play their part. They are no longer capital. Withdrawn from circulation, they become petrified into a hoard, and though they remained in that state till doomsday, not a single farthing would accrue to them. If, then, the expansion of value is once aimed at, there is just the same inducement to augment the value of the £110 as that of the £100; for both are but limited expressions for exchange-value, and therefore both have the same vocation to approach, by quantitative increase, as near as possible to absolute wealth. Momentarily, indeed, the value originally advanced, the £100 is distinguishable from the surplus-value of £10 that is annexed to it during circulation; but the distinction vanishes immediately. At the end of the process, we do not receive with one hand the original £100, and with the other, the surplus-value of £10. We simply get a value of £110, which is in exactly the same condition and fitness for commencing the expanding process, as the original £100 was. Money ends the movement only to begin it again. Therefore, the final result of every separate circuit, in which a purchase and consequent sale are completed, forms of itself the starting-point of a new circuit. The simple circulation of commodities – selling in order to buy – is a means of carrying out a purpose unconnected with circulation, namely the appropriation of use-values, the satisfaction of wants. The circulation of money as capital is, on the contrary, an end in itself, for the expansion of value takes place only within this constantly renewed movement. The circulation of capital has therefore no limits.

As the conscious representative of this movement, the possessor of money becomes a capitalist. His person, or rather his pocket, is the point from which the money starts and to which it returns. The expansion of value, which is the objective basis or main-spring of the circulation M–C–M, becomes his subjective aim, and it is only in so far as the appropriation of ever more and more wealth in the abstract becomes the sole motive of his operations, that he functions as a capitalist, that is, as capital personified and endowed with consciousness and a will. Use-values must therefore never be looked upon as the real aim of the capitalist; neither must the profit on any single transaction. The restless never-ending process of profit-making alone is what he aims at. This boundless greed after riches, this passionate chase after exchange-value, is common to the capitalist and the miser; but while the miser is merely a capitalist gone mad, the capitalist is a rational miser. The never-ending augmentation of exchange-value, which the miser strives after, by seeking to save his money from circulation, is attained by the more acute capitalist, by constantly throwing it afresh into circulation.

The independent form, that is, the money-form, which the value of commodities assumes in the case of simple circulation, serves only one purpose, namely their exchange, and vanishes in the final result of the movement. On the other hand, in the circulation M–C–M, both the money and the commodity represent only different modes of existence of value itself, the money its general mode, and the commodity its particular, or, so to say, disguised mode. It is constantly changing from one form to the other without thereby becoming lost, and thus assumes an automatically active character. If now we take in turn each of the two different forms which self-expanding value successively assumes in the course of its life, we then arrive at these two propositions: Capital is money: Capital is commodities. In truth, however, value is here the active factor in a process, in which, while constantly assuming the form in turn of money and commodities, it at the same time changes in magnitude, differentiates itself by throwing off surplus-value from itself; the original value, in other words, expands spontaneously. For the movement, in the course of which it adds surplus-value, is its own movement, its expansion, therefore, is automatic expansion. Because it is value, it has acquired the occult quality of being able to add value to itself. It brings forth living offspring, or, at the least, lays golden eggs.

Value, therefore, being the active factor in such a process, and assuming at one time the form of money, at another that of commodities, but through all these changes preserving itself and expanding, it requires some independent form, by means of which its identity may at any time be established. And this form it possesses only in the shape of money. It is under the form of money that value begins and ends, and begins again, every act of its own spontaneous generation. It began by being £100, it is now £110, and so on. But the money itself is only one of the two forms of value. Unless it takes the form of some commodity, it does not become capital. There is here no antagonism, as in the case of hoarding, between the money and commodities. The capitalist knows that all commodities, however scurvy they may look, or however badly they may smell, are in faith and in truth money, inwardly circumcised Jews, and what is more, a wonderful means whereby out of money to make more money.

In simple circulation, C–M–C, the value of commodities attained at the most a form independent of their use-values, that is, the form of money; but that same value now in the circulation M–C–M, or the circulation of capital, suddenly presents itself as an independent substance, endowed with a motion of its own, passing through a life-process of its own, in which money and commodities are mere forms which it assumes and casts off in turn. Nay, more: instead of simply representing the relations of commodities, it enters now, so to say, into private relations with itself. It differentiates itself as original value from itself as surplus-value; as the father differentiates himself from himself *quâ* the son, yet both are one and of one age: for only by the surplus-value of £10 does the £100 originally advanced become capital, and so soon as this takes place, so soon as the son, and by the son, the father, is begotten, so soon does their difference vanish, and they again become one, £110.

Value therefore now becomes value in process, money in process, and, as such, capital. It comes out of circulation, enters into it again, preserves and multiplies itself within its circuit, comes back out of it with expanded bulk, and begins the same round ever afresh. M–M′, money which begets money, such is the description of Capital from the mouths of its first interpreters, the Mercantilists.

Buying in order to sell, or, more accurately, buying in order to sell dearer, M–C–M′, appears certainly to be a form peculiar to one kind of capital alone, namely merchants' capital. But industrial capital too is money, that is changed into commodities, and by the sale of these commodities, is re-converted into more money. The events that take place outside the sphere of circulation, in the interval between the buying and selling, do not affect the form of this movement. Lastly, in the case of interest-bearing capital, the circulation M–C–M′ appears abridged. We have its result without the intermediate stage, in the form M–M′, 'en style lapidaire' so to say, money that is worth more money, value that is greater than itself.

M–C–M′ is therefore in reality the general formula of capital as it appears *prima facie* within the sphere of circulation.

Part III: The production of absolute surplus-value

Chapter VII: The labour-process and the process of producing surplus-value

Section 1: The labour-process or the production of use-values

The capitalist buys labour-power in order to use it; and labour-power in use is labour itself. The purchaser of labour-power consumes it by setting the seller of it to work. By working, the latter becomes actually, what before he only was potentially, labour-power in action, a labourer. In order that his labour may re-appear in a commodity, he must, before all things, expend it on something useful, on something capable of satisfying a want of some sort. Hence, what the capitalist sets the labourer to produce, is a particular use-value, a specified article. The fact that the production of use-values, or goods, is carried on under the control of a capitalist and on his behalf, does not alter the general character of that production. We shall, therefore, in the first place, have to consider the labour-process independently of the particular form it assumes under given social conditions.

Labour is, in the first place, a process in which both man and Nature participate, and in which man of his own accord starts, regulates, and controls the material re-actions between himself and Nature. He opposes himself to Nature as one of her own forces, setting in motion arms and legs, head and hands, the natural forces of his body, in order to appropriate Nature's productions in a form adapted to his own wants. By thus acting on the external world and changing it, he at the same time changes his own nature. He develops his slumbering powers and compels them to act in obedience to his sway. We are not now dealing with those primitive instinctive forms of labour that remind us of the mere animal. An immeasurable interval of time separates the state of things in which a man brings his labour-power to market for sale as a commodity, from that state in which human labour was still in its first instinctive stage. We pre-suppose labour in a form that stamps it as exclusively human. A spider conducts operations that resemble those of a weaver, and a bee puts to shame many an architect in the construction of her cells. But what distinguishes the worst architect from the best of bees is this, that the architect raises his structure in imagination before he erects it in reality. At the end of every labour-process, we get a result that already existed in the imagination of the labourer at its commencement. He not only effects a change of form in the material on which he works, but he also realises a purpose of his own that gives the law to his *modus operandi*, and to which he must subordinate his will. And this subordination is no mere momentary act. Besides the exertion of the bodily organs, the process demands that, during the whole operation, the workman's will be steadily in consonance with his purpose. This means close attention. The less he is attracted by the nature of the work, and the mode in which it is carried on, and the less, therefore, he enjoys it as something which gives play to his bodily and mental powers, the more close his attention is forced to be. The elementary factors of the labour-process are (1) the personal activity of man, that is, work itself, (2) the subject of that work, and (3) its instruments. The soil (and this, economically speaking, includes water) in the virgin state in which it supplies man with necessaries or the means of subsistence ready to hand, exists independently of him, and is the universal subject of human labour. All those things which labour merely separates from immediate connexion with their environment, are subjects of labour spontaneously provided by Nature. Such are fish which we catch and take from their element, water, timber which we fell in the virgin forest, and ores which we extract from their veins. If, on the other hand, the subject of labour has, so to say, been filtered through previous labour, we call it raw material; such is ore already extracted and ready for washing. All raw material is the subject of labour, but not every subject of labour is raw material: it can only become so, after it has undergone some alteration by means of labour.

An instrument of labour is a thing, or a complex of things, which the labourer interposes between himself and the subject of his labour, and which serves as the conductor of his activity. He makes use of the mechanical, physical, and chemical properties of some substances in order to make other substances subservient to his aims. Leaving out of consideration such ready-made means of subsistence as fruits, in gathering which a man's own limbs serve as the instruments of his labour, the first thing of which the labourer possesses himself is not the subject of labour but its instrument. Thus, Nature becomes one of the organs of his activity, one that he annexes to his own bodily organs, adding stature to himself in spite of the Bible. As the earth is his original larder, so too it is his original tool house. It supplies him, for instance, with stones for throwing, grinding, pressing, cutting, etc. The earth itself is an instrument of labour, but when used as such in agriculture implies a whole series of other instruments and a comparatively high development of labour. No sooner does labour undergo the least development, than it requires specially prepared instruments. Thus, in the oldest caves we find stone implements and weapons. In the earliest period of human history domesticated animals, that is, animals which have been bred for the purpose, and have undergone modifications by means of labour, play the chief part as instruments of labour along with specially prepared stones, wood, bones, and shells. The use and fabrication of instruments of labour, although existing in the germ among certain species of animals, is specifically characteristic of the human labour-process, and Franklin therefore defines man as a tool-making animal. Relics of bygone instruments of labour possess the same importance for the investigation of extinct economic forms of society, as do fossil bones for the determination of extinct species of animals. It is not the articles made, but how they are made, and by what instruments, that enables us to distinguish different economic epochs. Instruments of labour not only supply a standard of the degree of development to which human labour has attained, but they are also indicators of the social conditions under which that labour is carried on. Among the instruments of labour, those of a mechanical nature, which, taken as a whole, we may call the bone and muscles of production, offer much more decided characteristics of a given epoch of production, than those which, like pipes, tubs, baskets, jars, etc., serve only to hold the materials for labour, which latter class, we may in a general way, call the vascular system of production. The latter first begins to play an important part in the chemical industries. In a wider sense we may include among the instruments of labour, in addition to those things that are used for directly transferring labour to its subject, and which therefore, in one way or another, serve as conductors of activity, all such objects as are necessary for carrying on the labour-process. These do not enter directly into the process, but without them it is either impossible for it to take place at all, or possible only to a partial extent. Once more we find the earth to be a universal instrument of this sort, for it furnishes a *locus standi* to the labourer and a field of employment for his activity. Among instruments that are the result of previous labour and also belong to this class, we find workshops, canals, roads, and so forth.

In the labour-process, therefore, man's activity, with the help of the instruments of labour, effects an alteration, designed from the commencement, in the material worked upon. The process disappears in the product, the latter is a use-value, Nature's material adapted by a change of form to the wants of man. Labour has incorporated itself with its subject: the former is materialised, the latter transformed. That which in the labourer appeared as movement, now appears in the product as a fixed quality without motion. The blacksmith forges and the product is a forging.

If we examine the whole process from the point of view of its result, the product, it is plain that both the instruments and the subject of labour, are means of production, and that the labour itself is productive labour.

Though a use-value, in the form of a product, issues from the labour-process, yet other use-values, products of previous labour, enter into it as means of production. The same-use-value is both the product of a previous process, and a means of production in a later process. Products are therefore not only results, but also essential conditions of labour.

With the exception of the extractive industries, in which the material for labour is provided immediately by Nature, such as mining, hunting, fishing, and agriculture (so far as the latter is confined to breaking up virgin soil), all branches of industry manipulate raw material, objects already filtered through labour, already products of labour. Such is seed in agriculture. Animals and plants, which we are accustomed to consider as products of Nature, are in their present form, not only products of, say last year's labour, but the result of a gradual transformation, continued through many generations, under man's superintendence, and by means of his labour. But in the great majority of cases, instruments of labour show even to the most superficial observer, traces of the labour of past ages.

Raw material may either form the principal substance of a product, or it may enter into its formation only as an accessory. An accessory may be consumed by the instruments of labour, as coal under a boiler, oil by a wheel, hay by draft-horses, or it may be mixed with the raw material in order to produce some modification thereof, as chlorine into unbleached linen, coal with iron, dye-stuff with wool, or again, it may help to carry on the work itself, as in the case of the materials used for heating and lighting workshops. The distinction between principal substance and accessory vanishes in the true chemical industries, because there none of the raw material re-appears, in its original composition, in the substance of the product.

Every object possesses various properties, and is thus capable of being applied to different uses. One and the same product may therefore serve as raw material in very different processes. Corn, for example, is a raw material for millers, starch-manufacturers, distillers, and cattlebreeders. It also enters as raw material into its own production in the shape of seed; coal, too, is at the same time the product of, and a means of production in, coal-mining. Again, a particular product may be used in one and the same process, both as an instrument of labour and as raw material. Take, for instance, the fattening of cattle, where the animal is the raw material, and at the same time an instrument for the production of manure.

A product, though ready for immediate consumption, may yet serve as raw material for a further product, as grapes when they become the raw material for wine. On the other hand, labour may give us its product in such a form, that we can use it only as raw material, as is the case with cotton, thread, and yarn. Such a raw material, though itself a product, may have to go through a whole series of different processes: in each of these in turn, it serves, with constantly varying form, as raw material, until the last process of the series leaves it a perfect product, ready for individual consumption, or for use as an instrument of labour.

Hence we see, that whether a use-value is to be regarded as raw material, as instrument of labour, or as product, this is determined entirely by its function in the labour-process, by the position it there occupies: as this varies, so does its character.

Whenever therefore a product enters as a means of production into a new labour-process, it thereby loses its character of product, and becomes a mere factor in the process. A spinner treats spindles only as implements for spinning, and flax only as the material that he spins. Of course it is impossible to spin without material and spindles; and therefore the existence of these things as products, at the commencement of the spinning operation, must be presumed: but in the process itself, the fact that they are products of previous labour, is a matter of utter indifference; just as in the digestive process, it is of no importance whatever, that bread is the produce of the previous labour of the farmer, the miller, and the baker. On the contrary, it is generally by their imperfections as products, that the means of production in any process assert themselves in their character of products. A blunt knife or weak thread forcibly remind us of Mr A, the cutler, or Mr B, the spinner. In the finished product the labour by means of which it has acquired its useful qualities is not palpable, has apparently vanished.

A machine which does not serve the purposes of labour, is useless. In addition, it falls a prey to the destructive influence of natural forces. Iron rusts and wood rots. Yarn with which we neither weave nor knit, is cotton wasted. Living labour must seize upon these things and rouse them from their death-sleep, change them from mere possible use-values into real and effective ones. Bathed in the fire of labour, appropriated as part and parcel of labour's organism, and, as it were, made alive for the performance of their functions in the process, they are in truth consumed, but consumed with a purpose, as elementary constituents of new use-values, of new products, ever ready as means of subsistence for individual consumption, or as means of production for some new labour-process.

If then, on the one hand, finished products are not only results, but also necessary conditions, of the labour-process, on the other hand, their assumption into that process, their contact with living labour, is the sole means by which they can be made to retain their character of use-values, and be utilised.

Labour uses up its material factors, its subject and its instruments, consumes them, and is therefore a process of consumption. Such productive consumption is distinguished from individual consumption by this, that the latter uses up products, as means of subsistence for the living individual; the former, as means whereby alone, labour, the labour-power of the living individual, is enabled to act. The product, therefore, of individual consumption, is the consumer himself; the result of productive consumption, is a product distinct from the consumer.

In so far then, as its instruments and subjects are themselves products, labour consumes products in order to create products, or in other words, consumes one set of products by turning them into means of production for another set. But, just as in the beginning, the only participators in the labour-process were man and the earth, which latter exists independently of man, so even now we still employ in the process many means of production, provided directly by Nature, that do not represent any combination of natural substances with human labour.

The labour-process, resolved as above into its simple elementary factors, is human action with a view to the production of use-values, appropriation of natural substances to human requirements; it is the necessary condition for effecting exchange of matter between man and Nature; it is the everlasting Nature-imposed condition of human existence, and therefore is independent of every social phase of that existence, or rather, is common to every such phase. It was, therefore, not necessary to represent our labourer in connexion with other labourers; man and his labour on one side, Nature and its materials on the other, sufficed. As the taste of the porridge does not tell you who grew the oats, no more does this simple process tell you of itself what are the social conditions under which it is taking place, whether under the slave-owner's brutal lash, or the anxious eye of the capitalist, whether Cincinnatus carries it on in tilling his modest farm or a savage in killing wild animals with stones.

Let us now return to our would-be capitalist. We left him just after he had purchased, in the open market, all the necessary factors of the labour-process – its objective factors, the means of production, as well as its subjective factor, labour-power. With the keen eye of an expert, he has selected the means of production and the kind of labour-power best adapted to his particular trade, be it spinning, bootmaking, or any other kind. He then proceeds to consume the commodity, the labour-power that he has just bought, by causing the labourer, the impersonation of that labour-power, to consume the means of production by his labour. The general character of the labour-process is evidently not changed by the fact, that the labourer works for the capitalist instead of for himself; moreover, the particular methods and operations employed in bootmaking or spinning are not immediately changed by the intervention of the capitalist. He must begin by taking the labour-power as he finds it in the market, and consequently be satisfied with labour of such a kind as would be found in the period immediately preceding the rise of capitalists. Changes in the methods of production by the subordination of labour to capital, can take place only at a later period, and therefore will have to be treated of in a later chapter.

The labour-process, turned into the process by which the capitalist consumes labour-power, exhibits two characteristic phenomena. First, the labourer works under the control of the capitalist to whom his labour belongs; the capitalist taking good care that the work is done in a proper manner, and that the means of production are used with intelligence, so that there is no unnecessary waste of raw material, and no wear and tear of the implements beyond what is necessarily caused by the work.

Second, the product is the property of the capitalist and not that of the labourer, its immediate producer. Suppose that a capitalist pays for a day's labour-power at its value; then the right to use that power for a day belongs to him, just as much as the right to use any other commodity, such as a horse that he has hired for the day. To the purchaser of a commodity belongs its use, and the seller of labour-power, by giving his labour, does no more, in reality, than part with the use-value that he has sold. From the instant he steps into the workshop, the use-value of his labour-power, and therefore also its use, which is labour, belongs to the capitalist. By the purchase of labour-power, the capitalist incorporates labour, as a living ferment, with the lifeless constituents of the product. From his point of view, the labour-process is nothing more than the consumption of the commodity purchased, that is, of labour-power; but this consumption cannot be effected except by supplying the labour-power with the means of production. The labour-process is a process between things that the capitalist has purchased, things that have become his property. The product of this process belongs, therefore, to him, just as much as does the wine which is the product of a process of fermentation completed in his cellar.

Section 2: The production of surplus-value

The product appropriated by the capitalist is a use-value, as yarn, for example, or boots. But, although boots are, in one sense, the basis of all social progress, and our capitalist is a decided 'progressist', yet he does not manufacture boots for their own sake. Use-value is, by no means, the thing 'qu'on aime pour lui-même' in the production of commodities. Use-values are only produced by capitalists, because, and in so far as, they are the material substratum, the depositories of exchange-value. Our capitalist has two objects in view: in the first place, he wants to produce a use-value that has a value in exchange, that is to say, an article destined to be sold, a commodity; and second, he desires to produce a commodity whose value shall be greater than the sum of the values of the commodities used in its production, that is, of the means of production and the labour-power, that he purchased with his good money in the open market. His aim is to produce not only a use-value, but a commodity also; not only use-value, but value; not only value, but at the same time surplus-value.

It must be borne in mind, that we are now dealing with the production of commodities, and that, up to this point, we have only considered one aspect of the process. Just as commodities are, at the same time, use-values and values, so the process of producing them must be a labour-process, and at the same time, a process of creating value.

Let us now examine production as a creation of value.

We know that the value of each commodity is determined by the quantity of labour expended on and materialised in it, by the working-time necessary, under given social conditions, for its production. This rule also holds good in the case of the product that accrued to our capitalist, as the result of the labour-process carried on for him. Assuming this product to be 10 lbs of yarn, our first step is to calculate the quantity of labour realised in it.

For spinning the yarn, raw material is required; suppose in this case 10 lbs of cotton. We have no need at present to investigate the value of this cotton, for our capitalist has, we will assume, bought it at its full value, say of ten shillings. In this price the labour required for the production of the cotton is already expressed in terms of the average labour of society. We will further assume that the wear and tear of the spindle, which, for our present purpose, may represent all other instruments of labour employed, amounts to the value of two shillings. If, then, twenty-four hours' labour, or two working-days, are required to produce the quantity of gold represented by twelve shillings, we have here, to begin with, two days' labour already incorporated in the yarn.

We must not let ourselves be misled by the circumstance that the cotton has taken a new shape while the substance of the spindle has to a certain extent been used up. By the general law of value, if the value of 40 lbs of yarn = the value of 40 lbs of cotton + the value of a whole spindle, that is, if the same working-time is required to produce the commodities on either side of this equation, then 10 lbs of yarn are an equivalent for 10 lbs of cotton, together with one-fourth of a spindle. In the case we are considering the same working-time is materialised in the 10 lbs of yarn on the one hand, and in the 10 lbs of cotton and the fraction of a spindle on the other. Therefore, whether value appears in cotton, in a spindle, or in yarn, makes no difference in the amount of that value. The spindle and cotton, instead of resting quietly side by side, join together in the process, their forms are altered, and they are turned into yarn; but their value is no more affected by this fact than it would be if they had been simply exchanged for their equivalent in yarn.

The labour required for the production of the cotton, the raw material of the yarn, is part of the labour necessary to produce the yarn, and is therefore contained in the yarn. The same applies to the labour embodied in the spindle, without whose wear and tear the cotton could not be spun.

Hence, in determining the value of the yarn, or the labour-time required for its production, all the special processes carried on at various times and in different places, which were necessary, first to produce the cotton and the wasted portion of the spindle, and then with the cotton and spindle to spin the yarn, may together be looked on as different and successive phases of one and the same process. The whole of the labour in the yarn is past labour; and it is a matter of no importance that the operations necessary for the production of its constituent elements were carried on at times which, referred to the present, are more remote than the final operation of spinning. If a definite quantity of labour, say thirty days, is requisite to build a house, the total amount of labour incorporated in it is not altered by the fact that the work of the last day is done twenty-nine days later than that of the first. Therefore, the labour contained in the raw material and the instruments of labour can be treated just as if it were labour expended in an earlier stage of the spinning process, before the labour of actual spinning commenced.

The values of the means of production, that is, the cotton and the spindle, which values are expressed in the price of twelve shillings, are therefore constituent parts of the value of the yarn, or, in other words, of the value of the product. Two conditions must nevertheless be fulfilled. First, the cotton and spindle must concur in the production of a use-value; they must in the present case become yarn. Value is independent of the particular use-value by which it is borne, but it must be embodied in a use-value of some kind. Second, the time occupied in the labour of production must not exceed the time really necessary under the given social conditions of the case. Therefore, if no more than 1 lb of cotton be requisite to spin 11 lbs of yarn, care must be taken that no more than this weight of cotton is consumed in the production of 11 lbs of yarn; and similarly with regard to the spindle. Though the capitalist have a hobby, and use a gold instead of a steel spindle, yet the only labour that counts for anything in the value of the yarn is that which would be required to produce a steel spindle, because no more is necessary under the given social conditions. We now know what portion of the value of the yarn is owing to the cotton and the spindle. It amounts to twelve shillings or the value of two days' work. The next point for our consideration is, what portion of the value of the yarn is added to the cotton by the labour of the spinner.

We have now to consider this labour under a very different aspect from that which it had during the labour-process; there, we viewed it solely as that particular kind of human activity which changes cotton into yarn; there, the more the labour was suited to the work, the better the yarn, other circumstances remaining the same. The labour of the spinner was then viewed as specifically different from other kinds of productive labour, different on the one hand in its special aim, namely spinning, different, on the other hand, in the special character of its operations, in the special nature of its means of production and in the special use-value of its product. For the operation of spinning, cotton and spindles are a necessity, but for making rifled cannon they would be of no use whatever. Here, on the contrary, where we consider the labour of the spinner only so far as it is value-creating, that is, a source of value, his labour differs in no respect from the labour of the man who bores cannon, or (what here more nearly concerns us), from the labour of the cotton-planter and spindle-maker incorporated in the means of production. It is solely by reason of this identity, that cotton planting, spindle making, and spinning, are capable of forming the component parts differing only quantitatively from each other, of one whole, namely the value of the yarn. Here, we have nothing more to do with the quality, the nature, and the specific character of the labour, but merely with its quantity. And this simply requires to be calculated. We proceed upon the assumption that spinning is simple, unskilled labour, the average labour of a given state of society. Hereafter, we shall see that the contrary assumption would make no difference.

While the labourer is at work, his labour constantly undergoes a transformation: from being motion, it becomes an object without motion; from being the labourer working, it becomes the thing produced. At the end of one hour's spinning, that act is represented by a definite quantity of yarn; in other words, a definite quantity of labour namely that of one hour, has become embodied in the cotton. We say labour, that is, the expenditure of his vital force by the spinner, and not spinning labour, because the special work of spinning counts here, only so far as it is the expenditure of labour-power in general, and not in so far as it is the specific work of the spinner.

In the process we are now considering it is of extreme importance, that no more time be consumed in the work of transforming the cotton into yarn than is necessary under the given social conditions. If under normal, that is, average social conditions of production, *a* lbs of cotton ought to be made into *b* lbs of yarn by one hour's labour, then a day's labour does not count as twelve hours' labour unless 12*a* lbs of cotton have been made into 12*b* lbs of yarn; for in the creation of value, the time that is socially necessary alone counts.

Not only the labour, but also the raw material and the product now appear in quite a new light, very different from that in which we viewed them in the labour-process pure and simple. The raw material serves now merely as an absorbent of a definite quantity of labour. By this absorption it is in fact changed into yarn, because it is spun, because labour-power in the form of spinning is added to it; but the product, the yarn, is now nothing more than a measure of the labour absorbed by the cotton. If in one hour $1\frac{2}{3}$ lbs of cotton can be spun into $1\frac{2}{3}$ lbs of yarn, then 10 lbs of yarn indicate the absorption of six hours' labour. Definite quantities of product, these quantities being determined by experience, now represent nothing but definite quantities of labour, definite masses of crystallised labour-time. They are nothing more than the materialisation of so many hours or so many days of social labour. We are here no more concerned about the facts, that the labour is the specific work of spinning, that its subject is cotton and its product yarn, than we are about the fact that the subject itself is already a product and therefore raw material. If the spinner, instead of spinning, were working in a coal mine, the subject of his labour, the coal, would be supplied by Nature; nevertheless, a definite quantity of extracted coal, a hundredweight for example, would represent a definite quantity of absorbed labour.

We assumed, on the occasion of its sale, that the value of a day's labour-power is three shillings, and that six hours' labour is incorporated in that sum; and consequently that this amount of labour is requisite to produce the necessaries of life daily required on an average by the labourer. If now our spinner by working for one hour, can convert $1\frac{2}{3}$ lbs of cotton into $1\frac{2}{3}$ lbs of yarn, it follows that in six hours he will convert 10 lbs of cotton into 10 lbs of yarn. Hence, during the spinning process, the cotton absorbs six hours' labour. The same quantity of labour is also embodied in a piece of gold of the value of three shillings. Consequently by the mere labour of spinning, a value of three shillings is added to the cotton.

Let us now consider the total value of the product, the 10 lbs of yarn. Two and a half days' labour has been embodied in it, of which two days were contained in the cotton and in the substance of the spindle worn away, and half a day was absorbed during the process of spinning. This two and a half days' labour is also represented by a piece of gold of the value of fifteen shillings. Hence, fifteen shillings is an adequate price for the 10 lbs of yarn, or the price of one pound is eighteen pence.

Our capitalist stares in astonishment. The value of the product is exactly equal to the value of the capital advanced. The value so advanced has not expanded, no surplus-value has been created, and consequently money has not been converted into capital. The price of the yarn is fifteen shillings, and fifteen shillings were spent in the open market upon the constituent elements of the product, or, what amounts to the same thing, upon the factors of the labour-process; ten shillings were paid for the cotton, two shillings for the substance of the spindle worn away, and three shillings for the labour-power. The swollen value of the yarn is of no avail, for it is merely the sum of the values formerly existing in the cotton, the spindle, and the labour-power: out of such a simple addition of existing values, no surplus-value can possibly arise. These separate values are now all concentrated in one thing; but so they were also in the sum of fifteen shillings, before it was split up into three parts, by the purchase of the commodities.

There is in reality nothing very strange in this result. The value of one pound of yarn being eighteen pence, if our capitalist buys 10 lbs of yarn in the market, he must pay fifteen shillings for them. It is clear that, whether a man buys his house ready built, or gets it built for him, in neither case will the mode of acquisition increase the amount of money laid out on the house.

Our capitalist, who is at home in his vulgar economy, exclaims: 'Oh! but I advanced my money for the express purpose of making more money.' The way to Hell is paved with good intentions, and he might just as easily have intended to make money, without producing at all. He threatens all sorts of things. He won't be caught napping again. In future he will buy the commodities in the market, instead of manufacturing them himself. But if all his brother capitalists were to do the same, where would he find his commodities in the market? And his money he cannot eat. He tries persuasion. 'Consider my abstinence; I might have played ducks and drakes with the 15 shillings; but instead of that I consumed it productively, and made yarn with it'. Very well, and by way of reward he is now in possession of good yarn instead of a bad conscience; and as for playing the part of a miser, it would never do for him to relapse into such bad ways as that; we have seen before to what results such asceticism leads. Besides, where nothing is, the king has lost his rights; whatever may be the merit of his abstinence, there is nothing wherewith specially to remunerate it, because the value of the product is merely the sum of the values of the commodities that were thrown into the process of production. Let him therefore console himself with the reflection that virtue is its own reward, But no, he becomes importunate. He says: 'The yarn is of no use to me: I produced it for sale'. In that case let him sell it, or, still better, let him for the future produce only things for satisfying his personal wants, a remedy that his physician MacCulloch has already prescribed as infallible against an epidemic of over-production. He now gets obstinate. 'Can the labourer', he asks, 'merely with his arms and legs, produce commodities out of nothing? Did I not supply him with the materials, by means of which, and in which alone, his labour could be embodied? And as the greater part of society consists of such ne'er-do-wells, have I not rendered society incalculable service by my instruments of production, my cotton and my spindle, and not only society, but the labourer also, whom in addition I have provided with the necessaries of life? And am I to be allowed nothing in return for all this service?' Well, but has not the labourer rendered him the equivalent service of changing his cotton and spindle into yarn? Moreover, there is here no question of service. A service is nothing more than the useful effect of a use-value, be it of a commodity, or be it of labour. But here we are dealing with exchange-value. The capitalist paid to the labourer a value of three shillings, and the labourer gave him back an exact equivalent in the value of three shillings, added by him to the cotton: he gave him value for value. Our friend, up to this time so purse-proud, suddenly assumes the modest demeanour of his own workman, and exclaims: 'Have I myself not worked? Have I not performed the labour of superintendence and of overlooking the spinner? And does not this labour, too, create value?' His overlooker and his manager try to hide their smiles. Meanwhile, after a hearty laugh, he re-assumes his usual mien. Though he chanted to us the whole creed of the economists, in reality, he says, he would not give a brass farthing for it. He leaves this and all such like subterfuges and juggling tricks to the professors of Political Economy, who are paid for it. He himself is a practical man; and though he does not always consider what he says outside his business, yet in his business he knows what he is about.

Let us examine the matter more closely. The value of a day's labour-power amounts to three shillings, because on our assumption half a day's labour is embodied in that quantity of labour-power, that is, because the means of subsistence that are daily required for the production of labour-power, cost half a day's labour. But the past labour that is embodied in the labour-power, and the living labour that it can call into action; the daily cost of maintaining it, and its daily expenditure in work, are two totally different things. The former determines the exchange-value of the labour-power, the latter is its use-value. The fact that half a day's labour is necessary to keep the labourer alive during twenty-four hours, does not in any way prevent him from working a whole day. Therefore, the value of labour-power, and the value which that labour-power creates in the labour-process, are two entirely different magnitudes; and this difference of the two values was what the capitalist had in view, when he was purchasing the labour-power. The useful qualities that labour-power possesses, and by virtue of which it makes yarn or boots, were to him nothing more than a *conditio sine qua non*; for in order to create value, labour must be expended in a useful manner. What really influenced him was the specific use-value which this commodity possesses of being a source not only of value, but of more value than it has itself. This is the special service that the capitalist expects from labour-power, and in this transaction he acts in accordance with the 'eternal laws' of the exchange of commodities. The seller of labour-power, like the seller of any other commodity, realises its exchange-value, and parts with its use-value. He cannot take the one without giving the other. The use-value of labour-power, or in other words, labour, belongs just as little to its seller, as the use-value of oil after it has been sold belongs to the dealer who has sold it. The owner of the money has paid the value of a day's labour-power; his, therefore, is the use of it for a day; a day's labour belongs to him. The circumstance that, on the one hand, the daily sustenance of labour-power costs only half a day's labour, while, on the other hand, the very same labour-power can work during a whole day, that consequently the value which its use during one day creates, is double what he pays for that use, this circumstance is, without doubt, a piece of good luck for the buyer, but by no means an injury to the seller.

Our capitalist foresaw this state of things, and that was the cause of his laughter. The labourer therefore finds, in the workshop, the means of production necessary for working, not only during six, but during twelve hours. Just as during the six hours' process our 10 lbs of cotton absorbed six hours' labour, and became 10 lbs of yarn, so now, 20 lbs of cotton will absorb twelve hours' labour and be changed into 20 lbs of yarn. Let us now examine the product of this prolonged process. There is now materialised in this 20 lbs of yarn the labour of five days, of which four days are due to the cotton and the lost steel of the spindle, the remaining day having been absorbed by the cotton during the spinning process. Expressed in gold, the labour of five days is thirty shillings. This is therefore the price of the 20 lbs of yarn, giving, as before, eighteenpence as the price of a pound. But the sum of the values of the commodities that entered into the process amounts to twenty-seven shillings. The value of the yarn is thirty shillings. Therefore, the value of the product is one-ninth greater than the value advanced for its production; twenty-seven shillings have been transformed into thirty shillings; a surplus-value of three shillings has been created. The trick has at last succeeded; money has been converted into capital.

Every condition of the problem is satisfied, while the laws that regulate the exchange of commodities, have been in no way violated. Equivalent has been exchanged for equivalent. For the capitalist as buyer paid for each commodity, for the cotton, the spindle and the labour-power, its full value. He then did what is done by every purchaser of commodities; he consumed their use-value. The consumption of the labour-power, which was also the process of producing commodities, resulted in 20 lbs of yarn, having a value of thirty shillings. The capitalist, formerly a buyer, now returns to market as a seller, of commodities. He sells his yarn at eighteen pence a pound, which is its exact value. Yet, for all that he withdraws three shillings more from circulation than he originally threw into it. This metamorphosis, this conversion of money into capital, takes place both within the sphere of circulation and also outside it; within the circulation, because conditioned by the purchase of the labour-power in the market; outside the circulation, because what is done within it is only a stepping-stone to the production of surplus-value, a process which is entirely confined to the sphere of production. Thus, 'tout est pour le mieux dans le meflleur des mondes possibles'.

By turning his money into commodities that serve as the material elements of a new product, and as factors in the labour-process, by incorporating living labour with their dead substance, the capitalist at the same time converts value, that is, past, materialised, and dead labour into capital, into value big with value, a live monster that is fruitful and multiplies.

If we now compare the two processes of producing value and of creating surplus-value, we see that the latter is nothing but the continuation of the former beyond a definite point. If, on the one hand, the process be not carried beyond the point, where the value paid by the capitalist for the labour-power is replaced by an exact equivalent, it is simply a process of producing value; if, on the other hand, it be continued beyond that point, it becomes a process of creating surplus-value.

If we proceed further, and compare the process of producing value with the labour-process, pure and simple, we find that the latter consists of the useful labour, the work, that produces use-values. Here we contemplate the labour as producing a particular article; we view it under its qualitative aspect alone, with regard to its end and aim. But viewed as a value-creating process, the same labour-process presents itself under its quantitative aspect alone. Here it is a question merely of the time occupied by the labourer in doing the work; of the period during which the labour-power is usefully expended. Here, the commodities that take part in the process, do not count any longer as necessary adjuncts of labour-power in the production of a definite, useful object. They count merely as depositories of so much absorbed or materialised labour; that labour, whether previously embodied in the means of production, or incorporated in them for the first time during the process by the action of labour-power, counts in either case only according to its duration; it amounts to so many hours or days as the case may be.

Moreover, only so much of the time spent in the production of any article is counted, as, under the given social conditions, is necessary. The consequences of this are various. In the first place, it becomes necessary that the labour should be carried on under normal conditions. If a self-acting mule is the implement in general use for spinning, it would be absurd to supply the spinner with a distaff and spinning wheel. The cotton too must not be such rubbish as to cause extra waste in being worked, but must be of suitable quality. Otherwise the spinner would be found to spend more time in producing a pound of yarn than is socially necessary, in which case the excess of time would create neither value nor money. But whether the material factors of the process are of normal quality or not, depends not upon the labourer, but entirely upon the capitalist. Then again, the labour-power itself must be of average efficacy. In the trade in which it is being employed, it must possess the average skill, handiness, and quickness prevalent in that trade, and our capitalist took good care to buy labour-power of such normal goodness. This power must be applied with the average amount of exertion and with the usual degree of intensity; and the capitalist is as careful to see that this is done, as that his workmen are not idle for a single moment. He has bought, the use of the labour-power for a definite period, and he insists upon his rights. He has no intention of being robbed. Lastly, and for this purpose our friend has a penal code of his own, all wasteful consumption of raw material or instruments of labour is strictly forbidden, because what is so wasted, represents labour superfluously expended, labour that does not count in the product or enter into its value. We now see, that the difference between labour, considered, on the one hand, as producing utilities, and on the other hand, as creating value, a difference which we discovered by our analysis of a commodity, resolves itself into a distinction between two aspects of the process of production.

The process of production, considered, on the one hand, as the unity of the labour-process and the process of creating value, is production of commodities; considered, on the other hand, as the unity of the labour-process and the process of producing surplus-value, it is the capitalist process of production, or capitalist production of commodities.

We stated, on a previous page, that in the creation of surplus-value it does not in the least matter, whether the labour appropriated by the capitalist be simple unskilled labour of average quality or more complicated skilled labour. All labour of a higher or more complicated character than average labour is expenditure of labour-power of a more costly kind, labour-power whose production has cost more time and labour, and which therefore has a higher value, than unskilled or simple labour-power. This power being higher-value, its consumption is labour of a higher class, labour that creates in equal times proportionally higher values than unskilled labour does. Whatever difference in skill there may be between the labour of a spinner and that of a jeweller, the portion of his labour by which the jeweller merely replaces the value of his own labour-power, does not in any way differ in quality from the additional portion by which he creates surplus-value. In the making of jewellery, just as in spinning, the surplus-value results only from a quantitative excess of labour, from a lengthening-out of one and the same labour-process, in the one case, of the process of making jewels, in the other of the process of making yarn. But on the other hand, in every process of creating value, the reduction of skilled labour to average social labour, for example, one day of skilled to six days of unskilled labour, is unavoidable. We therefore save ourselves a superfluous operation, and simplify our analysis, by the assumption, that the labour of the workman employed by the capitalist is unskilled average labour.

Part VII: The accumulation of capital

Chapter XXV: The general law of capitalist accumulation

Section 1: The increased demand for labour-power that accompanies accumulation, the composition of capital remaining the same

In this chapter we consider the influence of the growth of capital on the lot of the labouring class. The most important factor in this inquiry is the composition of capital and the changes it undergoes in the course of the process of accumulation.

The composition of capital is to be understood in a two-fold sense. On the side of value, it is determined by the proportion in which it is divided into constant capital or value of the means of production, and variable capital or value of labour-power, the sum total of wages. On the side of material, as it functions in the process of production, all capital is divided into means of production and living labour-power. This latter composition is determined by the relation between the mass of the means of production employed, on the one hand, and the mass of labour necessary for their employment on the other. I call the former the *value-composition*, the latter the *technical composition* of capital. Between the two there is a strict correlation. To express this, I call the value-composition of capital, in so far as it is determined by its technical composition and mirrors the changes of the latter, the *organic composition* of capital. Wherever I refer to the composition of capital, without further qualification, its organic composition is always understood.

The many individual capitals invested in a particular branch of production have, one with another, more or less different compositions. The average of the individual compositions gives us the composition of the total capital in this branch of production. Lastly, the average of these averages, in all branches of production, gives us the composition of the total social capital of a country, and with this alone are we, in the last resort, concerned in the following investigation.

Growth of capital involves growth of its variable constituent or of the part invested in labour-power. A part of the surplus-value turned into additional capital must always be re-transformed into variable capital, or additional labour-fund. If we suppose that, all other circumstances remaining the same, the composition of capital also remains constant (i.e. that a definite mass of means of production constantly needs the same mass of labour-power to set it in motion), then the demands for labour and the subsistence-fund of the labourers clearly increase in the same proportion as the capital, and the more rapidly, the more rapidly the capital increases. Since the capital produces yearly a surplus-value, of which one part is yearly added to the original capital; since this increment itself grows yearly along with the augmentation of the capital already functioning; since lastly, under special stimulus to enrichment, such as the opening of new markets, or of new spheres for the outlay of capital in consequence of newly developed social wants, etc., the scale of accumulation may be suddenly extended, merely by a change in the division of the surplus-value or surplus-product into capital and revenue, the requirements of accumulating capital may exceed the increase of labour-power or of the number of labourers; the demand for labourers may exceed the supply, and, therefore, wages may rise. This must, indeed, ultimately be the case if the conditions supposed above continue. For since in each year more labourers are employed than in its predecessor, sooner or later a point must be reached, at which the requirements of accumulation begin to surpass the customary supply of labour, and, therefore, a rise of wages takes place. A lamentation on this score was heard in England during the whole of the fifteenth, and the first half of the eighteenth centuries. The more or less favourable circumstances in which the wage-working class supports and multiplies itself, in no way alter the fundamental character of capitalist production. As simple reproduction constantly reproduces the capital-relation itself, that is, the relation of capitalists on the one hand, and wage-workers on the other, so reproduction on a progressive scale, that is, accumulation, reproduces the capital-relation on a progressive scale, more capitalists or larger capitalists at this pole, more wage-workers at that. The reproduction of a mass of labour-power, which must incessantly re-incorporate itself with capital for that capital's self-expansion; which cannot get free from capital, and whose enslavement to capital is only concealed by the variety of individual capitalists to whom it sells itself, this reproduction of labour-power forms, in fact, an essential of the reproduction of capital itself. Accumulation of capital is, therefore, increase of the proletariat.

...

The law of capitalist production, that is at the bottom of the pretended 'natural law of population', reduces itself simply to this: The correlation between accumulation of capital and rate of wages is nothing else than the correlation between the unpaid labour transformed into capital, and the additional paid labour necessary for the setting in motion of this additional capital. It is therefore in no way a relation between two magnitudes, independent one of the other: on the one hand, the magnitude of the capital; on the other, the number of the labouring population; it is rather, at bottom, only the relation between the unpaid and the paid labour of the same labouring population. If the quantity of unpaid labour supplied by the working class, and accumulated by the capitalist class, increases so rapidly that its conversion into capital requires an extraordinary addition of paid labour, then wages rise, and, all other circumstances remaining equal, the unpaid labour diminishes in proportion. But as soon as this diminution touches the point at which the surplus-labour that nourishes capital is no longer supplied in normal quantity, a reaction sets in: a smaller part of revenue is capitalised, accumulation lags, and the movement of rise in wages receives a check. The rise of wages therefore is confined within limits that not only leave intact the foundations of the capitalistic system, but also secure its reproduction on a progressive scale. The law of capitalistic accumulation, metamorphosed by economists into a pretended law of Nature, in reality merely states that the very nature of accumulation excludes every diminution in the degree of exploitation of labour, and every rise in the price of labour, which could seriously imperil the continual reproduction, on an ever-enlarging scale, of the capitalistic relation. It cannot be otherwise in a mode of production in which the labourer exists to satisfy the needs of self-expansion of existing values, instead of, on the contrary, material wealth existing to satisfy the needs of development on the part of the labourer. As, in religion, man is governed by the products of his own brain, so in capitalistic production, he is governed by the products of his own hand.

Section 3: Progressive production of a relative surplus-population or industrial reserve army

The accumulation of capital, though originally appearing as its quantitative extension only, is effected, as we have seen, under a progressive qualitative change in its composition, under a constant increase of its constant, at the expense of its variable constituent.

The specifically capitalist mode of production, the development of the productive power of labour corresponding to it, and the change thence resulting in the organic composition of capital, do not merely keep pace with the advance of accumulation, or with the growth of social wealth. They develop at a much quicker rate, because mere accumulation, the absolute increase of the total social capital, is accompanied by the centralisation of the individual capitals of which that total is made up; and because the change in the technological composition of the additional capital goes hand in hand with a similar change in the technological composition of the original capital. With the advance of accumulation, therefore, the proportion of constant to variable capital changes. If it was originally say $1:1$, it now becomes successively $2:1$, $3:1$, $4:1$, $5:1$, $7:1$, etc., so that, as the capital increases, instead of $1/2$ of its total value, only $1/3$, $1/4$, $1/5$, $1/6$, $1/8$, etc., is transformed into labour-power, and, on the other hand, $2/3$, $3/4$, $4/5$, $5/6$, $7/8$, into means of production. Since the demand for labour is determined not by the amount of capital as a whole, but by its variable constituent alone, that demand falls progressively with the increase of the total capital, instead of, as previously assumed, rising in proportion to it. It falls relatively to the magnitude of the total capital, and at an accelerated rate, as this magnitude increases. With the growth of the total capital, its variable constituent or the labour incorporated in it, also does increase, but in a constantly diminishing proportion. The intermediate pauses are shortened, in which accumulation works as simple extension of production, on a given technical basis. It is not merely that an accelerated accumulation of total capital, accelerated in a constantly growing progression, is needed to absorb an additional number of labourers, or even, on account of the constant metamorphosis of old capital, to keep employed those already functioning. In its turn, this increasing accumulation and centralisation becomes a source of new changes in the composition of capital, of a more accelerated diminution of its variable, as compared with its constant constituent. This accelerated relative diminution of the variable constituent, that goes along with the accelerated increase of the total capital, and moves more rapidly than this increase, takes the inverse form, at the other pole, of an apparently absolute increase of the labouring population, an increase always moving more rapidly than that of the variable capital or the means of employment. But in fact, it is capitalistic accumulation itself that constantly produces, and produces in the direct ratio of its own energy and extent, a relatively redundant population of labourers, that is, a population of greater extent than suffices for the average needs of the self-expansion of capital, and therefore a surplus-population.

Considering the social capital in its totality, the movement of its accumulation now causes periodical changes, affecting it more or less as a whole, now distributes its various phases simultaneously over the different spheres of production. In some spheres a change in the composition of capital occurs without increase of its absolute magnitude, as a consequence of simple centralisation; in others the absolute growth of capital is connected with absolute diminution of its variable constituent, or of the labour-power absorbed by it; in others again, capital continues growing for a time on its given technical basis, and attracts additional labour-power in proportion to its increase, while at other times it undergoes organic change, and lessens its variable constituent; in all spheres, the increase of the variable part of capital, and therefore of the number of labourers employed by it, is always connected with violent fluctuations and transitory production of surplus-population, whether this takes the more striking form of the repulsion of labourers already employed, or the less evident but not less real form of the more difficult absorption of the additional labouring population through the usual channels. With the magnitude of social capital already functioning, and the degree of its increase, with the extension of the scale of production, and the mass of the labourers set in motion, with the development of the productiveness of their labour, with the greater breadth and fullness of all sources of wealth, there is also an extension of the scale on which greater attraction of labourers by capital is accompanied by their greater repulsion; the rapidity of the change in the organic composition of capital, and in its technical form increases, and an increasing number of spheres of production become involved in this change, now simultaneously, now alternately. The labouring population therefore produces, along with the accumulation of capital produced by it, the means by which itself is made relatively superfluous, is turned into a relative surplus-population; and it does this to an always increasing extent. This is a law of population peculiar to the capitalist mode of production; and in fact every special historic mode of production has its own special laws of population, historically valid within its limits alone. An abstract law of population exists for plants and animals only, and only in so far as man has not interfered with them.

But if a surplus labouring population is a necessary product of accumulation or of the development of wealth on a capitalist basis, this surplus-population becomes, conversely, the lever of capitalistic accumulation, nay, a condition of existence of the capitalist mode of production. It forms a disposable industrial reserve army, that belongs to capital quite as absolutely as if the latter had bred it at its own cost. Independently of the limits of the actual increase of population, it creates, for the changing needs of the self-expansion of capital, a mass of human material always ready for exploitation. With accumulation, and the development of the productiveness of labour that accompanies it, the power of sudden expansion of capital grows also; it grows, not merely because the elasticity of the capital already functioning increases, not merely because the absolute wealth of society expands, of which capital only forms an elastic part, not merely because credit, under every special stimulus, at once places an unusual part of this wealth at the disposal of production in the form of additional capital; it grows, also, because the technical conditions of the process of production themselves – machinery, means of transport, etc. – now admit of the rapidest transformation of masses of surplus-product into additional means of production. The mass of social wealth, overflowing with the advance of accumulation, and transformable into additional capital, thrusts itself frantically into old branches of production, whose market suddenly expands, or into newly formed branches, such as railways, etc., the need for which grows out of the development of the old ones. In all such cases, there must be the possibility of throwing great masses of men suddenly on the decisive points without injury to the scale of production in other spheres. Over-population supplies these masses. The course characteristic of modern industry, namely a decennial cycle (interrupted by smaller oscillations), of periods of average activity, production at high pressure, crisis and stagnation, depends on the constant formation, the greater or less absorption, and the re-formation of the industrial reserve army or surplus-population. In their turn, the varying phases of the industrial cycle recruit the surplus-population, and become one of the most energetic agents of its reproduction. This peculiar course of modern industry, which occurs in no earlier period of human history, was also impossible in the childhood of capitalist production. The composition of capital changed but very slowly. With its accumulation, therefore, there kept pace, on the whole, a corresponding growth in the demand for labour. Slow as was the advance of accumulation compared with that of more modern times, it found a check in the natural limits of the exploitable labouring population, limits which could only be got rid of by forcible means to be mentioned later. The expansion by fits and starts of the scale of production is the preliminary to its equally sudden contraction; the latter again evokes the former, but the former is impossible without disposable human material, without an increase in the number of labourers independently of the absolute growth of the population. This increase is effected by the simple process that constantly 'sets free' a part of the labourers; by methods which lessen the number of labourers employed in proportion to the increased production. The whole form of the movement of modern industry depends, therefore, upon the constant transformation of a part of the labouring population into unemployed or half-employed hands. The superficiality of Political Economy shows itself in the fact that it looks upon the expansion and contraction of credit, which is a mere symptom of the periodic changes of the industrial cycle, as their cause. As the heavenly bodies, once thrown into a certain definite motion, always repeat this, so is it with social production as soon as it is once thrown into this movement of alternate expansion and contraction. Effects, in their turn, become causes, and the varying accidents of the whole process, which always reproduces its own conditions, take on the form of periodicity. When this periodicity is once consolidated, even Political Economy then sees that the production of a relative surplus population – that is, surplus with regard to the average needs of the self-expansion of capital – is a necessary condition of modern industry.

... Even Malthus recognises over-population as a necessity of modern industry, though, after his narrow fashion, he explains it by the absolute over-growth of the labouring population, not by their becoming relatively supernumerary. He says: 'Prudential habits with regard to marriage, carried to a considerable extent among the labouring class of a country mainly depending upon manufactures and commerce, might injure it. ... From the nature of a population, an increase of labourers cannot be brought into market in consequence of a particular demand till after the lapse of sixteen or eighteen years, and the conversion of revenue into capital, by saving, may take place much more rapidly; a country is always liable to an increase in the quantity of the funds for the maintenance of labour faster than the increase of population.' After Political Economy has thus demonstrated the constant production of a relative surplus-population of labourers to be a necessity of capitalistic accumulation, she very aptly, in the guise of an old maid, puts in the mouth of her 'beau ideal' of a capitalist the following words addressed to those supernumeraries thrown on the streets by their own creation of additional capital: 'We manufacturers do what we can for you, whilst we are increasing that capital on which you must subsist, and you must do the rest by accommodating your numbers to the means of subsistence'.

Capitalist production can by no means content itself with the quantity of disposable labour-power which the natural increase of population yields. It requires for its free play an industrial reserve army independent of these natural limits.

Up to this point it has been assumed that the increase or diminution of the variable capital corresponds rigidly with the increase or diminution of the number of labourers employed.

The number of labourers commanded by capital may remain the same, or even fall, while the variable capital increases. This is the case if the individual labourer yields more labour, and therefore his wages increase, and this although the price of labour remains the same or even falls, only more slowly than the mass of labour rises. Increase of variable capital, in this case, becomes an index of more labour, but not of more labourers employed. It is the absolute interest of every capitalist to press a given quantity of labour out of a smaller, rather than a greater number of labourers, if the cost is about the same. In the latter case, the outlay of constant capital increases in proportion to the mass of labour set in action; in the former that increase is much smaller. The more extended the scale of production, the stronger this motive. Its force increases with the accumulation of capital.

We have seen that the development of the capitalist mode of production and of the productive power of labour – at once the cause and effect of accumulation – enables the capitalist, with the same outlay of variable capital, to set in action more labour by greater exploitation (extensive or intensive) of each individual labour-power. We have further seen that the capitalist buys with the same capital a greater mass of labour-power, as he progressively replaces skilled labourers by less skilled, mature labour-power by immature, male by female, that of adults by that of young persons or children.

On the one hand, therefore, with the progress of accumulation, a larger variable capital sets more labour in action without enlisting more labourers; on the other, a variable capital of the same magnitude sets in action more labour with the same mass of labour-power; and finally, a greater number of inferior labour-powers by displacement of higher.

The production of a relative surplus-population, or the setting free of labourers, goes on therefore yet more rapidly than the technical revolution of the process of production that accompanies, and is accelerated by, the advance of accumulation; and more rapidly than the corresponding diminution of the variable part of capital as compared with the constant. If the means of production, as they increase in extent and effective power, become to a less extent means of employment of labourers, this state of things is again modified by the fact that in proportion as the productiveness of labour increases, capital increases its supply of labour more quickly than its demand for labourers. The overwork of the employed part of the working class swells the ranks of the reserve, whilst conversely the greater pressure that the latter by its competition exerts on the former, forces these to submit to over-work and to subjugation under the dictates of capital. The condemnation of one part of the working class to enforced idleness by the over-work of the other part, and the converse, becomes a means of enriching the individual capitalists, and accelerates at the same time the production of the industrial reserve army on a scale corresponding with the advance of social accumulation. How important is this element in the formation of the relative surplus-population, is shown by the example of England. Her technical means for saving labour are colossal. Nevertheless, if to-morrow morning labour generally were reduced to a rational amount, and proportioned to the different sections of the working class according to age and sex, the working population to hand would be absolutely insufficient for the carrying on of national production on its present scale. The great majority of the labourers now 'unproductive' would have to be turned into 'productive' ones.

Taking them as a whole, the general movements of wages are exclusively regulated by the expansion and contraction of the industrial reserve army, and these again correspond to the periodic changes of the industrial cycle. They are, therefore, not determined by the variations of the absolute number of the working population, but by the varying proportions in which the working class is divided into active and reserve army, by the increase or diminution in the relative amount of the surplus-population, by the extent to which it is now absorbed, now set free. For Modern Industry with its decennial cycles and periodic phases, which, moreover, as accumulation advances, are complicated by irregular oscillations following each other more and more quickly, that would indeed be a beautiful law, which pretends to make the action of capital dependent on the absolute variation of the population, instead of regulating the demand and supply of labour by the alternate expansion and contraction of capital, the labour-market now appearing relatively under-full, because capital is expanding, now again over-full, because it is contracting. Yet, this is the dogma of the economists. According to them, wages rise in consequence of accumulation of capital. The higher wages stimulate the working population to more rapid multiplication, and this goes on until the labour-market becomes too full, and therefore capital, relatively to the supply of labour, becomes insufficient. Wages fall, and now we have the reverse of the medal. The working population is little by little decimated as the result of the fall in wages, so that capital is again in excess relatively to them, or, as others explain it, falling wages and the corresponding increase in the exploitation of the labourer again accelerates accumulation, whilst, at the same time, the lower wages hold the increase of the working class in check. Then comes again the time, when the supply of labour is less than the demand, wages rise, and so on. A beautiful mode of motion this for developed capitalist production! Before, in consequence of the rise of wages, any positive increase of the population really fit for work could occur, the time would have been passed again and again, during which the industrial campaign must have been carried through, the battle fought and won.

...

The industrial reserve army, during the periods of stagnation and average prosperity, weighs down the active labour-army; during the periods of over-production and paroxysm, it holds its pretensions in check. Relative surplus-population is therefore the pivot upon which the law of demand and supply of labour works. It confines the field of action of this law within the limits absolutely convenient to the activity of exploitation and to the domination of capital.

This is the place to return to one of the grand exploits of economic apologetics. It will be remembered that if through the introduction of new, or the extension of old, machinery, a portion of variable capital is transformed into constant, the economic apologist interprets this operation which 'fixes' capital and by that very act sets labourers 'free', in exactly the opposite way, pretending that it sets free capital for the labourers. Only now can one fully understand the effrontery of these apologists. What are set free are not only the labourers immediately turned out by the machines, but also their future substitutes in the rising generation, and the additional contingent, that with the usual extension of trade on the old basis would be regularly absorbed. They are now all 'set free', and every new bit of capital looking out for employment can dispose of them. Whether it attracts them or others, the effect on the general labour demand will be nil, if this capital is just sufficient to take out of the market as many labourers as the machines threw upon it. If it employs a smaller number, that of the supernumeraries increases; if it employs a greater, the general demand for labour only increases to the extent of the excess of the employed over those 'set free'. The impulse that additional capital, seeking an outlet, would otherwise have given to the general demand for labour, is therefore in every case neutralised to the extent of the labourers thrown out of employment by the machine. That is to say, the mechanism of capitalistic production so manages matters that the absolute increase of capital is accompanied by no corresponding rise in the general demand for labour. And this the apologist calls a compensation for the misery, the sufferings, the possible death of the displaced labourers during the transition period that banishes them into the industrial reserve army! The demand for labour is not identical with increase of capital, nor supply of labour with increase of the working class. It is not a case of two independent forces working on one another. *Les dés sont pipés.* Capital works on both sides at the same time. If its accumulation, on the one hand, increases the demand for labour, it increases on the other the supply of labourers by the 'setting free' of them, whilst at the same time the pressure of the unemployed compels those that are employed to furnish more labour, and therefore makes the supply of labour, to a certain extent, independent of the supply of labourers. The action of the law of supply and demand of labour on this basis completes the despotism of capital. As soon, therefore, as the labourers learn the secret, how it comes to pass that in the same measure as they work more, as they produce more wealth for others, and as the productive power of their labour increases, so in the same measure even their function as a means of the self-expansion of capital becomes more and more precarious for them; as soon as they discover that the degree of intensity of the competition among themselves depends wholly on the pressure of the relative surplus-population; as soon as, by Trades' Unions, etc., they try to organize a regular co-operation between employed and unemployed in order to destroy or to weaken the ruinous effects of this natural law of capitalistic production on their class, so soon capital and its sycophant, Political Economy, cry out at the infringement of the 'eternal' and so to say 'sacred' law of supply and demand. Every combination of employed and unemployed disturbs the 'harmonious' action of this law. But, on the other hand, as soon as (in the colonies, for example) adverse circumstances prevent the creation of an industrial reserve army and, with it, the absolute dependence of the working class upon the capitalist class, capital, along with its commonplace Sancho Panza, rebels against the 'sacred' law of supply and demand, and tries to check its inconvenient action by forcible means and State interference.

Section 4: Different forms of the relative surplus-population – the general law of capitalistic accumulation

...

... Pauperism is the hospital of the active labour-army and the dead weight of the industrial reserve army. Its production is included in that of the relative surplus-population, its necessity in theirs; along with the surplus-population, pauperism forms a condition of capitalist production, and of the capitalist development of wealth. It enters into the *faux frais* of capitalist production; but capital knows how to throw these, for the most part, from its own shoulders on to those of the working class and the lower middle class.

The greater the social wealth, the functioning capital, the extent and energy of its growth, and, therefore, also the absolute mass of the proletariat and the productiveness of its labour, the greater is the industrial reserve army. The same causes which develop the expansive power of capital, develop also the labour-power at its disposal. The relative mass of the industrial reserve army increases therefore with the potential energy of wealth. But the greater this reserve army in proportion to the active labour-army, the greater is the mass of a consolidated surplus-population, whose misery is in inverse ratio to its torment of labour. The more extensive, finally, the lazarus-layers of the working class, and the industrial reserve army, the greater is official pauperism. *This is the absolute general law of capitalist accumulation.* Like all other laws it is modified in its working by many circumstances, the analysis of which does not concern us here.

The folly is now patent of the economic wisdom that preaches to the labourers the accommodation of their number to the requirements of capital. The mechanism of capitalist production and accumulation constantly effects this adjustment. The first word of this adaptation is the creation of a relative surplus-population, or industrial reserve army. Its last word is the misery of constantly extending strata of the active army of labour, and the dead weight of pauperism.

The law by which a constantly increasing quantity of means of production, thanks to the advance in the productiveness of social labour, may be set in movement by a progressively diminishing expenditure of human power, this law, in a capitalist society – where the labourer does not employ the means of production, but the means of production employ the labourer – undergoes a complete inversion and is expressed thus: the higher the productiveness of labour, the greater is the pressure of the labourers on the means of employment, the more precarious, therefore, becomes their condition of existence, namely the sale of their own labour-power for the increasing of another's wealth, or for the self-expansion of capital. The fact that the means of production, and the productiveness of labour, increase more rapidly than the productive population, expresses itself, therefore, capitalistically in the inverse form that the labouring population always increases more rapidly than the conditions under which capital can employ this increase for its own self-expansion.

We saw in Part IV, when analysing the production of relative surplus-value: within the capitalist system all methods for raising the social productiveness of labour are brought about at the cost of the individual labourer; all means for the development of production transform themselves into means of domination over, and exploitation of, the producers; they mutilate the labourer into a fragment of a man, degrade him to the level of an appendage of a machine, destroy every remnant of charm in his work and turn it into a hated toil; they estrange from him the intellectual potentialities of the labour-process in the same proportion as science is incorporated in it as an independent power; they distort the conditions under which he works, subject him during the labour-process to a despotism the more hateful for its meanness; they transform his life-time into working-time, and drag his wife and child beneath the wheels of the Juggernaut of capital. But all methods for the production of surplus-value are at the same time methods of accumulation; and every extension of accumulation becomes again a means for the development of those methods. It follows therefore that in proportion as capital accumulates, the lot of the labourer, be his payment high or low, must grow worse. The law, finally, that always equilibrates the relative surplus-population, or industrial reserve army, to the extent and energy of accumulation, this law rivets the labourer to capital more firmly than the wedges of Vulcan did Prometheus to the rock. It establishes an accumulation of misery, corresponding with accumulation of capital. Accumulation of wealth at one pole is, therefore, at the same time accumulation of misery, agony of toil, slavery, ignorance, brutality, mental degradation, at the opposite pole, that is, on the side of the class that produces its own product in the form of capital.

...

Part VIII: The so-called primitive accumulation

Chapter XXVI: The secret of primitive accumulation

We have seen how money is changed into capital; how through capital surplus-value is made, and from surplus-value more capital. But the accumulation of capital pre-supposes surplus-value; surplus-value pre-supposes capitalistic production; capitalistic production pre-supposes the pre-existence of considerable masses of capital and of labour-power in the hands of producers of commodities. The whole movement, therefore, seems to turn in a vicious circle, out of which we can only get by supposing a primitive accumulation (previous accumulation of Adam Smith) preceding capitalistic accumulation; an accumulation not the result of the capitalist mode of production but its starting point.

This primitive accumulation plays in Political Economy about the same part as original sin in theology. Adam bit the apple, and thereupon sin fell on the human race. Its origin is supposed to be explained when it is told as an anecdote of the past. In times long gone by there were two sorts of people; one, the diligent, intelligent, and above all, frugal elite; the other, lazy rascals, spending their substance, and more, in riotous living. The legend of theological original sin tells us certainly how man came to be condemned to eat his bread in the sweat of his brow; but the history of economic original sin reveals to us that there are people to whom this is by no means essential. Never mind! Thus it came to pass that the former sort accumulated wealth, and the latter sort had at last nothing to sell except their own skins. And from this original sin dates the poverty of the great majority that, despite all its labour, has up to now nothing to sell but itself, and the wealth of the few that increases constantly although they have long ceased to work. Such insipid childishness is every day preached to us in the defence of property. M. Thiers, for example, had the assurance to repeat it with all the solemnity of a statesman, to the French people, once so *spirituel*. But as soon as the question of property crops up, it becomes a sacred duty to proclaim the intellectual food of the infant as the one thing fit for all ages and for all stages of development. In actual history it is notorious that conquest, enslavement, robbery, murder, briefly force, play the great part. In the tender annals of Political Economy, the idyllic reigns from time immemorial. Right and 'labour' were from all time the sole means of enrichment, the present year, of course, always excepted. As a matter of fact, the methods of primitive accumulation are anything but idyllic.

In themselves money and commodities are no more capital than are the means of production and of subsistence. They want transforming into capital. But this transformation itself can only take place under certain circumstances that centre in this, namely, that two very different kinds of commodity-possessors must come face to face and into contact; on the one hand, the owners of money, means of production, means of subsistence, who are eager to increase the sum of values they possess, by buying other people's labour-power; on the other hand, free labourers, the sellers of their own labour-power, and therefore the sellers of labour. Free labourers, in the double sense that neither they themselves form part and parcel of the means of production, as in the case of slaves, bondsmen, etc., nor do the means of production belong to them, as in the case of peasant-proprietors; they are, therefore, free from, unencumbered by, any means of production of their own. With this polarisation of the market for commodities, the fundamental conditions of capitalist production are given. The capitalist system pre-supposes the complete separation of the labourers from all property in the means by which they can realise their labour. As soon as capitalist production is once on its own legs, it not only maintains this separation, but reproduces it on a continually extending scale. The process, therefore, that clears the way for the capitalist system, can be none other than the process which takes away from the labourer the possession of his means of production; a process that transforms, on the one hand, the social means of subsistence and of production into capital, on the other, the immediate producers into wage-labourers. The so-called primitive accumulation, therefore, is nothing else than the historical process of divorcing the producer from the means of production. It appears as primitive, because it forms the pre-historic stage of capital and of the mode of production corresponding with it.

The economic structure of capitalistic society has grown out of the economic structure of feudal society. The dissolution of the latter set free the elements of the former.

The immediate producer, the labourer, could only dispose of his own person after he had ceased to be attached to the soil and ceased to be the slave, serf, or bondman of another. To become a free seller of labour-power, who carries his commodity wherever he finds a market, he must further have escaped from the regime of the guilds, their rules for apprentices and journeymen, and the impediments of their labour regulations. Hence, the historical movement which changes the producers into wage-workers, appears, on the one hand, as their emancipation from serfdom and from the fetters of the guilds, and this side alone exists for our bourgeois historians. But, on the other hand, these new freedmen became sellers of themselves only after they had been robbed of all their own means of production, and of all the guarantees of existence afforded by the old feudal arrangements. And the history of this, their expropriation, is written in the annals of mankind in letters of blood and fire.

The industrial capitalists, these new potentates, had on their part not only to displace the guild masters of handicrafts, but also the feudal lords, the possessors of the sources of wealth. In this respect their conquest of social power appears as the fruit of a victorious struggle both against feudal lordship and its revolting prerogatives, and against the guilds and the fetters they laid on the free development of production and the free exploitation of man by man. The *chevaliers d'industrie*, however, only succeeded in supplanting the chevaliers of the sword by making use of events of which they themselves were wholly innocent. They have risen by means as vile as those by which the Roman freedman once on a time made himself the master of his *patronus*.

The starting-point of the development that gave rise to the wage-labourer as well as to the capitalist, was the servitude of the labourer. The advance consisted in a change of form of this servitude, in the transformation of feudal exploitation into capitalist exploitation. To understand its march, we need not go back very far. Although we come across the first beginnings of capitalist production as early as the fourteenth or fifteenth century, sporadically, in certain towns of the Mediterranean, the capitalistic era dates from the sixteenth century. Wherever it appears, the abolition of serfdom has been long effected, and the highest development of the middle ages, the existence of sovereign towns, has been long on the wane.

In the history of primitive accumulation, all revolutions are epoch-making that act as levers for the capitalist class in course of formation; but, above all, those moments when great masses of men are suddenly and forcibly torn from their means of subsistence, and buried as free and 'unattached' proletarians on the labour-market. The expropriation of the agricultural producer, of the peasant, from the soil, is the basis of the whole process. The history of this expropriation, in different countries, assumes different aspects, and runs through its various phases in different orders of succession, and at different periods. In England alone, which we take as our example, has it the classic form.

Chapter XXXII: Historical tendency of capitalist accumulation

What does the primitive accumulation of capital, that is, its historical genesis, resolve itself into? In so far as it is not immediate transformation of slaves and serfs into wage-labourers, and therefore a mere change of form, it only means the expropriation of the immediate producers, that is, the dissolution of private property based on the labour of its owner. Private property, as the antithesis to social, collective property, exists only where the means of labour and the external conditions of labour belong to private individuals. But according as these private individuals are labourers or not labourers, private property has a different character. The numberless shades, that it at first sight presents, correspond to the intermediate stages lying between these two extremes. The private property of the labourer in his means of production is the foundation of petty industry, whether agricultural, manufacturing, or both; petty industry, again, is an essential condition for the development of social production and of the free individuality of the labourer himself. Of course, this petty mode of production exists also under slavery, serfdom, and other states of dependence. But it flourishes, it lets loose its whole energy, it attains its adequate classical form, only where the labourer is the private owner of his own means of labour set in action by himself: the peasant of the land which he cultivates, the artisan of the tool which he handles as a virtuoso. This mode of production pre-supposes parcelling of the soil, and scattering of the other means of production. As it excludes the concentration of these means of production, so also it excludes co-operation, division of labour within each separate process of production, the control over, and the productive application of the forces of Nature by society, and the free development of the social productive powers. It is compatible only with a system of production, and a society, moving within narrow and more or less primitive bounds. To perpetuate it would be, as Pecqueur rightly says, 'to decree universal mediocrity'. At a certain stage of development it brings forth the material agencies for its own dissolution. From that moment new forces and new passions spring up in the bosom of society; but the old social organisation fetters them and keeps them down. It must be annihilated; it is annihilated. Its annihilation, the transformation of the individualised and scattered means of production into socially concentrated ones, of the pigmy property of the many into the huge property of the few, the expropriation of the great mass of the people from the soil, from the means of subsistence, and from the means of labour, this fearful and painful expropriation of the mass of the people forms the prelude to the history of capital. It comprises a series of forcible methods, of which we have passed in review only those that have been epoch-making as methods of the primitive accumulation of capital. The expropriation of the immediate producers was accomplished with merciless Vandalism, and under the stimulus of passions the most infamous, the most sordid, the pettiest, the most meanly odious. Self-earned private property, that is based, so to say, on the fusing together of the isolated, independent labouring-individual with the conditions of his labour, is supplanted by capitalistic private property, which rests on exploitation of the nominally free labour of others, that is, on wage-labour.

As soon as this process of transformation has sufficiently decomposed the old society from top to bottom, as soon as the labourers are turned into proletarians, their means of labour into capital, as soon as the capitalist mode of production stands on its own feet, then the further socialisation of labour and further transformation of the land and other means of production into socially exploited and, therefore, common means of production, as well as the further expropriation of private proprietors, takes a new form. That which is now to be expropriated is no longer the labourer working for himself, but the capitalist exploiting many labourers. This expropriation is accomplished by the action of the immanent laws of capitalistic production itself, by the centralisation of capital. One capitalist always kills many. Hand in hand with this centralisation, or this expropriation of many capitalists by a few, develop, on an ever-extending scale, the co-operative form of the labour-process, the conscious technical application of science, the methodical cultivation of the soil, the transformation of the instruments of labour into instruments of labour only usable in common, the economising of all means of production by their use as the means of production of combined, socialised labour, the entanglement of all peoples in the net of the world-market, and with this, the international character of the capitalistic regime. Along with the constantly diminishing number of the magnates of capital, who usurp and monopolise all advantages of this process of transformation, grows the mass of misery, oppression, slavery, degradation, exploitation; but with this too grows the revolt of the working class, a class always increasing in numbers, and disciplined, united, organised by the very mechanism of the process of capitalist production itself. The monopoly of capital becomes a fetter upon the mode of production, which has sprung up and flourished along with, and under it. Centralisation of the means of production and socialisation of labour at last reach a point where they become incompatible with their capitalist integument. This integument is burst asunder. The knell of capitalist private property sounds. The expropriators are expropriated.

The capitalist mode of appropriation, the result of the capitalist mode of production, produces capitalist private property. This is the first negation of individual private property, as founded on the labour of the proprietor. But capitalist production begets, with the inexorability of a law of Nature, its own negation. It is the negation of negation. This does not re-establish private property for the producer, but gives him individual property based on the acquisitions of the capitalist era: that is, on co-operation and the possession in common of the land and of the means of production.

The transformation of scattered private property, arising from individual labour, into capitalist private property is, naturally, a process, incomparably more protracted, violent, and difficult, than the transformation of capitalistic private property, already practically resting on socialised production, into socialised property. In the former case, we had the expropriation of the mass of the people by a few usurpers; in the latter, we have the expropriation of a few usurpers by the mass of the people.

Part 4

The Marginal Revolution

Introduction

Socialism – or Socialism, Romanticism, and Anarchism – were not the only responses to both Classical Political Economy and the new economic system which the Classical economists were seeking to both explicate and promote. Another response – actually a response to both Classical Political Economy and Socialism – was that of the so-called marginal revolution of the 1870s. Still another was the historical approach of schools in England and Germany.

By roughly 1870, political economy, or economics as it was increasingly coming to be called, exhibited something of an identity crisis. The crisis, which remains largely unresolved well over a century later, had several elements: (1) The name of the discipline: political economy or economics – surely a central aspect of identity. (2) The status of the founding fathers: Quesnay, Smith, Ricardo, the other Classical economists – surely another central aspect of identity. (3) Ambiguity and conflict in value theory, the field deemed by many to be central to the discipline, the core of economic theory. (4) The multiplicity and diversity of schools of economic thought – a further aspect of confused identity. (5) The threat of Marxian economics and philosophy, and of socialism in general, to economics and to the Western economic, political and social system; and the status of the status quo – increasingly defined in economic terms – in general. Where economics stood on all this. (6) The identity of economics as a science: (a) its epistemological, or methodological, character; (b) its central problem of analysis; and (c) its own identity (supra). (7) Disagreements over fundamental terms, for example, capital, money, investment, and so on.

The marginalist response germinating in the 1870s led to the discipline, now largely called economics, having certain structural and substantive characteristics in the twentieth century, especially after the 1940s. The structural characteristics included: (1) the hegemony of neoclassical economics; (2) the heterogeneity of neoclassical economics; (3) the heterogeneity of an array of heterodox schools of economic thought; and (4) the resultant heterogeneity of economics as a whole, neoclassical hegemony notwithstanding. The heterogeneity was a consequence of the efforts of different schools and of different factions (on particular substantive and methodological issues) within individual schools working out the elements of the identity crisis differently from each other.

The substantive characteristics of the increasingly ascendent neoclassicism – equated by many within the school with economics as such – included: (1) Formal price theory replaced value theory, founded upon (a) the general but not ubiquitous demise of belief in some absolute and invariant basis of price and (b) the rise of the demand and supply model incorporating both cost of production and utility theories, formerly of value but now of their respective curves (functions). Other schools, such as the Austrians and the Marxists, retained a belief in value theory as distinct from price theory; and the institutionalists had quite different ideas, some holding a technological theory of value and others analyzing the values ensconced within the working rules of law and morals. (2) Economics as the explication of the market mechanism, largely devoid of considerations of social and institutional structure and change. Neoclassicism eventually adopted the model of a pure abstract conceptual a-institutional market economy, in marked contrast to the view of those, largely but not solely of an institutionalist persuasion, that markets were a function of and gave effect to the institutions which formed and operated through them. The neoclassical model, which earlier had been treated as a set of conceptual tools with which to then analyze the economy, increasingly became treated as a definition of economic reality itself. (3) Economic categories became increasingly narrow. As neoclassical economics increasingly centered on pure exchange, considerations of social structure evaporated; for example, what the Classical economists identified as social classes, the neoclassicists called factors of production: land, labor, and capital. (4) The neoclassical focus was on what eventually came to be called microeconomic analysis: on the role of the price mechanism in the allocation of resources, accompanied by theories of abstract households and firms. (5) The conduct of microeconomic analysis in largely, though not entirely, partial static equilibrium terms, supplemented by a concept of general equilibrium, all formulated differently by different economists. (6) The development of a neoclassical research protocol calling for the creation of unique determinate optimal equilibrium solutions for all problems – in contrast with the earlier Marshallian (see below) approach in which economics is the science of conflicting tendencies, not unique solutions which also were deemed optimal. (7) The development of period analysis – especially short run and long run; eventually year one and year two – as conceptual tools. (8) The development of the theory of distribution on two levels: (a) particular theories of particular factors of production, multiple in number; and (b) generalized theories encompassing all factors of production: opportunity cost and marginal productivity theories.

The neoclassicism which emerged relatively triumphant after the 1960s was given a variety of central meanings or problems. These included analysis of: (1) the pure market, or price mechanism; (2) the allocation of resources; (3) constrained-maximization decision-making; and (4) the logic of choice. Such heterogeneity is not surprising, given that marginalism itself had several different connotations, including: (1) the marginal utility theory of value; (2) constrained maximization; and (3) marginal adjustments.

The heterogeneous structure and diverse substantive content of economics in the twentieth century resulted from different ways of trying to resolve the identity crisis of the late nineteenth century. Although still not resolved, it seems that developments had certain motivations, but conscious and unarticulated. These included: (1) The quest for social status, especially to have economics recognized as a science. This was complicated by the fact that the concept "science" meant different things to different people. It was advanced, in part, by those who wanted economists to speak with one voice – of course, theirs – and to be safe in a world of controversy and ideological subversion. (2) The desire for the social role of the expert, the man (as the discipline mainly encompassed) of knowledge. The combination of (1) and (2) gave rise to a tension between objectivity and advocacy. (3) The desire to have something authoritative to say about the economic role of government, that is, as to "sound" economic policy.

In all that economics increasingly came to perform three social roles: (1) the provision of authoritative economic knowledge, both for its own sake and as a basis for policy; (2) the provision of psychic balm, in the form of claims of harmony and optimality, of coherence and of meaningfulness, in the face of apparent conflict and confusion; and (3) the provision of social control, in the form of (a) putatively definitive answers to questions of policy and (b) legitimation of some idealized model of the modern, market economic system.

The marginal revolution had multiple sources and indeed multiple precursors. The precursors were primarily economists who had earlier adopted the subjective utility theory of value or applied the analysis of the margin to production and supply – including Mountifort Longfield, Jules Dupuit, Augustin Cournot, Johann Heinrich von Thünen, and Hermann Heinrich Gossen. The principal sources were the writings of several men: the English economist William Stanley Jevons; the Austrian School economist Carl Menger – together with several others, including Eugen von Böhm-Bawerk and Friedrich von Wieser; the French economist Leon Walras; and the English economist Alfred Marshall – and others, such as Francis Y. Edgeworth and Arthur Cecil Pigou.

References and further reading

Black, R.D.C. *et al.*, eds (1972) *The Marginal Revolution in Economics*, Durham, NC: Duke University Press.

Fisher, Robert M. (1986) *The Logic of Scientific Discovery: Neoclassical Economics and the Marginal Revolution*, New York: Columbia University Press.

Hennings, Klaus and Samuels, Warren J., eds (1989) *Neoclassical Economic Theory, 1870–1930*, Boston: Kluwer.

Howey, R.S. (1960) *The Rise of the Marginal Utility School, 1870–1899*, Lawrence, KS: University Press of Kansas.

Hutchison, T.W. (1953) *A Review of Economic Doctrines, 1870–1929*, New York: Oxford University Press.

——(1978) *On Revolutions and Progress in Economic Knowledge*, Cambridge: Cambridge University Press.

Kauder, E. (1965) *A History of Marginal Utility Theory*, Princeton: Princeton University Press.

Jaffé, William (1976) "Menger, Jevons and Walras De-Homogenized," *Economic Inquiry* 14 (December): 511–24.

Mirowski, Philip (1989) *More Heat Than Light: Economics as Social Physics, Physics as Nature's Economics*, Cambridge: Cambridge University Press.

Stigler, George J. (1941) *Production and Distribution Theories: The Formative Period*, New York: Macmillan.

WILLIAM STANLEY JEVONS (1835–1882)

William Stanley Jevons was born in Liverpool and educated at University College, London, where, due to his family's financial misfortunes, his studies were interrupted by a five-year period during which he served as assayer to the Mint in Sydney, Australia. His early education was in mathematics and chemistry, but his return to England saw him broaden his studies to include logic and economics. After completing his M.A. in 1862, he held academic positions at Owens College, Manchester, and, from 1876, University College, London. Jevons died by drowning at the age of forty-six.

Jevons was one of the foremost virtuoso economists of all time. Although he technically reduced economics – or economic theory, often equated with economics – to the mechanics of utility and self-interest, he did economics, and did it remarkably well, in a variety of ways. He wrote on pure theory, especially advocating the marginal utility theory of value. He conducted historical and statistical studies of the coal industry and of currency and finance, and historical and institutional analysis of the state in relation to labor as well as on social reform. He did empirical work on business cycles. And he wrote on the philosophy of science and logic.

Unlike Alfred Marshall, who, although a major participant in the "marginal revolution," saw himself as putting forth a body of theory consistent with that of his classical predecessors, Jevons was self-consciously revolutionary in attempting to promulgate a body of theory to replace what he saw as the erroneous ideas of Ricardo and, especially, J.S. Mill.

The excerpts from Jevons's *Theory of Political Economy* reprinted here are illustrative of his desire to build upon Bentham's calculus of pleasure and pain and to center this "new" economics on the principle of marginal utility (called "final degree of utility" by Jevons). His attempt to distance himself from the classical approach is evidenced in his marginal utility theory of value. The last part of this reading introduces the reader to Jevons's famous analysis of the labor supply decision in terms of balancing the marginal utility of the produce of labor against the marginal disutility of the labor itself.

References and further reading

Black, R.D.C. (1972) "Jevons, Bentham and De Morgan," *Economica* 39: 119–34.

——(1987) "Jevons, William Stanley," in John Eatwell, Murray Milgate, and Peter Newman (eds), *The New Palgrave: A Dictionary of Economics*, Vol. 2, London: Macmillan, 1008–13.

Hutchison, T.W. (1982) "The Politics and Philosophy in Jevons's Political Economy," *The Manchester School* 50 (4): 366–79.

Jevons, W.S. (1865) *The Coal Question*, London: Macmillan.

——(1875) *Money and the Mechanism of Exchange*, London: C. Kegan & Paul.

——(1882) *The State in Relation to Labour*, London: Macmillan.

——(1972–1981) *Papers and Correspondence of William Stanley Jevons*, 7 vols, edited by R.D.C. Black and R. Könekamp, London: Macmillan for the Royal Economic Society.

Keynes, J.M. (1936) "William Stanley Jevons, 1835–1882: A Centenary Allocution on His Life and Work as Economist and Statistician," reprinted in J.M. Keynes, *Essays in Biography*, London: Rupert Hart-Davis, 1951, 255–308.

Laidler, David (1982) "Jevons on Money," *The Manchester School* 50 (4): 326–53.

Peach, Terry (1987) "Jevons as an Economic Theorist," in John Eatwell, Murray Milgate, and Peter Newman (eds), *The New Palgrave: A Dictionary of Economics*, Vol. 2, London: Macmillan, 1014–19.

Peart, Sandra (1996) *The Economics of W.S. Jevons*, London: Routledge.

Robbins, Lionel (1936) "The Place of Jevons in the History of Economic Thought," reprinted in Lionel Robbins, *The Evolution of Modern Economic Theory*, 1970, 169–88.

Schabas, Margaret (1990) *A World Ruled by Number: William Stanley Jevons and the Rise of Mathematical Economics*, Princeton: Princeton University Press.

Warke, Tom (2000) "Mathematical Fitness in the Utility Concept from Bentham to Jevons to Marshall," *Journal of the History of Economic Thought* 22 (March): 5–27.

The Theory of Political Economy (1871)

Chapter I: Introduction

The science of Political Economy rests upon a few notions of an apparently simple character. Utility, wealth, value, commodity, labour, land, capital, are the elements of the subject; and whoever has a thorough comprehension of their nature must possess or be soon able to acquire a knowledge of the whole science. As almost every economic writer has remarked, it is in treating the simple elements that we require the most care and precision, since the least error of conception must vitiate all our deductions. Accordingly, I have devoted the following pages to an investigation of the conditions and relations of the above-named notions.

Repeated reflection and inquiry have led me to the somewhat novel opinion, that *value depends entirely upon utility*. Prevailing opinions make labour rather than utility the origin of value; and there are even those who distinctly assert that labour is the *cause* of value. I show, on the contrary, that we have only to trace out carefully the natural laws of the variation of utility, as depending upon the quantity of commodity in our possession, in order to arrive at a satisfactory theory of exchange, of which the ordinary laws of supply and demand are a necessary consequence. This theory is in harmony with facts; and, whenever there is any apparent reason for the belief that labour is the cause of value, we obtain an explanation of the reason. Labour is found often to determine value, but only in an indirect manner, by varying the degree of utility of the commodity through an increase or limitation of the supply.

These views are not put forward in a hasty or ill-considered manner. All the chief points of the theory were sketched out ten years ago; but they were then published only in the form of a brief paper communicated to the Statistical or Economic Section of the British Association at the Cambridge Meeting, which took place in the year 1862. A still briefer abstract of that paper was inserted in the report of the meeting, and the paper itself was not printed until June 1866. Since writing that paper, I have, over and over again, questioned the truth of my own notions, but without ever finding any reason to doubt their substantial correctness.

Mathematical character of the science

It is clear that Economics, if it is to be a science at all, must be a mathematical science. There exists much prejudice against attempts to introduce the methods and language of mathematics into any branch of the moral sciences. Many persons seem to think that the physical sciences form the proper sphere of mathematical method, and that the moral sciences demand some other method – I know not what. My theory of Economics, however, is purely mathematical in character. Nay, believing that the quantities with which we deal must be subject to continuous variation, I do not hesitate to use the appropriate branch of mathematical science, involving though it does the fearless consideration of infinitely small quantities. The theory consists in applying the differential calculus to the familiar notions of wealth, utility, value, demand, supply, capital, interest, labour, and all the other quantitative notions belonging to the daily operations of industry. As the complete theory of almost every other science involves the use of that calculus, so we cannot have a true theory of Economics without its aid.

To me it seems that *our science must be mathematical, simply because it deals with quantities*. Wherever the things treated are capable of being *greater or less*, there the laws and relations must be mathematical in nature. The ordinary laws of supply and demand treat entirely of quantities of commodity demanded or supplied, and express the manner in which the quantities vary in connection with the price. In consequence of this fact the laws *are* mathematical. Economists cannot alter their nature by denying them the name; they might as well try to alter red light by calling it blue. Whether the mathematical laws of Economics are stated in words, or in the usual symbols, $x, y, z, p, q,$ and so on, is an accident, or a matter of mere convenience. If we had no regard to trouble and prolixity, the most complicated mathematical problems might be stated in ordinary language, and their solution might be traced out by words. In fact, some distinguished mathematicians have shown a liking for getting rid of their symbols, and expressing their arguments and results in language as nearly as possible approximating to that in common use. In his *Système du Monde*, Laplace attempted to describe the truths of physical astronomy in common language; and Thomson and Tait interweave their great *Treatise on Natural Philosophy* with an interpretation in ordinary words, supposed to be within the comprehension of general readers.

These attempts, however distinguished and ingenious their authors, soon disclose the inherent defects of the grammar and dictionary for expressing complicated relations. The symbols of mathematical books are not different in nature from language; they form a perfected system of language, adapted to the notions and relations which we need to express. They do not constitute the mode of reasoning they embody; they merely facilitate its exhibition and comprehension. If, then, in Economics, we have to deal with quantities and complicated relations of quantities, we must reason mathematically; we do not render the science less mathematical by avoiding the symbols of algebra – we merely refuse to employ, in a very imperfect science, much needing every kind of assistance, that apparatus of appropriate signs which is found indispensable in other sciences.

...

Chapter II: Theory of pleasure and pain

Pleasure and pain as quantities

Proceeding to consider how pleasure and pain can be estimated as magnitudes, we must undoubtedly accept what Bentham has laid down upon this subject. 'To a person', he says, 'considered by *himself*, the value of a pleasure or pain, considered by *itself*, will be greater or less according to the four following circumstances:

1   Its *intensity*.
2   Its *duration*.
3   Its *certainty* or *uncertainty*.
4   Its *propinquity* or *remoteness*.

These are the circumstances which are to be considered in estimating a pleasure or a pain considered each of them by itself'.

Bentham goes on to consider three other circumstances which relate to the ultimate and complete result of any act or feeling; these are:

5   *Fecundity*, or the chance a feeling has of being followed by feelings of the same kind: that is, pleasures, if it be a pleasure; pains, if it be a pain.

6   *Purity*, or the chance it has of not being followed by feelings of an opposite kind.
7   *Extent*, or the number of persons to whom it extends, and who are affected by it.

These three last circumstances are of high importance as regards the theory of morals; but they will not enter into the more simple and restricted problem which we attempt to solve in Economics.

A feeling, whether of pleasure or of pain, must be regarded as having two dimensions, or modes of varying in regard to quantity. Every feeling must last some time, and it may last a longer or shorter time; while it lasts, it may be more or less acute and intense. If in two cases the duration of feeling is the same, that case will produce the greater quantity which is the more intense; or we may say that, with the same duration, the quantity will be proportional to the intensity. On the other hand, if the intensity of a feeling were to remain constant, the quantity of feeling would increase with its duration. Two days of the same degree of happiness are to be twice as much desired as one day; two days of suffering are to be feared twice as much. If the intensity ever continued fixed, the whole quantity would be found by multiplying the number of units of intensity into the number of units of duration. Pleasure and pain, then, are quantities possessing two dimensions, just as superficies possesses the two dimensions of length and breadth.

In almost every case, however, the intensity of feeling will change from moment to moment. Incessant variation characterizes our states of mind, and this is the source of the main difficulties of the subject. Nevertheless, if these variations can be traced out at all, or any approach to method and law can be detected, it will be possible to form a conception of the resulting quantity of feeling. We may imagine that the intensity changes at the end of every minute, but remains constant in the intervals. The quantity during each minute may be represented, as in Figure 1, by a rectangle whose base is supposed to correspond to the duration of a minute, and whose height is proportional to the intensity of the feeling during the minute in question. Along the line *ox* we measure *time*, and along parallels to the perpendicular line *oy* we measure *intensity*. Each of the rectangles between *pm* and *qn* represents the feeling of 1 minute. The aggregate quantity of feeling generated during the time *mn* will then be represented by the aggregate area of the rectangles between *pm* and *qn*. In this case the intensity of the feeling is supposed to be gradually declining.

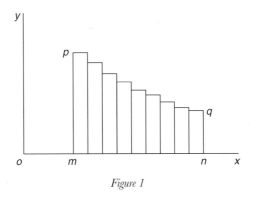

Figure 1

But it is an artificial assumption that the intensity would vary by sudden steps and at regular intervals. The error thus introduced will not be great if the intervals of time are very short, and will be less the shorter the intervals are made. To avoid all error, we must imagine the intervals of time to be infinitely short; that is, we must treat the intensity as varying continuously. Thus the proper representation of the variation of feeling is found in a curve of more or less complex character. In Figure 2 the height of each point of the curve *pq*, above the horizontal line *ox*, indicates the intensity of feeling in a moment of time; and the whole quantity of feeling

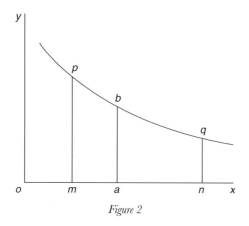

Figure 2

generated in the time *mn* is measured by the area bounded by the lines *pm*, *qn*, *mn*, and *pq*. The feeling belonging to any other time, *ma*, will be measured by the space *mabp* cut off by the perpendicular line *ab*.

Pain, the negative of pleasure

It will be readily conceded that pain is the opposite of pleasure; so that to decrease pain is to increase pleasure; to add pain is to decrease pleasure. Thus pleasure and pain treated as positive and negative quantities can be treated in algebra. The algebraic sum of a series of pleasures and pains will be obtained by adding the pleasures together and the pains together, and then striking the balance by subtracting the smaller amount from the greater. Our object will always be to maximize the resulting sum in the direction of pleasure, which we may fairly call the positive direction. This object we shall accomplish by accepting everything, and undertaking every action of which the resulting pleasure exceeds the pain which is undergone; we must avoid every object or action which leaves a balance in the other direction.

...

Chapter III: Theory of utility

Definition of terms

Pleasure and pain are undoubtedly the ultimate objects of the Calculus of Economics. To satisfy our wants to the utmost with the least effort – to procure the greatest amount of what is desirable at the expense of the least that is undesirable – in other words, *to maximize pleasure*, is the problem of Economics. But it is convenient to transfer our attention as soon as possible to the physical objects or actions which are the source to us of pleasures and pains. A very large part of the labour of any community is spent upon the production of the ordinary necessaries and conveniences of life, such as food, clothing, buildings, utensils, furniture, ornaments, and so on; and the aggregate of these things, therefore, is the immediate object of our attention.

It is desirable to introduce at once, and to define, some terms which facilitate the expression of the Principles of Economics. By a *commodity* we shall understand any object, substance, action, or service, which can afford pleasure or ward off pain. The name was originally abstract, and denoted the quality of anything by which it was capable of serving man. Having acquired, by a common process of confusion, a concrete signification, it will be well to retain the word entirely for that signification, and employ the term *utility* to denote the abstract quality whereby an object serves our purposes, and becomes entitled to rank as a commodity. Whatever can produce pleasure or prevent pain *may* possess utility. J.-B. Say has correctly and briefly defined utility as 'la faculté qu'ont les choses de pouvoir servir à l'homme, de quelque maniere que ce soit'. The food which prevents the pangs of hunger, the clothes which fend off the cold of winter, possess incontestable utility; but we must beware of restricting the meaning of the word by any moral considerations. Anything which an individual is found to desire and to labour for must be assumed to possess for him utility. In the science of Economics we treat men not as they ought to be, but as they are. Bentham, in establishing the foundations of Moral Science in his great *Introduction to the Principles of Morals and Legislation* (p. 3), thus comprehensively defines the term in question: 'By utility is meant that property in any object, whereby it tends to produce benefit, advantage, pleasure, good, or happiness (all this, in the present case, comes to the same thing), or (what comes again to the same thing) to prevent the happening of mischief, pain, evil, or unhappiness to the party whose interest is considered'.

This perfectly expresses the meaning of the word in Economics, provided that the will or inclination of the person immediately concerned is taken as the sole criterion, for the time, of what is or is not useful.

...

Utility is not an intrinsic quality

My principal work now lies in tracing out the exact nature and conditions of utility. It seems strange indeed that economists have not bestowed more minute attention on a subject which doubtless furnishes the true key to the problem of Economics.

In the first place, utility, though a quality of things, is *no inherent quality*. It is better described as *a circumstance of things* arising out of their relation to man's requirements. As Senior most accurately says, 'Utility denotes no intrinsic quality in the things which we call useful; it merely expresses their relations to the pains and pleasures of mankind'. We can never, therefore, say absolutely that some objects have utility and others have not. The ore lying in the mine, the diamond escaping the eye of the searcher, the wheat lying unreaped, the fruit ungathered for want of consumers, have no utility at all. The most wholesome and necessary kinds of food are useless unless there are hands to collect and mouths to eat them sooner or later. Nor, when we consider the matter closely, can we say that all portions of the same commodity possess equal utility. Water, for instance, may be roughly described as the most useful of all substances. A quart of water per day has the high utility of saving a person from dying in a most distressing manner. Several gallons a day may possess much utility for such purposes as cooking and washing; but after an adequate supply is secured for these uses, any additional quantity is a matter of comparative indifference. All that we can say, then, is, that water, up to to a certain quantity, is indispensable; that further quantities will have various degrees of utility; but that beyond a certain quantity the utility sinks gradually to zero; it may even become negative, that is to say, further supplies of the same substance may become inconvenient and hurtful.

Exactly the same considerations apply more or less clearly to every other article. A pound of bread per day supplied to a person saves him from starvation, and has the highest conceivable utility. A second pound per day has also no slight utility: it keeps him in a state of comparative plenty, though it be not altogether indispensable. A third pound would begin to be superfluous. It is clear, then, that *utility is not proportional to commodity*: the very same articles vary in utility according as we already possess more or less of the same article. The like may be said of other things. One suit of clothes per annum is necessary, a second convenient, a third desirable, a fourth not unacceptable; but we, sooner or later, reach a point at which further supplies are not desired with any perceptible force, unless it be for subsequent use.

Law of the variation of utility

Let us now investigate this subject a little more closely. Utility must be considered as measured by, or even as actually identical with, the addition made to a person's happiness. It is a convenient name for the aggregate of the favourable balance of feeling produced – the sum of the pleasure created and the pain prevented. We must now carefully discriminate between the *total utility* arising from any commodity and the utility attaching to any particular portion of it. Thus the total utility of the food we eat consists in maintaining life, and may be considered as infinitely great; but if we were to subtract a tenth part from what we eat daily, our loss would be but slight. We should certainly not lose a tenth part of the whole utility of food to us. It might be doubtful whether we should suffer any harm at all.

Let us imagine the whole quantity of food which a person consumes on an average during twenty-four hours to be divided into ten equal parts. If his food be reduced by the last part, he will suffer but little; if a second tenth part be deficient, he will feel the want distinctly; the subtraction of the third tenth part will be decidedly injurious; with every subsequent subtraction of a tenth part his sufferings will be more and more serious, until at length he will be upon the verge of starvation. Now, if we call each of the tenth parts *an increment*, the meaning of these facts is, that each increment of food is less necessary, or possesses less utility, than the previous one. To explain this variation of utility we may make use of space-representations, which I have found convenient in illustrating the laws of Economics in my college lectures in the past fifteen years (Figure 3).

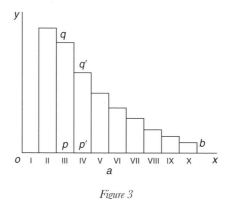

Figure 3

Let the line *ox* be used as a measure of the quantity of food, and let it be divided into ten equal parts to correspond to the ten portions of food mentioned above. Upon these equal lines are constructed rectangles, and the area of each rectangle may be assumed to represent the utility of the increment of food corresponding to its base. Thus the utility of the last increment is small, being proportional to the small rectangle on *x*. As we approach towards *o*, each increment bears a larger rectangle, that standing upon III being the largest complete rectangle. The utility of the next increment, II, is undefined, as also that of I, since these portions of food would be indispensable to life, and their utility, therefore, infinitely great.

We can now form a clear notion of the utility of the whole food, or of any part of it, for we have only to add together the proper rectangles. The utility of the first half of the food will be the sum of the rectangles on the line *oa*; that of the second, angles standing half will be represented I

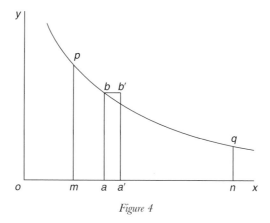

Figure 4

by the sum of the smaller rectangles between *a* and *b*. The total utility of the food will be the whole sum of the rectangles, and will be infinitely great.

The comparative utility of the several portions is, however, the most important point. Utility may be treated as *a quantity of two dimensions*, one dimension consisting in the quantity of the commodity, and another in the intensity of the effect produced upon the consumer. Now, the quantity of the commodity is measured on the horizontal line *ox*, and the intensity of utility will be measured by the length of the upright lines, or *ordinates*. The intensity of utility of the third increment is measured either by *pq*, or *p'q'*, and its utility is the product of the units in *pp'* multiplied by those in *pq*.

But the division of the food into ten equal parts is an arbitrary supposition. If we had taken twenty or a hundred or more equal parts, the same general principle would hold true, namely, that each small portion would be less useful and necessary than the last. The law may be considered to hold true theoretically, however small the increments are made; and in this way we shall at last reach a figure which is undistinguishable from a continuous curve. The notion of infinitely small quantities of food may seem absurd as regards the consumption of one individual; but, when we consider the consumption of a nation as a whole, the consumption may well be conceived to increase or diminish by quantities which are, practically speaking, infinitely small compared with the whole consumption. The laws which we are about to trace out are to be conceived as theoretically true of the individual; they can only be practically verified as regards the aggregate transactions, productions, and consumptions of a large body of people. But the laws of the aggregate depend of course upon the laws applying to individual cases.

The law of the variation of the degree of utility of food may thus be represented by a continuous curve *pbq* (Figure 4), and the perpendicular height of each point of the curve above the line *ox*, represents the degree of utility of the commodity when a certain amount has been consumed.

Thus, when the quantity *oa* has been consumed, the degree of utility corresponds to the length of the line *ab*; for if we take very little more food, *aa'*, its utility will be the product of *aa'* and *ab* very and more nearly the less is the magnitude of *aa'*. The degree of utility is thus properly measured by the height of a very narrow rectangle corresponding to a very small quantity of food, which theoretically ought to be infinitely small.

Total utility and degree of utility

We are now in a position to appreciate perfectly the difference between the *total utility* of any commodity and *the degree of utility* of the commodity at any point. These are, in fact, quantities of altogether different kinds, the first being represented by an area, and the second by a line.

We must consider how we may express these notions in appropriate mathematical language. Let *x* signify, as is usual in mathematical books, the quantity which varies independently – in this case the quantity of commodity. Let *u* denote the *whole utility* proceeding from the consumption of *x*. Then *u* will be, as mathematicians say, *a function* of *x*; that is, it will vary in some continuous and regular, but probably unknown, manner, when *x* is made to vary. Our great object at present, however, is to express the *degree of utility*.

Mathematicians employ the sign Δ prefixed to a sign of quantity, such as *x*, to signify that a quantity of the same nature as *x*, but small in proportion to *x*, is taken into consideration. Thus Δx means a small portion of *x*, and $x + \Delta x$ *is* therefore a quantity a little greater than *x*. Now, when *x* is a quantity of commodity, the utility of $x + \Delta x$ will be more than that of *x* as a general rule. Let the whole utility of $x + \Delta x$ be denoted by $u + \Delta u$; then it is obvious that the increment of utility Δu belongs to the increment of commodity Δx; and if, for the sake of argument, we suppose the degree of utility uniform over the whole of Δx, which is nearly true owing to its smallness, we shall find the corresponding degree of utility by dividing Δu by Δx.

We find these considerations fully illustrated by Figure 4, in which *oa* represents *x*, and *ab is* the degree of utility at the point *a*. Now, if we increase *x* by the small quantity *aa'*, or Δx, the utility is increased by the small rectangle *abb'a'*, or Δu; and, since a rectangle is the product of its sides, we find that the length of the line *ab*, the degree of utility, is represented by the fraction $\Delta u / \Delta x$.

As already explained, however, the utility of a commodity may be considered to vary with perfect continuity, so that we commit a small error in assuming it to be uniform over the whole increment Δx. To avoid this we must imagine Δx to be reduced to an infinitely small size, Δu decreasing with it. The smaller the quantities are the more nearly we shall have a correct expression for *ab*, the degree of utility at the point *a*. Thus the *limit* of this fraction $\Delta u / \Delta x$, or, as it is commonly expressed, du/dx, is the degree of utility corresponding to the quantity of commodity *x*. *The degree of utility is*, in mathematical language, *the differential coefficient of u considered as a function of x*, and will itself be another function of *x*.

We shall seldom need to consider the degree of utility except as regards the last increment which has been consumed, or, which comes to the same thing, the next increment which is about to be consumed. I shall therefore commonly use the expression *final degree of utility*, as meaning the degree of utility of the last addition, or the next possible addition of a very small, or infinitely small, quantity to the existing stock. In ordinary circumstances, too, the final degree of utility will not be great compared with what it might be. Only in famine or other extreme circumstances do we approach the higher degrees of utility. Accordingly, we can often treat the lower portions of the curves of variation (*pbq*, Figure 4) which concern ordinary commercial transactions, while we leave out of sight the portions beyond *p* or *q*. It is also evident that we may know the degree of utility at any point while ignorant of the total utility, that is, the area of the whole curve. To be able to estimate the total enjoyment of a person would be an interesting thing, but it would not be really so important as to be able to estimate the additions and subtractions to his enjoyment, which circumstances occasion. In the same way a very wealthy person may be quite unable to form any accurate statement of his aggregate wealth; but may nevertheless have exact accounts of income and expenditure, that is, of additions and subtractions.

Variation of the final degree of utility

The final degree of utility is that function upon which the Theory of Economics will be found to turn. Economists, generally speaking, have failed to discriminate between this function and the total utility, and from this confusion has arisen much perplexity. Many commodities which are most useful to us are esteemed and desired but little. We cannot live without water, and yet in ordinary circumstances we set no value on it. Why is this? Simply because we usually have so much of it that its final degree of utility is reduced nearly to zero. We enjoy, every day, the almost infinite utility of water, but then we do not need to consume more than we have. Let the supply run short by drought, and we begin to feel the higher degrees of utility, of which we think but little at other times.

The variation of the function expressing the final degree of utility is the all-important point in economic problems. We may state as a general law, that *the degree of utility varies with the quantity of commodity, and ultimately decreases as that quantity increases.* No commodity can be named which we continue to desire with the same force, whatever be the quantity already in use or possession. All our appetites are capable of *satisfaction* or *satiety* sooner or later, in fact, both these words mean, etymologically, that we have had *enough*, so that more is of no use to us. It does not follow, indeed, that the degree of utility will always sink to zero. This may be the case with some things, especially the simple animal requirements, such as food, water, air, and the like. But the more refined and intellectual our needs become, the less are they capable of satiety. To the desire for articles of taste, science, or curiosity, when once excited, there is hardly a limit.

...

Distribution of commodity in different uses

The principles of utility may be illustrated by considering the mode in which we distribute a commodity when it is capable of several uses. There are articles which may be employed for many distinct purposes: thus, barley may be used either to make beer, spirits, bread, or to feed cattle; sugar may be used to eat, or for producing alcohol; timber may be used in construction, or as fuel; iron and other metals may be applied to many different purposes. Imagine, then, a community in the possession of a certain stock of barley; what principles will regulate their mode of consuming it? Or, as we have not yet reached the subject of exchange, imagine an isolated family, or even an individual, possessing an adequate stock, and using some in one way and some in another. The theory of utility gives, theoretically speaking, a complete solution of the question.

Let s be the whole stock of some commodity, and let it be capable of two distinct uses. Then we may represent the two quantities appropriated to these uses by x_1, and y_1, it being a condition that $x_1 + y_1 = s$. The person may be conceived as successively expending small quantities of the commodity. Now it is the inevitable tendency of human nature to choose that course which appears to offer the greatest advantage at the moment. Hence, when the person remains satisfied with the distribution he has made, it follows that no alteration would yield him more pleasure; which amounts to saying that an increment of commodity would yield exactly as much utility in one use as in another. Let Δu_1, Δu_2, be the increments of utility, which might arise respectively from consuming an increment of commodity in the two different ways. When the distribution is completed, we ought to have $\Delta u_1 = \Delta u_2$; or at the limit we have the equation $du_1/dx = du_2/dy$, which is true when x, y are respectively equal to x_1, y_1. We must, in other words, have the *final degrees of utility* in the two uses equal.

The same reasoning which applies to uses of the same commodity will evidently apply to any two uses, and hence to all uses simultaneously, so that we obtain a series of equations less numerous by a unit than the number of ways of using the commodity. The general result is that commodity, if consumed by a perfectly wise being, must be consumed with a maximum production of utility.

We should often find these equations to fall. Even when x is equal to 99/100 of the stock, its degree of utility might still exceed the utility attaching to the remaining 1/100 part in either of the other uses. This would mean that it was preferable to give the whole commodity to the first use. Such a case might perhaps be said to be not the exception but the rule; for, whenever a commodity is capable of only one use, the circumstance is theoretically represented by saying, that the final degree of utility in this employment always exceeds that in any other employment.

Under peculiar circumstances great changes may take place in the consumption of a commodity. In a time of scarcity the utility of barley as food might rise so high as to exceed altogether its utility, even as regards the smallest quantity, in producing alcoholic liquors; its consumption in the latter way would then cease. In a besieged town the employment of articles becomes revolutionized. Things of great utility in other respects are ruthlessly applied to strange purposes. In Paris a vast stock of horses were eaten, not so much because they were useless in other ways, as because they were needed more strongly as food. A certain stock of horses had, indeed, to be retained as a necessary aid to locomotion, so that the equation of the degrees of utility never wholly failed.

...

Chapter IV: Theory of Exchange

Importance of exchange in economics

Exchange is so important a process in the maximizing of utility and the saving of labour, that some economists have regarded their science as treating of this operation alone. Utility arises from commodities being brought in suitable quantities and at the proper times into the possession of persons needing them; and it is by exchange, more than any other means, that this is effected. Trade is not indeed the only method of economizing: a single individual may gain in utility by a proper consumption of the stock in his possession. The best employment of labour and capital by a single person is also a question disconnected from that of exchange, and which must yet be treated in the science. But, with these exceptions, I am perfectly willing to agree with the high importance attributed to exchange.

It is impossible to have a correct idea of the science of Economics without a perfect comprehension of the Theory of Exchange; and I find it both possible and desirable to consider this subject before introducing any notions concerning labour or the production of commodities. In these words of J. S. Mill I thoroughly concur: 'Almost every speculation respecting the economical interests of a society thus constituted, implies some theory of Value: the smallest error on that subject infects with corresponding error all our other conclusions; and anything vague or misty in our conception of it creates confusion and uncertainty in everything else'. But when he proceeds to say, 'Happily, there is nothing in the laws of Value which remains for the present or any future writer to clear up; the theory of the subject is complete' – he utters that which it would be rash to say of any of the sciences.

Ambiguity of the term Value

I must, in the first place, point out the thoroughly ambiguous and unscientific character of the term *value*. Adam Smith noticed the extreme difference of meaning between *value in use* and *value in exchange*; and it is usual for writers on Economics to caution their readers against the confusion of thought to which they are liable. But I do not believe that either writers or readers can avoid the confusion so long as they use the word. In spite of the most acute feeling of the danger, I often detect myself using the word improperly; nor do I think that the best authors escape the danger.

Let us turn to Mill's definition of Exchange Value, and we see at once the misleading power of the term. He tells us, 'Value is a relative term. The value of a thing means the quantity of some other thing, or of things in general, which it exchanges for'. Now, if there is any fact certain about exchange value, it is, that it means not an object at all, but a circumstance of an object. Value implies, in fact, a relation; but if so, it cannot possibly be *some other thing*. A student of Economics has no hope of ever being clear and correct in his ideas of the science if he thinks of value as at all a *thing* or an *object*, or even as anything which lies in a thing or object. Persons are thus led to speak of such a nonentity as *intrinsic value*. There are, doubtless, qualities inherent in such a substance as gold or iron which influence its value; but the word Value, so far as it can be correctly used, merely expresses *the circumstance of its exchanging in a certain ratio for some other substance.*

Value expresses Ratio of Exchange

If a ton of pig-iron exchanges in a market for an ounce of standard gold, neither the iron is value nor the gold; nor is there value in the iron nor in the gold. The notion of value is concerned only in the fact or circumstance of one exchanging for the other. Thus it is scientifically incorrect to say that the value of the ton of iron is the ounce of gold: we thus convert value into a concrete thing; and it is, of course, equally incorrect to say that the value of the ounce of gold is the ton of iron. The more correct and safe expression is, that *the value of the ton of iron is equal to the value of the ounce of gold*, or that their values are as one to one.

Value in exchange expresses nothing but a ratio, and the term should not be used in any other sense. To speak simply of the value of an ounce of gold is as absurd as to speak of the *ratio of the number seventeen*. What is the ratio of the number seventeen? The question admits no answer, for there must be another number named in order to make a ratio; and the ratio will differ according to the number suggested. What is the value of iron compared with that of gold? – is an intelligible question. The answer consists in stating the ratio of the quantities exchanged.

Popular use of the term Value

In the popular use of the word value no less than three distinct though connected meanings seem to be confused together. These may be described as

1   Value in use;
2   Esteem, or urgency of desire;
3   Ratio of exchange.

Adam Smith, in the familiar passage already referred to, distinguished between the first and the third meanings. He said, 'The word value, it is to be observed, has two different meanings, and sometimes expresses the power of purchasing other goods which the possession of that object conveys. The one may be called "value in use"; the other "value in exchange". The things which have the greatest value in use have frequently little or no value in exchange; and, on the contrary, those which have the greatest value in exchange have frequently little or no value in use. Nothing is more useful than water: but it will purchase scarce anything; scarce anything can be had in exchange for it. A diamond, on the contrary, has scarce any value in use; but a very great quantity of other goods may frequently be had in exchange for it'.

It is sufficiently plain that, when Smith speaks of water as being highly useful and yet devoid of purchasing power, he means *water in abundance*, that is to say, water so abundantly supplied that it has exerted its full useful effect, or its *total utility*. Water, when it becomes very scarce, as in a dry desert, acquires exceedingly great purchasing power. Thus Smith evidently means by value in use, *the total utility of a substance of which the degree of utility has sunk very low, because the want of such substance has been well nigh satisfied*. By purchasing power he clearly means the ratio of exchange for other commodities. But here he fails to point out that the quantity of goods received in exchange depends just as much upon the nature of the goods received, as on the nature of those given for them. In exchange for a diamond we can get a great quantity of iron, or corn, or paving-stones, or other commodity of which there is abundance; but we can get very few rubies, sapphires, or other precious stones. Silver is of high purchasing power compared with zinc, or lead, or iron, but of small purchasing power compared with gold, platinum, or iridium. Yet we might well say in any case that diamond and silver are things of high value. Thus I am led to think that the word value is often used in reality to mean *intensity of desire or esteem for a thing*. A silver ornament is a beautiful object apart from all ideas of traffic; it may thus be valued or esteemed simply because it suits the taste and fancy of its owner, and is the only one possessed. Even Robinson Crusoe must have looked upon each of his possessions with varying esteem and desire for more, although he was incapable of exchanging with any other person. Now, in this sense value seems to be identical with the final degree of utility of a commodity, as defined in a previous page ... it is measured by the intensity of the pleasure or benefit which would be obtained from a new increment of the same commodity. No doubt there is a close connection between value in this meaning, and value as ratio of exchange. Nothing can have a high purchasing power unless it be highly esteemed in itself; but it may be highly esteemed apart from all comparison with other things; and, though highly esteemed, it may have a low purchasing power, because those things against which it is measured are still more esteemed.

Thus I come to the conclusion that, in the use of the word value, three distinct meanings are habitually confused together, and require to be thus distinguished:

1   Value in use = total utility;
2   Esteem = final degree of utility;
3   Purchasing power = ratio of exchange.

It is not to be expected that we could profitably discuss such matters as economic doctrines, while the fundamental ideas of the subject are thus jumbled up together in one ambiguous word. The only thorough remedy consists in substituting for the dangerous name *value* that one of the three stated meanings which is intended in each case. In this work, therefore, I shall discontinue the use of the word value altogether, and when, as will be most often the case in the remainder of the book, I need to refer to the third meaning, often called by economists *exchange or exchangeable value*, I shall substitute the wholly unequivocal expression *Ratio of Exchange*, specifying at the same time what are the *two articles* exchanged. When we speak of the ratio of exchange of pig-iron and gold, there can be no possible doubt that we intend to refer to the ratio of the number of units of the one commodity to the number of units of the other commodity for which it exchanges, the units being arbitrary concrete magnitudes, but the ratio an abstract number.

...

Definition of market

Before proceeding to the Theory of Exchange, it will be desirable to place beyond doubt the meanings of two other terms which I shall frequently employ.

By a *Market* I shall mean much what commercial men use it to express. Originally a market was a public place in a town where provisions and other objects were exposed for sale; but the word has been generalized, so as to mean any body of persons who are in intimate business relations and carry on extensive transactions in any commodity. A great city may contain as many markets as there are important branches of trade, and these markets may or may not be localized. The central point of a market is the public exchange, mart or auction rooms, where the traders agree to meet and transact business. In London, the Stock Market, the Corn Market, the Coal Market, the Sugar Market, and many others, are distinctly localized; in Manchester, the Cotton Market, the Cotton Waste Market, and others. But this distinction of locality is not necessary. The traders may be spread over a whole town, or region of country, and yet make a market, if they are, by means of fairs, meetings, published price lists, the post office, or otherwise, in close communication with each other. Thus, the common expression *Money Market* denotes no locality: it is applied to the aggregate of those bankers, capitalists, and other traders who lend or borrow money, and who constantly exchange information concerning the course of business.

In Economics we may usefully adopt this term with a clear and well-defined meaning. By a market I shall mean two or more persons dealing in two or more commodities, whose stocks of those commodities and intentions of exchanging are known to all. It is also essential that the ratio of exchange between any two persons should be known to all the others. It is only so far as this community of knowledge extends that the market extends. Any persons who are not acquainted at the moment with the prevailing ratio of exchange, or whose stocks are not available for want of communication, must not be considered part of the market. Secret or unknown stocks of a commodity must also be considered beyond reach of a market so long as they remain secret and unknown. Every individual must be considered as exchanging from a pure regard to his own requirements or private interests, and there must be perfectly free competition, so that any one will exchange with any one else for the slightest apparent advantage. There must be no conspiracies for absorbing and holding supplies to produce unnatural ratios of exchange. Were a conspiracy of farmers to withhold all corn from market, the consumers might be driven, by starvation, to pay prices bearing no proper relation to the existing supplies, and the ordinary conditions of the market would be thus overthrown.

The theoretical conception of a perfect market is more or less completely carried out in practice. It is the work of brokers in any extensive market to organize exchange, so that every purchase shall be made with the most thorough acquaintance with the conditions of the trade. Each broker strives to gain the best knowledge of the conditions of supply and demand, and the earliest intimation of any change. He is in communication with as many other traders as possible, in order to have the widest range of information, and the greatest chance of making suitable exchanges. It is only thus that a definite market price can be ascertained at every moment, and varied according to the frequent news capable of affecting buyers and sellers. By the mediation of a body of brokers a complete *consensus* is established, and the stock of every seller or the demand of every buyer brought into the market. It is of the very essence of trade to have wide and constant information. A market, then, is theoretically perfect only when all traders have perfect knowledge of the conditions of supply and demand, and the consequent ratio of exchange; and in such a market, as we shall now see, there can only be one ratio of exchange of one uniform commodity at any moment.

So essential is a knowledge of the real state of supply and demand to the smooth procedure of trade and the real good of the community, that I conceive it would be quite legitimate to compel the publication of any requisite statistics. Secrecy can only conduce to the profit of speculators who gain from great fluctuations of prices. Speculation is advantageous to the public only so far as it tends to equalize prices; and it is, therefore, against the public good to allow speculators to foster artificially the inequalities of prices by which they profit. The welfare of millions, both of consumers and producers, depends upon an accurate knowledge of the stocks of cotton and corn; and it would, therefore, be no unwarrantable interference with the liberty of the subject to require any information as to the stocks in hand. In Billingsgate fish market there was long ago a regulation to the effect that salesmen shall fix up in a conspicuous place every morning a statement of the kind and amount of their stock. The same principle has long been recognised in the Acts of Parliament concerning the collection of statistics of the quantities and prices of corn sold in English market towns. More recently similar legislation has taken place as regards the cotton trade, in the Cotton Statistics Act of 1868. Publicity, whenever it can thus be enforced on markets by public authority, tends almost always to the advantage of everybody except perhaps a few speculators and financiers.

Definition of trading body

I find it necessary to adopt some expression for any number of people whose aggregate influence in a market, either in the way of supply or demand, we have to consider. By a *trading body* I mean, in the most general manner, any body either of buyers or sellers. The trading body may be a single individual in one case; it may be the whole inhabitants of a continent in another; it may be the individuals of a trade diffused through a country in a third. England and North America will be trading bodies if we are considering the corn we receive from America in exchange for iron and other goods. The continent of Europe is a trading body as purchasing coal from England. The farmers of England are a trading body when they sell corn to the millers, and the millers both when they buy corn from the farmers and sell flour to the bakers.

We must use the expression with this wide meaning, because the principles of exchange are the same in nature, however wide or narrow may be the market considered. Every trading body is either an individual or an aggregate of individuals, and the law, in the case of the aggregate, must depend upon the fulfilment of law in the individuals. We cannot usually observe any precise and continuous variation in the wants and deeds of an individual, because the action of extraneous motives, or what would seem to be caprice, overwhelms minute tendencies. As I have already remarked … a single individual does not vary his consumption of sugar, butter, or eggs from week to week by infinitesimal amounts, according to each small change in the price. He probably continues his ordinary consumption until accident directs his attention to a rise in price, and he then, perhaps, discontinues the use of the articles altogether for a time. But the aggregate, or what is the same, the average consumption, of a large community will be found to vary continuously or nearly so. The most minute tendencies make themselves apparent in a wide average. Thus, our laws of Economics will be theoretically true in the case of individuals, and practically true in the case of large aggregates; but the general principles will be the same, whatever the extent of the trading body considered. We shall be justified, then, in using the expression with the utmost generality.

It should be remarked, however, that the economic laws representing the conduct of large aggregates of individuals will never represent exactly the conduct of any one individual. If we could imagine that there were a thousand individuals all exactly alike in regard to their demand for commodities, and their capabilities of supplying them, then the average laws of supply and demand deduced from the conduct of such individuals would agree with the conduct of any one individual. But a community is composed of persons differing widely in their powers, wants, habits, and possessions. In such circumstances the average laws applying to them will come under what I have elsewhere called the 'Fictitious Mean', that is to say, they are numerical results which do not pretend to represent the character of any existing thing. But average laws would not on this account be less useful, if we could obtain them; for the movements of trade and industry depend upon averages and aggregates, not upon the whims of individuals.

The Law of Indifference

When a commodity is perfectly uniform or homogeneous in quality, any portion may be indifferently used in place of an equal portion: hence, in the same market, and at the same moment, all portions must be exchanged at the same ratio. There can be no reason why a person should treat exactly similar things differently, and the slightest excess in what is demanded for one over the other will cause him to take the latter instead of the former. In nicely balanced exchanges it is a very minute scruple which turns the scale and governs the choice. A minute difference of quality in a commodity may thus give rise to preference, and cause the ratio of exchange to differ. But where no difference exists at all, or where no difference is known to exist, there can be no ground for preference whatever. If, in selling a quantity of perfectly equal and uniform barrels of flour, a merchant arbitrarily fixed different prices on them, a purchaser would of course select the cheaper ones; and where there was absolutely no difference in the thing purchased, even an excess of a penny in the price of a thing worth a thousand pounds would be a valid ground of choice. Hence follows what is undoubtedly true, with proper explanations, that *in the same open market, at any one moment, there cannot be two prices for the same kind of article.* Such differences as may practically occur arise from extraneous circumstances, such as the defective credit of the purchasers, their imperfect knowledge of the market, and so on.

The principle expressed above is a general law of the utmost importance in Economics, and I propose to call it *The Law of Indifference*, meaning that, when two objects or commodities are subject to no important difference as regards the purpose in view, they will either of them be taken instead of the other with perfect indifference by a purchaser. Every such act of indifferent choice gives rise to an equation of degrees of utility, so that in this principle of indifference we have one of the central pivots of the theory.

Though the price of the same commodity must be uniform at any one moment, it may vary from moment to moment, and must be conceived as in a state of continual change. Theoretically speaking, it would not usually be possible to buy two portions of the same commodity *successively* at the same ratio of exchange, because, no sooner would the first portion have been bought than the conditions of utility would be altered. When exchanges are made on a large scale, this result will be verified in practice. If a wealthy person invested £100,000 in the funds in the morning, it is hardly likely that the operation could be repeated in the afternoon at the same price. In any market, if a person goes on buying largely, he will ultimately raise the price against himself. Thus it is apparent that extensive purchases would best be made gradually, so as to secure the advantage of a lower price upon the earlier portions. In theory this effect of exchange upon the ratio of exchange must be conceived to exist in some degree, however small the purchases made may be. Strictly speaking, the ratio of exchange at any moment is that of dy to dx, of an infinitely small quantity of one commodity to the infinitely small quantity of another which is given for it. The ratio of exchange is really a differential coefficient. The quantity of any article purchased is a function of the price at which it is purchased, and the ratio of exchange expresses the rate at which the quantity of the article increases compared with what is given for it.

We must carefully distinguish, at the same time, between the Statics and Dynamics of this subject. The real condition of industry is one of perpetual motion and change. Commodities are being continually manufactured and exchanged and consumed. If we wished to have a complete solution of the problem in all its natural complexity, we should have to treat it as a problem of motion – a problem of dynamics. But it would surely be absurd to attempt the more difficult question when the more easy one is yet so imperfectly within our power. It is only as a purely statical problem that I can venture to treat the action of exchange. Holders of commodities will be regarded not as continuously passing on these commodities in streams of trade, but as possessing certain fixed amounts which they exchange until they come to equilibrium.

It is much more easy to determine the point at which a pendulum will come to rest than to calculate the velocity at which it will move when displaced from that point of rest. Just so, it is a far more easy task to lay down the conditions under which trade is completed and interchange ceases, than to attempt to ascertain at what rate trade will go on when equilibrium is not attained.

The difference will present itself in this form: dynamically we could not treat the ratio of exchange otherwise than as the ratio of dy and dx, infinitesimal quantities of commodity. Our equations would then be regarded as differential equations, which would have to be integrated. But in the statical view of the question we can substitute the ratio of the finite quantities y and x. Thus, from the self-evident principle … that there cannot, in the same market, at the same moment, be two different prices for the same uniform commodity, it follows that *the last increments in an act of exchange must be exchanged in the same ratio as the whole quantities exchanged.* Suppose that two commodities are bartered in the ratio of *x* for *y*; then every *m*th part of *x* is given for the *m*th part of *y*, and it does not matter for which of the *m*th parts. No part of the commodity can be treated differently from any other part. We may carry this division to an indefinite extent by imagining *m* to be constantly increased, so that, at the limit, even an infinitely small part of *x* must be exchanged for an infinitely small part of *y*, in the same ratio as the whole quantities. This result we may express by stating that the increments concerned in the process of exchange must obey the equation

$$\frac{dy}{dx} = \frac{y}{x}.$$

The use which we shall make of this equation will be seen in the next section.

The Theory of Exchange

The keystone of the whole Theory of Exchange, and of the principal problems of Economics, lies in this proposition – *The ratio of exchange of any two commodities will be the reciprocal of the ratio of the final degrees of utility of the quantities of commodity available for consumption after the exchange is completed.* When the reader has reflected a little upon the meaning of this proposition, he will see, I think, that it is necessarily true, if the principles of human nature have been correctly represented in previous pages.

Imagine that there is one trading body possessing only corn, and another possessing only beef. It is certain that, under these circumstances, a portion of the corn may be given in exchange for a portion of the beef with a considerable increase of utility. How are we to determine at what point the exchange will cease to be beneficial? This question must involve both the ratio of exchange and the degrees of utility. Suppose, for a moment, that the ratio of exchange is approximately that of ten pounds of corn for one pound of beef: then if, to the trading body which possesses corn, ten pounds of corn are less useful than one of beef, that body will desire to carry the exchange further. Should the other body possessing beef find one pound less useful than ten pounds of corn, this body will also be desirous to continue the exchange. Exchange will thus go on until each party has obtained all the benefit that is possible, and loss of utility would result if more were exchanged. Both parties, then, rest in satisfaction and equilibrium, and the degrees of utility have come to their level, as it were.

This point of equilibrium will be known by the criterion, that an infinitely small amount of commodity exchanged in addition, at the same rate, will bring neither gain nor loss of utility. In other words, if increments of commodities be exchanged at the established ratio, their utilities will be equal for both parties. Thus, if ten pounds of corn were of exactly the same utility as one pound of beef, there would be neither harm nor good in further exchange at this ratio.

It is hardly possible to represent this theory completely by means of a diagram, but Figure 5 may, perhaps, render it clearer. Suppose the line *pqr* to be a small portion of the curve of utility of one commodity, while the broken line *p'qr'* is the like curve of another commodity which has been reversed and superposed on the other. Owing to this reversal, the quantities of the first commodity are measured along the base line from *a* towards *b*, whereas those of the second must be measured in the opposite direction. Let units of both commodities be represented by equal lengths: then the little line *a'a* indicates an increase of the first commodity, and a decrease of the second. Assume the ratio of exchange to be that of unit for unit, or 1 to 1: then, by receiving the commodity *a'a* the person will gain the utility *ad*, and lose the utility *a'c*; or he will make a net gain of the utility corresponding to the mixtilinear figure *cd*. He will, therefore, wish to extend the

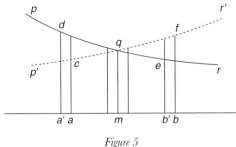

Figure 5

exchange. If he were to go up to the point b', and were still proceeding, he would, by the next small exchange, receive the utility be, and part with $b'f$; or he would have a net loss of ef. He would, therefore, have gone too far; and it is pretty obvious that the point of intersection, q, defines the place where he would stop with the greatest advantage. It is there that a net gain is converted into a net loss, or rather where, for an infinitely small quantity, there is neither gain nor loss. To represent an infinitely small quantity, or even an exceedingly small quantity, on a diagram is, of course, impossible; but on either side of the line mq I have represented the utilities of a small quantity of commodity more or less, and it is apparent that the net gain or loss upon the exchange of these quantities would be trifling.

Symbolic statement of the theory

To represent this process of reasoning in symbols, let Δx denote a small increment of corn, and Δy a small increment of beef exchanged for it. Now our Law of Indifference comes into play. As both the corn and the beef are homogeneous commodities, no parts can be exchanged at a different ratio from other parts in the same market: hence, if x be the whole quantity of corn given for y the whole quantity of beef received, Δy must have the same ratio to Δx as y to x; we have then,

$$\frac{\Delta y}{\Delta x} = \frac{y}{x}, \quad \text{or} \quad \Delta y = \frac{y}{x}\Delta x.$$

In a state of equilibrium, the utilities of these increments must be equal in the case of each party, in order that neither more nor less exchange would be desirable. Now the increment of beef, Δy, is y/x times as great as the increment of corn, Δx, so that, in order that their utilities shall be equal, the degree x of utility of beef must be x/y times as great as the degree of utility of corn. Thus we arrive at the principle that *the degrees of utility of commodities exchanged will be in the inverse proportion of the magnitudes of the increments exchanged.*

Let us now suppose that the first body, A, originally possessed the quantity a of corn, and that the second body, B, possessed the quantity b of beef. As the exchange consists in giving x of corn for y of beef, the state of things after exchange will be as follows:

> A holds $a - x$ of corn, and y of beef,
> B holds x of corn, and $b - y$ of beef.

Let $\phi_1(a - x)$ denote the final degree of utility of corn to A, and $\phi_2 x$ the corresponding function for B. Also let $\psi_1 y$ denote A's final degree of utility for beef, and $\psi_2(b - y)$ B's similar function. Then ... A will not be satisfied unless the following equation holds true:

$$\phi_1(a - x) \cdot dx = \psi_1 y \cdot dy;$$

or

$$\frac{\phi_1(a-x)}{\psi_1 y} = \frac{dy}{dx}.$$

Hence, substituting for the second member by the equation given [above] we have

$$\frac{\phi_1(a-x)}{\psi_1 y} = \frac{y}{x}.$$

What holds true of A will also hold true of B, *mutatis mutandis*. He must also derive exactly equal utility from the final increments, otherwise it will be for his interest to exchange either more or less, and he will disturb the conditions of exchange. Accordingly the following equation must hold true:

$$\psi_2(b-y) \cdot dy = \phi_2 x \cdot dx;$$

or, substituting as before,

$$\frac{\phi_2 x}{\psi_2(b-y)} = \frac{y}{x}.$$

We arrive, then, at the conclusion, that whenever two commodities are exchanged for each other, and *more or less can be given or received in infinitely small quantities*, the quantities exchanged satisfy two equations, which may be thus stated in a concise form:

$$\frac{\phi_1(a-x)}{\psi_1 y} = \frac{y}{x} = \frac{\phi_2 x}{\psi_2(b-y)}.$$

The two equations are sufficient to determine the results of exchange; for there are only two unknown quantities concerned, namely, x and y, the quantities given and received.

A vague notion has existed in the minds of economical writers, that the conditions of exchange may be expressed in the form of an equation. Thus, J.S. Mill has said: 'The idea of a *ratio*, as between demand and supply, is out of place, and has no concern in the matter: the proper mathematical analogy is that of an *equation*. Demand and supply, the quantity demanded and the quantity supplied, will be made equal'. Mill here speaks of an equation as only a proper mathematical *analogy*. But if Economics is to be a real science at all, it must not deal merely with analogies; it must reason by real equations, like all the other sciences which have reached at all a systematic character. Mill's equation, indeed, is not explicitly the same as any at which we have arrived above. His equation states that the quantity of a commodity given by A is equal to the quantity received by B. This seems at first sight to be a mere truism, for this equality must necessarily exist if any exchange takes place at all. The theory of value, as expounded by Mill, fails to reach the root of the matter, and show how the amount of demand or supply is caused to vary. And Mill does not perceive that, as there must be two parties and two quantities to every exchange, there must be two equations.

Nevertheless, our theory is perfectly consistent with the laws of supply and demand; and if we had the functions of utility determined, it would be possible to throw them into a form clearly expressing the equivalence of supply and demand. We may regard x as the quantity demanded on one side and supplied on the other; similarly, y is the quantity supplied on the one side and demanded on the other. Now, when we hold the two equations to be simultaneously true, we assume that the x and y of one equation equal those of the other. The laws of supply and demand are thus a result of what seems to me the true theory of value or exchange.

$$\ldots$$

Impediments to exchange

We have hitherto treated the Theory of Exchange as if the action of exchange could be carried on without trouble or cost. In reality, the cost of conveyance is almost always of importance, and it is sometimes the principal element in the question. To the cost of mere transport must be added a variety of charges of brokers, agents, packers, dock, harbour, light dues, and the like together with any customs duties imposed either on the importation or exportation of commodities. All these charges, whether necessary or arbitrary, are so many impediments to commerce, and tend to reduce its advantages. The effect of any one such charge, or of the aggregate of the costs of exchange, can be represented in our formulæ in a very simple manner.

In whatever modes the charges are payable, they may be conceived as paid by the surrender on importation of a certain fraction of the commodity received; for the amount of the charges will usually be proportional to the quantity of goods, and, if expressed in money, can be considered as turned into commodity.

Thus, if A gives x in exchange, this is not the quantity received by B; a part of x is previously subtracted, so that B receives say mx, which is less than x, and the terms of exchange must be adjusted on his part so as to agree with this condition. Hence the second equation will be

$$\frac{y}{mx} = \frac{\phi_2(mx)}{\psi_2(b-y)}.$$

Again, A, though giving x, will not receive the whole of y; but say ny, so that his equation similarly will be

$$\frac{\phi_1(a-x)}{\psi_1(ny)} = \frac{ny}{x}.$$

The result is, that there is not one ratio of exchange, but two ratios; and the more these differ, the less advantage there will be in exchange. It is obvious that A has either to remain satisfied with less of the second commodity than before, or has to give more of his own in purchasing it. By an obvious transfer of the factors m and n we may state the equations of impeded exchange in the concise form:

$$\frac{\phi_1(a-x)}{n \cdot \psi_1(ny)} = \frac{y}{x} = \frac{m \cdot \phi_2(mx)}{\psi_2(b-y)}.$$

Illustrations of the Theory of Exchange

As stated above, the Theory of Exchange may seem to be of a somewhat abstract and perplexing character; but it is not difficult to find practical illustrations which will show how it is verified in the actual working of a great market. The ordinary laws of supply and demand, when properly stated, are the practical manifestation of the theory. Considerable discussion has taken place concerning these laws, in consequence of Mr W.T. Thornton's writings upon the subject in the *Fortnightly Review*, and in his work on the *Claims of Labour*. Mill, although he had previously declared the Theory of Value to be complete and perfect ... was led by Mr Thornton's arguments to allow that modification was required.

For my own part, I think that most of Mr Thornton's arguments are beside the question. He suggests that there are no regular laws of supply and demand, because he adduces certain cases in which no regular variation can take place. Those cases might be indefinitely multiplied, and yet the laws in question would not be touched. Of course, laws which assume a continuity of variation are inapplicable where continuous variation is impossible. Economists can never be free from difficulties unless they will distinguish between a theory and the *application of a theory*. Because, in retail trade, in English or Dutch auction, or other particular modes of traffic, we cannot at once observe the operation of the laws of supply and demand, it is not in the least to be supposed that those laws are false. In fact, Mr Thornton seems to allow that, if prospective demand and supply are taken into account, they become substantially true. But, in the actual working of any market, the influence of future events should never be neglected, neither by a merchant nor an economist.

Though Mr Thornton's objections are mostly beside the question, his remarks have served to show that the action of the laws of supply and demand was inadequately explained by previous economists. What constitutes the demand and the supply was not investigated carefully enough. As Mr Thornton points out, there may be a number of persons willing to buy; but if their highest offer is ever so little short of the lowest price which the seller is willing to take, their influence is *nil*. If in an auction there are ten people willing to buy a horse at £20, but not higher, their demand instantly ceases when any one person offers £21. I am inclined not only to accept such a view, but to carry it further. Any change in the price of an article will be determined not with regard to the large numbers who might or might not buy it at other prices, but by the few who will or will not buy it according as a change is made close to the existing price.

The theory consists in carrying out this view to the point of asserting that it is only comparatively insignificant quantities of supply and demand which are at any moment operative on the ratio of exchange. This is practically verified by what takes place in any very large market – say that of the Consolidated Three Per Cent Annuities. As the whole amount of the English funds is nearly eight hundred millions sterling, the quantity bought or sold by any ordinary purchaser is inconsiderably small in comparison. Even £1000 worth of stock may be taken as an infinitesimally small increment, because it does not appreciably affect the total existing supply. Now the theory consists in asserting that the market price of the funds is affected from hour to hour not by the enormous amounts which *might* be bought or sold at extreme prices, but by the comparatively insignificant amounts which *are* being sold or bought at the existing prices. A change of price is always occasioned by the overbalancing of the inclinations of those who will or will not sell just about the point at which prices stand. When Consols are 93½, and business is in a tranquil state, it matters not how many buyers there are at 93, or sellers at 94. They are really off the market. Those only are operative who may be made to buy or sell by a rise or fall of an eighth. The question is, whether the price shall remain at 93½, or rise to 93⅝, or fall to 93⅜. This is determined by the sale or purchase of comparatively very small amounts. It is the purchasers who find a little stock more profitable to them than the corresponding sum of money who make the price rise by ⅛. When the price of the funds is very steady and the market quiescent, it means that the stocks are distributed among holders in such a way that the exchange of more or less at the prevailing price is a matter of indifference.

In practice, no market ever long fulfils the theoretical conditions of equilibrium, because, from the various accidents of life and business, there are sure to be people compelled to sell every day, or having sudden inducements to buy. There is nearly always, again, the influence of prospective supply or demand, depending upon the political intelligence of the moment. Speculation complicates the action of the laws of supply and demand in a high degree, but does not in the least degree arrest their action or alter their nature. We shall never have a science of Economics unless we learn to discern the operation of law even among the most perplexing complications and apparent interruptions.

···

Complex cases of the theory

We have hitherto considered the Theory of Exchange as applying only to two trading bodies possessing and dealing in two commodities. Exactly the same principles hold true, however numerous and complicated may be the conditions. The main point to be remembered in tracing out the results of the theory is, that the same pair of commodities in the same market can have only one ratio of exchange, which must therefore prevail between each body and each other, the costs of conveyance being considered as *nil*. The equations become rapidly more numerous as additional bodies or commodities are considered; but we may exhibit them as they apply to the case of three trading bodies and three commodities.

Thus, suppose that

> A possesses the stock a of cotton, and gives
> x_1 of it to B, x_2 to C.
> B possesses the stock b of silk, and gives
> y_1 to B, y_2 to C.
> C possesses the stock c of wool, and gives
> z_1 to A, z_2 to B.

We have here altogether six unknown quantities: $x_1, x_2, y_1, y_2, z_1, z_2$; but we have also sufficient means of determining them. They are exchanged as follows:

> A gives x_1 for y_1, and x_2 for z_1.
> B gives y_1 for x_1, and y_2 for z_2.
> C gives z_1 for x_2, and z_2 for y_2.

These may be treated as independent exchanges; each body must be satisfied in regard to each of its exchanges, and we must therefore take into account the functions of utility or the final degrees of utility of each commodity in respect of each body. Let us express these functions as follows:

> ϕ_1, ψ_1, χ_1 are the respective functions of utility for A.
> ϕ_2, ψ_2, χ_2 .... B.
> ϕ_3, ψ_3, χ_3 .... C.

Now A, after the exchange, will hold $a - x_1 - x_2$ of cotton and y_1 of silk; and B will hold x_1 of cotton and $b - y_1 - y_2$ of silk: their ratio of exchange, y_1 for x_1, will therefore be governed by the following pair of equations:

$$\frac{\phi_1(a - x_1 - x_2)}{\psi_1 y_1} = \frac{y_1}{x_1} = \frac{\phi_2 x_1}{\psi_2(b - y_1 - y_2)}.$$

The exchange of A with C will be similarly determined by the ratio of the degrees of utility of wool and cotton on each side subsequent to the exchange; hence we have

$$\frac{\phi_1(a - x_1 - x_2)}{x_1 z_1} = \frac{z_1}{x_2} = \frac{\phi_3 x_2}{x_3(c - z_1 - z_2)}.$$

There will also be interchange between B and C which will be independently regulated on similar principles, so that we have another pair of equations to complete the conditions, namely

$$\frac{\psi_2(b - y_1 - y_2)}{x_2 z_2} = \frac{z_2}{y_2} = \frac{\psi_3 y_2}{x_3(c - z_1 - z_2)}.$$

We might proceed in the same way to lay down the conditions of exchange between more numerous bodies, but the principles would be exactly the same. For every quantity of commodity which is given in exchange something must be received; and if portions of the same kind of commodity be received from several distinct parties, then we may conceive the quantity which is given for that commodity to be broken up into as many distinct portions. The exchanges in the most complicated case may thus always be decomposed into simple exchanges, and every exchange will give rise to two equations sufficient to determine the quantities involved. The same can also be done when there are two or more commodities in the possession of each trading body.

···

Acquired utility of commodities

The Theory of Exchange, as explained above, rests entirely on the consideration of quantities of utility, and no reference to labour or cost of production has been made. The *value* of a divisible commodity, if I may for a moment use the dangerous term, is measured, not, indeed, by its total utility, but by its final degree of utility, that is by the intensity of the need we have for *more* of it. But the power of exchanging one commodity for another greatly extends the range of utility. We are no longer limited to considering the degree of utility of a commodity as regards the wants of its immediate possessor; for it may have a higher usefulness to some other person, and can be transferred to that person in exchange for some commodity of a higher degree of utility to the purchaser. The general result of exchange is, that all commodities sink, as it were, to the same level of utility in respect of the last portions consumed.

In the Theory of Exchange we find that the possessor of any divisible commodity will exchange such a portion of it, that the next increment would have exactly equal utility with the increment of other produce which he would receive for it. This will hold good however various may be the kinds of commodity he requires. Suppose that a person possesses one single kind of commodity, which we may consider to be money, or income, and that p, q, r, s, t, and so on, are quantities of other commodities which he purchases with portions of his income. Let x be the uncertain quantity of money which he will desire not to exchange; what relation will exist between these quantities x, p, q, r, and so on? This relation will partly depend upon the ratio of exchange, partly on the final degree of utility of these commodities. Let us assume, for a moment, that, all the ratios of exchange are equalities or that a unit of one is always to be purchased with a unit of another. Then, plainly, we must have the degrees of utility equal, otherwise there would be advantage in acquiring more of that possessing the higher degree of utility. Let the sign ϕ denote the function of utility, which will be different in each case; then we have simply the equations:

$$\phi_1 x = \phi_2 p = \phi_3 q = \phi_4 r = \phi_5 s = \text{etc.}$$

But, as a matter of fact, the ratio of exchange is seldom or never that of unit for unit; and when the quantities exchanged are unequal, the degrees of utility will not be equal. If for one pound of silk I can have three of cotton, then the degree of utility of cotton must be a third that of silk, otherwise I should gain by exchange. Thus the general result of the facility of exchange prevailing in a civilized country is, that *a person procures such quantities of commodities that the final degrees of utility of any pair of commodities are inversely as the ratios of exchange of the commodities.*

Let x_1, x_2, x_3, x_4, and so on, be the portions of his income given for p, q, r, s, and so on, respectively, then we must have

$$\frac{\phi_2 p}{\phi_1 x} = \frac{x_1}{p}, \quad \frac{\phi_3 q}{\phi_1 x} = \frac{x_2}{q}, \quad \frac{\phi_4 r}{\phi_1 x} = \frac{x_3}{r},$$

and so on. The theory thus represents the fact, that a person distributes his income in such a way as to equalize the utility of the final increments of all commodities consumed. As water runs into hollows until it fills them up to the same level, so wealth runs into all the branches of expenditure. This distribution will vary greatly with different individuals, but it is self-evident that the want which an individual feels most acutely at the moment will be that upon which he will expend the next increment of his income. It obviously follows that *in expending a person's income to the greatest advantage, the algebraic sum of the quantities of commodity received or parted with, each multiplied by its final degree of utility* [*after the exchange*], *will be zero.*

We can now conceive, in an accurate manner, the utility of money, or of that supply of commodity which forms a person's income. Its final degree, of utility is measured by that of any of the other commodities which he consumes. What, for instance, is the utility of one penny to a poor family earning fifty pounds a year? As a penny is an inconsiderable portion of their income, it may represent one of the infinitely small increments, and its utility is equal to the utility of the quantity of bread, tea, sugar, or other articles which they could purchase with it, this utility depending upon the extent to which they were already provided with those articles. To a family possessing one thousand pounds a year, the utility of a penny may be measured in an exactly similar manner; but it will be much less, because their want of any given commodity will be satiated or satisfied to a much greater extent, so that the urgency of need for a pennyworth more of any article is much reduced.

The general result of exchange is thus to produce a certain equality of utility between different commodities, as regards the same individual; but between different individuals no such equality will tend to be produced. In Economics we regard only commercial transactions, and no equalization of wealth from charitable motives is considered. The degree of utility of wealth to a very rich man will be governed by its degree of utility in that branch of expenditure in which he continues to feel the most need of further possessions. His primary wants will long since have been fully satisfied; he could find food, if requisite, for a thousand persons, and so, of course, he will have supplied himself with as much as he in the least desires. But so far as is consistent with the inequality of wealth in every community, all commodities are distributed by exchange so as to produce the maximum benefit. Every person whose wish for a certain thing exceeds his wish for other things, acquires what he wants provided he can make a sufficient sacrifice in other respects. No one is ever required to give what he more desires for what he less desires, so that perfect freedom of exchange must be to the advantage of all.

...

The origin of value

The preceding pages contain, if I am not mistaken, an explanation of the nature of value which will, for the most part, harmonize with previous views upon the subject. Ricardo has stated, like most other economists, that utility is absolutely essential to value; but that 'possessing utility, commodities derive their exchangeable value from two sources: from their scarcity, and from the quantity of labour required to obtain them'. Senior, again, has admirably defined wealth, or objects possessing value, as 'those things, and those things only, which are transferable, are limited in supply, and are directly or in directly productive of pleasure or preventive of pain'. Speaking only of things which are transferable, or capable of being passed from hand to band, we find that two of the clearest definitions of value recognize *utility* and *scarcity* as the essential qualities. But the moment that we distinguish between the total utility of a mass of commodity and the degree of utility of different portions, we may say that it is scarcity which prevents the fall in the final degree of utility. Bread has the almost infinite utility of maintaining life, and when it becomes a question of life or death, a small quantity of food exceeds in value all other things. But when we enjoy our ordinary supplies of food, a loaf of bread has little value, because the utility of an additional loaf is small, our appetites being satiated by our customary meals.

I have pointed out the excessive ambiguity of the word Value, and the apparent impossibility of using it safely. When intended to express the mere fact of certain articles exchanging in a particular ratio, I have proposed to substitute the unequivocal expression – *ratio* of exchange. But I am inclined to believe that a ratio is not the meaning which most persons attach to the word Value. There is a certain sense of esteem or desirableness, which we may have with regard to a thing apart from any distinct consciousness of the ratio in which it would exchange for other things. I may suggest that this distinct feeling of value is probably identical with the final degree of utility. While Adam Smith's often quoted *value in use* is the total utility of a commodity to us, the *value in exchange* is defined by the terminal utility, the remaining desire which we or others have for possessing more.

There remains the question of labour as an element of value. Economists have not been wanting who put forward labour as the *cause of value*, asserting that all objects derive their value from the fact that labour has been expended on them; and it is thus implied, if not stated, that value will be proportional to labour. This is a doctrine which cannot stand for a moment, being directly opposed to facts. Ricardo disposes of such an opinion when he says: 'There are some commodities, the value of which is determined by their scarcity alone. No labour can increase the quantity of such goods, and therefore their value can not be lowered by an increased supply. Some rare statues and pictures, scarce books and coins, wines of a peculiar quality, which can be made only from grapes grown on a particular soil, of which there is a very limited quantity, are all of this description. Their value is wholly independent of the quantity of labour originally necessary to produce them, and varies with the varying wealth and inclinations of those who are desirous to possess them'.

The mere fact that there are many things, such as rare ancient books, coins, antiquities, and the like, which have high values, and which are absolutely incapable of production now, disperses the notion that value depends on labour. Even those things which are producible in any quantity by labour seldom exchange exactly at the corresponding values. The market price of corn, cotton, iron, and most other things is, in the prevalent theories of value, allowed to fluctuate above or below its natural or cost value. There may, again, be any discrepancy between the quantity of labour spent upon an object and the value ultimately attaching to it. A great undertaking like the Great Western Railway, or the Thames Tunnel, may embody a vast amount of labour, but its value depends entirely upon the number of persons who find it useful. If no use could be found for the *Great Eastern* steamship, its value would be *nil*, except for the utility of some of its materials. On the other hand, a successful undertaking, which happens to possess great utility, may have a value, for a time at least, far exceeding what has been spent upon it, as in the case of the [first] Atlantic Cable. The fact is, that *labour once spent has no influence on the future value of any article*: it is gone and lost for ever. In commerce bygones are for ever bygones; and we are always starting clear at each moment, judging the values of things with a view to future utility. Industry is essentially prospective, not retrospective; and seldom does the result of any undertaking exactly coincide with the first intentions of its promoters.

But though labour is never the cause of value, it is in a large proportion of cases the determining circumstance, and in the following way: *Value depends solely on the final degree of utility. How can we vary this degree of utility? – By having more or less of the commodity to consume. And how shall we get more or less of it? – By spending more or less labour in obtaining a supply.* According to this view, then, there are two steps between labour and value. Labour affects supply, and supply affects the degree of utility, which governs value, or the ratio of exchange. In order that there may be no possible mistake about these important series of relations, I will re-state it in a tabular form, as follows:

Cost of production determines supply;
Supply determines final degree of utility;
Final degree of utility determines value.

But it is easy to go too far in considering labour as the regulator of value; it is equally to be remembered that labour is itself of unequal value. Ricardo, by a violent assumption, founded his theory of value on quantities of labour considered as one uniform thing. He was aware that labour differs infinitely in quality and efficiency, so that each kind is more or less scarce, and is consequently paid at a higher or lower rate of wages. He regarded these differences as disturbing circumstances which would have to be allowed for; but his theory rests on the assumed equality of labour. This theory rests on a wholly different ground. I hold labour to be *essentially variable, so that its value must be determined by the value of the produce, not the value of the produce by that of the labour.* I hold it to be impossible to compare á priori the productive powers of a navy, a carpenter, an iron-puddler, a schoolmaster, and a barrister. Accordingly, it will be found that not one of my equations represents a comparison between one man's labour and another's. The equation, if there is one at all, is between the same person in two or more different occupations. The subject is one in which complicated action and reaction takes place, and which we must defer until after we have described, in the next chapter, the Theory of Labour.

Chapter V: Theory of Labour

Definition of labour

Adam Smith said, 'The real price of everything, what everything really costs to the man who wants to acquire it, is the toil and trouble of acquiring it. … Labour was the first price, the original purchase-money that was paid for all things'. If subjected to a very searching analysis, this celebrated passage might not prove to be so entirely true as it would at first sight seem to most readers. Yet it is substantially true, and luminously expresses the fact that labour is the beginning of the processes treated by economists as consumption is the end and purpose. Labour is the painful exertion which we undergo to ward off pains of greater amount, or to procure pleasures which leave a balance in our favour. Courcelle-Seneuil and Hearn have stated the problem of Economics with the utmost truth and brevity in saying, that it is *to satisfy our wants with the least possible sum of labour.*

In defining *labour* for the purposes of the economist we have a choice between two courses. In the first place, we may, if we like, include in it *all exertion of body or mind*. A game of cricket would, in this case, be labour; but if it be undertaken solely for the sake of the enjoyment attaching to it, the question arises whether we need take it under our notice. All exertion not directed to a distant and distinct end must be repaid simultaneously. There is no account of good or evil to be balanced at a future time. We are not prevented in any way from including such cases in our Theory of Economics; in fact, our Theory of Labour will, of necessity, apply to them. But we need not occupy our attention by cases which demand no calculus. When we exert ourselves for the sole amusement of the moment, there is but one rule needed, namely, to stop when we feel inclined – when the pleasure no longer equals the pain.

It will probably be better, therefore, to take the second course and concentrate our attention on such exertion as is not completely repaid by the immediate result. This would give us a definition nearly the same as that of Say, who defined labour as '*Action suivée, dirigée vers un but*'. Labour, I should say, is *any painful exertion of mind or body undergone partly or wholly with a view to future good*. It is true that labour may be both agreeable at the time and conducive to future good; but it is only agreeable in a limited amount, and most men are compelled by their wants to exert themselves longer and more severely than they would otherwise do. When a labourer is inclined to stop, he clearly feels something that is irksome, and our theory will only involve the point where the exertion has become so painful as to nearly balance all other considerations. Whatever there is that is wholesome or agreeable about labour before it reaches this point may be taken as a net profit of good to the labourer; but it does not enter into the problem. It is only when labour becomes effort that we take account of it, and, as Hearn truly says, 'such effort, as the very term seems to imply, is more or less troublesome'. In fact, we must, as will shortly appear, measure labour by the amount of pain which attaches to it.

Quantitative notions of labour

Let us endeavour to form a clear notion of what we mean by amount of labour. It is plain that duration will be one element of it; for a person labouring *uniformly* during two months must be allowed to labour twice as much as during one month. But labour may vary also in intensity. In the same time a man may walk a greater or less distance; may saw a greater or less amount of timber; may pump a greater or less quantity of water; in short, may exert more or less muscular and nervous force. Hence amount of labour will be a quantity of two dimensions, the product of intensity and time when the intensity is uniform, or the sum represented by the area of a curve when the intensity is variable.

But intensity of labour may have more than one meaning; it may mean the quantity of work done, or the painfulness of the effort of doing it. These two things must be carefully distinguished, and both are of great importance for the theory. The one is the reward, the other the penalty, of labour. Or rather, as the produce is only of interest to us so far as it possesses utility, we may say that there are three quantities involved in the theory of labour – the amount of painful exertion, the amount of produce, and the amount of utility gained. The variation of utility, as depending on the quantity of commodity possessed, has already been considered; the variation of the amount of produce will be treated in the next chapter; we will here give attention to the variation of the painfulness of labour.

Experience shows that as labour is prolonged the effort becomes as a general rule more and more painful. A few hours of work per day may be considered agreeable rather than otherwise; but so soon as the overflowing energy of the body is drained off, it becomes irksome to remain at work. As exhaustion approaches, continued effort becomes more and more intolerable. Jennings has so clearly stated this law of the variation of labour, that I must quote his words. 'Between these two points, the point of incipient effort and the point of painful suffering, it is quite evident that the degree of toilsome sensations endured does not vary directly as the quantity of work performed, but increases much more rapidly, like the resistance offered by an opposing medium to the velocity of a moving body'.

'When this observation comes to be applied to the toilsome sensations endured by the working classes, it will be found convenient to fix on a middle point, the average amount of toilsome sensation attending the average amount of labour, and to measure from this point the degrees of variation. If, for the sake of illustration, this average amount be assumed to be of ten hours' duration, it would follow that, if at any period the amount were to be supposed to be reduced to five hours, the sensations of labour would be found, at least by the majority of mankind, to be almost merged in the pleasures of occupation and exercise, whilst the amount of work performed would only be diminished by one-half; if, on the contrary, the amount were to be supposed to be increased to twenty hours, the quantity of work produced would only be doubled, whilst the amount of toilsome suffering would become insupportable. Thus, if the quantity produced, greater or less than the average quantity, were to be divided into any number of parts of equal magnitude, the amount of toilsome sensation attending each succeeding increment would be found greater than that which would attend the increment preceding; and the amount of toilsome sensation attending each succeeding decrement would be found less than that which would attend the decrement preceding'.

There can be no question of the general truth of the above statement, although we may not have the data for assigning the exact law of the variation. We may imagine the painfulness of labour in proportion to produce to be represented by some such curve as *abcd* in Figure 6. In this diagram the height of points above the line *ox* denotes pleasure, and depths below it pain. At the moment of commencing labour it is usually more irksome than when the mind and body are well bent to the work. Thus, at first, the pain is measured by *oa*. At *b* there is neither pain nor pleasure. Between *b* and *c* an excess of pleasure is represented as due to the exertion itself. But after *c* the energy begins to be rapidly exhausted, and the resulting pain is shown by the downward tendency of the line *cd*.

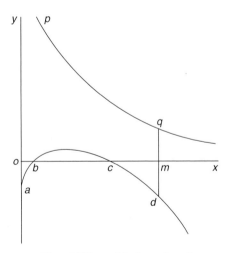

Figure 6 [Figure 9 in Jevons' text]

We may at the same time represent the degree of utility of the produce by some such curve as *pq*, the amount of produce being measured along the line *ox*. Agreeably to the theory of utility, already given, the curve shows that, the larger the wages earned, the less is the pleasure derived from a further increment. There will, of necessity, be some point *m* such that $qm = dm$, that is to say, such that the pleasure gained is exactly equal to the labour endured. Now, if we pass the least beyond this point, a balance of pain will result: there will be an ever-decreasing motive in favour of labour, and an ever-increasing motive against it. The labourer will evidently cease, then, at the point *m*. It would be inconsistent with human nature for a man to work when the pain of work exceeds the desire of possession, including all the motives for exertion.

We must consider the duration of labour as measured by the number of hours of work per day. The alternation of day and night on the earth has rendered man essentially periodic in his habits and actions. In a natural and wholesome condition a man should return each twenty-four hours to exactly the same state; at any rate, the cycle should be closed within the seven days of the week. Thus the labourer must not be supposed to be either increasing or diminishing his normal strength. But the theory might also be made to apply to cases where special exertion is undergone for many days or weeks in succession, in order to complete work, as in collecting the harvest. Adequate motives may lead to and warrant overwork, but, if long continued, excessive labour reduces the strength and becomes insupportable; and the longer it continues the worse it is, the law being somewhat similar to that of periodic labour.

CARL MENGER (1840–1921)

Carl Menger, by courtesy of The Warren J. Samuels Portrait Collection at Duke University.

Carl Menger was born in Poland and received a law degree from the University of Krakow in 1867. He became interested in economics while working in the office of the Prime Minister in Vienna and published his *Principles of Economics* in 1871, the same year that Jevons published his *Theory of Political Economy*. Apart from a three-year break serving as tutor to the Crown Prince of Austria, he was a professor at the University of Vienna from 1873 until 1903, when he resigned to devote his time fully to research and writing – in particular, fleshing out and extending the analysis first elaborated in his *Principles*. Unfortunately, he was unable to do so before his death in 1921.

Through his *Principles*, Menger made fundamental contributions to the economic theory of value and price, centering on the theory of utility and the complementarity relationships between consumer and producer goods. Menger's analysis did not use the pleasure–pain locus of Jevons, but, rather, the idea of subjectively felt human needs and the translation of these into consumer demands. He also emphasized the essential commonality between the value-determination processes of consumer ("lower order") and producer ("higher order") goods, and he did all of this sans the mathematical and diagrammatical apparatus that marks the work of Jevons and Walras. It is these themes that are dealt with in the excerpts from his *Principles*, reprinted below.

Menger was also a key player in the *Methodenstreit*, defending the use of pure theory against the German Historical School's advocacy of empirical and historical case studies. However, he simultaneously emphasized the importance of institutions and the complex manner in which they originated and evolved. He argued both that many important institutions evolved nondeliberatively, that is, without conscious design, and that these same institutions were and must be the object of deliberative critique and revision. Menger also worked in the field of monetary theory, where his writings became foundational works for the later elaboration of Austrian monetary theory in the hands of, for example, Ludwig von Mises.

References and further reading

Calwell, Bruce J., ed. (1990) *Carl Menger and His Legacy in Economics*, Durham, NC: Duke University Press.

Endres, A.M. (1995) "Carl Menger's Theory of Price Formation Reconsidered," *History of Political Economy* 27 (Summer): 261–87.

Hayek, F.A. (1981) "Carl Menger," introduction to Carl Menger, *Principles of Economics*, translated by James Dingwall and Bert F. Hoselitz, New York: New York University Press.

Hicks, J.R. and Weber, W. (eds) (1973) *Carl Menger and the Austrian School of Economics*, Oxford: Clarendon Press.

Menger, Carl (1934–1936) *The Collected Works of Carl Menger*, London: London School of Economics.

Mises, Ludwig von (1978) "Carl Menger and the Austrian School of Economics," in Ludwig von Mises, *The Clash of Group Interests and Other Essays*, New York: Center for Libertarian Studies.

Streissler, Eric (1972) "To What Extent Was the Austrian School Marginalist?" *History of Political Economy* 4 (Fall): 426–41.

Various Authors, "Carl Menger and Austrian Economics," *Atlantic Economic Journal* 6 (September): special issues.

Vaugh, Karen I. (1987) "Menger, Carl," in John Eatwell, Murray Milgate and Peter Newman (eds), *The New Palgrave: A Dictionary of Economics*, Vol. 3, London: Macmillan, 438–44.

Principles of Economics (1871)*

Chapter III: The theory of value

1. The nature and origin of value

If the requirements for a good, in a time period over which the provident activity of men is to extend, are greater than the quantity of it available to them for that time period, and if they endeavor to satisfy their needs for it as completely as possible in the given circumstances, men feel impelled to engage in the activity described earlier and designated *economizing*. But their perception of this relationship gives rise to another phenomenon, the deeper understanding of which is of decisive importance for our science. I refer to the value of goods.

If the requirements for a good are larger than the quantity of it available, and some part of the needs involved must remain unsatisfied in any case, the available quantity of the good can be diminished by no part of the whole amount, in any way practically worthy of notice, without causing some need, previously provided for, to be satisfied either not at all or only less completely than would otherwise have been the case. The satisfaction of some one human need is therefore dependent on the availability of each concrete, practically significant, quantity of all goods subject to this quantitative relationship. If economizing men become aware of this circumstance (i.e. if they perceive that the satisfaction of one of their needs, or the greater or less completeness of its satisfaction, is dependent on their command of each portion of a quantity of goods or on each individual good subject to the above quantitative relationship) these goods attain for them the significance we call *value*. Value is thus the importance that individual goods or quantities of goods attain for us because we are conscious of being dependent on command of them for the satisfaction of our needs.

The value of goods, accordingly, is a phenomenon that springs from the same source as the economic character of goods – that is, from the relationship, explained earlier, between requirements for and available quantities of goods. But there is a difference between the two phenomena. On the one hand, perception of this quantitative relationship stimulates our provident activity, thus causing goods subject to this relationship to become objects of our economizing (i.e. economic goods). On the other hand, perception of the same relationship makes us aware of the significance that command of each concrete unit of the available quantities of these goods has for our lives and well-being, thus causing it to attain *value* for us. Just as a penetrating investigation of mental processes makes the cognition of external things appear to be merely our consciousness of the impressions made by the external things upon our persons, and thus, in the final

---

* *Principles of Economics*, First, General Part, by Carl Menger, translated and edited by James Dingwall and Bert F. Hoselitz, with an Introduction by Frank H. Knight, The Free Press, Glencoe, Illinois, 1950.

analysis, merely the cognition of states of our own persons, so too, in the final analysis, is the importance that we attribute to things of the external world only an outflow of the importance to us of our continued existence and development (life and well-being). Value is therefore nothing inherent in goods, no property of them, but merely the importance that we first attribute to the satisfaction of our needs, that is, to our lives and well-being, and in consequence carry over to economic goods as the exclusive causes of the satisfaction of our needs.

From this, it is also clear why only economic goods have value to us, while goods subject to the quantitative relationship responsible for non-economic character cannot attain value at all. The relationship responsible for the non-economic character of goods consists in requirements for goods being smaller than their available quantities. Thus there are always portions of the whole supply of non-economic goods that are related to no unsatisfied human need, and which can therefore lose their goods-character without impinging in any way on the satisfaction of human needs. Hence no satisfaction depends on our control of any one of the units of a good having non-economic character, and from this it follows that definite quantities of goods subject to this quantitative relationship (non-economic goods) also have no value to us.

If an inhabitant of a virgin forest has several hundred thousand trees at his disposal while he needs only some twenty a year for the full provision of his requirements for timber, he will not consider himself injured in any way, in the satisfaction of his needs, if a forest fire destroys a thousand or so of the trees, provided he is still in a position to satisfy his needs as completely as before with the rest. In such circumstances, therefore, the satisfaction of none of his needs depends upon his command of any single tree, and for this reason a tree also has no value to him.

But suppose there are also in the forest ten wild fruit trees whose fruit is consumed by the same individual. Suppose too, that the amount of fruit available to him is not larger than his requirements. Certainly then, not a single one of these fruit trees can be burned in the fire without causing him to suffer hunger as a result, or without at least causing him to be unable to satisfy his need for fruit as completely as before. For this reason each one of the fruit trees has value to him.

If the inhabitants of a village need a thousand pails of water daily to meet their requirements completely, and a brook is at their disposal with a daily flow of a hundred thousand pails, a concrete portion of this quantity of water, one pail for instance, will have no value to them, since they could satisfy their needs for water just as completely if this partial amount were removed from their command, or if it were altogether to lose its goods-character. Indeed, they will let many thousands of pails of this good flow to the sea every day without in any way impairing satisfaction of their need for water. As long as the relationship responsible for the non-economic character of water continues, therefore, the satisfaction of none of their needs will depend upon their command of any one pail of water in such a way that the satisfaction of this need would not take place if they were not in a position to use that particular pail. For this reason a pail of water has no value to them.

If, on the other hand, the daily flow of the brook were to fall to five hundred pails daily due to an unusual drought or other act of nature, and the inhabitants of the village had no other source of supply, the result would be that the total quantity then available would be insufficient to satisfy their full needs for water, and they could not venture to lose any part of that quantity, one pail for instance, without impairing the satisfaction of their needs. Each concrete portion of the quantity at their disposal would certainly then have value to them.

Non-economic goods, therefore, not only do not have exchange value, as has previously been supposed in the literature of our subject, but no value at all, and hence no use value. I shall attempt to explain the relationship between exchange value and use value in greater detail later, when I have dealt with some of the principles relevant to their consideration. For the time being, let it be observed that exchange value and use value are two concepts subordinate to the general concept of value, and hence coordinate in their relations to each other. All that I have already said about value in general is accordingly as valid for use value as it is for exchange value.

If then, a large number of economists attribute use value (though not exchange value) to non-economic goods, and if some recent English and French economists even wish to banish the concept use value entirely from our science and see it replaced with the concept utility, their desire rests on a misunderstanding of the important difference between the two concepts and the actual phenomena underlying them.

Utility is the capacity of a thing to serve for the satisfaction of human needs, and hence (provided the utility is *recognized*) it is a general prerequisite of goods-character. Non-economic goods have utility as well as economic goods, since they are just as capable of satisfying our needs. With these goods also, their capacity to satisfy needs must be *recognized* by men, since they could not otherwise acquire goods-character. But what distinguishes a non-economic good from a good subject to the quantitative relationship responsible for economic character is the circumstance that the satisfaction of human needs does not depend upon the availability of concrete quantities of the former but does depend upon the availability of concrete quantities of the latter. For this reason the former possesses utility, but only the latter, in addition to utility, possesses also that significance for us that we call value.

Of course the error underlying the confusion of utility and use value has had no influence on the practical activity of men. At no time has an economizing individual attributed value under ordinary circumstances to a cubic foot of air or, in regions abounding in springs, to a pint of water. The practical man distinguishes very well the capacity of an object to satisfy one of his needs from its value. But this confusion has become an enormous obstacle to the development of the more general theories of our science.

The circumstance that a good has value to us is attributable, as we have seen, to the fact that command of it has for us the significance of satisfying a need that would not be provided for if we did not have command of the good. Our needs, at any rate in part, at least as concerns their origin, depend upon our wills or on our habits. Once the needs have come into existence, however, there is *no further arbitrary element* in the value goods have for us, for their value is then the necessary consequence of our knowledge of their importance for our lives or well-being. It would be impossible, therefore, for us to regard a good as valueless when we know that the satisfaction of one of our needs depends on having it at our disposal. It would also be impossible for us to attribute value to goods when we know that we are not dependent upon them for the satisfaction of our needs. The value of goods is therefore nothing arbitrary, but always the necessary consequence of human knowledge that the maintenance of life, of well-being, or of some ever so insignificant part of them, depends upon control of a good or a quantity of goods.

Regarding this *knowledge*, however, men can be in error about the value of goods just as they can be in error with respect to all other objects of human knowledge. Hence they may attribute value to things that do not, according to economic considerations, possess it in reality, if they mistakenly assume that the more or less complete satisfaction of their needs depends on a good, or quantity of goods, when this relationship is really non-existent. In cases of this sort we observe the phenomenon of *imaginary* value.

The value of goods arises from their relationship to our needs, and is not inherent in the goods themselves. With *changes in this relationship*, value arises and disappears. For the inhabitants of an oasis, who have command of a spring that abundantly meets their requirements for water, a certain quantity of water at the spring itself will have no value. But if the spring, as the result of an earthquake, should suddenly decrease its yield of water to such an extent that the satisfaction of the needs of the inhabitants of the oasis would no longer be fully provided for, each of their concrete needs for water would become dependent upon the availability of a definite quantity of it, and such a quantity would immediately attain value for each inhabitant. This value would, however, suddenly disappear if the old relationship were reestablished and the spring regained its former yield of water. A similar result would ensue if the population of the oasis should increase to such an extent that the water of the spring would no longer suffice for the satisfaction of all needs. Such a change, due to the increase of consumers, might even take place with a certain regularity at such times as the oasis was visited by numerous caravans.

Value is thus nothing inherent in goods, no property of them, nor an independent thing existing by itself. It is a judgment economizing men make about the importance of the goods at their disposal for the maintenance of their lives and well-being. Hence value does not exist outside the consciousness of men. It is, therefore, also quite erroneous to call a good that has value to economizing individuals a "value," or for economists to speak of "values" as of independent real things, and to objectify value in this way. For the entities that exist objectively are always only particular things or quantities of things, and their value is something fundamentally different from the things themselves; it is a judgment made by economizing individuals about the importance their command of the things has for the maintenance of their lives and well-being. Objectification of the value of goods, which is entirely *subjective* in nature, has nevertheless contributed very greatly to confusion about the basic principles of our science.

2. *The original measure of value*

In what has preceded, we have directed our attention to the nature and ultimate causes of value – that is, to the factors common to value in all cases. But in actual life, we find that the values of different goods are very different in magnitude, and that the value of a given good frequently changes. An investigation of the causes of differences in the value of goods and an investigation of the measure of value are the subjects that will occupy us in this section. The course of our investigation is determined by the following consideration.

The goods at our disposal have no value to us for their own sakes. On the contrary, we have seen that only the satisfaction of our needs has importance to us directly, since our lives and well-being are dependent on it. But I have also explained that men attribute this importance to the goods at their disposal if the goods ensure them the satisfaction of needs that would not be provided for if they did not have command of them – that is, they attribute this importance to economic goods. In the value of goods, therefore, we always encounter merely the significance we assign to the satisfaction of our needs – that is, to our lives and well-being. If I have adequately described the nature of the value of goods, if it has been established that in the final analysis only the satisfaction of our needs has importance to us, and if it has been established too that the value of all goods is merely an imputation of this importance to economic goods, then the *differences* we observe in the magnitude of value of different goods in actual life can only be founded on differences in the magnitude of importance of the satisfactions that depend on our command of these goods. To reduce the differences that we observe in the magnitude of value of different goods in actual life to their ultimate causes, we must therefore perform a double task. We must investigate: (i) to what extent different satisfactions have different degrees of importance to us (subjective factor), and (ii) which satisfactions of concrete needs depend, in each individual case, on our command of a particular good (objective factor). If this investigation shows that separate satisfactions of concrete needs have different degrees of importance to us, and that these satisfactions, of such different degrees of importance, depend on our command of particular economic goods, we shall have solved our problem. For we shall have reduced the economic phenomenon whose explanation we stated to be the central problem of this investigation to its ultimate causes. I mean differences in the magnitude of value of goods.

With an answer to the question as to the ultimate causes of differences in the value of goods, a solution is also provided to the problem of how it comes about that the value of each of the various goods is itself subject to change. All change consists of nothing but differences through time. Hence, with a knowledge of the ultimate causes of the differences between the members of a set of magnitudes in general, we also obtain a deeper insight into their changes.

A. Differences in the magnitude of importance of different satisfactions (subjective factor)

As concerns the differences in the importance that different satisfactions have for us, it is above all a fact of the most common experience that the satisfactions of greatest importance to men are usually those on which the maintenance of life depends, and that other satisfactions are graduated in magnitude of importance according to the degree (duration and intensity) of pleasure dependent upon them. Thus if economizing men must choose between the satisfaction of a need on which the maintenance of their lives depends and another on which merely a greater or less degree of well-being is dependent, they will usually prefer the former. Similarly, they will usually prefer satisfactions on which a higher degree of their well-being depends. With the same intensity, they will prefer pleasures of longer duration to pleasures of shorter duration, and with the same duration, pleasures of greater intensity to pleasures of less intensity.

The maintenance of our lives depends on the satisfaction of our need for food, and also, in our climate, on clothing our bodies and having shelter at our disposal. But merely a higher degree of well-being depends on our having a coach, a chessboard, etc. Thus we observe that men fear the lack of food, clothing, and shelter much more than the lack of a coach, a chessboard, etc. They also attribute a substantially higher importance to securing satisfaction of the former needs than they attribute to the satisfaction of needs on which, as in the cases just mentioned, only a passing enjoyment or increased comfort (i.e. merely a higher degree of their well-being) depends. But these satisfactions also have very different degrees of importance. The maintenance of life depends neither on having a comfortable bed nor on having a chessboard, but the use of these goods contributes, and certainly in very different degrees, to the increase of our well-being. Hence there can also be no doubt that, when men have a choice between doing without a comfortable bed or doing without a chessboard, they will forgo the latter much more readily than the former.

We have thus seen that different satisfactions are very unequal in importance, since some are satisfactions that have the full importance to men of maintaining their lives, others are satisfactions that determine their well-being in a higher degree, still others in a less degree, and so on down to satisfactions on which some insignificant passing enjoyment depends. But careful examination of the phenomena of life shows that these differences in the importance of different satisfactions can be observed not only with the satisfaction of needs of *different kinds* but also with the *more or less complete* satisfaction of one and the same need.

The lives of men depend on satisfaction of their need for food in general. But it would be entirely erroneous to regard all the foods they consume as being necessary for the maintenance of their lives or even their health (i.e. for their continuing well-being). Everyone knows how easy it is to skip one of the usual meals without endangering life or health. Indeed, experience shows that the quantities of food necessary to maintain life are only a small part of what well-to-do persons as a rule consume, and that men even take much more food and drink than is necessary for the full preservation of health. Men consume food for several reasons: above all, they take food to maintain life; beyond this, they take further quantities to preserve health, since a diet sufficient merely to maintain life is too sparing, as experience shows, to avoid organic disorders; finally, having already consumed quantities sufficient to maintain life and preserve health, men further partake of foods simply for the pleasure derived from their consumption.

The separate concrete acts of satisfying the need for food accordingly have very different degrees of importance. The satisfaction of every man's need for food up to the point where his life is thereby assured has the full importance of the maintenance of his life. Consumption exceeding this amount, again up to a certain point, has the importance of preserving his health (i.e. his continuing well-being). Consumption extending beyond even this point has merely the importance – as observation shows – of a progressively weaker pleasure, until it finally reaches a certain limit at which satisfaction of the need for food is so complete that every further intake of food contributes neither to the maintenance of life nor to the preservation of health – nor does it even give pleasure to the consumer, becoming first a matter of indifference to him, eventually a cause of pain, a danger to health, and finally a danger to life itself.

Similar observations can be made with respect to the more or less complete satisfaction of all other human needs. A room, or at least some place to sleep protected from the weather, is necessary in our climate for the maintenance of life, and reasonably spacious quarters for the preservation of health. In addition, however, men usually possess further accommodations, if they have the means, merely for purposes of pleasure (drawing rooms, ballrooms, playrooms, pavilions, hunting lodges, etc.). Thus it is not difficult to recognize that the separate concrete acts of satisfying the need for shelter have very different degrees of importance. Up to a certain point, our lives depend on satisfying our need for shelter. Beyond this, our health depends on a more complete satisfaction. And still further attempts to satisfy the same need will bring at first a greater and then a smaller enjoyment, until eventually a point can be conceived, for each person, at which the further *employment* of available accommodations would become a matter of complete indifference to him, and finally even burdensome.

It is possible, therefore, with respect to the more or less complete satisfaction of one and the same need, to make an observation similar to the one made earlier with respect to the different needs of men. We saw earlier that the different needs of men are very unequal in importance of satisfaction, being graduated from the importance of their lives down to the importance they attribute to a small passing enjoyment. We see now, in addition, that the satisfaction of any one specific need has, up to a certain degree of completeness, relatively the highest importance, and that further satisfaction has a progressively smaller importance, until eventually a stage is reached at which a more complete satisfaction of that particular need is a matter of indifference. Ultimately a stage occurs at which every act having the external appearance of a satisfaction of this need not only has no further importance to the consumer but is rather a burden and a pain.

In order to restate the preceding argument numerically, to facilitate comprehension of the subsequent difficult investigation, I shall designate the importance of satisfactions on which life depends with 10, and the smaller importance of the other satisfactions successively with 9, 8, 7, 6, etc. In this way we obtain a scale of the importance of *different* satisfactions that begins with 10 and ends with 1.

Let us now, for each of these different satisfactions, give numerical expression to the additional importance, diminishing by degrees from the figure indicating the extent to which the particular need is already satisfied, of further acts of satisfaction of that particular need. For satisfactions on which, up to a certain point, our lives depend, and on which, beyond this point, a well-being is dependent that steadily decreases with the degree of completeness of the satisfaction already achieved, we obtain a scale that begins with 10 and ends with 0. Similarly, for satisfactions whose highest importance is 9, we obtain a scale that begins with this figure and also ends with 0, and so on.

The ten scales obtained in this way are given in the following table:

I	II	III	IV	V	VI	VII	VIII	IX	X
10	9	8	7	6	5	4	3	2	1
9	8	7	6	5	4	3	2	1	0
8	7	6	5	4	3	2	1	0	
7	6	5	4	3	2	1	0		
6	5	4	3	2	1	0			
5	4	3	2	1	0				
4	3	2	1	0					
3	2	1	0						
2	1	0							
1	0								
0									

The Roman numerals in the top line of the table are symbols designating the different commodities (or classes of commodities) consumed by a single individual. The successive figures down each vertical column represent successive additions to total satisfaction resulting from increased consumption of the designated commodity. ... – TR.

Suppose that the scale in column I expresses the importance to some one individual of satisfaction of his need for food, this importance diminishing according to the degree of satisfaction already attained, and that the scale in column V expresses similarly the importance of his need for tobacco. It is evident that satisfaction of his need for food, up to a certain degree of completeness, has a decidedly higher importance to this individual than satisfaction of his need for tobacco. But if his need for food is already satisfied up to a certain degree of completeness (if, e.g. a further satisfaction of his need for food has only the importance to him that we designated numerically by the figure 6), consumption of tobacco begins to have the same importance to him as further satisfaction of his need for food. The individual will therefore endeavor, from this point on, to bring the satisfaction of his need for tobacco into equilibrium with satisfaction of his need for food. Although satisfaction of his need for food in general has a substantially higher importance to the individual in question than satisfaction of his need for tobacco, with the progressive satisfaction of the former a stage nevertheless comes (as is illustrated in the table) at which further acts of satisfaction of his need for food have a smaller importance to him than the first acts of satisfying his need for tobacco, which although less important in general is at this stage still wholly unsatisfied.

By this reference to an ordinary phenomenon of life, I believe I have clarified satisfactorily the meaning of the numbers in the table, which were chosen merely to facilitate demonstration of a difficult and previously unexplored field of psychology.

The varying importance that satisfaction of separate concrete needs has for men is not foreign to the consciousness of any economizing man, however little attention has hitherto been paid by scholars to the phenomena here treated. Wherever men live, and whatever level of civilization they occupy, we can observe how economizing individuals weigh the relative importance of satisfaction of their various needs in general, how they weigh especially the relative importance of the separate acts leading to the more or less complete satisfaction of each need, and how they are finally guided by the results of this comparison into activities directed to the fullest possible satisfaction of their needs (economizing). Indeed, this weighing of the relative importance of needs – this choosing between needs that are to remain unsatisfied and needs that are, in accordance with the available means, to attain satisfaction, and determining the degree to which the latter are to be satisfied – is the very part of the economic activity of men that fills their minds more than any other, that has the most far-reaching influence on their economic efforts, and that is exercised almost continually by every economizing individual. But human knowledge of the different degrees of importance of satisfaction of different needs and of separate acts of satisfaction is also the first cause of differences in the value of goods.

B. The dependence of separate satisfactions on particular goods (objective factor)

If, opposite each particular concrete need of men, there was but a single available good, and that good was suitable exclusively for the satisfaction of the one need (so that, on the one side, satisfaction of the need would not take place if the particular good were not at our disposal, and on the other side, the good would be capable of serving for the satisfaction of that concrete need and no other) the determination of the value of the good would be very easy; it would be equal to the importance we attribute to satisfaction of that need. For it is evident that whenever we are dependent, in satisfying a given need, on the availability of a certain good (i.e. whenever this satisfaction would not take place if we did not have the good at our disposal) and when that good is, at the same time, not suitable for any other useful purpose, it can attain the full but never any other importance than that which the given satisfaction has for us. Hence, according to whether the importance of the given satisfaction to us, in a case such as this, is greater or smaller, the value of the particular good to us will be greater or smaller. If, for instance, a myopic individual were cast away on a lonely island and found among the goods he had salvaged just *one* pair of glasses correcting his myopia but no second pair, there is no doubt that these glasses would have the full importance to him that he attributes to corrected eyesight, and just as certainly no greater importance, since the glasses would hardly be suitable for the satisfaction of other needs.

But in ordinary life the relationship between available goods and our needs is generally much more complicated. Usually not a single good but a *quantity* of goods stands opposite not a single concrete need but a *complex* of such needs. Sometimes a larger and sometimes a smaller number of satisfactions, of very different degrees of importance, depends on our command of a given quantity of goods, and each one of the goods has the ability to produce these satisfactions differing so greatly in importance.

An isolated farmer, after a rich harvest, has more than two hundred bushels of wheat at his disposal. A portion of this secures him the maintenance of his own and his family's lives until the next harvest, and another portion the preservation of health; a third portion assures him seed-grain for the next seeding; a fourth portion may be employed for the production of beer, whiskey, and other luxuries; and a fifth portion may be used for the fattening of his cattle. Several remaining bushels, which he cannot use further for these more important satisfactions, he allots to the feeding of pets in order to make the balance of his grain in *some* way useful.

The farmer is, therefore, dependent upon the grain in his possession for satisfactions of very different degrees of importance. At first he secures with it his own and his family's lives, and then his own and his family's health. Beyond this, he secures with it the uninterrupted operation of his farm, an important foundation of his continuing welfare. Finally, he employs a portion of his grain for purposes of pleasure, and in so doing is again employing his grain for purposes that are of very different degrees of importance to him.

We are thus considering a case – one that is typical of ordinary life – in which satisfactions of very different degrees of importance depend on the availability of a quantity of goods that we shall assume, for the sake of greater simplicity, to be composed of completely homogeneous units. The question that now arises is: what, under the given conditions, is the value of a certain portion of the grain to our farmer? Will the bushels of grain that secure his own and his family's lives have a higher value to him than the bushels that enable him to seed his fields? And will the latter bushels have a greater value to him than the bushels of grain he employs for purposes of pleasure?

No one will deny that the satisfactions that seem assured by the various portions of the available supply of grain are very unequal in importance, ranging from an importance of 10 to an importance of 1 in terms of our earlier designations. Yet no one will be able to maintain that some bushels of grain (those, for instance, with which the farmer will nourish himself and his family till the next harvest) will have a higher value to him than other bushels of the same quality (those, for instance, from which he will make luxury beverages).

In this and in every other case where satisfactions of different degrees of importance depend on command of a given quantity of goods, we are, above all, faced with the difficult question: which particular satisfaction is dependent on a particular portion of the quantity of goods in question?

The solution of this most important question of the theory of value follows from reflection upon human economy and the nature of value.

We have seen that the efforts of men are directed toward fully satisfying their needs, and where this is impossible, toward satisfying them *as completely as possible*. If a quantity of goods stands opposite needs of varying importance to men, they will first satisfy, or provide for, those needs whose satisfaction has the greatest importance to them. If there are any goods remaining, they will direct them to the satisfaction of needs that are next in degree of importance to those already satisfied. Any further remainder will be applied consecutively to the satisfaction of needs that come next in degree of importance.

If a good can be used for the satisfaction of several different kinds of needs, and if, with respect to each kind of need, successive single acts of satisfaction each have diminishing importance according to the degree of completeness with which the need in question has already been satisfied, economizing men will first employ the quantities of the good that are available to them to secure those acts of satisfaction, without regard to the kind of need, which have the highest importance for them. They will employ any remaining quantities to secure satisfactions of concrete needs that are next in importance, and any further remainder to secure successively less important satisfactions. The end result of this procedure is that the most important of the satisfactions that cannot be achieved have the same importance for every kind of need, and hence that all needs are being satisfied up to an equal degree of importance of the separate acts of satisfaction.

We have been asking what value a given unit of a quantity of goods possessed by an economizing individual has for him. Our question can be more precisely stated with respect to the nature of value if it is stated in this form: which satisfaction would not be attained if the economizing individual did not have the given unit at his disposal – that is, if he were to have command of a total amount smaller by that one unit? The answer, which follows from the previous exposition of the nature of human economy, is that every economizing individual would in this case, with the quantity of goods yet remaining to him, by all means satisfy his more important needs and forgo satisfaction of the less important ones. Thus, of all the satisfactions previously obtained, only the one that has the smallest importance to him would now be unattained.

Accordingly, (in every concrete case) of all the satisfactions secured by means of the whole quantity of a good at the disposal of an economizing individual, only those that have the least importance to him are dependent on the availability of a given portion of the whole quantity. Hence the value to this person of any portion of the whole available quantity of the good is equal to the importance to him of the satisfactions of least importance among those assured by the whole quantity and achieved with an equal portion.

Suppose that an individual needs 10 discrete units (or 10 measures) of a good for the full satisfaction of all his needs for that good, that these needs vary in importance from 10 to 1, but that he has only 7 units (or only 7 measures) of the good at his command. From what has been said about the nature of human economy it is directly evident that this individual will satisfy only those of his needs for the good that range in importance from 10 to 4 with the quantity at his command (7 units), and that the other needs, ranging in importance from 3 to 1, will remain unsatisfied. What is the value to the economizing individual in question of one of his 7 units (or measures) in this case? According to what we have learned about the nature of the value of goods, this question is equivalent to the question: what is the importance of the satisfactions that would be unattained if the individual concerned were to have only 6 instead of 7 units (or measures) at his command. If some accident were to deprive him of one of his seven goods (or measures), it is clear that the person in question would use the remaining 6 units to satisfy the more important needs and would neglect the least important one. Hence the result of losing one good (or one measure) would be that only the least of all the satisfactions assured by the whole available quantity of seven units (i.e. the satisfaction whose importance was designated as 4) would be lost, while those satisfactions (or acts of satisfying needs) whose importance ranges from 10 to 5 would take place as before. In this case, therefore, only a satisfaction whose importance was designated by 4 will depend on command of a single unit (or measure), and as long as the individual in question continues to have command of 7 units (or measures) of the good, the value of each unit (or measure) will be equal to the importance of this satisfaction. For it is only this satisfaction with an importance of 4 that depends on one unit (or measure) of the available quantity of the good. Other things being equal, if only 5 units (or measures) of the good were available to the economizing individual in question, it is evident that – as long as this economic situation persisted – each discrete unit or partial quantity of the good would have an importance to him expressed numerically by the figure 6. If he had 3 units, each one would have an importance to him expressed numerically by the figure 8. Finally, if he had but a single good, its importance would be equal to 10.

...

If we summarize what has been said, we obtain the following principles as the result of our investigation thus far:

1   The importance that goods have for us and which we call value is merely imputed. Basically, only satisfactions have importance for us, because the maintenance of our lives and well-being depend on them. But we logically impute this importance to the goods on whose availability we are conscious of being dependent for these satisfactions.

2   The magnitudes of importance that different satisfactions of concrete needs (the separate acts of satisfaction that can be realized by means of individual goods) have for us are unequal, and their measure lies in the degree of their importance for the maintenance of our lives and welfare.

3   The magnitudes of the importance of our satisfactions that are imputed to goods – that is, the magnitudes of their values – are therefore also unequal, and their measure lies in the degree of importance that the satisfactions dependent on the goods in question have for us.

4   In each particular case, of all the satisfactions assured by the whole available quantity of a good, only those that have the least importance to an economizing individual are dependent on command of a given portion of the whole quantity.

5   The value of a particular good or of a given portion of the whole quantity of a good at the disposal of an economizing individual is thus for him equal to the importance of the least

important of the satisfactions assured by the whole available quantity and achieved with any equal portion. For it is with respect to these least important satisfactions that the economizing individual concerned is dependent on the availability of the particular good, or given quantity of a good.

Thus, in our investigation to this point, we have traced the differences in the value of goods back to their ultimate causes, and have also, at the same time, found the ultimate, and original, measure by which the values of all goods are judged by men.

If what has been said is correctly understood, there can be no difficulty in solving any problem involving the explanation of the causes determining the differences between the values of two or more concrete goods or quantities of goods.

If we ask, for example, why a pound of drinking water has no value whatsoever to us under ordinary circumstances, while a minute fraction of a pound of gold or diamonds generally exhibits a very high value, the answer is as follows: Diamonds and gold are so rare that all the diamonds available to mankind could be kept in a chest and all the gold in a single large room, as a simple calculation will show. Drinking water, on the other hand, is found in such large quantities on the earth that a reservoir can hardly be imagined large enough to hold it all. Accordingly, men are able to satisfy only the most important needs that gold and diamonds serve to satisfy, while they are usually in a position not only to satisfy their needs for drinking water fully but, in addition, also to let large quantities of it escape unused, since they are unable to use up the whole available quantity. Under ordinary circumstances, therefore, no human need would have to remain unsatisfied if men were unable to command some particular quantity of drinking water. With gold and diamonds, on the other hand, even the least significant satisfactions assured by the total quantity available still have a relatively high importance to economizing men. Thus concrete quantities of drinking water usually have *no* value to economizing men but concrete quantities of gold and diamonds a *high* value.

All this holds only for the ordinary circumstances of life, when drinking water is available to us in copious quantities and gold and diamonds in very small quantities. In the desert, however, where the life of a traveller is often dependent on a drink of water, it can by all means be imagined that more important satisfactions depend, for an individual, on a pound of water than on even a pound of gold. In such a case, the value of a pound of water would consequently be greater, for the individual concerned, than the value of a pound of gold. And experience teaches us that such a relationship, or one that is similar, actually develops where the economic situation is as I have just described.

...

3. *The laws governing the value of goods of higher order*

A. The principle determining the value of goods of higher order

Among the most egregious of the fundamental errors that have had the most far-reaching consequences in the previous development of our science is the argument that goods attain value for us because goods were employed in their production that had value to us. Later, when I come to the discussion of the prices of goods of higher order, I shall show the specific causes that were responsible for this error and for its becoming the foundation of the accepted theory of prices (in a form hedged about with all sorts of special provisions, of course). Here I want to state, above all, that this argument is so strictly opposed to all experience ... that it would have to be rejected even if it provided a *formally* correct solution to the problem of establishing a principle explaining the value of goods.

But even this last purpose cannot be achieved by the argument in question, since it offers an explanation only for the value of goods we may designate as "products" but not for the value of all other goods, which appear as original factors of production. It does not explain the value of goods directly provided by nature, especially the services of land. It does not explain the value of labor services. Nor does it even, as we shall see later, explain the value of the services of capital. For the value of all these goods cannot be explained by the argument that goods derive their value from the value of the goods expended in their production. Indeed, it makes their value completely incomprehensible.

This argument, therefore, provides neither a formally correct solution nor one that conforms with the facts of reality, to the problem of discovering a universally valid explanation of the value of goods. On the one hand, it is in contradiction with experience; and on the other hand, it is patently inapplicable wherever we have to deal with goods that are not the product of the combination of goods of higher order. The value of goods of lower order cannot, therefore, be determined by the value of the goods of higher order that were employed in their production. On the contrary, it is evident that the value of goods of higher order is always and without exception determined by the prospective value of the goods of lower order in whose production they serve. The existence of our *requirements* for goods of higher order is dependent upon the goods they serve to produce having expected economic character ... and hence expected *value*. In securing our requirements for the satisfaction of our needs, we do not need command of goods that are suitable for the production of goods of lower order that have no expected value (since we have no requirements for them). We therefore have the principle that the value of goods of higher order is dependent upon the expected value of the goods of lower order they serve to produce. Hence goods of higher order can attain value, or retain it once they have it, only if, or as long as, they serve to produce goods that we expect to have value for us. If this fact is established, it is clear also that the value of goods of higher order cannot be the *determining* factor in the prospective value of the corresponding goods of lower order. Nor can the value of the goods of higher order already expended in producing a good of lower order be the determining factor in its present value. On the contrary, the value of goods of higher order is, in all cases, regulated by the prospective value of the goods of lower order to whose production they have been or will be assigned by economizing men.

The prospective value of goods of lower order is often – and this must be carefully observed – very different from the value that similar goods have in the present. For this reason, the value of the goods of higher order by means of which we shall have command of goods of lower order at some future time ... is by no means measured by the current value of similar goods of lower order, but rather by the prospective value of the goods of lower order in whose production they serve.

Suppose, for example, that we have the saltpetre, sulphur, charcoal, specialized labor services, appliances, etc., necessary for the production of a certain quantity of gunpowder, and that thus, by means of these goods, we shall have this quantity of gunpowder at our command in three months time. It is clear that the value this gunpowder is expected to have for us in three months time need not necessarily be equal to, but may be greater or less than, the value of an identical quantity of gunpowder at the present time. Hence also, the magnitude of the value of the above goods of higher order is measured, not by the value of gunpowder at present, but by the prospective value of their product at the end of the production period. Cases can even be imagined in which a good of lower or first order is completely valueless at present (ice in winter, for example), while simultaneously available corresponding goods of higher order that assure quantities of the good of lower order for a future time period (all the materials and implements necessary for the production of artificial ice, for example) have value with respect to this future time period – and vice versa.

Hence there is no necessary connection between the value of goods of lower or first order in the present and the value of currently available goods of higher order serving for the production of such goods. On the contrary, it is evident that the former derive their value from the relationship between requirements and available quantities in the present, while the latter derive their value from the prospective relationship between the requirements and the quantities that will be available at the future points in time when the products created by means of the goods of higher order will become available. If the prospective future value of a good of lower order rises, other things remaining equal, the value of the goods of higher order whose possession assures us future command of the good of lower order rises also. But the rise or fall of the value of a good of lower order available in the present has no necessary causal connection with the rise or fall of the value of currently available corresponding goods of higher order.

Hence the principle that the value of goods of higher order is governed, not by the value of corresponding goods of lower order of the present, but rather by the prospective value of the product, is the universally valid principle of the determination of the value of goods of higher order.

Only the satisfaction of our needs has direct and immediate significance to us. In each concrete instance, this significance is measured by the importance of the various satisfactions for our lives and well-being. We next attribute the exact quantitative magnitude of this importance to the specific goods on which we are conscious of being directly dependent for the satisfactions in question – that is, we attribute it to economic goods of first order, as explained in the principles of the previous section. In cases in which our requirements are not met or are only incompletely met by goods of first order, and in which goods of first order therefore attain value for us, we turn to the corresponding goods of the next higher order in our efforts to satisfy our needs as completely as possible, and attribute the value that we attributed to goods of first order in turn to goods of second, third, and still higher orders whenever these goods of higher order have economic character. The value of goods of *higher order* is therefore, in the final analysis, nothing but a special form of the importance we attribute to our lives and well-being. Thus, as with goods of first order, the factor that is ultimately responsible for the value of goods of higher order is merely the importance that we attribute to those satisfactions with respect to which we are aware of being dependent on the availability of the goods of higher order whose value is under consideration. But due to the causal connections between goods, the value of goods of higher order is not measured directly by the expected importance of the final satisfaction, but rather by the expected value of the corresponding goods of lower order.

...

C. The value of complementary quantities of goods of higher order

In order to transform goods of higher order into goods of lower order, the passage of a certain period of time is necessary. Hence, whenever economic goods are to be produced, *command of the services of capital is necessary for a certain period of time.* The length of this period varies according to the nature of the production process. In any given branch of production, it is longer the higher the order of the goods to be directed to the satisfaction of human needs. But some passage of time is inseparable from any process of production.

During these time periods, the quantity of economic goods of which I am speaking (capital) is fixed, and not available for other productive purposes. In order to have a good or a quantity of goods of lower order at our command at a future time, it is not sufficient to have fleeting possession of the corresponding goods of higher order at some single point in time, but instead necessary that we retain command of these goods of higher order for a period of time that varies in length according to the nature of the particular process of production, and that we *fix* them in this production process for the duration of that period.

In the preceding section, we saw that command of quantities of economic goods for given periods of time has value to economizing men, just as other economic goods have value to them. From this it follows that the aggregate present value of all the goods of higher order necessary for the production of a good of lower order can be set equal to the prospective value of the product to economizing men only if the value of the services of capital during the production period is included.

Suppose, for example, we wish to determine the value of the goods of higher order that assure us command of a given quantity of grain a year hence. The value of the seed grain, the services of land, the specialized agricultural labor services, and all the other goods of higher order necessary for the production of the given quantity of grain will indeed be equal to the *prospective* value of the grain at the end of the year ..., but only on condition that the value of a year's command of these economic goods to the economizing individuals concerned is included in the sum. The *present* value of these goods of higher order by themselves is therefore equal to the value of the prospective product minus the value of the services of the capital employed.

To express what has been said numerically, suppose that the prospective value of the product that will be available at the end of the year is 100, and that the value of a year's command of the necessary quantities of economic goods of higher order (the value of the services of capital) is 10. It is clear that the aggregate value of all the complementary goods of higher order required for the production of the product, excluding the services of capital, is equal not to 100, but only to 90. If the value of the services of capital were 15, the present value of the other goods of higher order would be only 85.

The value of goods to the economizing individuals concerned is, as I have already stated several times, the most important foundation of price formation. Now if, in ordinary life, we see that buyers of goods of higher order never pay the full prospective price of a good of lower order for the complementary means of production technically necessary for its production, that they are always only in a position to grant, and actually do grant, prices for them that are somewhat lower than the price of the product, and that the sale of goods of higher order thus has a certain similarity to discounting, the prospective price of the product forming the basis of the computation, these facts are explained by the preceding argument.

A person who has at his disposal the goods of higher order required for the production of goods of lower order does not, by virtue of this fact, have command of the goods of lower order immediately and directly, but only after the passage of a period of time that is longer or shorter according to the nature of the production process. If he wishes to exchange his goods of higher order immediately for the corresponding goods of lower order, or for what is the same thing under developed trade relations, a corresponding sum of money, he is evidently in a position similar to that of a person who is to receive a certain sum of money at a future point in time (after 6 months, for example) but who wants to obtain command of it immediately. If the owner of goods of higher order intends to transfer them to a third person and is willing to receive payment only after the end of the production process, naturally no "discounting" takes place. In fact, we can observe the prices of goods that are sold on credit rising higher (apart from the risk premium) the further the agreed-upon date of payment lies in the future. All this, however, explains at the same time why the productive activity of a people is greatly promoted by credit. In by far the greater number of cases, credit transactions consist in handing goods of higher order over to persons who transform them into corresponding goods of lower order. Production, or more extensive fabrication at least, is very often only possible through credit; hence the pernicious stoppage and curtailment of the productive activity of a people when credit suddenly ceases to flow.

The process of transforming goods of higher order into goods of lower or first order, provided it is economic in other respects, must also always be planned and conducted, with some economic purpose in view, by an economizing individual. This individual must carry through the economic computations of which I have just been speaking, and he must actually bring the goods of higher order, including technical labor services, together (or cause them to be brought together) for the purpose of production. The question as to which functions are included in this so-called *entrepreneurial activity* has already been posed several times. Above all we must bear in mind that an entrepreneur's own *technical* labor services are often among the goods of higher order that he has at his command for purposes of production. When this is the case, he assigns them, just like the services of other persons, their roles in the production process. The owner of a magazine is often a contributor to his own magazine. The industrial entrepreneur often works in his own factory. Each of them is an entrepreneur, however, not because of his technical participation in the production process, but because he makes not only the underlying economic calculations but also the actual decisions to assign goods of higher order to particular productive purposes. Entrepreneurial activity includes: (a) obtaining *information* about the economic situation; (b) economic calculation – all the various computations that must be made if a production process is to be efficient (provided that it is economic in other respects); (c) the *act of will* by which goods of higher order (or goods in general – under conditions of developed commerce, where any economic good can be exchanged for any other) are assigned to a particular production process; and finally (d) *supervision* of the execution of the production plan so that it may be carried through as economically as possible. In small firms, these entrepreneurial activities usually occupy but an inconsiderable part of the time of the entrepreneur. In large firms, however, not only the entrepreneur himself, but often several helpers, are fully occupied with these activities. But however extensive the activities of these helpers may be, the four functions listed above can always be observed in the actions of the entrepreneur, even if they are ultimately confined (as in corporations) to determining the allocation of portions of wealth to particular productive purposes only by general categories, and to the selection and control of persons. After what has been said, it will be evident that I cannot agree with Mangoldt, who designates "risk bearing" as the *essential* function of entrepreneurship in a production process, since this "risk" is only incidental and the chance of loss is counterbalanced by the chance of profit.

In the early stages of civilization and even later in the case of small manufactures, entrepreneurial activity is usually performed by the same economizing individual whose technical labor services also constitute one of the factors in the production process. With progressive division of labor and an increase in the size of enterprises, entrepreneurial activity often occupies his full time. For this reason, entrepreneurial activity is just as necessary a factor in the production of goods as technical labor services. It therefore has the character of a good of higher order, and value too, since like other goods of higher order it is also generally an economic good. Hence whenever we wish to determine the present value of complementary quantities of goods of higher order, the prospective value of the product determines the total value of all of them together only if the value of entrepreneurial activity is included in the total.

Let me summarize the results of this section. The aggregate present value of all the complementary quantities of goods of higher order (i.e. all the raw materials, labor services, services of land, machines, tools, etc.) necessary for the production of a good of lower or first order is equal to the prospective value of the product. But it is necessary to include in the sum not only the goods of higher order technically required for its production but also the services of capital and the activity of the entrepreneur. For these are as unavoidably necessary in every economic production of goods as the technical requisites already mentioned. Hence the *present* value of the technical factors of production by themselves is not equal to the full prospective value of the product, but always behaves in such a way that a margin for the value of the services of capital and entrepreneurial activity remains.

D. The value of individual goods of higher order

We have seen that the value of a particular good (or of a given quantity of goods) to the economizing individual who has it at his command is equal to the importance he attaches to the satisfactions he would have to forgo if he did not have command of it. From this we could infer, without difficulty, that the value of each unit of goods of higher order is likewise equal to the importance of the satisfactions assured by command of a unit if we were not impeded by the fact that a good of higher order cannot be employed for the satisfaction of human needs by itself but only in combination with other (the complementary) goods of higher order. Because of this, however, the opinion could arise that we are dependent, for the satisfaction of concrete needs, not on command of an individual concrete good (or concrete quantity of some one kind of good) of higher order, but rather on command of complementary quantities of goods of higher order, and that therefore only aggregates of complementary goods of higher order can independently attain value for an economizing individual.

It is, of course, true that we can obtain quantities of goods of lower order only by means of *complementary* quantities of goods of higher order. But it is equally certain that the various goods of higher order need not always be combined in the production process in fixed proportions (in the manner, perhaps, that is to be observed in the case of chemical reactions, where only a certain weight of one substance combines with an equally fixed weight of another substance to yield a given chemical compound). The most ordinary experience teaches us rather that a given quantity of some one good of lower order can be produced from goods of higher order that stand in very different quantitative relationships with one another. In fact, one or several goods of higher order that are complementary to a group of certain other goods of higher order may often be omitted altogether without destroying the capacity of the remaining complementary goods to produce the good of lower order. The services of land, seed, labor services, fertilizer, the services of agricultural implements, etc., are used to produce grain. But no one will be able to deny that a *given* quantity of grain can also be produced without the use of fertilizer and without employing a large part of the usual agricultural implements, provided only that the other goods of higher order used for the production of grain are available in correspondingly larger quantities.

If experience thus teaches us that some complementary goods of higher order can often be omitted entirely in the production of goods of lower order, we can much more frequently observe, not only that given products can be produced by varying quantities of goods of higher order, but also that there is generally a very wide range within which the proportions of goods applied to their production can be, and actually are, varied. Everyone knows that, even on land of homogeneous quality, a given quantity of grain can be produced on fields of very different sizes if more or less intensively tilled – that is, if larger or smaller quantities of the other complementary goods of higher order are applied to them. In particular, an insufficiency of fertilizer can be compensated for by the employment of a larger amount of land or better machines, or by the more intensive application of agricultural labor services. Similarly, a diminished quantity of almost every good of higher order can be compensated for by a correspondingly greater application of the other complementary goods.

But even where particular goods of higher order cannot be replaced by quantities of other complementary goods, and a diminution of the available quantity of some particular good of higher order causes a corresponding diminution of the product (in the production of some chemical, for instance), the corresponding quantities of the other means of production do not necessarily become valueless when this one production good is lacking. The other means of production can, as a rule, still be applied to the production of other consumption goods, and so in the last analysis to the satisfaction of human needs, even if these needs are usually less important than the needs that could have been satisfied if the missing quantity of the complementary good under consideration had been available.

As a rule, therefore, what depends on a given quantity of a good of higher order is not command of an exactly corresponding quantity of product, but only a portion of the product and often only its higher quality. Accordingly, the value of a given quantity of a particular good of higher order is not equal to the importance of the satisfactions that depend on the whole product it helps to produce, but is equal merely to the importance of the satisfactions provided for by the portion of the product that would remain unproduced if we were not in a position to command the given quantity of the good of higher order. Where the result of a diminution of the available quantity of a good of higher order is not a decrease in the quantity of product but a worsening of its quality, the value of a given quantity of a good of higher order is equal to the difference in importance between the satisfactions that can be achieved with the more highly qualified product and those that can be achieved with the less qualified product. In both cases, therefore, it is not satisfactions provided by the whole product that a given quantity of a particular good of higher order helps to produce that are dependent on command of it, but only satisfactions of the importance here explained.

Even where a diminution of the available quantity of a particular good of higher order causes the product (some chemical compound, for example) to diminish proportionately, the other complementary quantities of goods of higher order do not become valueless. Although their complementary factor of production is now missing, they can still be applied to the production of other goods of lower order, and thus directed to the satisfaction of human needs, even if these needs are, perhaps, somewhat less important than would otherwise have been the case. Thus in this case too, the full value of the product that would be lost to us for lack of a particular good of higher order is not the determining factor in its value. Its value is equal only to the difference in importance between the satisfactions that are assured if we have command of the good of higher order whose value we wish to determine and the satisfactions that would be achieved if we did not have it at our command.

If we summarize these three cases, we obtain a general law of the determination of the value of a concrete quantity of a good of higher order. Assuming in each instance that all available goods of higher order are employed in the most economic fashion, the value of a concrete quantity of a good of higher order is equal to the difference in importance between the satisfactions that can be attained when we have command of the given quantity of the good of higher order whose value we wish to determine and the satisfactions that would be attained if we did not have this quantity at our command.

This law corresponds exactly to the general law of value determination ... since the difference referred to in the law of the preceding paragraph represents the importance of the satisfactions that depend on our command of a given good of higher order.

If we examine this law with respect to what was said earlier ... about the value of the complementary quantities of goods of higher order required for the production of a consumption good, we obtain a corollary principle: the value of a good of higher order will be greater (1) the greater the prospective value of the product if the value of the other complementary goods necessary for its production remains equal, and (2) the lower, other things being equal, the value of the complementary goods.

...

LEON WALRAS (1834–1910)

Leon Walras, by Courtesy of Donald A. Walker.

Leon Walras, the son of economist Auguste Walras, was born in France and educated at the University of Paris. After a time studying engineering, working as a journalist and then in the railway and banking sectors, Walras received an appointment as a professor of political economy at the University of Lausanne.

Walras not only was a co-founder of the marginal utility approach to economic theory, he was the first economist to self-consciously and elaborately develop a mathematical model of general equilibrium – doing so in his *Elements of Pure Economics*, published in two parts in 1874 and 1877. Unlike Jevons' *Theory of Political Economy* and Menger's *Principles*, the *Elements* was largely ignored for a long time after its publication, in spite of Walras' extensive efforts to promote it. The book was simply too mathematically complex for many contemporary readers. On the other hand, the extent of the insight into the market process under idealized conditions evidenced in the *Elements* has resulted in it being far more read in the modern era than the works of Walras' fellow "revolutionaries."

Walras constructed his basic analytical structure of general equilibrium sequentially, beginning with the simplest of cases and gradually increasing the degree of complexity. The analysis starts with the case of two parties and two goods in a pure exchange (barter) system, where he derives the same consumer exchange equilibrium equations as Jevons but moved on to the derivation of downward-sloping consumer demands. From there, he moves to exchange involving multiple parties and multiple goods, then to the addition of production to the system, and lastly to the inclusion of credit and money. The result was an analytical system in which prices adjust through a process that Walras labeled *tâtonnement* to eliminate excess supplies and demands, with the end result being a system of prices such that all markets in the system clear simultaneously.

Walras was not interested solely in pure economic theory. He also wrote on monetary theory and reform, and concentrated as well on rational efforts to reform society along moderate socialist lines. In fact, he had hoped to write a major treatise on social and applied economics that was on a par with his *Elements*, but he never managed to compete it.

The excerpts from the *Elements* reprinted here illustrate the case of exchange with several commodities and the determination of general equilibrium in that context.

References and further reading

Arrow, Kenneth J. and Hahn, Frank H. (1971) *General Competitive Analysis*, San Francisco: Holden-Day.

Collard, David (1973) "Léon Walras and the Cambridge Caricature," *Economic Journal* 83 (June): 465–76.

Eatwell, John (1987) "Walras's Theory of Capital," in John Eatwell, Murray Milgate, and Peter Newman (eds), *The New Palgrave: A Dictionary of Economics*, Vol. 4, London: Macmillan, 868–72.

Friedman, Milton (1955) "Léon Walras and His Economic System," *American Economic Review* 45 (December) 900–9.

Ingrao, Bruna and Israel, Giorgio (1990) *The Invisible Hand: Economic Equilibrium in the History of Science*, Cambridge, MA: MIT Press.

Jaffé, William, ed. (1965) *Correspondence of Léon Walras and Related Papers*, 3 vols, Amsterdam: North Holland.

——(1981) "Another Look at Walras's Theory of Tâtonnement," *History of Political Economy* 13 (Summer): 313–36.

——(1984) "The Antecedents and Early Life of Léon Walras, edited by Donald A. Walker," *History of Political Economy* 16 (Spring): 1–57.

Morishima, Michio (1977) *Walras' Economics: Pure Theory of Capital and Money*, Cambridge: Cambridge University Press.

Patinkin, Don (1987) "Walras's Law," in John Eatwell, Murray Milgate, and Peter Newman (eds), *The New Palgrave: A Dictionary of Economics*, Vol. 4, London: Macmillan, 863–8.

Walker, Donald A. (1983) *William Jaffé's Essays on Walras*, Cambridge: Cambridge University Press.

——(1987) "Walras, Léon," in John Eatwell, Murray Milgate, and Peter Newman (eds), *The New Palgrave: A Dictionary of Economics*, Vol. 4, London: Macmillan, 852–63.

——(1996) *Walras's Market Models*, Cambridge: Cambridge University Press.

Weintraub, E. Roy (1983) "On the Existence of a Competitive Equilibrium: 1930–1954," *Journal of Economic Literature* 21 (March): 1–39.

——(1985) *General Equilibrium Analysis: Studies in Appraisal*, Cambridge: Cambridge University Press.

Elements of Pure Economics (1874)*

Lesson 11: Problem of exchange of several commodities for one another – the theorem of general equilibrium

104. We shall now pass from the study of the exchange of two commodities, (A) and (B), for each other to a study of the exchange of several commodities, (A), (B), (C), (D), ..., for one another. In this connection, all we need to do is to return to the case in which each party to the exchange is a holder of only one commodity and then generalize our formulae in a suitable way.

From now on, let $D_{a,b}$ designate the effective demand for (A) in exchange for (B), $D_{b,a}$ the effective demand for (B) in exchange for (A), $p_{a,b}$ the price of (A) in terms of (B) and $p_{b,a}$ the price of (B) in terms of (A). To relate the four unknowns $D_{a,b}$, $D_{b,a}$, $p_{a,b}$, and $p_{b,a}$ we have two equations of effective demand

$$D_{a,b} = F_{a,b}(p_{a,b}),$$
$$D_{b,a} = F_{b,a}(p_{b,a}),$$

and two equations expressing equality between effective demand and effective offer:

$$D_{b,a} = F_{a,b}p_{a,b},$$
$$D_{a,b} = D_{b,a}p_{b,a}.$$

As we have already seen, the first two of these equations can be represented geometrically by two curves, and the last two by inscribing two rectangles within these curves such that the base of each is equal to the inverse ratio of its altitude to the altitude of the other or to the direct ratio of its area to the area of the other.

105. Now, leaving the case of two commodities (A) and (B), we shall take the case of three commodities (A), (B), and (C). We shall imagine, therefore, some people coming to a market with commodity (A), of which they are prepared to give up one part for commodity (B) and another part for commodity (C); while others come to the same market with commodity (B) of which they are prepared to give up one part for commodity (A) and another part for commodity (C); and still others come with commodity (C) of which they are prepared to give up one part for commodity (A) and another part for commodity (B).

Under this supposition, let us take one of these people, say a holder of (B), and let us develop the reasoning which we outlined earlier in a way that is appropriate to the new situation. We shall find that here again the trader's schedule of this individual can be rigorously determined.

In fact, every holder of a quantity q_b of commodity (B), who comes to the market prepared to exchange a certain quantity $o_{h,a}$ of (B) for a certain quantity $d_{a,b}$ of (A) according to the equation of exchange

$$d_{a,b}v_a = o_{b,a}v_b,$$

* *Elements of Pure Economics or The Social Theory of Wealth*, translated by William Jaffé. Published for The American Economic Association and The Royal Economic Society by George Allen and Unwin Ltd., Museum Street, London. A translation of the Edition Definitive (1926) of the *Eléments d'économie politique pure*, annotated and collated with the previous editions. First edition 1874.

as well as a certain quantity $o_{b,a}$ of (B) for a certain quantity $d_{c,b}$ of (C) according to the equation of exchange

$$d_{c,b}v_c = o_{b,c}v_b,$$

will take away from the market a quantity $d_{a,b}$ of (A), a quantity $d_{c,b}$ of (C) and a quantity y of (B) equal to

$$q_b - o_{b,a} - o_{b,c} = q_b - d_{a,b}\frac{v_a}{v_b} - d_{c,b}\frac{v_c}{v_b}.$$

In general, the quantities q_b and v_a/v_b or $p_{a,b}$, $d_{a,b}$ and v_c/v_b or $p_{c,b}$, $d_{c,b}$ and y will always be related by the equation

$$q_b = y + d_{a,b}\, p_{a,b} + d_{c,b}\, p_{c,b}.$$

Before he reaches the market, our trader does not know what v_a/v_b or $p_{a,b}$ and what v_c/v_b or $p_{c,b}$ will be; but he is sure to find out as soon as he gets there. Once he discovers how high $p_{a,b}$ and $p_{c,b}$ are, he will decide upon the quantities $d_{a,b}$ and $d_{c,b}$ accordingly, whence a certain value of y results by virtue of the above equation. Surely, we must admit that the determination of $d_{a,b}$ is impossible unless $p_{a,b}$ is known as well as $p_{c,b}$ and that the determination of $d_{c,b}$ is impossible unless $p_{a,b}$ is known as well as $p_{c,b}$. At the same time, we have to agree that, when both $p_{a,b}$ and $p_{c,b}$ are known, this very knowledge makes possible the determination $d_{a,b}$ and $d_{c,b}$.

106. Now, again, nothing could be easier than to indicate mathematically the direct relationship of $d_{a,b}$ and $d_{c,b}$, that is, the effective demand for (A) and (C) in exchange for (B), to $p_{a,b}$ and $p_{c,b}$, that is, prices of these commodities. This relationship, which amounts to the trader's schedule of the individual we are considering, is rigorously defined by the two equations, $d_{a,b} = f_{a,b}(p_{a,b},p_{c,b})$ and $d_{c,b} = f_{c,b}(p_{a,b},p_{c,b})$. In like manner, we could obtain equations to express the several trader's schedules of all other holders of (B) for (A) and (C). Then, simply by adding these equations of individual demand, we obtain two equations of total demand

$$D_{a,b} = F_{a,b}(p_{a,b}, p_{c,b}),$$
$$D_{c,b} = F_{c,b}(p_{a,b}, p_{c,b}),$$

which express the trader's schedules of all holders of (B) taken together.

Similarly, we could obtain two equations of total demand

$$D_{a,c} = F_{a,c}(p_{a,c}, p_{b,c}),$$
$$D_{b,c} = F_{b,c}(p_{a,c}, p_{b,c}),$$

which express the trader's schedules of all holders of (C) taken together.

Finally, using the same procedure, we could obtain two equations of total demand

$$D_{b,a} = F_{b,a}(p_{b,a}, p_{c,a}),$$
$$D_{c,a} = F_{c,a}(p_{b,a}, p_{c,a}),$$

which express the trader's schedules of all holders of (A).

107. We have, besides, two equations of exchange of (B) for (A) and of (B) for (C)

$$D_{b,a} = D_{a,b}\, p_{a,b},$$
$$D_{b,c} = D_{c,b}\, p_{c,b}.$$

We have, also, two equations of exchange of (C) for (A) and of (C) for (B):

$$D_{c,a} = D_{a,c}\, p_{a,c},$$
$$D_{c,b} = D_{b,c}\, p_{b,c}.$$

And, last of all, we have two equations of exchange of (A) for (B) and of (A) for (C):

$$D_{a,b} = D_{b,a}\, p_{b,a},$$
$$D_{a,c} = D_{c,a}\, p_{c,a}.$$

Thus, we have in all twelve equations relating the following twelve unknowns: the six prices of the three commodities each expressed in terms of the other two, and the six total quantities of the three commodities which are exchanged for one another.

108. Now let us suppose a market in which there are m commodities: (A), (B), (C), (D), ... It is readily seen that by using, in this case, exactly the same reasoning which we used first in the case of two commodities and then in the case of three commodities and which it would be otiose to repeat here, we can immediately write, first, the $m - 1$ equations of effective demand for (B), (C), (D), ... in exchange for (A)

$$D_{b,a} = F_{b,a}(p_{b,a}, p_{c,a}, p_{d,a}, \ldots),$$
$$D_{c,a} = F_{c,a}(p_{b,a}, p_{c,a}, p_{d,a}, \ldots),$$
$$D_{d,a} = F_{d,a}(p_{b,a}, p_{c,a}, p_{d,a}, \ldots),$$
$$\ldots$$

then, the $m - 1$ equations of effective demand for (A), (C), (D), ... in exchange for (B)

$$D_{a,b} = F_{b,a}(p_{a,b}, p_{c,b}, p_{d,b}, \ldots),$$
$$D_{c,b} = F_{c,b}(p_{a,b}, p_{c,b}, p_{d,b}, \ldots),$$
$$D_{d,b} = F_{d,b}(p_{a,b}, p_{c,b}, p_{d,b}, \ldots),$$
$$\ldots$$

then, the $m - 1$ equations of effective demand for (A), (B), (D), ... in exchange for (C)

$$D_{a,c} = F_{a,c}(p_{a,c}, p_{b,c}, p_{d,c}, \ldots),$$
$$D_{b,c} = F_{b,c}(p_{a,c}, p_{b,c}, p_{d,c}, \ldots),$$
$$D_{d,c} = F_{d,c}(p_{a,c}, p_{b,c}, p_{d,c}, \ldots),$$
$$\ldots$$

then, the $m - 1$ equations of effective demand for (A), (B), (C), ... in exchange for (D)

$$D_{a,d} = F_{a,d}(p_{a,d}, p_{b,d}, p_{c,d}, \ldots),$$
$$D_{b,d} = F_{b,d}(p_{a,d}, p_{b,d}, p_{c,d}, \ldots),$$
$$D_{c,d} = F_{c,d}(p_{a,d}, p_{b,d}, p_{c,d}, \ldots),$$
$$\ldots$$

and so on. In all we have $m(m - 1)$ equations.

109. In addition, we can evidently write, without further explanation, the $m - 1$ equations of exchange of (A) for (B), (C), (D), ...

$$D_{a,b} = D_{b,a}p_{b,a} \quad D_{a,c} = D_{c,a}p_{c,a} \quad D_{a,d} = D_{d,a}p_{d,a}, \quad \ldots$$

the $m - 1$ equations of exchange of (B) for (A), (C), (D),...

$$D_{b,a} = D_{a,b}p_{a,b} \quad D_{b,c} = D_{c,b}p_{c,b} \quad D_{b,d} = D_{d,b}p_{d,b}, \quad \ldots$$

the $m - 1$ equations of exchange of (C) for (A), (B), (D), ...

$$D_{c,a} = D_{a,c}p_{a,c} \quad D_{c,b} = D_{b,c}p_{b,c} \quad D_{c,d} = D_{d,c}p_{d,c}, \quad \ldots$$

the $m - 1$ equations of exchange of (D) for (A), (B), (C), ...

$$D_{d,a} = D_{a,d}p_{a,d} \quad D_{d,b} = D_{b,d}p_{b,d} \quad D_{d,c} = D_{c,d}p_{c,d}, \quad \ldots$$

and so on. In all we have again $m(m - 1)$ equations.

These $m(m - 1)$ equations of exchange along with the $m(m - 1)$ equations of effective demand make a total of $2m(m - 1)$ equations. These equations connect precisely $2m(m - 1)$ unknowns, for there are $m(m - 1)$ prices and $m(m - 1)$ total quantities exchanged when the m commodities are considered two at a time.

110. In the special case of the exchange of two commodities for each other, and in the special case of the exchange of three commodities for one another, the problem can be solved either geometrically or algebraically, because in both these cases the demand functions can be represented geometrically. In the first of these special cases, the demand functions are functions of one variable and can be represented by two curves. In the second, the demand functions are functions of two variables and can be represented by six surfaces in space. In the first case we obtain a geometrical solution of the problem (of equilibrium) simply by inscribing rectangles within the curves; while in the second case we arrive at a geometrical solution by inscribing rectangles within curves obtained by the intersection of the six surfaces by planes.

In the general case, however, the demand functions are functions of $m - 1$ variables which are too numerous to be represented in space. It seems, therefore, that the problem when generalized can only be formulated and solved algebraically, not geometrically. It should be recalled, moreover, that what we have in mind throughout this volume is not to pose and solve the problem in question as if it were a real problem in a given concrete situation, but solely to formulate scientifically the nature of the problem which actually arises in the market where it is solved empirically. From our point of view, not only is the algebraic solution as good as the geometrical solution; but we may go so far as to say that in adopting the analytical form of mathematical expression we are using a form that is general and scientific *par excellence*.

111. The problem of the exchange of several commodities for one another now appears to be solved. Actually, it is only half solved. Under the conditions described above, there would indeed be a certain equilibrium in the market so far as the prices of commodities taken two at a time were concerned; but that equilibrium would be an imperfect equilibrium. *We do not have perfect or general market equilibrium unless the price of one of any two commodities in terms of the other is equal to the ratio of the prices of these two commodities in terms of any third commodity.* This remains to be proved. Let us begin by selecting three commodities out of the total number, say (A), (B) and (C), and let us suppose that the price $p_{c,b}$ is greater or smaller than the ratio of $p_{c,a}$ to $p_{b,a}$ and see what will happen.

In order to fix our ideas, we shall imagine that the place which serves as a market for the exchange of all the commodities (A), (B), (C), (D), ... for one another is divided into as many sectors as there are pairs of commodities exchanged. We should then have $m(m - 1)/2$ special markets, each identified by a signboard indicating the names of the two commodities exchanged there as well as their prices or rates of exchange which are mathematically determined in accordance with the system of equations developed above. For example, we should read: "Exchange of (A) for (B) and (B) for (A) at the reciprocal prices $p_{a,b}$ and $p_{b,a}$"; "Exchange of (A) for (C) and (C) for (A) at the reciprocal prices $p_{a,c}$ and $p_{c,a}$"; and "Exchange of (B) for (C) and (C) for (B) at the reciprocal prices $p_{b,c}$ and $p_{c,b}$." Under these assumptions, if each holder of (A) who wanted (B) and (C) simply traded his (A) for (B) and (C) on the first two of the above specially designated markets, if each holder of (B) who wanted some (A) and (C) simply traded his (B) for (A) and (C) on the first and third of these markets, and if each holder of (C) who wanted (A) and (B) simply traded his (C) for (A) and (B) on the last two of these markets, then equilibrium would remain unchanged [even though $p_{c,b}$ might be greater or less than the ratio of $p_{c,a}$ to $p_{b,a}$]. It is easy to show, however, that neither the holders of (A), nor those of (B), nor those of (C) will trade in this way. They will all go about it in another way which is more to their advantage.

112. Let us suppose, as we did before, that

$$p_{c,b} = \alpha \frac{p_{c,a}}{p_{b,a}},$$

or that

$$\frac{p_{c,b}\, p_{b,a}\, p_{a,c}}{\alpha} = 1,$$

where α is first assumed > 1.

It follows from this equation that the true price of (C) in terms of (B) will not be $p_{c,b}$ but $p_{c,b}/\alpha$, in view of the fact that for $p_{c,b}/\alpha$ units of (B) it is possible first to obtain $p_{c,b}\, p_{b,a}/\alpha$ units of (A) on the (A, B) market at the price $p_{a,b} = 1/p_{b,a}$ of (A) in terms of (B), and then to trade these $p_{c,b}\, p_{b,a}/\alpha$ units of (A) on the (A, C) market for $p_{c,b}\, p_{b,a}\, p_{a,c}/\alpha = 1$ unit of (C) at the price $p_{c,a} = 1/p_{a,c}$ of (C) in terms of (A).

It follows also that the true price of (B) in terms of (A) will not be $p_{b,a}$ but $p_{b,a}/\alpha$, in view of the fact that for $p_{b,a}/\alpha$ units of (A) it is possible first to obtain $p_{b,a}p_{a,c}/\alpha$ units of (C) on the (A, C) market at the price $p_{c,a} = 1/p_{a,c}$ of (C) in terms of (A), and then to trade these $p_{b,a}p_{a,c}/\alpha$ units of (C) on the (B, C) market for $p_{b,a}p_{a,c}p_{c,b}/\alpha = 1$ unit of (B) at the price $p_{b,c} = 1/p_{c,b}$ of (B) in terms of (C).

And finally it follows that the true price of (A) in terms of (C) will not be $p_{a,c}$ but $p_{a,c}/\alpha$, in view of the fact that for $p_{a,c}/\alpha$ units of (C) it is possible first to obtain $p_{a,c}p_{c,b}/\alpha$ units of (B) on (B, C) market, at the price $p_{b,c} = 1/p_{c,b}$ of (B) in terms of (C) and then to trade these $p_{a,c}p_{c,b}/\alpha$ units of (B) on the (A, B) market for $p_{a,c}p_{c,b}p_{b,a}/\alpha = 1$ unit of (A) at the price $p_{a,b} = 1/p_{b,a}$ of (A) in terms of (B).

113. In order to clarify this point with the aid of concrete numbers, let us suppose that $p_{c,b} = 4$, $p_{c,a} = 6$, and $p_{b,a} = 2$, which makes $\alpha = 1.33$. From the equation

$$\frac{4 \times 2 \times \frac{1}{6}}{1.33} = 1$$

we see that the true price of (C) in terms of (B) will not be 4, but $4/1.33 = 3$, in view of the fact that for 3 units of (B) [intended for the eventual purchase of (C)] it is possible first to obtain $3 \times 2 = 6$ units of (A) on the (A, B) market, where the price of (A) in terms of (B) is $1/2$ and then to trade these 6 units of (A) on the (A, C) market for $6 \times 1/6 = 1$ unit of (C), since the price there of (C) in terms of (A) is 6.

We see also from the above equation that the true price of (B) in terms of (A) will not be 2, but $2/1.33 = 1.50$, in view of the fact that for 1.50 units of (A) [intended for the eventual purchase of (B)] it is possible first to obtain $1.50 \times 1/6 = 1/4$ of a unit of (C) on the (A, C) market, where the price of (C) in terms of (A) is 6; and then to trade this $1/4$ of a unit of (C) on the (B, C) market for $1/4 \times 4 = 1$ unit of (B), since the price there of (B) in terms of (C) is $1/4$.

And finally we see that the true price of (A) in terms of (C) will not be $1/6$, but $1/6 \times 1.33 = 1/8$, in view of the fact that for $1/8$ of a unit of (C) [intended for the eventual purchase of (A)] it is possible first to obtain $1/8 \times 4 = 1/2$ of a unit of (B) on the (B, C) market, where the price of (B) in terms of (C) is $1/4$; and then to trade this $1/2$ of a unit of (B) on the (A, B) market for $1/2 \times 2 = 1$ unit of (A), since the price there of (A) in terms of (B) is $1/2$.

114. Clearly, no one of the holders of (A), or (B), or (C) will hesitate to resort to the expedient of substituting the indirect exchange of (A) against (C) and (C) against (B) for the direct exchange of (A) against (B); or the indirect exchange of (B) against (A) and (A) against (C) for the direct exchange of (B) against (C); or the indirect exchange of (C) against (B) and (B) against (A) for the direct exchange of (C) against (A). This indirect exchange is called *arbitrage*. As to the gains the trading parties realize by arbitrage, they will distribute them as they please according to their various wants, by purchasing a little more of one commodity or another in order to procure the largest possible sum total of satisfactions. The condition of this maximum, it is well to point out, is that the ratios of the intensities of the last wants satisfied be equal to the real prices resulting from arbitrage operations. But we shall not go into that now, for it suffices to note at this point that the supplementary demand [entailed in arbitrage operations] is part and parcel of the principal demand: when the holders of (A) exchange (A) against (C) and (C) against (B) but never (A) directly against (B); when the holders of (B) exchange (B) against (A) and (A) against (C) but never (B) directly against (C); and when the holders of (C) exchange (C) against (B) and (B) against (A) but never (C) directly against (A). Consequently, on the (A, B) market there will inevitably be a demand for (A) and an offer of (B), but no demand for (B) nor offer of (A); whence a fall in $p_{b,a}$. On the (A, C) market there will inevitably be a demand for (C) and an offer of (A), but no demand for (A) nor offer of (C); whence a rise $p_{c,a}$. And on the (B, C) market there will inevitably be a demand for (B) and an offer of (C), but no demand for (C) nor offer of (B); whence a fall in $p_{c,b}$.

115. It is evident from this that in the case where $p_{c,b} > p_{c,a}/p_{b,a}$, the market equilibrium will neither be final nor general and arbitrage operations will be effected with the result that $p_{c,b}$ will fall,

$p_{c,a}$ will rise and $p_{b,a}$ will fall. It is evident, also, that if the case were such that $p_{c,b} < p_{c,a}/p_{b,a}$, there would be arbitrage operations in the market, resulting in a rise in $p_{c,b}$, a fall in $p_{c,a}$ and a rise in $p_{b,a}$. In this second case we should find that

$$p_{c,b} = \alpha \frac{p_{c,a}}{p_{b,a}} \quad \text{or} \quad \alpha p_{b,c}\, p_{a,b}\, p_{c,a} = 1,$$

where $\alpha < 1$, in consequence of which the true price of (B) in terms of (C) would be $\alpha p_{b,c}$, provided that (C) was traded for (A) and (A) for (B); the true price of (A) in terms of (B) would be $\alpha p_{a,b}$, provided that (B) was traded for (C) and (C) for (A); and the true price of (C) in terms of (A) would be $\alpha p_{c,a}$, provided that (A) was traded for (B) and (B) for (C). Clearly, what has been said about the prices of (A), (B), and (C) is equally true of the prices of any three commodities whatsoever. Hence, if one wished to leave arbitrage operations aside and at the same time to generalize the equilibrium established for pairs of commodities in the market, it would be necessary to introduce the condition that the price of either one of any two commodities [chosen at random] expressed in terms of the other be equal to the ratio of the prices of each of these two commodities in terms of any third commodity. In other words, the following equations would have to be satisfied:

$$p_{a,b} = \frac{1}{p_{b,a}}, \quad p_{c,b} = \frac{p_{c,a}}{p_{b,a}}, \quad p_{d,b} = \frac{p_{d,a}}{p_{b,a}}, \cdots$$

$$p_{a,c} = \frac{1}{p_{c,a}}, \quad p_{b,c} = \frac{p_{b,a}}{p_{c,a}}, \quad p_{d,c} = \frac{p_{d,a}}{p_{c,a}}, \cdots$$

$$p_{a,d} = \frac{1}{p_{d,a}}, \quad p_{b,d} = \frac{p_{b,a}}{p_{d,a}}, \quad p_{c,d} = \frac{p_{c,a}}{p_{d,a}}, \cdots$$

$$\cdots$$

and so forth. We should have, in all, $(m-1)(m-1)$ equations of general equilibrium, which contained implicitly $m(m-1)/2$ equations expressing the reciprocal relationship between prices. The commodity in terms of which the prices of all the others are expressed is the '*numéraire*' [or *standard commodity*].

116. It goes without saying that the change to these $(m-1)(m-1)$ conditions calls for a reduction of our previously developed system of equations of demand and exchange by an equal number of equations. This is precisely the reduction which is effected when a single general market is substituted for the several special markets in such a way that the equations of exchange expressing equality between the demand and offer of each commodity in terms of and in exchange for each of the other commodities taken separately are replaced by the following equations of exchange expressing equality between the demand and offer of each commodity in terms of and in exchange for all the other commodities taken together:

$$D_{a,b} + D_{a,c} + D_{a,d} + \cdots = D_{b,a}p_{b,a} + D_{c,a}p_{c,a} + D_{d,a}p_{d,a} + \cdots$$
$$D_{b,a} + D_{b,c} + D_{b,d} + \cdots = D_{a,b}p_{a,b} + D_{c,b}p_{c,b} + D_{d,b}p_{d,b} + \cdots$$
$$D_{c,a} + D_{c,b} + D_{c,d} + \cdots = D_{a,c}p_{a,c} + D_{b,c}p_{b,c} + D_{d,c}p_{d,c} + \cdots$$
$$D_{d,a} + D_{d,b} + D_{d,c} + \cdots = D_{a,d}p_{a,d} + D_{b,d}p_{b,d} + D_{c,d}p_{c,d} + \cdots$$

$$\cdots$$

and so on, in all m equations. But these m equations reduce to $m-1$ equations. If we insert the values of the prices found in the general equilibrium equations and then designate the prices of (B), (C), (D), ... in terms of (A) simply by $p_b, p_c, p_d, \ldots$, and the above equations become:

$$D_{a,b} + D_{a,c} + D_{a,d} + P = D_{b,a}\, p_b + D_{c,a}p_c + D_{d,a}p_d + \cdots$$

$$D_{b,a} + D_{b,c} + D_{b,d} + P = D_{a,b} \frac{1}{p_b} + D_{c,b}\frac{p_c}{p_b} + D_{d,b}\frac{p_d}{p_b} + \cdots$$

$$D_{c,a} + D_{c,b} + D_{b,d} + p = D_{a,c}\frac{1}{p_c} + D_{b,c}\frac{p_b}{p_c} + D_{d,c}\frac{p_d}{p_c} + \cdots$$

$$D_{d,a} + D_{d,b} + D_{d,c} + p = D_{a,d}\frac{1}{p_d} + D_{b,d}\frac{p_b}{p_d} + D_{c,d}\frac{p_c}{p_d} + \cdots$$

...

And now, adding together all but the first of these m equations, after multiplying both sides of the first of the remaining $m-1$ equations by p_b, both sides of the second of these $m-1$ equations by p_c, both sides of the third by p_d, ..., and then cancelling out identical terms on both sides of the sum, we end up with the first equation of the above system. The first equation, may, therefore, be omitted, and the whole system reduces to the remaining $m-1$ equations. Thus, we have finally $m-1$ equations of exchange to which we add the $m(m-1)$ equations of demand and the $(m-1)(m-1)$ general equilibrium equations, making a total of $2m(m-1)$ equations the roots of which are the $m(m-1)$ prices of the m commodities in terms of one another and the $m(m-1)$ total quantities of the m commodities which are exchanged for one another. In this way, given the equations of demand, the prices are determined mathematically. Now there remains only to show – and this is the essential point – that the problem of exchange for which we have just given a theoretical solution is the selfsame problem that is solved empirically on the market by the mechanism of free competition. Before proceeding to this demonstration, however, we shall examine the case where the parties to the exchange come to the market each holding several commodities. This is the general case which the theorem of maximum satisfaction will enable us to deal with quite simply and easily.

Lesson 12: The general formula of the mathematical solution of the problem of exchange of several commodities for one another – the law of the establishment of commodity prices

117. In the case of the exchange of any number of commodities for one another, as in the case of the exchange of two commodities for each other, the individual effective demand equations are mathematically determined by the condition of maximum satisfaction of wants. What, exactly, is this condition of maximum satisfaction? It always consists in the attainment of equality between the ratio of the *raretés* of any two commodities and the price of one in terms of the other, for otherwise it would be advantageous to make further exchanges of these commodities for each other. If each of the parties to the exchange is a holder of one commodity only, and if, in order to furnish an occasion for arbitrage transactions, the $m(m-1)$ prices of the m commodities are cried as ratios of exchange between the commodities taken two at a time without reference to the condition of general equilibrium, then maximum satisfaction will be achieved by each party when the ratios of the *raretés* of the several commodities demanded to the *rareté* of the one commodity originally held are equal, not to prices as they are first cried, but to the true prices arrived at by arbitrage. But if each party is the holder of several commodities and if, in this case, the prices of $m-1$ of the m commodities are cried in terms of the mth, which is selected as the *numéraire*, in order to prevent arbitrage operations from taking place, then, provided that the price of one of any pair of the m commodities in terms of the other is equal to the ratio of their prices in terms of the *numéraire*, it is evident that maximum satisfaction will be achieved by each trader when the ratios of the *raretés* of the commodities not used as the *numéraire* to the *rareté* of the commodity so used equal the prices cried.

118. Now let party (1) be a holder of $q_{a,1}$ of (A), $q_{b,1}$ of (B), $q_{c,1}$ of (C), $q_{d,1}$ of (D), ... Let $r = \phi_{a,1}(q), r = \phi_{b,1}(q), r = \phi_{c,1}(q), r = \phi_{d,1}(q), \ldots$ be his equations of utility or want for commodities (A), (B), (C), (D), ... during a given period of time. Let $p_b, p_c, p_d, \ldots$ be the respective prices of commodities (B), (C), (D), ... in terms of (A). And let $x_1, y_1, z_1, w_1, \ldots$ be the quantities of (A), (B),

(C), (D), ... respectively which our individual will add to the original quantities held $q_{a,1}, q_{b,1}, q_{c,1}, q_{d,1}, \dots$ at prices $p_b, p_c, p_d, \dots$. These additions may be positive and consequently represent quantities demanded; or they may be negative so as to represent quantities offered. Inasmuch as the individual trader cannot possibly demand any of these commodities without offering in return a quantity of other commodities having the same value, we can be sure that if some of the quantities $x_1, y_1, z_1, w_1, \dots$ are positive, others are bound to be negative, and that the following relationship between these quantities will always hold:

$$x_1 + y_1 p_b + z_1 p_c + w_1 p_d + \dots = 0.$$

If we suppose maximum satisfaction to have been attained, the above quantities will evidently be related by the following system:

$$\phi_{b,1}(q_{b,1} + y_1) = p_b \phi_{a,1}(q_{a,1} + x_1),$$
$$\phi_{c,1}(q_{c,1} + z_1) = p_c \phi_{a,1}(q_{a,1} + x_1),$$
$$\phi_{d,1}(q_{d,1} + w_1) = p_d \phi_{a,1}(q_{a,1} + x_1),$$
$$\dots$$

constituting in all $m - 1$ equations, which together with the preceding equation give us a system of m equations. We may suppose that $m - 1$ of the m unknowns, $x_1, y_1, z_1, w_1, \dots$, are eliminated one after another from these equations so that we are left with only one equation expressing the mth unknown as a function of the prices. We should then have the following equations of demand or offer of (B), (C), (D),... by party (1):

$$y_1 = f_{b,1}(p_b, p_c, p_d, \dots),$$
$$z_1 = f_{c,1}(p_b, p_c, p_d, \dots),$$
$$w_1 = f_{d,1}(p_b, p_c, p_d, \dots),$$
$$\dots$$

while his demand or offer of (A) is given by the equation

$$x_1 = -(y_1 p_b + z_1 p_c + w_1 p_d + \dots).$$

Similarly, in the case of parties (2), (3), ... we could derive the following equations of demand or offer of (B), (C), (D), ... :

$$y_2 = f_{b,2}(p_b, p_c, p_d, \dots),$$
$$z_2 = f_{c,2}(p_b, p_c, p_d, \dots),$$
$$w_2 = f_{d,2}(p_b, p_c, p_d, \dots),$$
$$\dots$$
$$y_3 = f_{b,3}(p_b, p_c, p_d, \dots),$$
$$z_3 = f_{c,3}(p_b, p_c, p_d, \dots),$$
$$w_3 = f_{d,3}(p_b, p_c, p_d, \dots),$$
$$\dots$$

and so forth, while their respective demands or offers of (A) are given by the equations:

$$x_2 = -(y_2 p_b + z_2 p_c + w_2 p_d + \dots),$$
$$x_3 = -(y_3 p_b + z_3 p_c + w_3 p_d + \dots).$$
$$\dots$$

In this way everyone's trading schedule could be deduced from the utility which the various commodities have for him and from his original stocks of these commodities. Before proceeding further, however, we have a very important observation to make at this juncture.

119. It is possible for y_1 to be negative at certain values of $p_b, p_c, p_d, \dots$ which is the case when party (1) offers commodity (B) instead of demanding it. It is even possible for y_1 to be equal

to $-q_{b,1}$, when party (1) does not retain any of commodity (B) at all for himself. If we enter this value of y_1 in the system of $m-1$ equations of maximum satisfaction, we have

$$\phi_{b,1}(0) = p_b\phi_{a,1}(q_{a,1} + x_1),$$
$$\phi_{c,1}(q_{c,1} + z_1) = p_c\phi_{a,1}(q_{a,1} + x_1),$$
$$\phi_{d,1}(q_{d,1} + z_1) = p_d\phi_{a,1}(q_{a,1} + x_1),$$
$$\cdots$$

Substituting the values for $p_b, p_c, p_d, \ldots$ derived from the above equations into

$$x_1 + z_1 p_c + w_1 p_d + \cdots = q_{b,1} p_b,$$

we obtain

$$x_1\phi_{a,1}(q_{a,1} + x_1) + z_1\phi_{c,1}(q_{c,1} + z_1) + w_1\phi_{d,1}(q_{d,1} + w_1) + \cdots = q_{b,1}\phi_{b,1}(0).$$

This equation expresses a condition which can be translated into the following terms: *For the offer of one of the commodities to be equal to the quantity possessed of that commodity, it must be possible to inscribe such rectangles within the segments of the utility curves enclosing the areas which lie just above the bounded areas representing the wants [already] satisfied by the quantities possessed of the commodities to be demanded, that the sum of their areas is equal to the area of a rectangle the altitude of which represents the original stock of the commodity to be offered and the base the maximum intensity of want for that* commodity.

This condition may or may not be satisfied. If it is, party (1)'s offer of (B) may, under certain circumstances, be equal to the quantity $q_{b,1}$ which he holds to start with. In any case, the offer can never be greater than this quantity. The essential point which follows from this is that the demand or offer equation of (B) must be replaced by $y_1 = -q_{b,1}$ for all values of $p_b, p_c, p_d, \ldots$ which make y_1 negative and greater than $q_{b,1}$ in this equation.

120. But that is not all. In the first place, the same conclusion applies to the demand or offer equations of (C), (D), ... for such values of $p_b, p_c, p_d, \ldots$ which make $z_1, w_1, \ldots$ negative and larger than $q_{c,1}, q_{d,1}, \ldots$. In the second place, it is precisely when these equations have to be replaced by $z_1 = -q_{c,1}$, $w_1 = -q_{d,1}, \ldots$, that the demand or offer equation of (B) must be changed in consequence.

For example, if $z_1 = -q_{c,1}$, the system of equations determining party (1)'s demand or offer of (B) would be the following:

$$x_1 + y_1 p_b + z_1 p_c + w_1 p_d + \cdots = q_{c,1} p_c,$$
$$\phi_{b,1}(q_{b,1} + y_1) = p_b\phi_{a,1}(q_{a,1} + x_1),$$
$$\phi_{d,1}(q_{d,1} + w_1) = p_d\phi_{a,1}(q_{a,1} + x_1),$$
$$\cdots$$

$m-1$ equations in all, from which we could suppose $m-2$ unknowns, such as, $x_1, w_1, \ldots$, to be eliminated one after another, so that only one equation expressing y_1 as a function of $p_b, p_c, p_d, \ldots$ would remain. The procedure is the same when $w_1 = -q_{d,1}, \ldots$. It will be readily understood, without further demonstration, that the same procedure would apply not only in the case where offer equals the quantity possessed of one of the commodities (C), (D), ..., but also in the case where this equality holds for 2, 3, 4, ..., or, generally speaking, for any number of these commodities.

121. We have said nothing so far about the equation of the demand or offer of the *numéraire* commodity (A), because this equation takes on a special form. Evidently it too must be replaced by $x_1 = -q_{a,1}$ for values of $p_b, p_c, p_d, \ldots$ which would make x_1 negative and greater than $q_{a,1}$. In that case, moreover, the system of equations determining party (1)'s demand or offer of (B) would be the following:

$$y_1 p_b + z_1 p_c + w_1 p_d + \cdots = q_{a,1},$$
$$p_b\phi_{c,1}(q_{c,1} + z_1) = p_c\phi_{b,1}(q_{b,1} + y_1),$$
$$p_b\phi_{d,1}(q_{d,1} + w_1) = p_d\phi_{b,1}(q_{b,1} + y_1),$$
$$\cdots$$

in all, as before, $m - 1$ equations from which we could suppose $m - 2$ unknowns such as $z_1, w_1, \ldots$ to be eliminated one after another, so that only one equation expressing y_1 as a function *of* $p_b, p_c, p_d, \ldots$ would remain.

122. Undoubtedly, it would be more or less difficult to set out the demand and offer equations in such a way as to satisfy the restrictions described above; but it is none the less certain – and this is the important point – that, once certain prices, say $p_b', p_c', p_d', \ldots$ of (B), (C), (D), ... in terms of (A), have been cried, the quantities to be offered and demanded of all the commodities in question, even when we take into account the fact that offer may equal quantity possessed, are perfectly determinate. This is what we have to prove.

Let $q = \psi_{a,1}(r)$, $q = \psi_{b,1}(r)$, $q = \psi_{c,1}(r)$, $q = \psi_{d,1}(r)$, ... be the utility equations of party (1) for commodities (A), (B), (C), (D), ..., which are to be solved now for the quantities rather than the *raretés*. Upon the completion of all the exchange transactions, we have not only

$$q_{a,1} + x_1' = \psi_{a,1}(r_{a,1}'),$$
$$q_{a,1} + y_1' = \psi_{b,1}(r_{b,1}'),$$
$$q_{a,1} + z_1' = \psi_{c,1}(r_{c,1}'),$$
$$q_{d,1} + z_1' = \psi_{d,1}(r_{d,1}'),$$
$$\cdots$$

but also

$$q_{a,1} + p_b' q_{b,1} + p_c' q_{c,1} + p_d' q_{d,1} + \cdots = \psi_{a,1}(r_{a,1}') + p_b' \psi_{b,1}(p_b' r_{a,1}') + p_c' \psi_{c,1}(p_c' r_{a,1}') + p_d' \psi_{d,1}(p_d' r_{a,1}') + \cdots$$

by virtue of the condition of equality of the values of the quantities exchanged and the condition of maximum satisfaction. This last equation can be solved for $r_{a,1}'$. Knowing $r_{a,1}'$, we have $r_{b,1}', r_{c,1}', r_{d,1}', = \cdots$, and consequently $x_1', y_1', z_1', w_1', \ldots$. The only commodities which will be retained or acquired are those for which the intensity of the first want to be satisfied is greater than the product of price times $r_{a,1}'$.

If $r_{a,1}'$ is greater than the intensity of his first want for (A), party (1) will neither demand nor retain any of the commodity serving as the *numéraire*.

123. The equations of the demand or offer of (A), (B), (C), (D), ... by parties (1), (2), (3), ... having been appropriately set out *ex hypothesi* in such a way as to satisfy the restrictions described above, let $X, Y, Z, W, \ldots$ designate respectively the sums $x_1 + x_2 + x_3 + \cdots, y_1 + y_2 + y_3 + \cdots, z_1 + z_2 + z_3 + \cdots, w_1 + w_2 + w_3 + \cdots$, and let $F_b, F_c, F_d, \ldots$ designate respectively the sums of the functions $f_{b,1}, f_{b,2}, f_{b,3}, \ldots f_{c,1}, f_{c,2}, f_{c,3}, \ldots f_{d,1}, f_{d,2}, f_{d,3}, \ldots$ Since the condition of equality between the demand and the offer of (A), (B), (C), (D), ... is expressed by the equations $X = 0, Y = 0, Z = 0, W = 0, \ldots$ in the general case under discussion, we have the following equations for the determination of current equilibrium prices:

$$F_b(p_b, p_c, p_d, \ldots) = 0,$$
$$F_c(p_b, p_c, p_d, \ldots) = 0,$$
$$F_d(p_b, p_c, p_d, \ldots) = 0,$$
$$\cdots$$

making up, in all, $m - 1$ equations. Moreover, since $p_b, p_c, p_d, \ldots$ are by their nature positive, it is evident that, if the above equations are satisfied, that is, if $Y = 0, Z = 0, W = 0, \ldots$, we also have

$$X = -(Yp_b + Zp_c + Wp_d + \cdots) = 0.$$

124. Thus, $m - 1$ prices of $m - 1$ of the m commodities are determined mathematically in terms of the mth commodity which serves as the *numéraire*, when the following three conditions are satisfied: first that each and every party to the exchange obtain the maximum satisfaction of

his wants, the ratios of his *raretés* then being equal to the prices; second that each and every party give up quantities that stand in a definite ratio to the quantities received and vice versa, there being only one price in terms of the *numéraire* for each commodity, namely the price at which total effective demand equals total effective offer; and third that there be no occasion for arbitrage transactions, the equilibrium price of one of any two commodities in terms of the other being equal to the ratio of the prices of these two commodities in terms of any third commodity. Now let us see in what way this problem of the exchange of several commodities for one another to which we have just given a scientific solution is also the problem which is empirically solved in the market by the mechanism of competition.

125. First of all, what actually takes place in the market is that the $m(m-1)$ prices of m commodities in terms of one another are reduced through the employment of a *numéraire to m − 1* prices of $m-1$ of the m commodities in terms of the mth. This mth commodity is the *numéraire*. The $(m-1)(m-1)$ prices of the remaining commodities in terms of one another are presumed to be equal to the ratios of the prices of the commodities in terms of the *numéraire* in comformity with the condition of general equilibrium. Let p_b', p_c', p_d', ... of (B), (C), (D), ... in terms of (A) be $m-1$ prices cried in this way, at random. At these prices each party to the exchange decides upon his demand or offer of (A), (B), (C), (D), ... These decisions which are arrived at after some deliberation, but without refined calculation, are made as if they were reached by the mathematical solution of the system of equations of demand and offer and of maximum satisfaction subject to suitable constraints. Let x_1', x_2', x_3', ... y_1', y_2', y_3', ... w_1', w_2', w_3', ... be positive or negative, representing the individual demands or offers corresponding to the prices p_b', p_c', p_d', ... If the total demand equalled the total offer of each and every commodity, if, in other words, we immediately had $Y' = 0$, $Z' = 0$, $W' = 0$, ..., and, in consequence, $X' = 0$, the exchange would take place at these prices and the problem would be solved. Generally, however, the total demand will not equal the total offer of each and every commodity, so that we have $Y' \gtrless 0$, $Z' \gtrless 0$, $W' \gtrless 0'$, ..., and, in consequence, $X' \gtrless 0$. What will happen on the market then? If the demand for any one commodity is greater than the offer, the price of that commodity in terms of the *numéraire* will rise; if the offer is greater than the demand, the price will fall. What must we do in order to prove that the theoretical solution is identically the solution worked out by the market? Our task is very simple: we need only show that the upward and downward movements of prices solve the system of equations of offer and demand by a process of groping ['par tâtonnement'].

126. Let us recall that we have the equation

$$X' + Y' p_b' + Z' p_c' + W' p_d' + \cdots = 0,$$

which can be written

$$D_a' - O_a' + (D_b' - O_b')p_b' + (D_c' - O_c')p_c' + (D_d' - O_d')p_d' + \cdots = 0,$$

where $D_a', D_b', D_c', D_d', \ldots$, designate the sums of the positive x's, y's, z's, w's, ... and $O_a', O_b', O_c', O_d', \ldots$, designate the sums of the negative x's, y's, z's, w's, ... taken positively, the corresponding prices being p_b', p_c', p_d', ... We observe that, since p_b', p_c', p_d', ... are positive by their very nature, if some of the quantities $X' = D_a' - O_a'$, $Y' = D_b' - O_b'$, $Z' = D_c' - O_c'$, $W' = D_d' - O_d'$, ... are positive, others will be negative, and conversely, if some of these quantities are negative, others will be positive. This means that if at the prices p_b', p_c', p_d', ... the total demand for some commodities is greater (or smaller) than their offer, then the offer of some of the other commodities must be greater (or smaller) than the demand for them.

127. Let us now consider the inequality

$$F_b(p_b', p_c', p_d', \ldots) \gtrless 0,$$

and let us rewrite it in this form

$$\Delta_b(p_b', p_c', p_d', \cdots) \gtrless \Omega_b(p_b', p_c', p_d', \ldots),$$

where the function Δ_b is the sum of the positive y's, or D_b, and the function Ω_b is the sum of the negative y's, or O_b. Leaving p_c, p_d, ... to one side since these prices are assumed to have been previously determined, so that p_b alone remains to be determined, let us try to find how p_b must be adjusted between zero and infinity for the demand for (B) to equal its offer. Although neither the function F_b nor the functions Δ_b and Ω_b are known, we can, nevertheless, derive sufficient information for present purposes from the foregoing study of exchange to tell us how p_b can be brought to a value which, if it exists at all, will make the F_b function equal zero or the Δ_b and Ω_b functions equal to each other.

128. Starting, now, with the function Δ_b, which is the demand function of (B) in exchange for (A), (C), (D), ..., we know that it is positive when $p_b = 0$, that is, at zero prices of (B) in terms of (A), (C), (D), ... In fact, at these [zero] prices the total effective demand for (B) will be equal to the excess of the total extensive utility of (B) over the total quantity of (B) possessed, and this will be a positive excess if commodity (B) is scarce and forms part of social wealth. If p_b is allowed to increase in such a way that the various prices of (B) in terms of (A), (C), (D), ... all rise in the same proportion, the function Δ_b will decrease since it is a sum of decreasing functions. In fact, commodity (B) will become dearer and dearer in relation to commodities (A), (C), (D), ...; and it is unthinkable, under this hypothesis, that the demand for (B) should increase. It can only diminish. Moreover, we can always suppose the value of p_b, that is to say the prices of (B) in terms of (A), (C), (D), ..., to be so high, infinite if need be, that the demand for (B) is zero.

Turning our attention, next, to the function Ω_b, which is the offer function of (B) in exchange for (A), (C), (D), ..., we know that it is zero for $p_b = 0$, and even for certain positive values of p_b, that is, for the zero price and even certain positive prices of (B) in terms of (A), (C), (D), ... Indeed, just as we may suppose prices of (B) in terms of (A), (C), (D), ... so high that the demand for (B) is zero, so we may imagine prices of (A), (C), (D), ... in terms of (B) so high that the demand for these commodities is zero, in which case the offer of (B) must be zero. If p_b is allowed to increase in such a way that the various prices of (B) in terms of (A), (C), (D), ... all rise in the same proportion, the function Ω_b will first increase and then decrease, since it is a sum of functions which first increase and then decrease. In this case, the commodities (A), (C), (D), ... will become cheaper and cheaper in relation to commodity (B), and the demand for them will conform to the successive changes in the offer of (B). But this offer will not increase indefinitely; it passes through at least one maximum value which cannot be greater than the total quantity possessed. The offer of (B) must then diminish and return to zero if p_b is infinite, that is, if (A), (C), (D), ... are free goods.

129. Under these conditions there exists a certain value of p_b at which D_b and O_b are equal, except in the case where D_b falls to zero before O_b starts to rise above zero, in which case there is no solution. Such a case, however, will not occur as long as there are any parties to the exchange who are holders of more than one commodity. In order to find the [equilibrium] value of p_b, p_b' will have to rise whenever $\Upsilon' > 0$, that is, whenever $D_b' > O_b'$ at that price; and p_b' will have to fall whenever $\Upsilon' < 0$, that is, whenever $O_b' > D_b'$ at that price. Thus, we arrive at the equation

$$F_b(p_b'', p_c', p_d', \dots) = 0.$$

Once this operation has been carried out, the inequality

$$F_c(p_b', p_c', p_d', \dots) \gtrless 0.$$

becomes

$$F_c(p_b'', p_c'', p_d', \dots) \gtrless 0,$$

but this inequality can be turned into

$$F_c(p_b'', p_c'', p_d', \dots) = 0,$$

by increasing or decreasing p_c', according as $Z \gtrless 0$ (i.e. $D_c' \gtrless O_c'$) at that price.

In the same way we can obtain the equation

$$F_d(p''_b, p''_c, p'_d, \dots) = 0,$$

and so forth.

130. After these operations have been effected, we shall have

$$F_b(p''_b, p''_c, p''_d, \dots) \gtreqless 0.$$

It remains to be shown that this inequality is closer to equality than the inequality

$$F_b(p'_b, p'_c, p'_d, \dots) \gtreqless 0,$$

with which we started. This will appear probable if we remember that the change from p'_b to p''_b, which reduced the above inequality to an equality, exerted a direct influence that was invariably in the direction of equality at least so far as the demand for (B) was concerned; while the [consequent] changes from p'_c to p''_c, p'_d, to p''_d, ..., which moved the foregoing inequality farther away from equality, exerted indirect influences, some in the direction of equality and some in the opposite direction, at least so far as the demand for (B) was concerned, so that up to a certain point they cancelled each other out. Hence, the new system of prices $p''_b, p''_c, p''_d, \dots$ is closer to equilibrium than the old system of prices $p'_b, p'_c, p'_d, \dots$; and it is only necessary to continue this process along the same lines for the system to move closer and closer to equilibrium.

We are now in a position to formulate the law of the establishment of equilibrium prices in the case of the exchange of several commodities for one another through the medium of a *numéraire:* *Given several commodities, which are exchanged for one another through the medium of a* numéraire, *for the market to be in a state of equilibrium or for the price of each and every commodity in terms of the* numéraire *to be stationary, it is necessary and sufficient that at these prices the effective demand for each commodity equal its effective offer. When this equality is absent, the attainment of equilibrium prices requires a rise in the prices of those commodities the effective demand for which is greater than the effective offer, and a fall in the prices of those commodities the effective offer of which is greater than the effective demand.*

FRANCIS YSIDRO EDGEWORTH
(1845–1926)

Francis Ysidro Edgeworth, Photographer: Walter Stoneman, by courtesy of the National Portrait Gallery, London.

F.Y. Edgeworth, an Irishman, was educated at Trinity College, Dublin, and at Oxford. He practiced law for a time and then held a succession of academic posts in the areas of literature, logic, and political economy, culminating in his appointment as Drummond Professor of Political Economy at Oxford in 1891. In addition to his extensive writings in economics and pioneering work in mathematical statistics, Edgeworth also served, from 1891, as editor of the *Economic Journal*, which was sponsored by the Royal Economic Society.

Edgeworth was one of the first to restate utilitarian ethical and economic analysis in mathematical form, albeit, and not surprisingly, in rudimentary form; the mathematics was largely that of algebra and calculus. His analysis raised in a direct way the problem of barriers to reaching determinate answers, thus setting the stage for a century-long process of coming to grips with that problem, with mixed and controversial results. He also was the first to make use of indifference curves (which were very slow to catch on as tools of the trade) and formulated the notion of a "contract curve" as the locus of equilibrium curves of trades between economic actors with different combinations of initial entitlements – a view which, while it interfered with the attainment of unique determinant outcomes, effectively, if unconsciously, continued the Ricardian idea that allocation is influenced by distribution. Edgeworth's notion of the core of an exchange economy and, in the large numbers case, the correspondence between this and perfectly competitive equilibrium, has had a fundamentally important influence on the development of modern general equilibrium theory.

The excerpts here from Edgeworth's *Mathematical Psychics* show his elaboration of the exchange analysis for which he has become so well known. The reader's attention is also drawn to his discussion of the relation of the social sciences to the natural sciences – representative of the general desire in economics over this period to bring the analysis more into line with the methods of the more prestigious natural sciences.

References and further reading

Blaug, Mark, ed. (1992) *Alfred Marshall (1842–1924) and Francis Edgeworth (1845–1926)*, Aldershot: Edward Elgar Publishing.

Bowley, A.L. (1934) "Francis Ysidro Edgeworth," *Econometrica* 2: 113–24.

Creedy, John (1979) "Edgeworth's Contribution to the Theory of Exchange," *Scottish Journal of Political Economy* 26 (June): 163–81.

——(1986) *Edgeworth and the Development of Neoclassical Economics*, Oxford: Basil Blackwell.

——(1990) "Marshall and Edgeworth," *Scottish Journal of Political Economy* 37 (February): 18–39.

Edgeworth, F.Y. (1925) *Papers Relating to Political Economy*, 3 vols, London: Macmillan for the Royal Economic Society.

Keynes, J.M. (1951) "Francis Ysidro Edgeworth, 1845–1926," in J.M. Keynes (ed.), *Essays in Biography*, London: Rupert Hart-Davis, 218–38.

Newman, Peter (1987) "Edgeworth, Francis Ysidro," in John Eatwell, Murray Milgate, and Peter Newman (eds), *The New Palgrave: A Dictionary of Economics*, Vol. 2, London: Macmillan, 84–98

Stigler, Stephen M. (1987) "Edgeworth as a Statistician," in John Eatwell, Murray Milgate, and Peter Newman (eds), *The New Palgrave: A Dictionary of Economics*, Vol. 2, London: Macmillan, 98–9.

Mathematical Psychics (1881)*

The application of mathematics to *Belief*, the calculus of Probabilities, has been treated by many distinguished writers; the calculus of *Feeling*, of Pleasure and Pain, is the less familiar, but not in reality more paradoxical subject of this essay.

The subject divides itself into two parts; concerned respectively with principle and practice, root and fruit, the applicability and the application of Mathematics to Sociology.

Part I

In the first part it is attempted to prove an affinity between the moral and the admittedly mathematical sciences from their resemblance as to (1) a certain general complexion, (2) a particular salient feature.

1. The science of quantity is not alien to the study of man, it will be generally admitted, in so far as actions and effective desires can be *numerically* measured by way of statistics – that is, very far, as Professor Jevons anticipates. But in so far as our *data* may consist of estimates other than *numerical*, observations that some conditions are accompanied with greater or less pleasure than others, it is necessary to realise that mathematical reasoning is not, as commonly supposed, limited to subjects where numerical data are attainable. Where there are data which, though not *numerical* are *quantitative* – for example, that a quantity is *greater* or *less* than another, *increases* or *decreases*, is *positive* or *negative*, a *maximum* or *minimum*, there mathematical reasoning is possible and may be indispensable. To take a trivial instance: *a* is greater than *b*, and *b* is greater than *c*, therefore *a* is greater than *c*. Here is mathematical reasoning applicable to quantities which may not be susceptible of numerical evaluation. The following instance is less trivial, analogous indeed to an important social problem. It is required to distribute a given quantity of fuel, so as to obtain the greatest possible quantity of available energy, among a given set of engines, which differ in efficiency – *efficiency* being thus defined: one engine is more efficient than another if, whenever the total quantity of fuel consumed by the former is equal to that consumed by the latter, the total quantity of energy yielded by the former is greater than that yielded by the latter.

In the distribution, shall a larger portion of fuel be given to the more efficient engines? Always, or only in some cases? And, if so, in what sort of cases? Here is a very simple problem involving no numerical data, yet requiring, it may be safely said, mathematics for its complete investigation.

The latter statement may be disputed in so far as such questions may be solved by reasoning, which, though not symbolical, is strictly mathematical; answered more informally, yet correctly, by undisciplined common sense. But, first, the advocate of mathematical reasoning in social science is not concerned to deny that mathematical reasoning in social, as well as in physical, science may

* *Mathematical Psychics: An Essay on the Application of Mathematics to the Moral Sciences*. London: C. Kegan Paul & Co., 1881. Reprinted by Augustus M. Kelley, 1967.

be divested of symbol. Only it must be remembered that the question how far mathematics can with safety or propriety be divested of her peculiar costume is a very delicate question, only to be decided by the authority and in the presence of Mathematics herself. And, second, as to the sufficiency of common sense, the worst of such unsymbolic, at least unmethodic, calculations as we meet in popular economics is that they are apt to miss the characteristic advantages of deductive reasoning. He that will not verify his conclusions as far as possible by mathematics, as it were bringing the ingots of common sense to be assayed and coined at the mint of the sovereign science, will hardly realise the full value of what he holds, will want a measure of what it will be worth in however slightly altered circumstances, a means of conveying and making it current. When the given conditions are not sufficient to determinate the problem – a case of great importance in Political Economy – the ἀγεωμετρητπς is less likely to suspect this deficiency, less competent to correct it by indicating what conditions are necessary and sufficient. All this is evident at a glance through the instrument of mathematics, but to the naked eye of common sense partially and obscurely, and, as Plato says of unscientific knowledge, in a state between genuine Being and Not-Being.

The preceding problem, to distribute a given quantity of material in order to a maximum of energy, with its starting point *loose quantitative relations* rather than numerical data – its slippery though short path almost necessitating the support of mathematics – illustrates fairly well the problem of utilitarian distribution. To illustrate the economical problem of exchange, the maze of many dealers contracting and competing with each other, it is possible to imagine a mechanism of many parts where the law of motion, which particular part moves off with which, is not precisely given – with symbols, arbitrary functions, representing not merely *not numerical knowledge* but ignorance – where, though the mode of motion towards equilibrium is indeterminate, the position of equilibrium is mathematically determined.

Examples not made to order, taken from the common stock of mathematical physics, will of course not fit so exactly. But they may be found in abundance, it is submitted, illustrating the property under consideration – mathematical reasoning without numerical data. In Hydrodynamics, for instance, we have a Thomson or Tait reasoning 'principles' for 'determining P and Q will *be given later*. In the meantime it is obvious that *each decreases as X increases*. Hence the equations of motion show' – and he goes on to draw a conclusion of momentous interest that balls (properly) projected in an infinite incompressible fluid will move as if they were attracted to each other. And generally in the higher Hydrodynamics, in that boundless ocean of perfect fluid, swum through by vortices, where the deep first principles of Physics are to be sought, is not a similar *unnumerical*, or *hyperarithmetical* method there pursued? If a portion of perfect fluid so moves at any time that each particle has no motion of rotation, then that portion of the fluid will retain that property for all time; here is no application of the numerical measuring-rod.

No doubt it may be objected that these hydrodynamical problems employ some *precise* data; the very definition of Force, the conditions of fluidity and continuity. But so also have our social problems *some* precise data: for example, the property *of uniformity of price* in a market; or rather the (approximately realised) conditions of which that property is the deducible *effect*, and which bears a striking resemblance to the data of hydrodynamics: (1) the *fulness* of the market: that there *continues* to be up to the conclusion of the dealing an indefinite number of dealers; (2) the *fluidity* of the market, or infinite dividedness of the dealers' interests. Given this property of uniform price, Mr Marshall and M. Walras deduce mathematically, though not arithmetically, an interesting theorem, which Mill and Thornton failed with unaided reason to discern, though they were quite close to it – the theorem that the equation of supply to demand, though a necessary, is not a sufficient condition of market price.

To attempt to select representative instances from each recognised branch of mathematical inquiry would exceed the limits of this paper and the requirements of the argument. It must suffice, in conclusion, to direct attention to one species of Mathematics which seems largely affected with the property under consideration, the Calculus of Maxima and Minima, or (in a wide sense) *of Variations*. The criterion of a *maximum* turns, not upon the *amount*, but upon the *sign* of a certain quantity. We are continually concerned with the ascertainment of a certain *loose quantitative relation*, the *decrease-of-rate-of-increase* of a quantity. Now, this is the very quantitative relation which it is proposed to employ in mathematical sociology; given in such data as the *law of diminishing returns to capital and labour*, the *law of diminishing utility*, the *law of increasing fatigue*; the very same irregular, unsquared material which constitutes the basis of the Economical and the Utilitarian Calculus.

Now, it is remarkable that the principal inquiries in Social Science may be viewed as *maximum-problems*. For Economics investigates the arrangements between agents each tending to his own *maximum* utility; and Politics and (Utilitarian) Ethics investigate the arrangements which conduce to the *maximum* sum total of utility. Since, then, Social Science, as compared with the Calculus of Variations, starts from similar data – *loose quantitative relations* – and travels to a similar conclusion – determination of *maximum* – why should it not pursue the same method, Mathematics?

There remains the objection that in Physical Calculus there is always (as in the example quoted above from Thomson and Tait) a potentiality, an expectation, of measurement; while Psychics want the first condition of calculation, a *unit*. The following brief answer is diffidently offered.

Utility, as Professor Jevons says, has two dimensions, *intensity* and *time*. The unit in each dimension is the just perceivable increment. The implied equation to each other of each *minimum sensibile is* a first principle incapable of proof. It resembles the equation to each other of undistinguishable events or cases, which constitutes the first principle of the mathematical calculus of *belief*. It is doubtless a principle acquired in the course of evolution. The implied equatability of time-intensity units, irrespective of distance in time and kind of pleasure, is still imperfectly evolved. Such is the unit of *economical* calculus.

For moral calculus a further dimension is required; to compare the happiness of one person with the happiness of another, and generally the happiness of groups of different members and different average happiness.

Such comparison can no longer be shirked, if there is to be any systematic morality at all. It is postulated by distributive justice. It is postulated by the population question; that horizon in which every moral prospect terminates; which is presented to the far-seeing at every turn, on the most sacred and the most trivial occasions. You cannot spend sixpence utilitarianly, without having considered whether your action tends to increase the comfort of a limited number, or numbers with limited comfort; without having compared such alternative utilities.

In virtue of what *unit* is such comparison possible? It is here submitted: Any individual experiencing a unit of pleasure-intensity during a unit of time is to 'count for one'. Utility, then, has *three* dimensions; a mass of utility, 'lot of pleasure', is greater than another when it has more *intensity-time-number* units. The third dimension is doubtless an evolutional acquisition; and is still far from perfectly evolved.

Looking back at our triple scale, we find no peculiar difficulty about the third dimension. It is an affair of census. The second dimension is an affair of clockwork; assuming that the distinction here touched, between subjective and objective measure of time, is of minor importance. But the first dimension, where we leave the safe ground of the objective, equating to unity each *minimum sensibile*, presents indeed peculiar difficulties. *Atoms of pleasure* are not easy to distinguish and discern; more continuous than sand, more discrete than liquid; as it were nuclei of the just-perceivable, embedded in circumambient semi-consciousness.

We cannot *count* the golden sands of life; we cannot *number* the 'innumerable smile' of seas of love; but we seem to be capable of observing that there is here a *greater*, there a *less*, multitude of pleasure-units, mass of happiness; and that is enough.

2. The application of mathematics to the world of soul is countenanced by the hypothesis (agreeable to the general hypothesis that every psychical phenomenon is the concomitant, and in

some sense the other side of a physical phenomenon), the particular hypothesis adopted in these pages, that Pleasure is the concomitant of Energy. *Energy* may be regarded as the central idea of Mathematical Physics; *maximum energy* the object of the principal investigations in that science. By aid of this conception we reduce into scientific order physical phenomena, the complexity of which may be compared with the complexity which appears so formidable in Social Science.

Imagine a material Cosmos, a mechanism as composite as possible, and perplexed with all manner of wheels, pistons, parts, connections, and whose mazy complexity might far transcend in its entanglement the webs of thought and wiles of passion; nevertheless, if any given impulses be imparted to any definite points in the mechanism at rest, it is mathematically deducible that each part of the great whole will move off with a velocity such that the energy of the whole may be the greatest possible – the greatest possible consistent with the given impulses and existing construction. If we know *something* about the construction of the mechanism, if it is 'a mighty maze, but not without a plan'; if we have some quantitative though not numerical datum about the construction, we may be able to deduce a similarly indefinite conclusion about the motion. For instance, any number of cases may be imagined in which, if a datum about the construction is that certain parts are *less stiff* than others, a conclusion about the motion would be that those parts take on more energy than their stiffer fellows. This rough, indefinite, yet mathematical reasoning is analogous to the reasoning on a subsequent page, that in order to the greatest possible sum total of happiness, the more capable of pleasure shall take more means, more happiness.

In the preceding illustration the motion of a mechanism was supposed instantaneously generated by the application of given impulses at definite points (or over definite surfaces); but similar general views are attainable in the not so dissimilar case in which we suppose motion generated in time by finite forces acting upon, and interacting between, the particles of which the mechanism is composed. This supposition includes the celebrated problem of Many Bodies (attracting each other according to any function of the distance); in reference to which one often hears it asked what can be expected from Mathematics in social science, when she is unable to solve the problem of Three Bodies in her own department. But Mathematics can solve the problem of many bodies – not indeed numerically and explicitly, but practically and philosophically, affording approximate measurements, and satisfying the soul of the philosopher with the grandest of generalisations. By a principle 'discovered or improved by Lagrange, each particle of the however complex whole is continually so moving that the accumulation of energy, which is constituted by adding to each other the energies of the mechanism existing at each instant of time (technically termed *Action* – the time-integral of Energy) should be a maximum. By the discovery of Sir William Rowan Hamilton the subordination of the parts to the whole is more usefully expressed, the velocity of each part is regarded as derivable from the *action* of the whole; the action is connected by a *single*, although not an explicit or in general easily interpretable, relation with the given law of force. The many unknown are reduced to one unknown, the one unknown is connected with the known.

Now this accumulation (or time-integral) of energy which thus becomes the principal object of the physical investigation is analogous to that accumulation of pleasure which is constituted by bringing together in prospect the pleasure existing at each instant of time, the end of rational action, whether self-interested or benevolent. The central conception of Dynamics and (in virtue of pervading analogies it may be said) in general of Mathematical Physics is *other-sidedly identical* with the central conception of Ethics; and a solution practical and philosophical, although not numerical and precise, as it exists for the problem of the interaction of bodies, so is possible for the problem of the interaction of souls.

This general solution, it may be thought, at most is applicable to the utilitarian problem of which the object is the greatest possible sum total of universal happiness. But it deserves consideration that an object of Economics also, the arrangement to which contracting agents actuated only by self-interest is capable of being regarded upon the psychophysical hypothesis here entertained as the realisation of the maximum sum total of happiness, the *relative maximum*, or that which is *consistent with certain conditions*. There is dimly discerned the Divine idea of a power tending to the greatest possible quantity of happiness *under conditions*; whether the condition of that perfect disintegration and unsympathetic isolation abstractedly assumed in Economics, or those intermediate conditions of what Herbert Spencer might term integration on to that perfected utilitarian sympathy in which the pleasures of another are accounted equal with one's own. There are diversities of conditions, but one maximum-principle; many stages of evolution, but 'one increasing purpose'.

'Mécanique Sociale' may one day take her place along with 'Mécanique Celeste', throned each upon the double-sided height of one maximum principle, the supreme pinnacle of moral as of physical science. As the movements of each particle, constrained or loose, in a material cosmos are continually subordinated to one maximum sum-total of accumulated energy, so the movements of each soul, whether selfishly isolated or linked sympathetically, may continually be realising the maximum energy of pleasure, the Divine love of the universe.

'Mécanique Sociale', in comparison with her elder sister, is less attractive to the vulgar worshipper in that she is discernible by the eye of faith alone. The statuesque beauty of the one is manifest; but the fairylike features of the other and her fluent form are veiled. But Mathematics has long walked by the evidence of things not seen in the world of atoms (the methods whereof, it may incidentally be remarked, statistical and rough, may illustrate the possibility of social mathematics). The invisible energy of electricity is grasped by the marvellous methods of Lagrange; the invisible energy of pleasure may admit of a similar handling.

As in a system of conductors carrying electrical currents the energy due to electro-magnetic force is to be distinguished from the energy due to ordinary dynamical forces, for example, gravitation acting upon the conductors, so the energy of pleasure is to be distinguished not only from the gross energy of the limbs, but also from such nervous energy as either is not all represented in consciousness (*pace* G. H. Lewes), or is represented by *intensity of consciousness* not *intensity of pleasure*. As electro-magnetic force tends to a maximum energy, so also pleasure force tends to a maximum energy. The energy generated by pleasure force is the physical concomitant and measure of the conscious feeling of delight.

Imagine an electrical circuit consisting of two rails isolated from the earth connected at one extremity by a galvanic battery and bridged over at the other extremity by a steam-locomotive. When a current of electricity is sent through the circuit, there is an electro-magnetic force tending to move the circuit or any moveable part of it in such a direction that the number of lines of force (due to the magnetism of the earth) passing through the circuit in a positive direction may be a *maximum*. The electro-magnetic force therefore tends to move the locomotive along the rails in that direction. Now this delicate force may well be unable to move the ponderous locomotive, but it may be adequate to press a spring and turn a handle and let on steam and cause the locomotive to be moved by the steam-engine *in the direction of the electro-magnetic force*, either backwards or forwards according to the direction in which the electrical current flows. The delicate electro-magnetic force is placed in such a commanding position that she sways the movements of the steam-engine so as to satisfy her own yearning towards *maximum*.

Add now another degree of freedom; and let the steam-car governed move upon a *plane* in a direction tending towards the position of Minimum Potential Electro-Magnetic Energy. Complicate this conception; modify it by substituting for the principle of Minimum Force-Potential the principle of *Minimum Momentum-Potential*; imagine a comparatively gross mechanism of innumerable degrees of freedom *governed*, in the sense adumbrated, by a more delicate system – itself, however inconceivably diversified its degrees of freedom, obedient still to the great *Maximum Principles* of Physics, and amenable to mathematical demonstration, though at first sight as hopelessly incalculable as whatever is in life capricious and irregular – as the smiles of beauty and the waves of passion.

Similarly pleasure in the course of evolution has become throned among grosser subject energies – as it were explosive engines, ready to go off at the pressure of a hair-spring. Swayed by the first principle, she sways the subject energies so as to satisfy her own yearning towards *maximum*; 'her every air Of gesture and least motion' a law of Force to governed systems – a fluent form, a Fairy Queen guiding a most complicated chariot, wheel within wheel, the 'speculative and active instruments', the motor nerves, the limbs and the environment on which they act.

A system of such charioteers and chariots is what constitutes the object of Social Science. The attractions between the charioteer forces, the collisions and compacts between the chariots, present an appearance of quantitative regularity in the midst of bewildering complexity resembling in its general characters the field of electricity and magnetism. To construct a scientific hypothesis seems rather to surpass the powers of the writer than of Mathematics. 'Sin has ne possim naturæ accedere partes Frigidus obstiterit circum præcordia sanguis'; at least *the conception of Man as a pleasure machine* may justify and facilitate the employment of mechanical terms and Mathematical reasoning in social science.

Part II

Such are some of the preliminary considerations by which emboldened we approach the two fields into which the Calculus of Pleasure may be subdivided, namely Economics and Utilitarian Ethics. The Economical Calculus investigates the equilibrium of a system of hedonic forces each tending to maximum individual utility; the Utilitarian Calculus, the equilibrium of a system in which each and all tend to maximum universal utility. The motives of the two species of agents correspond with Mr Sidgwick's Egoistic and Universalistic Hedonism. But the correspondence is not perfect. For, first, upon the principle of 'self limitation' of a method, so clearly stated by Mr Sidgwick, so persistently misunderstood by critics, the Pure Utilitarian might think it most beneficent to sink his benevolence towards competitors; and the *Deductive Egoist* might have need of a Utilitarian Calculus. But further, it is possible that the moral constitution of the concrete agent would be neither Pure Utilitarian nor Pure Egoistic, but μικτήτις. For it is submitted that Mr Sidgwick's division of Hedonism – the class of 'Method' whose principle of action may be generically defined *maximising happiness* – is not exhaustive. For between the two extremes Pure Egoistic and Pure Universalistic there may be an indefinite number of impure methods; wherein the happiness of others as compared by the agent (in a calm moment) with his own, neither counts for nothing, not yet 'counts for one', but *counts for a fraction*.

Deferring controversy, let us glance at the elements of the *Economic Calculus*; observing that the connotation (and some of the reasoning) extends beyond the usual denotation; to the political struggle for power, as well as to the commercial struggle for wealth.

Economical calculus

Definitions

The first principle of Economics is that every agent is actuated only by self-interest. The workings of this principle may be viewed under two aspects, according as the agent acts *without*, or *with*, the consent of others affected by his actions. In wide senses, the first species of action may be called *war*; the second, *contract*. Examples: (1) A general, or fencer, making moves, a dealer lowering price, *without consent of rival*. (2) A set of co-operatives (labourers, capitalists, manager) agreed *nem. con.* to distribute the joint-produce by assigning to each *a certain function* of his sacrifice. The *articles* of contract are in this case the *amount* of sacrifice to be made by each, *and the principle of distribution*.

'Is it peace or war?' asks the lover of 'Maud', of economic *competition*, and answers hastily: It is both, *pax* or *pact* between contractors during contract, *war*, when some of the contractors *without the consent of others recontract*. Thus, an auctioneer having been in contact with the last bidder (to sell at such a price *if* no higher bid) *recontracts* with a higher bidder. So a landlord on expiry of lease recontracts, it may be, with a new tenant.

The *field of competition* with reference to a contract, or contracts, under consideration consists of all the individuals who are willing and able to recontract about the articles under consideration. Thus, in an auction the field consists of the auctioneer and all who are effectively willing to give a higher price than the last bid. In this case, as the transaction reaches determination, the field continually diminishes and ultimately vanishes. But this is not the case in general. Suppose a great number of auctions going on at the same point; or, what comes to the same thing, a market consisting of an indefinite number of dealers, say *X*s, in commodity *x*, and an indefinite number of dealers, say *Y*s, in commodity *y*. In this case, up to the determination of equilibrium, the field continues indefinitely large. To be sure it may be said to vanish at the position of equilibrium. But that circumstance does not stultify the definition. Thus, if one chose to define the *field of force* as the centres of force sensibly acting on a certain system of bodies, then in a continuous medium of attracting matter, the field might be continually of indefinite extent, might change as the system moved, might be said to vanish when the system reached equilibrium.

There is free communication throughout a *normal* competitive field. You might suppose the constituent individuals collected at a point, or connected by telephones – an ideal supposition, but sufficiently approximate to existence or tendency for the purposes of abstract science.

A *perfect* field of competition professes in addition certain properties peculiarly favourable to mathematical calculation; namely a certain indefinite *multiplicity* and *dividedness*, analogous to that *infinity* and *infinitesimality* which facilitate so large a portion of Mathematical Physics (consider the theory of Atoms, and all applications of the Differential Calculus). The conditions of a *perfect* field are four; the first pair referrible to the heading *multiplicity* or continuity, the second to *dividedness* or fluidity.

1   Any individual is free to *recontract* with any out of an indefinite number, for example, in the last example there are an indefinite number of *X*s and similarly of *Y*s.
2   Any individual is free to *contract* (at the same time) with an indefinite number; for example, any *X* (and similarly *Y*) may deal with any number of *Y*s. This condition combined with the first appears to involve the indefinite divisibility of each *article* of contract (if any *X* deal with an indefinite number of *Y*s he must give each an indefinitely small portion of *x*); which might be erected into a separate condition.
3   Any individual is free to *recontract* with another independently of, *without the consent* being required of, any third party, for example, there is among the *Y*s (and similarly among the *X*s) no *combination* or pre-contract between two or more contractors that none of them will recontract without the consent of all. Any *Y* then may accept the offer of any *X* irrespectively of other *Y*s.
4   Any individual is free to *contract* with another independently of a third party; for example, in simple exchange each contract is between two only, but *secus* in the entangled contract described in the example … where it may be a condition of production that there should be three at least to each bargain.

There will be observed a certain similarity between the relation of the first to the second condition, and that of the third to the fourth. The failure of the first involves the failure of the second, but not *vice versâ*; and the third and fourth are similarly related.

A *settlement* is a contract which cannot be varied with the consent of all the parties to it.

A *final settlement* is a settlement which cannot be varied by recontract, within the field of competition.

Contract is *indeterminate* when there are an indefinite number of *final settlements*.

The *Problem* to which attention is specially directed in this introductory summary is: *How far contract is indeterminate* – an enquiry of more than theoretical importance, if it show not only that indeterminateness tends to prevent widely, but also in what direction an escape from its evils is to be sought.

Demonstrations

The general answer is – (α) Contract without competition is indeterminate, (β) Contract with *perfect* competition is perfectly determinate, (γ) Contract with more or less perfect competition is less or more indeterminate.

α. Let us commence with almost the simplest case of contract – two individuals, X and Y, whose interest depends on two variable quantities, which they are agreed not to vary without mutual consent. Exchange of two commodities is a particular case of this kind of contract. Let x and y be the portions interchanged, as in Professor Jevons's example. Then the utility of one party, say X, may be written $\Phi_1(a - x) + \Psi_1(y)$; and the utility of the other party, say Y, $\Phi_2(x) + \Psi_2(b - y)$; where Φ and Ψ are the integrals of Professor Jevons's symbols ϕ and ψ. It is agreed that x and y shall be varied only by consent (not for example by violence).

More generally, let P, the utility of X, one party, $= F(x, y)$, and Π, the utility of Y, the other party, $= \Phi(x, y)$. If now it is inquired at what point they will reach equilibrium, one or both refusing to move further, to what *settlement* they will consent; the answer is in general that contract by itself does not supply sufficient conditions to determinate the solution; supplementary conditions as will appear being supplied by competition or ethical motives, Contract will supply only *one* condition (for the two variables), namely

$$\frac{dP}{dx}\frac{d\Pi}{dy} = \frac{dP}{dy}\frac{d\Pi}{dx},$$

(corresponding to Professor Jevons's equation

$$\frac{\phi_1(a-x)}{\psi_1(y)} = \frac{\phi_2(x)}{\psi_2(b-y)}.$$

Theory (p. 108), which it is proposed here to investigate.

Consider $P - F(x, y) = 0$ as a surface, P denoting the length of the ordinate drawn from any point on the plane of xy (say the plane of the paper) to the surface. Consider $\Pi - \Phi(x, y)$ similarly. It is required to find a point (xy) such that, *in whatever direction* we take an infinitely small step, P and Π do not increase together, but that, while one increases, the other decreases. It may be shown from a variety of points of view that the locus of the required point is

$$\frac{dP}{dx}\frac{d\Pi}{dy} - \frac{dP}{dy}\frac{d\Pi}{dx} = 0,$$

which locus it is here proposed to call the *contract-curve*.

1. Consider first in what directions X can take an indefinitely small step, say of length ρ, from any point (xy). Since the addition to P is

$$\rho\left[\left(\frac{dP}{dx}\right)\cos\theta + \left(\frac{dP}{dy}\right)\sin\theta\right],$$

$\rho\cos\theta$ being $= dx$, and $\rho\sin\theta = dy$, it is evident that X will step only on one side of a certain line, the *line of indifference*, as it might be called; its equation being

$$(\xi - x)\left(\frac{dP}{dx}\right) + (\eta - y)\left(\frac{dP}{\xi dy}\right) = 0.$$

And it is to be observed, in passing, that the direction in which X will *prefer* to move, the line of force or *line of preference*, as it may be termed, is perpendicular to the line of indifference. Similar remarks apply to Π. If then we enquire in what directions X and Y will consent to move *together*, the answer is, in any direction between their respective lines of indifference, in a direction *positive as it may be called for both*. At what point then will they refuse to move at all? When their *lines of indifference* are coincident (and *lines of preference* not only coincident, but in opposite directions); whereof the *necessary* (but *not sufficient*) condition is

$$\left(\frac{dP}{dx}\right)\left(\frac{d\Pi}{dy}\right) - \left(\frac{dP}{dy}\right)\left(\frac{d\Pi}{dx}\right) = 0.$$

2. The same consideration might be thus put. Let the complete variation of *P* be

$$DP = \rho\left[\left(\frac{dP}{dx}\right)\cos\theta + \left(\frac{dP}{dy}\right)\sin\theta\right]$$

and similarly for Π. Then in general θ can be taken, so that $DP/D\Pi$ should be positive, say $=g^2$, and so *P* and Π both increase together.

$$\tan\theta = -\frac{(dP/dx) - g^2(d\Pi/dx)}{(dP/dy) - g^2(d\Pi/dy)}.$$

But this solution fails when

$$\frac{(dP/dx)}{(dP/dy)} = \frac{(d\Pi/dx)}{(d\Pi/dy)}.$$

In fact, in this case $DP/D\Pi$ *is the same for all directions*.

If, then, that common value of $DP/D\Pi$ is negative, motion is impossible in any direction.

3. Or, again, we may consider that motion is possible so long as, one party not losing, the other gains. The point of equilibrium, therefore, may be described as a *relative maximum*, the point at which for example Π being constant, *P* is a maximum. Put $P = P - c(\Pi - \Pi')$, where *c* is a constant and Π' is the supposed given value of Π. Then *P* is a maximum only when

$$dx\left(\frac{dP}{dx} - c\frac{d\Pi}{dx}\right) + dy\left(\frac{dP}{dy} - c\frac{d\Pi}{dy}\right) = 0,$$

whence we have as before the *contract-curve*.

The same result would follow if we supposed Y induced to consent to the variation, not merely by the guarantee that he should not lose, or gain infinitesimally, but by the understanding that he should gain sensibly with the gains of *P*. For instance, let $\Pi = k^2 P$ where *k* is a constant, certainly not a very practicable condition. Or, more generally, let *P* move subject to the condition that $DP = \theta^2 \times D\Pi$, where θ is a function of the coordinates. Then *DP, subject to this condition*, vanishes only when

$$0 = \left(\frac{dP}{dx}\right)dx + \left(\frac{dP}{dy}\right)dy + c\left\{\left(\frac{dP}{dx}\right)dx + \left(\frac{dP}{dy}\right)dy - \theta^2\left[\left(\frac{d\Pi}{dx}\right)dx + \left(\frac{d\Pi}{dy}\right)dy\right]\right\},$$

where *c* is a constant; whence

$$\left(\frac{dP}{dx}\right)(1+c) - c\theta^2\left(\frac{d\Pi}{dx}\right) = 0$$

and

$$\left(\frac{\mathrm{d}P}{\mathrm{d}x}\right)(1+c)-c\,\theta^2\left(\frac{\mathrm{d}\Pi}{\mathrm{d}y}\right)=0,$$

whence as before

$$\left(\frac{\mathrm{d}P}{\mathrm{d}x}\right)\left(\frac{\mathrm{d}\Pi}{\mathrm{d}y}\right)-\left(\frac{\mathrm{d}P}{\mathrm{d}y}\right)\left(\frac{\mathrm{d}\Pi}{\mathrm{d}x}\right)=0.$$

No doubt the one theory which has been thus differently expressed could be presented by a professed mathematician more elegantly and scientifically. What appears to the writer the most philosophical presentation may be thus indicated.

4. Upon the hypothesis above shadowed forth, human action generally, and in particular the step taken by a contractor modifying articles of contract, may be regarded as the working of a gross force *governed*, let on, and directed by a more delicate pleasure-force. From which it seems to follow upon general dynamical principles applied to this special case that equilibrium is attained when the total *pleasure-energy of the contractors is a maximum relative*, or subject, to conditions; the conditions being here (i) that the pleasure-energy of X and Y considered each as a function of (certain values of) the variables x and y should be functions of the same values: in the metaphorical language above employed that the charioteer-pleasures should drive their teams together over the plane of xy; (ii) that the joint-team should never be urged in a direction contrary to the preferences of either individual; that the resultant line of force (and the momentum) of the gross, the chariot, system should be continually intermediate between the (positive directions of the) lines of the respective pleasure-forces. [We may without disadvantage make abstraction of sensible momentum, and suppose the by the condition joint-system to move towards equilibrium along a line of resultant gross force. Let it start from the origin. And let us employ an *arbitrary function* to denote the unknown *principle of compromise* between the parties; suppose the ratio of the sines of angles made by the resultant line with the respective lines of pleasure-force.] Then, by reasoning different from the preceding only in the point of view, it appears that the *total utility of the system is a relative maximum at any point on the pure contract-curve.*

It appears from (1) and (2) there is a portion of the locus

$$\left(\frac{\mathrm{d}P}{\mathrm{d}x}\right)\left(\frac{\mathrm{d}\Pi}{\mathrm{d}y}\right)-\left(\frac{\mathrm{d}\Pi}{\mathrm{d}x}\right)\left(\frac{\mathrm{d}P}{\mathrm{d}y}\right)=0,$$

where $DP/D\Pi$ is $+$, *not* therefore indicating immobility, *au contraire*, the im*pure* (part of the) contract-curve, as it might be called. This might be illustrated by two spheres, each having the plane of the paper as a diametral plane. The contract curve is easily seen to be the line joining the centres. Supposing that the distance between the centres is less than the less of the radii, part of the contract-curve is *impure*. If the index, as Mr Marshall might call it, be placed anywhere in this portion it will run up to a centre. But between the centres the contract-curve is *pure*; the index placed anywhere in this portion is immovable; and if account be taken of the portions of the spheres underneath the plane of the paper, the downward ordinates representing *negative pleasures*, similar statements hold, *mutatis mutandis*.

It appears that the pure and impure parts of the contract-curve are demarcated by the points where $DP/D\Pi$ changes sign, that is (in general) where either $DP/\mathrm{d}\sigma$ or $D\Pi/\mathrm{d}\sigma$ ($\mathrm{d}\sigma$ being an increment of the length of the contract-curve) either vanishes or becomes infinite. Accordingly the maxima and minima of P and Π present demarcating points; for example, the centre of each sphere, which corresponds to a maximum in reference to the upper hemisphere, a minimum in reference to the lower hemisphere. The impure contract curve is relevant to cases where the commodity of one party is a *discommodity* to the other.

But even in the pure contract-curve all points do not in the same sense indicate immobility. For, according to the consideration (3) (above, ...), the contract-curve may be treated as the locus where, Π being constant, P is *stationary*, either a *maximum or minimum*. Thus, any point in our case of two intersecting spheres affords a *maximum* in relation to the upper hemisphere; but the same point (it is only an accident that it should be *the same* point – it would not be the same point if you suppose slightly distorted spheres) affords a *minimum* in relation to the lower hemisphere. This *pure, but unstable* (part of the) contract-curve is exemplified in certain cases of that *unstable equilibrium of trade*, which has been pointed out by Principal Marshall and Professor Walras.

The preceding theory may easily be extended to several persons and several variables. Let $P_1 = F_1(xyz)$ denote the utility of one of three parties, utility depending on three variables, xyz; and similarly $P_2 = F_2$, $P_3 = F_3$. Then the *contract-settlement*, the arrangement for the alteration of which *the consent of all three parties* cannot be obtained, will be (subject to reservations analogous to those analysed in the preceding paragraphs) *the Eliminant*.

$$\frac{dP_1}{dx} \quad \frac{dP_1}{dy} \quad \frac{dP_1}{dz},$$

$$\frac{dP_2}{dx} \quad \frac{dP_2}{dy} \quad \frac{dP_2}{dz},$$

$$\frac{dP_3}{dx} \quad \frac{dP_3}{dy} \quad \frac{dP_3}{dz}.$$

In general let there be m contractors and n subjects of contract, n variables. Then by the principle (3) [above, ...] the state of equilibrium may be considered as such that the utility of any one contractor must be a maximum *relative to* the utilities of the other contractors being constant, or not decreasing; which may be thus mathematically expressed:

$D(l_1 P_1 + l_2 P_2 + \cdots + l_m P_m) = 0$, where D represents complete increment and $l_1, l_2, \ldots$, are indeterminate multipliers; whence, if there be n variables $x_1 x_2 \cdots x_n$, we have n equations of the form

$$l_1 \frac{dP_1}{dx_1} + l_2 \frac{dP_2}{dx_1} + \cdots + l_m \frac{dP_m}{dx_1} = 0,$$

from which, if n be not less than m, we can eliminate the ($m - 1$ independent) constants l and obtain the contract-system consisting of $n - (m - 1)$ equations.

The case of n being less than m may be sufficiently illustrated by a particular example. Let the abscissa x represent the single variable on which the utilities P and Π of two persons contracting depend. Then if p and π are the maximum points for the respective pleasure-curves (compare the reasoning, ...) it is evident that the tract of abscissa between π and p is of the nature of pure contract-curve; that the index being placed anywhere in that tract will be immovable; secus on either side beyond π and p. Similarly it may be shown that, if three individuals are in contract about two variables $x\,y$, the contract locus or region is (the space within) a curvilinear triangle in the plane $x\,y$ bounded by the *three* contract-curves presented by successively supposing each pair of individuals to be in contract with respect to x and y. And similarly for larger numbers in hyperspace.

It is not necessary for the purpose of the present study to carry the analysis further. To gather up and fix our thoughts, let us imagine a simple case – Robinson Crusoe contracting with Friday. The *articles* of contract: wages to be given by the white, labour to be given by the black. Let Robinson Crusoe $= X$. Represent y, the labour given by Friday, by a horizontal line measured *northward* from an assumed point, and measure x, the remuneration given by Crusoe, from the same point along an *eastward* line (see accompanying Figure 1). Then any point between these lines represents a contract. It will very generally be the interest of both parties to vary the articles of any contract taken at random. But there is a class of contracts to the variation of which the, consent of *both* parties cannot be obtained, of *settlements*. These settlements are represented by an *indefinite number* of points, a locus, the *contract-curve CC'*, or rather, a certain portion of it which may be supposed to be wholly in the space between our perpendicular lines in a direction trending from south-east to north-west. This available portion of the contract-curve lies between two points, say $\eta_0 x_0$ north-west, and $y_0 \xi_0$ south-east; which are, respectively, the intersections with the contract-curve of the *curves of indifference* for each party drawn through the origin. Thus, the utility of the contract represented by $\eta_0 x_0$ is for Friday zero, or rather, the same as if there was no contract. At that point he would as soon be off with the bargain – work by himself perhaps.

This simple case brings clearly into view the characteristic evil of indeterminate contract, *deadlock*, undecidable opposition of interests, ἄκριτός ἔρις καὶ ταραχή. It is the interest of both parties that there should be *some settlement*, one of the contracts represented by the contract-curve between the limits. But *which* of these contracts is arbitrary in the absence of arbitration, the interests of the two *adversâ pugnantia fronte* all along the contract-curve, Y desiring to get as far as possible south-east towards $y_0 \xi_0$, X north-west toward $\eta_0 x_0$. And it further appears from the preceding analysis that in the case of any number of *articles* (for instance, Robinson Crusoe to give Friday in the way of Industrial Partnership a *fraction* of the produce as well as wages, or again, *arrangements about the mode* of work), the *contract-locus* may still be represented as a sort of line, along which the pleasure-forces of the contractors are mutually antagonistic.

An accessory evil of indeterminate contract is the tendency, greater than in a full market, towards dissimulation and objectionable arts of higgling. As Professor Jevons says with reference to a similar case, 'Such a transaction must be settled upon other than strictly economical grounds. ... The art of bargaining consists in the buyer ascertaining the lowest price at which the seller is willing to part with his object, without disclosing, if possible, the highest price which he, the buyer, is willing to give'. Compare Courcelle-Seneuil's account of the contract between a hunter and a wood-man in an isolated region.

With this clogged and underground procedure is contrasted (β) the smooth machinery of the open market. As Courcelle-Seneuil says, 'à mesure que le nombre des concurrents augmente, les

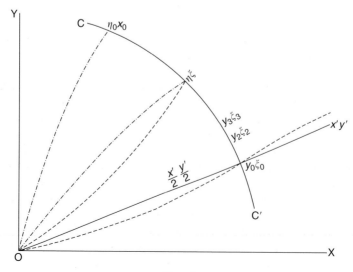

Figure 1

conditions d'échange deviennent plus nécessaires, plus impersonelles en quelque sorte.' You might suppose each dealer to write down his *demand*, how much of an article he would take at each price, without attempting to conceal his requirements; and these data having been furnished to a sort of market-machine, the *price* to be passionlessly evaluated.

That contract in a state of perfect competition is determined by demand and supply is generally accepted, but is hardly to be fully understood without mathematics. The mathematics of a perfect market have been worked out by several eminent writers, in particular Messrs Jevons, Marshall, Walras; to whose varied cultivation of the mathematical science, *Catallactics*, the reader is referred who wishes to dig down to the root of first principles, to trace out all the branches of a complete system, to gather fruits rare and only to be reached by a mathematical substructure.

There emerges amidst the variety of construction and terminology πολλῶν ὀνομάτων μορφή μία, an essentially identical graphical form or analytical formula expressing the equation of supply to demand; whereof the simplest type, the catallactic molecule, as it might be called, is presented in the case above described in the definition of perfect competition. The familiar pair of equations is deduced by the present writer from the first principle: Equilibrium is attained when the existing contracts can neither be varied without recontract with the consent of the existing parties, nor by recontract within the field of competition. The advantage of this general method is that it is applicable to the particular cases of imperfect competition; where the conceptions of *demand and supply at a price* are no longer appropriate.

The catallactic molecule is compounded, when we suppose the Xs and Ys dealing in respect each of *several* articles with several sets of Zs, As, Bs, etc.; a case resolved by M. Walras.

Thus, the actual commercial field might be represented by sets of entrepreneurs Xs, Ys, Zs, each X buying labour from among sets of labourers, As, Bs, Cs, use of capital from among sets of capitalists, Js, Ks, Ls, use of land from among sets of landowners, Ps, Qs, Rs, and selling products among a set of consumers consisting of the sum of the three aforesaid classes *and* the entrepreneurs of a species different from X, the Ys and Zs. As the demand of the labourer is deducible from considering his utility as a function of wages received and work done, so the demand of the entrepreneur is deducible from considering his utility as a function of (1) his expenditures on the agents of production; (2) his expenditures in the way of consumption; (3) his receipts from sale of produce; (4) his labour of superintendence. The last-named variable is not an article of contract; but there being supposed a definite relation connecting the produce with agents of production and entrepreneur's labour, the catallactic formulæ become applicable. This is a very abstract representation (abstracting, for example, risk, foreign trade, the migration from one employment to another, for example Xs becoming Ys, etc.), yet more concrete than that of M. Walras, who apparently makes the more abstract supposition of a sort of *frictionless* entrepreneur, 'faisant ni perte ni bénéfice'.

From the point of view just reached may with advantage be contemplated one of the domains most recently added to Economic Science – Mr Sidgwick's contribution to the 'Fortnightly Review', September, 1879. The *indirectness of the relation between wages and interest* which Mr Sidgwick has so clearly demonstrated in words is self-evident in symbols. The *pre-determinatedness of the wage-fund*, which has received its *coup de grâce* from Mr Sidgwick, must always, one would think, have appeared untenable from the humblest mathematical point of view, the consideration of the simplest types of perfect competition; from which also it must be added that Mr Sidgwick's – perhaps inadvertent, perhaps here misinterpreted – statement, that contract between employer and operative even in the case of what is here called *perfect* competition, is indeterminate, does not, it is submitted, appear tenable. It is further submitted that Mr Sidgwick's strictures on Prof Jevons are hasty; for that by a (compound) employment of the Jevonian (or an equivalent catallactic) formula, the complex relations between entrepreneur, capitalist and labourer are best made clear. And so 'there is *á priori* ground for supposing that industrial competition tends to equalize the rate of *profit* (as well as *interest*) on capitals of different amount'. That 'the labour of managing capital does not increase in proportion to the amount managed' is so far from creating any peculiar difficulty, that it is rather of the essence of the theory of exchange; quite congruent with the familiar circumstance that the *disutility* of (common) labour (labour subjectively estimated) does not increase in proportion to *work done* (labour objectively estimated). That the labour of managing capital increases not only *not at the same* but at a less rate-of-increase than the amount managed, as Mr Sidgwick seems to imply, is indeed a peculiar circumstance; but it is of a sort with which the Jevonian formula, the mathematical theory of catallactics, is quite competent to deal, with which in fact Mr Marshall has dealt in his *second class* of Demand-Curves.

But it is not the purport of the present study to attempt a detailed, much less a polemical, discussion of pure Catallactics, but rather (γ) to enquire how far contract is determinate in cases of imperfect competition. It is not necessary for this purpose to attack the *general problem of Contract qualified by Competition*, which is much more difficult than the general problem of unqualified contract already treated. It is not necessary to resolve analytically the composite mechanism of a *competitive field*. It will suffice to proceed synthetically, observing in a simple typical case the effect of continually introducing into the field additional competitors.

I. Let us start, then, from the abstract typical case above put ... an X and Y dealing respectively in *x* and *y*. Here *x* represents the *sacrifice objectively measured* of X; it may be manual work done, or commodity manufactured, or capital abstained from during a certain time. And *y* is the objectively measured remuneration of X. Hence it may be assumed, according to the two first axioms of the Utilitarian Calculus, the law of increasing labour, and the law of decreasing utility, that *P* being the utility of X, (1) dP/dx is continually *negative*, dP/dy *positive*; d_2P/dx^2, d_2P/dy^2, $d_2P/dxdy$, continually *negative*. (Attention is solicited to the interpretation of the third condition.) No doubt these latter conditions are subject to many exceptions, especially in regard to abstinence from capital, and in case of purchase not for consumption, but with a view to re-sale; and in the sort of cases comprised in Mr Marshall's Class II curves. Still, these exceptions, though they destroy the watertightness of many of the reasonings in this and the companion calculus, are yet perhaps of secondary importance to one taking a general abstract view.

This being premised, let us now introduce a second X and a second Y; so that the field of competition consists of two Xs and two Ys. And for the sake of illustration (not of the argument) let us suppose that the new X has the same requirements, the same nature as the old X; and similarly that the new Y is equal-natured with the old.

Then it is evident that there cannot be equilibrium unless (1) all the field is collected at one point; (2) that point is on the *contract-curve*. For (1) if possible let one couple be at one point, and another couple at another point. It will generally be the interest of the X of one couple and the Y of the other to rush together, leaving their partners in the lurch. And (2) if the common point is not on the contract-curve, it will be the interest of all *parties* to descend to the contract-curve.

The points of the contract-curve in the immediate neighbourhood of the limits $y_0\xi_0$ and η_0x_0 cannot be *final settlements*. For if the system be placed at such a point, say slightly north-west of $y_0\xi_0$, it will in general be possible for *one* of the Ys (without the consent of the other) to *recontract* with the two Xs, so that for all those three parties the recontract is more advantageous than the previously existing contract. For the right line joining the origin to (the neighbourhood of) $y_0\xi_0$ will in general lie altogether within the *indifference-curve* drawn from the origin to $y_0\xi_0$. For the indifference-curve is in general convex to the abscissa. For its differential equation is

$$-\frac{dy}{dx} = \frac{dF(xy)/dx}{dF(xy)/dy},$$

whence

$$\frac{d_2 y}{dx^2} = \frac{-\left[\left(\dfrac{d_2 F}{dx^2}\right)+\left(\dfrac{d_2 F}{dxdy}\right)\dfrac{dy}{dx}\right]\left(\dfrac{dF}{dy}\right)+\left(\dfrac{dF}{dx}\right)\left[\left(\dfrac{d_2 F}{dxdy}\right)+\dfrac{d_2 F}{dy^2}\dfrac{dy}{dx}\right]}{\left(\dfrac{dF}{dy}\right)^2},$$

which is perfectly *positive*. Therefore the indifference curve (so far as we are concerned with it) is convex to the abscissa.

Now, at the contract-curve the two indifference curves for X and Y touch. Thus, the Figure 1, is proved to be a correct representation, indicating that a point $x'y'$ can be found both more advantageous for Y than the point on the contract-curve $y_1\xi_1$ (on an *interior* indifference-curve, as it may be said), and also such that its co-ordinates are the sums (respectively) of the co-ordinates of two other points, both more advantageous for an X. These latter points to be occupied by X_1, and X_2, may be properly regarded (owing to the symmetry and competition) as *coincident*; with co-ordinates $\frac{x'}{2} \frac{y'}{2}$. Further, it appears from previous reasonings that there will be a *contract-relation* between $(x'y')$ and $\frac{x'}{2} \frac{y'}{2}$; namely

$$\frac{\Phi'_x (x'y')}{\Phi'_y (x'y')} = \frac{F'_x \left(\dfrac{x'}{2} \dfrac{y'}{2}\right)}{F'_y \left(\dfrac{x'}{2} \dfrac{y'}{2}\right)}; 1$$

where F'_x is put for the first partially derived function $(dF(xy)/dx)$.

When this relation is satisfied the system of three might remain in the position reached; but for Y_2 who has been left out in the cold. He will now strike in, with the result that the system will be worked down to the contract-curve again; to a point at least as favourable for the Xs as $\frac{x'}{2} \frac{y'}{2}$. Thus, the Ys will have lost some of their original advantage by competition. And a certain process of which this is an abstract typical representation will go on as long as it is possible to find a point $x'y'$ with the requisite properties. Attention to the problem will show that the process will come to a stop at a point on the contract-curve $y_2\xi_2$, such that if a line joining it to the origin intersect the curve, the *supplementary contract-curve.* as it might be called,

$$\frac{\Phi'_x(xy)}{\Phi'_y(xy)} = \frac{F'_x \left(\dfrac{x}{2} \dfrac{y}{2}\right)}{F'_y \left(\dfrac{x}{2} \dfrac{y}{2}\right)}; 2$$

in the point $x'y'$ then $\Phi(\xi_2 y_2) = \Phi(x'y')$, *provided that* $(\frac{x'}{2} \frac{y'}{2})$ falls within the indifference-curve for Y drawn through $(\xi_2 y_2)$. If otherwise, a slightly different system of equations must be employed.

If now a *third* X and third Y (still equal-natured) be introduced into the field, the system can be worked down to a point $\xi_3 y_3$; whose conditions are obtained from those just written by substituting for $\frac{x'}{2} \frac{y'}{2}$, $\frac{2x'}{3} \frac{2y'}{3}$. For this represents the last point at which 2 Ys can recontract with 3 Xs with advantage to all five. Analytical geometry will show that this point is lower down (in respect of the advantage of Y) than $\xi_2 y_2$. In the limit, when the Xs and Ys are indefinitely (equally) multiplied, we shall have $(x'y')$ coincident with $(\xi_\infty y_\infty)$, or as we may say for convenience $(\xi\eta)$, satisfying one or other of the *alternatives* corresponding to those just mentioned.

In case of the first alternative we have

$$\xi\Phi'_x(\xi\eta) + \eta\Phi'_y(\xi\eta) = 0.$$

For $\Phi(\xi\eta) = \Phi(X'y') = \Phi((1 + h)\xi(1 + h)\eta)$. In the limiting case h is infinitesimal. Whence by differentiating the above equation is obtained. And the second alternative ($\frac{x'}{2}$ $\frac{y'}{2}$) *not* falling within the indifference-curve of Y) is not to be distinguished from the first in the limiting case.

If this reasoning does not seem satisfactory, it would be possible to give a more formal proof; bringing out the important result that the common tangent to both indifference-curves at the point $\zeta\eta$ is the vector from the origin.

By a parity of reasoning it may be shown that, if the system had been started at the north-west extremity of (the available portion of the contract-curve, it would have been worked down by competition *between the* Xs to the same point; determined by the intersection with the contract-curve of $\xi F'_x + \eta F'_y = 0$; for the *same* point is determined by the intersection of *either* curve with the contract-curve. For the three curves evidently intersect in the same point.

Taking account of the two processes which have been described, the competing Ys being worked down for a certain distance towards the north-west, and similarly the competing Xs towards the south-east: we see that in general for any number short of the *practically infinite* (if such a term be allowed) there is a finite length of contract-curve, from $\xi_m y_m$ to $x_m \eta_m$, at any point of which if the system is placed, it cannot by contract or recontract, be displaced; that there are *an indefinite number of final settlements*, a quantity continually diminishing as we approach a perfect market. We are brought back again to case (β), on which some further remarks have been conveniently postponed to this place. (For additional illustrations see Appendix V [not provided here].)

The two conditions, $\xi\Phi'_x + \eta\Phi'_y = 0$ and $\xi F'_x + \eta F'_y = 0$, just obtained correspond to Professor Jevons's two equations of exchange. His formulæ are to be regarded as representing the transactions of two *individuals in, or subject to, the law* of, a market. Our assumed *unity of nature* in the midst of plurality of persons naturally brings out the same result. The represented two curves may be called *demand-curves*, as each expresses the amount of dealing which will afford to one of the dealers the maximum of advantage *at a certain rate of exchange a value of* y/x. This might be elegantly expressed in polar co-ordinates, $\tan\theta$ will then be the rate of exchange, and, if P be the utility of X, $(dP/d\rho) = 0$ is the demand-curve. By a well-known property of analysis $(dP/d\rho) = 0$ represents not only maximum points, but *minimum points*; the lowest depths of valley, as well as the highest elevations, which one moving continually in a fixed right line from the origin over the *utility-surface* would reach. This minimum portion of the demand-curve corresponds to Mr Marshall's Class II. We see that the dealer at any given rate of exchange, far from resting and having his end at a point on this part of the curve, will tend to move away from it. It has not the properties of a genuine demand-curve.

The dealing of an individual in an open market, in which there prevails what may be called the law of price, the relation between the individual's requirements and that quantity *collectively-demanded-at-a-price*, usually designated by the term *Demand*, between little d and big D in M. Walras's terminology, is elegantly exhibited by that author. Compare also Cournot on 'Concurrence'.

Here it is attempted to proceed without postulating the phenomenon of uniformity of price by the longer route of *contract-curve*. When we suppose plurality of natures as well as persons, we have to suppose a plurality of contract-curves (which may be appropriately conceived as grouped, according to the well-known logarithmic law, about an average). Then, by considerations analogous to those already employed, it may appear that the quantity of final settlements is diminished as the number of competitors is increased. To facilitate conception, let us suppose that the field consists of two Xs, not equally, but nearly equally, natured; and of two Ys similarly related. And (as in the fifth Appendix) let the indifference curves consist of families of concentric circles. Then, instead of a single contract-curve, we have a contract-region, or bundle of contract-curves; namely the four lines joining the centres of the circle-systems, the lines $C_1C'_1$, $C_1C'_2$,

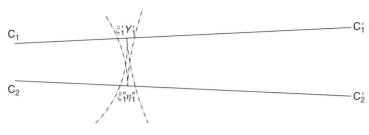

Figure 2

C_2C_1', C_2C_2'; wherein C_1C_2 are the centres of X_1 and X_2, supposed close together; and similarly C_1' and C_2' for the Ys.

What corresponds here to that *settlement of the whole field at a single point in the contract-curve*, which we had under consideration in reasoning about equal-natured Xs, may thus be indicated. Take a point $\xi_1'\eta_1'$ on one of the contract-lines, say C_1C_1'; and let X_1 and Y_1 be placed there. Let X_2Y_2 be placed at a neighbouring point, $\xi_1''\eta_1''$, on the line C_2C_2'; such that (1) $\xi_1''\eta_1''$ is outside the two indifference curves drawn for X_1 and Y_1 respectively through $\xi_1'\eta_1'$; (2) $\xi_1'\eta_1'$ is outside the two indifference curves drawn for X_2 and Y_2 respectively through $\xi_1''\eta_1''$ (Figure 2).

Then the settlement cannot be disturbed by an X and a Y simply changing partners, rushing into each other's arms, and leaving their deserted consorts to look out for new alliances. Re-contract can now proceed only by one Y moving off with the two Xs, as in the previous case; by which process the system may be worked down to a neighbourhood describable as $\xi_2 y_2$. In the limit, when the number of Xs and Ys are increased indefinitely, but not necessarily equally (suppose mX, and nY, where m and n are indefinitely large); if $x_r y_r$ represent the dealings of any X, namely X_r, and similarly ξ and η be employed for the dealings of the Ys, we should find for the $2m + 2n$ variables the following $2m + 2n$ equations:

1    $m + n$ equations indicating that each X and each Y *is on his individual demand-curve* …, for example

$$x_r \frac{\mathrm{d}F_r(x_r y_r)}{\mathrm{d}x_r} + y_r \frac{\mathrm{d}F_r(x_r y_r)}{\mathrm{d}y_r} = 0,$$

(the differentiation being of course partial).

2    $m + n - 1$ equations indicating *uniformity* of price $\dfrac{y_1}{x_1} = \dfrac{y_2}{x_2} = \cdots = \dfrac{\eta_1}{\xi_1} = \dfrac{\eta_2}{\xi_2} = \cdots$.

3   A last condition, which might perhaps be called *par excellence* the equation of Demand to Supply, namely *either* $Sx = \Sigma\xi$, *or* $Sy = \Sigma\eta$. Thus the dealings of each and all are completely determinate and determined.

If we transform to polar co-ordinates, we might write any individual demand-curve, as $\rho = f_r(\theta)$; and thence obtain two *collective demand-curves* $\rho = Sf(\theta)$ and $\rho = \Sigma\phi(\theta)$; substantially identical with those collective demand curves so scientifically developed by M. Walras, and so fruitfully applied by Mr Marshall.

Thus, proceeding by degrees from the case of two isolated bargainers to the limiting case of a perfect market, we see how *contract is more or less indeterminate according as the field is less or more affected with the first imperfection*, limitation of numbers.

II. Let there be equal numbers of equal-natured Xs and equal-natured Ys, subject to the condition that each Y can deal at the same time with only nXs, and similarly each X with only n'Ys. First let $n = n'$. Then, in the light of the conceptions lately won, it appears that contract is as indeterminate as if the field consisted of only nXs and nYs; that is to say, there areas many and the same *final settlements* as in that case, represented by the same portion of the contract-curve between (say) ξy and $x\eta$. Let n' increase. Contract becomes less indeterminate: ξ moving north-west, and the quantity of *final settlements* being thereby diminished. The subtracted final settlements are most favourable to the Ys. Let n' diminish. Contract becomes more indeterminate; ξ moving south-east, and the quantity of final settlements being thereby increased. The added final settlements are more favourable to the Ys than those previously existing.

The theorem admits of being extended to the general case of unequal numbers and natures.

III. Let there be an equal number N of equal-natured Xs and equal-natured Ys, and let each set be formed into equal *combinations*, there being nXs in each X combination, and n'Ys in each Y combination. First, let $n = n'$. Then contract is *as indeterminate* as if the field consisted of (N/n) Xs and (N/n) Ys; in the same sense as that explained in the last paragraph. Let n' diminish. Contract becomes *less indeterminate*, in the same sense as in the last paragraph. Let n' increase. Contract becomes more indeterminate; the added final settlements being more favourable to the Ys than those previously existing.

The theorem is typical of the general case in which numbers, natures, and combinations are unequal. Combination tends to introduce or increase indeterminateness; and the final settlements thereby added are more favourable to the combiners than the (determinate or indeterminate) final settlements previously existing. Combiners *stand to gain* in this sense.

The worth of this abstract reasoning ought to be tested by comparison with the unmathematical treatment of the same subject. As far as the writer is aware, a straightforward answer has never been offered to the abstract question, What is the effect of combinations on *contract* in an otherwise *perfect* state of competition, as here supposed? Writers either ignore the abstract question altogether, confining themselves to other aspects of Trade Unionism; its tendency to promote communication, mobility, etc.; in our terms, to render the competition more *normal*, and more perfect in respect of *extent* (diminishing our *first* imperfection, for such is the effect of increased mobility, alike of goods and men). Or, while they seem to admit that unionism would have the effect of raising the *rate of wages*, they yet deny that the *total remuneration* of the operatives, the *wage-fund* (in the intelligible sense of that term), can be increased. But if our reasonings be correct, the one thing from an abstract point of view visible amidst the jumble of catallactic molecules, the jostle of competitive crowds, is that those who form themselves into compact bodies by *combination* do not tend to lose, but *stand to gain* in the sense described, to gain in point of utility, which is a function not only of the (objective) remuneration, but also of the labour, and which, therefore, may increase, although the remuneration decrease; as Mr Fawcett well sees (in respect to the question of unproductive consumption – 'Manual', ch. iv.), though he gives so uncertain a sound about Trades Unionism. And if, as seems to be implied in much that has been written on this subject, it is attempted to enforce the argument against Trades Unionism by the consideration that it tends to diminish the *total national produce*, the obvious reply is that unionists, as 'economic men', are not concerned with the *total produce*. Because the total produce is diminished, it does not follow that the labourer's share is diminished (the loss may fall on the capitalist and the entrepreneur, whose compressibility has been well shown by Mr Sidgwick in the article already referred to); much less does it follow (as aforesaid) that there should be diminished that quantity which alone the rational unionist is concerned to increase – *the labourer's utility*. If this view be correct, it would seem as if, in the matter of *unionism*, as well as in that of the predeterminate *wage-fund*, the 'untutored mind' of the workman had gone more straight to the point than economic intelligence *misled by a bad method*, reasoning without mathematics upon mathematical subjects.

IV. Let there be an equal number N of equal natured Xs and Ys; subject to the condition that to every contract made by a Y at least n Xs must be parties, and similarly for an X n' Ys. First, let $n = n'$. Contract is as indeterminate as if the field consisted of (N/n) Xs and (N/n) Ys. Let n' increase. Contract becomes more indeterminate, and the Ys *stand to gain*. And conversely.

To appreciate the quantity of indeterminateness likely to result in fact from these imperfections (operating separately *and together*) would require a knowledge of concrete phenomena to which the writer can make no claim.

The *first* imperfection applies to *Monopolies*. It is perhaps chiefly important, as supplying a clue for the solution of the other cases.

The *second* imperfection may be operative in many cases of contract for personal service. Suppose a market, consisting of an equal number of masters and servants, offering respectively wages and service; subject to the condition that no man can serve two masters, no master employ more than one man; or suppose equilibrium already established between such parties to be disturbed by any sudden influx of wealth into the hands of the masters. Then there is no *determinate*, and very generally *unique*, arrangement towards which the system tends under the operation of, may we say, a law of Nature, and which would be predictable if we knew beforehand the real requirements of each, or of the average, dealer; but there are an indefinite number of arrangements à priori possible, towards one of which the system is urged *not* by the concurrence of innumerable (as it were) neuter atoms eliminating chance, but (abstraction being made of custom) by what has been called the Art of Bargaining – higgling dodges and designing obstinacy, and other incalculable and often disreputable accidents.

Now, if managerial work does not admit of being distributed over several establishments, of being sold in bits, it would seem that this species of indeterminateness affects the contract of an entrepreneur with foreman, of a co-operative association of workmen (or a *combination*) with a manager. This view must be modified in so far as managerial wages are determined by the *cost of production* (of a manager!), or more exactly by the equation between managerial wages and the remuneration in other occupations, where the remuneration is determined by a process of the nature of *perfect* competition; and by other practical considerations.

The *third* imperfection may have any degree of importance up to the point where a whole interest (labourers or entrepreneurs) is solidified into a single competitive unit. This varying result may be tolerably well illustrated by the case of a market in which an indefinite number of consumers are supplied by varying numbers of monopolists (a case properly belonging to our *first imperfection:* namely limited *number* of dealers). Starting with complete monopoly, we shall find the *price* continually diminish as the number of monopolists increases, until the point of complete fluidity is reached. This gradual 'extinction' of the influence of monopoly is well traced by Cournot in a discussion masterly, but limited by a particular condition, which may be called *uniformity of price, not (it is submitted) abstractedly necessary in cases of imperfect competition.* Going beyond Cournot, not without trembling, the present enquiry finds that, where the field of competition is sensibly imperfect, an indefinite number of *final settlements* are possible; that in such a case *different* final settlements would be reached if the system should run down from different *initial positions* or contracts. The sort of difference which exists between Dutch and English auction, theoretically unimportant in *perfect competition*, does correspond to different results, *different final settlements* in imperfect competition. And in general, and in the absence of imposed conditions, the said final settlements are *not on the demand-curve, but on the contract-curve.* That is to say, there *does not necessarily exist* in the case of imperfect as there does in the case of perfect competition a certain property (which some even mathematical writers may appear to take for granted), namely that – in the case all along supposed of Xs and Ys dealing respectively in x and y – if any X X give x in exchange for y_r, he gets no less and no more y than he is willing to take at the *rate of exchange y_r/x_r.*

If, however, this condition, though *not spontaneously generated by imperfect as by perfect competition*, should be introduced *ab extra*, imposed by custom and convenience, as no doubt would be very generally the case, nevertheless the property of *indeterminateness, plurality of final settlements*, will abide. Only the final settlements *will* now be by way of demand-curve, not contract-curve. *If*, for instance, powerful trades unions did not seek to fix the *quid pro quo*, the *amounts* of labour exchanged for wealth (which they would be quite competent to seek), but only the *rate of exchange*, it being left to each capitalist to purchase as much labour as he might demand at that rate, there would still be that sort of *indeterminateness favourable to unionists* above described. ...

The *fourth* imperfection would seem likely to operate in the case of *co-operative associations* up to the time when the competitive field shall contain a practically infinite number of such bodies; that is, perhaps for a long time. To fix the ideas, suppose associations of capitalist-workmen, consisting each of 100 members, 50 contributing chiefly capital, and 50 chiefly labour. Let the *field of competition* consist of 1000 individuals. The point here indicated is that, notwithstanding the numerical size of the field, contract will not be more determinate (owing to the fact that all the members of the association are *in contract with each other* – not, as now usual, each for himself contracting with employer) than if the field consisted of 10 individuals. And a similar result would hold if, with more generality, we suppose members contributing labour and capital in varying amounts, and remunerated for their sacrifices according to a *principle of distribution*; in the most, or, at any rate, a sufficiently general case, a *function* of the sacrifices, the form of the function being a contract-variable, or what comes to much the same thing, there being assumed a function of given form containing any number of constants, which are *articles of contract*, subject, of course, to the condition that the sum of the portions assigned is equal to the distribuend. And, similarly, if we introduce different kinds of labour and other concrete complications.

The Determinateness will depend not so much upon the number of individuals as upon the number of associations in the field. As co-operative association becomes more prevalent, no doubt, *cæteris paribus*, the indeterminateness here indicated would decrease. Nevertheless, in consequence of the great variety of cooperative experiments, the sundry kinds of contract and divers species of *articles*, the field of competition being thus broken up, it is submitted that the rise of co-operative association is likely to be accompanied with the prevalence of indeterminateness, whatever opinion we may form about the possible regularity in a distant future.

Altogether, if of two great coming institutions, trades unionism is affected with the *third* imperfection, and co-operative association with the *fourth*, and both with the *second*, it does not seem very rash to infer, if not for the present, at least in the proximate future, a considerable extent of indeterminateness.

Of this inference what would be the consequence. To impair, it may be conjectured, the reverence paid to *competition*; in whose results – as if worked out by a play of physical forces, impersonal, impartial – economists have complacently acquiesced. Of justice and humanity there was no pretence; but there seemed to command respect the majestic neutrality of Nature. But if it should appear that the field of competition is deficient in that *continuity of fluid*, that *multiety of atoms* which constitute the foundations of the uniformities of Physics; if competition is found wanting, not only the regularity of law, but even the impartiality of chance – the throw of a die loaded with villainy – economics would be indeed a 'dismal science', and the reverence for competition would be no more.

There would arise a general demand for a *principle of arbitration*.

And this aspiration of the commercial world would be but one breath in the universal sigh for articles of peace. For almost every species of social and political contract is affected with an indeterminateness like that which has been described; an evil which is likely to be much more felt when, with the growth of intelligence and liberty, the principle of *contract* shall have replaced both the appeal to force and the acquiescence in custom. Throughout the whole region of in a wide sense *contract*, in the general absence of a mechanism like perfect competition, the same essential indeterminateness prevails; in international, in domestic politics; between nations, classes, sexes.

The whole creation groans and yearns, desiderating a principle of arbitration, an end of strifes.

Corollary

Where, then, would a world weary of strife seek a principle of arbitration? In *justice*, replies the moralist; and a long line of philosophers, from Plato to Herbert Spencer, are ready to expound the principle. But their expositions, however elevating in moral tone, and of great hortative value for those who already know their duty, are not here of much avail, where the thing sought is a definite, even quantitative, criterion of what is to be done. *Equity* and 'fairness of division' are charming in the pages of Herbert Spencer, and delighted Dugald Stewart with the appearance of mathematical certainty; but how would they be applicable to the distribution of a joint product between co-operators? Nor is the *equity* so often invoked by a high authority on co-operation much more available; for *why* is the particular principle of distribution recommended by Mr Holyoake (operatives to take not product, paying therefrom a salary to manager, roughly speaking, and to say nothing of capital) more equitable than an indefinite number of other prin-ciples of distribution (e.g. operatives to take *any fraction* which might have been agreed upon, manager the remainder; *either* party, or *neither*, paying wages to the other).

Justice requires to be informed by some more definite principle, as Mill and Mr Sidgwick reason well. The star of justice affords no certain guidance – for those who have loosed from the moorings of custom – unless it reflect the rays of a superior luminary – utilitarianism.

But, even admitting a disposition in the purer wills and clearer intellects to accept the just as *finis litium*, and the useful as the definition of the just; admitting that there exists in the higher parts of human nature a tendency towards and feeling after utilitarian institutions; could we seri-ously suppose that these moral considerations were relevant to war and trade; could eradicate the 'controlless core' of human selfishness, or exercise an appreciable force in comparison with the impulse of self-interest. It would have to be first shown that the interest of all is the interest of each, an illusion to which the ambiguous language of Mill, and perhaps Bentham, may have lent some countenance, but which is for ever dispelled by the masterly analysis of Mr Sidgwick. Mr Sidgwick acknowledges two supreme principles – Egoism and Utilitarianism; of independent authority, conflicting dictates; irreconcilable, unless indeed by religion.

It is far from the spirit of the philosophy of pleasure to depreciate the importance of religion; but in the present enquiry, and dealing with the lower elements of human nature, we should have to seek a more obvious transition, a more earthy passage, from the principle of self-interest to the principle, or at least the practice, of utilitarianism.

Now, it is a circumstance of momentous interest – visible to common sense when pointed out by mathematics – that *one* of the in general indefinitely numerous *settlements* between contractors is the utilitarian arrangement of the articles of contract, the contract tending to the greatest pos-sible total utility of the contractors. In this direction, it may be conjectured, is to be sought the required principle. For the required basis of arbitration between economical contractors is evidently *some* settlement; and the utilitarian settlement may be selected, in the absence of any other principle of selection, in virtue of its moral peculiarities: its satisfying the sympathy (such as it is) of each with all, the sense of justice and utilitarian equity.

These considerations might be put clearest in a particular, though still very abstract, case. Let us suppose that in consequence of combinations competition fails to determine the contract between entrepreneur and operatives. The case becomes that described under (a) deadlock between two contracting parties. One of the *parties* is indeed here *collective*; but it is allowable for the sake of illustration to make abstraction of this circumstance, to abstract also the correlated bargains with capitalists, landowners, etc., and to suppose a single entrepreneur in dealing with a single operative. And, first, let it be attempted to arbitrate upon some principle of *doctrinaire justice* – some metaphysical dogma, for instance, of equality: that the entrepreneur shall have an 'equal' share of the produce. Now, there is no presumption that this 'fair division' is utilitarianian; in view of the different character of the entrepreneur's *sacrifice*, in view also (if one may be allowed to say so) of a possible difference in the entrepreneur's *capacity*: suppose, for instance, that a more highly nervous organisation required on the average a higher *minimum* of means to get up to the zero of utility. As there is no presumption that the proposed arrangement is utilitarian, so there is no presumption that it *is* on the contract-curve. Therefore, the self-interests of the two parties will *concur* to bulge away from the assumed position; and, bursting the cobwebs of doctrinaire justice, to descend with irresistible force to some point upon the contract-curve. Suppose that by repeated experiences of this sort the contract-curve has been roughly ascertained – a considerable number of *final settlements* statistically tabulated. Now these positions lie in a *reverse order of desirability* for each party; and it may seem to each that as he cannot have his own way, in the absence of any definite principle of selection, he has about as good a chance of one of the arrangements as another. But, rather than resort to some process which may virtually amount to tossing up, both parties may agree to commute their chance of any of the arrangements for the certainty of one of them, which has certain distinguishing features and peculiar attractions as above described – the utilitarian arrangement.

Or perhaps, considering the whole line of possible arrangements, they might agree to 'split the difference', and meet each other in the neighbourhood of the central point – the 'quantitative mean', as it might be called. Well, first, this quantitative mean would likely to be nearer than the extremes to the utilitarian point; and, further, this very notion of *mean* appears to be the outcome of a rudimentary 'implicit' justice, apt in a dialectical atmosphere to bloom into the 'qualitative mean' of utilitarian equity.

Or less specifically may we say that in the neighbourhood of the contract-curve *the forces of self-interest being neutralised*, the tender power of sympathy and right would become appreciable; as the gentler forces of the magnetic field are made manifest when terrestrial magnetism, by being opposed to itself, is eliminated.

Upon the whole – omitting what it is obvious to understand about the spirit in which very abstract reasonings are to be regarded: a star affording a general direction, not a finger-post to specify a by-path – there may appear, at however great a distance, a general indication that *competition requires to be supplemented by arbitration, and the basis of arbitration between self-interested contractors is the greatest possible sum-total utility.*

Thus, the *economical* leads up to the *utilitarian calculus*; the faint outlines of which, sketched in a previously published paper, may be accepted as the second subdivision of our Second Part.

Notes

1 Corrected version of equation; that published in the book is in error.
2 Corrected version of equation; that published in the book is in error.

ALFRED MARSHALL (1842–1924)

Alfred Marshall, Photographer: Walter Stoneman, by courtesy of the National Portrait Gallery, London.

Alfred Marshall was educated in mathematics at St John's College Cambridge, and was elected to a mathematics fellowship thereupon receiving his degree. He resigned this position in 1877 and took a position as professor of political economy at Bristol. He moved on to Balliol College, Oxford and, in 1885 returned to Cambridge, where he remained as professor of political economy until his retirement in 1908.

Unlike Jevons, who painted his economics as representing a strong break from the classical analysis, Marshall emphasized the strong degree of continuity between the classicals and his own theory. Yet, through his *Principles of Economics* (1890), as well as through the force of his personality in developing economics education at Cambridge, Marshall helped shape many of the principal elements of what became the microeconomic core of neoclassical economics: its static partial equilibrium analysis; the demand and supply model; the concern with the household and the firm as the basis of demand and supply, respectively; and a vast array of tools of partial-equilibrium analysis. The tools included: the principle of substitution, elasticity, long run and short run, internal and external economies of scale, prime and supplementary costs, consumers' surplus, quasi-rents, and the representative firm. For Marshall, however, these were strictly tools of analysis, not a body of concrete truth, not a model of some transcendent conceptual economic system, as it later became for neoclassicism, but an engine for the discovery of concrete truth also requiring close empirical and institutional analysis. For Marshall, too, economics was a science of tendencies, not a logic machine generating unique determinate optimal equilibrium results.

Marshall was one of those who used utility analysis, but not as a theory of value; for him it was part of the theory with which one could explain demand curves, another part being the principle of substitution. Indeed, Marshall's scissors analysis – which combined demand and supply, that is, utility and cost of production, as if two blades of a pair of scissors – not only transcended the conflict between Classical and Austrian theories of value but, equally if not more important, effectively removed the theory of value from center stage and replaced it with the theory of price; though the term "value" continued to be used, for most people it was a synonym for "price." Prices no longer were thought to gravitate toward some ultimate and absolute basis of price; prices were purely existential, a matter of a dance, as it were, between demand and supply, or, rather, between and among the factors and forces operating through demand and supply (only some of which, however, were thought to be within the purview of economists).

Marshall's approach to methodological issues was largely low key, or middlebrow. He emphasized deliberateness over selfishness and, sensitive to criticisms of economics as extolling selfishness, proposed to study man as he is rather than an abstract "economic" man; proposed a catholic definition of economics as the study of mankind in the ordinary business of life, earning a living; affirmed the limited use of mathematics in economic theory (e.g. in spite of his strong mathematical background, Marshall largely relegated mathematical analysis to footnotes and appendices in the *Principles*); combined habit with deliberateness in explaining economic behavior; identified economic laws as statements of tendency under certain, stipulated conditions, not absolute natural laws; emphasized objectivity through measurement, though he himself engaged in little quantitative study; combined quantitative empirical study with both pure theory and the study of institutions and behavior; was dubious about the practical and theoretical relevance of such grandiose notions as maximum satisfaction, the invisible hand, and *laissez faire*; and so on.

The core of Marshall's theory is the determination of price. Price, he argued, is a function of demand and supply, but could be analyzed differently on the basis of different conceptual time periods – especially the market period, short run and long run – understood as the different lengths of time it took for certain variables to work themselves out. In the short run, for example, price was heavily influenced by demand; in the long run, by cost of production. In all such periods, however, price was also influenced by whether the market was competitive or monopolistic.

Marshall's distribution theory was, like that of most other economists, eclectic. It included (1) a general theory of factor pricing, (2) different specific theories of wages, rent, interest and profit, and (3) attention to the different conditions of supply of the several factors of production – conditions which reflected class, custom, legal status and power structure. He thought that labor markets, especially on their supply side, were not like other markets; such markets had certain "peculiarities" which worked to labor's cumulatively disadvantageous position. While he urged caution in seeking major institutional reforms to improve the position of labor, he nonetheless argued that failure to attend to labor's problems was worse than making mistakes in doing so.

The excerpts from Marshall's *Principles* reprinted here are taken from his eighth edition, published in 1920. We are given a glimpse of his view of the nature and goals of economic analysis, the theory of increasing and diminishing returns in production, his elegant formulation of the apparatus of demand and supply, including his famous "scissors" analogy, and his introduction of period analysis into economic theory, where the reader might take note of the degree of correspondence between Marshall's long-period equilibrium and the concept of market equilibrium in the classical analysis.

References and further reading

Aldrich, John (1996) "The Course of Marshall's Theorizing about Demand," *History of Political Economy* 28 (Summer): 171–217.

Blaug, Mark, ed. (1992) *Alfred Marshall (1842–1924) and Francis Edgeworth (1845–1926)*, Aldershot: Edward Elgar Publishing.

Coase, R.H. (1975) "Marshall on Method," *Journal of Law and Economics* 18 (April): 25–31.

Friedman, Milton (1949) "The Marshallian Demand Curve," *Journal of Political Economy* 57 (December): 463–95.

Gordon, H. Scott (1973) "Alfred Marshall and the Development of Economics as a Science," in R.N. Glere and R.S. Westfall (eds), *Foundations of Scientific Method in the Nineteenth Century*, Bloomington, IN: Indiana University Press.

Groenewegen, Peter (1995) *A Soaring Eagle: Alfred Marshall, 1842–1924*, Aldershot: Edward Elgar Publishing.

Keynes, J.M. (1933) "Alfred Marshall, 1842–1924," in J.M. Keynes, *Essays in Biography*, London: Macmillan, 125–217.

Maloney, John (1985) *Marshall, Orthodoxy and the Professionalisation of Economics*, Cambridge: Cambridge University Press.

Marshall, Alfred (1879) *The Pure Theory of Foreign Trade. The Pure Theory of Domestic Values*, London: London School of Economics, 1930.

——(1919) *Industry and Trade*, London: Macmillan.

——(1923) *Money, Credit and Commerce*, London: Macmillan.

——(1961) *Principles of Economics*, 9th (Variorum) edn, edited by C.W. Guillebaud, 2 vols, London: Macmillan.

Marshall, Alfred and Marshall, Mary Paley (1979) *The Economics of Industry*, London: Macmillan.

Pigou, A.C. (1925) *Memorials of Alfred Marshall*, London: Macmillan.

Robbins, Lionel (1928) "The Representative Firm," *Economic Journal* 38: 387–404.

Robertson, D.H. (1952) *Utility and All That*, London: George Allen & Unwin.

Shove, Gerald (1942) "The Place of Marshall's Principles in the Development of Economic Theory," *Economic Journal* 52 (December): 294–329.

Sraffa, Piero (1926) "The Laws of Returns Under Competitive Conditions," *Economic Journal* 36 (December): 535–50.

Whitaker, J.K. (1975) *The Early Economic Writings of Alfred Marshall, 1867–1890*, 2 vols, London: Macmillan.

——(1987) "Marshall, Alfred," in John Eatwell, Murray Milgate, and Peter Newman (eds), *The New Palgrave: A Dictionary of Economics*, Vol. 3, London: Macmillan, 350–63.

Wood, John C. (1982) *Alfred Marshall: Critical Assessments*, London: Croom Helm.

——(1993) *Alfred Marshall: Critical Assessments*, second series, London: Routledge.

Principles of Economics (1890)*

Book I: Preliminary survey

Chapter I: Introduction

1. Political economy or economics is a study of mankind in the ordinary business of life; it examines that part of individual and social action which is most closely connected with the attainment and with the use of the material requisites of well-being.

Thus it is on the one side a study of wealth; and on the other, and more important side, a part of the study of man. For man's character has been moulded by his every-day work, and the material resources which he thereby procures, more than by any other influence unless it be that of his religious ideals; and the two great forming agencies of the world's history have been the religious and the economic. Here and there the ardour of the military or the artistic spirit has been for a while predominant: but religious and economic influences have nowhere been displaced from the front rank even for a time; and they have nearly always been more important than all others put together. Religious motives are more intense than economic, but their direct action seldom extends over so large a part of life. For the business by which a person earns his livelihood generally fills his thoughts during by far the greater part of those hours in which his mind is at its best; during them his character is being formed by the way in which he uses his faculties in his work, by the thoughts and the feelings which it suggests, and by his relations to his associates in work, his employers or his employees.

And very often the influence exerted on a person's character by the amount of his income is hardly less, if it is less, than that exerted by the way in which it is earned. It may make little difference to the fullness of life of a family whether its yearly income is £1000 or £5000; but it makes a very great difference whether the income is £30 or £150: for with £150 the family has, with £30 it has not, the material conditions of a complete life. It is true that in religion, in the family affections and in friendship, even the poor may find scope for many of those faculties which are the source of the highest happiness. But the conditions which surround extreme poverty, especially in densely crowded places, tend to deaden the higher faculties. Those who have been called the Residuum of our large towns have little opportunity for friendship; they know nothing of the decencies and the quiet, and very little even of the unity of family life; and religion often fails to reach them. No doubt their physical, mental, and moral ill-health is partly due to other causes than poverty: but this is the chief cause.

And, in addition to the Residuum, there are vast numbers of people both in town and country who are brought up with insufficient food, clothing, and house-room; whose education is broken

---

* *Principles of Economics*, Eighth Edition, London: Macmillan, 1920.

off early in order that they may go to work for wages; who thenceforth are engaged during long hours in exhausting toil with imperfectly nourished bodies, and have therefore no chance of developing their higher mental faculties. Their life is not necessarily unhealthy or unhappy. Rejoicing in their affections towards God and man, and perhaps even possessing some natural refinement of feeling, they may lead lives that are far less incomplete than those of many, who have more material wealth. But, for all that, their poverty is a great and almost unmixed evil to them. Even when they are well, their weariness often amounts to pain, while their pleasures are few; and when sickness comes, the suffering caused by poverty increases tenfold. And, though a contented spirit may go far towards reconciling them to these evils, there are others to which it ought not to reconcile them. Overworked and undertaught, weary and careworn, without quiet and without leisure, they have no chance of making the best of their mental faculties.

Although then some of the evils which commonly go with poverty are not its necessary consequences; yet, broadly speaking, 'the destruction of the poor is their poverty', and the study of the causes of poverty is the study of the causes of the degradation of a large part of mankind.

...

Book IV: The agents of production: Land, labour, capital and organization

Chapter XIII: Conclusion. Correlation of the tendencies to increasing and to diminishing return

1. At the beginning of the Book we saw how the extra return of raw produce which nature affords to an increased application of capital and labour, other things being equal, tends in the long run to diminish. In the remainder of the Book and especially in the last four chapters we have looked at the other side of the shield, and seen how man's power of productive work increases with the volume of the work that he does. Considering first the causes that govern the supply of labour, we saw how every increase in the physical, mental and moral vigour of a people makes them more likely, other things being equal, to rear to adult age a large number of vigorous children. Turning next to the growth of wealth, we observed how every increase of wealth tends in many ways to make a greater increase more easy than before. And lastly we saw how every increase of wealth and every increase in the numbers and intelligence of the people increased the facilities for a highly developed industrial organization, which in its turn adds much to the collective efficiency of capital and labour.

Looking more closely at the economies arising from an increase in the scale of production of any kind of goods, we found that they fell into two classes – those dependent on the general development of the industry, and those dependent on the resources of the individual houses of business engaged in it and the efficiency of their management; that is, into *external* and *internal* economies.

We saw how these latter economies are liable to constant fluctuations so far as any particular house is concerned. An able man, assisted perhaps by some strokes of good fortune, gets a firm footing in the trade, he works hard and lives sparely, his own capital grows fast, and the credit that enables him to borrow more capital grows still faster; he collects around him subordinates of more than ordinary zeal and ability; as his business increases they rise with him, they trust him and he trusts them, each of them devotes himself with energy to just that work for which he is specially fitted, so that no high ability is wasted on easy work, and no difficult work is entrusted to unskilful hands. Corresponding to this steadily increasing economy of skill, the growth of his business brings with it similar economies of specialized machines and plants of all kinds; every improved process is quickly adopted and made the basis of further improvements; success brings credit and credit brings success; credit and success help to retain old customers and to bring new ones; the increase of his trade gives him great advantages in buying; his goods advertise one another, and thus diminish his difficulty in finding a vent for them. The increase in the scale of his business increases rapidly the advantages which he has over his competitors, and lowers the price at which he can afford to sell. This process may go on as long as his energy and enterprise, his inventive and organizing power retain their full strength and freshness, and so long as the risks which are inseparable from business do not cause him exceptional losses; and if it could endure for a hundred years, he and one or two others like him would divide between them the whole of that branch of industry in which he is engaged. The large scale of their production would put great economies within their reach; and provided they competed to their utmost with one another, the public would derive the chief benefit of these economies, and the price of the commodity would fall very low.

But here we may read a lesson from the young trees of the forest as they struggle upwards through the benumbing shade of their older rivals. Many succumb on the way, and a few only survive; those few become stronger with every year, they get a larger share of light and air with every increase of their height, and at last in their turn they tower above their neighbours, and seem as though they would grow on for ever, and for ever become stronger as they grow. But they do not. One tree will last longer in full vigour and attain a greater size than another; but sooner or later age tells on them all. Though the taller ones have a better access to light and air than their rivals, they gradually lose vitality; and one after another they give place to others, which, though of less material strength, have on their side the vigour of youth.

And as with the growth of trees, so was it with the growth of businesses as a general rule before the great recent development of vast joint-stock companies, which often stagnate, but do not readily die. Now that rule is far from universal, but it still holds in many industries and trades. Nature still presses on the private business by limiting the length of the life of its original founders, and by limiting even more narrowly that part of their lives in which their faculties retain full vigour. And so, after a while, the guidance of the business falls into the hands of people with less energy and less creative genius, if not with less active interest in its prosperity. If it is turned into a joint-stock company, it may retain the advantages of division of labour, of specialized skill and machinery: it may even increase them by a further increase of its capital; and under favourable conditions it may secure a permanent and prominent place in the work of production. But it is likely to have lost so much of its elasticity and progressive force, that the advantages are no longer exclusively on its side in its competition with younger and smaller rivals.

When therefore we are considering the broad results which the growth of wealth and population exert on the economies of production, the general character of our conclusions is not very much affected by the fact that many of these economies depend directly on the size of the individual establishments engaged in the production, and that in almost every trade there is a constant rise and fall of large businesses, at any one moment some firms being in the ascending phase and others in the descending. For in times of average prosperity decay in one direction is sure to be more than balanced by growth in another.

Meanwhile an increase in the aggregate scale of production of course increases those economies, which do not directly depend on the size of individual houses of business. The most important of these result from the growth of correlated branches of industry which mutually assist one another, perhaps being concentrated in the same localities, but anyhow availing themselves of the modern facilities for communication offered by steam transport, by the telegraph and by the printing press. The economies arising from such sources as this, which are accessible to any branch of production, do not depend exclusively upon its own growth: but yet they are sure to grow rapidly and steadily with that growth; and they are sure to dwindle in some, though not in all respects, if it decays.

2. These results will be of great importance when we come to discuss the causes which govern the supply price of a commodity. We shall have to analyse carefully the normal cost of producing a commodity, relatively to a given aggregate volume of production; and for this purpose we shall have to study *the expenses of a representative producer* for that aggregate volume. On the one hand we shall not want to select some new producer just struggling into business, who works under many disadvantages, and has to be content for a time with little or no profits, but who is satisfied with the fact that he is establishing a connection and taking the first steps towards building up a successful business; nor on the other hand shall we want to take a firm which by exceptionally long-sustained ability and good fortune has got together a vast business, and huge well-ordered workshops that give it a superiority over almost all its rivals. But our representative firm must be one which has had a fairly long life, and fair success, which is managed with normal ability, and which has normal access to the economies, external and internal, which belong to that aggregate volume of production; account being taken of the class of goods produced, the conditions of marketing them and the economic environment generally.

Thus a representative firm is in a sense an average firm. But there are many ways in which the term 'average' might be interpreted in connection with a business. And a Representative firm is that particular sort of average firm, at which we need to look in order to see how far the economies, *internal and external*, of production on a large scale have extended generally in the industry and country in question. We cannot see this by looking at one or two firms taken at random: but we can see it fairly well by selecting, after a broad survey, a firm, whether in private or joint-stock management (or better still, more than one), that represents, to the best of our judgment, this particular average.

The general argument of the present Book shows that an increase in the aggregate volume of production of anything will generally increase the size, and therefore the internal economies possessed by such a representative firm; that it will always increase the external economies to which the firm has access; and thus will enable it to manufacture at a less proportionate cost of labour and sacrifice than before.

In other words, we say broadly that while the part which nature plays in production shows a tendency to diminishing return, the part which man plays shows a tendency to increasing return. The *law of increasing return* may be worded thus: An increase of labour and capital leads generally to improved organization, which increases the efficiency of the work of labour and capital.

Therefore in those industries which are not engaged in raising raw produce an increase of labour and capital generally gives a return increased more than in proportion; and further this improved organization tends to diminish or even override any increased resistance which nature may offer to raising increased amounts of raw produce. If the actions of the laws of increasing and diminishing return are balanced we have the *law of constant return*, and an increased produce is obtained by labour and sacrifice increased just in proportion.

For the two tendencies towards increasing and diminishing return press constantly against one another. In the production of wheat and wool, for instance, the latter tendency has almost exclusive sway in an old country, which cannot import freely. In turning the wheat into flour, or the wool into blankets, an increase in the aggregate volume of production brings some new economies, but not many; for the trades of grinding wheat and making blankets are already on so great a scale that any new economies that they may attain are more likely to be the result of new inventions than of improved organization. In a country however in which the blanket trade is but slightly developed, these latter may be important; and then it may happen that an increase in the aggregate production of blankets diminishes the proportionate difficulty of manufacturing by just as much as it increases that of raising the raw material. In that case the actions of the laws of diminishing and of increasing return would just neutralize one another; and blankets would conform to the law of constant return. But in most of the more delicate branches of manufacturing, where the cost of raw material counts for little, and in most of the modern transport industries the law of increasing return acts almost unopposed.

Increasing Return is a relation between a quantity of effort and sacrifice on the one hand, and a quantity of product on the other. The quantities cannot be taken out exactly, because changing methods of production call for machinery, and for unskilled and skilled labour of new kinds and in new proportions. But, taking a broad view, we may perhaps say vaguely that the output of a certain amount of labour and capital in an industry has increased by perhaps a quarter or a third in the last twenty years. To measure outlay and output in terms of money is a tempting, but a dangerous resource: for a comparison of money outlay with money returns is apt to slide into an estimate of the rate of profit on capital.

3. We may now sum up provisionally the relations of industrial expansion to social well-being. A rapid growth of population has often been accompanied by unhealthy and enervating habits of life in overcrowded towns. And sometimes it has started badly, outrunning the material resources of the people, causing them with imperfect appliances to make excessive demands on the soil; and so to call forth the stern action of the law of diminishing return as regards raw produce, without having the power of minimizing its effects. Having thus begun with poverty, an increase in numbers may go on to its too frequent consequences in that weakness of character which unfits a people for developing a highly organized industry.

These are serious perils: but yet it remains true that the collective efficiency of a people with a given average of individual strength and energy may increase more than in proportion to their numbers. If they can for a time escape from the pressure of the law of diminishing return by importing food and other raw produce on easy terms; if their wealth is not consumed in great wars, and increases at least as fast as their numbers; and if they avoid habits of life that would enfeeble them; then every increase in their numbers is likely *for the time* to be accompanied by a more than proportionate increase in their power of obtaining material goods. For it enables them to secure the many various economies of specialized skill and specialized machinery, of localized industries and production on a large scale: it enables them to have increased facilities of communication of all kinds; while the very closeness of their neighbourhood diminishes the expense of time and effort involved in every sort of traffic between them, and gives them new opportunities of getting social enjoyments and the comforts and luxuries of culture in every form. No doubt deduction must be made for the growing difficulty of finding solitude and quiet and even fresh air: but there is in most cases some balance of good.

Taking account of the fact that an increasing density of population generally brings with it access to new social enjoyments we may give a rather broader scope to this statement and say: An increase of population accompanied by an equal increase in the material sources of enjoyment and aids to production is likely to lead to a more than proportionate increase in the aggregate income of enjoyment of all kinds; provided firstly, an adequate supply of raw produce can be obtained without great difficulty, and secondly there is no such overcrowding as causes physical and moral vigour to be impaired by the want of fresh air and light and of healthy and joyous recreation for the young.

The accumulated wealth of civilized countries is at present growing faster than the population: and though it may be true that the wealth per head would increase somewhat faster if the population did not increase quite so fast; yet as a matter of fact an increase of population is likely to continue to be accompanied by a more than proportionate increase of the material aids to production: and in England *at the present time*, with easy access to abundant foreign supplies of raw material, an increase of population is accompanied by a more than proportionate increase of the means of satisfying human wants other than the need for light, fresh air, etc. Much of this increase is however attributable not to the increase of industrial efficiency but to the increase of wealth by which it is accompanied: and therefore it does not necessarily benefit those who have no share in that wealth. And further, England's foreign supplies of raw produce may at any time be checked by changes in the trade regulations of other countries, and may be almost cut off by a great war, while the naval and military expenditure which would be necessary to make the country fairly secure against this last risk, would appreciably diminish the benefits that she derives from the action of the law of increasing return.

Book V

Chapter III: Equilibrium of normal demand and supply

1. We have next to inquire what causes govern supply prices, that is prices which dealers are willing to accept for different amounts. In the last chapter we looked at the affairs of only a single day; and supposed the stocks offered for sale to be already in existence. But of course these stocks are dependent on the amount of wheat sown in the preceding year; and that, in its turn, was largely influenced by the farmers' guesses as to the price which they would get for it in this year. This is the point at which we have to work in the present chapter.

Even in the corn-exchange of a country town on a market-day the equilibrium price is affected by calculations of the future relations of production and consumption; while in the leading corn-markets of America and Europe dealings for future delivery already predominate and are rapidly weaving into one web all the leading threads of trade in corn throughout the whole world. Some of these dealings in 'futures' are but incidents in speculative manœuvres; but in the main they are governed by calculations of the world's consumption on the one hand, and of the existing stocks and coming harvests in the Northern and Southern hemispheres on the other. Dealers take account of the areas sown with each kind of grain, of the forwardness and weight of the crops, of the supply of things which can be used as substitutes for grain, and of the things for which grain can be used as a substitute. Thus, when buying or selling barley, they take account of the supplies of such things as sugar, which can be used as substitutes for it in brewing, and again of all the various feeding stuffs, a scarcity of which might raise the value of barley for consumption on the farm. If it is thought that the growers of any kind of grain in any part of the world have been losing money, and are likely to sow a less area for a future harvest; it is argued that prices are likely to rise as soon as that harvest comes into sight, and its shortness is manifest to all. Anticipations of that rise exercise an influence on present sales for future delivery, and that in its turn influences cash prices; so that these prices are indirectly affected by estimates of the expenses of producing further supplies.

But in this and the following chapters we are specially concerned with movements of prices ranging over still longer periods than those for which the most far-sighted dealers in futures generally make their reckoning: we have to consider the volume of production adjusting itself to the conditions of the market, and the normal price being thus determined at the position of stable equilibrium of normal demand and normal supply.

2. In this discussion we shall have to make frequent use of the terms *cost* and *expenses* of production; and some provisional account of them must be given before proceeding further.

We may revert to the analogy between the supply price and the demand price of a commodity. Assuming for the moment that the efficiency of production depends solely upon the exertions of the workers, we saw that 'the price required to call forth the exertion necessary for producing any given amount of a commodity may be called the supply price for that amount, with reference of course to a given unit of time'. But now we have to take account of the fact that the production of a commodity generally requires many different kinds of labour and the use of capital in many forms. The exertions of all the different kinds of labour that are directly or indirectly involved in making it; together with the abstinences or rather the waitings required for saving the capital used in making it: all these efforts and sacrifices together will be called the *real cost of production* of the commodity. The sums of money that have to be paid for these efforts and sacrifices will be called either its *money cost of production*, or, for shortness, its *expenses of production*; they are the prices which have to be paid in order to call forth an adequate supply *of* the efforts and waitings that are required for making it; or, in other words, they are its supply price.

The analysis of the expenses of production of a commodity might be carried backward to any length; but it is seldom worth while to go back very far. It is for instance often sufficient to take the supply price of the different kinds of raw materials used in any manufacture as ultimate facts, without analysing these supply prices into the several elements of which they are composed; otherwise indeed the analysis would never end. We may then arrange the things that are required for making a commodity into whatever groups are convenient, and call them its *factors of production*. Its expenses of production when any given amount of it is produced are thus the supply prices of the corresponding quantities of its factors of production. And the sum of these is the supply price of that amount of the commodity.

3. The typical modern market is often regarded as that in which manufacturers sell goods to wholesale dealers at prices into which but few trading expenses enter. But taking a broader view, we may consider that the supply price of a commodity is the price at which it will be delivered for sale to that group of persons whose demand for it we are considering; or, in other words, in the market which we have in view. On the character of that market will depend how many trading expenses have to be reckoned to make up the supply price. For instance, the supply price of wood in the neighbourhood of Canadian forests often consists almost exclusively of the price of the labour of lumber men: but the supply price of the same wood in the wholesale London market consists in a large measure of freights: while its supply price to a small retail buyer in an English country town is more than half made up of the charges of the railways and middlemen who have brought what he wants to his doors, and keep a stock of it ready for him. Again, the supply price of a certain kind of labour may for some purposes be divided up into the expenses of rearing, of general education and of special trade education. The possible combinations are numberless; and though each may have incidents of its own which will require separate treatment in the complete solution of any problem connected with it, yet all such incidents may be ignored, so far as the general reasonings of this Book are concerned.

In calculating the expenses of production of a commodity we must take account of the fact that changes in the amounts produced are likely, even when there is no new invention, to be accompanied by changes in the relative quantities of its several factors of production. For instance, when the scale of production increases, horse or steam power is likely to be substituted for manual labour; materials are likely to be brought from a greater distance and in greater quantities, thus increasing those expenses of production which correspond to the work of carriers, middlemen and traders of all kinds.

As far as the knowledge and business enterprise of the producers reach, they in each case choose those factors of production which are best for their purpose; the sum of the supply prices of those factors which are used is, as a rule, less than the sum of the supply prices of any other set of factors which could be substituted for them; and whenever it appears to the producers that this is not the case, they will, as a rule, set to work to substitute the less expensive method. And further on we shall see how in a somewhat similar way society substitutes one undertaker for another who is less efficient in proportion to his charges. We may call this, for convenience of reference, *The principle of substitution*.

The applications of this principle extend over almost every field of economic inquiry.

4. The position then is this: we are investigating the equilibrium of normal demand and normal supply in their most general form; we are neglecting those features which are special to

particular parts of economic science, and are confining our attention to those broad relations which are common to nearly the whole of it. Thus we assume that the forces of demand and supply have free play; that there is no close combination among dealers on either side, but each acts for himself, and there is much free competition; that is, buyers generally compete freely with buyers, and sellers compete freely with sellers. But though everyone acts for himself, his knowledge of what others are doing is supposed to be generally sufficient to prevent him from taking a lower or paying a higher price than others are doing. This is assumed provisionally to be true both of finished goods and of their factors of production, of the hire of labour and of the borrowing of capital. We have already inquired to some extent, and we shall have to inquire further, how far these assumptions are in accordance with the actual facts of life. But meanwhile this is the supposition on which we proceed; we assume that there is only one price in the market at one and the same time; it being understood that separate allowance is made, when necessary, for differences in the expense of delivering goods to dealers in different parts of the market; including allowance for the special expenses of retailing, if it is a retail market.

In such a market there is a demand price for each amount of the commodity, that is, a price at which each particular amount of the commodity can find purchasers in a day or week or year. The circumstances which govern this price for any given amount of the commodity vary in character from one problem to another; but in every case the more of a thing is offered for sale in a market the lower is the price at which it will find purchasers; or in other words, the demand price for each bushel or yard diminishes with every increase in the amount offered.

The unit of time may be chosen according to the circumstances of each particular problem: it may be a day, a month, a year, or even a generation: but in every case it must be short relatively to the period of the market under discussion. It is to be assumed that the general circumstances of the market remain unchanged throughout this period; that there is, for instance, no change in fashion or taste, no new substitute which might affect the demand, no new invention to disturb the supply.

The conditions of normal supply are less definite; and a full study of them must be reserved for later chapters. They will be found to vary in detail with the length of the period of time to which the investigation refers; chiefly because both the material capital of machinery and other business plant, and the immaterial capital of business skill and ability and organization, are of slow growth and slow decay.

Let us call to mind the 'representative firm', whose economies of production, internal and external, are dependent on the aggregate volume of production of the commodity that it makes; and, postponing all further study of the nature of this dependence, let us assume that the normal supply price of any amount of that commodity may be taken to be its normal expenses of production (including *gross* earnings of managements) by that firm. That is, let us assume that this is the price the expectation of which will just suffice to maintain the existing aggregate amount of production; some firms meanwhile rising and increasing their output, and others falling and diminishing theirs; but the aggregate production remaining unchanged. A price higher than this would increase the growth of the rising firms, and slacken, though it might not arrest, the decay of the falling firms; with the net result of an increase in the aggregate production. On the other hand, a price lower than this would hasten the decay of the falling firms, and slacken the growth of the rising firms; and on the whole diminish production: and a rise or fall of price would affect in like manner though perhaps not in an equal degree those great joint-stock companies which often stagnate, but seldom die.

5. To give definiteness to our ideas let us take an illustration from the woollen trade. Let us suppose that a person well acquainted with the woollen trade sets himself to inquire what would be the normal supply price of a certain number of millions of yards annually of a particular kind of cloth. He would have to reckon (i) the price of the wool, coal, and other materials which would

be used up in making it, (ii) wear-and-tear and depreciation of the buildings, machinery and other fixed capital, (iii) interest and insurance on all the capital, (iv) the wages of those who work in the factories, and (v) the gross earnings of management (including insurance against loss), of those who undertake the risks, who engineer and superintend the working. He would of course estimate the supply prices of all these different factors of production of the cloth with reference to the amounts of each of them that would be wanted, and on the supposition that the conditions of supply would be normal; and he would add them all together to find the supply price of the cloth. Let us suppose a list of supply prices (or a supply schedule) made on a similar plan to that of our list of demand prices: the supply price of each amount of the commodity in a year, or any other unit of time, being written against that amount. As the flow, or (annual) amount of the commodity increases, the supply price may either increase or diminish; or it may even alternately increase and diminish. For if nature is offering a sturdy resistance to man's efforts to wring from her a larger supply of raw material, while at that particular stage there is no great room for introducing important new economies into the manufacture, the supply price will rise; but if the volume of production were greater, it would perhaps be profitable to substitute largely machine work for hand work and steam power for muscular force; and the increase in the volume of production would have diminished the expenses of production of the commodity of our representative firm. But those cases in which the supply price falls as the amount increases involve special difficulties of their own; and they are postponed to Chapter XII of this Book.

6. When therefore the amount produced (in a unit of time) is such that the demand price is greater than the supply price, then sellers receive more than is sufficient to make it worth their while to bring goods to market to that amount; and there is at work an active force tending to increase the amount brought forward for sale. On the other hand, when the amount produced is such that the demand price is less than the supply price, sellers receive less than is sufficient to make it worth their while to bring goods to market on that scale; so that those who were just on the margin of doubt as to whether to go on producing are decided not to do so, and there is an active force at work tending to diminish the amount brought forward for sale. When the demand price is equal to the supply price, the amount produced has no tendency either to be increased or to be diminished; it is in equilibrium. When demand and supply are in equilibrium, the amount of the commodity which is being produced in a unit of time may be called the *equilibrium-amount*, and the price at which it is being sold may be called the *equilibrium-price*.

Such an equilibrium is *stable*; that is, the price, if displaced a little from it, will tend to return, as a pendulum oscillates about its lowest point; and it will be found to be a characteristic of stable equilibria that in them the demand price is greater than the supply price for amounts just less than the equilibrium amount, and vice versa. For when the demand price is greater than the supply price, the amount produced tends to increase. Therefore, if the demand price is greater than the supply price for amounts just less than an equilibrium amount; then, if the scale of production is temporarily diminished somewhat below that equilibrium amount, it will tend to return; thus the equilibrium is stable for displacements in that direction. If the demand price is greater than the supply price for amounts just less than the equilibrium amount, it is sure to be less than the supply price for amounts just greater and therefore, if the scale of production is somewhat increased beyond the equilibrium position, it will tend to return; and the equilibrium will be stable for displacements in that direction also.

When demand and supply are in stable equilibrium, if any accident should move the scale of production from its equilibrium position, there will be instantly brought into play forces tending to push it back to that position; just as, if a stone hanging by a string is displaced from its equilibrium position, the force of gravity will at once tend to bring it back to its equilibrium position. The movements of the scale of production about its position of equilibrium will be of a somewhat similar kind.[1]

But in real life such oscillations are seldom as rhythmical as those of a stone hanging freely from a string; the comparison would be more exact if the string were supposed to hang in the troubled waters of a mill-race, whose stream was at one time allowed to flow freely, and at another partially cut off. Nor are these complexities sufficient to illustrate all the disturbances with which the economist and the merchant alike are forced to concern themselves. If the person holding the string swings his hand with movements partly rhythmical and partly arbitrary, the illustration will not outrun the difficulties of some very real and practical problems of value. For indeed the demand and supply schedules do not in practice remain unchanged for a long time together, but are constantly being changed; and every change in them alters the equilibrium amount and the equilibrium price, and thus gives new positions to the centres about which the amount and the price tend to oscillate.

These considerations point to the great importance of the element of time in relation to demand and supply, to the study of which we now proceed. We shall gradually discover a great many different limitations of the doctrine that the price at which a thing can be produced represents its real cost of production, that is, the efforts and sacrifices which have been directly devoted to its production. For, in an age of rapid change such as this, the equilibrium of normal demand and supply does not thus correspond to any distinct relation of a certain aggregate of pleasures got from the consumption of the commodity and an aggregate of efforts and sacrifices involved in producing it: the correspondence would not be exact, even if normal earnings and interest were exact measures of the efforts and sacrifices for which they are the money payments. This is the real drift of that much quoted, and much misunderstood doctrine of Adam Smith and other economists that the normal, or 'natural', value of a commodity is that which economic forces tend to bring about *in the long run*. It is the average value which economic forces would bring about if the general conditions of life were stationary for a run of time long enough to enable them all to work out their full effect.

But we cannot foresee the future perfectly. The unexpected may happen; and the existing tendencies may be modified before they have had time to accomplish what appears now to be their full and complete work. The fact that the general conditions of life are not stationary is the source of many of the difficulties that are met with in applying economic doctrines to practical problems. Of course Normal does not mean Competitive. Market prices and Normal prices are alike brought about by a multitude of influences, of which some rest on a moral basis and some on a physical; of which some are competitive and some are not. It is to the persistence of the influences considered, and the time allowed for them to work out their effects that we refer when contrasting Market and Normal price, and again when contrasting the narrower and the broader use of the term Normal price.

7. The remainder of the present volume will be chiefly occupied with interpreting and limiting this doctrine that the value of a thing tends in the long run to correspond to its cost of production. In particular the notion of equilibrium, which has been treated rather slightly in this chapter, will be studied more carefully in Chapters V and XII of this Book: and some account of the controversy whether 'cost of production' or 'utility' governs value will be given in Appendix I. But it may be well to say a word or two here on this last point.

We might as reasonably dispute whether it is the upper or the under blade of a pair of scissors that cuts a piece of paper, as whether value is governed by utility or cost of production. It is true that when one blade is held still, and the cutting is effected by moving the other, we may say with careless brevity that the cutting is done by the second; but the statement is not strictly accurate, and is to be excused only so long as it claims to be merely a popular and not a strictly scientific account of what happens.

In the same way, when a thing already made has to be sold, the price which people will be willing to pay for it will be governed by their desire to have it, together with the amount they can afford to spend on it. Their desire to have it depends partly on the chance that, if they do not buy it, they will be able to get another thing like it at as low a price: this depends on the causes that govern the supply of it, and this again upon cost of production. But it may so happen that the stock to be sold is practically fixed. This, for instance, is the case with a fish market, in which the value of fish for the day is governed almost exclusively by the stock on the slabs in relation to the demand: and if a person chooses to take the stock for granted, and say that the price is governed by demand, his brevity may perhaps be excused so long as he does not claim strict accuracy. So again it may be pardonable, but it is not strictly accurate to say that the varying prices which the same rare book fetches, when sold and resold at Christie's auction room, are governed exclusively by demand.

Taking a case at the opposite extreme, we find some commodities which conform pretty closely to the law of constant return; that is to say, their average cost of production will be very nearly the same whether they are produced in small quantities or in large. In such a case the normal level about which the market price fluctuates will be this definite and fixed (money) cost of production. If the demand happens to be great, the market price will rise for a time above the level; but as a result production will increase and the market price will fall: and conversely, if the demand falls for a time below its ordinary level.

In such a case, if a person chooses to neglect market fluctuations, and to take it for granted that there will anyhow be enough demand for the commodity to insure that some of it, more or less, will find purchasers at a price equal to this cost of production, then he may be excused for ignoring the influence of demand, and speaking of (normal) price as governed by cost of production – provided only he does not claim scientific accuracy for the wording of his doctrine, and explains the influence of demand in its right place.

Thus we may conclude that, *as a general rule*, the shorter the period which we are considering, the greater must be the share of our attention which is given to the influence of demand on value; and the longer the period, the more important will be the influence of cost of production on value. For the influence of changes in cost of production takes as a rule a longer time to work itself out than does the influences of changes in demand. The actual value at any time, the market value as it is often called, is often more influenced by passing events and by causes whose action is fitful and short-lived, than by those which work persistently. But in long periods these fitful and irregular causes in large measure efface one another's influence; so that in the long run persistent causes dominate value completely. Even the most persistent causes are however liable to change. For the whole structure of production is modified, and the relative costs of production of different things are permanently altered, from one generation to another.

When considering costs from the point of view of the capitalist employer, we of course measure them in money; because his direct concern with the efforts needed for the work of his employees lies in the money payments he must make. His concern with the real costs of their effort and of the training required for it is only indirect, though a monetary assessment of his own labour is necessary for some problems, as will be seen later on. But when considering costs from the social point of view, when inquiring whether the cost of attaining a given result is increasing or diminishing with changing economic conditions, then we are concerned with the real costs of efforts of various qualities, and with the real cost of waiting. If the purchasing power of money, in terms of effort has remained about constant, and if the rate of remuneration for waiting has remained about constant, then the money measure of costs corresponds to the real costs: but such a correspondence is never to be assumed lightly. These considerations will generally suffice for the interpretation of the term Cost in what follows, even where no distinct indication is given in the context.

Chapter V: Equilibrium of normal demand and supply, continued, with reference to long and short periods

1. The variations in the scope of the term *Normal*, according as the periods of time under discussion are long or short, were indicated in Chapter III. We are now ready to study them more closely.

In this case, as in others, the economist merely brings to light difficulties that are latent in the common discourse of life, so that by being frankly faced they may be thoroughly overcome. For in ordinary life it is customary to use the word Normal in different senses, with reference to different periods of time; and to leave the context to explain the transition from one to another. The economist follows this practice of everyday life: but, by taking pains to indicate the transition, he sometimes seems to have created a complication which in fact he has only revealed.

Thus, when it is said that the price of wool on a certain day was abnormally high though the average price for the year was abnormally low, that the wages of coal-miners were abnormally high in 1872 and abnormally low in 1879, that the (real) wages of labour were abnormally high at the end of the fourteenth century and abnormally low in the middle of the sixteenth; everyone understands that the scope of the term normal is not the same in these various cases.

The best illustrations of this come from manufactures where the plant is long-lived, and the product is short-lived. When a new textile fabric is first introduced into favour, and there is very little plant suitable for making it, its normal price for some months may be twice as high as those of other fabrics which are not less difficult to make, but for making which there is an abundant stock of suitable plant and skill. Looking at long periods we may say that its normal price is on a par with that of the others: but if during the first few months a good deal of it were offered for sale in a bankrupt's stock we might say that its price was abnormally low even when it was selling for half as much again as the others. Everyone takes the context as indicating the special use of the term in each several case; and a formal interpretation clause is seldom necessary, because in ordinary conversation misunderstandings can be nipped in the bud by question and answer. But let us look at this matter more closely.

We have noticed how a cloth manufacturer would need to calculate the expenses of producing all the different things required for making cloth with reference to the amounts of each of them that would be wanted; and on the supposition in the first instance that the conditions of supply would be normal. But we have yet to take account of the fact that he must give to this term a wider or narrower range, according as he was looking more or less far ahead.

Thus in estimating the wages required to call forth an adequate supply of labour to work a certain class of looms, he might take the current wages of similar work in the neighbourhood: or he might argue that there was a scarcity of that particular class of labour in the neighbourhood, that its current wages there were higher than in other parts of England, and that looking forward over several years so as to allow for immigration, he might take the normal rate of wages at a rather lower rate than that prevailing there at the time. Or lastly, he might think that the wages of weavers all over the country were abnormally low relatively to others of the same grade, in consequence of a too sanguine view having been taken of the prospects of the trade half a generation ago. He might argue that this branch of work was overcrowded, that parents had already begun to choose other trades for their children which offered greater net advantages and yet were not more difficult; that in consequence a few years would see a falling-off in the supply of labour suited for his purpose; so that looking forward a long time he must take normal wages at a rate higher than the present average.

Again, in estimating the normal supply price of wool, he would take the average of several past years. He would make allowance for any change that would be likely to affect the supply in the immediate future; and he would reckon for the effect of such droughts as from time to time occur in Australia and elsewhere; since their occurrence is too common to be regarded as abnormal. But he would not allow here for the chance of our being involved in a great war, by which the Australian supplies might be cut off; he would consider that any allowance for this should come under the head of extraordinary trade risks, and not enter into his estimate of the normal supply price of wool.

He would deal in the same way with the risk of civil tumult or any violent and long-continued disturbance of the labour market of an unusual character; but in his estimate of the amount of work that could be got out of the machinery, etc. under normal conditions, he would probably reckon for minor interruptions from trade disputes such as are continually occurring, and are therefore to be regarded as belonging to the regular course of events, that is as not abnormal.

In all these calculations he would not concern himself specially to inquire how far mankind are under the exclusive influence of selfish or self-regarding motives. He might be aware that anger and vanity, jealousy and offended dignity are still almost as common causes of strikes and lock-outs, as the desire for pecuniary gain: but that would not enter into his calculations. All that he would want to know about them would be whether they acted with sufficient regularity for him to be able to make a reasonably good allowance for their influence in interrupting work and raising the normal supply price of the goods.

2. The element of time is a chief cause of those difficulties in economic investigations which make it necessary for man with his limited powers to go step by step; breaking up a complex question, studying one bit at a time, and at last combining his partial solutions into a more or less complete solution of the whole riddle. In breaking it up, he segregates those disturbing causes, whose wanderings happen to be inconvenient, for the time in a pound called *Cæteris Paribus*. The study of some group of tendencies is isolated by the assumption *other things being equal*: the existence of other tendencies is not denied, but their disturbing effect is neglected for a time. The more the issue is thus narrowed, the more exactly can it be handled: but also the less closely does it correspond to real life. Each exact and firm handling of a narrow issue, however, helps towards treating broader issues, in which that narrow issue is contained, more exactly than would otherwise have been possible. With each step more things can be let out of the pound; exact discussions can be made less abstract, realistic discussions can be made less inexact than was possible at an earlier stage.

Our first step towards studying the influences exerted by the element of time on the relations between cost of production and value may well be to consider the famous fiction of the 'Stationary state' in which those influences would be but little felt; and to contrast the results which would be found there with those in the modern world.

This state obtains its name from the fact that in it the general conditions of production and consumption, of distribution and exchange remain motionless; but yet it is full of movement; for it is a mode of life. The average age of the population may be stationary; though each individual is growing up from youth towards his prime, or downwards to old age. And the same amount of things per head of the population will have been produced in the same ways by the same classes of people for many generations together; and therefore this supply of the appliances for production will have had full time to be adjusted to the steady demand.

Of course we might assume that in our stationary state every business remained always of the same size, and with the same trade connection. But we need not go so far as that; it will suffice to suppose that firms rise and fall, but that the 'representative' firm remains always of about the same size, as does the representative tree of a virgin forest, and that therefore the economies resulting from its own resources are constant: and since the aggregate volume of production is constant, so also are those economies resulting from subsidiary industries in the neighbourhood, etc. [That is, its internal and external economies are both constant. The price, the expectation of which just induced persons to enter the trade, must be sufficient to cover in the long run the cost of building up a trade connection; and a proportionate share of it must be added in to make up the total cost of production.]

In a stationary state then the plain rule would be that cost of production governs value. Each effect would be attributable mainly to one cause; there would not be much complex action and reaction between cause and effect. Each element of cost would be governed by 'natural' laws, subject to some control from fixed custom. There would be no reflex influence of demand; no fundamental difference between the immediate and the later effects of economic causes. There would be no distinction between long-period and short-period normal value, at all events if we supposed that in that monotonous world the harvests themselves were uniform: for the representative firm being always of the same size, and always doing the same class of business to the same extent and in the same way, with no slack times, and no specially busy times, its normal expenses by which the normal supply price is governed would be always the same. The demand lists of prices would always be the same, and so would the supply lists; and normal price would never vary.

But nothing of this is true in the world in which we live. Here every economic force is constantly changing its action, under the influence of other forces which are acting around it. Here changes in the volume of production, in its methods, and in its cost are ever mutually modifying one another; they are always affecting and being affected by the character and the extent of demand. Further all these mutual influences take time to work themselves out, and, as a rule, no two influences move at equal pace. In this world therefore every plain and simple doctrine as to the relations between cost of production, demand and value is necessarily false: and the greater the appearance of lucidity which is given to it by skilful exposition, the more mischievous it is. A man is likely to be a better economist if he trusts his common sense, and practical instincts, than if he professes to study the theory of value and is resolved to find it easy.

3. The Stationary state has just been taken to be one in which population is stationary. But nearly all its distinctive features may be exhibited in a place where population and wealth are both growing, provided they are growing at about the same rate, and there is no scarcity of land: and provided also the methods of production and the conditions of trade change but little; and above all, where the character of man himself is a constant quantity. For in such a state by far the most important conditions of production and consumption, of exchange and distribution will remain of the same quality, and in the same general relations to one another, though they are all increasing in volume.

This relaxation of the rigid bonds of a purely stationary state brings us one step nearer to the actual conditions of life: and by relaxing them still further we get nearer still. We thus approach by gradual steps towards the difficult problem of the interaction of countless economic causes. In the stationary state all the conditions of production and consumption are reduced to rest: but less violent assumptions are made by what is, not quite accurately, called the *statical* method. By that method we fix our minds on some central point: we suppose it for the time to be reduced to a *stationary* state; and we then study in relation to it the forces that affect the things by which it is surrounded, and any tendency there may be to equilibrium of these forces. A number of these partial studies may lead the way towards a solution of problems too difficult to be grasped at one effort.

...

5. To go over the ground in another way. Market values are governed by the relation of demand to stocks actually in the market; with more or less reference to 'future' supplies, and not without some influence of trade combinations.

But the current supply is in itself partly due to the action of producers in the past; and this action has been determined on as the result of a comparison of the prices which they expect to get for their goods with the expenses to which they will be put in producing them. The range of expenses of which they take account depends on whether they are merely considering the extra expenses of certain extra production with their existing plant, or are considering whether to lay down new plant for the purpose. In the case, for instance, of an order for a single locomotive, which was discussed a little while ago, the question of readjusting the plant to demand would hardly arise: the main question would be whether more work could conveniently be got out of the existing plant. But in view of an order for a large number of locomotives to be delivered gradually over a series of years, some extension of plant 'specially' made for the purpose, and therefore truly to be regarded as prime marginal costs would almost certainly be carefully considered.

Whether the new production for which there appears to be a market be large or small, the general rule will be that unless the price is expected to be very low that portion of the supply which can be most easily produced, with but small prime costs, will be produced: that portion is not likely to be on the margin of production. As the expectations of price improve, an increased part of the production will yield a considerable surplus above prime costs, and the margin of production will be pushed outwards. Every increase in the price expected will, as a rule, induce some people who would not otherwise have produced anything, to produce a little; and those, who have produced something for the lower price, will produce more for the higher price. That part of their production with regard to which such persons are on the margin of doubt as to whether it is worth while for them to produce it at the price, is to be included together with that of the persons who are in doubt whether to produce at all; the two together constitute the marginal production at that price. The producers, who are in doubt whether to produce anything at all, may be said to lie altogether on the margin of production (or, if they are agriculturists, on the margin of cultivation). But as a rule they are very few in number, and their action is less important than that of those who would in any case produce something.

The general drift of the term normal supply price is always the same whether the period to which it refers is short or long; but there are great differences in detail. In every case reference is made to a certain given rate of aggregate production; that is, to the production of a certain aggregate amount daily or annually. In every case the price is that the expectation of which is sufficient and only just sufficient to make it worth while for people to set themselves to produce that aggregate amount; in every case the cost of production is marginal; that is, it is the cost of production of those goods which are on the margin of not being produced at all, and which would not be produced if the price to be got for them were expected to be lower. But the causes which determine this margin vary with the length of the period under consideration. For short periods people take the stock of appliances for production as practically fixed; and they are governed by their expectations of demand in considering how actively they shall set themselves to work those appliances. In long periods they set themselves to adjust the flow of these appliances to their expectations of demand for the goods which the appliances help to produce. Let us examine this difference closely.

6. The immediate effect of the expectation of a high price is to cause people to bring into active work all their appliances of production, and to work them full time and perhaps overtime. The supply price is then the money cost of production of that part of the produce which forces the undertaker to hire such inefficient labour (perhaps tired by working overtime) at so high a price, and to put himself and others to so much strain and inconvenience that he is on the margin of doubt whether it is worth his while to do it or not. The immediate effect of the expectation of a low price is to throw many appliances for production out of work, and slacken the work of others; and if the producers had no fear of spoiling their markets, it would be worth their while

to produce for a time for any price that covered the prime costs of production and rewarded them for their own trouble.

But, as it is, they generally hold out for a higher price; each man fears to spoil his chance of getting a better price later on from his own customers; or, if he produces for a large and open market, he is more or less in fear of incurring the resentment of other producers, should he sell needlessly at a price that spoils the common market for all. The marginal production in this case is the production of those whom a little further fall of price would cause, either from a regard to their own interest or by formal or informal agreement with other producers, to suspend production for fear of further spoiling the market. The price which, for these reasons, producers are just on the point of refusing, is the true marginal supply price for short periods. It is nearly always above, and generally very much above the special or prime cost for raw materials, labour and wear-and-tear of plant, which is immediately and directly involved by getting a little further use out of appliances which are not fully employed. This point needs further study.

In a trade which uses very expensive plant, the prime cost of goods is but a small part of their total cost; and an order at much less than their normal price may leave a large surplus above their prime cost. But if producers accept such orders in their anxiety to prevent their plant from being idle, they glut the market and tend to prevent prices from reviving. In fact however they seldom pursue this policy constantly and without moderation. If they did, they might ruin many of those in the trade, themselves perhaps among the number; and in that case a revival of demand would find little response in supply, and would raise violently the prices of the goods produced by the trade. Extreme variations of this kind are in the long run beneficial neither to producers nor to consumers; and general opinion is not altogether hostile to that code of trade morality which condemns the action of anyone who 'spoils the market' by being too ready to accept a price that does little more than cover the prime cost of his goods, and allows but little on account of his general expenses.

For example, if at any time the prime cost, in the narrowest sense of the word, of a bale of cloth is £100; and if another £100 are needed to make the cloth pay its due share of the general expenses of the establishment, including normal profits to its owners, then the practically effective supply price is perhaps not very likely to fall below £150 under ordinary conditions, even for short periods; though of course a few special bargains may be made at lower prices without much affecting the general market.

Thus, although nothing but prime cost enters *necessarily and directly* into the supply price for short periods, it is yet true that supplementary costs also exert some influence indirectly. A producer does not often isolate the cost of each separate small parcel of his output; he is apt to treat a considerable part of it, even in some cases the whole of it, more or less as a unit. He inquires whether it is worth his while to add a certain new line to his present undertakings, whether it is worth while to introduce a new machine and so on. He treats the extra output that would result from the change more or less as a unit beforehand; and afterwards he quotes the lowest prices, which he is willing to accept, with more or less reference to the whole cost of that extra output regarded as a unit.

In other words he regards an increase in his processes of production, rather than an individual parcel of his products, as a unit in most of his transactions. And the analytical economist must follow suit, if he would keep in close touch with actual conditions. These considerations tend to blur the sharpness of outline of the theory of value: but they do not affect its substance.

To sum up then as regards short periods. The supply of specialized skill and ability, of suitable machinery and other material capital, and of the appropriate industrial organization has not time to be fully adapted to demand; but the producers have to adjust their supply to the demand as best they can with the appliances already at their disposal. On the one hand there is not time materially to increase those appliances if the supply of them is deficient; and on the other, if the supply is excessive, some of them must remain imperfectly employed, since there is not time for the supply to be much reduced by gradual decay, and by conversion to other uses. Variations in the particular income derived from them do not *for the time* affect perceptibly the supply; and do not directly affect the price of the commodities produced by them. The income is a surplus of total receipts over prime cost; [that is, it has something of the nature of a rent as will be seen more clearly in Chapter VIII]. But unless it is sufficient to cover in the long run a fair share of the general costs of the business, production will gradually fall off. In this way a controlling influence over the relatively quick movements of supply price during short periods is exercised by causes in the background which range over a long period; and the fear of 'spoiling the market' often makes those causes act more promptly than they otherwise would.

7. In long periods on the other hand all investments of capital and effort in providing the material plant and the organization of a business, and in acquiring trade knowledge and special-ized ability, have time to be adjusted to the incomes which are expected to be earned by them: and the estimates of those incomes therefore directly govern supply, and are the true long-period normal supply price of the commodities produced.

A great part of the capital invested in a business is generally spent on building up its internal organization and its external trade connections. If the business does not prosper all that capital is lost, even though its material plans may realize a considerable part of its original cost. And anyone proposing to start a new business in any trade must reckon for the chance of this loss. If himself a man of normal capacity for that class of work, he may look forward ere long to his business being a representative one, in the sense in which we have used this term, with its fair share of the economies of production on a large scale. If the net earnings of such a representative business seem likely to be greater than he could get by similar investments in other trades to which he has access, he will choose this trade. Thus that investment of capital in a trade, on which the price of the commodity produced by it depends in the long run, is governed by estimates on the one hand of the outgoings required to build up and to work a representative firm, and on the other of the incomings, spread over a long period of time, to be got by such a price.

At any particular moment some businesses will be rising and others falling: but when we are taking a broad view of the causes which govern normal supply price, we need not trouble our-selves with these eddies on the surface of the great tide. Any particular increase of production may be due to some new manufacturer who is struggling against difficulties, working with insuf-ficient capital, and enduring great privations in the hope that he may gradually build up a good business. Or it may be due to some wealthy firm which by enlarging its premises is enabled to attain new economies, and thus obtain a larger output at a lower proportionate cost: and, as this additional output will be small relatively to the aggregate volume of production in the trade, it will not much lower the price; so that the firm will reap great gains from its successful adaptation to its surroundings. But while these variations are occurring in the fortunes of individual busi-nesses, there may be a steady tendency of the long-period normal supply price to diminish, as a direct consequence of an increase in the aggregate volume of production.

8. Of course there is no hard and sharp line of division between 'long' and 'short' periods. Nature has drawn no such lines in the economic conditions of actual life; and in dealing with practical problems they are not wanted. Just as we contrast civilized with uncivilized races, and establish many general propositions about either group, though no hard and fast division can be drawn between the two; so we contrast long and short periods without attempting any rigid demarcation between them. If it is necessary for the purposes of any particular argument to divide one case sharply from the other, it can be done by a special interpretation clause: but the occasions on which this is necessary are neither frequent nor important.

Four classes stand out. In each, price is governed by the relations between demand and supply. As regards *market* prices, Supply is taken to mean the stock of the commodity in question which is on hand, or at all events 'in sight'. As regards *normal* prices, when the term Normal is taken to relate to *short* periods of a few months or a year, Supply means broadly what can be produced for the price in question with the existing stock of plant, personal and impersonal, in the given time. As regards *normal* prices, when the term Normal is to refer to *long* periods of several years, Supply means what can be produced by plant, which itself can be remuneratively produced and applied within the given time; while lastly, there are very gradual or *Secular* movements of normal price, caused by the gradual growth of knowledge, of population and of capital, and the changing conditions of demand and supply from one generation to another.

. . .

Notes

1   Compare V.I.I. To represent the equilibrium of demand and supply geometrically we may draw the demand and supply curves together as in Fig. 19. If then *OR* represents the rate at which production is being actually carried on, and *Ed* the demand price is greater than *Rf* the supply price, the production is exceptionally profitable, and will be increased. *R*, the *amount-index*, as we may call it, will move to the right. On the other hand, if *Rd* is less than *Rs*, *R* will move to the left. If *Rd* is equal to *Rs*, that is, if *R* is vertically under a point of intersection of the curves, demand and supply are in equilibrium.

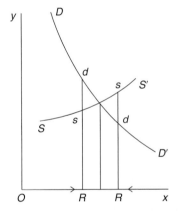

This may be taken as the typical diagram for stable equilibrium for a commodity that obeys the law of diminishing return. But if we had made *S'* a horizontal straight line, we should have represented the case of 'constant return', in which the supply price is the same for all amounts of the commodity. And if we made *SS'* inclined negatively, but less steeply than *DD'* (the necessity for this condition will appear more fully later on), we should have got a case of stable equilibrium for a commodity which obeys the law of increasing return. In either case the above reasoning remains unchanged without the alteration of a word or a letter; but the last case introduces difficulties which we have arranged to postpone.

EUGEN VON BÖHM-BAWERK (1851–1914)

Eugen von Böhm-Bawerk, by courtesy of The Warren J. Samuels Portrait Collection at Duke University.

Eugen von Böhm-Bawerk was born in Vienna and educated in law at the University there. He spent his career as a professor at the universities of Innsbruck and Vienna, sandwiched around fifteen years in the civil service, including three tours of duty as Minister of Finance. Böhm-Bawerk was a staunch critic of Karl Marx and, with Friedrich von Wieser, did a great deal to popularize the Austrian approach to economics, originally developed at the hands of Menger. His signal contributions are his theories of capital and interest, and these are built upon the notion of "roundaboutness" – the idea that the investment of physical capital lengthens the production process and positively impacts productivity.

Böhm-Bawerk was one of the first to treat the economic problems introduced by the passage of time in a significant way and as a central building block of the theory. Beyond the obvious fact that roundaboutness introduces an intertemporal element, Böhm-Bawerk pointed out that many consumption and production activities invariably occur over time and/or require a choice between present and future activities. He argued that there is a systematic tendency on the part of economic agents to excessively favor the present over the future, there by making interest rates positive. First, marginal utility of income is declining over time because they expect higher incomes in the future. Second, the marginal utility of a commodity diminishes the greater is the length of time that passes before it will be available to the agent. Taken together, these two ideas indicate a positive rate of time preference, which requires the payment of interest in return for the deferral of activities – productive or consumptive – into the future and the willingness to pay interest in order to command these activities in the present rather than in the future. The third rationale for a positive rate of interest in Böhm-Bawerk's analysis is what he calls "the technical superiority of present over future goods" and is derived from his theory of roundaboutness. Greater amounts of capital imply greater roundaboutness, both lengthening the production period and increasing the amount of the final product. This increase in productivity associated with capital, then, would result in a positive rate of interest even apart from the first two issues of time preference.

The following excerpts from Böhm-Bawerk's *The Positive Theory of Capital* lay out his notion of roundaboutness in production, his ideas regarding the evaluation of present versus future activities, and his theory of the determination of the rate of interest.

References and further reading

Blaug, Mark, ed. (1992) *Eugen von Böhm-Bawerk (1851–1914) and Friedrich von Wieser (1851–1926)*, Aldershot: Edward Elgar Publishing.

Böhm-Bawerk, Eugen von (1884) *Capital and Interest*, London: Macmillan, 1890.

——(1896) *Karl Marx and the Close of His System*, London: Fisher Unwin, 1898.

——(1962) *Shorter Classics*, South Holland, IL: Libertarian Press.

Dorfman, Robert (1959) "A Graphical Exposition of Böhm-Bawerk's Interest Theory," *Review of Economic Studies* 26 (February): 153–58.

——(1959) "Waiting and the Period of Production," *Quarterly Journal of Economics* 73 (August): 351–72.

Faber, M. (1979) *Introduction to Modern Austrian Capital Theory*, Berlin: Springer.

Garrison, Roger W. (1990) "Austrian Capital Theory: The Early Controversies," *History of Political Economy* 22 (Supplement): 133–54.

Hennings, K.H. (1987) "Böhm-Bawerk, Eugen von," in John Eatwell, Murray Milgate, and Peter Newman (eds), *The New Palgrave: A Dictionary of Economics*, Vol. 1, London: Macmillan, 254–59.

——(1997) *The Austrian Theory of Value and Capital: Studies in the Life and Work of Eugen von Böhm-Bawerk*, Aldershot: Edward Elgar.

Kuenne, R.E. (1971) *Eugen von Böhm-Bawerk*, New York: Columbia University Press.

The Positive Theory of Capital (1888)*

Book I: The nature and conception of capital

Chapter II: The nature of capital

The end and aim of all production is the making of things with which to satisfy our wants; that is to say, the making of goods for immediate consumption, or Consumption Goods. The method of their production we have already looked at in a general way. We combine our own natural powers and natural powers of the external world in such a way that, under natural law, the desired material good must come into existence. But this is a very general description indeed of the matter, and looking at it closer there comes in sight an important distinction which we have not as yet considered. It has reference to the distance which lies between the expenditure of human labour in the combined production and the appearance of the desired good. We either put forth our labour just before the goal is reached, or we, intentionally, take a roundabout way. That is to say, we may put forth our labour in such a way that it at once completes the circle of conditions necessary for the emergence of the desired good, and thus the existence of the good *immediately* follows the expenditure of the labour; or we may associate our labour first with the more remote causes of the good, with the object of obtaining, not the desired good itself, but a proximate cause of the good; which cause, again, must be associated with other suitable materials and powers, till, finally, – perhaps through a considerable number of intermediate members, – the finished good, the instrument of human satisfaction, is obtained.

The nature and importance of this distinction will be best seen from a few examples; and, as these will, to a considerable extent, form a demonstration of what is really one of the most fundamental propositions in our theory, I must risk being tedious.

A peasant requires drinking water. The spring is some distance from his house. There are various ways in which he may supply his daily wants. First, he may go to the spring each time he is thirsty, and drink out of his hollowed hand. This is the most direct way; satisfaction follows immediately on exertion. But it is an inconvenient way, for our peasant has to take his way to the well as often as he is thirsty. And it is an insufficient way, for he can never collect and store any great quantity such as he requires for various other purposes. Second, he may take a log of wood, hollow it out into a kind of pail, and carry his day's supply from the spring to his cottage. The advantage is obvious, but it necessitates a roundabout way of considerable length. The man must spend, perhaps, a day in cutting out the pail; before doing so he must have felled a tree in the forest; to do this, again, he must have made an axe, and so on. But there is still a third way; instead of felling one tree he fells a number of trees, splits and hollows them, lays them end for end, and

---

* Eugen v. Böhm-Bawerk, *The Positive Theory of Capital*, translated with a preface and analysis by William Smart, 1891. Reprinted New York: G.E. Stechert & Co., 1930.

so constructs a runnel or rhone which brings a full head of water to his cottage. Here, obviously, between the expenditure of the labour and the obtaining of the water we have a very roundabout way, but, then, the result is ever so much greater. Our peasant needs no longer take his weary way from house to well with the heavy pail on his shoulder, and yet he has a constant and full supply of the freshest water at his very door.

Another example. I require stone for building a house. There is a rich vein of excellent sandstone in a neighbouring hill. How is it to be got out? First, I may work the loose stones back and forward with my bare fingers, and break off what can be broken off. This is the most direct, but also the least productive way. Second, I may take a piece of iron, make a hammer and chisel out of it, and use them on the hard stone – a roundabout way, which, of course, leads to a very much better result than the former. Third method – Having a hammer and chisel I use them to drill a hole in the rock; next I turn my attention to procuring charcoal, sulphur, and nitre, and mixing them in a powder, then I pour the powder into the hole, and the explosion that follows splits the stone into convenient pieces – still more of a roundabout way, but one which, as experience shows, is as much superior to the second way in result as the second was to the first.

Yet another example. I am short-sighted, and wish to have a pair of spectacles. For this I require ground and polished glasses, and a steel framework. But all that nature offers towards that end is silicious earth and iron ore. How am I to transform these into spectacles? Work as I may, it is as impossible for me to make spectacles directly out of silicious earth as it would be to make the steel frames out of iron ore. Here there is no immediate or direct method of production. There is nothing for it but to take the roundabout way, and, indeed, a very roundabout way. I must take silicious earth and fuel, and build furnaces for smelting the glass from the silicious earth; the glass thus obtained has to be carefully purified, worked, and cooled by a series of processes; finally, the glass thus prepared – again by means of ingenious instruments carefully constructed beforehand – is ground and polished into the lens fit for short-sighted eyes. Similarly, I must smelt the ore in the blast furnace, change the raw iron into steel, and make the frame therefrom – processes which cannot be carried through without a long series of tools and buildings that, on their part again, require great amounts of previous labour. Thus, by an exceedingly roundabout way, the end is attained.

The lesson to be drawn from all these examples alike is obvious. It is – that a greater result is obtained by producing goods in roundabout ways than by producing them directly. Where a good can be produced in either way, we have the fact that, by the indirect way, a greater product can be got with equal labour, or the same product with less labour. But, beyond this, the superiority of the indirect way manifests itself in being the only way in which certain goods can be obtained; if I might say so, it is so much the better that it is often the only way!

That roundabout methods lead to greater results than direct methods is one of the most important and fundamental propositions in the whole theory of production. It must be emphatically stated that the only basis of this proposition is the experience of practical life. Economic theory does not and cannot show a priori that it must be so; but the unanimous experience of all the technique of production says that it is so. And this is sufficient; all the more that the facts of experience which tell us this are commonplace and familiar to everybody. But *why* is it so? The economist might quite well decline to answer this question. For the fact that a greater product is obtained by methods of production that begin far back is essentially a purely technical fact, and to explain questions of technique does not fall within the economist's sphere. For instance, that tropical lands are more fruitful than the polar zone; that the alloy of which coins is made stands more wear and tear than pure metal; that a railroad is better for transport than an ordinary turnpike road; – all these are matters of fact with which the economist reckons, but which his science does not call on him to explain. But this is exactly one of those cases where, in the economist's own interest – the interest he has in limiting and defining his own task – it is exceedingly desirable to go beyond the specific economic sphere. If the sober physical truth is once made clear, political economy cannot indulge in any fancies or fictions about it; and, in such questions, political economy has never been behind in the desire and the attempt to substitute its own imaginings! Although, then, this law is already sufficiently accredited by experience, I attach particular value to explaining its cause, and, after what has been said as to the nature of production, this should not be very difficult.

In the last resort all our productive efforts amount to shiftings and combinations of matter. We must know how to bring together the right forms of matter at the right moment, in order that from those associated forces the desired result, the product wanted, may follow. But, as we saw, the natural forms of matter are often so infinitely large, often so infinitely fine, that human hands are too weak or too coarse to control them. We are as powerless to overcome the cohesion of the wall of rock when we want building stone as we are, from carbon, nitrogen, hydrogen, oxygen, phosphor, potash, etc., to put together a single grain of wheat. But there are other powers which can easily do what is denied to us, and these are the powers of nature. There are natural powers which far exceed the possibilities of human power in greatness, and there are other natural powers in the microscopic world which can make combinations that put our clumsy fingers to shame. If we can succeed in making those forces our allies in the work of production, the limits of human possibility will be infinitely extended. And this we have done.

The condition of our success is, that we are able to control the materials on which the power that helps us depends, more easily than the materials which are to be transformed into the desired good. Happily this condition can be very often complied with. Our weak yielding hand cannot overcome the cohesion of the rock, but the hard wedge of iron can; the wedge and the hammer to drive it we can happily master with little trouble. We cannot gather the atoms of phosphorus and potash out of the ground, and the atoms of carbon and oxygen out of the atmospheric air, and put them together in the shape of the corn of wheat; but the organic chemical powers of the seed can put this magical process in motion, while we on our part can very easily bury the seed in the place of its secret working, the bosom of the earth. Often, of course, we are not able directly to master the form of matter on which the friendly power depends, but in the same way as we would like it to help us, do we help ourselves against it; we try to secure the alliance of a second natural power which brings the form of matter that bears the first power under our control. We wish to bring the well water into the house. Wooden rhones would force it to obey our will, and take the path we prescribe, but our hands have not the power to make the forest trees into rhones. We have not far to look, however, for an expedient. We ask the help of a second ally in the axe and the gouge; their assistance gives us the rhones; then the rhones bring us the water. And what in this illustration is done through the mediation of two or three members may be done, with equal or greater result, through five, ten, or twenty members. Just as we control and guide the immediate matter of which the good is composed by one friendly power, and that power by a second, so can we control and guide the second by a third, the third by a fourth, this, again, by a fifth, and so on, – always going back to more remote causes of the final result – till in the series we come at last to one cause which we can control conveniently by our own natural powers. This is the true importance which attaches to our entering on roundabout ways of production, and this is the reason of the result associated with them: every roundabout way means the enlisting in our service of a power which is stronger or more cunning than the human hand; every extension of the roundabout way means an addition to the powers which enter into the service of man, and the shifting of some portion of the burden of production from the scarce and costly labour of human beings to the prodigal powers of nature.

And now we may put into words an idea which has long waited for expression, and must certainly have occurred to the reader; the kind of production which works in these wise circuitous methods is nothing else than what economists call Capitalist Production, as opposed to that production which goes directly at its object, as the Germans say, '*mit der nackten Faust*'. And Capital is nothing but the complex of intermediate products which appear on the several stages of the roundabout journey.

It is in this way I interpret the most important fundamental conception in the theory of capital, and I should be very glad to stop here. But, like so many other conceptions in the theory of capital, this conception of capital itself has become a veritable apple of discord to the theorists. A perfectly amazing number of divergent interpretations here confront each other, and block the approach to the theory of capital with one of the most vexatious controversies in which our science could be involved. This uncertainty as to the conception of capital, bad enough in itself, becomes worse in proportion as Capital gives modern science new questions to consider and discuss. It is certainly very unfortunate when a science already earnestly, even acrimoniously engaged on the solution of questions which affect society to its depths – questions which all the world knows, ponders, and discusses as the great 'problems of capital' – is struck, as it were, by a second confusion of tongues, and becomes involved in an endless wrangle as to what kind of thing it is that properly is called Capital! Such a controversy at such a point is more than embarrassing; it is a calamity; and has been found so in the history of Political Economy. Almost every year there appears some new attempt to settle the disputed conception, but, unfortunately, no authoritative result has as yet followed these attempts. On the contrary, many of them have only served to put more combatants in the field and furnish more matter to the dispute.

I confess that, to me, the settlement of the real problems connected with the name of capital seems more important, and certainly is more attractive, than the cataloguing of controversies as to the proper use of the word. All the same the fact remains that the confusion about the name has brought a great amount of confusion into the matter; and, again, it might be open to misconstruction – and not without reason, – if the author of a somewhat comprehensive work on capital were to pass over the discussion of what is certainly the most noisy, if not the most weighty controversy about capital. On these two accounts I feel obliged again to tread the heated path of controversy, in the hope that impartial and sober inquiry into the matter in dispute may succeed in ending it.

Chapter IV: The true conception of capital

...

Capital in general we shall call a group of Products which serve as means to the Acquisition of Goods. Under this general conception we shall put that of Social Capital as a narrower conception. Social Capital we shall call a group of products, which serve as means to the socio-economical Acquisition of Goods; or, as this acquisition is only possible through production, we shall call it a group of products destined to serve towards further production; or, briefly, a group of Intermediate Products. Synonymous with the wider of the two conceptions, the term Acquisitive Capital may be very suitably used, or, less suitably but more in accordance with usage the term Private Capital. Social Capital again, the narrower of the two conceptions, may be well and concisely called Productive Capital. The following are my reasons for this classification.

Capital in its wider sense, and capital in its narrower sense, both mark out categories which, economically, are of the highest importance. 'Products which serve to acquisitive ends' possess a pre-eminent importance for the theory of income as being the source of interest; while the 'intermediate products' possess at least as great an importance for the theory of production. The distinction between production from hand to mouth and production which employs roundabout and fruitful methods, is so fundamental that it is eminently desirable that a special conception should be coined for the latter. This is done – if not, as we shall see, in the only possible way, yet in a way that is not inappropriate – in grouping together, under the conception of capital, the 'intermediate products' which come into existence in the course of this roundabout production.

Again, the solution suggested is the most conservative one. Without laying any particular weight on the fact that the historical origin of the word Capital indicates a relation to an acquisition or a gain, and that our reading remains true to this, it preserves the double relation – the relation to acquisition of interest on the one side, and to production on the other – which was imported into the conception of capital by Adam Smith, and since his time has been adopted in scientific usage. It is no inconsiderable advantage, then, that we do not require to create a majority in its favour by a revolution in terminology; the majority is already with us, and the conception may easily be carried unanimously if we add some new unbiassed members. Here, too, it is worthy of particular attention that those writers who have occupied themselves professedly and most profoundly with the investigation of the conception of capital and its problems, have ended, almost without exception, by adopting exactly the same conception, or at least one which comes very close to it.

Connected with this is the further advantage, that we avoid a puzzling change of name for the two classes of problems which are both treated of now under the name of problems of capital. The popular name is retained both for the 'factor of production' and for the 'source of interest'. And finally, it seems to me no small advantage that, notwithstanding the material difference there is between capital the factor of production, and capital the source of interest, it is not necessary in our reading of it to make two conceptions of capital that are entirely foreign to one another, and have nothing more in common than cat has with category. Our two conceptions have just enough in common to allow of their being formally coupled under one common definition, and then distinguished as narrower and wider conceptions. True, their connection is not an intimate one, and in the light of what has been said it cannot be so; it rests simply on the accidental circumstance that, for society as a whole, which cannot acquire except through producing, the goods which constitute the produced means of *acquisition* (capital in the wider sense) coincide with the goods which constitute the produced means of *production* (capital in the narrower sense, or Social Capital). It will be noted that I use the phrase Social Capital, and not the common expression National Capital I do so for this reason, that, for a limited community, the means of acquisition embrace not only productive goods but consumption goods lent to foreign countries. Those who hold by the conception of National Capital, then, must either take in the above-named consumption goods along with productive goods, thereby arriving at a very uninteresting conception indeed; or if they mean to confine it to productive goods only, they must build their national conception on a quite independent basis, and break off all logical connection with the other conception, – which would at any rate be a doubtful policy. Our 'Social Capital' avoids both these difficulties.

Book V: Present and future

Chapter I: Present and future in economic life

Present goods are, as a rule, worth more than future goods of like kind and number. This proposition is the kernel and centre of the interest theory which I have to present. All the lines of explanation, by which I hope to elucidate the phenomena of interest, run through this fact; and round it, both essentially and superficially, is grouped the whole of the theoretical work we have to do. The first part of our explanation will try to prove the truth of the proposition; the second will then show that, out of the fact, spring, naturally and necessarily, all the manifold forms which the phenomena of interest take. In the present book we have to take up the first part, and I shall try to go into it with that minuteness which is due to the cardinal importance of such a proposition. To this end we shall, first of all, make a general survey of the relations between present and future in human economy – a subject, obviously, of the highest importance, but one which, strangely enough, has up till now attracted but scanty scientific attention.

In the present we live and move, but our future is not a matter of indifference to us, and our desires are, with reason, directed towards a well-being not limited by the present. It is only as the logical carrying out of this general principle that we set before us, in our economical arrangements, the larger object of providing for our future as well as for our present well-being. As a fact, the future has a great place in our economical provision; a greater, indeed, than people usually think. It is, of course, a commonplace, but, all the same, it is a truth seldom seen in all its bearings, that our economical conduct has exceedingly little reference to the present, but is, almost entirely, taken up with the future.

Let us clearly understand what this latter statement means. It means that our anxiety in the present is to have at our disposal, in the future, means for the satisfaction of wants that will not emerge till the future. In other words, it means that pleasures or pains, which we will only experience in the future, determine us now to provide goods or services, which, again, will only assert their use in the future. But how is it possible that feelings which are not yet felt, and therefore feelings which, essentially, do not exist, can be motives to will and deed?

Now, as a suggestive writer has said, we do not indeed possess the gift of feeling future sensations, but we possess the other gift of anticipating them in imagination. Either it is that we have already in the past, once or many times, experienced the same want as we expect in the future, and retain a picture of it in our memory; or, at least, we have already experienced wants or feelings that bear a certain resemblance to the feelings we are expecting, and can, from such analogous reminiscences, construct for ourselves an imaginative picture which is more or less true. On such pictures of memory and imagination we base our economical calculations and our economical decisions. Certainly, as many a one will be apt to object, it is an unsafe and deceptive foundation, but, all the same, it is almost the only one that we have. It is the rarest possible thing for us to base a valuation of goods, or an economical decision, on a pain that we are feeling at the very moment. It is, indeed, one of the characteristics of a civilised community that it anticipates want by providing for it, and does not allow the pain of emptiness, which the unsatisfied want would involve, to get to its full height. We do not begin to prepare our meals when hunger has reached its highest point of torment: we do not wait till the flood has overwhelmed house and home before we think of putting up the dam: we do not delay building the fire-engine till the flames have broken over us. At the moment when we decide on an economical action, the wants which cause us to make the decision are, almost always, in the future, and so, however near that future may be, they are acting on us, not as actual feelings, but as simple anticipations. How many a man has never, even in the past, fully felt the want which makes him value the goods he daily uses! How many rich people know only from hearsay what real hunger is!

Hence it is obvious that, however deceitful and unsafe this gift of anticipation may be, and however far astray it may lead us in individual cases, we still have every cause to be heartily thankful that we have it. Otherwise, neither actually feeling the future wants, nor yet forewarned of them by anticipation, we could not, of course, provide for them in advance; once want had made itself felt, any measures we could take would be miserably inadequate to provide for it; and, poorer than the poorest savages, we should drag out a hazardous hand-to-mouth existence.

But economical action means something more than thinking generally about the wants which are to be provided for. As, indeed, all economising arises from the quantitative insufficiency of the means of satisfaction as compared with the wants requiring satisfaction, so it demands a constant selection, a constant choosing between those wants which can and should be provided for, and those others which cannot be provided for. The selection naturally proceeds on a comparison of the importance and urgency – or, as we may say, the intensity – of the feelings of pleasure and pain which are associated with individual wants and their satisfaction. Now, if it is seldom that, in the moment of an economical decision, we actually feel that *one* want to which it refers, it is much more seldom that, on the moment of our choice, we experience, as actual feelings, *all* those sensations of pleasure and pain between which we have to choose. Our comparisons must, almost invariably, be, partially and very often completely, made on imaginative anticipations which we make of future feelings. And this leads us to a fact which I should like to emphasise: The future feelings we imagine are commensurable. They are commensurable with present actually felt sensations, and they are commensurable with one another, and that too without reference to whether they belong to the same or to different levels of time. It is as easy for me to choose between a pleasure which seems desirable at the moment and another pleasure which I can obtain in eight days, as between two different pleasures which are both obtainable in eight days, or, again, as between two pleasures of which the one is obtainable in eight days, the other in eight months, or eight years.

The fact that we borrow from future sensations the motive for our present actions, is one side of our connection with the future. Another side is that, by our present actions, we prepare goods or material services for the benefit of the future. If we analyse the totality of goods which constitutes our wealth we shall find that by far the greater part has the character of what, for want of a better name, we may call 'future goods' (*Zukunftsgüter*). All productive goods, without exception, are destined altogether to the service of the future. Durable consumption goods give off only a fraction of their material services in the present, and all the remainder in the future. If a dwelling-house, for instance, remains occupied for a hundred years, and affords shelter and comfort all that time, only an infinitesimal fraction of these services is rendered today; a still very small fraction is rendered in the present year; the great bulk of the service is spread over remote future periods. Even in the case of those perishable goods, such as meat and drink, wood and candles, which we keep ready for immediate consumption in our domestic economy, only one portion of their use is, strictly speaking, devoted to the service of the moment; the greater part is carried over into the future, although it may be the immediate future. As, among our motives, future feelings are the dominant ones, so, among the goods we possess and use, 'future goods' occupy the larger place.

And there is yet another important analogy. As future feelings, whether they belong to the near or to the far future, are commensurable, alike with one another and with present feelings, so are future goods commensurable, alike with one another and with present goods. We can compare the value of a camellia which fades in an hour, with that of a ticket for a next week's concert, or with that of a bunch of next year's roses; or we can give one of these goods for the other. It makes no difference to the matter whether the 'future good', which we compare or barter, is at hand and ready for delivery now, or whether it is represented in bodily shape by nothing more than the means of production out of which it will come, or whether, at the moment, it is neither itself ready nor is capable of being palpably represented – is, that is to say, a 'future good', in the narrowest and strictest sense of that word. Thus we give present money in exchange, not only for the present consumption good Bread, but also for the present productive good Meal, in which the future good, bread, lies concealed. But just as easily can we buy from a farmer, for money down, his next year's harvest. In 'reserved seats' we buy the future services of actors and singers. In buying Consols we give our present money for a series of future payments. Future goods and services are to us – I have cause to emphasise this – entirely familiar objects of economic dealing, just as future feelings are entirely familiar economic motives. Both have their ultimate ground in the continuity of our personal life. What we shall experience in a week or a year hence affects *us* not less than what we experience today, and has, therefore, equal claims to be considered in our economic arrangements. Both arrangements have for their end *our* well-being.

Whether this theoretically similar claim of future and present is always fully recognised in practical life, is another question which will require much consideration.

Provision for the future makes no inconsiderable demands on our intellectual strength; makes some demands, even, on our moral strength; and these demands are not equally met by men at all stages of civilisation. The present always gets its rights. It forces itself upon us through our senses. To cry for food when hungry occurs even to a baby. But the future we must anticipate and picture. Indeed, to have any effect in the future, we must form a double series of anticipations. We must be able to form a mental picture of what will be the state of our wants, needs, feelings, at any particular point of time. And we must be able to form another set of anticipations as to the fate of those measures which we take at the moment with a view to the future. Our knowledge of causal processes must enable us beforehand to form an adequate picture of the forms which goods will take, of the quantity of them, and of the time when they will come to maturity as a result of those productive or commercial activities which we are now commencing. To make this double work of anticipating a comparatively remote future clear and true to fact, is not possible to the infant, and not much more than possible to the child and the savage. Civilisation of course teaches us this difficult art gradually. But, even among the most advanced peoples, the art is still very far from being perfect, and the practical economic provision for the future is correspondingly inadequate. But, be the degree of anticipation and provision for the future what it may, wherever it exists in the most general way – and that is even among the most barbarous tribes – future goods and future services are as much actual objects of economical dealing as present goods. We strive to get them; we produce them; we value them; we buy and sell them.

I say, we value them; and this is a point that must be looked more closely into. On what principles do we estimate the value of future goods? The answer is: On the same principles as we estimate the value of goods in general: that is, according to the marginal utility which they will bring us in the circumstances, of Want and Provision for want. But here, naturally, we have not to deal with the relations of want and provision that obtain at the moment, but with the want and provision of that future period when the goods in question will be at our disposal. To the inhabitants of a besieged town, threatened with starvation, grain that was promised for delivery a year after the raising of the siege would certainly not be valued and paid according to the standard of the moment's need; while, on the contrary, a brewer who, in January, concludes a purchase for a hundred cubic feet of ice to be delivered in July of the coming summer, will, just as certainly, not measure the value of the ice according to the over-supply that obtains at the moment when the bargain is concluded, but according to the scarcity which is likely to come with the summer.

Very frequently, however, there enters into the valuation of future goods an element which causes us to value them a little – or even a great deal – under their future marginal utility, but which – as I shall show presently – has no connection with the phenomenon of interest. This is the element of Uncertainty. To us nothing future is absolutely certain. However closely we may have bound present and future together in economical connection, and however much reason we may have to expect the future to bring certain goods into existence, or put them at our disposal, still the actual fulfilment of our expectations is never, in the strict sense of the word, certain: it is always more or less probable. Of course, the probability is often so great that, practically, it amounts to certainty: as, for instance, the expectation that payment will follow an acceptance by the Rothschilds. In such cases we do neglect the infinitely small amount that is wanting of full certainty, and deduct nothing from the valuation we put upon the acceptance on the ground of uncertainty. But, frequently, the probability falls considerably short of full certainty. The farmer, for instance, may have done everything in his power to obtain a harvest by ploughing, manuring, sowing, and so on: but the harvest may be destroyed, wholly or in part, by hail, frost, flooding, or insect ravages. Sometimes, indeed, the probability sinks to the level of a very faint possibility, as, for example, when a man holds one of a hundred tickets in a lottery where there is only a single prize.

Cases like these cause a certain amount of hesitation to economic men. Are they to value uncertain future sums of goods exactly as if they were certain? Impossible! For then every lottery ticket that carried the chance of winning £100 would be valued at £100, and every claim, even the most doubtful, at its full nominal amount; – a course which, obviously, would land the men who tried to do business on these lines in the bankruptcy court in the shortest possible time. Or are the uncertain future sums of goods not to have any value put upon them? Is no importance whatever to be attached to them with respect to our well-being? As impossible, and as ruinous! For then no man would give the smallest price for a chance in a lottery, or even for nine hundred and ninety-nine chances out of a thousand; no one would dare to make the slightest sacrifice to sow when harvest was uncertain. From this dilemma there is only one escape: we must ascribe to uncertain future sums of goods an importance as regards our well-being, but, at the same time, we must take account of the uncertainty of their acquisition according to the degree of that uncertainty. But, practically, this cannot be done otherwise than by transferring the gradation from where the gradation exists, but cannot be expressed – that is, from the degree of probability, – to where the gradation is not, but where alone it can be expressed – that is, the degree of the expected utility: thus equalising a greater, but less probable utility, to a less, but more probable utility, and this again to a still less but absolutely certain utility. In a word, we reduce all possibilities of utility to certainty, and restore the balance by deducting from this utility or value the amount we must add to the probability of the expected utility to raise it to certainty. Thus we reckon a claim on the Rothschilds at its full nominal value (disregarding for the moment the discount, as belonging to an entirely different sphere of phenomena), while one lottery ticket of a thousand, where the chance is a prize of £100, we value perhaps at 2s., one of a hundred at 20s., and one of ten, perhaps, at £10.

Strictly looked at, this kind of valuation – except where the certainty of the anticipated future utility is practically assured – is always incorrect. For, to recur to our illustration, the ticket will either draw the prize or it will draw a blank. In the former case it will have been, as the events show, worth a hundred pounds; in the latter, worth nothing at all. In no case will it have been worth 2s., or 20s., or £10. But, however false this method of valuation is in the individual case, it comes at least approximately right, according to the law of averages, over a great many cases; and, in the absence of any better method of valuation – which is denied us by the dullness of our imaginative forethought – it is well justified as a practical makeshift.

I repeat that the element of uncertainty, which is the cause of a lesser value being put upon particular classes of future goods, has no causal connection with the phenomenon of interest. The lesser valuation which is its effect is a special one, and extends to one class of future goods only, and there it bears the character of a deduction as premium for risk.

With the exception of this peculiarity, the valuation of present and future goods is made on identical principles. But, to conclude from this that the *amount* of value of present and future goods must be identical, would be too hasty. On the contrary, since present goods are available at a different time from future ones, and therefore come under different actual circumstances, and are intended for the service of a different set of wants, it is to be argued, from all we know about value, that the value of such goods must, as a rule, be different. And so it is in fact. We arrive thus at a proposition which is a fundamental one in our inquiry: As a rule present goods have a higher subjective value than future goods of like kind and number. And since the resultant of subjective valuations determines objective exchange value, present goods, as a rule, have a higher exchange value and price than future goods of like kind and number.

This phenomenon is the result of the co-operation of a number of causes; – causes which, individually, are of very different natures, but which, as it happens, work in the same direction. These causes we shall consider in order.

Chapter II: Differences in want and provision for want

The first great cause of difference in value between present and future goods consists in the different circumstances of want and provision (*Bedarf und Deckung*) in present and future. Present goods, as we know, receive their value from the circumstances of want and provision in the present: future goods from the same circumstances in those future periods of time when they will come into our disposal. If a person is badly in want of certain goods, or of goods in general, while he has reason to hope that, at a future period, he will be better off, he will always value a given quantity of immediately available goods at a higher figure than the same quantity of future goods. In economic life this occurs very frequently, and may be considered as typical in the two following cases. First, in all cases of immediate distress and necessity. A peasant who has had a bad harvest, or sustained loss by fire, an artisan who has had heavy expenses through illness or death in his family, a labourer who is starving; all these agree in valuing the present shilling, which lifts them out of direst need, ever so much more than the future shilling, – the proof being the usurious conditions to which such people often submit in order to raise money at the moment. Second, in the case of persons who have reason to look forward to economical circumstances of increasing comfort. Thus all kinds of beginners who have no means, such as young artists, lawyers, officials, budding doctors, men going into business, are only too ready, in return for a sum of present goods which assists them to start in the vocation they have chosen, and acts as foundation of their economical existence, to promise a considerably larger sum on the condition that they do not require to pay it until they are in receipt of a decent income.

Of course the contrary also occurs not unfrequently in economical life. There are persons who are comparatively well off at the moment, and who are likely to be worse off in the future. To this category belongs, among others, that very considerable number of people whose income is obtained, mostly or altogether, by personal exertions, and will, presumably, fall away at a later period of life when they become unfit for work. A merchant's clerk, for instance, who is in his fiftieth year, and has an income of £100, cannot expect to have anything better ten years later than, perhaps, a small retiring allowance of £30, or an annuity which he may secure by purchase at an assurance office. It is evident that to such people the marginal utility that depends on a shilling spent now is smaller than that depending on a shilling available in the more badly secured future. It would seem that, in such cases, a present shilling should be less valued than a future one. And so it would be if present goods were necessarily spent in the present, but that is not the case. Most goods, and among them, particularly, money, which represents all kinds of goods indifferently, are durable, and can, therefore, be reserved for the service of the future. The case, then, between present and future goods stands thus. The only possible uses of future goods are, naturally, future, while present goods have the same possibility of future use, and have besides – according to choice – either the present uses, or those future ones which may turn up in the time that intervenes between the present moment and the future point of time with which the comparison is being made.

Here then are two possibilities. Either it is the case that all those uses of the present and near future, which are generally taken into consideration as regards the good in question, are less important than the future uses; and in this case the present good will be reserved for these future uses, will derive its value from them, and will be just equal in value to a future good similarly available. Or it is the case that one of the earlier uses is more important; and then the present good gets its value from this use, and has, therefore, the advantage over the future good, which can only obtain its value from a less important future employment. But, usually, one never knows that some unforeseen occurrence in the near future may not give rise to some more urgent want. At any rate such a thing is possible, and it gives a chance of profitable employment to a good already on hand, such as, naturally, a good that will only come into our possession in the future has not got: a chance which, as we have seen, is calculated in the amount of the value, and assessed, according to practical although incorrect methods, as an increment graduated according to its probability. To put it in figures. With £100 which will come into my hands at the end of five years, I can only aim at a marginal utility determined by the situation of things in the year

1896; we shall put this utility down at 1000 ideal units. With £100 at my disposal now, I can, *at the least*, realise the same marginal utility of 1000 units, but if an urgent want, arising in the meantime, gives me an opportunity of obtaining a marginal utility of 1200, I may, possibly, realise it. Say, now, that the probability of such an opportunity occurring equals one-tenth, I shall estimate the value of the present £100 at 1000 units certain, and, beyond that, at one-tenth of the possible surplus of 200: that is, in all, at 1020 units. Present goods are, therefore, in the worst case, equal in value to future goods, and, as a rule, they have the advantage over them in being employed as a reserve. The only exception occurs in those comparatively rare cases where it is difficult or impracticable to keep the present goods till the time of worse provision comes. This happens, for instance, in the case of goods subject to rapid deterioration or decay, such as ice, fruit, and the like. Any fruit merchant in harvest time will put a considerably higher value on a bushel of grapes to be delivered in April than on a bushel of grapes in his store at the time. Or say that a rich man is anticipating a long period of arrest, during which his living will be conformed to the hard fare of prison regime, how willingly would he give the price of a hundred present luxurious meals if he could ensure ten such meals during his captivity!

We may, then, draw up the balance-sheet which shows the influence of the different circumstances of Want and its Provision in present and future as follows. A great many persons who are not so well provided for in the present as they expect to be in the future, set a considerably higher value on present goods than on future. A great many persons who are better provided for in the present than they expect to be in the future, but who have the chance of preserving present goods for the service of the future, and, moreover, of using them as a reserve fund for anything that may turn up in the meantime, value present goods either at the same figure as future, or a little higher. It is only in a fractional minority of cases, where communication between present and future is hindered or threatened by peculiar circumstances, that present goods have, for their owners, a lower subjective use value than future. This being the state of things, even if there was nothing else co-operating with this difference of want and provision in present and future, the resultant of the subjective valuations, which determines the objective exchange value, would obviously be such that present goods must maintain a proportionate advantage, a proportionate, agio over future. But, besides this, there are other co-operating circumstances which work, even more distinctly, in the same direction.

Chapter III: Underestimate of the future

It is one of the most pregnant facts of experience that we attach less importance to future pleasures and pains simply because they are future, and in the measure that they are future. Thus it is that, to goods which are destined to meet the wants of the future, we ascribe a value which is really less than the true intensity of their future marginal utility. We systematically underestimate future wants, and the goods which are to satisfy them.

Of the fact itself there can be no doubt; but, of course, in particular nations, at various stages of life, in different individuals, the phenomenon makes its appearance in very varying degree. We find it most frankly expressed in children and savages. With them the slightest enjoyment, if only it can be seized at the moment, outweighs the greatest and most lasting advantage. How many an Indian tribe, with careless greed, has sold the land of its fathers, the source of its maintenance, to the pale faces for a couple of casks of 'firewater'! Unfortunately very much the same may be seen in our own highly civilised countries. The working man who drinks on Sunday the week's wage he gets on Saturday, and starves along with wife and child the next six days, is not far removed from the Indian. But, to a smaller extent, and in more refined form, the same phenomenon is, I venture to assert, not quite unknown to any of us, however prudent, or cultured, or highly principled. Which of us has not been surprised to find that, under the pressure of momentary appetite, he was not able to refuse some favourite dish or cigar which the doctor had forbidden – knowing perfectly that he was doing an injury to his health, which, calm consideration would tell him, was much more considerable than the pleasure of that trifling indulgence? Or, which of us has not, to avoid a little momentary embarrassment or annoyance, plunged headlong into a much greater? Who is there that has never postponed some troublesome but unavoidable call, or business, or work which had to be done within a certain time, till the day was past when it could be done with little trouble, and has had to do it in more difficult circumstances, in haste and hurry, with over-exertion and ill-humour, to the displeasure of those who were injured or wounded by the delay? Any one who knows himself, and keeps his eyes open to what is going on around him, will find this fact of the underestimate of future pleasures and pains exhibited under a thousand forms in the midst of our civilised society.

Of the fact, then, there is no doubt. Why it should be so is more difficult to say. The entire psychological relations, indeed, through which future feelings in general act on our judgments and our actions, are still very obscure, and it will be understood that the same obscurity covers the reasons why future feelings act with greater weakness on our judgments and actions than present feelings. Without meaning to forestall the pronouncement of the psychologists, who seem to me more competent to decide on both questions than the economists, I venture to think that this phenomenon rests, not on one ground, but on the joint action of no less than three different grounds.

The first ground seems to me to be the incompleteness of the imaginations we form to ourselves of our future wants. Whether it be that our power of representation and abstraction is not strong enough, or whether it be that we will not take the necessary trouble, the consideration we give our future and, particularly, our far-away future wants, is more or less imperfect. Naturally, then, all those wants which we have not considered remain without influence on the valuation of such goods as are destined to serve those future wants, and, consequently, the marginal utility of such goods is put too low.

While this first ground is very much a peculiar defect in estimate, the second seems to me to rest on a defect in will. I believe it frequently occurs that a man, called on to make choice between a present and a future pleasure or pain, decides for the present pleasure although he knows perfectly, and is even conscious while choosing, that his future loss will outweigh his present gain, and that, taking his welfare as a whole, the choice is unprofitable. How well many a 'good fellow' knows the painful embarrassments and privations he is bringing on himself, by running through his salary on the day he gets it, and yet has not the strength to resist the temptation of the moment! Or, how often does a man, 'from weakness', let himself be hurried into taking some step, or making some promise, which he knows at the moment he will rue before twenty-four hours are over! The cause of such defects in conduct, I say, appears to me, in distinction from the former case, to rest, not on want of knowledge, but on defect of will. I should not be surprised, however, if the psychologists were to explain this case also as only a variation of the former: it may be that the weaker feeling of the moment prevails over the stronger feeling of the future only because the latter, while present in consciousness in a general way, is not lively enough and strong enough to take possession of the mind. For our purpose, however, it is a matter of no consequence.

Finally, as third ground, I am inclined to name the consideration of the shortness and uncertainty of life. In the case of future goods, their *objective* acquisition may be practically certain, and yet it is possible that we may not live to acquire them. This makes their utility a matter of uncertainty for us, and causes us – in perfect analogy with the case of objectively uncertain goods – to make a deduction from their value corresponding to the degree of uncertainty. A utility of 100, as to which there is 50 per cent of probability that we shall not live to see it, we certainly do not value so highly as a present utility of 100; probably we value it as we do a present utility of 50; and I am convinced that any of us who was promised, today, a cheque for £10,000 on his hundredth birthday, would be glad to exchange this large, but somewhat uncertain gift, for a very small sum in present money! ...

Chapter IV: The technical superiority of present goods

There is still a third reason why present goods are, as a rule, worth more than future. The fact on which it is based has long been known in a general way, but its essential nature has been thoroughly misunderstood. Hidden in a perfect wilderness of mistakes, economists ever since Say and Lauderdale have been in the habit of going to it, under the name 'productivity of capital', for their explanation and justification of Interest. This name, which has already been the cause of so many errors, and which, besides, does not altogether correspond with what it is intended to convey, I shall lay on one side, and shall confine myself to the facts of the case –pure and simple. These facts are as follows: – that, as a rule, present goods are, on technical grounds, preferable instruments for the satisfaction of human want, and assure us, therefore, a higher marginal utility than future goods.

It is an elementary fact of experience that methods of production which take time are more productive. That is to say, given the same quantity of productive instruments, the lengthier the productive method employed the greater the quantity of products that can be obtained. In previous chapters we went very thoroughly into this, showed the reasons of it, and illustrated and confirmed it by many examples. I venture to think we may now assume it as proved. If, then, we take an amount of productive instruments available at a certain point of time as given, we have to represent the product, which may be turned out by increasingly lengthy processes, under the picture of a series increasing in a certain ratio, regular or irregular. Suppose that, in the year 1888, we have command of a definite quantity of productive instruments, say, thirty days of labour, we may, in terms of the above proposition, assume something like the following. The month's labour, employed in methods that give a return immediately, and are, therefore, very unremunerative, will yield only 100 units of product: employed in a one year's process, it yields 200 units but, of course, yields them only for the year 1889: employed in a two years' process it yields 280 units – for this year 1890 – and so on in increasing progression; say, 350 units for 1891, 400 for 1892, 440 for 1893, 470 for 1894, and 500 for 1895.

Compare with this what we may get from a similar quantity of productive instruments, namely, a month's labour, under the condition that we do not get possession of the labour till a year later. A month's labour which falls due in the year 1889 evidently yields nothing for the economic year 1888. If any result is to be got from it in the year 1889 it can only be by employing it in the most unremunerative (because immediate) production, and that result will be, as above, 100 units. In 1890 it is possible to have a return of 200 units by employing it in a one year's method of production; in 1891 to have 280 units by employing it in a two years' process, and so on. In exactly the same way, with a month's labour falling due two years later, in 1890, nothing can be had to satisfy the wants of the economic years 1888 and 1889, while 100 units may be got for 1890 by an unremunerative immediate, process, 200 for 1891, 280 for 1892, and so on. ... Whatever period of time we take as our standpoint of comparison, the earlier (present) amount of productive instruments is seen to be superior, technically, to the equally great later (future) amount.

But is it superior also in the height of its marginal utility and value? Certainly it is. For if, in every conceivable department of wants for the supply of which we may or shall employ it, it puts more means of satisfaction at our disposal, it must have a greater importance for our well-being. Of course I am aware that the greater amount need not always have the greater value – a bushel of corn in a year of famine may be worth more than two bushels after a rich harvest; a silver shilling before the discovery of America was worth more than five shillings are now. But for one and the same person, at one and the same point of time, the greater amount has always the greater value; whatever may be the absolute value of the bushel or the shilling, this much is certain, that, for me, two shillings or two bushels which I have today are worth more than one shilling or one bushel which I have today. And in our comparison of the value of a present and a future amount of productive instruments the case is exactly similar. Possibly the 470 units of product which may be made from a month's labour in 1889 for the year 1895, are worth less than the 350 units which may be got from the same for the year 1892, and the latter, notwithstanding their numbers, may be the most valuable product which can be made out of a month of 1889 in general. In any case the 400 units which a man can gain by a month's labour of the year 1888 for the year 1892 are still more valuable, and therefore the superiority of the earlier (present) amount of productive instruments – here and everywhere, however the illustration may be varied – remains confirmed.

The truth of the proposition, that the technical superiority of present to future means of production must also be associated with a superiority in value, may be made absolutely convincing by mathematical evidence if the tabular comparison, which we have drawn out to show the technical productiveness of different years of productive instruments, be extended to the marginal utility and value of the same. And since we have to deal here with a proposition which will form the chief pillar in my interest theory, I prefer to err on the side of making it too plain rather than risk not making it plain enough, and I shall spare no pains to prove it in the most complete way. In other respects, too, the trouble it costs us will not be altogether lost: as we proceed we shall get an occasional glimpse into certain relations which are seldom or never taken thought of, and yet, none the less, have some importance towards giving us a complete and thorough grasp of the whole.

The marginal utility and value of means of production depend, as we know, on the anticipated marginal utility and value of their product. But the means of production of which we have been speaking, the month's labour, may be invested in a production that yields an immediate return, or in a one, two, three, or ten years' period of production, and, according as it is so invested, we may obtain the very different product of 100, 200, 280, 350 units, and so on. Which of these products is to be our standard? The foregoing chapters have already given us the answer. In the case of goods which may be employed in different ways yielding different marginal utilities, it is the highest marginal utility that is the standard. Therefore, in our present case, it is that product which produces the greatest amount of value. But this need not coincide with the largest product, the product which contains the greatest number of units; on the contrary, it seldom or never coincides with that. We should obtain the greatest number of units by an infinitely long production process, or a process lasting a hundred or two hundred years. But goods which first come into possession in the lifetime of our grandchildren or great-grandchildren, have, in our valuation of today, little or no value.

In determining which, of various possible products, has the highest value for us, we are guided by the two considerations of which we have just spoken. First, we are guided by the anticipated position of our provision at the various periods of time. If, for instance, a man is ill provided for in the present, or not provided for at all, the unit of product in the present may, on that very account, have so high a marginal utility and value, that the sum of value of 100 present units of product is greater to him than that of 500 units which he might have at his command in 1895. To another man, again, whose present is as well provided for, or nearly as well provided for, as his future, the advantage in numbers may give an advantage in value to the 500 units. The second consideration by which we are guided is, that our present valuation of a future good or product does not depend on its true marginal utility, but on our *subjective* estimation of the marginal utility. But, in forming this subjective estimate, there takes place, as we have already seen, a kind of perspective diminution; a diminution which is in direct ratio with the futurity of the time to which the good in question belongs. The amount of which we are in search, therefore, the greatest sum of value, will evidently belong to that one, among the various possible products, the number of whose items, multiplied by the value of the unit of product (as that value shows itself with regard to the relation of want and provision for want in the particular economic period, and with regard to the diminution which future goods undergo from perspective), gives the greatest amount of value.

...

But if we were also to abstract the difference in the circumstances of provision in different periods of time, the situation would receive the stamp of extreme improbability, even of self-contradiction. If the value of the unit of product were to be the same in all periods of time, however remote, the most abundant product would, naturally, at the same time be the most valuable. But since the most abundant product is obtained by the most lengthy and roundabout methods of production – perhaps extending over decades of years – the economic centre of gravity, for all present means of production, would, on this assumption, be found at extremely remote periods of time – which is entirely contrary to all experience. And, besides, if such a state of things were to emerge at any particular point of time, it would immediately bring its own correction. For if every employment of goods for future periods is, not only technically, but economically, more remunerative than the employment of them for the present or near future, of course men would withdraw their stocks of goods, to a great extent, from the service of the present, and direct them to the more remunerative service of the future. But this would immediately cause an ebb-tide in the provision for the present, and a flood in the provision for the future, for the future would then have the double advantage of having a greater amount of productive instruments directed to its service, and those instruments employed in more fruitful methods of production. Thus the difference in the circumstances of provision, which might have disappeared for the moment, would recur of its own accord.

But it is just at this point that we get the best proof that the superiority in question is independent of differences in the circumstances of provision: so far from being obliged to borrow its strength and activity from any such difference, it is, on the contrary, able, if need be, to call forth this very difference. – Thus we get, as a result of our digression, the assured conviction of two things; first, that the productive superiority of present goods assures them, not only a surplus in product, but a surplus in value, and, second, that, in this superiority, we have to deal with a third cause of the surplus value, and one which is independent of any of the two already mentioned.

We have now to ask: To what extent is this third cause active? Of this our former analyses give a poor and inadequate picture. What has been said is only sufficient to explain how present means of production are worth more than future means of production. But, from the same cause, as we have now to show, present consumption goods also obtain a preference over future consumption goods, so that, in this third cause, we have a quite universally valid reason for present goods having a greater value than future.

The connection is as follows. Command over a sum of present consumption goods provides us with the means of subsistence during the current economic period. This leaves the means of production, which we may have at our disposal during this period (Labour, Uses of Land, Capital), free for the technically more productive service of the future, and gives us the more abundant product attainable by them in longer methods of production. On the other hand, command over a sum of future consumption goods leaves, of course, the present unprovided for, and, consequently, leaves us under the necessity of directing the means of production that are at our command in the present, wholly or partially, to the service of the present. But this involves curtailment of the production process, and, as a consequence, a diminished product. The difference of the two products is the advantage connected with the possession of present consumption goods.

To illustrate this by an example as simple as it is well-worn: imagine, with Roscher, a tribe of fisher-folk without capital, subsisting on fish left in pools on the shore by the ebb-tide and caught with the bare hand. Here a labourer may catch and eat three fish a day. If he had a boat and net he could catch 30 fish a day, instead of three. But he cannot have these tools, for their making would cost him a month's time and labour, and, in the meantime, he would have nothing to live upon. To save himself from starvation he must continue his wretched and costly fishing by hand. But now some one cleverer than the rest borrows 90 fish, promising, against the loan, to give back 180 fish after one month. With the borrowed fish he supports himself during a month, makes a boat and net, and, during the next month, catches 900 fish instead of 90. From this take, not only can he make the stipulated payment of 180 fish, but he retains a considerable net gain to himself, and thereby affords a striking proof that the 90 (present) fish he borrowed were worth to him, not only much more than the 90, but even more than the 180 (future) fish he paid for them.

Now, of course, the differences in value are not always so great as in this example. They are greatest among people who live from hand to mouth. For them to get command over present consumption goods means the transition to capitalist production. Less striking, but always present, is the difference where people already possess a certain stock of goods. If, for example, their stock of goods is sufficient for three years, they may realise their means of production in an average three years' production process. If, now, by some means or other, they obtain another year's supply of present means of subsistence, they may extend their average production period from three to four years, and obtain thereby an increment of product which, absolutely, is always important, but, relatively, will be much less than in the first case.

We can see that here, again, the matter of fact, on which I base my conclusions, is an old and well-known one: even in the time of Adam Smith and Turgot, it was notorious that the possession of present consumption goods confers certain advantages. But as the older theory of capital was, generally speaking, a nest of warped conceptions and incorrect explanations, this fact also was put down in a form as singular as it was inappropriate. Consumption goods – goods for immediate consumption – were looked on as productive goods or means of production; as such they were counted capital; and then all the advantages inherent in them were explained by the productivity of capital. Indeed, a writer of the standing of Jevons, simply through dwelling on the great importance which attaches to the command over present goods, was misled into ascribing to consumption goods the high position of being the only capital! In the face of such misinterpretations our business now is to get at the truth of facts. And the facts are very simple. Consumption goods are not means of production: they are, therefore, not capital; and the advantages which they confer do not proceed from any productive power they possess. Everything turns on the simple fact that, according to the quite familiar laws of value, present goods, in virtue of the above stated casuistical connection of circumstances, are, normally, the means of obtaining a higher marginal utility, and receive thereby a higher value, than future goods.

Chapter V: Co-operation of the three factors

To put together the results at which we have arrived thus far. We have seen that there are three factors, each of which, independently of the other, is adequate to account for a difference in value between present and future goods in favour of the former. These three factors are: The difference in the circumstances of provision between present and future; the underestimate, due to perspective, of future advantages and future goods; and, finally, the greater fruitfulness of lengthy methods of production. …

…

Here we come to our last duty in this book: to show how the ratio that obtains between present and future goods in subjective valuations is transferred to their objective exchange value.

In the case of the single individual, extremely various subjective valuations will be formed, according as the one or the other of the above-mentioned factors is stronger or weaker. These encounter each other on the market where present goods are exchanged against the future. There are many such markets and they take many different forms. In the next book we shall more exactly examine their constitution. In the meantime we must be content to examine the method in which prices are formed in its most general and typical outlines. Indeed the formation of price here takes the same course as it does elsewhere. The divergence of the subjective valuations which encounter each other on the market makes possible, economically, the exchange of property between the two parties. Those who, on any subjective grounds, put a relatively high value on present goods, appear as buyers of present against future commodities; those who put a relatively low value, as sellers: and the market price will be settled between the subjective valuations of the last competitors who actually exchange, and the first competitors who are shut out, or, as we have put it, between the valuations of the two marginal pairs. We may represent the position of the market by the following scheme:

Intending buyers	Present goods in units		Next year's goods in units	Intending sellers	Present goods in units		Next year's goods in units
A_1 values	100	=	300	B_1 values	100	=	99
A_2	100		200	B_2	100		100
A_3	100		150	B_3	100		101
A_4	100		120	B_4	100		102
A_5	100		110	B_5	100		103
A_6	100		108	B_6	100		105
A_7	100		107	B_7	100		106
A_8	100		106	B_8	100		107
A_9	100		104	B_9	100		108
A_{10}	100		102	B_{10}	100		110

In the circumstances of the market which this scheme represents, A_7 and B_7 form the upper marginal pair, A_8 and B_8 the lower. The market price for 100 present units of goods will be fixed between 106 and 107, say at 106 $1/2$ next year's units, and this determines an agio of 6 $1/2$% in favour of present goods.

Once a market price of this kind for present goods has been established, it exerts a reflex levelling influence on the subjective valuations which were originally so strongly divergent. Even those who, from personal circumstances, would value future goods only a little under, or perhaps at equal terms with, present goods, now value present goods according to the higher exchange value which the position of the market lends to them. This is the reason, and the only reason, why, in practical life, scarcely any one would be willing to exchange present goods against an exactly equal sum of future ones. There are plenty of people whose circumstances of want and provision for want are of such a kind, that the subjective *use* value of present and future goods to them stands almost equal. But the general position of the market is, almost invariably, so strongly in favour of present goods, that it assures them a preference in *exchange* value, of which, naturally, every one takes advantage.

Developed market exchange, however, brings with it a levelling effect from another side; that is to say, it brings the amount of agio in favour of present goods, as against future goods which fall due at variously remote points of time, into one normal ratio with the length of the elapsing time. It might easily be the case that the causes which tend to the undervaluation of future goods might chance to be quite disproportionately effective on goods belonging to different periods of time. Indeed, in the very nature of several of those causes (for instance, the consideration of the shortness of human life) they would scarcely obtain at all as against goods of the near future, while, as against goods of remote periods, they would obtain strongly and irregularly. In itself, therefore, it might be quite possible that, while 100 present units of goods, as against 100 units of next year's goods, obtained, in the market, an agio of 5 units only, as against goods of the next year they might obtain an agio of more than twice that, say 20, and, as against the third year's goods, perhaps an agio of 40. But such disproportionate prices for goods of different periods of remoteness could not long hold. By a kind of time arbitrage they would very soon be brought into an equal ratio. If, for instance, the various market prices mentioned above were found quoted at one given moment, speculators would immediately appear on the scene, who would sell present goods against two years' goods, cover the purchase by buying present against next year's goods, and arrange for paying the latter a year later by a second purchase of present against next year's goods. The business would work out thus. In 1888 the speculator buys 1000 present units for 1050 units of the year 1889, and sells them at the same time for 1200 of the year 1890. In 1889 he has to deliver 1050 units, and he gets them by buying, again with a agio of 5%, the then present (1889) goods for the then next year's (1890) goods. For the 1050 units he requires to deliver he must thus give 1102 1/2 units of 1890. But, from the first transaction, he then receives 1200 of these very (1890) units. He has thus, on the whole business, a utility of about 100 units. Such arbitrage transactions must evidently bring the prices obtainable for goods of various future years to a level. The speculative demand for the much undervalued two years' goods must raise their price; the supply of next year's goods must depress *their* price; till such time as the agio is brought directly into proportion with the length of the time. When this happens – say, for example, that the agio has become equalised at 5% *per year*, it may hold on at that rate undisturbed. For then it is equally remunerative to exchange present goods against next year's goods for three years successively, or to exchange present goods directly against three years' goods, and the arbitrage we have just sketched has no further occasion to interfere in the formation of price.

Thus we may accept the following as positive result of the present book.

The relation between want and provision for want in present and future, the undervaluation of future pleasures and pains, and the technical advantage residing in present goods, have the effect that, to the overwhelming majority of men, the subjective use value of present goods is higher than that of similar future goods. From this relation of subjective valuations there follows, in the market generally, a higher objective exchange value and market price for present goods, and this, reflecting back on present goods, gives them a higher subjective (exchange) value even among those whose personal circumstances happen to be such that the goods would not naturally have any preference in subjective use value. Finally, the levelling tendencies of the market bring the reduced value of future goods into a regular proportion to their remoteness in time. In the economic community, then, we find universally that future goods have a less value, both subjective and objective, corresponding to the degree of their remoteness in time.

Book VI: The source of interest

Chapter IX: Results

We have traced all kinds and methods of acquiring interest to one identical source – the increasing value of future goods as they ripen into present goods. Thus it is with the profit of the undertakers, who transform labour – the future good which they purchase – into products for consumption. Thus it is with landlords, property-owners, and owners of durable goods generally, who allow the later services of the goods they possess to gradually mature, and pluck them when they have ripened into full value. Thus, finally, it is with the loan. Even here it is not the case, as one might easily think at first sight, that the enrichment of the capitalist comes from the creditor receiving more articles than he gives – for at first, indeed, the articles concerned are less in value – but from the fact that the loaned objects, at first lower in value, gradually increase in value, and on the moment of fruition enter into their complete higher present value.

What, then, are the capitalists as regards the community? – In a word, they are merchants who have present goods to sell. They are the fortunate possessors of a stock of goods which they do not require for the personal needs of the moment. They exchange this stock, therefore, into future goods of some form or another, and allow these to ripen in their hands again into present goods possessing full value. Many capitalists make this exchange once for all. One who builds a house with his capital, or buys a piece of land, or acquires a bond, or gives a loan at interest for fifty years, exchanges his present goods, wholly or in part, for goods or services which belong to a remote period of time, and consequently creates, as it were at a blow, the opportunity or condition of a permanent increment of value, and an income called interest which will last over this long period. One, again, who discounts a three months' bill, or enters on a one year's production, must frequently repeat the exchange. In three months or in one year the future goods thus acquired become full-valued present goods. With these present goods the business begins over again; new bills are bought, new raw material, new labour; these in their turn ripen into present goods, and so on again and again.

In the circumstances, then, it is very easily explained why capital bears an 'everlasting' interest. We may dismiss any idea of an inexhaustible 'productive power' in capital, assuring it eternal fruitfulness, – any idea of an eternal 'Use' given off, year out year in, to the end of time by a good perhaps long perished. It is because the stock of present goods is always too low that the conjuncture for their exchange against future goods is always favourable. And it is because time always stretches forward that the prudently purchased future commodity steadily becomes a present commodity, grows accordingly into the full value of the present, and permits its owner again and again to utilise the always favourable conjuncture.

I do not see that there is anything objectionable in this. For natural reasons, present goods are certainly more valuable commodities than future goods. If the owner of the more valuable commodity exchange it for a greater quantity of the less valuable, there is nothing more objectionable in this than that the owner of wheat should exchange a peck of wheat for more than a peck of oats or barley, or that a holder of gold should exchange a pound of gold for more than a pound of iron or copper. For the owner not to realise the higher value of his commodity would be an act of unselfishness and charity which could not possibly be translated into a general duty, and as a fact would not be so translated in regard to any other commodity.

. . .

In making this calculation it will not be overlooked that the institution of interest has its manifold uses; particularly as the prospect of interest induces saving and accumulation of capital, and thus, by making possible the adoption of more fruitful methods of production, becomes the cause of a more abundant provision for the whole people. In this connection the much-used and much-abused expression, 'Reward of Abstinence', is in its proper place. The existence of interest cannot be theoretically *explained* by it: one cannot hope in using it to say anything about the essential nature of interest: every one knows how much interest is simply pocketed without any 'abstinence' that deserves reward. But, just as interest sometimes has its injurious accompaniments, so in its train it brings others, fortunately, that are beneficent and useful; and to these it is due that interest, which has its origin in quite different causes, acts, among other things, as a wage and as an inducement to save. I know very well that private saving is not the only possible way to the accumulation of capital, and that, even in the Socialist state, capital may be accumulated and added to. But the fact remains that private accumulation of capital is a proved fact, while socialist accumulation is not; – and there are, besides, some very serious a priori doubts whether it can be.

. . .

Book VII: The rate of interest

Chapter I: The rate in isolated exchange

The exchange of present goods for future, in which interest has its origin, is only a special case of the exchange of goods in general. It goes, then, without saying that the formation of price in this case is subject to the same laws as govern the formation of price in economical exchange generally. The question whether present goods in general obtain an agio, and also the further question of the height of that agio, are both to be answered according to the rules laid down in Book IV. as regards prices of goods in general. What remains for us here is only to amplify and vivify the colourless scheme which demonstrated that the current price of goods is the resultant of subjective valuations coming together in a market, by pointing out those concrete circumstances which in this case – the exchange of present against future commodities – influence the mutual valuation of both.

As before, it is advisable to distinguish between isolated exchange and competitive exchange.

In the exchange which takes place between an owner of a present commodity and a suitor for it, the price, according to the formula laid down on p. 199, will be fixed somewhere between the value of the present good to its owner as under limit, and its value to the suitor as upper limit. If, for instance, £100 present money are worth to their owner exactly as much as £100 of next year's money, while to the suitor they are worth, on subjective grounds (say, on account of temporarily pressing circumstances), as much as £200 of next year's money, the price of £100 present money will be fixed somewhere between £100 and £200 of next year's money, and the agio at something between nothing and 100 per cent. The precise figure that is fixed, in the individual case, within these wide limits, depends on the skill and 'staying power' displayed by both parties in conducting the negotiations. As a rule, the owner of present goods will be in a position of advantage, because he can do without the exchange and yet suffer no loss, while the suitor is often driven to pay any price for present goods. Hence the familiar cases where, in the absence of competition, usuriously high rates of 50, 100, even 200 and 300 per cent, are extorted.

When we go farther, and inquire as to the deeper reasons which affect the subjective valuation of the suitors and thus affect the economic upper limit of the agio, we find them a little different in the case of the consumption loan from what they are in the production loan, to which latter the buying of labour is closely allied.

In the case of the consumption loan the determinants are – the urgency of want at the time, the probable provision at the time when the loan is to be paid back, and, finally, the degree of the suitor's underestimate of the future. The more urgently he requires the loan, the more easily he expects to be able to replace it; and the less he takes thought for the morrow, the higher the agio to which he will, in the worst case, consent and vice versa.

In the production loan we find different concrete determinants. Here the important thing is the difference in productiveness between the methods open to him who gets the loan, and those open to him who has to do without it. To recur to our old illustration. If the fisher, who has no capital, and can catch only 3 fish a day by hand, gets a loan of 90 fish, and is thus put in a position to make a boat and net in the course of a month, and with these to catch 30 fish a day for the remaining 11 months, the balance stands as follows: – without the loan he catches in a year $3 \times 365 = 1095$ fish; with the loan he catches nothing in the first month, but 30 per day for the other 11 months, that is, $335 \times 30 = 10,050$, or a surplus of 8955 fish. So long, then, as he has to give anything less than 8955 (next year's) fish for the borrowed 90 (present) fish, he gains by the transaction.

In this illustration the difference in possible return between the two productive methods, and, with it, the upper limit of the economically possible agio, is absurdly high – 8955 next year's units for 90 present units is something like 10,000 per cent. But there will always be a very important difference when the choice lies between capitalist production and hand-to-mouth production, as the latter is, of course, always extremely unremunerative. The difference, again, will tend to grow less when the choice lies between two different capitalist methods; and will become more rapidly less in proportion to the length of the process already secured without the loan. This fact is of very great importance as regards the, rate of interest, not only in isolated, but also in competitive exchange. If we put it in the clearest possible way now, it will give a good basis for what comes later.

In an earlier chapter I called attention to the well-attested fact that the lengthening of the capitalist process always leads to extra returns, but that, beyond a certain point, these extra returns are of decreasing amount. Take again the case of fishing. If what we might call the one month's production process of making of a boat and net leads to the return of the day's labour being increased from 3 to 30, – that is by 27 fish, – it is scarcely likely that the lengthening of the process to two or three months will double or treble the return. Certainly the lengthening it to 100 months will not increase the surplus by a hundredfold. The surplus return – for there will always be a surplus return – will increase by a slower progression than the production period. We may, therefore, with approximate correctness represent the increasing productivity of extending production periods by the following typical scheme.

Production period without capital (years)	Return per annum £15	Surplus —
1	35	£20
2	45	10
3	53	8
4	58	5
5	62	4
6	65	3
7	67	2
8	68:10s.	1:10s.
9	69:10s.	1
10	70	0:10s.

It must be understood that I do not attach any importance to these particular figures. Everybody knows that, in every branch of production and at every stage of technical knowledge, the figures will differ. In one branch the fall of surplus return may be slower, in another it may be more rapid. All I lay stress on is the fact that the figures express the general tendency of surplus returns to fall. Assume, to complete the hypothesis, that a worker needs £30 a year to maintain him in suitable circumstances, and let us try to find out on this basis the limit of the economically possible agio which a suitor for productive credit may, in the worst case, offer for a loan of £30 a year.

If the suitor has no capital whatever, he can get a return of only £15 without the loan: with the loan, in a one year's production period he can get a return of £35. In the most extreme case he may therefore, without altering his position for the worse by the transaction, offer an agio of £20; that is 66²/₃ per cent. If, on the other hand, the suitor already has a capital of £30 (whence he gets it – whether it is his own or advanced from other quarters – does not affect the case), he can, without borrowing, engage in a one year's process and obtain a product of £35, and all that depends on his getting the loan is the extension of the process from one year to two, and the raising of the return from £35 to £45; that is, a yearly surplus of £10. Here, then, the suitor can economically offer, at the most, an agio of £10 on £30; that is, an interest rate of 33¹/₃ per cent. Similarly, if the suitor, by whatever means, is already equipped for a two years' process, the loan of £30 is now the cause of a surplus return of £8 (£53 − £45) = 26²/₃ per cent. Thus the more ample the suitor's equipment is already – the more capital he has – the lower fall the surplus returns and the ratio of agio dependent on the loan. That is to say, the surplus falls to £5, £4, £3, £2, 30s., 20s., 10s., and the rate to $16^2/3$, $13^1/3$, 10, $6^2/3$, 5, $3^1/3$, $1^2/3$ per cent. This fall is bound to emerge unless the returns obtainable in 1, 2, 3, 4, x production periods should run, not, as we have assumed, in the progression of 35, 45, 53, 58, 62, etc., but steadily in the much sharper progression of 35, 45, 55, 65, 75 ... 105 ... 1005, etc. In this latter case, on every one-year extension of the production period made possible by the £30, there would depend a constant surplus return of £10, and the upper limit of the economically possible agio would remain uniform at $33^1/3$%. But a ratio of increase like this cannot in any case go beyond a few stages in some few productions; it cannot go on permanently and without limit in any production.

We come, then, to the important proposition that to intending producers, generally speaking, a present loan has less value in proportion to the length of the production periods already provided for from other sources. The proposition directly applies to the rate of interest in isolated exchange, inasmuch as the valuation of the borrower for productive purposes directly gives the upper limit of the economically possible rate. It also allows us, however, to judge in what direction this proposition must influence the rate of interest in competitive exchange, where the price is the resultant of the subjective valuations of individuals, of whom many are intending producers.

As has been said above, the case of productive credit is closely related to the case of the purchase of labour, the employment of productive labourers by the capitalists themselves. Here, however, there enter certain complications which may be as easily and briefly stated under competitive exchange. I shall not, therefore, discuss them separately, but shall go on at once to explain the rate of interest in developed competitive exchange.

Chapter II: The rate in market transactions

The character of the market in which present goods are exchanged against future goods has already been described. We now know the people who appear in that market as buyers and sellers. We know that the supply of present goods is represented by the community's current stock of wealth – with certain unimportant exceptions – and that the demand for them comes (1) from the suitors for productive credit who wish to equip themselves for their own work in production, (2) from the suitors for wage-paid labour, and (3) from the suitors for consumption credit. To these three categories we may add, under certain reservations, the maintenance of the landowners. Finally, it will be remembered that the resultant market price must, as a rule, be in favour of present goods, and must lead to an agio on the same. What we have now to do is to group together the causes which determine the height of this agio in one adequate and typical picture.

If we were to attempt all at once to draw a picture like this, covering, as it does, the whole area of the varied influences that cross and intersect each other on the market, we should meet with great, indeed insuperable difficulties, in the way of statement. I shall, therefore, act on the principle, *divide et impera*, and first consider how the price is determined under the assumption that, confronting the supply of present goods, there is one single branch of demand, though, in present circumstances, by far the most important branch, namely the demand of the Wage-Earners. Once we have drawn in broad clear lines the most important and difficult part of the whole picture, it will be relatively easy to define the kind and measure of the share which all the remaining market factors have in forming the resultant, and so gradually to make the picture true to the full complexity of practical life. For good reasons I also retain provisionally the former assumption, that the whole supply and the whole demand for present goods meet in one single market embracing the entire community. And, finally, we shall suppose meanwhile that all branches of production show the same productiveness, and also the same increment of productiveness on each extension of the production period: that is to say, we shall assume an identical scale of surplus returns.

Suppose, then, that in our community the stock of wealth in the market, as supply, amounts to £1500,000,000, and that there are 10,000,000 of wage-earners. Following the scheme [above], the annual product of each worker increases in all branches of production, in proportion to the length of the production period) from £35 (in a one year's process) to £70 (in a ten years' process). The question is – in these circumstances of the market how high will rise the agio on present goods?

It is quite certain, as we have already explained, that the agio will settle at that level where supply and demand exactly balance each other, and this lies between the subjective valuations of the last pair who actually exchange. But the fixing of these valuations here encounters a quite exceptional difficulty, and one which does not occur in any other exchange transaction, but has its basis in a special peculiarity of the commodity 'labour'. Every other commodity, that is to say, has a predetermined subjective value to the one who wishes to buy it. Labour has not, and for this reason. It is valued according to its prospective product, while the prospective product varies according as that labour is invested in a short or in a long production process. We said above that, in the subjective circumstances of the capitalist, a sum of present goods was, as a rule, worth as much as the same sum of future goods. The capitalist will, therefore, count the value of labour equal to just as many present shillings as it will bring him in in the future. But, according as this labour is invested in a short or a roundabout process, it may bring him in £35 or £58 or £70. At which of these figures is the capitalist to value it?

It may be answered: According to the product aimed at in entering upon the method of production which is, economically, the most reasonable. He will, therefore, value the year's labour at £35 if, on reasonable grounds, he meditates adopting a one year's process; at £70 if he considers a ten years' period the most suitable. This would be very well if only it was certain beforehand what period was the most suitable for the undertaker. But this is not certain: on the contrary, the length of the process is itself dependent on the rate of wage fixed as resultant price on the labour market. If the wage, for instance, stands at £25, a one year's process is the most favourable for the undertaker. At £25 he gains £10 in the year – or, to put it exactly, in the six months, since, on the average, the advance extends over only six months; that is, 80 per cent per annum. In a ten years' process for the £25 in wages he gets £70, and the surplus return of £45 is, absolutely, much greater, but, when divided as profit over an average of five years' gives only £9 for one year, or a profit of 36 per cent. On the other hand, if the year's wage is £50, it is quite clear that it would be as absurd to choose a one year's process, with its product of £35, as it was most reasonable in the previous circumstances, and only those longer production periods which show an annual product over £50 could be thought of.

The matter, therefore, stands as follows. Elsewhere, in the case of other commodities, the employment for which the buyers wish to acquire them is already determined. It is the fixed point – the thing which first of all helps to determine the price offered by the buyers, and then through that the resultant market price. Here, in the case of the commodity Labour on the contrary, the employment is an undetermined amount, an x, which is first determined by the resultant price. In these circumstances it is clear that the fixed point of the price transactions must be got somewhat differently from the ordinary way; not, of course, according to different principles or laws, but with a certain casuistical modification in detail which we have now to examine.

In place of the fixed point, which is not available because the employment of the labour itself is not fixed, we find a substitute in the fact that another amount, usually indetermined, is here fixed, namely, the quantities sold. It may be taken as certain that all the labour offered, like the whole sum of present goods offered, finds a market. The certainty of this is based on a peculiar circumstance. Exactly as, in the science of money, it is a familiar dogma that, in the long-run, any sum of money, be it great or small, is sufficient to do the work of circulation in a community, so is it true that any sum of present goods, be it great or small, is sufficient to buy up the whole supply of wage labour that exists in the community, and to pay its wages. All that requires to be done is to contract or extend the production period. If there are ten million wage workers, and fifteen hundred millions of capital, this stock is just sufficient to pay the ten million workers £30 a year each over a ten years' production process. If there are only five hundred millions of capital no labourers need go idle on that account: only, of course, they cannot have their maintenance advanced them for a ten years' process, but (at the same wage of £30) only for a three and a third years' process, and the average duration of the production period must be curtailed accordingly. Suppose there are only fifty millions of capital, all the labour could still be bought, but now only for a four months' process, and it must be secured, by a further shortening of the production period, that the scanty amount of present goods is renewed after every short period by the accession of fresh returns.

It is, therefore, always *possible* for the existing stock of wealth to buy all the labour, and there are certain reasons in this case that work very strongly towards always making the possible into the actual. Between capitalists and labourers the economic conditions are – with very few exceptions – extremely favourable to the effecting of exchange. The labourers urgently need present goods, and cannot, or can scarcely turn their own labour to any account; they will, therefore, to a man rather sell their labour cheaply than not sell it at all. But very much the same is true of the capitalists. In their peculiar circumstances of want and provision for want, their present goods – which they, in any case, would lay up against the future – are not worth more to them than a similar sum of future goods. They will, therefore, prefer any purchase of labour where there is an agio, however little it may be, rather than let their capital lie dead; and the consequence is that all capital, like all labour, actually comes to a sale. As a fact we see that, in all economic communities, although the quantitative relations between wealth and number of wage-earners are extremely various, these two amounts exactly buy up each other. There are everywhere a few labourers who have no work, and a few capitals which are not employed, but this is, of course, not in contradiction to what has been said. I need scarcely point out that the presence of such unemployed is never traceable to the purchasing power of capital being insufficient to the whole number of the labourers – in a poorer country, indeed, a capital of half the amount would have to pay the same number of labourers, and actually does pay them – but always to certain frictional and temporary disturbances of organisation, such as are inevitable in a mechanism so complicated as the industrial division of labour in a great country.

We may, therefore, assume it as certain that the whole supply of labour, and the whole supply of present goods, come to mutual exchange. In this fact the length of the production period, and thus the amount of product which the undertaker may obtain through the labour he buys, obtains a certain definiteness. That is to say, we must, in any case, assume such a period of production that, during its continuance, the entire disposable fund of subsistence is required for, and is sufficient to pay for, the entire quantity of labour offering itself. If the period were to be shorter than this, some capital would remain unemployed; if longer, all the workers could not be provided for over the whole period; the result would always be a supply of unemployed economic elements urgently offering their services, and this could not fail to upset the offending arrangements

But we are not yet finished with the subject. It is not one single definite production period that harmonises with the above assumption, but a great many different periods. Obviously, given the capital and the number of workers, a very varying number of years can be provided for according as the wage of labour is high or low. With a capital of fifteen hundred millions for instance, our ten million workers can be kept in work and wage for ten years at a wage of £30, or for five years at a wage of £60, or for six years at a wage of £50. Now which of these possible cases will be the one actually adopted? – This will be determined, by the play of the same egoistic motives as regulate the formation of price in competition generally, in the following way.

Assume for a moment that the usual wage is £30. A capitalist then with £1000 – for convenience sake we shall take this amount as the unit throughout the following discussion – may employ either 66.6 labourers in a one year's process, or 33.3 labourers in a two years' process, or 22.2 in a three years' process. Naturally he will choose the process which he finds most advantageous. Which process that is will be seen from the Table I, based on the former scheme of productivity ..., showing how many workers can be employed by £1000 in each production period, and how much annual profit may be got from that sum.

Table I Wage £30

Production period in years	Annual product	Annual profit per labourer	Number of employed	Total annual profit on the £1000
1	£35 0	£5 0	66.66	£333.30
2	45 0	15 0	33.33	500
3	53 0	23 0	22.22	511.11
4	58 0	28 0	16.66	466.66
5	62 0	32 0	13.33	426.66
6	65 0	35 0	11.11	388.85
7	67 0	37 0	9.52	352.24
8	68 10	38 10	8.33	320.82
9	69 10	39 10	7.4	292.5
10	70 0	40 0	6.66	266.66

The table I shows that, in the given circumstances of all the factors, it is most profitable for the undertakers to devote themselves to a three years' production period. They obtain thereby the very considerable rate of 51.1 per cent, while both in the longer and in the shorter processes the profit is lower. In these circumstances naturally all undertakers will seek to adopt this length of process. But to what does this lead? In a three years' process £1000 can employ 22.2 workers, and therefore to employ all the available capital in the community (viz. £1500,000,000) 33 1/3 million workers would be needed – while there are only ten millions. These ten million workers could be employed by a sum of four and a half million pounds, leaving capital to the amount of ten and a half millions lying idle. Of course these ten and a half millions of capital could not and would not remain so: they would compete for employment; attract labourers by offering higher wages; and the necessary result would be a rise of the rate of wages. The £30 rate, then, assuming the above position of the factors, cannot possibly be a permanent one.
  Suppose now that the rate of wages is £60, we get the following table.

Table II Wage £60

Production period in years	Annual product	Annual profit per labourer	Number of employed	Total profit on the £1000
1	£35 0	£25 0	33.33	Loss
2	45 0	15 0	16.66	Loss
3	53 0	7 0	11.11	Loss
4	58 0	2 0	8.33	Loss
5	62 0	2 0	6.66	£13.33
6	65 0	5 0	5.55	27.77
7	67 0	7 0	4.76	33.33
8	68 10	8 10	4.16	35.41
9	69 10	9 10	3.70	35.15
10	70 0	10 0	3.33	33.33

This table proves that, if we assume £60 as the rate of wages, production in anything *less* than a five years' period shows a positive loss, while, of the longer periods, the eight years' process is the most profitable. It yields the modest interest of 3.54 per cent, but, relatively speaking, it is the most favourable rate that can be got. It is easy to see, however, that it is as impossible for a wage of £60, as it was for £30, to be the definite resultant price of labour. Under the assumed circumstances of productivity the eight years' period is the most profitable length of process at a £60 rate of wage. By adopting it a capital of £1000 can employ only 4.16 labourers; consequently the entire capital of £1500,000,000 can employ only six and a quarter million workers; and the remaining three and three-quarter millions must starve. This again is impossible; the unemployed will offer their services in competition with each other; and wages will be pressed below the rate of £60.

At what point, then, will this overbidding and under-bidding, which come from unemployed capital when wage is too low and from unemployed labour when wage is too high, come to an end? Obviously it will be when the most reasonable production period exactly absorbs the wage fund on the one side, and the labour offered on the other. This will be the case, as the following table shows, at a wage of £50.

Table III Wage £50

Production period in years	Annual product	Annual profit per labourer	Number of employed	Total profit on the £1000
1	£35 0	£15 0	40	Loss
2	45 0	5 0	20	Loss
3	53 0	3 0	13.33	£40
4	58 0	8 0	10	80
5	62 0	12 0	8	96
6	65 0	15 0	6.66	100
7	67 0	17 0	5.71	97.07
8	68 10	18 10	5	92.5
9	69 10	19 10	4.44	86.66
10	70 0	20 0	4	80

At a wage of £50 the six years' production period proves the most profitable. It gives an interest of 10 per cent on the invested capital, while a five years' process would return only 9.6 per cent, and a seven years', 9.7 per cent. Moreover, as at that wage the £1000 employs 6²/3 labourers, the entire ten million workers and the entire fifteen hundred millions of capital find employment; and the point is reached where the formation of price may come to rest. All who have it in their power to disturb the settlement by further over or under bidding have no inducement to do so, and all who might have an inducement have not the power, as, on economic grounds, they are already excluded from competition. There is no idle capital which might be tempted to seek employment by overbidding, and there are no idle labourers who might be tempted to seek employment by underbidding. And, finally, the undertakers who have placed their production on the footing which makes this favourable position of things possible are rewarded by this arrangement being at the same time the most profitable for them, and they too have no inducement to make any change. Those undertakers, on the other hand, who might have wished to engage in longer or shorter processes, and would thus have made either capital or labour insufficient, are excluded from any such disturbing competition by the fact that such methods of production show either a loss or a smaller profit.

The price of labour, then, will and must settle at a wage of £50, and this involves, at the same time, an agio of 10 per cent on present goods. I say, it *must* do so, for, so long as this point is not reached, there are certain tendencies always at work to force the price towards it. If, for example, the wage were only a little higher, say £51, the six years' process would still be the most profitable, but only 9,800,000 labourers could be employed by the available capital of £1500,000,000; the unemployed, by the urgency of their circumstances, would exert a pressure on the price of labour, till such time as they also could be taken in, which would be the case when wage came down to £50. If, on the contrary, the wage were a little lower; say £49, the employment of the ten million workers would take up only £1470,000,000 of capital; the unemployed remainder would attract employment through overbidding; and the result again would be a rise of wage till such time as the point was reached at which equilibrium all round could take place.

In the assumed state of all the factors an agio of 10 per cent is therefore the economically necessary result. Why exactly 10 per cent? – The considerations hitherto presented can only answer *negatively* that the necessary equilibrium could have been reached at no other rate of interest. But we may now inquire whether our figures do not bring out some other circumstances which may *positively* indicate a rate of 10 per cent, and give us matter for a precise positive law of the interest rate.

To arrive at a position of equilibrium, the capital of the community had to be taken out of shorter processes where full employment could not be found for the existing stock of labour, and employed in gradually extending methods till all the labourers were fully occupied. This was arrived at in the six years' process. On the other hand, the adoption of still longer processes, for which again the capital is *not* sufficient, had, economically, to be prevented. In these circumstances the six years' producers are the last buyers, the 'marginal buyers'; the would-be seven years' producers are the most capable excluded suitors for means of subsistence; and, according to our well-known law, the price that results must fall between the subjective valuations of these two. How does it stand with these valuations?

What we have to look to simply is: What is the utility which, for those two sets of buyers, depends on the disposal over a definite sum of means of subsistence? Here, first of all, it may be put down generally that, on the disposal over each half year's wage – in the present case, £25 – depends on one year's extension of the production period per worker. Accordingly, with respect to the six years' producers, it specially depends on their possession or non-possession of the £25 whether, as regards one labourer, they can embark on or continue in the six years' process instead of the shorter five years' process. But according to our scheme of productivity the year's return of one worker in a five years' process amounts to only £62, while in a six years' process it amounts to £65. What, therefore, as regards the marginal buyer, depends on his having the disposal over £25, is the obtaining of a yearly surplus product of £3. On the other hand, those would-be producers who are trying to take means of subsistence out of the market in order to extend the production period to a seventh year, could gain by their extension only a surplus return of £2 (£67 − £65). For them, therefore, all that depends on their disposal over the £25 is a surplus of £2, and they are excluded from competition inasmuch as the resultant price has established an agio which exceeds the rate of 2 on 25 (8 per cent).

If therefore – and this is indispensable to equilibrium being reached – the extension of the production period is to halt at the limit of six years, the agio established by the fixing of the price must lie between the rate that represents the valuation of the last buyers (£3 on £25, or 12 per cent) as upper limit, and the rate representing the valuation of the competitors first excluded (8 per cent) as lower limit. And thus our former empirical and circumstantial demonstration of the rate of wage and the rate of interest at which equilibrium may be reached on the market, *must* point provisionally to the rate of 10 per cent. It must at least point to the zone between 8 per cent and 12 per cent. The fact that, within this zone, the rate of 10 per cent is exactly brought out, is due, of course, not to the limitations indicated by the valuations of the marginal pair, but ... simply to the quantitative effect of supply and demand. We shall see immediately, however, that the wide latitude (8 to 12 per cent) which our abstract scheme leaves for the narrowing action of supply and demand, looks considerable only on account of the figures accidentally chosen; in practical life the latitude given is almost always vanishingly small.

Meanwhile we may put the results at which we have arrived in general form as follows:-

The rate of interest – on the assumptions already made – is limited and determined by the productiveness of the last extension of process economically permissible, and of the further extension economically not permissible; in this way that the unit of capital, which makes this extension of process possible, must always bear an amount of interest less than the surplus return of the first-named, and more than the surplus return of the last-named extension. Within these marginal limits the price may be more exactly determined by the quantitative relation between wage fund and number of workers, according to the law of supply and demand.

In practical life, however, the latter method of determining price is seldom taken. It is true that in our abstract scheme there was an unusually wide latitude to come and go on, because we had assumed a sudden decrease of the surplus return from £3 to £2; that is, a fall of fully one-half. But in practical life sudden differences like this scarcely ever occur. The figures which represent the productiveness of the last permissible, and the first non-permissible extension come usually very close to each other, and, consequently, they are sufficient to limit the variations of the interest rate so strictly and sharply that the theoretically more exact determination by means of the relation of supply and demand is practically unimportant. Indeed, assuming that these two marginal limits are very near each other, one of them may even be left out of account without any serious inaccuracy, and the law be simply formulated thus: the rate is determined by the surplus return of the last permissible extension of production. This coincides almost to a word with Thünen's celebrated law which makes the rate of interest depend on the productiveness of the 'last applied dose of capital'.

Chapter III: The rate in market transactions (continued)

...

We have, then, over the sphere of our investigations so far, to record three elements or factors which act as decisive determinants of the rate of interest: the Amount of the national subsistence fund, the Number of workers provided for by it, and the Degree of productivity in extending production periods. And the way in which these three factors affect the rate may be put as follows: In a community interest will be high in proportion as the national subsistence fund is low, as the number of labourers employed by the same is great, and as the surplus returns connected with any further extension of the production period continue high. Conversely, interest will be low the greater the subsistence fund, the fewer tire labourers, and the quicker the fall of the surplus returns.

This is the way in which the interest rate should be formed, and the way in which it should alter, if our theory is correct. How is it in actual life? – Exactly as our formula predicts, and thus experience gives that formula the most complete verification. For, first, it is one of the best accredited and recognised facts of economic history that the increase of the subsistence fund, or, to use an expression not quite so accurate but yet roughly significant, the increase of the community's capital, has a tendency to depress the rate of interest. Second, it is no less familiar and self-evident that here we do not speak of the absolute amount of the national capital, but of the relation between that capital and the numbers of the population: in other words, we mean that an increase of population, without a simultaneous increase of capital, has a tendency to raise the interest rate. And, thirdly, it is also an acknowledged empirical fact that the discovery of new and more productive methods of production, outlets, business opportunities, etc., which conduce to check the fall of surplus returns, tend to raise the rate of interest, while the closing of former opportunities of production or sale, or other occurrences which end in a reduction of the previous degree of productiveness, tend to lower the interest rate. We find, therefore, that all those factors to which, on the lines of our former inquiry, we were forced to ascribe a decisive influence on the interest rate, do, as a fact, possess and exert that influence.

...

Part 5

The Development of Macroeconomics

Introduction

For about a century, Say's Law was seen as effectively ruling out serious economic instability, business cycles, and problems of unemployment. Yet, it was increasingly and uneasily combined with empirical and theoretical studies of business cycles and unemployment. As Paul Samuelson put it in a different connection, Economics exhibited schizophrenia: preaching stability and studying instability. Hundreds, if not thousands, of books and articles were published dealing with economic instability and its accompaniments. The fields of business cycle theory and empirical business cycle research became, in the early twentieth century, increasingly important.

In part, the subject-matter derived from the historical record: crises and cycles; and economists endeavored to make sense of them. In part, too, the work of economists centered on how they modeled the macroeconomy, that is, the general levels of output and employment. Part of the record is the use of monetary theory, particularly the quantity theory of money, as either an approach or a major element in the approach formulated.

Say's Law was formulated in several different ways: that supply creates its own demand, that is, that payments to input owners constitute the purchasing power for output; that production is coextensive with total use; and that all income is spent, that is, what is not spent on consumption (and government, then a minor spending category) is also spent, on investment goods. The basic logic of Say's Law made intuitive sense: people supplied goods in order to acquire the purchasing power with which to buy other goods. But this logic – and a system of logic, not of empirics, it was – depended on several assumptions; in fact, in the nineteenth century economists identified these assumptions often for the purpose of making the system work, that is, to yield inferences of stable output and employment. The assumptions include these: (1) that money is only a medium of exchange, (2) that the interest rate equates saving and investment, (3) that the prices of goods and the factors of production are flexible, and (4) that wants are insatiable. If these conditions applied, the economy should be stable, that is, without business cycles.

But the assumptions need not apply and, perhaps, typically did not. (1) Money was a store of value, not only a medium of exchange; people could have a desire to hold on to money balances or to put them in portfolio investment, which did not necessarily lead to the real investment required by the theory. (2) The interest rate equated the demand and supply of money, not saving and investment. (3) Prices either were not or were not necessarily flexible. Inflexible prices meant markets did not clear, leading to instability. Also, economists could not agree when prices were and were not flexible. (4) Insatiable wants proved somewhat metaphysical; eventually the riddle was solved by asking, not whether wants were in fact insatiable – who knew what "insatiable" meant? – but would consumers buy goods under any and all conditions, and would real investors buy investment goods no matter what the expected rate of profit? Putting the matter that way, it became obvious that, for example, even if businesspersons could accumulate plant and equipment without limit, there were in fact limits, which meant that, in combination with the other findings, the logic of Say's Law broke down. In addition, it eventually became widely felt that Say's Law misconstrued the income mechanism, misconceived the problem with which it dealt, and was empirically wrong, this unless one assumed that *any* achieved level of income is *ipso facto* the full employment level – an assumption with problems of its own.

Of the hundreds of economists who worked on these problems, three are included in this collection: Knut Wicksell, Irving Fisher, and John Maynard Keynes. Each made important advances on classical macroeconomic thinking, and each did so in quite different ways – and with rather different policy implications, as the following readings demonstrate.

KNUT WICKSELL (1851–1926)

One major contributor to this macroeconomics literature at the turn of the century was the Swedish economist Knut Wicksell (1851–1926). Wicksell was born in Stockholm and educated in mathematics at the University of Uppsala. Roughly a decade later, in 1885, he began to travel on the continent studying economics, and, in 1895, he earned his doctorate from Uppsala and, subsequent to that, a degree in law. He taught at the University of Lund (Sweden) from 1899 to 1916. But Wicksell's interests went far beyond the academic; he was also a social and political radical. He was deeply influenced by the Malthusian theory of population and wrote in the popular press on issues of population and family planning, feminism, alcoholism, and the monarchy.

On the economics front, Wicksell was much more the pure theorist than what his reformist activities might lead one to think. He wrote on a number of topics, including public finance (his doctoral thesis was on taxation), price theory, marginal productivity theory, and so on. Wicksell's theory that only unanimity in the voting process could guarantee that policy measures were welfare-improving was a major impetus for the development of modern public choice theory in the hands of James Buchanan and Gordon Tullock.

But Wicksell's major contribution was his attempt to explicate economic instability on the basis of differences between the "natural" (return on new capital) and "market" (what banks charge) rates of interest, doing so with an emphasis on what another Swedish economist, Gunnar Myrdal, later called "cumulative causation." The basic idea was that if the market rate of interest was below the posited natural rate, increased investment would take place, leading to both growth that could not be maintained and inflation, and thereby to a more or less serious adjustment process. Conversely, if the market rate of interest was above the natural rate, investment, output, and income would fall, leading to an adjustment process of the opposite kind, a recession or depression. Here, Wicksell moved the debate beyond the simple quantity theory that linked the price level directly to the supply of money. The Stockholm School of Economics, which included Bertil Ohlin, Myrdal, and Erik Lindahl, developed from his work.

Wicksell's "The influence of the interest rate on prices," reprinted here, gives a concise statement of his theory of the relationship between price-level fluctuations and the rate of interest – Wicksell's signal contribution to economic theory.

References and further reading

Blaug, Mark, ed. (1992) *Knut Wicksell (1851–1926)*, Aldershot: Edward Elgar Publishing.
Gårlund, Torsten (1958) *The Life of Knut Wicksell*, translated by Nancy Adler, Stockholm: Almqvist & Wiksell.
Hennipman, P. (1982) "Wicksell and Pareto: Their Relationship in the Theory of Public Finance," *History of Political Economy* 14 (Spring): 37–64.
Humphrey, Thomas M. (1997) "Fisher and Wicksell on the Quantity Theory," *Federal Reserve Bank of Richmond Economic Quarterly* 83 (Fall): 71–90.

Patinkin, Don (1972) *Studies in Monetary Economics*, New York: Harper & Row.

Pivetti, Massimo (1987) "Wicksell's Theory of Capital," in John Eatwell, Murray Milgate, and Peter Newman (eds), *The New Palgrave: A Dictionary of Economics*, Vol. 4, London: Macmillan, 912–15.

Samuelson, P.A. (1987) "Wicksell and Neoclassical Economics," in John Eatwell, Murray Milgate, and Peter Newman (eds), *The New Palgrave: A Dictionary of Economics*, Vol. 4, London: Macmillan, 908–10.

Uhr, C.G. (1960) *Economic Doctrines of Knut Wicksell*, Berkeley, CA: University of California Press.

——(1987) "Wicksell, Johan Gustav Knut," in John Eatwell, Murray Milgate, and Peter Newman (eds), *The New Palgrave: A Dictionary of Economics*, Vol. 4, London: Macmillan, 901–8.

Wicksell, Knut (1893) *Value, Capital and Rent*, translated by S.H. Frowein, London: Allen & Unwin, 1954.

——(1898) *Interest and Prices: A Study of the Causes Regulating the Value of Money*, translated by R.F. Kahn, London: Macmillan, 1936.

——(1938) *Lectures on Political Economy*, 2 vols, translated by E. Classen and edited with an introduction by Lionel Robbins, London: Routledge.

——(1958) *Selected Papers on Economic Theory*, edited by Erik Lindahl, Cambridge, MA: Harvard University Press.

——(1997) *Selected Essays in Economics*, Vol. I, edited by Bo Sandelin, London: Routledge.

——(1999) *Selected Essays in Economics*, Vol. II, edited by Bo Sandelin, London: Routledge.

"The Influence of the Rate of Interest on Prices" (1907)*

The thesis which I humbly submit to criticism is this. If, other things remaining the same, the leading banks of the world were to lower their rate of interest, say 1 per cent below its ordinary level, and keep it so for some years, then the prices of all commodities would rise and rise and rise without any limit whatever; on the contrary, if the leading banks were to *raise* their rate of interest, say 1 per cent above its normal level, and keep it so for some years, then all prices would *fall* and fall and fall without any limit except Zero.

Now this proposition cannot be proved directly by experience, because the fact required in its hypothesis never happens.

The supposition was that the banks were to lower or raise their interest, *other things remaining the same*, but that, of course, the banks never do; why, indeed, should they? Other things remaining the same, the bank-rate is sure to remain the same too, or if, by any chance, for example, by mistake, it were altered, it would very soon come round to its proper level. My thesis is, therefore, only an abstract statement, and somebody, perhaps, will ask: what is the use of it then? But I venture to assert that it may be of very great use all the same. Everybody knows the statement of Newton that, if the attraction of the sun were suddenly to cease, then the planets would leave their orbits in the tangential direction; this, too, of course, is only an abstract proposition, because the solar attraction never ceases, but it is most useful nevertheless; indeed, it is the very corner-stone of celestial mechanics; and in the same way I believe that the thesis here propounded, if proved to be true, will turn out to be the corner-stone of the mechanics of prices, or rather one of its corner-stones, the influence of the supply of precious metals and of the demand for commodities from the gold-producing countries being the other.

Before going further, however, we must answer one more question. Our supposition might be not only unreal as to facts, but even logically impossible; and then, of course, its use would be *nil*. According to the general opinion among economists, the interest on money is regulated in the long run by the profit on capital, which in its turn is determined by the productivity and relative abundance of real capital, or, in the terms of modern political economy, by its *marginal productivity*. This remaining the same, as, indeed, by our supposition it is meant to do, would it be at all possible for the banks to keep the rate of interest either higher or lower than its normal level, prescribed by the simultaneous state of the average profit on capital?

This question deserves very careful consideration, and, in fact, its proper analysis will take us a long way towards solving the whole problem.

Interest on money and profit on capital are not the same thing, nor are they *immediately* connected with each other; if they were, they could not differ at all, or could only differ a certain

* A paper read before the Economic Section of the British Association, 1906. Published in: *The Economic Journal*, 17 (June 1907): 213–20.

amount at every time. There is no doubt *some* connecting link between them, but the proper nature and extent of this connection is not so very easy to define.

If we look only at credit transactions between individuals, without any interference of banks, the connection between interest and profit indeed seems obvious. If by investing your capital in some industrial enterprise you can get, after due allowance for risk, a profit of, say, 10 per cent, then, of course, you will not lend it at a much cheaper rate; and if the borrower has no recourse but to individuals in the same situation as you, he will not be able to get the money much cheaper than that.

But it is a very different thing with the modern forms of credit, which almost always imply the mediation of some bank or professional money-lender. The banks in their lending business are not only not limited by their own capital; they are not, at least not immediately, limited by any capital whatever; by concentrating in their hands almost all payments, they themselves create the money required, or, what is the same thing, they accelerate *ad libitum* the rapidity of the circulation of money. The sum borrowed to-day in order to buy commodities is placed by the seller of the goods on his account at the same bank or some other bank, and can be lent the very next day to some other person with the same effect. As the German author, Emil Struck, justly says in his well-known sketch of the English money market: in our days demand and supply of money have become about the same thing, the demand to a large extent creating its own supply.

In a *pure* system of credit, where all payments were made by transference in the bank-books, the banks would be able to grant at any moment any amount of loans at any, however diminutive, rate of interest.

But then, what becomes of the connecting link between interest and profit? In my opinion there is no such link, except precisely *the effect on prices*, which would be caused by their difference.

When interest is low in proportion to the existing rate of profit, and if, as I take it, *the prices thereby rise*, then, of course, trade will require more sovereigns and bank-notes, and therefore the sums lent will *not* all come back to the bank, but part of them will remain in the boxes and purses of the public; in consequence, the bank reserves will melt away while the amount of their liabilities very likely has increased, which will force them to raise their rate of interest.

The reverse of all this, of course, will take place when the rate of interest has accidentally become too high in proportion to the average profit on capital. So far, you will easily remark, my proposition is quite in accordance with well-known facts of the money market. If it be not true, if, on the contrary, as Thomas Tooke asserted, and even Ricardo in his earlier writings seems to have believed, a low rate of interest, by cheapening, as they put it, one of the elements of production, would lower prices, and a high rate of interest raise them – a most specious argument, resting, however, on the unwarrantable assumption that the remuneration of the other factors of production could, under such circumstances, remain the same – then the policy of banks must be the very reverse of what it really is; they would lower their rates when prices were getting high and reserves becoming low, they would raise them in the opposite case.

A more direct proof of my thesis is required, however, and might be given in some such way as this. If as a merchant I have sold my goods to the amount of £100 against a bill or promissory note of three months, and I get it discounted at once by a bank or a bill broker, the rate of discount being 4 per cent per annum, then in fact I have received a cash price for my goods amounting to £99. If, however, the bill is taken by the bank at 3 per cent, then the cash price of my goods have *ipso facto* risen, if only a quarter of 1 per cent; very likely not even that, because competition probably will force me to cede part of my extra profit to the buyer of the goods. In other cases, however, when long-term credit comes into play, the immediate rise of prices might be very much greater than that. If the rate of discount remains low, the interest on long loans is sure to go down too; building companies and railway companies will be able to raise money, say at 4 per cent instead of 5 per cent, and therefore, other things being the same, they can offer, and by competition will be more or less compelled to offer for wages and materials, anything up to 25 per cent *more* than before, 4 per cent on £125 being the same as 5 per cent on £100.

But, further – and this is the essential point to which I would call your special attention – the upward movement of prices, whether great or small in the first instance, *can never cease* so long as the rate of interest is kept lower than its normal rate, that is, the rate consistent with the then existing marginal productivity of real capital. When all commodities have risen in price, a *new level of prices* has formed itself which in its turn will serve as basis for all calculations for the future, and all contracts. Therefore, if the bank-rate now goes up to its normal height, the level of prices will not go down; it will simply remain where it is, there being no forces in action which could press it down; and, consequently, if the bank-rate *remains lower* than its normal height, a new impetus towards forcing up the prices will follow, and so on. The opposite of all this will take place when the rate of interest has become too high in proportion to average profit, and so in both cases a difference between the two rates remaining, the movement of prices can never cease, just as the electric current never ceases as long as the difference of tension between the poles remains.

The proposition that a low rate of interest will raise prices, a high rate of interest lower prices, is in some respects anything but new; it has been stated more than once, but a formidable objection was always triumphantly brought against it in the shape of statistical facts; indeed, if you consider the figures given, for example, by Sauerbeck in his well-known tables in the *Journal of the Statistical Society*, you will generally find that high prices do not correspond with a low rate of interest, and vice versa; it rather comes the opposite way, interest and prices very often rising and falling together. But this objection quite loses its importance; nay, more, it turns into a positive support of our theory, as soon as we fix our eyes on the relativity of the conception of interest on money, its necessary connection with profit on capital. The rate of interest is never high or low in itself, but only in relation to the profit which people can make with the money in their hands, and this, of course, varies. In good times, when trade is brisk, the rate of profit is high, and, what is of great consequence, is generally expected to remain High; in periods of depression it is low, and expected to remain low. The rate of interest on money follows, no doubt, the same course, but not at once, not of itself; it is, as it were, dragged after the rate of profit by the movement of prices and the consequent changes in the state of bank reserve, caused by the difference between the two rates. In the meantime this difference acts on prices in just the same way as would be the case if, according to our original supposition, profit on capital were to remain constant, and interest on money were to rise or fall spontaneously. In one word, the interest on money is, in reality, very often low when it seems to be high, and high when it seems to be low. This I believe to be the proper answer to the objection stated above, as far as the influence of credit on prices is regarded; occasionally, of course, as in times of wild speculation or panics, the problem is complicated very much by the action of other factors, which need not here be taken into consideration.

Granted, then, our theory to be true in the main or in the abstract, what will be its practical consequences? To what extent would the leading money institutions be able to regulate prices?

A single bank, of course, has no such power whatever; indeed, it cannot put its rates, whether much higher or much lower than prescribed by the state of the market; if it did, it would in the former case lose all profitable business; in the latter case its speedy insolvency would be the inevitable consequence.

Not even all the banks of a single country united could do it in the long run; a too high or too low rate would influence its balance of trade, and thereby cause an influx or reflux of gold in the well-known way, so as to force the banks to apply their rates to the state of the universal money market.

But supposing, as, indeed, we have done, that all the leading banks of the commercial world were to follow the same course, then gold could have no reason to go to one place more than to another, and so the action exercised on prices would have its sway without any hindrance from the international movement of money. Still, even then it would, under the present circumstances, have its obvious limits. As I remarked at the outset, the influence of credit or the rate of interest is only one of the factors acting on prices; the other is the volume of metallic money itself, especially, in our times, the supply of gold, and so long as the gold itself remains the standard of value, this factor evidently will take the lead in the long run. Were the production of gold materially to diminish while the demand for money be unaltered, the banks no doubt, by lowering their rate of interest, might for a while profitably react against the otherwise inevitable pressure on prices, but only for a while, because, even if the rather unnecessary stiffness of present bank legislations could be slackened, the ever-growing demand for gold for industrial purposes would gradually reduce the bank stores, and could only be checked by raising the price of gold – that is, by lowering the average money prices.

The other extreme, which at present seems much more likely to occur: a plethora of gold supply, and the rise of prices thereby caused, could not be effectually met in any way, so long as free coinage of gold exists.[1]

On the other hand, if this most essential step on the way to a rational monetary system should be taken, if the free coining of gold, like that of silver, should cease, and eventually the bank-note itself, or rather the unity in which the accounts of banks are kept, should become the standard of value, then, and not till then, the problem of keeping the value of money steady, the average level of money prices at a constant height, which evidently is to be regarded as the fundamental problem of monetary science, would be solvable theoretically and practically to any extent. And the means of solving it need not be sought in some more or less fantastic scheme like that of a central issuing bank for all the world, as it is sometimes proposed, but simply in a proper manipulation of general bank-rates, lowering them when prices are getting low, and raising them when prices are getting high.

Nor would this system be at all artificial, because the point about which the rate of interest would then oscillate, and to which it would constantly gravitate, would be precisely what I have called above its normal level, that one prescribed by the simultaneous state of the marginal productivity of real capital, the alterations of which we, of course, cannot control, but only have to comply with.

PS – When this paper was read at the British Association meeting it was objected by Mr Palgrave that the banks could not possibly be charged with the regulation of prices, their liberty of action – if I understood him right – being, in his view, restricted by the necessity of protecting their own reserves as well from getting too low in consequence of an unfavourable balance of trade, as from running to an unprofitable height by an influx of gold. This, no doubt, is true, but it must not be forgotten that the international rate policy of banks has, as it were, *two degrees of freedom*, in so far as the international movement of gold can be checked or modified, not only by raising the rate of discount in the country *from* which the metal flows, but also by lowering it in the country, or countries, *to* which gold is flowing. In other words, the action of the banks against each other, which has for its object the proper distribution of money, or the levelling of the *niveau* of prices between different countries, might logically be concomitant with a *common* action for the purpose of keeping the universal value of money and level of prices at a constant height, which, however, under present circumstances only can be done within the limits prescribed by the general supply of gold.

On the other hand, it was remarked by Professor Edgeworth that if the free coinage of gold be suppressed, the Governments themselves have in their hand the regulating of general prices. This, too, is true, at any rate so long as the present large production of gold persists; and even if it should cease, and gold become scarce, the Governments, no doubt, might supplant the lack in currency by a judicious emission of paper-money. But a single Government has in this respect only the choice between two alternatives: it may try to keep the value of its money steady *towards the commodities*, but then it necessarily sacrifices the parity of its exchanges; or else it may manage to keep its exchanges strictly at par, but then it has of itself no power over the level of prices. Some international agreement, either regarding the amount of gold to be coined by each country or else involving a common rate-policy of the banks as described above, must needs come into play, shall both those purposes – the steadiness of the average value of money and the parity of exchanges – be fulfilled together; and it seems to me, although I may be mistaken, that for several reasons such agreements could be far more easily and effectually made by the banks, with the support, that is, of the Governments, than by the Governments themselves exclusive of the banks.

For a more detailed analysis of the practical side of the question and of the whole argument, I must refer to my book, *Geldzins und Güterpreise* (Jena: Gustav Fischer, 1898; being the further development of an article in Conrad's *Jahrbücher*, Bd. 13, 1897), as well as to my printed *University Lectures* (Bd. 1:2, 1906, in Swedish).

Notes

1 It is not easy to describe or imagine the exact manner in which an excess or deficiency in the ordinary gold supply affects prices, although its ultimate effect on them cannot well be doubted. As in our days the new gold generally finds its way as soon as possible to the banks, the common impression seems to be that it by so much increases the loanable funds of the banks, and therefore in the first instance causes the rate of interest to go down. This, no doubt, would be true if the new gold in its totality were deposited by its owners as *capital* for lending purposes, and in so far as this may be the case it indeed affords an illustration, and the only practical one, of the lowering of bank rates effecting a rise of prices. But mostly, I suppose, the gold comes to us not as lending capital, but as payment for the imports of the gold-producing countries, and if so its acting on the prices will be much more immediate and its effect on the rate of interest very slight. It is even possible that the rise of prices, caused by the increased demand for commodities from the gold countries, will *forerun* the arriving of the gold, the necessary medium of exchange being in the meantime supplied by an extension of the credit, so that the rate of interest perhaps will rise from the beginning. In any case the *ultimate* effect of an increased gold supply will be a *rise*, not a fall, in the rate of interest (and vice versa with a lacking supply of gold), because the large mining enterprises and the buying up of gold by the non-producing countries have actually destroyed large amounts of real capital and thereby given the rate of profit a tendency to rise. This all maybe the explanation of some rather perplexing features in economic history, a rise of prices even when apparently caused by a surplus of gold supply very seldom being accompanied by a low rate of interest, but generally by a high one.

IRVING FISHER (1867–1947)

Irving Fisher, by courtesy of Manuscripts and Archives, Yale University Library.

Irving Fisher was a leading US economist for many years and is thought by some to be the greatest US economist prior to Paul Samuelson and was certainly the US's foremost monetary economist. Educated at Yale, Fisher originally taught mathematics there, but moved over to economics in 1895 following the publication of his thesis, *Mathematical Investigations into the Theory of Value and Prices* attracted wide attention for its original and insightful contributions. He spent the remainder of his career at Yale, writing extensively in economics (and monetary theory in particular) and also promoting various causes – including prohibition, the scientific approach to healthy living, eugenics, and world peace – in which he was a passionate believer. Fisher was, along with Ragnar Frisch and Charles F. Roos, a founder of the Econometric Society and served as its first president.

Fisher was a virtuoso developer of the quantity theory, which, in his model, included both currency and bank credit – a major innovation. If Say's Law held, then the quantity theory meant that any change in the money supply, M, likely affected only the price level, P, in the equation $P = MV/T$. With the economy stable at full employment, the velocity of the use of money, V, would likely not change, nor would the level of transactions, T (or output, O, in a different formulation of the theory). Thus, Fisher and other monetary economists attempted to combat empirical instability by tinkering, even reconstructing in a major way, the monetary, or money and banking, system. Fisher was particularly adroit at identifying or imagining monetary reforms which hopefully would stabilize the economic system. His other most important technical contributions included his theory of interest (quite in the tradition of Böhm-Bawerk); the theory and practice of index numbers; price theory; capital theory; and so on, including the mathematicization of economic theory.

He combined pure theory, statistics, and nonquantitative empirical and institutional studies, in a manner reminiscent of, but arguably more advanced than, Jevons.

The excerpts from *The Purchasing Power of Money* reprinted here give the reader a nice elaboration of Fisher's resurrection and refinement of the quantity theory and the associated equation of exchange.

References and further reading

Barber, William J. (1999) "Irving Fisher (1867–1947): Career Highlights and Formative Influences," in Hans-E. Loef and Hans G. Monissen (eds), *The Economics of Irving Fisher: Reviewing the Scientific Work of a Great Economist*, Aldershot: Edward Elgar Publishing.

Blaug, Mark *et al.* (1995) *The Quantity Theory of Money: From Locke to Keynes and Friedman*, Aldershot: Edward Elgar Publishing.

Dimand, Robert A. (1998) "Fisher and Veblen: Two Paths for American Economics," *Journal of the History of Economic Thought* 20 (December): 449–65.

Fellner, William *et al.* (1967) *Ten Economic Studies in the Tradition of Irving Fisher*, New York: John Wiley & Sons.

Fisher, Irving (1892) *Mathematical Investigations in the Theory of Value and Prices*, reprinted, New York: Augustus M. Kelley, 1961.

——(1906) *The Nature of Capital and Income*, New York: Macmillan.

——(1922) *The Making of Index Numbers*, Boston: Houghton Mifflin.

——(1930) *The Theory of Interest*, New York: Macmillan.

——(1997) *The Works of Irving Fisher*, edited by William J. Barber, consulting editor James Tobin, London: Pickering and Chatto.

Fisher, I.N. (1956) *My Father Irving Fisher*, New York: Comet Press.

Loef, Hans-E. and Monissen, Hans G., eds (1999) *The Economics of Irving Fisher: Reviewing the Scientific Work of a Great Economist*, Cheltenham: Edward Elgar Publishing.

Samuelson, Paul A. (1967) "Irving Fisher and the Theory of Capital," in William Fellner *et al.* (eds), *Ten Economic Studies in the Tradition of Irving Fisher*, New York: John Wiley & Sons.

Tobin, James (1987) "Fisher, Irving," in John Eatwell, Murray Milgate, and Peter Newman (eds), *The New Palgrave: A Dictionary of Economics*, Vol. 2, London: Macmillan, 369–76.

The Purchasing Power of Money and Its Determination and Relation to Credit Interest and Crises (1911)*

Chapter II: Purchasing power of money as related to the equation of exchange

1

We define money as *what is generally acceptable in exchange for goods*. The facility with which it may thus be exchanged, or its general acceptability, is its distinguishing characteristic. The general acceptability may be reënforced by law, the money thus becoming what is known as "legal tender"; but such reënforcement is not essential. All that is necessary in order that any good may be money is that general acceptability attach to it. On the frontier, without any legal sanction, money is sometimes gold dust or gold nuggets. In the Colony of Virginia it was tobacco. Among the Indians in New England it was wampum. "In German New Guinea the bent tusks of a boar are used as money. In California red birds' heads have been used in the same way." Stone money and shell money are so used in Melanesia. "In Burmah Chinese gambling counters are used as money. Guttapercha tokens issued by street car companies in South America are said to be used in the same way." Not many years ago in a town in New York state, similar tokens got into local circulation until their issue was forbidden by the United States government. In Mexico large cacao beans of relatively poor quality were used as money, and on the west coast of Africa little mats were used. The list could be extended indefinitely. But whatever the substance of such a commodity, it is general exchangeability which makes it money.

On the other hand, even what is made legal tender may, by general usage, be deprived of its practical character as money. During the Civil War the government attempted to circulate fifty-dollar notes, bearing interest at 7.3 per cent, so that the interest amounted to the very easily computed amount of a cent a day. The notes, however, failed to circulate. In spite of the attempt to make their exchange easy, people preferred to keep them for the sake of the interest. Money never bears interest except in the sense of creating convenience in the process of exchange. This convenience is the special service of money and offsets the apparent loss of interest involved in keeping it in one's pocket instead of investing.

There are various degrees of exchangeability which must be transcended before we arrive at real money. Of all kinds of goods, perhaps the *least* exchangeable is real estate. Only in case some person happens to be found who wants it, can a piece of real estate be traded. A mortgage on real estate is one degree more exchangeable. Yet, even a mortgage is less exchangeable than a well known and safe corporation security; and a corporation security is less exchangeable than a government bond. In fact persons not infrequently buy government bonds as merely temporary investments, intending

---

* *The Purchasing Power of Money and Its Determination and Relation to Credit Interest and Crises*, New York: Macmillan, 1911. Second revised edition 1922.

to sell them again as soon as permanent investments yielding better interest are obtainable. One degree more exchangeable than a government bond is a bill of exchange; one degree more exchangeable than a bill of exchange is a sight draft; while a check is almost as exchangeable as money itself. Yet, no one of these is really money for none of them is "*generally* acceptable."

If we confine our attention to present and normal conditions, and to those means of exchange which either are money or most nearly approximate it, we shall find that money itself belongs to a general class of property rights which we may call "currency" or "circulating media." Currency includes any type of property right which, whether generally acceptable or not, does actually, for its chief purpose and use, serve as a means of exchange.

Circulating media are of two chief classes: (1) money; (2) bank deposits, which will be treated fully in the next chapter. By means of checks, bank deposits serve as a means of payment in exchange for other goods. A check is the "certificate" or evidence of the transfer of bank deposits. It is acceptable to the payee only by his consent. It would not be generally accepted by strangers. Yet by checks, bank deposits even more than money do actually serve as a medium of exchange. Practically speaking, money and bank deposits subject to check are the only circulating media. If post-office orders and telegraphic transfer are to be included, they may be regarded as certificates of transfer of special deposits, the post office or telegraph company serving the purpose, for these special transactions, of a bank of deposit.

But while a bank deposit transferable by check is included as circulating media, it is not money. A bank *note*, on the other hand, is both circulating medium and money. Between these two lies the final line of distinction between what is money and what is not. True, the line is delicately drawn, especially when we come to such checks as cashier's checks or certified checks, for the latter are almost identical with bank notes. Each is a demand liability on a bank, and each confers on the holder the right to draw money. Yet, while a note is *generally* acceptable in exchange, a check is *specially* acceptable only, that is, only by the consent of the payee. Real money rights are what a payee accepts without question, because he is induced to do so either by "legal tender" laws or by a well-established custom.

Of real money there are two kinds: primary and fiduciary. Money is called "primary" if it is a commodity which has just as much value in some use other than money as it has in monetary use. Primary money has its full value independently of any other wealth. Fiduciary money, on the other hand, is money the value of which depends partly or wholly on the confidence that the owner can exchange it for other goods, for example, for primary money at a bank or government office, or at any rate for discharge of debts or purchase of goods of merchants. The chief example of primary money is gold coin; the chief example of fiduciary money is bank notes. The qualities of primary money which make for exchangeability are numerous. The most important are portability, durability, and divisibility. The chief quality of fiduciary money which makes it exchangeable is its redeemability in primary money, or else its imposed character of legal tender.

Bank notes and all other fiduciary money, as well as bank deposits, circulate by certificates often called "tokens." "Token coins" are included in this description. The value of these tokens, apart from the rights they convey, is small. Thus, the value of a silver dollar, as wealth, is only about 40 cents; that is all that the actual silver in it is worth. Its value as property, however, is 100 cents; for its holder has a legal right to use it in paying a debt to that amount, and a customary right to so use it in payment for goods. Likewise, the property value of a 50-cent piece, a quarter, a 10-cent piece, a 5-cent piece, or a 1-cent piece is considerably greater than its value as wealth. The value of a paper dollar as wealth – for instance, a silver certificate – is almost nothing. It is worth just its value as paper, and no more. But its value as property is a hundred cents, that is, the equivalent of one gold dollar. It represents to that extent a claim of the holder on the wealth of the community.

Figure 1 indicates the classification of all circulating media in the United States. It shows that the total amount of circulating media is about $8\frac{1}{2}$ billions, of which about 7 billions are bank deposits subject to check, and $1\frac{1}{2}$ billions, money; and that of this $1\frac{1}{2}$ billions of money, 1 billion is fiduciary money and only about $\frac{1}{2}$ a billion, primary money.

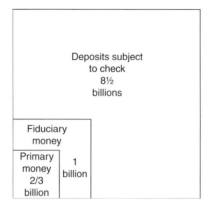

Figure 1

In the present chapter we shall exclude the consideration of bank deposits or check circulation and confine our attention to the circulation of money, primary and fiduciary. In the United States, the only primary money is gold coin. The fiduciary money includes (1) token coins, namely silver dollars, fractional silver, and minor coins ("nickels" and cents); (2) paper money, namely (a) certificates for gold and silver, and (b) promissory notes, whether of the United States government ("greenbacks"), or of the National banks.

Checks aside, we may classify exchanges into three groups: the exchange of goods against goods, or barter; the exchange of money against money, or *changing* money; and the exchange of money against goods, or *purchase and sale*. Only the last-named species of exchange makes up what we call the "circulation" of money. The circulation of money signifies, therefore, the aggregate amount of its transfers against goods. All money held for circulation, that is, all money, except what is in the banks and United States government's vaults, is called "money in circulation."

The chief object of this book is to explain the causes determining the purchasing power of money. The purchasing power of money is indicated by the quantities of other goods which a given quantity of money will buy. The lower we find the prices of goods, the larger the quantities that can be bought by a given amount of money, and therefore the higher the purchasing power of money. The higher we find the prices of goods, the smaller the quantities that can be bought by a given amount of money, and therefore the lower the purchasing power of money. In short, the purchasing power of money is the reciprocal of the level of prices; so that the study of the purchasing power of money is identical with the study of price levels.

2

Overlooking the influence of deposit currency, or checks, the price level may be said to depend on only three sets of causes: (1) the quantity of money in circulation; (2) its "efficiency" or velocity of circulation (or the average number of times a year money is exchanged for goods); and (3) the volume of trade (or amount of goods bought by money). The so-called "quantity theory,"[1] that is, that prices vary proportionately to money, has often been incorrectly formulated, but (overlooking checks) the theory is correct in the sense that the level of prices varies directly with the quantity of money in circulation, provided the velocity of circulation of that money and the volume of trade which it is obliged to perform are not changed.

The quantity theory has been one of the most bitterly contested theories in economics, largely because the recognition of its truth or falsity affected powerful interests in commerce and politics.

It has been maintained – and the assertion is scarcely an exaggeration – that the theorems of Euclid would be bitterly controverted if financial or political interests were involved.

The quantity theory has, unfortunately, been made the basis of arguments for unsound currency schemes. It has been invoked on behalf of irredeemable paper money and of national free coinage of silver at the ratio of 16 to 1. As a consequence, not a few "sound money men," believing that a theory used to support such vagaries must be wrong, and fearing the political effects of its propagation, have drifted into the position of opposing, not only the unsound propaganda, but also the sound principles by which its advocates sought to bolster it up. These attacks upon the quantity theory have been rendered easy by the imperfect comprehension of it on the part of those who have thus invoked it in a bad cause.

Personally, I believe that few mental attitudes are more pernicious, and in the end more disastrous, than those which would uphold sound practice by denying sound principles because some thinkers make unsound application of those principles. At any rate, in scientific study there is no choice but to find and state the unvarnished truth.

The quantity theory will be made more clear by the equation of exchange, which is now to be explained.

The equation of exchange is a statement, in mathematical form, of the total transactions effected in a certain period in a given community. It is obtained simply by adding together the equations of exchange for all individual transactions. Suppose, for instance, that a person buys 10 pounds of sugar at 7 cents per pound. This is an exchange transaction, in which 10 pounds of sugar have been regarded as equal to 70 cents, and this fact may be expressed thus: 70 cents = 10 pounds of sugar multiplied by 7 cents a pound. Every other sale and purchase may be expressed similarly, and by adding them all together we get the equation of exchange *for a certain period in a given community*. During this same period, however, the same money may serve, and usually does serve, for several transactions. For that reason the money side of the equation is of course greater than the total amount of money in circulation.

The equation of exchange relates to all the purchases made by money in a certain community during a certain time. We shall continue to ignore checks or any circulating medium not money. We shall also ignore foreign trade and thus restrict ourselves to trade within a hypothetical community. Later we shall reinclude these factors, proceeding by a series of approximations through successive hypothetical conditions to the actual conditions which prevail to-day. We must, of course, not forget that the conclusions expressed in each successive approximation are true solely on the particular hypothesis assumed.

The equation of exchange is simply the sum of the equations involved in all individual exchanges in a year. In each sale and purchase, the money and goods exchanged are *ipso facto* equivalent; for instance, the money paid for sugar is equivalent to the sugar bought. And in the grand total of all exchanges for a year, the total money paid is equal in value to the total value of the goods bought. The equation thus has a money side and a goods side. The money side is the total money paid, and may be considered as the product of the quantity of money multiplied by its rapidity of circulation. The goods side is made up of the products of quantities of goods exchanged multiplied by their respective prices.

The important magnitude, called the velocity of circulation, or rapidity of turnover, is simply the quotient obtained by dividing the total money payments for goods in the course of a year by the average amount of money in circulation by which those payments are effected. This velocity of circulation for an entire community is a sort of average of the rates of turnover of money for different persons. Each person has his own rate of turnover which he can readily calculate by dividing the amount of money he expends per year by the average amount he carries.

Let us begin with the money side. If the number of dollars in a country is 5,000,000, and their velocity of circulation is twenty times per year, then the total amount of money changing hands (for goods) per year is 5,000,000 times twenty, or $100,000,000. This is the *money* side of the equation of exchange.

Since the money side of the equation is $100,000,000, the *goods* side must be the same. For if $100,000,000 has been spent for goods in the course of the year, then $100,000,000 worth of goods must have been sold in that year. In order to avoid the necessity of writing out the quantities and prices of the innumerable varieties of goods which are actually exchanged, let us assume for the present that there are only three kinds of goods – bread, coal, and cloth; and that the sales are:

> 200,000,000 loaves of bread at $0.10 a loaf,
> 10,000,000 tons of coal at $5.00 a ton, and
> 30,000,000 yards of cloth at $1.00 a yard.

The value of these transactions is evidently $100,000,000, that is, $20,000,000 worth of bread plus $50,000,000 worth of coal plus $30,000,000 worth of cloth. The equation of exchange therefore (remember that the money side consisted of $5,000,000 exchanged 20 times) is as follows:

$$\$5,000,000 \times 20 \text{ times a year} = 200,000,000 \text{ loaves} \times \$0.10 \text{ a loaf}$$
$$+ 10,000,000 \text{ tons} \times \$5.00 \text{ a ton}$$
$$+ 30,000,000 \text{ yards} \times \$1.00 \text{ a yard.}$$

This equation contains on the money side two magnitudes, namely (1) the quantity of money and (2) its velocity of circulation; and on the goods side two *groups* of magnitudes in two columns, namely (1) the quantities of goods exchanged (loaves, tons, yards), and (2) the prices of these goods. The equation shows that these four sets of magnitudes are mutually related. Because this equation must be fulfilled, the prices must bear a relation to the three other sets of magnitudes, – quantity of money, rapidity of circulation, and quantities of goods exchanged. Consequently, these prices must, as a whole, vary proportionally with the quantity of money and with its velocity of circulation, and inversely with the quantities of goods exchanged.

Suppose, for instance, that the quantity of money were doubled, while its velocity of circulation and the quantities of goods exchanged remained the same. Then it would be quite impossible for prices to remain unchanged. The money side would now be $10,000,000 × 20 times a year or $200,000,000; whereas, if prices should not change, the goods would remain $100,000,000, and the equation would be violated. Since exchanges, individually and collectively, always involve an equivalent *quid pro quo*, the two sides *must* be equal. Not only must purchases and sales be equal in amount – since every article bought by one person is necessarily sold by another – but the total value of goods sold must equal the total amount of money exchanged. Therefore, under the given conditions, prices must change in such a way as to raise the goods side from $100,000,000 to $200,000,000. This doubling may be accomplished by an even or uneven rise in prices, but some sort of *a rise of prices there must be*. If the prices rise evenly, they will evidently all be exactly doubled, so that the equation will read:

$$\$10,000,000 \times 20 \text{ times a year} = 200,000,000 \text{ loaves} \times \$0.20 \text{ per loaf}$$
$$+ 10,000,000 \text{ tons} \times \$10.00 \text{ per ton}$$
$$+ 30,000,000 \text{ yards} \times \$2.00 \text{ per yard.}$$

If the prices rise unevenly, the doubling must evidently be brought about by compensation; if some prices rise by less than double, others must rise by enough more than double to exactly compensate.

But whether all prices increase uniformly, each being exactly doubled, or some prices increase more and some less (so as still to double the total money value of the goods purchased), the prices *are* doubled *on the average*. This proposition is usually expressed by saying that the "general level of prices" is raised twofold. From the mere fact, therefore, that the money spent for goods must equal the quantities of those goods multiplied by their prices, it follows that the level of prices must rise or fall according to changes in the quantity of money, *unless* there are changes in its velocity of circulation or in the quantities of goods exchanged.

If changes in the quantity of money affect prices, so will changes in the other factors – quantities of goods and velocity of circulation – affect prices, and in a very similar manner. Thus, a doubling in the velocity of circulation of money will double the level of prices, provided the quantity of money in circulation and the quantities of goods exchanged for money remain as before. The equation will become:

$$\$5,000,000 \times 40 \text{ times a year} = 200,000,000 \text{ loaves} \times \$0.20 \text{ a loaf}$$
$$+10,000,000 \text{ tons} \times \$10.00 \text{ a ton}$$
$$+30,000,000 \text{ yards} \times \$2.00 \text{ a yard},$$

or else the equation will assume a form in which some of the prices will more than double, and others less than double by enough to preserve the same total value of the sales.

Again, a doubling in the quantities of goods exchanged will not double, but halve, the height of the price level, *provided* the quantity of money and its velocity of circulation remain the same. Under these circumstances the equation will become:

$$\$5,000,000 \times 20 \text{ times a year} = 400,000,000 \text{ loaves} \times \$0.05 \text{ a loaf}$$
$$+20,000,000 \text{ tons} \times \$2.50 \text{ a ton}$$
$$+60,000,000 \text{ yards} \times \$0.50 \text{ a yard},$$

or else it will assume a form in which some of the prices are more than halved, and others less than halved, so as to preserve the equation.

Finally, if there is a simultaneous change in two or all of the three influences, that is, quantity of money, velocity of circulation, and quantities of goods exchanged, the price level will be a compound or resultant of these various influences. If, for example, the quantity of money is doubled, and its velocity of circulation is halved, while the quantity of goods exchanged remains constant, the price level will be undisturbed. Likewise, it will be undisturbed if the quantity of money is doubled and the quantity of goods is doubled, while the velocity of circulation remains the same. To double the quantity of money, therefore, is not always to double prices. We must distinctly recognize that the quantity of money is only one of three factors, all equally important in determining the price level.

3

The equation of exchange has now been expressed by an arithmetical illustration. It may be also represented visually, by a mechanical illustration. Such a representation is embodied in Figure 2. This represents a mechanical balance in equilibrium, the two sides of which symbolize, respectively, the money side and the goods side of the equation of exchange. The weight at the left, symbolized by a purse, represents the money in circulation; the "arm" or distance from the fulcrum at which this weight (purse) is hung represents the efficiency of this money, or its velocity of circulation. On the right side are three weights – bread, coal, and cloth, symbolized respectively by a loaf, a coal scuttle, and a roll of cloth. The arm, or distance of each from the fulcrum, represents its price. In order that the lever arms at the right may not be inordinately long, we have found it convenient to reduce the unit of measure of coal from tons to hundredweights, and that of cloth from yards to feet, and consequently to enlarge correspondingly the numbers of units (the measure of coal changing from 10,000,000 tons to 200,000,000 hundredweights, and that of the cloth from 30,000,000 yards to 90,000,000 feet). The price of coal in the new unit per hundredweight becomes 25 cents per hundredweight, and that of cloth in feet becomes 33 ⅓; cents per foot.

We all know that, when a balance is in equilibrium, the tendency to turn in one direction equals the tendency to turn in the other. Each weight produces on its side a tendency to turn,

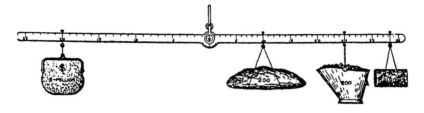

Figure 2

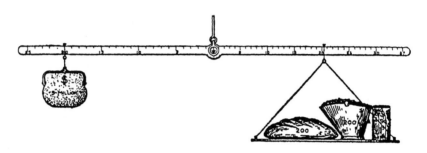

Figure 3

measured by the product of the weight by its arm. The weight on the left produces, on that side, a tendency measured by 5,000,000 × 20; while the weights on the right make a combined opposite tendency measured by 200,000,000 × 0.10 + 200,000,000 × 0.25 + 90,000,000 × 0.33⅓. The equality of these opposite tendencies represents the equation of exchange.

An increase in the weights or arms on one side requires, in order to preserve equilibrium, a proportional increase in the weights or arms on the other side. This simple and familiar principle, applied to the symbolism here adopted, means that if, for instance, the velocity of circulation (left arm) remains the same, and if the trade (weights at the right) remains the same, then any increase of the purse at the left will require a lengthening of one or more of the arms at the right, representing prices. If these prices increase uniformly, they will increase in the same ratio as the increase in money; if they do not increase uniformly, some will increase more and some less than this ratio, maintaining an average.

Likewise it is evident that if the arm at the left lengthens, and if the purse and the various weights on the right remain the same, there must be an increase in the arms at the right.

Again, if there is an increase in weights at the right, and if the left arm and the purse remain the same, there must "be a shortening of right arms."

In general, a change in one of the four sets of magnitudes must be accompanied by such a change or changes in one or more of the other three as shall maintain equilibrium.

As we are interested in the average change in prices rather than in the prices individually, we may simplify this mechanical representation by hanging all the right-hand weights at one average point, so that the arm shall represent the average prices. This arm is a "weighted average" of the three original arms, the weights being literally the weights hanging at the right.

This averaging of prices is represented in Figure 3, which visualizes the fact that the average price of goods (right arm) varies directly with the quantity of money (left weight), and directly with its velocity of circulation (left arm), and inversely with the volume of trade (right weight).

4

We now come to the strict algebraic statement of the equation of exchange. An algebraic state-ment is usually a good safeguard against loose reasoning; and loose reasoning is chiefly responsi-ble for the suspicion under which economic theories have frequently fallen. If it is worth while in geometry to demonstrate carefully, at the start, propositions which are almost self-evident, it is a hundredfold more worth while to demonstrate with care the propositions relating to price levels, which are less self-evident; which, indeed, while confidently assumed by many, are contemptu-ously rejected by others.

Let us denote the total circulation of money, that is, the amount of money expended for goods in a given community during a given year, by E (expenditure); and the average amount of money in circulation in the community during the year by M (money). M will be the simple arithmetical average of the amounts of money existing at successive instants separated from each other by equal intervals of time indefinitely small. If we divide the year's expenditures, E, by the average amount of money, M, we shall obtain what is called the average rate of turnover of money in its exchange for goods, E/M, that is, the velocity of circulation of money. This velocity may be denoted by V, so that $E/M=V$; then E may be expressed as MV. In words: the total circulation of money in the sense of money expended is equal to the total money in circulation multiplied by its velocity of circulation or turnover. E or MV, therefore, expresses the money side of the equation of exchange. Turning to the goods side of the equation, we have to deal with the prices of goods exchanged and quantities of goods exchanged. The average price of sale of any particular good, such as bread, purchased in the given community during the given year, may be represented by p (price); and the total quantity of it purchased, by Q (quantity); likewise the average price of another good (say coal) may be represented by p' and the total quantity of it exchanged, by Q'; the average price and the total quantity of a third good (say cloth) may be represented by p'' and Q'' respectively; and so on, for all other goods exchanged, however numerous. The equation of exchange may evidently be expressed as follows:[2]

$$MV = pQ + p'Q' + p''Q'' + \cdots$$

The right-hand side of this equation is the sum of terms of the form pQ – a price multiplied by a quantity bought. It is customary in mathematics to abbreviate such a sum of terms (all of which are of the same form) by using "Σ" as a symbol of summation. This symbol does not signify a *magnitude* as do the symbols M, V, p, Q, etc. It signifies merely the *operation* of addition and should be read "the sum of terms of the following type." The equation of exchange may therefore be written:

$$MV = \Sigma pq$$

That is, the magnitudes E, M, V, the p's and the Q's relate to the *entire* community and an *entire* year; but they are based on and related to corresponding magnitudes for the individual persons of which the community is composed and for the individual moments of time of which the year is composed.

The algebraic derivation of this equation is, of course, essentially the same as the arithmetical derivation previously given. It consists simply in *adding together the equations for all individual purchases within the community during the year.*

By means of this equation, $MV = \Sigma pq$, the three theorems set forth earlier in this chapter may be now expressed as follows:

1   If V and the Q's remain invariable while M varies in any ratio, the money side of the equa-tion will vary in the same ratio and therefore its equal, the goods side, must vary in that same ratio also; consequently, either the p's will all vary in that ratio or else some p's will vary more than in that ratio and others enough less to compensate and maintain the same average.

2   If M and the Q's remain invariable while V varies in any ratio, the money side of the equation will vary in the same ratio, and therefore its equal, the goods side, must vary in that ratio also; consequently, the p's will all vary in the same ratio or else some will vary more and others enough less to compensate.

3   If M and V remain invariable, the money side and the goods side will remain invariable; consequently, if the Q's all vary in a given ratio, either the p's must all vary in the inverse ratio or else some of them will vary more and others enough less to compensate.

We may, if we wish, further simplify the right side by writing it in the form PT where P is a weighted average of all the p's, and T is the sum of all the Q's. P then represents in one magnitude the level of prices, and T represents in one magnitude the volume of trade. This simplification is the algebraic interpretation of the mechanical illustration given in Figure 3, where all the goods, instead of being hung separately, as in Figure 2, were combined and hung at an average point representing their average price.

We have derived the equation of exchange, $MV = \Sigma pq$, by adding together, for the right side, the sums *expended* by different persons. But the same reasoning would have derived an equation of exchange by taking the sums *received* by different persons. The results of the two methods will harmonize if the community has no foreign trade; for, apart from foreign trade, what is expended by one person in the community is necessarily received by some other person in that community.

If we wish to extend the reasoning so as to apply to foreign trade, we shall have *two* equations of exchange, one based on money expended and the other on money *received* or accepted by members of the community. These will always be approximately equal and may or may not be exactly equal within a country according to the "balance of trade" between that country and others. The *right* side of the equation based on expenditures will include, in addition to the domestic quantities already represented there, the quantities of goods *imported* and their prices, but not those exported; while the reverse will be true of the equation based on receipts.

5

This completes our statement of the equation of exchange, except for the element of check payments, which is reserved for the next chapter. We have seen that the equation of exchange has as its ultimate basis the elementary equations of exchange pertaining to given persons and given moments, in other words, the equations pertaining to individual transactions. Such elementary equations mean that the money paid in any transaction is the equivalent of the goods bought at the price of sale. From this secure and obvious premise is derived the equation of exchange $MV = \Sigma pq$, each element in which is a sum or an average of the like elementary elements for different individuals and different moments, thus comprising all the purchases in the community during the year. Finally, from this equation we see that prices vary directly as M and V, and inversely as the Q's, provided in each case only one of these three sets of magnitudes varies, and the other two remain unchanged. Whether to change one of the three necessarily disturbs the others is a question reserved for a later chapter. Those who object to the equation of exchange as a mere truism are asked to defer judgment until they have read Chapter VIII.

To recapitulate, we find then that, under the conditions assumed, the price level varies (1) directly as the quantity of money in circulation (M), (2) directly as the velocity of its circulation (V), (3) inversely as the volume of trade done by it (T). The first of these three relations is worth emphasis. It constitutes the "quantity theory of money."

So important is this principle, and so bitterly contested has it been, that we shall illustrate it further. As already indicated, by "the quantity of money" is meant the number of dollars (or other given monetary units) in circulation. This number may be changed in several ways, of which the following three are most important. Their statement will serve to bring home to us the conclusions we have reached and to reveal the fundamental peculiarity of money on which they rest.

As a first illustration, let us suppose the government to double the *denominations* of all money; that is, let us suppose that what has been hitherto a half dollar is henceforth called a dollar, and that what has hitherto been a dollar is henceforth called two dollars. Evidently the number of "dollars" in circulation will then be doubled; and the price level, measured in terms of the new "dollars," will be double what it would otherwise be. Every one will pay out the *same coins* as though no such law were passed. But he will, in each case, be paying twice as many "dollars." For example, if $3 formerly had to be paid for a pair of shoes, the price of this same pair of shoes will now become $6. Thus, we see how the *nominal* quantity of money affects price levels.

A second illustration is found in a *debased currency*. Suppose a government cuts each dollar in two, coining the halves into new "dollars"; and, recalling all paper notes, replaces them with double the original number – two new notes for each old one of the same denomination. In short, suppose money not only to be *renamed*, as in the first illustration, but also *reissued*; prices in the debased coinage will again be doubled just as in the first illustration. The subdivision and recoinage is an immaterial circumstance, unless it be carried so far as to make counting difficult and thus to interfere with the *convenience* of money. Wherever a dollar had been paid before debasement, two dollars – that is, two of the old halves coined into two of the new dollars – will now be paid instead.

In the first illustration, the increase in quantity was simply nominal, being brought about by renaming coins. In the second illustration, besides renaming, the further fact of recoining is introduced. In the first case the number of actual pieces of money of each kind was unchanged, but their denominations were doubled. In the second case, the number of pieces is also doubled by splitting each coin and reminting it into two coins, each of the same nominal denomination as the original whole of which it is the half, and by similarly redoubling the paper money.

For a third illustration, suppose that, instead of doubling the number of dollars by splitting them in two and recoining the halves, the government *duplicates* each piece of money in existence and presents the duplicate to the possessor of the original. (We must in this case suppose, further, that there is some effectual bar to prevent the melting or exporting of money. Otherwise the quantity of money in circulation will not be doubled: much of the increase will escape.) If the quantity of money is thus doubled, prices will also be doubled just as truly as in the second illustration, in which there were exactly the same denominations. The only difference between the second and the third illustrations will be in the size and weight of the coins. The weights of the individual coins, instead of being reduced, will remain unchanged; but their number will be doubled. This doubling of coins must have the same effect as the 50 per cent debasement, that is, it must have the effect of doubling prices.

The force of the third illustration becomes even more evident if, in accordance with Ricardo's presentation, we pass back by means of a seigniorage from the third illustration to the second. That is, after duplicating all money, let the government abstract half of each coin, thereby reducing the weight to that of the debased coinage in the second illustration, and removing the only point of distinction between the two. This "seigniorage" abstracted will not affect the value of the coins, so long as their *number* remains unchanged.

In short, the quantity theory asserts that (provided velocity of circulation and volume of trade are unchanged) if we increase the number of dollars, whether by renaming coins, or by debasing coins, or by increasing coinage, or by any other means, prices will be increased in the same proportion. It is the number, and not the weight, that is essential. This fact needs great emphasis. It is a fact which differentiates money from all other goods and explains the peculiar manner in which its purchasing power is related to other goods. Sugar, for instance, has a specific desirability dependent on its quantity in pounds. Money has no such quality. The value of sugar depends on its *actual quantity*. If the quantity of sugar is changed from 1,000,000 pounds to 1,000,000 hundredweight, it does not follow that a hundredweight will have the value previously possessed by a pound. But if money in circulation is changed from 1,000,000 units of one weight to 1,000,000 units of another weight, the value of each unit will remain unchanged.

The quantity theory of money thus rests, ultimately, upon the fundamental peculiarity which money alone of all goods possesses – the fact that it has no power to satisfy human wants except a power *to purchase* things which do have such power.

Chapter VIII: Influence of quantity of money and other factors on purchasing power and on each other

1

The chief purpose of the foregoing chapters is to set forth the causes determining the purchasing power of money. This purchasing power has been studied as the effect of five, and only five, groups of causes. The five groups are money, deposits, their velocities of circulation, and the volume of trade. These and their effects, prices, we saw to be connected by an equation called the equation of exchange, $MV + M'V' = \Sigma pQ$. The five causes, in turn, we found to be themselves effects of antecedent causes lying entirely outside of the equation of exchange, as follows: the volume of trade will be increased, and therefore the price level correspondingly decreased by the differentiation of human wants; by diversification of industry; and by facilitation of transportation. The velocities of circulation will be increased, and therefore also the price level increased by improvident habits; by the use of book credit; and by rapid transportation. The quantity of money will be increased, and therefore the price level increased correspondingly by the import and minting of money, and, antecedently, by the mining of the money metal; by the introduction of another and initially cheaper money metal through bimetallism; and by the issue of bank notes and other paper money. The quantity of deposits will be increased, and therefore the price level increased by extension of the banking system and by the use of book credit. The reverse causes produce, of course, reverse effects.

Thus, behind the five sets of causes which alone affect the purchasing power of money, we find over a dozen antecedent causes. If we chose to pursue the inquiry to still remoter stages, the number of causes would be found to increase at each stage in much the same way as the number of one's ancestors increases with each generation into the past. In the last analysis myriads of factors play upon the purchasing power of money; but it would be neither feasible nor profitable to catalogue them. The value of our analysis consists rather in simplifying the problem by setting forth clearly the five proximate causes through which all others whatsoever must operate. At the close of our study, as at the beginning, stands forth the equation of exchange as the great determinant of the purchasing power of money. With its aid we see that normally the quantity of deposit currency varies directly with the quantity of money, and that therefore the introduction of deposits does not disturb the relations we found to hold true before. That is, it is still true that (1) prices vary directly as the quantity of money, provided the volume of trade and the velocities of circulation remain unchanged; (2) that prices vary directly as the velocities of circulation (if these velocities vary together), provided the quantity of money and the volume of trade remain unchanged; and (3) that prices vary inversely as the volume of trade, provided the quantity of money – and therefore deposits – and their velocities remain unchanged.

2

It is proposed in this chapter to inquire how far these propositions are really *causal* propositions. We shall study in detail the influence of each of the six magnitudes on each of the other five. This study will afford answers to the objections which have often been raised to the quantity theory of money.

To set forth all the facts and possibilities as to causation we need to study the effects of varying, one at a time, the various magnitudes in the equation of exchange. We shall in each case distinguish between the effects during transition periods and the ultimate or normal effects after the transition periods are finished. For simplicity we shall in each case consider the normal or ultimate effects first and afterward the abnormal or transitional effects.

Since almost all of the possible effects of changes in the elements of the equation of exchange have been already set forth in previous chapters, our task in this chapter is chiefly one of review and rearrangement.

Our first question therefore is: given (say) a doubling of the quantity of money in circulation (M), what are the normal or ultimate effects on the other magnitudes in the equation of exchange, namely: M', V, V', the p's and the Q's?

We have seen, in Chapter III, that normally the effect of doubling money in circulation (M) is to double deposits (M') because under any given conditions of industry and civilization deposits tend to hold a fixed or normal ratio to money in circulation. Hence, the ultimate effect of a doubling in M is the same as that of doubling both M and M'. We propose next to show that this doubling of M and M' does not normally change V, V', or the Q's, but only the p's. The equation of exchange of itself does not affirm or deny these propositions.

For aught the equation of exchange itself tells us, the quantities of money and deposits might even vary inversely as their respective velocities of circulation. Were this true, an increase in the quantity of money would exhaust all its effects in reducing the velocity of circulation, and could not produce any effect on prices. If the opponents of the "quantity theory" could establish such a relationship, they would have proven their case despite the equation of exchange. But they have not even attempted to prove such a proposition. As a matter of fact, the velocities of circulation of money and of deposits depend, as we have seen, on technical conditions and bear no discoverable relation to the quantity of money in circulation. Velocity of circulation is the average rate of "turnover," and depends on countless individual rates of turnover. These, as we have seen, depend on individual habits. Each person regulates his turnover to suit his convenience. A given rate of turnover for any person implies a given time of turnover – that is, an average length of time a dollar remains in his hands. He adjusts this time of turnover by adjusting his average quantity of pocket money, or till money, to suit his expenditures. He will try to avoid carrying too little lest, on occasion, he be unduly embarrassed; and on the other hand, to avoid encumbrance, waste of interest, and risk of robbery, he will avoid carrying too much. Each man's adjustment is, of course, somewhat rough, and dependent largely on the accident of the moment; but, in the long run and for a large number of people, the average rate of turnover, or what amounts to the same thing, the average time money remains in the same hands, will be very closely determined. It will depend on density of population, commercial customs, rapidity of transport, and other technical conditions, but not on the quantity of money and deposits nor on the price level. These may change without any effect on velocity. If the quantities of money and deposits are doubled, there is nothing, so far as velocity of circulation is concerned, to prevent the price level from doubling. On the contrary, doubling money, deposits, and prices would necessarily leave velocity quite unchanged. Each individual would need to spend more money for the same goods, and to keep more on hand. The ratio of money expended to money on hand would not vary. If the number of dollars in circulation and in deposit should be doubled and a dollar should come to have only half its former purchasing power, the change would imply merely that twice as many dollars as before were expended by each person and twice as many kept on hand. The ratio of expenditure to stock on hand would be unaffected.

If it be objected that this *assumes* that with the doubling in M and M' there would be also a doubling of prices, we may meet the objection by putting the argument in a slightly different form. Suppose, for a moment, that a doubling in the currency in circulation should not at once raise prices, but should halve the velocities instead; such a result would evidently upset for each individual the adjustment which he had made of cash on hand. Prices being unchanged, he now has double the amount of money and deposits which his convenience had taught him to keep on hand. He will then try to get rid of the surplus money and deposits by buying goods. But as somebody else must be found to take the money off his hands, its mere transfer will not diminish the amount in the community. It will simply increase somebody else's surplus. Everybody has money on his hands beyond what experience and convenience have shown to be necessary. Everybody will want to exchange this relatively useless extra money for goods, and the desire to do so must surely drive up the price of goods. No one can deny that the effect of every one's desiring to spend more money will be to raise prices. Obviously this tendency will continue until there is found another adjustment of quantities to expenditures, and the V's are the same as originally. That is, if there is no change in the quantities sold (the Q's), the only possible effect of doubling M and M' will be a doubling of the p's, for we have just seen that the V's cannot be permanently reduced without causing people to have surplus money and deposits, and there cannot be surplus money and deposits without a desire to spend it, and there cannot be a desire to spend it without a rise in prices. In short, the only way to get rid of a plethora of money is to raise prices to correspond.

So far as the surplus deposits are concerned, there might seem to be a way of getting rid of them by canceling bank loans, but this would reduce the normal ratio which M' bears to M, which we have seen tends to be maintained.

We come back to the conclusion that the velocity of circulation either of money or deposits is independent of the quantity of money or of deposits. No reason has been, or, so far as is apparent, can be assigned, to show why the velocity of circulation of money, or deposits, should be different, when the quantity of money, or deposits, is great, from what it is when the quantity is small.

There still remains one seeming way of escape from the conclusion that the sole effect of an increase in the quantity of money in circulation will be to increase prices. It may be claimed – in fact it has been claimed – that such an increase results in an increased volume of trade. We now proceed to show that (except during transition periods) the volume of trade, like the velocity of circulation of money, is independent of the quantity of money. An inflation of the currency cannot increase the product of farms and factories, nor the speed of freight trains or ships. The stream of business depends on natural resources and technical conditions, not on the quantity of money. The whole machinery of production, transportation, and sale is a matter of physical capacities and technique, none of which depend on the quantity of money. The only way in which the quantities of trade appear to be affected by the quantity of money is by influencing trades accessory to the creation of money and to the money metal. An increase of gold money will, as has been noted, bring with it an increase in the trade in gold objects. It will also bring about an increase in the sales of gold mining machinery, in gold miners' services, in assaying apparatus and labor. These changes may entail changes in associated trades. Thus, if more gold ornaments are sold, fewer silver ornaments and diamonds may be sold. Again the issue of paper money may affect the paper and printing trades, the employment of bank and government clerks, etc. In fact, there is no end to the minute changes in the Q's which the changes mentioned, and others, might bring about. But from a practical or statistical point of view they amount to nothing, for they could not add to nor subtract one-tenth of 1 per cent from the general aggregate of trade. Only a very few Q's would be appreciably affected, and those few very insignificant. Probably no one will deny this, but some objectors might claim that, though technique of production and trade determine most of these things, nevertheless the Q's – the actual quantities of goods *exchanged for money and deposit currency* – might conceivably vary according as barter is or is not resorted to. If barter were as convenient as sale-and-purchase, this contention would have force. There would then be little need of distinguishing between money as the generally acceptable medium of exchange and other property as not generally acceptable. If all property were equally acceptable, all property would be equally money; or if there were many kinds of property nearly as exchangeable as money, resort to barter would be so easy that some of the goods sold for money could be almost equally well bartered for something else. But as long as there were any preference at all for the use of money, resort to barter would be reluctantly made and as a temporary expedient only. We have seen this when studying transition periods. Under normal conditions and in the long run only a negligible fraction of modern trade can be done through barter. We conclude, therefore, that a change in the quantity of money will not appreciably affect the quantities of goods sold for money.

Since, then, a doubling in the quantity of money: (1) will normally double deposits subject to check in the same ratio, and (2) will not appreciably affect either the velocity of circulation of money or of deposits or the volume of trade, it follows necessarily and mathematically that the level of prices must double. While, therefore, the equation of exchange, of itself, asserts no causal relations between quantity of money and price level, any more than it asserts a causal relation between any other two factors, yet, when we take into account conditions known quite apart from that equation, namely that a change in M produces a proportional change in M', and no changes in V, V', or the Q's, there is no possible escape from the conclusion that a change in the quantity of money (M) must normally cause a proportional change in the price level (the p's).

One of the objectors to the quantity theory attempts to dispose of the equation of exchange as stated by Newcomb, by calling it a mere truism. While the equation of exchange is, if we choose, a mere "truism," based on the equivalence, in all purchases, of the money or checks expended, on the one hand, and what they buy, on the other, yet in view of supplementary knowledge as to the relation of M to M', and the non-relation of M to V, V', and the Q's, this equation is the means of demonstrating the fact that normally the p's vary directly as M, that is, demonstrating the quantity theory. "Truisms" should never be neglected. The greatest generalizations of physical science, such as that forces are proportional to mass and acceleration, are truisms, but, when duly supplemented by specific data, these truisms are the most fruitful sources of useful mechanical knowledge. To throw away contemptuously the equation of exchange because it is so obviously true is to neglect the chance to formulate for economic science some of the most important and exact laws of which it is capable.

We may now restate, then, in what causal sense the quantity theory is true. It is true in the sense that one of *the normal effects of an increase in the quantity of money is an exactly proportional increase in the general level of prices.*

To deny this conclusion requires a denial of one or more of the following premises upon which it rests:

1   The equation of exchange, $MV + M'V' = \Sigma pQ$.
2   An increase of M normally causes a proportional increase of M'.
3   An increase of M does not normally affect V, V', or the Q's.

If these three premises be granted, the conclusion must be granted. If any of the premises be denied, the objector must show wherein the fallacy lies. Premise (1) has been justified in Chapters II and III, and mathematically demonstrated in the Appendices to Chapters II and III. Premise (2) has been shown to be true in Chapter III and premise (3) in the present chapter.

So much pains has been taken to establish these premises and to emphasize the results of the reasoning based on them because it seems nothing less than a scandal in Economic Science that there should be any ground for dispute on so fundamental a proposition.

The quantity theory as thus stated does not claim that while money is increased in quantity, *other* causes may not affect M', V, V', and the Q's, and thus aggravate or neutralize the effect of M on the p's. But these are not the effects of M on the p's. So far as M *by itself* is concerned, its effect on the p's is strictly proportional.

The importance and reality of this proposition are not diminished in the least by the fact that these other causes do not historically remain quiescent and allow the effect on the *p*'s of an increase in *M* to be seen alone. The effects of *M* are blended with the effects of changes in the other factors in the equation of exchange just as the effects of gravity upon a falling body are blended with the effects of the resistance of the atmosphere.

Finally, it should be noted that, in accordance with principles previously explained, no great increase of money (*M*) in any one country or locality can occur without spreading to other countries or localities. As soon as local prices have risen enough to make it profitable to sell at the high prices in that place and buy at the low prices elsewhere, money will be exported. The production of gold in Colorado and Alaska first results in higher prices in Colorado and Alaska, then in sending gold to other sections of the United States, then in higher prices throughout the United States, then in export abroad, and finally in higher prices throughout the gold-using world.

3

We have emphasized the fact that the strictly proportional effect on prices of an increase in *M* is only the *normal* or *ultimate* effect after transition periods are over. The proposition that prices vary with money holds true only in comparing two imaginary periods for each of which prices are stationary or are moving alike upward or downward and at the same rate.

As to the periods of transition, we have seen that an increase in *M* produces effects not only on the *p*'s, but on all the magnitudes in the equation of exchange. We saw in Chapter IV on transition periods that it increases *M'* not only in its normal ratio to *M*, but often, temporarily, beyond that ratio. We saw that it also quickened *V* and *V'* temporarily.

As previously noted, while *V* and *V'* usually move in sympathy, they may move in opposite directions when a panic decreases confidence in bank deposits. Then people pay out deposits as rapidly as possible and money as slowly as possible – the last-named tendency being called hoarding.

We saw also that an increase of *M* during a period of rising prices stimulated the *Q*'s. Finally, we saw that a reduction in *M* caused the reverse effects of those above set forth, decreasing *V* and *V'*, decreasing *M'* not absolutely only, but in relation to *M*, and decreasing the *Q*'s partly because of the disinclination to sell at low money prices which are believed to be but temporary, partly because of a slight substitution of barter for sales; for if *M* should be very suddenly reduced, some way would have to be found to keep trade going, and barter would be temporarily resorted to in spite of its inconvenience. This would bring some relief, but its inconvenience would lead sellers to demand money whenever possible, and prospective buyers to supply themselves therewith. The great pressure to secure money would enhance its value – that is, would lower the prices of other things. This resultant fall of prices would make the currency more adequate to do the business required, and make less barter necessary. The fall would proceed until the abnormal pressure, due to the inconvenience of barter, had ceased. Practically, however, in the world of to-day, even such temporary resort to barter is trifling. The convenience of exchange by money is so much greater than the convenience of barter, that the price adjustment would be made almost at once. If barter needs to be seriously considered as a relief from money stringency, we shall be doing it full justice if we picture it as a safety-valve, working against a resistance so great as almost never to come into operation and then only for brief transition intervals. For all practical purposes and all normal cases, we may assume that money and checks are necessities for modern trade.

The peculiar effects during transition periods are analogous to the peculiar effects in starting or stopping a train of cars. Normally the caboose keeps exact pace with the locomotive, but when the train is starting or stopping this relationship is modified by the gradual transmission of effects through the intervening cars. Any special shock to one car is similarly transmitted to all the others and to the locomotive.

We have seen, for instance, that a sudden change in the quantity of money and deposits will temporarily affect their velocities of circulation and the volume of trade. Reversely, seasonal changes in the volume of trade will affect the velocities of circulation, and even, if the currency system is elastic, the quantity of money and deposits. In brisk seasons, as when "money is needed to move the crops," the velocity of circulation is evidently greater than in dull seasons. Money is kept idle at one time to be used at another, and such seasonal variations in velocity reduce materially the variations which otherwise would be necessary in the price level. In a similar way seasonal variations in the price level are reduced by the alternate expansion and contraction of an elastic bank currency. In this case temporarily, and to an extent limited by the amount of legal tender currency, money or deposits or both may be said to adapt themselves to the amount of trade. In these two ways, then, both the rise and fall of prices are mitigated. Therefore the "quantity theory" will not hold true strictly and absolutely during transition periods.

We have finished our sketch of the effects of M, and now proceed to the other magnitudes.

4

As to deposits (M'), this magnitude is always dependent on M. Deposits are payable on demand in money. They require bank reserves of money, and there must be some relation between the amount of money in circulation (M), the amount of reserves (μ), and the amount of deposits (M'). Normally we have seen that the three remain in given ratios to each other. But what is a normal ratio at one state of industry and civilization may not be normal at another. Changes in population, commerce, habits of business men, and banking facilities and laws may produce great changes in this ratio. Statistically, as will be shown in Chapter XII, the ratio M'/M has changed from 3.1 to 4.1 in fourteen years.

Since M' is normally dependent on M, we need not ask what are the effects of an increase of M'; for these effects have been included under the effects of M. But, since the ratio of M' to M may change, we do need to ask what are the effects of this change.

Suppose, as has actually been the case in recent years, that the ratio of M' to M increases in the United States. If the magnitudes in the equations of exchange in other countries with which the United States is connected by trade are constant, the ultimate effect on M is to make it less than what it would otherwise have been, by increasing the exports of gold from the United States or reducing the imports. In no other way can the price level of the United States be prevented from rising above that of other nations in which we have assumed this level and the other magnitudes in the equation of exchange to be quiescent. While the ultimate effect then is to increase the volume of circulating media, this increase is spread over the whole world. Although the extension of banking is purely local, its effects are international. In fact, not only will there be a redistribution of gold money over all gold countries, but there will be a tendency to melt coin into bullion for use in the arts.

The remaining effects are the same as those of an increase in M which have already been studied. That is, there will be no (ultimate) appreciable effect on V, V', or the Q's, but only on the p's, and these will rise, relatively to what they would otherwise have been, throughout the world. In foreign countries the normal effect will be proportional to the increase of money in circulation which they have acquired through the displacement of gold in the United States. In the United States the effect will not be proportional to the increase in M', since M has moved in the opposite direction. It will be proportional to the increase in $M + M'$ if V and V' are equal, and less than in that proportion if V is less than V', as is the actual fact.

In any case the effect on prices is extremely small, being spread over the whole commercial world. Taking the world as a whole, the ultimate effect is, as we have seen, to raise world prices slightly and to melt some coin. The only appreciable ultimate effect of increasing the ratio of M' to M in one country is to expel money from that country into others. All of these effects are exactly the same as those of increasing the issue of bank notes, so long as they continue redeemable in gold or other exportable money. An issue beyond this point results in isolating the issuing country and therefore in rapidly raising prices there instead of spreading the effect over other countries. This is what happened in the United States during the Civil War.

As to transitional effects, it is evident that, before the expulsion of gold from the United States, there must be an appreciable rise in prices there, of which traders will then take advantage by selling in the United States, shipping away money, and buying abroad. During the period of rising prices all the other temporary effects peculiar to such a period, effects which have been described at length elsewhere, will be in evidence.

Exactly opposite effects of course follow a decrease of M' relatively to M.

5

We come next to the effects of changes in velocities (V and V'). These effects are closely similar to those just described. The ultimate effects are on prices, and not on quantity of money or volume of trade. But a change in the velocity of circulation of money in any country, connected by international trade with other countries, will cause an opposite change in the quantity of money in circulation in that country. There will be a redistribution of money among the countries of the world and of money metal as between money and the arts.

The normal effect, then, of increasing V or V' in any country is to decrease M by export, to decrease M' proportionally, and to raise prices (p's) slightly throughout the world. There is no reason to believe that there will, normally, be any effects on the volume of trade. It is quite possible that a change in one of the two velocities will cause a corresponding change in the other, or, at any rate, that most of the causes which increase one will increase the other. Increased density of population, for instance, in all probability quickens the flow both of money and checks. Unfortunately, however, we have not sufficient empirical knowledge of the two sorts of velocity to assert, with confidence, any relations between them.

During transition periods the effects of changes in velocities are doubtless the same as the effects of increased currency.

6

Our next question is as to the effects of a general increase or decrease in the Q's, that is, in the volume of trade.

An increase of the volume of trade in any one country, say the United States, ultimately increases the money in circulation (M). In no other way could there be avoided a depression in the price level in the United States as compared with foreign countries. The increase in M brings about a proportionate increase in M'. Besides this effect, the increase in trade undoubtedly has some effect in modifying the habits of the community with regard to the proportion of check and cash transactions, and so tends somewhat to increase M' relatively to M; as a country grows more commercial the need for the use of checks is more strongly felt.

As to effects on velocity of circulation, we may distinguish three cases. The first is where the change in volume of trade corresponds to a change in population, as when there is an increase in trade from the settling of new lands, without any greater concentration in previously settled areas, and without any change in the per capita trade or in the distribution of trade among the elements of the population. Under such conditions no reason has been assigned, nor apparently can be assigned, to show why the velocity of circulation of money should be other for a condition in which the volume of trade is large than for a condition in which it is small.

The second case is where the increase in volume of trade corresponds to an increased *density* of population, but no change in per capita trade. In this case, the closer settlement may facilitate somewhat greater velocity. The third case is where the change in the volume of trade *does* affect the per capita trade or the distribution of trade in the population.

There are then several ways in which the velocity of circulation may conceivably be affected. First, any change in trade, implying a change in methods of transportation of goods, will imply a change in methods of transportation of money; quick transportation means usually more rapid circulation.

Second, a changed distribution of trade will alter the relative expenditures of different persons. If their rates of turnover are different, a change in their expenditures will clearly alter the relative importance or weighting of these rates in the general average, thus changing that average without necessarily changing the individual rates of turnover. For instance, an increased trade in the southern states, where the velocity of circulation of money is presumably slow, would tend to lower the average velocity in the United States, simply by giving more weight to the velocity in the slower portions of the country.

Third, a change in individual expenditures, when due to a real change in the quantity of goods purchased, may cause a change in individual velocities. It seems to be a fact that, at a given price level, the greater a man's expenditures the more rapid his turnover; that is, the rich have a higher rate of turnover than the poor. They spend money faster, not only absolutely but relatively to the money they keep on hand. Statistics collected at Yale University of a number of cases of individual turnover show this clearly. In other words, the man who spends much, though he needs to carry more money than the man who spends little, does not need to carry as much in proportion to his expenditure. This is what we should expect; since, in general, the larger any operation, the more economically it can be managed. Professor Edgeworth has shown that the same rule holds in banking. When two banks are consolidated, the reserve needed is less than the sum of the two previous reserves.

We may therefore infer that, if a nation grows richer per capita, the velocity of circulation of money will increase. This proposition, of course, has no reference to *nominal* increase of expenditure. As we have seen, a doubling of all prices and incomes would not affect anybody's rate of turnover of money. Each person would need to make exactly twice the expenditure for the same actual result and to keep on hand exactly twice the money in order to meet the same contingencies in the same way. The determinant of velocity is real expenditure, not nominal. But a person's real expenditure is only another name for his volume of trade. We conclude, therefore, that a change in the volume of trade, when it affects the *per capita* trade, affects velocity of circulation as well.

We find then that an increase in trade, unlike an increase in currency (M and M') or velocities (V and V') has other effects than simply on prices – effects, in fact, of increasing magnitudes on the opposite side of the equation, V and V', and (though only indirectly by affecting business convenience and habit) M' relatively to M. If these effects increase the left side as much as the increase in trade itself (the Q's) directly increases the right side, the effect on prices will be *nil*. If the effect on the left side exceeds that on the right, prices will rise. Only provided the effect on the left side is less than the increase in trade will prices fall, and then not proportionately to the increase in trade.

In a former chapter, it was shown that a change in trade, *provided currency* (M *and* M') *and velocities* (V *and* V') *remained the same*, produced an inverse change in prices. But now we find that the proviso is inconsistent with the premise; currency and velocities can remain the same only by the clumsy hypothesis that the various other causes affecting them shall be so changed as exactly to neutralize the increase in trade. If these various other causes remain the same, then currency and velocities will not remain the same.

This is the first instance in our study where we have found that normally, that is, apart from temporary or transitional effects, we reach different results by assuming *causes* to vary one at a time, than by assuming the algebraic *factors in the equation* to vary one at a time. The "quantity theory" still holds true – that prices (p's) vary with money (M) – when we assume that other *causes* remain the same, as well as when we assumed merely that other algebraic *factors* remain the same; and all the other theorems stated algebraically were found to hold causationally, excepting only the theorem as to variation in trade. While the main purpose of this chapter is to justify the "quantity theory" as expressing a causal as well as an algebraic relation, it is important to point out that causal and algebraic theorems are not always identical.

As to the transitional effects of a change in the volume of trade, these depend mainly on one of the two possible directions in which prices move. If they move upward, the transitional effects are similar to those we are already familiar with for periods of rising prices; if downward, they are similar to those incident to such a movement.

7

We have now studied the effects of variations in each of the factors in the equation of exchange (save one) on the other factors. We have found that in each case except in the case of trade (the Q's) the ultimate effect was on prices (the p's). The only group of factors which we have not yet studied as cause are the prices (p's) themselves. Hitherto they have been regarded solely as effects of the other factors. But the objectors to the quantity theory have maintained that prices should be regarded as causes rather than as effects. Our next problem, therefore, is to examine and criticize this proposition.

So far as I can discover, *except to a limited extent during transition periods, or during a passing season* (e.g. *the fall*), there is no truth whatever in the idea that the price level is an independent cause of changes in any of the other magnitudes M, M', V, V', or the Q's. To show the untenability of such an idea let us grant for the sake of argument that – in some other way than as the effect of changes in M, M', V, V', or the Q's – the prices in (say) the United States are changed to (say) double their original level, and let us see what effect this cause will produce on the other magnitudes in the equation.

It is clear that the equality between the money side and the goods side must be maintained somehow, and that if the prices are raised the quantity of money or the quantity of deposits or their velocities must be raised, or else the volume of business must be reduced. But examination will show that none of these solutions is tenable.

The quantity of money cannot be increased. No money will come from abroad, for we have seen that a place with high prices drives money away. The consequence of the elevation of prices in the United States will be that traders will sell in the United States where prices are high, and take the proceeds in money and buy abroad where prices are low. It will be as difficult to make money flow into a country with high prices as to make water run up hill.

For similar reasons money will not come in *via* the mint. Since bullion and gold coin originally had the same value relatively to goods, after the supposed doubling of prices, gold coin has lost half its purchasing power. No one will take bullion to the mint when he thereby loses half its value. On the contrary, as we saw in a previous chapter, the result of high prices is to make men melt coin.

Finally, the high prices will not stimulate mining, but on the contrary they will discourage it, nor will high prices discourage consumption of gold, but on the contrary they will stimulate it. These tendencies have all been studied in detail. Every principle we have found regulating the distribution of money among nations (the distribution of money metal as between money and the arts or the production and consumption of metals) works exactly opposite to what would be necessary in order to bring money to fit prices instead of prices to fit money.

It is equally absurd to expect high prices to increase the quantity of deposits (M'). We have seen that the effect would be to diminish the quantity of money in circulation (M), but this money is the basis of the deposit currency (M'), and the shrinkage of the first will entail the shrinkage of the second. The reduction of M and M' will not tend to favor, but on the contrary will tend to pull down the high prices we have arbitrarily assumed.

The appeal to the velocities (V and V') is no more satisfactory. These have already been adjusted to suit individual convenience. To double them might not be a physical possibility, and would certainly be a great inconvenience.

There is left the forlorn hope that the high prices will diminish trade (the Q's). But if all prices including the prices of services are doubled, there is no reason why trade should be reduced.

Since the average person will not only pay, but also receive high prices, it is evident that the high prices he gets will exactly make him able to stand the high prices he pays without having to reduce his purchases.

We conclude that the hypothesis of a doubled price level acting as an independent cause controlling the other factors in the equation of exchange and uncontrolled by them is untenable. Any attempt to maintain artificially high prices must result, as we have seen, not in adjusting the other elements in the equation of exchange to suit these high prices, but on the contrary in arousing their antagonism. Gold will go abroad and into the melting pot, will be produced less and consumed more until its scarcity as money will pull down the prices. *The price level is normally the one absolutely passive element in the equation of exchange*. It is controlled solely by the other elements and the causes antecedent to them, but exerts no control over them.

But though it is a fallacy to think that the price level in any community can, in the long run, affect the money in *that* community, it is true that the price level in one community may affect the money in *another* community. This proposition has been repeatedly made use of in our discussion, and should be clearly distinguished from the fallacy above mentioned. The price level in an outside community is an influence outside the equation of exchange of that community, and operates by affecting its money in circulation and not by directly affecting its price level. The price level outside of New York City, for instance, affects the price level in New York City only *via* changes in the money in New York City. Within New York City it is the money which influences the price level, and not the price level which influences the money. The price level is effect and not cause. Moreover, although the price level outside of New York is a proximate cause of changes of money in New York, that price level in turn is cause only in a secondary sense, being itself an effect of the other factors in the equation of exchange outside of New York City. For the world as a whole the price level is not even a secondary cause, but solely an effect – of the world's money, deposits, velocities, and trade.

We have seen that high prices in any *place* do not cause an increase of the money supply there; for money flows *away* from such a place. In the same way high prices at any *time* do not cause an increase of money at that time; for money, so to speak, flows *away* from that time. Thus, if the price level is high in January as compared with the rest of the year, bank notes will not tend to be issued in large quantities then. On the contrary, people will seek to avoid paying money at the high prices and wait till prices are lower. When that time comes they may need more currency; bank notes and deposits may then expand to meet the excessive demands for loans which may ensue. Thus, currency expands when prices are low and contracts when prices are high, and such expansion and contraction tend to lower the high prices and raise the low prices, thus working toward mutual equality. We see then that, so far from its being true that high prices cause increased supply of money, it is true that money avoids the place and time of high prices and seeks the place and time of low prices, thereby mitigating the inequality of price levels.

What has been said presupposes that purchasers have the option to change the place and time of their purchases. To the extent that their freedom to choose their market place or time is interfered with, the corrective adjustment of the quantity of money is prevented. The anomalous time of a panic may even be characterized by necessity to meet old contracts which afford no choice of deferring the payment. There may then be a "money famine" and a feverish demand for emergency currency needed to liquidate outstanding contracts which would never have been entered into if the situation had been foreseen. That such anomalous conditions do not negative the general thesis that prices are the effect and not the cause of currency (including deposit currency) is shown statistically by Minnie Throop England.

8

Were it not for the fanatical refusal of some economists to admit that the price level is in ultimate analysis effect and not cause, we should not be at so great pains to prove it beyond cavil. It is due our science to demonstrate its truths. The obligation to do this carries with it the obligation to explain if possible why so obvious a truth has not been fully accepted.

One reason has already been cited, the fear to give aid and comfort to the enemies of all sound economists – the unsound money men. Another may now receive attention, namely the fallacious idea that the price level cannot be determined by other factors in the equation of exchange because it is already determined by other causes, usually alluded to as "supply and demand." This vague phrase has covered multitudes of sins of slothful analysts in economics. Those who place such implicit reliance on the competency of supply and demand to fix prices, irrespective of the quantity of money, deposits, velocity, and trade, will have their confidence rudely shaken if they will follow the reasoning as to price causation of separate articles. They will find that there are always just one *too few equations* to determine the unknown quantities involved. The equation of exchange is needed in each case to supplement the equations of supply and demand.

It would take us too far afield to insert here a complete statement of price-determining principles. But the compatibility of the equation of exchange with the equations which have to deal with prices individually may be brought home to the reader sufficiently for our present purposes by emphasizing the distinction between (1) individual prices relatively to each other and (2) the price *level*. The equation of exchange determines the latter (the price level) only, and the latter only is the subject of this book. It will not help, but only hinder the reader to mix with the discussion of price levels the principles determining individual prices relatively to each other. It is amazing how tenaciously many people cling to the mistaken idea that an individual price, though expressed in money, may be determined wholly without reference to money. Others, more open-minded but almost equally confused, see the necessity of including the quantity of money among the causes determining prices, but in the careless spirit of eclecticism simply jumble it in with a miscellaneous collection of influences affecting prices, with no regard for their mutual relations. It should be clearly recognized that price *levels* must be studied independently of individual *prices*.

The legitimacy of separating the study of price levels from that of prices will be clearly recognized, when it is seen that individual prices cannot be fully determined by supply and demand, money cost of production, etc., without surreptitiously introducing the price level itself. We can scarcely overemphasize the fact that the "supply and demand" or the "cost of production" of goods in terms of money do not and cannot completely determine prices. Each phrase, fully expressed, already implies *money*. There is always hidden somewhere the assumption of a general price level. Yet, writers, like David A. Wells, have seriously sought the explanation of a general change in price levels in the individual price changes of various commodities considered separately. Much of their reasoning goes no farther than to explain one price in terms of other prices. If we attempt to explain the *money* price of a finished product in terms of the *money* prices of its raw materials and other *money* costs of prices of production, it is clear that we merely shift the problem. We have *still* to explain these antecedent prices. In elementary textbooks much emphasis is laid on the fact that "demand" and "supply" are incomplete designations and that to give them meaning it is necessary to add to each the phrase "at a price." But emphasis also needs to be laid on the fact that "demand at a price" and "supply at a price" are *still* incomplete designations, and that to give them meaning it is necessary to add "at a price level." The demand for sugar is not only relative to the price of sugar, but also to the general level of other things. Not only is the demand for sugar at 10 cents a pound greater than the demand at 20 cents a pound (at a given level of prices of other things), but the demand at 20 cents *at a high level of prices* is greater than the demand at 20 cents *at a low level of prices*. In fact if the price level is doubled, the demand at 20 cents a pound will be as great as the demand was before at 10 cents a pound, assuming that the doubling applies likewise to wages and incomes generally. The significance of a dollar lies in what it will buy; and the equivalence between sugar and dollars is at bottom an equivalence between sugar and *what dollars will buy*. A change in the amount of what dollars will buy is as important as a change in the amount of sugar. The price of sugar in dollars depends partly on sugar and partly on dollars – that is, on what dollars will buy – that is, on the price level. Therefore, beneath the price of sugar in particular there lies, as one of the bases of that particular price, the general level of prices. We have more need to study the price level preparatory to a study of the price of sugar than to study the price of sugar preparatory to a study of the price level. We cannot explain the level of the sea by the height of its individual waves; rather must we explain in part the position of these waves by the general level of the sea. Each "supply curve" or "demand curve" rests upon the unconscious assumption of a price level already existing. Although the curves relate to a commodity, they relate to it only as compared with money. A price is a ratio of exchange between the commodity and money. The money side of each exchange must never be forgotten nor the fact that money already stands in the mind of the purchaser for a general purchasing power. Although every buyer and seller who bids or offers a price for a particular commodity tacitly assumes a given purchasing power of the money bid or offered, he is usually as unconscious of so doing as the spectator of a picture is unconscious of the fact that he is using the background of the picture against which to measure the figures in the foreground. As a consequence, if the general level changes, the supply and demand curves for the particular commodity considered will change accordingly. If the purchasing power of the dollar is reduced to half its former amount, these curves will be doubled in height; for each person will give or take double the former money for a given quantity of the commodity. If, through special causes affecting a special commodity, the supply and demand curves of that commodity and their intersection are raised or lowered, then the supply and demand curves of some other goods must change in the reverse direction. That is, if one commodity rises in price (without any change in the quantity of it or of other things bought and sold, and without any change in the volume of circulating medium or in the velocity of circulation), then other commodities must *fall* in price. The increased money expended for this commodity will be taken from other purchases. In other words, the waves in the sea of prices have troughs. This can be seen from the equation of exchange. If we suppose the quantity of money and its velocity of circulation to remain unaltered, the left side of the equation remains the same, and therefore the right side must remain unaltered also. Consequently, any increase in one of its many terms, due to an increase of any individual price, must occur at the expense of the remaining terms.

It is, of course, true that a decrease in the price of any particular commodity will usually be accompanied by an increase in the amount of it exchanged, so that the product of the two may not decrease and may even increase if the amount exchanged increases sufficiently. In this case, since the right side of our equation remains the same, the effect of the increase in some terms will necessarily be a decrease in others; and the remaining terms of the right side must decrease to some extent. The effect may be a general or even a universal lowering of prices. Even in this case the reduction in the price level has no direct connection with the reduction in the price of the particular commodity, but is due to the increase in the amount of it exchanged.

The reactionary effect of the price of one commodity on the prices of other commodities must never be lost sight of. Much confusion will be escaped if we give up any attempt to reason directly from individual prices. Improvements in production will affect price levels simply as they affect the volume of business transacted. Any rational study of the influence of improvements in methods of production upon the level of prices should, therefore, fix attention, first, on the resulting volume of trade, and should aim to discover whether this, in turn, carries prices upwards or downwards.

One of the supposed causes of high prices to-day, much under discussion at the present time, is that of industrial and labor combinations. From what has been said, it must be evident that, other things remaining equal, trusts cannot affect the general level of prices through manipulating special commodities except as they change the amounts sold. If prices for one commodity are changed without a change in the number of sales, the effect on the price level will be neutralized by compensatory changes in other prices. If trade unions seek to raise prices of labor while trusts raise prices of commodities, the general level of everything may rise or fall; but it can rise only by a general decrease in the quantities of commodities, labor, etc., sold, or by an increase of currency, or by an increase in velocities of circulation. If there is neither an increase nor decrease in volume of business, and if the quantity and velocity of circulation of money and its substitutes remain unchanged, the price level cannot change. Changes in some parts of the price level may occur only at the expense of opposite changes in other parts.

We have seen that the price level is not determined by individual prices, but that, on the contrary, any individual price presupposes a price level. We have seen that the complete and only explanation of a price level is to be sought in factors of the equation of exchange and whatever antecedent causes affect those factors. The terms "demand" and "supply," used in reference to particular prices, have no significance whatever in explaining a rise or fall of price *levels*. In considering the influence affecting individual prices we say that an increase in supply lowers prices, but an increase in demand raises them. But in considering the influences affecting price *levels* we enter upon an entirely different set of concepts, and must not confuse the proposition that an increase in the *trade* (the Q's) tends to lower the price *level*, with the proposition that an increase in supply tends to lower an individual price. Trade (the Q's) is not supply – in fact is no more to be associated with supply than with demand. The Q's are the quantities finally sold by those who supply, and bought by those who demand.

We may here state a paradox which will serve to bring out clearly the distinction between the causation of individual prices relatively to each other and the causation of the general level of prices. The paradox is that although an increased demand for any individual commodity results in a greater consumption *at a higher price*, yet an increased general demand for goods will result in a greater, trade (the Q's) *at lower prices*.

We cannot, therefore, reason directly from particular to general prices; we can reason only indirectly by reference to the effects on quantities. Sometimes the rise in an individual price raises and at other times lowers the general price level. To draw a physical parallel let us suppose that a thousand piles have been driven in a quicksand and that the owner wishes to raise their level a foot. He gets hoisting apparatus and planting it on the piles pulls one of them up a foot. He then pulls up another and continues until he has pulled up each of the thousand. But if every time he has pulled one up a foot he has pushed down 999 over 1/999 of a foot, when he has finished, he will find his thousand piles lower than when he began. Each time a pile has risen, the average level of all has fallen.

The proposition that a general increase in demand, resulting in an increase in trade, tends to decrease and and [*sic*] not to increase the general level of prices, may be regarded as a sort of *pons asinorum* to test one's knowledge of the fundamental distinction between those influences affecting the general price level and those affecting the rise and fall of a particular price with respect to that level.

9

We have seen that the various factors represented in the equation of exchange do not stand on the same causal footing. Prices are the passive elements and their general level must conform to the other factors. The causal propositions we have found to be true normally, that is after transitions are completed, are in brief as follows:

1   An increase in the quantity of money (M) tends to increase deposits (M') proportionally, and the increase in these two (M and M') tends to increase prices proportionally.
2   An increase in the quantity of money in one country tends to spread to others using the same money metal, and to the arts, as soon as the price levels or the relative value of money and bullion differ enough to make export or melting of the money metal profitable and to raise slightly world prices.
3   An increase in deposits (M') compared with money (M) tends likewise to displace and melt coin, and to raise world prices.

4   An increase in velocities tends to produce similar effects.
5   An increase in the volume of trade (the Q's) tends, not only to decrease prices, but also to increase velocities and deposits relatively to money and through them to neutralize partly or wholly the said decrease in prices.
6   The price level is the effect and cannot be the cause of change in the other factors.
7   Innumerable causes *outside* the equation of exchange may affect M, M', V, V', and the Q's and through them affect the p's. Among these outside causes are the price levels in surrounding countries.
8   The causation of individual prices can only explain prices as compared among themselves. It cannot explain the general level of prices as compared with money.
9   Some of the foregoing propositions are subject to slight modification during transition periods. It is then true, for instance, that an increase in the quantity of money (M) besides having the effects above mentioned will change temporarily the ratio of M' to M and disturb temporarily V, V', and the Q's, making a credit cycle.

In general, then, our conclusion as to causes and effects is that normally the price level (the p's) is the effect of all the other factors in the equation of exchange (M, M', V, V', and the Q's); that among these other factors, deposits (M') are chiefly the effect of money, given the normal ratio of M' to M, that this ratio is partly the effect of trade (the Q's), that V and V' are also partly the effects of the Q's; and that all of the magnitudes, M, M', V, V', and the Q's are the effects of antecedent causes outside the equation of exchange, *ad infinitum*.

The main conclusion is that we find nothing to interfere with the truth of the quantity theory that variations in money (M) produce normally proportional changes in prices.

Notes

1   This theory, though often crudely formulated, has been accepted by Locke, Hume, Adam Smith, Ricardo, Mill, Walker, Marshall, Hadley, Fetter, Kemmerer, and most writers on the subject. The Roman Julius Paulus, about AD 200, stated his belief that the value of money depends on its quantity. See Zuckerkandl, *Theorie des Preises*; Kemmerer, *Money and Credit Instruments in their Relation to General Prices*, New York (Holt), 1909. It is true that many writers still oppose the quantity theory. See especially, Laughlin, *Principles of Money*, New York (Scribner), 1903.
2   An algebraic statement of the equation of exchange was made by Simon Newcomb in his able but little appreciated *Principles of Political Economy*, New York (Harper), 1885, p. 346. It is also expressed by Edgeworth, "Report on Monetary Standard." *Report of the British Association for the Advancement of Science*, 1887, p. 293, and by President Hadley, *Economics*, New York (Putnam), 1896, p. 197. See also Irving Fisher, "The Rôle of Capital in Economic Theory," *Economic Journal*, December, 1899, pp. 515–21, and E. W. Kemmerer, *Money and Credit Instruments in their Relation to General Prices*, New York (Holt), 1907, p. 13. While thus only recently given mathematical expression, the quantity theory has long been understood as a relationship among the several factors: amount of money, rapidity of circulation, and amount of trade. See Mill, *Principles of Political Economy*, Book III, Chapter VIII, §3. Ricardo probably deserves chief credit for launching the theory.

JOHN MAYNARD KEYNES (1883–1946)

John Maynard Keynes, Photographer: Ramsay and Muspratt, by courtesy of the National Portrait Gallery, London.

John Maynard Keynes was the son of John Neville Keynes (1852– 1949), himself a distinguished economist and colleague of Marshall's at the University of Cambridge. Keynes was educated at Cambridge, worked in the civil service, was an active member of the artistic and literary circle known as the Bloomsbury Group (which also included, for example, Lytton Strachey, Virginia Wolf, Bertrand Russell, and Clive and Vanessa Bell), and was the leading figure in economics at Cambridge at a time when Cambridge emerged as the center of the economics universe. Keynes served in numerous ways as an advisor to governments and governmental committees throughout his career, and was one of the architects of the post Second World War international monetary system. He also contributed regularly to the popular press and served as editor (with Edgeworth) of the *Economic Journal*.

By the time of the Great Depression, Keynes had become one of the world's great economists, perhaps its leading monetary theorist. Yet, even in the 1920s he held many then-unorthodox views: He early felt that the relationship between saving and investment, particularly their psychological underpinnings, were fragile. He rejected the so-called automaticity and benevolence of the gold standard in favor of monetary reform and central bank management of the money supply and price level independent of gold reserves. He felt that for all its highly touted advantages, notably for some people, the market economy, especially its *laissez-faire* form, was inadequate for attending to various important and disruptive social problems, for example, control of unemployment, inflation, and population. He was one of a group of monetary theorists who reformulated the quantity theory to give effect to motives for holding money, thereby deferring spending, which seriously compromised the relationship between the supply of money and the price level. Late in the 1920s he came to see that disequilibrium between saving and investment was the critical immediate cause of instability, but continued to think in the terms of traditional monetary theory, focusing on the effect of price-level changes on profit-and-loss balances. He continued to emphasize monetary management, focusing on deflation rather than recession or depression as the central problem and policy target.

In 1936, Keynes published his epochal G*eneral Theory of Employment, Interest and Money*. Keynes's target was traditional monetary and macroeconomic theory (though it was not yet so named), centering on the rejection of Say's Law and extending the revision of the quantity theory, generally along the lines summarized above. But now the focus was no longer on the price level; it was on the levels of real economic activity and of employment and unemployment.

Keynes's new theory was important in several ways: (1) He established a conviction among economists that a macroeconomic problem existed – the determination of the levels of income, output, and employment – which required analysis and should not be finessed by a theory whose assumptions excluded the possible sources of disequilibrium, instability, and equilibrium, as it were, at less than full employment. (2) He provided an extensive theory of the determination of the levels of income, output, and employment, as well as of the price level which constituted his version of that analysis. (3) He had a more complex, and even quite radical, view of saving than hitherto held. Saving had been held to be an unmixed blessing (perhaps except for the miser who died of malnutrition): it financed investment, enabled greater income, provided resources for a rainy day, retirement, and inheritance. Keynes argued that (a) that was largely true but (b) investment was also financed by bank credit as well as retained business earnings (not solely household saving), and (c) the economic significance of any level of saving depended on its relation to its correlative level of investment: if saving exceeded investment, the level of economic activity was likely to contract, and vice versa. (4) He argued that the role of the interest rate was not to equate saving and investment but something like the demand and supply of money, taking especial account of the demand to hold money (liquidity preference). (5) He maintained that government spending willy nilly was part of the income mechanism and raised the theoretical and practical-policy possibilities of using the relation of government spending to taxation as a means of countering or compensating for developments in the private sector deemed undesirable, for example, unemployment and inflation. (6) He argued that the traditional views of the benefits of reductions in price and wage levels were incomplete. A fall in the price level would increase the real value of cash balances, and possibly lead to the spending of excess balances to counter the recession which led to the fall in prices; but a serious recession might also lead people to want to hold greater real balances and to a fall in profit expectations. It was a matter, generally speaking, of the relative strength of the two tendencies (sometimes called the Pigou and the Keynes effects). As for wage cuts, such might well lead to increased employment at lower wage-rate levels; but such would also decrease effective demand by reducing the purchasing power of wage earners. Again it was a matter of the relative strength of the two tendencies.

Keynes's theory maintained that the levels of income, output, and employment, as well as of price, were a function of the level of spending, or aggregate demand. Changes in spending brought about changes in income. These changes came in the variables which comprised and undergirded spending (and in the function which related aggregate supply to employment): Consumption: the average and marginal propensity to consume, and especially consumer psychology. Investment: the expected rate of profit (called by him the marginal efficiency of capital) in relation to the interest rate (which was a function of the supply of money in relation to liquidity preference). Government: the policies, more or less coherent, which related the levels of spending and taxation.

All this was, especially as assembled by Keynes, quite unlike anything which had appeared before 1936. Much remained to be reformulated both theoretically and empirically and made subject to further criticism. But Keynes's "general theory" wrought a revolution in economics the likes of which had not been seen before – rivalled, perhaps, only by that slowly (and thus hardly a matter of revolution) brought about by Cantillon, Turgot, and Smith, as well as perhaps Ricardo. The fact of the Great Depression not only helped to motivate Keynes, it conditioned other economists to be receptive to his theory. The focus on unemployment also tended to obscure the fact that Keynes's theory could help account for inflation: inflation could result from businesses raising prices (as well as output, in whatever proportion) at less than full employment in response to increases in aggregate demand, or inflation would have to result from increases in aggregate demand at full employment. Finally, Keynes's analysis helped locate the sources of unemployment in the scarcity of jobs (due to inadequate effective demand) rather than in the unwillingness of labor to work (say, at lower wages and salaries).

Keynes was both and admirer and critic of the Western economic system then in place. Those who felt the sting of his criticism did not trust either his reforms or his theory. Those who comprehended his admiration felt that he was seeking to save capitalism, if only a reformed capitalism.

Reprinted here are three different excerpts from Keynes's writings. The first, "The end of *laissez-faire*," is an elegant statement of the case for what is commonly referred to as "government intervention." This is followed by a relatively brief statement of the ideas developed in *The General Theory* – taken from an article responding to his critics that Keynes wrote for the *Quarterly Journal of Economics* shortly after the book's publication. The last extract is from *The General Theory* itself – the concluding chapter, in which Keynes elaborates the implications of his theory.

References and further reading

Bateman, Bradley W. (1996) *Keynes's Uncertain Revolution*, Ann Arbor: University of Michigan Press.

Blaug, Mark, ed. (1991) *John Maynard Keynes (1883–1946)*, Aldershot: Edward Elgar Publishing.

Clarke, Peter (1988) *The Keynesian Revolution in the Making, 1924–1936*, New York: Oxford University Press.

Corry, B. (1978) "Keynes in the History of Economic Thought," in A.P. Thirwall (ed.) *Keynes and Laissez-Faire*, London: Macmillan.

Eatwell, John (1987) "Keynesianism," in John Eatwell, Murray Milgate, and Peter Newman (eds), *The New Palgrave: A Dictionary of Economics*, Vol. 3, London: Macmillan, 46–7.

Hansen, Alvin H. (1953) *A Guide to Keynes*, New York: McGraw-Hill.

Harrod, R.F. (1951) *The Life of John Maynard Keynes*, London: Macmillan.

Hicks, J.R. (1937) "Mr. Keynes and the Classics: A Suggested Reinterpretation," *Econometrica* 5 (April): 147–59.

Kahn, R.F. (1984) *The Making of Keynes' General Theory*, Cambridge: Cambridge University Press.

Keynes, J.M. (1919) *The Economic Consequences of the Peace*, London: Macmillan.

—— (1921) *A Treatise on Probability*, London: Macmillan.

—— (1923) *A Tract on Monetary Reform*, London: Macmillan.

—— (1930) *A Treatise on Money*, 2 vols, London: Macmillan.

—— (1971–1989) *The Collected Writings of John Maynard Keynes*, London: Macmillan for the Royal Economic Society.

Laidler, David E.W. (1999) *Fabricating the Keynesian Revolution*, Cambridge: Cambridge University Press.

Leijonhufvud, A. (1968) *On Keynesian Economics and the Economics of Keynes*, New York: Oxford University Press.

Lekachman, Robert (1966) *The Age of Keynes*, New York: Random House.

Milgate, Murray (1987) "Keynes's *General Theory*," in John Eatwell, Murray Milgate, and Peter Newman (eds), *The New Palgrave: A Dictionary of Economics*, Vol. 3, London: Macmillan, 42–6.

Moggridge, D.E. (1992) *Maynard Keynes: An Economist's Biography*, London: Routledge.

Patinkin, Don (1965) *Money, Interest, and Prices*, 2nd edn, New York: Harper & Row.

—— (1987) "Keynes, John Maynard," in John Eatwell, Murray Milgate, and Peter Newman (eds), *The New Palgrave: A Dictionary of Economics*, Vol. 3, London: Macmillan, 19–41.

Skidelsky, Robert (1983) *John Maynard Keynes, Vol. 1: Hopes Betrayed, 1883–1920*, New York: Viking Penguin.

Skidelsky, Robert (1988) *John Maynard Keynes, Vol. 2: The Economist as Savior, 1920–1937*, New York: Penguin.

—— (2001) *John Maynard Keynes Vol. 3: Fighting for Freedom, 1937–1946*, New York: Viking.

Tarshis, L. (1987) "Keynesian Revolution," in John Eatwell, Murray Milgate, and Peter Newman (eds), *The New Palgrave: A Dictionary of Economics*, Vol. 3, London: Macmillan, 47–50.

Thirwall, A.P. (ed.) (1978) *Keynes and Laissez-Faire*, London: Macmillan.

Weintraub, Sidney (1961) *Classical Keynesianism, Monetary Theory and the Price Level*, Philadelphia: Chilton.

Wood, J.C., ed. (1983) *John Maynard Keynes: Critical Assessments*, London: Croom Helm.

"The End of *Laissez-Faire*" (1926)*

Let us clear from the ground the metaphysical or general principles upon which, from time to time, *laissez-faire* has been founded. It is *not* true that individuals possess a prescriptive 'natural liberty' in their economic activities. There is *no* 'compact' conferring perpetual rights on those who Have or on those who Acquire. The world is *not* so governed from above that private and social interest always coincide. It is *not* so managed here below that in practice they coincide. It is *not* correct deduction from the Principles of Economics that enlightened self-interest always operates in the public interest. Nor is it true that self-interest generally *is* enlightened; more often individuals acting separately to promote their own ends are too ignorant or too weak to attain even these. Experience does *not* show that individuals, when they make up a social unit, are always less clear-sighted than when they act separately.

We cannot, therefore, settle on abstract grounds, but must handle on its merits in detail, what Burke termed 'one of the finest problems in legislation, namely to determine what the State ought to take upon itself to direct by the public wisdom, and what it ought to leave, with as little interference as possible, to individual exertion'. We have to discriminate between what Bentham, in his forgotten but useful nomenclature, used to term *Agenda* and *Non-Agenda*, and to do this without Bentham's prior presumption that interference is, at the same time, 'generally needless' and 'generally pernicious'. Perhaps the chief task of Economists at this hour is to distinguish afresh the *Agenda* of Government from the *Non-Agenda*, and the companion task of 'Politics is to devise forms of Government within a Democracy which shall be capable of accomplishing the *Agenda*'. I will illustrate what I have in mind by two examples.

1. I believe that in many cases the ideal size for the unit of control and organization lies somewhere between the individual and the modern State. I suggest, therefore, that progress lies in the growth and the recognition of semi-autonomous bodies within the State – bodies whose criterion of action within their own field is solely the public good as they understand it, and from whose deliberations motives of private advantage are excluded, though some place it may still be necessary to leave, until the ambit of men's altruism grows wider, to the separate advantage of particular groups, classes, or faculties – bodies which in the ordinary course of affairs are mainly autonomous within their prescribed limitations, but are subject in the last resort to the sovereignty of the democracy expressed through Parliament.

I propose a return, it may be said, towards mediaeval conceptions of separate autonomies. But, in England at any rate, corporations are a mode of government which has never ceased to be important and is sympathetic to our institutions. It is easy to give examples, from what already exists, of separate autonomies which have attained or are approaching the mode I designate – the

* In J.M. Keynes, *Essays in Persuasion*, New York: Harcourt, Brace, & Co., 1932.

Universities, the Bank of England, the Port of London Authority, even perhaps the Railway Companies.

But more interesting than these is the trend of Joint Stock Institutions, when they have reached a certain age and size, to approximate to the status of public corporations rather than that of individualistic private enterprise. One of the most interesting and unnoticed developments of recent decades has been the tendency of big enterprise to socialise itself. A point arrives in the growth of a big institution – particularly a big railway or big public utility enterprise, but also a big bank or a big insurance company – at which the owners of the capital, that is, the shareholders, are almost entirely dissociated from the management, with the result that the direct personal interest of the latter in the making of great profit becomes quite secondary. When this stage is reached, the general stability and reputation of the institution are more considered by the management than the maximum of profit for the shareholders. The shareholders must be satisfied by conventionally adequate dividends; but once this is secured, the direct interest of the management often consists in avoiding criticism from the public and from the customers of the concern. This is particularly the case if their great size or semi-monopolistic position renders them conspicuous in the public eye and vulnerable to public attack. The extreme instance, perhaps, of this tendency in the case of an institution, theoretically the unrestricted property of private persons, is the Bank of England. It is almost true to say that there is no class of persons in the Kingdom of whom the Governor of the Bank of England thinks less when he decides on his policy than of his shareholders. Their rights, in excess of their conventional dividend, have already sunk to the neighbourhood of zero. But the same thing is partly true of many other big institutions. They are, as time goes on, socialising themselves.

Not that this is unmixed gain. The same causes promote conservatism and a waning of enterprise. In fact, we already have in these cases many of the faults as well as the advantages of State Socialism. Nevertheless, we see here, I think, a natural line of evolution. The battle of Socialism against unlimited private profit is being won in detail hour by hour. In these particular fields – it remains acute elsewhere – this is no longer the pressing problem. There is, for instance, no so-called important political question so really unimportant, so irrelevant to the reorganisation of the economic life of Great Britain, as the Nationalisation of the Railways.

It is true that many big undertakings, particularly Public Utility enterprises and other business requiring a large fixed capital, still need to be semi-socialised. But we must keep our minds flexible regarding the forms of this semi-socialism. We must take full advantage of the natural tendencies of the day, and we must probably prefer semi-autonomous corporations to organs of the Central Government for which Ministers of State are directly responsible.

I criticise doctrinaire State Socialism, not because it seeks to engage men's altruistic impulses in the service of Society, or because it departs from *laissez-faire*, or because it takes away from man's natural liberty to make a million, or because it has courage for bold experiments. All these things I applaud. I criticise it because it misses the significance of what is actually happening; because it is, in fact, little better than a dusty survival of a plan to meet the problems of fifty years ago, based on a misunderstanding of what some one said a hundred years ago. Nineteenth-century State Socialism sprang from Bentham, free competition, etc., and is in some respects a clearer, in some respects a more muddled, version of just the same philosophy as underlies nineteenth-century individualism. Both equally laid all their stress on freedom, the one negatively to avoid limitations on existing freedom, the other positively to destroy natural or acquired monopolies. They are different reactions to the same intellectual atmosphere.

2. I come next to a criterion of *Agenda* which is particularly relevant to what it is urgent and desirable to do in the near future. We must aim at separating those services which are *technically social* from those which are *technically individual*. The most important *Agenda* of the State relate not to those activities which private individuals are already fulfilling, but to those functions which fall outside the sphere of the individual, to those decisions which are made by *no one* if the State does not make them. The important thing for Government is not to do things which individuals are doing already, and to do them a little better or a little worse; but to do those things which at present are not done at all.

It is not within the scope of my purpose on this occasion to develop practical policies. I limit myself, therefore, to naming some instances of what I mean from amongst those problems about which I happen to have thought most.

Many of the greatest economic evils of our time are the fruits of risk, uncertainty, and ignorance. It is because particular individuals, fortunate in situation or in abilities, are able to take advantage of uncertainty and ignorance, and also because for the same reason big business is often a lottery, that great inequalities of wealth come about; and these same factors are also the cause of the Unemployment of Labour, or the disappointment of reasonable business expectations, and of the impairment of efficiency and production. Yet, the cure lies outside the operations of individuals; it may even be to the interest of individuals to aggravate the disease. I believe that the cure for these things is partly to be sought in the deliberate control of the currency and of credit by a central institution, and partly in the collection and dissemination on a great scale of data relating to the business situation, including the full publicity, by law if necessary, of all business facts which it is useful to know. These measures would involve Society in exercising directive intelligence through some appropriate organ of action over many of the inner intricacies of private business, yet it would leave private initiative and enterprise unhindered. Even if these measures prove insufficient, nevertheless they will furnish us with better knowledge than we have now for taking the next step.

My second example relates to Savings and Investment. I believe that some co-ordinated act of intelligent judgement is required as to the scale on which it is desirable that the community as a whole should save, the scale on which these savings should go abroad in the form of foreign investments, and whether the present organisation of the investment market distributes savings along the most nationally productive channels. I do not think that these matters should be left entirely to the chances of private judgement and private profits, as they are at present.

My third example concerns Population. The time has already come when each country needs a considered national policy about what size of Population, whether larger or smaller than at present or the same, is most expedient. And having settled this policy, we must take steps to carry it into operation. The time may arrive a little later when the community as a whole must pay attention to the innate quality as well as to the mere numbers of its future members.

These reflections have been directed towards possible improvements in the technique of modern Capitalism by the agency of collective action. There is nothing in them which is seriously incompatible with what seems to me to be the essential characteristic of Capitalism, namely the dependence upon an intense appeal to the money-making and money-loving instincts of individuals as the main motive force of the economic machine. Nor must I, so near to my end, stray towards other fields. Nevertheless, I may do well to remind you, in conclusion, that the fiercest contests and the most deeply felt divisions of opinion are likely to be waged in the coming years not round technical questions, where the arguments on either side are mainly economic, but round those which, for want of better words, may be called psychological or, perhaps, moral.

In Europe, or at least in some parts of Europe – but not, I think, in the United States of America – there is a latent reaction, somewhat widespread, against basing Society to the extent that we do upon fostering, encouraging, and protecting the money-motives of individuals. A preference for arranging our affairs in such a way as to appeal to the money-motive as little as possible, rather than as much as possible, need not be entirely à priori, but may be based on the comparison of experiences. Different persons, according to their choice of profession, find the money-motive playing a large or a small part in their daily lives, and historians can tell us about other phases of social organisation in which this motive has played a much smaller part than it does now. Most religions and most philosophies deprecate, to say the least of it, a way of life mainly influenced by considerations of personal money profit. On the other hand, most men today reject ascetic notions and do not doubt the real advantages of wealth. Moreover, it seems obvious to them that one cannot do without the money motive, and that, apart from certain admitted abuses, it does its job well. In the result the average man averts his attention from the problem, and has no clear idea what he really thinks and feels about the whole confounded matter.

Confusion of thought and feeling leads to confusion of speech. Many people, who are really objecting to Capitalism as a way of life, argue as though they were objecting to it on the ground of its inefficiency in attaining its own objects. Contrariwise, devotees of Capitalism are often unduly conservative, and reject reforms in its technique, which might really strengthen and preserve it, for fear that they may prove to be first steps away from Capitalism itself. Nevertheless, a time may be coming when we shall get clearer than at present as to when we are talking about Capitalism as an efficient or inefficient technique, and when we are talking about it as desirable or objectionable in itself. For my part, I think that Capitalism, wisely managed, can probably be made more efficient for attaining economic ends than any alternative system yet in sight, but that in itself it is in many ways extremely objectionable. Our problem is to work out a social organisation which shall be as efficient as possible without offending our notions of a satisfactory way of life.

The next step forward must come, not from political agitation or premature experiments, but from thought. We need by an effort of the mind to elucidate our own feelings. At present our sympathy and our judgement are liable to be on different sides, which is a painful and paralysing state of mind. In the field of action reformers will not be successful until they can steadily pursue a clear and definite object with their intellects and their feelings in tune. There is no party in the world at present which appears to me to be pursuing right aims by right methods. Material Poverty provides the incentive to change precisely in situations where there is very little margin for experiments. Material Prosperity removes the incentive just when it might be safe to take a chance. Europe lacks the means, America the will, to make a move. We need a new set *of* convictions which spring naturally from a candid examination of our own inner feelings in relation to the outside facts.

"The General Theory of Employment" (1937)*

I

I am much indebted to the Editors of the Quarterly Journal for the four contributions relating to my *General Theory of Employment, Interest and Money* which appeared in the issue for November, 1936. They contain detailed criticisms, much of which I accept and from which I hope to benefit. There is nothing in Professor Taussig's comment from which I disagree. Mr Leontief is right, I think, in the distinction he draws between my attitude and that of the "orthodox" theory to what he calls the "homogeneity postulate." I should have thought, however, that there was abundant evidence from experience to contradict this postulate; and that, in any case, it is for those who make a highly special assumption to justify it, rather than for one who dispenses with it, to prove a general negative. I would also suggest that his idea might be applied more fruitfully and with greater theoretical precision in connection with the part played by the quantity of money in determining the rate of interest. For it is here, I think, that the homogeneity postulate primarily enters into the orthodox theoretical scheme.

My differences, such as they are, from Mr Robertson chiefly arise out of my conviction that both he and I differ more fundamentally from our predecessors than his piety will allow. With many of his points I agree, without, however, being conscious in several instances of having said (or, anyhow, meant) anything different. I am surprised he should think that those who make sport with the velocity of the circulation of money have much in common with the theory of the multiplier. I fully agree with the important point he makes … that the increased demand for money resulting from an increase in activity has a backwash which tends to raise the rate of interest; and this is, indeed, a significant element in my theory of why booms carry within them the seeds of their own destruction. But this is, essentially, a part of the liquidity theory of the rate of interest, and not of the "orthodox" theory. Where he states … that my theory must be regarded "not as a refutation of a common-sense account of events in terms of supply and demand for loanable funds, but as an alternative version of it," I must ask, before agreeing, for at least one reference to where this common-sense account is to be found.

There remains the most important of the four comments, namely Professor Viner's. In regard to his criticisms of my definition and treatment of involuntary unemployment, I am ready to agree that this part of my book is particularly open to criticism. I already feel myself in a position to make improvements, and I hope that, when I do so, Professor Viner will feel more content, especially as I do not think that there is anything fundamental between us here. In the case of his second section, however, entitled "The Propensity to Hoard" I am prepared to debate his points. There are passages which suggest that Professor Viner is thinking too much in the more familiar terms of the quantity of money actually hoarded, and that he overlooks the emphasis I seek to

* *Quarterly Journal of Economics* (February 1937): 209–23.

place on the rate of interest as being the inducement *not* to hoard. It is precisely because the facilities for hoarding are strictly limited that liquidity preference mainly operates by increasing the rate of interest. I cannot agree that "in modern monetary theory the propensity to hoard is generally dealt with, with results which in kind are substantially identical with Keynes', as a factor operating to reduce the 'velocity' of money." On the contrary, I am convinced that the monetary theorists who try to deal with it in this way are altogether on the wrong track. Again, when Professor Viner points out that most people invest their savings at the best rate of interest they can get and asks for statistics to justify the importance I attach to liquidity-preference, he is overlooking the point that it is the *marginal* potential hoarder who has to be satisfied by the rate of interest, so as to bring the desire for actual hoards within the narrow limits of the cash available for hoarding. When, as happens in a crisis, liquidity-preferences are sharply raised, this shows itself not so much in increased hoards – for there is little, if any, more cash which is hoardable than there was before – as in a sharp rise in the rate of interest, that is, securities fall in price until those, who would now like to get liquid if they could do so at the previous price, are persuaded to give up the idea as being no longer practicable on reasonable terms. A rise in the rate of interest is a means *alternative* to an increase of hoards for satisfying an increased liquidity-preference. Nor is my argument affected by the admitted fact that different types of assets satisfy the desire for liquidity in different degrees. The mischief is done when the rate of interest corresponding to the degree of liquidity of a given asset leads to a market-capitalization of that asset which is less than its cost of production.

There are other criticisms also which I should be ready to debate. But though I might be able to justify my own language, I am anxious not to be led, through doing so in too much detail, to overlook the substantial points which may, nevertheless, underlie the reactions which my treatment has produced in the minds of my critics. I am more attached to the comparatively simple fundamental ideas which underlie my theory than to the particular forms in which I have embodied them, and I have no desire that the latter should be crystallized at the present stage of the debate. If the simple basic ideas can become familiar and acceptable, time and experience, and the collaboration of a number of minds will discover the best way of expressing them. I would, therefore, prefer to occupy such further space, as the Editor of this Journal can allow me, in trying to reëxpress some of these ideas, than in detailed controversy which might prove barren. And I believe that I shall effect this best, even though this may seem to some as plunging straight off into the controversial mood from which I purport to seek escape, if I put what I have to say in the shape of a discussion as to certain definite points where I seem to myself to be most clearly departing from previous theories.

II

It is generally recognized that the Ricardian analysis was concerned with what we now call long-period equilibrium. Marshall's contribution mainly consisted in grafting on to this the marginal principle and the principle of substitution, together with some discussion of the passage from one position of long-period equilibrium to another. But he assumed, as Ricardo did, that the amounts of the factors of production in use were given and that the problem was to determine the way in which they would be used and their relative rewards. Edgeworth and Professor Pigou and other later and contemporary writers have embroidered and improved this theory by considering how different peculiarities in the shapes of the supply functions of the factors of production would affect matters, what will happen in conditions of monopoly and imperfect competition, how far social and individual advantage coincide, what are the special problems of exchange in an open system and the like. But these more recent writers like their predecessors were still dealing with a system in which the amount of the factors employed was given and the other relevant facts were known more or less for certain. This does not mean that they were dealing with a system in which change was ruled out, or even one in which the disappointment of expectation was ruled out. But at any given time facts and expectations were assumed to be given in a definite and calculable form; and risks, of which, though admitted, not much notice was taken, were supposed to be capable of an exact actuarial computation. The calculus of probability, though mention of it was kept in the background, was supposed to be capable of reducing uncertainty to the same calculable status as that of certainty itself; just as in the Benthamite calculus of pains and pleasures or of advantage and disadvantage, by which the Benthamite philosophy assumed men to be influenced in their general ethical behavior.

Actually, however, we have, as a rule, only the vaguest idea of any but the most direct consequences of our acts. Sometimes we are not much concerned with their remoter consequences, even though time and chance may make much of them. But sometimes we are intensely concerned with them, more so, occasionally, than with the immediate consequences. Now of all human activities which are affected by this remoter preoccupation, it happens that one of the most important is economic in character, namely Wealth. The whole object of the accumulation of Wealth is to produce results, or potential results, at a comparatively distant, and sometimes at an *indefinitely* distant, date. Thus, the fact that our knowledge of the future is fluctuating, vague, and uncertain, renders Wealth a peculiarly unsuitable subject for the methods of the classical economic theory. This theory might work very well in a world in which economic goods were necessarily consumed within a short interval of their being produced. But it requires, I suggest, considerable amendment if it is to be applied to a world in which the accumulation of wealth for an indefinitely postponed future is an important factor; and the greater the proportionate part played by such wealth-accumulation the more essential does such amendment become.

By "uncertain" knowledge, let me explain, I do not mean merely to distinguish what is known for certain from what is only probable. The game of roulette is not subject, in this sense, to uncertainty; nor is the prospect of a Victory bond being drawn. Or, again, the expectation of life is only slightly uncertain. Even the weather is only moderately uncertain. The sense in which I am using the term is that in which the prospect of a European war is uncertain, or the price of copper and the rate of interest twenty years hence, or the obsolescence of a new invention, or the position of private wealth-owners in the social system in 1970. About these matters there is no scientific basis on which to form any calculable probability whatever. We simply do not know. Nevertheless, the necessity for action and for decision compels us as practical men to do our best to overlook this awkward fact and to behave exactly as we should if we had behind us a good Benthamite calculation of a series of prospective advantages and disadvantages, each multiplied by its appropriate probability, waiting to be summed.

How do we manage in such circumstances to behave in a manner which saves our faces as rational, economic men? We have devised for the purpose a variety of techniques, of which much the most important are the three following:

1   We assume that the present is a much more serviceable guide to the future than a candid examination of past experience would show it to have been hitherto. In other words, we largely ignore the prospect of future changes about the actual character of which we know nothing.
2   We assume that the *existing* state of opinion as expressed in prices and the character of existing output is based on a *correct* summing up of future prospects, so that we can accept it as such unless and until something new and relevant comes into the picture.
3   Knowing that our own individual judgment is worthless, we endeavor to fall back on the judgment of the rest of the world which is perhaps better informed. That is, we endeavor to conform with the behavior of the majority or the average. The psychology of a society of individuals each of whom is endeavoring to copy the others leads to what we may strictly term a *conventional* judgment.

Now a practical theory of the future based on these three principles has certain marked characteristics. In particular, being based on so flimsy a foundation, it is subject to sudden and violent changes. The practice of calmness and immobility, of certainty and security, suddenly breaks down. New fears and hopes will, without warning, take charge of human conduct. The forces of disillusion may suddenly impose a new conventional basis of valuation. All these pretty, polite techniques, made for a well-panelled Board Room and a nicely regulated market, are liable to collapse. At all times the vague panic fears and equally vague and unreasoned hopes are not really lulled, and lie but a little way below the surface.

Perhaps the reader feels that this general, philosophical disquisition on the behavior of mankind is somewhat remote from the economic theory under discussion. But I think not. Though this is how we behave in the market place, the theory we devise in the study of how we behave in the market place should not itself submit to market-place idols. I accuse the classical economic theory of being itself one of these pretty, polite techniques which tries to deal with the present by abstracting from the fact that we know very little about the future.

I daresay that a classical economist would readily admit this. But, even so, I think he has overlooked the precise nature of the difference which his abstraction makes between theory and practice, and the character of the fallacies into which he is likely to be led.

This is particularly the case in his treatment of Money and Interest. And our first step must be to elucidate more clearly the functions of Money.

Money, it is well known, serves two principal purposes. By acting as a money of account it facilitates exchanges without its being necessary that it should ever itself come into the picture as a substantive object. In this respect it is a convenience which is devoid of significance or real influence. In the second place, it is a store of wealth. So we are told, without a smile on the face. But in the world of the classical economy, what an insane use to which to put it! For it is a recognized characteristic of money as a store of wealth that it is barren; whereas practically every other form of storing wealth yields some interest or profit. Why should anyone outside a lunatic asylum wish to use money as a store of wealth?

Because, partly on reasonable and partly on instinctive grounds, our desire to hold Money as a store of wealth is a barometer of the degree of our distrust of our own calculations and conventions concerning the future. Even though this feeling about Money is itself conventional or instinctive, it operates, so to speak, at a deeper level of our motivation. It takes charge at the moments when the higher, more precarious conventions have weakened. The possession of actual money lulls our disquietude; and the premium which we require to make us part with money is the measure of the degree of our disquietude.

The significance of this characteristic of money has usually been overlooked; and in so far as it has been noticed, the essential nature of the phenomenon has been misdescribed. For what has attracted attention has been the *quantity* of money which has been hoarded; and importance has been attached to this because it has been supposed to have a direct proportionate effect on the price-level through affecting the velocity of circulation. But the *quantity* of hoards can only be altered either if the total quantity of money is changed or if the quantity of current money-income (I speak broadly) is changed; whereas fluctuations in the degree of confidence are capable of having quite a different effect, namely in modifying not the amount that is actually hoarded, but the amount of the premium which has to be offered to induce people not to hoard. And changes in the propensity to hoard, or in the state of liquidity-preference as I have called it, primarily affect, not prices, but the rate of interest; any effect on prices being produced by repercussion as an ultimate consequence of a change in the rate of interest.

This, expressed in a very general way, is my theory of the rate of interest. The rate of interest obviously measures – just as the books on arithmetic say it does – the premium which has to be offered to induce people to hold their wealth in some form other than hoarded money. The quantity of money and the amount of it required in the active circulation for the transaction of current business (mainly depending on the level of money-income) determine how much is available for inactive balances, that is, for hoards. The rate of interest is the factor which adjusts at the margin the demand for hoards to the supply of hoards.

Now let us proceed to the next stage of the argument. The owner of wealth, who has been induced not to hold his wealth in the shape of hoarded money, still has two alternatives between which to choose. He can lend his money at the current rate of money-interest or he can purchase some kind of capital-asset. Clearly in equilibrium these two alternatives must offer an equal advantage to the marginal investor in each of them. This is brought about by shifts in the money-prices of capital-assets relative to the prices of money-loans. The prices of capital-assets move until, having regard to their prospective yields and account being taken of all those elements of doubt and uncertainty, interested and disinterested advice, fashion, convention, and what else you will which affect the mind of the investor, they offer an equal apparent advantage to the marginal investor who is wavering between one kind of investment and another.

This, then, is the first repercussion of the rate of interest, as fixed by the quantity of money and the propensity to hoard, namely on the prices of capital-assets. This does not mean, of course, that the rate of interest is the only fluctuating influence on these prices. Opinions as to their prospective yield are themselves subject to sharp fluctuations, precisely for the reason already given, namely the flimsiness of the basis of knowledge on which they depend. It is these opinions taken in conjunction with the rate of interest which fix their price.

Now for stage three. Capital-assets are capable, in general, of being newly produced. The scale on which they are produced depends, of course, on the relation between their costs of production and the prices which they are expected to realize in the market. Thus, if the level of the rate of interest taken in conjunction with opinions about their prospective yield raise the prices of capital-assets, the volume of current investment (meaning by this the value of the output of newly produced capital-assets) will be increased; while if, on the other hand, these influences reduce the prices of capital-assets, the volume of current investment will be diminished.

It is not surprising that the volume of investment, thus determined, should fluctuate widely from time to time. For it depends on two sets of judgments about the future, neither of which rests on an adequate or secure foundation – on the propensity to hoard and on opinions of the future yield of capital-assets. Nor is there any reason to suppose that the fluctuations in one of these factors will tend to offset the fluctuations in the other. When a more pessimistic view is taken about future yields, that is no reason why there should be a diminished propensity to hoard. Indeed, the conditions which aggravate the one factor tend, as a rule, to aggravate the other. For the same circumstances which lead to pessimistic views about future yields are apt to increase the propensity to hoard. The only element of self-righting in the system arises at a much later stage and in an uncertain degree. If a decline in investment leads to a decline in output as a whole, this may result (for more reasons than one) in a reduction of the amount of money required for the active circulation, which will release a larger quantity of money for the inactive circulation, which will satisfy the propensity to hoard at a lower level of the rate of interest, which will raise the prices of capital-assets, which will increase the scale of investment, which will restore in some measure the level of output as a whole.

This completes the first chapter of the argument, namely the liability of the scale of investment to fluctuate for reasons quite distinct (*a*) from those which determine the propensity of the individual to *save* out of a given income and (*b*) from those physical conditions of technical capacity to aid production which have usually been supposed hitherto to be the chief influence governing the marginal efficiency of capital.

If, on the other hand, our knowledge of the future was calculable and not subject to sudden changes, it might be justifiable to assume that the liquidity-preference curve was both stable and very inelastic. In this case a small decline in money-income would lead to a large fall in the rate of interest, probably sufficient to raise output and employment to the full. In these conditions we might reasonably suppose that the whole of the available resources would normally be employed; and the conditions required by the orthodox theory would be satisfied.

III

My next difference from the traditional theory concerns its apparent conviction that there is no necessity to work out a theory of the demand and supply of output *as a whole*. Will a fluctuation in investment, arising for the reasons just described, have any effect on the demand for output as a whole, and consequently on the scale of output and employment? What answer can the traditional theory make to this question? I believe that it makes no answer at all, never having given the matter a single thought; the theory of effective demand, that is the demand for output as a whole, having been entirely neglected for more than a hundred years.

My own answer to this question involves fresh considerations. I say that effective demand is made up of two items – investment-expenditure determined in the manner just explained and consumption-expenditure. Now what governs the amount of consumption-expenditure? It depends mainly on the level of income. People's propensity to spend (as I call it) is influenced by many factors such as the distribution of income, their normal attitude to the future, and – though probably in a minor degree – by the rate of interest. But in the main the prevailing psychological law seems to be that when aggregate income increases, consumption-expenditure will also increase but to a somewhat lesser extent. This is a very obvious conclusion. It simply amounts to saying that an increase in income will be divided in some proportion or another between spending and saving, and that when our income is increased it is extremely unlikely that this will have the effect of making us either spend less or save less than before. This psychological law was of the utmost importance in the development of my own thought, and it is, I think, absolutely fundamental to the theory of effective demand as set forth in my book. But few critics or commentators so far have paid particular attention to it.

There follows from this extremely obvious principle an important, yet unfamiliar, conclusion. Incomes are created partly by entrepreneurs producing for investment and partly by their producing for consumption. The amount that is consumed depends on the amount of income thus made up. Hence, the amount of consumption-goods which it will pay entrepreneurs to produce depends on the amount of investment-goods which they are producing. If, for example, the public are in the habit of spending nine-tenths of their income on consumption-goods, it follows that if entrepreneurs were to produce consumption-goods at a cost more than nine times the cost of the investment-goods they are producing, some part of their output could not be sold at a price which would cover its cost of production. For the consumption-goods on the market would have cost more than nine-tenths of the aggregate income of the public and would therefore be in excess of the demand for consumption-goods, which by hypothesis is only the nine-tenths. Thus, entrepreneurs will make a loss until they contract their output of consumption-goods down to an amount at which it no longer exceeds nine times their current output of investment goods.

The formula is not, of course, quite so simple as in this illustration. The proportion of their incomes which the public will choose to consume will not be a constant one, and in the most general case other factors are also relevant. But there is always a formula, more or less of this kind, relating the output of consumption-goods which it pays to produce to the output of investment-goods; and I have given attention to it in my book under the name of the *Multiplier*. The fact that an increase in consumption is apt in itself to stimulate this further investment merely fortifies the argument.

That the level of output of consumption-goods, which is profitable to the entrepreneur, should be related by a formula of this kind to the output of investment-goods depends on assumptions of a simple and obvious character. The conclusion appears to me to be quite beyond dispute. Yet, the consequences which follow from it are at the same time unfamiliar and of the greatest possible importance.

The theory can be summed up by saying that, given the psychology of the public, the level of output and employment as a whole depends on the amount of investment. I put it in this way, not because this is the only factor on which aggregate output depends, but because it is usual in a complex system to regard as the *causa causans* that factor which is most prone to sudden and wide fluctuation. More comprehensively, aggregate output depends on the propensity to hoard, on the policy of the monetary authority as it affects the quantity of money, on the state of confidence concerning the prospective yield of capital-assets, on the propensity to spend and on the social factors which influence the level of the money-wage. But of these several factors it is those which determine the rate of investment which are most unreliable, since it is they which are influenced by our views of the future about which we know so little.

This that I offer is, therefore, a theory of why output and employment are so liable to fluctuation. It does not offer a ready-made remedy as to how to avoid these fluctuations and to maintain output at a steady optimum level. But it is, properly speaking, a Theory of Employment because it explains *why*, in any given circumstances, employment is what it is. Naturally, I am interested not only in the diagnosis, but also in the cure; and many pages of my book are devoted to the latter. But I consider that my suggestions for a cure, which, avowedly, are not worked out completely, are on a different plane from the diagnosis. They are not meant to be definitive; they are subject to all sorts of special assumptions and are necessarily related to the particular conditions of the time. But my main reasons for departing from the traditional theory go much deeper than this. They are of a highly general character and are meant to be definitive.

I sum up, therefore, the main grounds of my departure as follows:

1. The orthodox theory assumes that we have a knowledge of the future of a kind quite different from that which we actually possess. This false rationalization follows the lines of the Benthamite calculus. The hypothesis of a calculable future leads to a wrong interpretation of the principles of behavior which the need for action compels us to adopt, and to an underestimation of the concealed factors of utter doubt, precariousness, hope, and fear. The result has been a mistaken theory of the rate of interest. It is true that the necessity of equalizing the advantages of the choice between owning loans and assets requires that the rate of interest should be *equal* to the marginal efficiency of capital. But this does not tell us at what *level* the equality will be effective. The orthodox theory regards the marginal efficiency of capital as setting the pace. But the marginal efficiency of capital depends on the price of capital-assets; and since this price determines the rate of new investment, it is consistent in equilibrium with only one given level of money-income. Thus, the marginal efficiency of capital is not determined, unless the level of money-income is given. In a system in which the level of money-income is capable of fluctuating, the orthodox theory is one equation short of what is required to give a solution. Undoubtedly, the reason why the orthodox system has failed to discover this discrepancy is because it has always tacitly assumed that income *is* given, namely at the level corresponding to the employment of all the available resources. In other words it is tacitly assuming that the monetary policy is such as to maintain the rate of interest at that level which is compatible with full employment. It is, therefore, incapable of dealing with the general case where employment is liable to fluctuate. Thus, instead of the marginal efficiency of capital determining the rate of interest, it is truer (though not a full statement of the case) to say that it is the rate of interest which determines the marginal efficiency of capital.

2. The orthodox theory would by now have discovered the above defect, if it had not ignored the need for a theory of the supply and demand of output as a whole. I doubt if many modern economists really accept Say's Law that supply creates its own demand. But they have not been aware that they were tacitly assuming it. Thus, the psychological law underlying the Multiplier has escaped notice. It has not been observed that the amount of consumption-goods which it pays entrepreneurs to produce is a function of the amount of investment-goods which it pays them to produce. The explanation is to be found, I suppose, in the tacit assumption that every individual spends the whole of his income either on consumption or on buying, directly or indirectly, newly produced capital goods. But, here again, whilst the older economists expressly believed this, I doubt if many contemporary economists really do believe it. They have discarded these older ideas without becoming aware of the consequences.

The General Theory of Employment, Interest and Money (1936)*

Chapter 24: Concluding notes on the social philosophy towards which the general theory might lead

I

The outstanding faults of the economic society in which we live are its failure to provide for full employment and its arbitrary and inequitable distribution of wealth and incomes. The bearing of the foregoing theory on the first of these is obvious. But there are also two important respects in which it is relevant to the second.

Since the end of the nineteenth century significant progress towards the removal of very great disparities of wealth and income has been achieved through the instrument of direct taxation – income tax and surtax, and death duties – especially in Great Britain. Many people would wish to see this process carried much further, but they are deterred by two considerations; partly by the fear of making skilful evasions too much worth while and also of diminishing unduly the motive towards risk-taking, but mainly, I think, by the belief that the growth of capital depends upon the strength of the motive towards individual saving and that for a large proportion of this growth we are dependent on the savings of the rich out of their superfluity. Our argument does not affect the first of these considerations. But it may considerably modify our attitude towards the second. For we have seen that, up to the point where full employment prevails, the growth of capital depends not at all on a low propensity to consume but is, on the contrary, held back by it; and only in conditions of full employment is a low propensity to consume conducive to the growth of capital. Moreover, experience suggests that in existing conditions saving by institutions and through sinking funds is more than adequate, and that measures for the redistribution of incomes in a way likely to raise the propensity to consume may prove positively favourable to the growth of capital.

The existing confusion of the public mind on the matter is well illustrated by the very common belief that the death duties are responsible for a reduction in the capital wealth of the country. Assuming that the State applies the proceeds of these duties to its ordinary outgoings so that taxes on incomes and consumption are correspondingly reduced or avoided, it is, of course, true that a fiscal policy of heavy death duties has the effect of increasing the community's propensity to consume. But inasmuch as an increase in the habitual propensity to consume will in general (i.e. except in conditions of full employment) serve to increase at the same time the inducement to invest, the inference commonly drawn is the exact opposite of the truth.

Thus, our argument leads towards the conclusion that in contemporary conditions the growth of wealth, so far from being dependent on the abstinence of the rich, as is commonly supposed, is more likely to be impeded by it. One of the chief social justifications of great inequality of wealth is, therefore, removed. I am not saying that there are no other reasons, unaffected by our theory, capable of justifying some measure of inequality in some circumstances. But it does dispose of the most important of the reasons why hitherto we have thought it prudent to move carefully. This particularly affects our attitude towards death duties: for there are certain justifications for inequality of incomes which do not apply equally to inequality of inheritances.

* London: Macmillan, 1936.

For my own part, I believe that there is social and psychological justification for significant inequalities of incomes and wealth, but not for such large disparities as exist to-day. There are valuable human activities which require the motive of money-making and the environment of private wealth-ownership for their full fruition. Moreover, dangerous human proclivities can be canalised into comparatively harmless channels by the existence of opportunities for money-making and private wealth, which, if they cannot be satisfied in this way, may find their outlet in cruelty, the reckless pursuit of personal power and authority, and other forms of self-aggrandisement. It is better that a man should tyrannise over his bank balance than over his fellow-citizens; and whilst the former is sometimes denounced as being but a means to the latter, sometimes at least it is an alternative. But it is not necessary for the stimulation of these activities and the satisfaction of these proclivities that the game should be played for such high stakes as at present. Much lower stakes will serve the purpose equally well, as soon as the players are accustomed to them. The task of transmuting human nature must not be confused with the task of managing it. Though in the ideal commonwealth men may have been taught or inspired or bred to take no interest in the stakes, it may still be wise and prudent statesmanship to allow the game to be played, subject to rules and limitations, so long as the average man, or even a significant section of the community, is in fact strongly addicted to the money-making passion.

II

There is, however, a second, much more fundamental inference from our argument which has a bearing on the future of inequalities of wealth; namely our theory of the rate of interest. The justification for a moderately high rate of interest has been found hitherto in the necessity of providing a sufficient inducement to save. But we have shown that the extent of effective saving is necessarily determined by the scale of investment and that the scale of investment is promoted by a *low* rate of interest, provided that we do not attempt to stimulate it in this way beyond the point which corresponds to full employment. Thus, it is to our best advantage to reduce the rate of interest to that point relatively to the schedule of the marginal efficiency of capital at which there is full employment.

There can be no doubt that this criterion will lead to a much lower rate of interest than has ruled hitherto; and, so far as one can guess at the schedules of the marginal efficiency of capital corresponding to increasing amounts of capital, the rate of interest is likely to fall steadily, if it should be practicable to maintain conditions of more or less continuous full employment – unless, indeed, there is an excessive change in the aggregate propensity to consume (including the State).

I feel sure that the demand for capital is strictly limited in the sense that it would not be difficult to increase the stock of capital up to a point where its marginal efficiency had fallen to a very low figure. This would not mean that the use of capital instruments would cost almost nothing, but only that the return from them would have to cover little more than their exhaustion by wastage and obsolescence together with some margin to cover risk and the exercise of skill and judgement. In short, the aggregate return from durable goods in the course of their life would, as in the case of short-lived goods, just cover their labour-costs of production *plus* an allowance for risk and the costs of skill and supervision.

Now, though this state of affairs would be quite compatible with some measure of individualism, yet it would mean the euthanasia of the rentier, and, consequently, the euthanasia of the cumulative oppressive power of the capitalist to exploit the scarcity-value of capital. Interest to-day rewards no genuine sacrifice, any more than does the rent of land. The owner of capital can obtain interest because capital is scarce, just as the owner of land can obtain rent because land is scarce. But whilst there may be intrinsic reasons for the scarcity of land, there are no intrinsic reasons for the scarcity of capital. An intrinsic reason for such scarcity, in the sense of a genuine sacrifice which could only be called forth by the offer of a reward in the shape of interest, would not exist, in the long run, except in the event of the individual propensity to consume proving to be of such a character that net saving in conditions of full employment comes to an end before capital has become sufficiently abundant. But even so, it will still be possible for communal saving through the agency of the State to be maintained at a level which will allow the growth of capital up to the point where it ceases to be scarce.

I see, therefore, the rentier aspect of capitalism as a transitional phase which will disappear when it has done its work. And with the disappearance of its rentier aspect much else in it besides will suffer a sea-change. It will be, moreover, a great advantage of the order of events which I am advocating, that the euthanasia of the rentier, of the functionless investor, will be nothing sudden, merely a gradual but prolonged continuance of what we have seen recently in Great Britain, and will need no revolution.

Thus, we might aim in practice (there being nothing in this which is unattainable) at an increase in the volume of capital until it ceases to be scarce, so that the functionless investor will no longer receive a bonus; and at a scheme of direct taxation which allows the intelligence and determination, and executive skill of the financier, the entrepreneur *et hoc genus omne* (who are certainly so fond of their craft that their labour could be obtained much cheaper than at present), to be harnessed to the service of the community on reasonable terms of reward.

At the same time we must recognise that only experience can show how far the common will, embodied in the policy of the State, ought to be directed to increasing and supplementing the inducement to invest; and how far it is safe to stimulate the average propensity to consume, without forgoing our aim of depriving capital of its scarcity-value within one or two generations. It may turn out that the propensity to consume will be so easily strengthened by the effects of a falling rate of interest, that full employment can be reached with a rate of accumulation little greater than at present. In this event a scheme for the higher taxation of large incomes and inheritances might be open to the objection that it would lead to full employment with a rate of accumulation which was reduced considerably below the current level. I must not be supposed to deny the possibility, or even the probability, of this outcome. For in such matters it is rash to predict how the average man will react to a changed environment. If, however, it should prove easy to secure an approximation to full employment with a rate of accumulation not much greater than at present, an outstanding problem will at least have been solved. And it would remain for separate decision on what scale and by what means it is right and reasonable to call on the living generation to restrict their consumption, so as to establish, in course of time, a state of full investment for their successors.

III

In some other respects the foregoing theory is moderately conservative in its implications. For whilst it indicates the vital importance of establishing certain central controls in matters which are now left in the main to individual initiative, there are wide fields of activity which are unaffected. The State will have to exercise a guiding influence on the propensity to consume partly through its scheme of taxation, partly by fixing the rate of interest, and partly, perhaps, in other ways. Furthermore, it seems unlikely that the influence of banking policy on the rate of interest will be sufficient by itself to determine an optimum rate of investment. I conceive, therefore, that a somewhat comprehensive socialisation of investment will prove the only means of securing an approximation to full employment; though this need not exclude all manner of compromises and of devices by which public authority will co-operate with private initiative. But beyond this no obvious case is made out for a system of State Socialism which would embrace most of the economic life of the community. It is not the ownership of the instruments of production which it is important for the State to assume. If the State is able to determine the aggregate amount of resources devoted to augmenting the instruments and the basic rate of reward to those who own them, it will have accomplished all that is necessary. Moreover, the necessary measures of social-isation can be introduced gradually and without a break in the general traditions of society.

Our criticism of the accepted classical theory of economics has consisted not so much in finding logical flaws in its analysis as in pointing out that its tacit assumptions are seldom or never satisfied, with the result that it cannot solve the economic problems of the actual world. But if our central controls succeed in establishing an aggregate volume of output corresponding to full employment as nearly as is practicable, the classical theory comes into its own again from this point onwards. If we suppose the volume of output to be given, that is, to be determined by forces outside the classi-cal scheme of thought, then there is no objection to be raised against the classical analysis of the manner in which private self-interest will determine what in particular is produced, in what pro-portions the factors of production will be combined to produce it, and how the value of the final product will be distributed between them. Again, if we have dealt otherwise with the problem of thrift, there is no objection to be raised against the modern classical theory as to the degree of con-silience between private and public advantage in conditions of perfect and imperfect competition, respectively. Thus, apart from the necessity or central controls to bring about an adjustment between the propensity to consume and the inducement to invest, there is no more reason to socialise economic life than there was before.

To put the point concretely, I see no reason to suppose that the existing system seriously misemploys the factors of production which are in use. There are, of course, errors of foresight; but these would not be avoided by centralising decisions. When 9,000,000 men are employed out of 10,000,000 willing and able to work, there is no evidence that the labour of these 9,000,000 men is misdirected. The complaint against the present system is not that these 9,000,000 men ought to be employed on different tasks, but that tasks should be available for the remaining 1,000,000 men. It is in determining the volume, not the direction, of actual employment that the existing system has broken down.

Thus, I agree with Gesell that the result of filling in the gaps in the classical theory is not to dispose of the 'Manchester System', but to indicate the nature of the environment which the free play of economic forces requires if it is to realise the full potentialities of production. The central controls necessary to ensure full employment will, of course, involve a large extension of the traditional functions of government. Furthermore, the modern classical theory has itself called attention to various conditions in which the free play of economic forces may need to be curbed or guided. But there will still remain a wide field for the exercise of private initiative and responsibility. Within this field the traditional advantages of individualism will still hold good.

Let us stop for a moment to remind ourselves what these advantages are. They are partly advantages of efficiency – the advantages of decentralisation and of the play of self-interest. The advantage to efficiency of the decentralisation of decisions and of individual responsibility is even greater, perhaps, than the nineteenth century supposed; and the reaction against the appeal to self-interest may have gone too far. But, above all, individualism, if it can be purged of its defects and its abuses, is the best safeguard of personal liberty in the sense that, compared with any other system, it greatly widens the field for the exercise of personal choice. It is also the best safeguard of the variety of life, which emerges precisely from this extended field of personal choice, and the loss of which is the greatest of all the losses of the homogeneous or totalitarian state. For this variety preserves the traditions which embody the most secure and successful choices of former generations; it colours the present with the diversification of its fancy; and, being the handmaid of experiment as well as of tradition and of fancy, it is the most powerful instrument to better the future.

Whilst, therefore, the enlargement of the functions of government, involved in the task of adjusting to one another the propensity to consume and the inducement to invest, would seem to a nineteenth-century publicist or to a contemporary American financier to be a terrific encroachment on individualism, I defend it, on the contrary, both as the only practicable means of avoiding the destruction of existing economic forms in their entirety and as the condition of the successful functioning of individual initiative.

For if effective demand is deficient, not only is the public scandal of wasted resources intolerable, but the individual enterpriser who seeks to bring these resources into action is operating with the odds loaded against him. The game of hazard which he plays is furnished with many zeros, so that the players *as a whole* will lose if they have the energy and hope to deal all the cards. Hitherto the increment of the world's wealth has fallen short of the aggregate of positive individual savings; and the difference has been made up by the losses of those whose courage and initiative have not been supplemented by exceptional skill or unusual good fortune. But if effective demand is adequate, average skill and average good fortune will be enough.

The authoritarian state systems of to-day seem to solve the problem of unemployment at the expense of efficiency and of freedom. It is certain that the world will not much longer tolerate the unemployment which, apart from brief intervals of excitement, is associated – and, in my opinion, inevitably associated – with present-day capitalistic individualism. But it may be possible by a right analysis of the problem to cure the disease whilst preserving efficiency and freedom.

IV

I have mentioned in passing that the new system might be more favourable to peace than the old has been. It is worth while to repeat and emphasise that aspect.

War has several causes. Dictators and others such, to whom war offers, in expectation at least, a pleasurable excitement, find it easy to work on the natural bellicosity of their peoples. But, over and above this, facilitating their task of fanning the popular flame, are the economic causes of war, namely the pressure of population and the competitive struggle for markets. It is the second factor, which probably played a predominant part in the nineteenth century, and might again, that is germane to this discussion.

I have pointed out in the preceding chapter that, under the system of domestic *laissez-faire* and an international gold standard such as was orthodox in the latter half of the nineteenth century, there was no means open to a government whereby to mitigate economic distress at home except through the competitive struggle for markets. For all measures helpful to a state of chronic or intermittent under-employment were ruled out, except measures to improve the balance of trade on income account.

Thus, whilst economists were accustomed to applaud the prevailing international system as furnishing the fruits of the international division of labour and harmonising at the same time the interests of different nations, there lay concealed a less benign influence; and those statesmen were moved by common sense and a correct apprehension of the true course of events, who believed that if a rich, old country were to neglect the struggle for markets its prosperity would droop and fail. But if nations can learn to provide themselves with full employment by their domestic policy (and, we must add, if they can also attain equilibrium in the trend of their population), there need be no important economic forces calculated to set the interest of one country against that of its neighbours. There would still be room for the international division of labour and for international lending in appropriate conditions. But there would no longer be a pressing motive why one country need force its wares on another or repulse the offerings of its neighbour, not because this was necessary to enable it to pay for what it wished to purchase, but with the express object of upsetting the equilibrium of payments so as to develop a balance of trade in its own favour. International trade would cease to be what it is, namely, a desperate expedient to maintain employment at home by forcing sales on foreign markets and restricting purchases, which, if successful, will merely shift the problem of unemployment to the neighbour which is worsted in the struggle, but a willing and unimpeded exchange of goods and services in conditions of mutual advantage.

V

Is the fulfilment of these ideas a visionary hope? Have they insufficient roots in the motives which govern the evolution of political society? Are the interests which they will thwart stronger and more obvious than those which they will serve?

I do not attempt an answer in this place. It would need a volume of a different character from this one to indicate even in outline the practical measures in which they might be gradually clothed. But if the ideas are correct – a hypothesis on which the author himself must necessarily base what he writes – it would be a mistake, I predict, to dispute their potency over a period of time. At the present moment people are unusually expectant of a more fundamental diagnosis; more particularly ready to receive it; eager to try it out, if it should be even plausible. But apart from this contemporary mood, the ideas of economists and political philosophers, both when they are right and when they are wrong, are more powerful than is commonly understood. Indeed the world is ruled by little else. Practical men, who believe themselves to be quite exempt from any intellectual influences, are usually the slaves of some defunct economist. Madmen in authority, who hear voices in the air, are distilling their frenzy from some academic scribbler of a few years back. I am sure that the power of vested interests is vastly exaggerated compared with the gradual encroachment of ideas. Not, indeed, immediately, but after a certain interval; for in the field of economic and political philosophy there are not many who are influenced by new theories after they are 25 or 30 years of age, so that the ideas which civil servants and politicians and even agitators apply to current events are not likely to be the newest. But, soon or late, it is ideas, not vested interests, which are dangerous for good or evil.

Part 6

Institutional Economics

Introduction

Institutional economics, akin to and somewhat influenced by the German Historical Schools, is nonetheless a distinctively US phenomenon, though it has several key figures – Gunnar Myrdal and A.W. Kapp – and numerous followers in Europe. Institutionalism was a very conspicuous part of economics in the US before the First World War and during the interwar years, when the distinction between institutionalism and neoclassicism was not very stark and when many if not most economists were eclectic and had their feet in both schools of economic thought.

Institutionalism has had three distinct facets. (1) It has generated a body of knowledge concerning the organization and control of the economic system considered as a whole and its evolution, including the roles of informal and formal social control. (2) It has protested both (a) aspects of the market economy, particularly those associated with the corporate system and its hegemony in both economy and polity and (b) mainstream economics for its myopic treatment of important factors and forces, and its service in rationalizing and legitimizing the capitalist-dominated form of the market economy. (3) It has provided an approach to problem-solving which is empirical, holistic, and multi-disciplinary, pragmatic, reformist, and pluralist with regard to both power structure and the interests given effect through policy. Its leading early figures included Richard T. Ely, Thorstein B. Veblen, Walton Hamilton, John R. Commons, Wesley C. Mitchell, and John Maurice Clark.

As a body of knowledge dealing with the organization and control of the economic system as a whole and its evolution, institutionalism has centered on markets as institutional complexes operating within and giving effect to other institutional complexes; on the importance of power structure and power play; on the critical importance of the economic role of government and, therefore, of those who control its making of policy; on the critical roles of technology, psychology, and belief system in economic organization, policy, and performance. Where institutional economics has dealt with the same general problem as neoclassical economics, for example, the allocation of resources, it has deployed a wider and deeper range of variables; but for the most part institutional economics has dealt with a different central problem, that of organization and control. In those respects, institutionalism has continued – it will be seen on the basis of many of the earlier readings in this collection – a dual tradition, as it were, in economics: the simultaneous "pure-theory" analysis of the operation of markets and the empirical and historical analysis of institutions and the economic order which they form. Some of the latter has been obscured – as also seen above – by some economists through their taking the institutional system to be part of the natural order of things.

Thus, institutionalist theory has had several important coordinates, including: (1) a theory of social change, including an activist orientation toward social institutions; (2) a theory of social control, with a focus on the importance of collective action through the legal–economic nexus; (3) the importance of technology and, thereby, of industrialization; (4) the market seen as functioning within and giving effect to institutions, including the fundamental theme that it is not markets which allocate resources but the institutional and organizational structure of the system; (5) a theory of value centering, not on the exchange ratios between commodities, but on the values ensconced within the working rules of law and of morals which structured, governed access to, and governed the performance of markets and other domains of economic activity, such as government. In other words, institutionalism, far from seeking unique determinate optimal equilibrium solutions, sought to identify the factors and forces operative in the process of working out solutions to problems; and far from postulating a pure conceptual abstract a-institutional economic system, sought to deal with institutionally driven economies and the processes through which those institutions were formed, changed and operated. In both of these respects and also in regard to the foregoing coordinates, institutionalism has been, by comparison with mainstream neoclassical economics, holistic, and empirical.

The Veblen and Commons approaches to economics had several differences. One was that Veblen and his disciples have generally thought that institutional and neoclassical economics were contradictory and mutually exclusive; whereas Commons and his followers have generally felt that the work of the two schools was supplementary to each other. Another was that the Veblenians have envisioned institutions as inhibitive of progressive technology; whereas those in the Commons tradition have considered both institutions and technology to be important in generating economic performance and working things out.

For further reading

Barber, William J. (1994) "The Divergent Fates of Two Strands of 'Institutionalist' Doctrine During the New Deal Years," *History of Political Economy* 26 (Winter): 569–87.

Dorfman, Joseph *et al.* (1963) *Institutional Economics*, Berkeley: University of California Press.

Gruchy, Allan G. (1947) *Modern Economic Thought*, New York: Prentice-Hall.

Hodgson, Geoffrey M., Samuels, Warren J., and Tool, Marc R. (1994) *The Elgar Companion to Institutional and Evolutionary Economics*, Aldershot: Edward Elgar Publishing.

Rutherford, Malcolm (1994) *Institutions in Economics: The Old and the New Institutionalism*, Cambridge: Cambridge University Press.

—— (2000) "Understanding Institutional Economics: 1918–1929," *Journal of the History of Economic Thought* 22 (September): 277–308.

—— (2001) "Institutional Economics: Then and Now," *Journal of Economic Perspectives* 15 (Summer): 173–94.

Samuels, Warren J. (1987) "Institutional Economics," in John Eatwell, Murray Milgate, and Peter Newman (eds), *The New Palgrave: A Dictionary of Economics*, Vol. 2, London: Macmillan, 864–6.

——, ed. (1988) *Institutional Economics*, 3 vols., Aldershot: Edward Elgar Publishing.

THORSTEIN B. VEBLEN (1857–1929)

Thorstein B. Veblen, by courtesy of Corbis, www.corbis.com.

Thorstein B. Veblen was perhaps the United States' most original social thinker. Born in Wisconsin to Norwegian immigrant parents, Veblen earned a PhD in philosophy from Yale and later studied economics at Cornell. Veblen subsequently taught at the University of Chicago, Stanford University, and the University of Missouri.

Veblen brought a critical anthropological attitude toward behavior and practices taken as given and natural by his contemporaries. He stressed the roles of custom and habit over against the strict hedonism of the mainstream's notion of rational economic man. He emphasized the importance of the instinct of workmanship and its subversion by business principles – and a parallel analysis of the subversion of universities ("the higher learning") by the introduction of business ideology and principles. He leveled a wide-ranging critique of the methodology, as well as the substantive doctrines, of neoclassical economics – the name apparently coined by him. He stressed the static character of the mainstream analysis of utility and markets, arguing instead for an evolutionary economics which, *inter alia*, paid attention to the multiplicity of psychological drives (in the language of his day he called them "instincts") and the dynamic role of institutions, maintaining that otherwise economics was little more than a defense of existing arrangements, arrangements which were, in fact, always in a process of change.

Veblen's critique covered capitalism as it was institutionalized as well as mainstream economics. He identified a nonproductive ruling leisure class – in relation to which he coined the term "conspicuous consumption" to describe practices which all classes undertook in pursuit of status emulation. He distinguished between activities which were essentially pecuniary (making money) and activities which were essentially industrial (making goods). He focused on the institutional and power dynamics of the business enterprise and was among the first to identify and examine the modern corporate system and corporate state.

Veblen's most well-known book is undoubtedly his *Theory of the Leisure Class*, from which the following excerpts are drawn.

References and further reading

Blaug, Mark, ed. (1992) *Thorstein Veblen (1857–1929)*, Aldershot: Edward Elgar Publishing.

Dorfman, Joseph (1934) *Thorstein Velben and His America*, New York: Viking.

Hamilton, David (1953) "Veblen and Commons: A Case of Theoretical Convergence," *Southwestern Social Science Quarterly* 34 (September): 43–50.

Hobson, J.A. (1936) *Veblen*, London: Chapman and Hall.

Rutherford, Malcolm (1984) "Thorstein Veblen and the Process of Institutional Change," *History of Political Economy* 16 (Fall): 331–48.

Seckler, David (1974) Thorstein Veblen and the Institutionalists, London: Macmillan.

Sowell, Thomas (1967) "On the 'Evolutionary' Economics of Thorstein Veblen," *Oxford Economic Papers* 19 (July): 177–98.

——(1987) "Veblen, Thorstein," in John Eatwell, Murray Milgate, and Peter Newman (eds), *The New Palgrave: A Dictionary of Economics*, Vol. 4, London: Macmillan, 799–800.

Tilman, Ric (1992) *Thorstein Velben and His Critics, 1891–1963*, Princeton, NJ: Princeton University Press.

Veblen, Thorstein (1904) *The Theory of Business Enterprise*, New York: Charles Scribner's Sons.

——(1919) *The Place of Science in Modern Civilization*, New York: Huebsch.

Walker, Donald A. (1977) "Thorstein Veblen's Economic System," *Economic Inquiry* 15 (April): 213–37.

The Theory of the Leisure Class (1899)*

Chapter two: Pecuniary emulation

In the sequence of cultural evolution the emergence of a leisure class coincides with the beginning of ownership. This is necessarily the case, for these two institutions result from the same set of economic forces. In the inchoate phase of their development they are but different aspects of the same general facts of social structure.

It is as elements of social structure – conventional facts – that leisure and ownership are matters of interest for the purpose in hand. An habitual neglect of work does not constitute a leisure class; neither does the mechanical fact of use and consumption constitute ownership. The present enquiry, therefore, is not concerned with the beginning of indolence, nor with the beginning of the appropriation of useful articles to individual consumption. The point in question is the origin and nature of a conventional leisure class, on the one hand, and the beginnings of individual ownership as a conventional right or equitable claim, on the other hand.

The early differentiation out of which the distinction between a leisure and a working class arises is a division maintained between men's and women's work in the lower stages of barbarism. Likewise the earliest form of ownership is an ownership of the women by the able bodied men of the community.

The facts may be expressed in more general terms and truer to the import of the barbarian theory of life, by saying that it is an ownership of the woman by the man.

There was undoubtedly some appropriation of useful articles before the custom of appropriating women arose. The usages of existing archaic communities in which there is no ownership of women is warrant for such a view. In all communities the members, both male and female, habitually appropriate to their individual use a variety of useful things; but these useful things are not thought of as owned by the person who appropriates and consumes them. The habitual appropriation and consumption of certain slight personal effects goes on without raising the question of ownership; that is to say, the question of a conventional, equitable claim to extraneous things.

The ownership of women begins in the lower barbarian stages of culture, apparently with the seizure of female captives. The original reason for the seizure and appropriation of women seems to have been their usefulness as trophies. The practice of seizing women from the enemy as trophies, gave rise to a form of ownership-marriage, resulting in a household with a male head.

This was followed by an extension of slavery to other captives and inferiors, besides women, and by an extension of ownership-marriage to other women than those seized from the enemy. The outcome of emulation under the circumstances of a predatory life, therefore, has been, on the one hand, a form of marriage resting on coercion, and, on the other hand, the custom of

* Macmillan, 1899.

ownership. The two institutions are not distinguishable in the initial phase of their development; both arise from the desire of the successful men to put their prowess in evidence by exhibiting some durable result of their exploits. Both also minister to that propensity for mastery which pervades all predatory communities.

From the ownership of women the concept of ownership extends itself to include the products of their industry, and so there arises the ownership of things as well as of persons.

In this way a consistent system of property in goods is gradually installed. And although in the latest stages of the development, the serviceability of goods for consumption has come to be the most obtrusive element of their value, still, wealth has by no means yet lost its utility as a honorific evidence of the owner's prepotence.

Wherever the institution of private property is found, even in a slightly developed form, the economic process bears the character of a struggle between men for the possession of goods.

It has been customary in economic theory, and especially among those economists who adhere with least faltering to the body of modernised classical doctrines, to construe this struggle for wealth as being substantially a struggle for subsistence. Such is, no doubt, its character in large part during the earlier and less efficient phases of industry. Such is also its character in all cases where the 'niggardliness of nature' is so strict as to afford but a scanty livelihood to the community in return for strenuous and unremitting application to the business of getting the means of subsistence. But in all progressing communities an advance is presently made beyond this early stage of technological development. Industrial efficiency is presently carried to such a pitch as to afford something appreciably more than a bare livelihood to those engaged in the industrial process. It has not been unusual for economic theory to speak of the further struggle for wealth on this new industrial basis as a competition for an increase of the comforts of life – primarily for an increase of the physical comforts which the consumption of goods affords.

The end of acquisition and accumulation is conventionally held to be the consumption of the goods accumulated – whether it is consumption directly by the owner of the goods or by the household attached to him and for this purpose identified with him in theory. This is at least felt to be the economically legitimate end of acquisition, which alone it is incumbent on the theory to take account of. Such consumption may of course be conceived to serve the consumer's physical wants – his physical comfort – or his so-called higher wants – spiritual, aesthetic, intellectual, or what not; the latter class of wants being served indirectly by an expenditure of goods, after the fashion familiar to all economic readers.

But it is only when taken in a sense far removed from its naive meaning that consumption of goods can be said to afford the incentive from which accumulation invariably proceeds. The motive that lies at the root of ownership is emulation; and the same motive of emulation continues active in the further development of the institution to which it has given rise and in the development of all those features of the social structure which this institution of ownership touches. The possession of wealth confers honour; it is an invidious distinction. Nothing equally cogent can be said for the consumption of goods, nor for any other conceivable incentive to acquisition, and especially not for any incentive to accumulation of wealth.

It is of course not to be overlooked that in a community where nearly all goods are private property the necessity of earning a livelihood is a powerful and ever-present incentive for the poorer members of the community. The need of subsistence and of an increase of physical comfort may for a time be the dominant motive of acquisition for those classes who are habitually employed as manual labour, whose subsistence is on a precarious footing, who possess little and ordinarily accumulate little; but it will appear in the course of the discussion that even in the case of these impecunious classes the predominance of the motive of physical want is not so decided as has sometimes been assumed.

On the other hand, so far as regards those members and classes of the community who are chiefly concerned in the accumulation of wealth, the incentive of subsistence or of physical comfort never plays a considerable part. Ownership began and grew into a human institution on grounds unrelated to the subsistence minimum. The dominant incentive was from the outset the invidious distinction attaching to wealth, and, save temporarily and by exception, no other motive has usurped the primacy at any later stage of the development.

Property set out with being booty held as trophies of the successful raid. So long as the group had departed and so long as it still stood in close contact with other hostile groups, the utility of things or persons owned lay chiefly in an invidious comparison between their possessor and the enemy from whom they were taken. The habit of distinguishing between the interests of the individual and those of the group to which he belongs is apparently a later growth. Invidious comparison between the possessor of the honorific booty and his less successful neighbours within the group was no doubt present early as an element of the utility of the things possessed, though this was not at the outset the chief element of their value. The man's prowess was still primarily the group's prowess, and the possessor of the booty felt himself to be primarily the keeper of the honour of his group. This appreciation of exploit from the communal point of view is met with also at later stages of social growth, especially as regards the laurels of war.

But as soon as the custom of individual ownership begins to gain consistency, the point of view taken in making the invidious comparison on which private property rests will begin to change.

Indeed, the one change is but the reflex of the other. The initial phase of ownership, the phase of acquisition by naive seizure and conversion, begins to pass into the subsequent stage of an incipient organisation of industry on the basis of private property (in slaves); the horde develops into a more or less self-sufficing industrial community; possessions then come to be valued not so much as evidence of successful foray, but rather as evidence of the prepotence of the possessor of these goods over other individuals within the community. The invidious comparison now becomes primarily a comparison of the owner with the other members of the group. Property is still of the nature of trophy, but, with the cultural advance, it becomes more and more a trophy of successes scored in the game of ownership carried on between the members of the group under the quasi-peaceable methods of nomadic life.

Gradually, as industrial activity further displaced predatory activity in the community's everyday life and in men's habits of thought, accumulated property more and more replaces trophies of predatory exploit as the conventional exponent of prepotence and success. With the growth of settled industry, therefore, the possession of wealth gains in relative importance and effectiveness as a customary basis of repute and esteem. Not that esteem ceases to be awarded on the basis of other, more direct evidence of prowess; not that successful predatory aggression or warlike exploit ceases to call out the approval and admiration of the crowd, or to stir the envy of the less successful competitors; but the opportunities for gaining distinction by means of this direct manifestation of superior force grow less available both in scope and frequency. At the same time opportunities for industrial aggression, and for the accumulation of property, increase in scope and availability. And it is even more to the point that property now becomes the most easily recognised evidence of a reputable degree of success as distinguished from heroic or signal achievement. It therefore becomes the conventional basis of esteem. Its possession in some amount becomes necessary in order to any reputable standing in the community. It becomes indispensable to accumulate, to acquire property, in order to retain one's good name. When accumulated goods have in this way once become the accepted badge of efficiency, the possession of wealth presently assumes the character of an independent and definitive basis of esteem. The possession of goods, whether acquired aggressively by one's own exertion or passively by transmission through inheritance from others, becomes a conventional basis of reputability. The possession of wealth, which was at the outset valued simply as an evidence of efficiency, becomes, in popular apprehension, itself a meritorious act. Wealth is now itself intrinsically honourable and confers honour on its possessor. By a further refinement, wealth acquired passively by transmission from ancestors or other antecedents presently becomes even more honorific than wealth acquired by the possessor's own effort; but this distinction belongs at a later stage in the evolution of the pecuniary culture and will be spoken of in its place.

Prowess and exploit may still remain the basis of award of the highest popular esteem, although the possession of wealth has become the basis of common place reputability and of a blameless social standing. The predatory instinct and the consequent approbation of predatory efficiency are deeply ingrained in the habits of thought of those peoples who have passed under the discipline of a protracted predatory culture. According to popular award, the highest honours within human reach may, even yet, be those gained by an unfolding of extraordinary predatory efficiency in war, or by a quasi-predatory efficiency in statecraft; but for the purposes of a commonplace decent standing in the community these means of repute have been replaced by the acquisition and accumulation of goods. In order to stand well in the eyes of the community, it is necessary to come up to a certain, somewhat indefinite, conventional standard of wealth; just as in the earlier predatory stage it is necessary for the barbarian man to come up to the tribe's standard of physical endurance, cunning, and skill at arms. A certain standard of wealth in the one case, and of prowess in the other, is a necessary condition of reputability, and anything in excess of this normal amount is meritorious.

Those members of the community who fall short of this, somewhat indefinite, normal degree of prowess or of property suffer in the esteem of their fellow-men; and consequently they suffer also in their own esteem, since the usual basis of self-respect is the respect accorded by one's neighbours. Only individuals with an aberrant temperament can in the long run retain their self-esteem in the face of the disesteem of their fellows. Apparent exceptions to the rule are met with, especially among people with strong religious convictions. But these apparent exceptions are scarcely real exceptions, since such persons commonly fall back on the putative approbation of some supernatural witness of their deeds.

So soon as the possession of property becomes the basis of popular esteem, therefore, it becomes also a requisite to the complacency which we call self-respect. In any community where goods are held in severalty it is necessary, in order for his own peace of mind, that an individual should possess as large a portion of goods as others with whom he is accustomed to class himself; and it is extremely gratifying to possess something more than others. But as fast as a person makes new acquisitions, and becomes accustomed to the resulting new standard of wealth, the new standard forthwith ceases to afford appreciably greater satisfaction than the earlier standard did. The tendency in any case is constantly to make the present pecuniary standard the point of departure for a fresh increase of wealth; and this in turn gives rise to a new standard of sufficiency and a new pecuniary classification of one's self as compared with one's neighbours. So far as concerns the present question, the end sought by accumulation is to rank high in comparison with the rest of the community in point of pecuniary strength. So long as the comparison is distinctly unfavourable to himself, the normal, average individual will live in chronic dissatisfaction with his present lot; and when he has reached what may be called the normal pecuniary standard of the community, or of his class in the community, this chronic dissatisfaction will give place to a restless straining to place a wider and ever-widening pecuniary interval between himself and this average standard. The invidious comparison can never become so favourable to the individual making it that he would not gladly rate himself still higher relatively to his competitors in the struggle for pecuniary reputability.

In the nature of the case, the desire for wealth can scarcely be satiated in any individual instance, and evidently a satiation of the average or general desire for wealth is out of the question. However widely, or equally, or 'fairly', it may be distributed, no general increase of the community's wealth can make any approach to satiating this need, the ground of which approach to satiating this need, the ground of which is the desire of every one to excel every one else in the accumulation of goods. If, as is sometimes assumed, the incentive to accumulation were the want of subsistence or of physical comfort, then the aggregate economic wants of a community might conceivably be satisfied at some point in the advance of industrial efficiency; but since the struggle is substantially a race for reputability on the basis of an invidious comparison, no approach to a definitive attainment is possible.

What has just been said must not be taken to mean that there are no other incentives to acquisition and accumulation than this desire to excel in pecuniary standing and so gain the esteem and envy of one's fellow-men. The desire for added comfort and security from want is present as a motive at every stage of the process of accumulation in a modern industrial community; although the standard of sufficiency in these respects is in turn greatly affected by the habit of pecuniary emulation. To a great extent this emulation shapes the methods and selects the objects of expenditure for personal comfort and decent livelihood.

Besides this, the power conferred by wealth also affords a motive to accumulation. That propensity for purposeful activity and that repugnance to all futility of effort which belong to man by virtue of his character as an agent do not desert him when he emerges from the naive communal culture where the dominant note of life is the unanalysed and undifferentiated solidarity of the individual with the group with which his life is bound up. When he enters upon the predatory stage, where self-seeking in the narrower sense becomes the dominant note, this propensity goes with him still, as the pervasive trait that shapes his scheme of life. The propensity for achievement and the repugnance to futility remain the underlying economic motive. The propensity changes only in the form of its expression and in the proximate objects to which it directs the man's activity. Under the regime of individual ownership the most available means of visibly achieving a purpose is that afforded by the acquisition and accumulation of goods; and as the self-regarding antithesis between man and man reaches fuller consciousness, the propensity for achievement – the instinct of workmanship – tends more and more to shape itself into straining to excel others in pecuniary achievement. Relative success, tested by an invidious pecuniary comparison with other men, becomes the conventional end of action. The currently accepted legitimate end of effort becomes the achievement of a favourable comparison with other men; and therefore the repugnance to futility to a good extent coalesces with the incentive of emulation. It acts to accentuate the struggle for pecuniary reputability by visiting with a sharper disapproval all shortcoming and all evidence of shortcoming in point of pecuniary success. Purposeful effort comes to mean, primarily, effort directed to or resulting in a more creditable showing of accumulated wealth. Among the motives which lead men to accumulate wealth, the primacy, both in scope and intensity, therefore, continues to belong to this motive of pecuniary emulation.

In making use of the term 'invidious', it may perhaps be unnecessary to remark, there is no intention to extol or depreciate, or to commend or deplore any of the phenomena which the word is used to characterise. The term is used in a technical sense as describing a comparison of persons with a view to rating and grading them in respect of relative worth or value – in an aesthetic or moral sense – and so awarding and defining the relative degrees of complacency with which they may legitimately be contemplated by themselves and by others. An invidious comparison is a process of valuation of persons in respect of worth.

Chapter three: Conspicuous leisure

If its working were not disturbed by other economic forces or other features of the emulative process, the immediate effect of such a pecuniary struggle as has just been described in outline would be to make men industrious and frugal. This result actually follows, in some measure, so far as regards the lower classes, whose ordinary means of acquiring goods is productive labour. This is more especially true of the labouring classes in a sedentary community which is at an agricultural stage of industry, in which there is a considerable subdivision of industry, and whose laws and customs secure to these classes a more or less definite share of the product of their industry.

These lower classes can in any case not avoid labour, and the imputation of labour is therefore not greatly derogatory to them, at least not within their class. Rather, since labour is their recognised and accepted mode of life, they take some emulative pride in a reputation for efficiency in their work, this being often the only line of emulation that is open to them. For those for whom acquisition and emulation is possible only within the field of productive efficiency and thrift, the struggle for pecuniary reputability will in some measure work out in an increase of diligence and parsimony. But certain secondary features of the emulative process, yet to be spoken of, come in to very materially circumscribe and modify emulation in these directions among the pecuniary inferior classes as well as among the superior class.

But it is otherwise with the superior pecuniary class, with which we are here immediately concerned. For this class also the incentive to diligence and thrift is not absent; but its action is so greatly qualified by the secondary demands of pecuniary emulation, that any inclination in this direction is practically overborne and any incentive to diligence tends to be of no effect. The most imperative of these secondary demands of emulation, as well as the one of widest scope, is the requirement of abstention from productive work. This is true in an especial degree for the barbarian stage of culture. During the predatory culture, labour comes to be associated in men's habits of thought with weakness and subjection to a master. It is therefore a mark of inferiority, and therefore comes to be accounted unworthy of man in his best estate. By virtue of this tradition labour is felt to be debasing, and this tradition has never died out. On the contrary, with the advance of social differentiation it has acquired the axiomatic force due to ancient and unquestioned prescription.

In order to gain and to hold the esteem of men it is not sufficient merely to possess wealth or power. The wealth or power must be put in evidence, for esteem is awarded only on evidence.

And not only does the evidence of wealth serve to impress one's importance on others and to keep their sense of his importance alive and alert, but it is of scarcely less use in building up and preserving one's self-complacency. In all but the lowest stages of culture the normally constituted man is comforted and upheld in his self-respect by 'decent surroundings' and by exemption from 'menial offices'. Enforced departure from his habitual standard of decency, either in the paraphernalia of life or in the kind and amount of his everyday activity, is felt to be a slight upon his human dignity, even apart from all conscious consideration of the approval or disapproval of his fellows.

The archaic theoretical distinction between the base and the honourable in the manner of a man's life retains very much of its ancient force even today. So much so that there are few of the better class who are not possessed of an instinctive repugnance for the vulgar forms of labour. We have a realising sense of ceremonial uncleanness attaching in an especial degree to the occupations which are associated in our habits of thought with menial service. It is felt by all persons of refined taste that a spiritual contamination is inseparable from certain offices that are conventionally required of servants. Vulgar surroundings, mean (that is to say, inexpensive) habitations, and vulgarly productive occupations are unhesitatingly condemned and avoided. They are incompatible with life on a satisfactory spiritual plane – with 'high thinking'. From the days of the Greek philosophers to the present, a degree of leisure and of exemption from contact with such industrial processes as serve the immediate everyday purposes of human life has ever been recognised by thoughtful men as a prerequisite to a worthy or beautiful, or even a blameless, human life. In itself and in its consequences the life of leisure is beautiful and ennobling in all civilised men's eyes.

This direct, subjective value of leisure and of other evidences of wealth is no doubt in great part secondary and derivative. It is in part a reflex of the utility of leisure as a means of gaining the respect of others, and in part it is the result of a mental substitution. The performance of labour has been accepted as a conventional evidence of inferior force; therefore it comes itself, by a mental short-cut, to be regarded as intrinsically base.

During the predatory stage proper, and especially during the earlier stages of the quasi-peaceable development of industry that follows the predatory stage, a life of leisure is the readiest and most conclusive evidence of pecuniary strength, and therefore of superior force; provided always that the gentleman of leisure can live in manifest ease and comfort. At this stage wealth consists chiefly of slaves, and the benefits accruing from the possession of riches and power take the form chiefly of personal service and the immediate products of personal service.

Conspicuous abstention from labour therefore becomes the conventional mark of superior pecuniary achievement and the conventional index of reputability; and conversely, since application to productive labour is a mark of poverty and subjection, it becomes inconsistent with a reputable standing in the community. Habits of industry and thrift, therefore, are not uniformly furthered by a prevailing pecuniary emulation. On the contrary, this kind of emulation indirectly discountenances participation in productive labour. Labour would unavoidably become dishonourable, as being an evidence indecorous under the ancient tradition handed down from an earlier cultural stage. The ancient tradition of the predatory culture is that productive effort is to be shunned as being unworthy of able-bodied men and this tradition is reinforced rather than set aside in the passage from the predatory to the quasi-peaceable manner of life.

Even if the institution of a leisure class had not come in with the first emergence of individual ownership, by force of the dishonour attaching to productive employment, it would in any case have come in as one of the early consequences of ownership.

And it is to be remarked that while the leisure class existed in theory from the beginning of predatory culture, the institution takes on a new and fuller meaning with the transition from the predatory to the next succeeding pecuniary stage of culture. It is from this time forth a 'leisure class' in fact as well as in theory. From this point dates the institution of the leisure class in its consummate form.

During the predatory stage proper, the distinction between the leisure and the labouring class is in some degree a ceremonial distinction only. The able bodied men jealously stand aloof from whatever is in their apprehension, menial drudgery; but their activity in fact contributes appreciably to the sustenance of the group. The subsequent stage of quasi-peaceable industry is usually characterised by an established chattel slavery, herds of cattle, and a servile class of herdsmen and shepherds; industry has advanced so far that the community is no longer dependent for its livelihood on the chase or on any other form of activity that can fairly be classed as exploit. From this point on, the characteristic feature of leisure class life is a conspicuous exemption from all useful employment.

The normal and characteristic occupations of the class in this mature phase of its life history are in form very much the same as in its earlier days. These occupations are government, war, sports, and devout observances. Persons unduly given to difficult theoretical niceties may hold that these occupations are still incidentally and indirectly 'productive'; but it is to be noted as decisive of the question in hand that the ordinary and ostensible motive of the leisure class in engaging in these occupations is assuredly not an increase of wealth by productive effort. At this as at any other cultural stage, government and war are, at least in part, carried on for the pecuniary gain of those who engage in them; but it is gain obtained by the honourable method of seizure and conversion. These occupations are of the nature of predatory, not of productive, employment.

Something similar may be said of the chase, but with a difference. As the community passes out of the hunting stage proper, hunting gradually becomes differentiated into two distinct employments. On the one hand it is a trade, carried on chiefly for gain; and from this the element of exploit is virtually absent, or it is at any rate not present in a sufficient degree to clear the pursuit of the imputation of gainful industry. On the other hand, the chase is also a sport – an exercise of the predatory impulse simply. As such it does not afford any appreciable pecuniary incentive, but it contains a more or less obvious element of exploit. It is this latter development of the chase – purged of all imputation of handicraft – that alone is meritorious and fairly belongs in the scheme of life of the developed leisure class.

Abstention from labour is not only a honorific or meritorious act, but it presently comes to be a requisite of decency. The insistence on property as the basis of reputability is very naive and very imperious during the early stages of the accumulation of wealth. Abstention from labour is the convenient evidence of wealth and is therefore the conventional mark of social standing; and this insistence on the meritoriousness of wealth leads to a more strenuous insistence on leisure. *Nota notae est nota rei ipsius.* According to well established laws of human nature, prescription presently seizes upon this conventional evidence of wealth and fixes it in men's habits of thought as something that is in itself substantially meritorious and ennobling; while productive labour at the same time and by a like process becomes in a double sense intrinsically unworthy.

Prescription ends by making labour not only disreputable in the eyes of the community, but morally impossible to the noble, freeborn man, and incompatible with a worthy life.

This tabu on labour has a further consequence in the industrial differentiation of classes. As the population increases in density and the predatory group grows into a settled industrial community, the constituted authorities and the customs governing ownership gain in scope and consistency. It then presently becomes impracticable to accumulate wealth by simple seizure, and, in logical consistency, acquisition by industry is equally impossible for high minded and impecunious men. The alternative open to them is beggary or privation. Wherever the canon of conspicuous leisure has a chance undisturbed to work out its tendency, there will therefore emerge a secondary, and in a sense spurious, leisure class – abjectly poor and living in a precarious life of want and discomfort, but morally unable to stoop to gainful pursuits. The decayed gentleman and the lady who has seen better days are by no means unfamiliar phenomena even now. This pervading sense of the indignity of the slightest manual labour is familiar to all civilised peoples, as well as to peoples of a less advanced pecuniary culture. In persons of a delicate sensibility who have long been habituated to gentle manners, the sense of the shamefulness of manual labour may become so strong that, at a critical juncture, it will even set aside the instinct of self-preservation. So, for instance, we are told of certain Polynesian chiefs, who, under the stress of good form, preferred to starve rather than carry their food to their mouths with their own hands. It is true, this conduct may have been due, at least in part, to an excessive sanctity or tabu attaching to the chief's person. The tabu would have been communicated by the contact of his hands, and so would have made anything touched by him unfit for human food. But the tabu is itself a derivative of the unworthiness or moral incompatibility of labour; so that even when construed in this sense the conduct of the Polynesian chiefs is truer to the canon of honorific leisure than would at first appear. A better illustration, or at least a more unmistakable one, is afforded by a certain king of France, who is said to have lost his life through an excess of moral stamina in the observance of good form. In the absence of the functionary whose office it was to shift his master's seat, the king sat uncomplaining before the fire and suffered his royal person to be toasted beyond recovery. But in so doing he saved his Most Christian Majesty from menial contamination. *Summum crede nefas animam praeferre pudori, Et propter vitam vivendi perdere causas.*

It has already been remarked that the term 'leisure', as here used, does not connote indolence or quiescence. What it connotes is non-productive consumption of time. Time is consumed non-productively (1) from a sense of the unworthiness of productive work, and (2) as an evidence of pecuniary ability to afford a life of idleness. But the whole of the life of the gentleman of leisure is not spent before the eyes of the spectators who are to be impressed with that spectacle of honorific leisure which in the ideal scheme makes up his life.

For some part of the time his life is perforce withdrawn from the public eye, and of this portion which is spent in private the gentleman of leisure should, for the sake of his good name, be able to give a convincing account. He should find some means of putting in evidence the leisure that is not spent in the sight of the spectators. This can be done only indirectly, through the exhibition of some tangible, lasting results of the leisure so spent – in a manner analogous to the familiar exhibition of tangible, lasting products of the labour performed for the gentleman of leisure by handicraftsmen and servants in his employ.

The lasting evidence of productive labour is its material product – commonly some article of consumption. In the case of exploit it is similarly possible and usual to procure some tangible result that may serve for exhibition in the way of trophy or booty. At a later phase of the development it is customary to assume some badge of insignia of honour that will serve as a conventionally accepted mark of exploit, and which at the same time indicates the quantity or degree of exploit of which it is the symbol. As the population increases in density, and as human relations grow more complex and numerous, all the details of life undergo a process of elaboration and selection; and in this process of elaboration the use of trophies develops into a system of rank, titles, degrees, and insignia, typical examples of which are heraldic devices, medals, and honorary decorations.

As seen from the economic point of view, leisure, considered as an employment, is closely allied in kind with the life of exploit; and the achievements which characterise a life of leisure, and which remain as its decorous criteria, have much in common with the trophies of exploit. But leisure in the narrower sense, as distinct from exploit and from any ostensibly productive employment of effort on objects which are of no intrinsic use, does not commonly leave a material product. The criteria of a past performance of leisure therefore commonly take the form of 'immaterial' goods. Such immaterial evidences of past leisure are quasi-scholarly or quasi-artistic accomplishments and a knowledge of processes and incidents which do not conduce directly to the furtherance of human life. So, for instance, in our time there is the knowledge of the dead languages and the occult sciences; of correct spelling; of syntax and prosody; of the various forms of domestic music and other household art; of the latest properties of dress, furniture, and equipage; of games, sports, and fancy-bred animals, such as dogs and race-horses. In all these branches of knowledge the initial motive from which their acquisition proceeded at the outset, and through which they first came into vogue, may have been something quite different from the wish to show that one's time had not been spent in industrial employment; but unless these accomplishments had approved themselves as serviceable evidence of an unproductive expenditure of time, they would not have survived and held their place as conventional accomplishments of the leisure class.

These accomplishments may, in some sense, be classed as branches of learning. Beside and beyond these there is a further range of social facts which shade off from the region of learning into that of physical habit and dexterity. Such are what is known as manners and breeding, polite usage, decorum, and formal and ceremonial observances generally. This class of facts are even more immediately and obtrusively presented to the observation, and they therefore more widely and more imperatively insisted on as required evidences of a reputable degree of leisure. It is worth while to remark that all that class of ceremonial observances which are classed under the general head of manners hold a more important place in the esteem of men during the stage of culture at which conspicuous leisure has the greatest vogue as a mark of reputability, than at later stages of the cultural development. The barbarian of the quasi-peaceable stage of industry is notoriously a more high-bred gentleman, in all that concerns decorum, than any but the very exquisite among the men of a later age. Indeed, it is well known, or at least it is currently believed, that manners have progressively deteriorated as society has receded from the patriarchal stage. Many a gentleman of the old school has been provoked to remark regretfully upon the under-bred manners and bearing of even the better classes in the modern industrial communities; and the decay of the ceremonial code – or as it is otherwise called, the vulgarisation of life – among the industrial classes proper has become one of the chief enormities of latter-day civilisation in the eyes of all persons of delicate sensibilities. The decay which the code has suffered at the hands of a busy people testifies – all depreciation apart – to the fact that decorum is a product and an exponent of leisure class life and thrives in full measure only under a regime of status.

The origin, or better the derivation, of manners is no doubt, to be sought elsewhere than in a conscious effort on the part of the well-mannered to show that much time has been spent in acquiring them. The proximate end of innovation and elaboration has been the higher effectiveness of the new departure in point of beauty or of expressiveness. In great part the ceremonial code of decorous usages owes its beginning and its growth to the desire to conciliate or to show goodwill, as anthropologists and sociologists are in the habit of assuming, and this initial motive is rarely if ever absent from the conduct of well-mannered persons at any stage of the later development.

Manners, we are told, are in part an elaboration of gesture, and in part they are symbolical and conventionalised survivals representing former acts of dominance or of personal service or of personal contact. In large part they are an expression of the relation of status – a symbolic pantomime of mastery, on the one hand, and of subservience, on the other. Wherever at the present time the predatory habit of mind, and the consequent attitude of mastery and of subservience, gives its character to the accredited scheme of life, there the importance of all punctilios of conduct is extreme, and the assiduity with which the ceremonial observance of rank and titles is attended to approaches closely to the ideal set by the barbarian of the quasi-peaceable nomadic culture. Some of the Continental countries afford good illustrations of this spiritual survival.

In these communities the archaic ideal is similarly approached as regards the esteem accorded to manners as a fact of intrinsic worth.

Decorum set out with being symbol and pantomime and with having utility only as an exponent of the facts and qualities symbolised; but it presently suffered the transmutation which commonly passes over symbolical facts in human intercourse.

Manners presently came, in popular apprehension, to be possessed of a substantial utility in themselves; they acquired a sacramental character, in great measure independent of the facts which they originally prefigured. Deviations from the code of decorum have become intrinsically odious to all men, and good breeding is, in everyday apprehension, not simply an adventitious mark of human excellence, but an integral feature of the worthy human soul. There are few things that so touch us with instinctive revulsion as a breach of decorum; and so far have we progressed in the direction of imputing intrinsic utility to the ceremonial observances of etiquette that few of us, if any, can dissociate an offence against etiquette from a sense of the substantial unworthiness of the offender. A breach of faith may be condoned, but a breach of decorum can not. 'Manners make the man'. None the less, while manners have this intrinsic utility, in the apprehension of the performer and the beholder alike, this sense of the intrinsic rightness of decorum is only the proximate ground of the vogue of manners and breeding. Their ulterior, economic ground is to be sought in the honorific character of that leisure or non-productive employment of time and effort without which good manners are not acquired. The knowledge and habit of good form come only by long-continued use. Refined tastes, manners, habits of life are a useful evidence of gentility, because good breeding requires time, application and expense, and can therefore not be compassed by those whose time and energy are taken up with work. A knowledge of good form is *prima facie* evidence that that portion of the well-bred person's life which is not spent under the observation of the spectator has been worthily spent in acquiring accomplishments that are of no lucrative effect. In the last analysis the value of manners lies in the fact that they are the voucher of a life of leisure.

Therefore, conversely, since leisure is the conventional means of pecuniary repute, the acquisition of some proficiency in decorum is incumbent on all who aspire to a modicum of pecuniary decency.

So much of the honourable life of leisure as is not spent in the sight of spectators can serve the purposes of reputability only in so far as it leaves a tangible, visible result that can be put in evidence and can be measured and compared with products of the same class exhibited by competing aspirants for repute.

Some such effect, in the way of leisurely manners and carriage, etc., follows from simple persistent abstention from work, even where the subject does not take thought of the matter and studiously acquire an air of leisurely opulence and mastery.

Especially does it seem to be true that a life of leisure in this way persisted in through several generations will leave a persistent, ascertainable effect in the conformation of the person, and still more in his habitual bearing and demeanour. But all the suggestions of a cumulative life of leisure, and all the proficiency in decorum that comes by the way of passive habituation, may be further improved upon by taking thought and assiduously acquiring the marks of honourable leisure, and then carrying the exhibition of these adventitious marks of exemption from employ-ment out in a strenuous and systematic discipline.

Plainly, this is a point at which a diligent application of effort and expenditure may materially further the attainment of a decent proficiency in the leisure-class properties. Conversely, the greater the degree of proficiency and the more patent the evidence of a high degree of habitua-tion to observances which serve no lucrative or other directly useful purpose, the greater the con-sumption of time and substance impliedly involved in their acquisition, and the greater the resultant good repute. Hence, under the competitive struggle for proficiency in good manners, it comes about that much pains is taken with the cultivation of habits of decorum; and hence the details of decorum develop into a comprehensive discipline, conformity to which is required of all who would be held blameless in point of repute. And hence, on the other hand, this con-spicuous leisure of which decorum is a ramification grows gradually into a laborious drill in deportment and an education in taste and discrimination as to what articles of consumption are decorous and what are the decorous methods of consuming them.

In this connection it is worthy of notice that the possibility of producing pathological and other idiosyncrasies of person and manner by shrewd mimicry and a systematic drill have been turned to account in the deliberate production of a cultured class – often with a very happy effect. In this way, by the process vulgarly known as snobbery, a syncopated evolution of gentle birth and breeding is achieved in the case of a goodly number of families and lines of descent. This syncopated gentle birth gives results which, in point of serviceability as a leisure-class factor in the population, are in no wise substantially inferior to others who may have had a longer but less arduous training in the pecuniary properties.

There are, moreover, measureable degrees of conformity to the latest accredited code of the punctilios as regards decorous means and methods of consumption. Differences between one person and another in the degree of conformity to the ideal in these respects can be compared, and persons may be graded and scheduled with some accuracy and effect according to a pro-gressive scale of manners and breeding. The award of reputability in this regard is commonly made in good faith, on the ground of conformity to accepted canons of taste in the matters con-cerned, and without conscious regard to the pecuniary standing or the degree of leisure practised by any given candidate for reputability; but the canons of taste according to which the award is made are constantly under the surveillance of the law of conspicuous leisure, and are indeed constantly undergoing change and revision to bring them into closer conformity with its require-ments. So that while the proximate ground of discrimination may be of another kind, still the pervading principle and abiding test of good breeding is the requirement of a substantial and patent waste of time. There may be some considerable range of variation in detail within the scope of this principle, but they are variations of form and expression, not of substance.

Much of the courtesy of everyday intercourse is of course a direct expression of consideration and kindly good-will, and this element of conduct has for the most part no need of being traced back to any underlying ground of reputability to explain either its presence or the approval with which it is regarded; but the same is not true of the code of properties. These latter are expressions of status. It is of course sufficiently plain, to any one who cares to see, that our bearing towards menials and other pecuniary dependent inferiors is the bearing of the superior member in a relation of status, though its manifestation is often greatly modified and softened from the original expression of crude dominance. Similarly, our bearing towards superiors, and in great measure towards equals, expresses a more or less conventionalised attitude of subservience. Witness the masterful presence of the high-minded gentleman or lady, which testifies to so much of dominance and independence of economic circumstances, and which at the same time appeals with such convincing force to our sense of what is right and gracious. It is among this highest leisure class, who have no superiors and few peers, that decorum finds its fullest and maturest expression; and it is this highest class also that gives decorum that definite formulation which serves as a canon of conduct for the classes beneath. And there also the code is most obviously a code of status and shows most plainly its incompatibility with all vulgarly productive work. A divine assurance and an imperious complaisance, as of one habituated to require subservience and to take no thought for the morrow, is the birthright and the criterion of the gentleman at his best; and it is in popular apprehension even more than that, for this demeanour is accepted as an intrinsic attribute of superior worth, before which the base-born commoner delights to stoop and yield.

As has been indicated in an earlier chapter, there is reason to believe that the institution of ownership has begun with the ownership of persons, primarily women. The incentives to acquiring such property have apparently been: (1) a propensity for dominance and coercion; (2) the utility of these persons as evidence of the prowess of the owner; (3) the utility of their services.

Personal service holds a peculiar place in the economic development. During the stage of quasi-peaceable industry, and especially during the earlier development of industry within the limits of this general stage, the utility of their services seems commonly to be the dominant motive to the acquisition of property in persons. Servants are valued for their services. But the dominance of this motive is not due to a decline in the absolute importance of the other two utilities possessed by servants. It is rather that the altered circumstance of life accentuate the utility of servants for this last-named purpose. Women and other slaves are highly valued, both as an evidence of wealth and as a means of accumulating wealth. Together with cattle, if the tribe is a pastoral one, they are the usual form of investment for a profit. To such an extent may female slavery give its character to the economic life under the quasi-peaceable culture that the women even comes to serve as a unit of value among peoples occupying this cultural stage – as for instance in Homeric times. Where this is the case there need be little question but that the basis of the industrial system is chattel slavery and that the women are commonly slaves. The great, pervading human relation in such a system is that of master and servant. The accepted evidence of wealth is the possession of many women, and presently also of other slaves engaged in attendance on their master's person and in producing goods for him.

A division of labour presently sets in, whereby personal service and attendance on the master becomes the special office of a portion of the servants, while those who are wholly employed in industrial occupations proper are removed more and more from all immediate relation to the person of their owner. At the same time those servants whose office is personal service, including domestic duties, come gradually to be exempted from productive industry carried on for gain.

This process of progressive exemption from the common run of industrial employment will commonly begin with the exemption of the wife, or the chief wife. After the community has advanced to settled habits of life, wife-capture from hostile tribes becomes impracticable as a customary source of supply. Where this cultural advance has been achieved, the chief wife is ordinarily of gentle blood, and the fact of her being so will hasten her exemption from vulgar employment. The manner in which the concept of gentle blood originates, as well as the place which it occupies in the development of marriage, cannot be discussed in this place. For the purpose in hand it will be sufficient to say that gentle blood is blood which has been ennobled by protracted contact with accumulated wealth or unbroken prerogative. The women with these antecedents is preferred in marriage, both for the sake of a resulting alliance with her powerful relatives and because a superior worth is felt to inhere in blood which has been associated with many goods and great power. She will still be her husband's chattel, as she was her father's chattel before her purchase, but she is at the same time of her father's gentle blood; and hence there is a moral incongruity in her occupying herself with the debasing employments of her fellow-servants.

However completely she may be subject to her master, and however inferior to the male members of the social stratum in which her birth has placed her, the principle that gentility is transmissible will act to place her above the common slave; and so soon as this principle has acquired a prescriptive authority it will act to invest her in some measure with that prerogative of leisure which is the chief mark of gentility. Furthered by this principle of transmissible gentility the wife's exemption gains in scope, if the wealth of her owner permits it, until it includes exemption from debasing menial service as well as from handicraft. As the industrial development goes on and property becomes massed in relatively fewer hands, the conventional standard of wealth of the upper class rises. The same tendency to exemption from handicraft, and in the course of time from menial domestic employments, will then assert itself as regards the other wives, if such there are, and also as regards other servants in immediate attendance upon the person of their master.

The exemption comes more tardily the remoter the relation in which the servant stands to the person of the master.

If the pecuniary situation of the master permits it, the development of a special class of personal or body servants is also furthered by the very grave importance which comes to attach to this personal service. The master's person, being the embodiment of worth and honour, is of the most serious consequence. Both for his reputable standing in the community and for his self-respect, it is a matter of moment that he should have at his call efficient specialised servants, whose attendance upon his person is not diverted from this their chief office by any by-occupation. These specialised servants are useful more for show than for service actually performed. In so far as they are not kept for exhibition simply, they afford gratification to their master chiefly in allowing scope to his propensity for dominance. It is true, the care of the continually increasing household apparatus may require added labour; but since the apparatus is commonly increased in order to serve as a means of good repute rather than as a means of comfort, this qualification is not of great weight. All these lines of utility are better served by a larger number of more highly specialised servants.

There results, therefore, a constantly increasing differentiation and multiplication of domestic and body servants, along with a concomitant progressive exemption of such servants from productive labour. By virtue of their serving as evidence of ability to pay, the office of such domestics regularly tends to include continually fewer duties, and their service tends in the end to become nominal only. This is especially true of those servants who are in most immediate and obvious attendance upon their master. So that the utility of these comes to consist, in great part, in their conspicuous exemption from productive labour and in the evidence which this exemption affords of their master's wealth and power.

After some considerable advance has been made in the practice of employing a special corps of servants for the performance of a conspicuous leisure in this manner, men begin to be preferred above women for services that bring them obtrusively into view. Men, especially lusty, personable fellows, such as footmen and other menials should be, are obviously more powerful and more expensive than women. They are better fitted for this work, as showing a larger waste of time and of human energy.

Hence, it comes about that in the economy of the leisure class the busy housewife of the early patriarchal days, with her retinue of hard-working handmaidens, presently gives place to the lady and the lackey.

In all grades and walks of life, and at any stage of the economic development, the leisure of the lady and of the lackey differs from the leisure of the gentleman in his own right in that it is an occupation of an ostensibly laborious kind. It takes the form, in large measure, of a painstaking attention to the service of the master, or to the maintenance and elaboration of the household paraphernalia; so that it is leisure only in the sense that little or no productive work is performed by this class, not in the sense that all appearance of labour is avoided by them. The duties performed by the lady, or by the household or domestic servants, are frequently arduous enough, and they are also frequently directed to ends which are considered extremely necessary to the comfort of the entire household. So far as these services conduce to the physical efficiency or comfort of the master or the rest of the household, they are to be accounted as productive work. Only the residue of employment left after deduction of this effective work is to be classed as a performance of leisure.

But much of the services classed as household cares in modern everyday life, and many of the 'utilities' required for a comfortable existence by civilised man, are of a ceremonial character. They are, therefore, properly to be classed as a performance of leisure in the sense in which the term is here used. They may be none the less imperatively necessary from the point of view of decent existence: they may be none the less requisite for personal comfort even, although they may be chiefly or wholly of a ceremonial character. But in so far as they partake of this character they are imperative and requisite because we have been taught to require them under pain of ceremonial uncleanness or unworthiness. We feel discomfort in their absence, but not because their absence results directly in physical discomfort; nor would a taste not trained to discriminate between the conventionally good and the conventionally bad take offence at their omission. In so far as this is true the labour spent in these services is to be classed as leisure; and when performed by others than the economically free and self-directed head of the establishment, they are to be classed as vicarious leisure.

The vicarious leisure performed by housewives and menials, under the head of household cares, may frequently develop into drudgery, especially where the competition for reputability is close and strenuous. This is frequently the case in modern life.

Where this happens, the domestic service which comprises the duties of this servant class might aptly be designated as wasted effort, rather than as vicarious leisure. But the latter term has the advantage of indicating the line of derivation of these domestic offices, as well as of neatly suggesting the substantial economic ground of their utility; for these occupations are chiefly useful as a method of imputing pecuniary reputability to the master or to the household on the ground that a given amount of time and effort is conspicuously wasted on that behalf.

In this way, then, there arises a subsidiary or derivative leisure class, whose office is the performance of a vicarious leisure for the behoof of the reputability of the primary or legitimate leisure class. This vicarious leisure class is distinguished from the leisure class proper by a characteristic feature of its habitual mode of life. The leisure of the master class is, at least ostensibly, an indulgence of a proclivity for the avoidance of labour and is presumed to enhance the master's own well-being and fulness of life; but the leisure of the servant class exempt from productive labour is in some sort a performance exacted from them, and is not normally or primarily directed to their own comfort. The leisure of the servant is not his own leisure. So far as he is a servant in the full sense, and not at the same time a member of a lower order of the leisure class proper, his leisure normally passes under the guise of specialised service directed to the furtherance of his master's fulness of life. Evidence of this relation of subservience is obviously present in the servant's carriage and manner of life.

The like is often true of the wife throughout the protracted economic stage during which she is still primarily a servant – that is to say, so long as the household with a male head remains in force. In order to satisfy the requirements of the leisure class scheme of life, the servant should show not only an attitude of subservience, but also the effects of special training and practice in subservience. The servant or wife should not only perform certain offices and show a servile disposition, but it is quite as imperative that they should show an acquired facility in the tactics of subservience – a trained conformity to the canons of effectual and conspicuous subservience. Even today it is this aptitude and acquired skill in the formal manifestation of the servile relation that constitutes the chief element of utility in our highly paid servants, as well as one of the chief ornaments of the well-bred housewife.

The first requisite of a good servant is that he should conspicuously know his place. It is not enough that he knows how to effect certain desired mechanical results; he must above all, know how to effect these results in due form. Domestic service might be said to be a spiritual rather than a mechanical function. Gradually there grows up an elaborate system of good form, specifically regulating the manner in which this vicarious leisure of the servant class is to be performed. Any departure from these canons of form is to be depreciated, not so much because it evinces a shortcoming in mechanical efficiency, or even that it shows an absence of the servile attitude and temperament, but because, in the last analysis, it shows the absence of special training. Special training in personal service costs time and effort, and where it is obviously present in a high degree, it argues that the servant who possesses it, neither is nor has been habitually engaged in any productive occupation.

It is *prima facie* evidence of a vicarious leisure extending far back in the past. So that trained service has utility, not only as gratifying the master's instinctive liking for good and skilful workmanship and his propensity for conspicuous dominance over those whose lives are subservient to his own, but it has utility also as putting in evidence a much larger consumption of human service than would be shown by the mere present conspicuous leisure performed by an untrained person. It is a serious grievance if a gentleman's butler or footman performs his duties about his master's table or carriage in such unformed style as to suggest that his habitual occupation may be ploughing or sheepherding. Such bungling work would imply inability on the master's part to procure the service of specially trained servants; that is to say, it would imply inability to pay for the consumption of time, effort, and instruction required to fit a trained servant for special service under the exacting code of forms. If the performance of the servant argues lack of means on the part of his master, it defeats its chief substantial end; for the chief use of servants is the evidence they afford of the master's ability to pay.

What has just been said might be taken to imply that the offence of an under-trained servant lies in a direct suggestion of inexpensiveness or of usefulness. Such, of course, is not the case. The connection is much less immediate. What happens here is what happens generally. Whatever approves itself to us on any ground at the outset, presently comes to appeal to us as a gratifying thing in itself; it comes to rest in our habits of thought as substantially right. But in order that any specific canon of deportment shall maintain itself in favour, it must continue to have the support of, or at least not be incompatible with, the habit or aptitude which constitutes the norm of its development. The need of vicarious leisure, or conspicuous consumption of service, is a dominant incentive to the keeping of servants. So long as this remains true it may be set down without much discussion that any such departure from accepted usage as would suggest an abridged apprenticeship in service would presently be found insufferable. The requirement of an expensive vicarious leisure acts indirectly, selectively, by guiding the formation of our taste – of our sense of what is right in these matters – and so weeds out unconformable departures by withholding approval of them.

As the standard of wealth recognised by common consent advances, the possession and exploitation of servants as a means of showing superfluity undergoes a refinement. The possession and maintenance of slaves employed in the production of goods argues wealth and prowess, but the maintenance of servants who produce nothing argues still higher wealth and position.

Under this principle there arises a class of servants, the more numerous the better, whose sole office is fatuously to wait upon the person of their owner, and so to put in evidence his ability unproductively to consume a large amount of service. There supervenes a division of labour among the servants or dependents whose life is spent in maintaining the honour of the gentleman of leisure. So that, while one group produces goods for him, another group, usually headed by the wife, or chief, consumes for him in conspicuous leisure; thereby putting in evidence his ability to sustain large pecuniary damage without impairing his superior opulence.

This somewhat idealised and diagrammatic outline of the development and nature of domestic service comes nearest being true for that cultural stage which has here been named the 'quasi-peaceable' stage of industry. At this stage personal service first rises to the position of an economic institution, and it is at this stage that it occupies the largest place in the community's scheme of life. In the cultural sequence, the quasi-peaceable stage follows the predatory stage proper, the two being successive phases of barbarian life. Its characteristic feature is a formal observance of peace and order, at the same time that life at this stage still has too much of coercion and class antagonism to be called peaceable in the full sense of the word. For many purposes, and from another point of view than the economic one, it might as well be named the stage of status. The method of human relation during this stage, and the spiritual attitude of men at this level of culture, is well summed up under the term. But as a descriptive term to characterise the prevailing methods of industry, as well as to indicate the trend of industrial development at this point in economic evolution, the term 'quasi-peaceable' seems preferable. So far as concerns the communities of the Western culture, this phase of economic development probably lies in the past; except for a numerically small though very conspicuous fraction of the community in whom the habits of thought peculiar to the barbarian culture have suffered but a relatively slight disintegration.

Personal service is still an element of great economic importance, especially as regards the distribution and consumption of goods; but its relative importance even in this direction is no doubt less than it once was. The best development of this vicarious leisure lies in the past rather than in the present; and its best expression in the present is to be found in the scheme of life of the upper leisure class. To this class the modern culture owes much in the way of the conservation of traditions, usages, and habits of thought which belong on a more archaic cultural plane, so far as regards their widest acceptance and their most effective development.

In the modern industrial communities the mechanical contrivances available for the comfort and convenience of everyday life are highly developed. So much so that body servants, or, indeed, domestic servants of any kind, would now scarcely be employed by anybody except on the ground of a canon of reputability carried over by tradition from earlier usage. The only exception would be servants employed to attend on the persons of the infirm and the feeble-minded. But such servants properly come under the head of trained nurses rather than under that of domestic servants, and they are, therefore, an apparent rather than a real exception to the rule.

The proximate reason for keeping domestic servants, for instance, in the moderately well-to-do household of to-day, is (ostensibly) that the members of the household are unable without discomfort to compass the work required by such a modern establishment. And the reason for their being unable to accomplish it is (1) that they have too many 'social duties', and (2) that the work to be done is too severe and that there is too much of it. These two reasons may be restated as follows: (1) Under the mandatory code of decency, the time and effort of the members of such a household are required to be ostensibly all spent in a performance of conspicuous leisure, in the way of calls, drives, clubs, sewing-circles, sports, charity organisations, and other like social functions. Those persons whose time and energy are employed in these matters privately avow that all these observances, as well as the incidental attention to dress and other conspicuous consumption, are very irksome but altogether unavoidable. (2) Under the requirement of conspicuous consumption of goods, the apparatus of living has grown so elaborate and cumbrous, in the way of dwellings, furniture, bric-a-brac, wardrobe and meals, that the consumers of these things cannot make way with them in the required manner without help. Personal contact with the hired persons whose aid is called in to fulfil the routine of decency is commonly distasteful to the occupants of the house, but their presence is endured and paid for, in order to delegate to them a share in this onerous consumption of household goods. The presence of domestic servants, and of the special class of body servants in an eminent degree, is a concession of physical comfort to the moral need of pecuniary decency.

The largest manifestation of vicarious leisure in modern life is made up of what are called domestic duties. These duties are fast becoming a species of services performed, not so much for the individual behoof of the head of the household as for the reputability of the household taken as a corporate unit – a group of which the housewife is a member on a footing of ostensible equality. As fast as the household for which they are performed departs from its archaic basis of ownership-marriage, these household duties of course tend to fall out of the category of vicarious leisure in the original sense; except so far as they are performed by hired servants. That is to say, since vicarious leisure is possible only on a basis of status or of hired service, the disappearance of the relation of status from human intercourse at any point carries with it the disappearance of vicarious leisure so far as regards that much of life. But it is to be added, in qualification of this qualification, that so long as the household subsists, even with a divided head, this class of non-productive labour performed for the sake of the household reputability must still be classed as vicarious leisure, although in a slightly altered sense. It is now leisure performed for the quasi-personal corporate household, instead of, as formerly, for the proprietary head of the household.

Chapter four: Conspicuous consumption

In what has been said of the evolution of the vicarious leisure class and its differentiation from the general body of the working classes, reference has been made to a further division of labour – that between the different servant classes. One portion of the servant class, chiefly those persons whose occupation is vicarious leisure, come to undertake a new, subsidiary range of duties – the vicarious consumption of goods.

The most obvious form in which this consumption occurs is seen in the wearing of liveries and the occupation of spacious servants' quarters. Another, scarcely less obtrusive or less effective form of vicarious consumption, and a much more widely prevalent one, is the consumption of food, clothing, dwelling, and furniture by the lady and the rest of the domestic establishment.

But already at a point in economic evolution far antedating the emergence of the lady, specialised consumption of goods as an evidence of pecuniary strength had begun to work out in a more or less elaborate system. The beginning of a differentiation in consumption even antedates the appearance of anything that can fairly be called pecuniary strength. It is traceable back to the initial phase of predatory culture, and there is even a suggestion that an incipient differentiation in this respect lies at the back of the beginnings of the predatory life. This most primitive differentiation in the consumption of goods is like the later differentiation with which we are all so intimately familiar, in that it is largely of a ceremonial character, but unlike the latter it does not rest on a difference in accumulated wealth.

The utility of consumption as an evidence of wealth is to be classed as a derivative growth. It is an adaption to a new end, by a selective process, of a distinction previously existing and well established in men's habits of thought.

In the earlier phases of the predatory culture the only economic differentiation is a broad distinction between an honourable superior class made up of the able-bodied men on the one side, and a base inferior class of labouring women on the other. According to the ideal scheme of life in force at the time it is the office of the men to consume what the women produce.

Such consumption as falls to the women is merely incidental to their work; it is a means to their continued labour, and not a consumption directed to their own comfort and fulness of life.

Unproductive consumption of goods is honourable, primarily as a mark of prowess and a perquisite of human dignity; secondarily it becomes substantially honourable to itself, especially the consumption of the more desirable things. The consumption of choice articles of food, and frequently also of rare articles of adornment, becomes tabu to the women and children; and if there is a base (servile) class of men, the tabu holds also for them.

With a further advance in culture this tabu may change into simple custom of a more or less rigorous character; but whatever be the theoretical basis of the distinction which is maintained, whether it be a tabu or a larger conventionality, the features of the conventional scheme of consumption do not change easily. When the quasi-peaceable stage of industry is reached, with its fundamental institution of chattel slavery, the general principle, more or less rigorously applied, is that the base, industrious class should consume only what may be necessary to their subsistence. In the nature of things, luxuries and the comforts of life belong to the leisure class. Under the tabu, certain victuals, and more particularly certain beverages, are strictly reserved for the use of the superior class.

The ceremonial differentiation of the dietary is best seen in the use of intoxicating beverages and narcotics. If these articles of consumption are costly, they are felt to be noble and honorific. Therefore, the base classes, primarily the women, practice an enforced continence with respect to these stimulants, except in countries where they are obtainable at a very low cost.

From archaic times down through all the length of the patriarchal regime it has been the office of the women to prepare and administer these luxuries, and it has been the perquisite of the men of gentle birth and breeding to consume them. Drunkenness and the other pathological consequences of the free use of stimulants therefore tend in their turn to become honorific, as being a mark, at the second remove, of the superior status of those who are able to afford the indulgence. Infirmities induced by over-indulgence are among some peoples freely recognised as manly attributes. It has even happened that the name for certain diseased conditions of the body arising from such an origin has passed into everyday speech as a synonym for 'noble' or 'gentle'.

It is only at a relatively early stage of culture that the symptoms of expensive vice are conventionally accepted as marks of a superior status, and so tend to become virtues and command the deference of the community; but the reputability that attaches to certain expensive vices long retains so much of its force as to appreciably lessen the disapprobation visited upon the men of the wealthy or noble class for any excessive indulgence. The same invidious distinction adds force to the current disapproval of any indulgence of this kind on the part of women, minors, and inferiors. This invidious traditional distinction has not lost its force even among the more advanced peoples of today. Where the example set by the leisure class retains its imperative force in the regulation of the conventionalities, it is observable that the women still in great measure practise the same traditional continence with regard to stimulants.

This characterisation of the greater continence in the use of stimulants practised by the women of the reputable classes may seem an excessive refinement of logic at the expense of common sense. But facts within easy reach of any one who cares to know them go to say that the greater abstinence of women is in some part due to an imperative conventionality; and this conventionality is, in a general way, strongest where the patriarchal tradition – the tradition that the woman is a chattel – has retained its hold in greatest vigour. In a sense which has been greatly qualified in scope and rigour, but which has by no means lost its meaning even yet, this tradition says that the woman, being a chattel, should consume only what is necessary to her sustenance – except so far as her further consumption contributes to the comfort or the good repute of her master. The consumption of luxuries, in the true sense, is a consumption directed to the comfort of the consumer himself, and is, therefore, a mark of the master. Any such consumption by others can take place only on a basis of sufferance. In communities where the popular habits of thought have been profoundly shaped by the patriarchal tradition we may accordingly look for survivals of the tabu on luxuries at least to the extent of a conventional deprecation of their use by the unfree and dependent class. This is more particularly true as regards certain luxuries, the use of which by the dependent class would detract sensibly from the comfort or pleasure of their masters, or which are held to be of doubtful legitimacy on other grounds. In the apprehension of the great conservative middle class of Western civilisation the use of these various stimulants is obnoxious to at least one, if not both, of these objections; and it is a fact too significant to be passed over that it is precisely among these middle classes of the Germanic culture, with their strong surviving sense of the patriarchal proprieties, that the women are to the greatest extent subject to a qualified tabu on narcotics and alcoholic beverages. With many qualifications – with more qualifications as the patriarchal tradition has gradually weakened – the general rule is felt to be right and binding that women should consume only for the benefit of their masters. The objection, of course, presents itself that expenditure on women's dress and household paraphernalia is an obvious exception to this rule; but it will appear in the sequel that this exception is much more obvious than substantial.

During the earlier stages of economic development, consumption of goods without stint, especially consumption of the better grades of goods – ideally all consumption in excess of the subsistence minimum – pertains normally to the leisure class. This restriction tends to disappear, at least formally, after the later peaceable stage has been reached, with private ownership of goods and an industrial system based on wage labour or on the petty household economy. But during the earlier quasi-peaceable stage, when so many of the traditions through which the institution of a leisure class has affected the economic life of later times were taking form and consistency, this principle has had the force of a conventional law. It has served as the norm to which consumption has tended to conform, and any appreciable departure from it is to be regarded as an aberrant form, sure to be eliminated sooner or later in the further course of development.

The quasi-peaceable gentleman of leisure, then, not only consumes of the staff of life beyond the minimum required for subsistence and physical efficiency, but his consumption also undergoes a specialisation as regards the quality of the goods consumed. He consumes freely and of the best, in food, drink, narcotics, shelter, services, ornaments, apparel, weapons and accoutrements, amusements, amulets, and idols or divinities. In the process of gradual amelioration which takes place in the articles of his consumption, the motive principle and proximate aim of innovation is no doubt the higher efficiency of the improved and more elaborate products for personal comfort and well-being. But that does not remain the sole purpose of their consumption. The canon of reputability is at hand and seizes upon such innovations as are, according to its standard, fit to survive. Since the consumption of these more excellent goods is an evidence of wealth, it becomes honorific; and conversely, the failure to consume in due quantity and quality becomes a mark of inferiority and demerit.

This growth of punctilious discrimination as to qualitative excellence in eating, drinking, etc. presently affects not only the manner of life, but also the training and intellectual activity of the gentleman of leisure. He is no longer simply the successful, aggressive male – the man of strength, resource, and intrepidity. In order to avoid stultification he must also cultivate his tastes, for it now becomes incumbent on him to discriminate with some nicety between the noble and the ignoble in consumable goods. He becomes a connoisseur in creditable viands of various degrees of merit, in manly beverages and trinkets, in seemly apparel and architecture, in weapons, games, dancers, and the narcotics. This cultivation of aesthetic faculty requires time and application, and the demands made upon the gentleman in this direction therefore tend to change his life of leisure into a more or less arduous application to the business of learning how to live a life of ostensible leisure in a becoming way. Closely related to the requirement that the gentleman must consume freely and of the right kind of goods, there is the requirement that he must know how to consume them in a seemly manner. His life of leisure must be conducted in due form. Hence arise good manners in the way pointed out in an earlier chapter. High-bred manners and ways of living are items of conformity to the norm of conspicuous leisure and conspicuous consumption.

Conspicuous consumption of valuable goods is a means of reputability to the gentleman of leisure. As wealth accumulates on his hands, his own unaided effort will not avail to suffi-ciently put his opulence in evidence by this method. The aid of friends and competitors is therefore brought in by resorting to the giving of valuable presents and expensive feasts and entertainments. Presents and feasts had probably another origin than that of naive ostentation, but they required their utility for this purpose very early, and they have retained that character to the present; so that their utility in this respect has now long been the substantial ground on which these usages rest. Costly entertainments, such as the potlatch or the ball, are peculiarly adapted to serve this end. The competitor with whom the entertainer wishes to institute a comparison is, by this method, made to serve as a means to the end. He consumes vicariously for his host at the same time that he is witness to the consumption of that excess of good things which his host is unable to dispose of single-handed, and he is also made to witness his host's facility in etiquette.

In the giving of costly entertainments, other motives of more genial kind, are of course also present. The custom of festive gatherings probably originated in motives of conviviality and reli-gion; these motives are also present in the later development, but they do not continue to be the sole motives. The latter-day leisure-class festivities and entertainments may continue in some slight degree to serve the religious need and in a higher degree the needs of recreation and con-viviality, but they also serve an invidious purpose; and they serve it none the less effectually for having a colorable non-invidious ground in these more avowable motives. But the economic effect of these social amenities is not therefore lessened, either in the vicarious consumption of goods or in the exhibition of difficult and costly achievements in etiquette.

As wealth accumulates, the leisure class develops further in function and structure, and there arises a differentiation within the class. There is a more or less elaborate system of rank and grades. This differentiation is furthered by the inheritance of wealth and the consequent inheri-tance of gentility. With the inheritance of gentility goes the inheritance of obligatory leisure; and gentility of a sufficient potency to entail a life of leisure may be inherited without the comple-ment of wealth required to maintain a dignified leisure. Gentle blood may be transmitted with-out goods enough to afford a reputably free consumption at one's ease. Hence results a class of impecunious gentlemen of leisure, incidentally referred to already. These half-caste gentlemen of leisure fall into a system of hierarchical gradations. Those who stand near the higher and the highest grades of the wealthy leisure class, in point of birth, or in point of wealth, or both, out-rank the remoter-born and the pecuniarily weaker. These lower grades, especially the impecu-nious, or marginal, gentlemen of leisure, affiliate themselves by a system of dependence or fealty to the great ones; by so doing they gain an increment of repute, or of the means with which to lead a life of leisure, from their patron. They become his courtiers or retainers, servants; and being fed and countenanced by their patron they are indices of his rank and vicarious consumer of his superfluous wealth. Many of these affiliated gentlemen of leisure are at the same time lesser men of substance in their own right; so that some of them are scarcely at all, others only partially, to be rated as vicarious consumers. So many of them, however, as make up the retainer and hangers-on of the patron may be classed as vicarious consumer without qualification. Many of these again, and also many of the other aristocracy of less degree, have in turn attached to their persons a more or less comprehensive group of vicarious consumer in the persons of their wives and children, their servants, retainers, etc.

Throughout this graduated scheme of vicarious leisure and vicarious consumption the rule holds that these offices must be performed in some such manner, or under some such circumstance or insignia, as shall point plainly to the master to whom this leisure or consumption pertains, and to whom therefore the resulting increment of good repute of right inures. The consumption and leisure executed by these persons for their master or patron represents an investment on his part with a view to an increase of good fame. As regards feasts and largesses this is obvious enough, and the imputation of repute to the host or patron here takes place immediately, on the ground of common notoriety. Where leisure and consumption is performed vicariously by henchmen and retainers, imputation of the resulting repute to the patron is effected by their residing near his person so that it may be plain to all men from what source they draw. As the group whose good esteem is to be secured in this way grows larger, more patent means are required to indicate the imputation of merit for the leisure performed, and to this end uniforms, badges, and liveries come into vogue. The wearing of uniforms or liveries implies a considerable degree of dependence, and may even be said to be a mark of servitude, real or ostensible. The wearers of uniforms and liveries may be roughly divided into two classes – the free and the servile, or the noble and the ignoble. The services performed by them are likewise divisible into noble and ignoble. Of course the distinction is not observed with strict consistency in practice; the less debasing of the base services and the less honorific of the noble functions are not infrequently merged in the same person. But the general distinction is not on that account to be overlooked. What may add some perplexity is the fact that this fundamental distinction between noble and ignoble, which rests on the nature of the ostensible service performed, is traversed by a secondary distinction into honorific and humiliating, resting on the rank of the person for whom the service is performed or whose livery is worn. So, those offices which are by right the proper employment of the leisure class are noble; such as government, fighting, hunting, the care of arms and accoutrements, and the like – in short, those which may be classed as ostensibly predatory employments. On the other hand, those employments which properly fall to the industrious class are ignoble; such as handicraft or other productive labour, menial services and the like. But a base service performed for a person of very high degree may become a very honorific office; as for instance the office of a Maid of Honor or of a Lady in Waiting to the Queen, or the King's Master of the Horse or his Keeper of the Hounds.

The two offices last named suggest a principle of some general bearing. Whenever, as in these cases, the menial service in question has to do directly with the primary leisure employments of fighting and hunting, it easily acquires a reflected honorific character. In this way great honor may come to attach to an employment which in its own nature belongs to the baser sort.

In the later development of peaceable industry, the usage of employing an idle corps of uniformed men-at-arms gradually lapses. Vicarious consumption by dependents bearing the insignia of their patron or master narrows down to a corps of liveried menials. In a heightened degree, therefore, the livery comes to be a badge of servitude, or rather servility. Something of an honorific character always attached to the livery of the armed retainer, but this honorific character disappears when the livery becomes the exclusive badge of the menial. The livery becomes obnoxious to nearly all who are required to wear it. We are yet so little removed from a state of effective slavery as still to be fully sensitive to the sting of any imputation of servility.

This antipathy asserts itself even in the case of the liveries or uniforms which some corporations prescribe as the distinctive dress of their employees. In this country the aversion even goes the length of discrediting – in a mild and uncertain way – those government employments, military and civil, which require the wearing of a livery or uniform.

With the disappearance of servitude, the number of vicarious consumers attached to any one gentleman tends, on the whole, to decrease. The like is of course true, and perhaps in a still higher degree, of the number of dependents who perform vicarious leisure for him. In a general way, though not wholly nor consistently, these two groups coincide. The dependent who was first delegated for these duties was the wife, or the chief wife; and, as would be expected, in the later development of the institution, when the number of persons by whom these duties are customarily performed gradually narrows, the wife remains the last. In the higher grades of society a large volume of both these kinds of service is required; and here the wife is of course still assisted in the work by a more or less numerous corps of menials. But as we descend the social scale, the point is presently reached where the duties of vicarious leisure and consumption devolve upon the wife alone. In the communities of the Western culture, this point is at present found among the lower middle class.

And here occurs a curious inversion. It is a fact of common observance that in this lower middle class there is no pretense of leisure on the part of the head of the household. Through force of circumstances it has fallen into disuse. But the middle-class wife still carries on the business of vicarious leisure, for the good name of the household and its master. In descending the social scale in any modern industrial community, the primary fact – the conspicuous leisure of the master of the household – disappears at a relatively high point. The head of the middle-class household has been reduced by economic circumstances to turn his hand to gaining a livelihood by occupations which often partake largely of the character of industry, as in the case of the ordinary business man of today. But the derivative fact – the vicarious leisure and consumption rendered by the wife, and the auxiliary vicarious performance of leisure by menials – remains in vogue as a conventionality which the demands of reputability will not suffer to be slighted. It is by no means an uncommon spectacle to find a man applying himself to work with the utmost assiduity, in order that his wife may in due form render for him that degree of vicarious leisure which the common sense of the time demands.

The leisure rendered by the wife in such cases is, of course, not a simple manifestation of idleness or indolence. It almost invariably occurs disguised under some form of work or household duties or social amenities, which prove on analysis to serve little or no ulterior end beyond showing that she does not occupy herself with anything that is gainful or that is of substantial use. As has already been noticed under the head of manners, the greater part of the customary round of domestic cares to which the middle-class housewife gives her time and effort is of this character. Not that the results of her attention to household matters, of a decorative and mundificatory character, are not pleasing to the sense of men trained in middle-class proprieties; but the taste to which these effects of household adornment and tidiness appeal is a taste which has been formed under the selective guidance of a canon of propriety that demands just these evidences of wasted effort. The effects are pleasing to us chiefly because we have been taught to find them pleasing. There goes into these domestic duties much solicitude for a proper combination of form and colour, and for other ends that are to be classed as aesthetic in the proper sense of the term; and it is not denied that effects having some substantial aesthetic value are sometimes attained. Pretty much all that is here insisted on is that, as regards these amenities of life, the housewife's efforts are under the guidance of traditions that have been shaped by the law of conspicuously wasteful expenditure of time and substance. If beauty or comfort is achieved – and it is a more or less fortuitous circumstance if they are – they must be achieved by means and methods that commend themselves to the great economic law of wasted effort. The more reputable, 'presentable' portion of middle-class household paraphernalia are, on the one hand, items of conspicuous consumption, and on the other hand, apparatus for putting in evidence the vicarious leisure rendered by the housewife.

The requirement of vicarious consumption at the hands of the wife continues in force even at a lower point in the pecuniary scale than the requirement of vicarious leisure. At a point below which little if any pretense of wasted effort, in ceremonial cleanness and the like, is observable, and where there is assuredly no conscious attempt at ostensible leisure, decency still requires the wife to consume some goods conspicuously for the reputability of the household and its head.

So that, as the latter-day outcome of this evolution of an archaic institution, the wife, who was at the outset the drudge and chattel of the man, both in fact and in theory – the producer of goods for him to consume – has become the ceremonial consumer of goods which he produces. But she still quite unmistakably remains his chattel in theory; for the habitual rendering of vicarious leisure and consumption is the abiding mark of the unfree servant.

This vicarious consumption practised by the household of the middle and lower classes cannot be counted as a direct expression of the leisure-class scheme of life, since the household of this pecuniary grade does not belong within the leisure class. It is rather that the leisure-class scheme of life here comes to an expression at the second remove. The leisure class stands at the head of the social structure in point of reputability; and its manner of life and its standards of worth therefore afford the norm of reputability for the community. The observance of these standards, in some degree of approximation, becomes incumbent upon all classes lower in the scale. In modern civilised communities the lines of demarcation between social classes have grown vague and transient, and wherever this happens the norm of reputability imposed by the upper class extends its coercive influence with but slight hindrance down through the social structure to the lowest strata. The result is that the members of each stratum accept as their ideal of decency the scheme of life in vogue in the next higher stratum, and bend their energies to live up to that ideal. On pain of forfeiting their good name and their self-respect in case of failure, they must conform to the accepted code, at least in appearance.

The basis on which good repute in any highly organised industrial community ultimately rests is pecuniary strength; and the means of showing pecuniary strength, and so of gaining or retaining a good name, are leisure and a conspicuous consumption of goods. Accordingly, both of these methods are in vogue as far down the scale as it remains possible; and in the lower strata in which the two methods are employed, both offices are in great part delegated to the wife and children of the household. Lower still, where any degree of leisure, even ostensible, has become impracticable for the wife, the conspicuous consumption of goods remains and is carried on by the wife and children. The man of the household also can do something in this direction, and indeed, he commonly does; but with a still lower descent into the levels of indigence – along the margin of the slums – the man, and presently also the children, virtually cease to consume valuable goods for appearances, and the woman remains virtually the sole exponent of the household's pecuniary decency. No class of society, not even the most abjectly poor, forgoes all customary conspicuous consumption. The last items of this category of consumption are not given up except under stress of the direst necessity. Very much of squalour and discomfort will be endured before the last trinket or the last pretense of pecuniary decency is put away. There is no class and no country that has yielded so abjectly before the pressure of physical want as to deny themselves all gratification of this higher or spiritual need.

From the foregoing survey of the growth of conspicuous leisure and consumption, it appears that the utility of both alike for the purposes of reputability lies in the element of waste that is common to both. In the one case it is a waste of time and effort, in the other it is a waste of goods. Both are methods of demonstrating the possession of wealth, and the two are conventionally accepted as equivalents. The choice between them is a question of advertising expediency simply, except so far as it may be affected by other standards of propriety, springing from a different source. On grounds of expediency the preference may be given to the one or the other at different stages of the economic development. The question is, which of the two methods will most effectively reach the persons whose convictions it is desired to affect. Usage has answered this question in different ways under different circumstances.

So long as the community or social group is small enough and compact enough to be effectually reached by common notoriety alone that is to say, so long as the human environment to which the individual is required to adapt himself in respect of reputability is comprised within his sphere of personal acquaintance and neighbourhood gossip – so long the one method is about as effective as the other. Each will therefore serve about equally well during the earlier stages of social growth. But when the differentiation has gone farther and it becomes necessary to reach a wider human environment, consumption begins to hold over leisure as an ordinary means of decency. This is especially true during the later, peaceable economic stage. The means of communication and the mobility of the population now expose the individual to the observation of many persons who have no other means of judging of his reputability than the display of goods (and perhaps of breeding) which he is able to make while he is under their direct observation.

The modern organisation of industry works in the same direction also by another line. The exigencies of the modern industrial system frequently place individuals and households in juxtaposition between whom there is little contact in any other sense than that of juxtaposition. One's neighbours, mechanically speaking, often are socially not one's neighbours, or even acquaintances; and still their transient good opinion has a high degree of utility. The only practicable means of impressing one's pecuniary ability on these unsympathetic observers of one's everyday life is an unremitting demonstration of ability to pay.

In the modern community there is also a more frequent attendance at large gatherings of people to whom one's everyday life is unknown; in such places as churches, theaters, ballrooms, hotels, parks, shops, and the like. In order to impress these transient observers, and to retain one's self-complacency under their observation, the signature of one's pecuniary strength should be written in characters which he who runs may read. It is evident, therefore, that the present trend of the development is in the direction of heightening the utility of conspicuous consumption as compared with leisure.

It is also noticeable that the serviceability of consumption as a means of repute, as well as the insistence on it as an element of decency, is at its best in those portions of the community where the human contact of the individual is widest and the mobility of the population is greatest. Conspicuous consumption claims a relatively larger portion of the income of the urban than of the rural population, and the claim is also more imperative. The result is that, in order to keep up a decent appearance, the former habitually live hand-to-mouth to a greater extent than the latter. So it comes, for instance, that the American farmer and his wife and daughters are notoriously less modish in their dress, as well as less urbane in their manners, than the city artisan's family with an equal income. It is not that the city population is by nature much more eager for the peculiar complacency that comes of a conspicuous consumption, nor has the rural population less regard for pecuniary decency. But the provocation to this line of evidence, as well as its transient effectiveness, is more decided in the city. This method is therefore more readily resorted to, and in the struggle to outdo one another the city population push their normal standard of conspicuous consumption to a higher point, with the result that a relatively greater expenditure in this direction is required to indicate a given degree of pecuniary decency in the city. The requirement of conformity to this higher conventional standard becomes mandatory. The standard of decency is higher, class for class, and this requirement of decent appearance must be lived up to on pain of losing caste.

Consumption becomes a larger element in the standard of living in the city than in the country. Among the country population its place is to some extent taken by savings and home comforts known through the medium of neighbourhood gossip sufficiently to serve the like general purpose of Pecuniary repute. These home comforts and the leisure indulged in – where the indulgence is found – are of course also in great part to be classed as items of conspicuous consumption; and much the same is to be said of the savings. The smaller amount of the savings laid by the artisan class is no doubt due, in some measure, to the fact that in the case of the artisan the savings are a less effective means of advertisement, relative to the environment in which he is placed, than are the savings of the people living on farms and in the small villages. Among the latter, everybody's affairs, especially everybody's pecuniary status, are known to everybody else. Considered by itself simply – taken in the first degree – this added provocation to which the artisan and the urban labouring classes are exposed may not very seriously decrease the amount of savings; but in its cumulative action, through raising the standard of decent expenditure, its deterrent effect on the tendency to save cannot but be very great.

A felicitous illustration of the manner in which this canon of reputability works out its results is seen in the practice of dram-drinking, 'treating', and smoking in public places, which is customary among the labourers and handicraftsmen of the towns, and among the lower middle class of the urban population generally Journeymen printers may be named as a class among whom this form of conspicuous consumption has a great vogue, and among whom it carries with it certain well-marked consequences that are often deprecated. The peculiar habits of the class in this respect are commonly set down to some kind of an ill-defined moral deficiency with which this class is credited, or to a morally deleterious influence which their occupation is supposed to exert, in some unascertainable way, upon the men employed in it. The state of the case for the men who work in the composition and press rooms of the common run of printing-houses may be summed up as follows.

Skill acquired in any printing-house or any city is easily turned to account in almost any other house or city; that is to say, the inertia due to special training is slight. Also, this occupation requires more than the average of intelligence and general information, and the men employed in it are therefore ordinarily more ready than many others to take advantage of any slight variation in the demand for their labour from one place to another. The inertia due to the home feeling is consequently also slight. At the same time the wages in the trade are high enough to make movement from place to place relatively easy. The result is a great mobility of the labour employed in printing; perhaps greater than in any other equally well-defined and considerable body of workmen. These men are constantly thrown in contact with new groups of acquaintances, with whom the relations established are transient or ephemeral, but whose good opinion is valued none the less for the time being. The human proclivity to ostentation, reinforced by sentiments of good fellowship, leads them to spend freely in those directions which will best serve these needs.

Here as elsewhere prescription seizes upon the custom as soon as it gains a vogue, and incorporates it in the accredited standard of decency. The next step is to make this standard of decency the point of departure for a new move in advance in the same direction – for there is no merit in simple spiritless conformity to a standard of dissipation that is lived up to as a matter of course by everyone in the trade.

The greater prevalence of dissipation among printers than among the average of workmen is accordingly attributable, at least in some measure, to the greater ease of movement and the more transient character of acquaintance and human contact in this trade. But the substantial ground of this high requirement in dissipation is in the last analysis no other than that same propensity for a manifestation of dominance and pecuniary decency which makes the French peasant-proprietor parsimonious and frugal, and induces the American millionaire to found colleges, hospitals, and museums. If the canon of conspicuous consumption were not offset to a considerable extent by other features of human nature, alien to it, any saving should logically be impossible for a population situated as the artisan and labouring classes of the cities are at present, however high their wages or their income might be.

But there are other standards of repute and other, more or less imperative, canons of conduct, besides wealth and its manifestation, and some of these come in to accentuate or to qualify the broad, fundamental canon of conspicuous waste. Under the simple test of effectiveness for advertising, we should expect to find leisure and the conspicuous consumption of goods dividing the field of pecuniary emulation pretty evenly between them at the outset. Leisure might then be expected gradually to yield ground and tend to obsolescence as the economic development goes forward, and the community increases in size; while the conspicuous consumption of goods should gradually gain in importance, both absolutely and relatively, until it had absorbed all the available product, leaving nothing over beyond a bare livelihood. But the actual course of development has been somewhat different from this ideal scheme. Leisure held the first place at the start, and came to hold a rank very much above wasteful consumption of goods, both as a direct exponent of wealth and as an element in the standard of decency, during the quasi-peaceable culture. From that point onward, consumption has gained ground, until, at present, it unquestionably holds the primacy, though it is still far from absorbing the entire margin of production above the subsistence minimum.

The early ascendency of leisure as a means of reputability is traceable to the archaic distinction between noble and ignoble employments. Leisure is honorable and becomes imperative partly because it shows exemption from ignoble labour. The archaic differentiation into noble and ignoble classes is based on an invidious distinction between employments as honorific or debasing; and this traditional distinction grows into an imperative canon of decency during the early quasi-peaceable stage. Its ascendency is furthered by the fact that leisure is still fully as effective an evidence of wealth as consumption.

Indeed, so effective is it in the relatively small and stable human environment to which the individual is exposed at that cultural stage, that, with the aid of the archaic tradition which deprecates all productive labour, it gives rise to a large impecunious leisure class, and it even tends to limit the production of the community's industry to the subsistence minimum. This extreme inhibition of industry is avoided because slave labour, working under a compulsion more vigorous than that of reputability, is forced to turn out a product in excess of the subsistence minimum of the working class. The subsequent relative decline in the use of conspicuous leisure as a basis of repute is due partly to an increasing relative effectiveness of consumption as an evidence of wealth; but in part it is traceable to another force, alien, and in some degree antagonistic, to the usage of conspicuous waste.

This alien factor is the instinct of workmanship. Other circumstances permitting, that instinct disposes men to look with favour upon productive efficiency and on whatever is of human use.

It disposes them to depreciate waste of substance or effort. The instinct of workmanship is present in all men, and asserts itself even under very adverse circumstances. So that however wasteful a given expenditure may be in reality, it must at least have some colourable excuse in the way of an ostensible purpose. The manner in which, under special circumstances, the instinct eventuates in a taste for exploit and an invidious discrimination between noble and ignoble classes has been indicated in an earlier chapter. In so far as it comes into conflict with the law of conspicuous waste, the instinct of workmanship expresses itself not so much in insistence on substantial usefulness as in an abiding sense of the odiousness and aesthetic impossibility of what is obviously futile. Being of the nature of an instinctive affection, its guidance touches chiefly and immediately the obvious and apparent violations of its requirements. It is only less promptly and with less constraining force that it reaches such substantial violations of its requirements as are appreciated only upon reflection.

So long as all labour continues to be performed exclusively or usually by slaves, the baseness of all productive effort is too constantly and deterrently present in the mind of men to allow the instinct of workmanship seriously to take effect in the direction of industrial usefulness; but when the quasi-peaceable stage (with slavery and status) passes into the peaceable stage of industry (with wage labour and cash payment) the instinct comes more effectively into play. It then begins aggressively to shape men's views of what is meritorious, and asserts itself at least as an auxiliary canon of self-complacency. All extraneous considerations apart, those persons (adult) are but a vanishing minority today who harbour no inclination to the accomplishment of some end, or who are not impelled of their own motion to shape some object or fact or relation for human use. The propensity may in large measure be overborne by the more immediately constraining incentive to a reputable leisure and an avoidance of indecorous usefulness, and it may therefore work itself out in make-believe only; as for instance in 'social duties', and in quasi-artistic or quasi-scholarly accomplishments, in the care and decoration of the house, in sewing-circle activity or dress reform, in proficiency at dress, cards, yachting, golf, and various sports. But the fact that it may under stress of circumstances eventuate in inanities no more disproves the presence of the instinct than the reality of the brooding instinct is disproved by inducing a hen to sit on a nestful of china eggs.

This latter-day uneasy reaching-out for some form of purposeful activity that shall at the same time not be indecorously productive of either individual or collective gain marks a difference of attitude between the modern leisure class and that of the quasi-peaceable stage. At the earlier stage, as was said above, the all-dominating institution of slavery and status acted resistlessly to discountenance exertion directed to other than naively predatory ends. It was still possible to find some habitual employment for the inclination to action in the way of forcible aggression or repression directed against hostile groups or against the subject classes within the group; and this sewed to relieve the pressure and draw off the energy of the leisure class without a resort to actually useful, or even ostensibly useful employments. The practice of hunting also sewed the same purpose in some degree. When the community developed into a peaceful industrial organisation, and when fuller occupation of the land had reduced the opportunities for the hunt to an inconsiderable residue, the pressure of energy seeking purposeful employment was left to find an outlet in some other direction. The ignominy which attaches to useful effort also entered upon a less acute phase with the disappearance of compulsory labour; and the instinct of workmanship then came to assert itself with more persistence and consistency.

The line of least resistance has changed in some measure, and the energy which formerly found a vent in predatory activity, now in part takes the direction of some ostensibly useful end.

Ostensibly purposeless leisure has come to be deprecated, especially among that large portion of the leisure class whose plebeian origin acts to set them at variance with the tradition of the *otium cum dignitate*. But that canon of reputability which discountenances all employment that is of the nature of productive effort is still at hand, and will permit nothing beyond the most transient vogue to any employment that is substantially useful or productive. The consequence is that a change has been wrought in the conspicuous leisure practiced by the leisure class; not so much in substance as in form. A reconciliation between the two conflicting requirements is effected by a resort to make-believe. Many and intricate polite observances and social duties of a ceremonial nature are developed; many organisations are founded, with some specious object of amelioration embodied in their official style and title; there is much coming and going, and a deal of talk, to the end that the talkers may not have occasion to reflect on what is the effectual economic value of their traffic. And along with the make-believe of purposeful employment, and woven inextricably into its texture, there is commonly, if not invariably, a more or less appreciable element of purposeful effort directed to some serious end.

In the narrower sphere of vicarious leisure a similar change has gone forward. Instead of simply passing her time in visible idleness, as in the best days of the patriarchal regime, the housewife of the advanced peaceable stage applies herself assiduously to household cares. The salient features of this development of domestic service have already been indicated.

Throughout the entire evolution of conspicuous expenditure, whether of goods or of services or human life, runs the obvious implication that in order to effectually mend the consumer's good fame it must be an expenditure of superfluities. In order to be reputable it must be wasteful. No merit would accrue from the consumption of the bare necessaries of life, except by comparison with the abjectly poor who fall short even of the subsistence minimum; and no standard of expenditure could result from such a comparison, except the most prosaic and unattractive level of decency. A standard of life would still be possible which should admit of invidious comparison in other respects than that of opulence; as, for instance, a comparison in various directions in the manifestation of moral, physical, intellectual, or aesthetic force. Comparison in all these directions is in vogue today; and the comparison made in these respects is commonly so inextricably bound up with the pecuniary comparison as to be scarcely distinguishable from the latter. This is especially true as regards the current rating of expressions of intellectual and aesthetic force or proficiency; so that we frequently interpret as aesthetic or intellectual a difference which in substance is pecuniary only.

The use of the term 'waste' is in one respect an unfortunate one. As used in the speech of everyday life the word carries an undertone of deprecation. It is here used for want of a better term that will adequately describe the same range of motives and of phenomena, and it is not to be taken in an odious sense, as implying an illegitimate expenditure of human products or of human life. In the view of economic theory the expenditure in question is no more and no less legitimate than any other expenditure. It is here called 'waste' because this expenditure does not serve human life or human well-being on the whole, not because it is waste or misdirection of effort or expenditure as viewed from the standpoint of the individual consumer who chooses it. If he chooses it, that disposes off the question of its relative utility to him, as compared with other forms of consumption that would not be deprecated on account of their wastefulness. Whatever form of expenditure the consumer chooses, or whatever end he seeks in making his choice, has utility to him by virtue of his preference. As seen from the point of view of the individual consumer, the question of wastefulness does not arise within the scope of economic theory proper. The use of the word 'waste' as a technical term, therefore, implies no deprecation of the motives or of the ends sought by the consumer under this canon of conspicuous waste.

But it is, on other grounds, worth noting that the term 'waste' in the language of everyday life implies deprecation of what is characterised as wasteful. This common-sense implication is itself an outcropping of the instinct of workmanship. The popular reprobation of waste goes to say that in order to be at peace with himself the common man must be able to see in any and all human effort and human enjoyment an enhancement of life and well-being on the whole. In order to meet with unqualified approval, any economic fact must approve itself under the test of impersonal usefulness – usefulness as seen from the point of view of the generically human. Relative or competitive advantage of one individual in comparison with another does not satisfy the economic conscience, and therefore competitive expenditure has not the approval of this conscience.

In strict accuracy nothing should be included under the head of conspicuous waste but such expenditure as is incurred on the ground of an invidious pecuniary comparison. But in order to bring any given item or element under this head it is not necessary that it should be recognised as waste in this sense by the person incurring the expenditure. It frequently happens that an element of the standard of living which set out with being primarily wasteful, ends with becoming, in the apprehension of the consumer, a necessary of life; and it may in this way become as indispensable as any other item of the consumer's habitual expenditure. As items which sometimes fall under this head, and are therefore available as illustrations of the manner in which this principle applies, may be cited carpets and tapestries, silver table service, waiter's services, silk hats, starched linen, many articles of jewelry and of dress. The indispensability of these things after the habit and the convention have been formed, however, has little to say in the classification of expenditures as waste or not waste in the technical meaning of the word. The test to which all expenditure must be brought in an attempt to decide that point is the question whether it serves directly to enhance human life on the whole – whether it furthers the life process taken impersonally.

For this is the basis of award of the instinct of workmanship, and that instinct is the court of final appeal in any question of economic truth or adequacy. It is a question as to the award rendered by a dispassionate common sense. The question is, therefore, not whether, under the existing circumstances of individual habit and social custom, a given expenditure conduces to the particular consumer's gratification or peace of mind; but whether, aside from acquired tastes and from the canons of usage and conventional decency, its result is a net gain in comfort or in the fullness of life. Customary expenditure must be classed under the head of waste in so far as the custom on which it rests is traceable to the habit of making an invidious pecuniary comparison – in so far as it is conceived that it could not have become customary and prescriptive without the backing of this principle of pecuniary reputability or relative economic success.

It is obviously not necessary that a given object of expenditure should be exclusively wasteful in order to come in under the category of conspicuous waste. An article may be useful and wasteful both, and its utility to the consumer may be made up of use and waste in the most varying proportions. Consumable goods, and even productive goods, generally show the two elements in combination, as constituents of their utility; although, in a general way, the element of waste tends to predominate in articles of consumption, while the contrary is true of articles designed for productive use. Even in articles which appear at first glance to serve for pure ostentation only, it is always possible to detect the presence of some, at least ostensible, useful purpose; and on the other hand, even in special machinery and tools contrived for some particular industrial process, as well as in the rudest appliances of human industry, the traces of conspicuous waste, or at least of the habit of ostentation, usually become evident on a close scrutiny. It would be hazardous to assert that a useful purpose is ever absent from the utility of any article or of any service, however, obviously its prime purpose and chief element is conspicuous waste; and it would be only less hazardous to assert of any primarily useful product that the element of waste is in no way concerned in its value, immediately or remotely.

Chapter five: The pecuniary standard of living

For the great body of the people in any modern community, the proximate ground of expenditure in excess of what is required for physical comfort is not a conscious effort to excel in the expansiveness of their visible consumption, so much as it is a desire to live up to the conventional standard of decency in the amount and grade of goods consumed. This desire is not guided by a rigidly invariable standard, which must be lived up to, and beyond which there is no incentive to go. The standard is flexible; and especially it is indefinitely extensible, if only time is allowed for habituation to any increase in pecuniary ability and for acquiring facility in the new and larger scale of expenditure that follows such an increase. It is much more difficult to recede from a scale of expenditure once adopted than it is to extend the accustomed scale in response to an accession of wealth. Many items of customary expenditure prove on analysis to be almost purely wasteful, and they are therefore honorific only, but after they have once been incorporated into the scale of decent consumption, and so have become an integral part of one's scheme of life, it is quite as hard to give up these as it is to give up many items that conduce directly to one's physical comfort, or even that may be necessary to life and health. That is to say, the conspicuously wasteful honorific expenditure that confers spiritual well-being may become more indispensable than much of that expenditure which ministers to the 'lower' wants of physical well-being or sustenance only. It is notoriously just as difficult to recede from a 'high' standard of living as it is to lower a standard which is already relatively low; although in the former case the difficulty is a moral one, while in the latter it may involve a material deduction from the physical comforts of life.

But while retrogression is difficult, a fresh advance in conspicuous expenditure is relatively easy; indeed, it takes place almost as a matter of course. In the rare cases where it occurs, a failure to increase one's visible consumption when the means for an increase are at hand is felt in popular apprehension to call for explanation, and unworthy motives of miserliness are imputed to those who fall short in this respect. A prompt response to the stimulus, on the other hand, is accepted as the normal effect. This suggests that the standard of expenditure which commonly guides our efforts is not the average, ordinary expenditure already achieved; it is an ideal of consumption that lies just beyond our reach, or to reach which requires some strain. The motive is emulation – the stimulus of an invidious comparison which prompts us to outdo those with whom we are in the habit of classing ourselves. Substantially the same proposition is expressed in the common-place remark that each class envies and emulates the class next above it in the social scale, while it rarely compares itself with those below or with those who are considerably in advance. That is to say, in other words, our standard of decency in expenditure, as in other ends of emulation, is set by the usage of those next above us in reputability; until, in this way, especially in any community where class distinctions are somewhat vague, all canons of reputability and decency, and all standards of consumption, are traced back by insensible gradations to the usages and habits of thought of the highest social and pecuniary class – the wealthy leisure class.

It is for this class to determine, in general outline, what scheme of Life the community shall accept as decent or honorific; and it is their office by precept and example to set forth this scheme of social salvation in its highest, ideal form. But the higher leisure class can exercise this quasi-sacerdotal office only under certain material limitations. The class cannot at discretion effect a sudden revolution or reversal of the popular habits of thought with respect to any of these ceremonial requirements. It takes time for any change to permeate the mass and change the habitual attitude of the people; and especially it takes time to change the habits of those classes that are socially more remote from the radiant body. The process is slower where the mobility of the population is less or where the intervals between the several classes are wider and more abrupt.

But if time be allowed, the scope of the discretion of the leisure class as regards questions of form and detail in the community's scheme of life is large; while as regards the substantial principles of reputability, the changes which it can effect lie within a narrow margin of tolerance. Its example and precept carries the force of prescription for all classes below it; but in working out the precepts which are handed down as governing the form and method of reputability – in shaping the usages and the spiritual attitude of the lower classes – this authoritative prescription constantly works under the selective guidance of the canon of conspicuous waste, tempered in varying degree by the instinct of workmanship. To those norms is to be added another broad principle of human nature – the predatory animus – which in point of generality and of psychological content lies between the two just named. The effect of the latter in shaping the accepted scheme of life is yet to be discussed.

The canon of reputability, then, must adapt itself to the economic circumstances, the traditions, and the degree of spiritual maturity of the particular class whose scheme of life it is to regulate. It is especially to be noted that however high its authority and however true to the fundamental requirements of reputability it may have been at its inception, a specific formal observance can under no circumstances maintain itself in force if with the lapse of time or on its transmission to a lower pecuniary class it is found to run counter to the ultimate ground of decency among civilised peoples, namely serviceability for the purpose of an invidious comparison in pecuniary success.

It is evident that these canons of expenditure have much to say in determining the standard of living for any community and for any class. It is no less evident that the standard of living which prevails at any time or at any given social altitude will in its turn have much to say as to the forms which honorific expenditure will take, and as to the degree to which this 'higher' need will dominate a people's consumption. In this respect the control exerted by the accepted standard of living is chiefly of a negative character; it acts almost solely to prevent recession from a scale of conspicuous expenditure that has once become habitual.

A standard of living is of the nature of habit. It is an habitual scale and method of responding to given stimuli. The difficulty in the way of receding from an accustomed standard is the difficulty of breaking a habit that has once been formed. The relative facility with which an advance in the standard is made means that the life process is a process of unfolding activity and that it will readily unfold in a new direction whenever and wherever the resistance to self-expression decreases. But when the habit of expression along such a given line of low resistance has once been formed, the discharge will seek the accustomed outlet even after a change has taken place in the environment whereby the external resistance has appreciably risen. That heightened facility of expression in a given direction which is called habit may offset a considerable increase in the resistance offered by external circumstances to the unfolding of life in the given direction. As between the various habits, or habitual modes and directions of expression, which go to make up an individual's standard of living, there is an appreciable difference in point of persistence under counteracting circumstances and in point of the degree of imperativeness with which the discharge seeks a given direction.

That is to say, in the language of current economic theory, while men are reluctant to retrench their expenditures in any direction, they are more reluctant to retrench in some directions than in others; so that while any accustomed consumption is reluctantly given up, there are certain lines of consumption which are given up with relatively extreme reluctance. The articles or forms of consumption to which the consumer clings with the greatest tenacity are commonly the so-called necessaries of life, or the subsistence minimum. The subsistence minimum is of course not a rigidly determined allowance of goods, definite and invariable in kind and quantity; but for the purpose in hand it may be taken to comprise a certain, more or less definite, aggregate of consumption required for the maintenance of life.

This minimum, it may be assumed, is ordinarily given up last in case of a progressive retrenchment of expenditure. That is to say, in a general way, the most ancient and ingrained of the habits which govern the individual's life – those habits that touch his existence as an organism – are the most persistent and imperative. Beyond these come the higher wants – later-formed habits of the individual or the race – in a somewhat irregular and by no means invariable gradation. Some of these higher wants, as for instance the habitual use of certain stimulants, or the need of salvation (in the eschatological sense), or of good repute, may in some cases take precedence of the lower or more elementary wants. In general, the longer the habituation, the more unbroken the habit, and the more nearly it coincides with previous habitual forms of the life process, the more persistently will the given habit assert itself. The habit will be stronger if the particular traits of human nature which its action involves, or the particular aptitudes that find exercise in it, are traits or aptitudes that are already largely and profoundly concerned in the life process or that are intimately bound up with the life history of the particular racial stock.

The varying degrees of ease with which different habits are formed by different persons, as well as the varying degrees of reluctance with which different habits are given up, goes to say that the formation of specific habits is not a matter of length of habituation simply. Inherited aptitudes and traits of temperament count for quite as much as length of habituation in deciding what range of habits will come to dominate any individual's scheme of life. And the prevalent type of transmitted aptitudes, or in other words the type of temperament belonging to the dominant ethnic element in any community, will go far to decide what will be the scope and form of expression of the community's habitual life process. How greatly the transmitted idiosyncrasies of aptitude may count in the way of a rapid and definitive formation of habit in individuals is illustrated by the extreme facility with which an all-dominating habit of alcoholism is sometimes formed; or in the similar facility and the similarly inevitable formation of a habit of devout observances in the case of persons gifted with a special aptitude in that direction. Much the same meaning attaches to that peculiar facility of habituation to a specific human environment that is called romantic love.

Men differ in respect of transmitted aptitudes, or in respect of the relative facility with which they unfold their life activity in particular directions; and the habits which coincide with or proceed upon a relatively strong specific aptitude or a relatively great specific facility of expression become of great consequence to the man's well-being. The part played by this element of aptitude in determining the relative tenacity of the several habits which constitute the standard of living goes to explain the extreme reluctance with which men give up any habitual expenditure in the way of conspicuous consumption. The aptitudes or propensities to which a habit of this kind is to be referred as its ground are those aptitudes whose exercise is comprised in emulation; and the propensity for emulation – for invidious comparison – is of ancient growth and is a pervading trait of human nature. It is easily called into vigorous activity in any new form, and it asserts itself with great insistence under any form under which it has once found habitual expression. When the individual has once formed the habit of seeking expression in a given line of honorific expenditure – when a given set of stimuli have come to be habitually responded to in activity of a given kind and direction under the guidance of these alert and deep-reaching propensities of emulation – it is with extreme reluctance that such an habitual expenditure is given up. And on the other hand, whenever an accession of pecuniary strength puts the individual in a position to unfold his life process in larger scope and with additional reach, the ancient propensities of the race will assert themselves in determining the direction which the new unfolding of life is to take. And those propensities which are already actively in the field under some related form of expression, which are aided by the pointed suggestions afforded by a current accredited scheme of life, and for the exercise of which the material means and opportunities are readily available – these will especially have much to say in shaping the form and direction in which the new accession to the individual's aggregate force will assert itself. That is to say, in concrete terms, in any community where conspicuous consumption is an element of the scheme of life, an increase in an individual's ability to pay is likely to take the form of an expenditure for some accredited line of conspicuous consumption.

With the exception of the instinct of self-preservation, the propensity for emulation is probably the strongest and most alert and persistent of the economic motives proper. In an industrial community this propensity for emulation expresses itself in pecuniary emulation; and this, so far as regards the Western civilised communities of the present, is virtually equivalent to saying that it expresses itself in some form of conspicuous waste. The need of conspicuous waste, therefore, stands ready to absorb any increase in the community's industrial efficiency or output of goods, after the most elementary physical wants have been provided for. Where this result does not follow, under modern conditions, the reason for the discrepancy is commonly to be sought in a rate of increase in the individual's wealth too rapid for the habit of expenditure to keep abreast of it; or it may be that the individual in question defers the conspicuous consumption of the increment to a later date – ordinarily with a view to heightening the spectacular effect of the aggregate expenditure contemplated. As increased industrial efficiency makes it possible to procure the means of livelihood with less labour, the energies of the industrious members of the community are bent to the compassing of a higher result in conspicuous expenditure, rather than slackened to a more comfortable pace.

The strain is not lightened as industrial efficiency increases and makes a lighter strain possible, but the increment of output is turned to use to meet this want, which is indefinitely expandable, after the manner commonly imputed in economic theory to higher or spiritual wants. It is owing chiefly to the presence of this element in the standard of living that J. S. Mill was able to say that 'hitherto it is questionable if all the mechanical inventions yet made have lightened the day's toil of any human being'. The accepted standard of expenditure in the community or in the class to which a person belongs largely determines what his standard of living will be. It does this directly by commending itself to his common sense as right and good, through his habitually contemplating it and assimilating the scheme of life in which it belongs; but it does so also indirectly through popular insistence on conformity to the accepted scale of expenditure as a matter of propriety, under pain of disesteem and ostracism. To accept and practice the standard of living which is in vogue is both agreeable and expedient, commonly to the point of being indispensable to personal comfort and to success in life. The standard of living of any class, so far as concerns the element of conspicuous waste, is commonly as high as the earning capacity of the class will permit – with a constant tendency to go higher. The effect upon the serious activities of men is therefore to direct them with great singleness of purpose to the largest possible acquisition of wealth, and to discountenance work that brings no pecuniary gain. At the same time the effect on consumption is to concentrate it upon the lines which are most patent to the observers whose good opinion is sought; while the inclinations and aptitudes whose exercise does not involve a honorific expenditure of time or substance tend to fall into abeyance through disuse.

Through this discrimination in favour of visible consumption it has come about that the domestic life of most classes is relatively shabby, as compared with the éclat of that overt portion of their life that is carried on before the eyes of observers. As a secondary consequence of the same discrimination, people habitually screen their private life from observation. So far as concerns that portion of their consumption that may without blame be carried on in secret, they withdraw from all contact with their neighbours. Hence, the exclusiveness of people, as regards their domestic life, in most of the industrially developed communities; and hence, by remoter derivation, the habit of privacy and reserve that is so large a feature in the code of proprieties of the better class in all communities. The low birthrate of the classes upon whom the requirements of reputable expenditure fall with great urgency is likewise traceable to the exigencies of a standard of living based on conspicuous waste. The conspicuous consumption, and the consequent increased expense, required in the reputable maintenance of a child is very considerable and acts as a powerful deterrent. It is probably the most effectual of the Malthusian prudential checks.

The effect of this factor of the standard of living, both in the way of retrenchment in the obscurer elements of consumption that go to physical comfort and maintenance, and also in the paucity or absence of children, is perhaps seen at its best among the classes given to scholarly pursuits. Because of a presumed superiority and scarcity of the gifts and attainments that characterise their life, these classes are by convention subsumed under a higher social grade than their pecuniary grade should warrant. The scale of decent expenditure in their case is pitched correspondingly high, and it consequently leaves an exceptionally narrow margin disposable for the other ends of life. By force of circumstances, their habitual sense of what is good and right in these matters, as well as the expectations of the community in the way of pecuniary decency among the learned, are excessively high – as measured by the prevalent degree of opulence and earning capacity of the class, relatively to the non-scholarly classes whose social equals they nominally are. In any modern community where there is no priestly monopoly of these occupations, the people of scholarly pursuits are unavoidably thrown into contact with classes that are pecuniarily their superiors. The high standard of pecuniary decency in force among these superior classes is transfused among the scholarly classes with but little mitigation of its rigour; and as a consequence there is no class of the community that spends a larger proportion of its substance in conspicuous waste than these.

JOHN R. COMMONS (1862–1945)

John R. Commons received his education at Oberlin College and Johns Hopkins University and spent the majority of his career as a professor at the University of Wisconsin, where he was a founder of what became known as the "Wisconsin school" of institutional economics.

Commons had, as it were, several careers. First, Commons became the first historian and theoretician of the labor movement in the United States. He envisioned labor unions as legitimate means of securing the legitimate interests of workers and both labor relations legislation and protective labor legislation as providing legal protection for labor interests in a manner paralleling the protection given to other interests under the name of private property.

Second, Commons analyzed the evolution of the introduction – over many centuries –, organization and control of the modern economic system, exploring what he called the legal foundations of capitalism. His analysis encompassed a model of interpersonal relations specified in quasi-legal terms; a behavioristic theory of psychology; theories of social control and social change; a theory of the nature, formation and roles of the working rules of law and morals; a theory of language and its role in the social construction of reality, including the sense of continuity provided by using the same term – such as freedom and property – even though its relevant substantive content changed over time; theories of system and institutional organization, especially of property, markets, government and business firms; a theory of power structure and a theory of the legal–economic nexus, including a theory of conflict resolution.

Third, Commons was involved in a series of experiments, both directly and through his students, at both state and national levels, in which legislation was crafted and enacted to promote hitherto neglected interests. These were in the areas of public utility regulation, workmen's compensation, civil service reform, control of working conditions and other areas of protective labor legislation, unemployment insurance, social security, and so on. Commons was also actively involved in monetary reform and antitrust enforcement.

Fourth, Commons sought to extend his legal–economic analysis and to combine it with both his interpretation of mainstream economics and still other bodies of knowledge, with the objective of producing a general institutional-economics theory. This was his least successful activity.

Commons essay on "Institutional Economics," reprinted here, gives a concise overview of what he believed the institutional approach to economic analysis could add to economic theory.

References and further reading

Commons, John R. (1924) *Legal Foundations of Capitalism*, New York: Macmillan.
——(1934) *Institutional Economics*, New York: Macmillan.
——(1950) *The Economics of Collective Action*, Madison: University of Wisconsin Press.
Harter, Lafayette G. (1962) *John R. Commons: His Assault on Laissez-Faire*, Corvallis: Oregon State University Press.

Mitchell, Wesley C. (1935) "Commons on Institutional Economics," *American Economic Review* 25 (December): 635–52.

Rutherford, Malcolm (1983) "John R. Commons's Institutional Economics," *Journal of Economic Issues* 17 (September): 721–44.

Samuels, Warren J. (1987) "Commons, John Rogers," in John Eatwell, Murray Milgate, and Peter Newman (eds), *The New Palgrave: A Dictionary of Economics*, Vol. 1, London: Macmillan, 506–507.

"Institutional Economics" (1931)*

An institution is defined as collective action in control, liberation and expansion of individual action. Its forms are unorganized custom and organized going concerns. The individual action is participation in bargaining, managing and rationing transactions, which are the ultimate units of economic activity. The control by custom or concerns consists in working rules which govern more or less what the individual can, must, or may do or not do. These are choices, resolved into performance, forbearance or avoidance while participating in transactions. The working rule of the Supreme Court is due process of law. The universal principles, that is, similarities of cause, effect, or purpose, discoverable in all transactions, are scarcity, efficiency, futurity, working rules and limiting factors under volitional control. These reveal themselves in a negotiational, or behavioristic, psychology of persuasion and coercion in bargaining transactions, command and obedience in managerial transactions, argument and pleading in rationing transactions.

Transactions determine legal control, while the classical and hedonic economics was concerned with physical control. Legal control is future physical control. The three social relations implicit in transactions are conflict, dependence and order. Social philosophies differ economically according to the kind of transactions which they place uppermost.

The difficulty in defining a field for the so-called institutional economics is the uncertainty of meaning of an institution. Sometimes an institution seems to mean a framework of laws or natural rights within which individuals act like inmates. Sometimes it seems to mean the behavior of the inmates themselves. Sometimes anything additional to or critical of the classical or hedonic economics is deemed to be institutional. Sometimes anything that is "economic behavior" is institutional. Sometimes anything that is "dynamic" instead of "static," or a "process" instead of commodities, or activity instead of feelings, or mass action instead of individual action, or management instead of equilibrium, or control instead of laissez faire, seems to be institutional economics.

All of these notions are doubtless involved in institutional economics, but they may be said to be metaphors or descriptions, whereas a *science* of economic behavior requires analysis into similarities of cause, effect or purpose, and a synthesis in a unified system of principles. And institutional economics, furthermore, cannot separate itself from the marvellous discoveries and insight of the classical and psychological economists. It should incorporate, however, in addition, the equally important insight of the communistic, anarchistic, syndicalistic, fascistic, cooperative and unionistic economists. Doubtless it is the effort to cover by enumeration all of these uncoordinated activities of the various schools which gives to the name institutional economics that reputation of a miscellaneous, nondescript yet merely descriptive, character of so-called "economic behavior," which has long since relegated the crude Historical School.

* *American Economic Review* 21 (December 1931), pp. 648–57.

If we endeavor to find a universal circumstance, common to all behavior known as institutional, we may define an institution as collective action in control, liberation and expansion of individual action.

Collective action ranges all the way from unorganized custom to the many organized going concerns, such as the family, the corporation, the trade association, the trade union, the reserve system, the state. The principle common to all of them is greater or less control, liberation and expansion of individual action by collective action.

This control of the acts of one individual always results in, and is intended to result in, a gain or loss to another or other individuals. If it be the enforcement of a contract, then the debt is exactly equal to the credit created for the benefit of the other person. A debt is a duty enforced collectively, while the credit is a corresponding right created by creating the duty. The resulting social relation is an economic status, consisting of the expectations towards which each party is directing his economic behavior. On the debt and duty side it is the status of conformity to collective action. On the credit and right side it is a status of security created by the expectation of the said conformity. This is known as "incorporeal" property.

Or, the collective control takes the form of a *tabu* or prohibition of certain acts, such as acts of interference, infringement, trespass; and this prohibition creates an economic status of liberty for the person thus made immune. But the liberty of one person may be accompanied by prospective gain or loss to a correlative person, and the economic status thus created is exposure to the liberty of the other. An employer is exposed to the liberty of the employee to work or not to work, and the employee is exposed to the liberty of the employer to hire or fire. The typical case of liberty and exposure is the goodwill of a business. This is coming to be distinguished as "intangible" property.

Either the state, or a corporation, or a cartel, or a holding company, or a cooperative association, or a trade union, or an employers' association, or a trade association, or a joint trade agreement of two associations, or a stock exchange, or a board of trade, may lay down and enforce the rules which determine for individuals this bundle of correlative and reciprocal economic relationships. Indeed, these collective acts of economic organizations are at times more powerful than the collective action of the political concern, the state.

Stated in the language of ethics and law, to be developed below, all collective acts establish relations of rights, duties, no rights and no duties. Stated in the language of individual behavior, what they require is performance, avoidance, forbearance by individuals. Stated in the language of the resulting economic status of individuals, what they provide is security, conformity, liberty and exposure. Stated in language of cause, effect or purpose, the common principles running through all of them are the principles of scarcity, efficiency, futurity, the working rules of collective action and the limiting and complementary factors of economic theory. Stated in language of the operation of working rules on individual action, they are expressed by the auxiliary verbs of what the individual can, cannot, must, must not, may or may not *do*. He "can" or "cannot," because collective action will or will not compel him. He "may," because collective action will permit him and protect him. He "may not," because collective action will prevent him.

It is because of these volitional auxiliary verbs that the familiar term "working rules" is appropriate to indicate the universal principles of cause, effect or purpose, common to all collective action. Working rules are continually changing in the history of an institution, and they differ for different institutions; but, whatever their differences, they have this similarity that they indicate what individuals can, must, or nay, do or not do, enforced by collective sanctions.

Analysis of these collective sanctions furnishes that correlation of economics, jurisprudence and ethics which is prerequisite to a theory of institutional economics. David Hume found the unity of these three social sciences in the principle of scarcity and the resulting conflict of interest, contrary to Adam Smith who isolated economics from the others on assumptions of divine providence, earthly abundance and the resulting harmony of interest. Institutional economics goes back to Hume. Taking our cue from Hume and the modern use of such a term as "business ethics," ethics deals with the rules of conduct arising from conflict of interests, arising, in turn, from scarcity and enforced by the *moral* sanctions of collective *opinion*; but economics deals with the same rules of conduct enforced by the collective economic sanctions of *violence*. Institutional economics is continually dealing with the relative merits and efficiency of these three types of sanctions.

From this universal principle of collective action in control, liberation and expansion of individual action arise not only the ethical concepts of rights and duties and the economic concepts of security, conformity, liberty and exposure, but also of assets and liabilities. In fact, it is from the field of corporation finance, with its changeable assets and liabilities, rather than from the field of wants and labor, or pains and pleasures, or wealth and happiness, or utility and disutility, that institutional economics derives a large part of its data and methodology. Institutional economics is the assets and liabilities of concerns, contrasted with Adam Smith's *Wealth of Nations*.

But collective action is even more universal in the unorganized from of custom than it is in the organized form of concerns. Custom has not given way to free contract and competition, as was asserted by Sir Henry Maine. Customs have merely changed with changes in economic conditions, and they may today be even more mandatory than the decrees of a dictator, who perforce is compelled to conform to them. The business man who refuses or is unable to make use of the modern customs of the credit system, by refusing to accept or issue checks on solvent banks, although they are merely private arrangements and not legal tender, simply cannot continue in business by carrying on transactions. These instruments are customary tender, instead of legal tender, backed by the powerful sanctions of profit, loss and competition, which compel conformity. Other mandatory customs might be mentioned, such as coming to work at seven o'clock and quitting at six.

If disputes arise, then the officers of an organized concern – a credit association, the manager of a corporation, a stock exchange, a board of trade, a commercial or labor arbitrator, or finally the courts of law up to the Supreme Court of the United States – reduce the custom to precision by adding an organized sanction.

This is the common-law method of making law by the decision of disputes. The decisions, by becoming precedents, become the working rules, for the time being, of the particular organized concern. The historic "common law" of Anglo-American jurisprudence is only a special case of the universal principle common to all concerns that survive, of making new law by deciding conflicts of interest, and thus giving greater precision and organized compulsion to the unorganized working rules of custom. The common-law *method* is universal in all collective action, but the technical "common-law" of the lawyers is a body of decisions. In short, the common-law method is itself a custom, with variabilities, like other customs. It is the way collective action acts on individual action in time of conflict.

Thus collective action is more than *control* of individual action – it is, by the very act of control, as indicated by the aforesaid auxiliary verb, a *liberation* of individual action from coercion, duress, discrimination, or unfair competition by other individuals.

And collective action is more than control and liberation of individual action – it is *expansion* of the will of the individual far beyond what he can do by his own puny acts. The head of a great corporation gives orders whose obedience, enforced by collective action, executes his will at the ends of the earth.

Thus an institution is collective action in control, liberation and expansion of individual action.

These individual actions are really *trans*-actions instead of either individual behavior or the "exchange" of commodities. It is this shift from commodities and individuals to transactions and working rules of collective action that marks the transition from the classical and hedonic schools to the institutional schools of economic thinking. The shift is a change in the ultimate unit of economic investigation. The classic and hedonic economists, with their communistic and anarchistic offshoots, founded their theories on the relation of man to nature, but institutionalism is a relation of man to man. The smallest unit of the classic economists was a commodity produced by labor. The smallest unit of the hedonic economists was the same or similar commodity enjoyed by ultimate consumers. One was the objective side, the other the subjective side, of the same relation between the individual and the forces of nature. The outcome, in either case, was the materialistic metaphor of an automatic equilibrium, analogous to the waves of the ocean, but personified as "seeking their level."

But the smallest unit of the institutional economists is a *unit of activity* – a transaction, with its participants. Transactions intervene between the labor of the classic economists and the pleasures of the hedonic economists, simply because it is society that controls access to the forces of nature, and transactions are, not the "exchange of commodities," but the alienation and acquisition, between individuals, of the *rights* of property and liberty created by society, which must therefore be negotiated between the parties concerned before labor can produce, or consumers can consume, or commodities be physically exchanged.

Transactions, as derived from a study of economic theories and of the decisions of courts, may be reduced to three economic activities, distinguishable as bargaining transactions, managerial transactions and rationing transactions. The participants in each of them are controlled and liberated by the working rules of the particular type of moral, economic or political concern in question.

The bargaining transaction derives from the familiar formula of a market, which, at the time of negotiation, before goods are exchanged, consists of the best two buyers and the best two sellers on that market. The others are potential. Out of this formula arise four relations of possible conflict of interest, on which the decisions of courts have built four classes of working rules.

1   The two buyers are competitors and the two sellers are competitors, from whose competition the courts, guided by custom, have constructed the long line of rules on fair and unfair competition.
2   One of the buyers will buy from one of the sellers, and one of the sellers will sell to one of the buyers, and, out of this economic choice of opportunities, both custom and the courts have constructed the rules of equal or unequal opportunity, which, when reduced to decisions of disputes, become the collective rules of reasonable and unreasonable discrimination.
3   At the close of the negotiations, one of the sellers, by operation of law, transfers title to one of the buyers, and one of the buyers transfers title to money or a credit instrument to one of the sellers. Out of this double alienation and acquisition of title arises the issue of equality or inequality of bargaining power, whose decisions create the rules of fair and unfair price, or reasonable and unreasonable value.
4   But even the decisions themselves on these disputes, or the legislative or administrative rules prescribed to guide the decisions, may be called in question, under the American System, by an appeal to the Supreme Court, on the ground that property or liberty has been "taken" by the governing or judicial authority "without due process of law." Due process of law is the working rule of the Supreme Court for the time being, which changes with changes in custom and class dominance, or with changes in judges, or changes in the opinions of judges, or with changes in the customary meanings of property and liberty.

Hence the four economic issues arising out of that unit of activity, the bargaining transaction, are competition, discrimination, economic power and working rules.

The habitual assumption back of the decisions in the foregoing classes of disputes is the assumption of equality of willing buyers and willing sellers in the bargaining transactions by which the ownership of wealth is transferred by operation of law. Here the universal principle is scarcity.

But the assumption back of managerial transactions, by which the wealth itself is produced, is that of superior and inferior. Here the universal principle is efficiency, and the relation is between *two* parties, instead of the *four* parties of the bargaining transaction. The master, or manager, or foreman, or other executive, gives orders – the servant or workman or other subordinate must obey. Yet a change in working rules, in course of time, as modified by the new collective action of court decisions, may distinguish between reasonable and unreasonable commands, willing and unwilling obedience.

Finally the rationing transactions differ from managerial transactions in that the superior is a collective superior while the inferiors are individuals. Familiar instances are the log-rolling activities of a legislature in matters of taxation and tariff; the decrees of communist or fascist dictatorships; the budget-making of a corporate board of directors; even the decisions of a court or arbitrator; all of which consist in rationing either wealth or purchasing power to subordinates without bargaining, although the negotiations are sometimes mistaken for bargaining, and without managing, which is left to executives. They involve negotiation, indeed, but in the form of argument, pleading, or eloquence, because they come under the rule of command and obedience instead of the rule of equality and liberty. On the borderline are partnership agreements which ration to the partners the benefits and burdens of a joint enterprise. These rationing transactions, likewise, in the American system, are subject finally to the working rules (due process of law) of the Supreme Court.

In all cases we have variations and hierarchies of the universal principle of collective action controlling, liberating and expanding individual action in all the economic transactions of bargaining, managing and rationing.

Since institutional economics is behavioristic, and the behavior in question is none other than the behavior of individuals while participating in transactions, institutional economics must make an analysis of the economic behavior of individuals. The peculiar quality of the human will in all its activities, distinguishing economics from the physical sciences, is that of choosing between alternatives. The choice may be voluntary, or it may be an involuntary choice imposed by another individual or by collective action. In any case the choice is the whole mind and body in action – that is, the will – whether it be physical action and reaction with nature's forces, or the economic activity of mutually inducing others in the transaction.

Every choice, on analysis, turns out to be a three-dimensional act, which, as may be derived from the issues arising in disputes, is at one and the same time, a performance, an avoidance, and a forbearance. Performance is the exercise of power over nature or others; avoidance is its exercise in one direction rather than the next available direction; while forbearance is the exercise, not of the total power except at a crisis, but the exercise of a limited degree of one's possible moral, physical or economic power. Thus forbearance is the limit placed on performance; performance is the actual performance; and avoidance is the alternative performance rejected or avoided – all at one and the same point of time.

It is from forbearance that the doctrine of reasonableness arises, while performance means either rendering a service, compelling a service, or paying a debt, but avoidance is non-interference with the performance, forbearance or avoidance of others. Each may be a duty or a liberty, with a corresponding right or exposure of others, and each may be enforced, permitted, or limited by collective action according to the then working rules of the particular concern.

If institutional economics is volitional it requires an institutional psychology to accompany it. This is the psychology of transactions, which may properly be named negotiational psychology. Nearly all historic psychologies are individualistic, since they are concerned with the relation of individuals to nature, or to other individuals, treated, however, not as citizens with rights, but as objects of nature without rights or duties. This is true all the way from Locke's copy psychology, Berkeley's idealistic psychology, Hume's skeptical psychology, Bentham's pleasure–pain psychology, the hedonistic marginal utility psychology, James's pragmatism, Watson's behaviorism, and the recent Gestalt psychology. All are individualistic. Only Dewey's is socialistic.

But the psychology of transactions is the psychology of negotiations. Each participant is endeavoring to influence the other towards performance, forbearance or avoidance. Each modifies the behavior of the other in greater or less degree. This is the psychology of business, of custom, of legislatures, of courts, of trade associations, of trade unions. In popular language it resolves into the *persuasions* or *coercions* of bargaining transactions, the *commands* and *obedience* of managerial transactions, or the *arguments* and *pleadings* of rationing transactions. All of these are negotiational psychology. It may be observed that they are a behavioristic psychology.

But these are only names and descriptions. A scientific understanding of negotiational psychology resolves it into the smallest number of general principles, that is, similarities of cause, effect or purpose, to be found in all transactions, but in varying degree. First is the personality of participants, which, instead of the assumed equality of economic theory, is all the differences among individuals in their powers of inducement and their responses to inducements and sanctions.

Then are the similarities and differences of circumstance in which personalities are placed. First is scarcity or abundance of alternatives. This is inseparable from efficiency, or the capacity to bring events to happen. In all cases negotiations are directed towards future time, the universal principle of futurity. Working rules are always taken into account, since they are the expectations of what the participants can, must or may do or not do, as controlled, liberated or expanded by collective action. Then, in each transaction is always a limiting factor whose control by the sagacious negotiator, salesman, manager or politician, will determine the outcome of complementary factors in the immediate or remote future.

Thus negotiational psychology is the transactional psychology which offers inducements and sanctions according to the variable personalities and the present circumstances of scarcity, efficiency, expectation, working rules and limiting factors.

Historically this transactional psychology may be seen to have changed, and is changing continuously, so that the whole philosophies of capitalism, fascism or communism are variabilities of it. In the common-law decisions it is the changing distinctions between persuasion and coercion or duress, persuasion being considered the outcome of a reasonable status of either equality of opportunity, or fair competition, or equality of bargaining power, or due process of law. But economic coercion and physical duress are denials of these economic ideals, and nearly every case of economic conflict becomes an assumption or investigation, under its own circumstances, of the negotiational psychology of persuasion and coercion. Even the managerial and rationing negotiations come under this rule of institutional change, for the psychology of command and obedience is changed with changes in the status of conformity, security, liberty or exposure. The modern "personnel" management is an illustration of this kind of change in negotiational psychology.

All of this rests on what may be distinguished as three social relations implicit in every transaction, the relations of conflict, dependence and order. The parties are involved in a conflict of interests on account of the universal principle of scarcity. Yet they depend on each other for reciprocal alienation and acquisition of what the other wants but does not own. Then the working rule is not a foreordained harmony of interests, as assumed in the hypotheses of natural rights or mechanical equilibrium of the classical and hedonic schools, but it actually creates, out of conflict of interests, a workable mutuality and orderly expectation of property and liberty. Thus conflict, dependence and order become the field of institutional economics, built upon the principles of scarcity, efficiency, futurity and limiting factors derived from the older schools, but correlated under the modern notions of working rules of collective action controlling, liberating and expanding individual action.

What then becomes of the "exchange" of physical commodities and the production of wealth, as well as the consumption of wealth and satisfaction of wants by consumers, which furnished the starting points of the classical, hedonic, communist and other schools of economists? They are merely *transferred to the future*. They become expectations of the immediate or remote future, secured by the collective action, or "institution," of property and liberty, and available only after the conclusion of a transaction. Transactions are the means, under operation of law and custom, of acquiring and alienating legal control of commodities, or legal control of the labor and management that will produce and deliver or exchange the commodities and services, forward to the ultimate consumers.

Institutional economics is not divorced from the classical and psychological schools of economists – it transfers their theories to the *future* when goods will be produced or consumed or exchanged as an outcome of present transactions. That future may be the engineering economics of production of the classical economists or the home economics of consumption of the hedonic economists, which depend on *physical* control. But institutional economics is *legal* control of commodities and labor, where the classical and hedonic theories dealt only with physical control. *Legal control is future physical control.* Future physical control is the field of engineering and home economics.

Thus it may be seen how it was that the natural rights ideas of the economists and lawyers created the illusion of a framework, supposed to be constructed in the past, within which present individuals are supposed to act. It was because they did not investigate collective action. They assumed the fixity of existing rights of property and liberty. But if rights, duties, liberties and exposures are simply the changeable working rules of all kinds of collective action, looking towards the future, then the framework analogy disappears in the actual collective action of controlling, liberating and expanding individual action for the immediate or remote future production, exchange, and consumption of wealth.

Consequently the final social philosophy, or "ism" – which is usually a belief regarding human nature and its goal – towards which institutional economics trends is not something foreordained by divine or natural "right," or materialistic equilibrium, or "laws of nature" – it may be communism, fascism, capitalism. If managerial and rationing transactions are the starting point of the philosophy, then the end is the command and obedience of communism or fascism. If bargaining transactions are the units of investigation then the trend is towards the equality of opportunity, the fair competition, the equality of bargaining power, and the due process of law of the philosophy of liberalism and regulated capitalism. But there may be all degrees of combination, for the three kinds of transactions are interdependent and variable in a world of collective action and perpetual change, which is the uncertain future world of institutional economics.

Index